Brief Contents

W9-AQN-550

www.wileyplus.com

ALL THE HELP, **RESOURCES**, AND PERSONAL **SUPPORT** YOU AND YOUR STUDENTS NEED!

www.wileyplus.com/resources

2-Minute Tutorials and all of the resources you & your students need to get started.

Student support from an experienced student user.

Collaborate with your colleagues, find a mentor, attend virtual and live events, and view resources.
www.WhereFacultyConnect.com

Pre-loaded, ready-to-use assignments and presentations. Created by subject matter experts.

Technical Support 24/7 FAQs, online chat, and phone support.
www.wileyplus.com/support

Your *WileyPLUS* Account Manager. Personal training and implementation support.

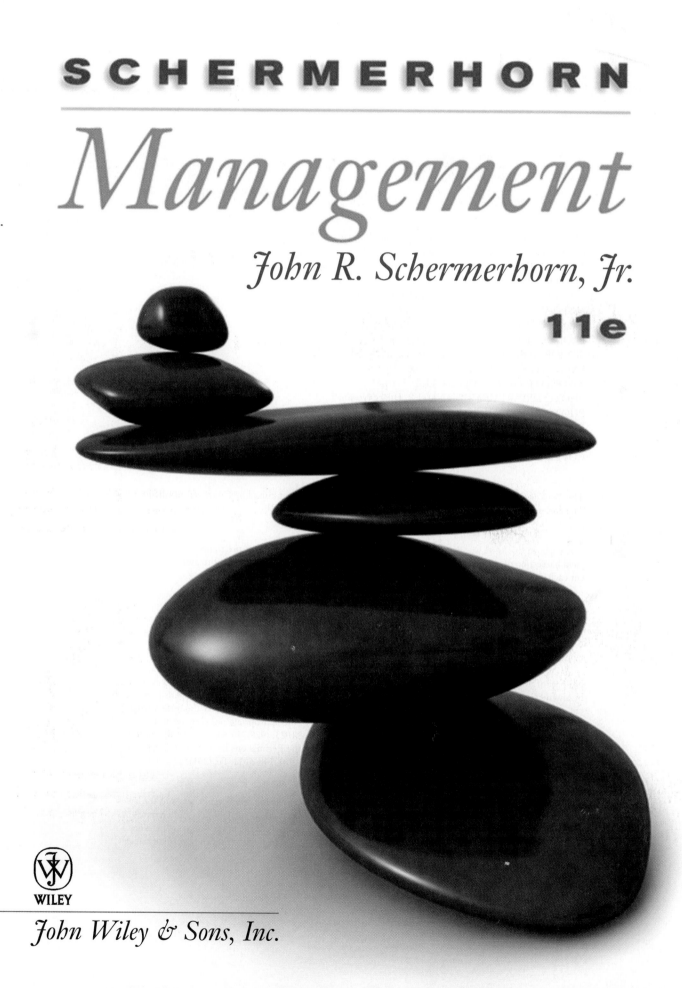

SCHERMERHORN

Management

John R. Schermerhorn, Jr.

11e

WILEY

John Wiley & Sons, Inc.

VICE PRESIDENT & PUBLISHER George Hoffman
EXECUTIVE EDITOR Lisé Johnson
ASSISTANT EDITOR Sarah Vernon
EDITOR Susan McLaughlin
ASSOCIATE DIRECTOR OF MARKETING Amy Scholz
ASSISTANT MARKETING MANAGER Laura Finley
PRODUCTION MANAGER Dorothy Sinclair
PRODUCTION EDITOR Sandra Dumas
SENIOR DESIGNER Maddy Lesure
EXECUTIVE MEDIA EDITOR Allison Morris
ASSOCIATE MEDIA EDITOR Elena Santa Maria
PHOTO DEPARTMENT MANAGER Hilary Newman
PHOTO EDITOR Teri Stratford
ILLUSTRATION EDITOR Anna Melhorn
PRODUCTION MANAGEMENT SERVICES Ingrao Associates
COVER IMAGE © Mark Evans/iStockphoto

This book was typeset in 10/12 Janson Text at Aptara and printed and bound by Courier/Kendallville. The cover was printed by Courier/Kendallville.

The paper in this book was manufactured by a mill whose forest management programs include sustained yield harvesting of its timberlands. Sustained yield harvesting principles ensure that the number of trees cut each year does not exceed the amount of new growth.

This book is printed on acid-free paper.

ISBN 13 978-0470-53051-1
ISBN 13 978-0470-91751-0
Printed in the United States of America.
10 9 8 7 6 5 4 3 2 1

To my sons, John Christian and Charles Porter

While you played
I wrote.
But always,
I was listening
and loving
you.
• 1984

It's later now.
Don't worry.
Time
means love shared,
by you
and me.
• 1986

Think
of all the fun
we have.
Here, there, everywhere,
doing things
together.
• 1989

Home,
now and forever,
will always be
wherever
I can be
with you.
• 1992

Time
has its ways,
doesn't it?
Not enough,
not enough,
I often say.
• 1996

Hurry home
when you can.
Come laughing, sons.
Tell us
your
wonderful stories.
• 1999

Songs riding winds.
Mimi,
Uncle George,
Uncle Nelson.
Whispers and choirs.
Silence speaks.
• 2002

On the mountain,
by Irish lakes,
find beauty and
peace.
Fairies dance
there.
• 2004

Mom loves
us, cats
and rainy days.
Nana and Poppy
loved us
too.
• 2007

Bookstores, museums,
stories, paintings.
And dreams.
We travel,
we laugh,
joined in life.
• 2009

While you work,
I'm starting to play
again.
Still listening,
and loving
you.
• 2011

About the **A**uthor

Dr. John R. Schermerhorn, Jr. is the Charles G. O'Bleness Professor of Management Emeritus in the College of Business at Ohio University, where he teaches graduate and undergraduate courses in management. Dr. Schermerhorn earned a Ph.D. in organizational behavior from Northwestern University, an MBA (with distinction) in management and international business from New York University, and a BS in business administration from the State University of New York at Buffalo. He previously taught at Tulane University, the University of Vermont, and Southern Illinois University at Carbondale, where he also served as head of the Department of Management and associate dean of the College of Business Administration.

Dr. Schermerhorn focuses on bridging the gap between the theory and practice of management in both the classroom and in his textbooks. Because of his instructional excellence and teaching innovations, Ohio University named Dr. Schermerhorn a University Professor. This is the university's highest campus-wide honor for excellence in undergraduate teaching.

International experience adds a unique global dimension to Dr. Schermerhorn's teaching and writing. He holds an honorary doctorate from the University of Pécs in Hungary. He was a visiting professor of management at the Chinese University of Hong Kong, on-site coordinator of the Ohio University MBA and Executive MBA programs in Malaysia, and Kohei Miura visiting professor at Chubu University in Japan. He has served as adjunct professor at the National University of Ireland at Galway, a member of the graduate faculty at Bangkok University in Thailand, and advisor to the Lao-American College in Vientiane, Laos. And at Ohio University, he has twice been Director of the Center for Southeast Asian Studies.

An enthusiastic scholar, Dr. Schermerhorn is a member of the Academy of Management, where he served as chairperson of the Management Education and Development Division. Management educators and students alike know him as author of *Exploring Management* 2e (Wiley, 2009), *Management* 10e (Wiley, 2009), and senior co-author of *Organizational Behavior* 11e (Wiley, 2010) and *Core Concepts of Organizational Behavior* (Wiley, 2004). Dr. Schermerhorn has also published numerous articles, including ones in the *Academy of Management Journal*, *Academy of Management Review*, *Academy of Management Executive*, *Organizational Dynamics*, *Asia-Pacific Journal of Management*, the *Journal of Management Development*, and the *Journal of Management Education*.

Dr. Schermerhorn is a popular guest speaker at colleges and universities. He is available for student lectures and classroom visits, as well as for faculty workshops on journal manuscript development, textbook writing, and instructional approaches and innovations.

Preface

From the beautiful cover of this book to the realities of organizations today, great accomplishments are much like inspired works of art. Whether one is talking about arranging stones or bringing together people and other resources in organizational systems, it is a balancing act. But the results are spectacular when goals and talent combine to create a lasting and positive impact.

Just as artists find inspiration in all the senses that bring our world to life, managers find inspiration in daily experiences, from the insights of management scholars, through relationships with other people, and among the goals that guide organizations in an ever more demanding society. And like artists, managers must master many challenges as they strive to create the future from the resources of the present.

While a beautiful formation of stones can offer the beholder a sense of balance and harmony in a compelling masterpiece, a well-managed workplace can build, mix, and integrate all the beauties of human talent with great success. This capacity for positive impact is the goal bound into the pages of *Management 11e*. It is an opportunity to gain knowledge, find inspiration, and engage practices that can prepare each of us to help build the organizations we need to forge a better world.

MANAGEMENT 11E PHILOSOPHY

Today's students are tomorrow's leaders and managers. They are our hope for the future. When well prepared, they can be major contributors during this time of social transformation. But the workplace is rapidly changing, and so too must our teaching and learning environments change from the comforts and successes of days gone by. New values and management approaches are appearing; organizations are changing forms and practices; jobs are being redefined and relocated; the age of information is a major force in our lives; and the intricacies of globalization are presenting major organizational and economic challenges.

Management 11e is designed for this new world of work. It is crafted to help students not just explore the essentials of the management discipline, but also to understand their great personal potential and accept their responsibilities for developing useful career skills. The content, pedagogy, and features of this edition were carefully blended to support management educators who want their courses to:

- enhance our students' career readiness
- make our students more attractive as intern and job candidates
- improve our students' confidence in critical thinking
- raise our students' awareness of timely social and organizational issues
- inspire our students to embrace life-long learning for career success

MANAGEMENT 11E PEDAGOGY

The pedagogical foundations of *Management 11e* are based on four constructive balances that are essential to higher education for business and management.

- *The balance of research insights with formative education.* As educators we must be willing to make choices when bringing the theories and concepts of our discipline to the attention of the introductory student. We cannot do everything in one course. The goal should be to make good content choices and to set the best possible foundations for lifelong learning.

- *The balance of management theory with management practice.* As educators we must understand the compelling needs of students to learn and appreciate the applications of the material they are reading and thinking about. We must continually bring to their attention good, interesting, and recognizable examples.

- *The balance of present understandings with future possibilities.* As educators we must continually search for the directions in which the real world of management is heading. We must select and present materials that can both point students in the right directions and help them develop the confidence and self-respect needed to best pursue them.

- *The balance of what "can" be done with what is, purely and simply, the "right" thing to do.* As educators we are role models; we set the examples. We must be willing to take stands on issues such as managerial ethics and social responsibility. We must be careful not to let the concept of "contingency" betray the need for positive "action" and "accountability" in managerial practice.

Today, more than ever before, our students have pressing needs for direction as well as suggestion. They have needs for application as well as information. They have needs for integration as well as presentation. And they have needs for confidence built upon solid understanding. Our instructional approaches and materials must deliver on all of these dimensions and more. My goal is to put into your hands and into those of your students a learning resource that can help meet these needs. *Management 11e* and its supporting online resources are my contributions to the future careers of your students and mine.

MANAGEMENT 11E HIGHLIGHTS

Management 11e introduces the essentials of management as they apply within the contemporary work environment and a complex global society. The subject matter is carefully chosen to meet AACSB accreditation guidelines, while still allowing extensive flexibility to fit various course designs and class sizes.

Organization and Content The following chapter realignment makes the new edition as useful and flexible as possible in meeting a wide variety of course objectives. All chapters have also been updated and enriched with new materials and examples from the latest current events.

- **Part 1: Management**—Three chapters introducing management in terms of present-day dynamics and historical foundations—Introducing Management, Management Learning Past to Present, and Ethics and Social Responsibility.

- **Part 2: Environment**—Three chapters setting the environmental context within which today's managers function—Environment, Sustainability and Innovation, Global Management and Cultural Diversity, and Entrepreneurship and New Ventures.

- **Part 3: Planning**—Three-chapter sequence covering Information and Decision Making, Planning Processes and Techniques, and Strategy and Strategic Management.

- **Part 4: Organizing**—Three chapters on the essential building blocks of organizations—Organization Structures and Design, Organizational Culture and Change, and Human Resource Management.
- **Part 5: Leading**—Five chapters exploring key leadership skills and competencies—Leading and Leadership Development, Individual Behavior, Motivation Theory and Practice, Teams and Teamwork, and Communication and Collaboration.
- **Part 6: Controlling**—Two chapters on Control Processes and Systems, and Operations and Services Management.

Integrated Learning Model *Management 11e* is written with an integrated learning model. From the chapter opener, through chapter content, to end–chapter support, learning model text:

- guides students to best read and study for exams,
- encourages self-reflection about personal management skills and competencies,
- engages students in critical thinking and active learning,
- informs students how management issues and themes apply both in their careers and in current events that affect everyday living.

Reading and Studying Each chapter begins with *Study Questions* that are linked to the major headings in the chapter. These headings and their major contents are highlighted in a *Visual Chapter Overview* that precedes the text discussion. A *Learning Check* follows each major section as a point of self-assessment prior to continuing with the reading.

A *Study Question Summary* and a *Chapter Self-Test* tie things together at the end of the chapter. Well designed *Figures* provide back-up to solidify student comprehension as concepts, theories, and terms are introduced. Where appropriate, *Small Boxed Figures and Summaries* are embedded with the discussion to help summarize and clarify major points.

Self-Reflection Each chapter also opens with *Learning About Yourself*, a feature that focuses on a critical personal skill or characteristic relevant to chapter content—such as "self-awareness"—in Chapter 1. Students are provided information and insight on the topic, and then asked to engage in a process of self-reflection. An integrated "Get to Know Yourself Better" box sets forth a personal development challenge and directs students toward self-assessment instruments at the end of the chapter and in the online resources.

The end-of-chapter *Self-Assessment* section has three components to further consolidate the self-reflection process. *Back to Yourself* reminds students about how chapter discussion relates back to the chapter opening Learning About Yourself segment. *Further Reflection* provides a self-assessment instrument, along with scoring and interpretation, for additional personal insights relevant to the chapter. And, students are reminded where to find more *Online Self-Assessment* resources.

Critical Thinking and Active Learning Special chapter features engage students in timely examples, current events, and applications of chapter material. *Real Ethics* challenges students to respond to an ethics problem or dilemma. *Real People* presents exemplars and raises awareness about success in career and work situations. *Research Brief* summarizes recent research on a chapter topic and asks students to consider further research of their own.

Management Cases for Critical Thinking is a rich and useful learning resource. It contains *Case Studies* for each chapter that asks students to answer questions relating the case to chapter content. These questions are of three types—discussion, problem solving, and further research. They are useful for in-class discussions, as well as both individual and team writing and presentation assignments.

Management Cases for Critical Thinking also contains a *Running Video Case—Greensburg, Kansas*. Each section of the case is linked to a book part, and explores management concepts and issues in the context of the economic renewal of a small town in middle America. Greensburg, Kansas, was hit by a devastating tornado in May of 2007. It killed 11 people and destroyed 95 percent of the buildings in the town. The community bonded together and, through shared visions and problem solving, made a commitment to rebuild as a model green community.

Practical Applications *Learning from Others* opens each chapter with an example that places chapter content in the context of real people and organizations. The examples are chosen to both capture student interest and remind them how insights into chapter topics and themes can be found in everyday experiences. An embedded *Do the Benchmarking* box summarizes a management lesson or applications question based on the example used.

Within a chapter, *Management Smarts* offers a bullet list summary of applications for a chapter concept or theory. Frequent *Embedded Examples* introduce or highlight a content issue or theory, and many carry small photos to attract the attention of student readers. And at the end of the chapter, the *Team Exercise* and *Case Study* have been carefully chosen to further extend the students' understanding and abilities in applying chapter content to real situations.

MANAGEMENT 11E TEACHING AND LEARNING RESOURCES

Instructor's Resource Manual Prepared by Francis Green of Pennsylvania State University, Brandywine, the Instructor's Resource Manual offers helpful teaching ideas. It has advice on course development, sample assignments, and recommended activities. It also offers chapter-by-chapter text highlights, learning objectives, lecture outlines, class exercises, lecture notes, answers to end-of-chapter material, and tips on using cases.

Test Bank Prepared by Joe Hanson of the Des Moines Area Community College, this comprehensive Test Bank (available on the instructor portion of the *Management 11e* Web site) has more than 175 questions per chapter. The true/false, multiple-choice, and short-answer questions are designed to vary in degree of difficulty by Bloom's Taxonomy and match AASCB guidelines. The computerized test bank allows instructors to modify and add questions to the master bank, and to customize their exams.

Web Quizzes An online study guide with quizzes of varying levels of difficulty helps students evaluate their progress through a chapter. It is available on the student portion of the Schermerhorn, *Management 11e* Web site.

Pre- and Post-Lecture Quizzes Prepared by Dianne Weinstein of Hofstra University and included in WileyPLUS, the Pre- and Post-Lecture Quizzes focus on the key terms and concepts. They can be used as stand-alone quizzes, or in combination to evaluate students' progress before and after lectures.

PowerPoint Presentation Slides Prepared by Susan Verhulst of Des Moines Area Community College, this robust set of slides can be accessed on the instructor portion of the *Management 11e* Web site. Lecture notes accompany each slide.

Lecture Launcher Videos Prepared by Susan Verhulst of Des Moines Area Community College, these short video clips developed from CBS source materials provide an excellent starting point for lectures or for general class discussion.

Movies and Music For those interested in integrating popular culture and the humanities into their management courses, the special teaching supplement *Art Imitates*

Life, prepared by Robert L. Holbrook of Ohio University, offers a world of options. This popular supplement provides innovative teaching ideas and scripts for integrating movies and music into day-to-day classroom activities. It is widely praised for increasing student involvement and enthusiasm for learning.

Personal Response System The Personal Response System (PRS) questions for each chapter are designed to spark classroom discussion and debate. For more information on PRS, please contact your local Wiley sales representative.

MP3 Downloads A complete playlist of MP3 downloads provides easy-to-access and ever-ready audio files that overview key chapter topics, terms, and potential test materials.

Student Portfolio Builder This special guide to building a student portfolio is complete with professional résumé and competency documentation templates. It is on the student Companion Web site.

Companion Website The *Management 11e* Web site at http://www.wiley.com/college/schermerhorn contains a myriad of tools and links to aid both teaching and learning, including resources described above.

Business Extra Select Online Courseware System This program provides an instructor with millions of content resources from an extensive database of cases, journals, periodicals, newspapers, and supplemental readings.

WileyPLUS

WileyPLUS is an innovative, research-based, online environment for effective teaching and learning.

What do students receive with *WileyPLUS*?

A Research-based Design. *WileyPLUS* provides an online environment that integrates relevant resources, including the entire digital textbook, in an easy-to-navigate framework that helps students study more effectively.

- *WileyPLUS* adds structure by organizing textbook content into smaller, more manageable "chunks."
- Related media, examples, and sample practice items reinforce the learning objectives.
- Innovative features such as calendars, visual progress tracking, and self-evaluation tools improve time management and strengthen areas of weakness.

One-on-one Engagement. With *WileyPLUS* for Management, 11th Edition, students receive 24/7 access to resources that promote positive learning outcomes. Students engage with related examples (in various media) and sample practice items, including:

- Animated Figures
- CBS/BBC videos
- Self-assessments quizzes students can use to test themselves on topics such as emotional intelligence, diversity awareness, and intuitive ability.
- Management Calendar including daily Management tips
- iPhone Applications for Download
- Flash Cards
- Hot Topic Modules
- Crossword Puzzles
- Self-Study Questions

Measurable Outcomes. Throughout each study session, students can assess their progress and gain immediate feedback. *WileyPLUS* provides precise reporting of strengths and weaknesses, as well as individualized quizzes, so that students are confident they are spending their time on the right things. With *WileyPLUS*, students always know the exact outcome of their efforts.

What do instructors receive with *WileyPLUS*?

WileyPLUS provides reliable, customizable resources that reinforce course goals inside and outside of the classroom as well as visibility into individual student progress. Pre-created materials and activities help instructors optimize their time:

Customizable Course Plan: *WileyPLUS* comes with a pre-created Course Plan designed by a subject matter expert uniquely for this course. Simple drag-and-drop tools make it easy to assign the course plan as-is or modify it to reflect your course syllabus.

Pre-created Activity Types Include:

- Questions
- Readings and resources
- Presentation
- Print Tests
- Concept Mastery
- Project

Course Materials and Assessment Content:

- Lecture Notes PowerPoint Slides
- Classroom Response System (Clicker) Questions
- Image Gallery
- Instructor's Manual
- Gradable Reading Assignment Questions (embedded with online text)
- Question Assignments: all end-of-chapter problems
- Testbank
- Pre and Post Lecture Quizzes
- Web Quizzes
- Video Teaching Notes—includes questions geared toward applying text concepts to current videos

Gradebook: *WileyPLUS* provides instant access to reports on trends in class performance, student use of course materials and progress toward learning objectives, helping inform decisions, and drive classroom discussions.

WileyPLUS. Learn More. www.wileyplus.com.

Powered by proven technology and built on a foundation of cognitive research, *WileyPLUS* has enriched the education of millions of students, in over 20 countries around the world.

Acknowledgments

Management 11e was initiated and completed with the support of my inspiring, talented, and dedicated development editor Susan McLaughlin, Acquisitions Editor Lise Johnson who never failed to support the project and the entire team through all of its ups and downs, and ever-helpful Assistant Editor Sarah Vernon. We have all benefitted from the further support of an expert Wiley team that includes George Hoffman (publisher), Madelyn Lesure (designer), Hilary Newman (photo research), Suzanne Ingrao (Ingrao Associates), Sandra Dumas (production), Amy Scholz (marketing), as well as the help of Teri Stratford (photos). As always, I have been fortunate during this revision to have worked with the support and encouragement of my wife Ann. She perseveres even when "the book" overwhelms many of life's opportunities. I am also grateful to be working in a college and university that values teaching most highly, and to have the special advantages of scholarly challenge and inspiration from my colleagues Lenie Holbrook and Will Lamb.

I thank the following colleagues whose help with this book at various stages of its life added to my understanding.

Jim Cashman, *University of Alabama*
Larry Chasteen, *Stephen F. Austin State University*
Samuel Hazen, *Tarleton State University*
Shane Spiller, *Western Kentucky University*
Jiaqin Yang, *Georgia College and State University*
Bruce Charnov, *Hofstra University*
Linda Ferraro, *Central Connecticut State University*
Susan Manring, *Elon University*
Jon Bryan, *Bridgewater State University*
Dan Hallock, *University of North Alabama*

Val D. Miskin, *Washington State University*
Brien N. Smith, *Ball State University*
Susan L. Verhulst, *Des Moines Area Community College*
Augustine Obiaku, *Allegheny County Community College*
Todd Allessandri, *Northeastern University*
Fernando Pargas, *James Madison University*
Jud Faurer, *Metropolitan State University*
Camille Johnson, *San Jose State University*
Michael Okrent, *Southern Connecticut State University*

Carl Adams, *University of Minnesota*; Allen Amason, *University of Georgia*; Lydia Anderson, *Fresno City College*; Hal Babson, *Columbus State Community College*; Marvin Bates, *Benedictine University*; Joy Benson, *University of Wisconsin–Green Bay*; Santanu Borah, *University of Northern Alabama*; Peggy Brewer, *Eastern Kentucky University*; Jim Buckenmyer, *Southeast Missouri State University*; Michael Buckley, *University of Oklahoma–Norman*; Barry Bunn, *Valencia Community College*; William Clark, *Leeward Community College*; Frederick Collett, *Mercy College*; Jeanie Diemer, *Ivy Tech State College*; Richard Eisenbeis, *Colorado State University–Pueblo*; Phyllis Flott, *Tennessee State University*; Dwight Frink, *Mississippi State University*; Shelly Gardner, *Augustana College*; Tommy Georgiades, *DeVry University*; Marvin Gordon, *University of Illinois–Chicago*; Fran Green, *Pennsylvania State University–Brandywine*; Joe Hanson, *Des Moines Area Community College*; Carol Harvey, *Assumption College*; Lenie Holbrook, *Ohio University*; Gary Insch, *West Virginia University*; Kathleen Jones, *University of North Dakota*; Marvin Karlins, *University of South Florida*; John Lipinski, *University of Pittsburgh*; Beverly Little, *Western Carolina University*; Kristie Loescher, *University of Texas*; James LoPresti, *University of Colorado–Boulder*; Kurt Martsolf, *California State University–Hayward*; Brian Maruffi, *Fordham University*; Brenda McAleer and Grace McLaughlin, *University of California–Irvine*; Donald Mosley, *University of South Alabama*; Behnam Nakhai, *Millersville University of Pennsylvania*; Robert Nale, *Coastal Carolina University*; John Overby, *The University of Tennessee–Martin*; Javier Pagan, *University of Puerto Rio—Piedras*; Diana Page, *University of West Florida*; Richard Pena, *University of Texas–San Antonio*; Wendy Pike, *Benedictine University*; Newman Pollack, *Florida Atlantic University*; Anthony Racka, *Oakland Community College*; Jenny Rink, *Community College of Philadelphia*; Joseph Santora, *Essex County College*; Rajib Sanyal, *The College of New Jersey*; Roy Shin, *Indiana University*; Shanthi Srinivas, *California State Polytechnic University–Pomona*; Howard Stanger, *Canisius College*; Jerry Stevens, *Texas Tech University*; William Stevens, *Missouri Southern State College*; Chuck Stubbart, *Southern Illinois University*; Harry Stucke, *Long Island University*; Thomas Thompson, *University of Maryland*; Judy Thompson, *Briar Cliff University*; Michael Troyer, *University of Wisconsin–Green Bay*; Jeffrey Ward, *Edmonds Community College*; Marta White, *Georgia State University*; James Whitney, *Champlain College*; Garland Wiggs, *Radford University*; Eric Wiklendt, *University of Northern Iowa*; Greg Yon, *Florida State University*; Yichuan Zhao, *Dalian Maritime University*.

Brief Contents

Contents

PART TWO ENVIRONMENT

PART THREE PLANNING

PART FOUR ORGANIZING

PART FIVE LEADING

PART SIX CONTROLLING

Features

Introducing

Management

1

Chapter 1 Study Questions

1 What are the challenges of working today?

2 What are organizations like in the new workplace?

3 Who are managers and what do they do?

4 What is the management process?

5 How do you learn managerial skills and competencies?

Learning From Others

Smart People Create Their Own Futures

Sure it's been a tough economy for job seekers. But isn't it time to take the future in your own hands? A good start for new college graduates is browsing online career sites like Monster.com, Yahoo!hotjobs, or Careerbuilder.com. For those with job experience, LinkedIn.com has become the place to post a career profile. There's been a major shift toward online recruiting practices and you'll need to join in and use your social media skills to reap the benefits. According to John Campagnino, head of consulting firm Accenture's global recruiting, being on the web is the way to get his attention; "this is the future of recruiting for our company," he says. *Fortune* magazine goes even further in advising its executive audience: "Facebook is for fun. Tweets have short life. If you're serious about managing your career the only social site that really matters is LinkedIn."[1]

Of course not everyone wants to work for someone else. Starting your own business can also be a great career choice. After all, Monster.com began when founder Jeff Taylor, shown here, jotted an idea on a sketch pad, made an early morning trip to a coffee shop, and turned his notes into a business concept.[2] As college sophomores Aaron Levie and Dylan Smith launched the online collaboration tool Box.net. It has attracted $14.5 million in venture capital and now has 50 employees. And, Eric and Susan Koger started their online indie clothing store ModCloth while freshmen at Carnegie Mellon University. It's now headed toward $15 million in annual sales.[3]

Whatever your career direction, entrepreneurship—corporate employer—nonprofit manager, there's one thing to be sure about—the future is yours. But, you have to go after it; you have to keep developing and even reinventing yourself with every passing day. This book and your management course offer many ways to explore your career skills and capabilities. Why not take good advantage of the opportunity? The timing is right. What happens next is up to you!

do the benchmarking

You don't need to create your own company in order to achieve career success. What you must do, however, is discover the learning "monster" within yourself. Look around and identify positive role models. Tap your full potential by investing your talents to achieve both academic success and career development. **Remind yourself every day that smart people create their own futures!**

Learning **A**bout **Y**ourself

Self-Awareness

When it comes to doing well as a student and in a career, a lot rests on how well you know yourself and what you do with this knowledge. **Self-Awareness** helps us build on strengths and overcome weaknesses, and it helps us avoid tendencies toward self-enhancement— viewing ourselves more favorably than is justified. Although an important career skill, self-awareness can be easy to talk about but hard to master.[4]

What do you really know about yourself? How often do you take a critical look at your attitudes, behaviors, skills, personal characteristics, and accomplishments? Do you ever realistically assess your strengths and weaknesses from a career perspective—both as you see them and as others do? After all, how others perceive us can sometimes be more accurate than our own assessment.

This figure, called the *Johari Window,* offers a way of comparing what we know about ourselves with what others know about us.[5] The "open" areas known to ourselves and others are often small. The "blind spot," "the unknown," and the "hidden" areas can be quite large; they challenge our willingness and capacities for self-discovery.

There are lots of personal insights available in the Johari Window. But to gain them you must be willing to open up to the perceptions of others, probe the unknown, and uncover your blind spots.

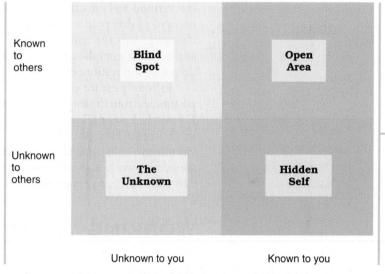

A high degree of self-awareness is essential for personal adaptability, to be able to learn, grow, and develop in changing times. It sets a strong foundation for stepping forward and making adjustments so that we can always move confidently toward the future. But remember that true self-awareness means not just knowing your idealized self, the person you want or hope to be. It also means knowing who you really are as defined by your actions.

get to know yourself better

Put the Johari Window to work by thinking about your career skills and personal characteristics. Make notes about your "Open Area" and "Hidden Self." Try to confront "The Unknown" by speculating what might be listed there. Ask friends, family members, and co-workers to comment on your "Blind Spot." Analyze the results in a short self-reflection paper that sets goals for personal and professional development. **Also take advantage of the end-of-chapter Self-Assessment feature to further reflect on your self-awareness and career readiness.**

Study Question 1	Study Question 2	Study Question 3	Study Question 4	Study Question 5
Working Today	**Organizations**	**Managers**	**The Management Process**	**Learning How to Manage**
• Talent • Technology • Globalization • Ethics • Diversity • Careers	• What is an organization? • Organizations as systems • Organizational performance • Changing nature of organizations	• What is a manager? • Levels of managers • Types of managers • Managerial performance • Changing nature of managerial work	• Management functions • Managerial roles and activities • Managerial agendas and networks	• Essential managerial skills • Developing managerial skills and competencies
Learning Check 1	**Learning Check 2**	**Learning Check 3**	**Learning Check 4**	**Learning Check 5**

Welcome to *Management 11/e* and its themes of personal development and career readiness. We live and work in a very complex world. Job scarcities, ethical miscues by business and government leaders, financial turmoil and uncertainties, great environmental challenges, complex economics, and global politics are regularly in the news. Today's organizations are fast changing, as is the nature of work itself. In most jobs learning, quality, and speed are in; habit, complacency, and even security are out. And, the global economy is driven by innovation, cost competitiveness, and high technology.

In your quest for career success, you must learn how to sort the really good opportunities from the mediocre and even bad ones. As described by James O'Toole and Edward E. Lawler III in their book *The New American Workplace*,[6] the best employers value people! They provide creative and inspiring leadership and supportive work environments built around themes of respect, participation, empowerment, involvement, teamwork, and self-management. All of this, and more, is what *Management 11/e* and your management course are about.

WORKING TODAY

We've just lived through a major recession in which unemployment was the highest it's been in 25 years. There are few guarantees of long-term employment, and jobs are increasingly earned and re-earned every day through one's performance accomplishments. Careers are being redefined along the lines of "flexibility," "free agency," "skill portfolios," and "entrepreneurship." Amidst it all, the pathways of career advancement demand lots of initiative and self awareness, as well as continuous learning. The question is: Are you ready?

TALENT

In a study of high-performing companies, management scholars Charles O'Reilly and Jeffrey Pfeffer report that they achieve success by being better than competitors at getting extraordinary results from the people working for them. "These companies have won the war for talent," they say, "not just by being great places to work—although they are that—but by figuring out how to get the best out of all of their people, every day."[7]

People and their talents—what they know, what they learn, and what they do with it—are the ultimate foundations of organizational performance. They represent what managers call **intellectual capital**, the collective brainpower or shared

Intellectual capital is the collective brainpower or shared knowledge of a workforce.

knowledge of a workforce that can be used to create value.[8] For organizations, intellectual capital is a strategic asset. It is the pathway to performance through human creativity, insight, and decision making. For individuals, intellectual capital is a personal asset. It is the package of intellect, skills, and capabilities that differentiates us from others and that makes us valuable to potential employers.

When we talk in the chapter openers about getting to know yourself better, the focus is really on developing your intellectual capital. Think about it in terms of this **intellectual capital equation**: Intellectual Capital = Competency × Commitment.[9] Competency represents your talents or job-relevant capabilities, while commitment represents your willingness to work hard in applying them to important tasks. Both are essential; one without the other is not enough to meet anyone's career needs or any organization's performance requirements.

Max DePree, former CEO of the innovative furniture maker Herman Miller once said: "Being successful is meeting goals in a good way—being exceptional is reaching your potential."[10] To be exceptional you must be willing to reach for the heights of personal accomplishment in a workplace now dominated by **knowledge workers**—persons whose minds, not just their physical capabilities, are critical assets.[11] Futurist Daniel Pink says that we are entering the *conceptual age* which belongs to people with "whole mind" competencies that are both "high concept"—creative and good with ideas, and "high touch"—joyful and good with relationships.[12] Management scholar and consultant Gary Hamel says we have a *creative economy* "where even knowledge itself is becoming a commodity" and "the most important differentiator will be how fast you can create something new."[13] Such challenges will be best mastered by those who develop multiple skill sets that always keep personal competencies well aligned with emerging job trends.[14]

> ● The **Intellectual Capital Equation states:** Intellectual Capital = Competency × Commitment.

> ● A **knowledge worker** is someone whose mind is a critical asset to employers.

TECHNOLOGY

Technology is continuously testing our talents. We are well into the expanded social media universe of Web 2.0, and you might be reading this book on an Amazon Kindle or iPad. What will it be tomorrow?

It is essential to build and maintain what we might call a high **Tech IQ**—a person's ability to use technology at work and everyday living, and a commitment to stay informed on the latest technological developments.[15] Tech IQ is required in basic operations of organizations, whether one is checking inventory, making a sales transaction, ordering supplies, or analyzing customer preferences. It is required in new ways of working as more and more people spend at least part of their work time "telecommuting" or "working from home" or in "mobile offices" that free them from the constraints of the normal "8–5" schedules. It is also

> ● **Tech IQ** is ability to use technology and commitment to stay informed on the latest technological developments.

Teach for America Is Worth a Look

Teach for America was founded by Wendy Kopp and based on ideas described in her undergraduate thesis at Princeton University. The nonprofit organization's mission "is to build the movement to eliminate educational inequity by enlisting our nation's most promising future leaders in the effort." Teach for America recruits recent college graduates to serve for two years as teachers in urban and rural public schools. Over 4,000 new teachers joined the corps in 2010. Kopp says: "We believe that education is the great enabler [and that] it's the foundation for life opportunity."

required in the rapidly growing numbers of "virtual teams" whose members hold meetings, access common databases, share information and files, make plans, and solve problems together—all without ever meeting face to face.

Even the process of job seeking and employment screening is increasingly technology driven. The chapter opener introduced Monster.com and LinkedIn.com as online career sites used by job hunters and employers. To take advantage you have to be online and also use the right protocols—Tech IQ again.[16] Poor communication like "Hey dude, you got any jobs in California?" doesn't work in the world of electronic job searches.[17] But, filling your online profile with the right key words does work; many employers even use special software to scan online profiles for indicators of real job skills and experiences that fit their needs.[18] And don't forget, some 44% or more of recruiters say they are now checking social media sites to spot negative indicators about their job applicants.[19]

GLOBALIZATION

Japanese management consultant Kenichi Ohmae points out that the national boundaries of world business have largely disappeared.[20] At last count there were some 5.3 million or 3.5% of Americans working in the United States for foreign employers.[21] We buy foreign cars like Toyota, Nissan, and Mercedes-Benz that are assembled in America. We buy appliances from the Chinese firm Haier and Eight O'Clock Coffee from India's Tata Group. Top managers at Starbucks, IBM, Sony, Ford, and other global corporations have little need for the word "overseas" or "international" in everyday business vocabulary. They operate as global businesses that serve customers and suppliers wherever in the world they may be located, and that hire talent from around the world wherever it may be available at the lowest costs.

● **Globalization** is the worldwide interdependence of resource flows, product markets, and business competition.

These are among the many faces of **globalization**, the worldwide interdependence of resource flows, product markets, and business competition that characterizes our economy. It is a process in which "improvements in technology—especially in communications and transportation, combine with the deregulation of markets and open borders to bring about vastly expanded flows of people, money, goods, services, and information."[22] In our global world, government leaders now worry about the competitiveness of nations, just as corporate leaders worry about business competitiveness.[23] Countries and people are not just interconnected through the news, in travel, and lifestyles; they are interconnected in labor markets and employment patterns, and in financial and business dealings.

Salesforce.com Puts Software in Cloud

Cloud computing, or software and storage on demand through the Internet, is the power behind Salesforce.com. Created by Marc Neioff and a colleague in a San Francisco apartment, the firm provides software that companies use to track potential customers, keep track of existing ones, and track sales performance. The beauty is that all is done "in the cloud" with no required software resident on company computers. This means users save on costs and complications. Also, the products keep getting better as Salesforce.com constantly seeks feedback from its users and tweaks products to best fit their needs.

Coke's Secret Formula a Tantalizer

Scene: *Corporate headquarters of PepsiCo.* A young executive is gesturing excitedly, and three more obviously senior ones listen attentively. The CEO sits at her desk, swiveling occasionally in the chair while listening carefully to the conversation.

YOUNG EXECUTIVE, *acting a bit proud to be there*

It started with a telephone call. I agreed to meet with a former employee of Coca-Cola at his request. We met and, lo and behold, he offered me the "secret formula."

ONE OF THE SENIOR EXECUTIVES, *cautiously*

Let me be sure I understand. You received a call from someone who said they used to work at Coke, and that person was requesting a face-to-face meeting. Correct?

YOUNG EXECUTIVE, *quickly and proudly*

Right!

THE SENIOR EXECUTIVE, *with a bit of challenge*

Why? Why would you meet with someone that said they just left Coke?

Young EXECUTIVE, *tentative now*

Well . . . I . . . uh . . . It seemed like a great chance to get some competitive information and maybe even hire someone who really knows their strategies.

SECOND SENIOR EXECUTIVE

So, what happened next?

YOUNG EXECUTIVE, *excited again*

Well, after just a minute or two conversing, he said that he had the formula!

SECOND SENIOR EXECUTIVE

AND . . .?

YOUNG EXECUTIVE, *uncertain all of a sudden and now speaking softly*

He said it was "for sale."

THIRD SENIOR EXECUTIVE, *with a bit of edge in her voice*

So what did you say?

YOUNG EXECUTIVE, *looking down and shuffling slightly backward*

I said that I'd take it "up the ladder." I'm supposed to call him back . . .

CEO, *breaking into the conversation*

And we're glad you did "bring it up the ladder," as you say. But now that you have, what do you propose we do about this opportunity to buy Coke's most important secret?

As CEO speaks, other senior executives move over to stand behind her. Everyone looks in the direction of the young executive.

You Decide

This young executive's career prospects might depend on his answer. What do you think he will recommend? Perhaps more importantly, what would you do? What are the key ethical tradeoffs that need to be considered here?

Author Thomas Friedman summarizes globalization in these comments by one of India's business entrepreneurs: "Any activity where we can digitize and decompose the value chain, and move the work around, will get moved around."[24] At a time when more Americans find that their customer service call is answered in Ghana, their CAT scan read by a radiologist in India, and their tax return prepared by an accountant in the Philippines, the fact that globalization offers both opportunities and challenges is quite clear indeed.

ETHICS

When Bernard Madoff was sentenced to 150 years in jail for a fraudulent Ponzi scheme that cost investors billions of dollars, the message was crystal clear: Commit white-collar crime and you will be punished.[25] His crime did terrible harm to individuals who lost lifelong and retirement savings, foundations that lost millions in charitable gifts, and employees who lost jobs. If this was a unique or limited case of bad behavior by business executives, it would be one thing, but the problem is bigger. Almost every week we learn about more scandals affecting banks and other financial institutions, as well as businesses and organizations of many other types.

● **Ethics** set moral standards of what is "good" and "right" in one's behavior.

The issue raised here goes beyond criminal behavior to embrace the broader notion of **ethics**—a code of moral principles that sets standards for what is "good" and "right" as opposed to "bad" and "wrong" in the conduct of a person or group.[26] At the end of the day we depend on individual people, working at all levels of organizations, to act ethically in all aspects of their jobs and in all their working relationships.

In his book *The Transparent Leader*, the former CEO of Dial Corporation, Herb Baum argues that integrity is a key to leadership success and that the responsibility for setting the ethical tone of an organization begins at the top. Believing that most CEOs are overpaid, he once gave his annual bonus to the firm's lowest paid workers. Baum also tells the story of a rival CEO, Reuben Mark, of Colgate Palmolive. Mark called him one day to say that a newly hired executive had brought to Colgate a disk containing Dial's new marketing campaign. Rather than read it, he returned the disk to Baum—an act Baum called "the clearest case of leading with honor and transparency I've witnessed in my career."[27]

Chapter 3 is devoted to topics of ethics and social responsibility in management, and Chapter 4 extends the discussion to issues of environment and sustainability. Elsewhere, you will find this book full of people and organizations that are exemplars of ethical behavior and integrity. And, each chapter has a Real Ethics feature—see "Coke's Secret Formula"—that helps you to think through and consider ethical challenges from everyday life and work situations.

DIVERSITY

● **Workforce diversity** describes differences among workers in gender, race, age, ethnicity, religion, sexual orientation, and able–bodiedness.

The term **workforce diversity** describes the composition of a workforce in terms of such differences among people as gender, age, race, ethnicity, religion, sexual orientation, and able-bodiedness.[28] Diversity trends of changing demographics in society are well recognized. Minorities now constitute more than one-third of the U.S. population, and the proportion is growing. The U.S. Census Bureau predicts that by 2050 whites will be in the minority, and the combined populations of African American, American Indians, Asians, and Hispanics will be the new majority. By 2030 more than 20% of the population will be aged 65+ years, and right now women may already outnumber men in the U.S. workforce.[29]

Even though our society is diverse, the way we deal with diversity in the workplace remains an issue. Women now lead global companies like PepsiCo, Xerox, and Kraft, but they hold only 2% of top jobs in American firms and 5% in Great Britain.[30] Why do so few women make it to the top?[31] And, what about people of color? In a research study, résumés with white-sounding first names, such as Brett, received 50% more responses from potential employers than those with black-sounding first names, such as Kareem.[32] Why? Given that the résumés were created equal, do the results show diversity bias?

● **Prejudice** is the display of negative, irrational attitudes toward members of diverse populations.

Prejudice, or the holding of negative, irrational opinions and attitudes regarding members of diverse populations, sets the stage for diversity bias. An example is prejudice that still lingers against working mothers. The nonprofit Families and Work Institute reports that in 1977 only 49% of men and 71% of women believed that mothers can be good employees; by 2008 the figures had risen to 67% and 80%, respectively.[33] Don't you wonder why the figures aren't 100% in support of working mothers?

● **Discrimination** actively denies minority members the full benefits of organizational membership.

Prejudice becomes active **discrimination** when minority members are unfairly treated and denied the full benefits of organizational membership. An example is when a manager fabricates reasons not to interview a minority job candidate, or refuses to promote a working mother on the belief that "she has too many parenting responsibilities to do a good job at this level." Such thinking underlies a subtle form of discrimination called the **glass ceiling effect**, an invisible barrier or "ceiling" that prevents women and minorities from rising above a certain level of organizational

● The **glass ceiling effect** is an invisible barrier limiting career advancement of women and minorities.

responsibility. Scholar Judith Rosener warns that the loss caused by any form of discriminatory practices is "undervalued and underutilized human capital."[34]

A female vice president at Avon once posed the diversity challenge this way: "Consciously creating an environment where everyone has an equal shot at contributing, participating, and most of all advancing."[35] And, many voices call diversity a "business imperative," meaning that today's increasingly diverse and multicultural workforce should be an asset that, if tapped, creates opportunities for performance gains. Even with such awareness existing, consultant R. Roosevelt Thomas says that too many employers still address diversity with the goal of "making their numbers," rather than truly valuing and managing diversity.[36]

CAREERS

For most college students, an immediate challenge is getting the first full-time job. Especially when the economy is down and employment markets are tight, the task of finding a career entry point can be daunting. It always pays to remember the importance of online résumés and job searches, and the power of social networking with established professionals. It's also helpful to pursue internships as pathways to first-job placements. Picture yourself in an interview situation. The person sitting across the table is asking this question: "What can you do for us?" How do you reply?

Today's career challenge isn't just finding your first job; it's also about successful career planning. British scholar and consultant Charles Handy uses the analogy of the **shamrock organization** to describe the implications.[37] The first leaf in the shamrock is a core group of permanent, full-time employees who follow standard career paths. And, the number of people in this first leaf is shrinking.[38] They are being replaced in part by a second leaf consisting of "freelancers" and "independent contractors" that provide organizations with specialized skills and talents on a contract basis, and then change employers when projects are completed.[39] Full-time employees are also being replaced by a growing third leaf of temporary part-timers. They often work without benefits and are the first to lose their jobs when an employer runs into economic difficulties.

If current trends continue, you will have to succeed in a **free-agent economy** where people change jobs more often and work on flexible contracts with a shifting mix of employers over time. This means skills like those in Management Smarts 1.1 must be up-to-date, portable, and always of value.[40] Job skills can't be gained once and then forgotten; they must be carefully maintained and upgraded all the time. This once again places a premium on your capacity for **self-management**, being able to realistically assess yourself and actively manage your personal development.

● A **shamrock organization** operates with a core group of full-time long-term workers supported by others who work on contracts and part-time.

● In a **free-agent economy** people change jobs more often, and many work on independent contracts with a shifting mix of employers.

● **Self-management** is the ability to understand oneself, exercise initiative, accept responsibility, and learn from experience.

Management Smarts 1.1

Early career survival skills

Mastery: You need to be good at something; you need to be able to contribute something of value to your employer.

Networking: You need to know people; links with peers and others within and outside the organization are essential to get things done.

Entrepreneurship: You must act as if you are running your own business, spotting ideas and opportunities and acting to embrace them.

Love of technology: You have to embrace technology; you must be willing and able to fully utilize what becomes newly available.

Marketing: You need to be able to communicate your successes and progress, both yours personally and those of your work team.

Passion for renewal: You need to be continuously learning and changing, always updating yourself to best meet future demands.

Be sure you can ☑ describe how intellectual capital, ethics, diversity, globalization, technology, and the changing nature of careers influence working in the new economy ☑ define *intellectual capital, workforce diversity,* and *globalization* ☑ explain how prejudice, discrimination, and the glass ceiling can hurt people at work

Learning Check ☑

Study Question 1
What are the challenges of working today?

ORGANIZATIONS IN THE NEW WORKPLACE

As pointed out earlier, what happens from this point forward in your career is largely up to you. So, let's start with organizations. In order to make good employment choices and perform well in a career, you need to understand the nature of organizations and how they work as complex systems.

WHAT IS AN ORGANIZATION?

● An **organization** is a collection of people working together to achieve a common purpose.

An **organization** is a collection of people working together to achieve a common purpose. It is a unique social phenomenon that enables its members to perform tasks far beyond the reach of individual accomplishment. This description applies to organizations of all sizes and types that make up the life of any community, from large corporations to small businesses, and nonprofit organizations such as schools, government agencies, and community hospitals.

The broad purpose of any organization is to provide goods or services of value to customers and clients. Indeed, a clear sense of purpose tied to "quality products and services," "customer satisfaction," and "social responsibility" is an important source of organizational strength and performance advantage. At Skype, founders Niklas Zennstrom and Janus Friis began with a straightforward sense of purpose: They wanted the whole world to be able to talk by telephone for free. When you open Skype on your computer and notice millions of users making calls, you'll see the appeal of what Zennstrom and Friis set out to accomplish. And when you shop at Whole Foods, the influence of founder John Mackey's values on his company's purpose are also obvious. "I think that business has a noble purpose," he says. "It means that businesses serve society. They produce goods and services that make people's lives better." On the Whole Foods website this is stated as a commitment to "Whole Foods—Whole People—Whole Planet."[41]

ORGANIZATIONS AS SYSTEMS

● An **open system** transforms resource inputs from the environment into product outputs.

All organizations are **open systems** that interact with their environments. They do so in a continual process of obtaining resource inputs—people, information, resources, and capital, and transforming them into outputs in the form of finished goods and services for customers.[42]

As shown in Figure 1.1, feedback from the environment indicates how well an organization is doing and provides opportunities for constructive adjustments. When Starbucks started a customer blog, for example, requests for speedier service quickly popped up. The company made changes that included eliminating customer signatures on credit card charges less than $25. Salesforce.com is another

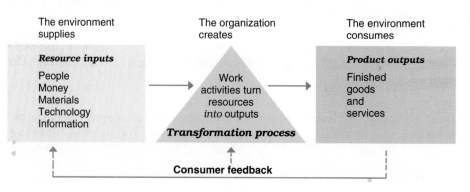

FIGURE 1.1 Organizations as open systems interacting with their environments.

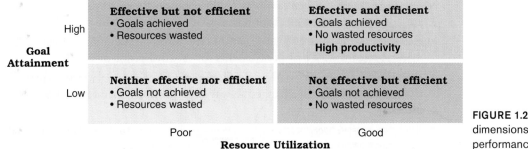

FIGURE 1.2 Productivity and the dimensions of organizational performance.

company that thrives on feedback. Featured in an earlier photo essay, it uses a website called IdeaExchange to get customer suggestions, even asking them at one point to vote on a possible name change—the response was "No!"[43] Gathering and listening to such feedback is important; when customers stop buying a firm's products it is hard to stay in business for long unless something soon changes for the better. Anytime you hear or read about bankruptcies, they are stark testimonies to this fact of the marketplace: Without loyal customers, a business can't survive.

ORGANIZATIONAL PERFORMANCE

Using resources well and serving customers is a process of value creation through organizational performance. When operations add value to the original cost of resource inputs, then (1) a business organization can earn a profit—that is, sell a product for more than the costs of making it—or (2) a nonprofit organization can add wealth to society—that is, provide a public service like fire protection that is worth more than its cost. One of the most common ways to assess performance by and within organizations is **productivity**. It measures the quantity and quality of outputs relative to the cost of inputs. And as Figure 1.2 shows, productivity involves two common performance dimensions: effectiveness and efficiency.

Performance effectiveness is an output measure of task or goal accomplishment. If you are working as a software engineer for a computer game developer, performance effectiveness may mean that you meet a daily production target in terms of the quantity and quality of lines of code written. This productivity helps the company meet customer demands for timely delivery of high-quality gaming products.

Performance efficiency is an input measure of the resource costs associated with goal accomplishment. Returning to the gaming example, the most efficient software production is accomplished at a minimum cost in materials and labor. If you are producing fewer lines of code in a day than you are capable of, this amounts to inefficiency; if you make a lot of mistakes that require extensive rewrites, this is also inefficient work. All such inefficiencies drive up costs and reduce productivity.

● **Productivity** is the quantity and quality of work performance, with resource utilization considered.

● **Performance effectiveness** is an output measure of task or goal accomplishment.

● **Performance efficiency** is an input measure of resource cost associated with goal accomplishment.

CHANGING NATURE OF ORGANIZATIONS

Change is a continuing theme in society at large, and organizations are certainly undergoing dramatic changes today. Although not exhaustive, the following list of organizational trends and transitions is relevant to your study of management.[44]

- *Renewed belief in human capital:* The premium is on high-involvement work settings that rally the knowledge, experience, and commitment of all members.

- *Demise of "command-and-control":* Traditional top-down "do as I say" bosses are giving way to participatory bosses that treat people with respect.
- *Emphasis on teamwork:* Organizations are more horizontal in focus, and driven by teamwork that pools talents for creative problem solving.
- *Preeminence of technology:* New developments in computer and information technology continually change the way organizations operate and how people work.
- *Importance of networking:* Organizations and their members are networked for intense, real-time communication and coordination.
- *New workforce expectations:* A new generation of workers is less tolerant of hierarchy, more informal, attentive to performance merit, and concerned for work-life balance.
- *Valuing sustainability:* Issues of sustainability direct attention toward the environment and climate justice, preservation of natural resources for future generations, and how work affects human well-being.

Learning Check

Study Question 2

What are organizations like in the new workplace?

Be sure you can ☑ describe how organizations operate as open systems ☑ explain productivity as a measure of organizational performance ☑ distinguish between performance effectiveness and performance efficiency ☑ list several ways in which organizations are changing today

MANAGERS IN THE NEW WORKPLACE

This chapter opened with an emphasis on people, their talents, and intellectual capital, as key foundations of organizational success. In an article entitled "Putting People First for Organizational Success," Jeffrey Pfeffer and John F. Veiga argue forcefully that organizations perform better when they treat their members better.[45] "Managers" in these high-performing organizations don't treat people as costs to be controlled; they treat them as valuable strategic assets to be carefully nurtured and developed. So, who are these managers and just what do they do?

WHAT IS A MANAGER?

● A **manager** is a person who supports, activates, and is responsible for the work of others.

You find them in all organizations. They work with a wide variety of job titles—team leader, department head, supervisor, project manager, president, administrator, and more. We call them **managers**, people in organizations who directly support, supervise, and help activate the work efforts and performance accomplishments of others.[46] Whether they are called direct reports, team members, work associates, or subordinates, these "other people" are the essential human resources whose contributions represent the real work of the organization. And as pointed out by management theorist Henry Mintzberg, being a manager remains an important and socially responsible job.

No job is more vital to our society than that of the manager. It is the manager who determines whether our social institutions serve us well or whether they squander our talents and resources. It is time to strip away the folklore about managerial work, and time to study it realistically so that we can begin the difficult task of making significant improvement in its performance.[47]

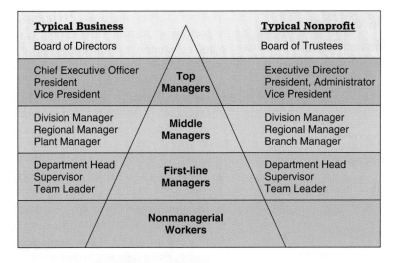

LEVELS OF MANAGERS

At the highest levels of business organizations, as shown in Figure 1.3, we find a **board of directors** whose members are elected by stockholders to represent their ownership interests. In nonprofit organizations such as a hospital or university, this level is often called a *board of trustees,* and it may be elected by local citizens, appointed by government bodies, or invited by existing members. In both business and the public sector, the basic responsibilities of board members are the same—to oversee the performance of the organization and make sure that it is always being run right.

Just below the board level, common job titles are chief executive officer (CEO), chief operating officer (COO), chief financial officer (CFO), chief information officer (CIO), president, and vice president. These **top managers** constitute an executive team that reports to the board and is responsible for the performance of an organization as a whole or for one of its larger parts.

Top managers are supposed to set strategy and lead the organization consistent with its purpose and mission. They should pay special attention to the external environment and be alert to potential long-run problems and opportunities. Procter & Gamble's former CEO, A.G. Lafley, says the job of top managers is to "link the external world with the internal organization . . . make sure the voice of the consumer is heard . . . shape values and standards." The best top managers are strategic thinkers able to make good decisions under highly competitive and even uncertain conditions. As Lafley points out, they have to be constantly "balancing the need for performance in the short term with the need to invest for the longer term."[48]

Reporting to top managers are **middle managers** that are in charge of relatively large departments or divisions consisting of several smaller work units. Examples are clinic directors in hospitals; deans in universities; and division managers, plant managers, and regional sales managers in businesses. Middle managers work with top managers, coordinate with peers, and support lower levels to develop and pursue action plans that implement organizational strategies to accomplish key objectives.

A first job in management typically involves serving as a **team leader** or supervisor—someone in charge of a small work group composed of nonmanagerial workers. Typical job titles at this level include department head, team leader, and supervisor. For example, the leader of an auditing team is considered a first-line manager as is the head of an academic department in a university. Even though most people enter the workforce as technical specialists such as engineer, market researcher, or systems analyst, sooner or later they often advance to positions of initial managerial responsibility. And they serve key performance roles.[49]

● Members of a **board of directors** or board of trustees are supposed to make sure an organization is run right.

● **Top managers** guide the performance of the organization as a whole or of one of its major parts.

● **Middle managers** oversee the work of large departments or divisions.

● **Team leaders** report to middle managers and supervise nonmanagerial workers.

Management Smarts 1.2

Ten responsibilities of team leaders

1. Plan meetings and work schedules.
2. Clarify goals and tasks, and gather ideas for improvement.
3. Appraise performance and counsel team members.
4. Recommend pay increases and new assignments.
5. Recruit, train, and develop team members.
6. Encourage high performance and teamwork.
7. Inform team members about organizational goals.
8. Inform higher levels of team needs and accomplishments.
9. Coordinate activities with other teams.
10. Support team members in all aspects of their work.

● **Line managers** directly contribute to producing the organization's goods or services.

● **Staff managers** use special technical expertise to advise and support line workers.

● **Functional managers** are responsible for one area such as finance, marketing, production, personnel, accounting, or sales.

● **General managers** are responsible for complex, multifunctional units.

● An **administrator** is a manager in a public or nonprofit organization.

● **Accountability** is the requirement to show performance results to a supervisor.

● **Corporate governance** occurs when a board of directors holds top management accountable for organizational performance.

● An **effective manager** helps others achieve high performance and satisfaction at work.

● **Quality of work life** is the overall quality of human experiences in the workplace.

At the large medical technology firm Medtronics, Justine Fritz led a 12-member team to launch a life-altering product. She says, "I've just never worked on anything that so visibly, so dramatically changes the quality of someone's life."[50] Management Smarts 1.2 offers useful advice on the basic responsibilities of team leaders and other first-line managers.

TYPES OF MANAGERS

In addition to serving at different levels of authority, managers work in different capacities within organizations. **Line managers** are responsible for work that makes a direct contribution to the organization's outputs. For example, the president, retail manager, and department supervisors of a local department store all have line responsibilities. Their jobs in one way or another are directly related to the sales operations of the store. **Staff managers**, by contrast, head units that use special technical expertise to advise and support the efforts of line workers. In a department store chain, the director of human resources and chief financial officer would have staff responsibilities.

In business, **functional managers** have responsibility for a single area of activity such as finance, marketing, production, human resources, accounting, or sales. **General managers** are responsible for activities covering many functional areas. An example is a plant manager who oversees purchasing, manufacturing, warehousing, sales, personnel, and accounting functions. In public or nonprofit organizations, it is common for managers to be called **administrators**. Examples include hospital administrators, public administrators, and city administrators.

MANAGERIAL PERFORMANCE

All managers help people, working individually and in teams, to perform. They do this while being personally "accountable" for results achieved. **Accountability** is the requirement of one person to answer to a higher authority for performance results in his or her area of work responsibility.

In the traditional organizational pyramid, accountability flows upward. The team leader is accountable to a middle manager, the middle manager is accountable to a top manager, and even the top manager is accountable to a board of directors or board of trustees. This was demonstrated when the board at General Motors removed Fritz Henderson as CEO of the firm after only eight months on the job. The board was not satisfied with GM's progress after emerging from bankruptcy. Other members of the top management team were removed as well. Board Chairman Ed Whitacre said: "I want to give people more responsibility and authority deeper in the organization and then hold them accountable."[51] Whether the GM board turns out to be right or wrong in its decisions, it was trying to fulfill its responsibility for **corporate governance**. This occurs when the board holds top management accountable for organizational performance.

But what, you might ask, actually constitutes excellence in managerial performance? When is a manager "effective"? A good answer is that **effective managers** successfully help others achieve both high performance *and* satisfaction in their work. This dual concern for performance and satisfaction introduces the concept of **quality of work life** as an indicator of the overall quality of human experiences at work. A "high-QWL" workplace offers such things as fair pay, safe working conditions, opportunities to learn and use new skills, room to grow and progress in a career, and protection of individual rights and wellness.

Scholar Jeffrey Pfeffer has recently argued that such QWL issues should be part of societal concerns for "sustainability" practices in organizations, something discussed in Chapter 4. Why, Pfeffer asks, don't we add to our concerns for natural environment sustainability further concerns for human sustainability and "organizational effects on employee health and mortality"?[52] In the present context we can ask more specifically: Should managers be held accountable not just for performance accomplished in their areas of supervisory responsibility, but also for the impact of their behavior and practices on human sustainability among those who work with and for them? In other words, shouldn't productivity and quality of working life go hand in hand?

CHANGING NATURE OF MANAGERIAL WORK

Cindy Zollinger, president and CEO of Cornerstone Research, directly supervises over 20 people. But she says: "I don't really manage them in a typical way; they largely run themselves. I help them in dealing with obstacles they face, or in making the most of opportunities they find."[53] As Cindy's comments suggest, we are in a time when the best managers are known more for "helping" and "supporting" than for "directing" and "order giving." The words "coordinator," "coach," and "team leader" are heard as often as "supervisor" or "boss." The best managers are well informed regarding the needs of those reporting to or dependent on them. They can often be found providing advice and developing the support needed for others to perform to the best of their abilities.

The concept of the **upside-down pyramid** shown in Figure 1.4 fits well with the changing mindset of managerial work today. Notice that the operating and front-line workers are at the top of the upside-down pyramid, just below the customers and clients they serve. They are supported in their work efforts by managers below them. These managers clearly aren't just order-givers; they are there to mobilize and deliver the support others need to do their jobs best and serve

● The **upside-down pyramid** view of organizations shows customers at the top being served by workers who are supported by managers.

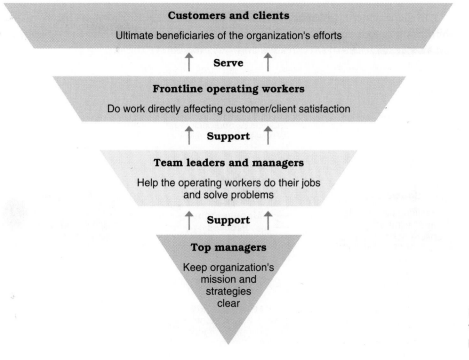

FIGURE 1.4 The organization viewed as an upside-down pyramid.

customer needs. Sitting at the bottom are top managers and executives; their jobs are to support the work of everyone above them. The upside-down pyramid view leaves no doubt that the whole organization is devoted to serving customers and that the job of managers is to support the workers.

THE MANAGEMENT PROCESS

● The **management process** is planning, organizing, leading, and controlling the use of resources to accomplish performance goals.

If productivity in the form of high levels of performance effectiveness and efficiency is a measure of organizational success, managers are largely responsible for its achievement. The ultimate "bottom line" in every manager's job is to help an organization achieve high performance by best utilizing its human and material resources. This is accomplished through the four functions of management that together constitute what is called the **management process** of planning, organizing, leading, and controlling.

FUNCTIONS OF MANAGEMENT

The four management functions of planning, organizing, leading, and controlling, and their interrelationships, are shown in Figure 1.5. All managers, regardless of title, level, type, and organizational setting, are responsible for the four functions. However, they are not accomplished in a linear, step-by-step fashion. The reality is that these functions are continually engaged as a manager moves from task to task and opportunity to opportunity in his or her work.

Planning

● **Planning** is the process of setting objectives and determining what should be done to accomplish them.

In management, **planning** is the process of setting performance objectives and determining what actions should be taken to accomplish them. Through planning, a manager identifies desired results and ways to achieve them.

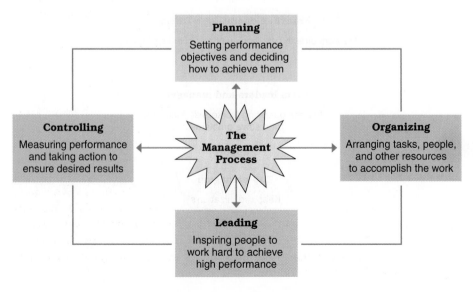

FIGURE 1.5 Four functions of management—planning, organizing, leading, and controlling.

Indra Nooyi leads Pepsi with talent, style, and a sharp eye

The *Financial Times* calls her one of the top women business leaders in the world. But the best advice she ever got, says Indra Nooyi, PepsiCo's Chairman and CEO, came from her father. Calling him "an absolutely wonderful human being" she says: "From him I learned to always assume positive intent. Whatever anybody says or does, assume positive intent. You will be amazed at how your whole approach to a person or problem becomes very different . . . You are trying to understand and listen because at your basic core you are saying, 'Maybe they are saying something to me that I am not hearing'."

That advice has carried Nooyi to the top ranks of global business—only the 12th woman to head a Fortune 500 firm at the time of her appointment. It's also taken her a long way from her early years in Chennai, India, and her first university degree in chemistry. After coming to the U.S., a country she says "likes to see others succeed," she earned a Master in Management from Yale before joining the Boston Consulting Group. She eventually ended up at PepsiCo where in just 12 years she moved through a variety of management positions to become the CEO.

BusinessWeek describes her "prescient business sense" as behind many of the firm's strategic and successful moves, including the spin off of its fast food businesses Taco Bell,

Pizza Hut, and KFC, a merger with Quaker Oats, and the purchase of Tropicana. Through it all Nooyi has maintained a style and presence that allows her personality to shine. Former CEO Roger Enrico says "Indra can drive as deep and hard as anyone I've ever met, but she can do it with a sense of heart and fun." ABC News described her as a blend of "Indian culture mixed in with the traditional American working mom."

There is no doubt that Nooyi is facing many challenges in leading her firm forward in the global economic turmoil. She refuses to think negative and says that CEOs should be realistic and visible during bad times, while communicating a sense of realism combined with confidence that the right moves will be taken for the future. Among her initiatives is a push toward healthier snacks and beverage selections, as well as a commitment to environmental sustainability. She believes that the bottom line of business should be redefined to focus on profits after costs to society have been deducted; "that's your real profit," she says.

Take, for example, an Ernst & Young initiative that was developed to better meet the needs of the firm's female professionals. This initiative grew out of top management's concern about the firm's retention rates for women.[54] Then-chairman Philip A. Laskawy launched a Diversity Task Force with the planning objective to reduce turnover rates for women. When the task force began its work, this turnover was running some 22% per year, and it cost the firm about 150% of a departing employee's annual salary to hire and train each replacement. Laskawy considered this performance unacceptable and put plans in place to improve it.

Organizing

Once plans are set, they must be implemented. This begins with **organizing**, the process of assigning tasks, allocating resources, and coordinating the activities of individuals and groups to accomplish plans. Organizing is how managers turn plans into actions by defining jobs, assigning personnel, and supporting them with technology and other resources.

At Ernst & Young, Laskawy organized by convening and personally chairing a Diversity Task Force to meet his planning objective. He also established a new Office of Retention and hired Deborah K. Holmes, now serving as global director of corporate responsibility, to head it. As retention problems were identified in various parts of the firm, Holmes also organized special task forces to tackle them and recommend location-specific solutions.

● **Organizing** is the process of assigning tasks, allocating resources, and coordinating work activities.

Research Brief

Worldwide Study Identifies Success Factors in Global Leadership

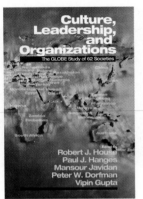

Robert J. House and colleagues developed a network of 170 researchers to study leadership around the world. Over a 10-year period they investigated cultural frameworks, cultural differences, and their leadership implications as part of Project GLOBE. The results are summarized in the book *Culture, Leadership and Organizations: The GLOBE Study of 62 Societies.*

Data from over 17,000 managers working in 62 national cultures were collected and analyzed. The researchers found that the world's cultures do have some differences in what constitutes leadership effectiveness. But they also share some universal facilitators to leadership success—such as leaders being honest and trustworthy, and impediments—such as leaders being self-protective and dictatorial. In terms of leadership development, the GLOBE researchers concluded that global mind-sets, tolerance for ambiguity, cultural adaptability, and flexibility are essential as leaders seek to influence persons whose cultural backgrounds are different from their own. Personal aspects that seemed most culturally sensitive in terms of leadership effectiveness were being individualist, being status conscious, and being open to risk.

You Be the Researcher

Take a survey of workers at your university, your place of employment, or a local organization. Ask them to describe their best and worst leaders. Use the results to answer the question: How closely do local views of leadership match with findings of the GLOBE study?

Don't you agree that we still have a lot more to learn about how leadership success is viewed in the many cultures of the world? The links between culture and leadership seem particularly important, not only in a business context, but also as governments try to work together both bilaterally and multilaterally in forums such as the United Nations.

Universal facilitators of leadership effectiveness.
- Trustworthy, honest, just
- Foresight, ability to plan ahead
- Positive, dynamic, encouraging, motivating
- Communicative, informed, integrating

Universal impediments to leadership effectiveness
- Loner, asocial, self-protective
- Non-cooperative, irritable
- Dictatorial and autocratic

Reference: Robert J. House, P. J. Hanges, Mansour Javidan, P. Dorfman, and V. Gupta (eds.). *Culture, Leadership and Organizations: The GLOBE Study of 62 Societies* (Thousand Oaks, CA: Sage Publications, 2004); Mansour Javidan, Peter W. Dorfman, Mary Sully de Luque, and Robert J. House, *Academy of Management Perspective,* vol. 20 (2006), pp. 67–90.

Leading

● **Leading** is the process of arousing enthusiasm and inspiring efforts to achieve goals.

In management, **leading** is the process of arousing people's enthusiasm and inspiring their efforts to work hard to fulfill plans and accomplish objectives. As leaders, managers build commitments to a common vision, encourage activities that support goals, and influence others to do their best work on the organization's behalf.

Deborah K. Holmes actively pursued her leadership responsibilities at Ernst & Young. She noticed that, in addition to stress caused by intense work at the firm, women often faced more stress because their spouses also worked. She became a champion for improved work-life balance and pursued it relentlessly. She started "call-free holidays," when professionals did not check voice mail or e-mail on weekends and holidays. She also started a "travel sanity" program that limited staffers' travel to four days a week so that they could get home for weekends. And, she started a Woman's Access Program to provide mentoring and career development.

Controlling

● **Controlling** is the process of measuring performance and taking action to ensure desired results.

The management function of **controlling** is the process of measuring work performance, comparing results to objectives, and taking corrective action as needed. Through controlling, managers stay in active contact with people as they work, gather and interpret reports on performance, and use this information to make constructive changes. Control is indispensable in the management process. Things don't always go as anticipated, and plans must often be modified and redefined to best fit new circumstances.

At Ernst & Young, Laskawy and Holmes documented what the firm's retention rates for women were when they started the new programs. This gave them a clear baseline against which they were able to track progress. They regularly measured retention rates for women and compared them to the baseline. By comparing results with plans and objectives, they were able to identify successes and also pinpoint where they needed to further adjust their work-life balance programs. Over time, turnover rates for women were reduced at all levels in the firm.

MANAGERIAL ROLES AND ACTIVITIES

Although the management process may seem straightforward, the responsibilities for planning, organizing, leading, and controlling are more complicated than they appear at first glance. In his classic book *The Nature of Managerial Work*, for example, Henry Mintzberg describes the daily work of corporate chief executives as follows: "There was no break in the pace of activity during office hours. The mail . . . telephone calls . . . and meetings . . . accounted for almost every minute from the moment these executives entered their offices in the morning until they departed in the evenings."[55] Today we would complicate things even further by adding ever-present e-mail, text messages, and social media to Mintzberg's list of executive preoccupations.

Managerial Roles

In trying to better understand and describe the nature of managerial work, Mintzberg identified a set of 10 roles commonly filled by managers.[56] The roles fall into the three categories shown in Figure 1.6: informational, interpersonal, and decisional roles.

A manager's informational roles involve the giving, receiving, and analyzing of information. A manager fulfilling these roles will be a *monitor*, scanning for information; a *disseminator*, sharing information; and a *spokesperson*, acting as official communicator. The interpersonal roles involve interactions with people inside and outside the work unit. A manager fulfilling these roles will be a *figurehead*, modeling and setting forth key principles and policies; a *leader*, providing direction and instilling enthusiasm; and a *liaison*, coordinating with others. The decisional roles involve using information to make decisions to solve problems or address opportunities. A manager fulfilling these roles will be a *disturbance handler*, dealing with problems and conflicts; a *resource allocator*, handling budgets and distributing resources; a *negotiator*—making deals and forging agreements; and an *entrepreneur*—developing new initiatives.

Interpersonal roles	Informational roles	Decisional roles
How a manager interacts with other people • Figurehead • Leader • Liaison	How a manager exchanges and processes information • Monitor • Disseminator • Spokesperson	How a manager uses information in decision making • Entrepreneur • Disturbance handler • Resource allocator • Negotiator

FIGURE 1.6 Mintzberg's managerial roles—interpersonal, informational, and decisional.

Managerial Activities

Managers must not only master the four management functions and these roles; they must implement them in intense and complex work settings. And without any doubt, managerial work is busy, demanding, and stressful at all levels of responsibility. The managers Mintzberg studied had little free time to themselves; in fact, unexpected problems and continuing requests for meetings consumed almost all available time. Their workdays were hectic, and the pressure for continuously improving performance was all-encompassing. Mintzberg summarized his observations this way: "The manager can never be free to forget the job, and never has the pleasure of knowing, even temporarily, that there is nothing else to do. . . . Managers always carry the nagging suspicion that they might be able to contribute just a little bit more. Hence they assume an unrelenting pace in their work."[57] Continuing research on the nature of managerial work offers this important reminder.[58]

- Managers work long hours.
- Managers work at an intense pace.
- Managers work at fragmented and varied tasks.
- Managers work with many communication media.
- Managers accomplish much work through interpersonal relationships.

MANAGERIAL AGENDAS AND NETWORKS

On his way to a meeting, a general manager bumped into a staff member who did not report to him. Using this opportunity, in a two-minute conversation he (a) asked two questions and received the information he needed; (b) reinforced their good relationship by sincerely complimenting the staff member on something he had recently done; and (c) got the staff member to agree to do something that the general manager needed done.

This brief incident provides a glimpse of an effective general manager in action.[59] It also portrays two activities that consultant and scholar John Kotter considers critical to a manager's success: agenda setting and networking.

● **Agenda setting** develops action priorities for accomplishing goals and plans.

Through **agenda setting**, good managers develop action priorities that include goals and plans spanning long and short time frames. These agendas are usually incomplete and loosely connected in the beginning, but they become more specific as the manager utilizes information continually gleaned from many different sources. The agendas are always present in the manager's mind and are "played out" or "pushed ahead" whenever an opportunity arises, as in the preceding example.

● **Networking** is the process of creating positive relationships with people who can help advance agendas.

● **Social capital** is a capacity to get things done with the support and help of others.

Good managers implement their agendas by working with many people inside and outside the organization. This is made possible by **networking**, the process of building and maintaining positive relationships with people whose help may be needed to implement one's agendas. Such networking creates **social capital**—a capacity to attract support and help from others in order to get things done. In Kotter's example, the general manager received help from a staff member who did not report directly to him. His networks and social capital would also include relationships with peers, a boss, higher-level executives, subordinates, and members of their work teams, as well as with external customers, suppliers, and community representatives.

Learning Check

Study Question 4

What is the management process?

Be sure you can ☑ define and give examples of each of the management functions—*planning, organizing, leading,* and *controlling* ☑ explain Mintzberg's view of what managers do, including the 10 key managerial roles ☑ explain Kotter's points on how managers use agendas and networks to fulfill their work responsibilities

LEARNING HOW TO MANAGE

Today's turbulent times reinforce the point that your career success depends on a real commitment to **learning**—changing behavior through experience. The learning focus in management is on developing skills and competencies to deal with the complexities of human behavior and problem solving in organizations. Indeed, managerial skills and competencies often top the list when alumni and corporate recruiters speak with business school deans and faculties about their academic programs. This is one of the reasons why the Learning from Others and Learning about Yourself features that begin each chapter in this book are so useful. When you read them be sure to ask probing questions on how to best develop your career readiness. And, don't forget that it's not just formal learning in the classroom that counts. The long-term difference in career success may well rest with **lifelong learning**—the process of continuous learning from all of our daily experiences and opportunities.

● **Learning** is a change in behavior that results from experience.

● **Lifelong learning** is continuous learning from daily experiences.

ESSENTIAL MANAGERIAL SKILLS

A **skill** is the ability to translate knowledge into action that results in desired performance.[60] Harvard scholar Robert L. Katz described the essential, or baseline, skills of managers in three categories: technical, human, and conceptual.[61] He suggests that all three sets of skills are necessary for management success, and that their relative importance varies by level of managerial responsibility as shown in Figure 1.7.

● A **skill** is the ability to translate knowledge into action that results in desired performance.

Technical Skills

A **technical skill** is the ability to use a special proficiency or expertise to perform particular tasks. Your college major is designed to enhance your technical skills, and you should also be adding a high Tech IQ to the mix as well. Accountants, engineers, market researchers, financial planners, and systems analysts, for example, possess technical skills within their areas of expertise. Knowing how to write a business plan, use statistics to analyze data from a market survey, prepare visual aids and deliver a persuasive oral presentation, and find useful information on the Internet are also technical skills. Although initially acquired through formal education, they should be nurtured and further developed by training and job experience.

● A **technical skill** is the ability to use expertise to perform a task with proficiency.

Figure 1.7 shows that technical skills are very important at job entry and early career levels. From a developmental perspective you might take a quick inventory of your technical skills. Make a list of those things you could tell a prospective employer about with confidence by saying in a job interview: "This is what I can do for you."

Human and Interpersonal Skills

The ability to work well in cooperation with other persons is a **human skill**. As pointed out in Figure 1.7, the interpersonal nature of managerial work makes

● A **human skill** or interpersonal skill is the ability to work well in cooperation with other people.

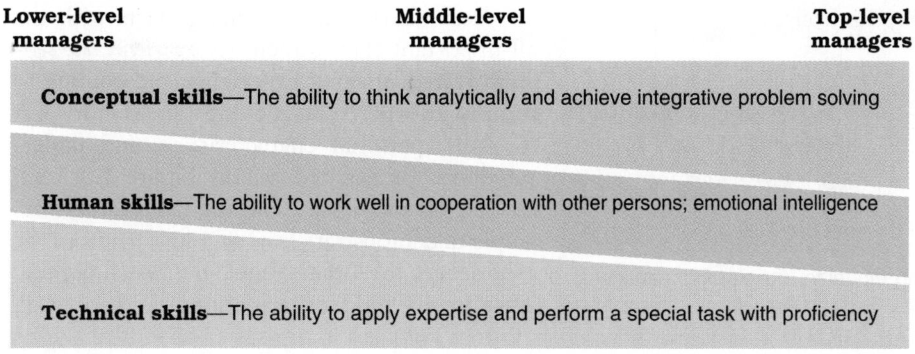

Lower-level managers	Middle-level managers	Top-level managers
Conceptual skills—The ability to think analytically and achieve integrative problem solving		
Human skills—The ability to work well in cooperation with other persons; emotional intelligence		
Technical skills—The ability to apply expertise and perform a special task with proficiency		

FIGURE 1.7 Katz's essential managerial skills—technical, human, and conceptual.

human skills consistently important across all levels of managerial responsibility. They are demonstrated in the workplace as a capacity to communicate, to collaborate and network, and to engage others through interpersonal relationships with a spirit of trust, enthusiasm, and positive engagement.

A manager with good human skills will have a high degree of self-awareness, as discussed in the chapter opening Learning about Yourself feature. Human skills also include a capacity to understand or empathize with the feelings of others. This creates something called **emotional intelligence**, defined by scholar and consultant Daniel Goleman as the "ability to manage ourselves and our relationships effectively."[62]

Strength or weakness in emotional intelligence is reflected in how well you recognize, understand, and manage feelings while interacting and dealing with others. Someone high in emotional intelligence will know when her or his emotions are about to become disruptive, and act to control them. This same person will sense when another person's emotions are negatively influencing a relationship, and act to understand and better deal with them.[63] Put your interpersonal skills and emotional intelligence to a developmental test by asking and answering this question: "Just how well do I relate with and work with others?"

> ● **Emotional intelligence** is the ability to manage ourselves and our relationships effectively.

Conceptual and Analytical Skills

The ability to think critically and analytically is a **conceptual skill**. It involves the capacity to break problems into smaller parts, to see the relations between the parts, and to recognize the implications of any one problem for others. We often call this "critical thinking," a diagnostic skill based on **cognitive intelligence**—a competency to think systematically, identify cause and effect links, and recognize patterns in events and data.[64]

Figure 1.7 shows that conceptual skills gain in relative importance as one moves from lower to higher levels of management. This is because the problems faced at higher levels of responsibility are often ambiguous and unstructured, full of complications and interconnections, and posing longer-term consequences. The end-of-book section with management cases for critical thinking is there to help you further develop strong conceptual skills in management. And in respect to personal development, the question to ask is: "Am I developing the strong critical thinking and problem-solving capabilities I will need for long-term career success?"

> ● A **conceptual skill** is the ability to think analytically to diagnose and solve complex problems.
>
> ● **Cognitive intelligence** is the ability to think systematically and identify cause-effect patterns in data and events.

DEVELOPING MANAGERIAL SKILLS AND COMPETENCIES

Management 11/e is written and organized to help you learn managerial skills and competencies while deepening your understanding of the key concepts, theories, and research upon which they are based. The pedagogy of *Management 11/e* and its underlying learning model are designed to help you accomplish these goals. In fact, you have already experienced them by reading this first chapter.

Real management learning starts with the all-important commitment to *experience and self-assessment*—engaging experience and coming to terms with where you presently stand in respect to skills, personal characteristics, and understandings. As pointed out in Figure 1.8, each chapter opens with a Learning from Others example to demonstrate how we can learn from the experiences of others, and by benchmarking what people and organizations do very well.

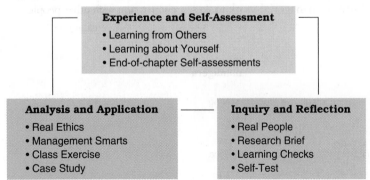

FIGURE 1.8 *Management 11/e* learning model for developing managerial skills and competencies.

Each chapter also opens with a Learning about Yourself section that engages you in active personal inquiry. This ties in with an end-of-chapter Management Skills and Competencies section that includes both Back to Yourself—a reflection on how the focus of the chapter opener fits with chapter content—and Further Reflection—offering additional self-assessments that can be taken to gain added personal insights.

Next in the learning model is *inquiry and reflection*—the process of discovering, thinking about, and understanding the knowledge base of management. The chapter content is interspersed with many examples to help show the relevance of the theories and concepts to real-world settings. The Real People feature brings chapter content to life in terms of a person's actual career accomplishments. Also, a Research Brief illustrates the types of questions researchers are trying to answer in their scientific inquiries. Learning Checks at the end of each major heading are chances to pause and check understanding before reading further. The end-of-chapter Management Learning Review includes a Study Questions Summary and a Self-Test with multiple-choice, short answer, and essay questions to further check comprehension and exam readiness.

The process of *analysis and application* completes the *Management 11/e* learning model. It is facilitated by a Real Ethics feature that presents real ethics dilemmas, and then asks you to engage in critical thinking about how to best deal with them. Management Smarts provide bullet list pointers on how to put the theories and concepts into practice. And, the end-of-chapter Class Exercise and recommended Case Study offer further opportunities to wrestle with theory-into-practice applications and test your problem-solving capabilities in management.

Be sure you can ☑ define three essential managerial skills—*technical, human,* and *conceptual skills* ☑ explain Katz's view of how these skills vary in importance across management levels ☑ define *emotional intelligence* as an important human skill ☑ list and give examples of personal competencies important for managerial success	**Learning Check** ☑ **Study Question 5** How do you learn management skills and competencies?

Management **L**earning **R**eview

Study Questions Summary

1 What are the challenges of working in the new economy?

- Work in the new economy is increasingly knowledge based, and intellectual capital is the foundation of organizational performance.
- Organizations must value the talents of a workforce whose members are increasingly diverse with respect to gender, age, race and ethnicity, able-bodiedness, and lifestyles.
- The forces of globalization are bringing increased interdependencies among nations and economies, as customer markets and resource flows create intense business competition.
- Ever-present developments in information technology are reshaping organizations, changing the nature of work, and increasing the value of knowledge workers.
- Society has high expectations for organizations and their members to perform with commitment to high ethical standards and in socially responsible ways.

- Careers in the new economy require great personal initiative to build and maintain skill "portfolios" that are always up-to-date and valuable in a free agent economy.

FOR DISCUSSION **How is globalization creating career risks and opportunities for today's college graduates?**

2 What are organizations like in the new workplace?

- Organizations are collections of people working together to achieve a common purpose.
- As open systems, organizations interact with their environments in the process of transforming resource inputs into product and service outputs.
- Productivity is a measure of the quantity and quality of work performance, with resource costs taken into account.

- High-performing organizations achieve both performance effectiveness in terms of goal accomplishment, and performance efficiency in terms of resource utilization.

FOR DISCUSSION **Is it ever acceptable to sacrifice performance efficiency for performance effectiveness?**

3 Who are managers and what do they do?

- Managers directly support and facilitate the work efforts of other people in organizations.
- Top managers scan the environment, create strategies, and emphasize long-term goals; middle managers coordinate activities in large departments or divisions; team leaders and supervisors support performance of front-line workers at the team or work-unit level.
- Functional managers work in specific areas such as finance or marketing; general managers are responsible for larger multifunctional units; administrators are managers in public or nonprofit organizations.
- The upside-down pyramid view of organizations shows operating workers at the top, serving customer needs while being supported from below by various levels of management.
- The changing nature of managerial work emphasizes being good at "coaching" and "supporting" others, rather than simply "directing" and "order-giving."

FOR DISCUSSION **In what ways could we expect the work of a top manager to differ from that of a team leader?**

4 What is the management process?

- The management process consists of the four functions of planning, organizing, leading, and controlling.

- Planning sets the direction; organizing assembles the human and material resources; leading provides the enthusiasm and direction; controlling ensures results.
- Managers implement the four functions in daily work that is often intense and stressful, involving long hours and continuous performance pressures.
- Managerial success requires the ability to perform well in interpersonal, informational, and decision-making roles.
- Managerial success also requires the ability to build interpersonal networks and use them to accomplish well-selected task agendas.

FOR DISCUSSION **How might the upside-down pyramid view of organizations affect a manager's approach to planning, organizing, leading, and controlling?**

5 How do you learn the essential managerial skills and competencies?

- Careers in the new economy demand continual attention to lifelong learning from all aspects of daily experience and job opportunities.
- Skills considered essential for managers are broadly described as technical—ability to use expertise; human—ability to work well with other people; and conceptual—ability to analyze and solve complex problems.
- Human skills are equally important for all management levels; while conceptual skills gain importance at higher levels and technical skills gain importance at lower levels.

FOR DISCUSSION **Among the various managerial skills and competencies, which do you consider the most difficult to develop, and why?**

Self-Test

Multiple-Choice Questions

1. The process of management involves the functions of planning, _____, leading, and controlling.
   (a) accounting   (b) creating   (c) innovating   (d) organizing

2. An effective manager achieves both high-performance results and high levels of _____ among people doing the required work.
   (a) turnover   (b) effectiveness   (c) satisfaction   (d) stress

3. Performance efficiency is a measure of the _____ associated with task accomplishment.
   (a) resource costs   (b) goal specificity   (c) product quality   (d) product quantity

4. The requirement that a manager answer to a higher-level boss for results achieved by a work team is called _____.
   (a) dependency   (b) accountability   (c) authority   (d) empowerment

5. Productivity is a measure of the quantity and _____ of work produced, with resource utilization taken into account.
   (a) quality   (b) cost   (c) timeliness   (d) value

6. _____ managers pay special attention to the external environment, looking for problems and opportunities and finding ways to deal with them.
   (a) Top   (b) Middle   (c) Lower   (d) First-line

7. The accounting manager for a local newspaper would be considered a _____ manager, whereas the plant manager in a manufacturing firm would be considered a _____ manager.
   (a) general, functional   (b) middle, top   (c) staff, line   (d) senior, junior

8. When a team leader clarifies desired work targets and deadlines for a work team, he or she is fulfilling the management function of _____.
   (a) planning   (b) delegating   (c) controlling   (d) supervising

9. The process of building and maintaining good working relationships with others who may help implement a manager's work agendas is called _____.

   (a) governance   (b) networking   (c) authority   (d) entrepreneurship

10. In Katz's framework, top managers tend to rely more on their _____ skills than do first-line managers.

    (a) human   (b) conceptual   (c) decision-making   (d) technical

11. The research of Mintzberg and others concludes that managers _____.

    (a) work at a leisurely pace   (b) have blocks of private time for planning   (c) always live with the pressures of performance responsibility   (d) have the advantages of short workweeks

12. When someone with a negative attitude toward minorities makes a decision to deny advancement opportunities to a Hispanic worker, this is an example of _____.

    (a) discrimination   (b) emotional intelligence   (c) control   (d) prejudice

13. Among the trends in the new workplace, one can expect to find _____.

    (a) more order-giving   (b) more valuing people as human assets   (c) less teamwork   (d) reduced concern for work-life balance

14. The manager's role in the "upside-down pyramid" view of organizations is best described as providing _____ so that operating workers can directly serve _____.

    (a) direction, top management   (b) leadership, organizational goals   (c) support, customers   (d) agendas, networking

15. The management function of _____ is being performed when a retail manager measures daily sales in the women's apparel department and compares them with daily sales targets.

    (a) planning   (b) agenda setting   (c) controlling   (d) delegating

Short-Response Questions

16. Discuss the importance of ethics in the relationship between managers and the people they supervise.

17. Explain how "accountability" operates in the relationship between (a) a team leader and her team members, and (b) the same team leader and her boss.

18. Explain how the "glass ceiling effect" may disadvantage newly hired African American college graduates in a large corporation.

19. What is globalization, and what are its implications for working in the new economy?

Essay Question

20. You have just been hired as the new head of an audit team for a national accounting firm. With four years of experience, you feel technically well prepared for the assignment. However, this is your first formal appointment as a "manager." Things are complicated at the moment. The team has 12 members of diverse demographic and cultural backgrounds, as well as work experience. There is an intense workload and lots of performance pressure. How will this situation challenge you to develop and use essential managerial skills and related competencies to successfully manage the team to high levels of auditing performance?

Management **S**kills and **C**ompetencies

Self-Assessment

Back to Yourself: **Self-Awareness**

The chapter opener used the Johari Window to introduce you to possible "blind spots" and other facets of your **self-awareness**. Now that you have had the chance to think about current trends in the workplace, how organizations are changing today, and the nature of managerial work, the importance of self-awareness to your career should be very evident. Its only through a willingness to discover the "real" self that we can identify strengths and understand weaknesses that can help us perform better in the future. And it's very important to remember that we have a tendency to form overly favorable impressions of ourselves, ones that often don't hold up when compared with how others perceive us.[65] True self-awareness is achieved only when we are able to objectively see ourselves through the eyes of others. That's why it is such an important starting point for getting to know yourself better during this introductory study of management. After you complete the following self-assessment on Career Readiness, don't forget to check your Emotional Intelligence and gain more self-awareness of your tendencies in dealing with emotions and handling relationships.

> **Self-Awareness** helps us build on strengths and overcome weaknesses; it helps us avoid tendencies toward self-enhancement, viewing ourselves more favorably than is justified.

Further Reflection: **Career Readiness**

Instructions

Use the following scale to rate yourself on personal characteristics.[66]

S = Strong, I am very confident with this one.
G = Good, but I still have room to grow.
W = Weak, I really need work on this one.
U = Unsure, I just don't know.

1. *Inner work standards:* The ability to personally set and work to high performance standards.
2. *Initiative:* The ability to actively tackle problems and take advantage of opportunities.
3. *Cognitive intelligence:* The ability to think systematically and identify cause-effect patterns in data and events.
4. *Tolerance for uncertainty:* The ability to get work done even under ambiguous and uncertain conditions.
5. *Social objectivity:* The ability to act free of racial, ethnic, gender, and other prejudices or biases.
6. *Social intelligence:* The ability to understand another person's needs and feelings.
7. *Emotional intelligence:* The ability to exercise self-awareness and self-management of emotions.
8. *Stamina:* The ability to sustain long work hours.
9. *Resistance to stress:* The ability to get work done even under stressful conditions.
10. *Adaptability:* The ability to be flexible and adapt to changes.
11. *Self-confidence:* The ability to be consistently decisive and willing to take action.
12. *Self-objectivity:* The ability to evaluate personal strengths and weaknesses and motives and skills relative to a job.
13. *Impression management:* The ability to create and sustain a positive impression in the eyes of others.
14. *Introspection:* The ability to learn from experience, awareness, and self-study.

Scoring

Give yourself 1 point for each S, and 1/2 point for each G. Do not give yourself points for W and U responses. Total your points and enter the result here [PMF _____].

Interpretation

This assessment offers a self-described Profile of your Personal Management Foundations (PMF)—things that establish strong career readiness. Are you a perfect 10, or is your PMF score something less than that? There shouldn't be too many 10s around. Ask someone you know to also assess you on this instrument. You may be surprised at the differences between your PMF score as you described it and your PMF score as described by someone else. Most of us, realistically speaking, must work hard to grow and develop continually in these and related management foundations. This list is a good starting point as you consider where and how to further pursue the development of your managerial skills and competencies.

Team Exercise

My Best Manager

Preparation

Working alone, make a list of the *behavioral attributes* that describe the "best" manager you have ever had. This could be someone you worked for in a full-time or part-time job, summer job, volunteer job, student organization, or elsewhere. If you have trouble identifying an actual manager, make a list of behavioral attributes of the manager you would most like to work for in your next job.

Instructions

Form into groups as assigned by your instructor, or work with a nearby classmate. Share your list of attributes and listen to the lists of others. Be sure to ask questions and make comments on items of special interest. Work together to create a master list that combines the unique attributes of the "best" managers experienced by members of your group. Have a spokesperson share that list with the rest of the class for further discussion.

Case Study: Trader Joe's

Go to *Management Cases for Critical Thinking* to find the recommended case for Chapter 1— "Trader Joe's: Keeping a Cool Edge."

Management Learning Past to Present

2

1 What can be learned from classical management thinking?

2 What are the insights of the behavioral management approaches?

3 What are the foundations of modern management thinking?

Learning From Others

There Are Many Pathways to Goal Achievement

Here are two names you are probably familiar with—Facebook, the popular social-media site, and Zappos, an online merchandiser recently bought by Amazon.com. Both were entrepreneurial start-ups that made it big. But interestingly, they differ in approaches to employee hiring and retention.[1] Is one right and the other wrong?

According to Facebook's founder and CEO Mark Zuckerberg, shown here, the firm wants to hire "hackers" with an entrepreneurial side. He's interested in people who want to create new things quickly rather than those who want long-term employment. He likens Facebook to great collegiate sports schools where athletes go to play and excel, while also preparing for later careers in professional sports. When it comes to Internet-based products, he considers Facebook the best place for talented people to learn while they are doing great things. These are the "hackers," and, according to Zuckerberg, the great ones don't "want to stay at one place forever."

Over at Zappos, CEO Tony Hsieh says that "We have a different approach from what Mark was talking about at Facebook. We actually want our employees to stay with the company for a long time, for 10 years, maybe for their entire life." Hsieh invests heavily in staff training and mentoring to help employees on career pathways toward the top. In fact, his hope is that within five to seven years new hires are already making a big impact in senior management. The key, according to Hsieh, is "constant growth" along with a strong dose of satisfaction. Internal career paths are clear at Zappos, promotions are frequent, and time off for personal affairs is not a problem. And always, Hsieh tries to lead the firm with inspiration that focuses on vision, purpose, and passion, as well as profits.

do the benchmarking

Working at Facebook or working at Zappos; that's quite a contrast isn't it? Which firm might you be most comfortable in joining? What does this choice say about your career needs and aspirations, as well as your criteria for selecting future employers? By the way, don't think that one of these CEOs—Zuckerberg or Hsieh—has to be "right" and the other "wrong." **Organizations act as systems and there are often many pathways to achieving a goal.**

Learning About Yourself

Learning Style

Speaking about foundations for performance success, what about you? Now is a good time to examine your **learning style**, how you like to learn through receiving, processing, and recalling new information. Some people learn by watching; they observe others and model what they see. Others learn by doing; they act and experiment, learning as they go. Some people are feelers for whom emotions and values count a lot; others are thinkers that emphasize reason and analysis.[2]

These preferences come together in the learning styles shown here. Look at the figure and then "shade" in each circle to show the degree to which you believe that description applies to you.

After you have turned the figure into your personal learning style profile, ask: "What are the implications of my learning style for how I perform academically and how well I perform at work? Ask also: "How does my learning style influence my relationships with others in study groups and work teams, including persons having different learning styles?"

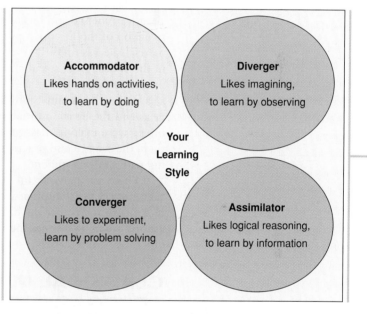

Every person a manager deals with is unique, most problem situations are complex, and things are always changing. Success only comes to managers who thrive on learning. It's a personal challenge to learn something new every day, and it's a big managerial challenge to consistently help others learn things as well. A senior PepsiCo executive says: "I believe strongly in the notion that enhancing managers' knowledge of their strengths and particularly their weaknesses is integral to ensuring long-term sustainable performance improvement and executive success."[3]

get to know yourself better

Why not take the Pepsi executive's words to heart and start building a personal learning scorecard? Make lists of your learning strengths and learning weaknesses based on past experiences in school, at work, in sports, and even at leisure. Use this awareness to write a set of goals that will help you take full advantage of the learning available from this book, your management course, and your academic program of studies. **Also make use of the end-of-chapter Self-Assessment feature to further reflect on your learning style and assess your managerial assumptions about people and how they work.**

2 Management Learning Past to Present

Study Question 1	Study Question 2	Study Question 3
Classical Management Approaches	**Behavioral Management Approaches**	**Modern Management Foundations**
• Scientific management • Administrative principles • Bureaucratic organization	• Organizations as communities • The Hawthorne studies • Maslow's theory of human needs • McGregor's Theory X and Theory Y • Argyris's theory of adult personality	• Quantitative analysis and tools • Organization as systems • Contingency thinking • Quality management • Knowledge management and organizational learning • Evidence-based management
Learning Check 1	**Learning Check 2**	**Learning Check 3**

In *The Evolution of Management Thought*, Daniel Wren traces management as far back as 5000 B.C., when ancient Sumerians used written records to assist in governmental and business activities.[4] Management was important to the construction of the Egyptian pyramids, the rise of the Roman Empire, and the commercial success of 14th-century Venice. By the time of the Industrial Revolution in the 1700s, great social changes had helped prompt a major leap forward in the manufacturing of basic staples and consumer goods. Industrial development was accelerated by Adam Smith's ideas of efficient production through specialized tasks and the division of labor. At the turn of the 20th century, Henry Ford and others were making mass production a mainstay of the emerging economy. Since then, the science and practices of management have been on a rapid and continuing path of development.[5]

There are many useful lessons in the history of management thought. Rather than naively believing that we are always reinventing management practice today, it is wise to remember the historical roots of many modern ideas and admit that we are still trying to perfect them.

CLASSICAL MANAGEMENT APPROACHES

Our study of management begins with the classical approaches: (1) scientific management, (2) administrative principles, and (3) bureaucratic organization.[6] Figure 2.1 associates each with a prominent person in the history of management thought—Taylor, Weber, and Fayol. The figure also shows that the classical approaches share

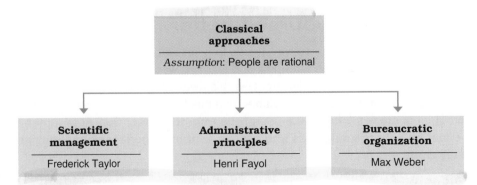

FIGURE 2.1 Major branches in the classical approach to management.

a common assumption: People at work rationally consider opportunities made available to them and do whatever is necessary to achieve the greatest personal and monetary gain.[7]

SCIENTIFIC MANAGEMENT

In 1911, Frederick W. Taylor published *The Principles of Scientific Management*, in which he made the following statement: "The principal object of management should be to secure maximum prosperity for the employer, coupled with the maximum prosperity for the employee."[8] Taylor, often called the father of scientific management, noticed that many workers did their jobs their own ways and without a clear and consistent approach. He believed this caused inefficiency and low performance. He also believed that this problem could be corrected if workers were taught and then helped by supervisors to always do their jobs in the right ways.

Taylor's goal was to improve the productivity of people at work. He used the concept of "time study" to analyze the motions and tasks required in any job and to develop the most efficient ways to perform them. He then linked these job requirements to both training for the worker and support from supervisors in the form of proper direction, work assistance, and monetary incentives. Taylor's approach is known as **scientific management** and includes four guiding action principles.

● **Scientific management** emphasizes careful selection and training of workers and supervisory support.

1. Develop for every job a "science" that includes rules of motion, standardized work implements, and proper working conditions.
2. Carefully select workers with the right abilities for the job.
3. Carefully train workers to do the job and give them the proper incentives to cooperate with the job "science."
4. Support workers by carefully planning their work and by smoothing the way as they go about their jobs.

Although Taylor called his approach "scientific" management, contemporary scholars have questioned both his veracity in reporting exactly what was done in his studies and the scientific rigor underlying them.[9] Nevertheless, Taylor's ideas have influenced management thinking along the lines described in Management Smarts 2.1.[10] A ready example of its present-day influence can be seen at United Parcel Service where many workers are guided by carefully calibrated productivity standards. Sorters at regional centers are timed according to strict task requirements and are expected to load vans at a set number of packages per hour. GPS technology plots the shortest delivery routes; stops are studied and carefully timed; supervisors generally know within a few minutes how long a driver's pickups and deliveries will take. Industrial engineers also devise precise routines for drivers, who are trained to knock on customers' doors rather than spend even a few seconds looking for the doorbell. At UPS, and in classic scientific management fashion, the point is that savings of seconds on individual stops adds up to significant increases in productivity.[11]

Management Smarts 2.1

Practical insights from scientific management

- Make results-based compensation a performance incentive.
- Carefully design jobs with efficient work methods.
- Carefully select workers with the abilities to do these jobs.
- Train workers to perform jobs to the best of their abilities.
- Train supervisors to support workers so they can perform to the best of their abilities.

One of the most enduring legacies of the scientific management approach grew out of Taylor's first principle and involves **motion study**, the science of reducing a job or task to its basic physical motions. Two of Taylor's contemporaries, Frank and Lillian Gilbreth, pioneered the use of motion studies as a management tool.[12]

● **Motion study** is the science of reducing a task to its basic physical motions.

In one famous case they reduced the number of motions used by bricklayers and tripled their productivity. The Gilbreths' work led to later advances in the areas of job simplification, work standards, and incentive wage plans—all techniques still used in the modern workplace. At Worthington Industries, an Ohio-based steel producer, for example, a drive to improve productivity has focused on time clocks that have been installed at workstations. Work teams track how long it takes to perform tasks using time clocks that display both a goal for the task—say 22 minutes—and actual time elapsed—say 24 minutes and 37 seconds. CEO John McConnell says that the idea for the clocks came from the workers and that "everybody is actively trying to improve that aspect of their jobs."[13]

ADMINISTRATIVE PRINCIPLES

In 1916, after a career in French industry, Henri Fayol published *Administration Industrielle et Générale*.[14] The book outlines his views on the proper management of organizations and of the people within them. It identifies the following five "rules" or "duties" of management, which are foundations for the four functions of management—planning, organizing, leading, and controlling—that we talk about today:

1. *Foresight*—to complete a plan of action for the future.
2. *Organization*—to provide and mobilize resources to implement the plan.
3. *Command*—to lead, select, and evaluate workers to get the best work toward the plan.
4. *Coordination*—to fit diverse efforts together and to ensure information is shared and problems solved.
5. *Control*—to make sure things happen according to plan and to take necessary corrective action.

Importantly, Fayol believed that management could be taught. He was very concerned about improving the quality of management and set forth a number of "principles" to guide managerial action. A number of them are still part of the management vocabulary. They include the *scalar chain principle*—there should be a clear and unbroken line of communication from the top to the bottom in the organization; *the unity of command principle*—each person should receive orders from only one boss; and the *unity of direction principle*—one person should be in charge of all activities that have the same performance objective.

UPS Uses Scientific Management

UPS is known for more than its "big brown" identity reflected in the color of its delivery trucks, popular TV ads, and the #88 NASCAR team. In management it uses many highly efficient operations based on current applications of scientific management principles. Package sorters are timed and expected to load vans at a set number of packages per hour. GPS technology plots the shortest delivery routes. And industrial engineers devise precise routines for drivers who are even trained to knock on customers' doors rather than spend extra seconds looking for the doorbell.

BUREAUCRATIC ORGANIZATION

Max Weber was a late-19th-century German intellectual whose insights have had a major impact on the field of management and the sociology of organizations. His ideas developed in reaction to his belief that the organizations of his day often failed to reach their performance potential. Among other things, Weber was concerned that people were in positions of authority not because of their job-related capabilities, but because of their social standing or "privileged" status in German society.

At the heart of Weber's thinking was a specific form of organization he believed could correct the problems just described—a **bureaucracy**.[15] For him it was an ideal, intentionally rational, and very efficient form of organization founded on principles of logic, order, and legitimate authority. The defining characteristics of Weber's bureaucratic organization are as follows:

- *Clear division of labor:* Jobs are well defined, and workers become highly skilled at performing them.
- *Clear hierarchy of authority:* Authority and responsibility are well defined for each position, and each position reports to a higher-level one.
- *Formal rules and procedures:* Written guidelines direct behavior and decisions in jobs, and written files are kept for historical record.
- *Impersonality:* Rules and procedures are impartially and uniformly applied, with no one receiving preferential treatment.
- *Careers based on merit:* Workers are selected and promoted on ability, competency, and performance, and managers are career employees of the organization.

● A **bureaucracy** is a rational and efficient form of organization founded on logic, order, and legitimate authority.

Weber believed that bureaucracies would have the advantages of efficiency in utilizing resources, and of fairness or equity in the treatment of employees and clients. These are his words.[16]

> The purely bureaucratic type of administrative organization . . . is, from a purely technical point of view, capable of attaining the highest degree of efficiency. . . . It is superior to any other form in precision, in stability, in the stringency of its discipline, and in its reliability. It thus makes possible a particularly high degree of calculability of results for the heads of the organization and for those acting in relation to it.

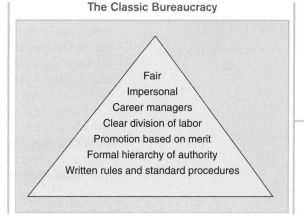
The Classic Bureaucracy

Fair
Impersonal
Career managers
Clear division of labor
Promotion based on merit
Formal hierarchy of authority
Written rules and standard procedures

This is the ideal side of bureaucracy. However, the terms *bureaucracy* and *bureaucrat* are now often used with negative connotations. The possible disadvantages of bureaucracy include excessive paperwork or "red tape," slowness in handling problems, rigidity in the face of shifting customer or client needs, resistance to change, and employee apathy.[17] These disadvantages are most likely to cause problems for organizations that must be flexible and quick in adapting to changing circumstances—a common situation today. Current trends in management include many innovations that seek the same goals as Weber but use different approaches to how organizations can be structured.

Be sure you can ☑ state the underlying assumption of the classical management approaches ☑ list the principles of Taylor's scientific management ☑ list three of Fayol's "principles" for guiding managerial action ☑ list the key characteristics of bureaucracy and explain why Weber considered it an ideal form of organization ☑ identify possible disadvantages of bureaucracy in today's environment

Learning Check
Study Question 1
What can be learned from classical management thinking?

BEHAVIORAL MANAGEMENT APPROACHES

During the 1920s, an emphasis on the human side of the workplace began to influence management thinking. Major branches in these behavioral or human resource approaches to management are shown in Figure 2.2. They include Follett's notion of organizations as communities, the famous Hawthorne studies, and Maslow's theory of human needs, as well as related ideas of Douglas McGregor and Chris Argyris. The behavioral approaches maintain that people are social and self-actualizing. People at work are assumed to seek satisfying social relationships, respond to group pressures, and search for personal fulfillment. The historical foundations set by this set of approaches are now well evidenced in the field of **organizational behavior**, which is devoted to the study of individuals and groups in organizations.

● **Organizational behavior** is the study of individuals and groups in organizations.

FOLLETT'S ORGANIZATIONS AS COMMUNITIES

The work of Mary Parker Follett was part of an important transition from classical thinking into behavioral management. As summarized in *Mary Parker Follett— Prophet of Management: A Celebration of Writings from the 1920s*, it is a good reminder of the wisdom of history. Although Follett wrote in a different day and age, her ideas are rich with foresight. She taught respect for the experience and knowledge of workers, warned against the dangers of too much hierarchy, and called for visionary leadership. Follett was eulogized upon her death in 1933 as "one of the most important women America has yet produced in the fields of civics and sociology."[18]

In her writings, Follett views organizations as "communities" in which managers and workers should labor in harmony without one party dominating the other, and with the freedom to talk over and truly reconcile conflicts and differences. For her, groups were mechanisms through which diverse individuals could combine their talents for a greater good. And she believed it was the manager's job to help people in organizations cooperate with one another and achieve an integration of interests.

Follett's emphasis on groups and her commitment to human cooperation are still highly relevant themes today.[19] Follett believed that making every employee an owner in a business would create feelings of collective responsibility. Today, we address the same issues under such labels as "employee ownership," "profit sharing," and "gain-sharing plans." Follett believed that business problems involve a wide

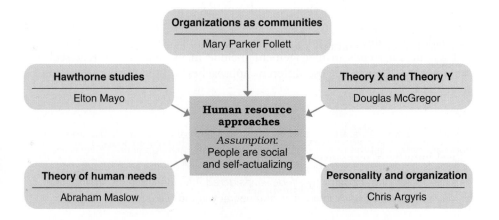

FIGURE 2.2 Foundations in the behavioral or human resource approaches to management.

Cisco CEO Calls for New Leadership Style

John Chambers, chairman and CEO of Cisco Systems, describes his leadership style this way. "I'm a command-and-control person. I like being able to say 'turn right,' and we truly have 67,000 people turn right. But that's the style of the past. . . . Today's world requires a different leadership style—moving more into a collaboration and teamwork, including how to use Web 2.0 technology."

variety of factors that must be considered in relationship to one another. Today, we talk about "systems" and "contingency thinking." Follett also believed that businesses were service organizations and that private profits should always be considered vis-à-vis the public good. Today, we pursue the same issues under the labels "managerial ethics" and "corporate social responsibility."

THE HAWTHORNE STUDIES

The shift toward behavioral thinking in management was given an important boost when in 1924 the Western Electric Company commissioned a research program to study individual productivity at the Hawthorne Works of the firm's Chicago plant.[20] The initial Hawthorne studies had a scientific management perspective and sought to determine how economic incentives and physical conditions of the workplace affected the output of workers. An initial focus was on the level of illumination in the manufacturing facilities; it seemed reasonable to expect that better lighting would improve performance. After failing to find this relationship, however, the researchers concluded that unforeseen "psychological factors" somehow interfered with their illumination experiments. This finding and later Hawthorne studies directed research attention toward better understanding human interactions in the workplace.

Social Setting and Human Relations

A team led by Harvard's Elton Mayo set out to examine the effect of worker fatigue on output. Care was taken to design a scientific test that would be free of the psychological effects thought to have confounded the earlier illumination studies. Six workers who assembled small electrical relays were isolated for intensive study in a special test room. They were given various rest pauses, as well as workdays and workweeks of various lengths, and production was regularly measured. Once again, researchers failed to find any direct relationship between changes in physical working conditions and output. Productivity increased regardless of the changes made.

Mayo and his colleagues concluded that the new "social setting" created for workers in the test room accounted for the increased productivity. Two factors were singled out as having special importance. One was the group atmosphere. The workers shared pleasant social relations with one another and wanted to do a good job. The other was more participative supervision. Test-room workers were made to feel important, were given a lot of information, and were frequently asked for their opinions. This was not the case in their regular jobs back in the plant. A general conclusion was that good "human relations" in the test room resulted in higher productivity.

CEO Compensation—Is It Excessive?

In corporate America today, CEO compensation is over 260 times greater than the compensation provided to the median full-time employee. A typical CEO will earn more in one workday than the average worker will earn all year.

In support of CEO salaries, the argument is that you have to pay a lot to attract the best executive talent; and, you have to pay for performance. However, pay levels are now so high that most CEOs are assured of getting rich no matter how the company performs. In fact, over 80% of executives receive bonuses even during down years for the stock market.

In the midst of the recent economic downturn, one might expect the CEO-worker pay gap to be significantly reduced.

But that has not occurred, and many people continue to be shocked by exorbitant salaries and bonuses received by some top executives. Especially at times when their firms are laying off employees and freezing salaries among lower-level workers, "CEO pay" is a hot button topic.

You Decide

Is it morally right for a CEO to accept multi-million dollar compensation when front-line employees are given minimal or even zero raises? Should CEO pay be capped at some multiple of the average worker's pay? Should CEOs be forced to take pay cuts during difficult financial times? If you were the CEO of a company that was laying off thousands of employees, would you voluntarily give up some of your compensation?

Employee Attitudes and Group Processes

Mayo's research continued until the worsening economic conditions of the Depression forced their termination in 1932. By then, interest in the human factor had broadened to include employee attitudes, interpersonal relations, and group dynamics. In one study, over 21,000 employees were interviewed to learn what they liked and disliked about their work environment. "Complex" and "baffling" results led the researchers to conclude that the same things (e.g., work conditions or wages) could be sources of satisfaction for some workers and of dissatisfaction for others.

The final Hawthorne study was conducted in the bank wiring room and centered on the role of the work group. A finding here was that people would restrict their output in order to avoid the displeasure of the group, even if it meant sacrificing pay that could otherwise be earned by increasing output. The researchers concluded that groups can have strong negative, as well as positive, influences on individual productivity.

Lessons of the Hawthorne Studies

As scholars now look back, they criticized the Hawthorne studies for poor research design, weak empirical support for the conclusions drawn, and the tendency of researchers to overgeneralize their findings.[21] Yet their significance as turning points in the evolution of management thought remains intact. The studies helped shift the attention of managers and researchers away from the technical and structural concerns of the classical approach and toward social and human concerns as keys to productivity. They brought visibility to the notions that people's feelings, attitudes, and relationships with coworkers affected their work, and that groups were important influences on individuals. They also identified the **Hawthorne effect**—the tendency of people who are singled out for special attention to perform as anticipated because of expectations created by the situation.

The Hawthorne studies contributed to the emergence of the **human relations movement,** which influenced management thinking during the 1950s and 1960s. This movement was largely based on the viewpoint that managers who used good human relations in the workplace would achieve productivity. Importantly, this

● The **Hawthorne effect** is the tendency of persons singled out for special attention to perform as expected.

● The **human relations movement** suggested that managers using good human relations will achieve productivity.

movement set the stage for what evolved into the field of organizational behavior, the study of individuals and groups in organizations.

MASLOW'S THEORY OF HUMAN NEEDS

The work of psychologist Abraham Maslow in the area of human "needs" has also had a major impact on the behavioral approach to management.[22] He described a **need** as a physiological or psychological deficiency a person feels the compulsion to satisfy, suggesting that needs create tensions that can influence a person's work attitudes and behaviors. He also placed needs in the five levels shown in Figure 2.3. From lowest to highest in order, they are physiological, safety, social, esteem, and self-actualization needs.

Maslow's theory is based on two underlying principles. The first is the **deficit principle**—a satisfied need is not a motivator of behavior. People act to satisfy "deprived" needs, those for which a satisfaction "deficit" exists. The second is the **progression principle**—the five needs exist in a hierarchy of "prepotency." A need at any level is activated only when the next-lower-level need is satisfied. According to Maslow, people try to satisfy the five needs in sequence. They progress step by step from the lowest level in the hierarchy up to the highest. Along the way, a deprived need dominates individual attention and determines behavior until it is satisfied. Then, the next-higher-level need is activated. At the level of self-actualization, the deficit and progression principles cease to operate. The more this need is satisfied, the stronger it grows.

Consistent with human relations thinking, Maslow's theory implies that managers who understand and help people satisfy their important needs at work will achieve productivity. Although scholars now recognize that things are more complicated than this, Maslow's ideas are still relevant. Consider, for example, the case of volunteer workers at the local Red Cross or other community organizations. They don't receive any monetary compensation. Managers in such nonprofit organizations have to offer jobs and work environments that satisfy the many

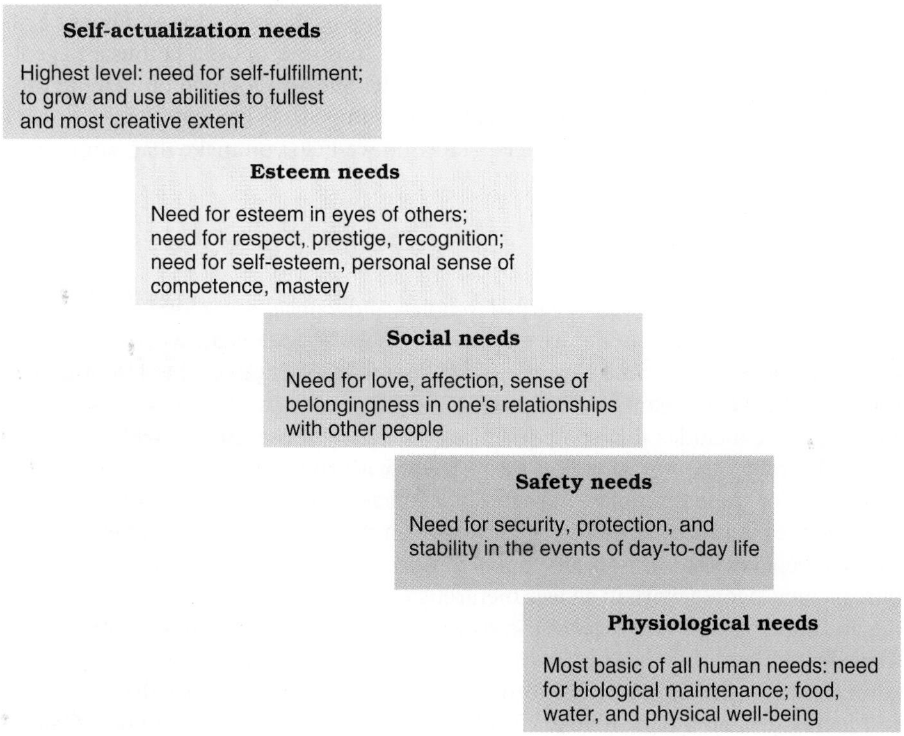

● A **need** is a physiological or psychological deficiency that a person wants to satisfy.

● According to the **deficit principle** a satisfied need does not motivate behavior.

● According to the **progression principle** a need is activated only when the next lower level need is satisfied.

Self-actualization needs

Highest level: need for self-fulfillment; to grow and use abilities to fullest and most creative extent

Esteem needs

Need for esteem in eyes of others; need for respect, prestige, recognition; need for self-esteem, personal sense of competence, mastery

Social needs

Need for love, affection, sense of belongingness in one's relationships with other people

Safety needs

Need for security, protection, and stability in the events of day-to-day life

Physiological needs

Most basic of all human needs: need for biological maintenance; food, water, and physical well-being

FIGURE 2.3 Maslow's hierarchy of human needs.

different needs of volunteers. If their work isn't fulfilling, the volunteers will lose interest and probably redirect their efforts elsewhere.

MCGREGOR'S THEORY X AND THEORY Y

Douglas McGregor was heavily influenced by both the Hawthorne studies and Maslow. His classic book, *The Human Side of Enterprise*, advances the thesis that managers should give more attention to the social and self-actualizing needs of people at work.[23] McGregor called upon managers to shift their view of human nature away from a set of assumptions he called Theory X and toward ones he called Theory Y. You can check your managerial assumptions by completing the self-assessment at the end of the chapter.

● **Theory X** assumes people dislike work, lack ambition, act irresponsibly, and prefer to be led.

● **Theory Y** assumes people are willing to work, like responsibility, and are self-directed and creative.

● **A self-fulfilling prophecy** occurs when a person acts in ways that confirm another's expectations.

According to McGregor, managers holding **Theory X** assumptions approach their jobs believing that those who work for them generally dislike work, lack ambition, are irresponsible, are resistant to change, and prefer to be led rather than to lead. McGregor considers such thinking inappropriate. He argues instead for **Theory Y** assumptions in which the manager believes people are willing to work, capable of self-control, willing to accept responsibility, imaginative and creative, and capable of self-direction.

An important aspect of McGregor's ideas is his belief that managers who hold either set of assumptions can create **self-fulfilling prophecies**—that is, through their behavior they create situations where others act in ways that confirm the original expectations.[24] Managers with Theory X assumptions, for example, act in a very directive "command-and-control" fashion that gives people little personal say over their work. These supervisory behaviors create passive, dependent, and reluctant subordinates, who tend to do only what they are told to or required to do. This reinforces the original Theory X viewpoint.

In contrast to Theory X, managers with Theory Y assumptions tend to behave in "participative" ways that allow subordinates more job involvement, freedom, and responsibility. This creates opportunities to satisfy esteem and self-actualization needs; workers tend to perform as expected with initiative and high performance. The self-fulfilling prophecy thus becomes a positive one.[25] Betsy Holden, former president and CEO of Kraft Foods, Inc., for example, showed a lot of Theory Y in her approach to leadership. She was praised for a "positive, upbeat, enthusiastic, collaborative, and team–oriented" management style. She also focused on helping others with questions like these: "What skills do you need? What experiences do you need? What development do you need? How do we help you make that happen?"[26]

ARGYRIS'S THEORY OF ADULT PERSONALITY

Ideas set forth by the well-regarded scholar and consultant Chris Argyris also reflect the belief in human nature advanced by Maslow and McGregor. In his book *Personality and Organization*, Argyris contrasts the management practices found in traditional and hierarchical organizations with the needs and capabilities of mature adults.[27] He concludes that some practices, especially those influenced by the classical management approaches, are inconsistent with the mature adult personality.

Consider these examples. In scientific management, the principle of specialization assumes that people will work more efficiently as tasks become better defined. Argyris believes that this limits opportunities for self-actualization. In Weber's bureaucracy, people work in a clear hierarchy of authority, with higher levels directing and controlling lower levels. Argyris worries that this creates dependent, passive workers who feel they have little control over their work environments. In Fayol's administrative principles, the concept of unity of direction assumes that efficiency will increase when a person's work is planned and directed by a supervisor. Argyris

Real People

Former Microsoft Executive Fights Illiteracy

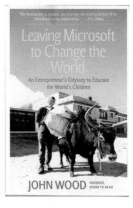

There are many ways to help build a better society. John Wood's choice is social entrepreneurship that promotes literacy for children of the developing world. During a successful career as Microsoft executive, his life changed after he went on a trekking vacation to the Himalayas of Nepal. While there Wood was shocked at the lack of schools and poor access to children's reading materials. He pledged to collect books for a Nepalese school that he visited and returned a year later with 3,000. But the impact didn't end there. As a result of the experience he found the inspiration to accomplish much more through nonprofit work.

Now in what he calls the "second chapter" in his life, Wood's passion is to provide the lifelong benefits of education to poor children. He quit his Microsoft job to found a nonprofit organization called Room to Read. It builds libraries and schools in poor nations like Nepal, Cambodia, Vietnam, and Laos, and publishes local language books to help fill them.

Picture this scene in Laos, one of the world's poorest nations. Children sit happily in a small library full of books reading a story with their teacher. It's a Room to Read project. So far the organization has put in place over 700 libraries and built 140 schools in this small land-locked Southeast Asian country. Laos has just over 8,000 primary schools nation-wide and the majority offer only incomplete educational experiences.

The Room to Read model is so efficient that it can build schools for as little as $6,000 and is now setting up 5–6 new libraries each day. Over 10,000 libraries are already in place in Asia and Sub-Saharan Africa.

Time magazine called Wood and his team "Asian Heroes," and *Fast Company* magazine gave Room to Read its Social Capitalist Award. Noting that one-seventh of the global population can't read or write, Wood says: "I don't see how we are going to solve the world's problems without literacy."

---

suggests that this may create conditions for psychological failure; conversely, psychological success occurs when people define their own goals.

Like McGregor, Argyris believes that managers who treat people positively and as responsible adults will achieve the highest productivity. His advice is to expand job responsibilities, allow more task variety, and adjust supervisory styles to allow more participation and promote better human relations. He believes that the common problems of employee absenteeism, turnover, apathy, alienation, and low morale may be signs of a mismatch between management practices and mature adult personalities.

Be sure you can ☑ explain Follett's concept of organizations as communities ☑ define the *Hawthorne effect* ☑ explain how the Hawthorne findings influenced the development of management thought ☑ explain how Maslow's hierarchy of needs operates in the workplace ☑ distinguish between Theory X and Theory Y assumptions, and explain why McGregor favored Theory Y ☑ explain Argyris's criticism that traditional organizational practices are inconsistent with mature adult personalities

Learning Check ☑

Study Question 2
What insights come from the behavioral management approaches?

MODERN MANAGEMENT FOUNDATIONS

The concepts, models, and ideas discussed so far helped set the stage for continuing developments in management thought. The many themes reflected throughout this book build from them as well as from modern management foundations that include the use of quantitative analysis and tools, a systems view of organizations, contingency thinking, commitment to quality, the role of knowledge management learning organizations, and the importance of evidence-based management.

QUANTITATIVE ANALYSIS AND TOOLS

● **Analytics** is the systematic use and analysis of data to solve problems and make informed decisions.

● **Management science** and **operations research** use quantitative analysis and applied mathematics to solve problems.

● **Operations management** is the study of how organizations produce goods and services.

In our world of vast computing power and the easy collection and storage of data, there is renewed emphasis on how to really use available data to make better management decisions. This is an area known as **analytics**, the use of data to solve problems and make informed decisions using systematic analysis.[28] And in respect to analytics, scholars are very interested in how managers can make use of mathematical tools to conduct quantitative and statistical analyses.

Quantitative applications are often described in academic programs and management practice by the terms **management science, operations research**, and **operations management**. In Chapter 19, for example, you'll find that the field of operations management uses such quantitative approaches and applied mathematics to systematically examine how organizations in manufacturing and service settings can produce goods and services most efficiently and effectively. Topics include value chain analysis, supply chain management, inventory management, and quality control, as well as business process analysis.

A typical quantitative approach to managerial problem solving proceeds as follows. A problem is encountered, it is systematically analyzed, appropriate mathematical models and computations are applied, and an optimum solution is identified. At Google, for example, a math formula has been developed to aid in talent planning. It pools information from performance reviews and surveys, promotions, and pay histories to identify employees who might feel underutilized and be open to offers from other firms. Human resource management plans are then developed to try and retain them.[29]

Consider these other examples of real management problems and how they can be addressed by using analytics and quantitative tools.

Problem: An oil exploration company is worried about future petroleum reserves in various parts of the world. *Quantitative approach—Mathematical forecasting* helps make future projections for reserve sizes and depletion rates that are useful in the planning process.

Problem: A "big box" retailer is trying to deal with pressures on profit margins by minimizing costs of inventories, but must also avoid going "out of stock" for customers. *Quantitative approach—Inventory analysis*, discussed in Chapter 19 on operations and services management, helps control inventories by mathematically determining how much to automatically order and when.

Problem: A grocery store is getting complaints from customers that waiting times are too long for checkouts during certain times of the day. *Quantitative approach—Queuing theory* helps allocate service personnel and workstations based on alternative workload demands and in a way that minimizes both customer waiting times and costs of service workers.

Problem: A manufacturer wants to maximize profits for producing three different products on three different machines, each of which can be used for different periods of times and run at different costs. *Quantitative approach—Linear programming* is used to calculate how best to allocate production among different machines.

Problem: A real estate developer wants to control costs and finish building a new apartment complex on time. *Quantitative approach—Network models*, such as the simplified Gantt chart pictured here and discussed further in Chapter 18 on control processes and systems, break large tasks into smaller components. This allows project managers to better analyze, plan, and control timetables for completion of many different activities.

Simplified Gantt Chart for Building Project

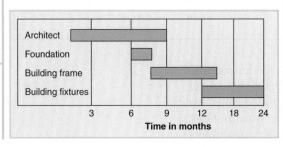

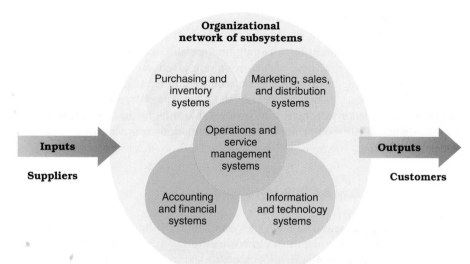

FIGURE 2.4 Organizations as complex networks of interacting subsystems.

ORGANIZATIONS AS SYSTEMS

Organizations have long been described as cooperative systems that achieve great things by integrating the contributions of many individuals to achieve a common purpose. But the reality is that cooperation among the many people and parts is often imperfect and can be improved upon. This is why we need to understand the full complexity of an organization as a **system** of interrelated parts or **subsystems** that work together to achieve a common purpose.[30]

In Chapter 1 organizations were described as **open systems** that interact with their environments in the continual process of transforming inputs—people, technology, information, money, and supplies—into outputs—goods and services for their customers and clients. Figure 2.4 also shows that an organization can also be viewed internally as an interlocking network of critical subsystems whose activities individually and collectively support the work of the larger system and make things happen. In the figure, the operations and service management subsystems center the transformation process while integrating with other subsystems such as purchasing, accounting, sales, and information. High performance by the organization occurs only when each subsystem both performs its tasks well and works well in cooperation with others.

● A **system** is a collection of interrelated parts working together for a purpose.

● A **subsystem** is a smaller component of a larger system.

● An **open system** interacts with its environment and transforms resource inputs into outputs.

CONTINGENCY THINKING

Modern management is situational in orientation; that is, it attempts to identify practices that are best fits with the demands of unique situations. This requires **contingency thinking** that tries to match managerial responses with the problems and opportunities specific to different settings, particularly those posed by individual and environmental differences. There is no expectation that one can or should find the "one best way" to manage in all circumstances. Rather, the contingency perspective tries to help managers understand situational differences and respond to them in ways appropriate to their unique characteristics.[31]

Contingency thinking is an important theme in this book, and its implications extend to all of the management functions—from planning and controlling for diverse environmental conditions, to organizing for different strategies, to leading in different performance

● **Contingency thinking** tries to match management practices with situational demands.

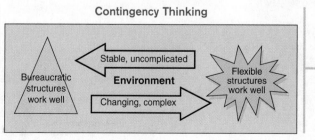

situations. To clarify the concept here, however, consider the concept of bureaucracy. Weber offered it as an ideal form of organization. But from a contingency perspective, the bureaucratic form is only one possible way of organizing things. What turns out to be the "best" structure in any given situation will depend on many factors, including environmental uncertainty, an organization's primary technology, and the strategy being pursued. As the figure suggests, a tight bureaucracy works best when the environment is relatively stable and operations are predictable and uncomplicated. In complex and changing situations more flexible structures are needed.[32]

QUALITY MANAGEMENT

The work of W. Edwards Deming is a cornerstone of the quality movement in management.[33] His story begins in 1951 when he was invited to Japan to explain quality control techniques that had been developed in the United States. The result was a lifelong relationship epitomized in the Deming Application Prize, which is still awarded annually in Japan for companies achieving extraordinary excellence in quality.

"When Deming spoke," we might say, "the Japanese listened." The principles he taught the Japanese were straightforward and they worked: tally defects, analyze and trace them to the source, make corrections, and keep a record of what happens afterward. Deming's approach to quality emphasizes constant innovation, use of statistical methods, and commitment to training in the fundamentals of quality assurance.[34]

One outgrowth of Deming's work was the emergence of **total quality management**, or TQM. This is a process that makes quality principles part of the organization's strategic objectives, applying them to all aspects of operations and striving to meet customers' needs by doing things right the first time. Most TQM approaches begin with an insistence that the total quality commitment applies to everyone and everything in an organization—from resource acquisition and supply chain management, through production and into the distribution of finished goods and services, and ultimately to customer–management relationship.

Joseph Juran was one of Deming's contemporaries in the quality movement, and his long career also included consultations at major companies around the world.[35] Juran is known for the slogan "There is always a better way" and for his three guiding principles—"plan, control, improve."[36] This

Total quality management is an organization-wide commitment to continuous improvement, product quality, and customer needs.

The *Outliers*–Read and Succeed

When Bill Gates was a kid he attended a school that gave him access to a computer. He learned programming, had thousands of hours to practice, and, as we all know, went on to found Microsoft. Was it abundance of intelligence or the thousands of hours of practice that most accounts for his success? Malcolm Gladwell, depicted here and author of the popular book *Outliers*, is a strong advocate of practice-practice-practice. He offers this "10,000 hour rule" of advice–you need to spend 10,000 hours of practice to reach the top in any field. Anything less just doesn't cut it.

search for and commitment to quality is now tied to the emphasis modern management gives to **continuous improvement**—always looking for new ways to improve on current performance. The notion is that one can never be satisfied; something always can and should be improved upon.

An indicator of just how important quality objectives have become is the value given to **ISO certification** by the International Standards Organization in Geneva, Switzerland. It has been adopted by many countries of the world as a quality benchmark. Businesses that want to compete as "world-class companies" are increasingly expected to have ISO certification at various levels. To do so, they must refine and upgrade quality in all operations, and then undergo a rigorous assessment by outside auditors to determine whether they meet ISO requirements.

● **Continuous improvement** involves always searching for new ways to improve work quality and performance.

● **ISO certification** indicates conformance with a rigorous set of international quality standards.

KNOWLEDGE MANAGEMENT AND ORGANIZATIONAL LEARNING

Our technology-driven world is both rich with information and demanding in the pace and uncertainty of change so much so in fact that the noted management scholar Peter Drucker issues this warning: "knowledge constantly makes itself obsolete."[37] His message suggests that neither people nor organizations can afford to rest on past laurels; future success will be earned only by those who continually build and use knowledge to the fullest extent possible.

The term **knowledge management** describes the processes through which organizations use information technology to develop, organize, and share knowledge to achieve performance success.[38] You can spot the significance of knowledge management with the presence of an executive job title—chief knowledge officer. The CKO is responsible for energizing learning processes and making sure that an organization's portfolio of intellectual assets is well managed and continually enhanced. These assets include such things as patents, intellectual property rights, trade secrets, and special processes and methods, as well as the accumulated knowledge and understanding of the entire workforce.

● **Knowledge management** is the process of using intellectual capital for competitive advantage.

● A **learning organization** continuously changes and improves, using the lessons of experience.

An emphasis on knowledge management is characteristic of what consultant Peter Senge calls a **learning organization**, popularized in his book *The Fifth Discipline*.[39] A learning organization, he says, is one that "by virtue of people, values, and systems is able to continuously change and improve its performance based upon the lessons of experience." He describes learning organizations as encouraging and helping all members to learn continuously, while emphasizing information sharing, teamwork, empowerment, and participation. As an example, Google's principles for knowledge management and organizational learning are shown in Management Smarts 2.2.[40]

Management Smarts 2.2

Google's principles for knowledge management and organizational learning

Hire by committee—let great people hire other great people.

Cater to every need—make sure nothing gets in anyone's way.

Make coordination easy—put people close to one another, physically and electronically.

Encourage creativity—give people time for projects they choose.

Seek consensus—get inputs before decisions are made.

Use data—make informed decisions based on solid quantitative analysis.

Don't be evil—create a climate of respect, tolerance, and ethical behavior.

Organizations can learn from many sources. They can learn from their own experience. They can learn from their members and employees. They can learn from the experiences of their contractors, suppliers, partners, and customers. And they can learn from firms in unrelated businesses. All of this, of course, depends on creating an organizational culture in which people are enthusiastic about learning opportunities and in which information sharing is an expected and valued work behavior. Senge believes that those meeting his criteria for learning organizations tend to display the following characteristics:

1. Mental models—everyone sets aside old ways of thinking.
2. Personal mastery—everyone becomes self-aware and open to others.
3. Systems thinking—everyone learns how the whole organization works.
4. Shared vision—everyone understands and agrees to a plan of action.
5. Team learning—everyone works together to accomplish the plan.

EVIDENCE-BASED MANAGEMENT

Looking back on the historical foundations of management, one thing that stands out is criticism by today's scholars of the scientific rigor of some historical corner-stones—among them Taylor's scientific management approach and the Hawthorne studies. The worry is that we may be too quick in accepting as factual the results of studies that are based on weak or questionable evidence. And if some studies are flawed, extra care needs to be exercised when trying to apply scholarly insights to improve management practices. This problem isn't limited to the distant past.

When Tom Peters and Robert Waterman published *In Search of Excellence: Lessons from America's Best-Run Companies* in 1982, the book helped kindle interest in the attributes of organizations that achieve performance excellence.[41] Peters and Waterman highlighted things like "closeness to customers," "bias toward action," "simple form and lean staff," and "productivity through people," all of which make good sense. Later findings, however, showed that many of the companies deemed to be "excellent" at the time encountered future problems.[42] Was there something fundamentally wrong with Peters' and Waterman's understanding of what created excellence? Or were there other factors at play that made long-term success a more complicated set of issues? A more recent book by Jim Collins, *Good to Great*, faced similar difficulties. It also achieved great acclaim and rose to best-seller status with descriptions of highly successful organizations.[43] But Collins's methods and findings have since been criticized by researchers.[44] And after the recent economic recession revealed problems at many firms he previously considered to be "great," Collins published a follow-up book called *How the Mighty Fall*.[45]

HOW THE MIGHTY FALL

AND WHY SOME COMPANIES NEVER GIVE IN

JIM COLLINS

BESTSELLING AUTHOR OF *GOOD TO GREAT*

Facts Show Greatness Isn't Forever

When Jim Collins wrote *Good to Great* and described the characteristics of high-performing companies, you have to wonder if he realized that his next best-seller would be titled *How the Mighty Fall*. In this new book he attempts to understand why some of his previous picks for greatness had major problems during the recent economic downturn. He also sets out a framework that describes failure as developing from such things as management egos that create excessive pride in past accomplishments and fuel excessive risks in the pursuit of future growth.

Research Brief

Setting Personal Goals Improves Academic Performance

University graduates out-earn and suffer less unemployment that non-completers. But, as many as 25% of U.S. students that begin college fail to graduate. Even among those that do graduate, only about 35% do so in four years of study, while only 57% graduate after six years. What can schools do to fight this problem?

Dominique Morisano, Jacob Hirsh, Jordan Peterson, Robert Phil, and Bruce Shore set out to determine if a goal-setting intervention could help by improving students' academic performance. They used longitudinal research to study the impact of a structured online personal goal-setting program on student grades, enrolled credits, and motivation. The basic hypothesis was that students engaged in personal goal setting would show academic improvement.

Participants in the study were 85 self-nominated undergraduate students from one university that met three criteria: full-time course load, have been on academic probation or have a cumulative GPA under 3.0, and having academic problems. They were assigned to intervention and control groups, with the intervention group doing online goal-setting while the control group did online questionnaires on personal characteristics. GPA and credit enrollment data was gathered both before and after the online activities, and a motivational questionnaire was completed at the end of the study.

Results, as shown in the figure, showed that students in the goal-setting intervention had higher GPAs after the intervention. The researchers conclude that: "This low-cost intervention could potentially be used by academic institutions to help 1st-year students establish goals and increase their academic prospects; it could also be used as a treatment for students on academic probation."

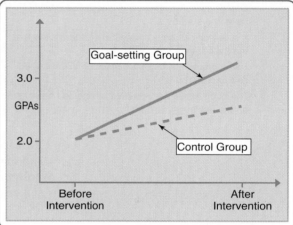

You Be the Researcher

Is the conclusion of this study sufficiently evidence-based for department heads and deans to seriously consider starting personal goal-setting interventions to improve their students' academic performance? What weaknesses can you spot in the study design? If you were to replicate this study at your college or university, what would you change to result in even better evidence-based ideas to improve students' grades, retention, and graduation rates?

Reference: Dominique Morisano, Jacob B. Hirsh, Jordan B. Peterson, Robert O. Phil, and Bruce M. Shore, "Setting, Elaborating, and Reflecting on Personal Goals Improves Academic Performance," *Journal of Applied Psychology,* Vol. 95, No. 2 (2010), pp. 255–264.

All of this is not meant to discredit what keen observers of management practice report, but it is meant to make you cautious and a bit skeptical when it comes to separating fads from facts and conjecture from informed insight. After all, managers are always searching for solid answers to questions on how to deal with day-to-day management dilemmas and situations. For example: What is the best way to do performance appraisals? How do you select members for high-performance teams? How should a merit pay system be designed and implemented? When does directive leadership work best? How do you structure organizations for innovation? Furthermore, when such questions are posed, the goal is to answer them with empirically sound and scientifically supported findings that stand up well to scholarly scrutiny.[46]

● **Evidence-based management** involves making decisions based on hard facts about what really works.

In this regard a book by Jeffrey Pfeffer and Robert Sutton makes the case for **evidence-based management**, or EBMgt. It is described as the process of making management decisions on "hard facts"—that is about what really works, rather than on "dangerous half-truths"—things that sound good but lack empirical substantiation.[47] Pfeffer and Sutton are talking about managers who are informed and discerning as they apply knowledge and insights to make their decisions. In this sense, EBMgt is about managers "making decisions through the conscientious, explicit, and judicious use of four sources of information: practitioner expertise and judgment, evidence from the local context, a critical evaluation of the best available research evidence, and the perspectives of those people who might be affected by the decision."[48] Management scholars help to inform EBMgt by pursuing solid and meaningful research using scientific methods, and by rigorously examining and reporting case studies and insights based on practitioner experiences.[49]

The Research Brief feature found in each chapter of *Management 11/e* introduces the types of studies that are being done and the types of evidence that are being accumulated and debated among management scholars. By staying abreast of such developments and findings, managers can have more confidence that they are approaching decisions from solid foundations of evidence rather than on mere speculation or hearsay. Pfeffer, for example, has studied the link between human resource management and organizational performance.[50] Using data from a sample of some 1,000 firms, he and a colleague found that firms using a mix of positive practices had more sales per employee and higher profits per employee than those that didn't. The positive human resource management practices included employment security, selective hiring, self-managed teams, high wages based on performance merit, training and skill development, minimal status differences, and shared information. With evidence like this available, managers have lots of insights to draw upon when trying to build and lead high-performing teams and organizations.

Basic Scientific Methods Used in Management Research

- A research question or problem is identified
- One or more hypotheses, or possible explanations, are stated
- A research design is created to systematically test the hypotheses
- Data gathered through the research are analyzed and interpreted
- The hypotheses are accepted or rejected based on the evidence

---

☑ **Learning Check**
Study Question 3
What are the foundations of modern management thinking?

Be sure you can ☑ define *system, subsystem,* and *open system* ☑ apply these concepts to describe the operations of an organization in your community ☑ define *contingency thinking, knowledge management,* and *learning organization* ☑ list characteristics of learning organizations ☑ describe evidence-based management and its link with scientific methods

---

Management **L**earning **R**eview

Study Questions Summary

1 What can be learned from classical management thinking?

● Frederick Taylor's four principles of scientific management focused on the need to carefully select, train, and support workers for individual task performance.

● Henri Fayol suggested that managers should learn what are now known as the management functions of planning, organizing, leading, and controlling.

● Max Weber described bureaucracy with its clear hierarchy, formal rules, and well-defined jobs as an ideal form of organization.

FOR DISCUSSION **Should Weber's notion of the ideal bureaucracy be scrapped altogether, or is it still relevant today?**

2 What are the insights of the behavioral management approaches?

- The behavioral approaches shifted management attention toward the human factor as a key element in organizational performance.
- Mary Parker Follett describes organizations as communities within which people combine talents to work for a greater good.
- The Hawthorne studies suggested that work behavior is influenced by social and psychological forces and that work performance may be improved by better "human relations."
- Abraham Maslow's hierarchy of human needs introduced the concept of self-actualization and the potential for people to experience self-fulfillment in their work.
- Douglas McGregor urged managers to shift away from Theory X and toward Theory Y thinking, which views people as independent, responsible, and capable of self-direction in their work.
- Chris Argyris pointed out that people in the workplace are adults and may react negatively when constrained by strict management practices and rigid organizational structures.

FOR DISCUSSION **How can a manager still benefit by using insights from Maslow's hierarchy of needs theory?**

3 What are the foundations of modern management thinking?

- Analytics that use advanced quantitative analysis techniques in decision sciences and operations management can help managers solve complex problems.
- Organizations are open systems that interact with their external environments, while consisting of many internal subsystems that must work together in a coordinated way to support the organization's overall success.
- Contingency thinking avoids "one best way" arguments, instead recognizing the need to understand situational differences and respond appropriately to them.
- Quality management focuses on making a total commitment to product and service quality throughout an organization, maintaining continuous improvement and meeting worldwide quality standards such as ISO certification.
- Knowledge management is a process for developing, organizing, sharing, and using knowledge to facilitate organizational performance and create an environment for ongoing organizational learning.
- Evidence-based management uses findings from rigorous scientific research to identify management practices for high performance.

FOR DISCUSSION **Can system and subsystem dynamics help describe and explain performance problems for an organization in your community?**

Self-Test

Multiple-Choice Questions

1. The assumption that people are complex with widely varying needs is most associated with the _____ management approaches.
   (a) classical   (b) neoclassical   (c) behavioral   (d) modern

2. The father of scientific management is _____.
   (a) Weber   (b) Taylor   (c) Mintzberg   (d) Katz

3. When the registrar of a university deals with students by an identification number rather than a name, which characteristic of bureaucracy is being displayed and what is its intended benefit?
   (a) division of labor . . . competency   (b) merit-based careers . . . productivity   (c) rules and procedures . . . efficiency   (d) impersonality . . . fairness

4. If an organization was performing poorly and Henri Fayol was called in as a consultant, what would he most likely suggest to improve things?
   (a) teach managers to better plan and control   (b) teach workers more efficient job methods   (c) promote to management only the most competent workers   (d) find ways to increase corporate social responsibility

5. One example of how scientific management principles are applied in organizations today would be:
   (a) a results-based compensation system.   (b) a bureaucratic structure.   (c) training in how to better understand worker attitudes.   (d) focus on groups and teamwork rather than individual tasks.

6. The Hawthorne studies are important because they raised awareness of the important influences of _____ on productivity.
   (a) structures   (b) human factors   (c) physical work conditions   (d) pay and rewards

7. Advice to study a job, carefully train workers to do that job, and link financial incentives to job performance would most likely come from _____.
   (a) scientific management   (b) contingency management   (c) Henri Fayol   (d) Abraham Maslow

8. The highest level in Maslow's hierarchy includes _____ needs.
   (a) safety   (b) esteem   (c) self-actualization   (d) physiological

9. Conflict between the mature adult personality and a rigid organization was a major concern of _____.
   (a) Argyris   (b) Follett   (c) Gantt   (d) Fuller

10. When people perform in a situation as they are expected to, this is sometimes called the _____ effect.
    (a) Hawthorne   (b) systems   (c) contingency   (d) open-systems

11. Resource acquisition and customer satisfaction are important when an organization is viewed as a(n) _____.
    (a) bureaucracy   (b) closed system   (c) open system   (d) pyramid

12. When your local bank or credit union is viewed as an open system, the loan-processing department would be considered a _____.
    (a) subsystem   (b) closed system   (c) resource input   (d) value center

13. When a manager notices that Sheryl has strong social needs and assigns her a job in customer relations, while also being sure to give Kwabena lots of praise because of his strong ego needs, the manager is displaying _____.
    (a) systems thinking   (b) Theory X   (c) motion study   (d) contingency thinking

14. In a learning organization, as described by Peter Senge, one would expect to find _____.
    (a) priority placed on following rules and procedures   (b) promotions based on seniority   (c) employees who are willing to set aside old thinking and embrace new ways   (d) a strict hierarchy of authority

15. When managers try to avoid hearsay and make decisions based on solid facts and information, this is known as _____.
    (a) continuous improvement   (b) evidence-based management   (c) TQM   (d) Theory X management

Short-Response Questions

16. Explain how McGregor's Theory Y assumptions can create self-fulfilling prophecies consistent with the current emphasis on participation and involvement in the workplace.

17. How do the deficit and progression principles operate in Maslow's hierarchy-of-needs theory?

18. Define contingency thinking and give an example of how it might apply to management.

19. Explain why the external environment is so important in the open-systems view of organizations.

Essay Question

20. Enrique Temoltzin has just been appointed the new manager of your local college bookstore. Enrique would like to make sure the store operates according to Weber's bureaucracy. Describe the characteristics of bureaucracy and answer this question: Is the bureaucracy a good management approach for Enrique to follow? Discuss the possible limitations of bureaucracy and the implications for managing people as key assets of the store.

Management Skills and Competencies

Back to Yourself: Learning Style

People tend to learn in different ways, and the chapter opener was a chance for you to think about your **learning style**, about how you like to learn through receiving, processing, and recalling new information. Because learning is any change of behavior that results from experience, one of our most significant challenges is to always embrace experiences at school, at work, and in everyday living, and try our best to learn from it. And when it comes to experience as a foundation for learning, let's always remember the wisdom of the past. This chapter is a reminder about the importance of management history and how the achievements of the past can still provide insights that can help us deal with the present. After you complete the following self-assessment on Managerial Assumptions, don't forget to go online for the Learning Tendencies self-assessment. It's an opportunity to gain more useful insights into how you learn.

> Each of us has a preferred **learning style**, a set of ways that we've become comfortable using as we learn by receiving, processing, and recalling new information.

Further Reflection: Managerial Assumptions

Instructions

Read the following statements. Use the space in the margins to write "Yes" if you agree with the statement, or "No" if you disagree with it. Force yourself to take a Yes or No position.

1. Is good pay and a secure job enough to satisfy most workers?
2. Should a manager help and coach subordinates in their work?
3. Do most people like real responsibility in their jobs?
4. Are most people afraid to learn new things in their jobs?
5. Should managers let subordinates control the quality of their work?
6. Do most people dislike work?
7. Are most people creative?
8. Should a manager closely supervise and direct the work of subordinates?
9. Do most people tend to resist change?
10. Do most people work only as hard as they have to?
11. Should workers be allowed to set their own job goals?
12. Are most people happiest off the job?
13. Do most workers really care about the organization they work for?
14. Should a manager help subordinates advance and grow in their jobs?

Scoring

Count the number of yes responses to items 1, 4, 6, 8, 9, 10, 12; write that number here as [X = _____]. Count the number of yes responses to items 2, 3, 5, 7, 11, 13, 14; write that score here as [Y = _____].

Interpretation

This assessment provides insight into your orientation toward Douglas McGregor's Theory X (your "X" score) and Theory Y (your "Y" score) assumptions as discussed earlier in the chapter. You should review the discussion of McGregor's thinking in this chapter and consider further the ways in which you are likely to behave toward other people at work. Think, in particular, about the types of "self-fulfilling prophecies" you are likely to create.

Evidence-Based Management Quiz

Instructions

1. For each of the following questions answer "T" (true) if you believe the statement is backed by solid research evidence, or "F" (false) if you do not believe it is an evidence-based statement.[51]

T F 1.   Intelligence is a better predictor of job performance than having a conscientious personality.

T F 2.   Screening job candidates for values results in higher job performance than screening for intelligence.

T F 3.   A highly intelligent person will have a hard time performing well in a low-skill job.

T F 4.   "Integrity tests" are good predictors of whether employees will steal, be absent, or take advantage of their employers in other ways.

T F 5.   Goal setting is more likely to result in improved performance than is participation in decision making.

T F 6.   Errors in performance appraisals can be reduced through proper training.

T F 7.   People behave in ways that show pay is more important to them than what they indicate on surveys.

T F 8.   People hired through employee referrals have better retention rates than those hired from other recruiting sources.

T F 9.   Workers who get training and development opportunities at work tend to have lower desires to change employers.

T F 10. Being "realistic" in job interviews and telling prospective employees about both negative and positive job aspects improves employee retention.

2. Share your answers with others in your assigned group. Discuss the reasons members chose the answers they did; arrive at a final answer to each question for the group as a whole.

3. Compare your results with these answers "from the evidence."

4. Engage in a class discussion of how common-sense answers can sometimes differ from answers provided by evidence. Ask: What are the implications of this discussion for management practice?

Case Study: Zara International

Go to *Management Cases for Critical Thinking* to find the recommended case for Chapter 2–
"Zara International: Fashion at the Speed of Light."

Ethics and Social Responsibility

3

Learning From Others

Everyone Gains When Our Planet Is a Priority

"Business is the most powerful force in the world," says Gary Hirshberg. "I believe that virtually every problem in the world exists because business hasn't made finding a solution a priority."

Gary Hirshberg is the co-founder, president, and CEO of Stonyfield Farm, the world's largest producer of organic yogurt. He is also the author of *Stirring It Up: How to Make Money and Save the World* and was named one of "America's Most Promising Social Entrepreneurs" by *BusinessWeek* magazine. Hirshberg has always been at the forefront of movements for environmental and social transformation. He studied climate change at Hampshire College, built energy-producing windmills, and worked at a nonprofit research center that published studies on organic farming, aquaculture, and renewable energy sources.

The mission of Stoneyfield Farm is straight-forward: "Offer a pure and healthy product that tastes good and earn a profit without harming the environment." Hirshberg says "We factor the planet into all our decisions."

Stonyfield Farm is committed to managing the triple bottom line of being economically, socially, and environmentally responsible. The company only uses dairy-farm suppliers who pledge not to use bovine growth hormone (BGH), installed solar panels on the factory roof, and built a water treatment plant. Under Hirshberg's leadership, it has recycled over 18 million pounds of material in the past 10 years and offset 100 percent of the greenhouse gases from its facility energy use. Hirshberg is also involved in programs to install healthy snack-food vending machines in schools.

"It's a simple strategy but a powerful one," says Hirshberg proudly. "Going green is not just the right thing to do, but a great way to build a successful business." Stonyfield Farm is now the number one maker of organic yogurt in the world.[1]

do the benchmarking

It is easy to appreciate Stonyfield's focus on the triple bottom line of profits, people, and planet. But can something like this only be done as a straight start-up, as in Hirshberg's case? Or, can an existing firm be refocused in this direction? **What does it take to manage people and organizations in ways that create a work culture of ethics and social responsibility?**

Learning About Yourself

Individual Character

There is no doubt that **Individual character** is a foundation for all that we do. It establishes our personal integrity and provides an ethical anchor for how we behave at work and in life overall. Persons of high character are confident in the self-respect it provides, even in difficult situations. Those who lack it have lots of insecurity, act inconsistently, and suffer not only in self-esteem but also in the esteem of others.

You can think of individual character in terms of demonstrated honesty, civility, caring, and sense of fair play. And, indeed, the ethics and social responsibility issues facing organizations today put individual character to the test. We need to know ourselves well enough to make principled decisions that we can be proud of and that others will respect. After all, it's the character of the people making key decisions that determines whether our organizations act in socially responsible or irresponsible ways.

Research suggests that the behavior of some individuals changes greatly when they enter into the business arena. That is, the demands that the business world makes on individuals to be successful may cause them to act less ethically than otherwise. For instance, there is evidence that generosity, temperance, and sociability are reduced when one is operating in the business arena.[2]

One trait that can undermine individual character is hypercompetitiveness. Individuals who are hypercompetitive tend to think that winning—or getting ahead—is the only thing that matters. They hate to lose and tend to judge themselves more on the outcomes they achieve than on the methods used to get there. And, they may be quicker to put aside virtues in competitive situations like the business world.[3]

Signs of Hypercompetitiveness
• Winning makes me feel powerful and increases my perception of self-worth
• I hate to lose an argument
• I turn everything into a contest
• I am not satisfied in a competition unless I win
• If it helps me win, I am willing to take actions to obstruct my opponent

Although competitiveness is highly valued in many business situations, individuals who are too competitive may ignore ethical boundaries in their attempts to come out on top. They may even take actions that are unfair, damage society, or perhaps are even illegal.

get to know yourself better

Check yourself on the facets of hypercompetitiveness.[4] Identify three situations that presented you with some ethical test. Put yourself in the position of being your parent, a loved one, or a good friend. Using their vantage points, write a letter to yourself that critiques your handling of each incident and summarizes the implications in terms of your individual character. **Also take advantage of the end-of-chapter Self-Assessment to further reflect on your terminal and instrumental values.**

Study Question 1	Study Question 2	Study Question 3	Study Question 4
What Is Ethical Behavior?	**Ethics in the Workplace**	**Maintaining High Ethical Standards**	**Social Responsibility and Corporate Governance**
• Laws and values as determinants of ethical behavior • Alternative views of ethics • Cultural issues in ethical behavior	• Ethical dilemmas at work • Influences on ethical decision making • Rationalizations for unethical behavior	• Ethics training • Codes of ethical conduct • Moral management • Whistleblower protection	• Stakeholder Management • Perspectives on corporate social responsibility • Evaluating corporate social performance • Corporate governance
Learning Check 1	**Learning Check 2**	**Learning Check 3**	**Learning Check 4**

The opening example of Stonyfield Farm should get you thinking about ethics, social responsibility, and principled leadership. Look around; there are many cases of people and organizations operating in admirable ways. Some are quite well known—Ben and Jerry's, Burt's Bees, Tom's of Maine, and Whole Foods Markets, for example. Surely there are others right in your local community. But as you think of the organizations, don't forget the people that run them—the ones whose behavior ultimately influences their organizations' performance. Consider also this reminder from Desmond Tutu, archbishop of Capetown, South Africa, and winner of the Nobel Peace Prize.

> You are powerful people. You can make this world a better place where business decisions and methods take account of right and wrong as well as profitability.... You must take a stand on important issues: the environment and ecology, affirmative action, sexual harassment, racism and sexism, the arms race, poverty, the obligations of the affluent West to its less-well-off sisters and brothers elsewhere.[5]

WHAT IS ETHICAL BEHAVIOR?

● **Ethics** establish standards of good or bad, or right or wrong, in one's conduct.

● **Ethical behavior** is "right" or "good" in the context of a governing moral code.

For our purposes, **ethics** is defined as the moral code of principles that sets standards of good or bad, or right or wrong, in one's conduct.[6] A person's moral code is influenced by a variety of sources including family, friends, local culture, religion, educational institutions, and individual experiences.[7] Ethics guide and help people make moral choices among alternative courses of action. And in practice, **ethical behavior** is that which is accepted as "good" and "right" as opposed to "bad" or "wrong" in the context of the governing moral code.

LAWS AND VALUES AS DETERMINANTS OF ETHICAL BEHAVIOR

Individuals often assume that anything that is legal should be considered ethical. Slavery was once legal in the United States, and laws once permitted only men to vote.[8] But that doesn't mean the practices were ethical. Sometimes legislation lags behind changes in moral positions within a society. The delay makes it possible for something to be legal during a time when most people think it should be illegal.[9]

By the same token, just because an action is not strictly illegal doesn't make it ethical.[10] Living up to the "letter of the law" is not sufficient to guarantee that one's actions will or should be considered ethical. Is it truly ethical, for example, for an employee to take longer than necessary to do a job? To call in sick so that you can take a day off work for leisure? To fail to report rule violations by a coworker? Although none of these acts is strictly illegal, many would consider them to be unethical.

Most ethical problems in the workplace arise when people are asked to do, or find they are about to do, something that violates their personal beliefs. For some, if the act is legal, they proceed without worrying about it. For others, the ethical test goes beyond legality and into personal **values**—the underlying beliefs and attitudes that help determine individual behavior.

The psychologist Milton Rokeach makes a distinction between "terminal" and "instrumental" values.[11] **Terminal values** are preferences about desired ends, such as the goals one strives to achieve in life. Examples of terminal values considered important by managers include self-respect, family security, freedom, and happiness. **Instrumental values** are preferences regarding the means for accomplishing these ends. Among the instrumental values held important by managers are honesty, ambition, imagination, and self-discipline.

The value pattern for any one person is very enduring, but values vary from one person to the next. And to the extent that they do, we can expect different interpretations of what behavior is ethical or unethical in a given situation. When commenting on cheating tendencies, an ethics professor at Insead in France once told business school students: "The academic values of integrity and honesty in your work can seem to be less relevant than the instrumental goal of getting a good job."[12] And when at Duke about 10% of an MBA class was caught cheating on a take-home final exam, some said that we should expect such behavior from students who are taught to collaborate and work in teams and utilize the latest communication technologies. For others, the instrumental values driving such behavior are unacceptable—it was an individual exam, the students cheated, and they should be penalized.[13]

- **Values** are broad beliefs about what is appropriate behavior.
- **Terminal values** are preferences about desired end states.
- **Instrumental values** are preferences regarding the means to desired ends.

ALTERNATIVE VIEWS OF ETHICS

Figure 3.1 shows four views of ethical behavior—the utilitarian, individualism, moral rights, and justice views.[14] Depending on which perspective one adopts in a given situation, the resulting behaviors may be considered ethical or unethical.

Utilitarian View

The **utilitarian view** considers ethical behavior to be that which delivers the greatest good to the greatest number of people. Based on the work of 19th-century philosopher John Stuart Mill, this results-oriented point of view assesses the moral implications of actions in terms of their consequences. Business decision makers, for example, are inclined to use profits, efficiency, and other performance criteria to judge what is best for the most people. In a recession or when a firm is suffering through hard times, an executive may make a decision to cut 30% of the workforce in order to keep the company profitable and save the remaining jobs. She could justify this decision based on a utilitarian sense of business ethics.

- In the **utilitarian view** ethical behavior delivers the greatest good to the most people.
- In the **individualism view** ethical behavior advances long-term self-interests.

Individualism view
Does a decision or behavior promote one's long-term self-interests?

Moral rights view
Does a decision or behavior maintain the fundamental rights of all human beings?

Justice view
Does a decision or behavior show fairness and impartiality?

Utilitarian view
Does a decision or behavior do the greatest good for the most people?

Individualism View

The **individualism view** of ethical behavior is based on the belief that one's primary commitment is to the long-term advancement of self-interests. The basic idea of this approach is that society will

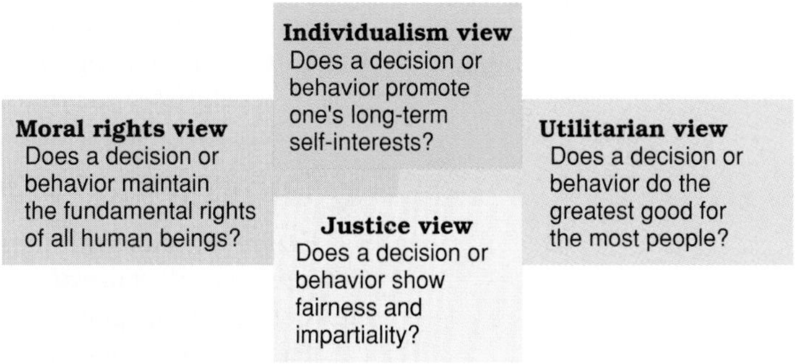

FIGURE 3.1 Four views of ethical behavior.

be best off if everyone acts in a way that maximizes his or her own utility or happiness. According to this viewpoint, people supposedly become self-regulating as they pursue long-term individual advantage. For example, lying and cheating for short-term gain should not be tolerated because if everyone behaves this way then no one's long-term interests will be served. The individualism view is supposed to promote honesty and integrity. But in business practice it may result in greed, a pecuniary ethic, described by one executive as the tendency to "push the law to its outer limits" and "run roughshod over other individuals to achieve one's objectives."[15]

Moral Rights View

● In the **moral rights view** ethical behavior respects and protects fundamental rights.

Ethical behavior under a **moral rights view** is that which respects and protects the fundamental rights of people. From the teachings of John Locke and Thomas Jefferson, for example, the rights of all people to life, liberty, and fair treatment under the law are considered inviolate. In organizations, the moral rights concept extends to ensuring that employees are protected in rights to privacy, due process, free speech, free consent, health and safety, and freedom of conscience. The issue of human rights, a major ethical concern in the international business environment, is central to this perspective. The United Nations, as indicated in the accompanying box, stands by the Universal Declaration of Human Rights passed by the General Assembly in 1948.[16]

Selections from Universal Declaration of Human Rights

- All human beings are born free and equal in dignity and rights.
- Everyone has the right to life, liberty, and security of person.
- No one shall be held in slavery or servitude.
- No one shall be subjected to torture or to cruel, inhuman, or degrading treatment or punishment.
- All are equal before the law and are entitled without any discrimination to equal protection of the law.

Justice View

● In the **justice view** ethical behavior treats people impartially and fairly.

The **justice view** of moral behavior is based on the belief that ethical decisions treat people impartially and fairly, according to legal rules and standards. This approach evaluates the ethical aspects of any decision on the basis of whether it is "equitable" for everyone affected.[17] Justice issues in organizations are often addressed on four dimensions—procedural, distributive, interactional, and commutative.[18]

● **Procedural justice** is concerned that policies and rules are fairly applied.

Procedural justice involves the degree to which policies and rules are fairly applied to all individuals. For example, does a sexual harassment charge levied against a senior executive receive the same full hearing as one made against a first-level supervisor? Does a woman with the same qualifications and experience as a man receive the same consideration for decisions regarding hiring or promotion?

● **Distributive justice** focuses on the degree to which outcomes are distributed fairly.

Distributive justice involves the degree to which outcomes are allocated fairly among people and without respect to individual characteristics based on ethnicity, race, gender, age, or other particularistic criteria. For example, are members of minority groups adequately or proportionately represented in senior management positions? Do universities allocate a proportionate share of athletic scholarships to males and females? **Interactional justice** involves the degree to which people treat one another with dignity and respect. For example, does a bank loan officer take the time to fully explain to an applicant why he or she was turned down for a loan?[19] **Commutative justice** focuses on the fairness of exchanges or transactions. According to this principle, the exchange is deemed to be fair if all parties enter into it freely, have access to relevant and available information, and obtain some type of benefit from the transaction.[20]

● **Interactional justice** is the degree to which others are treated with dignity and respect.

● **Commutative justice** is the degree to which an exchange or a transaction is fair to all parties.

Contrasts and Drawbacks

Examining issues through all four viewpoints helps to provide a more complete picture of the ethicality of a decision than merely relying on a single point of view. However, each viewpoint has some drawbacks that should be recognized.

The utilitarian view relies on the assessment of future outcomes that are often difficult to predict and that are tough to measure accurately. What is the economic value of a human life when deciding how rigid safety regulations need to be, especially when it is unclear exactly how many individuals might be affected? The individualism view presumes that individuals are self-regulating; however, not everyone has the same capacity or desire to control their behaviors. Even if only a few individuals take advantage of the freedom allowed under this perspective, such instances can disrupt the degree of trust that exists within a business community and make it difficult to predict how others will act.

The moral rights view provides for individual rights, but does not ensure that the outcomes associated with protecting those rights are beneficial to the majority of society. What happens when someone's right to privacy makes the workplace less safe for everyone? Finally, the justice view places an emphasis on fairness and equity, but this viewpoint raises the question of which type of justice is paramount. Is it more important to ensure that everyone is treated exactly the same way (procedural justice) or to ensure that those from different backgrounds are adequately represented in terms of the final outcome (distributive justice)?

CULTURAL ISSUES IN ETHICAL BEHAVIOR

● **Cultural relativism** suggests there is no one right way to behave; ethical behavior is determined by its cultural context.

● **Universalism** suggests ethical standards apply absolutely across all cultures.

Picture the situation: a 12-year-old boy is working in a garment factory in Bangladesh. He is the sole income earner for his family. He often works 12-hour days and was once burned quite badly by a hot iron. One day he is fired. His employer had been given an ultimatum by a major American customer: "no child workers if you want to keep our contracts." The boy says: "I don't understand. I could do my job very well. I need the money."

Should the boy be allowed to work? This difficult and perplexing situation is one example of the many ethics challenges faced in international business. Former Levi Strauss CEO Robert Haas once said that an ethical problem "becomes even more difficult when you overlay the complexities of different cultures and values systems that exist throughout the world."[21]

Those who believe that behavior in foreign settings should be guided by the classic rule of "when in Rome, do as the Romans do" reflect an ethical position known as **cultural relativism**.[22] This is the belief that there is no one right way to behave and that ethical behavior is always determined by its cultural context. An American international business executive guided by rules of cultural relativism, for example, would argue that the use of child labor is acceptable in another country as long as it is consistent with local laws and customs.

Figure 3.2 contrasts cultural relativism with **universalism**. Universalism is an absolutist ethical position suggesting that if a behavior or practice is not okay in one's home environment, it is not an acceptable

Child Labor Controversies

Child labor is a very complicated issue. In the United States, there are strict laws that govern the employment of children. However, child labor is a common practice in other cultures and many families are dependent on the income that children provide. The photo shows a young African child carrying goods which are to be sold in the market. Should child labor be outlawed in such circumstances?

Cultural relativism	Universalism
No culture's ethics are superior. The values and practices of the local setting determine what is right or wrong.	Certain absolute truths apply everywhere. Universal values transcend cultures in determining what is right or wrong.
When in Rome, do as the Romans do.	*Don't do anything you wouldn't do at home.*

FIGURE 3.2 Cultural relativism and universalism in international business ethics.
Source: Developed from Thomas Donaldson, "Values in Tension: Ethics Away from Home," *Harvard Business Review*, vol. 74 (September–October 1996), pp. 48–62.

● **Ethical imperialism** is an attempt to impose one's ethical standards on other cultures.

practice anywhere else. In other words, ethical standards are universal and should apply absolutely across cultures and national boundaries. In the former example, the American executive would not do business in a setting where child labor was used, since it is unacceptable at home. Critics of such a universal approach claim that it is a form of **ethical imperialism**, an attempt to impose one's ethical standards on others.

Business ethicist Thomas Donaldson finds fault with both cultural relativism and ethical imperialism. He argues instead that certain fundamental rights and ethical standards can be preserved at the same time that values and traditions of a given culture are respected.[23] The core values or "hyper-norms" that should transcend cultural boundaries focus on human dignity, basic rights, and good citizenship. Donaldson believes international business behaviors can be tailored to local and regional cultural contexts while still upholding these core values. In the case of child labor, the American executive might take steps so that any children working in a factory under contract to his or her business would be provided daily scheduled schooling as well as employment.[24]

Learning Check
Study Question 1
What is ethical behavior?

Be sure you can ☑ define ethics ☑ explain why obeying the law is not always the same as behaving ethically ☑ explain the difference between terminal and instrumental values ☑ identify the four alternative views of ethics ☑ contrast cultural relativism with universalism

ETHICS IN THE WORKPLACE

A college student gets a job offer and accepts it, only to get a better offer two weeks later. Is it right for her to renege on the first job to accept the second? A student knows that in a certain course his roommate submitted a term paper purchased on the Internet. Is it right for him not to tell the instructor? One student tells another that a faculty member promised her a high final grade in return for sexual favors. Is it right for him to inform the instructor's department head?

The real test of ethics occurs when individuals encounter a situation that challenges their personal values and standards. Often ambiguous and unexpected, these ethical challenges are inevitable. Everyone has to be prepared to deal with them, even students.

● An **ethical dilemma** is a situation that offers potential benefit or gain and that may also be considered unethical.

ETHICAL DILEMMAS

An **ethical dilemma** is a situation that requires a choice regarding a possible course of action that, although offering the potential for personal or organizational benefit, or both, may be considered unethical. It is often a situation in which action must be taken but for which there is no clear consensus on what is "right" and "wrong." An engineering manager speaking from experience sums it up this way: "I define an unethical situation as one in which I have to do something I don't feel good about."[25] Some examples of ethical dilemmas that managers face include:[26]

- *Discrimination*—Your boss suggests that it would be a mistake to hire a job candidate due to the individual's race, religion, gender, or age because your traditional customers might be uncomfortable with the individual.

- *Sexual harassment*—A female subordinate asks you to discipline a coworker that she claims is making inappropriate sexual remarks that make her feel uncomfortable. The coworker, your friend, says that he was just kidding around and asks you not to take any action that would go on his permanent record.

- *Conflicts of interest*—You are working in a foreign country and are offered an expensive gift in return for making a decision favorable to the gift giver. You know that such exchanges are common practice in this particular culture and that several of your colleagues have accepted similar gifts in the past.

- *Product safety*—Your company is struggling financially and can make one of its major products more cheaply by purchasing lower-quality materials, although doing so would marginally increase the risk of consumer injury.

- Use of *organizational resources*—Your company provides you with a laptop computer so that you can do work at home after hours. Your wife likes that computer better than hers, and asks if she can use it for her online business during the evening and on weekends.

It is almost too easy to confront ethical dilemmas from the safety of a textbook or a classroom discussion. In real life it's often a lot harder to consistently choose ethical courses of action. We end up facing ethical dilemmas at unexpected and inconvenient times, the events and facts can be ambiguous, and other performance pressures can be unforgiving and intense. Is it any surprise, then, that 56% of U.S. workers in one survey reported feeling pressured to act unethically in their jobs? Or that 48% said they had committed questionable acts within the past year?[27]

Management Smarts 3.1 presents a seven-step checklist for dealing with an ethical dilemma. It is a way to double-check the ethics of decisions before taking action. Step 6 highlights a key test: the risk of public disclosure. Asking and answering the recommended *spotlight questions* is a powerful way to test whether a decision is consistent with your personal ethical standards. They're worth repeating: "How will I feel if my family finds out about my decision, or if it's reported in the local newspaper or posted on the Internet?"

Management Smarts 3.1

Checklist for dealing with ethical dilemmas

Step 1. Recognize the ethical dilemma.

Step 2. Get the facts.

Step 3. Identify your options.

Step 4. Test each option: Is it legal? Is it right? Is it beneficial?

Step 5. Decide which option to follow.

Step 6. Double-check with the *spotlight questions*:
"How will I feel if my family finds out about my decision?"
"How will I feel about this if my decision is reported in the local newspaper or posted on the Internet?"

Step 7. Take action.

INFLUENCES ON ETHICAL DECISION MAKING

Increased awareness of the typical influences on ethical decision making can help you better deal with ethical pressures and dilemmas. These influences come from personal factors, the situational context, organizational culture, and the external environment.

Influences on ethical decision making

An **ethical framework** is a personal rule or strategy for making ethical decisions.

Personal Factors and Moral Development

Standing up for what you believe in isn't always easy, especially in a social context full of contradictory or just plain bad advice. Consider these words from a commencement address delivered some years ago at a well-known school of business administration. "Greed is all right," the speaker said. "Greed is healthy. You can be greedy and still feel good about yourself." The students, it is reported, greeted these remarks with laughter and applause. The speaker was Ivan Boesky, once considered the "king of the arbitragers."[28] It wasn't long after his commencement speech, however, that Boesky was arrested, tried, convicted, and sentenced to prison for trading on inside information.

Values, family, religion, and personal needs all help determine a person's ethics. Managers who lack a strong and clear set of personal ethics will find that their decisions vary from situation to situation. Those with solid **ethical frameworks**, ones that provide personal rules or strategies for ethical decision making, will act more consistently and confidently. The foundations for these frameworks rest with individual character and personal values that give priority to such virtues as honesty, fairness, integrity, and self-respect. These moral anchors can help us make ethical decisions even when circumstances are ambiguous and situational pressures are difficult.

Lawrence Kohlberg describes the three levels of moral development shown in Figure 3.3—preconventional, conventional, and postconventional.[29] There are two stages in each level, and Kohlberg believes that we move step by step through them as we grow in maturity and education. Most people operate either from a preconventional or conventional level of moral development; very few consistently operate at the postconventional level. And because individuals make decisions from different levels of moral development, they may approach the same ethical dilemma very differently.

In Kohlberg's *preconventional level* of moral development the individual is self-centered. Moral thinking is largely limited to issues of punishment, obedience, and personal interest. Decisions made in the preconventional stages of moral development are likely to be directed toward achieving personal gain or avoiding punishment and are based on obedience to rules.

In the *conventional level* of moral development, the individual is more social-centered. Decisions made in these stages are likely to be based on following social norms, meeting the expectations of others, and living up to agreed upon obligations.

At the *postconventional level* of moral development, the individual is strongly principle-centered. This is where a strong ethics framework is evident and the individual is willing to break with norms and conventions, even laws, to make decisions consistent with personal principles. Kohlberg believes that only a small percentage of people progress to the postconventional stages. An example might be the student who passes on an opportunity to cheat on a take-home examination because he or she believes it is wrong, even though the individual knows that most of the other students will cheat, that there is almost no chance of getting caught, and that the consequence of not cheating will be getting a lower grade on the test. Another example might be someone who refuses to use pirated computer software easily

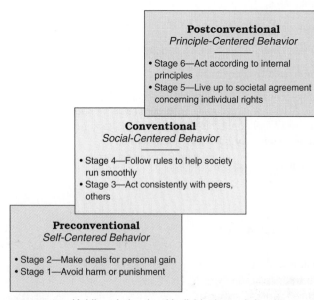

FIGURE 3.3 Kohlberg's levels of individual moral development.

available through the Internet and social networks, preferring to purchase them and respect others' intellectual property rights.

Situational Context and Ethics Intensity

Ethical dilemmas often appear unexpectedly or in ambiguous conditions; we're caught off guard and struggle to respond. Other times, we might even fail to see that an issue or a situation has an ethics component. This may happen, for example, when students find cheating so commonplace on campus that it becomes an accepted standard of behavior. Scholars use the concept of **ethics intensity** or **issue intensity** to describe the extent to which a situation is perceived to pose important ethics challenges.[30]

The conditions that raise the ethics intensity of a situation include the magnitude, probability, and immediacy of any potential harm, the proximity and concentration of the effects, and social consensus. A decision situation will elicit greater ethical attention when the potential harm is perceived as great, likely, and imminent, the potential victims are visible and close by, and there is more social agreement on what is good or bad about what is taking place. For example, how does the issue of pirated music downloads stack up on each of these ethics intensity factors? Can we say that low ethics intensity contributes to the likelihood of music pirating? In general, the greater the ethical intensity of the situation, the more aware the decision maker is about ethics issues and the more likely that his or her behavior will be ethical.

● **Ethics intensity** or **issue intensity** indicates the degree to which an issue or a situation is recognized to pose important ethical challenges.

Organizational Culture

The culture and values of an organization are important influences on ethics in the workplace. How a supervisor acts, what he or she requests, and what is rewarded or punished can certainly affect how others behave. The expectations of peers and group norms are likely to have a similar impact. In some cases, members will not be fully accepted as part of the team if they do not participate in actions that outsiders might consider unethical—for example, slacking off or abusing phone privileges. In other cases, the ethics culture sets high standards and may even push people to behave more ethically than they otherwise would.

Some organizations try to set the ethics culture by issuing formal policy statements and guidelines. Consider the story behind The Body Shop, quite well known for its entrepreneurial beginnings and socially responsible business model. Right from her first store in Brighton, England, the late founder Dame Anita Roddick built an organizational culture around the value of "profits with principles." She created an 11-point charter to guide the company's employees. It included this statement: "Honesty, integrity and caring form the foundations of the company and should flow through everything we do—we will

Anita Roddick Showed Way to Profits with Principles

Anita Roddick founded The Body Shop and grew the company from a single store to a global retail chain of over 2000 stores. The company is known for selling cosmetics and body creams that are produced in a socially responsible manner. As The Body Shop grew, so did Roddick's focus on social issues and her passion for environmental and human rights. She published several books including "Body and Soul: Profits with Principles" and "Take it Personally: How to Make Conscious Choices to Change the World" before her untimely death from a brain hemorrhage in 2007.

demonstrate our care for the world in which we live by respecting fellow human beings, by not harming animals, by preserving our forests."[31] Now owned by L'Oreal, The Body Shop's charter still communicates corporate expectations to employees in more than 2,100 shops in 55 countries.[32]

External Environment, Government Regulation, and Industry Norms

Wherever they operate, domestically or internationally, organizations are influenced by government laws and regulations as well as social norms and expectations. Laws interpret social values to define appropriate behaviors for organizations and their members; regulations help governments monitor these behaviors and keep them within acceptable standards. For example, the Sarbanes-Oxley Act of 2002 makes it easier for U.S. corporate executives to be tried and sentenced to jail for financial misconduct. It also created the Public Company Accounting Oversight Board and set a new standard for auditors to verify reporting processes in the companies they audit.

The climate of competition in an industry also sets a standard of behavior for those who hope to prosper within it. Sometimes the pressures of competition contribute to the ethical dilemmas of managers. Former American Airlines president Robert Crandall once telephoned Howard Putnam, then president of the now-defunct Braniff Airlines. Both companies were suffering from money-losing competition on routes from their home base of Dallas. A portion of their conversation follows.[33] Putnam: Do you have a suggestion for me? Crandall: Yes . . . Raise your fares 20 percent. I'll raise mine the next morning. Putnam: Robert, we— Crandall: You'll make more money and I will, too. Putnam: We can't talk about pricing. Crandall: Oh, Howard. We can talk about anything we want to talk about. In fact, the U.S. Justice Department strongly disagreed with Crandall. It alleged that his suggestion of a 20% fare increase amounted to an illegal attempt to monopolize airline routes. The suit was later settled when Crandall agreed to curtail future discussions with competitors about fares.

RATIONALIZATIONS FOR UNETHICAL BEHAVIOR

Consider the possibility of being asked to place a bid for a business contract using insider information, paying bribes to obtain foreign business, or falsifying expense account bills. "How," you should be asking, "do people explain doing things like this?" In fact, there are at least four common rationalizations that may be used to justify misconduct in situations that pose ethical dilemmas.[34]

- Convincing yourself that a behavior is not really illegal.
- Convincing yourself that a behavior is in everyone's best interests.
- Convincing yourself that nobody will ever find out what you've done.
- Convincing yourself that the organization will "protect" you.

After doing something that might be considered unethical, a rationalizer says: "*It's not really illegal.*" This expresses a mistaken belief that one's behavior is acceptable, especially in ambiguous situations. When dealing with shady or borderline situations in which you are having a hard time precisely determining right from wrong, the advice is quite simple: When in doubt about a decision to be made or an action to be taken, don't do it.

Another common statement by a rationalizer is "*It's in everyone's best interests.*" This response involves the mistaken belief that because someone can be found to benefit from the behavior, the behavior is also in the individual's or the organization's best interests. Overcoming this rationalization depends in part on the ability to look beyond short-run results to address longer-term implications, and to look beyond results in general to the ways in which they are obtained. In response to the

Real Ethics

No Super Bowl Advertisements from Pepsi

The Super Bowl is TV's priciest showcase in terms of advertisements, with commercials costing between $2 and $3 million for a 30-second spot. However, it's also an iconic event that draws a very large and attentive audience. Big name advertisers ante up to gain exposure to a huge pool of viewers, while ad agencies line up to get the big-dollar super bowl business. For them the chance to work on a Super Bowl advertising spot is not just a one-time revenue gain; if the ad is a major hit it's a reputation booster that pays off for the future as well.

Situation: In previous years, Pepsi used the Super Bowl to launch ad spots starring celebrities such as Britney Spears, Cindy Crawford, and Ozzy Osbourne. But after experiencing a drop in sales, the company decided it was time to sit on the sidelines of the big game. Saying "no" to Super Bowl advertising was an attractive place to cut costs.

But, like most business decisions, there's more to the story. Even though Pepsi cut its ad budget drastically in order to trim costs, it didn't cut back on some other expenses. In fact, the company decided to spend $20 million in philanthropy to provide grant money to be awarded to fund community projects. As advertising costs were reduced, philanthropic contributions increased.

You Decide

Who is likely to be helped and who is likely to be hurt by Pepsi's decision to do no Super Bowl advertising at this time? Is the firm acting in the best interest of its shareholders by cutting its advertising budget while spending $20 million on philanthropy?

While Pepsi's philanthropy might help communities that receive new grants, its reduction in advertising expenditures might hurt some of the ad agencies that it has worked closely with in the past. Some may even have to cut back on staff due to the loss of business. What are the ethics of Pepsi's action?

question "How far can I push matters to obtain this performance goal?" the best answer may be, "Don't try to find out."

Sometimes rationalizers tell themselves that *"no one will ever know about it."* They mistakenly believe that a questionable behavior is really "safe" and will never be found out or made public. Unless it is discovered, the argument implies, no crime was really committed. Lack of accountability, unrealistic pressures to perform, and a boss who prefers "not to know" can all reinforce such thinking. In this case, the best deterrent is to make sure that everyone knows that wrongdoing will be punished whenever it is discovered.

Finally, rationalizers may proceed with a questionable action because of a mistaken belief that *"the organization will stand behind me."* This is misperceived loyalty. The individual believes that the organization's best interests stand above all others. In return, the individual believes that top managers will condone the behavior and protect the individual from harm. But loyalty to the organization is not an acceptable excuse for misconduct; it should not stand above the law and social morality.

Be sure you can ☑ define *ethical dilemma* and give workplace examples ☑ identify Kohlberg's stages of moral development ☑ explain how ethics intensity influences ethical decision making ☑ explain how ethics decisions are influenced by an organization's culture and the external environment ☑ list four common rationalizations for unethical behavior

Learning Check ☑
Study Question 2
How do ethical dilemmas complicate the workplace?

MAINTAINING HIGH ETHICAL STANDARDS

Item: Bernard Madoff masterminded the largest fraud in history by swindling billions of dollars from thousands of investors. Item: Company admits overcharging consumers and insurers more than $13 million for repairs to damaged rental cars. Item: Former Tyco CEO Dennis Kozlowski convicted on 22 counts of grand larceny, fraud, conspiracy, and falsifying business records. Item: U.S. lawmakers charge that BP was negligent in inspecting oil pipelines, and that workers complained of excessive cost-cutting and pressures to falsify maintenance records. Item: Alcoa charged with paying illegal "kickbacks" to an official in Bahrain.[35]

We all know that news from the corporate world is not always positive when it comes to ethics. But as quick as we are to recognize the bad, we shouldn't forget that there is a lot of good news, too. There are many organizations, like Stonyfield Farm as featured in the chapter opener, whose leaders and members set high ethics standards for themselves and others.

ETHICS TRAINING

● **Ethics training** seeks to help people understand the ethical aspects of decision making and to incorporate high ethical standards into their daily behavior.

Ethics training takes the form of structured programs to help participants understand the ethical aspects of decision making. It is designed to help people incorporate high ethical standards into their daily behaviors. The Lockheed Martin Company, an aerospace, defense, security, and technology firm based in Maryland, requires all its employees to complete ethics awareness training on an annual basis. The company also produces short videos called the "Integrity Minute" as a complement to the training. The videos highlight key ethics topics such as harassment, conflicts of interest, gifts, and business courtesies. The company also shows its commitment to ethics and ethics training by appointing a vice president of ethics and business conduct as well as local ethics officers.[36]

There are lots of options in ethics training. College curricula include course work on ethics, and seminars on the topic are popular in the corporate world. But regardless of where or how the ethics training is conducted, it is important to keep things in perspective. Training is an ethics development aid; it isn't a guarantee of ethical behavior. A banking executive once summed things up this way: "We aren't teaching people right from wrong—we assume they know that. We aren't giving people moral courage to do what is right—they should be able to do that anyhow. We focus on dilemmas."[37]

CODES OF ETHICAL CONDUCT

● A **code of ethics** is a formal statement of values and ethical standards.

Ethics training often includes the communication of a **code of ethics**, a formal statement of an organization's values and ethical principles. Such codes are important anchor points in professions such as engineering, medicine, law, and public accounting. In organizations, they identify expected behaviors in such areas as general citizenship, the avoidance of illegal or improper acts in one's work, and good relationships with customers. Specific guidelines are often set for bribes and

Bernie Madoff's Ponzi Scheme

Bernard (Bernie) Madoff, a stock broker and financial advisor, founded the Wall Street firm Madoff Investment Securities LLC in 1960. He was its chairman until his arrest for securities fraud in December of 2008. Madoff is the admitted operator of what has been described as the largest Ponzi scheme in history. He defrauded thousands of investors out of billions of dollars. Madoff pleaded guilty to 11 federal offenses including securities fraud, wire fraud, and money laundering. In June of 2009 he was sentenced to 150 years in prison and is now prisoner number 61727-054 at Butner Federal Correctional Institute.

kickbacks, political contributions, honesty of books or records, customer–supplier relationships, coworker relationships, and confidentiality of corporate information.

Ethics codes are common in the complicated world of international business. For example, global manufacturing at Gap, Inc., is governed by a Code of Vendor Conduct.[38] The document addresses discrimination—"Factories shall employ workers on the basis of their ability to do the job, not on the basis of their personal characteristics or beliefs"; forced labor—"Factories shall not use any prison, indentured or forced labor"; working conditions—"Factories must treat all workers with respect and dignity and provide them with a safe and healthy environment"; and freedom of association—"Factories must not interfere with workers who wish to lawfully and peacefully associate, organize or bargain collectively."

But even though they have ethics codes in place, it is hard for even the most ethically committed global firms to police practices when they have many, even hundreds, of suppliers from different parts of the world. You might remember the recall of some 25 million toys, the large majority of which were made in China. Toy sellers like Wal-Mart have ethics codes and the U.S. government has toy safety regulations. Yet, the tainted toys got through to customers. Wal-Mart responded to the crisis by tightening its code and requiring suppliers to meet safety standards that are even higher than U.S. government requirements.[39]

MORAL MANAGEMENT

Although ethics training and codes of ethical conduct are helpful, they cannot guarantee ethical behavior in organizations. Ultimately, the issue boils down to individual character; there is no replacement for effective management practices that staff organizations with honest people. And, there is no replacement for having ethical leaders that set positive examples and always act as ethical role models.

Management scholar Archie Carroll makes a distinction between immoral, amoral, and moral managers.[40] The **immoral manager** chooses to behave unethically. He or she does something purely for personal gain and knowingly disregards the ethics of the action or situation. The **amoral manager** also disregards the ethics of an act or a decision, but does so unintentionally or unknowingly. This manager simply fails to consider the ethical consequences of his or her actions, and typically uses the law as a guideline for behavior. The **moral manager** considers ethical behavior as a personal goal. He or she makes decisions and acts in full consideration of ethical issues. In Kohlberg's terms, this manager is likely to be operating at the postconventional or principled level of moral development.[41]

Think about these three types of managers and how common they are in the real world of work. Although it may seem surprising, Carroll suggests that most managers act amorally. Though well intentioned, they remain mostly uninformed or undisciplined in considering the ethical aspects of our behavior. The moral manager, like Gary Hirshberg in the chapter opener, by contrast, is an ethics leader who always serves as a positive role model.

An **immoral manager** chooses to behave unethically.

An **amoral manager** fails to consider the ethics of her or his behavior.

A **moral manager** makes ethical behavior a personal goal.

WHISTLEBLOWER PROTECTION

- Agnes Connolly pressed her employer to report two toxic chemical accidents.
- Dave Jones reported that his company was using unqualified suppliers in the construction of a nuclear power plant.
- Margaret Newsham revealed that her firm was allowing workers to do personal business while on government contracts.
- Herman Cohen charged that the ASPCA in New York was mistreating animals.
- Barry Adams complained that his hospital followed unsafe practices.[42]

● A **whistleblower** exposes the misdeeds of others in organizations.

These persons from different work settings and linked to different issues share two important things in common. First, each was a **whistleblower** that exposed misdeeds in their organizations in order to preserve ethical standards and protect against further wasteful, harmful, or illegal acts.[43] Second, each was fired from their job.

At the same time that we can admire whistleblowers for their ethical stances, there is no doubt that they face risks of impaired career progress and other forms of organizational retaliation, up to and including termination. Although laws such as the Whistleblower Protection Act of 1989 offer some defense against "retaliatory discharge," legal protections for whistleblowers are continually being tested in court and many consider them inadequate.[44] Laws vary from state to state, and federal laws mainly protect government workers.

Research by the Ethics Resource Center has found that some 44% of workers in the United States fail to report the wrongdoings they observe at work. The top reasons are "(1) the belief that no corrective action would be taken and (2) the fear that reports would not be kept confidential."[45] Within an organization, furthermore, typical barriers to whistleblowing include a strict chain of command that makes it hard to bypass the boss; strong work group identities that encourage loyalty and self-censorship; and ambiguous priorities that make it hard to distinguish right from wrong.[46]

☑ **Learning Check**
Study Question 3
How can high ethical standards be maintained?

Be sure you can ☑ compare and contrast ethics training and codes of ethical conduct as methods for encouraging ethical behavior in organizations ☑ differentiate between amoral, immoral, and moral management ☑ define *whistleblower* ☑ identify common barriers to whistleblowing and the factors to consider when determining whether whistleblowing is appropriate

---

SOCIAL RESPONSIBILITY AND CORPORATE GOVERNANCE

● **Sustainability** in management means acting in ways that support a high quality of life for present and future generations.

Sustainability is an important word in management these days, and Procter & Gamble defines it as acting in ways that help ensure "a better quality of life for everyone now and for generations to come."[47] Think sustainability opportunities when you hear terms like alternative energy, recycling, and waste avoidance; think sustainability problems when you ponder the aftermath of the enormous Gulf of Mexico oil spill or read about hazardous chemicals in our medicines and food sources. We'll talk more about such issues in the next chapter on environment, sustainability, and innovation. But for now, they are all part and parcel of an important management concept known as **corporate social responsibility**. Also called CSR for short, it describes the obligation of an organization to act in ways that serve both its own interests and the interests of society at large.

● **Corporate social responsibility** is the obligation of an organization to serve the interests of society in addition to its own interests.

● The **triple bottom line** evaluates organizational performance on economic, social, and environmental criteria.

It is common for managers to make decisions while paying attention to what accountants call the "bottom line"—that is, considering how the decision will affect the profitability of the firm. But as introduced in the chapter opening example of Stonyfield Farm, more and more today we talk about the **triple bottom line**—a concept that focuses on a firm's economic, social, and environmental performance.[48] Some call this triple bottom line the concern for the "3 P's"—profit, people, and planet.[49] You might think of it more generally as acting with a sense of corporate social responsibility. And, by the way, that's most likely how you'd like your future employers to behave. "Students nowadays want to work for companies that help enhance the quality of life in their surrounding community," says one observer.[50] And in one survey 70% of students report that "a company's reputation and ethics" was "very important" when deciding whether or not to accept a job offer; in another survey 79% of 13–25 year olds say they "want to work for a company that cares about

Cue from Nature Leads to Sustainable Enterprise

"If nature designed an industrial process, what might it look like?" That is the question asked when executives at Interface, a Georgia company that produces high-quality carpets and flooring, decided to rethink their entire production process. For years Interface followed traditional manufacturing processes based on a "take, make, and waste" mindset. Although productive, it gave little thought to negative side effects on the environment. Historically, making carpet has always required a lot of raw materials, consumed a lot of energy, and emitted a large amount of pollution. And, carpet almost always ended up in a landfill at the end of its lifespan.

Things changed at Interface when Ray Anderson, company founder and chairman, realized that there had to be a more environmentally friendly way to make the company's products. Rather than settling for modest improvements, Anderson dedicated Interface to becoming a completely sustainable enterprise. The aim of a project called "Mission Zero" is to eliminate any negative impact on the environment by 2020.

Interface began by trying to design an environmentally friendly process that runs on renewable energy, does not create waste, and recycles almost everything. Anderson suggests

that the changes made so far have not only been good for the environment, but that they have been good for business as well. Innovation has helped to reduce costs and eliminate waste. Interface is also seen as a more desirable place to work, making it easier to attract and retain the best employees.

In cooperation with its stakeholders, Interface is making progress toward its vision of operating in a completely sustainable manner. Anderson hopes its actions and his commitment as CEO will influence other organizations to operate sustainably as well.

how it affects or contributes to society."[51] Here are some examples that seem to meet this test.[52]

- Trish Karter, who co-founded the Dancing Deer Bakery in Boston, found a winning recipe for social entrepreneurship. She hires people who lack skills, trains them, and provides them with a financial stake in the company. She also donates 35% of company proceeds to fund action programs to end family homelessness.
- Ori Sivan started a Chicago company called Greenmaker Building Supply. It supplies builders with a variety of green products—including kitchen tiles from coal combustion residue, countertops from recycled paper, and insulation made from old blue jeans.
- Carol Tienken worked 18 years for Polaroid Corporation before joining the nonprofit Greater Boston Food Bank. It serves 83,000 people each week. Tienken says: "At Polaroid, it was cameras and film. Nobody was going to die or go hungry. This business does make a difference."
- Deborah Sardone owns a housekeeping service in Texas. Noticing that clients with cancer really struggled with chores, she started Cleaning for a Reason. The nonprofit organization networks with cleaning firms around the country to provide free home cleaning to cancer patients.

STAKEHOLDER MANAGEMENT

Any discussion of social responsibility needs to recognize that organizations exist in a network of **stakeholders**. These are the persons, groups, and other organizations that are directly affected by the behavior of the organization and that hold a stake in its performance.[53] Typical organizations have many stakeholders such as

Stakeholders are the persons, groups, and other organizations that are directly affected by the behavior of the organization and that hold a stake in its performance.

Sample Stakeholder Map: Tom's of Maine

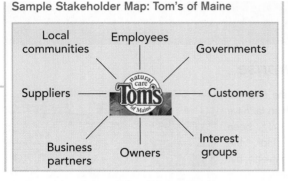

owners or shareholders, employees, customers, suppliers, business partners, government representatives and regulators, and community members. It can be helpful to identify them on a stakeholder map, such as the one in the Tom's of Maine example.

A key difficulty in stakeholder management is dealing with multiple stakeholders who make conflicting demands on the organization. For example, customers may demand low-cost products, while environmental activists may pressure the company to utilize manufacturing processes that make products more expensive. Or, shareholders may push the company to cut employment costs in order to improve the organization's financial performance, while employees may demand higher levels of healthcare benefits or protection against layoffs.

One way that managers can deal with conflicting stakeholder demands is to evaluate those demands along three criteria—the power of the stakeholder, the legitimacy of the demand, and the urgency of the issue.[54] **Stakeholder power** refers to the capacity of the stakeholder to positively or negatively affect the operations of the organization. **Demand legitimacy,** which reflects the extent to which the stakeholder's demand is perceived as valid and the extent to which the demand comes from a party with a legitimate stake in the organization. **Issue urgency** deals with the extent to which the issues require immediate attention or action.

● **Stakeholder power** refers to the capacity of the stakeholder to positively or negatively affect the operations of the organization.

● **Demand legitimacy** indicates the validity and legitimacy of a stakeholder's interest in the organization.

● **Issue urgency** indicates the extent to which a stakeholder's concerns need immediate attention.

Corporate social responsibility gets lots of stakeholder attention. Consumers, activist groups, nonprofit organizations, employees, and governments are often vocal and influential in pushing organizations toward socially responsible practices. In today's information age, business activities are increasingly transparent. Irresponsible practices are difficult to hide for long, no matter where in the world they take place. Not only do news organizations find and disseminate information on bad practices, activist organizations do the same. They also lobby, campaign, and actively pressure organizations to respect and protect everything from human rights to the natural environment.[55]

PERSPECTIVES ON CORPORATE SOCIAL RESPONSIBILITY

It may seem that corporate social responsibility is one of those concepts that most everyone agrees upon. But stakeholders can hold differing views on the ethicality of an organization's actions.[56] When the pros and cons of CSR are debated in academic and public-policy circles, those holding to a classical view take a stand against making corporate social responsibility a business priority while those holding to a socioeconomic view advocate for it.[57]

Classical View

● The **classical view of CSR** is that business should focus on profits.

The **classical view of CSR** holds that management's only responsibility in running a business is to maximize profits. In other words, "the business of business is business," and the principal obligation of management should always be to owners and shareholders. This classical view takes a very narrow stakeholder perspective and puts the focus on the single bottom line of financial performance. It is supported by Milton Friedman, a respected economist and Nobel Laureate. He says: "Few trends could so thoroughly undermine the very foundations of our free society as the acceptance by corporate officials of social responsibility other than to make as much money for their stockholders as possible."[58]

The arguments against corporate social responsibility include fears that its pursuit will reduce business profits, raise business costs (reducing competitiveness with foreign firms), dilute business purpose, and/or give business too much social

Research Brief

Prioritizing Stakeholders for Organizational Action

Journal of Business Ethics

Springer

Writing in the *Journal of Business Ethics,* Milena M. Parent and David L. Deephouse discuss how organizations can identify which stakeholder demands should get the most attention. Organizations typically cannot carry out all of the requests of stakeholders. Some are too expensive and time consuming, while others would interfere with an organization's ability to effectively conduct its business. Thus, it becomes important for organizations to discern which stakeholders should be listened to and how such requests should be prioritized.

Parent and Deephouse wanted to see if managers actually determine the importance of stakeholder demands based on the characteristics of power, legitimacy, and urgency. They studied organizations handling two major athletic contests, the Jeux de la Francophonie (Francophone Games) and the Pan American Games. Both organizations had to deal with a large number of stakeholders and a wide variety of demands in order to be successful.

The researchers found that having more than one of the characteristics of power, urgency, and legitimacy increased the importance of the stakeholder to managers. They also found that power was the single most important characteristic, followed by urgency and then legitimacy. Stakeholders with a lot of power relative to the organization are likely to be listened to; stakeholders with urgent requests were also given a reasonable amount of attention. In contrast, even legitimate demands were likely to be ignored when they lacked urgency and were made by relatively nonpowerful stakeholders. Because managers at different levels often evaluated stakeholder demands in a variety of ways, Parent and Deephouse recommend that more than one manager rate the stakeholders in order to increase the reliability with which such judgments are made.

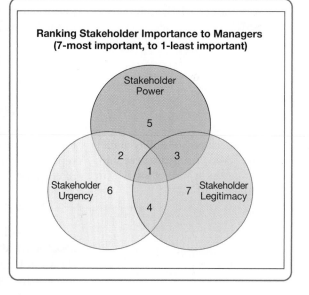

Ranking Stakeholder Importance to Managers (7-most important, to 1-least important)

You Be the Researcher

Think of the important stakeholders associated with the organization at which you work or volunteer. Which of the stakeholders would be viewed as powerful? Which have demands that would be seen as legitimate or as urgent? For specific demands, examine each of the three characteristics to see which demand is most likely to be viewed as important to your manager. Check to see if other members of your organization agree with your findings.

Reference: Milena M. Parent and David L. Deephouse, "A Case Study of Stakeholder Identification and Prioritization by Managers," *Journal of Business Ethics* (September 2007), pp. 1–23.

---

power without any specific accountability to the public. Although not against corporate social responsibility in its own right, Friedman and other proponents of the classical view believe that society's interests are best served in the long run by executives who focus on maximizing their firm's profits.

Socioeconomic View

The **socioeconomic view of CSR** holds that managers must be concerned with the organization's effect on the broader social welfare and not just with corporate profits. This view takes a broad stakeholder perspective and puts the focus on an expanded (triple) bottom line that includes not just financial performance but also social and environmental performance. It is supported by Paul Samuelson, another distinguished economist and Nobel Laureate. He says: "A large corporation these days not only may engage in social responsibility, it had damn well better try to do so."[59]

● The **socioeconomic view of CSR** is that business should focus on broader social welfare as well as profits.

Among the arguments in favor of corporate social responsibility are that it will enhance long-run profits, improve the public image of the business, make the organization a more attractive place to work, and help avoid government regulation. Furthermore, because society has provided the infrastructure that allows businesses to operate, businesses need to take actions that are in alignment with society's best interests. Thus, business executives have ethical obligations to ensure that their firms act responsibly and in the interests of society at large.

There is little doubt today that the public at large wants businesses and other organizations to act with genuine social responsibility. Also, a growing body of research links social responsibility and financial performance. One report showed that S&P 500 firms with strong commitments to corporate philanthropy outperform in respect to operating earnings.[60] More generally, research indicates that social responsibility is often associated with strong financial performance; at worst, corporate social responsibility appears to have no adverse financial impact.[61] Thus, the argument that acting with a commitment to social responsibility will negatively affect the "bottom line" is hard to defend. Instead, evidence points toward a **virtuous circle** in which corporate social responsibility leads to improved financial performance for the firm, and this in turn leads to more socially responsible actions in the future.[62]

● The **virtuous circle** occurs when CSR improves financial performance, which leads to more CSR.

EVALUATING CORPORATE SOCIAL PERFORMANCE

If we are to get serious about social responsibility, we need to get rigorous about measuring corporate social performance and holding business leaders accountable for the results. A **social responsibility audit** can be used at regular intervals to report on and systematically assess an organization's performance in various areas of corporate social responsibility.

● A **social responsibility audit** assesses an organization's accomplishments in areas of social responsibility.

Criteria for Social Performance

The social performance of business firms ranges from *compliance*—acting to avoid adverse consequences—to *conviction*—acting to create positive impact.[63] As shown in Figure 3.4, this performance can be evaluated on four criteria for evaluating socially responsible practices: economic, legal, ethical, and discretionary.[64]

1. Economic responsibility—Is the organization profitable?
2. Legal responsibility—Is the organization obeying the law?
3. Ethical responsibility—Is the organization doing what is "right"?
4. Discretionary responsibility—Is the organization contributing to the broader community?

An organization is meeting its *economic responsibility* when it earns a profit through the provision of goods and services desired by customers. While it might seem unusual to focus on economic performance, this is the foundation on which all the other types of responsibility rest. If a firm is not financially viable, it will not be able to take care of its owners or employees or engage in any of the other aspects of CSR. *Legal responsibility* is fulfilled when an organization operates within the law and according to the requirements of various external regulations. An organization meets its *ethical responsibility* when its actions voluntarily conform not only to legal expectations but also to

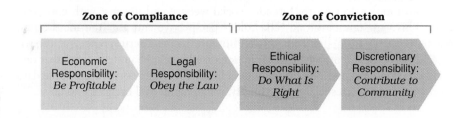

FIGURE 3.4 Criteria for evaluating corporate social performance.

the broader values and moral expectations of society. The highest level of social performance comes through the satisfaction of *discretionary responsibility*. At this level, the organization moves beyond basic economic, legal, and ethical expectations to provide leadership in advancing the well-being of individuals, communities, and society as a whole.

Social Responsibility Strategies

The decisions of people working at all levels in organizations ultimately determine whether or not practices are socially responsible. At the executive level these are "strategic" decisions designed to move the organization forward in its environment according to a long-term plan.[65] Figure 3.5 describes four corporate social responsibility strategies, with the commitment to social performance increasing as the strategy shifts from "obstructionist" at the lowest end to "proactive" at the highest.[66]

The **obstructionist strategy** ("Fight social demands") focuses mainly on economic priorities in respect to social responsibility. Social demands lying outside the organization's perceived self-interests are resisted. If the organization is criticized for wrongdoing, it can be expected to deny the claims. For example, cigarette manufacturers in the United States tried to minimize the negative health effects of smoking for decades until indisputable evidence became available.

● An **obstructionist strategy** avoids social responsibility and reflects mainly economic priorities.

A **defensive strategy** ("Do the minimum legally required") seeks to protect the organization by doing the minimum legally necessary to satisfy expectations. Corporate behavior at this level conforms only to legal requirements, competitive market pressure, and perhaps activist voices. If criticized, wrongdoing on social responsibility matters is likely to be denied. For example, car dealers are required to provide certain information to customers concerning loans they may be receiving. Some car dealers make sure their customers fully understand the information while other dealers gloss over the detailed information in hopes the customer will not realize the negative aspects of the car loan.

● A **defensive strategy** seeks protection by doing the minimum legally required.

Organizations pursuing an **accommodative strategy** ("Do the minimum ethically required") accept their social responsibilities. They try to satisfy economic, legal, and ethical criteria. Corporate behavior at this level is consistent with society's prevailing norms, values, and expectations, often reflecting the demands of outside pressures. An oil firm, for example, may be willing to "accommodate" with appropriate cleanup activities when a spill occurs; yet it may remain quite slow in taking actions to prevent spills in the first place.

● An **accommodative strategy** accepts social responsibility and tries to satisfy economic, legal, and ethical criteria.

The **proactive strategy** ("Take leadership in social initiatives") is designed to meet all prior criteria of social performance, and it also requires engaging in discretionary actions related to CSR. Corporate behavior at this level takes preventive action to avoid adverse social impacts from company activities, and it takes the lead in identifying and responding to emerging social issues. Interface's effort to proactively restructure its production processes in order to avoid having a negative effect on the environment is an example of this type of strategy.

● A **proactive strategy** meets all the criteria of social responsibility, including discretionary performance.

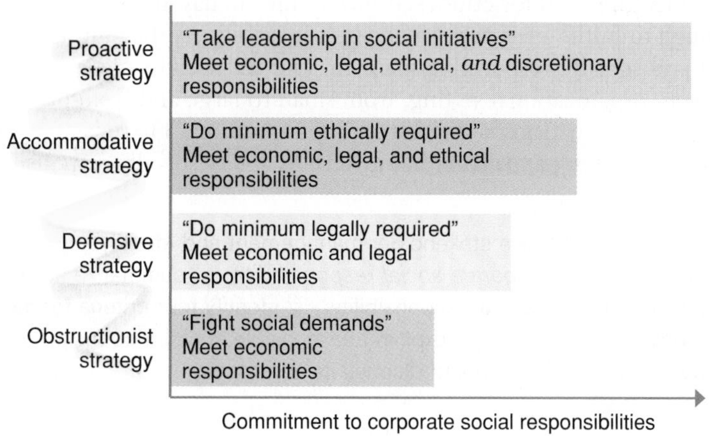

Proactive strategy	"Take leadership in social initiatives" Meet economic, legal, ethical, *and* discretionary responsibilities
Accommodative strategy	"Do minimum ethically required" Meet economic, legal, and ethical responsibilities
Defensive strategy	"Do minimum legally required" Meet economic and legal responsibilities
Obstructionist strategy	"Fight social demands" Meet economic responsibilities

Commitment to corporate social responsibilities

FIGURE 3.5 Four strategies of corporate social responsibility—from obstructionist to proactive behavior.

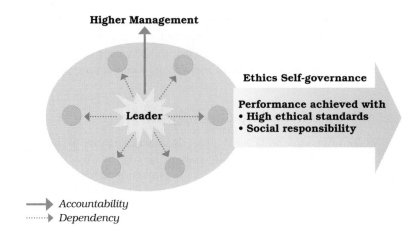

Higher Management

Ethics Self-governance

Performance achieved with
• **High ethical standards**
• **Social responsibility**

Leader

→ *Accountability*
┄┄► *Dependency*

FIGURE 3.6 Ethics self-governance in leadership and the managerial role.

● **Corporate governance** is the oversight of top management by a board of directors.

CORPORATE GOVERNANCE

When you read and hear about business ethics failures and poor corporate social responsibility, issues relating to **corporate governance** are often raised. The term refers to the active oversight of management decisions and company actions by boards of directors.[67] Businesses are required by law to have boards of directors that are elected by stockholders to represent their interests. The governance exercised by these boards most typically involves hiring, firing, and compensating the CEO; assessing strategy; and verifying financial records. The expectation is that board members will hold management accountable for ethical and socially responsible leadership.[68]

It is tempting to think that corporate governance is a clear-cut way to ensure that organizations exhibit social responsibility and that their members always act ethically. But the recent financial crisis and related banking scandals show once again that corporate governance can be inadequate and in some cases ineffectual. Where, you might ask, were the boards when such situations were first developing?

When corporate failures and controversies occur, weak governance often gets blamed. And when it does, you will sometimes see government stepping in to try to correct things for the future. In addition to holding hearings, as in the case of "bail-out" loans to U.S. automakers and banks, governments also pass laws and establish regulating agencies in attempts to better control and direct business behavior. The Sarbanes-Oxley Act, mentioned earlier, was passed by Congress in response to public outcries over major ethics and business scandals. Its goal is to ensure that top managers properly oversee and are held accountable for the financial conduct of their organizations.

Even as one talks about corporate governance reform and the accountability of top management, it is important to remember that all managers must accept personal responsibility for doing the "right" things.[69] Figure 3.6 highlights what might be called the need for ethics self-governance in day-to-day work behavior. It is not enough to fulfill one's performance accountabilities; they must be fulfilled in an ethical and socially responsible manner. The full weight of this responsibility holds in every organizational setting, from small to large and from private to non-profit, and at every managerial level from top to bottom. There is no escaping the ultimate reality—being a manager at any level is a very socially responsible job!

☑ **Learning Check**

Study Question 4
What are corporate social responsibility and governance?

Be sure you can ☑ discuss stakeholder management and identify key organizational stakeholders ☑ define *corporate social responsibility* ☑ summarize arguments for and against corporate social responsibility ☑ identify four criteria for measuring corporate social performance ☑ explain four possible social responsibility strategies ☑ define *corporate governance* and discuss its importance

Management Learning Review

Study Questions Summary

1 What is ethical behavior?

- Ethical behavior is that which is accepted as "good" or "right" as opposed to "bad" or "wrong."
- Because an action is not illegal does not necessarily make it ethical in a given situation.
- Because values vary, the question "What is ethical behavior?" may be answered differently by different people.
- The utilitarian, individualism, moral-rights, and justice views offer alternative ways of thinking about ethical behavior.
- Cultural relativism argues that no culture is ethically superior to any other; universalism argues that certain ethical standards apply everywhere.

FOR DISCUSSION **Is there ever a justification for cultural relativism in international business ethics?**

2 How do ethical dilemmas complicate the workplace?

- An ethical dilemma occurs when someone must decide whether to pursue a course of action that, although offering the potential for personal or organizational benefit or both, may be unethical.
- Managers report that their ethical dilemmas often involve conflicts with superiors, customers, and subordinates over such matters as dishonesty in advertising and communications, as well as pressure from bosses to do unethical things.
- Common rationalizations for unethical behavior include believing the behavior is not illegal, is in everyone's best interests, will never be noticed, or will be supported by the organization.

FOR DISCUSSION **Are ethical dilemmas always problems, or can they also be opportunities?**

3 How can high ethical standards be maintained?

- Ethics training can help people better deal with ethical dilemmas in the workplace.
- Written codes of ethical conduct formally state what an organization expects of its employees regarding ethical behavior at work.
- Immoral managers intentionally choose to behave unethically; amoral managers do not really pay attention to or think through the ethics of their actions or decisions; moral managers consider ethical behavior a personal goal.
- Whistleblowers expose the unethical acts of others in organizations, even while facing career risks for doing so.

FOR DISCUSSION **Is it right for organizations to require employees to sign codes of conduct and undergo ethics training?**

4 What are social responsibility and corporate governance?

- Social responsibility is an obligation of the organization to act in ways that serve both its own interests and the interests of its many stakeholders.
- An organization's social performance can be evaluated on how well it meets economic, legal, ethical, and discretionary responsibilities.
- Corporate strategies in response to demands for socially responsible behavior include obstruction, defense, accommodation, and proaction.
- Corporate governance is the responsibility of a board of directors to oversee the performance of the organization's top management.

FOR DISCUSSION **What questions would you include on a social audit for an organization in your community?**

Self-Test

Multiple-Choice Questions

1. Values are personal beliefs that help determine whether a behavior will be considered ethical or unethical. An example of a terminal value is _____.
   (a) ambition   (b) self-respect   (c) courage   (d) imagination

2. Under the _____ view of ethical behavior, a business owner would be considered ethical if she reduced a plant's workforce by 10% in order to cut costs to keep the business from failing and thus save jobs for the other 90%.
   (a) utilitarian   (b) individualism   (c) justice   (d) moral rights

3. A manager's failure to enforce a late-to-work policy the same way for all employees is an ethical violation of _____ justice.
   (a) ethical   (b) moral   (c) distributive   (d) procedural

4. The Sarbanes-Oxley Act of 2002 makes it easier for corporate executives to _____.
   (a) protect themselves from shareholder lawsuits   (b) sue employees who commit illegal acts   (c) be tried and sentenced to jail for financial misconduct   (d) shift blame for wrongdoing to boards of directors

5. Two "spotlight" questions for conducting the ethics double-check of a decision are (a) "How would I feel if my family found out about this?" and (b) "How would I feel if _____?"
   (a) my boss found out about this   (b) my subordinates found out about this   (c) this was printed in the local newspaper   (d) this went into my personnel file

6. Research on ethical dilemmas indicates that _____ is/are often the cause of unethical behavior by people at work.
   (a) declining morals in society   (b) lack of religious beliefs   (c) the absence of whistleblowers   (d) pressures from bosses and superiors

7. Customers, investors, employees, and regulators are examples of _____ that are important in the analysis of corporate social responsibility.
   (a) special-interest groups   (b) stakeholders   (c) ethics advocates   (d) whistleblowers

8. A(n) _____ is someone who exposes the ethical misdeeds of others.
   (a) whistleblower   (b) ethics advocate   (c) ombudsman   (d) stakeholder

9. A proponent of the classical view of corporate social responsibility would most likely agree with which of these statements?
   (a) Social responsibility improves the public image of business.   (b) The primary responsibility of business is to maximize business profits.   (c) By acting responsibly, businesses avoid government regulation.   (d) Businesses can and should do "good" while doing business.

10. An amoral manager _____.
    (a) always acts in consideration of ethical issues   (b) chooses to behave unethically   (c) makes ethics a personal goal   (d) takes action without considering whether or not the behavior is ethical

11. An organization that takes the lead in addressing emerging social issues is being _____, showing the most progressive corporate social responsibility strategy.
    (a) accommodative   (b) defensive   (c) proactive   (d) obstructionist

12. The criterion of _____ responsibility identifies the highest level of conviction by an organization to operate in a responsible manner.
    (a) economic   (b) legal   (c) ethical   (d) discretionary

13. Which ethical position has been criticized as a source of "ethical imperialism"?
    (a) individualism   (b) absolutism   (c) utilitarianism   (d) relativism

14. A manager supports an organization's attempts at self-governance when he or she always tries to achieve performance objectives in ways that are _____.
    (a) performance effective   (b) cost efficient   (c) quality oriented   (d) ethical and socially responsible

15. The potential for greed to influence decisions is most likely when one follows the _____ approach to ethics.
    (a) moral rights   (b) utilitarian   (c) individualism   (d) justice

Short-Response Questions

16. Explain the difference between the individualism and justice views of ethical behavior.

17. List four common rationalizations for unethical managerial behavior.

18. What are the major arguments for and against corporate social responsibility?

19. What is the primary difference between immoral and amoral management?

Essay Question

20. A small outdoor clothing company has just received an attractive offer from a business in Bangladesh to manufacture its work gloves. The offer would allow for substantial cost savings over the current supplier. The company manager, however, has read reports that some Bangladeshi businesses break their own laws and operate with child labor. How would differences in the following corporate responsibility strategies affect the manager's decision regarding whether to accept the offer: obstruction, defense, accommodation, and proaction?

Management **S**kills and **C**ompetencies

Self-Assessment

Back to Yourself: Individual Character

Character is something that people tend to think more about during presidential election years or when famous people, such as professional athletes or politicians, commit ethical transgressions. As suggested in the chapter opener, however, **individual character** and its underlying foundation of personal integrity isn't something that should only be an occasional concern; it deserves more than passing and even reluctant attention. The ethics and social responsibility issues facing organizations today put individual character to the test. Ethical dilemmas can arise on any given day. To deal with them we have to know ourselves well enough to make principled decisions that we can be proud of and that others will respect. After all, it's the character of people making key decisions that determines whether our organizations act in socially responsible or irresponsible ways. By giving in to things like hypercompetitiveness, we can damage or lose our individual character in personal and business situations. But if we can hold on to individual character, it is an anchor that builds a strong base of confidence and self-respect—both of which serve us very well in difficult work and decision situations. After you complete the following self-assessment on terminal values—a look at the "ends" you pursue in life, don't forget to go on-line for the instrumental values test—a look at the "means" you favor to achieve your goals.

> A person's **individual character** is reflected in their tendencies toward honesty, civility, caring, and sense of fair play.

Further Reflection: Terminal Values

Instructions

Rate each of the following values in terms of its importance to you. Think about each value in terms of its importance as a guiding principle in your life. Consider each value in relation to all the other values listed in the survey.[70]

Terminal Values

1. A comfortable life	Less important	1 2 3 4 5 6 7	More important
2. An exciting life	Less important	1 2 3 4 5 6 7	More important
3. A sense of accomplishment	Less important	1 2 3 4 5 6 7	More important
4. A world at peace	Less important	1 2 3 4 5 6 7	More important
5. A world of beauty	Less important	1 2 3 4 5 6 7	More important
6. Equality	Less important	1 2 3 4 5 6 7	More important
7. Family security	Less important	1 2 3 4 5 6 7	More important
8. Freedom	Less important	1 2 3 4 5 6 7	More important
9. Happiness	Less important	1 2 3 4 5 6 7	More important
10. Inner harmony	Less important	1 2 3 4 5 6 7	More important
11. Mature love	Less important	1 2 3 4 5 6 7	More important
12. National security	Less important	1 2 3 4 5 6 7	More important
13. Pleasure	Less important	1 2 3 4 5 6 7	More important
14. Salvation	Less important	1 2 3 4 5 6 7	More important
15. Self-respect	Less important	1 2 3 4 5 6 7	More important
16. Social recognition	Less important	1 2 3 4 5 6 7	More important
17. True friendship	Less important	1 2 3 4 5 6 7	More important
18. Wisdom	Less important	1 2 3 4 5 6 7	More important

Interpretation

Terminal values reflect a person's preferences concerning the "ends" to be achieved. They are the goals individuals would like to achieve in their lifetimes. Different value items receive different weights in this scale. (Example: "A comfortable life" receives a weight of "5" while "Freedom" receives a weight of "1.") Subtract your Social Values score from your Personal Values score to determine your Terminal Values score.

Scoring

To score this instrument, multiply your score for each item times a "weight"—for example, (#3 × 5) = your new question 3 score.

1. Calculate your Personal Values Score as:
   (#1 × 5) + (#2 × 4) + (#3 × 4) + (#7) + (#8) + (#9 × 4) + (#10 × 5) + (#11 × 4) + (#13 × 5) + (#14 × 3) + (#15 × 5) + (#16 × 3) + (#17 × 4) + (#18 × 5)
2. Calculate your Social Values Score as (#4 × 5) + (#5 × 3) + (#6 × 5) + (#12 × 5)
3. Calculate your Terminal Values Score as Personal Values-Social Values

---

Team Exercise

Confronting Ethical Dilemmas

Preparation

Read and indicate your response to each of the following situations.

1. Ron Jones, vice president of a large construction firm, receives in the mail a large envelope marked "personal." It contains a competitor's cost data for a project that both firms will be bidding on shortly. The data are accompanied by a note from one of Ron's subordinates saying: "This is the real thing!" Ron knows that the data could be a major advantage to his firm in preparing a bid that can win the contract. What should he do?

2. Kay Smith is one of your top-performing subordinates. She has shared with you her desire to apply for promotion to a new position just announced in a different division of the company. This will be tough on you since recent budget cuts mean you will be unable to replace anyone who leaves, at least for quite some time. Kay knows this and, in all fairness, has asked your permission before she submits an application. It is rumored that the son of a good friend of your boss is going to apply for the job. Although his credentials are less impressive than Kay's, the likelihood is that he will get the job if she doesn't apply. What will you do?

3. Marty Jose got caught in a bind. She was pleased to represent her firm as head of the local community development committee. In fact, her supervisor's boss once held this position and told her in a hallway conversation, "Do your best and give them every support possible." Going along with this, Marty agreed to pick up the bill (several hundred dollars) for a dinner meeting with local civic and business leaders. Shortly thereafter, her supervisor informed everyone that the entertainment budget was being eliminated in a cost-saving effort. Marty, not wanting to renege on supporting the community development committee, was able to charge the dinner bill to an advertising budget. Eventually, an internal auditor discovered the charge and reported it to you, the personnel director. Marty is scheduled to meet with you in a few minutes. What will you do?

Instructions

Working alone, make the requested decisions in each of these incidents. Think carefully about your justification for the decision. Meet in a group assigned by your instructor. Share your decisions and justifications in each case with other group members. Listen to theirs. Try to reach a group consensus on what to do in each situation and why. Be prepared to share the group decisions, and any dissenting views, in general class discussion.

Case Study: Patagonia

Go to *Management Cases for Critical Thinking* to find the recommended case for Chapter 3—"Patagonia: Turning a Profit Without Losing Your Soul."

Environment, Sustainability, and Innovation

4

Chapter 4 Study Questions

1 What is in the environment of organizations?

2 What are key issues in organization–environment relationships?

3 What are the emerging challenges of sustainability and the environment?

4 How do organizations accomplish innovation?

Learning From Others

A Keen Eye Will Spot Lots of Opportunities

Who would have predicted that something called "cloud computing" would challenge the way software firms traditionally serve business customers? Marc Benioff did. He saw the great potential of offering software services through the Internet and started Salesforce.com, now a powerhouse in business-to-business computing. It sells online services that allow firms to track sales, update accounts, bill customers, and handle an expanding variety of customer relationship functions.

Cloud computing frees users from costly in-house hardware and software ownership. Instead, they basically "rent" services delivered from remote servers maintained by firms such as Salesforce.com.

Benioff's genius in anticipating this market scored a bull's eye. His business model of on-demand computer services quickly moved from the fashion-forward stage to dead center in a popular and increasingly competitive industry.

Forward looking and confident in taking risk, Benioff recognized the opportunity in leading a shift away from selling business software as a product and toward selling it as a service. *The Wall Street Journal* now calls Salesforce.com "the pioneer in cloud computing." Customers buy what they want, have the opportunity to provide constant feedback, and can drop the service if they become dissatisfied. Salesforce.com even has a website called IdeaExchange where customers provide suggestions and comments to spur continued improvements. At one point they were asked to vote on a possible name change for the firm; they responded—"don't change it, we like Salesforce.com." And when the firm ran into difficulty handling computer crashes at one point, Benioff turned to a strategy of full disclosure and transparency so that customers always knew what was happening.[1]

you do the benchmarking

Some look at conditions in our world and see hopeless problems; others look and see endless opportunities. Some read environmental trends and spot innovation potential; some don't look at all. Marc Benioff's accomplishment in creating Salesforce.com is a great example of business innovation in the face of risk and uncertainty. Think about it. **Could this be your story someday—perhaps working in a different industry and setting, but still showing the same forward-thinking quest for innovation?**

Learning About Yourself

Risk Taking

Have you noticed the interest today in adventure sports—in things like ice climbing, river running, cliff parachuting, and more? Some say it's a quest for the adrenaline rush that comes from risk; others claim the "thrill" from such pastimes is addictive. For us it introduces the topic of **risk taking** and the degree to which we are uncomfortable or comfortable taking action in situations that are high in uncertainty. At issue here are the psychology of risk and the question of why some of us are risk takers while others are not.

Most consider tendencies toward risk taking as good for managers and organizational leaders. After all, isn't this the way to step forward and try new things that offer great potential returns in the future?

But there's need for caution as well. Research finds that risk taking by executives in higher performing organizations is motivated by confidence. This helps them adapt and deal positively with problems as they arise. In lower performing organizations, executives are motivated to take risks more by desperation to escape existing difficulties. Because they lack confidence when problems arise, they are more likely to quickly jump from one option to the next without making real gains.

> **Walking the fine line of Risk Taking**
>
> **Positive Side of Risk-Taking Behavior**
> Risk taking from base of performance success; motivated by confidence in moving to even better situation; able to deal with problems as they arise; lots of staying power
>
> Risk Line --- Risk Line
>
> **Negative Side of Risk-Taking Behavior**
> Risk taking from position of performance difficulty; motivated by desperation to get out of bad situation; hard time dealing with problems without losing focus; little staying power

The question, as suggested in the accompanying box, comes down to this: On which side of the "risk line" do you most often fall? Are you on the positive side where risk taking is motivated by confidence and is likely to have positive staying power? Or are you on the negative side where risk taking is motivated by desperation and the likelihood is to falter when problems are encountered? As a final thought, research also links high risk taking with boredom and dissatisfaction. Does this explain what you or friends experience when engaging in risky sports or personal behaviors?[2]

get to know yourself better

Make a commitment to carefully monitor your risk patterns. Which side of the risk line are you on most often? When you take risks in your coursework, is it confidence motivation that drives the risk taking or desperation? Think about how your current risk-taking tendencies might play out in future work and personal situations. **Also take advantage of the end-of-chapter Self-Assessment feature to further reflect on your Tolerance for Ambiguity, and examine your risk tendencies in conditions of Turbulence and Uncertainty.**

4 Environment, Sustainability, and Innovation

Study Question 1	Study Question 2	Study Question 3	Study Question 4
Environments of Organizations	Organization–Environment Relationships	Environment and Sustainability	Environment and Innovation
• General or macro-environment • Specific or task environment	• Competitive advantage • Uncertainty, complexity, and change • Organizational effectiveness	• Sustainability goals • Sustainable development • Green management • Human sustainability	• Types of innovations • The innovation process • Characteristics of innovative organizations
Learning Check 1	Learning Check 2	Learning Check 3	Learning Check 4

"I'm deeply sorry for any accident that Toyota drivers have experienced . . . I myself, as well as Toyota, am not perfect. We never run away from our problems or pretend we don't notice them." Toyota President Akio Toyoda, testifying before U.S. Congress

"Every single Toyota owner deserves a full accounting of what happened and what went wrong . . . The U.S. government has to do a much better job of keeping the American people safe." Senator Jay Rockefeller, Chairman, U.S. Senate Commerce Committee

When Toyota recalled millions of vehicles for accelerator problems and quality defects, it wasn't just customers and the marketplace that reacted; U.S. lawmakers did too.[3] Toyota's president felt the full brunt of American anger when called to testify before the Senate Commerce Committee. Although he apologized and pledged a full and complete response by the firm, Akio Toyoda was met by claims that his firm had acted with "greed and insensitivity."

ENVIRONMENTS OF ORGANIZATIONS

Interactions between business and lawmakers are just one example of the complex relationship that organizations maintain with their external environments. Top executives like Toyoda, and all managers, must understand what is taking place in the external environment and then make good decisions on how to run the organization and position its products and services for success.

THE GENERAL OR MACROENVIRONMENT

● The **general environment** is comprised of economic, legal-political, technological, sociocultural, and natural environment conditions.

With regard to the **general environment** of organizations, we are talking about all external conditions that set the context for managerial decision making. You might think of it as a broad envelope of dynamic forces that surround and influence an organization. We most often classify these forces as economic, legal-political, technological, sociocultural, and natural environment conditions, as shown by the Starbucks example in Figure 4.1.

Economic Conditions

Managers must be concerned about *economic conditions in the general environment*, particularly those that influence customer spending, resource supplies, and investment capital. Things like the overall health of the economy—domestic and global, in terms of financial markets, inflation, income levels, and job outlook are always important. All such economic conditions affect the prospects for individual

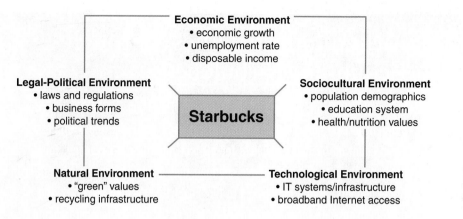

FIGURE 4.1 Sample general environment conditions faced by firms like Starbucks.

companies, the spending patterns and lifestyles of consumers, and even a nation's priorities. They are key factors to be assessed, forecasted, and considered when executives make decisions about the strategies and operations of their organizations.

Consider the practice of **offshoring**, which involves the outsourcing of work and jobs to lower cost foreign locations. One of the dominant trends over the past decade, it has resulted in the loss of many domestic jobs and been a source of great political debate and social concern. But economic signals are now showing signs of another shift; **onshoring** or **reshoring** is moving some jobs back home. Rising labor costs in foreign countries, higher shipping costs, complicated logistics, complaints about poor customer service, public criticisms about destroying local jobs, and economic incentives offered by communities are causing some global firms to transfer jobs from foreign locations and create new jobs at home.[4]

Another economic trend facing executives of national and global brands is the growing number of communities around the country that are advocating "buy local" themes. Activist citizens and government leaders are claiming that the local economy benefits more in job gains and amount of money circulating when people shop at "local" businesses as opposed to outside "big chains." Starbucks is among those trying to address this challenge through a practice known as **unbranding**—where stores owned by chains are advertised with local nonbranded names.[5] If you go to 15th Ave. Coffee & Tea in Seattle, for example, it's really a Starbucks-owned café, even though this corporate ownership isn't noticeable to a customer. Starbucks spokesperson Ann Kim-Williams says that the strategy of unbranding offers an "amplified focus on local relevance" and that "we hope customers will feel an enhanced sense of community."[6]

- **Offshoring** is the outsourcing of jobs to foreign locations.

- **Onshoring** or **reshoring** is the return of jobs from foreign locations as companies establish new domestic operations.

- **Unbranding** occurs when stores owned by major national and global chains are advertised with local nonbranded names.

Legal-Political Conditions

Managers must also stay abreast of developments in *legal-political conditions in the general environment.* These are represented by existing and proposed laws and regulations, government policies, and the philosophy and objectives of political parties. In the aftermath of economic recession, U.S. lawmakers are discussing many issues such as regulation of banks and the financial services industry, foreign trade agreements, and protection of U.S. jobs and industries. Corporate executives follow such debates to monitor trends that can affect the regulation and oversight of their businesses. As a result of Toyota's quality problems, featured earlier, U.S. lawmakers quickly decided to tighten car safety regulations and consider legislation that would require all cars sold in the United States to have "black boxes" that would record crash data.[7]

Legal-political conditions in the global business environment vary from one country to the next. Just as foreign firms like Toyota have to learn to deal with U.S. laws and political conditions, so too must U.S. firms adjust to the legal-political environments of foreign countries. Not too long ago, for example, the European

Airline Industry Flies Through Economic Turbulence

One of the lingering impacts of the economic recession is a continuing commitment to cost control by organizations. It used to be that most airlines could count on business travelers for 50% or more of their revenue. Tough times and new technologies have changed that. Many companies are cutting travel budgets, asking employees to fly "coach" when they do travel, and making it possible for them to travel a lot less by using videoconferencing. Airlines have resorted to a variety of new pricing schemes, including baggage and preferred seating charges, to try and reverse the revenue losses.

● **Internet censorship** is the deliberate blockage and denial of public access to information posted on the Internet.

Union fined Microsoft $1.35 billion for antitrust violations involving the practice of bundling media and Windows software and making the source code for interoperability unavailable to competitors.[8]

National policies on **Internet censorship**—the deliberate blockage and denial of public access to information posted on the Internet, also vary around the world. And, global firms face many dilemmas in dealing with them.[9] Google faced a running series of problems dealing with Chinese laws that restrict access within China to Internet sites deemed off limits by the government—things with political content or pornography, for example. When Google complied by engaging in censorship of its Google.cn site, the firm was criticized for reneging on its avowed commitments to information freedom.[10] When Google decided to stop censoring and leave China, others, including some Chinese citizens, criticized the firm for abandoning efforts to promote information access in the country. A Google spokesperson said: "We have a delicate balancing act between being a platform for free expression and also obeying local laws around the world."[11]

Technological Conditions

Speaking of the Internet, perhaps nothing gets as much attention these days as developments in the *technological conditions in the general environment.* Nobody doubts that we are in the midst of a continuing technological revolution that affects everything from the way we work to how we live and how we raise our children.

The role of technology in organizations is advancing as rapidly as the use of YouTube, Facebook, Google Maps, and "apps" on our smartphones. Did you know that customers of USAA, a financial services firm for military families, can take photos of checks, use an iPhone app to send them to the bank, and then spend the money from their account within minutes?[12] And are you aware that we are now spending more time in the world of social media than with e-mail?[13] Indeed, one of the growing concerns of employers is just how much time their "tech savvy" employees spend browsing the Web and engaging in online diversionary pastimes. After finding out that 70% of workers spent over an hour a day watching Web-based videos, one employer said: "I almost fell out of my chair when I saw how many people were doing it."[14]

Social media are now all the rage, but for employers it's both a problem and an opportunity. In a survey of 1,400 chief information officers, only one out of ten said his or her firm allowed employees full access to networking sites while on the job.[15] One concern is for too much "social *not*working," while another is for protecting the privacy of privileged information and communications. The term **Enterprise 2.0** describes how organizations use social networking and blog technologies to open up communications, while still keeping the focus on work and protecting the privacy of information exchanges. An example is Yammer, a corporate communication tool built around the question: "What are you working on?"

● **Enterprise 2.0** is the use of social networking and blog technologies in the workplace.

Also on the employee side of the technology equation is the issue of work-life balance. Do you realize how easily technology drives the penetration of work responsibilities into our non–work lives? How often, for example, do you hear people complaining that they're "never free from the job," and that their work follows them home, on vacation, and just about everywhere in the form of the ubiquitous notebook or netbook computer and smartphone device? And, don't forget that technology is playing an ever-increasing role in recruiting. A CareerBuilder.com survey reports that some 45% of executives said they visited social-network sites of job candidates and about one-third of them found information that caused them to not hire the person.[16] On the other side of the issue, U.S. Cellular reports that it saved $1 million in just one year by using LinkedIn.com to find job candidates rather than hiring through headhunter firms.[17]

Sociocultural Conditions

The *sociocultural conditions in the general environment* take meaning as norms, customs, and demographics of a society or region, as well as social values on such matters as ethics, human rights, gender roles, and life styles. Patterns and trends in these sociocultural factors can have major consequences for organizations and how they are managed.[18]

In respect to age demographics, managers should stay abreast of differences among **generational cohorts**—people born within a few years of one another and who experience somewhat similar life events during their formative years.[19] On the issue of technology, for example, the aging Baby Boomer generation is a "digital immigrant" group that has had to learn about technology as it became available. But the Millennials or Gen Ys, along with their younger counterparts the iGeneration, are "digital natives" who grew up and are growing up in technology-enriched homes, schools, and friendship environments. This affects everything from how they listen to music and watch TV and movies, to how they shop, to how they work and learn. Characteristics often described for the digital natives are ease of multitasking, desire for immediate gratification, continuous contact with others, and less concern with knowing things than with knowing where to find out about things.[20]

● **Generational cohorts** consist of people born within a few years of one another and who experience somewhat similar life events during their formative years.

In respect to social values, managers should be aware of how shifting currents and trends affect such things as reputation management, product development, and advertising messages. There was a time, for example, when the pay of American CEOs wouldn't have gotten a lot of public attention. No more. With a depressed economy and wide gaps between the average worker's pay and the average CEO's, complaints are flying. Public values are showing increasing intolerance of perceived pay inequities. We have reached the point where Congressional discussions have been held on executive pay, many articles are regularly published to report the pay of corporate executives, and a growing number of firms are facing shareholder resolutions asking for more input on executive compensation.[21] And on the customer side of things, it wasn't too long ago that research was reporting that only about 10% of consumers would "go out of their way to purchase environmentally sound products."[22] But dramatic shifts in energy prices and increased attention on global warming seem to be quickly increasing consumer preferences for "green" products— everything from automobiles to energy to building materials to the food we eat. Research also shows that many consumers are now willing to pay more for ethical products such as fair trade coffee.[23]

Generations Show Differences on Important Values

With our economy facing the implications of dealing with an aging workforce, scholars Jean Twenge, Stacy Campbell, Brian Hoffman, and Charles Lance decided to investigate value differences across generational cohorts—groups of individuals born about the same time and experiencing similar life events during their development years. The authors recognize that with a large number of retirements looming and with more seniors remaining in the workforce, it is important to understand how values may differ among generations in the same workplace and what the implications might be for managing them.

Twenge et al. focused their attention on comparing Baby Boomers (born 1946–1964, grew up during the Vietnam War and civil rights movement) with Generation X (born 1965–1981, saw fall of the Soviet Union and advent of the AIDS epidemic) with Generation Y or the Millennials (born 1982–1999, grew up digital and saw major corporate ethics scandals). They examined data gathered as part of a program called Monitoring the Future, which has surveyed high school seniors each year since 1976.

The main findings of the study were in values toward leisure, with GenX increasing over Boomers and Millennials further increasing over GenX. The researchers interpret this as a growing desire for work–life balance. Extrinsic values for money and status, however, increased for GenX and then decreased for Millennials. Data for intrinsic (meaning from work), altruistic (helping others), and social (relationships) values all showed a similar decline from Boomers to GenX to Millennials.

Because values are important influences on behavior, the researchers conclude that different generations may need different handling in the workplace. GenX and Millennials may be attracted to work settings that offer work–life balance and support leisure pursuits, things often associated with alternative and more flexible work scheduling. The researchers do caution that the data are old and that we shouldn't assume that values within the generational cohorts haven't shifted with time.

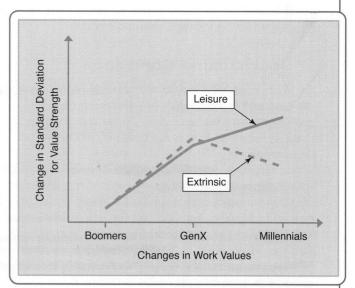

Reference: Jean M. Twenge, Stacy M. Campbell, Brian J. Hoffman, and Charles E. Lance, "Generational Difference in Work Values: Leisure and Extrinsic Values Increasing, Social and Intrinsic Values Decreasing," *Journal of Management Online First* (March 1, 2010): www.jom.sagepub.com.

NATURAL ENVIRONMENT CONDITIONS

The latter discussion leads directly into consideration of *natural environment conditions.* Debates about being "carbon neutral," "green," and "sustainable" are big issues on our campuses, in our communities, and in our everyday lives. You can look around and easily spot any number of initiatives to reduce paper usage, recycle, use local produce, and adopt energy saving practices. In business you'll find that industries like renewable power are creating new job opportunities in "green-collar" employment. New business practices are also emerging. For example, Timberland is labeling shoes with a carbon rating to show how much greenhouse gas was released during production, while SABMiller has set a goal of reducing by 25% the amount of water needed to brew a liter of beer.[24]

Without doubt, we increasingly expect businesses to supply us with environmentally friendly products and to operate in ways that preserve and respect the environment. When they don't, public criticism is likely to be vocal and harsh. Just recall the outrage that quickly surfaced over the disastrous BP oil spill in the Gulf of Mexico and subsequent calls for stronger government oversight and control over corporate practices that put our natural world at risk.[25]

There is now growing interest in the notion of **sustainable business**, where firms operate in ways that both meet the needs of customers and protect or advance the well-being of the natural environment. What makes a business "sustainable" is that how it operates and what it produces have minimum negative impact on the environment and helps preserve it for future generations.[26] A truly sustainable business operates in harmony with nature rather than by exploiting nature. Hallmarks of sustainable business practices include less waste, less toxic materials, resource efficiency, energy efficiency, and renewable energy. We'll explore these issues of environment and sustainability further in a later section of this chapter. For now, Management Smarts 4.1 shows that a commitment to environmental social responsibility offers benefits to both organizations and society.[27]

Management Smarts 4.1

Strategic goals engaged by environmental social responsibility (ESR) practices

Goal: **Increase market share**—advertise and publicize ESR activities to gain reputation; innovate in ESR to offer green products; use ESR to raise rivals' costs.

Goal: **Increase productivity**—innovate in ESR to gain operating efficiencies through green processes; raise worker morale by valuing and engaging in ESR activities.

Goal: **Increase human capital**—use ESR commitments as well as activities to recruit and retain employees, as well as to attract managers and executives with sustainability values.

Goal: **Increase competitiveness**—use ESR activities to attract investors, gain market reputation, and raise costs for competitors within the industry.

● **Sustainable business** both meets the needs of customers and protects the natural environment for future generations.

THE SPECIFIC OR TASK ENVIRONMENT

In contrast to the general environment conditions, organizations and their managers deal everyday with the **specific environment** or **task environment**. It comprises the actual organizations, groups, and persons with whom an organization interacts and conducts business. You can picture it as standing between the level of the general environment and the boundary of the organization itself.

● The **specific environment**, or **task environment**, includes the people and groups with whom an organization interacts.

● **Stakeholders** are the persons, groups, and institutions directly affected by an organization.

Organizational Stakeholders

Members of the specific or task environment are often described as **stakeholders**, first described in Chapter 3 as the persons, groups, and institutions affected by the organization's performance.[28] Stakeholders are key constituencies that have a stake in how an organization operates; they are influenced by it, and they can influence it in return. Figure 4.2 shows that the important stakeholders for most organizations include customers, suppliers, competitors, regulators, advocacy groups, investors or owners, and employees. "Society at large" and "future generations" are also part of the stakeholder map; they introduce, among other things, concerns for sustainability and the natural environment.

Top-level decisions are often made with an analysis of the extent to which the organization is creating value for and satisfying the needs of

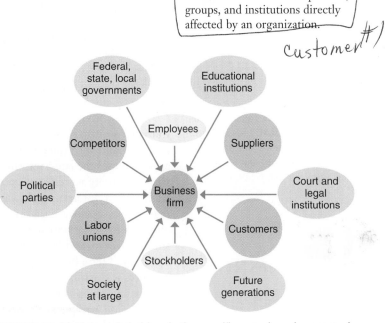

FIGURE 4.2 Multiple stakeholders in the specific or task environment of a typical business firm.

its multiple stakeholders. For example, businesses create value for customers through product pricing and quality; for owners the value is represented in realized profits and losses. Businesses can create stakeholder value for suppliers through the benefits of long-term business relationships. For local communities this value can be found in such areas as the citizenship that businesses display when they use and contribute to public services. For employees, value creation takes such forms as wages earned and job satisfaction. Businesses can even create value for competitors by stimulating markets and innovations that didn't exist before.

The interests of multiple stakeholders are sometimes conflicting, and management decisions may have to address different priorities and trade-offs among them. Some years ago, for example, researchers asked MBA students what a business's top priorities should be. Some 75% answered "maximizing shareholder value," and 71% responded "satisfying customers." Only 25% mentioned "creating value for communities," and only 5% noted "concern for environmentalism."[29] It would be interesting to repeat the survey to see if today's students would give more priority to society at large and future generations as stakeholders, and to more sustainable business practices.

Customers and Suppliers as Stakeholders

Question: What's your job?

Answer: I run the cash register and sack groceries.

Question: But isn't it your job to serve the customer?

Answer: I guess, but it's not in my job description.

This conversation illustrates what often becomes the missing link in the quest for business success: customer service.[30] Contrast it with the case of a customer who once called the Vermont Teddy Bear Company to complain that her new mail-order teddy bear had a problem. The company responded promptly, she said, and arranged to have the bear picked up and replaced. She wrote the firm to say "thank you for the great service and courtesy you gave me."[31]

Customers are always key stakeholders, and they can be very demanding in desires for low price, high quality, on-time delivery, and great service. A *Harvard Business Review* survey reports that American business leaders rank customer service and product quality as the first and second most important goals in the success of their organizations. A survey by the market research firm Michelson & Associates showed poor service and product dissatisfaction ranking first and second as the reasons customers abandon a retail store.[32] Imagine the ramifications if every customer or client contact with an organization were positive. Not only would these people return again and again as customers, but they would also tell others and expand the company's customer base.

● **Customer relationship management,** or **CRM**, uses information technologies to communicate with customers and gather data tracking their needs and desires.

Many organizations now use the principles of **customer relationship management** to establish and maintain high standards of customer service. Known as CRM and introduced in the chapter-opening example of Salesforce.com, this approach uses the latest information technologies to maintain intense communication with customers as well as to gather and utilize data regarding their needs and desires. At Marriott International, for example, CRM is supported by special customer management software that tracks information on customer preferences. When you check in to a Marriott hotel, your past requests for things like a king-size bed, no smoking room, and Internet access are likely already in your record. Says Marriott's chairman: "It's a big competitive advantage."[33]

Just as organizations need to manage their customers on the output side, supplier relationships on the input side must also be well managed. Any organization deals with a complex set of suppliers who provide it with finances, information, and material resources. How well the supplier relationships are managed can have a major impact on operating efficiencies and business profits. The concept of

supply chain management, or SCM, involves the strategic management of all operations linking an organization and its suppliers through purchasing, transportation logistics, and inventory management.[34] The goal of SCM is to achieve efficiency in all aspects of the supply chain while ensuring on-time availability of quality resources for customer-driven operations. As retail sales are made at Wal-Mart, for example, an information system updates inventory records and sales forecasts. Suppliers access this information electronically, allowing them to adjust their operations and rapidly ship replacement products to meet the retailer's needs.

> **Supply chain management**, or **SCM**, involves management of all operations linking an organization and its suppliers, such as purchasing, transportation logistics, and inventory management.

Be sure you can ☑ list key elements in the general and specific environments of organizations ☑ define *sustainable business* ☑ describe how a business can create value for four key stakeholders ☑ give examples of potential conflicting interests among stakeholders for a business in your community ☑ explain *customer relationship management* and *supply chain management*

Learning Check
Study Question 1
What is in the external environment of organizations?

ORGANIZATION–ENVIRONMENT RELATIONSHIPS

Understanding an organization's external environment is one thing; making good decisions to best deal with the opportunities and threats it poses is quite another. In today's challenging times, managers continually wrestle with the notion of competitive advantage, the challenges of environmental uncertainty, and the quest for organizational effectiveness.

COMPETITIVE ADVANTAGE

One of the goals in managing the organization–environment interface is to achieve **competitive advantage**—something that an organization does extremely well and that gives it an advantage over competitors in the marketplace.[35] This concept is discussed further in Chapter 9 on strategic management. For now, the notion of competitive advantage may be best summed up as an answer to this question: "What does my organization do best?"

> **Competitive advantage** is something that an organization does extremely well, is difficult to copy, and gives it an advantage over competitors in the marketplace.

Legendary investor Warren Buffett is often quoted as saying "sustainable competitive advantage" is what he first looks for in a potential investment. Examples of what might attract Buffett as an investor and that represent the essence of competitive advantage include Wal-Mart's inventory management technology, which enables a low-cost structure, and Coca-Cola's brand management, which helps maintain a loyal customer base. As a prelude to further discussion in Chapter 9, you should recognize that competitive advantage in general can be pursued in the following ways.[36]

- *Competitive advantage can be achieved through costs*—finding ways to operate with lower costs than one's competitors and thus earn profits with prices that one's competitors have difficulty matching.

- *Competitive advantage can be achieved through quality*—finding ways to create products and services that are of consistently higher quality for customers than what is offered by one's competitors.

- *Competitive advantage can be achieved through delivery*—finding ways to outperform competitors by delivering products and services to customers faster and on time, and by developing timely new products.

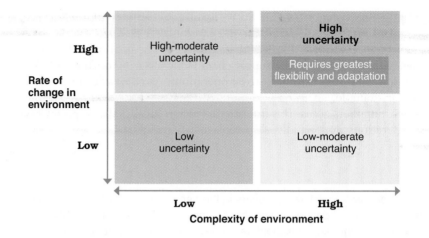

FIGURE 4.3 Dimensions of uncertainty in the external environments of organizations.

- *Competitive advantage can be achieved through flexibility*—finding ways to adjust and tailor products and services to fit customer needs in ways that are difficult for one's competitor to match.

UNCERTAINTY, COMPLEXITY, AND CHANGE

● **Environmental uncertainty** is a lack of information regarding what exists in the environment and what developments may occur.

As managers pursue competitive advantage, their decision making is often complicated by **environmental uncertainty**—a lack of complete information regarding what exists in the environment and what developments may occur. This uncertainty makes it difficult to analyze general and task environment conditions and deal with stakeholders' needs. The more uncertain the environment, the harder it is to predict future states of affairs and understand their potential implications for the organization.

Two dimensions of environmental uncertainty are shown in Figure 4.3.[37] The first is the *degree of complexity*, or the number of different factors in the environment. An environment is typically classified as relatively simple or complex. The second is the *rate of change* in and among these factors. An environment is typically classified as stable or dynamic. The most challenging and uncertain situation is an environment that is both complex and dynamic. This is perhaps what faces automobile, financial, and housing industry executives today. High-uncertainty environments require flexibility and adaptability in organizational designs and work practices, as well as an ability of decision makers to respond quickly as new circumstances arise and new information becomes available.

ORGANIZATIONAL EFFECTIVENESS

● **Organizational effectiveness** is a measure of how well an organization performs while using resources to accomplish mission and objectives.

A basic indicator of management success in dealing with complex and changing environments is **organizational effectiveness**. It is a measure of how well an organization performs while using resources to accomplish its mission and objectives. Theorists analyze organizational effectiveness from different vantage points.[38]

- The *goal approach* looks at the output side and defines organizational effectiveness in terms of achievement of key operating objectives such as profits and market share.
- The *systems resource approach* looks at the input side and defines organizational effectiveness in terms of success in acquiring needed resources from the organization's environment.

- The *internal process approach* looks at the transformation process and defines organizational effectiveness in terms of how efficiently resources are utilized to produce goods and services.
- The *strategic constituencies approach* looks at the external environment and defines organizational effectiveness in terms of the organization's impact on key stakeholders and their interests.

All approaches to organizational effectiveness—goal, systems resource, internal process, and strategic constituencies—should be assessed as a package in order to gain a full picture of the organization's performance. If we go back to the Toyota case of massive vehicle recalls, for example, "effectiveness" was a core theme when the firm's CEO, Akio Toyoda, issued his public apologies while testifying before the U.S. Congress. Toyoda said: "I would like to point out here that Toyota's priority has traditionally been the following: first, safety; second, quality; and third, volume. These priorities became confused, and we were not able to stop, think, and make improvements as much as we were able to before." He later suggested that the volume goal became inappropriately dominant in corporate decision making as Toyota expanded rapidly while trying to gain market share around the globe.[39] If anything, this case suggests that goals pursued without consideration of strategic constituencies and customers may cause executives to falsely conclude that all is well even when it is not.

Organizational effectiveness also needs to be evaluated on a time line, rather than as just one point in time.[40] In the short run, the focus is on performance effectiveness in goal accomplishment and performance efficiency in resource utilization. In the medium term, effectiveness involves adaptability in the face of changing environments and development of people and systems to meet new challenges. And in the long run, effectiveness may be described as achieving continued prosperity under conditions of uncertainty.

Be sure you can ☑ define *competitive advantage* and give examples of how a business might achieve it ☑ analyze the uncertainty of an organization's external environment using degree of complexity and rate of change ☑ describe the systems resource, internal process, goal, and strategic constituencies approaches to organizational effectiveness

Learning Check
Study Question 2
What are key issues in organization–environment relationships?

ENVIRONMENT AND SUSTAINABILITY

Climate change, carbon footprints, alternative energy—renew, recycle, conserve, and preserve; the link between people, environment, and sustainability has many facets. So, should some assessment of environmental impact be included in a full-range definition of organizational effectiveness? At PepsiCo, for example, CEO Indra Nooyi has said that her firm's "real profit" should be assessed in the following way: Revenue less Cost of Goods Sold less Costs to Society. "All corporations operate with a license from society," says Nooyi. "It's critically important that we take that responsibility very, very seriously; we have to make sure that what corporations do doesn't add costs to society."[41]

SUSTAINABILITY GOALS

The notion of "costs to society" raised by Nooyi links back to the **triple bottom line** of organizational responsibility discussed in Chapter 3—assessing economic, social, and environmental performance.[42] You might recall it as a

● The **triple bottom line** assesses the economic, social, and environmental performance of organizations.

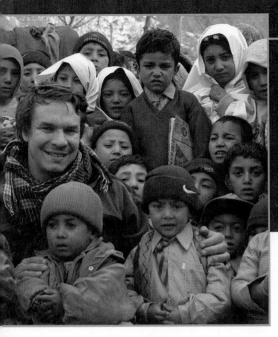

Nonprofit Rallies Pennies for Peace

Can you imagine an American building rural schools in the tribal regions of Pakistan and Afghanistan? Meet Greg Mortensen who founded the Central Asia Institute and Pennies for Peace to do just that. Author of best-sellers *Three Cups of Tea* and *Stones into Schools*, Mortensen turned a mountain-climbing adventure into a lifelong commitment. His nonprofit organizations are focused on human sustainability. They have helped more than 28,000 children, 18,000 of them girls, who receive education in places where a Westerner has to tread carefully and with cultural awareness.

● The **3 Ps of organizational performance** are Profit, People, and Planet.

● **ISO 14001** is an international quality standard requiring organizations to set environmental objectives and targets, account for environmental impacts, and continuously improve environmental performance.

focus on **3 Ps of organizational performance**: Profit, People, and Planet. The relevance of the 3 P's to the present discussion of environment and sustainability is highlighted by **ISO 14001**, a global quality standard that requires certified organizations to set environmental objectives and targets, account for the environmental impact of their activities, products, or services, and continuously improve environmental performance.[43] Its relevance is also reflected in one of the guiding Principles for Management Education as set forth in a United Nations' sponsored forum of global educational leaders: "We will develop the capabilities of students to be future generators of sustainable value for business and society at large and to work for an inclusive and sustainable global economy."[44]

What, for example, do you think of when you read or hear about J. W. Marriott Corporation? For most of us, it's a hotel chain focused on customers and profits. But for residents in Boa Frente, an isolated village in Brazil's interior Amazon region, Marriott is a sponsor of better education and health care. It's a partner in a United Nations plan that rallies the support of global businesses to help save the remaining rain forests through a program called REDD—Rules for Reducing Emissions from Deforestation and Degradation.[45] In Boa Frente this means not only getting new schools, health clinics, and infrastructure, it also means continuing education for the citizens about the natural environment and sustainability. Aderbal de Oliveira, a village leader, says: "The forest has riches. We must be its guardians." And in respect to its role in the project, Marriott's Vice President Arne M. Sorenson says: "We decided to be a leader in this space. It makes us a better brand and increases customer loyalty."[46]

SUSTAINABLE DEVELOPMENT

Rising oil prices, concerns for greenhouse-gas emissions and use of toxins, public values on climate change and clean energy, poverty and income disparities—all of these forces and more are driving the conversation about our planet and sustainable development today.[47] The range of issues stands at the interface between how people live and how organizations operate, and the capacity of the natural environment to support them. We want prosperity, convenience, comfort, and luxury in our everyday lives. But, we are also aware that more and more attention must be given to the costs of these aspirations and how those costs can be borne in a way that doesn't impair the future.

The term **sustainable development** describes practices that make use of environmental resources to support society today while also preserving and

● **Sustainable development** makes use of environmental resources to support societal needs today while also preserving and protecting them for future generations.

Real Ethics

Corporate Greens Take on Global Warming

Get ready—you'll be reading and hearing a lot more about "corporate greens." No, we're not talking about a new political party; we're talking about a growing voice from the business community that it really does care about global warming and is going to do its share to respond to the threats. There's emerging consensus not only that global warming is harming our planet even faster than expected, but that sustainable innovations by business are needed to deal with it.

As concerns for global warming build, so, too, do pressures for change in traditional business methods. More business leaders seem to be taking the challenge seriously. Ryan Wright is manager in charge of utility and sustainability at the Bellisio Foods plant in Jackson, Ohio. You may not think there's a lot that can be done to "green up" a manufacturing facility, but he's found the way. A large treatment plant digests food waste, using bio-organisms to create the methane that becomes fuel to run the factories' boilers. Wright believes the process cuts CO_2 output by 43,000 tons per year by saving

on costs of natural gas and transporting waste to a landfill. Although the price of the system was $4.65 million, he says: "It's a great project; we're proud of it: it's the right thing to do."

You Decide

Is it ethical for a business to pursue anything but "carbon neutrality" in today's world? Should businesses sacrifice profits by doing more than is legally required to fight global warming?

Alternatively, is it ethical for a firm to highlight its environmentally friendly practices if they are undertaken primarily to avoid government regulation or adverse publicity? In other words, does it make a difference from an ethics standpoint if a firm does "good things" for selfish reasons?

protecting the environment for use by future generations. The World Business Council for Sustainable Development, whose membership includes the CEOs of global corporations, defines sustainable development as "forms of progress that meet the needs of the present without compromising the ability of future generations to meet their needs."[48]

Conversations about sustainable development often refer to **environmental capital** or **natural capital**.[49] It represents the available storehouse of natural resources that exist in the form of atmosphere, land, water, and minerals, that we use to sustain life and produce goods and services for society. In this sense, sustainable development practices in management would be evaluated on the basis of their contributions to preserving environmental capital for future generations while tapping it for the present. The possibilities range from investments in alternative energy sources such as solar, wind, and algal biofuels, to water conservation efforts, to electronically monitoring energy usage for better decision making and control, to using more energy efficient building designs and materials, to changing work styles and schedules to be more energy efficient, to use of teleconferences to replace physical travel, to many more options.[50]

● **Environmental capital** or **natural capital** is the storehouse of natural resources—atmosphere, land, water, and, minerals, that we use to sustain life and produce goods and services for society.

GREEN MANAGEMENT

The importance of environment and sustainability was highlighted by the theme for the 2009 annual meeting of the Academy of Management—"Green Management Matters." **Green management** is defined as managing people and organizations in ways that demonstrate and achieve "responsible stewardship of the natural environment." Another way to put it is that green management treats people and resources in ways that give high priority to sustainable development and nurturing of environmental capital.[51]

You will find green management reflected in a wide variety of *green projects* ranging from the use of new technologies to reduce energy consumption to

● **Green management** is managing people and organizations in ways that achieve responsible stewardship of the natural environment.

changes in basic operations and practices to avoid or minimize adverse environmental impact. Procter & Gamble estimates that it has reduced energy use by 40% and cut 3 million sheets of paper from its annual consumption by outsourcing with Xerox to provide what is called "managed print services."[52] And, each Disney movie studio now gets quarterly performance scorecards on waste created as well as energy and water consumed.[53]

You will also find green management reflected in an increasing variety of *green products*. A notable example is the fully electric vehicle, which some suggest will make up 40% of new car sales by 2050.[54] You will also find green management reflected in *green marketing*, which is pursued by companies hoping to better educate a full range of stakeholders about the importance of sustainability. Robert Iger, CEO of Disney, says: "When you have the unique opportunity that our company has [to reach millions of children], and you can teach them the importance of behaving in a more responsible way from an environmental perspective—it adds up."[55]

HUMAN SUSTAINABILITY

Before leaving this discussion, it's important to recognize that the notion of sustainability in management can be made much broader than a focus on the natural environment alone. Scholar Jeffrey Pfeffer offers a strong case in favor of giving management attention not only to issues of ecological and environmental sustainability—traditional green management themes, but also to social and human sustainability—the People part of the 3 Ps.[56] He says: "Just as there is concern for protecting natural resources, there could be a similar level of concern for protecting human resources . . . Being a socially responsible business ought to encompass the effect of management practices on employee physical and psychological well-being."[57]

Pfeffer's concerns for human sustainability link back to the importance of employees as stakeholders, and to managerial concerns for their job satisfaction and quality of work life. Specifically, he calls attention to issues and practices like those highlighted in Management Smarts 4.2. They illustrate how management actions can have major consequences for the health and mortality of the people whose everyday work fuels the organizations of our society.[58] You should find many ideas in the chapters ahead that reflect Pfeffer's call for managers to respect and value people in organizations, and to recognize that good managers can make a positive difference on human sustainability.

Management Smarts 4.2

Assessing organizational impact on human sustainability

Get a start on assessing human sustainability by asking:
To what extent do management decisions and organizational practices help support and advance human health and well-being?

- Provision of health insurance to employees?
- Provision of health and wellness programs for employees?
- Avoiding job layoffs?
- Structuring work hours to reduce stress?
- Structuring work hours to avoid and minimize work-family conflict?
- Designing jobs to reduce stress?
- Designing jobs to give people control over their work?
- Being transparent and fair in handling wage and status inequalities?

Learning Check
Study Question 3
What are the emerging issues of sustainability and the environment?

Be sure you can ☑ explain the triple bottom line and 3 Ps of organizational performance ☑ explain the link between business activities and sustainability goals ☑ define the terms *sustainable development* and *environmental capital* ☑ give examples of sustainability issues today ☑ explain and give examples of *green management* ☑ discuss human sustainability as a management concern

ENVIRONMENT AND INNOVATION

If competitive advantage and sustainability are goals when executives and leaders manage the organization–environment interface, innovation is one of the major keys to accomplishing them. **Innovation** is the process of coming up with new ideas and putting them into practice.[59] And to stay successful, individuals and organizations alike must change and adapt through innovation even as the environment changes around them. As IBM's CEO Samuel J. Palmisano says: "The way you will thrive in this environment is by innovating—innovating in technologies, innovating in strategies, innovating in business models."[60]

Top CEOs know that innovation doesn't come easily; it has to be nurtured, championed, and supported as a core organizational value. Innovation killers like lengthy development times, poor coordination, risk-averse cultures, avoidance of customer feedback, and more, have to be dealt with. Mechanisms and resources that allow innovation to prosper have to be put into place. For example, BMW relocates engineers and designers to a central location for face-to-face product development; GE measures and tracks innovation records; 3M expects its "old timers" to pass along stories and values associated with the firm's long-standing commitments to innovation; and Procter & Gamble has created a new vice-president position for innovation and knowledge.[61]

> ● **Innovation** is the process of taking a new idea and putting it into practice.

TYPES OF INNOVATIONS

When you think innovation, products like the iPad, Kindle e-reader, Post-It Notes, and even a Super-Soaker water gun might come to mind. Or you might think about self-scanning checkouts at the grocery store, online check-ins for air travel, or your favorite smartphone app. All are part and parcel of a whole host of business innovations that are convenient tools to streamline tasks, increase communication, and provide entertainment. But don't forget about innovations that tackle social responsibility. Some seek sustainability in relationship with our natural environment, while others address social problems such as poverty and disease.

Business Innovations

Innovation in and by organizations has traditionally been addressed in three broad forms. (1) **Product innovations** result in the creation of new or improved goods and services. (2) **Process innovations** result in better ways of doing things. (3) **Business model innovations** result in new ways of making money for the firm. Consider these examples taken from annual listings of the world's most innovative companies.[62]

> ● **Product innovations** result in new or improved goods or services.
>
> ● **Process innovations** result in better ways of doing things.
>
> ● **Business model innovations** result in ways for firms to make money.

- *Product Innovation*—The Blackberry from Research in Motion ushered in a new era of handheld mobile devices; Apple introduced us to the iPod, iPhone, and iPad world; Amazon brought us the Kindle and launched a new era of e-readers; Facebook made social media part of everyday life; Tata Group of India introduced a $2,500 car—the Nano—for low-income earners.

- *Process Innovation*—Southwest Airlines continues to improve operations supporting its low-cost business strategy; IKEA transformed retail shopping for furniture and fixtures; Amazon.com keeps improving the online shopping experience; Procter & Gamble added design executives to its top management circle; LG Electronics keeps improving its world-class supply chain.

- *Business Model Innovation*—Virgin Group Ltd. uses "hip lifestyle" to brand over 200 companies, from airlines to communications to space travel; Starbucks continues to turn coffee selling into a global branding business;

eBay created the world's largest online marketplace; Google thrives on advertising revenues driven by Web technology; Salesforce.com sells software not as a product, but as a service.

Sustainable Innovations

> ● **Sustainable innovations** or **green innovations** help reduce the carbon footprints and environmental impacts of organizations, their practices, and products.

More and more today you will also hear and read about **sustainable innovations** or **green innovations**. They occur as businesses create new products and production methods that tackle the sustainability issues just discussed in the last section. The goal is to have minimal negative impact on the natural environment or, even better, actually improve it.[63]

At Procter & Gamble, for example, researchers found that customers' major energy consumption of its laundry products occurred as they used warm or hot water for washing.[64] The firm created Tide Cold Water laundry detergents to eliminate the need for hot water washes. P&G's goal is to have $20 billion in sustainable innovation products on the market by 2012. At Vodafone, estimates are that in one year new videoconferencing technologies eliminated the need for 13,500 flights and lowered carbon emissions by some 5,000 tons. Sierra Nevada Brewing Company blends purchased natural gas with biogas from its water treatment plant to fuel generators for heat; when solar power is added to the mix, the firm generates 80% of its power and also reduces air pollution. And at Wal-Mart, CEO Lee Scott has set a very high green innovation goal; he wants Wal-Mart to eliminate waste totally.[65]

Real People

Muhammad Yunus Fights Poverty with Social Business Model

For Muhammad Yunus, Nobel Prize winner and noted social entrepreneur from Bangladesh, a world without poverty may be a dream, but it's a dream that he has long been pursuing. He's CEO of Grameen Bank, an innovator in microfinance that provides loans to poor people with no collateral. The bank has loaned over $7.5 billion to date and now employs 27,000+ people.

Poverty is, unfortunately, a part of our global environment. You can find it in your local community, and it's an international concern. A large proportion of the world's population lives in poverty–at least a billion people live on less than one dollar per day. According to Yunus, two-thirds of the world's population has no access to banks. He says: "The way the banking institutions have been designed and built is based on certain criteria which poor people don't fulfill."

As an economist in Bangladesh, Yunus developed the Grameen Bank to help poor people start and operate small businesses. Recognizing that many poor couldn't get regular bank loans because they didn't have sufficient collateral, Yunus came up with the "microcredit" idea to lend small amounts of money at very low interest rates and with the goal of promoting self-sufficiency through operating small enterprises.

By design, the vast majority of loan recipients, 97%, are women. Yunus says: "we saw real benefits of money going straight to women–children benefited directly and women had long-term vision for escaping poverty." Each loan recipient becomes part of a local group of similar borrowers who agree to support and encourage one another. They pay the loans off in weekly installments and a borrower only gets another loan when the first is paid off successfully. The system works; the repayment rate is 98%.

The Grameen Bank model has been replicated in more than 40 countries, including the United States. Yunus continues to pursue poverty initiatives, including a commitment to "social business." In his book *Creating a World Without Poverty*, he defines a social business as one that accomplishes a social goal and in which profits are reinvested in the business rather than distributed as dividends to the owners.--

Social Business Innovations

Although the tendency is to view innovation in a business and economic context, it's important to remember that it applies equally well when we talk about the world's social problems—poverty, famine, literacy, diseases, and the general conditions for economic and social development. As Dipak C. Jain, the former dean of Northwestern's Kellogg School of Management, says: "Our primary goal should be producing leaders of real substance who put their knowledge to work in ways that make the world a better place."[66]

Check the profile of Mohammad Yunus and the Grameen Bank featured in the Real People box. On one level what Yunus has accomplished is a business model innovation—microcredit lending. But at another level it is a **social business innovation**—which might be described as pursuing business innovation with a social conscience. Yunus did this by using microcredit lending to help create small enterprises and fight poverty. In this case the underlying business model directly addresses a social problem. And it's a very good benchmark. As management consultant Peter Drucker once said: "Every single social and global issue of our day is a business opportunity in disguise."[67]

> ● **Social business innovation** finds ways to use business models to address important social problems.

THE INNOVATION PROCESS

Whatever the goal, whether it be new product, improved process, unique business model, sustainability, or social benefit, the innovation process begins with *invention*—the act of discovery—and ends with *application*—the act of use. Consultant Gary Hamel describes it in these five steps of what he calls the *wheel of innovation*.[68] Step 1 is *imagining*—thinking about new possibilities. Step 2 is *designing*—building initial models, prototypes, or samples. Step 3 is *experimenting*—examining practicality and financial value through experiments and feasibility studies. Step 4 is *assessing*—identifying strengths and weaknesses, potential costs and benefits, and potential markets or applications. Step 5 is *scaling*—implementing what has been learned and commercializing new products or services.

One of the newer developments in the innovation process is **reverse innovation**. Sometimes called *trickle-up innovation*, it recognizes the potential for valuable innovations to be launched from lower organizational levels and diverse locations.[69] The concept got its start in the world of global business where firms take products and services

> ● **Reverse innovation** recognizes the potential for valuable innovations to be launched from lower organizational levels and diverse locations, including emerging markets.

Infosys Innovates by Improvisation

India's Bangalore-based Infosys Technologies is one of the top technology firms in the world. It also thrives on a classic Indian approach to innovation known as *jugaad*. A slang word in the local dialect of Hindi, *jugaad* means innovating through improvisation and focusing on meeting immediate customer needs. When an Indian villager turns an irrigation pump into a diesel engine that he can use to drive a farm vehicle, this is *jugaad*—nothing fancy, based on available resources, and yet good enough to get the job done. It's all about "affordability and scale," says one Indian executive.

developed in emerging markets, often subject to poorer economies with pricing constraints, and use them elsewhere. GE, for example, has found expanded markets for handheld and portable electrocardiogram and ultrasound machines that sell for a fraction of the price of larger units. The smaller units were first developed in India and China, and then moved through reverse innovation into the United States where both their mobility and low prices made them popular with emergency units. Management scholar C. K. Prahalad praises reverse innovation while calling emerging market settings "laboratories for radical innovation."[70]

Commercializing Innovation

> ● The process of **commercializing innovation** turns new ideas into actual products, services, or processes to increase profits through greater sales or reduced costs.

In business, **commercializing innovation** turns new ideas into actual products, services, or processes that can increase profits through greater sales or reduced costs. For example, 3M Corporation generates as much as one-third or more of its revenues from products that didn't exist four years ago. Product innovation is a way of life for the firm, and its success relies on the imagination of employees like Art Fry. His creativity turned an adhesive that "wasn't sticky enough" into the blockbuster product known worldwide today as Post-It Notes.

Figure 4.4 shows the typical steps of commercializing innovation. It's tempting to think that the process for a product like the Post-It Note is easy, straightforward, even a "no brainer." But it isn't necessarily so. Fry and his colleagues had to actively "sell" the Post-It idea to 3M's marketing group and then to senior management before getting substantial support for its development as a salable product. And at Patagonia, its Common Threads innovation—collecting old garments and breaking them down to create reusable fibers—was almost four years in development from idea to implementation.[71]

CHARACTERISTICS OF INNOVATIVE ORGANIZATIONS

Innovative organizations such as 3M, Google, and Apple Computer have the capacity to move fast with innovations, a skill that helps deliver competitive advantage. But how do you view Microsoft? Do you see a firm whose strategy and culture drive an innovation powerhouse? Or do you see what *PC World* describes as "a stodgy old corporation churning out boring software"?[72] Even though 72% of executives in one survey considered innovation a top priority at their firms, about one-third said they were not happy with how fast companies innovate.[73] Such data, along with the

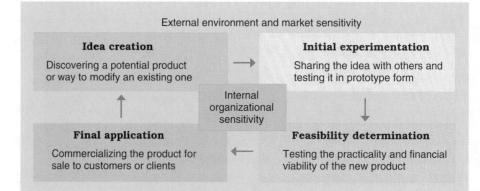

FIGURE 4.4 The process of commercializing innovation: an example of new-product development.

Microsoft example, raise an important question: What does it take to create a highly innovative organization? The answers boil down most often to strategy, culture, structure, top management, and staffing.

Strategy and Culture

In highly innovative organizations, the strategy and culture support innovation. The strategies of the organization, the visions and values of senior management, and the framework of policies and expectations all emphasize an entrepreneurial spirit. The culture is driven by values that let everyone know that innovation is expected, failure is accepted, and the organization is willing to take risks. For example, one of the world's most successful low-fare airlines is AirAsia. Based in Malaysia, it is the brainchild of CEO Tony Fernandes who took his original entrepreneurial cues from the successes of America's Southwest Airlines and Ireland's Ryanair. About his firm's track record with innovations, Fernandes says: "Unlike most Asian companies, we have controlled anarchy in AirAsia. I'd rather have 6,000 brains working for me than just 10."[74]

Similar commitments to supportive strategies and cultures are found at other firms known for valuing innovation. Johnson & Johnson's former CEO James Burke once said: "I try to give people the feeling that it's okay to fail, that it's important to fail." His point is that managers should eliminate risk-averse climates and replace them with organizational cultures in which innovation is the norm. Jack Welch, former CEO of GE, says that innovation occurs when "the whole organization buys into a mindset . . . that innovation is so deeply ingrained in everyone's job . . . that employees arrive each day thinking, 'Is there a better way to do everything we do around here'?" And when he took over as CEO at Sony, Howard Stringer was concerned that the firm was not as innovative as it could be. He placed a large part of the blame on a cumbersome corporate culture and told the executives: "I'm asking you to get mad" and pointedly said he wanted their businesses run in more "energetic," "bold," and "imaginative" ways.[75]

Structures

In highly innovative organizations, structures support innovation. One way is to form special creative units (stars in the boxed diagram) that are set free from the normal structure (shown as pyramids in the figure). Sometimes called **skunkworks**, these units are often given separate locations, special resources, their own managers, and a clear goal—innovation, innovation, innovation. Yahoo!, for example, has created a skunkworks known as the Brickhouse. It is

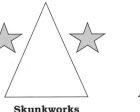

Skunkworks
Gives creative units freedom; separates from organization structure

Ambidextrous organization
Gives creative units freedom; integrates into organization structure

basically an idea incubator set up in a separate facility where staffers, some in bean bag chairs and others playing with Nerf balls, work on ideas submitted from all over the company. "The goal," says Salim Ismail who heads Brickhouse, "is to take the idea, develop it, and make sure it's seen by senior management quickly."[76] In other words, Brickhouse exists so that good ideas don't get lost in Yahoo!'s bureaucracy.

Another approach to structuring organizations for innovation has been advanced by scholars Charles O'Reilly and Michael Tushman. They describe an **ambidextrous organization** that is simultaneously good at both producing and creating.[77] Rather than assigning innovation to a separate creative unit such as a skunkworks, this approach scatters creative project teams throughout an organization. O'Reilly and Tushman suggest that by integrating the creative units, as

● **skunkworks** are special units given separate locations, special resources, and their own managers so that they can succeed with innovation.

● An **ambidextrous organization** uses integrated creative teams to simultaneously be good at both producing and creating.

opposed to separating them, ambidextrous organizations are often more successful than skunkworks in coming up with breakthrough innovations.

Systems

In highly innovative organizations, special information and knowledge management systems support innovation. Internally, the systems use the latest technologies to break traditional barriers of structures, time, and physical distance, and help employees collaborate. They link people and help them become known to one another, post and share information, and stay abreast of each other's expertise and latest thinking. IBM, for example, uses an internal version of Facebook known as BeeHive. Employees post profiles on BeeHive and engage in networking through the site. IBM has a program called SmallBlue that searches internal blogs, e-mail, instant messages, and files to maintain an up-to-date database of experts that can be contacted by other employees.[78]

Externally, the systems focus in innovative organizations is often on setting up mechanisms for customers to provide ideas and then getting these ideas considered for possible innovations. At Starbucks, for example, CEO Howard Schultz created the MyStarbucksIdea.com website for customers to provide suggestions on how the company could improve. Based on "Ideas" software from Salesforce.com, the site is monitored by 48 "idea partners" who facilitate the discussion and then act as idea champions within the firm. Results have led to ice cubes made of coffee so that iced coffees aren't diluted as added ice melts; shelves in bathroom cubicles to hold drink cups; and hole plugs in coffee lids to prevent splashing.[79]

Staffing and Management

In highly innovative organizations, staffing supports innovation. Step one is making creativity an important criterion when hiring and moving people into positions of responsibility. Step two is allowing their creative talents to fully operate by following through on the practices just discussed—strategy, culture, structure, and systems. Google engineers, for example, are allowed to spend 20% of their time on projects of their own choosing. The firm's CEO, Eric Schmidt, is considered a master at fueling innovation. He says: "The story of innovation has not changed. It has been a small team of people who have a new idea, typically not understood by people around them and their executives. This is a systematic way of making sure that a middle manager does not eliminate that innovation."[80]

In highly innovative organizations, top management makes innovation a high priority and does its best to fully support the innovation process. Such support is evident in strategy, culture, structures, systems, and staffing. In the case of 3M, many top managers have been the innovators and product champions in the company's past. They understand the innovation process, are tolerant of criticisms and differences of opinion, and take all possible steps to keep innovation goals clear and prominent. And, they lead in ways that encourage and allow the creative potential of people to operate fully. As GE's former CEO Jack Welch maintains, "often innovation doesn't arrive like a thunderbolt. It emerges incrementally, in bits and chugs, forged by a mixed bag of coworkers from up, down, and across an organization."[81]

☑ **Learning Check**

Study Question 4

How do organizations accomplish innovation?

Be sure you can ☑ define *innovation* ☑ discuss differences between process, product, business model, and social business innovations ☑ list the five steps in Hamel's wheel of innovation ☑ explain how innovations get commercialized ☑ list and explain the characteristics of innovative organizations

Management Learning Review

1 What is in the environment of organizations?

- The general environment includes background economic, sociocultural, legal-political, technological, and natural environment conditions.
- The specific environment or task environment consists of suppliers, customers, competitors, regulators, and other groups with which an organization interacts.
- Organizations exist in complex relationships with multiple stakeholders in the specific environment; they are the people, groups, and other organizations that are affected by an organization's performance.
- Customer relationship management (CRM) and supply chain management (SCM) are ways to improve how organizations interact with customers and suppliers as key stakeholders.

FOR DISCUSSION **If interests of a firm's owners/investors conflict with those of the community, which stakeholder gets preference?**

2 What are the key issues in organization–environment relationships?

- A competitive advantage is achieved when an organization does something very well and that allows it to outperform competitors.
- Environmental uncertainty is created by the rate of change of factors in the external environment and the complexity of this environment in terms of the numbers of factors that are relevant and important.
- The performance effectiveness of organizations can be assessed in different ways, including the systems resource, internal process, goal, and strategic constituency approaches.

FOR DISCUSSION **Which among the two or three stores that you shop at weekly has the strongest competitive advantage, and why?**

3 What are the emerging challenges of sustainability and the environment?

- The concept of the triple bottom line evaluates how well organizations perform on economic, social, and environmental performance criteria; this is also called the 3 Ps of organizational performance—profits, people, planet.

- ISO 14001, a world quality standard that requires certified organizations to set environmental objectives and targets, account for the environmental impact of their activities, products, or services, and continuously improve environmental performance.
- The concept of sustainable development refers to using environmental resources to support societal needs today while also preserving and protecting the environment for use by future generations.
- Green management describes managing in ways that support sustainability and help build and nurture environmental capital.

FOR DISCUSSION **When the costs of pursuing sustainability goals reduce business profits, which stakeholder interests should take priority, business owners or society at large?**

4 How do organizations accomplish innovation?

- Product innovations deliver new products and services to customers; process innovations improve operations; and business model innovations find new ways of creating value and making profits.
- Social business innovations and social business models help address social problems while doing business.
- Sustainable or green innovations minimize negative impact and maximize positive impact on the natural environment, while improving operating efficiencies by reducing energy and natural resource consumption.
- The innovation process involves moving from the stage of invention that involves discovery and idea creation all the way to final application that involves actual use of what has been created.
- The process of commercializing innovation turns new ideas into outcomes that add value or increase profits for organizations.
- Highly innovative organizations have supportive cultures, strategies, structures, systems, staffing, and management.

FOR DISCUSSION **Can a creative person prosper in an organization that doesn't have an innovation-driven culture?**

Multiple-Choice Questions

1. The general environment of an organization would include _____.
   (a) population demographics   (b) activist groups   (c) competitors   (d) customers

2. Issues such as Internet censorship faced in foreign countries by firms such as Google are examples of how differences in _____ factors in the general environment can cause complications for global business executives.
   (a) economic (b) legal-political (c) natural environment (d) demographic

3. The trend for organizations to develop in-house versions of social media platforms such as Facebook and Twitter is part of developments in an area known as _____.
   (a) cloud computing (b) app development (c) Enterprise 2.0 (d) video conferencing

4. If the term *offshoring* is used to describe an aspect of the economic environment that involves outsourcing of work and jobs to foreign locations, what is it called when firms like Caterpillar move jobs back into the United States from foreign locations?
   (a) protectionism (b) reshoring (c) relocating (d) upscaling

5. As a rule of thumb, organizations should recognize that customers as key stakeholders are very concerned about at least four things when they purchase goods and services—price, quality, delivery time, and _____.
   (a) style (b) packaging (c) labels (d) service

6. When Wal-Mart's suppliers electronically access inventory data and sales forecasts in the stores and automatically ship replacement products, this is an example of _____.
   (a) supply chain management (b) customer relationship management (c) total quality management (d) strategic constituencies analysis

7. The chapter-opening example of Salesforce.com shows how new technology is helping organizations better deal with stakeholders through excellence in the area of _____.
   (a) labor negotiations (b) customer relationship management (c) lobbying for reduced government regulation (d) control over external news media

8. Two dimensions that determine the level of environmental uncertainty are the number of factors in the external environment and the _____ of these factors.
   (a) location (b) rate of change (c) importance (d) interdependence

9. An organization that does very well in supply chain management might be considered "effective" according to which of the following assessment approaches?
   (a) systems resource (b) goal (c) internal process (d) strategic constituencies

10. One of the ways that corporations might better take into account their responsibility for being good environmental citizens is to redefine the notion of profit as: revenue less cost of goods sold less _____.
    (a) operating expenses (b) fossil-based energy consumption (c) costs to society (d) costs of sustainable innovation

11. What organizational stakeholder would be considered most important if a corporate board was having a serious discussion regarding how the firm could fulfill its obligations in respect to sustainable development?
    (a) owners or investors (b) customers (c) suppliers (d) future generations

12. Apps for an Apple iPhone or Google Android phone are examples of _____ innovations, whereas the use of robotics in performing manufacturing tasks previously done by humans is an example of _____ innovation.
    (a) cost-benefit, process (b) product, cost-benefit (c) value-driven, service-driven (d) product, process

13. The first step in Hamel's wheel of innovation is _____.
    (a) imagining (b) assessing (c) experimenting (d) scaling

14. When a new product is first developed in an emerging market such as China or India and then moved with cost and pricing advantages into an established market like the United States, this is known as _____.
    (a) skunkworks (b) ambidextrous organization (c) initial experimentation (d) reverse innovation

15. When Yahoo! set up a unit called the "Brickhouse," this was an example of top management using a _____ to support the innovation process.
    (a) technology (b) strategy (c) skunkworks (d) management team

Short-Response Questions

16. Who and/or what should be considered as key stakeholders by a business executive when mapping the task environment for her organization?

17. Exactly how should "sustainability" be best defined when making it part of a goal statement or performance objective for a business or an organization?

18. How do product, process, and business model innovations differ from one another?
19. How does the process of reverse innovation work?

Essay Question

20. At a reunion of graduates from a college of business at the local university, two former roommates engaged in a discussion about environment and sustainability. One is a senior executive with a global manufacturer, and the other owns a sandwich shop in the college town.

> Global executive: "We include sustainability in our corporate mission and have a Chief Sustainability Officer on the senior management team. The CSO is really good and makes sure that we don't do anything that could cause a lack of public confidence in our commitment to sustainability."

> Sandwich shop owner: "That's all well and good, but what are you doing on the positive side in terms of environmental care. It sounds like you do just enough to avoid public scrutiny. Shouldn't the CSO be a real advocate for the environment rather than just a protector of the corporate reputation? We, for example, use only natural foods and ingredients, recycle everything that is recyclable, and compost all possible waste."

Question: If you were establishing a new position called Corporate Sustainability Officer, what would you include in the job description as a way of both clarifying the responsibilities of the person hired and establishing clear accountability for what sustainability means to your organization?

Management Skills and Competencies

Self-Assessment

Back to Yourself: Risk Taking

The chapter opener highlighted the importance of understanding our tendencies toward **risk taking** and its potential to work for us or against us. As you ponder the many complexities of the external environment of organizations discussed in this chapter, including the challenges of sustainability and innovation, would you agree that it's important to stop and ask: How do we individually, organizationally, and as a society deal with risk, and how can we do better? After you complete the following self-assessment on Tolerance for Ambiguity, don't forget to go online to take the Turbulence Tolerance Test.

> Each of us has some personal tendency toward more or less **risk taking**. For some, risk is unsettling and a source of anxiety; for others, it is something to be welcomed as a source of potential new opportunities.

Further Reflection: Tolerance for Ambiguity

Instructions

To determine your level of tolerance for ambiguity, rate each of the following items on this 7-point scale.[82]

1	2	3	4	5	6	7
strongly disagree		slightly disagree		slightly agree		strongly agree

___ 1. An expert who doesn't come up with a definite answer probably doesn't know too much.

___ 2. There is really no such thing as a problem that can't be solved.

___ 3. I would like to live in a foreign country for a while.

___ 4. People who fit their lives to a schedule probably miss the joy of living.

___ 5. A good job is one where what is to be done and how it is to be done are always clear.

___ 6. In the long run it is possible to get more done by tackling small, simple problems rather than large, complicated ones.

___ 7. It is more fun to tackle a complicated problem than it is to solve a simple one.

___ 8. Often the most interesting and stimulating people are those who don't mind being different and original.

___ 9. What we are used to is always preferable to what is unfamiliar.

___ 10. A person who leads an even, regular life in which few surprises or unexpected happenings arise really has a lot to be grateful for.

___ 11. People who insist upon a yes or no answer just don't know how complicated things really are.

___ 12. Many of our most important decisions are based on insufficient information.

___ 13. I like parties where I know most of the people more than ones where most of the people are complete strangers.

___ 14. The sooner we all acquire ideals, the better.

___ 15. Teachers or supervisors who hand out vague assignments give a chance for one to show initiative and originality.

___ 16. A good teacher is one who makes you wonder about your way of looking at things.

___   Total Score

Scoring

To obtain a score, first *reverse* the scale score for the eight "reverse" items, 3, 4, 7, 8, 11, 12, 15, and 16 (i.e., a rating of 1 = 7, 2 = 6, 3 = 5, etc.), then add up the rating scores for all 16 items.

Interpretation

Individuals with a *higher* tolerance for ambiguity are more likely to be able to function effectively in organizations and contexts in which there is a high turbulence, a high rate of change, and less certainty about expectations, performance standards, what needs to be done, and so on. They are likely to "roll with the punches" as organizations, environmental conditions, and demands change rapidly. Individuals with a lower tolerance for ambiguity are more likely to be unable to adapt or adjust quickly in turbulence, uncertainty, and change. These individuals are likely to become rigid, angry, stressed, and frustrated when there is a high level of uncertainty and ambiguity in the environment.

Team Exercise

Organization Commitment to Sustainability Scorecard

Instructions

In your assigned work teams do the following.

1. Agree on a definition of "sustainability" that should fit the operations of any organization.

2. Brainstorm and agree on criteria for an Organizational Commitment to Sustainability Scorecard (OCSS) that can be used to audit the sustainability practices of an organization. Be sure that an organization being audited would not only receive scores on individual dimensions or categories of sustainability performance, but also receive a total overall "Sustainability Score" that can be compared with results for other organizations.

3. Present and defend OCSS to the class at large.

4. Use feedback received from the class presentation to revise your OCSS to be used in an actual organizational sustainability audit.

5. Use your OCSS to conduct a sustainability audit for a local organization.

6. Present the results of your audit to the instructor and class at large. Be sure to include in the presentation not only the audit scores and total, but also (a) recommendations for how this organization could improve its sustainability practices in the future and (b) any benchmarks from this organization that might be considered as sustainability "best practices" for others to follow.

Case Study: Global Green USA

Go to *Management Cases for Critical Thinking* to find the recommended case for Chapter 4– "Global Green USA: Greener Cities for a Cooler Planet."

Global Management and Cultural Diversity

5

Learning From Others

With Globalization, Businesses Are World Travelers

This is a shopping test. What do Victoria's Secret, C. O. Bigelow, Bath & Body Works, White Barn Candle Co., La Senza, and Henri Bendel have in common? The answer is they all trace their roots back to 1963 and a small women's clothing store in Columbus, Ohio. That single store has grown into a global company known as one of the world's most admired fashion retailers—Limited Brands.

The Limited's founder, chairman, and CEO, Leslie Wexner, is a member of the retail CEOs all-star team. He's called a "pioneer of specialty brands" and someone with special retailing "vision and focus." All this has been achieved in a competitive industry described as challenged by "logistics, merchandising, marketing, human resources, property and, in some cases, global expansion." Wexner sums up his business success this way: "Better brands, best brands—I don't believe bigger is better; I believe better is better. Period."

This is a global business test. Where does The Limited get its products? The answer is anywhere in the world where it can get quality at low cost. Under Wexner's leadership the firm has been a major participant in the world of global sourcing. But problems can develop if a firm's suppliers in other countries do things that hurt the brand.

To ensure quality and protect its brand, Limited's supplier and subcontractor relationships are guided by a "What We Stand For" policy designed to ensure ethical operations. The policy states: "We will not do business with individuals or suppliers that do not meet our standards. We expect our suppliers to promote an environment of dignity, respect and opportunity; provide safe and healthy working conditions; offer fair compensation through wages and other benefits; hire workers of legal age, who accept employment on a voluntary basis; and maintain reasonable working hours."[1]

do the benchmarking

There is more to Limited Brands than its many retail stores. Standing behind the displays and the fashion is a large operation that depends on vast worldwide networks of suppliers and subcontractors. But as with other international firms, the Limited's global reach must be well managed, and its ethical standards must be maintained. **Any misstep in global management will quickly be met by bad press, public criticism, damaged reputation, and consumer defections.**

Learning About Yourself

Cultural Awareness

The complications and dramas of global events are ever-present reminders that **cultural awareness** is one of the great challenges of our century. Consultant Richard Lewis warns of "cultural spectacles" that limit our vision, causing us to see and interpret things with the biases of our own culture.[2] Each of us has a responsibility to take off the blinders that limit our vision to the culture in which we were raised. We need to broaden our cultural horizons to embrace the full diversity of the world's peoples—that's what the concept of cultural awareness is all about.

> **Cultural Awareness—Confucian Values in Asian Cultures**
>
> * *Harmony*—works well in a group, doesn't disrupt group order, puts group before self-interests
> * *Hierarchy*—accepts authority and hierarchical nature of society, doesn't challenge superiors
> * *Benevolence*—acts kindly and understandingly toward others; paternalistic, willing to teach and help subordinates
> * *Loyalty*—loyal to organization and supervisor, dedicated to job, grateful for job and supportive of superior
> * *Learning*—eager for new knowledge, works hard to learn new job skills, strives for high performance

Many say this will be the "Asian" century. We're dealing with rising economic and geopolitical powers in China and India. It's hard to pass a day without bumping into one of these forces in the garments we wear and the customer services we seek.

Yet, it's a fact that even the most active global businesses don't always pass the cultural awareness test. In China, Nike once featured NBA star LeBron James in a TV ad where he played the role of kung-fu master and battled dragons and Chinese symbols. The ad had to be pulled when Chinese critics claimed it wounded the "national dignity." Also in China, McDonald's aired an ad that showed a Chinese man asking for a discount. It was pulled after locals considered the ad "humiliating."[3]

How informed are you regarding Asian cultures and how they might differ from both yours and those in other parts of the world? Are you aware, for example, that in Japan, China, and Korea, Confucian values such as those shown in the box are very influential? When our business and government leaders venture into Asia, they must be high in cultural awareness and well informed about how cultural dynamics can affect international business and politics. And as to the rest of us, doesn't a call for broad cultural awareness apply in our workplaces and everyday living?

get to know yourself better

The college campus is a great place to build competencies in cultural awareness. Monitor yourself as you meet, interact with, and otherwise come into contact with persons from other cultures. Jot down notes on what you perceive as cultural differences. Note your "first tendencies" in reacting to these differences and consider their implications for your relationships. **Also take advantage of the end-of-chapter Self-Assessment feature to further reflect on your Global Intelligence and examine your cultural tendencies on Time Orientation.**

Study Question 1	Study Question 2	Study Question 3	Study Question 4
Management and Globalization	Global Businesses	Culture and Global Diversity	Global Management Learning
• Global management • Why companies go global • How companies go global • Global business environments	• Types of global businesses • Pros and cons of global businesses • Ethics challenges for global businesses	• Cultural intelligence • Silent languages of culture • Values and national cultures	• Are management theories universal? • Cultural influences on management
Learning Check 1	Learning Check 2	Learning Check 3	Learning Check 4

Our global community is rich with information, opportunities, controversies, and complications. The Internet and television bring on-the-spot news from around the world into our homes and onto our cell phones; we play online games with competitors and partners from other countries; and our colleges and universities offer a growing variety of study-abroad programs.

Speaking of traveling the globe, companies like Limited Brands featured in the chapter opener are travelers too. IBM employs more than 40,000 software developers in India. Anheuser-Busch, maker of "America's King of Beers," is owned by the Belgian firm InBev. Ben & Jerry's Ice Cream is owned by the British-Dutch firm Unilever; and if you drink Tetley Tea or Eight-O'Clock Coffee you are buying from India's Tata Group. In autos, Mercedes builds M-class vehicles in Alabama; Italy's Fiat owns a large part of Chrysler; Ford Motor Company sells its Fiesta model around the world; and Japan's Honda, Nissan, and Toyota get 80 to 90% of their profits from sales in America.[4] As to Boeing's new 787 Dreamliner, the front fuselage is made by a Japanese company while some 60% of the plane's components are made by foreign firms. And, Nike's complex worldwide web of contractors includes more than 120 factories in China alone.[5]

MANAGEMENT AND GLOBALIZATION

• In the **global economy**, resources, markets, and competition are worldwide in scope.

• **Globalization** is the process of growing interdependence among elements of the global economy.

This is the age of the **global economy**, in which resource supplies, product markets, and business competition are worldwide rather than local or national in scope.[6] It is also a time heavily influenced by the forces of **globalization**, defined as the process of growing interdependence among the components in the global economy. Although the forces of globalization are both criticized and praised, there is no doubt that worldwide economic integration not only isn't going away, but will continue to grow in future significance.[7]

Right now the world's fastest growing economies are in the "BRIC" countries of Brazil, Russia, India, and China. Savvy investors are as interested in "emerging" markets in places like the Middle East, Latin America, Central Europe, and Africa, as they are in "established" markets of Western Europe and North America. And, the playing field of globalization isn't restricted to big corporations such as the Wal-Marts and Sonys and McDonald's of the world. Think of the many small and medium sized businesses that make up our communities. Where do their products come from? What are their ties to the global economy?

Have you ever wondered about the common everyday t-shirt? Where did you buy it? Where was it made? Where will it end up? In a fascinating book called *The*

Travels of a T-Shirt in the Global Economy, economist Pietra Rivoli tracks the origins and disposition of a t-shirt that she bought while on a vacation to Florida.[8]

As shown in the accompanying figure, it turns out that Rivoli's t-shirt lived a complicated and very global life. That life begins with cotton grown in Texas. It next moves to China where the cotton is processed and white t-shirts are manufactured. The t-shirts are sold to a firm in the United States that silk-screens them and sells them to retail shops

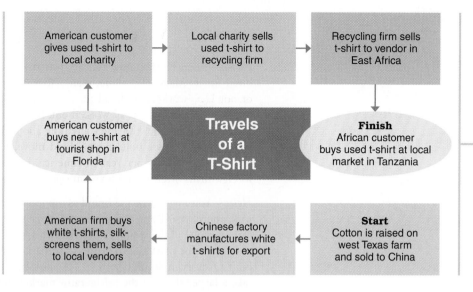

for resale to American customers. These customers eventually donate the used t-shirts to a charity that sells them to a recycler. The recycler sells them to a vendor in Africa who distributes them to local markets where they are sold yet again to local customers.

It's quite a story, this t-shirt that travels the commercial highways and byways of the world. Little doubt that Harvard scholar and consultant Rosabeth Moss Kanter describes globalization as "one of the most powerful and pervasive influences on nations, businesses, workplaces, communities, and lives."[9] This fact was well evidenced as the adverse effects of the recent financial crisis spread with lightning speed from country to country. Everything and everyone are already connected somehow by the forces of globalization. As columnist Thomas Friedman says in his book *Hot, Flat, and Crowded*:[10]

> "We live in a world in which globalization is now a fact: More people are connecting and competing with more other people in more ways on more days than ever before. But when you have this many people on the planet connecting and competing through free markets, the effects can be staggering. Their consumption can devour forests, rivers, and ocean life so swiftly as to change the climate and the landscape at unprecedented speeds. And when you have such an interconnected world, where financial contagions can spread so quickly and capsize dozens of economies at once, it is obvious that our overarching goal has to be "sustainable globalization."

GLOBAL MANAGEMENT

The term used to describe management in businesses and organizations with interests in more than one country is **global management**. Procter & Gamble, for example, pursues a global strategy with a presence in more than 70 countries. And, the majority of McDonald's sales are now coming from outside the United States, with the "Golden Arches" prominent on city streets from Moscow to Tokyo to Budapest to Rio de Janiero.

● **Global management** involves managing operations in more than one country.

As the leaders of these and other companies press forward with global initiatives, the management challenges and opportunities of working across national and cultural borders must be mastered. A new breed of manager, the **global manager**, is increasingly sought after. This is someone who has a strong global perspective, is culturally aware, and always stays informed about international developments. As expected, global managers face unique challenges. Consider, for

● A **global manager** is culturally aware and informed on international affairs.

example, two short cases—one rather a success story, and the other more of a "work in progress."

> *Honda*—Allen Kinzer, now retired, was the first American manager Honda hired for its Marysville, Ohio, plant. Although people were worried whether or not U.S. workers could adapt to the Japanese firm's production methods, technology, and style, it all worked out. Says Kinzer: "It wasn't easy blending the cultures; anyone who knew anything about the industry at the time would have to say it was a bold move." Bold move, indeed! Honda now produces almost 500,000 cars per year in America. It is only one among hundreds of foreign firms offering employment opportunities to U.S. workers.[11]

> *Haier*—You may know the brand as a popular name in dorm-room refrigerators; there's hardly a consumer in China that doesn't know it—the Haier Group is one of the country's best-known appliance makers. With goals to become a major player in the American market, Zhang Ruimin, Haier's CEO, built a factory in South Carolina. The idea was to manufacture in America and take a larger share of the refrigerator market. But the plant was expensive by Chinese standards, and it started production just at the time when the U.S. economy was heading down. Furthermore, Haier's organizational culture had a top-down management style and required work hats that showed different ranks and seniority that didn't fit well with American workers. But Zhang is committed to global expansion for his firm. "First the hard, then smooth," he says. "That's the way to win."[12]

WHY COMPANIES GO GLOBAL

John Chambers, chairman and CEO of Cisco Systems Inc., has said: "I will put my jobs anywhere in the world where the right infrastructure is, with the right educated workforce, with the right supportive government."[13] Cisco, Honda, Haier, and other firms like them are heavily involved in **international business** and conduct for-profit transactions of goods and services across national boundaries. International business is the foundation of world trade, helping to move raw materials, finished products, and specialized services from one country to another in the global economy.

Nike is one of the brands that may come to mind when you think of prominent players in international business. The Nike swoosh is one of the world's most recognized brands. But did you know that Nike does no domestic manufacturing? All of its products come from sources abroad. Its competitor New Balance, however, takes a different approach. Even though making extensive use of global suppliers and licensing its products internationally, New Balance still produces at factories in the United States.[14] Although competing in the same industry, Nike and New Balance are pursuing somewhat different global strategies. But, each is also well aware of the following reasons for pursuing international business.

> *Profits*—Global operations offer new and greater profit potential.
> *Customers*—Global operations offer new markets to sell products.
> *Suppliers*—Global operations offer access to needed products and services.
> *Capital*—Global operations offer access to financial resources.
> *Labor*—Global operations offer access to lower labor costs.
> *Risk*—Global operations spread assets among multiple countries.

Today you can add to this list *economic development*—where a global firm does business in foreign countries with direct intent to advance local economic development. An example is found with coffee giants Green Mountain Coffee

● An **international business** conducts for-profit transactions of goods and services across national boundaries.

Coffee Roaster Supports Free Trade

Green Mountain Coffee supports a free trade business model seeking fair prices and economic independence for coffee producers. One of the events in its "Be Fair" campaign was a cooking competition that featured four Boston chefs creating dishes with fair trade products. "We want to show that Fair Trade Certified™ products—including coffee—are high-quality, delicious, and easily available," said Sandy Yusen, Director of Public Relations for GMCR's Specialty Coffee Business Unit.

Roasters, Peet's Coffee & Tea, and Starbucks, all working in Rwanda with the nonprofit TechnoServe. Their goal is to help raise the incomes of African coffee farmers by improving their production and marketing methods. The global firms send advisers to teach coffee growers how to meet standards so that their products can be sold worldwide. It's a win-win: the global coffee company gets a quality product at a good price, the coffee growers gain skills and market opportunities, and the local economy improves.[15]

HOW COMPANIES GO GLOBAL

The common forms of international business are shown in Figure 5.1. When a business is just getting started internationally, global sourcing, exporting/importing, and licensing and franchising are the usual ways to begin. These are *market-entry strategies* that involve the sale of goods or services to foreign markets without expensive investments. Strategic alliances, joint ventures, and wholly owned subsidiaries are *direct investment strategies*. They require major capital commitments, but also create rights of ownership and control over operations in the foreign country.

Global Sourcing

A common first step into international business is **global sourcing**—the process of purchasing materials, manufacturing components, or business services from around the world. It is an international division of labor in which activities are performed in countries where they can be done well at the lowest cost. In auto manufacturing, global sourcing may mean local assembly but using, for example, instrument panels from Mexico and electrical components from Vietnam. In the service sector, it may mean setting up toll-free customer support call centers in the Philippines, or contracting for research and development by computer software engineers in Russia, or hiring physicians in India to read medical X-rays.

● In **global sourcing**, materials or services are purchased around the world for local use.

Market entry strategies			Direct investment strategies	
Global sourcing	Exporting and importing	Licensing and franchising	Joint ventures	Foreign subsidiaries

⟶ Increasing involvement in ownership and control of foreign operations

FIGURE 5.1 Common forms of international business—from market entry to direct investment strategies.

China Manufactures for the World
- 70% world's umbrellas
- 60% world's buttons
- 72% U.S. shoes
- 50% U.S. appliances
- 80% U.S. toys

Firms selling toys, shoes, electronics, furniture, and clothing are among those that make extensive use of global sourcing. The goal is to take advantage of international wage gaps by sourcing products in countries that can produce them at the lowest costs.[16] China, as suggested by the box, is a major outsourcing destination and in many areas of manufacturing has become the factory for the world.[17] If you use an Apple iPod, for example, chances are it was manufactured by a Taiwanese-owned company called Hon Hai and located in Shenzen, China. The plant employs over 200,000 workers to produce products not just for Apple, but for other firms like Sony and Hewlett-Packard.[18]

Exporting and Importing

- In **exporting**, local products are sold abroad to foreign customers.

- **Importing** involves the selling in domestic markets of products acquired abroad.

A second form of international business involves **exporting**—selling locally made products in foreign markets. The flip side of exporting is **importing**—buying foreign-made products and selling them in domestic markets.

Because the growth of export industries creates local jobs, governments often offer special advice and assistance to businesses that are trying to develop or expand their export markets. After visiting a U.S. government-sponsored trade fair in China, Bruce Boxerman, president of a small Cincinnati firm Richards Industries, decided to take advantage of the growing market for precision valves. In 10 years he doubled export sales to the point where they account for one-half the firm's revenues. One of his employees says: "It wasn't long ago that guys looked at globalization like it is going to cause all of us to lose our jobs. Now it's probably going to save our jobs."[19]

Licensing and Franchising

- In a **licensing agreement** a local firm pays a fee to a foreign firm for rights to make or sell its products.

Another form of international business is the **licensing agreement** whereby foreign firms pay a fee for rights to make or sell another company's products in a specified region. The license typically grants access to a unique manufacturing technology, special patent, or trademark. But, such licensing involves potential risk.[20] New Balance, for example, licensed a Chinese supplier to produce one of its brands. Even after New Balance revoked the license, the supplier continued to produce and distribute the shoes around Asia. New Balance ended up facing costly and complex litigation in China's courts.[21]

- In **franchising**, a fee is paid to a foreign business for rights to locally operate using its name, branding, and methods.

Franchising is a form of licensing in which the foreign firm buys the rights to use another's name and operating methods in its home country. The international version operates similar to domestic franchising agreements. Firms such as McDonald's, Wendy's, and Subway, for example, sell facility designs, equipment, product ingredients and recipes, and management systems to foreign investors, while retaining certain product and operating controls.

Joint Ventures and Strategic Alliances

Sooner or later, some firms decide to make substantial investments in global operations. Foreign direct investment, or FDI, involves setting up and buying all or part of a business in another country. And, for many countries, the ability to attract foreign business investors has been a key to succeeding in the global economy. The term **insourcing** is often used to describe local job creation that results from foreign direct investment. Over 5 million U.S. jobs, for example, are linked to insourcing.[22]

- **Insourcing** is job creation through foreign direct investment.

- A **joint venture** operates in a foreign country through co-ownership by foreign and local partners.

When foreign firms do invest in a new country, a common way to start is with a **joint venture**. This is a co-ownership arrangement in which the foreign and local partners agree to pool resources, share risks, and jointly operate the new business. Sometimes the joint venture is formed when a foreign partner buys part ownership in an existing local firm. In other cases it is formed as an entirely new operation that the foreign and local partners jointly invest in and start up together.

less struct

International joint ventures are types of **global strategic alliances** in which foreign and domestic firms work together for mutual benefit. Each partner hopes to gain through cooperation things they couldn't do or would have a hard time doing alone. For the local partner, an alliance may bring access to technology and opportunities to learn new skills. For the outside partner, an alliance may bring access to new markets and the expert assistance of locals that understand them and the local business context.

> ● A **global strategic alliance** is a partnership in which foreign and domestic firms share resources and knowledge for mutual gains.

Joint ventures and strategic alliances pose potential risks, and partners must be carefully chosen.[23] Sometimes the goals of partners may not match, for example, when the foreign firm seek profits and cost efficiencies while the local firm seeks maximum employment and acquisition of new technology.[24] Dishonesty and loss of business secrets are also risks. Not long ago GM executives noticed that a new car from a fast-growing local competitor, partially owned by GM's Chinese joint venture partner, looked very similar to one of its models. GM claims its design was copied. The competitor denied it and even pursued plans to export the cars, called "Cherys," for sale in the United States.[25]

How to Choose a Joint Venture Partner

- Familiar with firm's major business
- Employs a strong local workforce
- Values its customers
- Has potential for future expansion
- Has strong local market
- Has good profit potential
- Has sound financial standing

Foreign Subsidiaries

One way around some of the risks and problems associated with joint ventures and strategic alliances is full ownership of the foreign operation. A **foreign subsidiary** is a local operation completely owned and controlled by a foreign firm. These subsidiaries may be built ground up by so-called greenfield investments. They can also be established by acquisition, in which the outside firm purchases a local operation in its entirety.

> ● A **foreign subsidiary** is a local operation completely owned by a foreign firm.

Volkswagon

Although a foreign subsidiary represents the highest level of involvement in international operations, it can make very good business sense. When Nissan opened a plant in Canton, Mississippi, an auto analyst said: "It's a smart strategy to shift production to North America . . . building more in their regional markets, as well as being able to meet consumers' needs more quickly."[26] The analyst should have also pointed out another important benefit—by having this plant, Nissan can claim reputational benefits and deal with American customers as a "local" employer and not just a "foreign" company.

GLOBAL BUSINESS ENVIRONMENTS

When Nissan comes to America or GM goes to China, a lot of what takes place in the foreign business environment is very different from what is common at home. Not only must global managers master the demands of operating with worldwide suppliers, distributors, customers, and competitors, they must deal successfully with a variety of general environment forces that can pose unique challenges. Among those forces are differences in legal and political systems, complexities in trade agreements and barriers, and the roles of regional economic alliances.

Legal and Political Systems

Some of the biggest risk in international business comes from differences in legal and political systems. Global firms are expected to abide by local laws, some of which may be unfamiliar. And, the more home-country and host-country laws differ the harder it is for international businesses to adapt to local ways. Intel, for example, was fined $1.45 billion by the European Union for breaking its antitrust laws. Neelie Kroes, the EU's antitrust regulator, said: "Intel has harmed millions of European consumers by deliberately acting to keep competitors out of the market for computer chips for many years."[27]

Common legal problems faced by international businesses involve incorporation practices and business ownership; negotiation and implementation of contracts with foreign parties; handling of foreign exchange; and intellectual property rights—patents, trademarks, and copyrights. You might know the intellectual property issue best in terms of movie and music downloads, photocopying of books and journals, and sale of fake designer fashions. Companies like Microsoft, Sony, and Louis Vuitton know it as lost profits due to their products or designs being copied and sold as imitations by foreign firms. Not too long ago and working with Chinese police, Hewlett-Packard investigators tracked counterfeit ink cartridges to 14 warehouses in China. They seized $88 million of equipment and materials, and obtained jail sentences for two local manufacturers.[28]

Political turmoil, violence, and government changes constitute a further area of concern known as **political risk**—the potential loss in value of an investment in or managerial control over a foreign asset because of instability and political changes in the host country. The major threats of political risk today come from terrorism, civil wars, armed conflicts, and new government systems and policies. For example, Venezuela's President Hugo Chávez once threatened to take over the local operations of both Toyota and General Motors if the firms didn't produce cars suitable for rural driving and also transfer more technology to locals. "We'll take it, we'll expropriate it, we'll pay them what it is worth and immediately call on the Chinese," he said.[29] Although such things can't be prevented, they can be anticipated. Most global firms use a planning technique called **political-risk analysis** to forecast the probability of disruptive events that can threaten the security of a foreign investment.

Trade Agreements and Trade Barriers

When international businesses believe they are being mistreated in foreign countries, or when local companies believe foreign competitors are disadvantaging them, their respective governments might take the cases to the **World Trade Organization**. The WTO is a global organization established to promote free trade and open markets around the world. Its member nations, presently 151 of them, agree to negotiate and resolve disputes about tariffs and trade restrictions.[30]

WTO members are supposed to give one another **most favored nation status**—the most favorable treatment for imports and exports. Yet trade barriers are still common. They include outright **tariffs**, which are basically taxes that governments impose on imports. They also include **nontariff barriers** that discourage imports in nontax ways such as quotas, import restrictions, and other forms of **protectionism** that give favorable treatment to domestic businesses. Lately, for example, foreign firms have been complaining that the Chinese government is creating barriers that make it hard for them to succeed. A spokesperson for the U.S. Chamber of Commerce says that American multinationals like Caterpillar, Boeing, Motorola, and others,

---

● **Political risk** is the potential loss in value of a foreign investment due to instability and political changes in the host country.

● **Political-risk analysis** tries to forecast political disruptions that can threaten the value of a foreign investment.

● **World Trade Organization** member nations agree to negotiate and resolve disputes about tariffs and trade restrictions.

● **Most favored nation status** gives a trading partner most favorable treatment for imports and exports.

● **Tariffs** are taxes governments levy on imports from abroad.

● **Nontariff barriers** to trade discourage imports in nontax ways such as quotas and government import restrictions.

● **Protectionism** is a call for tariffs and favorable treatments to protect domestic firms from foreign competition.

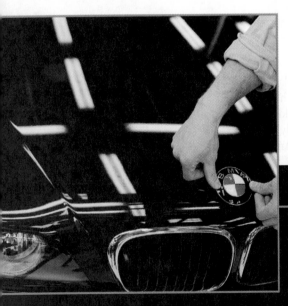

BMW Ups Its Investment in China

BMW AG is building its second manufacturing plant in China as it plans to tap further into the local demand for luxury cars with global brands. Its Chinese joint venture partner is Brilliance Automotive Holdings, and the new plant will bring BMW's annual production up to 100,000 cars annually. China is now the largest auto market in the world and is BMW's fourth largest customer destination. BMW and Brilliance have worked together before and their joint venture is investing $800+ million in the new plant.

Victor Fung Warns against Drift toward Protectionism

Li & Fung. You've probably never heard the name, but *Fast Company* magazine says the "middle-man consumer-products business has its prints on just about anything with a 'Made in China' label." Founded in 1906 in Guangzhou, China, by Fung Pak-liu and Li To-ming, Li & Fung Limited is now a $20 billion conglomerate headquartered in Hong Kong and with core businesses in export trading, distribution, and retailing. The export sourcing firm is one of the world's largest supply chain management companies, handling production for firms like Toys "Я" Us, Timberland, and Liz Claiborne.

Dr. Victor Fung is chairman of the Li & Fung group of companies. He is Fung Pak-liu's grandson and holds a doctorate in business administration and bachelor's and master's degrees from MIT. In addition to running his conglomerate, Fung is chairman of the International Chamber of Commerce. It is in this role that he has been speaking out with a "please deliver" message to global business leaders.

Fung publicly warned the Group of 20 industrialized nations not to drift into protectionism during the global financial and economic crisis. He expressed worry about President Nicolas Sarkozy's call to keep auto jobs in France and the chorus of voices supporting "Buy America" in the United States.

"If we take away what we've nurtured all these years in the multilateral trading systems, then we do so at our peril," he said. Pointing to the Great Depression, he observes that the protectionism it spawned actually caused a loss of jobs around the world and made the crisis worse. According to Fung, "Protectionism actually serves to destroy jobs in the economy."

Noting also that the Chinese word for "crisis" is a combination of "danger" and "opportunity," he also urged business leaders to take steps now to gain advantage when the economic rebound comes.

---

have been hurt by "systematic efforts by China to develop policies that build their domestic enterprises at the expense of U.S. firms."[31]

The goal of most tariffs and protectionism is to protect local firms from foreign competition and save jobs for local workers. You will see such issues reflected in political campaigns and debates. And the issues aren't easy. Government leaders face the often conflicting goals of seeking freer international trade while still protecting domestic industries. Such political dilemmas create controversies for the WTO in its role as a global arbiter of trade issues. In one claim filed with the WTO, for example, the United States complained that China's "legal structure for protecting and enforcing copyright and trademark protections" was "deficient" and not in compliance with WTO rules. China's official response was that the suit was out of line with WTO rules and that "we strongly oppose the U.S. attempt to impose on developing members through this case."[32]

Regional Economic Alliances

Speaking of political debates, **NAFTA** was a hot issue in the recent elections for the U.S. presidency. It is one example of many regional alliances or regional trading zones that now dot the global economy. This alliance, officially called the North American Free Trade Agreement, was formed in 1994 by the United States, Canada, and Mexico. It creates a trade zone with minimal barriers that free the flows of goods and services, workers, and investments among the three countries.

One direct result of NAFTA was the movement of production facilities from the United States to Mexico by many American businesses, largely to take advantage of lower wages paid to skilled Mexican workers. These job shifts have pros and cons. Arguments on the positive side of NAFTA include greater cross-border trade, greater productivity of U.S. manufacturers, and reform of the Mexican business environment. Arguments on the negative side blame NAFTA for substantial

● **NAFTA** is the North American Free Trade Agreement linking Canada, the United States, and Mexico in an economic alliance.

equal status
Bill Clinton
for free trade between
the three

job losses to Mexico, lower wages being paid at home to American workers wanting to keep their jobs, and a wider trade deficit with Mexico.[33]

Another well-known regional alliance, both economic and political, is the **European Union** or EU. It now links 27 countries that agree to support mutual economic growth by removing barriers that previously limited cross-border trade and business development. A common currency, the **Euro**, has grown to the point where it is a major alternative and competitor to the U.S. dollar in the global economy.

When one looks toward Asia, the Asia Pacific Economic Cooperation (APEC) was established to promote free trade and investment in the Pacific region. It has 21 members, including the United States and Australia. The 10 nations of Southeast Asia also belong to the Association of Southeast Asian Nations (ASEAN) with a stated goal of promoting economic growth and progress. More recently, foundations for the *China-ASEAN Free Trade Agreement* have been set. It will be the third largest regional trading agreement by value after NAFTA and the EU, and the largest in terms of population—spanning close to 2 billion people.[34]

Africa also makes business headlines.[35] The region's economies are growing, and there is a promising rise in entrepreneurship.[36] Says Coby Asmah, who runs a successful design and printing business in Ghana: "It's a young economy, and anyone who looks into that will see returns on investment here are 20% higher than anywhere else."[37] The *Southern Africa Development Community* (SADC) links 14 countries of southern Africa in trade and economic development efforts. The SADC website posts this vision: "a future in a regional community that will ensure economic well-being, improvement of the standards of living and quality of life, freedom and social justice, and peace and security for the peoples of Southern Africa."[38]

> ● The **European Union** is a political and economic alliance of European countries.
>
> ● The **Euro** is now the common European currency.

[handwritten notes in margin: 1.25 vs our Dollars / Debt in Greece Ireland France making Euro shaky / Soviet Union 1989 Disappeared / Turkey want to join the European Union / Asia / Europe]

☑ **Learning Check**	*Be sure you can* ☑ define *globalization* and discuss its implications for international
Study Question 1	management ☑ list five reasons companies pursue international business opportunities
What are the management challenges of globalization?	☑ describe and give examples of global sourcing, exporting/importing, franchising/licensing, joint ventures, and foreign subsidiaries ☑ discuss how differences in legal environments can affect businesses operating internationally ☑ explain the goals of the WTO ☑ discuss the significance of regional economic alliances such as NAFTA, the EU, ASEAN, and SADC

GLOBAL BUSINESSES

Big Mac Index 2010

United States	$3.58
Australia	$3.98
China	$1.83
Euro area	$4.84
Malaysia	$2.08
Mexico	$2.50
Norway	$7.02
Russia	$2.34
South Africa	$2.46
Turkey	$3.83

● A **global corporation** is a multinational enterprise (MNE) or multinational corporation (MNC) that conducts commercial transactions across national boundaries.

If you travel abroad these days, many of your favorite brands and products will travel with you. You can have a McDonald's sandwich in 119 countries, follow it with a Haagen-Dazs ice cream in some 50 countries, and then brush up with Procter & Gamble's Crest toothpaste in 80 countries. Economists even use the "Big Mac" index to track purchasing power parity among the world's currencies. The index, as shown in the box, compares the U.S. dollar price of the McDonald's sandwich around the world.[39]

Global corporations, also called **multinational enterprises** (MNEs) and **multinational corporations** (MNCs), are business firms with extensive international operations in many foreign countries. The largest global corporations are identified in annual listings such as *Fortune* magazine's Global 500 and the *Financial Times*' FT Global 500. They include familiar names such as Wal-Mart, BP, Toyota, Nestlé, BMW, Hitachi, Caterpillar, Sony, and Samsung, as well as others you might not recognize, such as the big oil and gas producers PetroChina (China), Gazprom (Russia), and Total (France).

In the last 10 years the geographical distribution of the world's largest and most powerful companies has shifted, with those from North America and Japan showing declines, while ones from countries like China, Russia, India, South Korea, and Mexico

[handwritten note at bottom: Tyco main office Bermuda for tax purpose]

Katie Durant

show substantial gains.[40] Also important on the world scene are *multinational organizations* (MNOs) that have nonprofit missions. Examples include the International Federation of Red Cross and Red Crescent Societies, the United Nations, and the World Bank.

TYPES OF GLOBAL BUSINESSES

Is there any doubt in your mind that Hewlett-Packard and Dell are American firms, Sony and Honda are Japanese, and BMW and Daimler are German? Most likely not; yet that may not be how their executives want the firms to be viewed. Each of these and many other global firms are acting more like **transnational corporations**. That is, they try to operate as "borderless firms" with worldwide presences and without being identified with one national home.[41]

Executives of transnationals view the entire world as their domain for acquiring resources, locating production facilities, marketing goods and services, and communicating brand image. They seek total integration of global operations, try to operate across borders without home-based prejudices, make major decisions from a global perspective, distribute work among worldwide points of excellence, and employ senior executives from many different countries. When shopping at an Aldi in Peoria, Illinois, would you know it's a German company? When buying a Nestlé product or learning that a new neighbor works for ABB in Columbus, Ohio, would you know that both are registered Swiss companies? And, which company is really more American— the Indian giant Tata which gets 51.4% revenues from North America, or IBM and McDonald's that get some 65% of their revenues outside of the United States?[42]

> ● A **transnational corporation** is a global corporation or MNE that operates worldwide on a borderless basis.

NATO = European military Union?

PROS AND CONS OF GLOBAL BUSINESSES

The recent global economic downturn raised important questions that relate, in part at least, to the growth of the "transnational" concept of global business. Does a company's nationality matter to the domestic economy? Does it matter to an American whether local jobs come from a domestic giant like IBM or a foreign one like Honda? And what about what some call the globalization gap? Is it wrong for large multinationals to gain disproportionately from the forces of globalization, while many smaller firms and many countries do not?[43]

Large global firms hold one-third of the world's productive assets and control 70% of world trade; more than 50 of the largest 100 economies in the world are multinational corporations; more than 90% of MNCs are based in the Northern Hemisphere.[44] Such facts can be very threatening to small and less developed countries, and to their domestic industries.

Host-Country Issues

Global corporations and the countries that "host" their foreign operations should ideally both reap benefits. But as shown in Figure 5.2, things can go right and wrong in these relationships.[45] The potential host-country benefits include larger tax bases, increased employment opportunities, technology transfers, introduction of new industries, and development of local resources. The potential host-country costs include complaints that global corporations extract excessive profits, dominate the local economy, interfere with the local government, do not respect local customs and laws, fail to help domestic firms develop, hire the most talented of local personnel, and fail to transfer their most advanced technologies.

Home-Country Issues

Global corporations may also encounter difficulties in their home country, the one where they were founded and where their headquarters is located. Even as

What should go right in MNC host-country relationships	What can go wrong in MNC host-country relationships	
Mutual benefits	**Host-country complaints about MNCs**	**MNC complaints about host countries**
Shared opportunities with potential for • Growth • Income • Learning • Development	• Excessive profits • Economic domination • Interference with government • Hire best local talent • Limited technology transfer • Disrespect for local customs	• Profit limitations • Overpriced resources • Exploitative rules • Foreign exchange restrictions • Failure to uphold contracts

FIGURE 5.2 What should go right and what can go wrong in global corporation and host-country relationships.

many global firms try to operate as transnationals, home-country governments and citizens still tend to identify them with local and national interests. They also expect the global firms to act as good domestic citizens.[46] Whenever a global business outsources home-country jobs, or cuts back or closes a domestic operation in order to shift work to lower-cost international destinations, the loss is controversial. Corporate decision makers are likely to be engaged by government and community leaders in critical debates about a firm's domestic social responsibilities. Other home-country criticisms of global firms include complaints about sending capital investments abroad and engaging in corrupt practices in foreign settings.

ETHICS CHALLENGES FOR GLOBAL BUSINESSES

In just one March day, the *Wall Street Journal* contained articles reporting on Brazil—where Alcoa is spending over $35 million on health services, a water system, and technical training for local residents in the area of a mine it wants to expand; Indonesia—where locals suffer shortages of coal, natural gas, and palm oil at the same time that exports of the same commodities are increasing to China, India, and Japan; and China—where the government's harsh treatment of Tibetan unrest dampened prospects for foreign direct investments in the region.[47] Take a moment to think about where you stand on the underlying issues in these examples, and think also about other ethics challenges that face global corporations.

Corruption

● **Corruption** involves illegal practices to further one's business interests.

Corruption—engaging in illegal practices to further one's business interests—is a source of continuing controversy in any setting.[48] The issue can be especially acute in the global business context. One American executive working in Russia, for example, says that payoffs are needed to get shipments through customs and that "we use customs brokers, and they build bribes into the invoice."[49] Bribery and other forms of corruption can pose significant challenges as such global managers travel the world. Whereas Transparency International scores Somalia, Iraq, Myanmar, and Sudan among the worst countries in respect to corruption, the best include Denmark, New Zealand, Sweden, and Singapore.[50]

● The **Foreign Corrupt Practices Act (FCPA)** makes it illegal for U.S. firms and their representatives to engage in corrupt practices overseas.

In the United States, the **Foreign Corrupt Practices Act (FCPA)** makes it illegal for U.S. firms and their representatives to engage in corrupt practices overseas.[51] They are not supposed to pay or offer bribes or excessive commissions, including nonmonetary gifts, to foreign officials or employees of state-run companies in return for business favors. Lucent Technologies, for example, was fined $2.5 million for paying travel expenses for executives of Chinese government-owned

Isreal largest recipent of our foreign aide

telecom companies to visit Disney World and other U.S. tourist spots. The trips were entered into the company's official records as "factory tours."[52]

The FCPA ban on such corrupt practices makes sense, but critics claim that it fails to recognize the realities of business as practiced in many foreign nations. They believe it puts U.S. companies at a competitive disadvantage because they can't offer the same "deals" or "perks" as businesses from other nations—deals that the locals may regard as standard business practices. However, other nations are starting to pass similar laws and the U.S. Department of Justice isn't backing down. A recent case involves claims that Hewlett-Packard violated the FCPA by using its German subsidiary and a complicated set of shell companies to handle millions of dollars in bribes paid to Russian officials. An HP spokesperson says the firm "is fully cooperating with U.S. and German authorities on the matter."[53]

Child Labor and Sweatshops

Complex networks of outsourcing contracts are now common as manufacturers follow the world's low-cost labor supplies from country to country. The many players in these supply chains are often difficult to identify, let alone control.

A major ethics issue in global sourcing is **child labor**, the employment of children to perform work otherwise done by adults. You've surely heard about the use of child labor to manufacture handmade carpets in countries such as India and Pakistan. But, what about your favorite Apple device whose components are largely made by foreign suppliers?[54] When an internal audit by Apple Inc. discovered that three of its foreign contractors had used underage workers, an Apple spokesperson said that the firm regularly audits suppliers "to make sure they comply with Apple's strict standards" and also conducts "extensive training programs to educate workers about their right to a safe and respectful work environment."[55]

Child labor isn't the only labor issue facing global managers. **Sweatshops**— business operations that employ workers at low wages for long hours in poor working conditions—are another concern. Microsoft, for example, is investigating

Transparency International— Global Corruption Index

Least Corrupt Countries
- New Zealand
- Denmark
- (tie) Singapore
- (tie) Sweden
- Switzerland

Most Corrupt Countries
- Somalia
- Afghanistan
- Myanmar
- Sudan
- Iraq

○ **Child labor** is the employment of children for work otherwise done by adults.

○ **Sweatshops** employ workers at very low wages for long hours in poor working conditions.

Real Ethics

E-Waste Travels to Graveyards in Africa and Asia

When you toss that old stereo, out-of-date television, or slow computer into the trash or the recycling bin, where does it ultimately end up? It very well may end up making its way to a poor community in some faraway country like Ghana, China, or Vietnam. Electronic waste arrives there on barges and sits in gigantic piles, contaminating the soil and water with toxic chemicals.

E-waste is a growing industry in these and other countries. However, because it is often too expensive to dispose of or recycle the used electronics safely, they frequently end up in huge dumps where their impact on the environment and individuals' health can be devastating. Women and children work at these sites, burning plastic in order to salvage scrap metal from the electronic equipment and burning motherboards to collect minute amounts of gold. But at what price are these materials being recovered? The fumes the women and children inhale are loaded with toxic lead. The nearby streams are being polluted with plastic and metal wastes. The streets are cluttered with electronic debris. A growing industry indeed!

You Decide

Many developing countries are becoming digital dumping grounds. Host governments seem to look the other way when confronted with the environmental and human consequences of this big business. But whose responsibility is it to handle, dispose of, and recycle e-waste? Developed countries pay to dispose of this waste, but do they have a further obligation to ensure that it is done safely? Do you, as a consumer, have an obligation to reduce the amount of waste you create or to make sure that the waste you dispose of is handled in an environmentally friendly manner?

complaints about workers being abused in a factory in China that supplies some of its electronic devices. The National Labor Committee, a U.S.-based human rights advocacy organization, claims that the Chinese factory owners were overworking employees and housing them in bad conditions. The NLC's director went so far as to say "the factory was really run like a minimum security prison." Microsoft's response was to send independent auditors "to conduct a complete and thorough investigation."[56]

Be sure you can ☑ differentiate a multinational corporation from a transnational corporation ☑ list at least three host-country complaints and three home-country complaints about global business operations ☑ give examples of corruption, sweatshops, and child labor in international businesses

CULTURE AND GLOBAL DIVERSITY

Here's the situation. A U.S. executive goes to meet a business contact in Saudi Arabia. He sits in the office with crossed legs and the sole of his shoe exposed. Both are unintentional signs of disrespect in the local culture. He passes documents to the host using his left hand, which Muslims consider unclean. He declines when coffee is offered, which suggests criticism of the Saudi's hospitality. What is the price for these cultural miscues? A $10 million contract is lost to a Korean executive better versed in Arab ways.[57]

"Culture" matters, as we often say, and here are its basic terms and considerations. **Culture** is the shared set of beliefs, values, and patterns of behavior common to a group of people.[58] **Culture shock** is the confusion and discomfort a person experiences when in an unfamiliar culture. A look at Management Smarts 5.1 is a reminder that these feelings must be mastered to travel comfortably and do business around the world.

Management Smarts 5.1

Culture shock: Stages in adjusting to a new culture

- *Confusion*: First contacts with the new culture leave you anxious, uncomfortable, and in need of information and advice.
- *Small victories*: Continued interactions bring some "successes," and your confidence grows in handling daily affairs.
- *The honeymoon*: A time of wonderment, cultural immersion, and even infatuation, with local ways viewed positively.
- *Irritation and anger*: A time when the "negatives" overwhelm the "positives," and the new culture becomes a target of your criticism.
- *Reality*: A time of rebalancing; you are able to enjoy the new culture while accommodating its less desirable elements.

CULTURAL INTELLIGENCE

The American's behavior in Saudi Arabia showed **ethnocentrism**, a tendency to view one's culture as superior to that of others. It was self-centered; he ignored and showed no concern for the culture of his Arab host. Some might excuse him as suffering from culture shock. Perhaps he was exhausted after a long international flight. Maybe he was so uncomfortable upon arrival in Saudi Arabia that all he could think about was offering his contract and leaving as quickly as possible. Still others might give him the benefit of the doubt. It could have been that he was well intentioned but didn't have time to learn enough about Saudi culture before making the trip. But regardless of the possible reasons for the cultural miscues, they still worked to this executive's disadvantage. They also showed a lack of something critical to success in global management—**cultural intelligence**, the ability to adapt and adjust to new cultures.[59]

People with cultural intelligence have high cultural awareness as discussed in the chapter-opening Learning about Yourself feature. They are flexible in dealing

Culture is a shared set of beliefs, values, and patterns of behavior common to a group of people.

Culture shock is the confusion and discomfort a person experiences when in an unfamiliar culture.

Ethnocentrism is the tendency to consider one's culture superior to others.

Cultural intelligence is the ability to accept and adapt to new cultures.

with cultural differences and willing to learn from what is unfamiliar. They also use that learning to modify their behaviors to act with sensitivity toward another culture's ways. In other words, someone high in cultural intelligence views cultural differences not as threats but as learning opportunities. And, the presence or absence of this quality is a good indicator of someone's potential for success in international assignments and in working with persons of different cultures.[60]

Executives at China's Haier Group showed cultural intelligence in the way they responded to problems that popped up at the firm's new factory in South Carolina.[61] As part of Haier's commitment to quality, workers who make mistakes in its Chinese factories are made to stand on special footprints and publicly criticize themselves. They are supposed to point out what they did wrong and what lessons they have learned. When this practice was implemented at the U.S. factory, however, the American workers protested—they thought it was humiliating. Although caught off guard, Haier executives didn't force the practice; instead, they changed their approach. They kept the footprints and used them to reinforce the firm's quality commitment. But American workers now stand in the footprints as a form of public recognition when they do exceptional work, not when they do something wrong. By listening and learning from the initial bad experience, the Chinese managers ended up with a local practice that fits both corporate values and the local culture.

SILENT LANGUAGES OF CULTURE

The capacities to listen, observe, and learn are building blocks of cultural intelligence. These skills and competencies can be developed by better understanding what anthropologist Edward T. Hall calls the "silent" languages of culture.[62] He believes that these silent languages are found in a culture's approach to context, time, and space.

Context

If we look and listen carefully, Hall believes we should recognize that cultures differ in how their members use language in communication.[63] In **low-context cultures** most communication takes place via the written or spoken word. This is common in the United States, Canada, and Germany, for example. As the saying goes, Americans say or write what they mean and mean what they say. Things aren't this way in many parts of the world.

In **high-context cultures** what is actually said or written may convey only part, and sometimes a very small part, of the real message. The rest must be interpreted from nonverbal signals and the situation as a whole, including body language, the physical setting, and even past relationships among the people involved. Dinner parties, social gatherings, and golf outings in high-context cultures such as Thailand and Malaysia, for example, are ways for potential business partners to get to know one another. Only after the social relationships are established and a context for communication exists is it possible to begin the discussions needed to make business deals.

● **Low-context cultures** emphasize communication via spoken or written words.

● **High-context cultures** rely on nonverbal and situational cues as well as on spoken or written words in communication.

Time

The way people approach and deal with time varies across cultures. You might think of this issue in terms of punctuality and sticking to schedules. Hall takes it a step further and describes differences between "monochronic" and "polychronic" cultures.

A **monochronic culture** is one in which people tend to do one thing at a time. This is typical of the United States, where most businesspeople schedule meetings with specific people invited to focus on an agenda for an allotted time.[64] And if someone is late for one of those meetings or brings an uninvited guest, we tend not to like it. Promptness is highly valued in monochronic cultures. But, members of a

● In **monochronic cultures** people tend to do one thing at a time.

Research Brief

Stable Personality Traits and Behavioral Competencies Linked with Expatriate Effectiveness

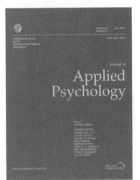

A research collaboration brought together teams of scholars from Hong Kong and the United States to investigate the effectiveness of expatriate workers. The results of three empirical studies reported in the *Journal of Applied Psychology* by Margaret Shaffer and her colleagues show that individual differences have an impact on expatriate effectiveness.

When organizations send employees to work as expatriates in foreign countries, the assignments can be challenging, and the expatriate's performance can turn out lower than anticipated. Nevertheless, many employers fail to make fully informed decisions on expatriate assignments.

The researchers propose a model in which expatriate effectiveness is a function of individual differences in personalities and competencies. Specifically, they address stable dispositions in terms of the "Big Five" personality traits: conscientiousness, emotional stability, agreeableness, intellectance, and extroversion; and the dynamic competencies of cultural flexibility, task orientation, people orientation, and ethnocentrism.

The research model was tested in samples of expatriates working in Hong Kong and among Korean expatriates working in other nations. Results show that each of the Big Five traits, except conscientiousness, predicts some aspect of expatriate effectiveness. Emotional stability was the strongest predictor of withdrawal cognitions, while intellectance was the only predictor of task and contextual performance. Results were less uniform with respect to the link between dynamic competencies and performance, and the researchers believe that study design and/or the presence of unmeasured moderator variables might account for the mixed findings. One of their suggestions is that future research look at the entire model in the context of one well-designed study.

Expatriate Effectiveness Model

Individual Differences
- Stable dispositions
- Dynamic competencies

Expatriate Effectiveness
- Adjustment
- Withdrawal cognitions
- Performance

You Be the Researcher

Chances are that there are international students in your class or on campus who have worked with or as expatriates. You may also have family and friends with expatriate experience. Why not interview them to gather their views about how expatriates adapt and perform in foreign cultures? Compare the results of your investigation with the model and findings of this research study.

Reference: Margaret A. Shaffer, David A. Harrison, Hal Gregersen, J. Steward Black, and Lori A. Ferzandi, "You Can Take It with You: Individual Differences and Expatriate Effectiveness," *Journal of Applied Psychology*, vol. 91 (2006), pp. 109–125.

● In **polychronic cultures** time is used to accomplish many different things at once.

polychronic culture are more flexible toward time. They often try to work on many different things at once, perhaps not in any particular order, and are responsive to distractions and interruptions. A monochronic American visitor to the office of a polychronic Egyptian client may be frustrated, for example, by the lack of singular attention she receives as the client greets and deals with a continuous stream of people flowing in and out of his office.

Space

Hall also considers the use of space as part of the silent language of culture. He describes these cultural tendencies in terms of **proxemics**, the study of how people use space to communicate.[65] Americans, for example, tend to like and value their own space, perhaps as much space as they can get. We like big offices, big cars, big homes, and big yards. We get uncomfortable in tight spaces and when others stand too close to us in lines. When someone "talks right in our face," we don't like it; the behavior

● **Proxemics** is how people use space to communicate.

may even be interpreted as an expression of anger. Members of other cultures may view such things quite differently. In many Latin cultures the *abrazzo*, or strong embrace, is a common greeting. In Vietnam, men often hold hands or link arms when talking with one another. And if you visit Japan you should notice very quickly that space is precious. Small homes, offices, and shops are the norm; gardens are tiny, but immaculate; public spaces are carefully organized for most efficient use; privacy is highly valued and protected. Indeed, Google ran into problems with its Japanese version of "street view" in Google Earth. It had to reshoot its images using cameras mounted 15 inches lower after local bloggers complained that the original shots looked over fence tops and invaded people's privacy at home.[66]

VALUES AND NATIONAL CULTURES

The work of Geert Hofstede is often considered a benchmark for how cultural differences can influence management and organizational practices. After studying employees of a global corporation operating in 40 countries, Hofstede identified four cultural dimensions: power distance, uncertainty avoidance, individualism–collectivism, and masculinity–femininity.[67] Later studies added a fifth: time orientation.[68]

Figure 5.3 shows how national cultures can vary on these dimensions. Imagine what these cultural differences might mean when international business executives try to make deals around the world, or when representatives of national governments meet to work out problems. But also remember that this model is just a starting point for developing cross-cultural awareness. In fact, Hofstede warns against the **ecological fallacy** acting with the mistaken assumption that a generalized cultural value, such as individualism in American culture or masculinity in Japanese culture, applies equally to all members of the culture.[69]

● The **ecological fallacy** assumes that a generalized cultural value applies equally well to all members of the culture.

Power Distance

Power distance is the degree to which a society accepts or rejects the unequal distribution of power among people in organizations and the institutions of society. In high-power-distance cultures such as India or Malaysia, we expect to find great respect for age, status, and titles. People in these cultures tend to be tolerant of power; they are prone to follow orders and accept differences in rank. Picture an American businesswoman visiting her firm's joint venture partner in high-power-distance Malaysia. Could her tendencies toward informality by using first names to address superiors and dressing casually in the office create discomfort for local executives less accustomed to such practices?

● **Power distance** is the degree to which a society accepts unequal distribution of power.

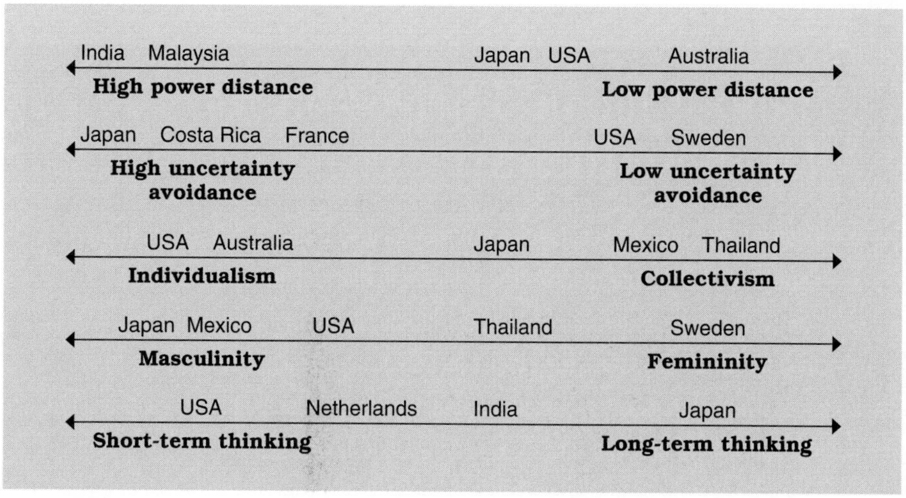

FIGURE 5.3 How countries compare on Hofstede's dimensions of national culture.

Individualism-Collectivism

● **Individualism–collectivism** is the degree to which a society emphasizes individuals and their self-interests.

Individualism-collectivism is the degree to which a society emphasizes individual accomplishments and self-interests versus collective accomplishments and the interests of groups.[70] In Hofstede's data, the United States had the highest individualism score of any country. Think about it; don't you find the "I" and "me" words used a lot in our conversations and meetings, or even when students are making team presentations in class? Such expressions reflect a cultural tendency toward individualism. Contrast this with the importance placed on group harmony in the Confucian cultures of Asia, as pointed out in the chapter opener. What are the implications when those of us from more individualistic settings try to work with colleagues from more collectivist national cultures? How, for example, are individualistic Americans perceived on work teams that include members from Japan or Thailand?

Uncertainty Avoidance

● **Uncertainty avoidance** is the degree to which a society tolerates risk and uncertainty.

Uncertainty avoidance is the degree to which a society is uncomfortable with risk, change, and situational uncertainty, versus having tolerance for them. Members of low-uncertainty-avoidance cultures display openness to change and innovation. In high-uncertainty-avoidance cultures such as France, by contrast, one would expect to find a preference for structure, order, and predictability. Persons in these cultures may have difficulties dealing with ambiguity, tend to follow rules, and prefer structure in their lives. Could high uncertainty avoidance be one of the reasons why Europeans seem to favor employment practices that provide job security? Could the entrepreneurial tendencies toward business risks that are characteristic of Hong Kong Chinese reflect a low-uncertainty-avoidance culture?

Masculinity–Femininity

● **Masculinity–femininity** is the degree to which a society values assertiveness and materialism.

Masculinity–femininity is the degree to which a society values assertiveness and materialism versus feelings, relationships, and quality of life.[71] You might think of it as a tendency for members of a culture to show stereotypical masculine or feminine traits and reflect different attitudes toward gender roles. Visitors to Japan, with the highest masculinity score in Hofstede's research, may be surprised at how restricted career opportunities can be for women. The *Wall Street Journal* comments: "In Japan, professional women face a set of socially complex issues—from overt sexism to deep-seated attitudes about the division of labor." One female Japanese manager says: "Men tend to have very fixed ideas about what women are like."[72]

Yahoo! Japan Thrives on Its Japanese Identity

Google is Number 2? Yes, believe it or not, Google trails Yahoo! Japan in the Japanese Web search market. The problem is that Google is viewed as a "foreign" company and has to struggle to gain its normal popular footing. Even though Yahoo! Japan is 35% owned by California-based Yahoo! belongs to the well-known local telecommunications firm Softbank. "Yahoo! Japan is a Japanese company," says a local analyst, "and most of their employees are Japanese people who fluently understand how the Japanese mind-set and business work."

Time Orientation

Time orientation is the degree to which a society emphasizes short-term or long-term goals and gratifications.[73] American tendencies toward impatience and desire for quick, even instantaneous, gratifications, show short-term thinking. Even our companies are expected to achieve short-term results; those failing to meet quarterly financial targets often suffer immediate stock price declines. Many Asian cultures are quite the opposite, displaying more Confucian values of persistence, thrift, patience, and willingness to work for long-term success. This might help explain why Japan's auto executives were more willing than their American counterparts to years ago invest in hybrid engine technologies and stick with them, even though market demand was very low at first and any return on the investments would take a long time to materialize.

● **Time orientation** is the degree to which a society emphasizes short-term or long-term goals.

Be sure you can ☑ define *culture* ☑ explain how ethnocentrism can create difficulties for people working across cultures ☑ differentiate between low-context and high-context cultures, and monochronic and polychronic cultures ☑ list and illustrate Hofstede's five dimensions of value differences among national cultures

Learning Check ☑

Study Question 3
How can we benefit from global management learning?

GLOBAL MANAGEMENT LEARNING

The management process of planning, organizing, leading, and controlling is as relevant to international operations as to domestic ones. Yet as the preceding discussions of global business environments and cultures should suggest, just how these functions are applied may vary somewhat from one country and culture to the next. Scholars in the area of **comparative management** study how management perspectives and practices systematically differ among countries and cultures.[74] And in today's highly globalized world, their work is increasingly important.

● **Comparative management** studies how management practices differ among countries and cultures.

ARE MANAGEMENT THEORIES UNIVERSAL?

An important question in global management is: "Are management theories universal?" Geert Hofstede, whose framework for understanding national cultures was just discussed, believes the answer is clearly "no." He worries that many theories are ethnocentric and fail to take into account cultural differences.[75] Hofstede argues, for example, that the American emphasis on participation in leadership reflects the culture's moderate stance on power distance. National cultures with lower scores, such as Sweden and Israel,

Feng Shui Brings Energy to McDonald's

Managers with cultural intelligence are open to collaboration and learning in their global business networks. At McDonald's the Chinese practice of *Feng Shui*, 風水, has been embraced in redesigning the firm's restaurants. *Feng Shui* involves arranging spaces and choosing locations to maximize harmony and balance, and bring positive energy to work and living places. Look for this influence in terms of color tones, seating arrangements, use of plants, and even the presence of water.

are characterized by even more "democratic" leadership initiatives. By contrast, the cultures of France and some Asian countries with higher power-distance scores are comfortable with hierarchy and less concerned with participative leadership.

Hofstede also points out that the management theories of American scholars tend to value individual performance. This is consistent with the high individualism found in Anglo-American countries such as the United States, Canada, and the United Kingdom. In other countries, where values are more collectivist, the theories may be less applicable. Sweden, for example, has a history of redesigning jobs for groups of workers rather than for individuals.

When it comes to casting the global learning net, it is important to both identify the potential merits of management practices in other countries and understand how cultural differences can affect their success when applied elsewhere. Consider the earlier example of "quality footprints" at Haier's Chinese and South Carolina factories. Instead of just taking a "best practice" from China and forcing it into the U.S. operation, Haier's managers showed cultural intelligence and modified the practice to find a better fit with the American workers.[76]

Without any doubt we should always be looking everywhere for new management ideas. But we should hesitate to accept any practice, no matter how well it appears to work somewhere else, as a universal prescription to action. The goal of comparative management studies is not to find universal principles. It is to engage in critical thinking about the way managers around the world do things and about whether they can and should be doing them better. As Hofstede states: "Disregard of other cultures is a luxury only the strong can afford . . . increase in cultural awareness represents an intellectual and spiritual gain."[77]

CULTURAL INFLUENCES ON MANAGEMENT

In an effort to integrate and extend insights on cultural influences on management, a team of international researchers led by Robert House convened to study leadership, organizational practices, and diversity among world cultures.[78] They called the effort Project GLOBE, short for Global Leadership and Organizational Behavior Effectiveness. By studying data from 170,000 managers in 62 countries, the GLOBE researchers sorted these countries into 10 culture clusters.[79] As shown in Figure 5.4, the researchers found practices based on nine cultural dimensions tended to be more similar among countries within a cluster than across them.

Two of the GLOBE culture dimensions are direct fits with Hofstede's framework. They are *power distance*, which is higher in Confucian Asia and lower in Nordic Europe, and *uncertainty avoidance*, which is high in Germanic Europe and low in the Middle East.

Four other GLOBE dimensions are similar to Hofstede's. *Gender egalitarianism* is the degree to which a culture minimizes gender inequalities. Similar to Hofstede's masculinity–femininity, it is high in the cultures of Eastern and Nordic Europe and low in those of the Middle East. *Future orientation* is the degree to which members of a culture are willing to look ahead, delay gratifications, and make investments in the expectation of longer-term payoffs. It is similar to Hofstede's time orientation. Germanic and Nordic Europe are high on future orientation; Latin America and the Middle East are low. *Institutional collectivism* is the extent to which a society emphasizes and rewards group action and accomplishments versus individual ones. It is similar to Hofstede's individualism–collectivism. Confucian Asia and Nordic Europe score high in institutional collectivism, whereas Germanic and Latin Europe score low. *In-group collectivism* is the extent to which people take pride in their families, small groups, and organizational memberships, acting loyally and cohesively regarding them. This form of

Universal Facilitators of Leadership Success

- Acting trustworthy, just, honest
- Showing foresight, planning
- Being positive, dynamic, motivating
- Inspiring confidence
- Being informed and communicative
- Being a coordinator and team builder

Universal Inhibitors of Leadership Success

- Being a loner
- Acting uncooperative
- Being irritable
- Acting autocratic

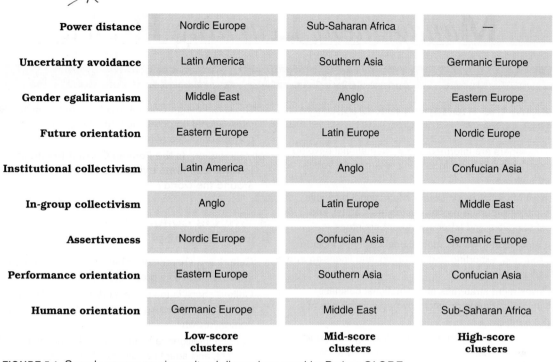

	Low-score clusters	Mid-score clusters	High-score clusters
Power distance	Nordic Europe	Sub-Saharan Africa	—
Uncertainty avoidance	Latin America	Southern Asia	Germanic Europe
Gender egalitarianism	Middle East	Anglo	Eastern Europe
Future orientation	Eastern Europe	Latin Europe	Nordic Europe
Institutional collectivism	Latin America	Anglo	Confucian Asia
In-group collectivism	Anglo	Latin Europe	Middle East
Assertiveness	Nordic Europe	Confucian Asia	Germanic Europe
Performance orientation	Eastern Europe	Southern Asia	Confucian Asia
Humane orientation	Germanic Europe	Middle East	Sub-Saharan Africa

FIGURE 5.4 Sample scores on nine cultural dimensions used by Project GLOBE.

collectivism runs high in Latin America and the Middle East, but tends to be low in Anglo and Germanic Europe cultures.

The remaining three GLOBE dimensions offer additional cultural insights. *Assertiveness* is the extent to which a culture emphasizes competition and assertiveness in social relationships, valuing behavior that is tough and confrontational as opposed to modest and tender. Cultures in Eastern and Germanic Europe score high in assertiveness; those in Nordic Europe and Latin America score low. *Performance orientation* is the degree of emphasis on performance excellence and improvements. Anglo and Confucian Asian cultures tend to be high in performance orientation. Countries in these clusters can be expected to reward performance accomplishments and invest in training to encourage future performance gains. *Humane orientation* reflects tendencies toward fairness, altruism, generosity, and caring as people deal with one another. It tends to be high in Southern Asia and Sub-Saharan Africa, and to be low in Latin and Germanic Europe.

The GLOBE research is a timely, systematic, and empirical look at culture and management across a large sample of countries. And as the small box on universal facilitators and inhibitors of leadership success shows, it adds to evidence on the universality of some management practices.[80] Yet, as with other cross-cultural research, the GLOBE project is insightful but not definitive. It should be used along with the insights of Hall, Hofstede, and others to help us better understand the diversity of global cultures.[81]

*Cultural Inf
Family
Religion
Education
Community
Business Organization*

Be sure you can ☑ answer this question: "Do management theories apply universally around the world?" ☑ describe the concept of global organizational learning ☑ identify the major components in Project GLOBE's model of cultural differences

Learning Check   ☑

Study Question 4
What is culture, and how does it impact global management?

Management Learning Review

Study Questions Summary

1 What are the management challenges of globalization?

- Global managers are informed about international developments and are competent in working with people from different cultures.
- The forces of globalization create international business opportunities to pursue profits, customers, capital, and low-cost suppliers and labor in different countries.
- Market entry strategies for international business include global sourcing, exporting and importing, and licensing and franchising.
- Direct investment strategies of international business establish joint ventures or wholly owned subsidiaries in foreign countries.
- General environment differences, including legal and political systems, often complicate international business activities.
- Regional economic alliances such as NAFTA, the EU, and SADC link nations of the world with the goals of promoting economic development.
- The World Trade Organization (WTO) is a global institution that promotes free trade and open markets around the world.

FOR DISCUSSION **What aspects of the U.S. legal-political environment could prove difficult for a Chinese firm setting up a factory in America?**

2 What are global businesses, and what do they do?

- A global corporation is a multinational enterprise or multinational corporation with extensive operations in multiple foreign countries.
- A transnational corporation tries to operate globally without a strong national identity and with a worldwide mission and strategies.
- Global corporations can benefit host countries by offering broader tax bases, new technologies, and employment opportunities.
- Global corporations can cause problems for host countries if they interfere in local government, extract excessive profits, and dominate the local economy.

- The U.S. Foreign Corrupt Practices Act prohibits American multinational corporations from engaging in bribery and corrupt practices abroad.

FOR DISCUSSION **Is the Foreign Corrupt Practices Act unfair to American firms trying to compete for business around the world?**

3 What is culture, and how does it impact global management?

- Culture is a shared set of beliefs, values, and behavior patterns common to a group of people.
- Culture shock is the discomfort people sometimes experience when interacting with persons from cultures different from their own.
- Cultural intelligence is an individual capacity to understand, respect, and adapt to cultural differences.
- Hall's "silent" languages of culture include the use of context, time, and interpersonal space.
- Hofstede's five dimensions of value differences in national cultures are power distance, uncertainty avoidance, individualism–collectivism, masculinity–femininity, and time orientation.

FOR DISCUSSION **Should religion be included on Hall's list of the silent languages of culture?**

4 How can we benefit from global management learning?

- The field of comparative management studies how management is practiced around the world and how management ideas are transferred from one country or culture to the next.
- Project GLOBE is an extensive worldwide study of management and leadership that identified country clusters that varied on nine cultural dimensions.
- Because management practices are influenced by cultural values, global management learning must recognize that successful practices in one culture may work less well in others.

FOR DISCUSSION **Even though cultural differences are readily apparent, is the tendency today for the world's cultures to converge and become more alike?**

Self-Test

Multiple-Choice Questions

1. The reasons why businesses go international include gaining new markets and the search for _____.
   (a) political risk   (b) protectionism   (c) lower labor costs   (d) most favored nation status

2. When Rocky Brands decided to buy full ownership of a manufacturing company in the Dominican Republic, Rocky was engaging in which form of international business?
   (a) import/export   (b) licensing   (c) foreign subsidiary   (d) joint venture

3. A form of international business that falls into the category of a direct investment strategy is _____.
   (a) exporting   (b) joint venture   (c) licensing   (d) global sourcing

4. The World Trade Organization, or WTO, would most likely become involved in disputes between countries over _____.
   (a) exchange rates   (b) ethnocentrism   (c) nationalization   (d) tariffs

5. Business complaints about copyright protection and intellectual property rights in some countries illustrate how differences in _____ can impact international operations.
   (a) legal environments   (b) political stability   (c) sustainable development   (d) economic systems

6. In _____ cultures, members tend to do one thing at a time; in _____ cultures, members tend to do many things at once.
   (a) monochronic, polychronic   (b) polycentric, geocentric   (c) collectivist, individualist   (d) neutral, affective

7. A culture that places great value on meaning expressed in the written or spoken word would be described as _____ by Hall.
   (a) monochronic   (b) proxemic   (c) collectivist   (d) low-context

8. It is common in Malaysian culture for people to value teamwork and to display great respect for authority. Hofstede would describe this culture as high in both _____.
   (a) uncertainty avoidance and feminism   (b) universalism and particularism   (c) collectivism and power distance
   (d) long-term orientation and masculinity

9. In Hofstede's study of national cultures, America was found to be the most _____ compared with other countries in his sample.
   (a) individualistic   (b) collectivist   (c) feminine   (d) long-term oriented

10. It is _____ when a foreign visitor takes offense at a local custom such as dining with one's fingers, considering it inferior to practices of his or her own culture.
    (a) universalist   (b) prescriptive   (c) monochronic   (d) enthnocentric

11. When Limited Brands buys cotton in Egypt, has tops sewn from it in Sri Lanka according to designs made in Italy, and then offers them for sale in the United States, this form of international business is known as _____.
    (a) licensing   (b) importing   (c) joint venturing   (d) global sourcing

12. The difference between an international business and a transnational corporation is that the transnational _____.
    (a) tries to operate without a strong national identity   (b) does business in only one or two foreign countries
    (c) is led by managers with ethnocentric attitudes   (d) is ISO 14000 certified

13. The Foreign Corrupt Practices Act makes it illegal for _____.
    (a) Americans to engage in joint ventures abroad   (b) foreign businesses to pay bribes to U.S. government officials
    (c) U.S. businesses to make "payoffs" abroad to gain international business contracts   (d) foreign businesses to steal intellectual property from U.S. firms operating in their countries

14. In a culture described by Project GLOBE as high in _____, one would expect to find men and women treated equally in terms of job and career opportunities.
    (a) humane orientation   (b) institutional collectivism   (c) gender egalitarianism   (d) performance orientation

15. Hofstede would describe a culture whose members respect age and authority and whose workers defer to the preferences of their supervisors as _____.
    (a) low masculinity   (b) high particularism   (c) high power distance   (d) monochronic

Short-Response Questions

16. Why do host countries sometimes complain about how global corporations operate within their borders?
17. Why is the "power-distance" dimension of national culture important in management?
18. What is the difference between institutional collectivism and in-group collectivism as described by Project GLOBE?
19. How do regional economic alliances impact the global economy?

Essay Question

20. Kim has just returned from her first business trip to Japan. While there, she was impressed with the intense use of work teams. Now back in Iowa, she would like to totally reorganize the workflows and processes of her canoe manufacturing company and its 75 employees around teams. There has been very little emphasis on teamwork, and she now believes this is "the way to go." Based on the discussion of culture and management in this chapter, what advice would you offer Kim?

Management Skills and Competencies

Self-Assessment

Back to Yourself: Cultural Awareness

The forces of globalization are often discussed in respect to job migration, outsourcing, currency fluctuations, and the fortunes of global corporations. These and other aspects of globalization are best understood and dealt with in a context of cultural awareness. It's only natural that we become habitual and used to the ways of our culture. But, many of these same values and patterns of behavior can be called into question when we work and interact with persons from different cultures. Although comfortable to us, our ways of doing things may seem strange and even, at the extreme, offensive to others who come from different cultural backgrounds. And it's only natural for cultural differences to be frustrating and even threatening when we come face to face with them. The models discussed in this chapter are a good basis for cultural understanding. National economies are now global; business is now global; our personal thinking must be global as well. After you complete the following self-assessment on Global Intelligence, don't forget to go online for the Time Orientation self-assessment.

> To achieve high levels of **cultural awareness**, we need to broaden our cultural horizons, embrace the full diversity of the world's peoples, and find pleasure in understanding the rich variety of global cultures.

Further Reflection: Global Intelligence

Instructions

Use the following scale to rate yourself on each of these 10 items:[82]

1 Very Poor   2 Poor   3 Acceptable   4 Good   5 Very Good

1. I understand my own culture in terms of its expectations, values, and influence on communication and relationships.
2. When someone presents me with a different point of view, I try to understand it rather than attack it.
3. I am comfortable dealing with situations where the available information is incomplete and the outcomes are unpredictable.
4. I am open to new situations and am always looking for new information and learning opportunities.
5. I have a good understanding of the attitudes and perceptions toward my culture as they are held by people from other cultures.
6. I am always gathering information about other countries and cultures and trying to learn from them.
7. I am well informed regarding the major differences in the government, political, and economic systems around the world.
8. I work hard to increase my understanding of people from other cultures.
9. I am able to adjust my communication style to work effectively with people from different cultures.
10. I can recognize when cultural differences are influencing working relationships, and I adjust my attitudes and behavior accordingly.

Interpretation

To be successful in the global economy, you must be comfortable with the cultural diversity that it holds. This requires a global mind-set that is receptive to and respectful of cultural differences, global knowledge that includes the continuing quest to know and learn more about other nations and cultures, and global work skills that allow you to work effectively across cultures.

Scoring

The goal is to score as close to a perfect "5" as possible on each of the three dimensions of global intelligence. Develop your scores as follows:

1. Items (1 + 2 + 3 + 4)/4 5 Global Mind-set Score
2. Items (5 + 6 + 7)/3 5 Global Knowledge Score
3. Items (8 + 9 + 10)/3 5 Global Work Skills Score

Team Exercise

American Football

Instructions

Form into groups as assigned by the instructor. In the group do the following:

1. Discuss "American Football"—the rules, the way the game is played, the way players and coaches behave, and the roles of owners and fans.
2. Use "American Football" as a metaphor to explain the way U.S. corporations run and how they tend to behave in terms of strategies and goals.
3. Prepare a class presentation for a group of visiting Japanese business executives. In this presentation, use the metaphor of "American Football" to (1) explain American business strategies and practices to the Japanese, and (2) critique the potential strengths and weaknesses of the American business approach in terms of success in the global marketplace.

Case Study: Harley-Davidson

Go to *Management Cases for Critical Thinking* to find the recommended case for Chapter 5—
"Harley-Davidson: Style and Strategy Have Global Reach."

Entrepreneurship and New Ventures

6

Chapter 6 Study Questions

1 What is entrepreneurship?

2 What is special about small business entrepreneurship?

3 How do entrepreneurs start and finance new ventures?

Learning From Others

Entrepreneurs Are Changing Our World

Chances are you are already heavily involved in what many are now calling the new "app economy." Those tiny programs that fuel our fun and productivity on smartphones and devices such as the iPad have already created an annual market exceeding $1 billion, and growing fast. The money is made selling the apps, selling products through the apps, and selling advertising space within the apps.

Among the app players that have made it big is Zynga, the brainchild of Marc Pincus.[1] Zynga's revenues jumped to $150+ million in just three years. Pincus is self-described as having one part the DNA of an entrepreneur and a second part the DNA of a competitive gamer. The company's mission is to connect the world through online games such as its wildly popular FarmVille. And the connection has been made; some 120 million people play Zynga games each day.

Like its apps, Zynga isn't the typical business. Perhaps it's the Google influence, or perhaps it's Pincus's instincts; or maybe it's both. His firm operates with a fun culture that is heavy on the creativity side and very light on the corporate control side. Chefs cook two meals a day for Zynga's employees—why waste time going out for food? A masseuse is on staff—who needs stress? And then there are the keg parties and poker tournaments—remember, it's a company that is based on having fun! And, yes, you can bring your pet to work.

As for Pincus, he's the guy in jeans and loose shirt—one among other casually dressed staffers. But don't let appearances fool you; he's all business. There's a lot at stake as the app economy grows bigger and more competitive every day. Zynga faces competition from the likes of Playfish and Playdom, and from the thousands of app programmers around the world. For now, Pincus is betting on Zynga's internal culture where freedom inspires teams of employees to work a tremendous number of hours together while creating what they each hope will be the next best fun app that everyone is clamoring to download.

do the benchmarking

Zynga is building a foundation for success based on a fun and flexible corporate culture. Don't you wonder if this could be the model for more organizations, not just those in the tech industries? And let's not forget another side of this story; there are thousands of people out there creating apps—on their own time and using their own creativity. **Opportunities for entrepreneurship are everywhere; you just have to recognize them.**

Learning About Yourself

Self-Management

The many complex challenges of work and everyday living in our uncertain times call significantly upon one's capacities for **self-management**. It's an ability to use an objective understanding of one's strengths and weaknesses to continuously improve and adapt to meet life's challenges. Self-management is an essential skill that asks you to dig deep and continually learn from experience. After all, how are you going to take the best advantage of what experience offers, including possible entrepreneurship, if you don't know yourself well enough?

Think of it this way. In order to be strong in self-management you must have the ability to understand yourself individually and in the social context, to assess personal strengths and weaknesses, to exercise initiative, to accept responsibility for accomplishments, to work well with others, and to adapt by continually learning from experience in the quest for self-improvement.

Some self-management ideas are shown in the box. These and other foundations for career success are within everyone's grasp. But the motivation and the effort required to succeed must come from within. Only you can make the commitment to take charge of your destiny and become a self-manager.

According to author and consultant Steven Covey, you can move your career forward by (1) behaving like an entrepreneur, (2) seeking feedback on your performance continually, (3) setting up your own mentoring systems, (4) getting comfortable with teamwork, (5) taking risks to gain experience and learn new skills, (6) being a problem solver, and (7) keeping your life in balance.[2]

Self-Management for Career Success

Lesson one: There is no substitute for high performance. No matter what the assignment, you must work hard to quickly establish your credibility and work value.

Lesson two: Be and stay flexible. Don't hide from ambiguity. Don't wait for structure. You must always adapt to new work demands, new situations, and new people.

Lesson three: Keep the focus. You can't go forward without talent. You must be a talent builder—always adding to and refining your talents to make them valuable to an employer.

Lesson four: Figure out what you love to do and then do it, do it, do it. Practice makes perfect. Like a professional golfer, you have to hit lots and lots of practice balls in order to make perfect shots during the match.

Lesson five: Don't give up; certainly never give up too soon. You have to stick with it, even during tough times. Remember—resilience counts. If you have the talent and know what you love, go for it. Self-management is a way to realize your dreams.

get to know yourself better

One of the best ways check your capacity for self-management is to examine how you approach college, your academic courses, and the rich variety of development opportunities available on and off campus. Test yourself. What activities are you involved in? How well do you balance them with academic and personal responsibilities? Do you miss deadlines or turn in assignments pulled together at the last minute? Do you accept poor or mediocre performance? Do you learn from mistakes? **Take advantage of the end-of-chapter Self-Assessment feature to further reflect on your Entrepreneurship Orientation.**

6 Entrepreneurship, Social Enterprise, and New Ventures

Study Question 1	Study Question 2	Study Question 3
Nature of Entrepreneurship	**Entrepreneurship and Small Business**	**New Venture Creation**
• Who are the entrepreneurs?	• Why and how to get started	• Life cycles of entrepreneurial firms
• Characteristics of entrepreneurs	• Internet entrepreneurship	• Writing the business plan
• Diversity and entrepreneurship	• Family businesses	• Choosing the form of ownership
• Social entrepreneurship	• Why small businesses fail	• Financing the new venture
	• Small business development	
Learning Check 1	**Learning Check 2**	**Learning Check 3**

Need a job? Why not create one? That's what Jennifer Wright did after the financial crisis shut down her work as a credit analyst. While back at school in an MBA program she tweaked a friend's idea for a better pizza box and entered it in a b-school entrepreneurship competition. The "green box" as she calls it breaks into plates and a storage container before it goes for recycling. She says the feedback was "so incredibly positive I felt I'd be crazy not to pursue this."

Retired, feeling a bit old, and want to do more? Not to worry; people aged 55-64 are the most entrepreneurially active in the U.S. Realizing that he needed "someplace to go and something to do" after retirement, Art Koff, now 74, started RetireBrains.com. It's a Job board for retirees and gets thousands of hits a day. It also employs 7 people and keeps Koff as busy as he wants to be.

Struggling with work-life balance as a mother? You might find flexibility and opportunity in entrepreneurship. Denise Devine was a financial executive with Campbell Soup Co. Now she has her own line of fiber-rich juice drinks for kids. Called *mompreneurs*, women like Devine find opportunity in market niches for healthier products they spot as moms. Says Devine: "As entrepreneurs we're working harder than we did, but we're doing it on our own schedules."[3]

Female, thinking about starting a small business, but don't have the money? Get creative and reach out. You might find help with organizations like Count-Me-In. Started by co-founders Nell Merlino and Irish Burnett, it offers "microcredit" loans of $500 to $10,000 to help women start and expand small businesses. Borrowers qualify by a unique credit scoring system that doesn't hold against them things such as a divorce, time off to raise a family, or age—all things that might discourage conventional lenders. Merlino says: "Women own 38% of all businesses in this country, but still have far less access to capital than men because of today's process."[4]

Think about it. These examples should be inspiring. In fact, this is really a chapter of examples. The goal is not only to inform, but to also get you thinking about starting your own business, becoming your own boss, and making your own special contribution to society. What about it? Can we count you in to join the world of entrepreneurship and small business management?

THE NATURE OF ENTREPRENEURSHIP

● **Entrepreneurship** is risk-taking behavior that results in new opportunities.

The term **entrepreneurship** describes strategic thinking and risk-taking behavior that results in the creation of new opportunities. H. Wayne Huizenga, who started Waste Management with just $5,000 and once owned the Miami Dolphins says: "An important part of being an entrepreneur is a gut instinct that allows you to believe in your heart that something will work even though everyone else says it will not.[5]

WHO ARE THE ENTREPRENEURS?

A **classic entrepreneur** is a risk-taking individual who takes action to pursue opportunities others fail to recognize, or may even view as problems or threats. Some people become **serial entrepreneurs** in that they start and run new ventures over and over again, moving from one interest and opportunity to the next. We find such entrepreneurs both in business and nonprofit settings.

On the business side, H. Wayne Huizenga, mentioned earlier, is a serial entrepreneur who made his fortune founding and selling businesses like Blockbuster Entertainment, Waste Management, and AutoNation. A member of the Entrepreneurs' Hall of Fame, he describes being an entrepreneur this way: "We're looking for something where we can make something happen: an industry where the competition is asleep, hasn't taken advantage. It's going to be hard to find another Blockbuster, but that doesn't mean you can't have three good companies growing. The point is, we're going to be busy."[6]

On the nonprofit side, Scott Beale is more of a classic entrepreneur. He quit his job with the U.S. State Department to start Atlas Corps, something he calls a "Peace Corps in reverse." The organization brings nonprofit managers from India and Colombia to the United States to volunteer for local nonprofits while improving their management skills. After a year they return to a nonprofit in their home countries. "I am just like a business entrepreneur," Beale says, "but instead of making a big paycheck I try to make a big impact."[7]

Both Huizenga and Beale show entrepreneurial skill with **first-mover advantage**, moving quickly to spot, exploit, and deliver a product or service to a new market or an unrecognized niche in an existing one. Here are some other business entrepreneurs who were willing to take risks and sharp enough to spot the chance for first-mover advantage. Although each is unique as an individual, they share something in common that we all might aspire to—each built a successful business from good ideas and hard work.[8]

● A **classic entrepreneur** is someone willing to pursue opportunities in situations others view as problems or threats.

● A **serial entrepreneur** starts and runs businesses and nonprofits over and over again, moving from one interest and opportunity to the next.

● A **first-mover advantage** comes from being first to exploit a niche or enter a market.

Mary Kay Ash

After a career in sales, Mary Kay Ash "retired" to write a book that she hoped would help women compete in the male-dominated business world. Then she realized she was writing a business plan. Her retirement lasted a month and she turned the plan into Mary Kay Cosmetics. Launched with an investment of $5,000, the company now operates worldwide and has been named one of the best companies to work for in America. Mary Kay's goal from the beginning was "to help women everywhere reach their full potential."

Caterina Fake

From idea to buyout only took 16 months. That's quite a benchmark for would-be Internet entrepreneurs. Welcome to the world of Flickr, started by

Caterina Fake and her husband Stewart Butterfield. They took the notion of online photo sharing and turned Flickr in real-time into an almost viral Internet phenomenon. They also built the firm in the online environment without needing start-up capital; their families, friends, and angel investors provided the necessary financing. The payoff came when Yahoo! bought them out for $30 million. Fake's latest venture is Hunch.com, a website designed to help people make decisions such as: "Should I buy that new BMW?"

Earl Graves

With a vision and a $175,000 loan, Earl Graves started *Black Enterprise* magazine in 1970. That success grew into the diversified business information company Earl G. Graves, Ltd., including BlackEnterprise.com. Today the business school at his college alma mater, Baltimore's Morgan State University, is named after him. Graves says: "I feel that a large part of my role as publisher of *Black Enterprise* is to be a catalyst for black economic development in this country."

David Thomas

Have you had your Wendy's today? A lot of people have, and there's quite a story behind it. The first Wendy's restaurant opened in Columbus, Ohio, in 1969. It's  still there, although there are also about 5,000 others now operating around the world. What began as founder David Thomas's dream to own one restaurant grew into a global enterprise. He became one of the world's best-known entrepreneurs and "the world's most famous hamburger cook." But there's more to Wendy's than profits and business performance. The company strives to help its communities, with a special focus on schools and schoolchildren. An adopted child, Thomas founded the Dave Thomas Foundation for Adoption.

CHARACTERISTICS OF ENTREPRENEURS

Is there something in your experience that could be a pathway to business or non-profit entrepreneurship? A common image of an entrepreneur is as the founder of a new enterprise that achieves large-scale success like the ones just mentioned. But that's only part of the story. Entrepreneurs and entrepreneurship are everywhere and there is no age prerequisite to join them.

Consider the stories of two "young" entrepreneurs. At the age of 22, Richard Ludlow turned down a full-time job offer and an MBA admission to start New York's Academic Earth. It's an online location for posting and sharing faculty lectures and other educational materials. His goal is to both make a profit and help society by lowering the cost of education. While in high school Jasmine Lawrence created her own natural cosmetics after having problems with a purchased hair relaxer. Products from her firm Eden Body Works can now be found at Wal-Mart and Whole Foods.[9]

There are lots of entrepreneurs to be found in any community. Just look around. Those who take the risk of buying a local McDonald's or Subway Sandwich or Papa John's franchise, open a small retail shop selling used video games or bicycles, start a self-employed service business such as financial planning or management consulting, or establish a nonprofit organization to provide housing for the homeless or deliver hot meals to house-bound senior citizens, are entrepreneurs in their own ways.[10] Entrepreneurs are found within larger organizations as well. Called **intrapreneurs**, they are people who step forward and take risk to introduce a new product or process, or pursue innovations that can change the organization in significant ways.

● **Intrapreneurs** display entre-preneurial behavior as employees of larger firms.

Attitudes and Personal Interests

Research suggests that entrepreneurs tend to share certain attitudes and personal characteristics. The general profile is of an individual who is very self-confident, determined, resilient, adaptable, and driven by excellence.[11] You should be able to identify these attributes in the prior examples.

As shown in Figure 6.1, typical personality traits and characteristics of entrepreneurs include the following.[12]

- *Internal locus of control:* Entrepreneurs believe that they are in control of their own destiny; they are self-directing and like autonomy.
- *High energy level:* Entrepreneurs are persistent, hardworking, and willing to exert extraordinary efforts to succeed.
- *High need for achievement:* Entrepreneurs are motivated to accomplish challenging goals; they thrive on performance feedback.
- *Tolerance for ambiguity:* Entrepreneurs are risk takers; they tolerate situations with high degrees of uncertainty.
- *Self-confidence:* Entrepreneurs feel competent, believe in themselves, and are willing to make decisions.
- *Passion and action orientation:* Entrepreneurs try to act ahead of problems; they want to get things done and not waste valuable time.
- *Self-reliance and desire for independence:* Entrepreneurs want independence; they are self-reliant; they want to be their own bosses, not work for others.
- *Flexibility:* Entrepreneurs are willing to admit problems and errors, and are willing to change a course of action when plans aren't working.

FIGURE 6.1 Personality traits and characteristics of entrepreneurs.

Background, Experiences, and Interests

Entrepreneurs tend to have unique backgrounds and personal experiences.[13] *Childhood experiences and family environment* seem to make a difference. Evidence links entrepreneurs with parents who were entrepreneurial and self-employed. And entrepreneurs are often raised in families that encourage responsibility, initiative, and independence. Another issue is *career or work history*. Entrepreneurs who try one venture often go on to others. Prior work experience in the business area or industry being entered is helpful.

Entrepreneurs also tend to emerge during certain *windows of career opportunity*. Most start their businesses between the ages of 22 and 45, an age spread that seems to allow for risk taking. However, age shouldn't be viewed as a barrier. When Tony DeSio was 50, he founded the Mail Boxes Etc. chain. He sold it for $300 million when he was 67 and suffering heart problems. Within a year he launched PixArts, another franchise chain based on photography and art.[14]

A report in the *Harvard Business Review* further suggests that entrepreneurs may have unique and *deeply embedded life interests*. The article describes entrepreneurs as having strong interests in creative production—enjoying project initiation, working with the unknown, and finding unconventional solutions. They also have strong interests in enterprise control—finding enjoyment from running things. The combination of creative production and enterprise control is characteristic of people who want to start things and move things toward a goal.[15]

Management Smarts 6.1

Challenging the myths about entrepreneurs

- *Entrepreneurs are born, not made.*
Not true! Talent gained and enhanced by experience is a foundation for entrepreneurial success.

- *Entrepreneurs are gamblers.*
Not true! Entrepreneurs are risk takers, but the risks are informed and calculated.

- *Money is the key to entrepreneurial success.*
Not true! Money is no guarantee of success. There's a lot more to it than that; many entrepreneurs start with very little.

- *You have to be young to be an entrepreneur.*
Not true! Age is no barrier to entrepreneurship; with age often comes experience, contacts, and other useful resources.

- *You have to have a degree in business to be an entrepreneur.*
Not true! You may not need a degree at all. Although a business degree is not necessary, it helps to study and understand business fundamentals.

● **Necessity-based entrepreneurship** takes place because other employment options don't exist.

Undoubtedly, entrepreneurs seek independence and the sense of mastery that comes with success. That seems to keep driving Tony DeSio from the earlier example. When asked by a reporter what he liked most about entrepreneurship, he replied: "Being able to make decisions without having to go through layers of corporate hierarchy—just being a master of your own destiny."

To help keep things in perspective, Management Smarts 6.1 debunks some common myths about entrepreneurship.[16]

DIVERSITY AND ENTREPRENEURSHIP

When economists speak about entrepreneurs, they differentiate between those who are driven by the quest for new opportunities and those who are driven by absolute need.[17] Those in the latter group pursue **necessity-based entrepreneurship**, meaning that they start new ventures because they have few or no other employment and career options. Necessity-driven entrepreneurship is one way for people, often minorities and women who have hit the "glass ceiling" in their careers or are otherwise cut off from other employment choices, to strike out on their own and gain economic independence. In the case of Anita Roddick who founded the Body Shop, she says it began because she needed "to create a livelihood for myself and my two daughters, while my husband, Gordon, was trekking across the Americas."[18]

The National Foundation for Women Business Owners (NFWBO) reports that women own more than 9 million, about 38%, of all U.S. businesses and are starting new businesses at twice the rate of the national average.[19] Among women leaving private-sector employment to work on their own, 33% said they were not being taken seriously by their prior employer and 29% said they had experienced glass ceiling issues.[20] In *Women Business Owners of Color: Challenges and Accomplishments*, the NFWBO points out that the glass ceiling problems motivating women of color to pursue entrepreneurship include not being recognized or valued by their employers, not being taken seriously, and seeing others promoted ahead of them.[21]

Minority entrepreneurship is one of the fastest-growing sectors of our economy.[22] Businesses created by minority entrepreneurs now employ more than 4 million U.S. workers and generate over $500 billion in annual revenues. And the trend is upward. In the last census of small businesses, those owned by African Americans had grown by 45%, by Hispanics 31%, and by Asians 24%. Small businesses owned by women also had grown by 24%.[23]

SOCIAL ENTREPRENEURSHIP

● **Social entrepreneurship** is a unique form of ethical entrepreneurship that seeks new ways to solve pressing social problems.

Speaking of entrepreneurship, don't forget it can play an important role in tackling social issues: housing and job training for the homeless—bringing technology to poor families—improving literacy among disadvantaged youth—making small loans to start minority-owned businesses. These examples and others like them are all targets for **social entrepreneurship,** a unique form of ethical entrepreneurship that seeks novel ways to solve pressing social problems.

Real People

Entrepreneurs Find Rural Setting Fuels Solar Power

When she received the Ohio Department of Development's Keys to Success Award, Michelle Greenfield said, "It's exciting. It's kind of nice to be recognized as a good business owner. The goal is not to have the award, the goal is to have a good business and do well." She and her husband Geoff certainly do have a good business; it's called Third Sun Solar Wind and Power, Ltd.

Although the company's products are timely today, they were a bit ahead of the market in the beginning. The Greenfields began by building a home that used no electricity in rural Athens County, Ohio. Using solar power. They have yet to pay an electric utility bill. As friends became interested, they helped others get into solar power. The business kept growing from there. Third Sun has been ranked by *Inc.* magazine as the 32nd fastest growing energy business in the United States. It is the largest provider of solar energy systems in the Midwest and has experienced a 390% growth in three years. Quite a story for an idea that began with a sustainable home!

Michelle says that they lived very frugally in their rural home, and this helped them start the business on a low budget. Soon after its birth, Third Sun moved into the Ohio University Innovation Center, a business incubator dedicated to helping local firms grow and prosper. They have also benefited from

tapping the local workforce in a university town and from having MBA students work with their firm in consulting capacities.

As the company grew, Geoff focused on technical issues while Michelle spent most of her time on the business and managerial ones. She's now the CEO and, though primarily concerned with strategic issues as the firm grows, still keeps involved by helping the firm's 21 employees with other aspects of the business. "I do a lot of marketing," she says. "I do speaking engagements . . . I serve on the Board of Directors of Green Energy Ohio."

Michelle says that the name "Third Sun . . ." was chosen to represent a "third son" for the couple, one requiring lots of nurturing in order to help it grow big and strong. Even now, with a growing customer base, she says that the company is still in an "adolescent" stage where it still needs lots of attention, although the challenges of running the business at this stage are different from those in the start-up phase.

Social entrepreneurs that take risks to find new ways to solve social problems share many characteristics with other entrepreneurs. But, they are driven by a social mission and pursue innovations that help make lives better for people who are disadvantaged.[24] You can think of these problems as the likes of poverty, illiteracy, poor health, and even social oppression. *Fast Company* magazine tries to spot and honor social entrepreneurs that run organizations with "innovative thinking that can transform lives and change the world." Here are some recent winners on its prestigious annual Honor Roll of Social Enterprises of the Year.[25]

- Chip Ransler and Manoj Sinha—tackled the lack of power faced by many of India's poor villagers. As University of Virginia business students, they realized that 350 million people without reliable electricity lived in India's rice-growing regions. Noting that tons of rice husks were being discarded with every harvest, Ransler and Sinha started Husk Power Systems to create biogas from the husks and use the gas to fuel small power plants.
- Neal Keny-Guyer—tackled the crowded field of microfinance in Indonesia, where more than 50,000 micro lenders serve 50 million people. But with as many as 110 million Indonesians struggling to live on $2 per day, Keny-Guyer's organization Mercy Corps bought a local bank that was in trouble and restructured it to serve as a banker for micro lenders. The goal was to boost the impact of microfinance in Indonesia by supporting it with top-flight financial tools and technology, as well as capital.
- Rose Donna and Joel Selanikio—tackled public health problems in Sub-Saharan Africa. Realizing that developing nations are often bogged down in

● A **social entrepreneur** takes risks to find new ways to solve pressing social problems.

the paperwork of public health, they created software to make the process quicker and more efficient, while increasing the reliability of the resulting databases. The UN, the World Health Organization, and the Vodafone Foundation are now helping their firm, DataDyne, move the program into 22 other African nations.

When you think social entrepreneurship, don't neglect what is happening in your community. Lots of social entrepreneurship takes place without much notice, flying under the radar so to speak. Attention most often goes to business entrepreneurs making lots of money, or trying to do so. But you can find many examples of people who have made the commitment to social entrepreneurship. Deborah Sardone is one. As the owner of a housekeeping service in Texas, she noticed that her clients with cancer really struggled with everyday household chores. This realization prompted her to start Cleaning for a Reason. It's a nonprofit that builds networks of linkages with cleaning firms around the country that are willing to offer free home cleaning to cancer patients.[26]

ENTREPRENEURSHIP AND SMALL BUSINESS

● A **small business** has fewer than 500 employees, is independently owned and operated, and does not dominate its industry.

The U.S. Small Business Administration (SBA) defines a **small business** as one that has 500 or fewer employees, is independently owned and operated, and does not dominate its industry. Almost 99% of American businesses meet this definition, and some 87% of them employ fewer than 20 persons. Small businesses in the United States employ some 52% of private workers, provide 51% of private-sector output, receive 35% of federal government contract dollars, and provide as many as 7 out of every 10 new jobs in the economy.[27] Their importance was center stage when President Barack Obama used the following words to proclaim National Small Business Week in 2009, a time of major economic turmoil for America and the world.[28]

> Small businesses are the lifeblood of cities and towns across the country. Over the last decade, small businesses created 70 percent of new jobs, and they are responsible for half of all jobs in the private sector. They also help enhance the lives of our citizens by improving our quality of life and creating personal wealth. Small businesses will lead the way to prosperity, particularly in today's challenging economic environment.

WHY AND HOW TO GET STARTED

There are many reasons why entrepreneurs launch their own small businesses. One study reports the following motivations: number 1—wanting to be your own boss and control your future; number 2—going to work for a family-owned business; and number 3—seeking to fulfill a dream.[29] The publication of a Gallup-Healthways Well-Being Index provides additional incentive to start your own business. It show that self-employed business and store owners outrank working

Roger the Plumber Enjoys Being in Control

His name really is Roger, and the company really is Roger the Plumber. The 14-person firm in Overland Park, Kansas, was founded by Roger Peugeot, and he has seen all the ups and downs of small business ownership—from growth to staff cutbacks. Yet he's happy, saying "I'm still excited to get up and go to work every day. Even when things get tough I'm still in control." Peugeot is one of many self-employed business owners that outranked 10 other occupational groups in a Gallup survey of job satisfaction and overall quality of life.

adults in 10 other occupations—including professional, manager/executive, and sales, on such factors as job satisfaction and emotional and physical health.[30]

Once a decision is made to go the small business route, the most common ways to get involved are to start one, buy an existing one, or buy and run a **franchise**—where a business owner sells to another the right to operate the same business in another location. A franchise such as Subway, Quiznos, or Domino's Pizza runs under the original owner's business name and guidance. In return, the franchise parent receives a share of income or a flat fee from the franchisee.

In terms of small business **startups**, serial entrepreneur Steven Blank calls them temporary organizations that are trying "to discover a profitable, scalable business model." In other words, a startup is just that—a "start;" it's a new venture that the entrepreneur is hoping will take shape and prove successful as things move forward. Blank advises that the early goals of a startup should be to move fast and create a "minimum viable product" that will attract customers, and that can be further developed and made more sophisticated over time. He gives the example of Facebook which started with simple message sharing and keeps growing by moving into ever-more complex features. He also favors what are now being called **lean startups**. They take maximum advantage of things like open-source software and free Web services, while staying small and striving to keep all operations as simple as possible.[31]

INTERNET ENTREPRENEURSHIP

Today there are major opportunities in **Internet entrepreneurship** that makes direct use of the Internet to pursue entrepreneurial activities. The Interactive Advertising Bureau estimates that Internet-related businesses provide some three million jobs in the U.S. economy.[32] And although firms like Amazon.com, Yahoo!, Google, and Netflix may jump to mind, the role of smaller Internet businesses is also significant. Just take a look at the action on eBay and imagine how many people are now running small trading businesses from their homes.

In our age of open-source software and ever-expanding access to high-speed broadband connections, the opportunities to pursue Internet-based entrepreneurship continue to grow. Some of the proven business models include the following.

- **Advertising model**—this is the great Google play; you build a website that is attractive to visitors, and then advertisers pay you to be displayed on the site and become known to its visitors.
- **Subscription model**—this is the *New York Times* online play; you offer something of value that visitors to your website are willing to pay to view.

A **franchise** is when one business owner sells to another the right to operate the same business in another location.

A **startup** is a new and temporary venture that is trying to discover a profitable business model for future success.

Lean startups use things like open-source software, while staying small and striving to keep operations as simple as possible.

Internet entrepreneurship is the use of the Internet to pursue an entrepreneurial venture.

Internet entrepreneurship through the **advertising model** creates a website attractive to visitors, and then advertisers pay to be displayed on it.

Internet entrepreneurship through the **subscription model** creates a website offering value that visitors are willing to pay to view.

● Internet entrepreneurship through the **intermediary model** creates a website that collects a fee for bringing buyers and sellers together.

● Internet entrepreneurship through the **transaction model** creates a website to sell something that customers are willing to buy.

- **Intermediary model**—this is the eBay play; you build a website that brings buyers and sellers together, and collect a fee or commission for the service.
- **Transaction model**—this is the Amazon.com play; you sell something through a website that customers are willing to buy.

The Small Business Administration states that some 85% of small firms are already conducting business over the Internet.[33] For some, the old ways of operating from a bricks-and-mortar retail establishment have given way to entirely online business activities. That's what happened to Rod Spencer and his S&S Sportscards store in Worthington, Ohio. He closed his store, not because business was bad; it was really good. But the nature of the business was shifting into cyberspace. When sales over the Internet became much greater than in-store sales, Spencer decided to follow the world of e-commerce. He now works from his own home with a computer and high-speed Internet connection. This saves the cost of renting retail space and hiring store employees. "I can do less business overall," he says, "to make a higher profit."[34]

FAMILY BUSINESSES

In the little town of Utica, Ohio, there is a small child's desk in the corner of the president's office at Velvet Ice Cream Company. Its purpose is to help grow the next generation of leadership for the firm. "That's the way Dad did it," says Luconda Dager, the current head of the firm. "He exposed us all to the business at an early age." She and her two sisters, now both vice presidents, started working at the firm when they were 13 years old. And when it came time for Joseph Dager to retire and pass the business on to the next generation, he said: "It is very special for me to pass the baton to my oldest daughter. Luconda has been with us for 15 years. She understands and breathes the ice cream business, and there is no one better suited for this position.[35]

● A **family business** is owned and controlled by members of a family.

Velvet Ice Cream is the classic **family business**, one owned and financially controlled by family members. The Family Firm Institute reports that family businesses account for 78% of new jobs created in the United States and provide 60% of the nation's employment.[36] These family businesses must solve the same problems of other small or large businesses—meeting the challenges of strategy, competitive advantage, and operational excellence. When everything goes right, as in the Velvet Ice Cream case, the family firm is almost an ideal situation—everyone working together, sharing values and a common

DiFara's Pizza Is a Lesson in Love

In a small shop and at the postretirement age of 70+, Dominick DeMarco pursues his quest of making the perfect pizza. He makes all the pizzas, doesn't even start until he has an order, and grinds fresh Parmigiano Reggiano flown in from his native village in Italy. One newspaper reporter describes a DiFara's pizza as "a masterpiece, challenging my expectations every moment . . . I sighed, wondering how pizza could be so good." The difference is Dominick. "He flies in his cheese because he loves it," the reporter says." He stretches dough only after it's ordered because he loves it. He does not run a restaurant–he makes pizza because he loves it."

Research Brief

Do Founders of New Ventures Take Less Compensation than Other Senior Managers in Their Firms?

"Yes, but," says Noam Wasserman in an article published in the *Academy of Management Journal*. Wasserman examines two theories that might explain the founders' approaches to compensation. *Stewardship theory* argues that founders are likely to act as "stewards" of the firms they create, derive more psychic rewards from their roles in the enterprise, and, thus, take less monetary compensation. *Agency theory* argues that nonfounders are "agents" hired by founders to work in their behalf; agency costs are incurred because the interests of the founders and agents may diverge. Incentive compensation is one way of reducing those agency costs.

Wasserman hypothesized that founders will act more like stewards and nonfounder executives more like agents. He used data from 1,238 executives in 528 private companies to test his ideas. Of the executives, 41% were company founders. His results confirmed his hypotheses with an interesting twist. He found that founders and executives holding higher amounts of equity in a private firm earn less monetary compensation. In some cases (above 50%) founders even earned less than or equal to other executives reporting to them. He describes this as a "founder's discount" where they essentially "pay to be founders" and take more soft compensation in the form of psychic rewards.

Wasserman also found an interesting pattern in the data. As private firms grow in size, compensation for all executives increases. And as it does, the "founder's discount" becomes smaller.

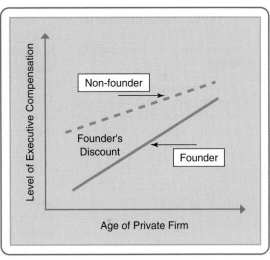

You Be the Researcher

Would you have predicted that founders will take less monetary compensation from their new ventures? It might seem likely since they own most of the assets and will thus profit more in the long run, especially if the company is sold. They should also be highly motivated to work hard and make these financial gains and firm success possible. Suppose founders gave more equity to other executives and lower-level employees? Is it possible that we would find that private firms where ownership is shared widely among employees have lower compensation but also tend to grow and prosper in contrast to others?

Reference: Noam Wasserman, "Stewards, Agents and the Founder Discount: Executive Compensation in New Ventures," *Academy of Management Journal,* vol. 49 (2006), pp. 960–76.

goal, and knowing that what they do benefits the family. But it doesn't always work out this way—or stay this way, as a business changes hands over successive generations. Indeed, family businesses often face quite unique problems.

"Okay, Dad, so he's your brother. But does that mean we have to put up with inferior work and an erratic schedule that we would never tolerate from anyone else in the business?"[37] This complaint introduces a problem that can all too often set the stage for failure in a family business—the **family business feud**. Simply put, members of the controlling family get into disagreements about work responsibilities, business strategy, operating approaches, finances, or other matters. The example is of an intergenerational problem, but the feud can be between spouses, among siblings, or between parents and children. It really doesn't matter. Unless family disagreements are resolved to the benefit of the business itself, the firm will have difficulty surviving in a highly competitive environment.

● A **family business feud** occurs when family members have major disagreements over how the business should be run.

FIGURE 6.2 Eight reasons why many small businesses fail.

● The **succession problem** is the issue of who will run the business when the current head leaves.

● A **succession plan** describes how the leadership transition and related financial matters will be handled.

Another common problem faced by family businesses is the **succession problem**—transferring leadership from one generation to the next. A survey of small and midsized family businesses indicated that 66% planned on keeping the business within the family.[38] But the management question is: how will the assets be distributed, and who will run the business when the current head leaves? Although this problem is not specific to the small firm, it is very important in the family business context. A family business that has been in operation for some time is often a source of both business momentum and financial wealth. Ideally, both are maintained in the succession process. But data on succession are eye-opening. About 30% of family firms survive to the second generation; only 12% survive to the third; and only 3% are expected to survive beyond that.[39]

Business advisers recommend having a **succession plan**—a formal statement that describes how the leadership transition and related financial matters will be handled when the time for changeover arrives. A succession plan should include at least procedures for choosing or designating the firm's new leadership, legal aspects of any ownership transfer, and financial and estate plans relating to the transfer. This plan should be shared and understood among all affected by it. And, the chosen successor should be prepared through experience and training to perform in the new role when the time comes.

WHY SMALL BUSINESSES FAIL

Small businesses have a high failure rate—one high enough to be intimidating. The SBA reports that as many as 60 to 80% of new businesses fail in their first five years of operation.[40] Part of this is a "counting" issue—the government counts as a "failure" any business that closes, whether it is because of the death or retirement of an owner, sale to someone else, or inability to earn a profit.[41] Nevertheless, the fact remains that a lot of small business startups don't make it. As shown in Figure 6.2, most of the failures are the result of insufficient financing, and bad judgment and management mistakes of several types.[42]

- *Insufficient financing*—not having enough money available to maintain operations while still building the business and gaining access to customers and markets.
- *Lack of experience*—not having sufficient know-how to run a business in the chosen market or geographical area.
- *Lack of expertise*—not having expertise in the essentials of business operations, including finance, purchasing, selling, and production.
- *Lack of strategy and strategic leadership*—not taking the time to craft a vision and mission, nor to formulate and properly implement a strategy.
- *Poor financial control*—not keeping track of the numbers, and failure to control business finances and use existing monies to best advantage.
- *Growing too fast*—not taking the time to consolidate a position, fine-tune the organization, and systematically meet the challenges of growth.
- *Lack of commitment*—not devoting enough time to the requirements of running a competitive business.
- *Ethical failure*—falling prey to the temptations of fraud, deception, and embezzlement.

SMALL BUSINESS DEVELOPMENT

Individuals who start small businesses face a variety of challenges. Even though the prospect of being part of a new venture is exciting, the realities of working through complex problems during setup and the early life of the business can be especially daunting. Fortunately, there is often some assistance available to help entrepreneurs and owners of small businesses get started.

One way that start-up difficulties can be managed is through participation in a **business incubator**. These are special facilities that offer space, shared administrative services, and management advice at reduced costs with the goal of helping new businesses become healthy enough to survive on their own. Some incubators are focused on specific business areas such as technology, light manufacturing, or professional services; some are located in rural areas, while others are urban based; some focus only on socially responsible businesses.

Regardless of their focus or location, business incubators share the common goal of increasing the survival rates for new start-ups. They want to help build new businesses that will create new jobs and expand economic opportunities in their local communities. An example is Y Combinator, an incubator located in Mountain View, California. It was founded by Paul Graham with a focus on Web start-ups, and supports about 10 start-ups at any given time. The entrepreneurs get offices, regular meetings with Graham and other business experts, and access to potential investors. They also receive $15,000 grants in exchange for the incubator taking a 6% ownership stake. Y Combinator hopes to capture a significant return on such investments as the new businesses succeed.[43]

Another source of assistance for small business development is the U.S. Small Business Administration. Because small business plays such a significant role in the economy, the SBA works with state and local agencies as well as the private sector to support a network of over 1,100 **Small Business Development Centers** (SBDCs) nationwide.[44] These SBDCs offer guidance to entrepreneurs and small business owners, actual and prospective, on how to set up and manage business operations. They are often associated with colleges and universities, and some give students a chance to work as consultants with small businesses at the same time that they pursue their academic programs.

● **Business incubators** offer space, shared services, and advice to help get small businesses started.

● **Small Business Development Centers** founded with support from the U.S. Small Business Administration provide advice to new and existing small businesses.

Be sure you can ☑ give the SBA definition of small business ☑ illustrate opportunities for entrepreneurship on the Internet ☑ discuss the succession problem in family-owned businesses and possible ways to deal with it ☑ list several reasons why many small businesses fail ☑ explain how business incubators work and how both they and SBDCs can help new small businesses

Learning Check
Study Question 2
What is special about small business entrepreneurship?

NEW VENTURE CREATION

Whether your interest is low-tech or high-tech, online or offline, opportunities for new ventures are always there for the true entrepreneur. To begin, you need good ideas and the courage to give them a chance. But then you must also be prepared to meet and master the test of strategy and competitive advantage. Can you identify a market niche on a new market that is being missed by other established firms? Can you generate first-mover advantage by exploiting a niche or entering a market before competitors? These are among the questions that entrepreneurs must ask and answer in the process of beginning a new venture.

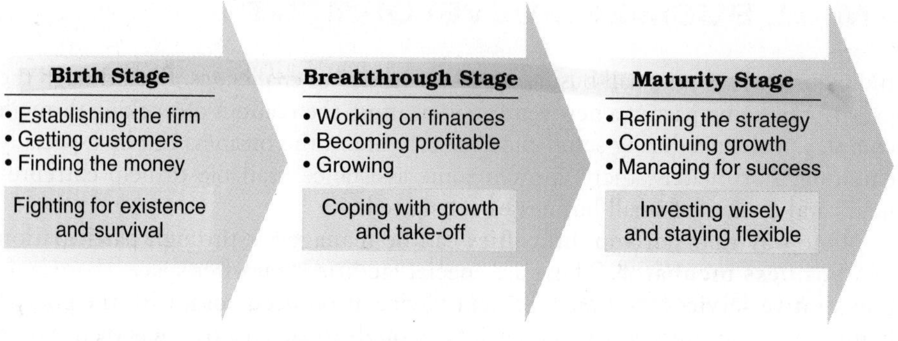

Birth Stage	Breakthrough Stage	Maturity Stage
• Establishing the firm • Getting customers • Finding the money	• Working on finances • Becoming profitable • Growing	• Refining the strategy • Continuing growth • Managing for success
Fighting for existence and survival	Coping with growth and take-off	Investing wisely and staying flexible

FIGURE 6.3 Stages in the life cycle of an entrepreneurial firm.

LIFE CYCLES OF ENTREPRENEURIAL FIRMS

Figure 6.3 describes the stages common to the life cycles of entrepreneurial companies. It shows the relatively predictable progression from birth to breakthrough to maturity.

The firm begins with the *birth stage*—where the entrepreneur struggles to get the new venture established and survive long enough to test the viability of the underlying business model in the marketplace. The firm then passes into the *breakthrough stage*—where the business model begins to work well, growth is experienced, and the complexity of managing the business operation expands significantly. Next comes the *maturity stage*—where the entrepreneur experiences the advantages of market success and financial stability, while also facing the continuing management challenge of remaining competitive in a changing environment.

Entrepreneurs often deal with substantial control and management dilemmas when their firms experience growth, including possible diversification or global expansion. They encounter a variation of the succession problem described earlier for family businesses. This time, the problem is transitioning from entrepreneurial leadership to professional strategic leadership. Entrepreneurial leadership brings the venture into being and sees it through the early stages of life. Professional strategic leadership manages and leads the venture into maturity as an ever-evolving and perhaps still-growing corporate enterprise. If the entrepreneur is incapable of meeting or unwilling to meet the firm's strategic leadership needs, continued business survival and success may well depend on the business being sold, or management control being passed to professionals.

WRITING THE BUSINESS PLAN

● A **business plan** describes the direction for a new business and the financing needed to operate it.

When people start new businesses or even launch new units within existing ones, they can benefit from a good **business plan**. This plan describes the details needed to obtain start-up financing and operate a new business.[45] Banks and other financiers want to see a business plan before they loan money or invest in a new venture; senior managers want to see a business plan before they allocate scarce organizational resources to support a new entrepreneurial project. And, there's good reason for this.

The detailed thinking required to prepare a business plan can contribute to the success of the new initiative. It forces the entrepreneur to think through important issues and challenges before starting out. Says Ed Federkeil, who founded a small business called California Custom Sport Trucks: "It gives you direction instead of haphazardly sticking your key in the door every day and saying—'What are we going to do?'"[46] More thoughts on why you need a business plan are presented in Management Smarts 6.2.

Although there is no single template, it is generally agreed that a good business plan includes an executive summary, covers certain business fundamentals, is well organized with headings and easy to read, and runs no more than about 20 pages in length. Here is a sample business plan outline.[47]

- *Executive summary*—overview of the business purpose and highlight of key elements of the plan.
- *Industry analysis*—nature of the industry, including economic trends, important legal or regulatory issues, and potential risks.
- *Company description*—mission, owners, and legal form.
- *Products and services description*—major goods or services, with competitive uniqueness.
- *Market description*—size of market, competitor strengths and weaknesses, five-year sales goals.
- *Marketing strategy*—product characteristics, distribution, promotion, pricing, and market research.
- *Operations description*—manufacturing or service methods, supplies and suppliers, and control procedures.
- *Staffing description*—management and staffing skills needed and available, compensation, and human resource systems.
- *Financial projection*—cash flow projections for one to five years, breakeven points, and phased investment capital.
- *Capital needs*—amount of funds needed to run the business, amount available, and amount requested from new sources.
- *Milestones*—a timetable of dates showing when key stages of the new venture will be completed.

Management Smarts 6.2
Why you need a business plan

- It makes you identify and confront the potential strengths and weaknesses of your proposed business.
- It makes you examine the market potential for your business's products or services.
- It makes you examine the strengths and weaknesses of the competitors for your proposed business.
- It helps you clarify the mission and key directions for the business, helping you to stay focused.
- It helps you determine how much money will be needed to launch and operate the business.
- It helps you communicate more confidently and credibly with potential lenders and investors.

CHOOSING THE FORM OF OWNERSHIP

One of the important choices that must be made in starting a new venture is the legal form of ownership. There are a number of alternatives, and the choice among them requires careful consideration of their respective advantages and disadvantages.

A **sole proprietorship** is simply an individual or a married couple pursuing business for a profit. This does not involve incorporation. One does business, for example, under a personal name—such as "Tiaña Lopez Designs." A sole proprietorship is simple to start, run, and terminate, and it is the most common form of small business ownership in the United States. However, the business owner is personally liable for business debts and claims.

A **partnership** is formed when two or more people agree to contribute resources to start and operate a business together. It is usually backed by a legal and written partnership agreement. Business partners agree on the contribution of resources and skills to the new venture, and on the sharing of profits and losses. The simplest and most common form is a *general partnership* where the partners share management responsibilities. A *limited partnership* consists of a general partner and one or more "limited" partners who do not participate in day-to-day business management. They share in the profits, but their losses are limited to the amount of their investment. A *limited liability partnership*, common among professionals such as accountants and attorneys, limits the liability of one partner for the negligence of another.

● A **sole proprietorship** is an individual pursuing business for a profit.

● A **partnership** is when two or more people agree to contribute resources to start and operate a business together.

TOMS Walks Pathways to Philanthropy

Would you buy shoes just because they're also pledged to philanthropy? Blake Mycoskie, founder of TOMS Shoes, wants you to. Back in 2002 he was participating with his sister in the reality TV show The Amazing Race. It whetted his appetite for travel and he visited Argentina in 2006. There he came face-to-face with lots of young children without shoes, and he had a revelation: he would return home and start a sustainable business that would help address the problem.

Blake launched TOMS (short he says for "better tomorrow") to sell shoes made in a classic Argentinean style. But there's a twist—for each pair of shoes it sells, TOMS donates a pair to needy children. Blake calls this One for One, a "move-

ment" that involves "people making everyday choices that improve the lives of children."

The TOMS business model can be described as caring capitalism, or profits with principles. Two other names associated with this approach are Ben & Jerry's Ice Cream and Tom's of Maine. But each of these firms was sold to a global enterprise—Unilever for Ben & Jerry's and Colgate-Palmolive for Tom's of Maine. The expectation was that the corporate buyers wouldn't compromise on the founder's core values and social goals. Who knows what the future holds for TOMS if it grows to the point where corporate buyers loom.

You Decide

What about it? Is the TOMS business model one that others should adopt? Is it ethical to link personal philanthropic goals with the products that your business sells? And if an entrepreneurial firm is founded on a caring capitalism model, is it ethical for a future buyer to reduce or limit the emphasis on social benefits?

● A **corporation** is a legal entity that exists separately from its owners.

A **corporation**, commonly identified by the "Inc." designation in a name, is a legal entity that is chartered by the state and exists separately from its owners. The corporation can be for-profit, such as Microsoft, Inc., or nonprofit, such as Count-Me-In, Inc.—a firm featured early in the chapter for helping women entrepreneurs get started with small loans. The corporate form offers two major advantages: (1) it grants the organization certain legal rights (e.g., to engage in contracts), and (2) the corporation becomes responsible for its own liabilities. This separates the owners from personal liability and gives the firm a life of its own that can extend beyond that of its owners. The disadvantage of incorporation rests largely with the cost of incorporating and the complexity of the documentation required to operate as an incorporated business.

● A **limited liability corporation** is a hybrid business form combining the advantages of the sole proprietorship, partnership, and corporation.

Recently, the **limited liability corporation**, or LLC, has gained popularity. A limited liability corporation combines the advantages of the other forms—sole proprietorship, partnership, and corporation. For liability purposes, it functions like a corporation and protects the assets of owners against claims made against the company. For tax purposes, it functions as a partnership in the case of multiple owners and as a sole proprietorship in the case of a single owner.

FINANCING THE NEW VENTURE

Have you seen the reality TV show *Shark Tank*? It pits entrepreneurs against potential investors called "sharks." The entrepreneurs present their ideas, and the sharks, people with money to invest, debate the worthwhileness of investing in their businesses. Brian Duggan went on the show to pitch his Element Bars, a custom energy bar he developed as an MBA student. He tried to get a bank loan, but failed. But the sharks were impressed and gave him $150,000 in return for 30% ownership in his business.[48]

While being part of a reality TV show isn't common, Brian Duggan's situation is characteristic of that faced by entrepreneurs. Starting a new venture takes money, and that money must often be raised. Realistically speaking, the cost of setting up a new business or expanding an existing one can easily exceed the amount a would-be entrepreneur has available from personal sources. Initial start-up financing might come from personal bank accounts and credit cards. Very soon, however, the chances are much more money will be needed to sustain and grow the business. There are two major ways an entrepreneur can obtain such outside financing for a new venture.

Debt financing involves going into debt by borrowing money from another person, bank, or financial institution. This loan must be paid back over time, with interest. It also requires collateral that pledges business assets or personal assets, such as a home, to secure the loan in case of default. The lack of availability of debt financing became a big issue during the recent financial crisis, and the problem hit entrepreneurs and small business owners especially hard. Andy Shallal, for example, owns a successful bookstore in the Washington, D.C., area. He employs 40 people and wanted to expand to other locations. But even with this track record he couldn't get a bank loan for the expansion without pledging his home as collateral, something he didn't want to do. Shallal says: "I want to have a loan that's really a business loan that's going to use my business as collateral. And I was told no, in these economic times it's very difficult for banks to give money this way."[49]

● **Debt financing** involves borrowing money that must be repaid over time, with interest.

Equity financing is an alternative to debt financing. It involves giving ownership shares in the business to outsiders in return for their cash investments. This money does not need to be paid back. It is an investment, and the investor assumes the risk for potential gains and losses. The equity investor gains some proportionate ownership control in return for taking that risk.

● **Equity financing** involves exchanging ownership shares for outside investment monies.

Equity financing is usually obtained from **venture capitalists**, companies and individuals that make investments in new ventures in return for an equity stake in the business. Most venture capitalists tend to focus on relatively large investments of $1 million or more, and they usually take a management role, such as a board of director's seat, in order to oversee business growth. The hope is that a fast-growing firm will gain a solid market base and be either sold at a profit to another firm or become a candidate for an **initial public offering**. This IPO is when shares of stock in the business are first sold to the public and begin trading on a stock exchange. When an IPO is successful and the share prices are bid up by the market, the original investments of the venture capitalist and entrepreneur rise in value. The quest for such return on investment is the business model of the venture capitalist.

● **Venture capitalists** make large investments in new ventures in return for an equity stake in the business.

● An **initial public offering**, or IPO, is an initial selling of shares of stock to the public at large.

When large amounts of venture capital aren't available to the entrepreneur, another financing option is the **angel investor**. This is a wealthy individual who is willing to make a personal investment in return for equity in a new venture. Angel investors are especially common and helpful in the very early start-up stage. Their presence can raise investor confidence and help attract additional venture funding that would otherwise not be available. For example, when Liz Cobb wanted to start her sales compensation firm, Incentive Systems, she contacted 15 to 20 venture capital firms. She was interviewed by 10 and turned down by all of them. After she located $250,000 from two angel investors, the venture capital firms got interested again. She was able to obtain her first $2 million in financing and has since built the firm into a 70-plus employee business.[50]

● An **angel investor** is a wealthy individual willing to invest in a new venture in return for equity in a new venture.

Be sure you can ☑ explain the concept of first-mover advantage ☑ illustrate the life cycle of an entrepreneurial firm ☑ identify the major elements in a business plan ☑ differentiate sole proprietorship, partnership, and corporation ☑ differentiate debt financing and equity financing ☑ explain the roles of venture capitalists and angel investors in new venture financing

Learning Check ☑

Study Question 3
How do entrepreneurs start and finance new ventures?

Management Learning Review

1 What is entrepreneurship?

- Entrepreneurship is risk-taking behavior that results in the creation of new opportunities.
- A classic entrepreneur is someone who takes risks to pursue opportunities in situations that others may view as problems or threats.
- A serial entrepreneur is someone who starts and runs businesses and other organizations one after another.
- Entrepreneurs tend to be creative people who are self-confident, determined, resilient, adaptable, and driven to excel; they like to be masters of their own destinies.
- Women and minorities are well represented among entrepreneurs, with some being driven by necessity or the lack of alternative career options.
- Social entrepreneurs pursue ethics goals in seeking novel ways to help solve social problems.

2 What is special about small business entrepreneurship?

- Entrepreneurship results in the founding of many small businesses that offer new jobs and other benefits to local economies.
- The Internet has opened a whole new array of entrepreneurial possibilities for small businesses.
- Family businesses, ones owned and financially controlled by family members, represent the largest percentage of businesses operating worldwide; they sometimes suffer from a succession problem.

- Small businesses have a high failure rate, with as many as 60 to 80% failing within five years; many failures are the result of poor management.
- Entrepreneurs and small business owners can often get help in the start-up stages by working with business incubators and Small Business Development Centers in their local communities.

3 How do entrepreneurs start and finance new ventures?

- Entrepreneurial firms tend to follow the life-cycle stages of birth, breakthrough, and maturity, with each stage offering different management challenges.
- A new start-up should be guided by a good business plan that describes the intended nature of the business, how it will operate, and how financing will be obtained.
- An important choice is the form of business ownership for a new venture, with the proprietorship, corporate, and limited liability forms offering different advantages and disadvantages.
- Two basic ways of financing a new venture are through debt financing—by taking loans, and equity financing—exchanging ownership shares in return for outside investment.
- Venture capitalists pool capital and make investments in new ventures in return for an equity stake in the business; an angel investor is a wealthy individual who is willing to invest money in return for equity in a new venture.

Multiple-Choice Questions

1. _____ is among the personality characteristics commonly found among entrepreneurs.
   (a) External locus of control   (b) Inflexibility   (c) Self-confidence   (d) Low self-reliance

2. When an entrepreneur is comfortable with uncertainty and willing to take risks, these are indicators of someone with a(n) _____.
   (a) high tolerance for ambiguity   (b) internal locus of control   (c) need for achievement   (d) action orientation

3. Almost _____ % of American businesses meet the definition of "small business" used by the Small Business Administration.
   (a) 40   (b) 99   (c) 75   (d) 81

4. When a business owner sells to another person the right to operate that business in another location, this is a _____.
   (a) conglomerate   (b) franchise   (c) joint venture   (d) limited partnership

5. A small business owner who is concerned about passing the business on to heirs after retirement or death should prepare a formal _____ plan.
(a) retirement   (b) succession   (c) franchising   (d) liquidation

6. Among the most common reasons that new small business start-ups often fail is _____.
(a) lack of business expertise   (b) strict financial controls   (c) slow growth   (d) high ethical standards

7. When a new business is quick to capture a market niche before competitors, this is called_____.
(a) intrapreneurship   (b) an initial public offering   (c) succession planning   (d) first-mover advantage

8. When a small business is just starting, the business owner is typically struggling to _____.
(a) gain acceptance in the marketplace   (b) find partners for expansion   (c) prepare an initial public offering
(d) bring professional skills into the management team

9. A venture capitalist who receives an ownership share in return for investing in a new business is providing _____ financing.
(a) debt   (b) equity   (c) corporate   (d) partnership

10. In _____ financing, the business owner borrows money as a loan that must eventually be paid, along with agreed-upon interest to the lender.
(a) debt   (b) equity   (c) partnership   (d) limited

11. _____ take ownership shares in a new venture in return for providing the entrepreneur with critical start-up funds.
(a) Business incubators   (b) Angel investors   (c) SBDCs   (d) Intrapreneurs

12. Among the forms of small business ownership, a _____ protects the owners from any personal liabilities for business losses.
(a) sole proprietorship   (b) franchise   (c) limited partnership   (d) corporation

13. The first component of a good business plan is usually _____.
(a) an industry analysis   (b) a marketing strategy   (c) an executive summary   (d) a set of milestones

14. Current trends in small business ownership in the United States would most likely show that _____.
(a) the numbers of women and minority-owned businesses are declining   (b) the majority of small businesses conduct some business by Internet   (c) large businesses create more jobs than small businesses   (d) very few small businesses engage in international import/export activities

15. If a new venture has reached the point where it is pursuing an IPO, the firm is most likely _____.
(a) going into bankruptcy   (b) trying to find an angel investor   (c) filing legal documents to become a LLC
(d) successful enough that the public at large will buy its shares

Short-Response Questions

16. What is the relationship between diversity and entrepreneurship?

17. What are the major stages in the life cycle of an entrepreneurial firm, and what are the management challenges at each stage?

18. What are the advantages of a limited partnership form of small business ownership?

19. What is the difference, if any, between a venture capitalist and an angel investor?

Essay Question

20. Assume for the moment that you have a great idea for a potential Internet-based start-up business. In discussing the idea with a friend, she advises you to be very careful to tie your business idea to potential customers and then describe it well in a business plan. "After all," she says, "you won't succeed without customers, and you'll never get a chance to succeed if you can't attract financial backers through a good business plan." With these words to the wise, you proceed. What questions will you ask and answer to ensure that you are customer-focused in this business? What are the major areas that you would address in writing your initial business plan?

Management Skills and Competencies

Self-Assessment

Back to Yourself: Self-Management

The pathway to entrepreneurship involves risk, confidence, insight, and more. But for those who have the desire to attempt new things and have strong **self-management** skills it's a path worth walking. Even in the absence of entrepreneurial aspirations, we need and depend upon self-management skills to do well in school, at work, and in everyday living. These are challenging times; what we are good at today may not serve us well tomorrow. There are lots of uncertainties. Now is the time to get in touch with your self-management skills. It's a good time to test what you really know about yourself individually and in a social context, to assess personal strengths and weaknesses, to actively try to make adjustments that better position you to achieve your goals and make positive contributions to your groups, organizations, and society at large. After you complete the following self-assessment on Entrepreneurship Orientation, don't forget to go online to further check on how you learn and how that learning can improve your self-management skills.

> **Self-management** Is a capacity to use an objective understanding of one's strengths and weaknesses to continuously improve and adapt to meet life's challenges.

Further Reflection: Entrepreneurship Orientation

Instructions

Answer each of the following questions.[51]

1. What portion of your college expenses did you earn (or are you earning)?
    (a) 50% or more   (b) less than 50%   (c) none

2. In college, your academic performance was/is
    (a) above average.   (b) average.   (c) below average.

3. What is your basic reason for considering opening a business?
    (a) I want to make money.   (b) I want to control my own destiny.   (c) I hate the frustration of working for someone else.

4. Which phrase best describes your attitude toward work?
    (a) I can keep going as long as I need to; I don't mind working for something I want.   (b) I can work hard for a while, but when I've had enough, I quit.   (c) Hard work really doesn't get you anywhere.

5. How would you rate your organizing skills?
    (a) super organized   (b) above average   (c) average   (d) I do well to find half the things I look for.

6. You are primarily a(n)
    (a) optimist.   (b) pessimist.   (c) neither.

7. You are faced with a challenging problem. As you work, you realize you are stuck. You will most likely
    (a) give up.   (b) ask for help.   (c) keep plugging; you'll figure it out.

8. You are playing a game with a group of friends. You are most interested in
    (a) winning.   (b) playing well.   (c) making sure that everyone has a good time.   (d) cheating as much as possible.

9. How would you describe your feelings toward failure?
    (a) Fear of failure paralyzes me.   (b) Failure can be a good learning experience.   (c) Knowing that I might fail motivates me to work even harder.   (d) "Damn the torpedoes! Full speed ahead."

10. Which phrase best describes you?
    (a) I need constant encouragement to get anything done.   (b) If someone gets me started, I can keep going, (c) I am energetic and hard-working—a self-starter.

11. Which bet would you most likely accept?
    (a) a wager on a dog race   (b) a wager on a racquetball game in which you play an opponent   (c) Neither. I never make wagers.

12. At the Kentucky Derby, you would bet on
    (a) the 100-to-1 long shot.   (b) the odds-on favorite,   (c) the 3-to-1 shot.   (d) none of the above.

Scoring

Give yourself 10 points each for answers 1a, 2a, 3c, 4a, 5a, 6a, 7c, 8a, 9c, 10c, 11b, 12c; total the scores and enter the result here [I = _____]. Give yourself 8 points each for answers 3b, 8b, 9b; enter total here [II = _____]. Give yourself 6 points each for answers 2b, 5b; enter total here [III = _____]. Give yourself 5 points for answer 1b; enter result here [IV = _____]. Give yourself 4 points for answer 5c; enter result here [V = _____]. Give yourself 2 points each for answers 2c, 3a, 4b, 6c, 9d, 10b, 11a, 12b; enter total here [VI = _____]. Any other answers are worth 0 points. Total your summary scores for I + II + III + IV + V + VI and enter the result here [EP = _____].

Interpretation

This assessment offers an impression of your *entrepreneurial profile (EP)*. It compares your characteristics with those of typical entrepreneurs, according to this profile: 100+ = Entrepreneur extraordinaire; 80–99 = Entrepreneur; 60–79 = Potential entrepreneur; 0–59 = Entrepreneur in the rough.

Team Exercise

Entrepreneurs Among Us

Michael Gerber, author and entrepreneur, says: "The entrepreneur in us sees opportunities everywhere we look, but many people see only problems everywhere they look."[52] The entrepreneurs he describes are everywhere. Some might live next door and one might be you; many own and operate the small businesses of your community.

Question

Who are the entrepreneurs in your community and what are they accomplishing?

Instructions

1. Think about your personal experiences and contacts in the local community. Identify those persons that you believe are good examples of respectable entrepreneurs. Try to identify more than one and also try to find entrepreneurs in various settings—retail, housing, etc.

2. In your teams, share and discuss the entrepreneurs in your community. Choose one entrepreneur as your team's "exemplar" and prepare to share it in class discussion. Focus on the entrepreneur as a person, the entrepreneur's business or nonprofit venture, and what factors account for success and/or failure in this case, and also what the entrepreneur contributes to the local community.

3. Further Research—turn this team exercise into a research project by doing the following.

   - Read the local news, talk to your friends and locals, consider where you shop. Make a list of the businesses and other organizations that have an entrepreneurial character. Be as complete as possible—look at both businesses and nonprofits.

   - For each of the organizations, do further research to identify the persons who are the entrepreneurs responsible for them.

   - Contact as many of the entrepreneurs as possible and interview them. Try to learn how they got started, why, what they encountered as obstacles or problems, what they learned about entrepreneurship that could be passed along to others. Add to these questions a list of your own—what do you want to know about entrepreneurship?

   - Analyze your results for class presentation and discussion. Look for patterns and differences in terms of entrepreneurs as persons, the entrepreneurial experience, and potential insights into business versus social entrepreneurship.

   - Consider writing short cases that summarize the "founding stories" of the entrepreneurs you find especially interesting.

Case Study: Sprinkles

Go to *Management Cases for Critical Thinking* to find the recommended case for Chapter 6—"Sprinkles: Leading a Sweet Trend."

Information and Decision Making

7

Chapter 7 Study Questions

1 What is the role of information in the management process?

2 How do managers use information to make decisions?

3 What are the steps in the decision-making process?

4 What are current issues in managerial decision making?

Learning From Others

Decisions Turn Potential into Achievement

Decisions . . . hunches . . . achievements? It's all about being tuned into the environment. That's a message that seems well learned by Tom Szaky. He has ridden the roller coaster of all roller coasters, taking ideas for "sustainability," "green," and "recycling" from dorm room banter to the shelves of Wal-Mart. If you read Tom Szaky's book *Revolution in a Bottle*, you enter the world of "upcycling"—the art, if you will, of turning waste that isn't recyclable into reusable packaging.[1]

Szaky is what many call an "eco-capitalist"—someone who brings environmentalism into the world of business and consumers. While a freshman at Princeton University, he ordered a million red worms with the goal of learning how to use them to recycle campus waste. In conversations with classmate Jon Beyer, the original idea shifted to creating and selling liquid fertilizer made from worm excrement. But they couldn't afford the expensive plastic bottles for packaging. More conversations, this time with entrepreneur Robin Tator, led to a new firm called TerraCycle with a mission to "find a meaningful use for waste materials."

Szaky's original liquid fertilizer became TerraCycle Plant Food. Now the firm upcycles a variety of waste products like cookie wrappers, drink containers, and discarded juice packs into usable products ranging from tote bags to containers of various sorts to pencil cases. And, yes, lots of them are found on Wal-Mart's shelves. Szaky says: "Unlike most companies, which spend years in product development and testing, TerraCycle moves through these stages very quickly. First we identify a waste stream, then we figure out what we can make from that material. This is our strength—creatively solving the 'what the hell do we make from it' issue. If a retailer bites, we are in full production in a matter of weeks."

do the benchmarking

Tom Szaky made many decisions as he moved into the entrepreneurial world of eco-capitalism. It could have ended when the experiment with red worms and campus recycling proved more difficult than expected. But Szaky and his friends didn't stop there; learning from the experience, they persevered and made changes—more than once. We all talk about the planet, sustainability, and social values. **But how often do we turn decisions into positive actions? Is there a bit of Tom Szaky in you?**

Learning About Yourself

Self-Confidence

Would you agree that confidence tends to put spring into your step and a smile on your face? It's a powerful force, something to be nurtured and protected. Managers must have the **self-confidence** not only to make decisions but to take the actions required to implement them. Too many of us find all sorts of excuses for doing everything but that. Lacking confidence, we have difficulty deciding how to decide, we have difficulty deciding, and we have difficulty acting.

Look at the situation in the box and choose how you would proceed. Would you choose option A, or B, or C?

Jeff McCracken was the chief engineer for the Norfolk Southern Railroad in this situation. He acted deliberately, with confidence, and in a collaborative fashion. After extensive consultations with the team, he decided to salvage the old track. They worked 24 hours a day and finished in less than a week. McCracken called it a "colossal job" and said the satisfaction came from "working with people from all parts of the company and getting the job done without anyone getting hurt."[2]

> ### Decision Time
>
> *Situation:* Hurricane Katrina has damaged a railroad bridge over Lake Ponchartrain. You are leading a repair team of 100. The bridge is important for relief efforts in devastated New Orleans. Two alternatives are on the table: rebuild using new tracks, or rebuild with old track salvaged from the lake.
>
> *Question:* How do you proceed?
>
> A. Decide to rebuild with new tracks; move quickly to implement.
>
> B. Decide to rebuild with old tracks; move quickly to implement.
>
> C. Consult with team; make decision; move quickly to implement.

Self-confidence doesn't have to mean acting alone, but it does mean being willing to act. Management consultant Ram Charan says that self-confidence involves a willingness to "listen to your own voice" and "speak your mind and act decisively." It is, he says, an "emotional fortitude" that counteracts "emotional insecurities."[3]

Fortunately, self-confidence is something we can nurture and develop. Consider the example set by Carole Clay Winters. She developed self-confidence in college by joining Students in Free Enterprise and participating in a team that taught business concepts to elementary school children. Her team was even chosen for a national competition judged by corporate leaders. They didn't win the competition, but Carole gained a lot in terms of self-confidence. "I felt my life had changed," she said. "I realized that if I could answer all the questions being posed by some of the country's most powerful executives, I had what I needed to become an executive myself." Carole went on to become a manager in the Washington, D.C. office of the accounting firm KPMG.[4]

get to know yourself better

Opportunities to improve your self-confidence abound, especially through involvement in student organizations and community activities. Do a self-check; make a list of things you could do to gain experience and add more self-confidence to your skills portfolio between now and graduation. Also take advantage of the end-of-chapter Self-Assessment feature to further reflect on your Cognitive Style and how you handle facts and inferences.

7 Information and Decision Making

Study Question 1	Study Question 2	Study Question 3	Study Question 4
Information, Technology, and Management	**Information and Managerial Decisions**	**The Decision-Making Process**	**Issues in Managerial Decision Making**
• What is useful information? • Information needs in organizations • Information systems • How information technology is changing organizations	• Managers as information processors • Managers as problem solvers • Types of managerial decisions • Decision conditions • Alternative decision conditions	• Identify problem • Examine alternatives • Make a decision • Implement decision • Evaluate results • Check ethical reasoning at all steps	• Decision errors and traps • Creativity in decision making
Learning Check 1	**Learning Check 2**	**Learning Check 3**	**Learning Check 4**

The opener referred to Hurricane Katrina and its disastrous impact on New Orleans. Another major disaster, the huge earthquake in Haiti, also became a test of human endurance and decision making. Nations and relief organizations rushed to help, but the scale of destruction made things difficult to coordinate. Days and lives were lost as everyone struggled to mobilize response capabilities, repair damage, and distribute aid to those in need. And in retrospect, it is clear that a lot of things could have been done differently to better deploy resources in the killer quake's aftermath.

When things are happening in "real time," it's not easy to do everything right. Information gets missed or lost or poorly used, mistakes get made, and even well-intended decisions can go wrong or prove inadequate to the task. Crises of this sort are the most extreme tests of our abilities to manage information and decision making.

INFORMATION, TECHNOLOGY, AND MANAGEMENT

Computer competency is the ability to understand computers and to use them to their best advantage.

Information competency is the ability to gather, analyze, and use information for decision making and problem solving.

Data are raw facts and observations.

Information is data made useful for decision making.

Management with analytics involves systematic gathering and processing of data to make it useful as information.

Our society is information-driven, digital, networked, and continuously evolving. Career success requires two "must have" competencies: **computer competency**—the ability to understand computers and to use them to their best advantage; and **information competency**—the ability to locate, gather, evaluate, organize, and analyze information for decision making and problem solving. How about it—are you ready?

WHAT IS USEFUL INFORMATION?

This sign should be on every manager's desk—Warning: data ≠ information. **Data are raw facts and observations. Information** is data made useful and meaningful for decision making. We all have lots of access to data, but we don't always turn it into useful information.

The term **management with analytics** is increasingly used to describe the systematic gathering and processing of data to make it useful as information. You might think of it as putting data to work for informed decision making.[5] Analytics is critically important in the management process of planning, organizing, leading, and controlling, but it often breaks down.

One of the key problems faced by complex organizations is making sure that data from different parts of the system find their way to other parts that can benefit from them. When a terrorist from Nigeria tried to set off an explosion on an airliner landing in Detroit, it turned out that data about his terrorist leanings had been provided to the U.S. embassy in Nigeria. But it wasn't properly shared with the airline and other parts of the national security system. And when Toyota faced a crisis over major quality defects and massive auto recalls, it turns out data on these problems had been available within the system a long time before action was taken. The top U.S. executive for the company said: "We did not hide it. But it was not properly shared."[6]

The bottom line is that managers need good information and they need it all the time. Information that is truly useful in management meets the test of these five criteria:

1. *Timely*—the information is available when needed; it meets deadlines for decision making and action.
2. *High quality*—the information is accurate, and it is reliable; it can be used with confidence.
3. *Complete*—the information is complete and sufficient for the task at hand; it is as current and up to date as possible.
4. *Relevant*—the information is appropriate for the task at hand; it is free from extraneous or irrelevant materials.
5. *Understandable*—the information is clear and easily understood by the user; it is free from unnecessary detail.

INFORMATION NEEDS IN ORGANIZATIONS

An important key to managerial performance is information technology, or IT, and the way it helps us acquire, store, process, analyze, and transmit information. In our computer-enriched world, where continual advances in technologies make more information about more things available to more people more quickly than ever before, the question is: how well do we take advantage of it?

Information and the External Environment

Driven largely by IT, information serves the variety of needs described in Figure 7.1. At the organization's boundaries, information in the external environment is accessed. Managers use this *intelligence information* to deal with customers,

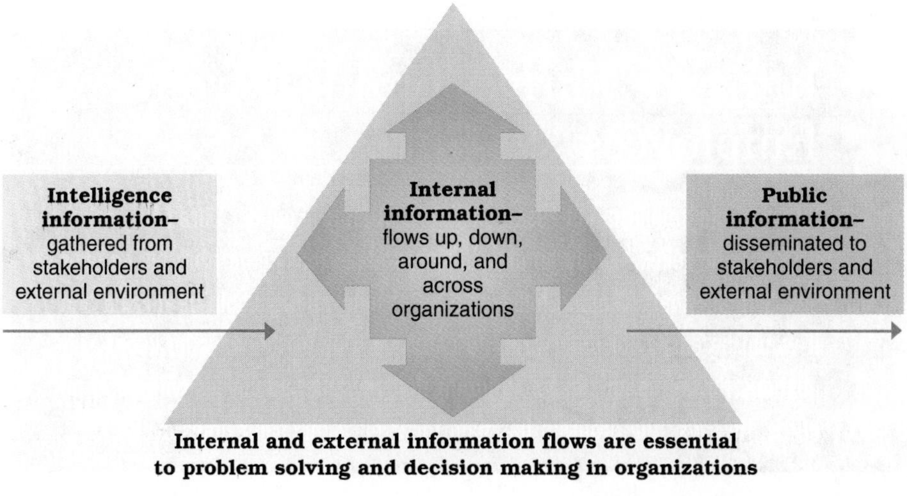

| **Intelligence information—** gathered from stakeholders and external environment | **Internal information—** flows up, down, around, and across organizations | **Public information—** disseminated to stakeholders and external environment |

Internal and external information flows are essential to problem solving and decision making in organizations

FIGURE 7.1 Internal and external information needs in organizations.

competitors, and other stakeholders such as government agencies, creditors, suppliers, and stockholders. Peter Drucker once said that "a winning strategy will require information about events and conditions outside the institution," and that organizations must have "rigorous methods for gathering and analyzing outside information."[7]

Organizations also send vast amounts of *public information* to stakeholders and the external environment. This often takes the form of advertising, public relations messages, and financial reports that serve a variety of purposes, ranging from image-building to product promotion to financial documentation. Today such public information is also being carried by the Internet and even social media such as Facebook and Twitter.

The way key executives and other members act as representatives of their organizations is also a form of public information, and it can have both benefits and detriments. This was a lesson learned by then CEOs of Chrysler, Ford, and General Motors when they were widely criticized for flying to Washington on private jets to beg for financial bailouts from the U.S. Congress. The way organizations handle public information is a very strategic issue. Soon after its CEO was criticized in Washington, for example, Ford, the strongest of the U.S. automakers, realized it was being hurt by being grouped in public perceptions with its much weaker rivals. The firm went on the offense with a successful ad campaign to tell the public a new "Ford Story" about corporate turnaround, sound finances, and great products.[8]

Information and the Internal Environment

Silicon Valley pioneer and Cisco Systems CEO John Chambers once pointed out that he always has the information he needs to be in control—be it information on earnings, expenses, profitability, gross margins, and more. He also said: "Because I have my data in that format, every one of my employees can make decisions that might have had to come all the way to the president. . . . Quicker decision making at lower levels will translate into higher profit margins. . . . Companies that don't do that will be noncompetitive."[9]

Within organizations, people need vast amounts of *internal information* to make decisions and solve problems in their daily work. They need information from their immediate work setting and from other parts of the organization. Internal information flows downward in such forms as goals, instructions, and feedback; it flows horizontally in ways that assist in cross-functional coordination and problem solving; and it flows upward in such forms as performance reports, suggestions for improvement, and even disputes. The ability of IT to gather and move information

Infosurv Thrives on Ideas from Employees

Infosurv is a small market-research firm in Atlanta. Founder Jared Heyman says that he relies heavily on new business ideas that come from his employees. Without their ideas he believes a lot of innovations would be missed and it would be easier for other firms to catch up. One of the ways he keeps suggestions flowing is an "Ideas" program that rewards employees with $150 gift cards. He says "the program has paid for itself a thousand times over."

quickly within an organization—up, down, and horizontal—can be a great asset to decision making. It helps top levels stay informed, while freeing lower levels to make speedy decisions and take the actions they need to best perform their jobs.

INFORMATION SYSTEMS

In order to perform well, people must have available to them the right information at the right time and in the right place. This is the function served by **information systems** that use the latest in information technology to collect, organize, and distribute data in such a way that they become meaningful as information. **Management information systems**, or MIS, meet the specific information needs of managers as they make a variety of day-to-day decisions. C.R. England, Inc., a long-haul refrigerated trucking company, for example, uses a computerized MIS to monitor more than 500 aspects of organizational performance. The system tracks everything from billing accuracy to arrival times to driver satisfaction with company maintenance on their vehicles. Says CEO Dan England: "Our view was, if we could measure it, we could manage it."[10]

- **Information systems** use IT to collect, organize, and distribute data for use in decision making.
- **Management information systems** meet the information needs of managers in making daily decisions.

HOW INFORMATION TECHNOLOGY IS CHANGING ORGANIZATIONS

Organizations today are not only using information technology; they are being changed by its use. Information departments or centers are now mainstream features on organization charts, and the CIO (chief information officer), or CKO (chief knowledge officer) or CTO (chief technology officer) are prominent members of top management teams. The number and variety of information career fields are rapidly expanding. And, as shown in Figure 7.2, IT helps break down barriers.[11]

IT is breaking barriers within organizations by helping people working in different departments, levels, and physical locations more easily communicate and share information. The new IT-intensive organizations are "flatter" and operate

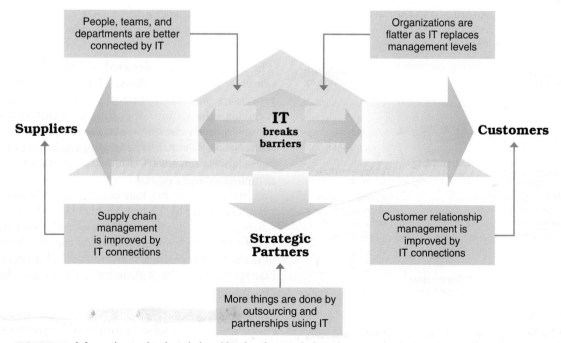

FIGURE 7.2 Information technology is breaking barriers and changing organizations.

with fewer levels than their more traditional organizational counterparts; computers replace people whose jobs were devoted primarily to moving information. This creates opportunities for faster decision making, better use of timely information, and better coordination of decisions and actions.

IT is also breaking barriers between organizations and key elements in the external environment. It plays an important role in customer relationship management by quickly and accurately providing information regarding customer needs, preferences, and satisfactions. It helps in supply chain management to better manage and control costs everywhere from initiation of purchase, to logistics and transportation, to point of delivery and ultimate use. And it helps maintain linkages with outsourcing clients and other strategic partners.

☑ **Learning Check**

Study Question 1
What is the role of information in the management process?

Be sure you can ☑ differentiate data and information ☑ list the criteria of useful information ☑ describe the role of information systems in organizations ☑ discuss how IT is breaking barriers within organizations and between organizations and their environments

---

INFORMATION AND MANAGERIAL DECISIONS

In a book entitled *Judgment: How Winning Leaders Make Great Calls*, scholars and consultants Noel M. Tichy and Warren G. Bennis discuss the importance of what leaders do before a decision is made, while making it, and when implementing it.[12] Information is the center point to all three phases—information helps a leader sense the need for a decision, frame an approach to the decision, and communicate about the decision with others. This is why the information competency described at the beginning of this chapter is so important.[13]

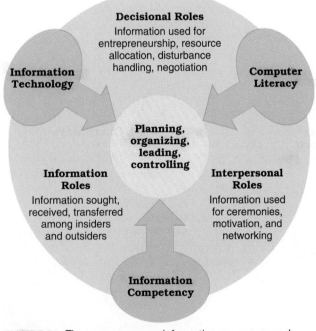

FIGURE 7.3 The manager as an information processor and nerve center for planning, organizing, leading, and controlling.

MANAGERS AS INFORMATION PROCESSORS

The manager's job is depicted in Figure 7.3 as a nerve center of information flows. Managers are information processors who are continually gathering, giving, and receiving information. And, this information processing is now as much electronic as it is face to face. Managers use technology at work the way we use it in our personal lives—always on, always connected, whether it be with a computer or smartphone.

In this high-technology context, all of the managerial roles identified by Henry Mintzberg and discussed in Chapter 1—interpersonal, decisional, and informational—benefit from new opportunities for communication and information processing.[14] So, too, do all aspects of the management process of planning, organizing, leading, and controlling.

- *Planning advantages of IT*—better and more timely access to useful information, involving more people in the planning process.

- *Organizing advantages of IT*—more ongoing and informed communication among all parts, improving coordination and integration.
- *Leading advantages of IT*—more frequent and better communication with staff and diverse stakeholders, keeping objectives clear.
- *Controlling advantages of IT*—more immediate measures of performance results, allowing real-time solutions to problems.

MANAGERS AS PROBLEM SOLVERS

Sometimes it's the big things—how to save General Motors. Other times, it's the smaller, but still consequential, things—how to handle July 4th holiday staffing when everyone on the team wants the day off. And some of the times it's being able to recognize and correct an outright mistake. What we are talking about here is a manager's skill with **problem solving**, the process of identifying a discrepancy between an actual and a desired state of affairs, and then taking action to resolve it.

Success in problem solving comes from using information to make good **decisions**—choices among alternative possible courses of action. Managers, in this sense, make decisions while facing a continuous stream of daily problems. The most obvious situation is a **performance threat** in which something is already wrong or has the potential to go wrong. This happens when actual performance is less than desired or is moving in an unfavorable direction. Examples are when turnover or absenteeism suddenly increases in the work unit, when a team member's daily output decreases, or when a customer complains about service delays. Another important situation emerges as a **performance opportunity** that offers the chance for a better future if the right steps are taken. This happens when an actual situation either turns out better than anticipated or offers the potential to do so.

- **Problem solving** involves identifying and taking action to resolve problems.
- A **decision** is a choice among possible alternative courses of action.
- A **performance threat** is a situation in which something is obviously wrong or has the potential to go wrong.
- A **performance opportunity** is a situation that offers the chance for a better future if the right steps are taken.

Openness to Problem Solving

Managers often differ in their openness to problem solving, that is, in their willingness to accept the responsibilities it entails. Some are *problem avoiders* who ignore information that would otherwise signal the presence of a performance opportunity or threat. They are passive in information gathering, not wanting to make decisions and deal with problems. Other managers are *problem solvers* who are willing to make decisions and try to solve problems, but only when forced by the situation. They are reactive in gathering information to solve problems after, but not before, they occur. They may deal reasonably well with performance threats, but miss many performance opportunities.

Changing Labels Caused Problems for Tropicana

Have you had your orange juice today? PepsiCo invests heavily in advertising to drive brand image and sales for its Tropicana line. After executives decided the classic image of the big juicy orange with a straw stuck in it was outdated, they hired a new advertising consultant to change the image and create all new packaging. But instead of rising, sales fell. Customers complained that without the big friendly orange on the label, they couldn't find their orange juice. Although the new image seemed like a good idea, it wasn't. Recognizing the problem, PepsiCo executives quickly canceled the campaign and brought back the big orange.

There is quite a contrast between the last two styles and *problem seekers.* These managers actively process information and constantly look for problems to solve. True problem seekers are proactive and forward thinking. They anticipate performance threats and opportunities, and they take action to gain the advantage. Success at problem seeking is one of the ways to distinguish exceptional managers from the merely good or even bad ones. In the case of Toyota's quality problems, as mentioned earlier, key data revealing the presence of problems apparently was avoided by top management. When the crisis hit, they switched to problem solving. But, customers and shareholders would have been better served by problem seeking managers who were continuously alert and acted to prevent product defects and the need for recalls.

Systematic and Intuitive Thinking

Managers also differ in their use of "systematic" and "intuitive" thinking as they try to solve problems and make decisions. In **systematic thinking** a person approaches problems in a rational, step-by-step, analytical fashion. The process is slow and analytical. Systematic thinking breaks a complex problem into smaller components and then addresses them in a logical and integrated fashion. Managers who are systematic can be expected to make a plan before taking action, and carefully search for information to facilitate problem solving in a step-by-step fashion.

Someone using **intuitive thinking** is more flexible and spontaneous in problem solving.[15] This process uses a quick and broad evaluation of the situation and the possible alternative courses of action. Managers who are intuitive can be expected to deal with many aspects of a problem at once, jump from one issue to another, and consider "hunches" based on experience or spontaneous ideas. This approach is often imaginative and tends to work best in situations where facts are limited and few decision precedents exist.[16]

Amazon.com's Jeff Bezos says that when it's not possible for the firm's top managers to make systematic fact-based decisions, "you have to rely on experienced executives who've honed their instincts" and are able to make good judgments.[17] In other words, there's a place for both systematic and intuitive decision making in management. It's important to recognize both the limits of intuition and the need to support it with good solid analysis, experience, and effort.[18]

- **Systematic thinking** approaches problems in a rational and analytical fashion.

- **Intuitive thinking** approaches problems in a flexible and spontaneous fashion.

Systematic versus Intuitive Thinking

Systematic thinker approaches problems in a step-by-step and linear fashion

Intuitive thinker approaches problems in flexible and spontaneous fashion

Multidimensional Thinking

Managers often deal with portfolios of problems that consist of multiple and interrelated issues. This requires **multidimensional thinking**, which is an ability to view many problems at once, in relationship to one another and across both long and short time horizons.[19] The best managers are able to "map" multiple problems into a network that can be actively managed over time as priorities, events, and demands continuously change. They are able to make decisions and take actions in the short run that benefit longer-run objectives. And they avoid being sidetracked while sorting through a shifting mix of daily problems. Harvard scholar Daniel Isenberg calls this skill **strategic opportunism**—the ability to remain focused on long-term objectives while being flexible enough to resolve short-term problems and opportunities in a timely manner.[20]

- **Multidimensional thinking** is an ability to address many problems at once.

- **Strategic opportunism** focuses on long-term objectives while being flexible in dealing with short-term problems.

Cognitive Styles

When US Airways Flight 1549 was in trouble and pilot Chesley Sullenberger decided to land in the Hudson River, he had both a clear head and a clear sense of what he had been trained to do. The landing was successful and no lives were lost. Called a "hero" for his efforts, Sullenberger described his thinking this way.[21]

> I needed to touch down with the wings exactly level. I needed to touch down with the nose slightly up. I needed to touch down at . . . a descent rate that was survivable. And I needed to touch down just above our minimum flying speed but not below it. And I needed to make all these things happen simultaneously.

This example points us toward consideration of **cognitive styles**, or the way individuals deal with information while making decisions. If you take the end-of-chapter self-assessment, it will examine your cognitive style as a contrast of tendencies toward information gathering—sensation vs. intuition, and information evaluation—feeling vs. thinking, in one's approach to problem solving. Most likely, pilot Sullenberger would score high in both sensation and thinking, and that is probably an ideal type for his job. But as the small figure shows, this is only one of four master cognitive styles.

People with different cognitive styles may approach problems and make decisions in quite different ways. Thus, it's helpful to understand the different styles and their characteristics both for yourself and as they are displayed by others.[22]

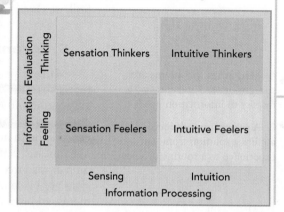

Cognitive Styles in Decision Making

● **Cognitive styles** are shown by the ways individuals deal with information while making decisions.

- *Sensation Thinkers*—STs tend to emphasize the impersonal rather than the personal and take a realistic approach to problem solving. They like hard "facts," clear goals, certainty, and situations of high control.
- *Intuitive Thinkers*—ITs are comfortable with abstraction and unstructured situations. They tend to be idealistic, prone toward intellectual and theoretical positions; they are logical and impersonal but also avoid details.
- *Intuitive Feelers*—IFs prefer broad and global issues. They are insightful and tend to avoid details, being comfortable with intangibles; they value flexibility and human relationships.
- *Sensation Feelers*—SFs tend to emphasize both analysis and human relations. They tend to be realistic and prefer facts; they are open communicators and sensitive to feelings and values.

Real People

New Parent Commits to Making Earth Friendly Products

It began, says John Vlahakis, when his daughter was born. "I realized that everything that was harming the environment would also be harming her," he says. "I felt I had to make a difference for her, to make the world a better place." He started Earth Friendly Products to make safe and environmentally friendly cleaning products for use at home. The firm's mission statement is to "create products for home and personal use that are derived from replenishable resources and we will conduct our business in a socially responsible manner that safe guards the earth, and all its inhabitants."

Vlahakis claims that "green" wasn't part of the normal business vocabulary at start-up time and that he had to conduct lots of analysis about chemicals and toxic ingredients. He began with just four products and tried to make them competitive on price and performance with non-green alternatives. That initial product list has grown to some 150 that are now distributed in the large grocery chains including Costco and Sam's Club, as well as in international markets including Mexico, South Korea, and the United Kingdom.

Sales now top $50 million annually, and Vlahakis says: "We're forcing established companies that didn't look at the environment responsibly to start paying attention."

TYPES OF MANAGERIAL DECISIONS

The bankruptcy of General Motors shocked the world. But an automobile industry analyst says we should have seen it coming, criticizing the firm for "decades of dumb decisions" that created unwarranted concessions to labor unions, poor styling and "look-alike" cars, bad acquisitions, and misguided bets on big SUVs.[23] Anyone who studies management knows that decision making is part of the job. They also know that not all decisions are going to be easy ones; some will always have to be made under tough conditions; and not all decisions will turn out right. Still, we should also admit that the goal is to do a lot better than was the case at GM.

Programmed and Nonprogrammed Decisions

> **Structured problems** are straightforward and clear with respect to information needs.

> A **programmed decision** applies a solution from past experience to a routine problem.

Managers sometimes face **structured problems** that are familiar, straightforward, and clear with respect to information needs. Because these problems are routine and occur over and over again, they can be dealt with by **programmed decisions** that use solutions or decision rules already available from past experience. Though not always predictable, routine problems can at least be anticipated. This means that decisions can be programmed in advance for use as needed. In human resource management, for example, problems are common whenever decisions are made on pay raises and promotions, vacation requests, committee assignments, and the like. Forward-looking managers use this understanding to decide in advance how to handle complaints and conflicts when and if they arise.

> **Unstructured problems** have ambiguities and information deficiencies.

> A **nonprogrammed decision** applies a specific solution crafted for a unique problem.

Managers also deal with **unstructured problems** that are new or unusual situations full of ambiguities and information deficiencies. These problems require **nonprogrammed decisions** that craft novel solutions to meet the demands of the unique situation at hand. Many, if not most, problems faced by higher-level managers are of this type, often involving the choice of strategies and objectives in situations of some uncertainty. In the recent financial crisis, for example, all eyes were on U.S. Treasury Secretary Timothy Geithner. His task was to solve the problems with billions of dollars in bad loans made by the nation's banks and restore stability to the financial markets. But it was uncharted territory; no programmed solutions were readily available. Geithner and his team crafted what they believed were the best possible solutions at the time. But only time would tell if these nonprogrammed decisions were the right ones.

Crisis Decisions

> A **crisis decision** occurs when an unexpected problem arises that can lead to disaster if not resolved quickly and appropriately.

An extreme type of nonprogrammed decision is the **crisis decision** that occurs when an unexpected problem arises and can lead to disaster if not resolved quickly and appropriately. Terrorism in a post-9/11 world, outbreaks of workplace violence, IT failures and security breaches, ethics scandals, and environmental catastrophes are examples. Fred Sawyers knows the crisis situation quite well. He was in New Orleans managing a Hilton hotel when Hurricane Katrina struck. But in what he describes as "the most harrowing week of his life," he excelled. Using common sense, quick perception, and solid hard work, Sawyers moved from decision to decision—motivating staff, keeping the damaged hotel as safe as possible, and feeding and sheltering 4,500 persons from the storm.[24]

The ability to handle crises may be the ultimate test of a manager's problem-solving capabilities.[25] Unfortunately, research indicates that managers may react to crises by doing the wrong things—isolating themselves and trying to solve the problem alone or in a small "closed" group.[26] In respect to Toyota's management of the massive recall crisis, for example, one observer said that "crisis management does not get any more woeful than this." Even though CEO Akio Toyoda eventually apologized in public and pledged a return to high quality standards, by the time he did so, customers and government regulators considered it too late and inadequate. He and the firm were criticized for "initially denying, minimizing and mitigating the problems." The poor crisis management was described as a fault of Toyota's insular corporate culture, one that discouraged early disclosure of quality problems and contributed to poor public relations when they reached crisis levels.[27]

It is getting more common for organizations to engage in formal crisis management training, using rules such as those in Management Smarts 7.1. These programs are designed to help managers and others prepare for unexpected high-impact events that threaten an organization's health and well-being. Anticipation is one aspect of crisis management; preparation is another. People can be assigned ahead of time to crisis management teams, and crisis management plans can be developed to deal with various contingencies. Just as police departments and community groups plan ahead and train to best handle civil and natural disasters, so, too, can managers and work teams plan ahead and train to best deal with organizational crises.

> ## Management Smarts 7.1
>
> ### Six rules for crisis management
>
> 1. *Figure out what is going on*–Take the time to understand what's happening and the conditions under which the crisis must be resolved.
>
> 2. *Remember that speed matters*–Attack the crisis as quickly as possible, trying to catch it when it is as small as possible.
>
> 3. *Remember that slow counts, too*–Know when to back off and wait for a better opportunity to make progress with the crisis.
>
> 4. *Respect the danger of the unfamiliar*–Understand the danger of all-new territory where you and others have never been before.
>
> 5. *Value the skeptic*–Don't look for and get too comfortable with agreement; appreciate skeptics and let them help you see things differently.
>
> 6. *Be ready to "fight fire with fire"*–When things are going wrong and no one seems to care, you may have to start a crisis to get their attention.

DECISION CONDITIONS

Figure 7.4 shows three different decision conditions or environments—certainty, risk, and uncertainty. Although managers make decisions in each, the conditions of risk and uncertainty are common at higher management levels where problems are more complex and unstructured.

Domino's Pizza CEO J. Patrick Boyle is a risk taker. He not only decided to change the firm's pizza recipe, he ran a television ad admitting that customers really disliked the old one because it was "totally devoid of flavor" and had a crust "like cardboard." Whereas some executives might want to hide or downplay such customer reviews, Boyle used them to help launch the new recipe. He says it was a "calculated risk" and that "we're proving to our customers that we are listening to them by brutally accepting the criticism that's out there."[28] When it comes to hybrid automobiles, General Motors wasn't a risk taker. The firm's former vice chairman, Bob Lutz, said in retrospect: "GM had the technology to do hybrids

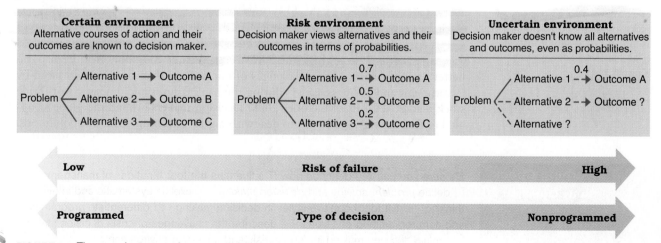

FIGURE 7.4 Three environments for managerial decision making.

back when Toyota was launching the first Prius, but we opted not to ask the board to approve a product program that'd be destined to lose hundreds of millions of dollars."[29]

Certain Environment

> A **certain environment** offers complete information on possible action alternatives and their consequences.

The decisions just described were made in conditions quite different from the relative predictability of a **certain environment**. This is an ideal decision situation in which factual information is available about the possible alternative courses of action and their outcomes. The decision maker's task is simple: study the alternatives and choose the best solution. Certain environments are nice, neat, and comfortable for decision makers. However, very few managerial problems are like this.

Risk Environment

> A **risk environment** lacks complete information but offers "probabilities" of the likely outcomes for possible action alternatives.

Looking back on decisions he made during the financial crisis, GE's CEO Jeffrey Immelt says that he did "things I never thought I would have to do. I am sure my board and investors frequently wondered what in the heck I was doing. I had to act without perfect knowledge."[30] In this statement Immelt is stating a basic fact of managerial decision making: Many management problems emerge in **risk environments**—ones where facts and information on action alternatives and their consequences are incomplete.

Decision making in risk environments requires the use of *probabilities* to estimate the likelihood that a particular outcome will occur (e.g., 4 chances out of 10). Because probabilities are only possibilities, some people have great difficulty acting under risk conditions. When considering possible investments in hybrid technologies, for example, GM executives either miscalculated the probabilities of positive payoffs or didn't believe the probabilities were high enough to justify the risk. Their Japanese competitors, facing the same risk environment, decided differently and gained advantage.

Entrepreneurs and highly innovative organizations have the personal characteristics that make them more open than others to decision making under risk conditions. Also, steps can sometimes be taken to reduce risk by gathering more and better information. In the case of new products like an energy drink or line of fashion purses, for example, firms often make "go-no-go" decisions only after consumer preferences are identified by extensive market testing with focus groups.

Uncertain Environment

> An **uncertain environment** lacks so much information that it is difficult to assign probabilities to the likely outcomes of alternatives.

When facts are few and information is so poor that managers are unable even to assign probabilities to the likely outcomes of alternatives, an **uncertain environment** exists. This is the most difficult decision condition. The high level of uncertainty forces managers to rely heavily on intuition, judgment, informed guessing, and hunches—all of which leave considerable room for error. Perhaps no better example exists of the challenges of uncertainty than the situation faced by government and business leaders during the bank failures and dramatic worldwide stock market sell-offs of October 2008. Decision makers around the globe struggled to find the right pathways to deal with highly uncertain economic conditions.

Be sure you can ☑ describe how IT influences the four functions of management ☑ define *problem solving* and *decision making* ☑ explain systematic and intuitive thinking ☑ list four cognitive styles in decision making ☑ differentiate programmed and nonprogrammed decisions ☑ describe the challenges of crisis decision making ☑ explain decision making in certain, risk, and uncertain environments

THE DECISION-MAKING PROCESS

Everyone who studies management knows that decision making is part of the job. They also know that not all decisions are going to be easy and some will always have to be made under tough conditions. All of those case studies, experiential exercises, class discussions, and even essay exam questions are intended to engage students in the complexities of managerial decision making, the potential problems and pitfalls, and even the pressures of crisis situations. From the classroom forward, however, it's all up to you. Only you can determine whether you step forward and make the best out of very difficult problems, or collapse under pressure.

Figure 7.5 describes five steps in the **decision-making process:** (1) identify and define the problem, (2) generate and evaluate alternative solutions, (3) choose a preferred course of action, (4) implement the decision, and (5) evaluate results.[31] Importantly, ethical reasoning should be double checked in all five steps. This process can be understood in the context of the following short case.

> The **decision-making process** begins with identification of a problem and ends with evaluation of implemented solutions.

> *The Ajax Case.* On December 31, the Ajax Company decided to close down its Murphysboro plant. Market conditions were forcing layoffs, and the company could not find a buyer for the plant. Some of the 172 employees had been with the company as long as 18 years; others as little as 6 months. All were to be terminated. Under company policy, they would be given severance pay equal to one week's pay per year of service.

This case reflects how competition, changing times, and the forces of globalization can take their toll on organizations, the people who work for them, and the communities in which they operate. Think about how you would feel as one of the affected employees. Think about how you would feel as the mayor of this small town. Think about how you would feel as a corporate executive having to make the difficult business decisions.

STEP 1—IDENTIFY AND DEFINE THE PROBLEM

The first step in decision making is to find and define the problem. Information gathering and deliberation are critical in this stage. The way a problem is defined can have a major impact on how it is resolved, and it is important to clarify exactly what a decision should accomplish. The more specific the goals, the easier it is to evaluate results after the decision is actually implemented. But, three common mistakes can occur in this critical first step in decision making.[32]

Mistake number 1 is defining the problem too broadly or too narrowly. To take a classic example, the problem stated as "build a better mousetrap" might be better defined as "get rid of the mice." Managers should define problems in ways that give them the best possible range of problem-solving options.

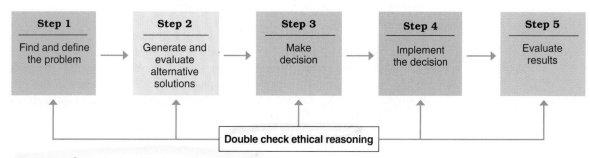

FIGURE 7.5 Steps in the decision-making process.

Is Fisker Automotive Worth Investors' Risks?

When the U.S. government loaned Fisker Automotive $529 million, one analyst called the move "a leap of faith". So what justifies the investment decision? Will Fisker Automotive's hybrid gas and electric sports car become a market favorite? Fisker is the brainchild of Henrik Fisker, former car designer for BMW. The Fisker Karma luxury hybrid is being built in Sweden and will sell for around $90,000 in the United States. Fisker has bought a former General Motors plant to build a family model that will sell for around $48,000.

Mistake number 2 is focusing on symptoms instead of causes. Symptoms are indicators that problems may exist, but they shouldn't be mistaken for the problems themselves. Although managers should be alert to spot problem symptoms (e.g., a drop in performance), they must also dig deeper to address root causes (such as discovering that a worker needs training in the use of a new computer system).

Mistake number 3 is choosing the wrong problem to deal with at a certain point in time. For example, here are three problems. Which would you address first on a busy workday? 1—An e-mail message from your boss is requesting a proposal "as soon as possible" on how to handle employees' complaints about lack of flexibility in their work schedules. 2—One of your best team members has just angered another by loudly criticizing her work performance. 3—Your working spouse has left a voice mail message that your daughter is sick at school and the nurse would like her to go home for the day. Choices like this are not easy. But we have to set priorities and deal with the most important problems first. In this case, perhaps the boss can wait while you telephone school to learn more about your daughter's illness and then spend some time with the employee who seems to be having "a bad day."

Back to the Ajax Case. Closing the Ajax plant will put a substantial number of people from the small community of Murphysboro out of work. The unemployment will have a negative impact on individuals, their families, and the town as a whole. The loss of the Ajax tax base will further hurt the community. The local financial implications of the plant closure will be great. The problem for Ajax management is how to minimize the adverse impact of the plant closing on the employees, their families, and the community.

STEP 2—GENERATE AND EVALUATE ALTERNATIVE COURSES OF ACTION

Once a problem is defined, it is time to assemble the facts and information that will solve it. This is where we clarify exactly what is known and what needs to be known. Extensive information gathering should identify alternative courses of action, as well as their anticipated consequences. Key stakeholders in the problem should be identified, and the effects of possible courses of action on each of them should be considered. During a time when General Motors was closing plants and laying off thousands of workers, for example, a union negotiator said: "While GM's continuing decline in market share isn't the fault of workers or our communities, it is these groups that will suffer."[33]

A useful approach for evaluating alternatives is a **cost-benefit analysis**—the comparison of what an alternative will cost in relation to the expected benefits. At a minimum, the benefits of an alternative should be greater than its costs, and it should be ethically sound. The following list includes costs, benefits, and other useful criteria for evaluating alternatives.

> **Cost-benefit analysis** involves comparing the costs and benefits of each potential course of action.

- *Costs:* What are the "costs" of implementing the alternative, including resource investments as well as potential negative side effects?
- *Benefits:* What are the "benefits" of using the alternative to solve a performance deficiency or take advantage of an opportunity?
- *Timeliness:* How fast can the alternative be implemented and a positive impact be achieved?
- *Acceptability:* To what extent will the alternative be accepted and supported by those who must work with it?
- *Ethical soundness:* How well does the alternative meet acceptable ethical criteria in the eyes of the various stakeholders?

Ultimately, any course of action can only be as good as the quality of the alternatives considered; the better the pool of alternatives, the more likely that any actions taken will help solve the problem at hand. A common decision-making error is abandoning the search for alternatives too quickly. This often happens under pressures of time and other circumstances. But just because an alternative is convenient doesn't make it the best. It could have damaging side effects, or it could be less good than others that might be discovered with extra effort. One way to minimize this error is through consultation and involvement. It often works out that bringing more people into the decision-making process brings more information and perspectives to bear on the problem, generates more alternatives, and results in a choice more appealing to everyone involved.

> *Back to the Ajax Case.* The Ajax plant is going to be closed. Among the possible alternatives that can be considered are (1) close the plant on schedule and be done with it; (2) delay the plant closing until all efforts have been made to sell it to another firm; (3) offer to sell the plant to the employees and/or local interests; (4) close the plant and offer transfers to other Ajax plant locations; or (5) close the plant, offer transfers, and help the employees find new jobs in and around Murphysboro.

STEP 3—DECIDE ON A PREFERRED COURSE OF ACTION

This is the point of choice where an actual decision is made to select a preferred course of action. Just how this is done and by whom must be successfully resolved in each problem situation. Management theory recognizes rather substantial differences between the classical and behavioral models of decision making as shown in Figure 7.6.

Classical Decision Model

The **classical decision model** views the manager as acting rationally in a certain world. The assumption is that a rational choice of the preferred course of action will be made by a decision maker who is fully informed about all possible alternatives. Here, the manager faces a clearly defined problem and knows all possible action alternatives, as well as their consequences. As a result, he or she makes an **optimizing decision** that gives the absolute best solution to the problem.

> The **classical decision model** describes decision making with complete information.

> An **optimizing decision** chooses the alternative giving the absolute best solution to a problem.

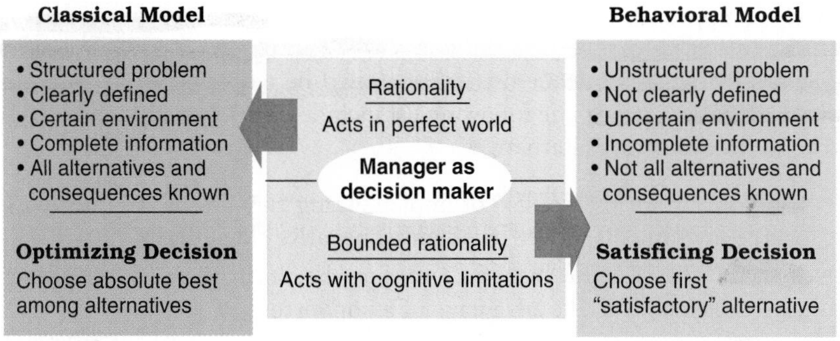

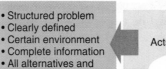
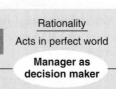

Classical Model

- Structured problem
- Clearly defined
- Certain environment
- Complete information
- All alternatives and consequences known

Optimizing Decision
Choose absolute best among alternatives

Rationality
Acts in perfect world

Manager as decision maker

Bounded rationality
Acts with cognitive limitations

Behavioral Model

- Unstructured problem
- Not clearly defined
- Uncertain environment
- Incomplete information
- Not all alternatives and consequences known

Satisficing Decision
Choose first "satisfactory" alternative

FIGURE 7.6 Differences in the classical and behavioral decision-making models.

● **Bounded rationality** describes making decisions within the constraints of limited information and alternatives.

● The **behavioral decision model** describes decision making with limited information and bounded rationality.

● A **satisficing decision** chooses the first satisfactory alternative that comes to one's attention.

Behavioral Decision Model

Behavioral scientists question the assumptions of perfect information underlying the classical model. Perhaps best represented by the work of scholar Herbert Simon, they instead recognize *cognitive limitations* to our human information—processing capabilities.[34] These limits make it hard for managers to become fully informed and make optimizing decisions. They create a **bounded rationality**, such that managerial decisions are rational only within the boundaries set by the available information and known alternatives, both of which are incomplete.

Because of cognitive limitations and bounded rationalities, the **behavioral decision model** assumes that people act with only partial knowledge about the available action alternatives and their consequences. Consequently, the first alternative that appears to give a satisfactory resolution of the problem is likely to be chosen. Simon, who won a Nobel Prize for his work, calls this the tendency to make **satisficing decisions**—choosing the first satisfactory alternative that comes to your attention. The behavioral model is useful in describing how many decisions get made in the ambiguous and fast-paced problem situations faced by managers.

> *Back to the Ajax Case*. Management at Ajax decided to close the plant, offer transfers to company plants in another state, and offer to help displaced employees find new jobs in and around Murphysboro.

STEP 4—IMPLEMENT THE DECISION

Once a decision is made, actions must be taken to fully implement it. Nothing new can or will happen unless action is taken to actually solve the problem. Managers not only need the determination and creativity to arrive at a decision, they also need the ability and willingness to implement it.

The "ways" in which decision-making steps 1, 2, and 3 are accomplished can have a powerful impact on how well decisions get implemented. Difficulties encountered at the point of implementation often trace to the **lack-of-participation error**. This is a failure to adequately involve in the process those persons whose support is necessary to implement the decision. Managers who use participation wisely get the right people involved in problem solving from the beginning. When they do, implementation typically follows quickly, smoothly, and to everyone's satisfaction. Participation in decision making makes everyone better informed and builds the commitments needed for implementation.

● **Lack-of-participation error** is failure to involve in a decision the persons whose support is needed to implement it.

Climber Left to Die on Mt. Everest

Some 40 climbers are winding their ways to the top of Mount Everest. About 1,000 feet below the summit sits a British mountain climber in trouble, collapsed in a shallow snow cave. Most of those on the way up just look while continuing their climbs. Sherpas from one passing team pause to give him oxygen before moving on. Within hours David Sharp, 34, is dead of oxygen deficiency on the mountain.

A climber who passed by says: "At 28,000 feet it's hard to stay alive yourself . . . he was in very poor condition . . . , it was a very hard decision . . . he wasn't a member of our team."

Someone who made the summit in the past says: "If you're going to go to Everest . . . I think you have to accept responsibility that you may end up doing something that's not ethically nice . . . you have to realize that you're in a different world."

After hearing about this case, the late Sir Edmund Hillary, who reached the top in 1953, said: "Human life is far more important than just getting to the top of a mountain."

You Decide

Who's right and who's wrong here? Should the climbers have ignored Sharp and continued on their way to the top of Mount Everest?

In our daily lives and careers we are all, in our own ways, seeking to achieve our dreams and realize our ambitions. These journeys often require us to make choices between what is best for us versus what is best for others. When we encounter others in trouble or struggling in some way, what are our ethical or moral obligations to them?

Back to the Ajax Case. Ajax ran ads in the local and regional newspapers. The ad called attention to an "Ajax skill bank" composed of "qualified, dedicated, and well-motivated employees with a variety of skills and experiences." Interested employers were urged to contact Ajax for further information.

STEP 5—EVALUATE RESULTS

The decision-making process is not complete until results are evaluated. If the desired outcomes are not achieved or if undesired side effects occur, corrective action should be taken. Evaluation is a form of managerial control. It involves gathering data to measure performance results and compare them against goals. If results are less than what was desired, it is time to reassess and return to earlier steps. In this way, problem solving becomes a dynamic and ongoing activity within the management process. Evaluation is always easier when clear goals, measurable targets, and timetables were established to begin with.

Back to the Ajax Case. The advertisement ran for some 15 days. The plant's industrial relations manager commented, "I've been very pleased with the results." That's all we know. How well did Ajax management do in dealing with this very difficult problem? You can look back on the case as it was described and judge for yourself. Perhaps you would have approached the situation and the five steps in decision making somewhat differently.

AT ALL STEPS—CHECK ETHICAL REASONING

The choices made at each step in the decision-making process often have a moral dimension that might easily be overlooked. Even in the heat of dealing with economic crisis, job eliminations such as those in the prior Ajax case might not be sufficiently considered for their implications on the persons, families, and community that will be affected.

If you look back to Figure 7.3, you'll see that each step in the decision-making process can and should be linked with ethical reasoning.[35] This helps to ensure that any underlying moral problems will be identified and dealt with in the best possible ways. One way to check ethical reasoning in decision making is to systematically ask and answer several pointed questions. Gerald Cavanagh and his associates, for example, suggest that we can proceed with the most confidence when a decision tests positive against these four ethics criteria.[36]

1. *Utility*—Does the decision satisfy all constituents or stakeholders?
2. *Rights*—Does the decision respect the rights and duties of everyone?
3. *Justice*—Is the decision consistent with the canons of justice?
4. *Caring*—Is the decision consistent with my responsibilities to care?

Another test of ethical reasoning basically exposes a decision to public scrutiny and forces the decision maker to consider it in the context of full transparency and the prospect of shame.[37] Three so-called **spotlight questions**, first introduced in Chapter 3 on ethics and social responsibility, can be powerful in this regard. Ask: "How would I feel if my family found out about this decision?" Ask: "How would I feel if this decision were published in the local newspaper or posted on the Internet?" Ask: "What would the person you know or know of who has the strongest character and best ethical judgment do in this situation?"

● The **spotlight questions** test the ethics of a decision by exposing it to scrutiny through the eyes of family, community members, and ethical role models.

☑ **Learning Check**

Study Question 3
What are the steps in the decision-making process.

Be sure you can ☑ list the steps in the decision-making process ☑ apply these steps to a sample decision-making situation ☑ explain cost-benefit analysis in decision making ☑ discuss differences between the classical and behavioral decision models ☑ define *optimizing* and *satisficing* ☑ explain how lack-of-participation error can hurt decision making ☑ list useful questions for double checking the ethical reasoning of a decision

ISSUES IN MANAGERIAL DECISION MAKING

Once we accept the fact that each of us is likely to make imperfect decisions at least some of the time, it makes sense to probe even further into the how's and why's of decision making in organizations. For sure it's important to understand possible causes of decision bias and error, as well as factors that enhance creativity in decision making and problem solving.

DECISION ERRORS AND TRAPS

Why do well-intentioned people sometimes make bad decisions? The reason can often be traced back to the simplifying strategies we often rely on when faced with limited information, time, and even energy. These strategies or rules of thumb are known as **heuristics**.[38] Although they can be helpful in dealing with complex and ambiguous situations, they are also common causes of decision-making errors.[39]

● **Heuristics** are strategies for simplifying decision making.

Availability Bias

The **availability bias** occurs when people assess a current event or situation by using information that is "readily available" from memory. An example is deciding not to invest in a new product based on your recollection of a recent product

● The **availability bias** bases a decision on recent information or events.

failure. The potential bias is that the readily available information is fallible and irrelevant. For example, the product that recently failed may have been a good idea that was released to market at the wrong time of year.

Representativeness Bias

The **representativeness bias** occurs when people assess the likelihood of something happening based on its similarity to a stereotyped set of occurrences. An example is deciding to hire someone for a job vacancy simply because he or she graduated from the same school attended by your last and most successful new hire. The potential bias is that the representative stereotype masks factors important and relevant to the decision. For instance, the abilities and career expectations of the person receiving the offer may not fit the job requirements.

● The **representativeness bias** bases a decision on similarity to other situations.

Anchoring and Adjustment Bias

The **anchoring and adjustment bias** occurs when decisions are influenced by inappropriate allegiance to a previously existing value or starting point. An example is a manager who sets a new salary level for an employee by simply raising her prior

● The **anchoring and adjustment bias** bases a decision on incremental adjustments from a prior decision point.

Research Brief

Escalation Increases Risk of Unethical Decisions

Journal of
Business
Ethics

Springer

That's the conclusion reached in an empirical study by Marc and Vera L. Street. They reviewed research confirming that escalating commitments to previously chosen courses of action cause many poor decisions in organizations. But they also point out that little has been done to investigate if escalation tendencies lead to unethical behaviors.

To address this void, the researchers conducted an experiment with 155 undergraduate students working on a computerized investment task. They found that exposure to escalation situations increases tendencies toward unethical acts and that the tendencies further increase with the magnitude of the escalation. Street and Street believe this link between escalation and poor ethics is driven by desires to get out of and avoid the increasing stress of painful situations.

Additional findings from the study showed that students with an external locus of control were more likely to choose an unethical decision alternative than their counterparts with an internal locus of control.

You Be the Researcher

This study was done in the college classroom and under simulated decision conditions. How would you design a study that tests the same hypotheses in the real world? Also, is it possible to design a training program that would use the "Spotlight Questions" to help people better deal with unethical decision options in escalation situations?

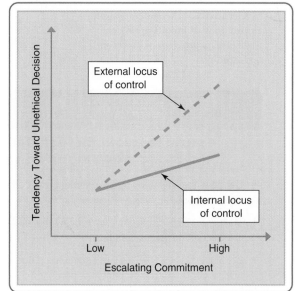

Reference: Marc Street and Vera L. Street, "The Effects of Escalating Commitment on Ethical Decision Making," *Journal of Business Ethics,* vol. 64 (2006), pp. 343–56.

year's salary by a small percentage amount. Although the increase may appear reasonable to the manager, the prior year's salary may have substantially undervalued the employee relative to the job market. The small incremental salary adjustment, reflecting anchoring and adjustment bias, may not satisfy her or keep her from looking for another job.

Framing Error

● **Framing error** is trying to solve a problem in the context in which it is perceived.

Sometimes managers suffer from **framing error** that occurs when a problem is evaluated and resolved in the context in which it is perceived—either positively or negatively. Suppose, for example, data show a product that has a 40% market share. A negative frame views the product as deficient because it is missing 60% of the market. The likely discussion would focus on: "What are we doing wrong?" Alternatively, the frame could be a positive one, looking at the 40% share as a good accomplishment. In this case the discussion is more likely to proceed with "How do we do things better?" Sometimes people use framing as a tactic for presenting information in a way that gets other people to think inside the desired frame. In politics, this is often referred to as "spinning" the data.

Confirmation Error

● A **confirmation error** occurs when focusing only on information that confirms a decision already made.

One of our tendencies after making a decision is to try and find ways to justify it. In the case of unethical acts, for example, Chapter 3 discussed ways we try to "rationalize" them after the fact. More generally, we can fall prey to **confirmation error.** This means that we notice, accept, and even seek out only information that confirms or is consistent with a decision we have just made. Contrary information that shows what we are doing is incorrect is downplayed or denied.

Escalating Commitment

● **Escalating commitment** is the continuation of a course of action even though it is not working.

● **Creativity** is the generation of a novel idea or unique approach that solves a problem or crafts an opportunity.

Another decision-making trap is **escalating commitment**. This occurs as a decision to increase effort and perhaps apply more resources to pursue a course of action that is not working.[40] Managers prone to escalation let the momentum of the situation overwhelm them. They are unable to "call it quits" even when facts and experience otherwise indicate that this is the best thing to do. This is a common decision error, perhaps one that you are personally familiar with.

Management Smarts 7.2 offers advice on how to avoid tendencies toward escalating commitments to previously chosen courses of action. NBC executives seem to have passed the test when they reversed a decision to move Jay Leno out of his popular Tonight Show at 11:35 p.m. and into a new show at 10 p.m. Leno attracted 29% fewer viewers at the new time while his replacement, Conan O'Brien, lost another 2 million viewers to David Letterman in the old time slot. With the facts in hand, NBC didn't escalate, but shifted Leno back into the Tonight Show.[41] Time will tell if things work out for the better.

Management Smarts 7.2

How to avoid the escalation trap in decision making

- Set advance limits on your involvement and commitment to a particular course of action; stick with these limits.

- Make your own decisions; don't follow the leads of others, since they are also prone to escalation.

- Carefully assess why you are continuing a course of action; if there are no good reasons to continue, don't.

- Remind yourself of what a course of action is costing; consider saving these costs as a reason to discontinue.

- Watch for escalation tendencies in your behaviors and those of others.

CREATIVITY IN DECISION MAKING

On the flip side of decision-making errors are decision-making successes. Consider the case of **creativity** in decision making, the generation of a novel idea or unique approach to solving problems or exploiting opportunities.[43] Creativity is one of our greatest personal assets, even though it may be too often unrecognized. In fact, we exercise creativity every day in lots of ways—solving problems at home, building something for the kids, or even finding ways to pack too many things into too small a suitcase. But are we creative when it would really help in solving workplace problems? Just imagine what can be accomplished with all the creative potential that exists in an organization. How do you turn that potential into creative decisions?

Personal Creativity Drivers

The three-component model shown in the small figure shows how task expertise, task motivation, and creativity skills each become personal creativity drivers.[44] The model is helpful because it points us in the direction of personal development in creativity as well as toward management actions that can be taken to boost creativity drivers in the work setting.

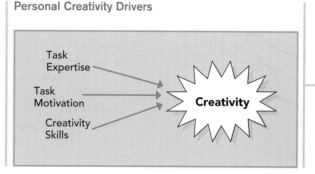
Personal Creativity Drivers

Creative decisions are more likely to occur when the person or team has a lot of *task expertise*. Creativity is an outgrowth of something one is good at or knows about, and typically extends it in new directions. Creativity is also more likely when someone is highly *task-motivated*. That is, creativity tends to occur in part because people work exceptionally hard to resolve a problem or exploit an opportunity.

Creative decisions are more likely when the people involved have strong *creativity skills*. There is general agreement, for example, that creative people tend to work with high energy, hold ground in face of criticism, and act resourceful even in difficult situations. They are also good at synthesizing and finding correct answers (convergent thinking), looking at diverse ways to solve problems (lateral thinking), and thinking "outside of the box" (divergent thinking).[45] Creativity consultant Edward De Bono offers this example.[46] Elevator riders in a new high-rise building were complaining about long waiting times. Building engineers recommended upgrading the entire system at substantial cost. When De Bono was called in to offer his advice, he suggested placing floor-to-ceiling mirrors by the elevators. People, he suspected, would not notice waiting times because they were distracted by their and others' reflections. He was right. His creativity broke the engineers' assumption that any solutions to slow elevators had to be mechanical ones.

Situational Creativity Drivers

If you mix creative people and traditional organization and management practices, what will you get? Perhaps not much; it takes more than individual creativity alone to make innovation a way of life in organizations. In this sense it is important to recognize situational creativity drivers like those shown in the small box.

Managers should, of course, try to make sure that their organizations are well staffed with creative members so that teams always have a solid foundation of *team creativity skills*. But in order to unlock the full potential of this creativity, they must also provide *management support* and build *organizational cultures* that are as conducive as possible to creativity in decision making. This can involve small things such as a team leader who has the patience to allow for creative processes to work themselves through a decision situation. It involves top management being willing to

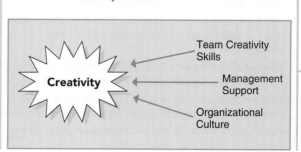
Situational Creativity Drivers

provide the resources—time, technology, and space that are helpful to the creative processes. It also involves valuing creativity and making it a top priority in the broader work climate and surrounding organizational culture.

Think creative the next time you see a young child playing with a really neat toy. It may be from *Fisher-Price Toys*—part of Mattel, Inc. In the firm's headquarters you'll find a special place called the "Cave," and it's not your typical office space. Picture bean-bag chairs, soft lighting, casual chairs, and couches. It's a place for brainstorming, where designers, marketers, engineers, and others can meet and join in freewheeling to come up with the next great toy for preschoolers. Consultants recommend that such innovation spaces be separated from the normal workplace and be large enough for no more than 15 to 20 people.[47]

Think creativity wasted the next time you watch TV on a beautiful, large, flat-panel screen. In 1964 George H. Heilmeier showed his employers at RCA Labs his new discovery—a liquid-crystal display, or LCD. They played with it until 1968 when RCA executives decided the firm was so heavily invested in color TV tubes that they weren't really interested. Today the market is dominated by Japanese, Korean, and Taiwanese producers, with not a single U.S. maker in the play. Ironically, Heilmeier received the Kyoto Prize, considered the Nobel Prize of Japan, for his pioneering innovation.[48]

☑	**Learning Check** **Study Question 4** What are the current issues in managerial decision making?	*Be sure you can* ☑ explain the availability, representativeness, anchoring, and adjustment heuristics ☑ illustrate framing error, confirmation error, and escalating commitment in decision making ☑ identify key personal and situational creativity drivers

Management **L**earning **R**eview

Study Questions Summary

1 What is the role of information in the management process?

- Competency in using technology to access, process, and share information is an essential career skill.
- Data are raw facts and figures; information is data made useful for decision making.
- Information useful in management is timely, high quality, complete, relevant, and understandable.
- Management information systems collect, organize, store, and distribute data to meet the information needs of managers.
- Managers play important roles in helping organizations meet their external and internal information needs.
- Information technology is breaking barriers within and between organizations to speed workflows and cut costs.

FOR DISCUSSION **What are the potential downsides to the ways IT is changing organizations?**

2 How do managers use information to make decisions?

- Managers serve as information nerve centers in the process of planning, organizing, leading, and controlling activities in organizations.
- Managers can display problem avoidance, problem solving, and problem seeking in facing problems.
- Managers vary in the use of systematic and intuitive thinking, and in tendencies toward multidimensional thinking.
- Managers must understand the different cognitive styles people use in decision making.
- Programmed decisions are routine solutions to recurring and structured problems; nonprogrammed decisions are unique solutions to novel and unstructured problems.
- Crisis problems occur unexpectedly and can lead to disaster if not handled quickly and properly.

● Managers face problems and make decisions under conditions of certainty, risk, and uncertainty.

FOR DISCUSSION **When would a manager be justified in acting as a problem avoider?**

3 What are the steps in the decision-making process?

● The steps in the decision-making process are (1) find and define the problem, (2) generate and evaluate alternatives, (3) decide on the preferred course of action, (4) implement the decision, and (5) evaluate the results.

● An optimizing decision, following the classical model, chooses the absolute best solution from a known set of alternatives.

● A satisficing decision, following the behavioral model, chooses the first satisfactory alternative to come to attention.

● To check the ethical reasoning of a decision at any step in the decision-making process, it is helpful to ask the ethics criteria questions of utility, rights, justice, and caring.

● To check the ethical reasoning of a decision at any step in the decision-making process, it is helpful to ask the spotlight questions that expose the decision to transparency in the eyes of family, community members, and ethical role models.

FOR DISCUSSION **Do the steps in the decision-making process have to be followed in order?**

4 What are current issues in managerial decision making?

● Common decision errors and traps include the availability, representation, and anchoring and adjustment biases, as well as framing error, confirmation error, and escalating commitment.

● Creativity in decision making can be enhanced by the personal creativity drivers of individual creativity skills, task expertise, and motivation.

● Creativity in decision making can be enhanced by the situational creativity drivers of group creativity skills, management support, and organizational culture.

FOR DISCUSSION **Which decision trap seems most evident as an influence on bad choices made by business CEOs today?**

Self-Test

Multiple-Choice Questions

1. Among the ways information technology is changing organizations today, _____ is one of its most noteworthy characteristics.
   (a) eliminating need for top managers   (b) reducing information available for decision making   (c) breaking down barriers internally and externally   (d) decreasing need for environmental awareness

2. Information technology assists with the management function of organizing because it _____.
   (a) gives more timely access to information   (b) allows for more immediate measures of performance results   (c) allows for better coordination among individuals and groups   (d) makes it easier to communicate with diverse stakeholders

3. A manager who is reactive and works hard to address problems after they occur is known as a _____.
   (a) problem seeker   (b) problem avoider   (c) problem solver   (d) problem manager

4. A(n) _____ thinker approaches problems in a rational and an analytic fashion.
   (a) systematic   (b) intuitive   (c) internal   (d) external

5. The assigning of probabilities for action alternatives and their consequences indicates the presence of _____ in the decision environment.
   (a) certainty   (b) optimizing   (c) risk   (d) satisficing

6. The first step in the decision-making process is to _____.
   (a) identify alternatives   (b) evaluate results   (c) find and define the problem   (d) choose a solution

7. Being asked to develop a plan to increase international sales of a product is an example of the types of _____ problems that managers must be prepared to deal with.
   (a) routine   (b) unstructured   (c) crisis   (d) structured

8. Costs, timeliness, and _____ are among the recommended criteria for evaluating alternative courses of action.
   (a) ethical soundness   (b) competitiveness   (c) availability   (d) simplicity

9. A common mistake made by managers facing crisis situations is that they _____.
   (a) try to get too much information before responding   (b) rely too much on group decision making   (c) isolate themselves to make the decision alone   (d) forget to use their crisis management plan

10. The _____ decision model views managers as making optimizing decisions, whereas the _____ decision model views them as making satisficing decisions.

    (a) behavioral, human relations   (b) classical, behavioral   (c) heuristic, humanistic   (d) quantitative, behavioral

11. When a manager makes a decision about someone's annual pay raise only after looking at his or her current salary, the risk is that the decision will be biased because of _____.

    (a) a framing error   (b) escalating commitment   (c) anchoring and adjustment   (d) strategic opportunism

12. When a problem is addressed according to the positive or negative context in which it is presented, this is an example of _____.

    (a) framing error   (b) escalating commitment   (c) availability and adjustment   (d) strategic opportunism

13. Among the environments for managerial decision making, certainty is the most favorable, and it can be addressed through _____ decisions.

    (a) programmed   (b) risk   (c) satisficing   (d) intuitive

14. When a manager decides to continue pursuing a course of action that facts otherwise indicate is failing to deliver desired results, this is called _____.

    (a) strategic opportunism   (b) escalating commitment   (c) confirmation error   (d) the risky shift

15. Personal creativity drivers include creativity skills, task expertise, and _____.

    (a) emotional intelligence   (b) management support   (c) organizational culture   (d) task motivation

Short-Response Questions

16. What is the difference between an optimizing decision and a satisficing decision?

17. How can a manager double-check the ethics of a decision?

18. How would a manager use systematic thinking and intuitive thinking in problem solving?

19. How can the members of an organization be trained in crisis management?

Essay Question

20. As a participant in a new mentoring program between your university and a local high school, you have volunteered to give a presentation to a class of sophomores on the challenges in the new "electronic office." The goal is to sensitize them to developments in information technology and motivate them to take the best advantage of their high school academics so as to prepare themselves for the workplace of the future. What will you say to them?

Management Skills and Competencies

Self-Assessment

Back to Yourself: Self-Confidence

Managers are decision makers. And if they are to make consistently good decisions, they must be skilled at gathering and processing information. Managers are also implementers. Once decisions are made, they are expected to rally people and resources to put them into action. This is how problems actually get solved and opportunities get explored. In order for all this to happen, managers must have the **self-confidence** to turn decisions into action accomplishments; they must believe in their decisions and the information foundations for them. A good understanding of the many topics in this chapter can improve your decision-making skills. A better understanding of your personal style in gathering and processing information can also go a long way toward building your self-confidence as a decision maker. After you complete the following self-assessment on Cognitive Style, don't forget to go online for the Decision-Making Biases and Intuitive Ability self-assessments. They are opportunities to learn more about your decision-making strengths and weaknesses.

> Managers must have the **self-confidence** to believe in their decisions and take the actions needed to turn decisions into real accomplishments.

Further Reflection: Cognitive Style

Instructions

This assessment is designed to get an impression of your cognitive style based on the work of psychologist Carl Jung.[49] For each of the following 12 pairs, place a "1" next to the statement that best describes you. Do this for each pair, even though the description you choose may not be perfect.

1. (a) I prefer to learn from experience.
   (b) I prefer to find meanings in facts and how they fit together.
2. (a) I prefer to use my eyes, ears, and other senses to find out what is going on.
   (b) I prefer to use imagination to come up with new ways to do things.
3. (a) I prefer to use standard ways to deal with routine problems.
   (b) I prefer to use novel ways to deal with new problems.
4. (a) I prefer ideas and imagination.
   (b) I prefer methods and techniques.
5. (a) I am patient with details, but get impatient when they get complicated.
   (b) I am impatient and jump to conclusions, but I am also creative, imaginative, and inventive.
6. (a) I enjoy using skills already mastered more than learning new ones.
   (b) I like learning new skills more than practicing old ones.
7. (a) I prefer to decide things logically.
   (b) I prefer to decide things based on feelings and values.
8. (a) I like to be treated with justice and fairness.
   (b) I like to be praised and to please other people.
9. (a) I sometimes neglect or hurt other people's feelings without realizing it.
   (b) I am aware of other people's feelings.
10. (a) I give more attention to ideas and things than to human relationships.
    (b) I can predict how others will feel.
11. (a) I do not need harmony; arguments and conflicts don't bother me.
    (b) I value harmony and get upset by arguments and conflicts.
12. (a) I am often described as analytical, impersonal, unemotional, objective, critical, hard-nosed, rational.
    (b) I am often described as sympathetic, people-oriented, unorganized, uncritical, understanding, ethical.

Scoring

Sum your scores as follows, and record them in the parentheses. (Note that the *Sensing* and *Feeling* scores will be recorded as negatives.)

- (−   ) *Sensing (S Type)* 5 1a 1 2a 1 3a 1 4a 1 5a 1 6a
- (   ) *Intuitive (N Type)* 5 1b 1 2b 1 3b 1 4b 1 5b 1 6b
- (   ) *Thinking (T Type)* 5 7a 1 8a 1 9a 1 10a 1 11a 1 12a
- (−   ) *Feeling (F Type)* 5 7b 1 8b 1 9b 1 10b 1 11b 1 12b

Interpretation

This assessment contrasts personal tendencies toward information gathering (sensation vs. intuition) and information evaluation (feeling vs. thinking) in one's approach to problem solving. The result is a classification of four master cognitive styles and their characteristics. Read the descriptions provided in the chapter text and consider the implications of your suggested style, including how well you might work with persons whose styles are very different.

Team Exercise

Lost at Sea

Consider This Situation[50]

You are adrift on a private yacht in the South Pacific when a fire of unknown origin destroys the yacht and most of its contents. You and a small group of survivors are now in a large raft with oars. Your location is unclear, but you estimate that you are about 1,000 miles south-southwest of the nearest land. One person has just found in her pockets five $1 bills and a packet of matches. Everyone else's pockets are empty. The items below are available to you on the raft.

	Individual ranking	Team ranking	Expert ranking
Sextant			
Shaving mirror			
5 gallons water			
Mosquito netting			
1 survival meal			
Maps of Pacific Ocean			
Floatable seat cushion			
2 gallons oil-gas mix			
Small transistor radio			
Shark repellent			
20 square feet black plastic			
1 quart 20-proof rum			
15 feet nylon rope			
24 chocolate bars			
Fishing kit			

Instructions

1. *Working alone*, rank the 15 items in order of their importance to your survival ("1" is most important and "15" is least important).
2. *Working in an assigned group*, arrive at a "team" ranking of the 15 items. Appoint one person as team spokesperson to report your team ranking to the class.
3. *Do not write in Column C* until your instructor provides the "expert" ranking.

Case Study: Amazon

Go to *Management Cases for Critical Thinking* to find the recommended case for Chapter 7—"Amazon: One E-Store to Rule Them All."

Planning
Processes and
Techniques

Chapter 8 Study Questions

1 Why and how do managers plan?

2 What types of plans do managers use?

3 What are the useful planning tools and techniques?

4 How can plans be well implemented?

Learning From Others

Think Now and Embrace the Future

It's easy to get so engrossed in the present that we forget about the future. Yet a rush to the future can go off track without solid reference points in the past. The trick is to blend past experiences with future aspirations, and a willingness to adjust as new circumstances arise.

Oprah Winfrey is a media star, corporate executive, and popular personality. Having grown up poor, Oprah says that she is grateful for getting a good education, calling it "the most vital aspect of my life." She's sharing that lesson through the Oprah Winfrey Leadership Academy for young women in South Africa. At the opening ceremony she said: "I wanted to give this opportunity to girls who had a light so bright that not even poverty could dim that light." She also talked about her past, mentioning that she "was a poor girl who grew up with my grandmother, like so many of these girls, with no water and electricity." As to the goal, she stated that she wanted the new academy to "be the best school in the world."

Nelson Mandela, first president of non-apartheid South Africa, spoke at the opening ceremony and praised her vision. "The key to any country's future is in educating its youth," said Mandela. "Oprah is therefore not only investing in a few young individuals, but in the future of our country." One of the first students said: "I would have had a completely different life if this hadn't happened to me."

Yet even with the best intentions things don't always go according to plan. Not long after the academy launched, it was hit by scandal. One of the dorm matrons was arrested for abusing one of the students. Oprah apologized to the students and their families, and rededicated herself to the school. "I think that crisis is there to teach you about life," she said. "The school is going to be even better because that happened." And looking even further ahead, she hasn't stopped dreaming or planning—her intention is to build yet another school for both young men and women.[1]

do the benchmarking

"The best plans often go wrong." "The problem is with the details." We often hear these expressions. But Oprah's experience in South Africa also shows that you can make great things happen with good insight, the right plans, and proper controls. **Even when things don't go as intended, plans and their implementation can often be adjusted to achieve important goals.**

Learning About Yourself

Time Management

When it comes to planning, one of the first things that may come to mind is time. It is one of our most precious resources, and **time management** is an essential skill in today's high-pressure and fast-paced world. Some 77% of managers in one survey said that the new digital age has increased the number of decisions they have to make; 43% complained there was less time available to make them. Another report notes that interruptions steal 28% of the average worker's day.[2] And, who hasn't complained or heard others complaining about a need for more work-life balance?

Don't you wonder about the time you waste dealing with e-mail, instant messages, voice and text messages, drop-in visits from coworkers and friends, waiting on the phone for customer service, and more?

Of course, you have to be careful in defining "waste." It isn't a waste of time to occasionally relax, take a breather from work or daily affairs, and find humor and pleasure in social interactions. Such breaks help us gather and replenish energies to do well in our tasks. But it is a waste to let friends dominate your time so that you don't work on a term paper until it is too late to write a really good one, or delay a decision to apply for an internship until the deadline is passed.

> **Time Management Planner**
>
> *List 1—What I have to do tomorrow*
> - (A) Most important, top priority—these are things you *must* do.
> - (B) Important, not top priority—these are things you *should* do.
> - (C) Least important, low priority—these are things you *might* do.
> - (D) Not important, no priority—these are things you *should not* do.
>
> *List 2—Time wasters*
> - (A) Things I can control—they won't happen if I don't let them.
> - (B) Things I can't control—they happen and I can't do anything about it.

Perhaps you are one of those who plan to do so many things in a day that you never get to the most important ones. Perhaps you hardly plan, letting events take you where they may. And perhaps on many days you end up not accomplishing much at all.

Learning to better manage your time can serve you very well in the future, both at work and in your personal life. Take a step forward in time management. Complete the lists requested in the boxed time management planner. Double-check all the List 1 "B" items. Reclassify any that are really "As" or "Cs." Look at your "As" and reclassify any that are really "Bs" or "Cs." Also check your time wasters in List 2. Make a commitment to take charge of the controllables and see if you really could do something about items marked "uncontrollable."

get to know yourself better

One of the best ways to improve time management is to keep a daily time log for a day or two—listing what you do and how long it takes. Make such a log, and then analyze it to determine where you seem to be wasting time and where you are using it well. **Also make use of the end-of-chapter Self-Assessment feature to better understand your Time Management Profile and think further about your Time Management Skills.**

8 Planning Processes and Techniques

Study Question 1	Study Question 2	Study Question 3	Study Question 4
Why and How Managers Plan	**Types of Plans Used by Managers**	**Planning Tools and Techniques**	**Implementing Plans**
• Importance of planning • The planning process • Benefits of planning • Planning and time management	• Long-range and short-range plans • Strategic and tactical plans • Operational plans	• Forecasting • Contingency planning • Scenario planning • Benchmarking • Staff planners	• Goal setting • Goal alignment • Participation and involvement
Learning Check 1	**Learning Check 2**	**Learning Check 3**	**Learning Check 4**

anagers need the ability to look ahead, make good plans, and help themselves and others meet the challenges of the future. But it can be easy to get so engrossed in the present that we forget about what lies ahead. Other times a mad rush to the future can go off track due to all sorts of uncertainties and lack of familiar reference points. The trick is to blend the lessons of past experiences with future aspirations, and with a willingness to adapt as new circumstances arise.

As the opening example of Oprah's Leadership Academy shows, no one knows for sure what the future holds. The likelihood is that even the best of plans will have to be adjusted and changed at some point. Thus, we need the insight and courage to be flexible, and the discipline to stay focused on goals even as complications and problems arise.

WHY AND HOW MANAGERS PLAN

> **Planning** is the process of setting objectives and determining how to accomplish them.

In Chapter 1 the management process was described as planning, organizing, leading, and controlling the use of resources to achieve performance objectives. The first of these functions, **planning**, sets the stage for the others by providing a sense of direction. It is a process of setting objectives and determining how best to accomplish them. Said a bit differently, planning involves deciding exactly what you want to accomplish and how best to go about it.

IMPORTANCE OF PLANNING

When planning is done well it creates a solid platform for the other management functions: organizing—allocating and arranging resources to accomplish tasks; leading—guiding the efforts of human resources to ensure high levels of task accomplishment; and controlling—monitoring task accomplishments and taking necessary corrective action. This centrality of planning in management is shown in Figure 8.1. Especially in today's demanding organizational and career environments, good planning helps us become better at what we are doing and to stay action-oriented. An Eaton Corporation annual report, for example, once stated: "Planning at Eaton means making the hard decisions before events force them upon you, and anticipating the future needs of the market before the demand asserts itself."[3]

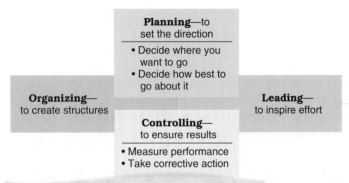

FIGURE 8.1 The roles of planning and controlling in the management process.

THE PLANNING PROCESS

Planning should focus attention on **objectives** and **goals** that identify the specific results or desired outcomes that one intends to achieve. But objectives and goals have to be good ones; they should push you to achieve substantial, not trivial, things. Jack Welch, former CEO of GE, believed in what he called **stretch goals**— performance targets that we have to work extra hard and really stretch to reach.[4] Would you agree that Welch's concept of stretch goals adds real strength to the planning process for both organizations and individuals?

It's important not to forget the action side of the planning process. It should always create a real and concrete **plan**, a statement of action steps to be taken in order to accomplish the objectives. And, planning should result in these plans being well implemented so that desired results are really accomplished.

Planning in the full sense of the responsibilities just described is an application of the decision-making process discussed in Chapter 7. The five basic steps in the planning process are:

1. *Define your objectives*—Identify desired outcomes or results in very specific ways. Know where you want to go; be specific enough that you will know you have arrived when you get there, or know how far off the mark you are at various points along the way.

2. *Determine where you stand vis-à-vis objectives*—Evaluate current accomplishments relative to the desired results. Know where you stand in reaching the objectives; know what strengths work in your favor and what weaknesses may hold you back.

3. *Develop premises regarding future conditions*—Anticipate future events. Generate alternative "scenarios" for what may happen; identify for each scenario things that may help or hinder progress toward your objectives.

4. *Analyze alternatives and make a plan*—List and evaluate possible actions. Choose the alternative most likely to accomplish your objectives; describe what must be done to follow the best course of action.

5. *Implement the plan and evaluate results*—Take action and carefully measure your progress toward objectives. Follow through by doing what the plan requires; evaluate results, take corrective action, and revise plans as needed.

The planning process probably seems simple and straightforward enough. But remember, planning is not something managers do while working alone in quiet rooms, free from distractions, and at scheduled times. It is an ongoing process, often continuously being done even while dealing with an otherwise busy and demanding work setting. And like other decision making in organizations, the best planning includes the active participation of those people whose work efforts will eventually determine whether or not the plans are well implemented.

- **Objectives** and **goals** are specific results that one wishes to achieve.

- **Stretch goals** are performance targets that we have to work extra hard and stretch to reach.

- A **plan** is a statement of intended means for accomplishing objectives.

Good Planning Helps Make Us

- *Priority oriented*—making sure the most important things get first attention;
- *Action oriented*—keeping a results-driven sense of direction;
- *Advantage oriented*—ensuring that all resources are used to best advantage;
- *Change oriented*—anticipating problems and opportunities so they can be best dealt with.

BENEFITS OF PLANNING

The pressures organizations face come from many sources. Externally, these include ethical expectations, government regulations, uncertainties of a global economy, changing technologies, and the sheer cost of investments in labor, capital, and other supporting resources. Internally, they include the quest for operating efficiencies, new structures and technologies, alternative work arrangements, greater workplace diversity, and concerns for work-life balance. As you would expect, planning in such conditions has a number of benefits for both organizations and individuals.

McDonald's President Sets Goals and Engineers a Winning Role

Some call Don Thompson, president and chief operating officer of McDonald's, the accidental executive. He's not only one of the youngest top managers in the Fortune 500, he also may have followed the most unusual career path.

After graduating from Purdue with a degree in electrical engineering, Thompson went to work for Northrop Grumman, a leading global security company. He did well, rose into engineering management, and one day received a call from a headhunter. Thompson listened, thinking the job being offered was at McDonnell Douglas (now owned by Boeing)—another engineering-centric firm. Upon finding out it was at McDonald's, he almost turned the opportunity down. But with encouragement, he took the interview and his career hasn't been the same since.

Thompson hit the ground running at McDonald's and did well, but became frustrated eventually when he failed to win the annual McDonald's president's award. He decided it might be time to move on. With the recommendation of the firm's diversity officer he spoke with Raymond Mines, at the time the firm's highest-ranking African American executive. When Thompson confided that he "wanted to have an impact on decisions," Mines told him to move out of engineering and into the operations side of the business. Thompson did and his work not only excelled, it got him the attention he needed to advance to ever-higher responsibilities that spanned restaurant operations, franchisee relations, and strategic management.

From his childhood on Chicago's South Side, Thompson rose to fill the president's chair at McDonald's world headquarters in Oak Brook, Illinois. He has a corner office, but no door; the building is configured with an open floor plan. And that fits well with Thompson's management style and personality. His former mentor Raymond Mines says: "he has the ability to listen, blend in, analyze and communicate. People feel at ease with him. A lot of corporate executives have little time for those below them. Don makes everyone a part of the process." As for Thompson, he says "I want to make sure others achieve their goals, just as I have."

Planning Improves Focus and Flexibility

Good planning improves focus and flexibility, both of which are important for performance success. An organization with focus knows what it does best, knows the needs of its customers, and knows how to serve them well. An individual with focus knows where he or she wants to go in a career or situation, and in life overall. An organization with flexibility is willing and able to change and adapt to shifting circumstances, and operates with an orientation toward the future rather than the past. An individual with flexibility adjusts career plans to fit new and developing opportunities.

Planning Improves Action Orientation

Planning is a way for people and organizations to stay ahead of the competition and become better at what they are doing. It keeps the future visible as a performance target and reminds us that the best decisions are often those made before events force problems upon us. Planning helps avoid the **complacency trap**—simply being carried along by the flow of events, and it directs our attention toward priorities. Management consultant Stephen R. Covey points out that the most successful executives "zero in on what they do that 'adds value' to an organization."[5] Instead of working on too many things, they work on the things that really count. Covey says that good planning makes managers more (1) results oriented—creating a performance-oriented sense of direction; (2) priority oriented—making sure the most important things get first attention; (3) advantage oriented—ensuring that all resources are used to best advantage; and (4) change oriented—anticipating problems and opportunities so they can be best dealt with.

● The **complacency trap** is being carried along by the flow of events.

⟋Planning Improves Coordination and Control

Planning improves coordination.[6] The different individuals, groups, and subsystems in organizations are each doing many different things at the same time. But their efforts must add up to meaningful contributions to the organization as a whole. Good plans help coordinate the activities of people and subsystems so that their combined accomplishments will advance performance for the organization.

When planning is done well it also facilitates control. The first step in the planning process—setting objectives and standards—is a prerequisite to effective control. The objectives set by planning make it easier to measure results and take action to improve things as necessary. In this way, planning and controlling work closely together in the management process. Without planning, control lacks objectives and standards for measuring how well things are going and what could be done to make them go better. Without control, planning lacks the follow-through needed to ensure that things work out as planned. With both, it's a lot easier to spot when things aren't going well and make the necessary adjustments. After launching a costly information technology upgrade, for example, executives at McDonald's realized that the system couldn't deliver on its promises. They stopped the project, took a loss of $170 million, and refocused the firm's plans and resources on projects with more direct impact on customers.[7]

x PLANNING AND TIME MANAGEMENT   ~calendar

Daniel Vasella is CEO of Novartis AG and responsible for operations spread across 140 countries. He's also calendar-bound. He says: "I'm locked in by meetings, travel and other constraints . . . I have to put down in priority things I like to do." Kathleen Murphy is CEO of ING US Wealth Management. She's also calendar-bound, with conferences and travel booked a year ahead. She schedules meetings at half-hour intervals, works 12-hour days, and spends 60% of her time traveling. She also makes good use of her time on planes. "No one can reach me by phone and I can get reading and thinking done."[8]

These are common executive stories—tight schedules, little time alone, lots of meetings and phone calls, and not much room for spontaneity. The keys to success in such classic management scenarios rest, in part at least, with another benefit of good planning—time management.

Management Smarts 8.1 offers useful tips on developing time management skills. And, a lot comes down to discipline and priorities. Lewis Platt, former chairman of Hewlett-Packard, once said: "Basically, the whole day is a series of choices."[9] These choices have to be made in ways that allocate your time to the most important priorities. Platt says that he was "ruthless about priorities" and that you "have to continually work to optimize your time."

Most of us have experienced the difficulties of balancing available time with our many commitments and opportunities. As suggested in the chapter opener, it is easy to lose track of time and fall prey to what consultants identify as "time wasters." All too often we allow our time to be dominated by other people or to be misspent on nonessential activities.[10] "To do" lists can help, but they have to contain the

Management Smarts 8.1

Personal time management tips

1. *Do* say "No" to requests that divert you from what you really should be doing.

2. *Don't* get bogged down in details that you can address later or leave for others.

3. *Do* have a system for screening telephone calls, e-mails, and requests for meetings.

4. *Don't let* drop-in visitors or instant messages use too much of your time.

5. *Do* prioritize what you will work on in terms of importance and urgency.

6. *Don't* become calendar-bound by letting others control your schedule.

7. *Do* follow priorities; work on the most important and urgent tasks first.

right things. In daily living and in management, it is important to distinguish between things that you must do (top priority), should do (high priority), would be nice to do (low priority), and really don't need to do (no priority).

TYPES OF PLANS USED BY MANAGERS

"I am the master of my fate: I am the captain of my soul." How often have you heard this phrase? The lines are from *Invictus*, written by British poet William Earnest Henley in 1875. He was sending a message, one of confidence and control, as he moved forward into the future. That notion, however, worries a scholar by the name of Richard Levin. His response to Henley is: "Not without a plan you're not."[11]

Managers use a variety of plans as they face different challenges in organizations. In some cases the planning environment is stable and quite predictable; in others, it is more dynamic and uncertain. Different needs call for different types of plans.

LONG-RANGE AND SHORT-RANGE PLANS

● **Long-term plans** typically look three or more years into the future.

● **Short-term plans** typically cover one year or less.

It used to be that **long-term plans** looked three or more years into the future, while **short-term plans** covered one year or less. But, the environmental turmoil of the past couple of years has put the concept of "long-term" planning to a stiff test. Would you agree that the complexities and uncertainties of today's environments challenge how we go about planning and how far ahead we can really plan? At the very least we can say that there is a lot less permanency to long-term plans today, and that they are subject to frequent revisions.

Even though the time frames of planning may be shrinking, top management is still responsible for setting longer-term plans and directions for the organization as a whole. They set the context for lower management to work on useful short-terms plans. And unless everyone understands an organization's long-term plans and objectives, there is always risk that the pressures of daily events will divert attention from important tasks. In other words, without a sense of long-term direction, people can end up working hard and still not achieve significant results. Auto industry executives know this only too well. Their firms are operating today in what used to be the far-off "future," and they have arrived here only to be in lots of trouble. Was it the inability to think long term that got them here, or was it an inability to anticipate, recognize, and adjust to changing events that led to their downfalls?

Management researcher Elliot Jaques suggests that people vary in their capability to think with different time horizons.[12] In fact, he believes that most people work comfortably with only 3-month time spans; a smaller group works well with a 1-year span; and only the very rare person can handle a 20-year time frame. These are provocative ideas and personally challenging. Although a team leader's planning may fall mainly in the weekly or monthly range, a chief executive is expected to have a vision extending years into the future. Career progress to higher management levels requires the conceptual skills to work well with longer-range time frames.

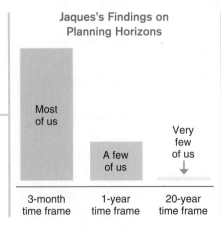

Jaques's Findings on Planning Horizons

Most of us

A few of us

Very few of us
↓

3-month time frame   1-year time frame   20-year time frame

STRATEGIC AND TACTICAL PLANS

Plans at the top of the traditional organizational pyramid, the ones senior executives deal mainly with, tend to be more "strategic." By contrast, middle and lower level managers deal with plans that are more "tactical."

Strategic Plans

When top managers plan for the organization as a whole or a major component, the focus is on **strategic plans**. These are longer-term plans that set broad directions for an organization and create a framework for allocating resources for maximum performance impact. Strategic planning is part of the strategic management process discussed in the next chapter. It begins with a **vision** that clarifies the mission or purpose of the organization and expresses what it hopes to be in the future, and it involves determining the goals and objectives that will be pursued in order to accomplish that vision.

> A **strategic plan** identifies long-term directions for the organization. *Broad + assets*
>
> A **vision** clarifies the purpose of the organization and expresses what it hopes to be in the future.

Even though strategic plans and visions are long term, they are also dynamic. Consider the example of Skype, which began as an entrepreneurial start-up founded by Niklas Zennstrom and Janus Friis. Their vision was to connect people through Internet telephony.[13] And, it wasn't their strategic plan to just start the company, move it fast, and sell quickly to the highest bidder. Says Zennstrom: "Our objective was to build the business." Once started, however, Skype quickly gained millions of users, became an acquisition target, and was bought by eBay for $2.6 billion. The deal was sealed after Zennstrom and Friis had a breakthrough meeting with eBay's CEO at the time, Meg Whitman. According to Zennstrom, it was an *Aha*! experience: "We went crazy on the whiteboard, mapping out ideas." But the realities of Skype's life within the eBay corporate umbrella didn't live up to the plan that brought the two firms together; the expected synergies didn't happen. When eBay finally sold the firm five years later at a loss, Skype's new private investors pledged to fulfill the founders' original vision by growing it again as an independent company dedicated to Internet telephony.

Tactical Plans

When a sports team enters a game or contest, it typically does so with a "strategy" in hand. Most often this strategy is set by the head coach in conjunction with assistants. The goal is clear: win the game or contest. As the game unfolds, however, situations arise that require actions to solve problems or exploit opportunities. They call for "tactics" that deal with a current situation in ways that advance the overall strategy for winning.

The same logic holds true for organizations. **Tactical plans** are developed and used to implement strategic plans. They specify how the organization's resources can be used to put strategies into action. In the sports context you might think of tactical plans as having "special teams" or as "special plays" ready to meet a particular threat or opportunity. In business, tactical plans often take the form of **functional plans** that indicate how different components of the enterprise will contribute to the overall strategy. Such functional plans might include:

> A **tactical plan** helps to implement all or parts of a strategic plan.
>
> **Functional plans** indicate how different operations within the organization will help advance the overall strategy.

- *Production plans*—dealing with work methods and technologies.
- *Financial plans*—dealing with money and capital investments.
- *Facilities plans*—dealing with facilities and work layouts.
- *Logistics plans*—dealing with suppliers and acquiring resource inputs.
- *Marketing plans*—dealing with selling and distributing goods or services.
- *Human resource plans*—dealing with building a talented workforce.

Research Brief

You've Got to Move Beyond Planning by the Calendar

Organizations today need executives who can make faster and better decisions, and that means strategic planning must be done continuously. Michael C. Mankins and Richard Steele, writing in the *Harvard Business Review*, express their concerns that planning is too often viewed as an annual activity focused more on documenting plans for the record than on action. Little wonder, they suggest, that only 11% of executives in a survey of 156 firms with sales of $1+ billion were highly satisfied that strategic planning is worthwhile.

The research, conducted in collaboration with Marakon Associates and the Economist Intelligence Unit, inquired as to how long-range strategic planning was conducted and how effective these planning activities were. Results showed that executives perceived a substantial disconnect between the way many firms approached strategic planning and the way they approached strategic decisions. Some 66% of the time, executives said that strategic planning at their firms was conducted only at set times, and very often was accomplished by a formal and structured process. Survey respondents also indicated that planning was often considered as only a "periodic event" and not something to be engaged in continuously. Mankins and Steele call such planning "calendar driven," and they question its effectiveness.

In calendar-driven planning, the researchers found that firms averaged only 2.5 major strategic decisions per year, with "major" meaning a decision that could move profits by more than 10%. They also point out that when planning is disconnected from the calendar, companies make higher-quality and more strategic decisions. The researchers call this alternative planning approach "continuous review" and argue it is more consistent with the way executives actually make decisions and business realities.

You Be the Researcher

Why is it that tying the planning process to certain calendar dates may be dysfunctional for a business? On the other hand, how can we plan almost continuously? Choose two or three organizations in your community for some field research. Arrange interviews with a senior executive at each. Find out if they plan on a set schedule and if so, what that schedule might be. Probe further to find out how effective they consider planning in their organization to be.

Planning and Decision Disconnects

Business Planning	*Executive Deciding*
66% – firms do strategic planning at set times	100% – executives make strategic decisions when needed
67% – planning done at business unit level	70% – executives make decisions issue-by-issue

Reference: Michael C. Mankins and Richard Steele, "Stop Making Plans; Start Making Decisions," *Harvard Business Review* (January 2006), reprint R0601F.

OPERATIONAL PLANS

● An **operational plan** identifies short-term activities to implement strategic plans.

Operational plans guide behavior and describe what needs to be done in the short term to support strategic and tactical plans. They include *standing plans* like policies and procedures that are used over and over again, and *single-use plans* like budgets that apply to one specific task or time period.

Policies and Procedures

● A **policy** is a standing plan that communicates broad guidelines for decisions and action.

A **policy** communicates broad guidelines for making decisions and taking action in specific circumstances. Organizations operate with lots of policies, and they set expectations for many aspects of employee behavior. Typical human resource policies cover things like employee hiring, termination, performance appraisals, pay increases, promotions, and discipline. For example, Judith Nitsch made sexual harassment a top priority when starting her engineering-consulting business.[14]

Office Romance Policies Vary

The former CEO of Boeing resigned after his relationship with a female executive became public. Just where do things stand when it comes to office romances? One survey shows employer policies on office relationships vary, with 4% prohibiting any such relationships, 24% prohibiting them among persons in the same department, 13% prohibiting them among persons who have the same supervisor, 80% prohibiting them between supervisors and subordinates, and 5% having no restrictions on office romances.

Nitsch defined a sexual harassment policy, took a hard line on its enforcement, and appointed both a male and a female employee for others to talk with about sexual harassment concerns.

Procedures describe rules for what actions are to be taken in specific situations. They are stated in employee handbooks and often called SOPs—standard operating procedures. Whereas a policy sets a broad guideline, procedures define precise actions to be taken. In the prior example, Judith Nitsch was right to establish a sexual harassment policy for her firm. But, she should also put into place procedures that ensure everyone receives fair, equal, and nondiscriminatory treatment under the policy. Everyone in her firm should know both how to file a sexual harassment complaint and just how that complaint will be handled.

● A **procedure** is a rule describing actions that are to be taken in specific situations.

Budgets

Budgets are single-use plans that commit resources for specific time periods to activities, projects, or programs. Managers typically spend a fair amount of time bargaining with higher levels to get adequate budgets to support the needs of their work units or teams. They are also expected to achieve work objectives while keeping within the allocated budget. To be "over budget" is generally bad; to come in "under budget" is generally good.

● A **budget** is a plan that commits resources to projects or activities.

Managers deal with and use a variety of budgets. *Financial budgets* project cash flows and expenditures; *operating budgets* plot anticipated sales or revenues against expenses; *nonmonetary budgets* allocate resources like labor, equipment, and space. A *fixed budget* allocates a stated amount of resources for a specific purpose, such as $50,000 for equipment purchases in a given year. A *flexible budget* allows resources to vary in proportion with various levels of activity, such as having extra money available to hire temporary workers when workloads exceed certain levels.

Because budgets link planned activities with the resources needed to accomplish them, they are useful for tracking and controlling performance. But budgets can get out of control, creeping higher and higher without getting sufficient critical attention. In fact, one of the most common budgeting problems is that resource allocations get "rolled over" from one time period to the next without a rigorous performance review; the new budget is simply an incremental adjustment to the previous one. In a major division of Campbell Soups, for example, managers once discovered that 10% of the marketing budget was going to sales promotions no longer relevant to current product lines. A **zero-based budget** deals with this problem by approaching each new budget period as it if were

● A **zero-based budget** allocates resources as if each budget were brand new.

brand new. In zero-based budgeting there is no guarantee that any past funding will be renewed; all proposals must compete for available funds at the start of each new budget cycle.

PLANNING TOOLS AND TECHNIQUES

The benefits of planning are best realized when the foundations are strong. Among the useful tools and techniques of managerial planning are forecasting, contingency planning, scenario planning, benchmarking, and the use of staff planners.

FORECASTING

Who would have predicted on New Year's Eve 2008 that in 2009 General Motors and Chrysler would declare bankruptcy; that the U.S. government would own large shares of both firms; that GM's Pontiac and Saturn brands would be discontinued; and, that China would become the largest car market in the world?[15] Who among us was prepared—individually and organizationally—for the recent financial crisis well before it actually hit? GE's CEO Jeffrey Immelt is frank about his failure in this regard. "I should have done more to anticipate the radical changes that occurred," he says.[16]

> **Forecasting** attempts to predict the future.

Planning in business and our personal lives often involves **forecasting**, the process of predicting what will happen in the future.[17] News media regularly report forecasts of economic conditions, interest rates, unemployment, trade deficits, and more. Some are based on *qualitative forecasting*, which uses expert opinions to predict the future. Others involve *quantitative forecasting*, which uses mathematical models and statistical analyses of historical data and surveys to predict future events.

Though useful, all forecasts should be treated cautiously. They are planning aids, not substitutes. It is said that a music agent once told Elvis Presley: "You ought to go back to driving a truck, because you ain't going nowhere." He was obviously mistaken, and that's the problem with forecasts. They rely on human judgment—and they can be wrong.

CONTINGENCY PLANNING

Picture the scene. A professional golfer is striding down the golf course with an iron in each hand. The one in her right hand is "the plan"; the one in her left is the "backup plan." Which club she uses will depend on how the ball lies on the fairway. One of her greatest strengths is being able to adjust to the situation by putting the right club to work in the circumstances at hand.

> **Contingency planning** identifies alternative courses of action to take when things go wrong.

Planning is often like that. By definition it involves thinking ahead. But the more uncertain the planning environment, the more likely that one's original forecasts and intentions may prove inadequate or wrong. The golfer deals with this by having backup clubs available. This amounts to **contingency planning**

Cola Wars Go Cross Cultural

Some American multinationals experienced backlash against their brands and products as a result of the Iraq War. Could Coca-Cola and Pepsi executives have anticipated the advent of new competitors like Mecca Cola and Qibla Cola that offered customers an alternative to the big U.S. brands? Qibla Cola was created by UK housewife Zahida Parveen to be "Muslim-friendly" and for customers wanting to "reject injustice and exploitation." The firm's CEO, Zafer Iqbal, once said: "The Qibla Cola Company is here to provide consumers from within the Muslim community and all people of conscience with a real alternative."

that identifies alternative courses of action that can be implemented if circumstances change. A really good contingency plan will even contain "trigger points" to indicate when to activate preselected alternatives. Given the uncertainties of our day, this is really an indispensable tool for managerial and personal planning.

The lack of adequate contingency planning was very much in the news when debates raged over the massive oil spill from a BP offshore well in the Gulf of Mexico. Everyone from the public at large to U.S. lawmakers to oil industry experts criticized BP not only for failing to contain the spill quickly, but also for failing to anticipate and have contingency plans in place to handle such a disaster. For its part, a BP spokesperson initially said: "You have here an unprecedented event . . . the unthinkable has become thinkable and the whole industry will be asking questions of itself." On the other hand, an industry expert responded: "There should be a technology that is pre-existing and ready to deploy at the drop of a hat . . . it shouldn't have to be designed and fabricated now, from scratch."

After experiencing the full brunt of the crisis, BP CEO Tony Hayward finally admitted: "There are some capabilities that we could have available to deploy instantly, rather than creating as we go."[18] The lesson here is hard-earned but very clear. Contingency planning can't prevent crises like this from occurring. But whenever acting in an environment of risk and uncertainty, it's essential to have good contingency plans available to help deal with crises if and when they do happen.

SCENARIO PLANNING

A long-term version of contingency planning, called **scenario planning**, involves identifying several alternative future scenarios or states of affairs that may occur. Plans are then made to deal with each scenario should it actually happen.[19]

Scenario planning typically involves discussions of both "worst case" and "best case" scenarios. A worst case scenario in respect to global resource planning, for example, is outright conflict where nations fight one another to secure increasingly scarce supplies of oil. A best case is where nations work together to find ways to meet current resource needs while supporting the sustainability of global resources. At Royal Dutch/Shell, scenario planning began years ago when top managers asked themselves: "What will Shell do after its oil supplies run out?" Although such planning can never be inclusive of all future possibilities, it can help executives to really think ahead and better prepare for "future shocks."[20]

● **Scenario planning** identifies alternative future scenarios and makes plans to deal with each.

What Really Works When Fighting World Poverty?

Developing countries send $100+ billion in aid to poor countries; private foundations and charities spend $70+billion more fighting poverty and its effects around the world. But, are these monies being well spent?

Not all of them, that's for sure. And that's a problem being tackled by the Poverty Action Lab at the Massachusetts Institute of Technology. The director, Abhijit Banerjee, a development economist, says: "We aren't really interested in the more-aid-less-aid debate. We're interested in seeing what works and what doesn't." The lab criticizes "feel good" evaluations and pushes for rigorous evaluations of poverty-fighting programs using scientific methods. Here's an example.

The Indian antipoverty group Seva Mandir was concerned about teacher absenteeism and low performance by rural school children. Its original plan was to pay extra tutors to assist teachers in 120 rural schools. The Poverty Lab Plan suggested paying extra tutors in 60 schools, making no changes in the

other 60, and then comparing outcomes to see if the plan worked. An evaluation of results showed no difference in children's performance, even with the higher costs of extra tutors.

A new plan was made to buy cameras for 60 teachers, have them take time/date-stamped photos with children at the start and end of each school day, and have the photos analyzed each month. Teachers would receive bonuses or fines based on their absenteeism and student performance. Again, no changes were made in the other 60 schools. Evaluation revealed that teacher absenteeism was 20% lower and student performance was significantly higher in the camera schools. With the Poverty Lab's help, Seva Mandir concluded that investing in closely monitored pay incentives could improve teacher attendance in rural schools.

You Decide

Look around your organization and at cases reported in the news. How often do we draw conclusions that "plans are working" based on feel-good evaluations or anecdotal reports rather than solid scientific evaluations? What are the consequences at work and in society when plans are implemented at great cost, but without defensible systems of evaluation? Even if the objectives of a project are honorable, what ethical issues arise in situations where it isn't clear that the project is having the intended benefit?

BENCHMARKING

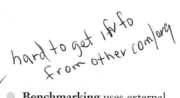

hard to get info to from other comp/org

● **Benchmarking** uses external and internal comparisons to plan for future improvements.

core pcompent

● **Best practices** are things people and organizations do that lead to superior performance.

Planners sometimes become too comfortable with the ways things are going and overconfident that the past is a good indicator of the future. It is often better to keep challenging the status quo and not simply accept things as they are. One way to do this is through **benchmarking**, or the use of external and internal comparisons to better evaluate one's current performance and identify possible ways to improve for the future.[21]

The purpose of benchmarking is to find out what other people and organizations are doing very well, and then plan how to incorporate these ideas into one's own operations. It is basically a way of learning from the successes of others. One benchmarking technique is to search for **best practices**—things people and organizations do that help them achieve superior performance.

Well-run organizations emphasize *internal benchmarking* that encourages members and work units to learn and improve by sharing one another's best practices. They also use *external benchmarking* to learn from competitors and non-competitors alike. Xerox, for example, has benchmarked L.L. Bean's warehousing and distribution methods, Ford's plant layouts, and American Express's billing and collections. Ford benchmarked BMW's 3 series because, says James D. Farley, Ford's global marketing head, "The ubiquity of the 3 series engenders trust in every part of the world, and its design always has a strong point of view."[22] And in the apparel industry, the Spanish retailer Zara has become a benchmark for excellence in "fast-fashion."[23] The firm's design and manufacturing systems allow it to get new fashions from

Plans Help Coach Adapt to Changing Times

The financial crisis and declining sales of Coach's high-end purses caused CEO Lew Frankfort to push top management to make better plans for how to adapt to changing times. "I've never worked harder," he says about the process of developing a new line that would maintain the firm's image while still being priced more affordably. The result was the more affordable Poppy collection and an increase of the number of bags that sell for under $300. Frankfort said that getting to the decision required a "mind shift" but that everyone also recognized that "the world will forever be different, and we need to acclimate ourselves."

design to stores in two weeks. Zara produces only in small batches that sell out and create impressions of scarcity. Shoppers know they have to buy now because an item will not be replaced. And if something doesn't sell at Zara, it's not a big problem; there wasn't a large stock of the item to begin with.

USE OF STAFF PLANNERS

As organizations grow, so do the planning challenges. Cisco Systems, for example, has been planning for quite some time that a lot of its growth will come from investments overseas. And it wasn't too long ago that China was the big target in Asia. It still is a big one, but when Cisco's planners analyzed their planning premises and projected future scenarios, India emerged as a strong competitor. It turns out that they found a lot to like about India: excellence in software design, need for Cisco's products, and weak local competition. They also found some major things to worry about in China, including a government favoring local companies and poor intellectual property protection.[24]

In many organizations, as with Cisco, staff planners are employed to help coordinate and energize planning. These specialists are experts in all steps of the planning process, as well as in the use of planning tools and techniques. They can help bring focus and expertise to a wide variety of planning tasks. But one risk is a tendency for a communication gap to develop between the staff planners and line managers. Unless everyone works closely together, the resulting plans may be based on poor information. Also, people may lack commitment to implement the plans, no matter how good they are.

Be sure you can ☑ define *forecasting, contingency planning, scenario planning,* and *benchmarking* ☑ explain the benefits of contingency planning and scenario planning ☑ describe pros and cons of using staff planners

Learning Check ☑
Study Question 3
What are some useful planning tools and techniques?

IMPLEMENTING PLANS TO ACHIEVE RESULTS

In a book entitled *Doing What Matters*, Jim Kilts, the former CEO of Gillette, quotes an old management adage: "In business, words are words, promises are promises, but only performance is reality."[25] The same applies to plans—plans, we might say, are words with promises attached. These promises are only fulfilled when plans are implemented so that their purposes are achieved. The implementation of plans is largely driven by solid management practices discussed throughout the rest of this book, from organizing to leading to controlling. But, the foundations for successful implementation begin with the processes of goal setting, goal alignment, and participation and involvement.

GOAL SETTING

In the dynamic and highly competitive technology industry, CEO T. J. Rodgers of Cypress Semiconductor Corp. values both performance goals and accountability. He supports a planning system where employees work with clear and quantified work goals that they help set. He believes this helps people find problems before they can interfere with performance. Says Rodgers: "Managers monitor the goals, look for problems, and expect people who fall behind to ask for help before they lose control of or damage a major project."[26]

Commitment to goals isn't unique among successful managers; in fact, it's standard practice. When Jim Kilts took over as CEO of Gillette he realized that the firm needed work.[27] In analyzing the situation, however, he was very disciplined in setting planning goals to deal with high priority problems. In respect to sales, Gillette's big brands were losing sales to competitors. Kilts made plans to *increase market shares* for these brands. In respect to earnings, the company had missed its estimates for 15 quarters in a row. Kilts made plans to *meet earnings estimates* and raise the company's stock price.

Although both Rodgers and Kilts make us aware of the importance of goal setting in management, they may make it look a bit too easy. The way goals are set can make a big difference in how well they do in pointing people in the right directions and inspiring them to work hard. One thing to remember is the importance of moving from having "no goals" or even just everyday run-of-the-mill "average goals" to having really "great goals"—goals that result in plans being successfully implemented. Great goals tend to have these characteristics.

1. *Specific*—clearly target key results and outcomes to be accomplished
2. *Timely*—linked to specific timetables and "due dates"
3. *Measurable*—described so results can be measured without ambiguity
4. *Challenging*—include a stretch factor that moves toward real gains
5. *Attainable*—although challenging, realistic and possible to achieve

GOAL ALIGNMENT

It is one thing to set great goals and make them part of a plan. It is quite another to make sure that goals and plans are well integrated across the many people, work units, and levels of an organization as a whole. Goals set everywhere in the organization should ideally help advance its overall mission or purpose. Yet, we sometimes work very hard to accomplish things that simply don't make much of a difference in organizational performance. This is why goal alignment is an important part of managerial planning.

Figure 8.2 shows how a **hierarchy of goals** or **hierarchy of objectives** helps with goal alignment. When such a hierarchy is well defined, the accomplishment of lower-level goals and objectives is the means to the accomplishment of higher-level

● In a **hierarchy of goals** or **hierarchy of objectives,** lower-level goals and objectives are means to accomplishing higher-level ones.

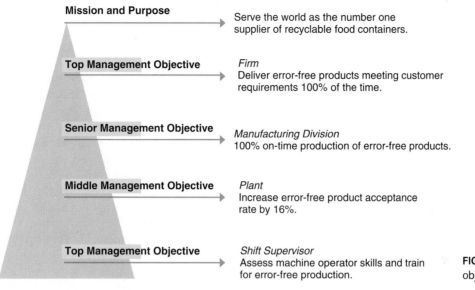

Mission and Purpose → Serve the world as the number one supplier of recyclable food containers.

Top Management Objective → *Firm* Deliver error-free products meeting customer requirements 100% of the time.

Senior Management Objective → *Manufacturing Division* 100% on-time production of error-free products.

Middle Management Objective → *Plant* Increase error-free product acceptance rate by 16%.

Top Management Objective → *Shift Supervisor* Assess machine operator skills and train for error-free production.

FIGURE 8.2 A sample hierarchy of objectives for quality management.

ones. The example in the figure is built around quality goals in a manufacturing setting. Strategic goals set by top management cascade down the organization step by step to become quality management objectives for lower levels. Ideally, everything works together in a consistent "means-end" fashion so that the organization, as stated in the figure, consistently performs as "the world's number one supplier of recyclable food containers."

Conversations between team leaders and team members or between supervisors and subordinates at each step in the hierarchy are essential to achieving the integration just described. Ideally, the conversations result in agreements on (1) performance objectives for a given time period, (2) plans through which they will be accomplished, (3) standards for measuring whether they have been accomplished, and (4) procedures for reviewing performance results. Sometimes this process is called *management by objectives* (MBO), but it is really just old-fashioned good management.[28]

As pointed out earlier, goal alignment conversations should focus on objectives that are specific, timely, measurable, challenging, and attainable. An example is the improvement objective for a team member "to reduce quality rejects by 10% within three months." Another is the personal development objective "to learn by April 15 the latest version of our supply chain management software package."

Goal Alignment Between Team Leader and Team Member

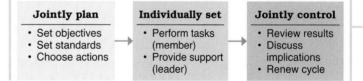

Jointly plan	Individually set	Jointly control
• Set objectives • Set standards • Choose actions	• Perform tasks (member) • Provide support (leader)	• Review results • Discuss implications • Renew cycle

One of the more difficult aspects of stating performance objectives is the need to make them as measurable as possible. Ideally, there is agreement on a *measurable end product*, for example, "to reduce travel expenses by 5% by the end of the fiscal year." But performance in some jobs, particularly managerial ones, can be hard to quantify. Rather than abandon the quest for a good objective in such cases, it is often possible to agree on *verifiable work activities*. Their accomplishment serves as an indicator of performance progress. An example is "to improve communications with my team in the next three months by holding weekly team meetings." Whereas it can be difficult to measure "improved communications," it is easy to document whether the "weekly team meetings" have been held.

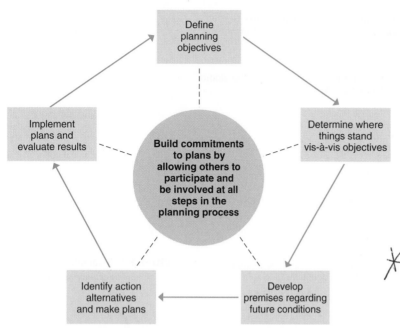

FIGURE 8.3 How participation and involvement help build commitment to plans.

● **Participatory planning** includes the persons who will be affected by plans and/or those who will implement them.

PARTICIPATION AND INVOLVEMENT

When 7-Eleven executives decided to offer new upscale products and services, such as selling fancy meals-to-go, they learned a planning lesson the hard way. Although their ideas sounded good at the top, franchise owners balked at the store level. The executives belatedly realized the value of taking time to involve the owners when making new plans for the stores.[29]

Planning is a process and not an event. And "participation" and "involvement" are two of its core components. **Participatory planning** includes in all planning steps the people who will be affected by the plans and asked to help implement them. One of the things that research is most clear about is that when people participate in setting goals they gain motivation to work hard to accomplish them.[30] Whether the planning is for a team, a large division, or the entire organization, involving people goes a long way toward gaining their commitments to work hard and support the implementation of plans.

This role of participation and involvement in the planning process is shown in Figure 8.3, and there are many benefits when and if it can be followed in practice. Participation can increase the creativity and information available for planning. It can also increase the understanding and acceptance of plans, as well as commitment to their success. And even though participatory planning takes more time, it can improve results by improving implementation.

☑ **Learning Check**

Study Question 4
How can plans be well implemented?

Be sure you can ☑ list the criteria of great goals   ☑ describe the value of a hierarchy of objectives   ☑ give examples of improvement and personal development objectives   ☑ explain how goal alignment can take place between a team leader and team members

Management **L**earning **R**eview

Study Questions Summary

1 Why and how do managers plan?

● Planning is the process of setting performance objectives and determining what should be done to accomplish them.

● A plan is a set of intended actions for accomplishing important goals and objectives.

● Five steps in the planning process are: (1) define your objectives, (2) determine where you stand vis-à-vis your objectives, (3) develop your premises regarding future conditions, (4) identify and choose among alternative ways of accomplishing objectives, and (5) implement action plans and evaluate results.

● The benefits of planning include better focus and flexibility, action orientation, coordination, control, and time management.

FOR DISCUSSION **Which step in the planning process is likely to cause the most difficulties for managers?**

2 What types of plans do managers use?

● Short-range plans tend to cover a year or less; long-range plans extend up to three years or more.

● Strategic plans set critical long-range directions; operational plans are designed to implement strategic plans.

- Policies, such as a sexual harassment policy, are plans that set guidelines for the behavior of organizational members.
- Procedures and rules are plans that describe actions to be taken in specific situations, such as the steps to be taken when persons believe they have been subjected to sexual harassment.
- Budgets are plans that allocate resources to activities or projects.

FOR DISCUSSION **Is there any real value to long-term planning in today's rapidly changing environment?**

3 What are the useful planning tools and techniques?

- Forecasting, which attempts to predict what might happen in the future, is a planning aid but not a planning substitute.
- Contingency planning identifies alternative courses of action that can be implemented if and when circumstances change.
- Scenario planning analyzes the implications of alternative versions of the future.
- Planning through benchmarking utilizes external and internal comparisons to identify best practices for possible adoption.

- Staff planners with special expertise are often used to assist in the planning process, but the risk is a lack of involvement by managers and others who must implement the plans.

FOR DISCUSSION **Shouldn't all plans be supported by contingency plans?**

4 How can plans be well implemented?

- Great goals are specific, timely, measurable, challenging, and attainable.
- A hierarchy of objectives helps to align goals from top to bottom in organizations.
- Goal alignment is facilitated by a participative process that clarifies performance objectives for individuals and teams, and identifies support that can and should be provided by managers.
- Participation and involvement open the planning process to valuable inputs from people whose efforts are essential to the effective implementation of plans.

FOR DISCUSSION **Given its potential advantages, why isn't goal alignment a characteristic of all organizations?**

Self-Test

Multiple-Choice Questions

1. Planning is the process of _____ and _____.
   (a) developing premises about the future, evaluating them   (b) measuring results, taking corrective action   (c) measuring past performance, targeting future performance   (d) setting objectives, deciding how to accomplish them

2. The benefits of planning include _____.
   (a) improved focus   (b) lower labor costs   (c) more accurate forecasts   (d) guaranteed profits

3. In order to implement its strategy, a business firm would likely develop a (an) _____ plan for the marketing department.
   (a) functional   (b) single-use   (c) production   (d) zero-based

4. _____ planning identifies alternative courses of action that can be taken if and when certain situations arise.
   (a) Zero-based   (b) Participative   (c) Strategic   (d) Contingency

5. The first step in the control process is to_____.
   (a) measure actual performance   (b) establish objectives and standards   (c) compare results with objectives   (d) take corrective action

6. A sexual harassment policy is an example of _____ plans used by organizations.
   (a) long-range   (b) single-use   (c) standing-use   (d) operational

7. When a manager is asked to justify a new budget proposal on the basis of projected activities rather than past practices, this is an example of _____ budgeting.
   (a) zero-based   (b) variable   (c) fixed   (d) contingency

8. One of the benefits of participatory planning is _____.
   (a) reduced time for planning   (b) less need for forecasting   (c) greater attention to contingencies   (d) more commitment to implementation

9. In a hierarchy of objectives, the ideal situation is that plans set at lower levels become the _____ for accomplishing higher-level plans.
   (a) means   (b) ends   (c) scenarios   (d) benchmarks

10. When managers use the benchmarking approach to planning, they _____.
    (a) use flexible budgets   (b) identify best practices used by others   (c) are seeking the most accurate forecasts that are available   (d) focus more on the short term than the long term

11. One of the problems in relying too much on staff planners is _____.
(a) a communication gap between planners and implementers   (b) lack of expertise in the planning process   (c) short-term rather than long-term focus   (d) neglect of budgets as links between resources and activities

12. The planning process isn't complete until _____.
(a) future conditions have been identified   (b) stretch goals have been set   (c) plans are implemented and results evaluated   (d) budgets commit resources to plans

13. Who should set an individual's performance objectives?
(a) the job holder   (b) the job holder's supervisor   (c) the job holder and the supervisor   (d) the job holder, the supervisor, and a lawyer

14. A good performance objective is written in such a way that it _____.
(a) has no precise timetable   (b) is general and not too specific   (c) is almost impossible to accomplish   (d) can be easily measured

15. Which type of plan most directly links resource allocations with long-term advancement of the organization's mission or purpose?
(a) tactical   (b) operational   (c) strategic   (d) functional

Short-Response Questions

16. List five steps in the planning process and give examples of each.
17. How might planning through benchmarking be used by the owner of a local bookstore?
18. How does planning help to improve focus?
19. Why does participatory planning facilitate implementation?

Essay Question

20. Put yourself in the position of a management trainer. You have been asked to make a short presentation to the local Small Business Enterprise Association at its biweekly luncheon. The topic you are to speak on is "How Each of You Can Use Objectives to Achieve Better Planning and Control." What will you tell them and why?

Management Skills and Competencies

Self-Assessment

Back to Yourself: Time Management

Time management is consistently rated one of the top "must-have" skills for new graduates entering fast-paced and complicated careers in business and management. As suggested in the chapter opener, many, perhaps most, of us keep To Do lists. But it's the rare person who is consistently successful in living up to one. Time management is a form of planning, and planning can easily suffer the same fate as the To Do lists—put together with the best of intentions, but with little or nothing to show as results at the end of the day. There were a lot of good ideas in this chapter on how to plan, both in management and in our personal lives. Now is a good time to get in touch with your time management skills and to start improving your capabilities to excel with planning as a key management function. After you complete the following self-assessment on your Time Management Profile, don't forget to go online for the Turbulence Tolerance Test to explore your comfort zones in challenging planning situations.

> **Time management** is a form of planning, and it is a must-have skill for those entering today's fast-paced careers.

Further Reflection: Time Management Profile

Instructions

Complete the following questionnaire by indicating "Y" (yes) or "N" (no) for each item. Be frank and allow your responses to create an accurate picture of how you tend to respond to these kinds of situations.

1. When confronted with several items of urgency and importance, I tend to do the easiest first.
2. I do the most important things during that part of the day when I know I perform best.

3. Most of the time I don't do things someone else can do; I delegate this type of work to others.
4. Even though meetings without a clear and useful purpose upset me, I put up with them.
5. I skim documents before reading and don't finish any that offer little value for my time.
6. I don't worry much if I don't accomplish at least one significant task each day.
7. I save the most trivial tasks for that time of day when my creative energy is lowest.
8. My workspace is neat and organized.
9. My office door is always "open"; I never work in complete privacy.
10. I schedule my time completely from start to finish every workday.
11. I don't like "to do" lists, preferring to respond to daily events as they occur.
12. I "block" out a certain amount of time each day or week that is dedicated to high-priority activities.

Scoring

Count the number of "Y" responses to items 2, 3, 5, 7, 8, 12. Enter that score here [   ]. Count the number of "N" responses to items 1, 4, 6, 9, 10, 11. Enter that score here [   ]. Add the two scores together here [   ].

Interpretation

The higher the total score, the closer your behavior matches recommended time management guidelines. Reread those items where your response did not match the desired one. Why don't they match? Do you have reasons why your behavior in this instance should be different from the recommended time management guideline? Think about what you can do to adjust your behavior to be more consistent with these guidelines.

Team Exercise

Personal Career Planning

Preparation

Complete the following activities and bring the results to class. Your work should be in a written form suitable for grading.

Activity 1 Strengths and Weaknesses Inventory   Different occupations require special talents, abilities, and skills. Each of us, you included, has a repertoire of existing strengths and weaknesses that are "raw materials" we presently offer a potential employer. Actions can (and should!) be taken over time to further develop current strengths and to turn weaknesses into strengths. Make a list identifying your most important strengths and weaknesses in relation to the career direction you are likely to pursue upon graduation. Place a * next to each item you consider most important to focus on for continued personal development.

Activity 2 Five-Year Career Objectives   Make a list of three career objectives that you hope to accomplish within five years of graduation. Be sure they are appropriate given your list of personal strengths and weaknesses.

Activity 3 Five-Year Career Action Plans   Write a specific action plan for accomplishing each of the five objectives. State exactly what you will do, and by when, in order to meet each objective. If you will need special support or assistance, identify it and state how you will obtain it. An outside observer should be able to read your action plan for each objective and end up feeling confident that he or she knows exactly what you are going to do and why.

Instructions

Form into groups as assigned by the instructor. Share your personal career-planning analysis with the group and listen to the analyses of others. Participate in a discussion that examines any common patterns and major differences among group members. Take advantage of any opportunities to gather feedback and advice from others. Have one group member be prepared to summarize the group discussion for the class as a whole.

Case Study: Land's End

Go to *Management Cases for Critical Thinking* to find the recommended case for Chapter 8— "Lands' End: Living the Golden Rule."

Strategy and Strategic Management

9

Chapter 9 Study Questions

1 What is strategic management?

2 What are the essentials of strategic analysis?

3 What are corporate-level strategies, and how are they formulated?

4 What are business-level strategies, and how are they formulated?

5 What are the foundations for strategy implementation?

Get and Stay Ahead With Strategy

When Disney's CEO Robert A. Iger announced that the firm was paying $4 billion to buy Marvel Entertainment, everyone from moviegoers to superhero lovers to financial analysts debated the move. Not everyone thought it was a good idea. But, Disney's chief financial officer at the time, Tom Staggs, said: "Marvel is worth more inside Disney than outside Disney."[1]

Under Iger's leadership, Disney has grown as an entertainment conglomerate. Steven Spielberg's DreamWorks, Steve Jobs's animation brainchild Pixar Studios, and now Marvel Entertainment are all in the Disney stable. It's "pure genius," claims Rick Sands, former chief operating officer of MGM. But it's also a lot to manage if the growth strategy is to succeed.

Each aspect of Disney has its own brand identity and customers, and each has unique management challenges. Iger tries to balance strategic control with strategic autonomy. He lets top executives of the major brands and divisions make their own decisions while taking advantage of corporate resources in areas such as marketing, which is a major and an increasingly expensive area.

As to the Marvel question, Disney's size and experience give it lots of power in turning brands and characters into moneymakers. Being part of Disney unlocks access to resources that can turn comic book heroes like Spider-Man and X-Men into brand legacies. Smaller players have a hard time matching such marketing muscle.

As for the strategic plan, Iger wants to leverage the Marvel brand through alliances with other Disney divisions. He also wants to access Marvel's younger demographic and tap their interests with Disney movies, toys, apparel, and video games.

do the benchmarking

Sure Disney has done well in the past. But is this a marriage that will last? Will this strategy create the blowout successes that Iger anticipates? **Behind every strategy is the need for great execution, and even the best strategies deliver high-performance results only when they are well implemented.**

Learning About Yourself

Critical Thinking

Strategic management such as described in the prior case of Disney is one of the most significant planning challenges faced by managers. It requires them to deal with an array of forces while trying to move an organization forward with success in situations that often involve lots of complexities and uncertainties. This is just one example of why **critical thinking** skills are so important. They represent an ability to gather, organize, analyze, and interpret information to make good decisions in the many problem and opportunity situations we face.

With all the uncertainties that exist today, we rarely have the luxury of making decisions with full information that is boxed up to digest and analyze in a nice neat format. So, just how good are you at making critical connections in unusual situations? Take a stab at these two puzzles. Get help from a friend if you have trouble finding the solutions.[2]

A good way to develop critical thinking skills is through case studies and problem-solving projects in your courses. But beware—one of the risks of our information-rich environment is overreliance on what we hear or read, especially when it comes from the Web. A lot of what circulates is anecdotal, superficial, irrelevant, and even just plain inaccurate. You must be disciplined, cautious, and discerning in interpreting the credibility and usefulness of information.

Whether you are searching the Web, talking with others, listening to presentations, or browsing reports and other information sources, critical thinking demands more than the ability to read and hear. Accessing information is one thing; sorting through it to identify what is solid and what is weak or pure nonsense is quite another. Also, determining what information is useful in a specific problem context is one thing; analyzing and integrating that information to make it useful for solid problem solving is yet another. Once you understand this and are willing to invest the time for critical thinking, the returns can be great.

Puzzle 1
Divide this shape into four shapes that are exactly the same size as one another.

Puzzle 2
Draw no more than four lines that cross all nine dots; don't lift your pencil while drawing.

get to know yourself better

Sometimes careers can be a lot like puzzles; everything looks pretty easy until you get down to the task. Is your personal career strategy well attuned to the future job market, not just the present one? Are you showing strong critical thinking skills as you make academic choices and prepare for your career? Make a list of information you need to best make solid career choices. Identify where you can obtain this information and how credible the sources might be. Write a short plan that uses this information and commits you to activities in this academic year that can improve your career readiness. **Also take advantage of the end-of-chapter Self-Assessment feature to further reflect on your Intuitive Ability.**

Study Question 1	Study Question 2	Study Question 3	Study Question 4	Study Question 5
Strategic Management	**Foundations of Strategic Analysis**	**Corporate-Level Strategy Formulation**	**Business-Level Strategy Formulation**	**Strategy Implementation**
• Competitive advantage • Strategy and strategic intent • Levels of strategy • Strategic management process	• Analysis of mission, values, objectives • SWOT analysis of organization and environment • Five forces analysis of industry attractiveness	• Portfolio planning model • Growth and diversification strategies • Retrenchment and restructuring strategies • Global strategies • Cooperation strategies	• Competitive strategies model • Differentiation strategy • Cost leadership strategy • Focus strategy	• Management practices and systems • Corporate governance • Strategic control • Strategic leadership
Learning Check 1	**Learning Check 2**	**Learning Check 3**	**Learning Check 4**	**Learning Check 5**

Set the opening story on Disney aside for a moment and switch to another global name—Wal-Mart. Its master plan is elegant in its simplicity: to attract customers by delivering consistently low prices and high-quality customer service.[3] This plan is supported by use of the latest technology and sophisticated logistics; inventories are monitored around the clock; world-class distribution ensures that stores are rarely out of the items customers are seeking; all systems and people are rallied to deliver on the objectives—low prices and quality service. At least, that's the plan.

As with Disney, times keep changing and Wal-Mart can't rest on past laurels. It's been challenged on everything from its wage levels to employee benefits, to its impact on competition in local communities, to the sustainability of its low-price business model, to the clutter and lack of attractiveness of its stores. Not too long ago, Wal-Mart's competitors were consistently asking: "How can we keep up?" Now Target has become not just a competitor, but a copy-cat nemesis that offers low prices, supersize stores, and even groceries.[4] And then there's Amazon.com and the threat it poses to Wal-Mart's push to become the nation's dominant web retailer.[5]

Even though sticking with its master plan, Wal-Mart is constantly making adjustments to stay in tune with economic trends, customer tastes, and the challenges of competition.[6] Among conversations in Wal-Mart's Barksdale, Arkansas, headquarters, you're likely to hear the strategists asking: "Are we still ahead, and if so, how can we stay ahead?"

STRATEGIC MANAGEMENT

The forces and challenges evident in the opening examples confront managers in all organizations and industries. The result is that today's management environment places a great premium on "competitive advantage" and how it is achieved, or not, through "strategy" and "strategic management."[7] And, the issues to be addressed in today's complex world of business relate to many of the themes discussed so far in this book, from productivity to innovation to sustainability and beyond.

COMPETITIVE ADVANTAGE

One of Wal-Mart's major strengths is its ability to cut costs, or "drive them out of the system," as its CEO says. The retailer makes aggressive use of the latest computer technologies to gain efficiencies in its supply chains, track sales, and quickly adjust orders and inventories to match buying trends. This is all part of Wal-Mart's quest for **competitive advantage**, operating with a combination of attributes that allow it to outperform rivals. You should remember this term from earlier chapters. It is an ability to use resources so well that the organization performs better than the competition. Typical sources of competitive advantage are:[8]

- *Cost and quality*—operating with greater efficiency and product or service quality.
- *Knowledge and speed*—doing better at innovation and speed of delivery to market for new ideas.
- *Barriers to entry*—creating a market stronghold that is protected from entry by others.
- *Financial resources*—having better investments or loss absorption potential than competitors.

Finding and holding on to competitive advantage is a stiff challenge. Even as organizations do things very well, rivals try to duplicate and copy the success stories. Thus, the goal becomes creating **sustainable competitive advantage**. This is a competitive advantage that is durable and difficult or costly for others to copy or imitate. It's a major concern for top managers. Not even Google, the undisputed king of search and click advertising, can rest on its laurels. The Googlers are constantly reassessing and innovating to stay ahead. Udi Manber, vice president of engineering and head of Google's search quality group says, "My worry is we could be stuck on top of a hill and it's not the right hill."[9]

> **Competitive advantage** is the ability to do something so well that one outperforms competitors.

> **Sustainable competitive advantage** is the ability to outperform rivals in ways that are difficult or costly to imitate.

STRATEGY AND STRATEGIC INTENT

If sustainable competitive advantage is the goal, "strategy" is the means to its achievement.[10] A **strategy** is a comprehensive action plan that identifies the long-term direction for an organization and guides resource utilization to achieve sustainable competitive advantage. It is a "best guess" about what must be done for future success in the face of rivalry and changing conditions. *Fast Company* magazine once said: "If you want to make a difference as a leader, you've got to make time for strategy."[11]

Everything happens so fast today that the life cycle of a strategy is becoming ever shorter. As it does, the challenges to the strategist become even greater. It used to be that companies could count on traditional "build-and-sell" business models that largely put them in control of their markets and made strategies long lasting. In the early days of the automobile industry Henry Ford once said: "The customer can have any color he wants as long as it's black." His firm, quite literally, was in the driver's seat. But that was yesterday. Today's executives must come up with strategies that are driven by customers and economic realities. Stephen Haeckel, former director of strategic studies at IBM's Advanced Business Institute, describes the shift in strategic thinking this way: "It's a difference between a bus, which follows a set route, and a taxi, which goes where customers tell it to go."[12]

Just as with our personal resources, organizational resources such as time, money, and people can sometimes get wasted on things that don't really add up to much value. A strategy helps ensure that resources are used with consistent **strategic intent**, that is, with all energies directed toward accomplishing a long-term

> **A strategy** is a comprehensive plan guiding resource allocation to achieve long-term organization goals.

> **Strategic intent** focuses and applies organizational energies on a unifying and compelling goal.

target or goal.[13] At Coca-Cola, for example, strategic intent has been described as "to put a Coke within 'arm's reach' of every consumer in the world." Given this intent we would not expect to find Coca-Cola investing in snack and convenience foods, as does its archrival PepsiCo. Yet such investments are consistent with Pepsi's strategic intent of being "the world's premier consumer products company focused on convenient food and beverages."[14]

LEVELS OF STRATEGIES

Three levels of strategy can be found in most organizations. Shown in Figure 9.1, they are corporate-level strategy, business-level strategy, and functional strategy.

Corporate-Level Strategy

> A **corporate strategy** sets long-term direction for the total enterprise.

The level of **corporate strategy** directs the organization as a whole toward sustainable competitive advantage. It describes the scope of operations by answering this *corporate-level strategic question*: "In what industries and markets should we compete?"

The purpose of corporate strategy is to set direction and guide resource allocations for the entire enterprise. In large, complex organizations, it identifies how to compete across multiple industries and markets. General Electric, for example, owns over 100 businesses in a wide variety of areas, including aircraft engines, appliances, capital services, medical systems, broadcasting, and power systems. Typical strategic decisions for GE at the corporate level relate to things like acquisitions, expansions, and cutbacks across this complex portfolio.

Business-Level Strategy

> A **business strategy** identifies how a division or strategic business unit will compete in its product or service domain.

Business strategy is the strategy for a single business unit or product line. It involves asking and answering this *business-level strategic question*: "How are we going to compete for customers in this industry and market?"

Typical business strategy decisions include choices about product and service mix, facilities locations, new technologies, and the like. In single-product enterprises, business strategy is the corporate strategy. But in large conglomerates such as General Electric, a variety of business strategies will be followed. The term *strategic business unit* (SBU) is often used to describe a business firm that is part of a larger enterprise. Whereas the enterprise on a whole will have a corporate strategy, each SBU will have its own business strategy.

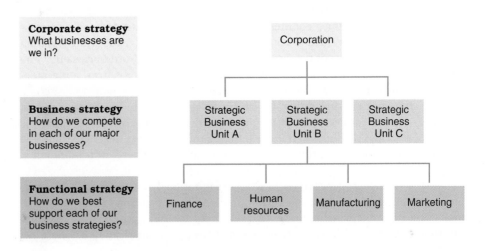

FIGURE 9.1 Three levels of strategy in organizations—corporate, business, and functional strategies.

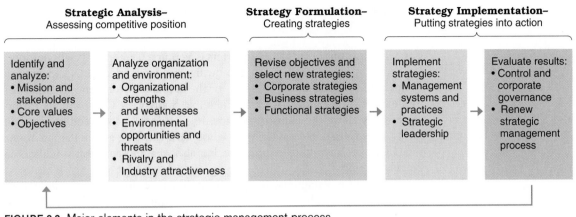

FIGURE 9.2 Major elements in the strategic management process.

Functional Strategy

Functional strategy guides the use of organizational resources to implement business strategy. This level of strategy focuses on activities within a specific functional area such as marketing, manufacturing, finance, or human resources. The *functional-level strategic question* is: "How can we best utilize resources within a function to implement our business strategy?" Answers to this question typically involve the choice of management practices to improve things like operating efficiency, product quality, customer service, or innovativeness.

✝ A **functional strategy** guides activities within one specific area of operations.

THE STRATEGIC MANAGEMENT PROCESS

Developing strategy for a business may seem a deceptively simple task: find out what customers want, provide it for them at the best prices and service, and make sure competitors can't copy what you are doing well. In practice, things can get very complicated.[15] The reality is that strategies don't just happen; they must be developed and then be well implemented. And at the same time that managers in one organization are doing all this, their competitors are trying to do the same—only better.

Strategic management is the process of formulating and implementing strategies to accomplish long-term goals and sustain competitive advantage. You can think of it as making decisions that allocate an organization's resources so as to consistently outperform rivals. As shown in Figure 9.2, the process begins with **strategic analysis** to assess the organization, its environment, its competitive positioning, and its current strategies. Next comes **strategy formulation**, the process of developing a new or revised strategy. The final phase is **strategy implementation**, using resources to put strategies into action, and then evaluating results so that the implementation can be improved or the strategy itself changed. As the late management consultant and guru Peter Drucker once said: "The future will not just happen if one wishes hard enough. It requires decision—now. It imposes risk—now. It requires action—now. It demands allocation of resources, and above all, it requires work—now."[16]

● **Strategic management** is the process of formulating and implementing strategies.

● **Strategic analysis** is the process of analyzing the organization, the environment, and the organization's competitive position and current strategies.

● **Strategy formulation** is the process of crafting strategies to guide the allocation of resources.

● **Strategy implementation** is the process of putting strategies into action.

ESSENTIALS OF STRATEGIC ANALYSIS

Can you name this firm? Its headquarters is Ventura, California. It sells outdoor clothing and gear, and its products are top-quality and high-priced. It is known for a commitment to sustainability and respect for the natural environment. Its larger competitors include The North Face and Columbia Sportswear Company. Its earnings are consistently above the industry average. Its workforce is loyal and inspired, and you are as likely to find its founder Yvon Chouinard climbing a mountain in Yosemite or the Himalayas as working in the office. It is also what most analysts would call a strategic success story.[17]

The firm is Patagonia. Keep it in mind as we now examine the essentials of strategic analysis. Think too about this set of questions that Peter Drucker often asked of his clients when consulting with them about strategic management: (1) What is your business mission? (2) Who are your customers? (3) What do your customers value? (4) What have been your results? (5) What is your plan?[18]

ANALYSIS OF MISSION, VALUES, AND OBJECTIVES

The strategic management process begins with a strategic analysis of mission, values, and objectives. This sets the stage for assessing the organization's resources and capabilities, as well as competitive opportunities and threats in its external environment.

Mission and Stakeholders

A statement of **mission** expresses the organization's reason for existence in society.

As first discussed in Chapter 1, the **mission** or purpose of an organization describes its reason for existence in society.[19] Strategy consultant Michael Hammer believes that a mission should represent what the strategy or underlying business model is trying to accomplish. To clarify mission he suggests asking: "What are we moving to?" "What is our dream?" "What kind of a difference do we want to make in the world?" "What do we want to be known for?"[20] For example, Starbucks's mission is to be "the premier purveyor of the finest coffee in the world, while maintaining our uncompromising principles as we grow." At Mary Kay, Inc., the mission is "to enrich women's lives." The mission of the American Red Cross is to "provide relief to victims of disasters and help people prevent, prepare for, and respond to emergencies."

The mission at Patagonia is to "Build the best product, cause no unnecessary harm, use business to inspire and implement solutions to the environmental

Patagonia Values Wild and Beautiful Places

Patagonia's mission is to "build the best product, cause no unnecessary harm, use business to inspire and implement solutions to the environmental crisis." The firm's values are evidenced in statements like these from the corporate website: "We know that our business activity–from lighting stores to dyeing shirts–creates pollution as a by-product. So we work steadily to reduce those harms" and "For us at Patagonia, a love of wild and beautiful places demands participation in the fight to save them."

FIGURE 9.3 External stakeholders as strategic constituencies in an organization's mission statement.

crisis."[21] In this mission one finds not only a business direction but also a distinctive value commitment, one that gives Patagonia a unique identity as it competes with much larger rivals in its industry. Such a clear sense of mission helps managers inspire the support and respect of an organization's **stakeholders**. You should recall that these are individuals and groups—including customers, shareholders, employees, suppliers, creditors, community groups, and others—who are directly affected by the organization and its accomplishments. Figure 9.3 gives an example of how stakeholder interests can be linked with the mission of a business firm.

Stakeholders are individuals and groups directly affected by the organization and its strategic accomplishments.

Core Values

In the strategic management process, core values and the organizational culture should be analyzed to determine how well they align with and support the organization's mission.[22] **Core values** are broad beliefs about what is or is not appropriate behavior. Patagonia founder and chairman Yvon Chouinard says: "Most people want to do good things, but don't. At Patagonia it's an essential part of your life."[23] He leads Patagonia with a personal commitment to sustainability and expects the firm to live up to his values. You should find, for example, that Patagonia's clothes use only organic rather than pesticide-intensive cotton."[24]

Core values are broad beliefs about what is or is not appropriate behavior.

The presence of strong core values helps build a clear organizational identity and give it a sense of character as seen through the eyes of its employees and external stakeholders. This character is part of what we call the **organizational culture** or predominant value system of the organization as a whole.[25] The organizational culture helps back up the mission by guiding the behavior of organization members in ways consistent with core values. When browsing Patagonia's Web site for job openings, for example, the message about the corporate culture is clear: "We're especially interested in people who share our love of the outdoors, our passion for quality, and our desire to make a difference."[26]

How to Turn Passion into Profit

"I have an M.B.A. Theory of Management: Management by Absence. I take off for weeks at a time and never call in. We hire the best people we can and then leave them to do their jobs."–Yves Chouinard

Organizational culture is the predominant value system for the organization as a whole.

Objectives

Whereas a mission statement sets forth an organization's purpose and core values establish standards for accomplishing it, **operating objectives** direct activities toward key performance areas. Typical operating objectives of a business include the following.[27]

Operating objectives are specific results that organizations try to accomplish.

- *Profitability*—operating with a net profit.
- *Financial health*—acquiring capital; earning positive returns.

- *Cost efficiency*—using resources well to operate at low cost.
- *Customer service*—meeting customer needs and maintaining loyalty.
- *Product quality*—producing high-quality goods or services.
- *Market share*—gaining a specific share of possible customers.
- *Human talent*—recruiting and maintaining a high-quality workforce.
- *Innovation*—developing new products and processes.
- *Social responsibility*—making a positive contribution to society.

Well chosen operating objectives turn a broad sense of mission into specific performance targets. In the case of Patagonia, the mission, values, and operating objectives seem to fit well together as a coherent whole. Chouinard says that he wants to run Patagonia "so that it's here 100 years from now and always makes the best-quality stuff." Although one of the firm's objectives is growth, for Chouinard this doesn't mean growth at any cost; the objective is modest, not extreme or uncontrolled, growth. At present, Patagonia is growing about 5% per year.[28]

SWOT ANALYSIS OF ORGANIZATION AND ENVIRONMENT

> A **SWOT analysis** examines organizational strengths and weaknesses and environmental opportunities and threats.

After the assessment of mission, values, and objectives, the next step in the strategic management process is to analyze the organization and its environment using a technique known as **SWOT analysis**. As shown in Figure 9.4, this is an internal analysis of *organizational strengths and weaknesses* as well as the external analysis of *environmental opportunities and threats*.

Organizational Strengths and Weaknesses

> A **core competency** is a special strength that gives an organization a competitive advantage.

A SWOT analysis begins with a systematic evaluation of the organization's resources and capabilities—its basic strengths and weaknesses. You can think of this as an analysis of organizational capacity to achieve its objectives. A major goal is to identify **core competencies**—things that the organization has or does exceptionally well in comparison with competitors. They are capabilities that by virtue of being rare, costly to imitate, and nonsubstitutable, become potential sources of competitive advantage.[29] Core competencies may be found in special knowledge or

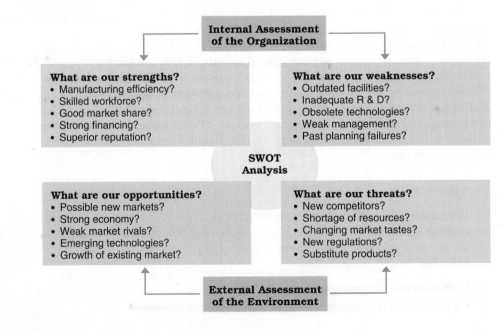

FIGURE 9.4 SWOT analysis of strengths, weaknesses, opportunities, and threats.

expertise, superior technologies, or unique distribution systems, among many other possibilities.

Organizational weaknesses are the other side of the picture. The goal here is to identify things that inhibit performance and hold the organization back from fully accomplishing its objectives. Examples might be outdated products, lack of capital, shortage of talented workers, or poor technology. When weaknesses are identified plans can be set to eliminate or reduce them, or possibly to turn them into strengths. Even if some weaknesses cannot be corrected, they need to be understood. Strategies should ideally build on organizational strengths and minimize the negative impact of weaknesses.

Environmental Opportunities and Threats

No SWOT analysis is complete until opportunities and threats in the external environment are also assessed. As shown in Figure 9.4, opportunities may exist as possible new markets, a strong economy, weaknesses in competitors, and emerging technologies. Environmental threats may be such things as the emergence of new competitors, resource scarcities, changing customer tastes, new government regulations, and a weak economy. Imagine the threats faced by airline executives when the U.S. and global economies went into recession and oil prices rose sharply. These forces upset existing strategies and caused major rethinking about what to do next. Some airlines adjusted tactically by reduced flight schedules, fleet cutbacks, and employee layoffs. Others made strategy shifts. For example, the large legacy carriers Northwest and Delta merged because their executives believed conditions in the industry favored consolidation and larger carriers.

> **Make SWOT Analysis Work for You**
> - Build on and use strengths to create core competencies
> - Avoid relying on weaknesses that can't be turned into strengths
> - Move toward opportunities to capture advantage
> - Avoid threats or act in ways that minimize their impact

FIVE FORCES ANALYSIS OF INDUSTRY ATTRACTIVENESS

The ideal condition for a firm is to operate in *monopoly conditions* as the only player in an industry—that is, to have no rivals to compete with for resources or customers. Although the firm's strategy is largely unchallenged due to its monopoly status, this ideal is rare except in highly regulated settings. The reality for most businesses is rivalry and competition that unfolds either under conditions of *oligopoly*—facing just a few competitors—such as in a consolidated airline industry, or *hypercompetition*— fast food facing several direct competitors, such as in the fast-food industry.[30] Both oligopoly and hypercompetition are strategically challenging, and hypercompetition is especially so because any competitive advantage tends to be short lived.

Harvard scholar and consultant Michael Porter describes the following five forces as a framework for competitive industry analysis.[31] An understanding of these forces can help managers make strategic choices that best position a firm within its industry.

1. *Industry competition*—the intensity of rivalry among firms in the industry and the ways they behave competitively toward one another.
2. *New entrants*—the threat of new competitors entering the market, based on the presence or absence of barriers to entry.
3. *Substitute products or services*—the threat of substitute products or services, or ability of customers to get what they want from other sellers.
4. *Bargaining power of suppliers*—the ability of resource suppliers to influence the price that one has to pay for their products or services.
5. *Bargaining power of customers*—the ability of customers to influence the price that they will pay for the firm's products or services.

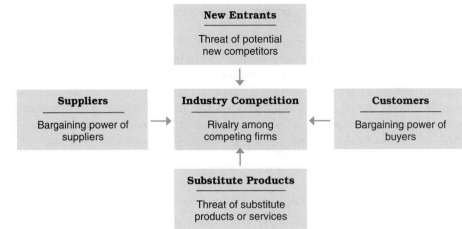

FIGURE 9.5 Porter's model of five strategic forces affecting industry competition.

Five Forces Analysis

Attractive Industry	Unattractive Industry
• Few competitors	• Many competitors
• High barriers to entry	• Low barriers to entry
• Few substitute products	• Many substitute products
• Low power of suppliers	• High power of suppliers
• Low power of customers	• High power of customers

The five competitive forces shown in Figure 9.5 constitute what Porter calls the "industry structure," and it establishes the industry's attractiveness or potential to generate long-term returns. The less attractive the industry structure, the harder it will be to make good strategic choices and realize a sustained competitive advantage relative to rivals. According to a five forces analysis, an *unattractive industry* is one in which rivalry among competitors is intense, substantial threats exist in the form of possible new entrants and substitute products, and suppliers and buyers are very powerful in bargaining over such things as prices and quality. An *attractive industry*, by contrast, has less existing competition, few threats from new entrants or substitutes, and low bargaining power among suppliers and buyers.

✓ **Learning Check**
Study Question 2
What are the essentials of strategic analysis?

Be sure you can ☑ explain what a mission statement is and illustrate how a good mission statement helps organizations ☑ list several operating objectives of organizations ☑ define *core competency* ☑ explain SWOT analysis ☑ explain how Porter's five forces model can be used to assess the attractiveness of an industry

CORPORATE-LEVEL STRATEGY FORMULATION

The CEO and the senior management team in a business are supposed to plot the overall direction of the organization in the competitive setting of its industry, something that is often easier said than done. If we had spoken with GM executives even just five years ago and asked about their strategy, "growth" would have been the ready answer. Today "restructuring" has been the goal as GM struggles to gain a fresh start after suffering through bankruptcy.[32] And if you go back just 10 years, one of the big business stories was the merger of AOL and Time Warner to create what was supposed to be the multimedia company of the future. Now the news is a corporate "divorce" as AOL and Time Warner go their separate ways. In these and the many other examples of organizations choosing and then changing courses of action, the challenge is finding the best strategy—one that keeps moving an organization forward in a complex and ever-changing competitive environment.

PORTFOLIO PLANNING MODEL

The global conglomerate General Electric owns a large portfolio of diverse businesses. CEO Jeffrey Immelt faces a difficult strategic question all the time: How should GE's resources be allocated across this mix of businesses in order to advance the success of the conglomerate as a whole?[33] If you think about it, Immelt's strategic management problem is similar to what we face while managing our personal assets. How, for example, do you manage a mix of cash, stocks, bonds, and real estate investments? What do you increase, what do you sell, and what do you hold? These are the same questions that Immelt and other executives ask. They are *portfolio-planning* questions, and they have major strategic implications. Shouldn't they be made systematically rather than haphazardly?[34]

The Boston Consulting Group has proposed a strategic portfolio planning approach shown in Figure 9.6 and known as the **BCG Matrix**. Although more complicated models are available, this is the foundation and a good place to start. The BCG Matrix asks managers to analyze business and product strategies based on two major issues: (1) the industry or market growth rate, and (2) the market share held by the firm.[35] This analysis sorts businesses or products into four strategic types: Dogs, Stars, Question Marks, and Cash Cows. Each type is then associated with a core or master strategy that is the most appropriate guide for resource allocations—growth, stability, or retrenchment.[36]

> The **BCG matrix** analyzes business opportunities according to market growth rate and market share.

Stars in the BCG Matrix have high-market-shares in high-growth markets. They produce large profits through substantial penetration of expanding markets. The preferred strategy for stars is growth and the BCG Matrix recommends making further resource investments in them. Stars are not only high performers in the present, but they offer similar potential for the future.

Cash cows have high-market shares in low-growth markets. They produce large profits and a strong cash flow, but with little upside potential. Because the markets offer little growth opportunity, the preferred strategy for cash cows is stability or modest growth. Like real dairy cows, the BCG Matrix advises firms to "milk" these businesses to generate cash for investing in other more promising areas.

Question marks have low-market shares in high-growth markets. Although they may not generate much profit at the moment, the upside potential is there because of the growing markets. Question marks make for difficult strategic decision

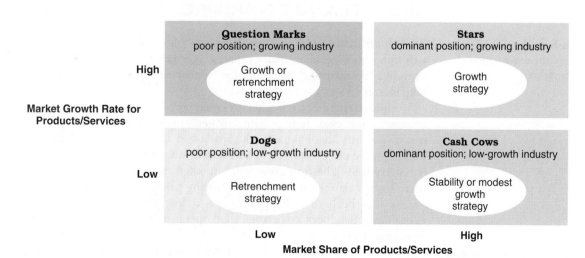

FIGURE 9.6 The BCG matrix approach for portfolio planning in corporate-level strategy formulation.

Ursula Burns Sets Pace in the Fortune 500

"Frankness," "sharp humor," "willingness to take risks," "deep industry knowledge," "technical prowess." These are all adjectives used to describe Ursula Burns, the new CEO of Xerox Corporation. She began her career with the company as an intern in 1980. Now Burns is the first African American woman to head a Fortune 500 firm as well as the first to succeed another woman in the CEO spot. Her predecessor, Anne Mulcahy, was also a company veteran who had worked her way to the top over a 27-year career. Ilene Lang, who heads Catalyst, a non-profit supporting women in business, says: "Most companies have one woman who might be a possibility to become CEO, Xerox has a range of them."

Burns took over Xerox at the height of financial crisis and faced declining sales and profits, as well as a stock price that had lost half of its value in a year's time. But her experience and leadership skills may be just what the firm now needs to address competitive challenges. And the challenges are many: less paper being used in offices, less equipment being bought or leased, and falling prices. Yet Burns conveys confidence with a smile, intending to pursue more sales in emerging markets, better efficiencies, and more sales of high margin services.

In her prior role as president, Burns made tough decisions on downsizing, closed Xerox manufacturing operations, and changed the product mix. She also knows how to work well with the firm's board. Board member Robert A. McDonald says, "She understands the technology and can communicate it in a way that a director can understand it."

Burns is a working mother and spouse with a teenage daughter and 20-year old stepson. She was raised by a single mom in New York City public housing and eventually earned a master's degree in engineering from Columbia University. Pride in her achievements comes across loud and clear in a speech to the YWCA in Cleveland. "I'm in this job because I believe I earned it through hard work and high performance," she said. "Did I get some opportunities early in my career because of my race and gender? Probably . . . I imagine race and gender got the hiring guys' attention. And then the rest was really up to me."

---

making. The BCG Matrix recommends targeting only the most promising question marks for growth, while retrenching those that are less promising.

Dogs have low-market shares in low-growth markets. They produce little if any profit, and they have low potential for future improvement. The preferred strategy for dogs in the BCG Matrix is straightforward: retrenchment.

GROWTH AND DIVERSIFICATION STRATEGIES

● A **growth strategy** involves expansion of the organization's current operations.

Growth strategies seek to expand the size and scope of operations in respect to such things as total sales, market shares, and operating locations. When you hear terms like "acquisition," "merger," and "global expansion," for example, the underlying master strategy is one of growth.

Although there is a tendency to equate growth with effectiveness, that is not necessarily the case. It is possible to get caught in an "expansion trap" where growth outruns an organization's capacity to run effectively. Mark Zuckerberg, founder and chief executive at Facebook, knows the challenges of a growth strategy pretty well. The firm grew fast, but when spending outran revenues the *Wall Street Journal* claimed the firm had "growing pains." Zuckerberg asked: "Is being a CEO always this hard?" His response was to hire an experienced Google vice president, Sheryl Sandberg, to become chief operating officer and lead Facebook's continued expansion.[37]

● Growth through **concentration** is within the same business area.

Organizations have a variety of strategic options in how to pursue growth strategies. One approach is growth through **concentration**, where expansion is within the same business area. McDonald's, Wal-Mart, Starbucks, and others pursue growth strategies while concentrating on their primary businesses. And as their domestic markets become saturated, they are aggressively expanding around the world in attempts to push further sales growth.[38]

Growth can also be pursued through **diversification**, where expansion takes place in new and different business areas. A strategy of *related diversification* pursues growth by acquiring new businesses or entering business areas that are related to what one already does. An example is the acquisition of Tropicana by PepsiCo. Although Tropicana specializes in fruit juices, the business is related to PepsiCo's expertise in the beverages industry. A strategy of *unrelated diversification* pursues growth by acquiring businesses or entering business areas that are different from what one already does. Tata Group, for example, is a $30 billion Indian conglomerate and FT Global 500 company. It started as a textile firm, but now owns 98 companies in diverse industries such as steel, telecommunications, communications and outsourcing, hotels, and automobiles—with brands including Jaguar and Land Rover. As Tata continues to grow and diversify, Chairman Ratan N. Tata says: "We have been thinking bigger . . . we have been bolder . . . we have been more aggressive in the marketplace."[39]

Diversification can also take the form of **vertical integration**, where a business acquires suppliers—*backward vertical integration*—or distributors—*forward vertical integration*. Backward vertical integration is evident at Apple Computer where the firm has bought chip manufacturers to give it more privacy and sophistication in developing microprocessors for products like the iPad. And it's also evident at Rolex where the firm owns a foundry that produces the precious metals for its luxury watches. Forward vertical integration is found in the beverage industry, where both Coca-Cola and PepsiCo have purchased some of their major bottlers.[40]

RETRENCHMENT AND RESTRUCTURING STRATEGIES

When organizations are in trouble, perhaps experiencing problems brought about by a bad economy or too much growth and diversification, the goal shifts toward **retrenchment and restructuring strategies** that pursue radical changes to solve problems. At the extreme, a firm may be insolvent and unable to pay its bills. In such cases, restructuring may take the form of **bankruptcy**, which under U.S. law gives firms Chapter 11 protection while they reorganize to restore solvency. Both Chrysler and General Motors used this strategy during

● Growth through **diversification** is by acquisition of or investment in new and different business areas.

● Growth through **vertical integration** occurs by acquiring suppliers or distributors.

● **Retrenchment and restructuring strategies** pursue radical changes to solve problems.

● Chapter 11 **bankruptcy** under U.S. law protects a firm from creditors while management reorganizes to restore solvency.

Sergio Marchionne Leads the "New" Chrysler

Many believed there wasn't much left to save of the old Chrysler when it emerged from bankruptcy. But Sergio Marchionne saw a chance to turn the troubled carmaker around after his firm, Fiat, bought into the restructured company. Chrysler's new CEO, Marchionne took his time crafting a turnaround strategy, one he called "a genuine transformation," "ambitious," "serious," and "a plan for which this management team ultimately wants to be held accountable." So far so good, it seems. One of Chrysler's board members says, "Sergio has an amazing ability to create loyalties."

● **Liquidation** is where a business closes and sells its assets to pay creditors.

● A **downsizing strategy** decreases the size of operations.

● **Divestiture** sells off parts of the organization to refocus attention on core business areas.

● A **turnaround strategy** tries to fix specific performance problems.

the recent economic crisis. Sometimes an insolvent firm goes into outright **liquidation**, where business ceases and assets are sold to pay creditors.

Short of the prior alternatives are a variety of situations where organizations try some form of strategic restructuring to get back on a high-performance track. Restructuring by **downsizing** decreases the size of operations, often by reducing the workforce.[41] The recent recession generated many examples, such as Delta's voluntary severance plan for 30,000 workers and the release of 53,000 by Citigroup.[42] Such cutbacks are most successful when done in targeted ways that advance specific performance objectives, rather than being simple "across the board cuts." The term *rightsizing* is sometimes used to describe downsizing with a clear strategic focus.[43]

Restructuring by **divestiture** sells off parts of the organization to refocus on core competencies, cut costs, and improve operating efficiency. This strategy is followed when organizations become overdiversified and have problems managing so much complexity. An example is eBay's sale of Skype for close to a $2 billion loss on its original investment. Originally the goal was integrating Skype's Internet telephony with eBay online auctions, but at the time of the sale eBay CEO John Donahoe said: "Skype is a strong standalone business, but it does not have synergies with our e-commerce and online payments business."[44] In other words, the original purchase was a costly and bad idea.

Restructuring by **turnaround** focuses on fixing specific performance problems. When McDonald's executives realized they were largely missing the boom in coffee sales led by Starbucks, for example, they crafted a turnaround strategy called Plan to Win. It added wireless Internet to restaurants along with a new internal décor and seating to encourage more of a "coffeehouse" atmosphere. The coffee blend was also changed and specialty coffees were added to menus. Plan to Win delivered as hoped, with McDonald's experiencing rising coffee sales.[45]

GLOBAL STRATEGIES

A key aspect of corporate strategy today is how the firm approaches the global economy and its mix of business risks and opportunities.[46] An easy way to spot differences in global strategies is to notice how products are developed and advertised around the world. A firm pursuing a **globalization strategy** tends to view the world as one large market, making most decisions from the corporate home base and trying as much as possible to standardize products and advertising for use everywhere. The latest Gillette razors, for example, are likely to be sold and advertised similarly around the world.

● A **globalization strategy** adopts standardized products and advertising for use worldwide.

Firms using a **multidomestic strategy** try to customize products and their advertising as much as possible to fit the local needs of different countries or regions. Local and regional managers are given authority to provide this differentiation. Many consumer goods companies, such as Bristol Myers, Procter & Gamble, and Unilever, take this strategic view and vary their products to fit consumer preferences in different countries and cultures. McDonald's is another example. Although you can get your standard fries and Big Mac in most locations, you can have a McVeggie in India, a McArabia Kofta in Saudi Arabia, and a Croque McDo in France.

● A **multidomestic strategy** customizes products and advertising to best fit local needs.

A third approach is the **transnational strategy** where a firm tries to operate without a strong national identity and blend seamlessly with the global economy. Resources are acquired worldwide. Manufacturing and other business functions are performed wherever in the world they can be done best at lowest cost. Ford, for example, draws upon design, manufacturing, and distribution expertise all over the world to build car platforms that can then be modified to meet regional tastes. Called the "one Ford" strategy, it helps Ford gain operating efficiencies while tapping customer markets and employee talents around the world.

● A **transnational strategy** seeks efficiencies of global operations with attention to local markets.

Real Ethics

Cutting Costs by Moving Jobs Overseas

Many companies relocate their manufacturing operations overseas in order to reduce their costs. While the wage differentials in various locations are often cited as one of the primary motivations, there are other potential cost savings as well.

Lower costs can arise from the less stringent, and possibly nonexistent, safety laws found in some countries. In these locations, manufacturers can produce goods more cheaply because they do not have to invest as much in safety processes or equipment. For instance, protective clothing and training that is required for operations in the United States may not be required when operating in another, typically poorer, country.

Some argue that the failure to provide equal training and protection to workers in other countries is exploitative and unethical and that it represents a disregard for human lives and safety. Others claim that such actions are appropriate as long as they are consistent with the host country's culture and laws.

You Decide

The world of global business strategy is complicated. Should companies comply with their own country's laws even when operating abroad? What if doing so increases costs to the point that it makes the company less competitive with its global rivals? Is imposing the home country's standards when doing business in another country a kind of cultural imperialism? If you were responsible for your company's financial well-being, would you incur the extra expenses required to protect workers in all of your company's operating locations?

COOPERATIVE STRATEGIES

Another trend today is toward **strategic alliances** in which two or more organizations join in partnership to pursue an area of mutual interest. One way to cooperate strategically is through *outsourcing alliances*—contracting to purchase important services from another organization. Some organizations, for example, are outsourcing their IT function to firms such as EDS, Infosys, and IBM in the belief that these services are better provided by a firm with specialized expertise. Cooperation in the supply chain takes the form of *supplier alliances*, in which preferred supplier relationships guarantee a smooth and timely flow of quality supplies among alliance partners. Another approach is cooperation in *distribution alliances*, where firms join together to sell and distribute products or services.

Cooperation also takes place as **co-opetition**, or strategic alliances among competitors.[47] For example, United Airlines and Lufthansa are major international competitors, but they also cooperate in the "Star Alliance." The alliance provides their customers code-sharing on flights and shared frequent flyer programs. Likewise, luxury car competitors Daimler and BMW are cooperating to co-develop new motors and components for hybrid cars.

● In a **strategic alliance**, organizations join in partnership to pursue an area of mutual interest.

● **Co-opetition** is the strategy of working with rivals on projects of mutual benefit.

Be sure you can ☑ describe the BCG matrix as a strategic portfolio planning tool ☑ list and explain the major types of growth and diversification strategies ☑ list and explain the major types of retrenchment and restructuring strategies ☑ list and give examples of global strategies ☑ define *strategic alliance* and explain cooperation as a business strategy

Learning Check ☑

Study Question 3

What are corporate-level strategies and how are they formulated?

BUSINESS-LEVEL
STRATEGY FORMULATION

Michael Porter says that "the company without a strategy is willing to try anything."[48] But with a good strategy in place, he believes a business can achieve superior profitability or above-average returns within its industry. The key question in formulating business-level strategy is: "How can we best compete for customers in our market and with our products or services?"

COMPETITIVE STRATEGIES MODEL

Figure 9.7 shows the model Porter proposes for making choices among possible competitive strategies. Porter bases these business-level strategic decisions on two main considerations: (1) market scope of the product or service, and (2) source of competitive advantage for the product or service.

In respect to *market scope* the strategic planner asks: "How broad or narrow is the market or target market?" In respect to *source of competitive advantage*, the question is: "Do we seek competitive advantage primarily through low price or product uniqueness?" When these questions are answered and the results analyzed in the matrix shown in Figure 9.7, three business-level strategies are possible—cost leadership, differentiation, and focus. The focus strategy exists in two combinations: focused cost leadership and focused differentiation.

DIFFERENTIATION STRATEGY

● A **differentiation strategy** offers products that are unique and different from the competition.

Organizations pursuing a **differentiation strategy** seek competitive advantage through uniqueness. They try to develop goods and services that are clearly different from those of the competition or that, through successful advertising, are perceived as clearly different. The objective is to build a strong base of customers that are loyal to the organization's products and lose interest in those of competitors.

To succeed with a differentiation strategy an organization must have strengths in research and development, marketing, and advertising. An example in the apparel industry is Polo Ralph Lauren, retailer of upscale classic fashions and accessories. In Ralph Lauren's words, "Polo redefined how American style and quality is perceived. Polo has always been about selling quality products by creating worlds and inviting our customers to be part of our dream."[49] In soft drinks, as shown in

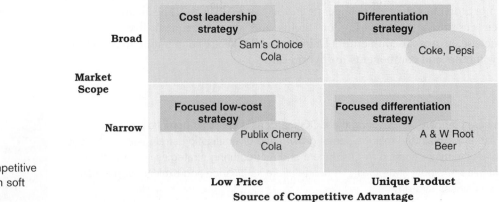

FIGURE 9.7 Porter's competitive strategies framework with soft drink industry examples.

Figure 9.7, the differentiation examples are Coke and Pepsi. The two are always battling for customer attention and loyalty. Although part of their product differentiation may be in actual taste, another very important part is pure perception. And that is driven by advertising. Coke and Pepsi spend enormous amounts on advertising to create and maintain perceptions that their products are somehow unique from one another.

COST LEADERSHIP STRATEGY

Organizations pursuing a **cost leadership strategy** try to have low costs so that they can sell products and services at low prices. The low-cost structure allows them to make profits even when selling at lower prices than competitors. Success with the cost leadership strategy requires a continuing search for innovations that increase operating efficiencies.

The classic benchmark for cost leadership in discount retailing is Wal-Mart. The firm is a master at using technology, mass purchasing, and retail savvy to keep its costs so low that it can offer customers the lowest prices and still make a reasonable profit. Whereas most discounters operate with 18 to 20% gross margins, Wal-Mart can accept less and still make good returns. Wal-Mart's cost leadership strategy in soft drinks is represented in Figure 9.7 by Sam's Choice Colas. In the financial services industry, the Vanguard Group is another benchmark for cost leadership. By keeping costs low, it attracts customers by offering mutual funds with low expense ratios and minimum fees.

You might be wondering at this point about a possible combination of cost leadership and differentiation. Porter believes that it is hard for a firm to do this because differentiation most often drives up costs. "You can compete on price or you can compete on product, but you can't compete on both," the marketers tend to say. And Porter generally agrees. He refers to this strategy combination as *stuck in the middle* and believes it is rarely successful.

> ● A **cost leadership strategy** seeks to operate with low cost so that products can be sold at low prices.

> **Porter's Competitive Strategies**
> - *Differentiation*—make products that are unique and different.
> - *Cost leadership*—produce at lower cost and sell at lower price
> - *Focused differentiation*—use differentiation and target needs of a special market.
> - *Focused cost leadership*—use cost leadership and target needs of a special market.

FOCUS STRATEGY

Organizations pursuing **focus strategies** concentrate on a special market segment in the form of a niche customer group, geographical region, or product or service line. The objective is to serve the needs of the segment better than anyone else. Competitive advantage is achieved by combining focus with either differentiation or cost leadership.[50]

In airlines, NetJets focuses on private, secure, and luxury air services for those who can pay a high fee, such as wealthy media stars and executives. This is a **focused differentiation** strategy because the firm sells a unique product to a special niche market. Also in airlines you find carriers such as Ryan Air and Easy Jet in Europe offering heavily discounted fares and "no frills" flying. This is a **focused cost leadership** strategy because it offers low prices to attract budget travelers. The airlines still make profits by keeping costs low; they fly to regional airports and cut out free services such as bag checks and in-flight snacks.

Figure 9.7 shows how these focus strategies play out in the soft drink industry. Specialty drinks such as A&W Root Beer, Dr. Pepper, and Mountain Dew represent the focused differentiation strategy. Each focuses on a special market segment and tries to compete on the basis of product uniqueness. Other drinks such as Sam's Diet Cola, Publix Cherry Cola, and Big K Cola with Lime represent

> ● A **focus strategy** concentrates on serving a unique market segment better than anyone else.

> ● A **focused differentiation strategy** offers a unique product to a special market segment.

> ● A **focused cost leadership** strategy seeks the lowest costs of operations within a special market segment.

the focused cost leadership strategy. They also focus on special market segments, but try to compete on the base of low prices made possible by low costs.

Be sure you can ☑ list and explain the four competitive strategies in Porter's model ☑ clarify the roles of both price and cost in a cost leadership strategy ☑ explain the differences between focused differentiation and focused cost leadership strategies ☑ illustrate how Porter's competitive strategies apply to products in a market familiar to you

STRATEGY IMPLEMENTATION

A discussion of the corporate history on Patagonia, Inc.'s website includes this statement: "During the past thirty years, we've made many mistakes but we've never lost our way for very long."[51] Not only is the firm being honest in its public information, it is also communicating an important point about strategic management—mistakes will be made. Sometimes those mistakes will be in poor strategy selection. Other times those mistakes will be implementation failures.

MANAGEMENT PRACTICES AND SYSTEMS

The rest of *Management 11/e* is really all about strategy implementation. In order to successfully put strategies into action, the entire organization and all of its resources must be mobilized in support of them. This, in effect, involves the complete management process—from planning and controlling through organizing and leading. No matter how well or elegantly planned, a strategy requires supporting structures and workflow designs staffed by talented people. The strategy needs leaders who are capable of motivating everyone so that individuals and teams work to its best advantage. And the strategy needs to be properly monitored and controlled to ensure that the desired results are being achieved.

● **Lack of participation error** is a failure to include key persons in strategic planning.

Poor management practices hinder strategy implementation in a number of ways. *Failures of substance* show up in poor strategic analysis and bad strategy formulation. *Failures of process* reflect poor handling of the ways in which strategic management is accomplished. A common process failure is the **lack of participation error**. This failure to include key persons in the strategic planning process shows up as a lack of commitment to all-important action and follow-through.[52] Process failure also occurs with too much centralization of planning in top management or too much reliance on staff planners or separate planning departments. Another process failure is *goal displacement*. This is the tendency to get so bogged down in details that the planning process becomes an end in itself, instead of a means to an end.

CORPORATE GOVERNANCE

● **Corporate governance** is the system of control and performance monitoring of top management.

Organizations today are experiencing lots of pressures at the level of **corporate governance**. This is the system of control and monitoring of top management performance exercised by boards of directors and boards of trustees.

Boards are supposed to make sure that the strategic management of the enterprise is successful.[53] But they are sometimes too compliant and uncritical in endorsing or confirming the strategic initiatives of top management. Such weak corporate governance means top management isn't subjected to rigorous oversight and accountability. As a result, organizations can end up doing the wrong or bad things, or just performing poorly.

Dell Computer Faces Strategic Challenges

For years, Dell's founder Michael S. Dell rode the wave of success with a strategy driven by excellence in logistics and supply chain management—one that seemed hard to beat. Then things started to go wrong. Rivals like HP and IBM were transforming, and Dell rapidly lost ground. Now Michael Dell claims the firm is developing new competencies based on "flexibility, customer focus, and innovation." But many wonder if Dell's attempted turnaround is too little and too late? Consultant Warren Bennis says, "He's got tremendous challenges ahead of him, because he's in an industry that is undergoing rapid, sweeping change."

When governance fails, blame may be placed on the individual board members or on the composition of the board overall. Controversies can arise over the role of *inside directors* who are chosen from the senior management of the organization, and *outside directors* who are chosen from other organizations and positions external to the organization. In some cases insiders may have too much control; in others the outsiders may be selected because they are friends of top management or at least sympathetic to them.

One area where corporate governance has been criticized is CEO pay, specifically for allowing excessive pay. The words out of Washington and other world capitals during the financial crisis were that corporate board members better exercise stronger governance over such matters or the governments will start doing the job for them. CEO John Mackey of Whole Foods pushes the issue further into the realm of *self-governance*, saying: "I do think it's the responsibility of the leadership of an organization to constrain itself for the good of the organization."[54] Shareholder activists are also increasingly vocal in proposing "say-on-pay" resolutions at annual corporate meetings. Apple and Pfizer are among the firms where such resolutions have passed. But when AT&T's retiree association supported a say-on-pay vote, it was defeated. The association's president, Carole Lovell, said: "AT&T's executive compensation policies continue to exhibit all the worst excesses and abuses."[55]

STRATEGIC CONTROL

Top managers probably feel more performance accountability today than ever before to boards and other stakeholder groups. They are expected to exercise **strategic control**, always making sure strategies are well implemented and that poor strategies are scrapped or modified to quickly meet performance demands of changing conditions. Basic management practice would have CEOs and other senior executives always "in control" in the sense of measuring results, evaluating the success of existing strategies, and taking action to improve things in the future. Yet many critics believe that the financial crisis showed strategic control was inadequate at many firms, especially the automakers and big banks.

Perhaps the best evidence for strategic control problems emerged in congressional hearings where three CEOs at the time—Robert Nardelli of Chrysler, Alan Mulally of Ford, and Richard Wagoner of GM—asked the government for $25 billion bail-out loans to save them from bankruptcy. One critic said that the firms were "already bankrupt," their troubles were caused by decision-making failures, and the CEOs should be held accountable. The low point in the hearing came when Representative Brad Sherman of California asked if any of the CEOs had

● **Strategic control** makes sure strategies are well implemented and that poor strategies are scrapped or modified.

Research Brief

Female Directors on Corporate Boards Linked with Positive Management Practices

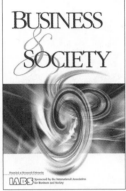

A growing body of research links the composition of boards of directors with both the financial performance of the firms and their social responsibility behaviors. Building on prior studies, Richard Vernardi, Susan Bosco, and Katie Vassill examined gender diversity of board membership and corporate performance.

The research question guiding their article in *Business and Society* was: "Do firms listed in *Fortune*'s '100 Best Companies to Work For' have a higher percentage of female directors than do Fortune 500 companies?" The researchers chose the "100 Best" listing because it includes firms whose employees consider them to have positive organizational cultures and supportive work practices. The evaluations were measured on a 225-item Great Place to Work Trust Index, sent to a random sample of employees in each company. Documentation of female board representatives was obtained by examining company annual reports.

Results confirmed expectations: the percentage of female directors was higher for firms on the "100 Best" list than for those in the Fortune 500 overall. In discussing the finding, the researchers suggest that gender diversity on boards of directors may bring about positive organizational changes that make firms better places to work. They also cite the growing presence of women on corporate boards as evidence that firms are changing board memberships to be "more representative of its employee and customer pools."

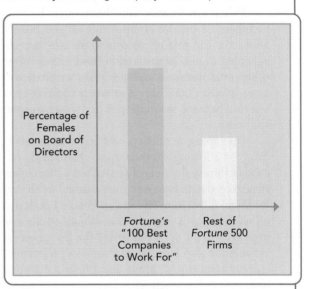

You Be the Researcher

Why would the presence of more female directors on a board result in a better workplace? Does board diversity, including minorities and women, lead to different agendas, deliberations, concerns, and strategies? Does it lead to better strategy implementation through greater employee involvement and loyalty? Look at organizations with which you are familiar. Can you see where greater membership diversity in general, not just at the top, makes a difference in the way an organization performs?

Reference: Richard A. Vernardi, Susan M. Bosco, and Katie M. Vassill, "Does Female Representation on Boards of Directors Associate with *Fortune*'s, '100 Best Companies to Work For' List? *Business and Society,* vol. 45 (June 2006), pp. 235–48.

flown into Washington by commercial airline. "Let the record show," he said, "that no hands went up." The estimated cost of the private jet travel was $20,000 per CEO compared to $500 for a standard economy fare round-trip ticket. This left a negative impression on the CEOs' abilities to exercise strategic control and reinforced concerns about their decision-making abilities. It didn't make sense to most at the hearing for the CEOs to spend that kind of money and then beg for huge bail-out assistance from the government.[56]

STRATEGIC LEADERSHIP

Of the three auto CEOs just mentioned, only Mulally of Ford survived to lead his firm's restructuring strategy. Paul Ingrassia, an auto analyst, says that Ford's success would be "one of the great turnarounds in corporate history" and praises Mulally's efforts "to simplify, relentlessly and systematically, a business that had grown way too complicated and costly to be managed effectively."[57] What Mulally is showing at Ford is all-important **strategic leadership**—the capability to inspire people to successfully engage in a process of continuous change, performance enhancement, and implementation of organizational strategies.[58]

● **Strategic leadership** inspires people to continuously change, refine, and improve strategies and their implementation.

One of the big lessons learned in studying how business firms fared in the economic crisis is that a *strategic leader has to maintain strategic control*. This means that the CEO and other top managers should always be in touch with the strategy, how well it is being implemented, whether the strategy is generating performance success or failure, and the need for the strategy to be tweaked or changed. Other key responsibilities of strategic leadership have been described in these ways.[59]

- *A strategic leader has to be the guardian of trade-offs.* It is the leader's job to make sure that the organization's resources are allocated in ways consistent with the strategy. This requires the discipline to sort through many competing ideas and alternatives, to stay on course, and not to get sidetracked.

- *A strategic leader needs to create a sense of urgency.* The leader can't allow the organization and its members to grow slow and complacent. Even when doing well, the leader keeps the focus on getting better and being alert to conditions that require adjustments to the strategy.

- *A strategic leader needs to make sure that everyone understands the strategy.* Unless strategies are understood, the daily tasks and contributions of people lose context and purpose. Everyone might work very hard, but without alignment to strategy the impact is dispersed and fails to advance common goals.

- *A strategic leader needs to be a teacher.* It is the leader's job to teach the strategy and make it a "cause." In order for strategy to work it must become an ever-present commitment throughout the organization. This means that a strategic leader must be a great communicator. Everyone must understand the strategy and how it makes their organization different from others.

Be sure you can ☑ explain how the management process supports strategy implementation ☑ define *corporate governance* ☑ explain why boards of directors sometimes fail in their governance responsibilities ☑ define *strategic control* and *strategic leadership* ☑ list the responsibilities of a strategic leader in today's organizations

Learning Check ☑

Study Question 5
What are the foundations for strategy implementation?

Management **L**earning **R**eview

Study Questions Summary

1 What is strategic management?

- Competitive advantage is achieved by operating in ways that allow an organization to outperform its rivals; a competitive advantage is sustainable when it is difficult for competitors to imitate.

- A strategy is a comprehensive plan that sets long-term direction and guides resource allocation for sustainable competitive advantage.

- Corporate strategy sets direction for an entire organization; business strategy sets direction for a business division or product/service line; functional strategy sets direction for the operational support of business and corporate strategies.

- Strategic management is the process of formulating and implementing strategies that achieve goals in a competitive environment.

FOR DISCUSSION **Can an organization have a good strategy and still fail to achieve competitive advantage?**

2 What are the essentials of strategic analysis?

- The strategic management process begins with analysis of mission, clarification of core values, and identification of objectives.

- A SWOT analysis systematically assesses organizational strengths and weaknesses, and environmental opportunities and threats.

- Porter's five forces model analyzes industry attractiveness in terms of competitive rivalry, new entrants, substitute products, and the bargaining powers of suppliers and buyers.

FOR DISCUSSION **Would a monopoly get a perfect score for industry attractiveness in Porter's five forces model?**

3 What are corporate-level strategies, and how are they formulated?

- Growth strategies pursue greater sales and broader markets by concentration that expands in related product or business areas, and diversification that expands in new and different product and business areas.
- Restructuring strategies pursue ways to correct performance problems by such means as liquidation, bankruptcy, downsizing, divestiture, and turnaround.
- Global firms take advantage of international business opportunities through globalization, multi-domestic, and transnational strategies.
- Cooperative strategies create strategic alliances with other organizations to achieve mutual gains, including such things as outsourcing alliances, supplier alliances, and even co-opetition among competitors.
- The BCG matrix is a portfolio planning approach that classifies businesses or product lines as "stars," "cash cows," "question marks," or "dogs" for purposes of strategy formulation.

FOR DISCUSSION **Is it good news or bad news for investors when a firm announces that it is restructuring?**

4 What are business-level strategies, and how are they formulated?

- Potential sources of competitive advantage in business-level strategy formulation are found in things like lower costs, better quality, more knowledge, greater speed, and strong financial resources.
- Porter's model of competitive strategy bases the choice of business-level strategies on two major considerations—market scope of product or service, and source of competitive advantage for the product or service.

- A differentiation strategy seeks competitive advantage by offering unique products and services that are clearly different from those of competitors.
- A cost leadership strategy seeks competitive advantage by operating at low costs that allow products and services to be sold to customers at low prices.
- A focus strategy seeks competitive advantage by serving the needs of a special market segment or niche better than anyone else; it can be done as focused differentiation or focused cost leadership.

FOR DISCUSSION **Can a business ever be successful with a combined cost leadership and differentiation strategy?**

5 What are the foundations for strategy implementation?

- Management practices and systems—including the functions of planning, organizing, leading, and controlling—must be mobilized to support strategy implementation.
- Pitfalls that inhibit strategy implementation include failures of substance—such as poor analysis of the environment; and failures of process—such as lack of participation by key players in the planning process.
- Boards of directors play important roles in control through corporate governance, including monitoring how well top management fulfills strategic management responsibilities.
- Top managers exercise strategic control by making sure strategies are well implemented, and are changed if not working.
- Strategic leadership inspires the process of continuous evaluation and improvement of strategies and their implementation.

FOR DISCUSSION **Is strategic leadership by top managers capable of making up for poor corporate governance by board members?**

Self-Test

Multiple-Choice Questions

1. The most appropriate first question to ask in strategic planning is _____.
   (a) "Where do we want to be in the future?" (b) "How well are we currently doing?" (c) "How can we get where we want to be?" (d) "Why aren't we doing better?"

2. The ability of a firm to consistently outperform its rivals is called _____.
   (a) vertical integration (b) competitive advantage (c) incrementalism (d) strategic intent

3. In a complex conglomerate business such as General Electric, a(n) _____ level strategy sets strategic direction for a strategic business unit.
   (a) institutional (b) corporate (c) business (d) functional

4. An organization that is downsizing to reduce costs is implementing a grand strategy of _____.
   (a) growth (b) cost differentiation (c) restructuring (d) stability

5. The _____ is a predominant value system for an organization as a whole.
   (a) strategy (b) core competency (c) mission (d) corporate culture

6. A _____ in the BCG matrix would have a high market share in a low-growth market.
   (a) dog (b) cash cow (c) question mark (d) star

7. In Porter's five forces framework, having _____ increases industry attractiveness.
   (a) many rivals (b) many substitute products (c) low bargaining power of suppliers (d) few barriers to entry

8. When PepsiCo acquired Tropicana, a maker of orange juice, the firm's strategy was growth by _____.
   (a) related diversification (b) concentration (c) vertical integration (d) cooperation

9. Cost efficiency and product quality are two examples of _____ objectives of organizations.
   (a) official (b) operating (c) informal (d) institutional

10. Restructuring by Chapter 11 bankruptcy is a _____ strategy.
    (a) turnaround (b) growth (c) concentration (d) incremental

11. Among the global strategies that might be pursued by international businesses, the _____ strategy is the most targeted on local needs, local management, and local products.
    (a) ethnocentric (b) transnational (c) geocentric (d) multidomestic

12. According to Porter's model of competitive strategies, a firm that wants to compete with its rivals in a broad market by selling a very low-priced product would need to successfully implement a _____ strategy.
    (a) retrenchment (b) differentiation (c) cost leadership (d) diversification

13. When Coke and Pepsi spend millions on ads trying to convince customers that their products are unique, they are pursuing a/an _____ strategy.
    (a) transnational (b) concentration (c) diversification (d) differentiation

14. The role of the board of directors as an oversight body that holds top executives accountable for the success of business strategies is called _____.
    (a) strategic leadership (b) corporate governance (c) logical incrementalism (d) strategic opportunism

15. An example of a process failure in strategic planning is _____.
    (a) lack of participation (b) poorly worded mission (c) incorrect core values (d) insufficient financial resources

Short-Response Questions

16. What is the difference between corporate strategy and functional strategy?
17. What would a manager look at in a SWOT analysis?
18. What is the difference between focus and differentiation as competitive strategies?
19. What is strategic leadership?

Essay Question

20. Kim Harris owns and operates a small retail store selling the outdoor clothing of an American manufacturer to a predominately college-student market. Lately, a large department store outside of town has started selling similar, but lower-priced clothing manufactured in China, Thailand, and Bangladesh. Kim believes she is starting to lose business to this store. Assume you are part of a student team assigned to do a management class project for Kim. Her question for the team is: "How can I best deal with my strategic management challenges in this situation?" How will you reply?

Management Skills and Competencies

Self-Assessment

Back to Yourself: Critical Thinking

Strategic management is one of the most significant planning challenges faced by managers. Managers deal with a complex array of forces and uncertainties, all of which must be consolidated and integrated to craft a strategy that moves an organization forward with success. **Critical thinking**, introduced in the opener, is an essential foundation for success in strategic management. The same critical thinking that is part of a rigorous class discussion or case study in your course is what helps strategic leaders create strategies that result in competitive advantage. But with all the uncertainties that exist today, managers rarely have the luxury of full information that is boxed up for analysis in a nice neat case format. Critical thinking in the real world must be multidimensional and embrace both the systematic and intuitive aspects of decision making. After you complete the following self-assessment on Intuitive Ability, don't forget to go online for the Facts and Inferences self-assessment. It's an opportunity to learn how strong you are in interpreting ambiguous situations.

> **Critical thinking** is a "must have" for success in strategic management, enabling you to gather and interpret information for decision making in problem settings that often include lots of complexity and uncertainties.

Further Reflection: Intuitive Ability

Instructions

Complete this survey as quickly as you can. Be honest with yourself. For each question, select the response that most appeals to you.[60]

1. When working on a project, do you prefer to
   (a) be told what the problem is but be left free to decide how to solve it?   (b) get very clear instructions for how to go about solving the problem before you start?

2. When working on a project, do you prefer to work with colleagues who are
   (a) realistic?   (b) imaginative?

3. Do you most admire people who are
   (a) creative?   (b) careful?

4. Do the friends you choose tend to be
   (a) serious and hard working?   (b) exciting and often emotional?

5. When you ask a colleague for advice on a problem you have, do you
   (a) seldom or never get upset if he or she questions your basic assumptions?   (b) often get upset if he or she questions your basic assumptions?

6. When you start your day, do you
   (a) seldom make or follow a specific plan?   (b) usually first make a plan to follow?

7. When working with numbers, do you find that you
   (a) seldom or never make factual errors?   (b) often make factual errors?

8. Do you find that you
   (a) seldom daydream during the day and really don't enjoy doing so when you do it?   (b) frequently daydream during the day and enjoy doing so?

9. When working on a problem, do you
   (a) prefer to follow the instructions or rules that are given to you?   (b) often enjoy circumventing the instructions or rules that are given to you?

10. When you are trying to put something together, do you prefer to have
    (a) step-by-step written instructions on how to assemble the item?   (b) a picture of how the item is supposed to look once assembled?

11. Do you find that the person who irritates you *the most* is the one who appears to be
    (a) disorganized?   (b) organized?

12. When an unexpected crisis comes up that you have to deal with, do you
    (a) feel anxious about the situation?   (b) feel excited by the challenge of the situation?

Scoring

Total the number of "a" responses selected for questions 1, 3, 5, 6, 11; enter the score here [a = ____]. Total the number of "b" responses for questions 2, 4, 7, 8, 9, 10, 12; enter the score here [b = ____]. Add your "a" and "b" scores and enter the sum here [a + b = ____]. This is your intuitive score. The highest possible intuitive score is 12; the lowest is 0.

Interpretation

In his book *Intuition in Organizations* (Newbury Park, CA: Sage, 1989), pp. 10–11, Weston H. Agor states, "Traditional analytical techniques . . . are not as useful as they once were for guiding major decisions. . . . If you hope to be better prepared for tomorrow, then it only seems logical to pay some attention to the use and development of intuitive skills for decision making." Agor developed the preceding survey to help people assess their tendencies to use intuition in decision making. Your score offers a general impression of your strength in this area. It may also suggest a need to further develop your skill and comfort with more intuitive decision-making approaches.

Team Exercise

Strategic Scenarios

Preparation

In today's turbulent economics it is no longer safe to assume that an organization that was highly successful yesterday will continue to be so tomorrow—or that it will even be in existence. Changing times exact the best from strategic planners. Think about the situations currently facing the following well-known organizations. Think, too, about the futures they may face.[61]

McDonald's	Domino's Pizza	Sony
Apple Computer	Nordstrom	Electronic Arts
Yahoo.com	National Public Radio	AT&T
Ann Taylor	*New York Times*	Federal Express

Instructions

Form into groups as assigned by your instructor. Choose one or more organizations from the prior list (or as assigned) and answer for the organization the following questions:

1. What in the future might seriously threaten the success, perhaps the very existence, of this organization? As a group, develop at least three such *future scenarios*.

2. Estimate the probability (0 to 100%) of each future scenario occurring.

3. Develop a strategy for each scenario that will enable the organization to deal with it successfully.

Thoroughly discuss these questions within the group and arrive at your best possible consensus answers. Be prepared to share and defend your answers in general class discussion.

Case Study: Dunkin' Donuts

Go to *Management Cases for Critical Thinking* to find the recommended case for Chapter 9—"Dunkin' Donuts: Betting Dollars on Donuts."

Organization Structures and Design

Chapter 10 Study Questions

1 What is organizing as a management function?

2 What are the traditional organization structures?

3 What are the types of horizontal organization structures?

4 How are organizational designs changing the workplace?

Learning From Others

It's All About How You Put The Pieces Together

The next time you're in the mall check out what's happening in the Build-A-Bear store. You'll see lots of activity, excitement, and fun as kids and parents work together building memories. Started by Maxine Clark in 1996, Build-A-Bear Workshop, Inc., grew rapidly, attracted venture capital, and now operates more than 150 stores in up-scale shopping malls in the United States and Canada.

The Build-A-Bear concept is simple but elegant: Pick out a bear or bunny or turtle shell that you like, add stuffing, and then outfit your pet with clothing, shoes, and accessories. Each pet is unique—soccer player, girl scout . . . you name it, personalized to the user's tastes and interests. Kids and accompanying adults love it.

Each Build-A-Bear store is carefully organized. Guest Bear Builders move along the Bear Pathway from the Choose Me computer workstation on to Stuff Me and finally to Name Me as their personal creation takes shape. Sounds a lot like organizations, doesn't it? Until you get to the "making it personal" part. That's where organizations often struggle—how to bring together hundreds, thousands, even hundreds of thousands of people in arrangements that make sense and still allow for personal talents to shine through.

Maxine Clark obviously had the talent, creativity, and drive to build a successful business. Some consider the Build-A-Bear concept to be brilliant, as even a quick stop into one of the stores or a look at the fascinating options available on the Web storefront would confirm. Clark's career began with May Company and children's marketing. By the time she resigned to start Build-A-Bear, she was president of the May subsidiary Payless ShoeSource. While there, she was named "one of the 30 Most Powerful People in Discount Store Retailing."

Children can now find Build-A-Bear stores internationally in places like Ireland and Japan, and expansion continues to be in the cards. Clark's current challenge is to manage the growth by continually adapting and redesigning her company to best meet its new global opportunities. When you think about it, it's a lot like her young customers who love to build their own bears.[1]

do the benchmarking

Build-A-Bear's founding story is one of classic entrepreneurship. Its continued success is classic management—good plans, a great design, following through with the details, and tackling opportunities and problems as they arise. But it's not easy to stay on course while adding people, changing structures, and building brands for competitive advantage. **With good organizing skills and strong values growth can be managed without compromising strategy and principles.**

Learning About Yourself

Empowerment

It takes a lot of trust to be comfortable with **empowerment**—letting others make decisions and exercise discretion in their work. But if you aren't willing and able to empower others, you may try to do too much on your own and end up accomplishing too little.

How often are you stressed out by group projects at school, feeling like you're doing all the work? Do you seem to be always rushing while your peers have time for coffee and chats? If so, perhaps you have a problem "letting go," or being willing to let others do their share of the work.

If the prior description fits you, your assumptions probably align with those in the upper left box in the Empowerment Quick Test. Alternatively, you could be in the lower right box and perhaps find that you work smarter and better while making others happier, too.

The beauty of organizations is synergy—bringing together the contributions of many people to achieve something that is much greater than what any individual can accomplish alone. Empowerment gives synergy a chance. It means joining with others to get things done; allowing and even helping them to do things that you might be very good at doing yourself.

EMPOWERMENT QUICK TEST

In a team situation, which square best describes your beliefs and behaviors?

It's faster to do things myself than explain how to do them to others

Some things are just too important not to do yourself

?

People make mistakes, but they also learn from them

Many people are ready to take on more work, but are too shy to volunteer

One of the common impediments to empowerment is that many of us suffer from control anxiety. We don't empower others because we fear losing control. Being "unwilling to let go," we try to do too much and end up running the risk of missed deadlines and even poor performance. This behavior denies others opportunities to contribute. We end up losing the benefits of their talents and often alienate them in the process.

get to know yourself better

Are you someone who easily and comfortably empowers others? Or, do you suffer from control anxiety and lack the willingness to delegate? The next time you are in a study or work group, be a self-observer. Write a short narrative that would accurately describe your behavior to someone who wasn't present. Compare that narrative with where you stand on the Empowerment Quick Test. **Also take advantage of the end-of-chapter Self-Assessment feature to further reflect on your strengths when it comes to Empowering Others.**

10 Organization Structures and Designs

Study Question 1	Study Question 2	Study Question 3	Study Question 4
Organizing as a Management Function	**Traditional Organization Structures**	**Horizontal Organization Structures**	**Organizational Designs**
• What is organization structure? • Formal structures • Informal structures	• Functional structures • Divisional structures • Matrix structures	• Team structures • Network structures • Boundaryless structures	• Contingency in organizational design • Mechanistic and organic designs • Organization design trends
Learning Check 1	**Learning Check 2**	**Learning Check 3**	**Learning Check 4**

I t is much easier to talk about high-performing organizations than to actually create them. In the context of the opening example, we might just say that it's a lot harder to build an organization than build a bear! And in true contingency fashion there is no one best way to do things; no one organizational form meets the needs of all circumstances. What works well at one moment in time can quickly become outdated or even dysfunctional in another. This is why you often read and hear about organizations making changes and reorganizing in an attempt to improve their performance.

Management scholar and consultant Henry Mintzberg points out that people need to understand how their organizations work if they are to work well within them.[2] Whenever job assignments and reporting relationships change, whenever the organization grows or shrinks, whenever old ways of doing things are reconfigured, people naturally struggle to understand the new ways of working. They ask questions such as: "Who's in charge?" "How do the parts connect to one another?" "How should processes and people come together?" "Whose ideas have to flow where?" They also worry about the implications of the new arrangements for their jobs and careers. These and related questions raise critical issues about organization structures and how well they meet an organization's performance needs.

ORGANIZING AS A MANAGEMENT FUNCTION

Organizing arranges people and resources to work toward a goal.

Organizing is the process of arranging people and other resources to work together to accomplish a goal. As one of the basic functions of management, it creates a division of labor and then coordinates results to achieve a common purpose.

Figure 10.1 shows the central role that organizing plays in the management process. Once plans are created, the manager's task is to see to it that they are carried out. Given a clear mission, core values, objectives, and strategy, organizing begins the process of implementation by clarifying jobs and working relationships. It identifies who is to do what, who is in charge of whom, and how different people and parts of the organization relate to and work with one another. All of this, of course, can be done in different ways. The strategic management challenge is to choose the best organizational form to fit the strategy and other situational demands.

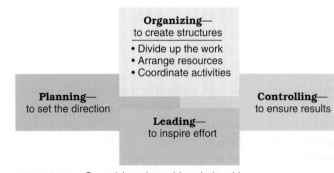

FIGURE 10.1 Organizing viewed in relationship with the other management functions.

WHAT IS ORGANIZATION STRUCTURE?

The way in which the various parts of an organization are formally arranged is usually referred to as the **organization structure**. It is the system of tasks, workflows, reporting relationships, and communication channels that link together the work of diverse individuals and groups. Any structure should both allocate tasks through a division of labor and provide for the coordination of performance results. A structure that does both of these things well is an important asset, helping to implement an organization's strategy.[3] Unfortunately, it is easier to talk about good structures than it is to actually create them.

* **Organization structure** is a system of tasks, reporting relationships, and communication linkages.

FORMAL STRUCTURES

You may know the concept of structure best in the form of an **organization chart**. This is a diagram that shows reporting relationships and the formal arrangement of work positions within an organization.[4] A typical organization chart identifies various positions and job titles, as well as the lines of authority and communication between them. It shows the **formal structure**, or the structure of the organization in its official state. This is how the organization is intended to function. By reading an organization chart, you can learn the basics of an organization's formal structure, including:

* An **organization chart** describes the arrangement of work positions within an organization.

* **Formal structure** is the official structure of the organization.

- *Division of work*—Positions and titles show work responsibilities.
- *Supervisory relationships*—Lines show who reports to whom.
- *Communication channels*—Lines show formal communication flows.
- *Major subunits*—Positions reporting to a common manager are shown.
- *Levels of management*—Vertical layers of management are shown.

But, sometimes you try to read an organization chart and it just doesn't make sense in terms of the circumstances faced by the organization. This happened to Carol Bartz, Yahoo!'s new CEO. Before taking the job, she asked to see the organization chart. Her reaction was "It was like a Dilbert cartoon. It was very odd." Her response was: "You need management here."[5]

INFORMAL STRUCTURES

Behind every formal structure typically lies an **informal structure**. This is a "shadow" organization made up of the unofficial, but often critical, working relationships between organizational members. If the informal structure could be drawn, it would show who talks to and interacts regularly with whom, regardless of their formal titles and relationships. The lines of the informal structure would cut across levels and move from side to side. They would show people meeting for coffee, in exercise groups, and in friendship cliques. No organization can be fully understood without gaining insight into the informal structure as well as the formal one.[6]

* **Informal structure** is the set of unofficial relationships among an organization's members.

A tool known as **social network analysis** is one way of identifying informal structures and their embedded social relationships. Such an analysis typically asks people to identify others whom they turn to for help most often, and with whom they communicate regularly, and who energizes and deenergizes them.[7] Social networks are then drawn with lines running from person to person according to frequency and type of relationship maintained. The result is an organizational map that shows how a lot of work really gets done in organizations, in contrast to the formal arrangements depicted on organization charts. This information is useful for redesigning the formal structure for better performance, and it also legitimates the informal networks people use in their daily work.

* **Social network analysis** identifies the informal structures and their embedded social relationships that are active in an organization.

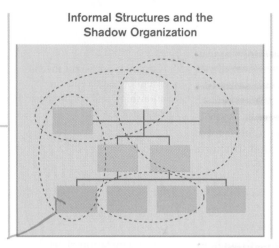

Informal Structures and the
Shadow Organization

Informal structures and social networks are in many ways essential to organizational success. They allow people to make contacts with others who can help them get things done. They also stimulate informal learning as people work and interact together throughout the workday. And, informal structures are sources of emotional support and friendship that satisfy important social needs. All of these things are especially helpful during times of change, when out-of-date formal structures may fail to provide the support people need to deal with new or unusual situations.

Of course, informal structures have potential disadvantages. Because they exist outside the formal authority system, informal structures can be susceptible to rumor, carry inaccurate information, breed resistance to change, and even divert work efforts from important objectives. The Society for Human Resource Management reported that after the bad economy caused massive job losses, firms experienced an increase in workplace eavesdropping and in "gossip and rumors about downsizings and layoffs."[8] Another problem sometimes linked to informal structures is the perception by some members that they are "outsiders" and not part of the informal groupings. As a result, they may become less engaged in their work and more dissatisfied. Some American managers of Japanese firms, for example, have complained about being excluded from what they call the "shadow cabinet" consisting of Japanese executives who hold the real power and sometimes interact with one another while excluding others.[9]

Learning Check
Study Question 1
What is organizing as a management function?

Be sure you can ☑ define *organizing* as a management function ☑ explain the difference between formal and informal structures ☑ discuss the potential advantages and disadvantages of informal structures in organizations

TRADITIONAL ORGANIZATION STRUCTURES

Departmentalization is the process of grouping people and jobs into work units.

A basic principle of organizing is that performance should improve when people are allowed to specialize and become experts in specific jobs or tasks. Given this division of labor, however, decisions must be made regarding **departmentalization**—how to group work positions into formal teams or departments that are linked together in a coordinated way. These decisions have traditionally resulted in three major types of organizational structures—functional, divisional, and matrix.[10]

FUNCTIONAL STRUCTURES

A **functional structure** groups together people with similar skills who perform similar tasks.

In **functional structures**, people with similar skills and performing similar tasks are grouped together into formal work units. Members of functional departments share technical expertise, interests, and responsibilities. The first example in Figure 10.2 shows a functional structure common in business firms, with top management arranged by the functions of marketing, finance, production, and human resources. In this functional structure, manufacturing problems are the responsibility of the production vice president, marketing problems are the responsibility of the marketing vice president, and so on. The key point is that members of a function work within their areas of expertise. If each function does its work properly, the expectation is that the business as a whole will operate successfully.

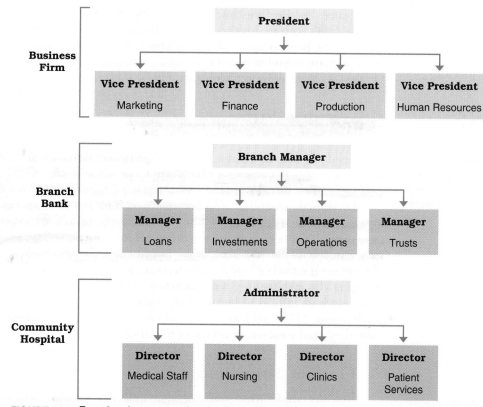

FIGURE 10.2 Functional structures in a business, branch bank, and community hospital.

Advantages of Functional Structures

Functional structures are not limited to businesses. Figure 10.2 also shows how they are used in other types of organizations such as banks and hospitals. Most typically, functional structures work well for smaller organizations dealing with only one or a few products or services. They also tend to work best in relatively stable environments where problems are predictable and the demands for change and innovation are limited. The major advantages of functional structures include the following:

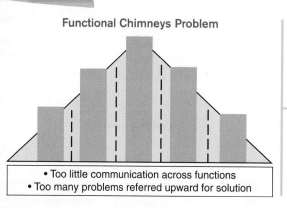

Functional Chimneys Problem

- Too little communication across functions
- Too many problems referred upward for solution

- Economies of scale with efficient use of resources.
- Task assignments consistent with expertise and training.
- High-quality technical problem solving.
- In-depth training and skill development within functions.
- Clear career paths within functions.

Disadvantages of Functional Structures

There are also potential disadvantages of functional structures. Common problems include difficulties in pinpointing responsibilities for things like cost containment, product or service quality, and innovation. A significant concern is with the **functional chimneys problem**. Sometimes also called the *functional silos problem*, this is a lack of communication, coordination, and problem solving across functions. It occurs because the functions become formalized not only on the organization chart, but also in the mind-sets of people. The sense of common purpose then gets lost to self-centered and narrow viewpoints.[11] Yahoo!'s CEO Carol

● The **functional chimneys problem** is a lack of communication and coordination across functions.

Bartz once described the functional chimneys problem this way: "The homepage people didn't want to drive traffic to the finance page because they wanted to keep them on the home page."[12] When problems like this occur, they are often persistent and harm organizational performance until, as in the case of Bartz at Yahoo!, an alert manager steps in to correct things.

DIVISIONAL STRUCTURES

East/West ✗

● A **divisional structure** groups together people working on the same product, in the same area, with similar customers, or on the same processes.

A second organizing alternative is the **divisional structure**. As illustrated in Figure 10.3, it groups together people who work on the same product or process, serve similar customers, or are located in the same area or geographical region.

Divisional structures are common in complex organizations with diverse operations that extend across many products, territories, customers, and work processes.[13] The idea is to use the divisional focus to overcome the disadvantages of a functional structure, such as the functional chimneys problem. For example, Toyota shifted toward a divisional structure in its North American operations by bringing the engineering, manufacturing, and sales functions together under a common boss instead of having each report to a top executive of its own. One analyst said: "The problem is every silo reported back to someone different, but now they need someone in charge of the whole choir."[14]

Product Structures

✗

● A **product structure** groups together people and jobs focused on a single product or service.

Product structures group together jobs and activities focused on a single product or service. They clearly link costs, profits, problems, and successes in a market area with a central point of accountability. This prompts managers to be responsive to changing market demands and customer tastes. Common in large organizations, product structures may even extend into global operations. When Fiat took over Chrysler, for example, CEO Sergio Marchionne said he wanted a "leaner, flatter structure" to "speed decision making and improve communication flow." His choice was to use product divisions. Each of the firm's three brands—

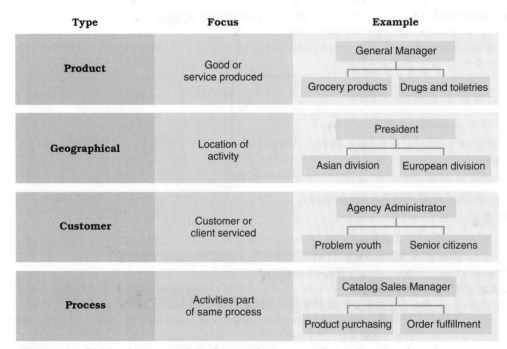

Type	Focus	Example
Product	Good or service produced	General Manager → Grocery products / Drugs and toiletries
Geographical	Location of activity	President → Asian division / European division
Customer	Customer or client serviced	Agency Administrator → Problem youth / Senior citizens
Process	Activities part of same process	Catalog Sales Manager → Product purchasing / Order fulfillment

FIGURE 10.3 Divisional structures based on product, geography, customer, and process.

Chrysler, Jeep, and Dodge—was given its own chief executive and assigned responsibility for its own profits and losses.[15] The "new" General Motors took the same approach, organizing around four product divisions—Buick, Cadillac, Chevrolet, and GMC, when it emerged from bankruptcy protection. The firm's CEO at the time, Fritz Henderson, said: "100 percent of our product, technology and marketing spending will now be focused behind the four core brands."[16]

Geographical Structures

Geographical structures, sometimes called *area structures*, group together jobs and activities being performed in the same location. They are typically used when there is a need to differentiate products or services in various locations, such as in different parts of a country. They are also quite common in international operations, where they help focus attention on the unique cultures and requirements of particular regions. As United Parcel Service operations expanded worldwide, for example, the company announced a change from a product structure to a geographical structure. Two geographical divisions were created—the Americas and Europe/Asia. Each area was given responsibility for its own logistics, sales, and other business functions.

A **geographical structure** groups together people and jobs performed in the same location.

Customer Structures

Customer structures group together jobs and activities that are serving the same customers or clients. The goal is to best serve the special needs of the different customer groups. This is a common structure in the consumer products industry.

women, men dept

A **customer structure** groups together people and jobs that serve the same customers or clients.

Real People

Patricia Karter Tackles Growth with Values

At least that's what Patricia Karter, the CEO of Dancing Deer Baking hopes for when a customer is digging into a Cherry Almond Ginger Chew cookie. The company sells about $8 million of them and other confectionary concoctions. Every product is made with all natural ingredients; they're packaged in recycled materials; and, they're all produced in inner-city Boston.

Dancing Deer began with a $20,000 investment and two ovens in a former pizza shop. A growth strategy soon emerged as the bakery prospered. When Dancing Deer was recognized on national TV as having the "best cake in the nation," that led to more expansion into mail-order sales.

Growth can cause problems for any organization as managers try to adjust practices, structures, and staffing to deal with increasing size. Dancing Deer is no exception. But for Patricia Karter the pathways to growth have been clear—let core values be the guide. All of Dancing Deer's employees get stock options and free lunches; 35% of profits from the firm's Sweet Home cakes are donated to help the homeless find accommodations and jobs. "There's more to life than selling cookies," says the firm's website, "but it's not a bad way to make a living."

Throughout all of Dancing Deer's success, Karter has been determined to stick with her principles and market a brand with values. She is steadfastly committed to low-income Roxbury, Massachusetts, as Dancing Deer's home territory. And when offered a chance to make a large cookie sale to Williams-Sonoma, she declined; the contract would have required use of preservatives. Williams-Sonoma was so impressed with her products and principles that it contracted for the sale of her bakery mixes. Instead of lost opportunity, Karter's principles guided the firm to more sales and further growth. Now her goal is to hit and surpass $50 million in sales. At that point she says the firm will be "big enough to make an impact, to be a social economic force."

Dancing Deer's web site sums up the firm's story this way: "It has been an interesting journey. Our successes are due to luck, a tremendous amount of dedication and hard work, and a commitment to having fun while being true to our principles. We have had failures as well—and survived them with a sense of humor."

3M Corporation structures itself to focus attention on such diverse markets as consumer and office, specialty materials, industrial, health care, electronics and communications, and safety. Customer structures are also useful in services. Banks, for example, use them to give separate attention to consumer and commercial customers for loans. Figure 10.3 also shows a government agency using the customer structure to serve different client populations.

Process Structures

● A **work process** is a group of related tasks that collectively creates a valuable work product.

● A **process structure** groups jobs and activities that are part of the same processes.

A **work process** is a group of related tasks that collectively creates something of value to a customer.[17] An example is order fulfillment by a catalog retailer, a process that takes an order from point of initiation by the customer to point of fulfillment by a delivered product. A **process structure** groups together jobs and activities that are part of the same processes. Figure 10.3 shows how this might take the form of product-purchasing teams and order-fulfillment teams for a mail-order catalog business.

Advantages and Disadvantages of Divisional Structures

Organizations use divisional structures for a variety of reasons, including the desire to avoid the functional chimneys problem and other disadvantages of functional structures. The potential advantages of divisional structures include:

- More flexibility in responding to environmental changes.
- Improved coordination across functional departments.
- Clear points of responsibility for product or service delivery.
- Expertise focused on specific customers, products, and regions.
- Greater ease in changing size by adding or deleting divisions.

As with other structural alternatives, there are also potential disadvantages to divisional structures. They can reduce economies of scale and increase costs through the duplication of resources and efforts across divisions. They can also create unhealthy rivalries as divisions compete for resources and top management attention, and as they emphasize division needs over the goals of the organization as a whole.

MATRIX STRUCTURES

● A **matrix structure** combines functional and divisional approaches to emphasize project or program teams.

The **matrix structure**, often called the *matrix organization*, combines the functional and divisional structures. In effect, it is an attempt to gain the advantages and minimize the disadvantages of each. This is accomplished in the matrix by using permanent teams that cut across functions to support specific products, projects, or programs.[18] As shown in Figure 10.4, workers in a matrix structure belong to at least two formal groups at the same time—a functional group and a product, program, or project team. They also report to two bosses—one within the function and the other within the team.

The matrix organization has gained a strong foothold in the workplace, with applications in such diverse settings as manufacturing (e.g., aerospace, electronics, pharmaceuticals), service industries (e.g., banking, brokerage, retailing), professional fields (e.g., accounting, advertising, law), and the nonprofit sector (e.g., city, state, and federal agencies, hospitals, universities). Matrix structures are also found in multinational corporations, where they offer the flexibility to deal with regional differences while still handling multiple product, program, or project needs.

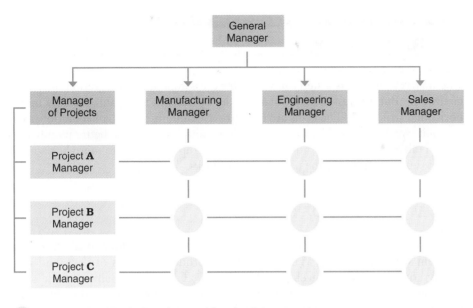

FIGURE 10.4 Matrix structure in a small, multiproject business firm.

Persons assigned to both projects and functional departments

Advantages and Disadvantages of Matrix Structures

The main benefits of matrix structures rest with the teams whose members work closely together to share expertise and information in a timely manner. This goes a long way toward eliminating the functional chimneys problem and poor cross-functional communication as discussed earlier. The potential advantages of matrix structures include:

- Better communication and cooperation across functions.
- Improved decision making; problem solving takes place at the team level where the best information is available.
- Increased flexibility in adding, removing, or changing operations to meet changing demands.
- Better customer service; there is always a program, product, or project manager informed and available to answer questions.
- Better performance accountability through the program, product, or project managers.
- Improved strategic management; top managers are freed from lower-level problem solving to focus time on more strategic issues.

Predictably, matrix structures also have potential disadvantages. The two-boss system is susceptible to power struggles if functional supervisors and team leaders compete with one another to exercise authority. The two-boss system can be frustrating if it creates task confusion and conflicting work priorities. Team meetings in the matrix can take lots of time, and the teams may develop "groupitis"—strong team loyalties that cause a loss of focus on larger organizational goals. And, the requirement of adding the team leaders to a matrix structure can result in higher costs.

Be sure you can ☑ explain the differences between functional, divisional, and matrix structures ☑ list advantages and disadvantages of a functional structure, divisional structure, and matrix structure ☑ draw charts to show how each type of traditional structure is used in organizations familiar to you

Learning Check

Study Question 2
What are the traditional organization structures?

HORIZONTAL ORGANIZATION STRUCTURES

The matrix structure is a step toward better cross-functional integration in an organization. But it is just one part of a broader movement to organize around more horizontal structures. The goals are to improve communication, collaboration, and flexibility by decreasing hierarchy, increasing empowerment, and better mobilizing human talents.[19] And as traditional vertical structures give way to more horizontal ones, teams are serving as the basic building blocks.[20]

TEAM STRUCTURES

It's no secret that Microsoft had a bad experience with the functional chimneys problem while developing Windows XP; the product had lots of flaws and was widely criticized. When developing Windows 7, CEO Steve Ballmer made sure that the focus was on collaboration and teamwork both within the firm and between the firm and its customers. He wanted walls limiting communication to be broken down, and he wanted mind-sets focused on the "whole" product, not just on its individual parts. Teamwork was one of the ways to get all this done. Whereas programmers stuck to their silos when working on XP—with the result that the system was full of conflicts and bugs as different devices like printers and graphics cards struggled to work together, Windows 7 was developed in a team-work-intensive way. The team leader for the touch technology in Windows 7 says: "Instead of it being a plan owned by one team, our plan was a part of all the teams."[21]

> A **team structure** uses permanent and temporary cross-functional teams to improve lateral relations.

Organizations with **team structures** make extensive use of both permanent and temporary teams to solve problems, complete special projects, and accomplish day-to-day tasks.[22] As illustrated in Figure 10.5, these are often **cross-functional teams** composed of members drawn from different areas of work responsibility.[23] Like the matrix structure, the intention is to break down functional chimneys and create more effective lateral relations around and across the organization.

> A **cross-functional team** brings together members from different functional departments.

> **Project teams** are convened for a particular task or project and disband once it is completed.

Team structures also make use of many **project teams** that are convened to complete a specific task or "project," such as handle the changeover to a new information system. These project teams are temporary and disband once the task is completed. The intention is to convene a team of people who have the needed talents, focus their efforts intensely to solve a problem or take advantage of a special opportunity, and then release them once the project is finished.

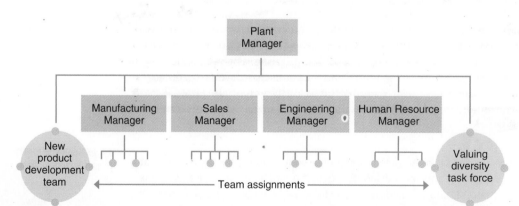

FIGURE 10.5 How a team structure uses cross-functional teams for improved lateral relations.

Advantages and Disadvantages of Team Structures

The advantages of team structures largely trace to the fact that team assignments break down barriers as people from different parts of an organization get to know one another. This can also boost morale. People working in teams often experience a greater sense of involvement and identification, and this increases their enthusiasm for the job. Because teams focus shared knowledge and expertise on specific problems, they can also improve the speed and quality of decisions in many situations. After a research team at Polaroid Corporation developed a new medical imaging system in one-half the predicted time, a senior executive said: "Our researchers are not any smarter, but by working together they get the value of each other's intelligence almost instantaneously."[24]

The complexities of teams and teamwork contribute to the potential disadvantages of team structures. These include conflicting loyalties for persons with both team and functional assignments. They also include issues of time management and group process. By their very nature, teams spend a lot of time in meetings. Not all of this time is productive. How well team members spend their time together often depends on the quality of interpersonal relations, group dynamics, and team management. But, as described in Chapter 16 on teams and teamwork, all of these concerns are manageable.

NETWORK STRUCTURES

Organizations using a **network structure**, like the one in Figure 10.6, have a central core of full-time employees surrounded by "networks" composed of outside contractors and partners that supply essential services.[25] Because the central core is relatively small and the surrounding networks can be expanded or shrunk as needed, the network structure helps lower costs and improve flexibility in dealing with changing environments.[26] It is quite a contrast to the old model in which organizations basically owned everything they needed.

Instead of doing everything for itself with full-time employees, the network organization employs a minimum staff and contracts out as much work as possible. It makes use of **strategic alliances**, which are cooperation agreements with other firms to pursue business activities of mutual interest. Some are *outsourcing strategic*

● A **network structure** uses information technologies to link with networks of outside suppliers and service contractors.

● A **strategic alliance** is a cooperation agreement with another organization to jointly pursue activities of mutual interest.

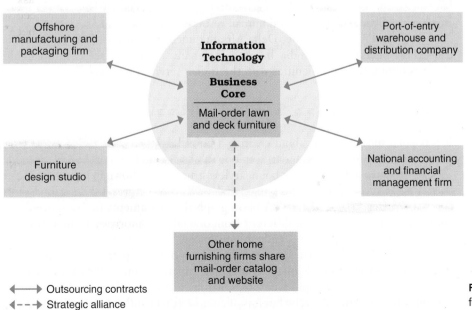

→ Outsourcing contracts
◄--→ Strategic alliance

FIGURE 10.6 A network structure for a Web-based retail business.

alliances in which they contract to purchase important services from another organization. Others may be *supplier strategic alliances* that link businesses in preferred supplier-customer relationships that guarantee a smooth and timely flow of quality supplies among the partners.

The example in Figure 10.6 shows how a network structure might work for a mail-order company selling lawn and deck furniture through a catalog. The firm is very small, consisting of relatively few full-time core employees. Beyond that, it is structured as a network of outsourcing and partner relationships that are maintained by the latest in information technology. Merchandise is designed on contract with a furniture designer—which responds quickly as designs are shared and customized via computer networking. The furniture is manufactured and packaged by subcontractors located around the world—wherever materials are found at the lowest cost and best quality. Stock is maintained and shipped from a contract warehouse—ensuring quality storage and on-time expert shipping. Accounting and financial details are contracted with an outside firm—providing better technical expertise than the merchandiser could afford to employ on a full-time basis. The quarterly catalog is produced cooperatively as a strategic alliance with two other firms that sell different home furnishings with a related price appeal. All of this is supported by a company website and information system maintained by an outside contractor.

Advantages and Disadvantages of Network Structures

In respect to advantages, network structures are lean and streamlined. They help organizations stay cost-competitive by reducing overhead and increasing operating efficiency. Network concepts allow organizations to employ outsourcing strategies and contract out specialized business functions. Within the operating core of a network structure, furthermore, interesting jobs are created for those who coordinate the entire system of relationships.

The potential disadvantages of network structures lie largely with the demands of new management responsibilities. The more complex the business or mission of the organization, the more complicated it is to control and coordinate the network of contracts and alliances. If one part of the network breaks down or fails to deliver, the entire system suffers. Also, there is the potential to lose control over activities contracted out and to experience a lack of loyalty among contractors who are used infrequently rather than on a long-term basis. Some worry that outsourcing can become so aggressive as to be dangerous to the firm, especially when critical activities such as finance, logistics, and human resources management are outsourced.[27] Not too long ago, for example, Delta Air announced that it was shutting down its call-center operations in India because too many customers were complaining about communication difficulties with the Indian service providers.[28]

BOUNDARYLESS STRUCTURES

A **boundaryless organization** eliminates internal boundaries among subsystems and external boundaries with the external environment.

It is popular today to speak about creating a **boundaryless organization** that eliminates many of the internal boundaries among subsystems and external boundaries with the external environment.[29] The boundaryless structure, as shown in Figure 10.7, can be viewed as a combination of the team and network structures just described, with the addition of "temporariness." A photograph that documents this organization's configuration today will look different from one taken tomorrow, as the form naturally adjusts to new pressures and circumstances.

Internal to the boundaryless organization, spontaneous teamwork and communication replace formal lines of authority. Meetings and information sharing happen continuously. People work together in teams that form and disband as needed. There is little hierarchy but lots of empowerment and technology utilization;

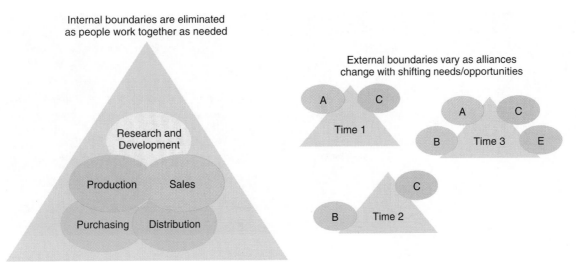

FIGURE 10.7 The boundaryless organization eliminates internal and external barriers.

impermanence is accepted. Knowledge sharing is both a goal and an essential component. At consulting giant PricewaterhouseCoopers, for example, knowledge sharing brings together 160,000 partners spread across 150 countries in a vast, virtual-learning and problem-solving network. Partners collaborate electronically through online databases, where information is stored, problems are posted, and questions are asked and answered in real time by those with experience and knowledge relevant to the problem at hand.[30]

The **virtual organization** takes the boundaryless concept to the extreme.[31] It operates as a shifting network of alliances that are engaged as needed using IT and the Internet. The virtual organization calls an alliance into action to meet specific operating needs and objectives; when the work is complete, the alliance rests until next called into action. This mix of mobilized alliances is continuously shifting, and an expansive pool of potential alliances is always ready to be called upon. Do you see similarities, for example, with the MySpace, Facebook, or LinkedIn communities? Isn't the virtual organization concept similar to how we manage our relationships online—signing on, signing off, getting things done as needed with different people and groups, and all taking place instantaneously, temporarily, and without the need for face-to-face contacts?

● A **virtual organization** uses IT and the Internet to engage a shifting network of strategic alliances.

Be sure you can ☑ describe how organizations can use cross-functional teams and project teams in their structures ☑ define *network structure* ☑ illustrate how a new retail venture might use a network structure to organize its various operations ☑ discuss the potential advantages and disadvantages of a network structure ☑ explain the concept of the boundaryless organization

Learning Check ☑

Study Question 3
What are the types of horizontal organization structures?

ORGANIZATIONAL DESIGNS

Organizational design is the process of choosing and implementing structures to accomplish the organization's mission and objectives.[32] Because every organization faces its own set of unique problems and opportunities, no one design applies in all circumstances. The best design at any moment is the one that achieves a good match between structure and situational contingencies—including task, technology, environment, and people.[33] The choices among organizational design alternatives are broadly framed in the distinction between mechanistic or bureaucratic designs at one extreme, and organic or adaptive designs at the other.

● **Organizational design** is the process of creating structures that accomplish mission and objectives.

Cisco Systems Fights Bureaucracy While Pursuing Growth

At a shareholder meeting of Cisco Systems, an investor came right out and asked CEO John Chambers, "At what size does Cisco become so big and diverse that its growth and profitability will plateau?" Chambers admits that one of Cisco's problems is managing growth and fighting the forces of bureaucracy. He tries to break bureaucracy and keep decisions flowing to fuel his growth strategy by using a series of 48 management councils. Their members are empowered to make major decisions without his approval.

● A **bureaucracy** emphasizes formal authority, order, fairness, and efficiency.

CONTINGENCY IN ORGANIZATIONAL DESIGN

As first introduced in the discussion of management history in Chapter 2, a **bureaucracy** is a form of organization based on logic, order, and the legitimate use of formal authority.[34] It is a classic vertical structure, and its distinguishing features include a clear-cut division of labor, strict hierarchy of authority, formal rules and procedures, and promotion based on competency.

According to sociologist Max Weber, bureaucracies were supposed to be orderly, fair, and highly efficient.[35] Yet, the bureaucracies that we know are often associated with "red tape." And instead of being orderly and fair, they are often seen as cumbersome and impersonal to customer or client needs.[36] But rather than view all bureaucratic structures as inevitably flawed, management theory asks the contingency questions: When is a bureaucratic form a good choice for an organization? What alternatives exist when it is not a good choice?

Pioneering research conducted in England during the early 1960s by Tom Burns and George Stalker helps answer these questions.[37] After investigating 20 manufacturing firms they concluded that two quite different organizational forms could be successful, depending on the nature of a firm's external environment. A more bureaucratic form, which Burns and Stalker called "mechanistic," thrived when the environment was stable. But it experienced difficulty when the environment was rapidly changing and uncertain. In these dynamic situations, a much less-bureaucratic form, called "organic," performed best. Figure 10.8 portrays these two approaches as opposite extremes on a continuum of organizational design alternatives.

MECHANISTIC AND ORGANIC DESIGNS

● A **mechanistic design** is centralized, with many rules and procedures, a clear-cut division of labor, narrow spans of control, and formal coordination.

Organizations with more **mechanistic designs** are highly bureaucratic. As shown in the figure, they are vertical structures that typically operate with centralized authority, many rules and procedures, a precise division of labor, narrow spans of control, and formal means of coordination. They can be described as "tight" structures of the traditional pyramid form.[38]

Mechanistic designs work best for organizations doing routine tasks in stable environments. For a good example, visit your local fast-food restaurant. Each store is a relatively small operation that operates quite like others in the franchise chain and according to rules established by the corporate management. Service personnel work in orderly and disciplined ways, guided by training, rules and procedures, and by close supervision of crew leaders who work alongside them.

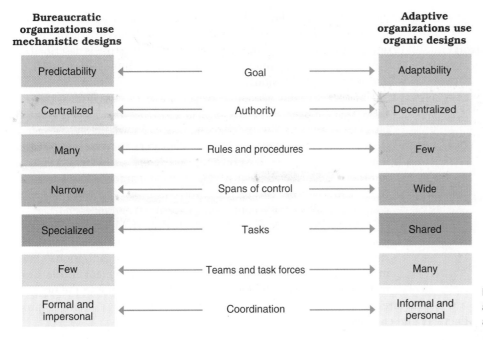

Bureaucratic organizations use mechanistic designs		Adaptive organizations use organic designs
Predictability	Goal	Adaptability
Centralized	Authority	Decentralized
Many	Rules and procedures	Few
Narrow	Spans of control	Wide
Specialized	Tasks	Shared
Few	Teams and task forces	Many
Formal and impersonal	Coordination	Informal and personal

FIGURE 10.8 Organizational design alternatives: from bureaucratic to adaptive organizations.

Even their appearance is carefully regulated, with everyone working in uniform. These restaurants perform well as they repetitively deliver items that are part of their standard menus. You quickly encounter the limits, however, if you try to order something not on the menu. The chains also encounter difficulty when consumer tastes change. Making adjustments to these mechanistic systems takes a long time.

When organizations operate in dynamic and often uncertain environments, their effectiveness depends on being able to change with the times. This requires more **organic designs** as described in Figure 10.8.[39] These are horizontal structures with decentralized authority, fewer rules and procedures, less precise division of labor, wider spans of control, and more personal means of coordination.

Organic designs create **adaptive organizations** that work well in environments that demand flexibility in dealing with changing conditions. They are relatively "loose" systems where a lot of work gets done through informal structures and networking.[40] And, they are built on a foundation of trust that people will do the right things on their own initiative. This means letting workers actively participate in production scheduling and setting up control systems; it means letting workers use their ideas for problem solving; and it means giving workers the freedom to do what they can do best—get the job done. This helps create what has been described in earlier chapters as a *learning organization*, one designed for continuous adaptation through problem solving, innovation, and learning.[41]

opposite of mechanistic designs

● An **organic design** is decentralized, with fewer rules and procedures, open divisions of labor, wide spans of control, and more personal coordination.

● An **adaptive organization** operates with a minimum of bureaucratic features and encourages worker empowerment and teamwork.

TRENDS IN ORGANIZATIONAL DESIGNS

The complexity, uncertainty, and change inherent in today's environment are prompting more and more organizations to shift toward horizontal structures and organic designs. As they do so, a number of trends in organizational design are evident.

Fewer Levels of Management

7-10 JPPI

A typical organization chart shows the **chain of command**, or the line of authority that vertically links each position with successively higher levels of management. When organizations grow in size, they tend to get taller as more and more levels of management are added to the chain of command. Yet, high-

● The **chain of command** links all persons with successively higher levels of authority.

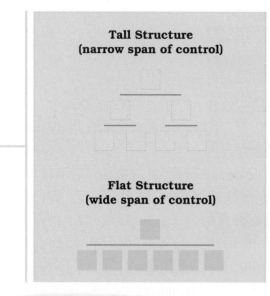

**Tall Structure
(narrow span of control)**

**Flat Structure
(wide span of control)**

X ● **Span of control** is the number of subordinates directly reporting to a manager. *7–10 people larso*

X ● **Tall structures** have narrow spans of control and many hierarchical levels.

X ● **Flat structures** have wide spans of control and few hierarchical levels.

performing firms like Nucor, a North Carolina-based steel producer, show preferences for fewer management levels. Nucor's management hierarchy is extremely compact. Its structure is described as "simple" and "streamlined" in order to "allow employees to innovate and make quick decisions."[42]

One of the influences on management levels is **span of control**—the number of persons directly reporting to a manager. **Tall structures** have narrow spans of control and many levels of management. Because tall organizations have more managers, they are more costly. They also tend to be less efficient, less flexible, and less customer-sensitive. **Flat structures** have wider spans of control and fewer levels of management, and this reduces overhead costs. The wider spans of control also allow workers more empowerment and independence.[43]

When Procter & Gamble's CEO, Robert McDonald, was appointed, one of his first announcements was that he would be taking steps to "create a simpler, flatter and more agile organization." This involved cutting the number of levels of management in the firm from nine to seven. McDonald stated that streamlining the organization structure was important "because simplification reduces cost, improves productivity and enhances employee satisfaction."[44]

Trend: Organizations are cutting unnecessary levels of management and shifting to wider spans of control. Managers are taking responsibility for larger numbers of subordinates who operate with less direct supervision.

Real Ethics

Flattened into Exhaustion

Dear Stress Doctor:

My boss has come up with this great idea of laying off some managers, assigning more workers to those of us who remain, and calling us "coaches" instead of supervisors. She says this is all part of a new management approach to operate with a flatter structure and more empowerment.

For me this means a lot more work coordinating the activities of 17 operators instead of the six that I previously supervised. I can't get everything cleaned up on my desk most days, and I end up taking a lot of paperwork home.

As my organization "restructures" and cuts back staff, it puts a greater burden on those of us that remain. We get exhausted, and our families get short-changed and even angry. I even feel guilty now taking time to watch my daughter play soccer on Saturday mornings. Sure, there's some decent pay involved, but that doesn't make up for the heavy price in terms of lost family time.

But you know what? My boss doesn't get it. I never hear her ask: "Camille, are you working too much; don't you think it's time to get back on a reasonable schedule?" No! What I often hear instead is "Look at Andy; he handles our new management model really well, and he's a real go-getter. I don't think he's been out of here one night this week before 8 PM."

What am I to do, just keep it up until everything falls apart one day? Is a flatter structure with fewer managers always best? Am I missing something in regard to this "new management?"

Sincerely,
Overworked in Cincinnati

You Decide

Is it ethical to restructure operations by cutting numerous employees and then simply expecting the remaining employees to do more work for the same pay? At what point do a manager's expectations regarding employee work hours become unreasonable? Do managers have an obligation to help employees maintain a reasonable work–life balance, or is a manager's only obligation to ensure that the company benefits from the employee's work efforts?

Macy's CEO Tries Decentralization with Centralization

Can Macy's succeed by becoming more centralized and decentralized at the same time? CEO Terry Lundgren thinks so; he wants a stronger local focus to allow stores and regions to cater more to tastes in their immediate customer areas. And he wants centralized buying, planning, and marketing to gain efficiencies and save costs. So far the results are good for the program he calls "My Macy's." The firm has saved millions in costs by cutting back on regional staff and transferring decision making so that the firm's stores, all 800+ of them, can now stock locally and buy centrally.

More Delegation and Empowerment

All managers must decide what work they should do themselves and what should be left for others. At issue here is **delegation**—the process of entrusting work to others by giving them the right to make decisions and take action. A classical principle of organization warns managers not to delegate without giving the other person sufficient authority to perform. The *authority-and-responsibility principle* states that authority should equal responsibility when work is delegated from a supervisor to a subordinate. When done well the process of delegation involves these three action steps.

- *Step 1*—the manager assigns responsibility by carefully explaining the work or duties someone else is expected to do. This responsibility is an expectation for the other person to perform assigned tasks.
- *Step 2*—the manager grants authority to act. Along with the assigned task, the right to take necessary actions (for example, to spend money, direct the work of others, or use resources) is given to the other person.
- *Step 3*—the manager creates accountability. By accepting an assignment, the person takes on a direct obligation to the manager to complete the job as agreed.

On those days when you complain that "I just can't get everything done" the real problem may be that you are trying to do everything yourself. Unwillingness to delegate is a common management failure. Whether this comes from a lack of trust in others or from personal inflexibility, it can still be damaging. Too little delegation overloads the manager with work that could be done by others; it also denies others many opportunities to fully utilize their talents on the job.

When done well, delegation leads to **empowerment**. This concept was defined in the chapter opener as letting others make decisions and exercise discretion in their work. Empowerment results when delegation moves decisions to people who are most capable of doing the work. It builds performance potential by allowing people freedom to use their talents, contribute ideas, and do their jobs in the best possible ways. And because empowerment creates a sense of ownership, it also increases commitment to decisions and work goals.

Trend: Managers are delegating more. They are finding ways to empower people at all levels to make more decisions that affect themselves and their work.

Decentralization with Centralization

Should most decisions be made at the top levels of an organization, or should they be dispersed by extensive delegation throughout all levels of management? The former approach is referred to as **centralization**; the latter is called **decentralization**.

● **Delegation** is the process of distributing and entrusting work to other persons.

● **Empowerment** allows others to make decisions and exercise discretion in their work.

● **Centralization** is the concentration of authority for most decisions at the top level of an organization.

● **Decentralization** is the dispersion of authority to make decisions throughout all organization levels.

Research Brief

Making Schools Work Better with Organizational Design

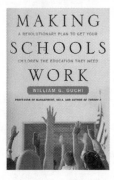

Scholar and consultant William Ouchi believes that our public schools can be improved through organizational design. In his book *Making Schools Work: A Revolutionary Plan to Get Your Children the Education They Need*, Ouchi points out that as organizations grow in size, they tend to "bulk up" with staff personnel and higher-level managers that are distant from customers and operating workers. He finds many less-successful schools following this pattern.

Ouchi's study of 223 school districts suggests that adding administrative weight and cost at the top does little to improve organizational performance and can actually harm it. Even though most school districts are highly centralized, he finds that decentralization is a characteristic of the more successful ones. The better districts in his study had fewer central office staff personnel per student and allowed maximum autonomy to school principals. Ouchi advocates redesigning schools so that decision making is more decentralized. He believes in allowing principals more autonomy to control school budgets and work with their staffs, and in allowing teachers more freedom to solve their own problems.

You Be the Researcher

Does Ouchi offer us a general organizational design principle—systems perform best with streamlined designs and greater decentralization? Or can you come up with examples of organizations that perform well with large staffs and lots of centralization?

Don't you wonder how School District B justifies its large administrative staff while School District A has a reputation for success? What is the ratio of administrative to instructional staff at your university? Could "performance" be improved along lines suggested by Ouchi?

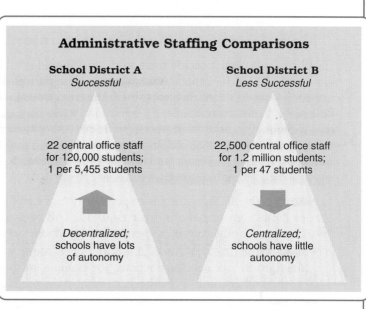

Administrative Staffing Comparisons

School District A
Successful

22 central office staff
for 120,000 students;
1 per 5,455 students

*Decentralized;
schools have lots
of autonomy*

School District B
Less Successful

22,500 central office staff
for 1.2 million students;
1 per 47 students

*Centralized;
schools have little
autonomy*

Reference: William Ouchi, *Making Schools Work: A Revolutionary Plan to Get Your Children the Education They Need* (New York: Simon & Schuster, 2003); and Richard Riordan, Linda Lingle, and Lyman Porter, "Making Public Schools Work: Management Reform as the Key," *Academy of Management Journal,* vol. 48, no. 6 (2005), pp. 929–40.

But the management issue here doesn't have to be framed as an either/or choice. Today's organizations can use information technology to operate with greater decentralization without giving up centralized control.[45]

With computer networks and advanced information systems, managers at higher levels can more easily stay informed about a wide range of day-to-day performance matters. Because they have information on results readily available, they can allow more decentralization in decision making. If something goes wrong, the information systems should sound an alarm and allow corrective action to be taken quickly.

> *Trend:* Delegation, empowerment, and horizontal structures are contributing to more decentralization in organizations; at the same time, advances in information technology are allowing for adequate centralized control.

Reduced Use of Staff

● **Staff positions** provide technical expertise for other parts of the organization.

When it comes to coordination and control in organizations, the issue of line—staff relationships is important. Chapter 1 described **staff positions** as providing expert advice and guidance to line personnel. They basically perform a technical service or provide special problem-solving expertise for other parts of the organization. In a large retail chain, for example, line managers in each store typically make daily operating decisions regarding direct sales of merchandise. But, staff specialists at the corporate or regional levels often provide direction and support so that all the stores operate with the same credit, purchasing, employment, marketing, and advertising procedures.

Problems in line–staff distinctions can and do arise, and organizations sometimes find that staff size grows to the point where it costs more than it is worth. This is why staff cutbacks are common in downsizing and other turnaround efforts. There is no one best solution to the problem of how to divide work between line and staff responsibilities. What is best for any organization will be a cost-effective staff component that satisfies, but doesn't overreact to, needs for specialized technical assistance to line operations.

Trend: Organizations are reducing the size of staff. They are lowering costs and increasing efficiency by employing fewer staff personnel and using smaller staff units.

Be sure you can ☑ define *organizational design* ☑ describe the characteristics of mechanistic and organic designs ☑ explain when the mechanistic design and the organic design work best ☑ describe trends in levels of management, delegation and empowerment, decentralization and centralization, and use of staff

Learning Check ☑

Study Question 4
How are organizational designs changing the workplace?

Management Learning Review

Study Questions Summary

1 What is organizing as a management function?

- Organizing is the process of arranging people and resources to work toward a common goal.
- Organizing decisions divide up the work that needs to be done, allocate people and resources to do it, and coordinate results to achieve productivity.
- Structure is the system of tasks, reporting relationships, and communication that links people and positions within an organization.
- The formal structure, such as that shown on an organization chart, describes how an organization is supposed to work.
- The informal structure of an organization consists of the unofficial relationships that develop among members.

FOR DISCUSSION **If organization charts are imperfect, why bother with them?**

2 What are the traditional organization structures?

- In functional structures, people with similar skills who perform similar activities are grouped together under a common manager.

- In divisional structures, people who work on a similar product, work in the same geographical region, serve the same customers, or participate in the same work process are grouped together under common managers.
- A matrix structure combines the functional and divisional approaches to create permanent cross-functional project teams.

FOR DISCUSSION **Why use functional structures if they are prone to functional chimneys problems?**

3 What are the types of horizontal organization structures?

- Team structures use cross-functional teams and task forces to improve lateral relations and problem solving at all levels.
- Network structures use contracted services and strategic alliances to support a core organizational center.
- Boundaryless structures or boundaryless organizations combine team and network structures with the advantages of technology to accomplish tasks and projects.
- Virtual organizations utilize information technology to mobilize a shifting mix of strategic alliances to accomplish tasks and projects.

FOR DISCUSSION **How can problems with group decision making hurt team structures?**

4 How are organizational designs changing the workplace?

- Contingency in organizational design basically means finding a design that best fits situational features.
- Mechanistic designs are bureaucratic and vertical, performing best for routine and predictable tasks.

- Organic designs are adaptive and horizontal, performing best in conditions requiring change and flexibility.
- Key organizing trends include fewer levels of management, more delegation and empowerment, decentralization with centralization, and fewer staff positions.

FOR DISCUSSION **Which of the organizing trends is most subject to change under current conditions?**

Self-Test

Multiple-Choice Questions

1. The main purpose of organizing as a management function is to _____.
   (a) make sure that results match plans   (b) arrange people and resources to accomplish work   (c) create enthusiasm for the work to be done   (d) match strategies with operational plans

2. _____ is the system of tasks, reporting relationships, and communication that links together the various parts of an organization.
   (a) Structure   (b) Staff   (c) Decentralization   (d) Differentiation

3. Transmission of rumors and resistance to change are potential disadvantages often associated with _____.
   (a) virtual organizations   (b) informal structures   (c) delegation   (d) specialized staff

4. An organization chart showing vice presidents of marketing, finance, manufacturing, and purchasing all reporting to the president is depicting a _____ structure.
   (a) functional   (b) matrix   (c) network   (d) product

5. The "two-boss" system of reporting relationships is found in the _____ structure.
   (a) functional   (b) matrix   (c) network   (d) product

6. A manufacturing business with a functional structure has recently developed two new product lines. The president of the company might consider shifting to a/an _____ structure to gain a stronger focus on each product.
   (a) virtual   (b) informal   (c) divisional   (d) network

7. Better lower-level teamwork and more top-level strategic management are among the expected advantages of a _____ structure.
   (a) divisional   (b) matrix   (c) geographical   (d) product

8. "Tall" organizations tend to have long chains of command and _____ spans of control.
   (a) wide   (b) narrow   (c) informal   (d) centralized

9. The functional chimneys problem occurs when people in different functions _____.
   (a) fail to communicate with one another   (b) try to help each other work with customers   (c) spend too much time coordinating decisions   (d) focus on products rather than functions

10. _____ structure tries to combine the best elements of the functional and divisional forms.
    (a) Virtual   (b) Boundaryless   (c) Team   (d) Matrix

11. A student volunteers to gather information on a company for a group case analysis project. The other members of the group agree, and tell her to go ahead and choose the information sources. In terms of delegation, this group is giving the student _____ to fulfill the agreed-upon task.
    (a) responsibility   (b) accountability   (c) authority   (d) decentralization

12. The current trend in the use of staff in organizations is to _____.
    (a) give staff personnel more authority over operations   (b) reduce the number of staff personnel   (c) remove all staff from the organization   (d) combine all staff functions in one department

13. The bureaucratic organization described by Max Weber is similar to the _____ organization described by Burns and Stalker.
    (a) adaptive   (b) mechanistic   (c) organic   (d) adhocracy

14. Which type of organization design best fits an uncertain and changing environment?
    (a) mechanistic   (b) bureaucratic   (c) organic   (d) traditional

15. Which type of organization structure is most likely to use lots of external strategic alliances?
    (a) functional   (b) network   (c) matrix   (d) mechanistic

Short-Response Questions

16. What symptoms might indicate that a functional structure is causing problems for the organization?
17. Explain by example the concept of a network organization structure.
18. Explain the practical significance of this statement: "Organizational design should be done in contingency fashion."
19. Describe two trends in organizational design and explain their importance to managers.

Essay Question

20. Faisal Sham supervises a group of seven project engineers. His unit is experiencing a heavy workload, as the demand for different versions of one of his firm's computer components is growing. Faisal finds that he doesn't have time to follow up on all design details for each version. Up until now he has tried to do this all by himself. Two of the engineers have shown interest in helping him coordinate work on the various designs. As a consultant, how would you advise Faisal in terms of delegating work to them?

Management Skills and Competencies

Self-Assessment

Back to Yourself: Empowerment

Structures help bring order to organizational complexity; they put people together in ways that, on paper at least, make good sense in terms of getting tasks accomplished. But although there are many structural alternatives, as described in this chapter, they all struggle for success at times. Things can change so fast that you might think of today's structures as solutions to yesterday's problems. This puts a great burden on people to fill in the gaps and deal spontaneously with things that structures don't or can't cover at any point in time. **Empowerment** is a way of unlocking talent and motivation so that people can act in ways that make a performance difference; it gives them freedom to make decisions about how they work. Many managers fail when it comes to empowerment. And when they do, their organizations often underperform. After you complete the following self-assessment on Empowering Others, don't forget to go online to check your Organization Design Preferences.

> Managers have a lot to gain from **empowerment** that lets other people use their expertise to make decisions and exercise discretion in their work.

Further Reflection: Empowering Others

Instructions

Think of times when you have been in charge of a group in a work or student situation. Complete the following questionnaire by recording how you feel about each statement according to this scale:[46]

1 Strongly disagree   2 Disagree   3 Neutral   4 Agree   5 Strongly agree

When in charge of a team, I find that:

1. Most of the time other people are too inexperienced to do things, so I prefer to do them myself.
2. It often takes more time to explain things to others than to just do them myself.
3. Mistakes made by others are costly, so I don't assign much work to them.
4. Some things simply should not be delegated to others.
5. I often get quicker action by doing a job myself.
6. Many people are good only at very specific tasks, so they can't be assigned additional responsibilities.
7. Many people are too busy to take on additional work.
8. Most people just aren't ready to handle additional responsibilities.
9. In my position, I should be entitled to make my own decisions.

Scoring

Total your responses to get an overall score. Possible scores range from 9 to 45.

Interpretation

The lower your score, the more willing you appear to be to delegate to others. Willingness to delegate is an important managerial characteristic. It is how you, as a manager, can "empower" others and give them opportunities to assume responsibility and exercise self-control in their work. With the growing importance of horizontal organizations and empowerment in the new workplace, your willingness to delegate is worth thinking about seriously.

Team Exercise

The Future Workplace

Instructions

Form groups as assigned by the instructor. Brainstorm to develop a master list of the major workplace characteristics you expect to find in the year 2020. Use this list as background for completing the following tasks:

1. Write a one-paragraph description of what the typical "Workplace 2020" manager's workday will be like.
2. Draw a "picture" representing what the Workplace 2020 organization will look like.
3. State why your Workplace 2020 organization does or does not conform with current organizational design trends.
4. Write a "short story" (10-sentence maximum) that portrays a manager in trouble in your Workplace 2020 workplace because of a failure to empower others.
5. Choose a spokesperson to share your results with the class as a whole and explain their implications for the class members.

Case Study: Nike

Go to *Management Cases for Critical Thinking* to find the recommended case for Chapter 10–"Nike: Spreading Out to Stay Together."

Organization Culture and Change

Chapter 11 Study Questions

1 What is organizational culture?

2 What is a multicultural organization?

3 What is the nature of organizational change?

Learning From Others

New Thinking Thrives in the Right Culture

If you ask friends and neighbors to identify the most exciting piece of mail they've received lately, it may well turn out to be a delivery from Netflix; personalized home entertainment in a small red and white envelope. On any given day there are over 45,000 DVD and Blu-ray titles in transit serving a customer base that is 8 million strong and growing.[1]

CEO Reed Hastings says that it's a commitment to customer service that keeps the Los Gatos, California, company on top of its game. Behind the great service is a pool of human ingenuity supported by the latest technology. And with the move toward video downloads, Netflix is already a hit with its Instant Viewing service. Netflix-ready gadgets are growing in number and already include Xbox 360s, TiVos, and some Blu-ray players.

Hastings is always trying to put people together with his vision and new technology. *Wired* magazine describes him as "a quiet disrupter, sabotaging business models silently and irretrievably." The article with this quote was entitled "Netflix Everywhere: Sorry Cable, You're History."

The company's work culture fits its founder—unique and high-performance oriented. Says Hastings: "At most companies, average performers get an average raise. At Netflix they get a generous severance package." The firm allows employees to choose how much of their salary is paid in cash and how much in stock options; they get as much time off as they want for vacation; and day-to-day work rules are kept to a minimum to maximize individual freedom on the job. As described by *Wired* magazine, Hastings is "a quiet, hands-off leader . . . sets the tone and objectives and lets his employees figure out how to execute them."

Of course change is always an issue, and Hastings is well aware of the need to avoid complacency. "If one thinks of Netflix as a DVD rental business," he says, "one is right to be scared." His view is different and dynamic; and he sees Netflix as "an online movie service with multiple delivery models." There's no room for stability in that notion of the Netflix world. Stay tuned in to see if Hastings is able to keep delivering on his promises.

do the benchmarking

Think about Netflix, its strategy, and CEO Hastings's view of management the next time you watch a movie. All too often, today's executives and organizations lose their grips on customers and markets. They either neglect to learn and change over time, or they are incapable of doing so because of personal and organizational constraints. There's a lot to think about when it comes to mastering the challenges of managing organizational culture and change.

Learning About Yourself

Tolerance for Ambiguity

Even through creativity and problem solving can be exciting, change and uncertainty also evoke anxiety. Change breaks us from past habits and conditions; uncertainty moves many things out of our direct control. Depending on your **tolerance for ambiguity**, you may be comfortable or uncomfortable dealing with these realities.

Consider the Tolerance for Ambiguity Double Check in the box. Which alternatives best describe how you respond to different courses and instructors? What are the insights for your tolerance for ambiguity?

It takes personal flexibility and lots of confidence to cope well with unpredictability, whether in a college course or a work situation. Some people, probably many, are uneasy when dealing with the unfamiliar. They prefer to work with directions that provide clear decision-making rules and minimize ambiguity. They like the structure of mechanistic organizations with bureaucratic features. They tend to get comfortable with fixed patterns in life and can be afraid of anything "new."

Does the latter description apply to you? Or are you among those who are willing, able, and happy to work in less structured settings—ones that allow lots of flexibility in responding to changing situations? Such people like the freedom and spontaneity allowed in organic organizations that are designed for innovation and adaptation. They are excited by the prospects of change and new opportunities.

Many management challenges today fall into the change category, and many personal challenges do so as well. In this regard it's important to find a good fit between your personal preferences and the pace and nature of change in organizations in which you choose to work. To achieve this fit, you have to understand your tolerance for ambiguity and how you react in change situations. The best time to explore all this is now, before you take your first or next job.

Tolerance for Ambiguity Double Check

An instructor who gives precise assignments and accepts no deviations,

or,

one who gives open-ended assignments and lets students suggest alternatives?

In a typical course, do you prefer...

An instructor who gives out a general syllabus and then modifies it over time based on student feedback,

or,

one who gives out a detailed syllabus and sticks to it?

get to know yourself better

Write a short narrative describing your "ideal" employer in terms of structure, culture, management styles, and frequency of major changes. Add a comment that explains how this ideal organization fits your personality, including insights from self-assessments completed in earlier chapters. What does this say about your capability to be a change leader? **Also take advantage of the end-of-chapter Self-Assessment feature to further reflect on your Tolerance for Ambiguity, as well as your capacity for Organizational Change Leadership.**

11 Organization Culture and Change

Study Question 1	Study Question 2	Study Question 3
Organizational Cultures	**Multicultural Organizations**	**Organizational Change**
• Understanding organizational culture • The observable culture • Values and the core culture	• Multicultural organizations and performance • Organizational subcultures • Diversity and organizational subcultures	• Models of change leadership • Incremental and transformational change • Phases of planned change • Change strategies • Resistance to change
Learning Check 1	Learning Check 2	Learning Check 3

According to Harvard scholars Michael Beer and Nitin Nohria, "The new economy has ushered in great business opportunities and great turmoil. Not since the Industrial Revolution have the stakes of dealing with change been so high. Most traditional organizations have accepted, in theory at least, that they must either change or die."[2] John Chambers, CEO of Cisco Systems, says "Companies that are successful will have cultures that thrive on change even though change makes most people uncomfortable."[3]

There's little doubt that discomfort with change can bog organizations and their leaders down, making it hard for them to keep pace with new environmental challenges. When General Motors board chairman Ed Whitacre fired then CEO Fritz Henderson, he did so in part because of frustration with the slow pace of change at GM. Whitacre and the board wanted more measurable progress as the firm came out of bankruptcy; they wanted the firm and its executives to take more risks; and, they held Henderson accountable for his inability to make that change happen. Notably, they were critical of what has been called "GM's cautious culture."[4]

ORGANIZATIONAL CULTURES

> **Organizational culture** is the system of shared beliefs and values that guides behavior in organizations.

Think of the stores where you shop; the restaurants that you patronize; the place where you work. What is the "climate" like? Do you notice, for example, that the stores of major retailers like Anthropologie, Gap, Hollister, and Banana Republic have atmospheres that seem to fit their brands and customer identities?[5] Such aspects of the internal environments of organizations are important in management, and the term used to describe them is **organizational culture**. This is the system of shared beliefs and values that shapes and guides the behavior of its members.[6] It is also often called the *corporate culture*, and through its influence on employees and customers it can have a strong impact on performance.[7]

At Zappos.com, a popular e-tailer of shoes, CEO Tony Hsieh has built a fun, creative, and customer-centered culture. He says: "The original idea was to add a little fun," and then everyone joined in the idea that "We can do it better." Now the notion of an unhappy Zappos customer is almost unthinkable. "They may only call once in their life," says Hsieh, "but that is our chance to wow them."[8] Amazon.com CEO Jeff Bezos likes Zappos so much he bought the company, and the Girl Scouts send executives to study Zappos' culture and bring back ideas for improving their own. Hsieh's advice is that if you "get the culture right, most of the other stuff, like brand and the customer service, will just happen."[9]

UNDERSTANDING ORGANIZATIONAL CULTURE

The organizational culture is what you see and hear when walking around an organization as a visitor, a customer, or an employee. Look carefully, check the atmosphere, and listen to the conversations. Whenever someone, for example, speaks of "the way we do things here," that person is shedding insight into the organization's culture. Just as nations, ethnic groups, and families have cultures, organizations also have cultures that create unique identities and help to distinguish them from one another.

Management Smarts 11.1 offers ideas for reading organizational cultures based on things such as innovation and risk taking, teamwork, people orientation, and emphasis on outcomes. For example, consider how executive headhunters described corporate cultures that they avoid when recruiting candidates for top jobs: British Airways—"like working for the FBI," General Mills—"patrician culture of conflict avoidance," Occidental Petroleum—"autocratic environment," and Oracle—"a company full of men who would walk over their mothers to get to the top."[10]

> ### *Management Smarts 11.1*
>
> **Questions for reading an organization's culture**
>
> - How tight or loose is the structure?
> - Do most decisions reflect change or the status quo?
> - What outcomes or results are most highly valued?
> - What is the climate for risk taking and innovation?
> - How widespread are empowerment and worker involvement?
> - What is the competitive style, internal and external?
> - What value is placed on people, as customers and employees?
> - Is teamwork a way of life in this organization?

The best organizations, as already suggested in the Zappos.com example, are likely to have positive cultures that respect members while being customer driven and performance oriented.[11] Have you visited Disneyland or Disney World? Think about how the employees acted, how the park ran, and how consistently and positively all visitors were treated. Strong organizational cultures like Disney's are clear, well defined, and widely shared among members. They encourage positive work behaviors and discourage dysfunctional ones. They also commit members to doing things for and with one another that are in the best interests of the organization.

One of the ways organizations build strong and positive cultures is through **socialization**. This is the process of helping new members learn the culture and values of the organization, as well as the behaviors and attitudes that are shared among its members.[12] Such socialization often begins in an anticipatory sense with one's education, such as teaching business students the importance of professional appearance and interpersonal skills. It then continues with an employer's orientation and training programs, which, when well done, can have a strong influence on the new member. Disney is one of those employers that invests heavily in socialization and training of its new hires. Founder Walt Disney is quoted as saying: "You can dream, create, design and build the most wonderful place in the world, but it requires people to make the dream a reality."[13]

> **Socialization** is the process through which new members learn the culture of an organization.

THE OBSERVABLE CULTURE OF ORGANIZATIONS

Organizational culture is usually described from the perspective of the two levels shown in Figure 11.1. The outer level is the "observable" culture, and the inner level is the "core" culture.[14] As suggested by the figure, you might think of this in terms of an iceberg. What lies below the surface and is harder to see is the core culture. That which stands out above the surface and is more visible to the discerning eye is the observable culture.

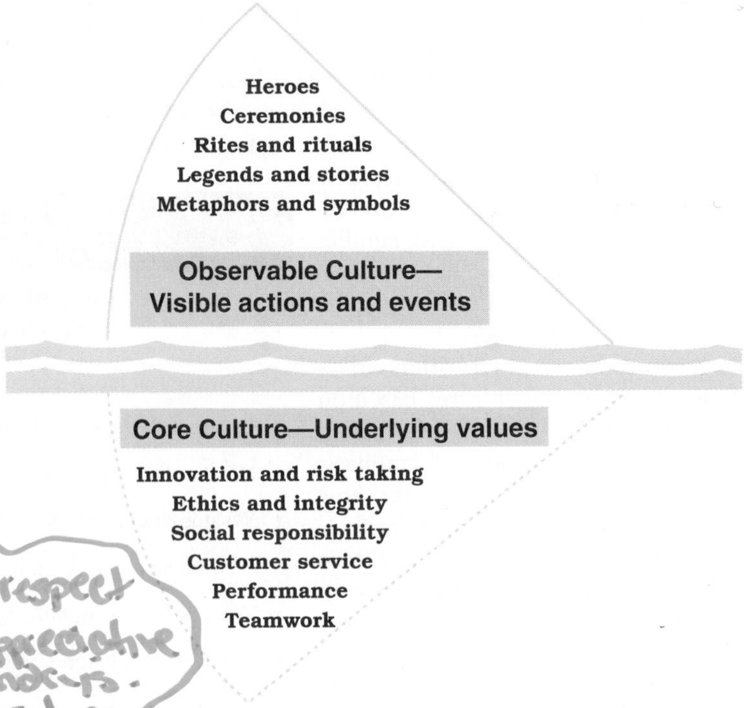

Heroes
Ceremonies
Rites and rituals
Legends and stories
Metaphors and symbols

**Observable Culture—
Visible actions and events**

Core Culture—Underlying values

Innovation and risk taking
Ethics and integrity
Social responsibility
Customer service
Performance
Teamwork

FIGURE 11.1 Levels of organizational culture–observable culture and core culture in the organizational "iceberg."

...is disrespect & unappreciative @ landr-rs.

● The **observable culture** is what one sees and hears when walking around an organization as a visitor, a customer, or an employee.

The **observable culture** is visible and readily apparent at the surface of every organization. It is expressed in the way people dress at work, how they arrange their offices, how they speak to and behave toward one another, the nature of their conversations, and how they talk about and treat their customers. Test this out the next time you go in a store, restaurant, or service establishment. How do people look, act, and behave? How do they treat one another? How do they treat customers? What's in their conversations? Are they enjoying themselves? When you answer these questions, you are starting to identify the observable culture of the organization.

The observable culture is also found in the stories, heroes, rituals, and symbols that are part of daily organizational life. In the university it includes the pageantry of graduation and honors ceremonies; in sports teams it's the pregame rally, sidelines pep talk, and all the "thumping and bumping" that takes place after a good play. In workplaces like Apple, Hewlett-Packard, Zappos, and Amazon, it's in the stories told about the founders and the firm's history, as well as spontaneous celebrations of a work accomplishment or personal milestone such as a coworker's birthday. When you are trying to understand the observable culture, for example, look for the following.[15]

- *Heroes*—the people singled out for special attention and whose accomplishments are recognized with praise and admiration; they include founders and role models.
- *Ceremonies, rites, and rituals*—the ceremonies and meetings, planned and spontaneous, that celebrate important occasions and performance accomplishments.
- *Legends and stories*—oral histories and tales, told and retold among members, about dramatic sagas and incidents in the life of the organization.
- *Metaphors and symbols*—the special use of language and other nonverbal expressions that communicate important themes and values of the organization.

The presence or absence of these aspects of the observable culture and the ways they are practiced can say a lot about an organization. When absent they indicate an organization without a strong cultural anchor. When present they communicate and carry the culture over time, keeping it visible and clear in all members' eyes. New members learn the organization's culture through them; all members keep the culture alive by sharing and joining in them.

VALUES AND THE CORE CULTURE OF ORGANIZATIONS

The second and deeper level of organizational culture is the **core culture**. As is also shown in the iceberg model, it consists of the **core values** or underlying assumptions and beliefs that shape and guide people's behaviors. This influence extends from the highest level executives through all managerial levels down to the workers who create the products or deliver the services of the organization. You know core values, so to speak, when you experience them. This may be when you are trying to claim lost luggage at an airline counter and are treated really well, or are returning a product to a retail store and are greeted with a smile and "no questions asked." Values set in the core culture are a strong influence on how such transactions play out. And when customer experiences aren't as positive as these, the culprit may well be weak or just plain bad core values.

Values in some of the best companies have been found to emphasize performance excellence, innovation, social responsibility, integrity, worker involvement, customer service, and teamwork.[16] Examples of values driving strong-culture firms include "service above all else" at Nordstrom; "science-based innovation" at Merck; "encouraging individual initiative and creativity" at Sony; and "fanatical attention to consistency and detail" at Disney.[17]

When trying to read or understand an organization's core culture, however, don't be fooled by values statements alone. It's easy to write a set of values, post them on the Web, and talk about them. It's a lot harder to live up to them. If an organization's stated values are to have any positive effects, everyone in the organization from top to bottom must reflect the values in day-to-day actions. In this sense managers have a special responsibility to "walk the values talk" and make the expressed values real. After all, how might you react if you found out senior executives in your organization talked up values such as honesty and ethical behavior, but then acted quite differently, perhaps by spending company funds on lavish private parties and vacations?

● The **core culture** consists of the core values, or underlying assumptions and beliefs that shape and guide people's behaviors in an organization.

● **Core values** are beliefs and values shared by organization members.

● **Value-based management** actively develops, communicates, and enacts shared values.

Value-Based Management

The term **value-based management** describes managers who actively help develop, communicate, and enact shared values within an organization.

Core Values Drive Herman Miller Designs

Core values support a strong culture at the innovative furniture maker Herman Miller. The stated values include • Making a meaningful contribution to our customers, • Cultivating community, participation, and people development, • Creating economic value for shareholders and employee-owners, • Responding to change through design and innovation, and • Living with integrity and respecting the environment and career development.

Alan Mulally Makes His Mark on Ford's Culture

Why is it that a CEO brought in from outside the industry fared the best as the big three automakers went into crisis mode during the economic downturn? That's a question that Ford Motor Company's chairman, William Clay Ford Jr., is happy to answer. And the person he's talking about is Alan Mulally, a former Boeing executive hired by Ford to retool the firm and put it back on a competitive track.

Many wondered at the time if an "airplane guy" could run an auto company. It isn't easy to come in from outside an industry and successfully lead a huge firm. But Mulally's management experience and insights are proving well up to the task. One consultant remarked: "the speed with which Mulally has transformed Ford into a more nimble and healthy operation has been one of the more impressive

jobs I've seen." He went on to say that without Mulally's impact Ford might well have gone out of business.

In addition to many changes to modernize plants and streamline operations, Mulally has tackled the bureaucratic problems common to many extremely large organizations—particularly functional chimneys and a lack of open communication. William Ford says that the firm had a culture that "loved to meet" and in which managers got together to discuss the message they wanted to communicate to the top executives. Mulally changed all that by pushing transparency and data-based decision making, cooperation between Ford's divisions, and global operations that build vehicles to sell in many markets. When some of the senior executives balked and tried to go directly to Ford with their complaints, he refused to listen. "I didn't permit it," he says, thus reinforcing his authority to run the firm his way.

As for Mulally's success, time will only tell how Ford does in the future. For now, Ford is outperforming GM and Chrysler, and Mulally has gained lots of respect for his executive prowess. One of his senior managers says: "I'm going into my fourth year on the job. I've never had such consistency of purpose before."

Although you might tend to associate value-based management with top management, the responsibility extends to all managers and team leaders. Like the organization as a whole, any work team or group will have a culture. How well this culture operates to support the group and its performance objectives will depend in part on the strength of the core values and the team leader's role as a values champion. The following criteria are a good test of the value-based management of any organization or team. *Relevance*—Core values support key performance objectives. *Integrity*—Core values provide clear, consistent ethical anchors. *Pervasiveness*—Core values are understood by all members. *Strength*—Core values are accepted by all members.[18]

An incident at Tom's of Maine provides a good example of value-based management.[19] After a big investment in a new deodorant, founder Tom Chappell was dismayed when he learned that customers were very dissatisfied with it. But having founded the company on values that include fairness and honesty in all matters, he decided to reimburse customers and pull the product from the market. Even though it cost the company more than $400,000, Tom did what he believed was the right thing. He was living up to the full spirit of the company's values and also setting a positive example for others in the firm to follow.

Symbolic Leadership

A strong **symbolic leader** is someone who uses symbols well to communicate values and maintain the organization's core culture. Symbolic managers and leaders both act and talk the "language" of the organization. Like Tom Chappell at Tom's of Maine, they are always careful to behave in ways that live up to core values. They are ever-present role models for others to emulate and follow. And, they use spoken and written words to describe people, events, and even the

● A **symbolic leader** uses symbols to communicate values that help create a desired organizational culture.

competition in ways that reinforce and communicate the culture. Language metaphors—the use of positive examples from another context—are very powerful in this regard. For example, newly hired workers at Disney World and Disneyland are counseled to always think of themselves as more than employees; they are key "members of the cast," and they work "on stage." After all, they are told, Disney isn't just any business; it is an "entertainment" business.

Good symbolic leaders take all opportunities to highlight and even dramatize core values and the observable culture. They tell key stories over and over again, and they encourage others to tell them. They may refer to the "founding story" about the entrepreneur whose personal values set a key tone for the enterprise. They remind everyone about organizational heroes, past and present, whose performances exemplify core values. They also use rites and rituals to glorify the performance of the organization and its members. At Mary Kay Cosmetics, for example, gala events at which top sales performers share their tales of success are legendary. So, too, are the lavish incentive awards presented at these ceremonies, especially the pink luxury cars given to the most successful salespeople.[20]

● **Workplace spirituality** creates meaning and shared community among organizational members.

Workplace Spirituality

It is becoming popular to discuss **workplace spirituality** along with value-based management. Although the first tendency might be to associate "spirituality" with religion, the term is used more broadly in management to describe an organizational culture in which people are able to find meaning in their work and experience a sense of shared community through their role in the organization. The foundations for workplace spirituality are set in management practices that respect and nurture the full value of human beings. The guiding principle is that people are inwardly enriched by meaningful work and a sense of personal connection with others inside and outside of the organization.[21]

Sample Values in Spiritual Organizational Cultures

- Meaningful purpose
- Trust and respect
- Honesty and openness
- Personal growth and development
- Worker friendly practices
- Ethics and social responsibility

The core values in a culture of workplace spirituality will have strong ethics foundations, recognize human dignity, respect diversity, and focus on linking jobs with an organization's contributions to society. When someone works in a culture of workplace spirituality, in other words, the person should derive pleasure from knowing that what is being accomplished is personally meaningful, created through community, and valued by others. Meeting these standards for workplace spirituality isn't easy, and not all organizational cultures will hold up to the test. But the prior case of decision making at Tom's of Maine by CEO Tom Chappell is a good model. Even though his decision to recall the product had a high monetary cost for the company, it lived up to his sense of ethics and social responsibility.[22]

Symbols and Traditions Set Disney Culture

Organizational culture is a core competency at Disney, Inc. The importance of people to the Disney strategy is evident right from the beginning when each new hire attends a program called traditions. It informs them on the company history, its language and lore, and its founding story. The goal is to make sure people learn the culture and commit to making the Disney dream a reality. And it works. Walt Disney's legacy has even endured to the point where the Disney Institute offers similar training for other employers.

Be sure you can ☑ define *organizational culture* and explain the importance of strong cultures to organizations ☑ define and explain the process of *socialization* ☑ distinguish between the observable and core cultures ☑ explain how value-based management helps build strong culture organizations ☑ describe how symbolic leadership and workplace spirituality relate to organizational culture

MULTICULTURAL ORGANIZATIONS

In his book *Beyond Race and Gender*, consultant R. Roosevelt Thomas Jr. makes the link between organizational culture and diversity.[23] He believes that the way people are treated at work—with respect and inclusion, or with disrespect and exclusion—is a direct reflection of the organization's culture and its leadership.

● **Multiculturalism** in organizations involves inclusiveness, pluralism, and respect for diversity.

● A **multicultural organization** has a culture with core values that respect diversity and support multiculturalism.

The term **multiculturalism** refers to inclusiveness, pluralism, and respect for diversity in the workplace. In a truly **multicultural organization** the organizational culture communicates and supports core values that respect and empower the full diversity of its members. Such a multicultural organization has these characteristics.[24]

- *Pluralism*—Members of both minority cultures and majority cultures are influential in setting key values and policies.
- *Structural integration*—Minority-culture members are well represented in jobs at all levels and in all functional responsibilities.
- *Informal network integration*—Various forms of mentoring and support groups assist in the career development of minority-culture members.
- *Absence of prejudice and discrimination*—A variety of training and task-force activities address the need to eliminate culture-group biases.
- *Minimum intergroup conflict*—Diversity does not lead to destructive conflicts between members of majority and minority cultures.

MULTICULTURAL ORGANIZATIONS AND PERFORMANCE

R. Roosevelt Thomas, mentioned above, argues that organizational cultures that respect diversity gain performance advantages from the mixture of talents and perspectives they can draw upon. The *Gallup Management Journal* also reports that a racially and ethnically inclusive workplace is good for morale. And in a study of 2,014 American workers, those who felt included were more likely to stay with their employers and recommend them to others. Survey questions asked such things as "Do you always trust your company to be fair to all employees?" "At work, are all employees always treated with respect?" "Does your supervisor always make the best use of employees' skills?"[25]

In researching the business case for diversity, however, Thomas Kochan and his colleagues at MIT found that the presence of diversity alone does not guarantee a positive performance impact. Only when diversity is leveraged through training and supportive human resource practices are the advantages gained. In other words, only when respect for diversity is embedded in the organizational culture can we expect positive performance impact. Kochan et al. summarize their findings with this guidance on diversity and organizational culture.[26]

To be successful in working with and gaining value from diversity requires a sustained, systemic approach and long-term commitment. Success is facilitated by a perspective that considers diversity to be an opportunity for everyone in an organization to learn from each other how better to accomplish their work and an occasion that requires a supportive and cooperative organizational culture as well as group leadership and process skills that can facilitate effective group functioning.

ORGANIZATIONAL SUBCULTURES

Like society as a whole, organizations contain a mixture of **organizational subcultures**. These are cultures common to groups of people that share similar values and beliefs based on their work responsibilities and personal characteristics. Subcultures often complicate the task of creating truly multicultural organizations. Just as with life in general, **ethnocentrism**—the belief that one's membership group or subculture is superior to all others—can creep into the workplace and adversely affect the way people relate to one another.

● **Organizational subcultures** are groups of people who share similar beliefs and values based on their work or personal characteristics.

● **Ethnocentrism** is the belief that one's membership group or subculture is superior to all others.

Occupations and Functions

The many possible subcultures in organizations include **occupational subcultures** that form among persons that share the same professions and skills.[27] Examples are lawyers, scientists, engineers, and accountants. Such professionals often have special needs for work autonomy and empowerment that may conflict with traditional management methods of top-down direction and control. Unless these needs are recognized and properly dealt with, salaried professionals may prove difficult to integrate into the culture of the larger organization.

There are also **functional subcultures** that form among people who work together in the same functional area. And, people from different functions may have difficulty understanding and working well with one another. Employees in a business firm, for example, may consider themselves "systems people" or "marketing people" or "manufacturing people" or "finance people." When such identities are overemphasized, members of the functional groups may spend most of their time with each other, develop a shared "jargon" or technical language, and view their roles in the organization as more important than those of the other functions.

● **Occupational subcultures** form among persons who share the same professions and skills.

● **Functional subcultures** form among people who work together in the same functional area, such as marketing, sales, and finance.

Ethnicity and National Cultures

Differences in **ethnic subcultures** or **national subcultures** form in the workplace among people sharing the same background in terms of ethnic community, home countries, or world regions. We all know that it can sometimes be hard to work well with persons whose national cultures are different from our own. The best cross-cultural understanding is most likely gained through direct contact and from being open-minded. The same advice holds true more generally for diverse cultural communities. Although one may speak in everyday conversations about "African American" or "Latino" or "Anglo" cultures, current events often demonstrate how difficult it can be for members of these cultures to understand and respect one another.[28] Just look back, for example, to some of the political conversation that took place during Barack Obama's candidacy for U.S. president. If improved cross-cultural understandings can help people work better across national boundaries, can the same understanding help people from different ethnic or racial subcultures work better together?

● **Ethnic subcultures** or **national subcultures** form among people who work together and have roots in the same ethnic community, country, or region of the world.

Gender and Generations

Issues based on **gender subcultures** whose members share gender identities can also complicate the workplace. Research shows that when men work together, a group culture may form around a competitive atmosphere where sports metaphors are common and games and stories often deal with winning and losing.[29] When women work together, a rather different culture may form with more emphasis on personal relationships and collaboration.[30]

● **Gender subcultures** form among persons who work together and share the same gender identities.

● **Generational subcultures** form among persons who work together and share similar ages, such as Millennials and Baby Boomers.

Tips for Working with the Millennial Generation

• Challenge them—give meaningful work.
• Reward them with responsibility and recognition for accomplishments.
• Ask their opinion, avoid command-and-control approaches.
• Link them with an experienced mentor.
• Give frequent feedback; they're used to instantaneous gratification.

We also live at a time when **generational subcultures** that exist among persons in similar age groups are often a topic for workplace conversations. Up to five generational subcultures may be represented in an organization today: Traditionalists born pre-1945, Baby Boomers born 1945–early 1960s, X-ers born 1965–1990, Y's or Millennials born 1980–1995, and the Internet Gen born after 1995.[31] Members of these generations grew up in quite different worlds and were influenced by different values and opportunities. Someone who is 60 years old today, a common age for senior managers, was a teenager in the 1960s. She or he may have difficulty understanding, working with, and leading younger managers who were teens during the 1980s or 1990s, let alone the early 2000s. See the small box for tips on working with the millennial generation.[32]

DIVERSITY AND ORGANIZATIONAL SUBCULTURES

The very term "diversity" basically means the presence of differences. But what happens when those differences are distributed unequally among organizational subcultures and in the governing power structures? That is, what happens when one subculture is in "majority" status while others become "minorities"?

Glass Ceilings

● The **glass ceiling** is an invisible barrier to advancement by women and minorities in organizations.

Even though organizations are changing today, there is likely to be more workforce diversity at lower and middle levels than at the top. Look at Figure 11.2. It depicts the **glass ceiling**, defined in Chapter 1 as an invisible barrier that limits the advancement of women and minorities in some organizations. What are the implications for minority members, such as women or persons of color, seeking to advance and prosper in an organization where the majority culture consists of white males? How easy is it for them to continue to move up when promotions and higher authority are controlled by decision makers who are part of an alternative and dominant culture?

Take the case of women. They now constitute more than 50% of the U.S. workforce and by 2011 there will be 2.5 million more women than men studying at universities. But although women are increasingly well represented in college, at work, and in management, they hold only about 2% of top jobs in American firms. In 2009 only 12 CEOs of Global 500 firms were female and only one of them was African-American—Ursula Burns of Xerox.[33]

Why aren't more women getting to the top? One answer is that the glass ceiling still causes many to drop out at earlier career stages. This glass ceiling isn't always based on outright gender prejudice. But it may trace to male-dominant organizational cultures and executive mindsets that have a hard time tolerating women who want both families and careers, thus making it hard for them to resolve the "produce or reproduce dilemma."[34] Even as employers put into place female-friendly human resource policies such as flexible hours or work arrangements, some women may feel forced at times to choose between career or family. Some 24% in one sample, for example, said they worried about adverse career impact if they turned down a job opportunity due to their family responsibilities.[35]

Harassment and Discrimination

The daily work challenges faced by minorities and women can range from misunderstandings and lack of sensitivity on the one hand to glass ceiling limitations

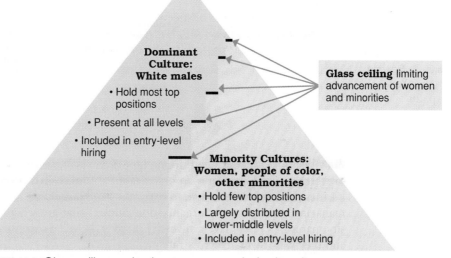

FIGURE 11.2 Glass ceilings as barriers to women and minority cultures in traditional organizations.

and even outright harassment and discrimination on the other. Data from the U.S. Equal Employment Opportunity Commission (EEOC), for example, show that a growing number of bias suits are being filed by workers and that sex discrimination is a factor in some 30% of them.[36] The EEOC also reports an increase in pregnancy discrimination complaints.[37] Pay discrimination is another issue. A senior executive in the computer industry reported her surprise at finding out that the top performer in her work group, an African American male, was paid 25% less than anyone else. This wasn't because his pay had been cut to that level, she said. It was because his pay increases had always trailed those given to his white coworkers. The differences added up significantly over time, but no one noticed or stepped forward to make the appropriate adjustment.[38]

Sexual harassment in the form of unwanted sexual advances, requests for sexual favors, and sexually laced comments is a problem female employees in particular may face. It's not uncommon for minority workers to be targets of cultural jokes; one survey reports some 45% of respondents had encountered such abuse. Sometimes members of minority cultures try to adapt through tendencies toward **biculturalism.** This is the display of majority culture characteristics that seem necessary to succeed in the work environment. For example, one might find gays and lesbians hiding their sexual orientation from coworkers out of fear of prejudice or discrimination. Similarly, one might find an African American carefully training herself to not use certain words or phrases at work that might be considered as subculture slang by white coworkers.

● **Biculturalism** is when minority members adopt characteristics of majority cultures in order to succeed.

Diversity Leadership

There should be no doubt that minority workers want the same things everyone wants—respect for their talents and a work setting that allows them to achieve their full potential. It takes an inclusive organizational culture and the best in diversity leadership at all levels of organizational management to meet these expectations.

R. Roosevelt Thomas describes the continuum of leadership approaches to diversity shown in Figure 11.3. The first is *affirmative action,* in which leadership commits the organization to hiring and advancing minorities and women. The second is *valuing diversity,* in which leadership commits the organization to education and training programs designed to help people better understand and respect

FIGURE 11.3 Leadership approaches to diversity—from affirmative action to managing diversity. *Source:* Developed from R. Roosevelt Thomas Jr., *Beyond Race and Gender* (New York: AMACOM, 1991), p. 28.

Affirmative Action
Create upward mobility for minorities and women

Valuing Differences
Build quality relationships with respect for diversity

Managing Diversity
Achieve full utilization of diverse human resources

● **Managing diversity** is a leadership approach that creates an organizational culture that respects diversity and supports multiculturalism.

individual differences. The third and most comprehensive is **managing diversity**, in which leadership creates an organizational culture that allows all members, minorities and women included, to reach their full potential.[39] Leaders committed to managing diversity build organization cultures that are what Thomas calls diversity mature.[40] They have a diversity mission as well as an organizational mission, and they view diversity as a strategic imperative.

✓ **Learning Check** **Study Question 2** What is a multicultural organization?	*Be sure you can* ☑ explain multiculturalism and the concept of a multicultural organization ☑ identify common organizational subcultures ☑ discuss glass ceilings and employment problems faced by minorities and women ☑ explain Thomas's concept of managing diversity

ORGANIZATIONAL CHANGE

What if the existing culture of an organization doesn't drive high performance and needs to be changed? What if organizational subcultures are clashing and changes must be made? What if diversity leadership requires that organization members change the ways they behave toward one another?

We use the word "change" so much that the tendency may be to make organizational changes like these seem easy, almost a matter of routine. But the realities of trying to change organizations and the behaviors of people within them can be quite different.[41] Former British Airways CEO Sir Rod Eddington once said that "Altering an airline's culture is like trying to perform an engine change in flight."[42] When Angel Martinez became CEO of Rockport, he tried to shift the firm away from traditional ways that were not aligned with future competition. Rather than embrace the changes he sponsored, employees resisted. Martinez said they "gave lip service to my ideas and hoped I'd go away."[43] And after Bank of America announced a large quarterly operating loss, the new CEO at the time, Samuel Armacost, complained about the lack of "agents of change" among his top managers. Claiming that managers seemed more interested in taking orders than initiating change, he said: "I came away quite distressed from my first couple of management meetings. Not only couldn't I get conflict, I couldn't even get comment. They were all waiting to see which way the wind blew."[44]

MODELS OF CHANGE LEADERSHIP

→ change agents

● A **change leader** takes initiative in trying to change the behavior of another person or social system.

A **change leader** is someone who takes leadership initiative to change the existing pattern of behavior of another person or social system. These are managers who act as *change agents* and make things happen, even when inertia has made systems and people reluctant to embrace new ways of doing things. Managers who are

Hidden Agendas in Organizational Change

There are a variety of ways to initiate change in an organization. Using force, using persuasion, and sharing power are common approaches that managers utilize to implement change. Each approach has its own advantages and drawbacks.

Sharing power means that subordinates are given a role in decision making and are involved throughout all stages of the change process. Although this can help generate employee "buy in" and support for the proposed change, it can also lead to resentment and negative attitudes if some of their ideas are not used. In addition, giving subordinates real power to initiate change can also be risky. What if their ideas end up taking the organization down what you believe is the wrong path?

Some managers try to minimize this risk while still highlighting the fact that employees played an important role in the change process. They follow hidden agendas by basically handpicking the team members responsible for proposing change, selecting those most likely to initiate desired changes, and excluding others more likely to resist and propose alternative ideas. This way the manager ensures that organization change heads in the preferred direction while giving the appearance of inclusion and empowerment.

You Decide

Although this situation happens frequently in organizations, does that make it right? What are the ethical issues involved? When is such an approach more or less likely to be ethical? As a manager, would you handpick the leaders of a change effort in order to get your way—even if that meant that alternative points of view were excluded from the process? What if your boss selected you to represent your department on a task force just because you agreed with his or her favored approach? If you knew that most people in your department disagreed, would you do what your boss wanted or would you try to represent the wishes of the majority of your department?

---

strong change leaders are alert to situations or to people needing change, open to good ideas and opportunities, and ready and able to support the implementation of new ideas in actual practice.

In theory, every manager should act as a change leader. But the reality is that people in organizations show major tendencies toward the status quo—accepting things as they are and not wanting to change. Figure 11.4 contrasts a true "change leader" with a "status quo manager." Whereas the status quo manager is backward-looking, reactive, and comfortable with habit, the change leader is forward-looking, proactive, supportive of new ideas, and open to criticism. At Xerox, for example, CEO Ursula Burns talks about the "Xerox family" when referring to her firm's corporate culture. But when speaking to employees as a change leader, she also says: "When we're in the family, you don't have to be as nice as when you're outside the family. I want us to stay civil and kind, but we have to be frank—and the reason we can be frank is because we're all in the same family."[45]

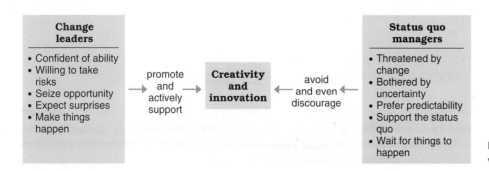

FIGURE 11.4 Change leaders versus status quo managers.

Top-Down Change

● In **top-down change**, the change initiatives come from senior management.

resistance

Top-down change is where senior managers initiate changes with the goal of improving organizational performance. Although it sounds straightforward, research indicates that some 70% or more of large-scale change efforts in American firms actually fail; only 20% of European firms report "substantial success" with large-scale change, while 63% report "occasional" success.

The most common reason for the failure of top-down change is poor implementation.[46] And this raises once again the benefits of participatory planning as discussed in Chapter 8—people are more committed to implement plans that they have played a part in creating. Change programs have little chance of success without the support of those who must implement them. Any change that is driven from the top and perceived as insensitive to the needs of lower-level personnel can easily fail. As the lessons in Management Smarts 11.2 show, successful top-down change is led in ways that earn the support of others throughout the organization.[47]

Management Smarts 11.2

How to lead organizational change

- Establish a sense of urgency for change.
- Form a powerful coalition to lead the change.
- Create and communicate a change vision.
- Empower others to move change forward.
- Celebrate short-term "wins" and recognize those who help.
- Build on success; align people and systems with the new ways.
- Stay with it; keep the message consistent; champion the vision.

Bottom-Up Change

● In **bottom-up change**, change initiatives come from all levels in the organization.

Bottom-up change tries to unlock ideas and initiative at lower organizational levels and let them percolate upward. Such change is made possible by management commitments to empowerment, involvement, and participation.

Many organizations are huge and it is easy for ideas about change to get lost in the bureaucracy. One way to unlock the potential for bottom-up change is through "diagonal slice meetings" where top managers meet with samples of workers from across functions and levels to get their ideas about what might be wrong and what changes might be made to improve things. Another way is to build an organizational culture around the belief that workers should be encouraged to use their job knowledge and common sense to improve things.

At General Electric, former CEO Jack Welch followed an integrated approach to change leadership. He began with an aggressive top-down restructuring that led to major workforce cuts and a trimmer organization structure. Next, he started bottom-up change, using a widely benchmarked program called Work-Out to gain employee involvement in a process of continuous assessment. In Work-Out sessions employees confront their managers in a "town meeting" format, with the manager in front listening to suggestions. The managers are expected to respond immediately and support positive change initiatives raised during the session. Welch felt that approaches like this facilitate change because they "bring an innovation debate to the people closest to the products, services, and processes."[48]

INCREMENTAL AND TRANSFORMATIONAL CHANGE

One way to consider change leadership is in respect to what is called an *organizational change pyramid*.[49] In this view, planned changes at top levels are likely to be large-scale and strategic repositioning changes focused on big issues that affect the organization as a whole. Middle-level changes often deal with major adjustments in structures, systems, technologies, products, and people to support strategic positioning. At the lower levels, frequent and smaller-scale changes seek continuous improvements in performance. Both incremental change and transformational change are important in this organizational change pyramid. Incremental changes keep things tuned up (like the engine on a car) in between transformations (as when the old car is replaced with a new one).

Incremental change is modest, frame-bending change. It basically bends or nudges existing systems and practices to better align them with emerging problems and opportunities. The intent isn't to break and remake the system, but to move it forward through continuous improvements. Common incremental changes in organizations involve evolutions in products, processes, technologies, and work systems.

Transformational change is radical or frame-breaking change that results in a major and comprehensive redirection of the organization.[50] It is usually led from the top and creates fundamental shifts in strategies, culture, structures, and even the underlying sense of purpose or mission.

As you might expect, transformation change is intense, highly stressful, and very complex to achieve. When leading a transformation of General Motors after its bankruptcy, for example, CEO Ed Whitacre made five major changes: 1—removing five senior executives, 2—changing the firm's advertising strategy, 3—cancelling a planned sale of Opel, 4—selling Saab and killing Pontiac and the Hummer, and, 5—vowing to pay back billions loaned during the bailout by the U.S. and Canadian Governments. In a message to employees who were getting nervous under the massive change conditions he said: "I want to reassure you that the major leadership changes are behind us."[51]

● **Incremental change** bends and adjusts existing ways to improve performance.

● **Transformational change** results in a major and comprehensive redirection of the organization.

Organizational Change Pyramid

PHASES OF PLANNED CHANGE

Managers seeking to lead change in organizations can benefit from a simple but helpful model developed many years ago by the psychologist Kurt Lewin. He recommends that any planned change be viewed as a process with the three phases. Phase 1 is *unfreezing*—preparing a system for change; phase 2 is *changing*—making actual changes in the system; and phase 3 is *refreezing*—stabilizing the system after change.[52] In today's fast-paced organizational environments we can also talk about another phase called *improvising*—making adjustments as needed while change is taking place.[53]

Unfreezing

Any planned change has a better chance for success when people are ready for it and open to doing things differently. **Unfreezing** is the phase in which a situation is prepared for change and felt needs for change are developed. The goal is to get people to view change as a way of solving a problem or pursuing an opportunity.

Some call unfreezing the "burning bridge" phase of change, arguing that in order to get people to jump off a bridge you might just have to set it on fire. Managers can simulate the burning bridge by engaging people with facts and information that communicate the need for change—environmental pressures, declining performance, and examples of benchmarks or alternative approaches. And as you have probably experienced, conflict can help people to break old habits and recognize new ways of thinking about or doing things. Common errors at the unfreezing stage include not creating a sense of urgency for change and neglecting to build a coalition of influential persons who support it.

● **Unfreezing** is the phase during which a situation is prepared for change.

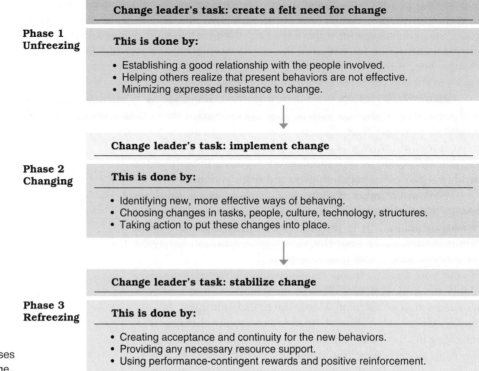

	Change leader's task: create a felt need for change
Phase 1 **Unfreezing**	**This is done by:** • Establishing a good relationship with the people involved. • Helping others realize that present behaviors are not effective. • Minimizing expressed resistance to change.

	Change leader's task: implement change
Phase 2 **Changing**	**This is done by:** • Identifying new, more effective ways of behaving. • Choosing changes in tasks, people, culture, technology, structures. • Taking action to put these changes into place.

	Change leader's task: stabilize change
Phase 3 **Refreezing**	**This is done by:** • Creating acceptance and continuity for the new behaviors. • Providing any necessary resource support. • Using performance-contingent rewards and positive reinforcement.

FIGURE 11.5 Lewin's three phases of planned organizational change.

Changing

● **Changing** is the phase where a planned change actually takes place.

Figure 11.5 shows that unfreezing is followed by the **changing** phase, where something new takes place in a system and change is actually implemented. This is the point where changes are made in such organizational targets as tasks, people, culture, technology, and structure. The changing phase is ideally pursued only after a good diagnosis of a problem and a careful examination of alternatives.

Lewin believes that many change agents commit the error of entering the changing phase prematurely. Too quick to change things, they end up creating harmful resistance. When change takes place before people and systems are ready for it, the likelihood of resistance and change failure is much greater. In this sense the change process is like building a house; you need to put a good foundation in place before you begin the framing. The lesson is that if you try to implement change before people are prepared and feel a need for it, there is an increased likelihood of failure.

Refreezing

● **Refreezing** is the phase at which change is stabilized.

The final phase in Lewin's planned change process is **refreezing**. Here, the manager is concerned about stabilizing the change and creating the conditions for its long-term continuity. Refreezing is accomplished by linking change with appropriate rewards, positive reinforcement, and resource support. It is important in this phase to evaluate results, provide feedback to the people involved, and make any required modifications in the original change.

When refreezing is done well, change should last longer because people have incorporated it into their normal routines. When it is done poorly, changes are too easily forgotten or abandoned with the passage of time. The most common error at the refreezing stage is declaring victory too soon and withdrawing support before the change is really fixed in normal routines. Also, in today's dynamic environments there may not be a lot of time for refreezing before things are ready to change again. We end up preparing for more change even before the present one is fully implemented.

Improvising

Although Lewin's model depicts change as a linear, step-by-step process, the reality is that change is dynamic and complex. Managers must not only understand each phase of planned change, they must be prepared to deal with them simultaneously. They should also be willing to engage the process of **improvisational change** where adjustments are continually made as things are being implemented.[54]

Consider the case of technological change. Because new technologies are often designed external to the organization in which they are to be used, the implications for local applications may be hard to anticipate. A technology that is attractive in concept may appear complicated to the new users; the full extent of its benefits or inadequacies may not become known until it is tried. Thus, the change leader should continually gather and process information relating to the change, and be willing to improvise by customizing the new technology to best meet local needs.

● **Improvisational change** makes continual adjustments as changes are being implemented.

CHANGE STRATEGIES

When a manager actually tries to move people and systems toward change, the issue boils down to change strategy. Figure 11.6 summarizes three common change strategies—force-coercion, rational persuasion, and shared power.[55] Managers, as change agents and leaders, should understand each strategy and its likely results.

Force-Coercion Strategies

A **force-coercion strategy** uses formal authority as well as rewards and punishments as the primary inducements to change. A change agent that seeks to create change through force-coercion believes that people are motivated by self-interest and by what the situation offers in terms of potential personal gains or losses.[56] In *direct forcing*, the change agent takes direct and unilateral action to "command" that change take place. In *political maneuvering*, the change agent works indirectly to gain special advantage over other persons and thereby make them change. This involves bargaining, obtaining control of important resources, forming alliances, or granting small favors.

● A **force-coercion strategy** pursues change through formal authority and/or the use of rewards or punishments.

Change Strategy	Power Bases	Managerial Behavior	Likely Results
Force–Coercion Using formal authority to create change by decree and position power	Legitimacy Rewards Punishments	*Direct forcing* and unilateral action *Political maneuvering* and indirect action	Faster, but low commitment and only temporary compliance
Rational Persuasion Creating change through rational persuasion and empirical argument	Expertise	*Informational efforts* using credible knowledge, demonstrated facts, and logical argument	
Shared power Developing support for change through personal values and commitments	Reference	*Participative efforts* to share power and involve others in planning and implementing change	Slower, but high commitment and longer-term internalization

FIGURE 11.6 Alternative change strategies and their leadership implications.

The force-coercion strategy of change usually produces limited results. Although it can be quickly tried, most people respond to this strategy out of fear of punishment or hope for a reward. The likely result is temporary compliance with the change agent's desires. That is, the new behavior continues only as long as the rewards and punishments are present. For this reason, force-coercion may be most useful as an unfreezing strategy that helps people break old patterns and gain impetus to try new ones. The earlier example of General Electric's Work-Out program applies here.[57] Jack Welch started Work-Out to create a forum for active employee empowerment of continuous change. But he didn't make the program optional; participation in Work-Out was mandatory. Part of Welch's commitment to change leadership was a willingness to use authority to unfreeze the situation and get Work-Out started. Once the program was under way, he was confident it would survive and prosper on its own—and it did.

Rational Persuasion Strategies

* A **rational persuasion strategy** pursues change through empirical data and rational argument.

Change agents using a **rational persuasion strategy** attempt to bring about change through persuasion backed by special knowledge, empirical data, and rational argument. A change agent following this strategy believes that people are inherently rational and guided by reason. Once a specific course of action is demonstrated by information and facts, the change agent assumes that reason and rationality will cause the person to adopt it. When successful, a rational persuasion strategy helps both unfreeze and refreeze a change situation. Although slower than force-coercion, it can result in longer-lasting and more internalized change.

To succeed with the rational persuasion strategy, a manager must convince others that a change will leave them better off than before. This persuasive power can come directly from the change agent if she or he has personal credibility as an "expert." It can also be borrowed in the form of consultants and other outside experts, or gained from credible demonstration projects and identified benchmarks. Many firms, for example, use Disney as a benchmark to demonstrate to their own employees the benefits of a customer-oriented culture. A Ford vice president says: "Disney's track record is one of the best in the country as far as dealing with customers."[58] In this sense, the power of rational persuasion is straightforward: if the culture works for Disney, why can't it work for us?

* A **shared power strategy** pursues change by participation in assessing change needs, values, and goals.

Shared Power Strategies

A **shared power** strategy uses collaboration to identify values, assumptions, and goals from which support for change will naturally emerge. Sometimes called a *normative-reeducative strategy*, this approach is empowerment based and highly

IDEO's Tim Brown Pursues Change by Design

In his book *Change by Design*, IDEO's CEO Tim Brown says that organizations that unlock "design thinking" can achieve radical and highly beneficial changes that improve performance dramatically. He describes design thinking as combining "the designer's creative problem-solving skills" with the "larger strategic initiatives" of the organization. IDEO's work with Kaiser Permanente health centers resulted in reengineering the ways nurses staff shifts. The changes came about through the efforts of a team that brought together design experts, nurses, and technologists.

participative. It involves others in examining personal needs and values, group norms, and operating goals as they relate to the issues at hand. Power is shared as the change agent and others work together to develop consensus to support needed change. Because it entails a high level of involvement, this strategy is often slow and time consuming. But power sharing is likely to result in longer-lasting, internalized change.

A change agent who shares power begins by recognizing that people have varied needs and complex motivations. Changes in organizations are understood to involve changes in attitudes, values, skills, and significant relationships, not just changes in knowledge, information, or practices. Thus, this change agent is sensitive to the way group pressures can support or inhibit change. In working with people, every attempt is made to gather their opinions, identify their feelings and expectations, and incorporate them fully into the change process.

The great "power" of sharing power in the change process lies with unlocking the creativity and experience of people within the system. Some managers hesitate to engage this strategy for fear of losing control or of having to compromise on important organizational goals. But, Harvard scholar Teresa M. Amabile points out that they should have the confidence to share power regarding means and processes, if not overall goals. "People will be more creative," she says, "if you give them freedom to decide how to climb particular mountains. You needn't let them choose which mountains to climb."[59]

RESISTANCE TO CHANGE

You may have heard the adage that "change can be your best friend." At this point, however, we should probably add: "but only if you deal with resistance in the right ways."

When people resist change, they are most often defending something important to them that now appears threatened. A change leader can learn a lot by listening to resistance and then using it as a resource for improving the change and change process.[60] A change of work schedules for workers in ON Semiconductor's Rhode Island plant, for example, may not have seemed like much of an issue to top management. But to the workers it was significant enough to bring about an organizing attempt by the Teamsters union. When management delved into the issues, they found that workers viewed changes in weekend work schedules as threatening to their personal lives. The problem was resolved when a new schedule was developed with input from the workers.[61]

Why People Resist Change

There are a number of reasons why people in organizations may resist planned change. Change is often viewed as a threat to something of value, as a source of uncertainty, or as something that is high in cost or limited in benefits. These and other common sources of resistance are shown in Management Smarts 11.3. Surely you've seen some or all of them. And honestly, haven't you been a resistor at times?

Management Smarts 11.3

Why people may resist change

- *Fear of the unknown*—not understanding what is happening or what comes next.
- *Disrupted habits*—feeling upset to see the end of the old ways of doing things.
- *Loss of confidence*—feeling incapable of performing well under the new ways of doing things.
- *Loss of control*—feeling that things are being done "to" you rather than "by" or "with" you.
- *Poor timing*—feeling overwhelmed by the situation or that things are moving too fast.
- *Work overload*—not having the physical or emotional energy to commit to the change.
- *Loss of face*—feeling inadequate or humiliated because the "old" ways weren't "good" ways.
- *Lack of purpose*—not seeing a reason for the change and/or not understanding its benefits.

Research Brief

Top Management Must Get—and Stay—Committed in Order for Shared Power to Work in Tandem with Top-Down Change

Harry Sminia and Antonie Van Nistelrooij's case study of a public-sector organization in the Netherlands sheds light on what happens when top-down change and organization development based on shared power are used simultaneously.

Writing in the *Journal of Change Management*, they describe how top management initiated a strategic change involving organization design, procedures, work standards, and systems. Called the "project strand," this change was well structured with deadlines and a management hierarchy. Simultaneously, a "change strand" was initiated with organization development interventions to develop information and create foundations helpful to the success of the project strand. The change strand involved conferences, workshops, and meetings. The goal was for both strands to operate in parallel and eventually converge in joint implementation.

What the researchers found was that top management favored the project strand and resisted challenges to its decision-making prerogatives that came from the change strand. Eventually, the shared power aspects of the change pretty much disappeared and activities centered around completing the project on schedule. Sminia and Van Nistelrooij conclude that the change was hampered by "management refusal to share power with the employees."

You Be the Researcher

Is it realistic to expect that top-down and bottom-up changes can operate simultaneously? Can any shared power change strategy be successful without full and continuing support from top management? How would you design research projects to test these questions?

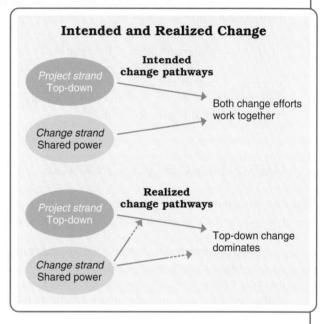

Reference: Harry Sminia and Antonie Van Nistelrooij, "Strategic Management and Organizational Development: Planned Change in a Public Sector Organization," *Journal of Change Management*, vol. 6 (March 2006), pp. 99–113.

Dealing with Resistance to Change

Change leaders and managers can view resistance as something that must be "overcome" in order for change to be successful. But as noted earlier, resistance is better viewed as feedback. The presence of resistance usually means that something can be done to achieve a better "fit" among the planned change, the situation, and the people involved. Use of the following basic checkpoints can help greatly in dealing with resistance and in leading successful organizational changes.[62]

1. *Check the benefits*—make sure the people involved see a clear advantage in making the change. People should know "what is in it for me" or "what is in it for our group or the organization as a whole."
2. *Check the compatibility*—keep the change as close as possible to the existing values and ways of doing things. Minimizing the scope of change helps keep it more acceptable and less threatening.

3. *Check the simplicity*—make the change as easy as possible to understand and use. People should have access to training and assistance to make the transition to new ways as easy as possible.

4. *Check the triability*—allow people to try the change little by little, making adjustments as they go. Don't rush the change, and be sure to adjust the timing to best fit work schedules and cycles of high/low workloads.

In addition to these checkpoints, other techniques can also be used when dealing with resistance to change.[63] *Education and communication* uses discussions, presentations, and demonstrations to educate people beforehand about a change. *Participation and involvement* allows others to contribute ideas and help design and implement the change. *Facilitation and support* provides encouragement and training, actively listens to problems and complaints, and finds ways to reduce performance pressures. *Negotiation and agreement* provides incentives to gain support from those who are actively resisting or ready to resist.

There are two other approaches to managing resistance, but they are risky in terms of potential negative side effects. *Manipulation and co-optation* tries to covertly influence others by selectively providing information and structuring events in favor of the desired change. *Explicit and implicit coercion* forces people to accept change by threatening resistors with undesirable consequences if they don't do what is being asked.

Be sure you can ☑ define *change leader* and *change agent* ☑ discuss pros and cons of top-down change and bottom-up change ☑ differentiate incremental and transformational change ☑ describe Lewin's three phases of planned change ☑ discuss pros and cons of the force-coercion, rational persuasion, and shared power change strategies ☑ list several reasons why people resist change ☑ describe strategies for dealing with resistance to change

Learning Check ☑

Study Question 3
What is the nature of organizational change?

Management **L**earning **R**eview

Study Questions Summary

1 What is organizational culture?

- Organizational culture is an internal environment that establishes a personality for the organization and influences the behavior of members.

- The observable culture is found in the rites, rituals, stories, heroes, and symbols of the organization; the core culture consists of the core values and fundamental beliefs on which the organization is based.

- In organizations with strong cultures, members behave with shared understandings and act with commitment to core values.

- Key dimensions of organizational culture include such things as innovation and risk taking, team emphasis, concern for people, and performance orientation.

- Among trends in managing organizational cultures, value-based management, workplace spirituality, and symbolic leadership are popular directions and considerations.

FOR DISCUSSION **Of the various dimensions of organizational culture, which are most important to you as an employee?**

2 What is a multicultural organization?

- Multicultural organizations operate with internal cultures that value pluralism, respect diversity, and build strength from an environment of inclusion.

- Organizations have many subcultures, including those based on occupational, functional, ethnic, age, and gender differences.

- Challenges faced by members of minority subcultures in organizations include sexual harassment, pay discrimination, job discrimination, and the glass ceiling effect.
- Managing diversity is the process of developing an inclusive work environment that allows everyone to reach their full potential.

FOR DISCUSSION **What can a manager do, at the work team level, to reduce diversity bias in the workplace?**

3 What is the nature of organizational change?

- Change leaders are change agents who take initiative to change the behavior of people and organizational systems.
- Organizational change can proceed with a top-down emphasis, with a bottom-up emphasis, or a combination of both.

- Incremental change makes continuing adjustments to existing ways and practices; transformational change makes radical changes in organizational directions.
- Lewin's three phases of planned change are unfreezing–preparing a system for change; changing–making a change; and refreezing–stabilizing the system.
- Change agents should understand the force-coercion, rational persuasion, and shared power change strategies.
- People resist change for a variety of reasons, including fear of the unknown and force of habit.
- Good change agents deal with resistance in a variety of ways, including education, participation, support, and facilitation.

FOR DISCUSSION **Can the refreezing stage of planned change ever be satisfied in today's dynamic environments?**

Self-Test

Multiple-Choice Questions

1. Pluralism and the absence of discrimination and prejudice in policies and practices are two important hallmarks of _____.
   (a) the glass ceiling effect (b) a multicultural organization (c) quality circles (d) affirmative action

2. When members of minority cultures feel that they have to behave in ways similar to the majority culture, this is called _____.
   (a) biculturalism (b) symbolic leadership (c) the glass ceiling effect (d) inclusivity

3. An executive pursuing transformational change would give highest priority to which one of these change targets?
   (a) an out-of-date policy (b) the organizational culture (c) a new MIS (d) job designs in a customer service department

4. A manager using a force-coercion strategy will rely on _____ to bring about change.
   (a) expertise (b) benchmarking (c) formal authority (d) information

5. The most participative of the planned change strategies is _____.
   (a) force-coercion (b) rational persuasion (c) shared power (d) command and control

6. Trying to covertly influence others, offering only selective information and structuring events in favor of the desired change, is a way of dealing with resistance by _____.
   (a) participation (b) manipulation and co-optation (c) force-coercion (d) facilitation

7. Stories, rituals, and heroes are most associated with the _____ culture of an organization.
   (a) observable (b) hidden (c) core (d) dominant

8. The presence or absence of a felt need for change is a key issue in the _____ phase of the planned change process.
   (a) improvising (b) evaluating (c) unfreezing (d) refreezing

9. The concept of empowerment is most often associated with the _____ strategy of planned change.
   (a) market-driven (b) rational persuasion (c) direct forcing (d) normative reeducative

10. Engineers, scientists, and information systems specialists are likely to become part of separate _____ subcultures in an organization.
    (a) ethnic (b) generational (c) functional (d) occupational

11. The quality concept of continuous improvement is most consistent with the notion of _____.
    (a) incremental change (b) transformational change (c) radical change (d) reactive change

12. True internalization and commitment to a planned change is most likely to occur when a manager uses a(n) _____ change strategy.
    (a) education and communication (b) rational persuasion (c) manipulation and co-optation (d) shared power

13. When a manager listens to users, makes adaptations, and continuously tweaks and changes a new MIS as it is being implemented, the approach to technological change can be described as _____.
    (a) top-down   (b) improvisational   (c) organization development   (d) frame breaking

14. In change management, the recommendation is to view resistance to change as _____.
    (a) feedback of potential value   (b) an indicator of political maneuvering   (c) a sign that change is moving too slowly
    (d) a warning that force-coercion may be needed

15. When members of a dominant subculture, such as white males, make it hard for members of minority subcultures, such as women, to advance to higher level positions in the organization, this is called the _____ effect.
    (a) dominator   (b) glass ceiling   (c) brick wall   (d) end-of-line

Short-Response Questions

16. What core values might be found in high-performance organizational cultures?

17. Why is it important for managers to understand subcultures in organizations?

18. What are the three phases of change described by Lewin, and what are their implications for change leadership?

19. What are the major differences in potential outcomes of using the force-coercion, rational persuasion, and shared power strategies of planned change?

Essay Question

20. Two businesswomen, former college roommates, are discussing their jobs and careers over lunch. You overhear one saying to the other: "I work for a large corporation, while you own a small retail business. In my company there is a strong corporate culture and everyone feels its influence. In fact, we are always expected to act in ways that support the culture and serve as role models for others to do so as well. This includes a commitment to diversity and multiculturalism. Because of the small size of your firm, things like corporate culture, diversity, and multiculturalism are not so important to worry about." Do you agree or disagree with this statement? Why?

Management Skills and Competencies

Self-Assessment

Back to Yourself: Tolerance for Ambiguity

The next time you are driving somewhere and following a familiar route only to find a "detour" sign ahead, test your **tolerance for ambiguity**. Is the detour just a minor inconvenience and you go forward without any further thought? Or is it a big deal, perhaps causing anxiety and anger, and showing your tendencies to resist change in your normal routines? The chapter opener links tolerance for ambiguity with organizational cultures and the processes of organizational change. People are being asked today to be ever more creative and innovative in their work; organizations are too. Managers are expected to support change initiatives launched from the top; they are also expected to be change leaders in their own teams and work units. This is a good time to check your readiness to meet the challenges of change in organizations.

> Your **tolerance for ambiguity** is a good predictor of how you deal with situations involving change and uncertainty. It also suggests the type of organizational culture you best fit.

After you complete the following self-assessment on your Change Leadership IQ, don't forget to go online to further examine your Tolerance for Ambiguity.

Further Reflection: Change Leadership IQ

Instructions

Indicate whether each of the following statements is true (T) or false (F).[64]

   T F   1. People invariably resist change.

   T F   2. One of the most important responsibilities of any change effort is that the leader clearly describes the expected future state.

   T F   3. Communicating what will remain the same after change is as important as communicating what will be different.

T F 4. Planning for change should be done by a small, knowledgeable group, and then that group should communicate its plan to others.

T F 5. Managing resistance to change is more difficult than managing apathy about change.

T F 6. Complaints about a change effort are often a sign of change progress.

T F 7. Leaders find it more difficult to change organizational goals than to change the ways of reaching those goals.

T F 8. Successful change efforts typically involve changing reward systems to support change.

T F 9. Involving more members of an organization in planning a change increases commitment to making the change successful.

T F 10. Successful organizational change requires certain significant and dramatic steps or "leaps," rather than moderate or "incremental" ones.

Scoring

Questions 2, 3, 6, 8, 9, 10 are true; the rest are false. Tally the number of correct items to indicate the extent to which your change management assumptions are consistent with findings from the discipline.

Team Exercise

Force-Field Analysis

Instructions

1. Form into your class discussion groups and review this model of **force-field analysis**—the consideration of forces driving in support of a planned change and forces resisting the change.

2. Use force-field analysis and make lists of driving and resisting forces for one of the following situations:

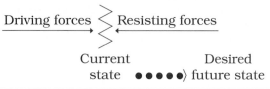

(a) Because of rapid advances in Web-based computer technologies, the possibility exists that the course you are presently taking could be, in part, offered online. This would mean a reduction in the number of required class sessions but an increase in students' responsibility for completing learning activities and assignments through computer mediation. The dean wants all faculty to put at least part of their courses online.

(b) A new owner has just taken over a small walk-in-and-buy-by-the-slice pizza shop in a college town. There are presently eight employees, three of whom are full-time and five of whom are part-time. The shop is open seven days a week from 10:30 a.m to midnight. The new owner believes there is a market niche available for late-night pizza and would like to stay open each night until 4 a.m. She wants to make the change as soon as possible.

(c) A situation assigned by the instructor.

3. Choose the three driving forces that are most significant for the proposed change. For each force, develop ideas on how it could be further increased or mobilized in support of the change.

4. Choose the three resisting forces that are most significant for the proposed change. For each force, develop ideas on how it could be reduced or turned into a driving force.

5. Be prepared to participate in a class discussion led by your instructor.

Case Study: Apple, Inc.

Go to *Management Cases for Critical Thinking* to find the recommended case for Chapter 11— "Apple Inc.: People and Design Create the Future."

Human Resource Management

12

Chapter 12 Study Questions

1 What is human resource management?

2 How do organizations attract a quality workforce?

3 How do organizations develop a quality workforce?

4 How do organizations maintain a quality workforce?

Learning From Others

Great Employers Respect Diversity and Value People

Working Mother magazine's annual listing of the "100 Best Companies for Working Mothers" has become an important management benchmark—both for employers that want to be able to say that they are among the best and for potential employees who only want to work for the best.

Twenty-four companies—including American Express, Hallmark, IBM, Merck, Patagonia, and Procter and Gamble—are included in the magazine's Hall of Fame for being recognized in the rankings for at least 15 years. A full 100% of the listed companies offer telecommuting and flextime schedules, 98% offer job-sharing, and 94% offer compressed workweeks. These companies are also committed to helping working parents with their child-care needs: 86% provide backup child care and 62% provide sick-child care.

The magazine is a major supporter of mothers with careers. Monthly topics range from kids to health to personal motivation, and more. One article reports how a 4½-day workweek quickly became a big favorite for employees at Bayer, a Pittsburgh, Pennsylvania-based pharmaceutical company. According to Beth Adams, Site Services administrator, "This option has worked out very well, especially for scheduling errands or doctor appointments, because the flex day is almost always the same day each week. And, I actually feel that my nine hours each day are more productive since there are no interruptions for such appointments." She explained further that "when the weekend comes there is more free time to have fun."[1]

Self-described as helping women "integrate their professional lives, their family lives and their inner lives," *Working Mother* mainstreams coverage of work–life balance issues and needs for women. The magazine is part of Working Mother Media, Inc., a conglomerate that is headed by President and CEO Carol Evans and also operates NAFE, the National Association for Female Executives— the country's largest women's professional organization. NAFE focuses on "education, networking, and public advocacy, to empower its members to achieve career success and financial security."

do the benchmarking

Pick up a copy of *Working Mother* magazine or browse the online version. It's a chance to learn more about the complexities of work–life balance, including the challenges faced by women blending motherhood with a career. Take time to learn how to match your goals and talents with employers that do a great job of respecting diversity and valuing people.

Learning About Yourself

Professionalism

It isn't just a word; it's a commitment. Speak the word aloud: **professionalism**. Ask: What does it really mean? And more importantly, ask: What does being "professional" mean to me?

Accounting, engineering, medicine, and law are examples of occupations governed by professional codes. We take some comfort in knowing that those who practice in these fields are held accountable by peers for meeting professional standards. Professionalism is also part of management careers, and we are expected to be and act just as professional in a management job as an attorney is in hers.

Take a moment and picture yourself in your ideal job. Then check off the items in the box that best describe you and how you expect to work in that job.[2] While doing so, think about how a real professional would act in that job.

Professionalism Self-Check How I Work
• Like to make own decisions
• Believe in my competence
• Want to help society through my work
• Feel responsible for good work
• Rate job significance above pay received
• Enjoy learning and training
• Willing to be judged by peers
• Willing to judge my peers
• Accept external standards of excellence
• Like to read journal articles

The code of ethics of the Society for Human Resource Management offers a framework for professionalism that is worth considering.[3] SHRM, as the association is often called, describes "Professional Responsibility" as: adding value to your organization; contributing to its ethical success; serving as a leadership role model for ethical conduct; accepting personal responsibility for decisions and actions; promoting fairness and justice in the workplace; being truthful in communications; protecting the rights of individuals; striving to meet high standards of excellence; and always strengthening your competencies.

Most colleges and universities have a branch of SHRM, and it is a strong force for professionalism in human resource management practice. But all students can also learn to behave with professional standards as they work on projects in management courses. Managers should display similar commitments in their work. But as we all know, they don't.

How about you? Can you say that professionalism will always be evident in the ways you approach your future jobs and career?

get to know yourself better

If you checked off each of the items in the short "How I Work" exercise, you're on the right path—the items are indicators of professionalism. Put yourself in the employer's seat. Think again about your ideal job. Write a list of questions that you, as the employer, would ask of a candidate for this job and that would help you get a fix on his or her professionalism. **Also make use of the end-of-chapter Self-Assessment feature to further reflect on your Performance Appraisal Assumptions and tendencies in handling Feedback and Assertiveness.**

Human Resource Management	Attracting a Quality Workforce	Developing a Quality Workforce	Maintaining a Quality Workforce
• Human resource management process • Strategic human resource management • Legal environment of human resource management	• Human resource planning • Recruiting techniques • Selection techniques	• Orientation and socialization • Training and development • Performance management	• Flexibility and work–life balance • Compensation and benefits • Retention and turnover • Labor–management relations
Learning Check 1	Learning Check 2	Learning Check 3	Learning Check 4

The key to managing people in ways that lead to profit, productivity, innovation, and real organizational learning ultimately lies in how you think about your organization and its people. . . . When you look at your people, do you see costs to be reduced? . . . Or, when you look at your people do you see intelligent, motivated, trustworthy individuals—the most critical and valuable strategic assets your organization can have?

With these words from his book *The Human Equation: Building Profits by Putting People First*, scholar Jeffrey Pfeffer challenges managers to invest in people and their talents.[4] He believes, and has research evidence to back up his claims, that organizations that invest more in people outperform those that don't. High-performing organizations thrive on strong foundations of **human capital**, first defined in Chapter 1 as the economic value of people with job-relevant abilities, knowledge, experience, ideas, energies, and commitments. This chapter explores how organizations build human capital by managing their human resources in ways that unlock and respect talents and value diversity.

● **Human capital** is the economic value of people with job-relevant abilities, knowledge, ideas, energies, and commitments.

HUMAN RESOURCE MANAGEMENT

● **Human resource management** is a process of attracting, developing, and maintaining a talented work force.

A marketing manager at IDEO, a Palo Alto-based consulting design firm, once said: "If you hire the right people . . . if you've got the right fit . . . then everything will take care of itself."[5] This is what **human resource management**, or HRM, is all about—attracting, developing, and maintaining a talented and energetic work force. If an organization can't do this well and therefore doesn't have talented and committed people available to do the required work, it has very little chance of long-term success.

There are many career opportunities in a wide variety of areas in human resource management. HRM specialists within organizations and human resource in consulting firms deal with hiring, compensation and benefits, training, employee relations, and more. Specific job titles include human resource planner, corporate recruiter, training and development specialist, compensation analyst, salary and benefits manager, and director of diversity. HRM expertise is highly important in an environment complicated by legal issues, economic turmoil, new corporate strategies, and changing social values. Scholar and consultant Edward E. Lawler III argues that the HRM staff should be experts "on the state of an organization's work force and its ability to perform."[6]

A key concept in HRM is "fit." In fact, an organization's HRM approach should always seek to ensure a good fit between the employee and the specific job to be accomplished, and between the employee and the overall culture of the organization. Hiring the wrong person can be a very expensive mistake. **Person–job fit** is the extent to which an individual's skills, interests, and personal characteristics are consistent with the requirements of their work.[7] **Person–organization fit** is the extent to which an individual's values, interests, and behavior are consistent with the culture of the organization.[8]

HUMAN RESOURCE MANAGEMENT PROCESS

The goal of human resource management is to enhance organizational performance capacity through people. All managers, not just human resource specialists, share this responsibility to ensure that highly capable and enthusiastic people are always in the right positions and working with the support they need to be successful. The three major tasks in human resource management are typically described as

1. *Attracting a quality workforce*—human resource planning, employee recruitment, and employee selection.
2. *Developing a quality workforce*—employee orientation, training and development, and performance management.
3. *Maintaining a quality workforce*—career development, work–life balance, compensation and benefits, retention and turnover, and labor–management relations.

STRATEGIC HUMAN RESOURCE MANAGEMENT

When Sheryl Sandberg left her senior management post with Google to become Facebook's chief operating officer, one of her first steps was to strengthen the firm's human resource management systems. She updated the approach for employee performance reviews, established new recruiting methods, and launched new management training programs.[9] Sandberg's initiatives are consistent with the concept of **strategic human resource management**—mobilizing human capital through the HRM process to best implement organizational strategies.[10]

Human resource management should always be fully integrated into the strategic management process. Strategic HRM translates the strategic goals of the organization into human resource plans to ensure the organization always has the right people in the right places at the right times. How else would the organization successfully implement its strategies and accomplish its objectives?

Human Resource Management Process

One indicator that HRM is truly strategic to an organization is when it is headed by a senior executive reporting directly to the chief executive officer. When Denis Donovan became Home Depot's first executive vice president for human resources, he said: "CEOs and boards of directors are learning that human resources can be one of your biggest game-changers in terms of competitive advantage."[11] The strategic importance of HRM has been further accentuated by the spate of corporate ethics scandals. "It was a failure of people and that isn't lost on those in the executive suite," says Susan Meisinger, former president of the Society for Human Resource Development.[12]

- **Person–job fit** is the extent to which an individual's skills, interests, and personal characteristics are consistent with the requirements of their work.
- **Person–organization fit** is the extent to which an individual's values, interests, and behavior are consistent with the culture of the organization.
- **Strategic human resource management** mobilizes human capital to implement organizational strategies.

Online Career Sites Now Center Stage for Recruiting

More and more recruiters are turning to the Web and social media sites to disseminate job openings and search for qualified applicants. Monster.com and LinkedIn are two examples of the online career sites frequently used by job hunters and employers. When going online with your résumés be sure to fill your online profile with the key words that both display your skills and match employer interests. Many use special software to scan online profiles for indicators that applicants possess real job skills and experiences that fit their organizations' needs.

LEGAL ENVIRONMENT OF HUMAN RESOURCE MANAGEMENT

In terms of human resource management practices, managers and employers can't simply do whatever they please. Everything must be done within the framework of laws and regulations that govern employment practices.

Laws against Employment Discrimination

"Why didn't I get invited for a job interview—is it because my first name is Abdul? Why didn't I get the promotion—is it because I'm so visibly pregnant?" These are questions that relate to possible **discrimination** in employment. It occurs when someone is denied a job or a job assignment for reasons that are not job-relevant. The possibilities raised in these questions shouldn't happen, and Figure 12.1 provides a sample of major U.S. laws prohibiting job discrimination. The legal protections are quite extensive, as the following examples further show.

● **Discrimination** occurs when someone is denied a job or job assignment for reasons that are not job-relevant.

Disabilities—The *Americans with Disabilities Act of 1990* (ADA) outlaws discrimination against qualified individuals with disabilities—physical or mental impairments that substantially limit one or more major life activities, and requires employers to provide reasonable accommodations for disabled employees.[13]

Age—The *Age Discrimination in Employment Act* (ADEA) *of 1967 as amended in 1978 and 1986* prohibits employment discrimination against persons 40 years of age or older.[14] Age discrimination occurs when a qualified individual is adversely affected by a job action that replaces him or her with a younger worker. The ADEA includes a broad ban against age discrimination, and specifically outlaws discrimination in hiring, promoting, compensating, or firing. It forbids statements in job notices or advertisements of age preference and limitations. It also prohibits mandatory retirement ages in most employment sectors.

Pregnancy—The *Pregnancy Discrimination Act of 1978* protects women from discrimination because of pregnancy. This law forbids discrimination when it comes to any aspect of employment, including hiring, firing, pay, job assignments, promotions, layoffs, training, fringe benefits, such as leave and health insurance, and any other term or condition of employment.[15] Pregnancy discrimination is the fastest growing type of discrimination in the United States. In fiscal year 2009, the EEOC received 6,196 charges of pregnancy-based discrimination and recovered $16.8 million in monetary benefits.[16]

Equal Pay Act of 1963	Requires equal pay for men and women performing equal work in an organization.	✓
Title VII of the Civil Rights Act of 1964 (as amended) *Pres Johnson*	Prohibits discrimination in employment based on race, color, religion, sex, or national origin.	✓
Age Discrimination in Employment Act of 1967 *Pilot 65 age restriction commerical*	Prohibits discrimination against persons over 40; restricts mandatory retirement.	✓
Occupational Health and Safety Act of 1970 *OHSA*	Establishes mandatory health and safety standards in workplaces.	
Pregnancy Discrimination Act of 1978	Prohibits employment discrimination against pregnant workers.	✓
Americans with Disabilities Act of 1990 *ADA cost of construction increase by 15-20%*	Prohibits discrimination against a qualified individual on the basis of disability.	✓
Civil Rights Act of 1991	Reaffirms Title VII of the 1964 Civil Rights Act; reinstates burden of proof by employer, and allows for punitive and compensatory damages.	✓
Family and Medical Leave Act of 1993	Allows employees up to 12 weeks of unpaid leave with job guarantees for childbirth, adoption, or family illness.	✓

FIGURE 12.1 Sample of U.S. laws against employment discrimination.

Family matters—The *Family and Medical Leave Act of 1993* (FMLA) entitles eligible employees to take up to 12 weeks of unpaid, job-protected leave in a 12-month period for specified family and medical reasons such as childbirth, adoption, or serious health conditions involving the employee or his/her family member. To be eligible, an employee must have worked for a covered employer for 12 months and at least 1,250 hours over the previous 12 months. Employers must have at least 50 employees to be covered by this act.[17]

Gender equity in education—*Title IX of the Educational Amendments of 1972 as amended in 1987* bans sex discrimination in schools receiving federal aid, whether it be in academics or athletics. Title IX governs the overall equity of treatment and opportunity in athletics while giving schools the flexibility to choose sports based on student body interest, geographic influence, budget restraints, and gender ratio. Three primary areas determine whether an institution is in compliance with the law—athletic financial assistance proportional to the ratio of male and female athletes; accommodation of athletic interests and abilities when selecting sports; and other program areas such as equipment, practice time, or opportunity to receive academic tutoring.[18]

Equal Employment Opportunity

The foundations of our legal protection against discrimination in employment rest with Title VII of the Civil Rights Act of 1964, as amended by the Equal Employment Opportunity Act of 1972 and the Civil Rights Act of 1991. These acts provide for **equal employment opportunity**—the requirement that employment decisions be made without regard to race, color, national origin, religion, gender, age, or disability status. The intent is to ensure all citizens the right to gain and keep employment based only on ability to do the job and performance once on the job. This right is federally enforced by the Equal Employment Opportunity

Equal employment opportunity is the requirement that employment decisions be made without regard to race, color, national origin, religion, gender, age, or disability status.

Commission, or EEOC. This agency has the power to file civil lawsuits against organizations that do not provide timely resolution of discrimination charges lodged against them. The laws generally apply to all public and private organizations employing 15 or more people.

Under Title VII, organizations are expected to show **affirmative action** in setting goals and having plans to ensure equal employment opportunity for members of protected groups, those historically underrepresented in the workforce. The purpose of affirmative action plans is to ensure that women and minorities are represented in the workforce in proportion to their labor market availability.[19] The pros and cons of affirmative action are debated at both the federal and state levels. Criticisms tend to focus on the use of group membership, such as female or minority status, as a criterion in employment decisions.[20] The issues include claims of reverse discrimination by members of majority populations. White males, for example, may claim that preferential treatment given to minorities interferes with their individual rights.

As a general rule, legal protections for equal employment opportunity do not restrict an employer's right to establish **bona fide occupational qualifications**. These are criteria for employment that can be clearly justified as being a reasonable necessity for the normal operation of a business and are clearly related to a person's capacity to perform a job. The use of bona fide occupational qualifications based on race and color is not allowed under any circumstances. Those based on sex, religion, age, and national origin are possible, but organizations must take great care to support these requirements.[21]

● **Affirmative action** is an effort to give preference in employment to women and minority group members who have traditionally been underrepresented.

● **Bona fide occupational qualifications** are employment criteria justified by capacity to perform a job.

Real Ethics

Are Employers Looking at Your Facebook Page?

When looking to hire a summer intern, the company's president went on Facebook and found out that an applicant listed smoking blunts (hollowed out cigars stuffed with marijuana) as one of his interests. "What kind of judgment does this person have?" wondered the president. "Why is he allowing this to be viewed online?"

It is a growing trend for recruiters to reject candidates and for HRM professionals to fire employees based on information obtained from web searches. Careerbuilder.com recently surveyed employers and found out that 20 percent of companies admitted to checking out candidate's profiles on social-networking sites before deciding to employ them; an additional 9 percent of companies planned on doing so in the future. Warren Ashton, group marketing manager at Microsoft, says: "For the first time ever, you suddenly have very public information about almost any candidate."

While a Facebook profile can be a treasure chest of information for recruiters and employers, it is less clear whether it is ethical for a firm to tap into this resource to measure a candidate's character and make employment decisions. Since when is one's Facebook profile meant to be an online résumé?

Sometimes negative decisions are made based on information involving relatively mild forms of questionable behavior. Other decisions may be based on information or pictures that the individual has little control over. What happens if a "friend" posts a picture of someone from a party that occurred years ago, or if untrue information is posted as a joke among friends?

You Decide

What are the ethical issues involved with regard to recruiters or managers searching out information posted on sites like Facebook? Should a manager search online sites to check up on what employees are doing outside of work? And, should what one does outside of work cost someone their job? On the other hand, in an accessible and public online forum, shouldn't individuals that knowingly post such information understand that it may end up in the hands of their employers?

Current Legal Issues

Because the legal environment is complex and dynamic, managers and human resource professionals have to stay informed about new laws and changes to existing ones. Failure to follow the laws is not only unjustified in civil society, it can also be an expensive mistake that results in fines and penalties. But things aren't always clear-cut and managers must be alert to issues of potential legal consequence. A brief sampler follows.

Sexual harassment occurs when a person experiences conduct or language of a sexual nature that affects his or her employment situation. The EEOC defines sexual harassment as behavior of a sexual nature that creates a hostile work environment, interferes with a person's ability to do a job, or impedes a person's promotion potential. *Quid pro quo sexual harassment* is where job decisions are made based on whether the employee submits to or rejects sexual advances. *Hostile work environment sexual harassment* occurs when any unwelcome form of sexual conduct (inappropriate touching, teasing, dirty jokes, vulgar conversations, or the display of sexually explicit pictures) creates an intimidating, hostile, or offensive working environment. Organizations should have clear sexual harassment policies in place, along with fair and equitable procedures for implementing them.

The Equal Pay Act of 1963 requires that men and women in the same organization be paid equally for doing work that is equivalent in terms of skills, responsibilities, and working conditions. But a lingering issue over gender disparities in pay involves **comparable worth**, the notion that persons performing jobs of similar importance should be paid at comparable levels. Why should a long-distance truck driver, for example, be paid more than an elementary teacher in a public school? Does it make any difference that truck driving is a traditionally male occupation and teaching is a traditionally female occupation? Advocates of comparable worth argue that such historical disparities result from gender bias. They would like to have the issue legally resolved.

The legal status and employee entitlements of part-time workers and **independent contractors** are also being debated. In today's era of downsizing and outsourcing, more and more persons are being hired as temporary workers who do not become part of an organization's permanent workforce. But even though they work only "as needed," many are engaged regularly by the same organization and become what some call "permatemps." Because these employees often work without benefits such as health insurance and pensions, legal cases are now being brought before the courts seeking to make independent contractors eligible for benefits.

Workplace privacy is the right of individuals to privacy on the job.[22] It is acceptable for employers to monitor the work performance and behavior of their employees. But employer practices can become invasive and cross legal and ethical lines, especially with the capabilities that information technology now provide. Computers can easily monitor e-mails and track Internet searches for unauthorized usage; they can identify who is called by telephone and how long conversations last; they can document work performance moment to moment; and they can do even more. All of this information, furthermore, can be stored in vast databases, even without the individual's permission. Until the legal status of electronic surveillance is cleared up, one consultant says the best approach is to "assume you have no privacy at work."[23]

• **Sexual harassment** is behavior of a sexual nature that affects a person's employment situation.

*EEOC
Equal Employment Opportunity Commission*

• **Comparable worth** holds that persons performing jobs of similar importance should be paid at comparable levels.

• **Independent contractors** are hired as needed and are not part of the organization's permanent workforce.

• **Workplace privacy** is the right to privacy while at work.

Be sure you can ☑ explain the human resource management process ☑ define *discrimination, equal employment opportunity, affirmative action,* and *bona fide occupational qualification* ☑ identify major laws that protect against discrimination in employment ☑ discuss legal issues of sexual harassment, comparable worth, independent contractors, and workplace privacy.

Learning Check
Study Question 1
What is human resource management?

ATTRACTING A QUALITY WORKFORCE

The first responsibility of human resource management is to attract to the organization a high-quality workforce whose talents match well with the jobs to be done. An advertisement once run by the Motorola Corporation clearly states the goal: "Productivity is learning how to hire the person who is right for the job." To attract the right people, an organization must first know exactly what it is looking for; it must have a clear understanding of the jobs to be done and the talents required to do them well. Then it must have the systems in place to excel at employee recruitment and selection.

HUMAN RESOURCE PLANNING

● **Human resource planning** analyzes staffing needs and identifies actions to fill those needs.

Human resource planning is the process of analyzing an organization's staffing needs and determining how to best fill them. As shown in Figure 12.2, human resource planning identifies staffing needs, assesses the existing workforce, and determines what additions or replacements are required for the future. The process becomes strategic when this is all done in specific reference to organizational mission, objectives, and strategies.

● A **job analysis** studies exactly what is done in a job, and why.

The foundations for human resource planning include **job analysis**—the orderly study of job facets to determine what is done when, where, how, why, and by whom.[24] Job analysis provides information that can then be used to write or update **job descriptions**. These are written statements of job duties and responsibilities. The information in a job analysis can also be used to create **job specifications**. These are lists of the qualifications—such as education, prior experience, and skills—needed by someone hired for a given job.

● A **job description** details the duties and responsibilities of a job holder.

● **Job specifications** list the qualifications required of a job holder.

RECRUITING TECHNIQUES

● **Recruitment** is a set of activities designed to attract a qualified pool of job applicants.

Recruitment is a set of activities designed to attract a qualified pool of job applicants to an organization. The word "qualified" is important. Recruiting should bring employment opportunities to the attention of people whose abilities and skills meet job specifications. Three steps in a typical recruitment process are: (1) advertisement

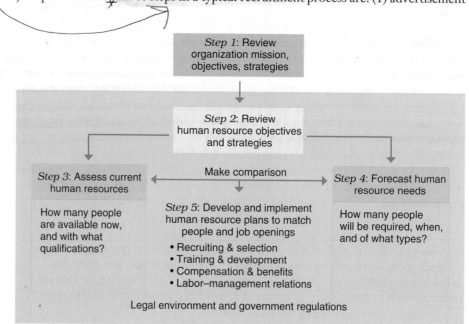

FIGURE 12.2 Steps in strategic human resource planning.

of a job vacancy, (2) preliminary contact with potential job candidates, and (3) initial screening to create a pool of qualified applicants.

External and Internal Recruitment

The recruiting that takes place on college campuses is one example of **external recruitment**, in which job candidates are sought from outside the hiring organization. Company websites or specialized recruiting websites such as HotJobs.com and Monster.com, newspapers and trade journals, employment agencies and headhunters, university job fairs and placement centers, personal contacts, employee referrals, and even persons in competing organizations are all sources of external recruits. **Internal recruitment**, by contrast, seeks applicants from inside the organization. Most organizations have a procedure for announcing vacancies through newsletters, electronic postings, and the like. They also rely on managers to recommend candidates for advancement.

Both recruitment methods have potential advantages and disadvantages. External recruitment brings in outsiders with fresh perspectives, expertise, and work experience. But less reliable information about the applicant is available and more training time will probably be required. External recruitment also tends to be time-consuming and expensive. Internal recruitment is usually quicker, less expensive, and focuses on persons whose performance records are well known. A history of internal recruitment also builds employees commitment and motivation by showing that opportunities exist to advance within the organization. Internal recruitment also helps to reduce turnover rates and aids the retention of high-quality employees. Yet, organizations often need skills and abilities that are more likely to be possessed by those outside the organization.

- **External recruitment** seeks job applicants from outside the organization. *fresh idea - change*

- **Internal recruitment** seeks job applicants from inside the organization. *moral*

Realistic Job Previews

In what may be called **traditional recruitment**, the emphasis is on selling the job and organization to applicants. The focus is on communicating the most positive features of the position, perhaps to the point where negatives are concealed. This may create unrealistic expectations that cause costly turnover when new hires become disillusioned and quit. The individual suffers a career disruption; the employer suffers lost productivity and the added costs of having to recruit again.

The alternative is to provide **realistic job previews** that give the candidate all pertinent information about the job and organization without distortion, and before the job is accepted.[25] Instead of "selling" the applicant on the positive features of the job or organization, realistic job previews try to be open and balanced. Both favorable and unfavorable aspects are covered. The interviewer in a realistic job preview might use phrases such as "Of course, there are some downsides. . . . " "Something that you will want to be prepared for is. . . ." "We have found that some new hires have difficulty with. . . ." Such conversations help candidates establish realistic expectations and better prepare for the inevitable "ups and downs" of a new job. Higher levels of early job satisfaction, greater trust in the organization, and less inclination to quit prematurely are among the expected benefits of realistic recruiting practices.

- **Traditional recruitment** focuses on selling the job and organization to applicants.

- **Realistic job previews** provide job candidates with all pertinent information about a job and an organization, both positive and negative.

SELECTION TECHNIQUES

Once a manager has a pool of qualified candidates, the next step is to select whom to hire. The process of **selection** as outlined in Figure 12.3 involves gathering and assessing information about job candidates and making a hiring decision. The selection process is a prediction exercise since the manager is trying to determine

- **Selection** is choosing individuals to hire from a pool of qualified job applicants.

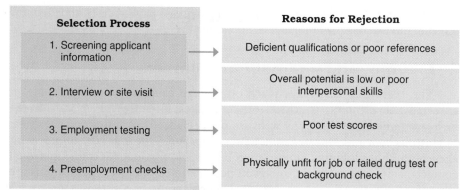

Selection Process	Reasons for Rejection
1. Screening applicant information	Deficient qualifications or poor references
2. Interview or site visit	Overall potential is low or poor interpersonal skills
3. Employment testing	Poor test scores
4. Preemployment checks	Physically unfit for job or failed drug test or background check

FIGURE 12.3 Steps in the selection process: the case of a rejected job applicant.

● **Reliability** means that a selection device gives consistent results over repeated measures.

● **Validity** means that scores on a selection device have demonstrated links with future job performance.

which applicants will perform well if hired. For this reason, selection techniques must demonstrate reliability and validity if they are to be effective predictors.

Reliability means that the selection technique is consistent in how it measures something. That is, it returns the same results time after time. For example, a personality test is reliable if the same individual receives a similar score when taking the test on two separate occasions. **Validity** means that there is a clear relationship between what the selection device is measuring and eventual job performance. That is, there is clear evidence that once on the job, individuals with high scores, on an employment test for example, outperform individuals with low scores.

Interviews

The traditional face-to-face interview remains the most common method of assessment in the selection process. Very few individuals are hired for professional positions without first sitting through one or more interviews. These interviews provide an opportunity for both the job applicant and the potential employer to learn a lot about one another.

● In **unstructured interviews** the interviewer does not work from a formal and preestablished list of questions that is asked of all interviewees.

It may surprise you to find out that interviews often have relatively low validity as a selection device. This is especially true of **unstructured interviews** where the interviewer does not work from a formal and preestablished list of questions that is asked of all interviewees. Some interviewers spend too much time discussing information that is unrelated to the key skills that will be needed in the job. Or, they dominate the conversation and spend more time talking about themselves or the organization than focusing on the extent to which the applicant is a good fit for the position. In addition, interviewee characteristics such as physical attractiveness and style of dress can disproportionately influence interviewers' assessments of job applicants.

Not all of the problems associated with interviews are the fault of the interviewer. Even well qualified job applicants may perform poorly. They may be unprepared for questions related to the specific organization with which they are interviewing. They may be nervous or may be poor communicators. And, they may be unfamiliar with an increasingly common and challenging interview setting—the telephone interview as highlighted in Management Smarts 12.1.

Management Smarts 12.1

How to succeed in a telephone interview

- *Prepare ahead of time*–study the organization; carefully list your strengths and capabilities.

- *Take the call in private*–make sure you are in a quiet room, with privacy and without the possibility of interruptions.

- *Dress as a professional*–don't be casual; dressing right increases confidence and sets a tone for your side of the conversation.

- *Practice your interview "voice"*–your impression will be made quickly; how you sound counts; it even helps to stand up while you talk.

- *Have reference materials handy*–your résumé and other supporting documents should be within easy reach.

- *Have a list of questions ready*–don't be caught hesitating; intersperse your best questions during the interview.

- *Ask what happens next*–find out how to follow up by telephone or e-mail; ask what other information you can provide.

The good news is that the predictive validity of interviews increases as the amount of structure increases. Also, behavioral interviews and situational interviews are much more effective at predicting successful job performance than the traditional interview.[26] **Behavioral interviews** ask job candidates about their past behavior, focusing specifically on behaviors that are likely to be important in the work environment. For example: "describe a situation in which you have been in conflict with a colleague and how you resolved that situation." **Situational interviews** ask applicants how they would react when confronted with specific work situations they would be likely to experience on the job. For example: "how would you handle two subordinates who do not get along with one another."[27]

> **Behavioral interviews** ask job applicants about past behaviors.
>
> **Situational interviews** ask job applicants how they would react in specific situations.

Employment Tests

Employment tests are often used to identify intelligence, aptitudes, personality, interests, and even ethics. But organizations need to be careful about the way that they use them and make sure that they are documented as valid predictors of job performance. **Biodata methods** usually take the form of multiple-choice, self-report questionnaires. They collect "hard" biographical information and also include "soft" items that inquire about more abstract things such as value judgments, aspirations, motivations, attitudes, and expectations. When used in conjunction with ability tests, this method can increase the reliability and validity of the selection process.[28] If you apply for a job at Google, for example, you may be asked to answer a biodata survey. The company will analyze your responses using an algorithm that compares your answers to those of existing top performers at the company.[29]

Other types of employment testing involve actual demonstrations of job-relevant skills and personal characteristics. An **assessment center** evaluates a person's potential by observing his or her performance in experiential activities designed to simulate daily work. When using **work sampling**, companies ask applicants to do actual job tasks while being graded by observers on their performance. Generally speaking, organizations should use a combination of methods in order to increase the predictive validity of the selection process.

> **Biodata methods** collect certain biographical information that has been proven to correlate with good job performance.
>
> An **assessment center** examines how job candidates handle simulated work situations.
>
> In **work sampling**, applicants are evaluated while performing actual work tasks.

Be sure you can ☑ explain the difference between internal recruitment and external recruitment ☑ discuss the value of realistic job previews to employers and job candidates ☑ differentiate reliability and validity as two criteria of selection devices ☑ discuss the use and validity of interviews and employment tests as selection devices

Learning Check
Study Question 2
How do organizations attract a quality workforce?

DEVELOPING A QUALITY WORKFORCE

When people join an organization, they must "learn the ropes" and become familiar with "the way things are done." It is important to help newcomers learn the organizational culture and fit into the work setting in a way that furthers their development and performance potential.

ORIENTATION AND SOCIALIZATION

The first formal experience of newcomers often begins with some form of **orientation**—a set of activities designed to familiarize new employees with their jobs, coworkers, and key aspects of the organization as a whole. A good orientation program clarifies the organization's mission and goals, explains the culture, and

> **Orientation** familiarizes new employees with jobs, coworkers, and organizational policies and services.

communicates key policies and procedures. At the Disney World Resort in Buena Vista, Florida, for example, new employees learn that everyone, regardless of her or his specific job title—be it entertainer, ticket seller, or groundskeeper—is a "cast member" there "to make the customer happy." A Disney HRM specialist says: "We want people who are enthusiastic, who have pride in their work, who can take charge of a situation without supervision."[30]

Socialization is a process of learning and adapting to the organizational culture.

Orientation is a form of **socialization**, a process that helps new members learn and adapt to the ways of the organization.[31] The socialization that occurs during the first six months or so of employment often determines how well someone is going to fit in and perform. When orientation is weak or neglected, socialization largely takes place informally as newcomers learn about the organization and their jobs through casual interactions with coworkers.[32] It is easy in such situations for even well-intentioned and capable people to learn the wrong things and pick up bad attitudes. By contrast, a good orientation program like Disney's helps ensure that socialization sets the right foundations for high performance, job satisfaction, and work enthusiasm.

TRAINING AND DEVELOPMENT

Training provides learning opportunities to acquire and improve job-related skills.

Training is a set of activities that helps people acquire and improve job-related skills. This applies both to initial training of an employee and to upgrading or improving skills to meet changing job requirements. Organizations committed to their employees invest in extensive training and development programs to ensure that everyone always has the capabilities needed to perform well.[33]

In **job rotation** people switch tasks to learn multiple jobs.

Coaching occurs as an experienced person offers performance advice to a less experienced person.

Mentoring assigns early-career employees as protégés to more senior ones.

Modeling uses personal behavior to demonstrate performance expected of others.

Management development is training to improve knowledge and skills in the management process.

On-the-job training takes place in the work setting while someone is doing a job. A common approach is **job rotation**, which allows people to spend time working in different jobs and thus expand the range of their job capabilities. LG Electronics, IBM, and McDonald's are some of the companies that are using job rotation.[34] Another approach is **coaching**, in which an experienced person provides performance advice to someone else. **Mentoring** is a form of coaching in which early-career employees are formally assigned as protégés to senior persons. The mentoring relationship gives them regular access to advice on developing skills and getting better informed about the organization. **Modeling** is a type of coaching in which someone demonstrates through behavior what is expected of others. An example might be senior managers who are always careful to act in ways that set the ethical culture and standards for other employees.

Off-the-job training is accomplished outside the work setting. An example is **management development**—formal training designed to improve a person's knowledge and skill in the fundamentals of management. Beginning managers often benefit from training that emphasizes team leadership and communication. Middle managers may benefit from training to better understand multifunctional viewpoints or techniques for motivating employees. Top managers may benefit from advanced management training to sharpen their decision-making and negotiating skills, as well as to expand their awareness of corporate strategy and direction.

PERFORMANCE MANAGEMENT

A **performance management system** sets standards, assesses results, and plans for performance improvements.

Performance appraisal is the process of formally evaluating performance and providing feedback to a job holder.

An important part of human resource management is the design and implementation of a successful **performance management system**. This system ensures that performance standards and objectives are set, that performance is regularly assessed, and that actions are taken to improve future performance.

Performance appraisal is the process of formally assessing someone's work accomplishments and providing feedback. It serves both evaluation and development purposes.[35] The *evaluation purpose* focuses on past performance

Research Brief

Racial Bias May Exist in Supervisor Ratings of Workers

That is a conclusion of a research study by Joseph M. Stauffer and M. Ronald Buckley reported in the *Journal of Applied Psychology*. The authors point out that it is important to have performance criteria and supervisory ratings that are free of bias. They cite a meta-analysis by Kraiger and Ford (1985) that showed white raters tending to rate white employees more favorably than black employees, whereas black raters rated blacks more favorably than did whites. They also cite a later study by Dackett and DuBois (1991) that disputed the finding that raters tended to favor members of their own racial groups.

In their study, Stauffer and Buckley re-analyzed the Dackett and DuBois data for possible interactions between rater and ratee. The data included samples of military and civilian workers, each of whom was rated by black and white supervisors. In both samples, white supervisors gave significantly higher ratings to white workers than they did to black workers; black supervisors also tended to favor white workers in their ratings.

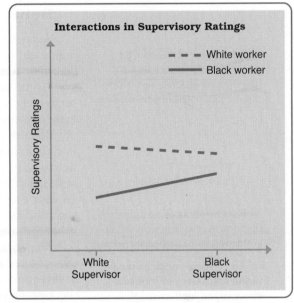

Stauffer and Buckley advise caution in concluding that the rating differences are the result of racial prejudice, saying the data aren't sufficient to address this issue. They call for future studies to examine both the existence of bias in supervisory ratings and the causes of such bias. In terms of present implications, the authors say: "If you are a White ratee, then it doesn't matter if your supervisor is Black or White. If you are a Black ratee, then it is important whether your supervisor is Black or White."

You Be the Researcher

Why would white supervisors rate black workers lower than white workers in this study if the ratings weren't based on racial prejudice? Why might black supervisors favor white workers over black workers in their ratings? What research questions come to mind that you would like to see definitively answered through rigorous scientific studies in the future? Is it possible that the present findings could be replicated with respect to teacher ratings of student performance? Suggest a study design that would examine this possibility.

References: Joseph M. Stauffer and M. Ronald Buckley, "The Existence and Nature of Racial Bias in Supervisory Ratings," *Journal of Applied Psychology*, vol. 90 (2005), pp. 586–91. Also cited: K. Kraiger and J. K. Ford, "A Meta-analysis of Ratee Race Effects in Performance Ratings," *Journal of Applied Psychology*, vol. 70 (1985), pp. 56–65; and P. R. Dackett and C. L. Z. DuBois, "Rater-Ratee Race Effects on Performance Evaluations: Challenging Meta-Analytic Conclusion," *Journal of Applied Psychology*, vol. 76 (1991), pp. 873–77.

and measures results against standards. Performance is documented for the record and for allocating rewards. The manager acts in a judgmental role and gives a direct evaluation of the subordinate's accomplishments. The *development purpose* focuses on future performance. Performance goals and obstacles are identified, along with areas where training or supervisory support may be needed. The manager acts in a counseling role and gives attention to the subordinate's developmental needs.

Organizations use a variety of performance appraisal methods and, just as with employment tests, they should be as reliable and valid as possible.[36] To be reliable, the method should consistently yield the same result over time or for different raters. To be valid, it should be unbiased and measure only factors directly relevant to job performance. At a minimum, written documentation of rigorous performance appraisals and a record of consistent past actions will be required to back up any

MBO
management
by objection

contested evaluations. In general, performance appraisal methods can be classified as focusing on traits, behaviors, results, or 360° feedbacks.

Trait-Based Performance Appraisals

Trait-based approaches are designed to measure the extent to which the employee possesses characteristics or traits that are considered important in the job. For example, trait-based measures often assess characteristics such as dependability, initiative, and leadership. One of the oldest and most widely used performance appraisal methods is a **graphic rating scale**. It is basically a checklist for rating an individual on traits or performance characteristics such as quality of work, job attitude, and punctuality. Although this approach is quick and easy, like other trait-based methods it tends to be very subjective and, as a result, has poor reliability and validity.

* A **graphic rating scale** uses a checklist of traits or characteristics to evaluate performance.

Behavior-Based Performance Appraisals

Behavior-based approaches evaluate employees on specific actions that are important parts of the job. The **behaviorally anchored rating scale**, or BARS, describes actual behaviors for various levels of performance achievement in a job. In the case of a customer-service representative illustrated in Figure 12.4, "extremely poor" performance is clearly defined as rude or disrespectful treatment of a customer.

Because performance assessments are anchored to specific descriptions of work behavior, the BARS is more reliable and valid than the graphic rating scale. Behavioral-based appraisals are also more consistent with a developmental purpose to performance appraisal since they provide specific feedback to employees on what they need to do better. But, one problem is that a BARS evaluation may be influenced by **recency bias**, the tendency for evaluations to focus on recent behaviors rather than on behavior that occurred throughout the evaluation period.

The **critical-incident technique** is a behavior-based approach that can reduce the influence of recency bias on evaluations. This technique keeps a running log or inventory of a person's effective and ineffective job behaviors. Using the case of the customer-service representative, a critical-incidents log might contain the following entries: Positive example—"Took extraordinary care of a customer who had purchased a defective item from a company store in another city;" negative example—"Acted rudely in dismissing the complaint of a customer who felt that

* A **behaviorally anchored rating scale** uses specific descriptions of actual behaviors to rate various levels of performance.

* **Recency bias** overemphasizes the most recent behaviors when evaluating individual performance.

* The **critical-incident technique** keeps a log of someone's effective and ineffective job behaviors.

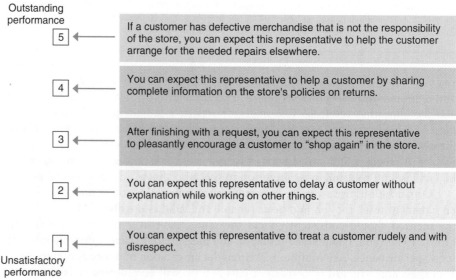

Outstanding performance

5 ← If a customer has defective merchandise that is not the responsibility of the store, you can expect this representative to help the customer arrange for the needed repairs elsewhere.

4 ← You can expect this representative to help a customer by sharing complete information on the store's policies on returns.

3 ← After finishing with a request, you can expect this representative to pleasantly encourage a customer to "shop again" in the store.

2 ← You can expect this representative to delay a customer without explanation while working on other things.

1 ← You can expect this representative to treat a customer rudely and with disrespect.

Unsatisfactory performance

FIGURE 12.4 Sample of a behaviorally anchored rating scale for performance appraisal.

Make Sure Performance Appraisals Work for You

Although each organization conducts performance appraisals in their own unique way, most employees receive them on an annual basis. And if they don't, they should ask for one. Performance appraisals are commonly used to provide feedback on past performance–the evaluation purpose, and to discuss ways to improve performance–the development purpose. They are often tied directly to the compensation system, used to determine training needs, and linked to decisions related to advancement or termination.

a sale item was erroneously advertised." Such a written record can be specifically discussed with the individual and used for both evaluative and developmental purposes.

Results-Based Performance Appraisals

Results-based approaches do just what their name implies. Rather than focusing on employee traits or specific behaviors, results-based assessments center on accomplishments. This type of assessment is typically quantitative and objective, making it ideal in some circumstances. But, results-based measures sometimes create more problems than they solve. In some jobs the things that are the easiest to measure quantitatively aren't the most important. In addition, results-based measures may ignore the impact of circumstances beyond the employee's control, such as economic conditions or poor performance by someone else. And when people are only evaluated on goal attainment, they may find unethical ways to accomplish the goals.[37]

Some performance appraisals use **multiperson comparisons** that formally compare one person's results with that of one or more others. Comparisons can be done in different ways. In *rank ordering*, all persons being rated are arranged in order of performance achievement. The best performer goes at the top of the list, the worst performer at the bottom; no ties are allowed. In *forced distribution*, each person is placed into a frequency distribution, which requires that a certain percentage of employees fall into specific performance classifications, such as top 10%, next 40%, next 40%, and bottom 10%. These systems are usually put in place to guard against supervisors giving their employees too lenient or overly positive evaluations.[38]

● A **multiperson comparison** compares one person's performance with that of others.

360-Degree Feedback

It is increasingly popular to include more than the immediate boss in the performance appraisal process.[39] **360-degree appraisals** are intended to gather feedback from multiple sources in order to provide a more comprehensive evaluation of the employee's performance. They typically include input not only from the employee's supervisor but from peers, subordinates, and even customers—individuals inside and outside the organization who depend on the job-holder's performance. Most 360-degree appraisals also include self-evaluations by the job holder to identify strengths, weaknesses, and development needs.[40]

● **360-degree appraisals** include superiors, subordinates, peers, and even customers in the appraisal process.

Be sure you can ☑ define *orientation* and *socialization* and describe their importance to organizations ☑ give examples of on-the-job and off-the-job training ☑ discuss strengths and weaknesses of trait-based, behavior-based, and results-based performance appraisals ☑ explain how 360-degree appraisals work

Learning Check ☑
Study Question 3
How do organizations develop a quality workforce?

MAINTAINING A QUALITY WORKFORCE

"Hiring good people is tough . . . keeping them can be even tougher" states an article in the *Harvard Business Review*.[41] The point is that it isn't enough to hire and train workers to meet an organization's immediate needs; they must also be successfully nurtured, supported, and retained. A Society for Human Resource Management survey of employers indicates that popular tools for maintaining a quality workforce include flexible work schedules and personal time off, competitive salaries, and good benefits—especially health insurance.[42]

FLEXIBILITY AND WORK–LIFE BALANCE

> **Work–life balance** involves balancing career demands with personal and family needs.

Today's fast-paced and complicated lifestyles have contributed to increased concerns about **work–life balance**—how people balance the demands of careers with their personal and family needs.[43] Not surprisingly, the "family-friendliness" of an employer is now frequently used as a screening criterion by job candidates. It is also used in "best employer" rankings found in magazines like *Working Mother* and *Fortune*.

Work–life balance is enhanced when workers have flexibility in scheduling work hours, work locations, and even such things as vacations and personal time off. Flexibility allows people to more easily balance personal affairs and work responsibilities. And it has been shown that workers who have flexibility, at least with start and stop times, are less likely to leave their jobs.[44] An example is Motorola, where all employees in its Chicago technology-acceleration group work flexible schedules at the office or from home. Another is Abbott Labs in Columbus, Ohio, where Wednesday is the only day employees have to be in the office; other days allow for flexible scheduling.[45]

Flexibility programs are becoming essential for many employers to attract and retain the talented workers they need. Some are helping workers handle family matters through such things as on-site day-care and elder-care, and concierge services for miscellaneous needs such as dry cleaning and gift purchasing. Others have moved into innovative programs like work sabbaticals—Schwab offers four weeks after five years employment, unlimited vacation days—a Dublin, Ohio, advertising agency lets workers take as many vacation days as they want, purchased vacation time—Xerox allows workers to buy vacation days using payroll deductions and on-call doctors—Microsoft sends doctors to employees' homes to keep them out of emergency rooms.[46]

COMPENSATION AND BENEFITS

> **Base compensation** is a salary or hourly wage paid to an individual.

Pay! It may be that no other work issue receives as much attention. **Base compensation** in the form of a market-competitive salary or hourly wage helps in hiring the right people. The way pay increases are subsequently handled can have a big impact on employees' job attitudes, motivation, and performance, and also influence their tendencies to "look around" for better jobs elsewhere.

Benefits! They rank right up there in importance with pay as a way of helping to attract and retain workers. How many times does a graduating college student hear "be sure to get a job with benefits!"?[47]

Merit Pay Systems

> **Merit pay** awards pay increases in proportion to performance contributions.

The trend in compensation today is largely toward "pay-for-performance."[48] If you are part of a **merit pay** system, your pay increases will be based on some assessment of how well you perform. The notion is that a good merit raise provides

Real People

Tony Hsieh Taps HRM to Keep Zappos.com One Step Ahead

As the CEO of Zappos.com, a popular online shoe store, Tony Hsieh (pronounced 'shay') has led the company through an amazing growth spurt. He's also forged a creative and unique approach to human resources management. Zappos' distinctive corporate culture gives it an edge over the competition, and Hsieh is determined to hire and retain only those employees who are truly committed to the values of the company.

Zappos now counts 1,600 "Zapponians" on its payroll. Despite this size, Hsieh goes out of his way to carefully screen and select new recruits. While he is shy and introverted, Hsieh focuses on hiring customer-service reps that are outgoing, creative, and open-minded.

Prospective hires go through two different interviews. In the first one, Hsieh assesses their technical proficiency. In the second one, he evaluates their ability to fit into the Zappos culture. Hsieh actually created the "cultural fit interview" himself. He included questions such as: "On a scale of 1 to 10, how weird are you?" "If they say 'one,' we won't hire them," says Hsieh. "If they're a 10, they're probably too psychotic for us. We like 7s or 8s." Hsieh, who figures he's an 8.5 says: "We want people who are passionate about what Zappos is about—service," says Hsieh.

Once hired, all employees, even executives, are required to go through a four-week customer loyalty training, where they not only spend time on the phone with customers but also work at the company's giant warehouse in Kentucky. They call

it the "KY Boot Camp." At the end of the boot camp, all trainees are offered a $2000 bonus to quit and walk away. When asked why he offers to pay new employees to leave the company, Hsieh says that he only wants people who are committed to his long-term vision. Interestingly, 97% of the trainees turn down the buyout.

Hsieh also believes in creating a "work hard, play hard" atmosphere. To keep Zapponians inspired, he throws a weekly costume party at the main office. Hsieh has also implemented several employee-friendly practices such as providing free food in the company's cafeterias and vending machines as well as paying 100% of medical and dental expenses for employees.

Although he sold Zappos to Amazon.com, Hsieh continues to run it as an independent unit. Even as part of a huge company like Amazon, he wants to maintain Zappos' culture and family-like atmosphere.

---

a positive signal to high performers while no merit raise or a low merit raise sends a negative signal to low performers, thus encouraging both to work hard in the future. Although this logic makes sense, merit systems are not problem-free. A survey reported by the *Wall Street Journal* found that only 23% of employees believed they understood their companies' reward systems.[49] Typical questions raised about merit pay plans include: Who assesses performance? What happens if the employee doesn't agree with the assessment? Is the system fair and equitable to everyone involved? Is there enough money available to make the merit increases meaningful?

A good merit pay system is based on a solid foundation of agreed-upon and well-defined performance measures. At the restaurant chain Applebee's International, Inc., managers know that part of their merit pay will be determined by what percentage of their best workers are retained. In an industry known for high turnover, Applebee's makes retention a high-priority goal for managers and makes their pay increases contingent on how well they do.[50] But this system can still break down if Applebee's managers don't perceive that it is administered in a fair, consistent, and credible fashion.

Bonuses and Profit-Sharing Plans

How would you like to someday receive a letter like this one, once sent to two top executives by Amazon.com's chairman Jeff Bezos? "In recognition and appreciation of your contributions," his letter read, "Amazon.com will pay you a special bonus in the amount of $1,000,000."[51] **Bonus pay** plans provide one-time or lump-sum payments to employees who meet specific performance targets or make some other

● **Bonus pay** plans provide one-time payments based on performance accomplishments.

extraordinary contribution, such as an idea for a work improvement. Bonuses have been most common at the executive level, but many companies now use them more extensively across all levels. At Applebee's, for example, "Applebucks" are small cash bonuses given to reward employee performance and raise loyalty to the firm.[52]

In contrast to straight bonuses, **profit-sharing** plans give employees a proportion of the net profits earned by the organization in a performance period. **Gain-sharing** plans extend the profit-sharing concept by allowing groups of employees to share in any savings or "gains" realized when their efforts or ideas result in measurable cost reductions or productivity increases. While all incentive systems can increase motivation, profit-sharing plans, gain-sharing plans, and bonus plans all have the advantage of helping to ensure that individual employees work hard and support the organization as a whole.

> **Profit-sharing** plans distribute to employees a proportion of net profits earned by the organization.

> **Gain-sharing** plans allow employees to share in cost savings or productivity gains realized by their efforts.

Stock Ownership and Stock Options

Some employers provide employees with ways to accumulate stock in their companies and thus develop a sense of ownership. The idea is that stock ownership will motivate employees to work hard so that the company stays successful. In an **employee stock ownership plan**, employees purchase stock directly through their employing companies and sometimes at special discounted rates. At Anson Industries, a Chicago construction firm, almost 95% of employees are stock owners.[53] An administrative assistant says it has made a difference in her job performance: "You have a different attitude . . . everyone here has the same attitude because it's our money." Of course, recent economic events show the risks of such ownership. When the company's market value falls, so too does the value of any employee-owned stock.

> **Employee stock ownership plans** help employees purchase stock in their employing companies.

Another approach is to grant employees **stock options** linked to their performance or as part of their hiring packages. Stock options give the owner the right to buy shares of stock at a future date at a fixed price. Employees gain financially if the stock price rises above the option price, but the stock options lose value if the stock price ends up lower. The logic is that option holders will work hard so that the company performs well and they reap some of the financial benefits. Some companies "restrict" stock options so that they come due only after designated periods of employment. This practice is meant to tie high performers to the employer and is often called the "golden handcuff." The Hay Group, a global human resource management consulting firm, reports that the most admired U.S. companies are also those that offer stock options to a greater proportion of their workforces.[54]

> **Stock options** give the right to purchase shares at a fixed price in the future.

Benefits

Employee benefits packages include nonmonetary forms of compensation that are intended to improve the work and personal lives of employees. In total, benefits packages can add as much as 30 to 40% to a typical worker's earnings. Some benefits are required by law, such as contributions to Social Security, unemployment insurance, and workers' compensation insurance. Also, some types of unpaid leave are mandated by the Family and Medical Leave Act. Most organizations also offer additional benefits in order to attract and retain highly qualified employees. These discretionary benefits include health care, retirement plans, pay for time not worked (personal days, vacations, and holidays), sick leave, and numerous other perks.

> **Employee benefits** are nonmonetary forms of compensation such as health insurance and retirement plans.

The ever-rising costs of benefits, especially medical insurance and retirement, are a major worry for employers. Many are attempting to gain control over health care expenses by shifting more of the insurance costs to the employee and by restricting choices among health care providers. Some are also encouraging healthy lifestyles as a way of decreasing health insurance claims.

Flexible benefits programs are increasingly common. They let the employee choose a set of benefits within a certain dollar amount. The trend is also toward more

> **Flexible benefits** programs allow employees to choose from a range of benefit options.

Googlers Enjoy Lots of Benefits

You've probably heard that working for Google not only pays, it can be a lot of fun. Start with the electric scooters that Googlers use to travel around the company's campus in Mountain View, California. Think next about them enjoying free gourmet food in on-campus cafeterias, having pet-friendly offices, and using recreation rooms when they need a work break. Employers like Google are finding that highly desirable perks that fit with today's employee preferences and lifestyles can be very helpful in attracting and retaining highly talented workers.

family-friendly benefits that help employees balance work and nonwork responsibilities. These include child care, elder care, flexible schedules, parental leave, and part-time employment options, among others. Increasingly common as well are **employee assistance programs** that help employees deal with troublesome personal problems. Such programs may offer assistance in dealing with stress, counseling on alcohol and substance abuse, referrals for domestic violence and sexual abuse, and sources for family and marital counseling.

● **Family-friendly benefits** help employees achieve better work–life balance.

RETENTION AND TURNOVER

The several steps in the human resource management process both conclude and recycle with retention and turnover. Some decisions transfer and promote people among positions; others involve terminations, layoffs, and retirements.

● **Employee assistance programs** help employees cope with personal stresses and problems.

Retirement is one of those things that can raise fears and apprehensions when it is close at hand. Many organizations offer special counseling and other forms of support for retiring employees, including advice on company benefits, money management, estate planning, and use of leisure time. Increasingly, you hear about **early retirement incentive programs**. These programs give workers financial incentives to retire early. The potential benefits for employers are opportunities to lower payroll costs by reducing positions, replacing higher-wage workers with less expensive newer hires, or creating openings that can be used to hire workers with different skills and talents.

● **Early retirement incentive programs** offer workers financial incentives to retire early.

The most extreme replacement decisions involve **termination**, or the involuntary and permanent dismissal of an employee. In some cases the termination is based on performance problems or violations of organizational policy. In other cases the persons involved may be performing well, but may be terminated as part of strategic restructuring by workforce reduction. In all cases, terminations should be handled fairly according to organizational policies and in full legal compliance.

● **Termination** is the involuntary dismissal of an employee.

Many employment relationships are governed by the **employment-at-will** doctrine. This principle assumes that employers can terminate employees at any time for any reason. Likewise, employees may quit their job at any time for any reason. In other cases, the principle of **wrongful discharge** gives workers legal protections against discriminatory firings, and employers must have bona-fide job-related reasons for a termination. In situations where workers belong to unions, terminations also become subject to labor contract rules and specifications.

● **Employment-at-will** means that employees can be terminated at any time for any reason.

● **Wrongful discharge** is a doctrine giving workers legal protections against discriminatory firings.

LABOR–MANAGEMENT RELATIONS

Labor unions are organizations to which workers belong and that deal with employers on the workers' behalf.[55] They are found in many industrial and business occupations, as well as among public-sector employees like teachers, police officers,

● A **labor union** is an organization that deals with employers on the workers' collective behalf.

and government workers. The National Labor Relations Act of 1935 (known as the Wagner Act) protects employees by recognizing their right to join unions and engage in union activities. It is enforced by the National Labor Relations Board (NLRB). The Taft-Hartley Act of 1947 protects employers from unfair labor practices by unions and allows workers to decertify unions. And, the Civil Service Reform Act of 1978 clarifies the right of government employees to join and be represented by labor unions.

Although union membership has been on the decline in the United States and now covers only about 12% of American workers, unions remain important forces in the workplace. At Verizon Communications, Inc., for example, 85,000 of the 103,000 workers in its telecom unit, or about 82%, belong to the Communications Workers of America and International Brotherhood of Electrical Workers unions.[56] Such unions serve as a collective "voice" for their members and act as bargaining agents to negotiate **labor contracts** with employers. These contracts specify the rights and obligations of employees and management with respect to wages, work hours, work rules, seniority, hiring, grievances, and other conditions of employment.

The foundation of any labor and management relationship is **collective bargaining**, the process through which labor and management representatives negotiate, administer, and interpret labor contracts. It typically involves face-to-face meetings between labor and management representatives. During this time, a variety of demands, proposals, and counterproposals are exchanged. Several rounds of bargaining may be required before a contract is reached or a dispute over a contract issue is resolved. As you might expect, the collective bargaining process is time-consuming and can lead to problems. Too often, labor and management sides view each other as "win-lose" adversaries. Ideally, the goal is a "win-win" outcome that offers benefits to labor in terms of fair treatment, and to management in terms of workforce quality.

> ● A **labor contract** is a formal agreement between a union and an employer about the terms of work for union members.
>
> ● **Collective bargaining** is the process of negotiating, administering, and interpreting a labor contract.

Learning Check
Study Question 4
How do organizations maintain a quality workforce?

Be sure you can ☑ define *work–life balance* ☑ explain why compensation and benefits are important elements in human resource management ☑ explain potential benefits and problems for merit pay plans ☑ differentiate between bonuses, profit sharing, and stock options ☑ define *flexible benefits plans* and discuss their advantages ☑ define *labor union* and *collective bargaining*

Management Learning Review

Study Questions Summary

1 What is human resource management?

● The human resource management process involves attracting, developing, and maintaining a quality workforce.

● Human resource management becomes strategic when it is integrated into the organization's strategic management process.

● Employees have legal protections against employment discrimination; equal employment opportunity requires that employment and advancement decisions be made without discrimination.

● Current legal issues in human resource management include sexual harassment, comparable worth, rights of independent contractors, and employee privacy.

FOR DISCUSSION **What gaps in legal protection against employment discrimination still exist?**

2 How do organizations attract a quality workforce?

● Human resource planning analyzes staffing needs and identifies actions to fill these needs over time.

- Recruitment is the process of attracting qualified job candidates to fill positions.
- Realistic job previews provide candidates with both positive and negative information about the job and organization.
- Selection involves gathering and assessing information about job candidates and making decisions about whom to hire.
- The selection process often involves screening applicants for qualifications, interviewing applicants, administering employment tests, and doing preemployment checks.

FOR DISCUSSION **Is it realistic to expect that a potential employer will give you a "realistic" job preview?**

3 How do organizations develop a quality workforce?

- Orientation is the process of formally introducing new employees to their jobs, performance expectations, and the organization.
- On-the-job training includes job rotation, coaching, modeling, and mentoring; off-the-job training includes things like management development programs.
- Performance appraisal serves both evaluation and development purposes.

- Common performance appraisal methods focus on evaluating employees' traits, behaviors, or performance achievements.

FOR DISCUSSION **What are some of the potential downsides of being on the receiving end of 360-degree feedback?**

4 How do organizations maintain a quality workforce?

- Complex demands of job and family responsibilities have made work–life balance programs increasingly important in human resource management.
- Compensation and benefits packages must be attractive so that an organization stays competitive in labor markets.
- Merit pay plans link compensation and performance; bonuses, profit sharing, and stock options are also forms of incentive compensation.
- Retention decisions in human resource management involve promotions, retirements, and/or terminations.
- The collective bargaining process and labor–management relations are carefully governed by law.

FOR DISCUSSION **Given current trends in globalization, is it likely that labor unions will gain in popularity?**

Self-Test

Multiple-Choice Questions

1. Human resource management is the process of _____, developing, and maintaining a high-quality workforce.
   (a) attracting (b) compensating (c) appraising (d) selecting

2. A _____ is a criterion that can be legally justified for use in screening candidates for employment.
   (a) job description (b) bona fide occupational qualification (c) job specification (d) BARS

3. _____ programs are designed to ensure equal employment opportunities for persons historically underrepresented in the workforce.
   (a) Realistic recruiting (b) External recruiting (c) Affirmative action (d) Employee assistance

4. If an employment test yields different results over time when taken by the same person, it lacks _____.
   (a) validity (b) specificity (c) realism (d) reliability

5. The assessment center approach to employee selection relies heavily on _____.
   (a) pencil-and-paper tests (b) simulations and experiential exercises (c) 360-degree feedback (d) formal one-on-one interviews

6. _____ is a form of on-the-job training wherein an individual learns by observing others who demonstrate desirable job behaviors.
   (a) Case study (b) Work sampling (c) Modeling (d) Simulation

7. The first step in strategic human resource planning is to _____.
   (a) forecast human resource needs (b) forecast labor supplies (c) assess the existing workforce (d) review organizational mission, objectives, and strategies

8. In the United States, the _____ Act of 1947 protects employers from unfair labor practices by unions.
   (a) Wagner (b) Taft-Hartley (c) Labor Union (d) Hawley-Smoot

9. Socialization of newcomers occurs during the _____ step of the staffing process.
   (a) recruiting (b) orientation (c) selecting (d) training

10. In human resource planning, a/an _____ is used to determine exactly what is done in an existing job.
    (a) critical-incident technique (b) assessment center (c) job analysis (d) multiperson comparison

11. In labor–management relations, the process of negotiating, administering, and interpreting a labor contract is known as _____.
    (a) arbitration   (b) mediation   (c) reconciliation   (d) collective bargaining

12. The _____ purpose of performance appraisal is being addressed when a manager describes training options that might help an employee improve future performance.
    (a) development   (b) evaluation   (c) judgment   (d) legal

13. When a team leader is required to rate 10% of team members as "superior," 80% as "good," and 10% as "unacceptable" for their performance on a project, this is an example of the _____ approach to performance appraisal.
    (a) graphic   (b) forced distribution   (c) behaviorally anchored rating scale   (d) realistic

14. An employee with domestic problems due to substance abuse would be pleased to learn that his employer had a(n) _____ plan to help on such matters.
    (a) employee assistance   (b) cafeteria benefits   (c) comparable worth   (d) collective bargaining

15. The critical-incident technique is one example of a _____ approach to performance appraisal.
    (a) trait-based   (b) behavior-based   (c) results-based   (d) realistic-job-preview-based

Short-Response Questions

16. What are the different advantages of internal and external recruitment?
17. Why is orientation an important part of the human resource management process?
18. Why is a BARS potentially superior to a graphic rating scale for use in performance appraisals?
19. How does mentoring work as a form of on-the-job training?

Essay Question

20. Sy Smith is not doing well in his job. The problems began to appear shortly after Sy's job was changed from a manual to a computer-based operation. He has tried hard but is just not doing well in learning to use the computer; as a result, he is having difficulty meeting performance expectations. As a 55-year-old employee with over 30 years with the company, Sy is both popular and influential among his work peers. Along with his performance problems, you have also noticed that Sy seems to be developing a more negative attitude toward his job. As Sy's manager, what options would you consider in terms of dealing with the issue of his retention in the job and in the company? What would you do, and why?

Management **S**kills and **C**ompetencies

Self-Assessment

Back to Yourself: **Professionalism**

Chances are that your school has a student branch of the Society for Human Resource Management. Introduced in the chapter opener, it's a great example of how **professionalism** plays a role in management. When students work together on SHRM projects, they are not just learning HRM techniques and practices; they are learning to behave with internalized commitments to external standards. All managers should show similar professionalism in their own areas of expertise and work responsibility. And, of course, they should be thoroughly professional in all aspects of human resource management discussed in this chapter. After you complete the following check of your Performance Appraisal Assumptions, don't forget to go online for the Feedback and Assertiveness self-assessment.

> Living up to **professionalism** in our work means accepting personal responsibility for our decisions and actions, behaving ethically, showing fairness, and performing at a high level.

Further Reflection: **Performance Appraisal Assumptions**

Instructions

In each of the following pairs, check the statement that best reflects your assumptions about performance evaluation.[57]

Performance evaluation is

1. (a) a formal process that is done annually.
   (b) an informal process done continuously.
2. (a) a process that is planned for subordinates.
   (b) a process that is planned with subordinates.
3. (a) a required organizational procedure.
   (b) a process done regardless of requirements.
4. (a) a time to evaluate subordinates' performance.
   (b) a time for subordinates to evaluate their manager.
5. (a) a time to clarify standards.
   (b) a time to clarify the subordinate's career needs.
6. (a) a time to confront poor performance.
   (b) a time to express appreciation.
7. (a) an opportunity to clarify issues and provide direction and control.
   (b) an opportunity to increase enthusiasm and commitment.
8. (a) only as good as the organization's forms.
   (b) only as good as the manager's coaching skills.

Scoring

There is no formal scoring for this assessment, but there may be a pattern to your responses.

Interpretation

The "a" responses represent a more traditional approach to performance appraisal that emphasizes its evaluation function. This role largely puts the supervisor in the role of documenting a subordinate's performance for control and administrative purposes. The "b" responses represent more emphasis on the counseling or development role. Here, the supervisor is concerned with helping the subordinate perform better and learn how he or she might be of help.

Team Exercise

Upward Appraisal

Instructions

Form into work groups as assigned by the instructor. After the instructor leaves the room, complete the following tasks.[58]

1. Create a master list of comments, problems, issues, and concerns about the course experience to date that members would like to communicate to the instructor.
2. Select one person from the group to act as the spokesperson who will give your feedback to the instructor when he or she returns to the classroom.
3. The spokespersons should meet to rearrange the room (placement of tables, chairs, etc.) for the feedback session. This arrangement should allow the spokespersons and instructor to communicate in view of the other class members.
4. While spokespersons are meeting, group members should discuss what they expect to observe during the feedback session.
5. The instructor should be invited in; spokespersons should deliver feedback while observers make notes.
6. After the feedback session is complete, the instructor will call on observers for comments, ask the spokespersons for their reactions, and engage the class in general discussion about the exercise and its implications.

Case Study: Netflix

Go to *Management Cases for Critical Thinking* to find the recommended case for Chapter 12–"Netflix: Making Movie Magic."

13 Leading and Leadership Development

Chapter 13 Study Questions

1 What is the nature of leadership?

2 What are the key leadership traits and behaviors?

3 What are the contingency approaches to leadership?

4 What are current issues in personal leadership development?

Learning From Others

Leaders Provide the Roadmaps

When Kraft Foods was bidding to buy Cadbury, Irene Rosenfeld was often in the news. As CEO of Kraft, she was leading a dramatic attempt to capture the British candy maker, against its wishes. It was all part of Rosenfeld's strategy to transform Kraft as a global power-house in snacks and confectionery.

Upon taking over as CEO, Rosenfeld said she found a firm that "was not living up to our potential." She's been relentless in engaging the firm's employees and stakeholders in frank discussions, and then embarking on strategies—such as the Cadbury acquisition—to meet her lofty goals.

One of Rosenfeld's leadership initiatives was to push decision authority down the hierarchy, such as letting managers of Kraft's major brands have control of their budgets and operations. She also built top management teams to bring perspectives in from all parts of the company. And she urged division managers to focus resources on what they did best in their customer markets. All the while, however, she stuck with the goal, pushing her turnaround strategy by communicating the ever present message of "Let's Get Growing!"

A former Kraft executive says that Rosenfeld "is a risk taker" and the Cadbury bid was "a pretty bold move." Rosenfeld describes key insights gained from experience with change leadership. First, she says you need to "get the right people on the bus." Rosenfeld replaced half her top team in the first year. Second, she says "give them a roadmap." This allowed a focus on implementation. Third, she says you have to "engage their hearts and minds." Her rallying cry of Let's Get Growing raised aspirations. Fourth, she says you must "move quickly." Facing the uncertainties of change, it was important to move faster than the resistance. And fifth, she says "communicate frequently, consistently and honestly."

do the benchmarking

There are a lot of great leaders around in all types of organizations, from large to small and from nonprofit to business. This example of Irene Rosenfeld is really a tickler, one designed to get you thinking about your leadership qualities and get you looking at the leadership models that abound in your experiences. Who are your leadership exemplars? Just who is the leader in you? **What can you do to keep yourself growing and confident as a leader in the days and years ahead?**

Learning About Yourself

Integrity

Whether you call it ethical leadership or moral leadership, the personal implications are the same: respect flows toward leaders who behave with **integrity**. You should understand that integrity is defined as being honest, credible, and consistent in all that we do. This description seems like a no-brainer. "This is what we have been taught since we were kids," you might say.

So, why do we find so many examples of leaders who act without integrity? Where, so to speak, does integrity go when some people find themselves in positions of leadership?

CEO coach Kenny Moore says: "Character is revealed by how we treat those with no power." Check it out by observing how people in leadership positions treat every-day workers—servers in restaurants, secretaries in the office, custodians and clerks, for example. Moore says that the ways we deal with people who are powerless "brings out our real dispositions."

Leadership and the Integrity Line

Consider also the notion of leadership and the "integrity line" as depicted in the figure. Notice the clear difference between where we should and should not be. Below the line you're likely to find leaders who are willing to lie, blame others for personal mistakes, want others to fail, and take credit for others' ideas. They're conceited, and they're also selfish. Above the line are honest, consistent, humble, and selfless leaders.

According to the late management guru Peter Drucker, leaders with integrity "are servants of the organization. Whether elected or appointed, whether the organization is a government, a government agency, a business, a hospital, a diocese, it's their duty to subordinate their likes, wishes, preferences to the welfare of the institution."[1]

get to know yourself better

How often have you worked for someone who behaved below the "integrity line" in the figure? How did you feel about it, and what did you do? Write a set of notes on your behavior in situations where your own leadership integrity could be questioned. What are the lessons for the future? **Also take advantage of the end-of-chapter Self-Assessment to further reflect on your Integrity and examine your leadership tendencies.**

Study Question 1	Study Question 2	Study Question 3	Study Question 4
Nature of Leadership	**Leadership Traits and Behaviors**	**Contingency Approaches to Leadership**	**Personal Leadership Development**
• Leadership and power • Leadership and vision • Leadership as service	• Leadership traits • Leadership behaviors • Classic leadership styles	• Fiedler's contingency model • Hersey-Blanchard situational model • Path–goal theory • Leader–member exchange theory • Leader–participation model	• Charismatic and transformational leadership • Emotional intelligence and leadership • Gender and leadership • Moral leadership • Drucker's "old-fashioned" leadership
Learning Check 1	**Learning Check 2**	**Learning Check 3**	**Learning Check 4**

The late Grace Hopper, management expert and the first female admiral in the U.S. Navy, once said: "You manage things; you lead people."[2] Leadership scholar and consultant Barry Posner believes that managers need to spend less time dealing with the status quo and focus more on "figuring out what needs to be changed." He says: "The present moment is the domain of managers. The future is the domain of leaders."[3] Consultant and author Tom Peters points out that the leader is "rarely—possibly never?—the best performer."[4] His point is that leaders thrive through and by the successes of others.

These are among many leadership insights that will be discussed in this chapter. If we go right to the heart of the matter, the consensus is that leaders become great by bringing out the best in people. The message is clear, but we also have to be realistic; the task isn't easy. When studying leadership and working on personal leadership development, it's important to remember that managers today often face daunting responsibilities. Resources are scarce and performance expectations are high. Time frames for getting things accomplished are becoming shorter, while problems to be resolved are complex, ambiguous, and multidimensional.[5]

It takes hard work to be a great leader. There are lots of challenges to be mastered. So, why not personalize this chapter and use it as an opportunity to find out more about the leader who resides in you?

THE NATURE OF LEADERSHIP

Leadership is the process of inspiring others to work hard to accomplish important tasks.

A glance at the shelves in your local bookstore will quickly confirm that **leadership**—the process of inspiring others to work hard to accomplish important tasks—is one of the most popular management topics.[6] As shown in Figure 13.1, it is also one of the four functions that constitute the management process. Planning sets the direction and objectives; organizing brings together resources to turn plans into action; leading builds the commitments and enthusiasm for people to apply their talents to help accomplish plans; and controlling makes sure things turn out right.

LEADERSHIP AND POWER

The foundation for leadership success rests with an ability to make things happen in ways that serve the goals of the team or organization. This is an issue of "power," and leadership essentially begins with the ways a manager uses power to influence the behavior of other people. Harvard professor Rosabeth Moss Kanter once called it "America's last great dirty word."[7] She was concerned that too many people, managers among them, are not only uncomfortable with the concept of power, but also they don't realize how indispensable it is to leadership.

Power is the ability to get someone else to do something you want done, or to make things happen the way you want. Although a need for power is essential to executive success, it is not a desire to control for the sake of personal satisfaction. It is a desire to influence and control others for the good of the group or organization as a whole.[8] This "positive" face of power is the foundation of effective leadership.

Figure 13.2 shows that leaders gain power both from the positions they hold and from their personal qualities.[9] Anyone holding a managerial position theoretically has power, but how well it is used will vary from one person to the next. The three bases of position power are reward power, coercive power, and legitimate power. The two bases of personal power are expertise and reference.

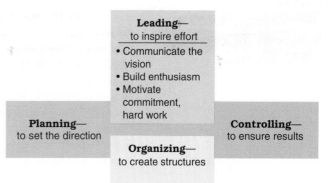

FIGURE 13.1 Leading viewed in relationship to the other management functions.

> **Power** is the ability to get someone else to do something you want done or to make things happen the way you want.

Position power

When it comes to power gained through the position of being a manager, **reward power** is the ability to influence through rewards. It is the capacity to offer something of value—a positive outcome—as a means of influencing another person's behavior. This involves use of incentives such as pay raises, bonuses, promotions, special assignments, and verbal or written compliments. To mobilize reward power, a manager says, in effect: "If you do what I ask, I'll give you a reward." And as you might expect, this approach can work well as long as people want the reward and the manager or leader makes it continuously available. But take the value of the reward or the reward itself away, and the power is quickly lost.

> **Reward power** is the capacity to offer something of value as a means of influencing other people.

Coercive power is the ability to influence through punishment. It is the capacity to punish or withhold positive outcomes as a way to influence the behavior of other people. A manager may attempt to coerce someone by threatening him or her with verbal reprimands, pay penalties, and even termination. To mobilize coercive power, a manager says, in effect: "If you don't do what I want, I'll punish you." How do you or would you feel when threatened in these ways? If you're like many, you'll most likely resent both the threat and the person making it. Sure, you might act as requested, or at least go through the motions. But you're unlikely to continue doing so once the threat no longer exists.

> **Coercive power** is the capacity to punish or withhold positive outcomes as a means of influencing other people.

Sources of power...

Power of the POSITION: *Based on things managers can offer to others.*	Power of the PERSON: *Based on how managers are viewed by others.*
Rewards: "If you do what I ask, I'll give you a reward."	**Expertise**—as a source of special knowledge and information.
Coercion: "If you don't do what I ask, I'll punish you."	**Reference**—as a person with whom others like to identify.
Legitimacy: "Because I am the boss; you *must* do as I ask."	

FIGURE 13.2 Sources of position power and personal power used by leaders.

Legitimate power is the capacity to influence other people by virtue of formal authority, or the rights of office.

Legitimate power is the ability to influence through authority—the right by virtue of one's organizational position or status to exercise control over persons in subordinate positions. To mobilize legitimate power, a manager says, in effect: "I am the boss; therefore, you are supposed to do as I ask." You can consider legitimate power in the context of your management course. When the instructor assigns homework, exams, and team projects, don't you most often do what is requested? Why? You do it because the requests seem legitimate in the context of the course. But if the instructor moves outside of the course boundaries, such as requiring you to attend a campus sports event, the legitimacy is lost and your compliance is much less likely.

Personal Power

After all is said and done, position power isn't going to be sufficient for any manager. How much personal power you can mobilize through expertise and reference may well make the difference someday between success and failure in a leadership situation, and even in your career.

Expert power is the capacity to influence other people because of specialized knowledge.

Expert power is the ability to influence through special expertise. It is the capacity to influence the behavior of other people because of one's knowledge and skills. Expertise derives from the possession of technical understanding or special information. In fact, the term *information power* is useful in this respect. Expert power is developed by acquiring relevant skills or competencies, and by accumulating and gaining access to useful information. It is maintained by protecting one's credibility and not overstepping the boundaries of true expertise. When a manager uses expert power, the implied message is: "You should do what I want because of my special expertise or information." Building such expertise, in fact, may be one of your biggest early career challenges.

Referent power is the capacity to influence other people because of their desire to identify personally with you.

Referent power is the ability to influence through identification. It is the capacity to influence the behavior of other people because they admire you and want to identify positively with you. Reference is a power derived from charisma or interpersonal attractiveness. The notions of *networking power* and *social capital* are relevant here, since both refer to a leader's ability to gain power by building and maintaining contacts with persons that can be of potential help in their work. You can think of reference power as something that can be developed and maintained through good interpersonal relationships, ones that encourage the admiration and respect of others. When a manager uses referent power, the implied message is: "You should do what I want in order to maintain a positive, self-defined relationship with me." Simply put, we can say that it's a lot easier to get people to do what you want when they like you than when they dislike you.

LEADERSHIP AND VISION

"Great leaders," it is said, "get extraordinary things done in organizations by inspiring and motivating others toward a common purpose."[10] In other words, they use their power exceptionally well. And that use of power is associated with **vision**—a future that one hopes to create or achieve in order to improve upon the present state of affairs. But simply having the vision of a desirable future is not enough. Truly exceptional leaders are really good at turning their visions into accomplishments.

Vision is a clear sense of the future.

Visionary leadership brings to the situation a clear sense of the future and an understanding of how to get there.

The term **visionary leadership** describes a leader who brings to the situation a clear and compelling sense of the future, as well as an understanding of the actions needed to get there successfully.[11] This means having a clear vision, communicating the vision, and getting people motivated and inspired to pursue the vision in their daily work. Think of it this way. Visionary leadership brings meaning

Lorraine Monroe's Leadership Turns Vision into Inspiration

Dr. Lorraine Monroe's career in the New York City schools began as a teacher. She went on to serve as assistant principal, principal, and vice-chancellor for curriculum and instruction. Then she founded the Frederick Douglass Academy, a public school in Harlem, where she grew up. Under her leadership as principal, the school became highly respected for educational excellence. The academy's namesake was an escaped slave who later became a prominent abolitionist and civil rights leader.

Through her experiences, Monroe formed a set of beliefs centered on a leader being vision-driven and follower-centered. She believes leaders must always start at the "heart of the matter" and that "the job of a good leader is to articulate a vision that others are inspired to follow."

Monroe believes in making sure all workers know they are valued and that their advice is welcome, and that workers and managers should always try to help and support one another. "I have never undertaken any project," she says, "without first imagining on paper what it would ultimately look like. . . . all the doers who would be responsible for carrying out my imaginings have to be informed and let in on the dream."

About her commitment to public leadership, Monroe states: "We can reform society only if every place we live—every school, workplace, church, and family—becomes a site of reform." She now serves as a leadership consultant and runs the Lorraine Monroe Leadership Institute. Its goal is to train educational leaders in visionary leadership and help them go forth to build high-performing schools that transform children's lives.

Lorraine Monroe's many leadership ideas are summarized in what is called the "Monroe Doctrine." It begins with this advice: "The job of the leader is to uplift her people—not just as members of and contributors to the organization, but as individuals of infinite worth in their own right."

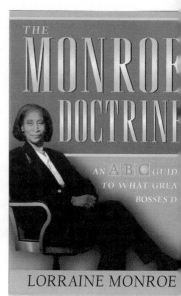

to people's work; it makes what they do seem worthy and valuable. As pointed out in the Real People feature, Lorraine Monroe brings visionary leadership to life at her Leadership Institute. "Leadership is about making a vision happen," she says: "The job of a good leader is to articulate a vision that others are inspired to follow. That leader makes everybody in an organization understand how to make the vision active."[12] Her views are consistent with those of the late John Wooden, former stand-out men's basketball coach at UCLA: "Effective leadership means having a lot of people working toward a common goal. And when you have that with no one caring who gets the credit, you're going to accomplish a lot."[13]

LEADERSHIP AS SERVICE

When thinking about leadership, power, and vision, it is important to revisit the issue of integrity as mentioned in the chapter opener. In the words of Peter Drucker, the concept of "service" is central to integrity, and leaders who have integrity act as "servants of the organization."[14] **Servant leadership** is leadership based on a commitment to serving others, to helping people use their talents to full potential while working together for organizations that benefit society.[15] You might think of servant leadership with this question in mind: Who is most important in leadership, the leader or the followers? For those who believe in servant leadership, there is no doubt about the correct answer: the followers. Servant leadership is "other-centered," and not "self-centered."

● **Servant leadership** is follower-centered and committed to helping others in their work.

If one shifts the focus away from the self and toward others, what does that generate in terms of leadership directions and opportunities? The answer is **empowerment**. As discussed in earlier chapters, this is the process through which managers enable and help others gain power and achieve influence within the organization. Servant leaders empower others by providing them with the

● **Empowerment** enables others to gain and use decision-making power.

information, responsibility, authority, and trust to make decisions and act independently. They expect that people who are empowered will follow through with commitment and high-quality work. Realizing that power in organizations is not a "zero-sum" quantity, they reject the idea that in order for one person to gain power someone else needs to give it up.[16] In this way servant leadership becomes empowering for everyone, and it makes the whole organization more powerful in pursuing its cause or mission.

Robert Greenleaf, who is credited with coining the term *servant leadership*, says: "Institutions function better when the idea, the dream, is to the fore, and the person, the leader, is seen as servant to the dream."[17] Max DePree of Herman Miller praises leaders who "permit others to share ownership of problems—to take possession of the situation."[18] And Lorraine Monroe says "The real leader is a servant of the people she leads. A really great boss is not afraid to hire smart people. You want people who are smart about things you are not smart about."[19]

Learning Check

Study Question 1
What is the nature of leadership?

Be sure you can ☑ define *power* ☑ illustrate three types of position power and discuss how managers use each ☑ illustrate two types of personal power and discuss how managers use each ☑ define *vision* ☑ explain the concept of visionary leadership ☑ define *empowerment* ☑ explain the notion and benefits of servant leadership

LEADERSHIP TRAITS AND BEHAVIORS

For centuries people have recognized that some persons perform very well as leaders, whereas others do not. The question still debated is why. Historically, the issue of leadership success has been studied from the perspective of the trait, behavioral, and contingency approaches. Each offers a slightly different explanation of leadership effectiveness and the pathways to leadership development.

LEADERSHIP TRAITS

An early direction in leadership research involved the search for universal traits or distinguishing personal characteristics that separated effective from ineffective leaders.[20] Sometimes called the "great person theory," the results of many years of research in this direction can be summarized as follows.

Physical characteristics such as a person's height, weight, and physique make no difference in determining leadership success. On the other hand, certain personal traits are common among the best leaders. A study of more than 3,400 managers, for example, found that followers rather consistently admired leaders who were honest, competent, forward looking, inspiring, and credible.[21] And, a comprehensive review by Shelley Kirkpatrick and Edwin Locke identifies these personal traits of many successful leaders:[22]

- *Drive*—Successful leaders have high energy, display initiative, and are tenacious.
- *Self-confidence*—Successful leaders trust themselves and have confidence in their abilities.
- *Creativity*—Successful leaders are creative and original in their thinking.
- *Cognitive ability*—Successful leaders have the intelligence to integrate and interpret information.
- *Job-relevant knowledge*—Successful leaders know their industry and its technical foundations.
- *Motivation*—Successful leaders enjoy influencing others to achieve shared goals.

- *Flexibility*—Successful leaders adapt to fit the needs of followers and the demands of situations.
- *Honesty and integrity*—Successful leaders are trustworthy; they are honest, predictable, and dependable.

LEADERSHIP BEHAVIORS

Moving on from the early trait studies, researchers next turned their attention to the issue of how leaders behave when dealing with followers.[23] If the most effective behaviors could be identified, the implications were straightforward and practical: Train leaders to become skilled at using them.

A stream of research that began in the 1940s, spearheaded by studies at Ohio State University and the University of Michigan, focused attention on two dimensions of leadership behavior: (1) concern for the task to be accomplished and (2) concern for the people doing the work. The Ohio State studies used the terms *initiating structure* and *consideration* for the respective dimensions; the University of Michigan studies called them *production-centered* and *employee-centered*.[24] But regardless of the terminology used, the characteristics of each dimension of leadership behavior were quite clear.

- *A leader high in concern for task*—plans and defines the work to be done, assigns task responsibilities, sets clear work standards, urges task completion, and monitors performance results.
- *A leader high in concern for people*—acts with warmth and supportiveness toward followers, maintains good social relations with them, respects their feelings, is sensitive to their needs, and shows trust in them.

The results of leader behavior research at first suggested that followers of people-oriented leaders would be the most productive and satisfied.[25] However, researchers eventually moved toward the position that truly effective leaders were high in concerns for both people and task. Figure 13.3 shows one of the popular versions of this conclusion—the Leadership Grid™ of Robert Blake and Jane Mouton.[26] It describes how leaders vary in tendencies toward people and production concerns. The preferred combination of "high-high" leadership is called the team manager. This leader shares decisions with team members, empowers them, encourages participation, and supports teamwork.

Leadership style is the recurring pattern of behaviors exhibited by a leader. *Jack Welch*

An **autocratic** leader acts in a command-and-control fashion.

A **human relations** leader emphasizes people over task.

A **laissez-faire** leader has a "do the best you can and don't bother me" attitude.

CLASSIC LEADERSHIP STYLES

Work in the leader behavior tradition made it easy to talk about different **leadership styles**—the recurring patterns of behaviors exhibited by leaders. Even today, when people talk about the leaders with whom they work, their vocabulary often describes classic styles of leadership relating back to the behavioral leadership theories.[27]

A leader identified with an **autocratic style**, Blake and Mouton's authority-obedience manager, emphasizes task over people, retains authority and information, and acts in a unilateral, command-and-control fashion. A leader with a **human relations style**, the country club manager in the grid, does just the opposite and emphasizes people over task. A leader with a **laissez-faire style**, the impoverished manager in the grid, shows little concern for the task, letting the group make

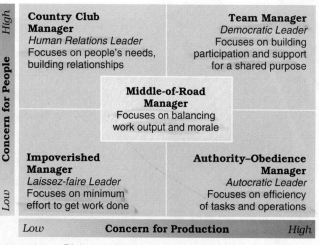

FIGURE 13.3 Blake and Mouton's Leadership Grid.

● A **democratic** leader emphasizes both tasks and people.

decisions and acting with a "do the best you can and don't bother me" attitude. A leader with a **democratic style**, Blake and Mouton's "high-high" team manager, is committed to both task and people. This leader tries to get things done while sharing information, encouraging participation in decision making, and otherwise helping others develop their skills and capabilities.

Be sure you can ☑ contrast the trait and leader-behavior approaches to leadership research ☑ identify five personal traits of successful leaders ☑ illustrate leader behaviors consistent with a high concern for task ☑ illustrate leader behaviors consistent with a high concern for people ☑ describe behaviors associated with four classic leadership styles

CONTINGENCY APPROACHES TO LEADERSHIP

As leadership research continued, scholars became increasingly uncomfortable with the notion that a "high-high" leader was always best. They eventually concluded that no one set of behaviors or style works best all of the time. This raised the question: When and under what circumstances is a leadership style preferable to others? In response, scholars developed a number of contingency approaches that try to explain the conditions for leadership success in different situations.

● The **least-preferred co-worker scale**, LPC, is used in Fiedler's contingency model to measure a person's leadership style.

FIEDLER'S CONTINGENCY MODEL

One of the first contingency leadership models was developed by Fred Fiedler. He proposed that good leadership depends on a match or fit between a person's leadership style and situational demands.[28]

Understanding Leadership Style

Leadership style in Fiedler's model is measured on the **least-preferred co-worker scale**, known as the LPC scale and found as the end-of-chapter self-assessment. It describes tendencies to behave either as a *task-motivated leader* (low LPC score) or *relationship-motivated leader* (high LPC score).

No Ego for César Conde at Univisión

At the age of 35 César Conde became president of Univisión Networks, the largest Spanish-language TV network in the U.S. Conde is the son of Peruvian and Cuban immigrants who he says arrived in America "with absolutely nothing except for spare change and the clothes they had on their back." He went on to earn an MBA from Wharton and is described by a close friend as "very approachable" and someone who "doesn't have an ego" and "never puts himself first." In leading Univisión he describes the goal as "to inform, entertain, and empower the Hispanic community."

Fiedler believes that leadership style is part of one's personality. This makes it relatively enduring and difficult to change. He doesn't place much hope in trying to train a task-motivated leader to behave in a relationship-motivated manner, or vice versa. Rather, he says that the key to leadership success is putting our existing styles to work in situations for which they are the best "fit." This requires both self-awareness of one's leadership style and awareness of the situational strengths and weaknesses of that style.[29]

Understanding Leadership Situations

In Fiedler's model, the amount of control a situation allows the leader is a critical issue in determining the correct style–situation fit. Three contingency variables are used to diagnose situational control. The *quality of leader–member relations* (good or poor) measures the degree to which the group supports the leader. The degree of *task structure* (high or low) measures the extent to which task goals, procedures, and guidelines are clearly spelled out. The amount of *position power* (strong or weak) measures the degree to which the position gives the leader power to reward and punish subordinates.

Figure 13.4 shows eight leadership situations that result from different combinations of these contingency variables. They range from the most favorable situation of high control (good leader–member relations, high task structure, strong in position power) to the least favorable situation of low control (poor leader–member relations, low task structure, weak in position power).

> **Three Factors of Situational Control**
>
> 1. Leader–member relations—support for leader is good or poor
> 2. Task structure—work to be done is high or low in structure
> 3. Position power—leader's authority is strong or weak.

Matching Leadership Style and Situation

In Fiedler's research neither the task-oriented nor the relationship-oriented leadership style proved effective all the time. Instead, each style seemed to work best when used in the right situation. His findings as summarized in Figure 13.4 can be stated as two propositions.

Proposition 1—A task-motivated leader will be most successful in either very favorable (high-control) or very unfavorable (low-control) situations.

Proposition 2—A relationship-motivated leader will be most successful in situations of moderate control.

Let's do some examples. Assume you are the leader of a team of market researchers. The researchers seem highly supportive of you, and their job is clearly defined regarding what needs to be done. You have the authority to evaluate their

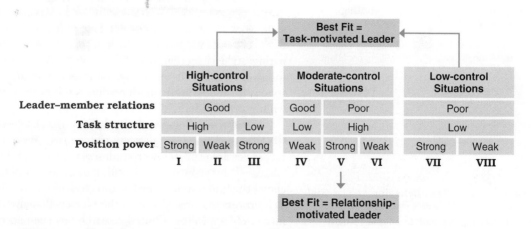

FIGURE 13.4 Predictions on style-situation fit from Fiedler's contingency leadership model.

performance and to make pay and promotion recommendations. This is a high-control situation consisting of good leader–member relations, high task structure, and high position power. Figure 13.4 shows that a task-motivated leader would be most effective in this situation.

Now, suppose that you are chairperson of a committee asked to improve student–faculty relations in a university. Although the goal is clear, no one can say for sure how to accomplish it. Task structure is low, and because committee members are free to quit any time they want, the chairperson has little position power. Because not all members believe the committee is necessary, poor leader–member relations are apparent. According to the figure, this low-control situation also calls for a task-motivated leader.

Finally, assume that you are the new head of a fashion section in a large department store. Because you were selected over one of the popular sales associates you now supervise, leader–member relations are poor. Task structure is high because the associate's job is well defined. Your position power is low because associates work under a seniority system and fixed wage schedule. Figure 13.4 shows that a relationship-motivated leader is the best fit for this moderate-control situation.

HERSEY-BLANCHARD SITUATIONAL LEADERSHIP MODEL

In contrast to Fiedler's notion that leadership style is hard to change, the Hersey-Blanchard situational leadership model suggests that successful leaders do adjust their styles. They do so contingently and relative to the task maturity or task readiness of followers, based on follower readiness to perform in a given situation.[30] "Maturity or readiness," in this sense, refers to how able and willing or confident followers are to perform required tasks.

As shown in Figure 13.5, the possible combinations of task-oriented and relationship-oriented behaviors in this model result in four leadership styles.

- *Delegating*—allowing the group to take responsibility for task decisions; a low-task, low-relationship style.
- *Participating*—emphasizing shared ideas and participative decisions on task directions; a low-task, high-relationship style.
- *Selling*—explaining task directions in a supportive and persuasive way; a high-task, high-relationship style.
- *Telling*—giving specific task directions and closely supervising work; a high-task, low-relationship style.

The delegating style works best in high-readiness situations with able, willing, and confident followers. The telling style works best at the other extreme of low readiness, where followers are unable and unwilling, or insecure. The participating style is recommended for low-to-moderate readiness followers—able but unwilling, or insecure. And, the selling style is for moderate-to-high readiness followers—unable, but willing or confident.

Hersey and Blanchard also believe that leadership styles should be adjusted as followers change over time. If the correct styles are used in lower-readiness situations, followers will "mature" and grow in ability, willingness, and confidence. This allows the leader to become less directive and more participative as followers mature. Although the Hersey-Blanchard model is intuitively appealing, limited research has been accomplished on it to date.[31]

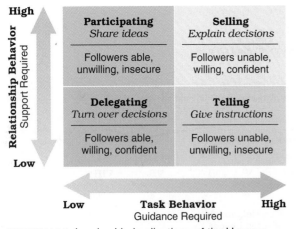

FIGURE 13.5 Leadership implications of the Hersey-Blanchard situational leadership model.

Real Ethics

Would You Put Your Boss Above Your Organization?

One of the primary duties of employees is to do what is in the best interest of their organization. Some aspects of a job are detailed in his or her job description. Because not all needs are foreseeable in advance, other job aspects are implied in a broad sense but not formally identified. Employees often have to rely on their boss's perception and interpretation of what actions are in the best interest of the organization.

Does this mean that you should always do what your boss requests? Obviously, there are many illegal or unethical actions that would clearly not pass the "in the best interests of the organization" test. However, there are also a lot of actions that are legal but that present an ethical challenge because it is not clear whether these actions really benefit the organization.

What if your boss wants to pay you overtime to make PowerPoint slides for a presentation he is giving at a conference and which you know he hopes will lead to a job offer from another organization? What if your boss asks you to spend part of your workday helping organize an event for a community group that he or she is a member of, but that has no connection to work?

By helping your supervisor with such requests, you may end up benefiting directly in the form of extra pay or indirectly in terms of building up goodwill. Likewise, your supervisor benefits by having the organization pay you to help on a project that isn't directly tied to work. But it's also clear that there is no direct benefit to the organization. In fact, the organization may end up being worse off.

You Decide

Is it ethical to help your supervisor in the situations described above? Are you doing a disservice to the organization's other stakeholders if you assist your supervisor in such cases? How far does a supervisor's authority extend? Is it acceptable for a supervisor to ask for help with things that are not directly tied to work? Where should you draw the line?

PATH–GOAL LEADERSHIP THEORY

A third contingency leadership approach is the path–goal theory advanced by Robert House.[32] Like Fiedler's approach, House's path–goal theory seeks the right fit between leadership and situation. But unlike Fiedler, House believes that a leader can use these four leadership styles and actually shift back and forth among them.

- *Directive leadership*—letting followers know what is expected; giving directions on what to do and how; scheduling work to be done; maintaining definite standards of performance; clarifying the leader's role in the group.
- *Supportive leadership*—doing things to make work more pleasant; treating team members as equals; being friendly and approachable; showing concern for the well-being of subordinates.
- *Achievement-oriented leadership*—setting challenging goals; expecting the highest levels of performance; emphasizing continuous improvement in performance; displaying confidence in meeting high standards.
- *Participative leadership*—involving team members in decision making; consulting with them and asking for suggestions; using these suggestions when making decisions.

Path–Goal Contingencies

The path–goal theory advises managers to use the prior leadership styles in ways that fit situational needs. The most critical thing is to use styles that add

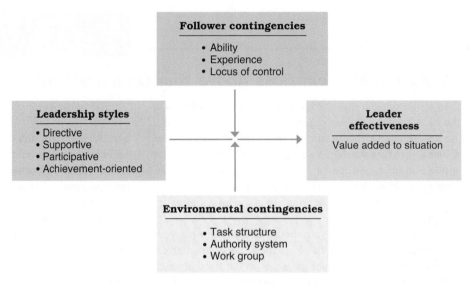

FIGURE 13.6 Contingency relationships in House's path–goal leadership theory.

value by contributing things that are missing from a situation or that need strengthening. Leaders should avoid being redundant by trying to do things that are already taken care of. For example, when team members are expert and competent at their tasks, it is unnecessary and even dysfunctional for the leader to tell them how to do things.

The details of path–goal theory, as summarized in Figure 13.6, provide a variety of research-based guidance on how to contingently match leadership styles with situational characteristics. When job assignments are unclear, *directive leadership* helps to clarify task objectives and expected rewards. When worker self-confidence is low, *supportive leadership* can increase confidence by emphasizing individual abilities and offering needed assistance. When task challenge is insufficient in a job, *achievement-oriented leadership* helps to set goals and raise performance aspirations. When performance incentives are poor, *participative leadership* might clarify individual needs and identify appropriate rewards.[33]

Substitutes for Leadership

Path–goal theory has contributed to the recognition of what are called **substitutes for leadership**.[34] These are aspects of the work setting and the people involved that can reduce the need for active leader involvement. In effect, they make leadership from the "outside" unnecessary because leadership is already provided from within the situation.

Possible substitutes for leadership include follower characteristics such as ability, experience, and independence; task characteristics such as the presence or absence of routine and the availability of feedback; and organizational characteristics such as clarity of plans and formalization of rules and procedures. When these substitutes for leadership are present, managers are advised in true path–goal fashion to avoid duplicating them. Instead, they should concentrate on making other and more important leadership contributions.

LEADER–MEMBER EXCHANGE THEORY

One of the things you may have noticed in your work and study groups is the tendency of leaders to develop "special" relationships with some team members, even to the point where not everyone is always treated in the same way. This notion is central to leader–member exchange theory, or LMX theory, as it is often called.[35]

● **Substitutes for leadership** are factors in the work setting that direct work efforts without the involvement of a leader.

Described in Figure 13.7, LMX theory recognizes that in many leadership situations not everyone is treated the same by the leader. People fall into "in-groups" and "out-groups," and the group you are in can have quite a significant influence on your experience with the leader. Those in the in-group are often considered the best performers. They enjoy special and trusted high-exchange relationships with the leaders and often get special assignments, privileges, and access to information. Those in the out-group may be marginalized or ignored. They get fewer benefits due to a low-exchange relationship with the leader.

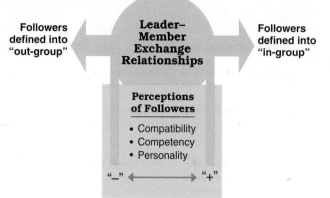

FIGURE 13.7 Elements of leader–member exchange (LMX) theory.

The premise underlying leader–member exchange theory is that as a leader and follower interact over time, their exchanges end up defining the follower's role.[36] For a follower in the leader's in-group, it's motivating and satisfying to be getting rewards, information, and other favorable treatments. For someone in the out-group, however, it can be frustrating to receive fewer rewards, less information, and little or no special attention.

Research on leader–member exchange theory places most value on its usefulness in describing leader–member relationships. Look around, and you're likely to see examples of this in classroom situations between instructors and certain students, and in work teams between leaders and certain members. The notion of leader in-groups and out-groups seems to make sense and corresponds to working realities experienced by many people. Also, research shows that members of leaders' in-groups get more positive performance evaluations and report higher levels of job satisfaction. They are also more loyal as followers and less prone to turnover than are members of out-groups.[37]

LEADER–PARTICIPATION MODEL

The Vroom-Jago leader-participation model links leadership success with choices among alternative decision-making methods. In true contingency fashion, the model suggests that leaders are most effective when the decision-making method used best fits the problem being faced.[38]

As shown in Figure 13.8, the leader's choices for making decisions fall into three categories—authority, consultative, or group decisions.[39] An **authority decision** is made by the leader and then communicated to the group. A **consultative decision** is made by the leader after gathering information and advice from others. A **group decision** is made by the group with the leader's support as a contributing member. The leader's choice among these decision-making methods is governed by three factors: (1) *decision quality*—based on who has the information needed for problem solving; (2) *decision acceptance*—based on the importance of follower acceptance of the decision to its eventual implementation; and (3) *decision time*—based on the time available to make and implement the decision.

Each of the decision methods is appropriate in certain situations, and each has its advantages and disadvantages in respect to these rules.[40] Thus, we should expect to find effective leaders continually shifting among individual, consultative, and group decisions as they deal with the problems and opportunities of daily events.[41]

- An **authority decision** is made by the leader and then communicated to the group.

- A **consultative decision** is made by a leader after receiving information, advice, or opinions from group members.

- A **group decision** is made by group members themselves.

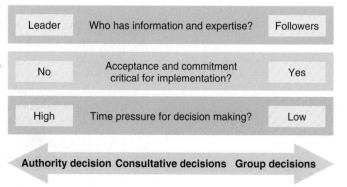

FIGURE 13.8 Leadership implications of Vroom-Jago leader participation model.

Management Smarts 13.1

Five ways for leaders to make decisions

1. *Decide alone*—This is an authority decision; the manager decides how to solve the problem and communicates the decision to the group.

2. *Consult individually*—The manager makes the decision after sharing the problem and consulting individually with group members to get their suggestions.

3. *Consult with group*—The manager makes the decision after convening the group, sharing the problem, and consulting with everyone to get their suggestions.

4. *Facilitate group*—The manager convenes the group, shares the problem, and facilitates discussion to make a decision.

5. *Delegate to group*—The manager convenes the group and delegates authority to define the problem and make a decision.

Authority decisions work best when leaders personally have the expertise needed to solve the problem, and are both confident and capable of acting alone. They also work best when others are likely to accept and implement the leader's decision and little or no time is available for group discussion.

Consultative and group decisions are best when the leader lacks sufficient expertise and information to solve the problem alone. They also work best when the problem is unclear and help is needed to clarify the situation, when acceptance of the decision and commitment by others are necessary for implementation, and, when adequate time is available to allow for true participation.

Although all decision methods shown in Management Smarts 13.1 are potentially useful, Vroom and Jago believe consultative and group decisions offer special benefits.[42] Participation helps improve decision quality by bringing more information to bear on the problem. It helps improve decision acceptance as participants gain understanding and become committed to the process. It also contributes to leadership development by allowing others to gain experience in the problem-solving process. But, a potential cost of consultative and group decisions is lost efficiency. Participation is time consuming, and leaders don't always have extra time available. When problems must be resolved immediately, the authority decision may be the only option.[43]

Learning Check

Study Question 3

What are the contingency approaches to leadership?

Be sure you can ☑ contrast the leader-behavior and contingency leadership approaches ☑ explain Fiedler's contingency model ☑ identify the four leadership styles in the Hersey–Blanchard situational model ☑ explain House's path–goal theory ☑ define *substitutes for leadership* ☑ explain LMX theory ☑ contrast the authority, consultative, and group decisions in the Vroom-Jago model

PERSONAL LEADERSHIP DEVELOPMENT

By now you should be thinking seriously about your leadership qualities, tendencies, styles, and effectiveness. You should also be thinking about your personal development as a leader. And if you consider the various theories just visited and also listen to what people say about leaders in their workplaces, you should be admitting that most of us have considerable room to grow. Fortunately, leadership research continues to bring to our attention many interesting insights and possibilities for personal leadership development.

CHARISMATIC AND TRANSFORMATIONAL LEADERSHIP

Leadership scholars James MacGregor Burns and Bernard Bass suggest that the research and models we have discussed so far give too little attention to a leader's

Martin Luther King, Jr. Shared His Dream

Martin Luther King, Jr. is well known for his famous "I Have a Dream" speech, delivered August 28, 1963, on the Washington Mall and to a massive audience of civil rights supporters. His choice of words and his emotional yet meaningful delivery are exemplars of transformational leadership skill. "I have a dream today," said Martin Luther King, "that my four little children will one day live in a nation where they will not be judged by the color of their skin but by the content of their character." Indeed! The U.S. Congress passed the Civil Rights Act in 1964, and King received the Nobel Peace Prize in 1965.

inspirational qualities, ones that bring "enthusiasm" and "emotion" to his or her relationships with followers.[44] Indeed, there is a great deal of interest today in "superleaders," persons whose visions and strong personalities have an extraordinary impact on others. They are often called **charismatic leaders** because of their special powers to inspire others in exceptional ways. Although often thought of as being limited to a few lucky persons who were born with it, charisma is now considered part of a broader set of personal leadership qualities that can be developed with foresight and practice.[45]

This notion of leaders with charismatic appeal is consistent with how Burns and Bass describe **transformational leadership**. It applies to someone who is truly inspiring as a leader, who is personally excited about what she or he is doing, and who arouses others to seek extraordinary performance accomplishments. A transformational leader raises aspirations and shifts people and organizational systems into new, high-performance patterns. The presence of transformational leadership is reflected in followers who are enthusiastic about the leader and his or her ideas, who work very hard to support them, who remain loyal and devoted, and who strive for superior performance accomplishments.

The goal of excellence in transformational leadership is a personal development challenge. It is not enough to possess leadership traits, know the leadership behaviors, and understand leadership contingencies. One must also be prepared to lead in an inspirational way and with a compelling personality. Charismatic and transformational leaders like Martin Luther King, Jr., as evidenced in his famous "I have a dream" speech, bring a strong sense of vision and a contagious enthusiasm to a situation. They substantially raise the confidence, aspirations, and performance commitments of followers through special qualities like the following.[46]

- *Vision*—having ideas and a clear sense of direction; communicating these to others; developing excitement about accomplishing shared "dreams."
- *Charisma*—using the power of personal reference and emotion to arouse others' enthusiasm, faith, loyalty, pride, and trust in themselves.
- *Symbolism*—identifying "heroes" and holding spontaneous and planned ceremonies to celebrate excellence and high achievement.
- *Empowerment*—helping others develop by removing performance obstacles, sharing responsibilities, and delegating truly challenging work.
- *Intellectual stimulation*—gaining the involvement of others by creating awareness of problems and stirring their imaginations.
- *Integrity*—being honest and credible, acting consistently out of personal conviction, and following through on commitments.

A **charismatic leader** inspires followers in extraordinary ways.

Transformational leadership is inspirational and arouses extraordinary effort and performance.

EMOTIONAL INTELLIGENCE AND LEADERSHIP

Emotional intelligence is the ability to manage our emotions in social relationships.

A popular issue in leadership development is **emotional intelligence**. Also called EI, it was first introduced in Chapter 1 as part of the essential human skills of managers. You should recall that Daniel Goleman defines EI as "the ability to manage ourselves and our relationships effectively."[47] His research links emotional intelligence with leadership effectiveness, especially in more senior management positions. In Goleman's words: "the higher the rank of the person considered to be a star performer, the more emotional intelligence capabilities showed up as the reason for his or her effectiveness."[48] This is a strong endorsement for considering whether or not EI is one of your leadership assets.

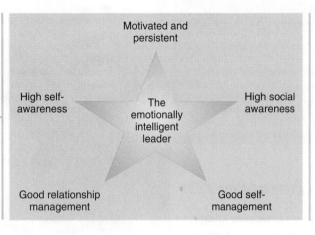

Goleman believes that a core set of emotional intelligence competencies can be learned.[49] A leader strong in emotional intelligence possesses *self-awareness*. This is the ability to understand our own moods and emotions, and to understand their impact on our work and on others. The emotionally intelligent leader is good at *self-management*, or self-regulation. This is the ability to think before we act and to control otherwise disruptive impulses. Emotional intelligence in leadership involves *motivation and persistence* in being willing to work hard for reasons other than money and status. Leaders who are high in emotional intelligence display *social awareness*, or empathy. They have the ability to understand the emotions of others and to use this understanding to better relate to them. And, a leader high in emotional intelligence is good at *relationship management*. This is the ability to establish rapport with others and to build social capital through relationships and networks.

GENDER AND LEADERSHIP

The **gender similarities hypothesis** holds that males and females have similar psychological properties.

Sara Levinson, former president of NFL Properties, Inc., and director of Macy's, once asked the all-male members of her NFL management team this question: "Is my leadership style different from a man's?" "Yes," they replied, suggesting that the very fact that she was asking the question was evidence of the difference. They also pointed out that her leadership style emphasized communication, as well as gathering ideas and opinions from others. When Levinson probed further by asking the men, "Is this a distinctly 'female' trait?" they said that they thought it was.[50]

Are there gender differences in leadership? In pondering the question, three background points deserve highlighting. First, social science research largely supports the **gender similarities hypothesis**. That is, males and females are very similar to one another in terms of psychological properties.[51] Second, research leaves no doubt that both women and men can be equally effective as leaders.[52] Third, research does show that men and women are sometimes perceived as using somewhat different styles, and perhaps arriving at leadership success from different angles.[53]

When men and women are perceived differently as leaders, the perceptions fit traditional stereotypes.[54] Men may be expected to act as "take-charge" leaders who are task-oriented, directive, and assertive while trying to get things done in traditional command-and-control ways. Women may be expected to act as "take-care" leaders who behave in supportive and nurturing ways. Studies report, for example, that female leaders are viewed as more participative than male leaders. And, they are rated by peers, subordinates, and supervisors as strong on motivating others, emotional intelligence, persuading, fostering communication, listening to others,

Research Brief

Charismatic Leaders Display Positive Emotions That Followers Find Contagious

When leaders show positive emotions, the effect on followers is positive, creating positive moods and also creating tendencies toward positive leader ratings and feelings of attraction to the leader. These are the major conclusions from four research studies conducted by Joyce E. Bono and Remus Ilies, and reported in *Leadership Quarterly*.

Bono and Ilies set out to examine how charismatic leaders "use emotion to influence followers." They advanced hypotheses as indicated in the figure. They expected to find that charismatic leaders display positive emotions, that positive leader emotions create positive follower moods, and that positive follower moods generate both positive ratings of the leader and attraction toward the leader. These hypotheses were examined in a series of four empirical studies.

The researchers concluded that positive emotions are an important aspect of charismatic leadership. They found that leaders who rated high in charisma chose words with more positive emotional content for vision statements and speeches. They also found that the positive emotions of leaders were transferred into positive moods among followers; that is, the positive leader moods were contagious. They also found that followers with positive moods had more positive perceptions of leader effectiveness.

One of the limitations of these studies, as pointed out by Bono and Ilies, is that they only focused on positive leader emotions. This leaves open the questions of how leaders use negative emotions and how these emotions affect followers. Also, the researchers suggest the need to examine the impact of leader moods on follower performance and creativity.

You Be the Researcher

While perhaps agreeing with the logic of emotional contagion, should we conclude that a leader can never have a "bad" day and can never communicate, verbally or nonverbally, anything other than positive emotional messages? Is it realistic for managers to live up to these expectations to always be positive?

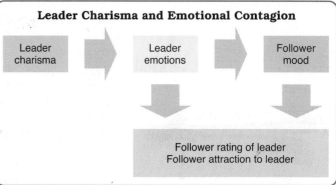

Leader Charisma and Emotional Contagion

Leader charisma → Leader emotions → Follower mood

Follower rating of leader
Follower attraction to leader

Reference: Joyce E. Bono and Remus Ilies, "Charisma, Positive Emotions and Mood Contagion," *Leadership Quarterly*, vol. 17 (2006), pp. 317–34.

---

mentoring, and supporting high-quality work.[55] In one study employing 360-degree assessments, women were rated more highly than men in all but one area of leadership—visioning. The researchers offered the possible explanation that because women are less directive as leaders, they aren't perceived as visionaries.[56]

The leadership style sometimes displayed by and attributed to women is called an **interactive leadership style**.[57] Leaders with this style are good communicators and typically act in a democratic and participative fashion—showing respect for others, caring for others, and sharing power and information with others. These leaders focus on using communication and involvement to build consensus and good interpersonal relations. And they display many qualities in common with transformational leadership.[58] An interactive leader tends to use personal power and gains influence over others through support and good interpersonal relationships. This contrasts with leadership that relies more on directive and assertive behaviors, and on using position power in traditional command-and-control ways.

If women tend to excel at interactive leadership, these comments by Rosabeth Moss Kanter are worth thinking about: "Women get high ratings on exactly those

● **Interactive leadership leaders** are strong communicators and act democratic and participative with followers.

skills required to succeed in the global information age, where teamwork and partnering are so important."[59] But one of the risks in any discussion of gender and leadership is falling prey to stereotypes that place individual men and women into leadership boxes in which they don't necessarily belong.[60] Perhaps we should set gender issues aside, accept the gender similarities hypothesis, and focus instead on the notion of interactive leadership. The likelihood is that an interactive leadership style is a very good fit with the needs of today's organizations and workers. Furthermore, there is no reason why men and women can't do it equally well.[61]

MORAL LEADERSHIP

X **Moral leadership** is always "good" and "right" by ethical standards.

As discussed many times in this book and also highlighted in the chapter opener, society expects organizations to be run with **moral leadership**. This is leadership with ethical standards that clearly meet the test of being "good" and "correct."[62] Ideally, anyone in a leadership position will practice high ethical standards of behavior, try to build and maintain an ethical organizational culture, and both help and require others to behave ethically in their work. But the facts don't always support this aspiration.

Would you be surprised to learn that a Harris Poll found only 37% of U.S. adults in a survey willing to describe their top managers as acting with "integrity and morality"?[63] Based on that result, it may not surprise you that a *Business Week* survey found that just 13% of top executives at large U.S. firms rated "having strong ethical values" as a top leadership characteristic.[64]

✓ Leaders show **integrity** by acting with honesty, credibility, and consistency in putting values into action.

Moral leadership begins with personal integrity, a concept fundamental to the notion of transformational leadership. As noted in the chapter opener, leadership **integrity** means acting in an honest, credible, and consistent manner in putting one's values into action. When a leader has integrity, he or she earns the trust of followers. And when followers believe leaders are trustworthy, they try to behave in ways that live up to the leader's expectations.

In his book *Transforming Leadership: A New Pursuit of Happiness*, James MacGregor Burns explains that transformational leadership creates significant, even revolutionary, change in social systems, while still based on integrity. Notably, he eliminates certain historical figures from this definition: Napoleon is out—too much order-and-obey in his style; Hitler is out—no moral foundations; Mao is out, too—no true empowerment of followers. Among Burns's positive role models from history are Mahatma Gandhi, George Washington, and both Eleanor and Franklin Delano Roosevelt. Burns firmly believes that great leaders follow agendas true to the wishes of their followers. He also says that wherever in the world great leadership is found, it will always have a moral anchor point.[65]

Nonviolence Was Moral Path for Mahatma Gandhi

Mohandas Karamchand Gandhi is praised as a moral leader who rallied nonviolent civil disobedience to support India's independence from Great Britain. He is most often addressed with the honorific "Mahatma" meaning great-souled. His example might prompt us to ask: where are the moral leaders today? A Harris interactive study reports that only 37% of workers believe their top managers display integrity and morality and only 39% believe leaders most often act in the best interests of the organization.

The concept of servant leadership is consistent with this thinking. So, too, is the notion of **authentic leadership** advanced by Fred Luthans and Bruce Avolio.[66] An authentic leader has a high level of self-awareness and clearly understands his or her personal values. This leader also acts consistent with those values, being honest and avoiding self-deceptions. Because of this the authentic leader is perceived as genuine, gains the respect of followers, and develops a capacity to positively influence their behaviors. Luthans and his colleagues believe that authentic leadership is activated by the positive psychological states of confidence, hope, optimism, and resilience. The result is positive self-regulation that helps authentic leaders clearly frame moral dilemmas, transparently respond to them, and consistently serve as ethical role models.[67]

> **Authentic leadership** activates positive psychological states to achieve self-awareness and positive self-regulation.

DRUCKER'S "OLD-FASHIONED" LEADERSHIP

The late and respected consultant Peter Drucker took a time-tested and very pragmatic view of leadership. It is based on what he refers to as a "good old-fashioned" look at the plain hard work it takes to be a successful leader. Consider, for example, his description of a telephone conversation with a potential consulting client: "We'd want you to run a seminar for us on how one acquires charisma," she said. Drucker's response was not what she expected. He advised her that there was more to leadership than the popular emphasis on personal "dash" or charisma. In fact, he said that "leadership is work."[68]

Drucker's many books and articles remind us that leadership effectiveness must have strong foundations. He believes that the basic building block is defining and establishing a sense of mission. A good leader sets the goals, priorities, and standards. And a good leader keeps them all clear and visible. In Drucker's words: "The leader's first task is to be the trumpet that sounds a clear sound." Next, Drucker believes in accepting leadership as a responsibility rather than a rank. Good leaders surround themselves with talented people. They are not afraid to develop strong and capable followers, and they do not blame others when things go wrong. The adage: "The buck stops here" is still good to remember.

Finally, Drucker stresses the importance of earning and keeping the trust of others. The key here is the leader's personal integrity, the point on which the chapter began. The followers of good leaders trust them. They believe the leader means what he or she says, and that his or her actions will be consistent with what is said. In Drucker's words again: "effective leadership is not based on being clever; it is based primarily on being consistent."[69]

Drucker's Leadership Wisdom
- Define and communicate a clear vision.
- Accept leadership as a responsibility, not a rank.
- Surround yourself with talented people.
- Don't blame others when things go wrong.
- Keep your integrity; earn the trust of others.
- Don't be clever, be consistent.

Be sure you can ☑ define *transformational leadership* ☑ explain how emotional intelligence contributes to leadership success ☑ discuss research insights on the relationship between gender and leadership ☑ define *interactive leadership* ☑ discuss integrity as a foundation for moral leadership ☑ list Drucker's essentials of good old-fashioned leadership

Learning Check
Study Question 4
What are current issues in personal leadership development?

Management Learning Review

Study Questions Summary

1 What is the nature of leadership?

- Leadership is the process of inspiring others to work hard to accomplish important tasks.
- The ability to communicate a vision—a clear sense of the future—is essential for effective leadership.
- Power is the ability to get others to do what you want them to do through leadership.
- Sources of position power include rewards, coercion, and legitimacy or formal authority; sources of personal power include expertise and reference.
- Effective leaders empower others, allowing them to make job-related decisions on their own.
- Servant leadership is follower-centered, focusing on helping others fully utilize their talents.

FOR DISCUSSION **When is a leader justified in using coercive power?**

2 What are the key leadership traits and behaviors?

- Traits that seem to have a positive impact on leadership include drive, integrity, and self-confidence.
- Research on leader behaviors has focused on alternative leadership styles based on concerns for the task and concerns for people.
- One suggestion of leader-behavior researchers is that effective leaders are team-based and participative, showing both high task and people concerns.

FOR DISCUSSION **Are any personal traits indispensable "must haves" for success in leadership?**

3 What are the contingency approaches to leadership?

- Contingency leadership approaches point out that no one leadership style always works best; the best style is one that properly matches the demands of each unique situation.
- Fiedler's contingency model matches leadership styles with situational differences in task structure, position power, and leader-member relations.
- The Hersey-Blanchard situational model recommends using task-oriented and people-oriented behaviors, depending on the "maturity" levels of followers.
- House's path-goal theory points out that leaders add value to situations by using supportive, directive, achievement-oriented, or participative styles.
- The Vroom-Jago leader-participation theory advises leaders to choose decision-making methods—individual, consultative, group—that best fit the problems to be solved.

FOR DISCUSSION **What are the career development implications of Fiedler's contingency model of leadership?**

4 What are the current issues in personal leadership development?

- Transformational leaders use charisma and emotion to inspire others toward extraordinary efforts and performance excellence.
- Emotional intelligence—the ability to manage our relationships and ourselves effectively—is an important leadership capability.
- The interactive leadership style emphasizes communication, involvement, and interpersonal respect.
- Managers are expected to be moral leaders who communicate high ethical standards and show personal integrity in all dealings with other people.

FOR DISCUSSION **Is transformational leadership always moral leadership?**

Self-Test

Multiple-Choice Questions

1. Someone with a clear sense of the future and the actions needed to get there is considered a _____ leader.
   (a) task-oriented   (b) people-oriented   (c) transactional   (d) visionary

2. Leader power = _____ power + _____ power.
   (a) reward, punishment   (b) reward, expert   (c) legitimate, position   (d) position, personal

3. A manager who says "because I am the boss, you must do what I ask" is relying on _____ power.
   (a) reward   (b) legitimate   (c) expert   (d) referent

4. The personal traits now considered important for managerial success include _____.
   (a) self-confidence   (b) gender   (c) age   (d) size

5. According to the Blake and Mouton leadership grid, the most successful leader is one who acts with _____.
   (a) high initiating structure (b) high consideration (c) high concern for task and high concern for people (d) low job stress and high task goals

6. In Fiedler's contingency model, both highly favorable and highly unfavorable leadership situations are best dealt with by a _____ leader.
   (a) task-motivated (b) laissez-faire (c) participative (d) relationship-motivated

7. Directive leadership and achievement-oriented leadership are among the options in House's _____ theory of leadership.
   (a) trait (b) path–goal (c) transformational (d) life-cycle

8. Vision, charisma, integrity, and symbolism are all on the list of attributes typically associated with _____ leaders.
   (a) contingency (b) informal (c) transformational (d) transactional

9. _____ leadership theory suggests that leadership success is achieved by correctly matching leadership style with situations.
   (a) Trait (b) Fiedler's (c) Transformational (d) Blake and Mouton's

10. In the leader-behavior approaches to leadership, someone who does a very good job of planning work, setting standards, and monitoring results would be considered a(n) _____ leader.
    (a) task-oriented (b) control-oriented (c) achievement-oriented (d) employee-centered

11. When a leader assumes that others will do as she asks because they want to positively identify with her, she is relying on _____ power to influence their behavior.
    (a) expert (b) reference (c) legitimate (d) reward

12. The interactive leadership style, sometimes associated with women, is characterized by _____.
    (a) inclusion and information sharing (b) use of rewards and punishments (c) command and control (d) emphasis on position power

13. A leader whose actions indicate an attitude of "do as you want, and don't bother me" would be described as having a(n) _____ leadership style.
    (a) autocratic (b) country club (c) democratic (d) laissez-faire

14. The critical contingency variable in the Hersey-Blanchard situational model of leadership is _____.
    (a) followers' maturity (b) LPC (c) task structure (d) LMX

15. A leader who _____ would be described as achievement-oriented in the path–goal theory.
    (a) works hard to achieve high performance (b) sets challenging goals for others (c) gives directions and monitors results (d) builds commitment through participation

Short-Response Questions

16. Why does a person need both position power and personal power to achieve long-term managerial effectiveness?

17. What is the major insight of the Vroom-Jago leader-participation model?

18. What are the three variables that Fiedler's contingency model uses to diagnose the favorability of leadership situations, and what does each mean?

19. How does Peter Drucker's view of "good old-fashioned leadership" differ from the popular concept of transformational leadership?

Essay Question

20. When Marcel Henry took over as leader of a new product development team, he was both excited and apprehensive. "I wonder," he said to himself on the first day in his new assignment, "if I can meet the challenges of leadership." Later that day, Marcel shared this concern with you during a coffee break. Based on the insights of this chapter, how would you describe to him the implications for his personal leadership development of current thinking on transformational leadership and moral leadership?

Management Skills and Competencies

Self-Assessment

Back to Yourself: Integrity

Even though we can get overly enamored with the notion of the "great" or "transformational" leader, it is just one among many leadership fundamentals that are enduring and important. This chapter covered a range of theories and models useful for leadership development. Each is best supported by a base of personal **integrity** that keeps the leader above the "integrity line" depicted in the chapter opener—high in honesty, consistency, humility, and selflessness. Servant leadership represents integrity; Drucker's notion of good old-fashioned leadership requires integrity; Gardner's concept of moral leadership is centered on integrity. Why is it then that in the news and in everyday experiences we so often end up wondering where leadership integrity has gone? After you complete the following Least-Preferred Co-Worker Scale, don't forget to go online and further examine your leadership tendencies using the T-t Leadership assessment.

> Leaders with **integrity** are honest, credible, humble, and consistent in all that they do; they "walk the talk" by living up to personal values in all their actions.

Further Reflection: Least-Preferred Co-Worker Scale

Instructions

Think of all the different people with whom you have ever worked—in jobs, in social clubs, in student projects, or whatever. Next think of the one person with whom you could work least well—that is, the person with whom you had the most difficulty getting a job done. This is the one person—a peer, boss, or subordinate—with whom you would least want to work. Describe this person by circling numbers at the appropriate points on each of the following pairs of bipolar adjectives. Work rapidly. There are no right or wrong answers.[70]

Pleasant	8 7 6 5 4 3 2 1	Unpleasant
Friendly	8 7 6 5 4 3 2 1	Unfriendly
Rejecting	1 2 3 4 5 6 7 8	Accepting
Tense	1 2 3 4 5 6 7 8	Relaxed
Distant	1 2 3 4 5 6 7 8	Close
Cold	1 2 3 4 5 6 7 8	Warm
Supportive	8 7 6 5 4 3 2 1	Hostile
Boring	1 2 3 4 5 6 7 8	Interesting
Quarrelsome	1 2 3 4 5 6 7 8	Harmonious
Gloomy	1 2 3 4 5 6 7 8	Cheerful
Open	8 7 6 5 4 3 2 1	Guarded
Backbiting	1 2 3 4 5 6 7 8	Loyal
Untrustworthy	1 2 3 4 5 6 7 8	Trustworthy
Considerate	8 7 6 5 4 3 2 1	Inconsiderate
Nasty	1 2 3 4 5 6 7 8	Nice
Agreeable	8 7 6 5 4 3 2 1	Disagreeable
Insincere	1 2 3 4 5 6 7 8	Sincere
Kind	8 7 6 5 4 3 2 1	Unkind

Scoring

Compute your "least-preferred co-worker" LPC, or score by totaling all the numbers you circled; enter that score here [LPC _____].

Interpretation

The LPC scale is used by Fred Fiedler to identify a person's dominant leadership style. He believes that this style is a relatively fixed part of our personality and is therefore difficult to change. Thus, he suggests the key to leadership success is finding (or creating) good "matches" between style and situation. If your score is 73 or above, Fiedler considers you a "relationship-motivated" leader. If your score is 64 or below, he considers you a "task-motivated" leader. If your score is between 65 and 72, Fiedler leaves it up to you to determine which leadership style is most like yours.

Team Exercise

Leading by Participation

Preparation

Read each of the following vignettes. Write in the margin the type of decision you think the leader should use to best handle the situation.[71]

I—an individual or authority decision   C—a consultative decision   G—a group decision

Vignette I

You are the leader of a large team laying an oil pipeline. It is now necessary to estimate your expected rate of progress in order to schedule material deliveries to the next field site. You know the nature of the terrain you will be traveling and have the historical data needed to compute the mean and variance in the rate of speed over the type of terrain. Given these two variables, it is a simple matter to calculate the earliest and latest times at which materials and support facilities will be needed at the next site. It is important that your estimate be reasonably accurate; underestimates result in idle teams, and overestimates result in materials being tied up for a period of time before they are to be used. Progress has been good, and your team stands to receive substantial bonuses if the project is completed ahead of schedule.

Vignette II

You are supervising the work of 12 engineers. Their formal training and work experience are very similar, permitting you to use them interchangeably on projects. Yesterday, your manager informed you that a request had been received from an overseas affiliate for 4 engineers to go abroad on extended loan for a period of 6 to 8 months. He argued and you agreed that for a number of reasons this request should be filled from your group. All your engineers are capable of handling this assignment, and from the standpoint of present and future projects, there is no particular reason that any one should be retained over any other. The problem is complicated by the fact that the overseas assignment is in what is generally regarded in the company as an undesirable location.

Vignette III

You are the head of a staff unit reporting to the vice president of finance. She has asked you to provide a report on the firm's current portfolio, including recommendations for changes in the selection criteria. Doubts have been raised about the efficiency of the existing system in the current market conditions, and there is dissatisfaction with rates of return. Your own specialty is the bond market, and it is clear to you that a detailed knowledge of the equity market, which you lack, would greatly enhance the value of the report. Four members of your staff are specialists in different segments of the equity market and possess a vast amount of knowledge about the intricacies of investment. However, they seldom agree on the best way to achieve anything when it comes to the stock market. Although conscientious as well as knowledgeable, they have major differences when it comes to investment philosophy and strategy. The report is due in 6 weeks. You have already begun to familiarize yourself with the firm's current portfolio and have been provided by management with a specific set of constraints that any portfolio must satisfy. Your immediate problem is to come up with some alternatives to the firm's present practices and select the most promising ones for detailed analysis in your report.

Instructions

Form groups as assigned by the instructor. Share your choices with other group members and try to achieve a consensus on how the leader should best handle each situation. Refer back to the Vroom-Jago leader–participation model presented in this chapter. Analyze each vignette according to the model and the three factors of decision quality, decision acceptance, and decision time. Do the group conclusions differ from your own? If so, why? Nominate a spokesperson to share results in general class discussion.

Case Study: Southwest Airlines

Go to *Management Cases for Critical Thinking* to find the recommended case for Chapter 13–"Southwest Airlines: How Herb Kelleher Led the Way."

Individual Behavior

Chapter 14 Study Questions

1 How do perceptions influence individual behavior?

2 What should we know about personalities in the workplace?

3 How do attitudes influence individual behavior?

What are the dynamics of emotions, moods, and stress?

Learning From Others

There Are Personalities Behind Those Faces

The headline reads: "Spanx queen leads from the bottom line." The story begins: Woman, unhappy with the way she looks in white pants, cuts the feet off a pair of panty hose, puts them on, and attends party feeling great. The story continues: Sara Blakely founds Spanx, Inc.

"I knew this could open up so many women's wardrobes," Blakely says, "All women have that clothing in the back of the closet that they don't wear because they don't like the way it looks." With $5,500 and the idea for "body-shaping" underwear, she set out to start a business. But the pathway to profits wasn't always a straight line; someone else with the same idea may not have succeeded. Yet Blakely did; her unique blend of skills and personality made it all work.

Blakely had experience with and a passion for direct selling, and she was diligent in researching patents and trademarks. When her first attempts to convince manufacturers to make product samples met with resistance—with one calling it "a crazy idea," she persisted until one agreed. She wanted to place Spanx in "high-end" department stores. When store after store turned her down, Blakely kept at it. Persistence paid off again when she persuaded a buyer at Neiman Marcus to give Spanx its first big chance.

Blakely traveled extensively and energetically, some might say exhaustively. "I'm the face of the brand," she says, "and we didn't have money to advertise. I had to be out. Sitting in the office wasn't helping." She sent Oprah Winfrey samples. And after Oprah voted Spanx "one of her favorite things," sales really took off.

As sales grew, Blakely realized additional skills were needed to handle the firm's fast-paced growth. She recognized her limits and "was eager to delegate my weaknesses." So, she turned day-to-day operations over to CEO Laurie Ann Goldman, leaving herself free to pursue creativity, new products, and brand development. She has since started the Sara Blakely Foundation with the express purpose of "supporting and empowering women around the world."[1]

do the benchmarking

Creative, outgoing, passionate, driven, persistent, and ambitious—these adjectives and more describe Sara Blakely and her personality. They can also go a long way in explaining how and why she was successful with Spanx. Any manager needs to understand people, both others and themselves. **When you look in the mirror, what and whom do you see?**

Learning About Yourself

Ambition

When it comes to understanding people at work, one of the differences that is often heard in conversations is **ambition**. You can think of it as the desire to achieve or to accomplish something. Ambition shows through in personality as a sense of competitiveness and a desire to be the best at something.[2] Sarah Blakely has it—it's a driving force in the Spanx story. Hopefully, you have it too.

Scholar and consultant Ram Charan believes that ambition is one of the personal traits that separates "people who perform from those who don't."[3] He calls these traits "personal differentiators." You shouldn't have any trouble admitting that ambition was a differentiator in the success of Susan Blakely and Spanx. Less ambitious persons could have gotten the same idea, but failed to pursue it as a business venture. Or they might have tried to make a business out of it, but ended up quitting when the first obstacles appeared.

Charan says that ambition "propels individual leaders and their companies to strive to reach their potential," and that "leaders need a healthy dose of it to push themselves and others." Ambition in this sense is a good thing, something to be admired and to be developed both in others and in ourselves.

Personal Traits Associated with People Who Perform
• Ambition—to achieve
• Drive—to solve
• Tenacity—to persevere
• Confidence—to act
• Openness—to experience
• Realism—to accept
• Learning—to grow
• Integrity—to fulfill

As you might expect, there's a potential downside to ambition as well. And this raises a word of caution, something to help us keep ambition in perspective. Charan points out that people can get blinded by ambition, that they can end up sacrificing substance for superficiality and even sacrificing right for wrong. People who are overly ambitious may overstate their accomplishments to themselves and others. They may also try to do too much and end up accomplishing little of real value. Ambitious people who lack integrity can also get trapped by corruption and misbehavior.[4]

get to know yourself better

Take a look at the "personal differentiators" in the small box. How do you score? Can you say that your career ambition is backed with a sufficient set of personal traits and skills to make success a real possibility? Ask others to comment on the ambition you display as you go about your daily activities. Write a short synopsis of two situations—one in which you showed ambition and one in which you did not. Consider the implications for your career development. **Also take advantage of the end-of-chapter Self-Assessment feature to further reflect on your tendencies when it comes to Internal/External Control.**

Study Question 1	Study Question 2	Study Question 3	Study Question 4
Perception	**Personality**	**Attitudes**	**Emotions, Moods, and Stress**
• Perception and psychological contracts • Perception and attribution • Perception tendencies and distortions • Perception and impression management	• Big 5 personality dimensions • Myers-Briggs personality types • Personal conception and emotional adjustment traits	• What is an attitude? • What is job satisfaction? • Job satisfaction and its outcomes	• Emotions • Moods • Stress • Sources of stress
Learning Check 1	**Learning Check 2**	**Learning Check 3**	**Learning Check 4**

In his books *Leadership Is an Art* and *Leadership Jazz*, Max DePree, former chairperson of furniture maker Herman Miller, Inc., talks about a millwright who worked for his father. When the man died, DePree's father, wishing to express his sympathy to the family, went to their home. There he listened as the widow read some beautiful poems which, to his father's surprise, the millwright had written. DePree says that he and his father often wondered, "Was the man a poet who did millwright's work, or a millwright who wrote poetry?" He summarizes the lesson this way: "It is fundamental that leaders endorse a concept of persons."[5]

Contrast that story with this one. Some years ago, Karen Nussbaum founded an organization called 9 to 5 devoted to improving women's salaries and promotion opportunities in the workplace. She started it after leaving her job as a secretary at Harvard University. Describing what she calls "the incident that put her over the edge," Nussbaum says: "One day I was sitting at my desk at lunchtime, when most of the professors were out. A student walked into the office and looked me dead in the eye and said, 'Isn't anyone here'?"[6] Nussbaum founded 9 to 5 to support her commitment to "remake the system so that it does not produce these individuals."

Such things as perceptions, personalities, attitudes, emotions, and moods influence individual behavior. When people work under conditions that fail to provide them with respect, as in Nussbaum's story, their behavior sets often tend toward low performance, poor customer service, absenteeism, and even antisocial behavior. But when people work in supportive settings and with caring bosses, more positive behavior sets—higher performance, less withdrawal and dysfunction, and helpful citizenship—are common. This relates to DePree's story. He says: "We need to give each other space so that we may both give and receive such beautiful things as ideas, openness, dignity, joy, healing, and inclusion."[7]

Individual Behavior Sets

Performance behaviors—task performance, customer service, productivity

Withdrawal behaviors—absenteeism, turnover, job disengagement

Citizenship behaviors—helping, volunteering, job engagement

Dysfunctional behaviors—antisocial behavior, intentional wrongdoing

PERCEPTION

● **Perception** is the process through which people receive, organize, and interpret information from the environment.

Perception is the process through which people receive and interpret information from the environment. It is the way we form impressions about ourselves, other people, and daily life experiences. It is also the way we process information to make the decisions that ultimately guide our actions.[8] Perception acts as a screen or filter through which information passes before it has an impact on communication, decision making, and behavior. Because perceptions are influenced by such things as cultural background, values, and other personal and situational circumstances,

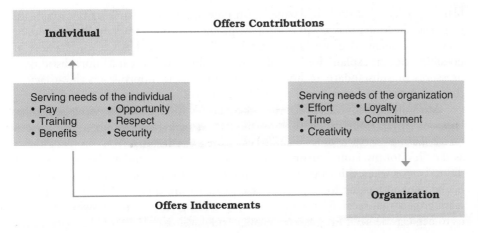

FIGURE 14.1 Components in the psychological contract.

people can and do perceive the same people, things, or situations differently. And importantly, people behave according to these perceptions.

PERCEPTION AND PSYCHOLOGICAL CONTRACTS

One way in which perception influences individual behavior is through the **psychological contract**, or set of expectations held by the individual about what will be given and received in the employment relationship.[9] Figure 14.1 shows that a healthy psychological contract offers a balance between individual contributions made to the organization and inducements received. Contributions are work activities, such as effort, time, creativity, and loyalty. Inducements are what the organization gives to the individual in exchange for these contributions. Typical inducements include pay, fringe benefits, training and opportunities for personal growth and advancement, and job security.

The ideal situation is one in which the exchange of values in the psychological contract is perceived as fair. Problems are likely when the psychological contract is perceived as unfair, unbalanced, or broken. Negative behaviors in the form of lower performance, withdrawal, and poor citizenship are likely when someone perceives that inducements are inadequate to compensate for contributions.

● A **psychological contract** is the set of individual expectations about the employment relationship.

PERCEPTION AND ATTRIBUTION

Perception also influences individual behavior through **attribution**, the process of developing explanations for events. The fact that people can perceive the same things quite differently has an important influence on attributions and their ultimate effect on behavior. What happens, for example, when you perceive that someone else in a job or student group isn't performing up to expectations? How do you explain it? Depending on the explanation, what do you do to try and correct things? And suppose that poor performer is you. How do you explain it?

In social psychology, attribution theory describes how people try to explain the behavior of themselves and other people.[10] **Fundamental attribution error** occurs when observers attribute another person's performance problems more to internal failures of the individual than external factors relating to the environment. In the case of someone producing poor-quality work, for example, a team leader might

● **Attribution** is the process of explaining events.

● **Fundamental attribution error** overestimates internal factors and underestimates external factors as influences on someone's behavior.

blame a lack of job skills or laziness—an unwillingness to work hard enough. In response, the leader may try to resolve the problem through training, motivation, or even replacement. Because fundamental attribution error leads to the neglect of possible external explanations for the poor-quality work, such as unrealistic time pressures or substandard technology, opportunities to improve on these factors through managerial action will probably be missed.

Attribution theory also recognizes tendencies toward **self-serving bias**. This happens when individuals blame their personal failures or problems on external causes and attribute their successes to internal causes. You can recognize it as the "It's not my fault!" error when something is wrong and as the "It was me, I did it!" error when things go right. Think of this, for example, the next time you blame your instructor for a poor course grade or are quick to claim credit for a team project that received a high grade. Self-serving bias is harmful when it causes us to neglect the need for personal change and development in problem situations.

● **Self-serving bias** explains personal success by internal causes and personal failures by external causes.

PERCEPTION TENDENCIES AND DISTORTIONS

In addition to attribution errors, a variety of perceptual tendencies and distortions also influence how people communicate and behave toward one another. They include the use of stereotypes, halo effects, selective perception, and projection.

Stereotypes

A **stereotype** occurs when someone is identified with a group or category, and then oversimplified attributes associated with the group or category are used to describe the individual. We all make use of stereotypes, and they are not always negative or ill-intended. But those based on such things as gender, age, and race can, and unfortunately do, bias perceptions.

Legitimate questions can be asked about *racial and ethnic stereotypes* and about the slow progress of minority managers into America's corporate mainstream.[11] And, women constitute only a small percentage of American managers sent abroad to work on international business assignments. Why? A Catalyst study of opportunities for women in global business points to *gender stereotypes* that assume women lack the ability or willingness to work abroad.[12] Although employment barriers caused by gender stereotypes are falling, even everyday

● A **stereotype** occurs when attributes commonly associated with a group are assigned to an individual.

No Age Stereotypes Allowed at BakBone Software

There's no generational stereotyping allowed at BakBone Software in San Diego, California. Teams are put together with an emphasis on skills and expertise, not just seniority. Times have changed, Senior Vice President Dan Woodward says, from "when a 23-year-old attended senior-level meetings and they were more often than not just taking notes." Now everyone is expected to be a contributor. According to Woodward, "The goal is to create an environment where the senior people recognize what the younger workforce brings to the table, and understands the value of each and every member of the team."

behavior may be misconstrued. Consider this example: "He's talking with coworkers" (interpretation: he's discussing a new deal); "she's talking with coworkers" (interpretation: she's gossiping).[13]

Ability stereotypes and *age stereotypes* also exist. A physically or mentally challenged candidate may be overlooked by a recruiter, even though her skills are perfect for the job. A talented older worker may not be promoted because a manager perceives older workers as cautious and tending to avoid risk. Interestingly, a Conference Board survey of workers 50 and older found that 72% felt they could take on additional responsibilities, and two-thirds were interested in further training and development.[14]

Halo Effects

A **halo effect** occurs when one attribute is used to develop an overall impression of a person or situation. When meeting someone new, for example, the halo effect may cause one trait, such as a pleasant smile, to result in a positive first impression. Or, a unique hairstyle or manner of dressing may create a negative perception. Such halo effects cause the same problem for managers as do stereotypes—individual differences become obscured. This is especially significant in performance evaluations. One factor, such as a person's punctuality, may become the "halo" for a positive overall performance assessment, even though high performance may or may not be true.

● A **halo effect** occurs when one attribute is used to develop an overall impression of a person or situation.

Selective Perception

Selective perception is the tendency to single out for attention those aspects of a situation or person that reinforce one's existing beliefs, values, or needs.[15] Information that makes us uncomfortable is screened out; comfortable information is allowed in. What this often means in organizations is that people from different departments or functions—such as marketing and manufacturing—see things from their own points of view and fail to recognize other points of view. One way to reduce this tendency and avoid the negative impact of selective perception is to be sure to gather and be open to inputs and opinions from many people.

● **Selective perception** is the tendency to define problems from one's own point of view.

Projection

Projection is a perceptual error that involves the assignment of personal attributes to other individuals. A classic projection error is to assume that other

● **Projection** is the assignment of personal attributes to other individuals.

Root Learning Celebrates Individual Differences

At Root Learning, a small management consulting firm in Sylvania, Ohio, and also ranked by the *Wall Street Journal* as one of America's Top Small Workplaces, the individual counts. Caricature drawings of each employee are prominently hung in the lobby with the goal of highlighting their interests and talents. CEO Jim Haudan sees this as a way of getting beyond stereotypes and making sure that everyone is viewed as a whole person. "If we pigeon-hole or just identify any of our people as a "proofer" or an "analyst," it grossly limits what they're capable of," he says.

Little Things Are Big Things for **Life Is Good**

Imagine! Yes, you can! Go for it! Life is good. Well make that: life is really good! These are thoughts that can turn dreams into realities. They're also part and parcel of the $80 million company that really is named Life Is Good.

It all began with two brothers—Bert and John Jacobs—making t-shirts for street sales. Now it's grown into a 200+ employee company selling a variety of fun apparel and related products in 14 or more countries. *Inc.* magazine calls it a "fine small business that only wants to make me happy."

Picture a card table set up at a Boston street fair and two young brothers setting out 48 t-shirts printed with a smiling face—Jake, and the words "Life is good." Then picture the cart empty, with all shirts sold for $10 apiece, and two brothers happily realizing they might, just might, have a viable business idea.

From that modest beginning, Bert–Chief Executive Optimist–and John–Chief Creative Optimist–built a company devoted to humor and humility. John says: "It's important that we're saying 'Life is good,' not 'Life is great' or 'Life is perfect,' there's a big difference. . . . Don't determine that you're going to be happy when you get the new car or the big promotion or meet that special person. You can decide that you're going to be happy today." According to Bert: "The little things in life are the big things." And that's the message of the Life Is Good brand.

So how did brothers Bert and John build a successful firm? Well, they didn't start with business degrees or experience, but their good instincts combined with creativity and positive views on life paved the road for prosperity. And they've learned as they've progressed, becoming good at things like marketing, supply chain management, distribution, and brand protection. Each step forward in the business was a chance to capture experience, learn from it, and keep getting better.

Bert and John have stuck to their values. They live the brand while enjoying leisure pursuits like kayaking and ultimate Frisbee. They support philanthropies like Camp Sunshine for children with serious illnesses and Project Joy for traumatized children. And, the company runs seasonal Life Is Good festivals to help raise money for charities.

persons share our needs, desires, and values. Suppose, for example, that you enjoy a lot of responsibility and challenge in your work. Suppose, too, that you are the newly appointed manager for a team whose jobs you consider dull and routine. You might move quickly to change the jobs so to give team members more responsibility and challenge. But this may not be a good decision. Instead of designing jobs to best fit members' needs, you have designed the jobs to fit your needs. The problem is that others may be quite satisfied doing jobs that, to you, seem routine. Projection errors can be controlled through self-awareness and a willingness to communicate and empathize with other persons. To do this you must try to see things through their eyes.

PERCEPTION AND IMPRESSION MANAGEMENT

Richard Branson, CEO of the Virgin Group, may be one of the richest and most famous executives in the world. One of his early business accomplishments was the successful start-up of Virgin Airlines, now a major competitor of British Airways (BA). In a memoir, the former head of BA, Lord King, said: "If Richard Branson had worn a shirt and tie instead of a goatee and jumper, I would not have underestimated him."[16] This shows how much impressions can count—both positive and negative. Knowing this, scholars emphasize the importance of **impression management**, the systematic attempt to influence how others perceive us.[17]

● **Impression management** is the systematic attempt to influence how others perceive us.

Impression management is a matter of routine in everyday life. We dress, talk, act, and surround ourselves with things that convey a desirable image to other persons. When well done, impression management can help us to advance in jobs and careers, form relationships with people we admire, and even create pathways to group memberships. And some basic tactics of impression management are worth remembering. Dress in ways that convey positive appeal—for example, know when to "dress up" and when to "dress down." Use words to flatter other people in ways that generate positive feelings toward you. Make eye contact and smile when engaged in conversations so as to create a personal bond. Display a high level of energy that is suggestive of lots of work commitment and initiative.[18]

Be sure you can ☑ define *perception* ☑ explain the benefits of a healthy psychological contract ☑ explain fundamental attribution error and self-serving bias ☑ define *stereotype, halo effect, selective perception*, and *projection* and illustrate how each can adversely affect work behavior ☑ explain impression management

Learning Check ☑

Study Question 1
How do perceptions influence individual behavior?

PERSONALITY

Think of how many times you've complained about someone's "bad personality" or told a friend how much you like someone else because they had such a "nice personality." Well, the same holds true at work. Perhaps you have been part of conversations like these: "I can't give him that job, with a personality like that there's no way he can work with customers." Or, "Put Erika on the project, her personality is perfect for the intensity that we expect from the team."

In management we use the term **personality** to describe the profile of enduring characteristics that makes each of us unique. As the prior examples suggest, as well as the chapter opener on Sarah Blakely of Spanx, this uniqueness can have consequences for how we behave and how that behavior is regarded by others.

● **Personality** is the profile of characteristics making a person unique from others.

BIG FIVE PERSONALITY DIMENSIONS

We all know that variations among personalities are both real and consequential in our relationships with everyone from family to friends to coworkers. Although there are many personality traits, scholars have identified a short list of five that are especially significant in the workplace. Known as the Big Five,[19] these personality traits are:

- *Extraversion*—the degree to which someone is outgoing, sociable, and assertive. An extravert is comfortable and confident in interpersonal relationships; an introvert is more withdrawn and reserved.
- *Agreeableness*—the degree to which someone is good-natured, cooperative, and trusting. An agreeable person gets along well with others; a disagreeable person is a source of conflict and discomfort for others.
- *Conscientiousness*—the degree to which someone is responsible, dependable, and careful. A conscientious person focuses on what can be accomplished and meets commitments; a person who lacks conscientiousness is careless, often trying to do too much and failing, or doing little.

● **Extraversion** is being outgoing, sociable, and assertive.

● **Agreeableness** is being good-natured, cooperative, and trusting.

● **Conscientiousness** is being responsible, dependable, and careful.

Is Personality Testing in Your Future?

Dear [your name goes here]:

I am very pleased to invite you to a second round of screening interviews with XYZ Corporation. Your on-campus session with our representative went very well, and we would like to consider you further for a full-time position. Please contact me to arrange a visit date. We will need a full day. The schedule will include several meetings with executives and your potential team members, as well as a round of personality tests.

Thank you again for your interest in XYZ Corp. I look forward to meeting you during the next step in our recruiting process.

Sincerely,
[signed]
Human Resource Director

Getting a letter like this is great news: a nice confirmation of your hard work and performance in college. You obviously made a good first impression. But have you thought about this "personality test" thing? What do you know about them and how they are used for employment screening?

A report in the *Wall Street Journal* advises that lawsuits can result when employers use personality tests that weren't specifically designed for hiring decisions. Some people might even consider their use an invasion of privacy.

You Decide

What are the ethical issues associated with the use of personality testing? In which situations might the use of personality tests be an invasion of privacy? Also, suppose that the specific personality test being used is not predictive of employee performance on the job. Could its use be termed unethical?

● **Emotional stability** is being relaxed, secure, and unworried.

● **Openness to experience** is being curious, receptive to new ideas, and imaginative.

- *Emotional stability*—the degree to which someone is relaxed, secure, and unworried. A person who is emotionally stable is calm and confident; a person lacking in emotional stability is anxious, nervous, and tense.
- *Openness to experience*—the degree to which someone is curious, open to new ideas, and imaginative. An open person is broad-minded, receptive to new things, and comfortable with change; a person who lacks openness is narrow-minded, has few interests, and is resistant to change.

A considerable body of literature links the personality dimensions of the Big Five model with work and career outcomes, as well as to life overall. For example, conscientiousness is a good predictor of job performance for most occupations, and extraversion is often associated with success in management and sales.[20] Indications are that extraverts tend to be happier than introverts in their lives overall, that conscientious people tend to be less risky, and that those more open to experience are more creative.[21]

You can easily spot the Big Five personality traits in people with whom you work, study, and socialize. But don't forget that they also apply to you. Others form impressions of your personality, and respond to it, just as you do with theirs. Managers often use personality judgments when making job assignments, building teams, and otherwise engaging in the daily social give-and-take of work.

Even though the Big Five model adds some discipline to personality assessments, it should still be considered and used with caution. Doug Conant, CEO of Campbell Soup Co., for example, surprised an interviewer when she asked him this personality-based question: "You describe yourself as an introvert, which does not seem like the right personality for a CEO. How do you make that work for you?" He answered: "In my opinion, more than half of all CEOs are introverts. They're internally driven . . . The most effective CEOs are not the ones trying to please everybody. They're driving the agenda."[22]

MYERS-BRIGGS TYPE INDICATOR

Another popular approach to personality assessment is the Myers-Briggs Type Indicator, a sophisticated questionnaire that probes into how people act or feel in various situations. Called the MBTI for short, it was developed by Katherine Briggs and her daughter Isabel Briggs-Myers from foundations set forth in the work of psychologist Carl Jung.[23]

Jung's model of personality differences included three main distinctions. First, he described personality differences in ways people relate with others—by extraversion or introversion, as just discussed. Second, Jung described how people vary in the way they gather information—by sensation (emphasizing details, facts, and routine) or by intuition (looking for the "big picture" and being willing to deal with various possibilities). Third, he described how people vary in ways of evaluating information—by thinking (using reason and analysis) or by feeling (responding to the feelings and desires of others).

Briggs and Briggs-Myers adopted Jung's three personality dimensions in their own work. But, they also added a fourth dimension that describes how people vary in the ways they relate to the outside world—judging or perceiving. These four personality dimensions constitute the Myers-Briggs Type Indicator. It can be briefly described as classifying, or typing, people in the following ways.[24]

- *Extraverted vs. introverted (E or I)*—social interaction: whether a person tends toward being outgoing and sociable or shy and quiet.
- *Sensing vs. intuitive (S or N)*—gathering data: whether a person tends to focus on details or on the big picture in dealing with problems.
- *Thinking vs. feeling (T or F)*—decision making: whether a person tends to rely on logic or emotions in dealing with problems.
- *Judging vs. perceiving (J or P)*—work style: whether a person prefers order and control or acts with flexibility and spontaneity.

Sample Myers-Briggs Types

- ESTJ (extraverted, sensing, thinking, judging)—decisive, logical, and quick to dig in; common among managers.
- EITJ (extraverted, intuitive, thinking, judging)—analytical, strategic, quick to take charge; common for leaders.
- ISJF (introverted, sensing, judging, feeling)—conscientious, considerate, and helpful; common among team players.
- IITJ (introverted, intuitive, thinking, judging)—insightful, free thinking, determined; common for visionaries.

Sixteen possible MBTI personality types result from combinations of these four dimensions. A sample of ones common in work settings is shown in the small box. The neat and understandable nature of the classification scheme has made the MBTI very popular in management training and development, although it receives mixed reviews from researchers.[25] Employers and trainers tend to like it because once a person is "typed" on the Myers-Briggs, for example as an ESTJ or ISJF, they can be trained to both understand their own styles and to learn how to work better with people having different styles.

PERSONAL CONCEPTION AND EMOTIONAL ADJUSTMENT TRAITS

In addition to the Big Five dimensions and the Myers-Briggs Type Indicator, psychologists have long studied many other personality traits. As shown in Figure 14.2, additional traits that have special relevance to people at work include the personal conception traits of locus of control, authoritarianism, Machiavellianism, and self-monitoring, as well as the emotional adjustment trait of Type A orientation.[26] In general, you can think of a *personal conception trait* as describing how people by personality tend to relate with the environment, while an *emotional adjustment trait* describes how they are inclined toward handling stress and uncomfortable situations.

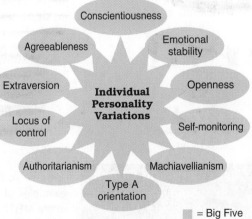

FIGURE 14.2 Common personality dimensions that influence human behavior at work.

Locus of Control

● **Locus of control** is the extent to which one believes that what happens is within one's control.

Scholars have a strong interest in **locus of control**, recognizing that some people believe they are in control of their destinies, whereas others believe that what happens to them is beyond their control.[27] "Internals" are more self-confident and accept responsibility for their own actions. "Externals" are more prone to blame others and outside forces for what happens to them. Research suggests that internals tend to be more satisfied and less alienated from their work.

Authoritarianism

● **Authoritarianism** is the degree to which a person tends to defer to authority.

Authoritarianism is the degree to which a person defers to authority and accepts status differences.[28] Someone with an authoritarian personality tends to act rigidly and be control-oriented when in a leadership capacity. This same person is likely to be subservient and follow the rules when in a follower capacity. The tendency of people with authoritarian personalities to obey orders can cause problems if they follow higher-level directives to the point of acting unethically or even illegally.

Machiavellianism

● **Machiavellianism** describes the extent to which someone is emotionally detached and manipulative.

In his 16th-century book, *The Prince*, Niccolo Machiavelli gained lasting fame for giving advice on how to use power to achieve personal goals.[29] The personality trait of **Machiavellianism** describes the extent to which someone is emotionally detached and manipulative in using power.[30] A person with a "high-Mach" personality is viewed as exploitative and unconcerned about others, often acting with the assumption that the end justifies the means. A person with a "low-Mach" personality, by contrast, would be deferential in allowing others to exert power over him or her.

Self-Monitoring

● **Self-monitoring** is the degree to which someone is able to adjust behavior in response to external factors.

Self-monitoring reflects the degree to which someone is able to adjust and modify behavior in response to the immediate situation and to external factors.[31] A person high in self-monitoring tends to be a learner, comfortable with feedback, and both willing and able to change. Because high self-monitors are flexible in changing behavior from one situation to the next, it may be hard to get a clear reading on where they stand. A person low in self-monitoring, by contrast, is predictable and tends to act consistently regardless of circumstances.

Type A Personality

● A **Type A personality** is a person oriented toward extreme achievement, impatience, and perfectionism.

It's quite common to hear people being described as "Type A's." A **Type A personality** is high in achievement orientation, impatience, and perfectionism. One of the important tendencies of Type A persons is to bring stress on themselves, even in situations others may find relatively stress free. You can spot Type A personality tendencies in yourself and others through the following patterns of behavior.[32]

- Always moving, walking, and eating rapidly.
- Acting impatient, hurrying others, put off by waiting.
- Doing, or trying to do, several things at once.
- Feeling guilty when relaxing.
- Hurrying or interrupting the speech of others.

✓ **Learning Check**
Study Question 2
What should we know about personalities in the workplace?

Be sure you can ☑ list the Big Five personality traits and give work-related examples of each ☑ list and explain the four dimensions used to assess personality in the MBTI ☑ list five personal conception and emotional adjustment personality traits and give work-related examples for each

ATTITUDES

At one time, Challis M. Lowe, as executive vice president at Ryder System, was one of only two African American women among the five highest-paid executives in over 400 U.S. companies.[33] She rose to the top after a 25-year career that included several changes of employers and lots of stressors—working-mother guilt, a failed marriage, gender bias on the job, and an MBA degree earned part-time. Through it all, she says: "I've never let being scared stop me from doing something. Just because you haven't done it before doesn't mean you shouldn't try." That, simply put, is what we would call a can-do attitude!

WHAT IS AN ATTITUDE?

An **attitude** is a predisposition to act in a certain way toward people and things in our environment.[34] Challis M. Lowe was predisposed to take risks and embrace challenges. This "positive" attitude influenced her behavior when dealing with the inevitable problems, choices, and opportunities of work and career.

● An **attitude** is a predisposition to act in a certain way.

To fully understand attitudes, positive or negative, you must recognize their three components as highlighted in the small box. First, the *cognitive component* reflects a belief or an opinion. You might believe, for example, that your management course is very interesting. Second, the *affective or emotional component* of an attitude reflects a specific feeling. For example, you might feel very good about being a management major. Third, the *behavioral component* of an attitude reflects an intention to behave in a manner consistent with the belief and feeling. Using the same example again, you might say to yourself: "I am going to work hard and try to get an A in all my management courses."

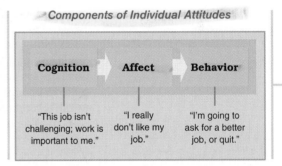

Components of Individual Attitudes

Cognition → Affect → Behavior

"This job isn't challenging; work is important to me."   "I really don't like my job."   "I'm going to ask for a better job, or quit."

Importantly, the intentions reflected in an attitude may or may not be confirmed in actual behavior. Despite having a positive attitude and all good intentions, for example, the demands of family, friends, or leisure activities might use up time you would otherwise devote to studying. So, you don't work hard enough to get an A in your management courses and fail to live up to your own expectations.

The psychological concept of **cognitive dissonance** describes the discomfort felt when one's attitude and behavior are inconsistent.[35] For most people, dissonance is very uncomfortable and results in changing the attitude to fit the behavior ("Oh, I really don't like management that much anyway"), changing future behavior to fit the attitude (dropping out of intramural sports to get extra study time), or rationalizing to force the two to be compatible ("Management is an okay major, but being a manager also requires the experience I'm gaining in my extracurricular activities").

● **Cognitive dissonance** is discomfort felt when attitude and behavior are inconsistent.

WHAT IS JOB SATISFACTION?

People hold attitudes about many things at work—bosses, each other, tasks, policies, goals, and more. One of the most discussed work attitudes is **job satisfaction**, the degree to which an individual feels positive or negative about various aspects of work.[36]

● **Job satisfaction** is the degree to which an individual feels positive or negative about a job.

Components of Job Satisfaction

Job satisfaction is something that we often express in conversations. It is something that managers often draw assumptions about for persons under their supervision. And it is an attitude that often gets measured through some form of questionnaire. These surveys usually probe beyond the more global questions of "job satisfaction—yes or no?" and make specific inquiries into just what aspects of a person's work are satisfying or not.

Two of the historically popular instruments that still underlie much of job satisfaction research are the Minnesota Satisfaction Questionnaire (MSQ) and the Job Descriptive Index (JDI).[37] They measure various facets of job satisfaction that give rise to positive or negative attitudes. Their use can give managers insights on how to take actions that increase levels of satisfaction. The following are among the job satisfaction facets most commonly measured.

- *Work itself*—Does the job offer responsibility, interest, challenge?
- *Quality of supervision*—Are task help and social support available?
- *Coworkers*—How much harmony, respect, friendliness exists?
- *Opportunities*—Are there avenues for promotion, learning, growth?
- *Pay*—is compensation, actual and perceived, fair and substantial?
- *Work conditions*—do conditions offer comfort, safety, support?
- *Security*—is the job and employment secure?

Job Satisfaction Trends

If you watch or read the news, you'll regularly find reports on job satisfaction. You'll also find lots of job satisfaction studies in the academic literature. The results don't always agree, but they do show a rather consistent trend.[38] Job satisfaction tends to be higher in small firms and lower in large ones, and job satisfaction tends to run together with overall life satisfaction. For a long while a majority of American workers responded to surveys by saying that they were basically satisfied, although a trend toward decreasing job satisfaction was also evident.

A recent survey conducted by The Conference Board confirmed the slide in reported job satisfaction. In 1987 about 61% of surveyed workers said they were satisfied, while in 2009, and in the midst of an economic downturn, only 45% were reporting job satisfaction.[39] The report states: "Fewer Americans are satisfied with all aspects of their employment and no age or income group is immune. In fact, the youngest cohort of employees (those currently under age 25) expresses the highest level of dissatisfaction ever recorded by the survey for that age group." Only 51% of workers in the survey said their jobs were interesting, versus 70% in 1987; and only 51% said they were satisfied with their bosses, versus 60% in 1987. In commenting on these data, Lynn Franco, director of the Consumer Research Center of The Conference Board, said: "The downward trend in job satisfaction could spell trouble for the engagement of U.S. employees and ultimately employee productivity."[40]

JOB SATISFACTION AND ITS OUTCOMES

Back in Chapter 1 we identified two primary goals for an effective manager—helping others achieve both high performance and job satisfaction. Surely you can accept that job satisfaction is important on quality of work life grounds alone; that is, people deserve to have satisfying work experiences. But now we also have to ask: Is job satisfaction important in other than a "feel good" sense? Here is what we know.

Job Satisfaction and Withdrawal Behaviors

● **Withdrawal behaviors** occur as temporary absenteeism and actual job turnover.

A strong relationship exists between job satisfaction and **withdrawal behaviors** in the forms of temporary absenteeism and actual job turnover. With regard to

Research Brief

Business Students More Satisfied with Lives Overall Perform Better

Wondering if "a happy student is a high-performing student," Joseph C. Rode, Marne L. Arthaud-Day, Christine H. Mooney, Janet P. Near, Timothy T. Baldwin, William H. Bommer, and Robert S. Rubin hypothesized that students' satisfaction with their life and student domains would, along with cognitive abilities, have a positive influence on academic performance.

A sample of 673 business students completed satisfaction and IQ questionnaires, and their academic performance was measured by self-reported GPAs and performance on a 3-hour simulation exercise. The findings confirmed the expected relationships between students' leisure and family satisfaction and overall life satisfaction. Also confirmed were links between both life satisfaction and IQ scores, and self-reported GPA and simulation performance. Expected relationships between students' university and housing satisfaction and overall life satisfaction proved not to be significant.

Rode et al. point out that "it is time to more fully acknowledge that college students also live 'integrated lives' and are heavily influenced by the milieu that surrounds them."

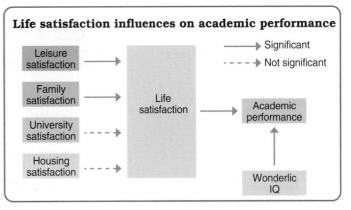

You Be the Researcher

Does your everyday experience as a student support these results or contradict them? Build a model that describes how you would predict student academic performance, not limiting yourself to directions used in this study. If it is true that students' academic performance is influenced by overall life satisfaction, what does this mean to an instructor or to a college administrator?

Reference: Joseph C. Rode, Marne L. Arthaud-Day, Christine H. Mooney, Janet P. Near, Timothy T. Baldwin, William H. Bommer, and Robert S. Rubin, "Life Satisfaction and Student Performance," *Academy of Management Learning & Education*, vol. 4 (2005), pp. 421–33.

absenteeism, workers who are more satisfied with their jobs are absent less often than those who are dissatisfied. With regard to *turnover,* satisfied workers are more likely to stay and dissatisfied workers are more likely to quit their jobs.[41]

Both findings are important. Absenteeism and turnover are costly in terms of the recruitment and training needed to replace workers, as well as in the productivity lost while new workers are learning how to perform up to expectations.[42] In fact, one study found that changing retention rates up or down results in magnified changes to corporate earnings. It also warns about the negative impact on corporate performance of declining employee loyalty and high turnover.[43]

Job Satisfaction and Employee Engagement

A survey of 55,000 American workers by the Gallup organization suggests that higher profits for employers arise when job satisfaction creates high levels of **employee engagement**.[44] This is a positive work attitude resulting in a strong sense of belonging or connection with one's job and employer. It shows up both in being willing to help others and always trying to do something extra to improve performance, and in feeling and speaking positively about the organization. Things that counted most toward employee engagement among workers in

● **Employee engagement** is willingness to help others do extra, and feeling positive about the organization.

the Gallup research were believing they had the opportunity to do their best every day, believing their opinions count, believing fellow workers are committed to quality, and believing there is a direct connection between their work and the company's mission.[45]

The employee engagement just described links with two other attitudes that also influence individual behavior at work. **Job involvement** is defined as the extent to which an individual is dedicated to a job. Someone with high job involvement psychologically identifies with her or his job, and, for example, would be expected to work beyond expectations to complete a special project. **Organizational commitment** reflects the degree of loyalty an individual feels toward the organization. Individuals with a high organizational commitment identify strongly with the organization and take pride in considering themselves a member. Researchers find that strong *emotional commitments* to the organization—based on values and interests of others—are as much as four times more powerful in positively influencing performance than are *rational commitments*—based primarily on pay and self-interests.[46]

● **Job involvement** is the extent to which an individual is dedicated to a job.

● **Organizational commitment** is the loyalty of an individual to the organization.

● **Organizational citizenship** is a willingness to "go beyond the call of duty" or "go the extra mile" in one's work.

Job Satisfaction and Organizational Citizenship

Have you ever wondered about those people who are always willing to "go beyond the call of duty" or "go the extra mile" in their work?[47] This is a set of behaviors that represent what we call **organizational citizenship** and it also links with job satisfaction.[48] A person who is a good organizational citizen does things that, though not required, help advance the performance of the organization. Examples are a service worker who goes to extraordinary lengths to take care of a customer, a team member who is always willing to take on extra tasks, or an employee who always volunteers to stay late at no pay just to make sure a key job is done right for his employer.

Two Dimensions of Organizational Commitment

1. Rational commitment—feelings that the job serves one's financial, developmental, professional interests.
2. Emotional commitment—feelings that what one does is important, valuable, and of real benefit to others.

Job Satisfaction and Performance

The job satisfaction and performance relationship is somewhat complicated.[49] Three different arguments are depicted in the small figure. One is that job satisfaction causes performance in the sense of "a happy worker is a productive worker." The second is that performance causes job satisfaction in the sense of "a productive worker is a happy worker." The third is that job satisfaction results when rewards follow performance, and that this satisfaction then influences future performance. Can you make a case for each argument based on personal experiences?

There is probably a modest link between job satisfaction and performance.[50] But keep the stress on the word "modest" in the last sentence. We need to be careful before rushing to conclude that making people happy is a sure-fire way to improve their job performance. The reality is that some people will like their jobs,

be very satisfied, and still will not perform very well. That's just part of the complexity regarding individual differences. When you think of this, remember a sign that once hung in a tavern near a Ford plant in Michigan: "I spend 40 hours a week here, am I supposed to work too?"

The relationship between performance and satisfaction holds pretty much to the same pattern. High-performing workers are likely to feel satisfied. But again, a realistic position is probably best; not everyone is likely to fit the model. Some people may get their jobs done and meet high performance expectations while still not feeling satisfied. Given that job satisfaction is a good predictor of

Arguments in the Job Satisfaction and Performance Relationship

"The happy worker is a productive worker."

Satisfaction ⟶ Performance

"The productive worker is a happy worker."

Performance ⟶ Satisfaction

"Performance followed by rewards creates satisfaction; satisfaction influences future performance."

Performance → Rewards → Satisfaction

absenteeism and turnover, managers might be well advised to worry about losing these highly productive but unhappy workers unless changes are made to increase their job satisfaction.

Finally, job satisfaction and job performance likely influence one another. But the relationship is also most likely to hold under certain "conditions" that are the subjects of a lot of research, particularly on the role of rewards. For example, job performance followed by rewards that are valued and perceived as fair will create job satisfaction, and this will likely increase motivation to work harder to achieve high performance in the future. The next chapter on motivation will explore such issues in respect to individual needs and the equity and expectancy theories.

Be sure you can ☑ define *attitude* and list the three components of an attitude ☑ define *job satisfaction* and list its components ☑ explain the potential consequences of high and low job satisfaction ☑ define *employee engagement, job involvement, organizational commitment*, and *organizational citizenship* ☑ explain three arguments on the satisfaction–performance relationship	**Learning Check** ☑ **Study Question 3** How do attitudes influence individual behavior?

EMOTIONS, MOODS, AND STRESS

Not long ago, Hewlett-Packard's CEO, Mark V. Hurd, faced an unusual corporate scandal. It involved a spy operation conducted to uncover what were considered to be information leaks by members of HP's board of directors. When trying to explain to the press the situation and resignation of the board's chair, Hurd called the actions "very disturbing" and said that "I could have and I should have" read an internal report that he had been given on the matter. The *Wall Street Journal* described him as speaking with "his voice shaking."[51] One might say that Hurd was emotional and angry that the incident was causing public humiliation for him and the company, that he was in a bad mood because of it, and that the whole episode was very stressful. In this one example we have wrapped up three aspects of individual psychology that are of interest to management scholars—emotions, moods, and stress.

EMOTIONS

As discussed in earlier chapters, **emotional intelligence** is an important human skill for managers and an essential leadership capability. Daniel Goleman defines "EI" as an ability to understand emotions in ourselves and in others and to use this understanding to manage relationships effectively.[52] His point is that we perform better when we are good at recognizing and dealing with emotions in ourselves and others. Simply put, we should avoid letting our emotions "get the better of us."[53] But what is an emotion, and how does it influence our behavior—positively and negatively?

● **Emotional intelligence** is an ability to understand emotions and manage relationships effectively.

● **Emotions** are strong feelings directed toward someone or something.

An **emotion** is a strong feeling directed toward someone or something. For example, you might feel positive emotion or elation when an instructor congratulates you on a fine class presentation; you might feel negative emotion or anger when an instructor criticizes you in front of the class. In both cases the object of your emotion is the instructor, but in each the impact of the instructor's behavior on your feelings is quite different. How you respond to the aroused emotions is likely to differ as well—perhaps breaking into a wide smile with the compliment, or making a nasty side comment after the criticism.

Understanding Emotions

"I was really mad when Prof. Nitpicker started criticizing my presentation."

- linked with a specific cause
- tends to be brief or episodic
- specific effect on attitude, behavior
- might turn into a mood

MOODS

● **Moods** are generalized positive and negative feelings or states of mind.

Whereas emotions tend to be short term and clearly targeted, **moods** are more generalized positive and negative feelings or states of mind that may persist for some time.[54] Everyone seems to have occasional moods, and we each know the full range of possibilities they represent. How often do you wake up in the morning and feel excited, refreshed, and just happy, or wake up feeling low, depressed, and generally unhappy? And, what are the consequences of these different moods for your behavior with friends and family, and at work or school?

● **Mood contagion** is the spillover of one's positive or negative moods onto others.

Researchers are increasingly interested in the influence of emotions and moods on workplace behaviors, particularly **mood contagion**—the spillover effects of one's mood onto others.[55] Positive and negative emotions can be "contagious," causing others to display similarly positive and negative moods. This contagion can easily extend to one's followers, co-workers and teammates, as well as family and friends. When a leader's mood contagion is positive, followers display more positive moods, report being more attracted to their leaders, and rate their leaders more highly.[56]

With regard to CEO moods, a *BusinessWeek* article claims "harsh is out, caring is in." In other words, it pays to be likable.[57] If a CEO goes to a meeting in a good mood and gets described as "cheerful," "charming," "humorous," "friendly," and "candid," she or he may be viewed as on the upswing. But if the CEO is in a bad mood and comes away perceived as "prickly," "impatient," "remote," "tough," "acrimonious," or even "ruthless," she or he may be seen as on the downhill slope. Some CEOs are even hiring executive coaches to help them manage emotions and moods so that they will come across as more personable and friendly in their relationships with others.

Understanding Moods

"I just feel lousy today and don't have any energy. I've been down all week."
- hard to identify cause
- tends to linger, be long-lasting
- general effect on attitude, behavior
- can be "negative" or "positive"

STRESS

● **Stress** is a state of tension caused by extraordinary demands, constraints, or opportunities.

Closely aligned with a person's emotions and moods is **stress**, a state of tension caused by extraordinary demands, constraints, or opportunities.[58] Any look toward the future and your work career would be incomplete without considering stress as a challenge that you are sure to encounter. In his book *The Future of Success*, for example, Robert Reich claims that "rewards are coming at the price of lives that are more frenzied, less secure, more economically divergent, more socially stratified."[59]

Consider these facts. In a recent survey of college graduates, 31% reported working over 50 hours per week, 60% rushed meals and 34% ate lunches "on the run," and 47% of those under 35 and 28% of those over 35 had feelings of job burnout.[60] A study by the Society for Human Resources Management found that 70% of those surveyed worked over and above scheduled hours, including putting in extra time on the weekends; over 50% said that the pressure to do the extra work was "self-imposed."[61]

SOURCES OF STRESS

● A **stressor** is anything that causes stress.

Stressors are things that cause stress. Whether they originate directly from work or nonwork situations, or from personality, stressors can influence our attitudes, emotions and moods, behavior, job performance, and even health.[62] Having the Type A personality discussed earlier is an example of a personal stressor. Stressful life situations include such things as family events (e.g., the birth of a new child), economics (e.g., a sudden loss of extra income), and personal affairs (e.g., a preoccupation with a bad relationship).

Tension Must Be Fine Tuned

When the tension on a violin string is just right, a talented artist can create a beautiful sound. But if the string is too loose the sound is weak, and if it's too tight the sound is shrill and the string can snap. Work is a lot like that, with stress sometimes offering the creative edge. But all too often there is too much tension on the system. We may work too many hours, eat too many lunches "on the run," miss too many family and leisure activities . . . and end up with feelings of burnout.

Work factors have an obvious potential to create job stress. Some 34% of workers in one survey said that their jobs were so stressful they were thinking of quitting.[63] We experience stress from long hours of work, excessive e-mails, unrealistic work deadlines, difficult bosses or coworkers, unwelcome or unfamiliar work, and unrelenting change. It is also associated with excessively high or low task demands, role conflicts or ambiguities, poor interpersonal relations, and career progress that is too slow or too fast. One common work-related stress syndrome is *set up to fail*—where the performance expectations are impossible or the support is totally inadequate to the task. Another is *mistaken identity*—where the individual ends up in a job that doesn't at all match talents, or that he or she simply doesn't like.[64]

Constructive Stress

Stress actually has two faces—one constructive and one destructive.[65] Consider the analogy of a violin.[66] When a violin string is too loose, the sound produced by even the most skilled player is weak and raspy. When the string is too tight, however, the sound gets shrill and the string might even snap. But when the tension on the string is just right, neither too loose nor too tight, a beautiful sound is created. With just enough stress, in other words, performance is optimized.

Constructive stress, sometimes called *eustress*, is personally energizing and performance-enhancing.[67] It encourages increased effort, stimulates creativity, and enhances diligence, while still not overwhelming the individual and causing negative outcomes. Individuals with a Type A personality, for example, are likely to work long hours and to be less satisfied with poor performance. For them, challenging task demands imposed by a supervisor may elicit higher levels of task accomplishment. Even nonwork stressors such as new family responsibilities may cause them to work harder in anticipation of greater financial rewards.

● **Constructive stress** acts in a positive way to increase effort, stimulate creativity, and encourage diligence in one's work.

Destructive Stress

Just like tuning the violin string, however, achieving the right balance of stress for each person and situation is difficult. **Destructive stress**, or *distress*, is dysfunctional. It occurs when intense or long-term stress overloads and breaks down a person's physical and mental systems.

Destructive stress can lead to **job burnout**—a form of physical and mental exhaustion that can be personally incapacitating. As shown in Figure 14.3, productivity suffers when people with exhaustion and burnout react through turnover, absenteeism, errors, accidents, dissatisfaction, and reduced performance. Another potential by-product of destructive stress is **workplace rage**—aggressive

● **Destructive stress** impairs the performance of an individual.

● **Job burnout** is physical and mental exhaustion from work stress.

● **Workplace rage** is aggressive behavior toward coworkers or the work setting.

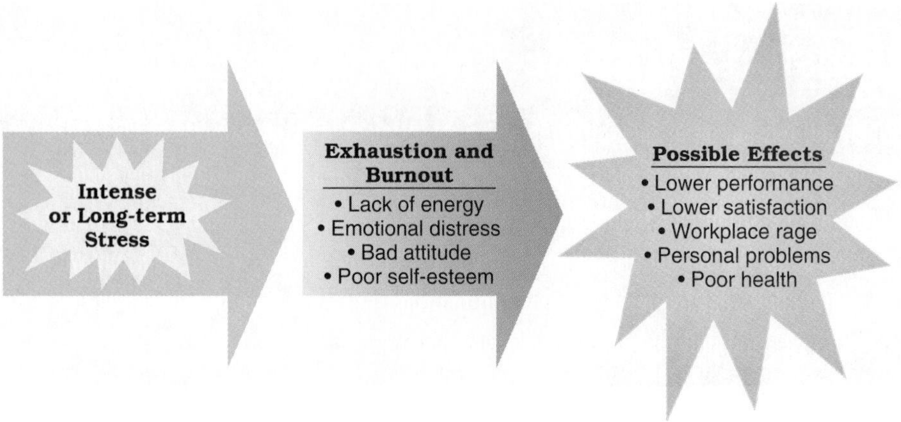

FIGURE 14.3 Potential negative consequences of a destructive job stress–burnout cycle.

behavior toward coworkers and the work setting in general. Lost tempers are common examples; the unfortunate extremes are tragedies that result in physical harm to others.[68] Medical research is concerned that too much stress causes poor health. It can reduce resistance to disease and increase the likelihood of physical and/or mental illness. Other possible health problems include hypertension, ulcers, substance abuse, overeating, depression, and muscle aches, among others.[69]

Like moods, the effects of stress at work can be contagious. Our responses can spill over on not only co-workers, but also on family and friends. The wife of a company controller, for example, went through a time when her husband was stressed by a boss who was overly critical. "He was angry, really angry when he came home," she says. His mood affected her and their young child, and created what she called "one of the worst times in our seven-year marriage."[70] Research on dual-career couples confirms that one partner's work experiences can have psychological consequences for the other; as one partner's work stress increases, the other is likely to experience stress too.[71]

Stress Management

The best stress management strategy is to prevent it from reaching excessive levels in the first place. A top priority is **personal wellness**. This means taking personal responsibility for your physical and mental health through a disciplined approach to such things as smoking, alcohol use, diet, exercise, and physical fitness.

● **Personal wellness** is the pursuit of one's full potential through a personal health-promotion program.

Stress can also be managed by taking actions to cope with and, hopefully, minimize the impact of personal and nonwork stressors. Family difficulties may be relieved by a change in work schedule, or the anxiety they cause may be reduced by an understanding supervisor. Work stress can sometimes be dealt with by role clarification through frank and open communication between bosses, subordinates, and coworkers. Jobs can sometimes be redesigned to eliminate poor fits between individual abilities and job demands. Some employers are even trying to curb tendencies to "work too much" as a way of helping people "do better work." The consulting firm KPMG, for example, uses a wellness scorecard to track and counsel workers who skip vacations and work excessive overtime. Harvard scholar Leslie Perlow says the goal is to avoid "a feeling of having no time truly free from work, no control over work and no opportunity to ask questions to clarify foggy priorities."[72]

Learning Check
Study Question 4
What are the dynamics of emotions, moods, and stress?

Be sure you can ☑ define *emotion, mood,* and *stress* ☑ explain how emotions and moods influence behavior ☑ identify the common stressors found in work and in personal life ☑ differentiate constructive and destructive stress ☑ define *job burnout* and *workplace rage* ☑ discuss personal wellness as a stress management strategy

Management Learning Review

1 How do perceptions influence individual behavior?

- Perception acts as a filter through which people receive and process information from the environment.
- Because people perceive things differently, a situation may be interpreted and responded to differently by different people.
- A healthy psychological contract occurs with perceived balance between work contributions, such as time and effort, and inducements received, such as pay and respect.
- Fundamental attribution error occurs when we blame others for performance problems while excluding possible external causes; self-serving bias occurs when we take personal credit for successes and blame failures on external factors.
- Stereotypes, projection, halo effects, and selective perception can distort perceptions and result in errors as people relate with one another.

FOR DISCUSSION **Are there times when self-serving bias is actually helpful?**

2 What should we know about personalities in the workplace?

- Personality is a set of traits and characteristics that cause people to behave in unique ways.
- The personality factors in the Big Five model are extraversion, agreeableness, conscientiousness, emotional stability, and openness to experience.
- The Myers-Briggs Type Indicator profiles personalities in respect to tendencies toward extraversion-introversion, sensing-intuitive, thinking-feeling, and judging-perceiving.
- Additional personality dimensions of work significance include the personal conception traits of locus of control, authoritarianism, Machiavellianism, and behavioral self-monitoring, as well as the emotional adjustment trait of Type A orientation.

FOR DISCUSSION **What dimension would you add to make the "Big Five" the "Big Six" personality model?**

3 How do attitudes influence individual behavior?

- An attitude is a predisposition to respond in a certain way to people and things.
- Cognitive dissonance occurs when a person's attitude and behavior are inconsistent.
- Job satisfaction is an important work attitude that reflects a person's evaluation of the job, coworkers, and other aspects of the work setting.
- Job satisfaction influences work attendance and turnover, and is related to other attitudes, such as job involvement and organizational commitment.
- Three possible explanations for the job satisfaction and performance relationship are: satisfaction causes performance, performance causes satisfaction, and rewards cause both performance and satisfaction.

FOR DISCUSSION **What should a manager do with someone who has high job satisfaction but is a low performer?**

4 What are the dynamics of emotions, moods, and stress?

- Emotions are strong feelings that are directed at someone or something; they influence behavior, often with intensity and for short periods of time.
- Moods are generalized positive or negative states of mind that can be persistent influences on one's behavior.
- Stress is a state of tension experienced by individuals facing extraordinary demands, constraints, or opportunities.
- Stress can be destructive or constructive; a moderate level of stress typically has a positive impact on performance.
- Stressors are found in a variety of personal, work, and non-work situations.
- Stress can be managed through both prevention and coping strategies, including a commitment to personal wellness.

FOR DISCUSSION **Is a Type A personality required for managerial success?**

Multiple-Choice Questions

1. In the psychological contract, job security is a/an _____, whereas loyalty is a/an _____.
   (a) satisfier factor, hygiene factor   (b) intrinsic reward, extrinsic reward   (c) inducement, contribution   (d) attitude, personality trait

2. Self-serving bias is a form of attribution error that involves _____.
   (a) blaming yourself for problems caused by others   (b) blaming the environment for problems you caused   (c) poor emotional intelligence   (d) authoritarianism

3. If a new team leader changes job designs for persons on her work team mainly "because I would prefer to work the new way rather than the old," the chances are that she is committing a perceptual error known as _____.
   (a) halo effect   (b) stereotype   (c) selective perception   (d) projection

4. If a manager allows one characteristic of a person, say a pleasant personality, to bias performance ratings of that individual overall, the manager is falling prey to a perceptual distortion known as _____.
   (a) halo effect   (b) stereotype   (c) selective perception   (d) projection

5. Use of special dress, manners, gestures, and vocabulary words when meeting a prospective employer in a job interview are all examples of how people use _____ in daily life.
   (a) projection   (b) selective perception   (c) impression management   (d) self-serving bias

6. A person with a/an _____ personality would most likely act unemotionally and manipulatively when trying to influence others to achieve personal goals.
   (a) extraverted   (b) sensation-thinking   (c) self-monitoring   (d) Machiavellian

7. When a person believes that he or she has little influence over things that happen in life, this indicates a/an _____ personality.
   (a) low emotional stability   (b) external locus of control   (c) high self-monitoring   (d) intuitive-thinker

8. Among the Big Five personality traits, _____ indicates someone who is responsible, dependable, and careful with respect to tasks.
   (a) authoritarianism   (b) agreeableness   (c) conscientiousness   (d) emotional stability

9. The _____ component of an attitude is what indicates a person's belief about something, whereas the _____ component indicates a specific positive or negative feeling about it.
   (a) cognitive, affective   (b) emotional, affective   (c) cognitive, attributional   (d) behavioral, attributional

10. The term used to describe the discomfort someone feels when his or her behavior is inconsistent with an expressed attitude is _____.
    (a) alienation   (b) cognitive dissonance   (c) job dissatisfaction   (d) person–job imbalance

11. Job satisfaction is known from research to be a good predictor of _____.
    (a) job performance   (b) job burnout   (c) conscientiousness   (d) absenteeism

12. A/an _____ represents a rather intense but short-lived feeling about a person or a situation, whereas a/an _____ describes a more generalized positive or negative state of mind.
    (a) stressor, role ambiguity   (b) external locus of control, internal locus of control   (c) self-serving bias, halo effect   (d) emotion, mood

13. Through _____, the stress people experience in their personal lives can create problems for them at work while the stress experienced at work can create problems for their personal lives.
    (a) eustress   (b) self-monitoring   (c) spillover effects   (d) selective perception

14. As a stress management strategy, better supervisor-subordinate communication might be especially useful in helping the subordinate deal with _____.
    (a) role conflicts   (b) workplace rage   (c) personal wellness   (d) resistance to change

15. What stress level is most functional or positive in terms of likely impact on individual performance?
    (a) zero   (b) low   (c) moderate   (d) high

Short-Response Questions

16. What is a healthy psychological contract?

17. What is the difference between self-serving bias and fundamental attribution error?

18. Which three of the Big Five personality traits do you believe most affect how well people work together in organizations, and why?

19. Why is it important for a manager to understand the Type A personality?

Essay Question

20. When Scott Tweedy picked up a magazine article on how to manage health care workers, he was pleased to find some advice. Scott was concerned about poor or mediocre performance on the part of several respiratory therapists in his clinic. The author of the article said that the "best way to improve performance is to make your workers happy." Scott was glad to have read this and made a pledge to himself to start doing a much better job of making workers happy. But should Scott follow this advice? What do we know about the relationship between job satisfaction and performance, and how can this apply to the performance problems at Scott's clinic?

Management **S**kills and **C**ompetencies

Back to Yourself: Ambition

People are different; personal styles vary in the way we work, in how we relate to others, and even in how we view ourselves. One of the differences you might observe when interacting with other people is in **ambition**, or the desire to succeed and reach for high goals. Ambition is one of those traits that can certainly have a big impact on individual behavior. As discussed in the chapter opener, it is evident in how we act and what we try to achieve at work, at home, and in leisure pursuits. The more we understand ambition in our lives, and the more we understand how personality traits like those in the Big Five model, the Myers-Briggs Type Indicator, and others influence our behavior, the more successful we're likely to be in accomplishing our goals and helping others do the same. After you complete the following self-assessment on Internal/External Control, don't forget to go online to take the Stress Self-Test.

> Someone's **ambition** reflects a desire to achieve or to accomplish something. It comes out in personality as competitiveness and desire to be the best at something.

Further Reflection: Internal/External Control

Instructions

Circle either (a) or (b) to indicate the item you most agree with in each pair of the following statements.[73]

1. (a) Promotions are earned through hard work and persistence.
   (b) Making a lot of money is largely a matter of breaks.
2. (a) Many times the reactions of teachers seem haphazard to me.
   (b) In my experience there is usually a direct connection between how hard I study and grades I get.
3. (a) The number of divorces indicates more and more people are not trying to make their marriages work.
   (b) Marriage is largely a gamble.
4. (a) It is silly to think that one can really change another person's basic attitudes.
   (b) When I am right, I can convince others.
5. (a) Getting promoted is really a matter of being a little luckier than the next guy.
   (b) In our society an individual's future earning power is dependent on his or her ability.
6. (a) If one knows how to deal with people, they are really quite easily led.
   (b) I have little influence over the way other people behave.
7. (a) In my case, the grades I make are the result of my own efforts; luck has little or nothing to do with it.
   (b) Sometimes I feel that I have little to do with the grades I get.
8. (a) People like me can change the course of world affairs if we make ourselves heard.
   (b) It is only wishful thinking to believe that one can really influence what happens in society at large.
9. (a) Much of what happens to me is probably a matter of chance.
   (b) I am the master of my fate.
10. (a) Getting along with people is a skill that must be practiced.
    (b) It is almost impossible to figure out how to please some people.

Scoring

Give yourself 1 point for 1a, 2b, 3a, 4b, 5b, 6a, 7a, 8a, 9b, 10a.

- 8–10 = high *internal* locus of control
- 6–7 = moderate *internal* locus of control
- 5 = mixed locus of control
- 3–4 = moderate *external* locus of control

Interpretation

This instrument offers an impression of your tendency toward an internal locus of control or an external locus of control. Persons with a high internal locus of control tend to believe they have control over their own destinies. They may appreciate opportunities for greater self-control at the workplace. Persons with a high external locus of control tend to believe that what happens to them is largely in the hands of external people or forces. They may be less comfortable with self-control and more responsive to external controls at work.

Team Exercise

Job Satisfaction Preferences

Preparation

Rank the following items for how important (1 = least important to 9 = most important) they are to your future job satisfaction.[74]

My job will be satisfying when it—

(a)   is respected by other people.

(b)   encourages continued development of knowledge and skills.

(c)   provides job security.

(d)   provides a feeling of accomplishment.

(e)   provides the opportunity to earn a high income.

(f)   is intellectually stimulating.

(g)   rewards good performance with recognition.

(h)   provides comfortable working conditions.

(i)   permits advancement to high administrative responsibility.

Instructions

Form into groups as designated by your instructor. Within each group, the men should develop a consensus ranking of the items as they think women ranked them. The reasons for the rankings should be shared and discussed so they are clear to everyone. The women in the group should not participate in this ranking task. They should listen to the discussion and be prepared to comment later in class discussions. A spokesperson for the men in the group should share the group's rankings with the class.

Optional Instructions

Form into groups consisting entirely of men or women. Each group should meet and decide which of the work values members of the opposite sex will rank first. Do this again for the work value ranked last. The reasons should be discussed, along with the reasons why each of the other values probably was not ranked first or last. A spokesperson for each group should share group results with the rest of the class.

Case Study: Facebook

Go to *Management Cases for Critical Thinking* to find the recommended case for Chapter 14– "Facebook: It's Not Just for Kids."

Motivation Theory and Practice

Chapter 15 Study Questions

1 How do individual needs influence motivation?

2 What are the process theories of motivation?

3 What role does reinforcement play in motivation?

What is the link between job design and motivation?

Learning From Others

Make People Your Top Priority

After 13 years being voted as one of *Fortune* magazine's "Best Companies to Work For," SAS, headquartered in North Carolina and the world's largest privately owned software firm, hit the number one spot in 2010. Just picture what it's like to be one of SAS's 4000+ headquarters employees.

> Typical workweek of 35 hours; no one monitors what time you show up; an in-house masseur is available for a fee at the company's fitness center; two SAS-owned day-care centers are on the premises; you can get dry cleaning, car detailing, and haircuts on site; and work–life or wellness centers provide everything from workout rooms to special programs in weight management to counseling on family issues.

Unlike other top high-tech names like Google, SAS offers no stock options and isn't even considered a top payer of its talent. Many wonder if all the pampering makes up for the lack of outright financial incentives. CEO Jim Goodnight, shown here, certainly thinks so. He's the brains behind SAS's unique culture and its emphasis on treating employees well, giving them freedom and support, and trusting them to act as responsible adults.

"My chief assets walk out the door every day," Goodnight says. "My job is to make sure they come back." And come back they do. The average employee turnover rate in the industry is 22% annually; SAS's is 2%. When the firm advertises a job opening, it expects to get at least 100 resumes. And when it comes to performance, SAS employee Bev Brown says: "Some may think that because SAS is family-friendly and has great benefits that we don't work hard, but people do work hard here because they're motivated to care for a company that takes care of them."

The SAS culture created and led by Goodnight emphasizes work–life balance, flexibility, and trust. He believes that more organizations should be run this way, investing in employees and giving them lots of work–life choices. "Contented cows give more milk," he says. "I'd rather spend the money on my employees than send it to Washington."[1]

do the benchmarking

What is it about SAS as an organization and Goodnight as a leader that might be inspiring to employees? Is it possible that organizations that really do "put people first", respect their needs and treat them as adults, will have highly motivated employees? **Who are the best employers in your community, and what do they do different from the "also ran's"?**

Learning About Yourself

Engagement

One of the hot topics in management these days is **engagement.** You might think of it in terms of personal initiative and willingness to "go the extra mile" in your work. According to Tim Galbraith, vice president of people development at Yum Brands, Inc., "A person who's truly engaged says 'I'm willing to give a little bit more; I'm willing to help my team member when I see they're in need.'"

The Conference Board, in reviewing the literature on engagement, defined it as "a heightened emotional connection" with the organization that influences an employee to "exert greater discretionary effort in his or her work." The report also describes the positive impact of engagement as greater retention, lower turnover, higher productivity, more loyalty to the employer, and better customer service.[2]

Engagement varies greatly among people at work, just as it does among students. Consider your experiences with airline travel. How well have you been taken care of by service workers when a plane is delayed, your bag is overweight, or your luggage is lost? Airline executives complain a lot about rising costs and falling profits; passengers also do lots of complaining about poor service.

Signs of High Engagement
• Willing to look for problems and fix them
• Willing to do more than just meeting job requirements
• Willing to stay late, start early, do the "extras"
• Willing to help others who are stuck or overwhelmed
• Willing to do things better; not accept the status quo
• Willing to think ahead, craft ideas, and plans for future

A book on the airline industry, *Up in the Air: How the Airlines Can Improve Performance by Engaging Their Employees*, makes the point that "a high level of engagement and a good labor relations system are the keys to increasing productivity and service quality." When the authors talk about engagement they link it to service workers' willingness "to use discretionary effort to solve problems for us as passengers." They further suggest that unlocking the powers of employee engagement requires two things: authority to act given from the company side and motivation shown on the worker side.[3]

In the technology industry, research shows that software programmers are up to 20% more efficient when they are allowed to spend part of their time working on job-related problems of their choice. Author Daniel Pink, in his book *Drive: The Surprising Truth about What Motivates Us*, argues that such results stem from intrinsic motivation that is unlocked when people are given autonomy and see purpose in their work; in other words, they find a sense of high engagement.[4]

get to know yourself better

How many signs of high engagement, shown in the box, apply to you—consistently and predictably? Draw up a set of examples that show you in "high-engagement situations" at work or school. Write a short description of the types of jobs and job settings that can bring out the best from you in terms of work engagement. **Also complete the end-of-chapter Student Engagement Survey to assess how your behavior as a student might reflect on your potential work with high engagement in your career.**

15 Motivation Theory and Practice

Study Question 1	Study Question 2	Study Question 3	Study Question 4
Individual Needs and Motivation	**Process Theories of Motivation**	**Reinforcement Theory**	**Motivation and Job Design**
• Hierarchy of needs theory • ERG theory • Two-factor theory • Acquired needs theory	• Equity theory • Expectancy theory • Goal-setting theory • Self-efficacy theory	• Reinforcement strategies • Positive reinforcement • Punishment	• Job simplification • Job rotation and job enlargement • Job enrichment • Alternative work schedules
Learning Check 1	**Learning Check 2**	**Learning Check 3**	**Learning Check 4**

D id you know that J. K. Rowling's first *Harry Potter* book was rejected by 12 publishers; that their "sound" cost the Beatles a deal with Decca Records; and that Walt Disney once lost a newspaper job because he supposedly "lacked imagination"?[5] Thank goodness they didn't give up. In fact, we might say that their "motivation" to stay engaged and confident with their work paid off handsomely—to them and to those who have enjoyed the fruits of their labors.

Why do some people work enthusiastically, persevere in the face of difficulty and often do more than required to turn out an extraordinary performance? Why do others hold back, quit at the first negative feedback, and do the minimum needed to avoid reprimand or termination? What can be done to ensure that the best possible performance is achieved by every person, in every job, on every workday?

Good answers to the prior questions begin with the discussion of engagement raised in the chapter opener. Studies show that as many as 17+% of U.S. workers report themselves as "disengaged" on any given workday; that up to 40% of workers say that they have trouble staying motivated; and that 25% of American employers believe their workers have low morale on the job.[6] Especially in times like these, when lots of organizations are running on reduced workforces and tight budgets, what can managers do to engage and motivate employees?[7]

INDIVIDUAL NEEDS AND MOTIVATION

● **Motivation** accounts for the level, direction, and persistence of effort expended at work.

The term **motivation** describes forces within the individual that account for the level, direction, and persistence of effort expended at work. Simply put, a highly motivated person works hard at a job while an unmotivated person does not. And, a manager who leads through motivation does so by creating conditions under which other people feel consistently inspired to work hard.

● A **need** is an unfulfilled physiological or psychological desire.

Most discussions of motivation begin with the concept of individual **needs**—the unfulfilled physiological or psychological desires of an individual. Although each of the following theories discusses a slightly different set of needs, all agree that needs cause tensions that influence attitudes and behavior. Their advice to managers is to help people satisfy important needs through their work, and try to eliminate obstacles that block need satisfaction.

HIERARCHY OF NEEDS THEORY

The theory of human needs developed by Abraham Maslow was introduced in Chapter 2 as an important foundation of the history of management thought. By

What satisfies higher-order needs?

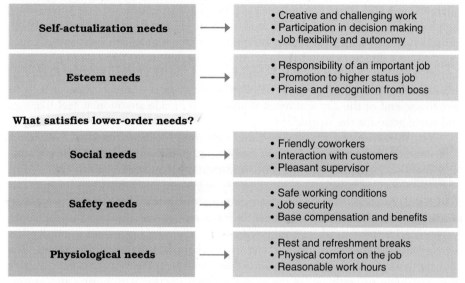

FIGURE 15.1 Opportunities for satisfaction in Maslow's hierarchy of human needs.

way of quick review, **lower-order needs** in his hierarchy include physiological, safety, and social concerns, and **higher-order needs** include esteem and self-actualization concerns.[8] Whereas lower-order needs are desires for social and physical well-being, the higher-order needs are desires for psychological development and growth.

Maslow uses two principles to describe how these needs affect human behavior. The **deficit principle** states that a satisfied need is not a motivator of behavior. People are expected to act in ways that satisfy deprived needs—that is, needs for which a "deficit" exists. The **progression principle** states that a need at one level does not become activated until the next-lower-level need is already satisfied. People are expected to advance step by step up the hierarchy in their search for need satisfactions. This principle ends at the level of self-actualization; the more these needs are satisfied, the stronger they are supposed to grow.

Figure 15.1 illustrates how managers can use Maslow's ideas to better meet the needs of the people with whom they work. Notice that higher-order self-actualization needs are served by things like creative and challenging work, and job autonomy; esteem needs are served by respect, responsibility, praise, and recognition. The satisfaction of lower-order social, safety, and physiological needs rests more with conditions of the work environment, such as compensation and benefits. A Harris interactive survey of American workers showed that the top two most valued benefits are health insurance and employer-matched 401(K) investments. And, 78% of respondents said that better benefits would increase their work motivation.[9]

- **Lower-order needs** are physiological, safety, and social needs in Maslow's hierarchy.

- **Higher-order** needs are esteem and self-actualization needs in Maslow's hierarchy.

- The **deficit principle** states that a satisfied need does not motivate behavior.

- The **progression principle** states that a need isn't activated until the next lower-level need is satisfied.

ERG THEORY

One of the most promising efforts to build on Maslow's work is the ERG theory proposed by Clayton Alderfer.[10] This theory collapses Maslow's five needs categories into three. **Existence needs** are desires for physiological and material well-being. **Relatedness needs** are desires for satisfying interpersonal relationships. **Growth needs** are desires for continued psychological growth and development.

Growth needs are essentially the higher-order needs in Maslow's hierarchy. They are evident in the following examples of motivated individuals doing

- **Existence needs** are desires for physical well-being.

- **Relatedness needs** are desires for good interpersonal relationships.

- **Growth needs** are desires for personal growth and development.

volunteer and nonprofit work. During the recession, Laine Seator lost her management job and started volunteering. She claims her time is well spent; she's helping others and is also gaining new skills in grant writing and strategic planning that should help with future job hunting. "In a regular job," she says, "you'd need to be a director or management staff to be able to do these types of things, but on a volunteer basis they welcome the help." As a United Way volunteer in Boise, Idaho, Rick Overton says: "It's hard to describe how much better it feels to get to the end of the day and, even if you haven't made any money, feel like you did some good for the world."[11]

● The **frustration-regression principle** states that an already satisfied need can become reactivated when a higher-level need is blocked.

The dynamics of ERG theory differ a bit from Maslow's thinking. ERG does not assume that certain needs must be satisfied before other needs become activated; any or all needs can influence individual behavior at a given time. Also, Alderfer does not believe that satisfied needs lose their motivational impact. His ERG theory contains a **frustration-regression principle**, through which an already satisfied lower-level need can become reactivated and influence behavior when a higher-level need cannot be satisfied. It might be argued, for example, that when labor unions representing factory workers bargain hard for things like shorter work weeks and better working conditions (responsive to existence needs), they are doing so partly out of the workers' dissatisfaction with boring and simplified jobs (frustrated growth needs).

TWO-FACTOR THEORY

Frederick Herzberg developed the two-factor theory of motivation from a pattern discovered in almost 4,000 interviews.[12] When asked what "turned them on" about their work, respondents talked mostly about things relating to the nature of the job itself. Herzberg calls these **satisfier factors**. When asked what "turned them off," they talked more about things relating to the work setting. Herzberg calls these **hygiene factors**. As shown in Figure 15.2, Herzberg suggests that these two-factors affect people in different ways.

● A **satisfier factor** is found in job content, such as a sense of achievement, recognition, responsibility, advancement, or personal growth.

● A **hygiene factor** is found in the job context, such as working conditions, interpersonal relations, organizational policies, and salary.

Hygiene factors are linked with job dissatisfaction. That is, job dissatisfaction goes up as hygiene quality goes down. The hygiene factors are found in the job context and include such things as working conditions, interpersonal relations, organizational policies and administration, technical quality of supervision, and base wage or salary. Herzberg argues that making improvements in these factors, such as by adding piped-in music or implementing a no-smoking policy, can make people less dissatisfied at work. But, it will not increase job satisfaction and motivation.

Satisfier factors, sometimes called motivator factors, are linked with job satisfaction. They include a sense of achievement, feelings of recognition, a sense of responsibility, the opportunity for advancement, and feelings of personal growth.

Herzberg believes that the more satisfier factors there are in job content, the higher the motivation to work, due to opportunities for high-order need satisfactions. To build such high content jobs, Herzberg suggests using the technique of *job enrichment*. It largely makes the job holder responsible for not just doing the work, but also planning and controlling its accomplishment. This job design technique will be discussed in more detail later in the chapter.

Scholars have criticized Herzberg's theory as being method-bound and difficult to replicate.[13] For his part, Herzberg

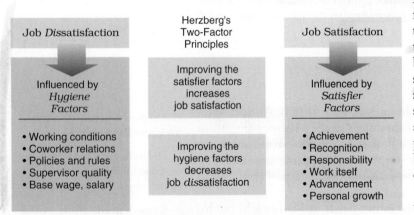

FIGURE 15.2 Elements in Herzberg's two-factor theory.

reports confirming studies around the world.[14] At the very least, the two-factor theory remains a useful reminder that all jobs have two important aspects: *job content*—what people do in terms of job tasks; and *job context*—the work setting in which they do it. And Herzberg's advice to managers makes good sense: (1) always correct poor job context to eliminate potential job dissatisfaction; and (2) be sure to build satisfier factors into job content to maximize job satisfaction.

ACQUIRED NEEDS THEORY

Another approach to human needs was developed by David McClelland and his colleagues. They began by asking people to view pictures and write stories about what they see.[15] The stories were then content-analyzed for themes that display the strengths of three needs—achievement, power, and affiliation. According to McClelland, people acquire or develop these needs over time as a result of individual life experiences. Because each need can be linked with a distinct set of work preferences, he encourages managers to understand these needs in themselves and in others, and try to create work environments responsive to them.

Need for achievement is the desire to do something better or more efficiently, to solve problems, or to master complex tasks. People with a high need for achievement like to put their competencies to work; they take moderate risks in competitive situations, and they are willing to work alone. As a result, the work preferences of high-need achievers include individual responsibility for results, achievable but challenging goals, and feedback on performance.

Need for power is the desire to control other people, to influence their behavior, or to be responsible for them. People with a high need for power are motivated to behave in ways that have a clear impact on other people and events. They enjoy being in control of a situation and being recognized for this responsibility. Importantly, though, McClelland distinguishes between two forms of the power need. The *need for personal power* is exploitative and involves manipulation for the pure sake of personal gratification. This type of power need is not successful in management. The *need for social power* involves the use of power in a socially responsible way, one that is directed toward group or organizational objectives rather than personal gains. This need for social power is essential to managerial leadership.

Need for affiliation is the desire to establish and maintain friendly and warm relations with other people. People with a high need for affiliation seek companionship, social approval, and satisfying interpersonal relationships. They tend to

● **Need for achievement** is the desire to do something better, to solve problems, or to master complex tasks.

Work Preferences of High-Need Achievers

- Challenging but achievable goals
- Feedback on performance
- Individual responsibility

● **Need for power** is the desire to control, influence, or be responsible for other people.

● **Need for affiliation** is the desire to establish and maintain good relations with people.

"Thank Yous" Motivate at Rockwell Collins

With monies for raises scarce, managers are seeking alternative ways to reward employees for extra work. Jenny Miller supervises 170 engineers at Rockwell Collins where the recession resulted in 1,600 lost jobs and a 15% increase in workload for those remaining. She uses $100 gift cards to reward those who volunteer to work holidays and weekends. The firm's vice president Steve Nieuwsma says that without the ability to give pay raises, gift cards are valued. "It's not so much the money," he says, but that employees know that someone "walked up to them and said, 'Thank you, you did a good job'."

like jobs that involve working with people and bring opportunities to receive social approval. This is consistent with managerial work. But, McClelland believes that managers must be careful that high needs for affiliation don't interfere with decision making. There are times when managers and leaders must decide and act in ways that other persons may disagree with. If the need for affiliation limits someone's ability to make these decisions, managerial effectiveness gets lost. The successful executive in McClelland's view is likely to possess a high need for social power that is greater than an otherwise strong need for affiliation.

Learning Check

Study Question 1

How do individual needs influence motivation?

Be sure you can ☑ define *motivation* and *needs* ☑ describe work practices that satisfy higher-order and lower-order needs in Maslow's hierarchy ☑ contrast Maslow's hierarchy with ERG theory ☑ describe work practices that influence hygiene factors and satisfier factors in Herzberg's two-factor theory ☑ explain McClelland's needs for achievement, affiliation, and power ☑ describe work conditions that satisfy a person with a high need for achievement

---

PROCESS THEORIES OF MOTIVATION

Although the details vary, each of the needs theories offers insights on individual differences and on how managers can deal positively with them. Another set of motivation theories, the process theories, add further to this understanding. They include the equity, expectancy, goal-setting, and self-efficacy theories.

EQUITY THEORY

What do you think when you hear or read news stories like these? In a year when retailer Abercrombie & Fitch's stock declined 79% in value and 9% of employees lost their jobs, CEO Michael Jeffries's pay went up 39%.[16] In 1965 the average CEO pay was 24 times that of the average worker; in 1994 it was 90 times; by 2006 it was 364 times. CEOs in America make 13 times more than their counterparts in other advanced countries.[17] "Equity" and "fairness" are probably two of the first words that come to mind.

The equity theory of motivation is best known through the work of J. Stacy Adams.[18] The theory is based on the logic of social comparisons and the notion that perceived inequity is a motivating state. In respect to pay and the prior examples, the equity question is: "In comparison with others, how fairly am I being compensated for the work that I do?" Equity theory holds that when people believe that they have been unfairly treated in comparison to others, they will be motivated to eliminate the discomfort and restore a sense of perceived equity to the situation.

Equity and Social Comparison

Figure 15.3 shows how the equity dynamic works. Perceived inequities occur whenever people feel that the rewards received for their work efforts are unfair, given the rewards others appear to be getting. Equity comparisons are especially common whenever managers allocate things such as pay raises, vacation schedules, preferred job assignments, work privileges, and office space. And, equity comparisons may be with coworkers, workers elsewhere in the organization, and even persons employed by other organizations.

A key point in the equity theory is that people behave according to their perceptions. What influences individual behavior is not the reward's absolute value or the manager's intentions; the recipient's perceptions determine the motivational outcomes. An individual who perceives that she or he is being treated unfairly in

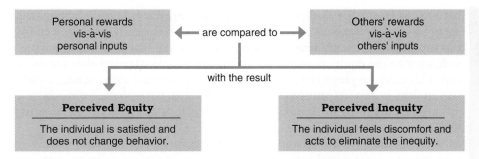

FIGURE 15.3 Equity theory and the role of social comparison.

comparison to others will be motivated to act in ways that reduce the perceived inequity. For example, when *perceived negative inequity* exists, Adams predicts that people will try to deal with it by:

- Changing their work inputs by putting less effort into their jobs—"If that's all I'm going to get, I'm going to do a lot less."
- Changing the rewards received by asking for better treatment—"Next stop, the boss's office; I should get what I deserve."
- Changing the comparison points to make things seem better—"Well, if I look at Marissa's situation, I'm still pretty well off."
- Changing the situation by leaving the job—"No way I'm going to stick around here if this is the way you get treated."

Equity Dynamics and Insights

Research on equity theory has largely been accomplished in the laboratory. It is most conclusive with respect to perceived negative inequity. Those who feel

Real Ethics

Information Goldmine Creates Equity Dilemma

A worker opens the top of the office photocopier and finds a document someone has left behind. It's a list of performance evaluations, pay, and bonuses for 80 coworkers.

She reads the document.

Lo and behold, someone considered a "nonstarter" by peers is getting paid more than others regarded as "super workers." New hires are being brought in at substantially higher pay and bonuses than are paid to existing staff.

And to make matters worse, she's in the middle of the list, not near the top where she would expect to be. She makes a lot less money than some others are getting.

Looking at the data, the worker wonders why she is spending extra hours on her laptop evenings and weekends at home, trying to do a really great job for the firm. The thought occurs to her—Why don't I pass this information around anonymously so that everyone knows what's going on? But then she asks—Or, should I just quit and find another employer who fully values me for my talents and hard work?

You Decide

What would you do? Would you hit "print," make about 80 copies, and then put them in everyone's mailboxes? That

would get the gossip chain started quickly. But would it be the right thing to do? What are the ethical issues that need to be considered?

In the real case, the worker decided to quit, saying: "I just couldn't stand the inequity." She also decided not to distribute the information to others in the office. "I couldn't give it to people who were still working there because it would make them depressed, like it made me depressed," she said. Okay, but is it wrong to withhold information from others, leaving them uninformed but treated inequitably?

they are underpaid, for example, may try to restore perceived equity by pursuing one or more of the actions described in the prior list, such as reducing work efforts to compensate for the missing rewards or even quitting the job.[19] There is also evidence that the equity dynamic occurs among people who feel they are over-paid. This time the perceived positive inequity is associated with a sense of guilt. The attempt to restore perceived equity may involve, for example, increasing the quantity or quality of work, taking on more difficult assignments, or working overtime.

Although no clear answers are available in equity theory, there are some very good insights. Managers should probably anticipate perceived negative inequities whenever especially visible rewards such as pay or promotions are allocated. One way of dealing with them is to try and manage perceptions. This might involve carefully communicating the intended value of rewards being given, clarifying the perform-ance appraisals on which they are based, and suggesting appropriate comparison points. This advice is especially relevant in organizations using merit-based pay-for-performance systems. The problem in these systems is that what constitutes "meri-torious" performance can be a source of considerable debate. Any disagreement over performance ratings makes problems due to negative equity dynamics more likely.

EXPECTANCY THEORY

Victor Vroom's expectancy theory of motivation asks the question: What deter-mines the willingness of an individual to work hard at tasks important to the organ-ization?[20] The theory answers that "people will do what they can do when they want to do it." More specifically, Vroom suggests that a person's motivation to

Real People

Pat Christen Fights Disease with Motivating Video Game

While many teens play video games just for fun, teens with cancer can now play a video game that can help them beat the disease. Picture a teenager dealing with the chal-lenges of cancer treatment and overwhelmed by trying to keep up with his medication schedules. Now picture him playing the video game Re-Mission and maneuvering a nanobot by the name of Roxxi through the body of a cancer patient to destroy cancer cells. Think also about an article in the med-ical journal *Pediatrics* reporting that patients who play the game at least one hour a week do a better job of holding to their medication schedules.

Roxxi is the brainchild of HopeLab, a nonprofit led by president and CEO Pat Christen with the mission of combining "rigorous research with innovative solutions to improve the health and quality of life of young people with chronic illness." The nonprofit was founded by Pam Omidyar, who as an im-munology researcher and gaming enthusiast saw the possible

link between games and fighting disease. The idea behind Re-Mission is to motivate kids to take their medications consis-tently, understand more about the disease, and keep their can-cer in remission.

Christen came to HopeLab after 20 years of nonprofit management experience, and focuses on strategic manage-ment and business development. Her goal is to keep finding innovative ways to improve the lives of young people fighting illnesses. Her previous positions included president and exec-utive director of the San Francisco AIDS Foundation and pres-ident of the Pangaea Global AIDS Foundation. In the latter capacity she helped found a state-of-the-art AIDS clinic and research center in Uganda. Her career began in Kenya, East Africa, where she served as a Peace Corps volunteer after graduating from Stanford University.

Re-Mission is one positive step in the war against child-hood cancer. With the founding vision of Pam Omidyar and the strategic leadership of Pam Christen, HopeLab received the Social Enterprise Award of the Year from *Fast Company* mag-azine. One of its current priorities is to unleash the power of video gaming to help in the fight against childhood obesity.

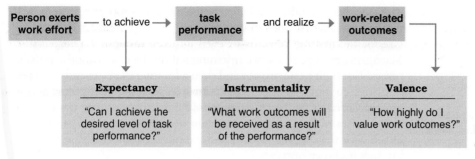

FIGURE 15.4 Elements in the expectancy theory of motivation.

work depends on the relationships between three expectancy factors depicted in Figure 15.4 and described here:

- **Expectancy**—a person's belief that working hard will result in a desired level of task performance being achieved (this is sometimes called effort-performance expectancy).
- **Instrumentality**—a person's belief that successful performance will be followed by rewards and other work-related outcomes (this is sometimes called performance-outcome expectancy).
- **Valence**—the value a person assigns to the possible rewards and other work-related outcomes.

> **Expectancy** is a person's belief that working hard will result in high task performance.

> **Instrumentality** is a person's belief that various outcomes will occur as a result of task performance.

> **Valence** is the value a person assigns to work-related outcomes.

Motivation = Expectancy × Instrumentality × Valence

In the expectancy theory, motivation (M), expectancy (E), instrumentality (I), and valence (V) are related to one another in a multiplicative fashion: that is, $M = E \times I \times V$. In other words, motivation is determined by expectancy times instrumentality times valence. Mathematically speaking, a zero at any location on the right side of the equation (that is, for E, I, or V) will result in zero motivation. In practice, this means that all three factors must be high and positive for motivation to also be high.[21]

Suppose, for example, that a manager is wondering whether or not the prospect of earning a promotion will be motivational to a job holder. Expectancy theory predicts that a person's motivation to work hard for a promotion will be low if any one or more of the following three conditions apply. First, if expectancy is low, motivation will suffer. This is the "If I try hard will I succeed?" question. The person may not believe that he or she can achieve the performance level necessary to get promoted. So why try? Second, if instrumentality is low, motivation will suffer. This is the "If I succeed will I be rewarded?" question. The person may lack confidence that a high level of task performance will result in being promoted. So why try? Third, if valence is low, motivation will suffer. This is the "What does the reward for this hard work and performance achievement mean to me?" question. The person may place little value on receiving a promotion; it simply isn't much of a reward. So, once again, why try?

Expectancy Theory Applications

Expectancy theory reminds managers that different people answer the question "Why should I work hard today?" in different ways. Every person deserves to be respected as an individual with unique needs, preferences, and concerns. Knowing this, a manager can try to customize work environments so that expectancies, instrumentalities, and valences all support motivation.

To maximize expectancy people must believe in their abilities. They must believe that if they try, they can perform. Managers can build positive expectancies by selecting workers with the right abilities for the jobs to be done, providing them

Managing by Expectancy Theory

Create high expectancies—select capable workers, train them well, support them with goals and resources

Create high instrumentalities—clarify rewards earned by performance, give rewards on performance-contingent basis

Create positive valences—identify individual needs, offer rewards that satisfy these needs

with the best training and development, and supporting them with resources so that the jobs can be done very well. *To maximize instrumentality people must see the link between high performance and work outcomes.* Managers can create positive instrumentalities by clarifying the possible rewards for high performance and then allocating these rewards on a performance-contingent basis. *To maximize positive valence people must value the outcomes associated with high performance.* Here, managers can use the content theories to help identify important needs. These needs can then be linked with rewards that create positive valences and that can be earned through high performance.

GOAL-SETTING THEORY

Steven A. Davis rose through a variety of management jobs to become CEO of Bob Evans Farms in Columbus, Ohio.[22] When he was a child, he got a lot of encouragement from his parents: "They never said that because you are an African-American, you can only go this far or do only this or that," he says, "they just said 'go for it'." Davis also says that when he graduated from college he set goals—to be a corporate vice president in 10 years and a president in 20. Using expectancy theory, Victor Vroom would point out that Davis's parents increased his motivation by creating high positive expectancy during his school years. Using goal-setting theory, Edwin Locke would add that Davis found lots of motivation through the goals he set as a college graduate.

Goal-Setting Essentials

> ## *Management Smarts 15.1*
>
> ### How to make goal setting work for you
>
> - *Set specific goals:* They lead to higher performance than do more generally stated ones, such as "do your best."
>
> - *Set challenging goals:* When viewed as realistic and attainable, more difficult goals lead to higher performance than do easy goals.
>
> - *Build goal acceptance and commitment:* People work harder for goals they accept and believe in; they resist goals forced on them.
>
> - *Clarify goal priorities:* Make sure that expectations are clear as to which goals should be accomplished first, and why.
>
> - *Provide feedback on goal accomplishment:* Make sure that people know how well they are doing with respect to goal accomplishment.
>
> - *Reward goal accomplishment:* Don't let positive accomplishments pass unnoticed; reward people for doing what they set out to do.

The basic premise of Locke's goal-setting theory is that task goals can be highly motivating if they are properly set and if they are well managed.[23] Goals give direction to people in their work. Goals clarify the performance expectations in supervisory relationships, between coworkers, and across subunits in an organization. Goals establish a frame of reference for task feedback. Goals also set a foundation for behavioral self-management. In these and related ways, goal setting can enhance individual work performance and job satisfaction.

To achieve the motivational benefits of goal setting, research by Locke and his associates indicates that managers and team leaders must work with themselves and others to set the right goals in the right ways. Things such as goal specificity, goal difficulty, goal acceptance, and goal commitment are among the goal-setting recommendations provided in Management Smarts 15.1.

Goal Setting and Participation

Participation is often a key to unlocking the motivational power of task goals. The concept of goal alignment as described in Chapter 8 is a good example. When team members communicate well with team leaders in a participative process of goal setting and performance review, members are likely to experience greater motivation. The participation increases understanding of specific and difficult task goals, and increases acceptance and commitment to them. The opportunity to receive feedback on goal accomplishment also adds to the motivational impact of goal alignment practices.

Managers should be aware of the participation options in goal setting. It isn't always possible to allow participation when selecting which goals need to be pursued. But it can be possible to allow participation in deciding how to best pursue them. Also, the constraints of time and other factors in some situations may not allow for participation. But, Locke's research suggests that workers will respond positively to externally imposed goals if supervisors assigning them are trusted and if workers believe they will be adequately supported in their attempts to achieve them.

SELF-EFFICACY THEORY

Closely related to both the expectancy and goal-setting approaches to motivation is self-efficacy theory, also referred to as social learning theory. Based on the work

Research Brief

Positive Psychological Capital Is an Important Influence on Performance and Satisfaction

A concept known as PsyCap, or psychological capital, is defined by Fred Luthans and his colleagues as "an individual's positive psychological state of development." This positive state is composed of (1) high personal confidence and self-efficacy in working on a task, (2) optimism about present and future success, (3) hope and perseverance in pursuing goals and adjusting them as needed, and (4) resiliency in responding to setbacks and problems.

A briefings report from the Gallup Leadership Institute points out that psychological capital deals with "who you are" and "who you are becoming." This is contrasted with human capital ("what you know") and social capital ("who you know"). The report also summarizes studies that address the measurement of PsyCap, and the impact of PsyCap on work attitudes and performance.

In samples of management students and managers, researchers report success with a training intervention designed to raise the level of PsyCap for participants. When performance measures were taken among the manager samples, increases in performance were associated with the PsyCap gains. In comparing the costs of the training intervention with the performance gains, the researchers calculated the return on investment as 270%. Overall conclusions for this stream of research are that the measurement of PsyCap is reliable and valid, and that PsyCap is positively related to individual performance and satisfaction.

You Be the Researcher

Does this concept of psychological capital make sense to you? Suppose you could rate others with whom you work or study on self-efficacy/confidence, optimism, hope, and resiliency. Is it reasonable to think that persons with high PsyCap will be more motivated and productive, whether we are talking about their work, academic performance, or approach to life overall?

Reference: "Psychological Capital (PsyCap) Measurement, Development, and Performance Impact," Briefings Report 2006–01 (Gallup Leadership Institute); and Fred Luthans, James B. Avey, Bruce J. Avolio, Steven M. Norman, and Gwendolyn M. Combs, "Psychological Capital Development: Toward a Micro-Intervention," *Journal of Organizational Behavior*, vol. 27 (2006), pp. 387–93.

● **Self-efficacy** is a person's belief that she or he is capable of performing a task.

of psychologist Albert Bandura, the notion of **self-efficacy** refers to a person's belief that she or he is capable of performing a task.[24] You can think of self-efficacy using such terms as confidence, competence, and ability. From a manager's perspective, the major point is that anything done to boost feelings of self-efficacy among people at work is likely to pay off with increased levels of motivation.

Mahatma Gandhi once said: "If I have the belief that I can do it, I shall surely acquire the capacity to do it, even if I may not have it at the beginning."[25] The essence of self-efficacy theory is that, when people believe themselves to be capable, they will be more motivated to work hard at a task. The *Wall Street Journal* has called this "the unshakable belief some people have that they have what it takes to succeed."[26] But self-efficacy is not an undifferentiated feeling of general confidence, it is a capability-specific belief in one's competency to perform a task.

There is a clear link between Bandura's ideas, elements of Vroom's expectancy theory, and Locke's goal-setting theory. With respect to Vroom, a person with higher self-efficacy will have higher expectancy that he or she can achieve a high level of task performance. With respect to Locke, a person with higher self-efficacy should be more willing to set challenging performance goals. In both respects, managers who help create feelings of self-efficacy in others should be boosting their motivation to work.

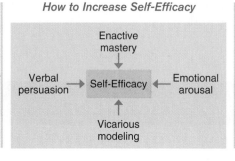

How to Increase Self-Efficacy

Bandura states that there are four major ways to enhance self-efficacy.[27] First is *enactive mastery*—when a person gains confidence through positive experience. The more you work at a task, so to speak, the more your experience builds and the more confident you become at doing it. Second is *vicarious modeling*—learning by observing others. When someone else is good at a task and we are able to observe how they do it, we gain confidence in being able to do it ourselves. Third is *verbal persuasion*—when someone tells us or encourages us that we can perform the task. Hearing others praise our efforts and link those efforts with performance successes is often very motivational. Fourth is *emotional arousal*—when we are highly stimulated or energized to perform well in a situation. A good analogy for arousal is how athletes get "psyched up" and highly motivated to perform in key competitions.

REINFORCEMENT THEORY

The motivation theories discussed so far are concerned with explaining "why" people do things in terms of satisfying needs, resolving felt inequities, evaluating expectancies, and pursuing task goals. Reinforcement theory, by contrast, views human behavior as determined by its environmental consequences. Instead of looking within the individual to explain motivation, this theory focuses on the external environment and its consequences.

● The **law of effect** states that behavior followed by pleasant consequences is likely to be repeated; behavior followed by unpleasant consequences is not.

The basic premises of reinforcement theory are based on what E. L. Thorndike called the **law of effect**. It states: Behavior that results in a pleasant outcome is likely to be repeated; behavior that results in an unpleasant outcome is not likely to be repeated.[28]

REINFORCEMENT STRATEGIES

Psychologist B. F. Skinner popularized the concept of **operant conditioning** as the process of applying the law of effect to control behavior by manipulating its consequences.[29] You may think of operant conditioning as learning by reinforcement. In management, the goal is to use reinforcement principles to systematically reinforce desirable work behavior and discourage undesirable work behavior.[30] The four strategies of reinforcement that can be used in operant conditioning are positive reinforcement, negative reinforcement, punishment, and extinction.

Positive reinforcement strengthens or increases the frequency of desirable behavior. It does so by making a pleasant consequence contingent on its occurrence. *Example*: A manager nods to express approval to someone who makes a useful comment during a staff meeting. **Negative reinforcement** also strengthens or increases the frequency of desirable behavior, but it does so by making the avoidance of an unpleasant consequence contingent on its occurrence. *Example*: A manager who has been nagging a worker every day about tardiness does not nag when the worker comes to work on time.

Punishment decreases the frequency of or eliminates an undesirable behavior. It does so by making an unpleasant consequence contingent on its occurrence. *Example*: A manager issues a written reprimand to an employee whose careless work is creating quality problems. **Extinction** also decreases the frequency of or eliminates an undesirable behavior, but does so by making the removal of a pleasant consequence contingent on its occurrence. *Example*: A manager observes that a disruptive employee is receiving social approval from coworkers; the manager counsels coworkers to stop giving this approval.

Figure 15.5 shows how the four reinforcement strategies can be used in management. The example applies the strategies to influence quality practices by employees. Note that both positive and negative reinforcement strategies strengthen desirable behavior when it occurs; punishment and extinction strategies weaken or eliminate undesirable behaviors.

- **Operant conditioning** is the control of behavior by manipulating its consequences.

- **Positive reinforcement** strengthens behavior by making a desirable consequence contingent on its occurrence.

- **Negative reinforcement** strengthens behavior by making the avoidance of an undesirable consequence contingent on its occurrence.

- **Punishment** discourages behavior by making an unpleasant consequence contingent on its occurrence.

- **Extinction** discourages behavior by making the removal of a desirable consequence contingent on its occurrence.

POSITIVE REINFORCEMENT

Positive reinforcement deserves special attention among the reinforcement strategies. It should be part of any manager's motivational tool kit. It should be part of our personal life strategies as well—as parents working with children, for example. Sir Richard Branson, well-known founder of Virgin Group, is a believer. "For the people who work for you or with you, you must lavish praise on them at all times," he says. "If a flower is watered, it flourishes. If not it shrivels up and dies." And

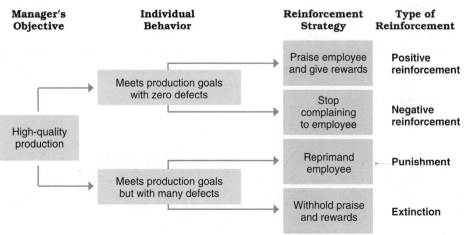

FIGURE 15.5 Four reinforcement strategies: case of total quality management.

● **Shaping** is positive reinforcement of successive approximations to the desired behavior.

● **Continuous reinforcement** rewards each time a desired behavior occurs.

● **Intermittent reinforcement** rewards behavior only periodically.

besides, he adds "It is much more fun looking for the best in people."[31] David Novak, CEO of Yum Brands, Inc., is also a believer. He claims that one of his most important tasks as CEO is "to get people fired up" and that "you can never underestimate the power of telling someone he's doing a good job."[32]

Guidelines for using positive reinforcement are presented in Management Smarts 15.2. One way to put it in action is through a process known as **shaping**. This is the creation of a new behavior by the positive reinforcement of successive approximations to it. A **continuous reinforcement** schedule administers a reward each time a desired behavior occurs. An **intermittent reinforcement** schedule rewards behavior only periodically. In general, continuous reinforcement works best to draw forth a desired behavior through shaping, while intermittent reinforcement works best to maintain it.

The power of positive reinforcement is governed by two important laws. First is the *law of contingent reinforcement*. It states that for a reward to have maximum reinforcing value, it must be delivered only if the desired behavior is exhibited. Second is the *law of immediate reinforcement*. It states that the more immediate the delivery of a reward after the occurrence of a desirable behavior, the greater the reinforcing value of the reward.

Rewards don't have to be large to achieve positive reinforcement effects. At the software firm Intuit, for example, Jennifer Lepird spent long hours over a several week period to complete a special project. When finished, her boss sent her an e-mail "thank you" note and a gift certificate. She said: "The fact that somebody took the time to recognize the effort just made the long hours melt away." Eric Mosley, founder and CEO of Globoforce, also gives frequent small awards as ways of recognizing performance. He says: "Even high earners can appreciate a small award if it is unexpected."[33]

PUNISHMENT

As a reinforcement strategy, punishment attempts to eliminate undesirable behavior by making an unpleasant consequence contingent on its occurrence. To punish an employee, for example, a manager may deny a valued reward—such as praise or merit pay, or administer an unpleasant outcome—such as a verbal reprimand or pay reduction. Like positive reinforcement, punishment can be done poorly or it can be done well. All too often, it is probably done both poorly and too frequently. Look at Management Smarts 15.3. It offers advice on how best to handle punishment as a reinforcement strategy.

☑ **Learning Check**
Study Question 3
What role does reinforcement play in motivation?

Be sure you can ☑ explain the law of effect and operant conditioning ☑ illustrate how positive reinforcement, negative reinforcement, punishment, and extinction influence work behavior ☑ explain the reinforcement technique of shaping ☑ describe how managers can use the laws of immediate and contingent reinforcement ☑ list guidelines for positive reinforcement and punishment

MOTIVATION AND JOB DESIGN

One area of practice in which the various motivation theories come into play is **job design**, the process of arranging work tasks for individuals and groups. Building jobs so that satisfaction and performance go hand in hand is in many ways an exercise in "fit" between task requirements and people's needs, capabilities, and interests.[34] Figure 15.6 shows how job designs vary in job scope and job depth to create the alternatives of job simplification, job rotation and enlargement, and job enrichment.

- **Job design** is arranging work tasks for individuals and groups.

JOB SIMPLIFICATION

A key aspect of Frederick Taylor's notion of scientific management, first discussed in Chapter 2 on the history of management thought, is the concept of **job simplification**.[35] It standardizes work procedures and employs people in well-defined and highly specialized tasks. The most extreme form of job simplification is **automation**, or the total mechanization of a job. One example is in manufacturing where robots are being used to perform tasks previously done by humans. Another is also evident each time you use an ATM machine; this technology is basically an automated replacement for a human teller.

Simplified jobs, such as those in classic automobile assembly lines, are narrow in *job scope*—that is, the number and variety of different tasks a person performs. The logic in using them is straightforward. Because the jobs don't require complex skills, workers should be easier and quicker to train, less difficult to supervise, and easy to replace if they leave. Because the tasks are well defined, workers should also become good at them by performing the same work over and over again.

Scholars Greg Oldham and J. Richard Hackman point out that the logic of using simplified jobs is to make people "just as interchangeable as standardized machine parts."[36] But, things don't always work out well in organizations using simplified job designs. The routine, structured, and repetitive tasks can cause problems if workers become bored and alienated. Productivity can go down when unhappy workers do poor work. And, costs can go up due to higher levels of absenteeism and turnover.

- **Job simplification** employs people in clearly defined and specialized tasks with narrow job scope.
- **Automation** is the total mechanization of a job.

JOB ROTATION AND JOB ENLARGEMENT

One step beyond simplification in job design is **job rotation**. This increases job scope by providing more task variety as workers periodically shift between jobs involving different task assignments. Job rotation can be done on a regular schedule such as every other day; it can also be done as opportunity or need exists. Also, it is often used as a training approach where people learn about jobs performed by others.

Another step up in job scope is **job enlargement**. This increases task variety by combining two or more tasks that were previously assigned to separate workers.

- **Job rotation** increases task variety by periodically shifting workers between different jobs.
- **Job enlargement** increases task variety by combining into one job two or more tasks previously done by separate workers.

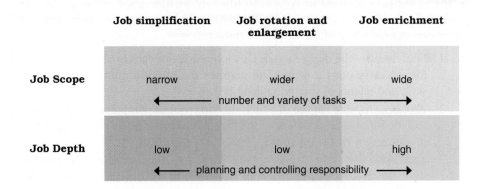

	Job simplification	Job rotation and enlargement	Job enrichment
Job Scope	narrow	wider	wide
	← number and variety of tasks →		
Job Depth	low	low	high
	← planning and controlling responsibility →		

FIGURE 15.6 Basic job design alternatives.

Quarterback Coach Goes from Assembly Line to Sideline

Ohio State's quarterback coach Mick Siciliano wasn't always destined for a career on the sidelines of big-time football. After struggling with college and facing some family hardships, he took a job with General Motors' Lordstown assembly plant for $19 an hour. "I wasn't crazy about school I have to admit," he says. "Then I went to work on the assembly line and, suddenly, I loved school." His career has certainly changed direction since then. But Siciliano respects his time in the factory, saying: "I know what it is to do a good day's work. . . . It makes you appreciate a lot of things."

Often these are tasks done immediately before or after the work performed in the original job. Job enlargement is sometimes called *horizontal loading*, which simply means making a job bigger by allowing the worker to do tasks from earlier and later stages in the workflow.

JOB ENRICHMENT

Frederick Herzberg, whose two-factor theory of motivation was discussed earlier, not only questions the motivational value of job simplification, he is also critical of job enlargement and rotation. "Why," he asks, "should a worker become motivated when one or more meaningless tasks are added to previously existing ones, or when work assignments are rotated among equally meaningless tasks?" By contrast, he says: "If you want people to do a good job, give them a good job to do."[37] Herzberg believes this is best done through **job enrichment** that expands job content and increases *job depth*—the extent to which planning and controlling duties are performed by the individual worker rather than the supervisor.

● **Job enrichment** increases job depth by adding work planning and evaluating duties normally performed by the supervisor.

Job Characteristics Model

Modern management theory takes job enrichment a step beyond Herzberg's suggestions. Most importantly, it adopts a contingency perspective and recognizes that job enrichment may not be good for everyone. This thinking is reflected in the job characteristics model developed by Hackman and Oldham and shown in Figure 15.7.[38]

The job characteristics models shows job satisfaction and performance influenced by three critical psychological states: (1) experienced meaningfulness of the work; (2) experienced responsibility for the outcomes of the work; and (3) knowledge of actual results of work activities. These, in turn, are influenced by the presence or absence of five core job characteristics.

1. *Skill variety*—the degree to which a job requires a variety of different activities to carry out the work, and involves the use of a number of different skills and talents of the individual.
2. *Task identity*—the degree to which the job requires completion of a "whole" and identifiable piece of work, one that involves doing a job from beginning to end with a visible outcome.
3. *Task significance*—the degree to which the job has a substantial impact on the lives or work of other people elsewhere in the organization, or in the external environment.

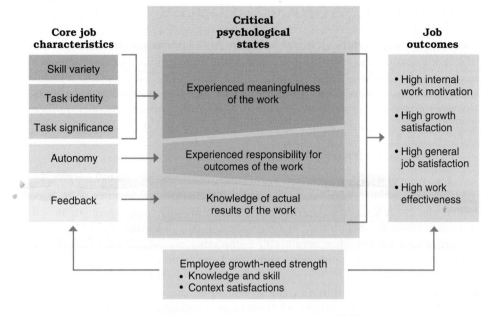

FIGURE 15.7 Designing jobs using the job characteristics model.

Source: Reprinted by permission from J. Richard Hackman and Greg R. Oldham, *Work Redesign* (Reading, MA: Addison-Wesley, 1980), p. 90.

4. *Autonomy*—the degree to which the job gives the individual freedom, independence, and discretion in scheduling work and in choosing procedures for carrying it out.

5. *Feedback from the job itself*—the degree to which work activities required by the job result in the individual obtaining direct and clear information on his or her performance.

A job that is high in these five core characteristics is considered enriched. The lower a job scores on these characteristics, the less enriched it is. But in true contingency fashion, an enriched job will not affect everyone in the same way. Generally speaking, people who respond most favorably to enriched jobs will have strong growth needs as described in Alderfer's ERG theory, appropriate job knowledge and skills, and be otherwise satisfied with job context. When people without these characteristics are given enriched jobs, there is a poor person-job fit and their satisfaction and performance may suffer.

Improving Job Characteristics

For those people and situations in which job enrichment is a good choice, Hackman and his colleagues recommend five ways to improve the core job characteristics. First, *form natural units of work*. Make sure that the tasks people perform are logically related to one another and provide a clear and meaningful task identity. Second, *combine tasks*. Expand job responsibilities by pulling together into one larger job a number of smaller tasks previously done by others. Third, *establish client relationships*. Put people in contact with others who, as clients inside or outside the organization, use the results of their work. Fourth, *open feedback channels*. Provide opportunities for people both to receive performance feedback as they work and to learn how performance changes over time. Fifth, *practice vertical loading* that gives people authority to perform the planning and controlling previously done by supervisors. In contrast to job enlargement and job rotation, which only make jobs bigger horizontally by expanding job scope, the small figure shows that job enrichment expands job depth to make jobs vertically bigger as well.

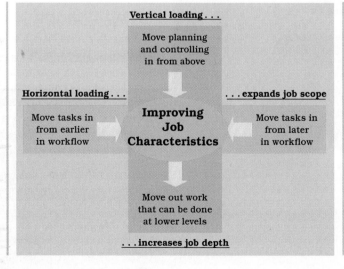

ALTERNATIVE WORK SCHEDULES

One thing learned from Herzberg's two-factor theory is that not only is the content of jobs important—the context is too. Among the more significant developments in managing job context is the emergence of alternative ways for people to schedule their work time.[39] "Flexibility" is the key word. Employers are finding that alternative work schedules can help attract and retain motivated workers by offering them flexibility to deal with the many complications of work–life balance.

Flexible Working Hours

● **Flexible working hours** give employees some choice in daily work hours.

The term **flexible working hours**, also called *flextime*, describes any work schedule that gives employees some choice in how to allocate their daily work hours. Flexible schedules of starting and ending times give employees greater autonomy while still meeting their work responsibilities. Some may choose to come in earlier and leave earlier, while still completing an 8-hour day; others may choose to start later in the morning and leave later. In between these extremes are opportunities to attend to personal affairs, such as dental appointments, home emergencies, visits to children's schools, and so on. Reports indicate that giving employees flexibility in dealing with their nonwork obligations reduces stress and lowers job turnover.[40] All top 100 companies in *Working Mother* magazine's list of best employers for working moms offer flexible scheduling.

Compressed Workweek

● A **compressed workweek** allows a full-time job to be completed in less than five days.

A **compressed workweek** is any work schedule that allows a full-time job to be completed in less than the standard five days of 8-hour shifts. Its most common form is the "4–40," that is, accomplishing 40 hours of work in four 10-hour days. A key feature of the 4–40 schedule is that the employee receives three consecutive days off from work each week. At USAA, a diversified financial services company that has been listed among the 100 best companies to work for in America, many employees are on a four-day schedule. Some work Monday through Thursday and others work Tuesday through Friday. Reported benefits of the compressed workweek include improved employee morale, lower overtime costs, less absenteeism, fewer days lost to sick leave, as well as lower costs of commuting.[41] Potential disadvantages of the compressed workweek include increased fatigue and family adjustment problems for the individual, as well as increased scheduling problems, possible customer complaints, and union objections.

Job Sharing

● **Job sharing** splits one job between two people.

Another alternative is **job sharing**, where one full-time job is split between two or more persons. This can be done on a variety of schedules, from half day to

Alternative Work Schedules Popular at Pitney Bowes

With changes in the economy, the mail service firm Pitney Bowes is increasing its already substantial commitment to alternative work schedules. The company uses online conference meetings to link employees working from remote sites and on flexible hours. Many workers are at the office only two days per week and spend another two days working from home and one day working from satellite locations. Carol Wallace, director of external communication, says: "It has worked out very well, people tend to get their weeks very organized."

weekly or monthly sharing arrangements. Organizations benefit by employing talented people who would otherwise be unable to work. A parent, for example, may be unable to stay away from home for a full workday, but may be able to work half a day. Job sharing allows two such persons to be employed as one, often to great benefit.

Telecommuting

It is increasingly popular for people to work by **telecommuting,** an arrangement that allows at least a portion of scheduled work hours to be completed outside the office. It is facilitated by computers and information technology that allow easy electronic links with customers and coworkers. New terms are even associated with telecommuting practices. We speak of *hoteling* when telecommuters come to the central office and use temporary office facilities; we also refer to *virtual offices* that include everything from an office at home to a mobile workspace in an automobile. When asked what they like, telecommuters tend to report increased productivity, fewer distractions, the freedom to be your own boss, and the benefit of having more time for themselves. On the negative side, they cite working too much, having less time to themselves, difficulty separating work and personal life, and having less time for family.[42] One telecommuter has this advice for others: "You have to have self-discipline and pride in what you do, but you also have to have a boss that trusts you enough to get out of the way."[43]

> ● **Telecommuting** involves using IT to work at home or outside the office.

Contingency and Part-Time Work

If there is one trend that has been reinforced by our tight economy, it's the use of more temporary and part time workers. Gerry Grabowski of Pittsburgh knows both the downside and the upside; he turned a temporary job in real-estate into a full-time one. Says Grabowski: "A lot of people say it's a raw deal, and I guess it can be. But if I were an entrepreneur, I would never do a straight hire. I would use a contractor or temp first . . ." And, if you wonder why, a business analyst says the appeal to the employer is "easy to lay off, no severance; no company funded retirement plan; pay own health insurance; get zero sick days and no vacation."[44]

Part-timers represent one-quarter of the U.S. workforce, and the number keeps growing. We call them **contingency workers,** or *permatemps*—persons who supplement the full-time workforce and work fewer than 35 hours per week for one employer, often on a long-term basis.[45] You'll hear them called freelancers and contract hires, as well as temps and part-timers. They provide just-in-time and as-needed work for employers who want to avoid the cost and responsibilities of hiring full-timers. It is now possible to hire on a part-time basis everything from executive support, such as a chief financial officer, to such special expertise in engineering, computer programming, and market research.

> ● **Contingency workers** are employed on a part-time and temporary basis to supplement a permanent workforce.

Because part-time or contingency workers can be easily hired, contracted with, and terminated in response to changing needs, many employers like the flexibility they offer in controlling labor costs and dealing with cyclical demand. Some say the cost saving is as much as 30% versus hiring a full-time worker.[46] But others worry that temporary workers lack the commitment of permanent workers and may lower productivity. Perhaps the most controversial issues associated with part-time workers are that they may be paid less than their full-time counterparts, can experience stress and anxiety from their part-time job status, and do not generally receive important benefits such as health care, life insurance, pension plans, and paid vacations.

Be sure you can ☑ illustrate a job designed by job simplification, rotation, and enlargement ☑ list and describe five core job characteristics ☑ describe advantages of the compressed workweek, flexible work hours, job sharing, and telecommuting ☑ discuss the role of part-time contingency workers in the economy

Learning Check ☑
Study Question 4
What is the link between job design and motivation?

Management Learning Review

1 How do individual needs influence motivation?

- Motivation predicts the level, direction, and persistence of effort expended at work; simply put, a highly motivated person works hard.
- Maslow's hierarchy of human needs suggests a progression from lower-order physiological, safety, and social needs to higher-order ego and self-actualization needs.
- Alderfer's ERG theory identifies existence, relatedness, and growth needs.
- Herzberg's two-factor theory describes the importance of both job content and job context to motivation and performance.
- McClelland's acquired needs theory identifies the needs for achievement, affiliation, and power, all of which may influence what a person desires from work.

FOR DISCUSSION **Is a high need for achievement always a good trait for managers?**

2 What are the process theories of motivation?

- Adams's equity theory recognizes that social comparisons take place when rewards are distributed in the workplace.
- People who feel inequitably treated are motivated to act in ways that reduce the sense of inequity; perceived negative inequity may result in someone working less hard in the future.
- Vroom's expectancy theory states that Motivation = Expectancy $\times$ Instrumentality $\times$ Valence.
- Locke's goal-setting theory emphasizes the motivational power of goals; task goals should be specific rather than ambiguous, difficult but achievable, and set through participatory means.
- Bandura's self-efficacy theory indicates that when people believe they are capable of performing a task, they experience a sense of confidence and will be more highly motivated to work hard at it.

FOR DISCUSSION **Can goals be motivational if they are set by the boss?**

3 What role does reinforcement play in motivation?

- Reinforcement theory recognizes that human behavior is influenced by its environmental consequences.
- The law of effect states that behavior followed by a pleasant consequence is likely to be repeated; behavior followed by an unpleasant consequence is unlikely to be repeated.
- Reinforcement strategies used by managers include positive reinforcement, negative reinforcement, punishment, and extinction.
- Positive reinforcement works best when applied according to the laws of contingent and immediate reinforcement.

FOR DISCUSSION **Is it possible for a manager or a parent to rely solely on positive reinforcement strategies?**

4 What is the link between job design and motivation?

- Job design is the process of creating or defining jobs by assigning specific work tasks to individuals and groups.
- Job simplification creates narrow and repetitive jobs consisting of well-defined tasks with many routine operations, such as the typical assembly-line job.
- Job enlargement allows individuals to perform a broader range of simplified tasks; job rotation allows individuals to shift among different jobs with similar skill levels.
- The job characteristics model of job design analyzes jobs according to skill variety, task identity, task significance, autonomy, and feedback; a job high in them is considered enriched.
- Alternative work schedules make work hours more convenient and flexible to better fit workers' needs and personal responsibilities; options include the compressed workweek, flexible working hours, job sharing, telecommuting, and part-time work.

FOR DISCUSSION **Can you enrich someone's job without increasing his or her pay as well?**

Multiple-Choice Questions

1. Lower-order needs in Maslow's hierarchy correspond to _____ needs in ERG theory.
   (a) growth   (b) affiliation   (c) existence   (d) achievement

2. A worker with a high need for _____ power in McClelland's theory tries to use power for the good of the organization.
   (a) position   (b) expert   (c) personal   (d) social

3. In the _____ theory of motivation, someone who perceives her- or himself as underrewarded relative to a coworker might be expected to reduce his or her performance in the future.
   (a) ERG   (b) acquired needs   (c) two-factor   (d) equity

4. Which of the following is a correct match?
   (a) McClelland—ERG theory   (b) Skinner—reinforcement theory   (c) Vroom—equity theory   (d) Locke—expectancy theory

5. The expectancy theory of motivation says that motivation = expectancy ×_____×_____.
   (a) rewards, valence   (b) instrumentality, valence   (c) equity, instrumentality   (d) rewards, valence

6. The law of _____ states that behavior followed by a positive consequence is likely to be repeated, whereas behavior followed by an undesirable consequence is not likely to be repeated.
   (a) reinforcement   (b) contingency   (c) goal setting   (d) effect

7. _____ is a positive reinforcement strategy that rewards successive approximations to a desirable behavior.
   (a) Extinction   (b) Negative reinforcement   (c) Shaping   (d) Merit pay

8. In Herzberg's two-factor theory, base pay is considered a(n) _____ factor.
   (a) valence   (b) satisfier   (c) equity   (d) hygiene

9. When someone has a high and positive "expectancy" in the expectancy theory of motivation, this means that the person _____.
   (a) believes he or she can meet performance expectations   (b) highly values the rewards being offered   (c) sees a link between high performance and available rewards (d) believes that rewards are equitable

10. In goal-setting theory, the goal of "becoming more productive in my work" would not be considered a source of motivation because it fails the criterion of goal _____.
    (a) acceptance   (b) specificity   (c) challenge   (d) commitment

11. B. F. Skinner would argue that "getting a paycheck on Friday" reinforces a person for coming to work on Friday, but it does not reinforce the person for having done an extraordinary job on Tuesday. This is because the Friday paycheck fails the law of _____ reinforcement.
    (a) negative   (b) continuous   (c) immediate   (d) intermittent

12. The addition of more planning and evaluating responsibilities to a job is an example of the _____ strategy of job design.
    (a) job enrichment   (b) job enlargement   (c) job rotation   (d) job sharing

13. Workers in a compressed workweek typically work 40 hours in _____ days.
    (a) 3   (b) 4   (c) 5   (d) a flexible number of

14. Another term used to describe part-time workers is _____.
    (a) contingency workers   (b) virtual workers   (c) flexible workers   (d) secondary workers

15. Hoteling is a development associated with the growing importance of _____ in the new workplace.
    (a) personal wellness   (b) telecommuting   (c) compressed work weeks   (d) Type A personalities

Short-Response Questions

16. What preferences does a person with a high need for achievement bring to the workplace?
17. Why is participation important to goal-setting theory?
18. What is the common ground in Maslow's, Alderfer's, and McClelland's views of human needs?
19. Why might an employer not want to offer employees the option of a compressed workweek schedule?

Essay Question

20. How can a manager combine the powers of goal setting and positive reinforcement to create a highly motivational work environment for a group of workers with high needs for achievement?

Management **S**kills and **C**ompetencies

Back to Yourself: **Engagement**

There's a lot of attention being given these days to the levels of **engagement** displayed by people at work. Differences in engagement are evident in a variety of ways. Is someone enthusiastic or lethargic, diligent or lazy, willing to do more than expected, or at best willing to do only what is expected? Managers obviously want high levels of engagement by members of their work units and teams, and the ideas of this chapter offer many insights on how to create engagement by using the content, process, and reinforcement theories of motivation. We also want engagement when our outcomes are dependent on how well others perform, say on a team project. Take a look around the classroom. What do you see and what would you predict for the future of your classmates based on the engagement they now show as students? After you complete the following Student Engagement Survey self-assessment, don't forget to go online to further examine your motivation preferences in respect to Job Design Choices.

> Someone shows **engagement** at work by demonstrating personal initiative, acting with enthusiasm, and being willing to do extra things or "go the extra mile" when performing his or her job.

Further Reflection: **Student Engagement Survey**

Instructions

Use the following scale to show the degree to which you agree with the following statements. Write your choices in the margin next to each question.[47]

1—No agreement
2—Weak agreement
3—Some agreement
4—Considerable agreement
5—Very strong agreement

1. Do you know what is expected of you in this course?
2. Do you have the resources and support you need to do your coursework correctly?
3. In this course, do you have the opportunity to do what you do best all the time?
4. In the last week, have you received recognition or praise for doing good work in this course?
5. Does your instructor seem to care about you as a person?
6. Is there someone in the course who encourages your development?
7. In this course, do your opinions seem to count?
8. Does the mission/purpose of the course make you feel your study is important?
9. Are other students in the course committed to doing quality work?
10. Do you have a best friend in the course?
11. In the last six sessions, has someone talked to you about your progress in the course?
12. In this course, have you had opportunities to learn and grow?

Scoring

Score the instrument by adding up all your responses. A score of 0–24 suggests you are "actively disengaged" from the learning experience; a score of 25–47 suggests you are "moderately engaged"; a score of 48–60 indicates you are "actively engaged."

Interpretation

This instrument is a counterpart to a survey used by the Gallup Organization to measure the "engagement" of American workers. The Gallup results are surprising—indicating that up to 19% of U.S. workers are actively disengaged, with the annual lost productivity estimated at some $300 billion per year. One has to wonder: What are the costs of academic disengagement by students?

Team Exercise

Why We Work

Preparation

Read this "ancient story."[48]

> In days of old, a wandering youth happened upon a group of men working in a quarry. Stopping by the first man, he said: "What are you doing?" The worker grimaced and groaned as he replied: "I am trying to shape this stone, and it is backbreaking work." Moving to the next man, the youth repeated the question. This man showed little emotion as he answered: "I am shaping a stone for a building." Moving to the third man, our traveler heard him singing as he worked. "What are you doing?" asked the youth. "I am helping to build a cathedral," the man proudly replied.

Instructions

In groups assigned by your instructor:

1. Discuss this short story.
2. Ask and answer the question: "What are the motivation and job design lessons of this ancient story?"
3. Have members of the group role-play each of the stonecutters as they answer this additional question: Why are you working?
4. Have someone prepared to report and share the group's responses with the class as a whole.

Case Study: The Three Doctors

Go to *Management Cases for Critical Thinking* to find the recommended case for Chapter 15—"The Three Doctors: Determined to Succeed."

Teams and Teamwork

16

Learning From Others

The Beauty Is in the Teamwork

What distinguishes a group of people from a high-performance team? For one, it's the way members work with one another to achieve common goals. A vivid example is a NASCAR pit crew. When a driver pulls in for a pit stop, the team must jump in to perform multiple tasks flawlessly and in perfect order and unison. A second gained or lost can be crucial to a NASCAR driver. Team members must be well trained and rehearsed to perform efficiently on race day.

The Daytona 500 is a premier race. And the difference between winning and losing often comes down to just seconds. Valuable time is easily lost—not just on the track but in the pits. "You can't win a race with a 12-second stop, but you can lose it with an 18-second stop," says Trent Cherry, the coach of Ryan Newman's pit crew.

Composed of former college and professional athletes, members of a pit crew are conditioned and trained to execute intricate maneuvers while taking care of tire changes, car adjustments, fueling, and related matters on a crowded pit lane. Each crew member is an expert at one task. But each is also fully aware of how that job fits into every other *task* that must be performed in a few-second pit-stop interval. The duties are carefully scripted for each individual's performance and equally choreographed to fit together seamlessly at the team level. Every task is highly specialized and interdependent; if the jacker is late, for example, the wheel changer can't pull the wheel.

Pit crews plan and practice over and over again, getting ready for the big test of race day performance. The crew chief makes sure that everyone is in shape, well trained, and ready to contribute to the team. "I don't want seven all-stars," Trent Cherry says, "I want seven guys who work as a team."[1]

do the benchmarking

We can't all be race car drivers or members of pit crews, but we're part of teams every day. The beauty of teams is accomplishing something far greater than what's possible for an individual alone. Like pit crews, great teams are built from a foundation of solid team contributors and leadership. Although teams can be hard work, they are worth it when things turn out right. **The question is: What should we do to make sure that a team achieves high performance and avoids just being an "also ran?"**

Learning About Yourself

Team Contributions

No one can deny that teams are indispensable in today's organizations. But the benefits of team performance aren't realized unless members make them happen through positive **team contributions**. These are the things people do to help teams succeed and help their members enjoy the team experience.

Scene—Hospital operating room:
Scholars notice that heart surgeons have lower death rates for similar procedures performed in hospitals where they do more operations than those performed where they do fewer operations.

"Must Have" Team Skills
• Encouraging and motivating others
• Accepting suggestions
• Listening to different points of view
• Communicating information and ideas
• Persuading others to cooperate
• Resolving and negotiating conflict
• Building consensus
• Fulfilling commitments
• Avoiding disruptive acts and words

Why? Researchers claim the operations go better because the doctors in the better hospitals spend more time working together with members of their surgery teams. It's not only the surgeon's skills that count, they say, ". . . the skills of the team, and of the organization, matter."[2]

Scene—NBA basketball court:
Scholars find that basketball teams win more games the longer the players have been together.

Why? Researchers claim it's a "teamwork effect." Teams whose members play together longest win more because the players get to know each other's moves and playing tendencies.[3]

There is no doubt that a large part of your career success will depend on how well you work in and lead teams. Take a look at the list of "must-have" team skills shown in the box. Do you have the skills portfolio and personal commitment to make truly valuable team contributions?

get to know yourself better

When you speak with others who know and work with you, what do they say about your performance as a team member? What suggestions do they have for how you could improve your team contributions? Take the recommended self-assessments and think about the results. If you were to make a presentation to a potential employer describing your team skills, what would you say? **Also make use of the end-of-chapter Self-Assessment feature to further reflect on your Team Leader Skills.**

16 Teams and Teamwork

Study Question 1	Study Question 2	Study Question 3	Study Question 4
Teams in Organizations	**Trends in the Use of Teams**	**How Teams Work**	**Decision Making in Teams**
• What is teamwork? • Teamwork pros • Teamwork cons • Meetings, meetings, meetings • Formal teams and informal groups	• Committees, project teams, task forces • Cross-functional teams • Virtual teams • Self-managing teams • Team building	• Team inputs • Stages of team development • Norms and cohesiveness • Task and maintenance roles • Communication networks	• Ways teams make decisions • Advantages and disadvantages of team decisions • Groupthink • Creativity in team decision making
Learning Check 1	**Learning Check 2**	**Learning Check 3**	**Learning Check 4**

"Sticks in a bundle are hard to break"—*Kenyan proverb*

"Teamwork is the fuel that allows common people to attain uncommon results"—*Andrew Carnegie*, industrialist and philanthropist

"Individual commitment to a group effort—that's what makes a team work, a society work, a civilization work"—*Vince Lombardi*, football coach

"Gettin' good players is easy. Gettin' 'em to play together is the hard part"—*Casey Stengel*, baseball manager

"I am a member of a team, and I rely on the team, I defer to it and sacrifice for it, because the team, not the individual, is the ultimate champion."—*Mia Hamm*, soccer player

From proverbs to sports to business, teams and teamwork are rich topics of conversation and major pathways to great accomplishments.[4] But even so, we have to admit that just the words "group" and "team" elicit both positive and negative reactions in the minds of many people. Although it is said that "two heads are better than one," we are also warned that "too many cooks spoil the broth." The true skeptic can be heard to say: "a camel is a horse put together by a committee."

Teams are both rich in performance potential and very complex in the way they work; they can be great successes and they can also be colossal failures.[5] Over 60% of the average worker's time is spent in a team environment, and for white-collar workers the figure goes over 80%.[6] But even though most workers spend time in teams, more than a third report dissatisfaction, and less than half say they receive training in group dynamics. Still, many people prefer to work in teams rather than independently.

TEAMS IN ORGANIZATIONS

Most tasks in organizations are well beyond the capabilities of individuals alone. Managerial success is always earned in part through mobilizing, leading, and supporting people as they work together in groups and teams. The new organizational designs and cultures require it, as does any true commitment to empowerment and employee involvement.[7] The question for managers, and the guiding theme of this chapter, thus becomes: how do we make sure that teams and teamwork are utilized to everyone's best advantage?

| Team leader | Network facilitator | Team member | External coach |

How managers get involved with teams and teamwork

FIGURE 16.1 Team and teamwork roles for managers.

WHAT IS TEAMWORK?

A **team** is a small group of people with complementary skills, who work together to accomplish shared goals while holding themselves mutually accountable for performance results.[8] **Teamwork** is the process of people working together to accomplish these goals.

As shown in Figure 16.1, managers must perform at least four important roles in order to fully master the challenges of teams and teamwork. These roles, along with examples, are *team leader*—serving as the appointed head of a team or work unit; *facilitator*—serving as the peer leader and networking hub for a special task force; *member*—serving as a helpful contributing member of a project team; and *coach*—serving as the external convener or sponsor of a problem-solving team staffed by others.

> A **team** is a collection of people who regularly interact to pursue common goals.

> **Teamwork** is the process of people actively working together to accomplish common goals.

TEAMWORK PROS

Teamwork in our society makes available everything from aircraft to the Internet, to music videos, to—as featured in the *Learning from Others* opener—a really successful pit stop for the leader of a NASCAR race. It all happens because of **synergy**, the creation of a whole that is greater than the sum of its parts.

Synergy pools individual talents and efforts to create extraordinary results. It occurs when a team uses its membership resources to the fullest and thereby achieves through collective action far more than could otherwise be achieved by individuals acting alone. When Jens Voigt, one of the top racers on the Tour de France, was asked to describe a "perfect cyclist," for example, he created a composite of his nine-member team: "We take the time trial legs of Fabian Cancellara, the speed of Stuart O'Grady, the climbing capacity of our leaders and my attitude." Voigt was confirming that the tour is way too hard for a single rider to win on his own talents; like so many other things in any workplace, the synergies made possible by teamwork are the keys to success.[9]

> **Synergy** is the creation of a whole greater than the sum of its individual parts.

Teams are good for organizations, and they are good for their members. Just as in life overall, being part of a work team or social group can strongly influence our attitudes and behaviors. The personal relationships and connections can help people do their jobs better—making contacts, sharing ideas, responding to favors, and bypassing roadblocks. And being part of a team often helps satisfy important needs that may be difficult to meet in the regular work setting or life overall, providing things like social relationships, a sense of security and belonging, or emotional support.[10] The many benefits of teams and teamwork can be summed up as follows.

- More resources for problem solving
- Improved creativity and innovation
- Improved quality of decision making
- Greater commitments to tasks
- Higher motivation through collective action
- Better control and work discipline
- More individual need satisfaction

TEAMWORK CONS

● **Social loafing** is the tendency of some people to avoid responsibility by "free-riding" in groups.

Experience has taught all of us that achieving synergy through teamwork isn't always easy and that things don't always work out as intended. Teams are not free from problems. Who, for example, hasn't encountered **social loafing**? This is the presence of "free-riders" who slack off because responsibility is diffused in teams and others are present to do the work.[11]

What can a leader or other concerned team members do when someone is free-riding? It's not easy, but the problem can be addressed. Actions can be taken to make individual contributions more visible, reward individuals for their contributions, make task assignments more interesting, and keep group size small so that free-riders are more subject to peer pressure and leader evaluation.[12]

Social loafing and other problems can easily turn the great potential of teams into frustration and failure.[13] Personality conflicts and individual differences in work styles can disrupt the team. Tasks are not always clear, and ambiguous agendas or ill-defined problems can cause teams to work too long on the wrong things. Not everyone is always ready to work. Sometimes the issue is lack of motivation, but it may also be conflicts with other deadlines and priorities. Low enthusiasm for group work may also be caused by a lack of team organization or success, as well as by meetings that lack purpose and members who come unprepared.[14]

MEETINGS, MEETINGS, MEETINGS

What do you think when someone says: "let's have a meeting?" Are you ready and willing, or apprehensive and even perturbed? Meetings are a hard fact of the workplace, especially in today's horizontal, flexible, and team-oriented structures. But many of us aren't always happy to get a request to add another meeting to our busy schedules. Consider the list of typical meeting problems described in Management Smarts 16.1.[15] You might even be able to add to the list from personal experience in student groups and work teams.

A survey by Office Team found that 27% of respondents viewed meetings as their biggest time wasters, ranking ahead of unnecessary interruptions.[16] "We have the most ineffective meetings of any company," says a technology executive. "We just seem to meet and meet and meet, and we never seem to do anything," says another in the package delivery industry. "We realize our meetings are unproductive. A consulting firm is trying to help us, but we've got a long way to go," says a corporate manager.[17]

As disconcerting as these data may sound, it's important to remember that meetings are not only necessary, but they can be run in effective and efficient ways. After all, face-to-face and virtual meetings are where lots of information is shared, decisions get made, and people gain understanding of issues and one another. All of this can be accomplished without "wasting" time. But as with all team activities in organizations, good meetings don't happen by chance. People have to work hard and work together to make them productive and rewarding. This is why knowing more about teams and teamwork can be very useful.

Management Smarts 16.1

Spotting the seven sins of deadly meetings

1. People arrive late, leave early, and don't take things seriously.

2. The meeting is too long, sometimes twice as long as necessary.

3. People don't stay on topic; they digress and are easily distracted.

4. The discussion lacks candor; people are unwilling to tell the truth.

5. The right information isn't available, so decisions are postponed.

6. Nothing happens when the meeting is over; no one puts decisions into action.

7. Things never get better; the same mistakes are made meeting after meeting.

Real Ethics

Social Loafing Isn't Going Away

1. *Psychology study:* A German researcher asked people to pull on a rope as hard as they could. First, individuals pulled alone. Second, they pulled as part of a group. The results showed that people pull harder when working alone than when working as part of a team. Such "social loafing" is the tendency to reduce effort when working in groups.

2. *Faculty office:* A student wants to speak with the instructor about his team's performance on the last group project. There were four members, but two did almost all of the work. The other two largely disappeared, showing up only at the last minute to be part of the formal presentation. His point is that the team was disadvantaged because two "free-riders" caused reduced performance capacity.

3. *Telephone call from the boss:* "John, I really need you to serve on this committee. Will you do it? Let me know tomorrow." In thinking about this, I ponder: I'm overloaded, but I don't want to turn down the boss. I'll accept but let the committee members know about my situation. I'll be active in discussions and try to offer viewpoints and

perspectives that are helpful. However, I'll let them know up front that I can't be a leader or volunteer for any extra work.

You Decide

Whether you call it "social loafing," "free-riding" or just plain old "slacking off," the question is the same: what are the ethical issues involved in team situations when some people sit back and let others do more of the work? When you join a group, do all members have an ethical obligation to do a similar amount of work–why or why not? When it comes to John, does the fact that he intends to be honest with the other committee members make any difference? Isn't he still going to be a social loafer while earning credit from his boss for serving on the committee? Is his approach ethical–or should he simply decline to participate on the committee?

FORMAL TEAMS AND INFORMAL GROUPS

The teams officially designated and supported by the organization are **formal teams**. They fulfill a variety of essential roles within the formal organizational structure. Rensis Likert, best known for his research on management styles, described organizations as interlocking networks of formal groups in which managers and leaders serve as important "linking pins."[18] Each manager or leader serves as a superior in one work group and as a subordinate in the next-higher-level one. Such formal groups exist in various sizes and go by different labels. They may be called departments (e.g., market research department), units (e.g., audit unit), teams (e.g., customer service team), or divisions (e.g., office products division), among other possibilities.

- A **formal team** is officially recognized and supported by the organization.

Although they are not depicted on organization charts, **informal groups** are also present and important in all organizations. They emerge from natural or spontaneous relationships among people. Some informal groups are *interest groups* in which workers band together to pursue a common cause such as better working conditions. Some emerge as *friendship groups* that develop for a wide variety of personal reasons, including shared nonwork interests. Others exist as *support groups*, in which the members basically help one another do their jobs or cope with common problems.

- An **informal group** is unofficial and emerges from relationships and shared interests among members.

Informal groups are very important for managers to understand. It's a mistake to assume they are necessarily bad; it's realistic to expect they can have a positive impact on work performance. The relationships and connections made possible by informal groups can help speed the workflow or allow people to "get things done" in ways not possible within the formal structure. Informal groups also help satisfy social needs that are otherwise thwarted or left unmet. Among other things, informal groups can offer their members social satisfactions, security, support, and a sense of belonging.

TRENDS IN THE USE OF TEAMS

The trend toward greater empowerment in organizations includes an emphasis on committees, project teams, task forces, and cross-functional teams. Organizations today also increasingly use computer-mediated or virtual teams, and self-managing teams.

COMMITTEES, PROJECT TEAMS, AND TASK FORCES

● A **committee** is designated to work on a special task on a continuing basis.

A **committee** brings people together outside of their daily job assignments to work in a small team for a specific purpose. The task agenda is typically narrow, focused, and ongoing. For example, organizations usually have a variety of permanent or standing committees dedicated to a wide variety of concerns, such as diversity and compensation. Committees are led by a designated head or chairperson, who is held accountable for performance results.

● A **project team** or **task force** is convened for a specific purpose and disbands when its task is completed.

Project teams or **task forces** bring people together to work on common problems, but on a temporary rather than on a permanent basis. The goals and task assignments for project teams and task forces are specific, and completion deadlines are clearly defined. Creativity and innovation may be important parts of the agendas. Project teams, for example, might be formed to develop a new product or service, redesign an office layout, or provide specialized consulting services for a client.[19]

CROSS-FUNCTIONAL TEAMS

● A **cross-functional team** operates with members who come from different functional units of an organization.

Cross-functional teams, ones whose members come from different functional units, are indispensable to matrix organizations and those that emphasize horizontal integration. They help avoid the functional chimneys problem discussed in Chapter 10 by eliminating the "walls" that otherwise separate departments and people in organizations.

Members of cross-functional teams work together on specific projects or tasks and with the needs of the whole organization in mind. They are expected to share information, explore new ideas, seek creative solutions, and meet project deadlines. At Tom's of Maine, for example, "Acorn Groups"—symbolizing the fruits of the stately oak tree—have been used to launch new products. They bring together members of all departments to work on new ideas from concept to finished product. The goal is to minimize problems and maximize efficiency through cross-departmental cooperation.[20] Target CEO Gregg Steinhafel also uses cross-functional teams in the "GO" apparel program. It unites talent from "merchandising, marketing, design, communications, presentation, supply chain and stores" to create and bring to customers new limited edition fashions.[21]

● An **employee involvement team** meets on a regular basis to help achieve continuous improvement.

Another application is the **employee involvement team** whose cross functional members meet on a regular basis, with the goal of applying their expertise

Teamwork Isn't Always Good for Productivity

A Microsoft survey of some 38,000 workers around the world raises concerns about teamwork and productivity. The chief culprits are bad meetings, poor communication, and unclear goals. The Microsoft survey found that the average worker spends 5.6 hours per week in meetings, 69% of meetings attended are considered ineffective, 32% of workers complained about poor team communication and unclear objectives, 31% complained about unclear priorities, and 29% complained about procrastination. How do these results fit your team experiences?

and attention to continuous improvement. One form of employee involvement team is the **quality circle**, a group of workers that meets regularly to discuss and plan specific ways to improve work quality.[22] After receiving special training in problem solving, team processes, and quality issues, members of the quality circle try to suggest ways to raise productivity through quality improvements.

VIRTUAL TEAMS

The constant emergence of new technologies is making virtual collaboration both easier and more common. At home it may be Facebook; at the office it's likely to be a wide variety of online meeting resources. **Virtual teams** whose members work together largely through computer-mediated, rather than face-to-face, interactions are increasingly common. Their use is changing the way many committees, task forces, and other problem-solving teams function. Virtual teams operate like other teams in respect to what gets done. It's the way they get things done that is different. And this difference can be a source of both potential advantages and disadvantages.[23]

In terms of potential advantages, virtual teams can save time and travel expenses. At IBM, for example, programming teams work together around the clock and around the world, often chopping months off of tasks.[24] Virtual teams can also be easily expanded to include more members, and the discussions and information shared among members can be stored online for continuous updating and access. Also, computer mediation helps virtual team members work collectively in a time-efficient fashion and without interpersonal difficulties that might otherwise occur—especially when the issues are controversial. A vice president for human resources at Marriott, for example, once called electronic meetings "the quietest, least stressful, most productive meetings you've ever had."[25]

When problems do occur in virtual teams, they often arise because members have difficulty establishing good working relationships. Lack of face-to-face interaction limits the role of emotions and nonverbal cues in the communication process, and relations among team members can become depersonalized.[26] But following some basic guidelines can help keep these problems to a minimum. Among tips for leading successful virtual teams are the following.[27]

- Select team members high in initiative and capable of self-starting.
- Select members who will join and engage the team with positive attitudes.
- Select members known for working hard to meet team goals.
- Begin with social messaging that allows members to exchange information about each other to personalize the process.
- Assign clear goals and roles so that members can focus while working alone and also know what others are doing.

● A **quality circle** is a team of employees who meet periodically to discuss ways of improving work quality.

● Members of a **virtual team** work together and solve problems through computer-based interactions.

- Gather regular feedback from members about how they think the team is doing and how it might do better.
- Provide regular feedback to team members about team accomplishments.

SELF-MANAGING TEAMS

● Members of a **self-managing work team** have the authority to make decisions about how they share and complete their work.

In a growing number of organizations, traditional work units consisting of first-level supervisors and their immediate subordinates are being replaced with **self-managing work teams**, as shown in Figure 16.2. Sometimes called *autonomous work groups*, these are teams of workers whose jobs have been redesigned to create a high degree of task interdependence, who have been given authority to make many decisions about how they work, and who accept collective responsibility for results.[28]

A key feature of any self-managing team is multitasking, in which team members each have the skills to perform several different jobs. And within a team the emphasis is always on participation. Self-managing teams operate with participative decision making, shared tasks, and responsibility for many of the managerial duties performed by supervisors in more traditional settings. The "self-management" responsibilities include planning and scheduling work, training members in various tasks, distributing tasks, meeting performance goals, ensuring high quality, and solving day-to-day operating problems. In some settings, the team's authority may even extend to "hiring" and "firing" members when necessary. Typical characteristics of self-managing teams include:

- Members are held collectively accountable for performance results.
- Members have discretion in distributing tasks within the team.
- Members have discretion in scheduling work within the team.
- Members are able to perform more than one job on the team.
- Members train one another to develop multiple job skills.
- Members evaluate one another's performance contributions.
- Members are responsible for the total quality of team products.

The expected advantages of self-managing teams include better performance, decreased costs, and higher morale. Of course, these results are not guaranteed. Managing the transition away from more traditional work settings isn't always easy.

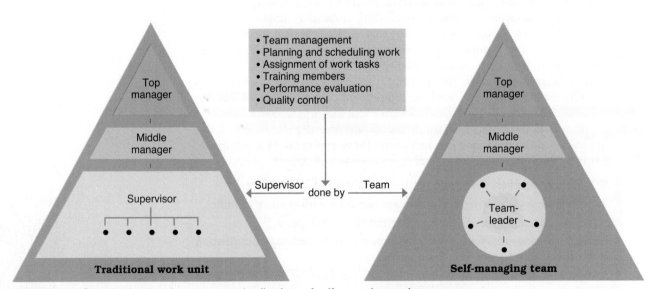

FIGURE 16.2 Organizational and management implications of self-managing work teams.

The switch to self-managing teams requires leadership committed to both empowerment and a lot of support for those learning to work in new ways. As the concept spreads globally, researchers are also examining the receptivity of different cultures to self-management concepts.[29] Such cultural dimensions as high-power distance and individualism, as discussed in Chapter 5, may generate resistance that must be considered when implementing team-based organizational practices.

TEAM BUILDING

The very best teams operate with characteristics like those shown in the accompanying box.[30] But real teamwork and high-performance results can't be left to chance. Just as in the world of sports, many things can go wrong and cause problems for work teams.

Team building is a sequence of planned activities used to analyze the functioning of a team and make constructive changes in how it operates.[31] The process begins with awareness that a problem may exist or may develop within the team. Members then work together to gather data and fully understand the problem, make and implement action plans, and evaluate results. As difficulties or new problems are discovered, the team-building process recycles.

● **Team building** is a sequence of activities to analyze a team and make changes to improve its performance.

There are many ways to gather data for team building, including structured and unstructured interviews, questionnaires, and team meetings. Regardless of the method used, however, the basic principle of team building remains the same: a careful and collaborative assessment of all aspects of the team ranging from how members work together to the results they achieve.

Characteristics of High-Performance Teams

- clear and elevating goals
- task-driven, results-oriented structure
- competent, hard-working members
- collaborative culture
- high standards of excellence
- external support and recognition
- strong, principled leadership

Team building can be done with consulting assistance or under managerial direction; it can also be done in the workplace or in outside locations. A popular approach is to bring team members together in special settings where their capacities for teamwork are put to the test in unusual and even physically demanding experiences. On one fall day, for example, a team of employees from American Electric Power (AEP) went to an outdoor camp for a day of team-building activities. They worked on problems such as how to get six members through a spider-web maze of bungee cords strung 2 feet above the ground. When her colleagues lifted Judy Gallo into their hands to pass her over the obstacle, she was nervous. But a trainer told the team this was just like solving a problem together at the office; the spider web was just another performance constraint, like the difficult policy issues or financial limits they might face at work. After "high-fives" for making it through the web, Judy's team jumped tree stumps together, passed hula hoops while

Reality Team Building Really Works

Chances are that you have probably tuned in to watch one of the many TV reality shows and wondered if they had a purpose. Surprisingly, some organizations are finding out that the "reality" notion is a great way to accomplish team building and drive innovation. Best Buy sent small teams to live together for 10 weeks in Los Angeles apartments. The purpose was to prove out new ideas and lay the groundwork for new lines of business as well as potential independent businesses. One participant says: "Living together and knowing we only had 10 weeks sped up our team-building process." From apartment living to outdoor training, novel approaches to team building are proving their worth.

holding hands, and more. Says one team-building trainer, "We throw clients into situations to try and bring out the traits of a good team."[32]

Learning Check

Study Question 2
What are current trends in the use of teams?

Be sure you can ☑ differentiate a committee from a task force ☑ explain the benefits of cross-functional teams ☑ explain potential advantages and disadvantages of virtual teams ☑ list the characteristics of self-managing work teams ☑ explain how self-managing teams are changing organizations ☑ describe the typical steps in team building

HOW TEAMS WORK

● An **effective team** achieves high levels of task performance, membership satisfaction, and future viability.

An **effective team** does three things well—perform its tasks, satisfy its members, and remain viable for the future.[33] On the *task performance* side, a work group or team is expected to transform resource inputs (such as ideas, materials, and information) into product outputs (such as a report, decision, service, or commodity). In respect to *member satisfaction*, members should take pleasure from both the team's performance accomplishments and their contributions toward making it happen. And as to *future viability*, the team should have a social fabric and work climate that makes its members willing and able to work well together in the future, again and again as needed.

Procter & Gamble's former CEO A. G. Lafley says that team effectiveness comes together when you have "the right players in the right seats on the same bus, headed in the same direction."[34] The open-systems model in Figure 16.3 shows that a team's effectiveness is influenced by inputs—"right players in the right seats," and by process—"on the same bus, headed in the same direction." You can remember the implications of this figure by the following **Team Effectiveness Equation**.[35]

● **Team Effectiveness Equation**
Team effectiveness = Quality of inputs + (Process gains − Process losses)

Team effectiveness = Quality of inputs + (Process gains − Process losses)

TEAM INPUTS

Among the important inputs that can influence team effectiveness are resources and setting, nature of the task, membership characteristics, and team size.[36] You can think of these as the things that "load" the team for action. A team with the right inputs has a greater chance of having a strong process and being effective.

Resources and Setting

The availability of resources and the nature of the organizational setting can affect how team members relate to one another and apply their skills to task accomplishment. A key issue is the support provided in terms of information, material resources, technology, organization structures, rewards, and work space. In this latter respect, many organizations are being architecturally designed to directly facilitate teamwork. At SEI Investments, employees work in a large, open space without cubicles or dividers; each has a private set of office furniture and fixtures—but all on wheels; all technology easily plugs and unplugs from suspended power beams that run overhead. This makes it easy for project teams to convene and disband as needed, and for people to meet and converse within the ebb and flow of daily work.[37]

Nature of the Task

The nature of the task is always an important input. It affects how well a team can focus its efforts and how intense the group process must be to get the job done. Clearly defined tasks make it easier for team members to combine their work efforts. Complex tasks require more information exchange and more intense interaction than do simpler tasks.[38] The next time you fly, check out the ground crews. You

Inputs

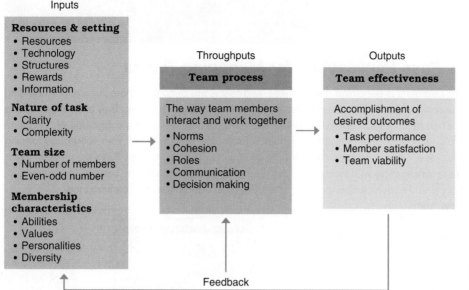

FIGURE 16.3 An open-systems model of team effectiveness.

should notice some similarities between them and teams handling pit stops for NASCAR racers. In fact, if you fly United Airlines, there's a good chance the members of the ramp crews have been through "Pit Crew U." United is among many organizations that are sending employees to Pit Instruction & Training in Mooresville, North Carolina. At this facility, where real racing crews train, United's ramp workers learn to work intensely and under pressure while meeting the goals of teamwork, safety, and job preparedness. The goal is better teamwork to reduce aircraft delays and service inadequacies.[39]

Team Size

Team size affects how members work together, handle disagreements, and make decisions. The number of potential interactions increases geometrically as teams increase in size and communications become more congested. Teams with odd numbers of members help prevent "ties" when votes need to be taken. Also, teams larger than about six or seven members can be difficult to manage for creative problem solving. Amazon.com's founder and CEO Jeff Bezos is a great fan of teams. But he also has a simple rule when it comes to sizing the firm's product development teams: No team should be larger than two pizzas can feed.[40]

Membership Characteristics

The blend of member characteristics on a team is also important. Teams need members with the right abilities, or skill sets, to master and perform tasks well. "The power of any group is in the mix," says Renee Wingo, former Chief People Officer at Virgin Mobile USA.[41] Teams must also have members whose attitudes, values, and personalities are sufficiently compatible for everyone to work well together. How often, for example, have you read or heard about college sports teams where a lack of the right "chemistry" among talented players meant sub-par team performance? As one of the chapter opening quotes said: "Gettin' good players is easy. Gettin' 'em to play together is the hard part."[42]

Team diversity, in the form of different values, personalities, experiences, demographics, and cultures among the membership, affects how teams work. It is easier to manage relationships among members of more *homogeneous teams*—ones whose members share similar characteristics. It is harder to manage relationships among members of more *heterogeneous teams*—ones whose members are quite dissimilar to one another. As team diversity increases, so does the complexity of interpersonal

● **Team diversity** is the differences in values, personalities, experiences, demographics, and cultures among the membership.

Research Brief

Demographic Faultlines Pose Implications for Managing Teams

Membership of organizations is becoming more diverse, and teams are becoming more important. According to Dora Lau and Keith Murnighan, these trends raise some important research issues. They believe that strong "faultlines" occur when demographic diversity results in the formation of two or more subgroups whose members are similar to and strongly identify with one another. Examples include teams with subgroups forming around age, gender, race, ethnic, occupational, or tenure differences. When strong faultlines are present, members tend to identify more strongly with their subgroups than with the team as a whole. Lau and Murnighan predict that this affects what happens within the team in terms of conflict, politics, and performance.

Using subjects from 10 organizational behavior classes at a university, the researchers created different conditions of faultline strengths by randomly assigning students to case work groups based on sex and ethnicity. After working on cases, the students completed questionnaires about group processes and outcomes. Results showed members of strong faultline groups evaluated those in their subgroups more favorably than did members of weak faultline groups. Members of strong faultline groups also experienced less conflict, more psychological safety, and more satisfaction than did those in weak faultline groups.

Strong faultline team
members identify more with subgroups than team
• more conflict
• less sense of safety
• less team satisfaction

Weak faultline team
members identify more with team than subgroups
• less conflict
• more sense of safety
• more team satisfaction

You Be the Researcher

How might faultlines operate in groups of different sizes and in the contexts of different organizational cultures? Are faultlines influencing the processes and outcomes of groups in which you participate—at the university and at work? And if you are a member or leader of a team with strong faultlines, what can you do to help minimize any negative effects?

References: Dora C. Lau and J. Keith Murnighan, "Interactions within Groups and Subgroups: The Effects of Demographic Faultlines," *Academy of Management Journal*, vol. 48 (2005), pp. 645–59; "Demographic Diversity and Faultlines: The Compositional Dynamics of Organizational Groups," *Academy of Management Review*, vol. 23 (1998), pp. 325–40.

relationships among members. But the complications of membership diversity also come with special performance opportunities. When the teams are well managed, the variety of ideas, perspectives, and experiences available on more heterogeneous teams can become valuable assets for problem solving and team performance.

STAGES OF TEAM DEVELOPMENT

● **Team process** is the way team members work together to accomplish tasks.

Although having the right inputs is important, it doesn't guarantee team effectiveness. **Team process** counts too. This is the way the members of any team actually work together as they transform inputs into output. Also called *group dynamics*, the process aspects of any group or team include how members develop norms and cohesiveness, share roles, communicate with one another, and make decisions.[43]

Depending upon how well processes and group dynamics are managed on a team, its effectiveness can go up or down. In the international arena, for example, culturally diverse work teams have more difficulty learning how to work well together than do culturally homogeneous teams.[44] If these problems are ignored or handled poorly, team performance suffers; if addressed and handled well, team

performance often gains substantially. We also know that teams experience different process challenges in these stages of team development.[45]

1. *Forming*—a stage of initial orientation and interpersonal testing.
2. *Storming*—a stage of conflict over tasks and working as a team.
3. *Norming*—a stage of consolidation around task and operating agendas.
4. *Performing*—a stage of teamwork and focused task performance.   *work get done*
5. *Adjourning*—a stage of task completion and disengagement.   *proletive*

Forming Stage

The forming stage involves the first entry of individual members into a team.
This is a stage of initial task orientation and interpersonal testing. When people
first come together, they ask questions: "What can or does the team offer me?"
"What will I be asked to contribute?" "Can my needs be met while my efforts serve
the task needs of the team?"

In the forming stage, people begin to identify with other members and with the
team itself. They are concerned about getting acquainted, establishing relationships,
discovering what is acceptable behavior, and learning how others perceive the
team's task. This may also be a time when some members rely on others who appear
"powerful" or especially "knowledgeable." Such things as prior experience with team
members in other contexts and individual impressions of organization philosophies,
goals, and policies may also affect emerging relationships. Difficulties in the forming
stage tend to be greater in more culturally and demographically diverse teams.

Storming Stage

The storming stage is a period of high emotionality and can be the most difficult
stage to pass through successfully. Tensions often emerge over tasks and interpersonal concerns. There may be periods of outright hostility
and infighting. Coalitions or cliques may form around personalities or interests. Subteams may form around areas of
agreement and disagreement. Conflict may develop as individuals compete to impose their preferences on others and to
become influential in groups.

Important changes occur in the storming stage as task
agendas become clarified and members begin to understand
one another's styles. Attention begins to shift toward obstacles that may stand in the way of task accomplishment.
Efforts are made to find ways to meet team goals while also
satisfying individual needs. The storming stage is part of a
"critical zone" in team development, where failures can create long-lasting problems, while success can set a strong
foundation for later effectiveness.

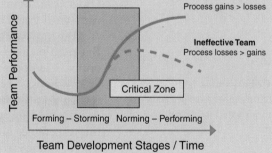

Norming Stage

Cooperation is an important issue in the norming stage. At this point, team members begin to become coordinated and operate with shared rules of conduct. The team
feels a sense of leadership, with each member starting to play useful roles. Interpersonal
hostilities start to give way to a precarious balancing of forces as norming builds initial
integration. Harmony is emphasized, but minority viewpoints may be discouraged.

The norming stage is also part of the critical zone of team development. Here,
members are likely to develop initial feelings of closeness, a division of labor, and
a sense of shared expectations. This helps protect the team from disintegration. In
fact, holding the team together may seem more important than successful task
accomplishment.

	Very poor			Very good	
1. Trust among members	1	2	3	4	5
2. Feedback mechanisms	1	2	3	4	5
3. Open communications	1	2	3	4	5
4. Approach to decisions	1	2	3	4	5
5. Leadership sharing	1	2	3	4	5
6. Acceptance of goals	1	2	3	4	5
7. Valuing diversity	1	2	3	4	5
8. Member cohesiveness	1	2	3	4	5
9. Support for each other	1	2	3	4	5
10. Performance norms	1	2	3	4	5

FIGURE 16.4 Criteria for assessing the maturity of a team.

Performing Stage

Teams in the performing stage are more mature, organized, and well-functioning. They score high on the criteria of team maturity shown in Figure 16.4.[46] Performing is a stage of total integration in which team members are able to deal in creative ways with complex tasks and any interpersonal conflicts. The team operates with a clear and stable structure, and members are motivated by team goals. The primary challenges are to continue refining the operations and relationships essential to working as an integrated unit.

Adjourning Stage

The final stage of team development is adjourning, when team members prepare to achieve closure and disband. Temporary committees, task forces, and project teams should disband with a sense that important goals have been accomplished. But adjourning may be an emotional period; when team members have worked together intensely for some time, breaking up may be painful. It is helpful here to acknowledge everyone for their contributions, praise them, and celebrate the team's success. Ideally, the team disbands with everyone feeling they would work with one another again sometime in the future.

NORMS AND COHESIVENESS

● A **norm** is a behavior, rule, or standard expected to be followed by team members.

A **norm** is a behavior expected of team members.[47] It is a "rule" or "standard" that guides behavior. The performance norm, which defines the level of work effort and performance that team members are expected to contribute, is an important example. Work groups and teams with positive performance norms are more successful in accomplishing task objectives than are teams with negative performance norms. Other team norms relate to such things as helpfulness, participation, timeliness, work quality, and creativity and innovation.

When violated, a norm may be enforced with reprimands and other sanctions. But team members vary in the degree to which they accept and adhere to group norms. Conformity to norms is largely determined by the strength of team **cohesiveness**, the degree to which members are attracted to and motivated to remain part of a team.[48] Persons in a highly cohesive team value their membership and strive to maintain positive relationships with other team members. Because they experience satisfaction from team identification, they tend to conform to the norms. In the extreme, violation of a norm can result in a member being expelled from a team or socially ostracized by other members.

● **Cohesiveness** is the degree to which members are attracted to and motivated to remain part of a team.

Managing Team Norms

Team leaders should help and encourage members to develop positive norms. During the forming and storming steps of development, for example, norms relating to membership issues such as expected attendance and levels of commitment are important. By the time the stage of performing is reached, norms relating to adaptability and change become relevant. Guidelines for building positive group norms include the following.[49]

- Act as a positive role model.
- Reinforce the desired behaviors with rewards.
- Control results by performance reviews and regular feedback.

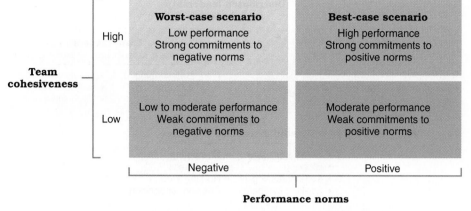

FIGURE 16.5 How cohesiveness and norms influence team performance.

- Train and orient new members to adopt desired behaviors.
- Recruit and select new members who exhibit the desired behaviors.
- Hold regular meetings to discuss progress and ways of improving.
- Use team decision-making methods to reach agreement.

Managing Team Cohesiveness

The power of group cohesiveness is shown in Figure 16.5. When the performance norm of a team is positive, high cohesion and the resulting conformity to norms have a beneficial effect on overall team performance. This is a "best-case" scenario. Competent team members work hard and reinforce one another's task accomplishments while experiencing satisfaction with the team. But when the performance norm is negative in a highly cohesive team, conformity to the norm can have undesirable results. The figure shows this as a "worst-case" scenario, where team performance suffers when members restrict their work efforts.

To achieve and maintain the best-case scenario shown in the figure, managers must be skilled at more than building positive norms. They must also be good at building high cohesiveness. This can be done in the following ways.

- Build agreement on team goals.
- Increase membership homogeneity.
- Increase interactions among members.
- Decrease team size.
- Introduce competition with other teams.
- Reward team rather than individual results.
- Provide physical isolation from other teams.

TASK AND MAINTENANCE ROLES

Research on the social psychology of groups identifies two types of roles or activities that are essential if team members are to work well together.[50] **Task activities** contribute directly to the team's performance purpose, while **maintenance activities** support the emotional life of the team as an ongoing social system.

Although the team leader or supervisor should give them special attention, the responsibility for both types of activities should also be shared and distributed among all team members. Anyone can help lead a team by acting in ways that satisfy its task and maintenance needs. This concept of **distributed leadership** in teams makes every member continually responsible for both recognizing when task or maintenance activities are needed and taking actions to provide them.

● A **task activity** is an action taken by a team member that directly contributes to the group's performance purpose.

● A **maintenance activity** is an action taken by a team member that supports the emotional life of the group.

● **Distributed leadership** is when all members of a team contribute helpful task and maintenance behaviors.

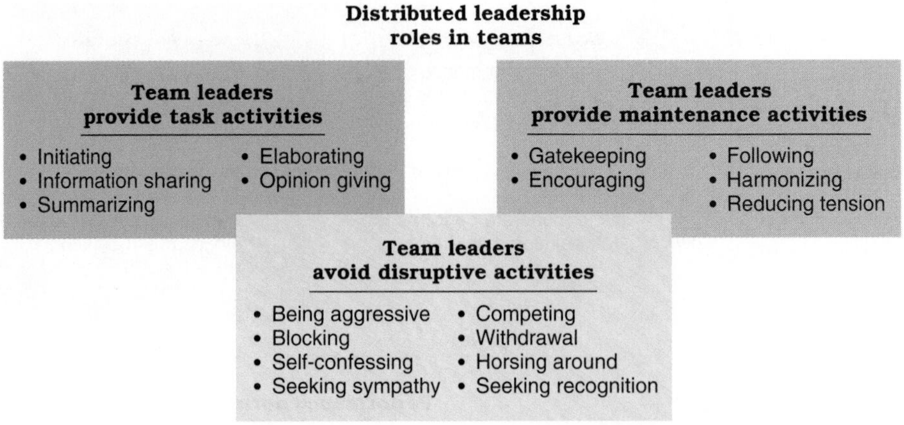

Distributed leadership roles in teams

Team leaders provide task activities		Team leaders provide maintenance activities	
• Initiating	• Elaborating	• Gatekeeping	• Following
• Information sharing	• Opinion giving	• Encouraging	• Harmonizing
• Summarizing			• Reducing tension

Team leaders avoid disruptive activities

• Being aggressive	• Competing
• Blocking	• Withdrawal
• Self-confessing	• Horsing around
• Seeking sympathy	• Seeking recognition

FIGURE 16.6 Distributed leadership helps teams meet task and maintenance needs.

Leading through task activities involves making an effort to define and solve problems and to advance work toward performance results. Without the relevant task activities, such as initiating agendas, sharing information, and others shown in Figure 16.6, teams will have difficulty accomplishing their objectives. Leading through maintenance activities, by contrast, helps strengthen the team as a social system. When maintenance activities such as encouraging others and reducing tensions are performed well, good interpersonal relationships are achieved and the ability of the team to stay together over the longer term is ensured.

Both team task and maintenance activities stand in distinct contrast to the **disruptive activities** also described in the figure. Activities such as showing incivility toward other members, withdrawing from the discussion, and fooling around are self-serving and detract from, rather than enhance, team effectiveness. Unfortunately, very few teams are immune to dysfunctional behavior by members. Everyone shares in the responsibility for minimizing its occurrence.

● **Disruptive activities** are self-serving behaviors that interfere with team effectiveness.

COMMUNICATION NETWORKS

There is considerable research on the interaction patterns and communication networks used by teams.[51] When team members must interact intensively and work closely together on tasks, this need is best met by a **decentralized communication network**. Sometimes called the *all-channel or star communication network*, this is where all members communicate directly with one another. At other times and in other situations, team members can work on tasks independently, with the required work being divided up among them. This creates a **centralized communication network**, sometimes called a *wheel or chain communication structure*. Its activities are coordinated and results pooled by a central point of control.

● A **decentralized communication network** allows all members to communicate directly with one another.

● In a **centralized communication network**, communication flows only between individual members and a hub, or center point.

● In a **restricted communication network** subgroups have limited communication with one another.

When teams are composed of subgroups experiencing issue-specific disagreements, such as a temporary debate over the best means to achieve a goal, the resulting interaction pattern often involves a **restricted communication network**. Here, polarized subgroups contest one another and may even engage in conflict. Communication between the subgroups is limited and biased, with negative consequences for group process and effectiveness.

The best teams use communication networks, as shown in Figure 16.7, in the right ways and at the right times. Centralized communication networks seem to work better on simple tasks.[52] These tasks require little creativity, information processing, and problem solving and lend themselves to more centralized control. The reverse is true for more complex tasks, where interacting groups do better. Here, the decentralized networks work well because they are able to support the more intense interactions and information sharing required to perform complicated tasks. When teams get complacent, the conflict that emerges from co-acting groups can be a source

Pattern	Diagram	Characteristics
Interacting Group Decentralized communication network		High interdependency around a common task Best at complex tasks
Co-acting Group Centralized communication network	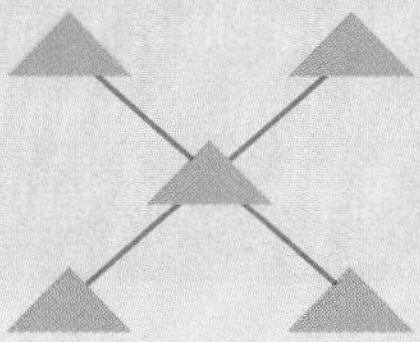	Independent individual efforts on behalf of common task Best at simple tasks
Counteracting Group Restricted communication network		Subgroups in disagreement with one another Slow task accomplishment

FIGURE 16.7 Interaction patterns and communication networks in teams.

Source: John R. Schermerhorn Jr., James G. Hunt, and Richard N. Osborn, *Organizational Behavior*, 8th ed. (Hoboken, NJ: Wiley, 2003), p. 347. Used by permission.

of creativity and critical evaluation. But when subgroups have difficulty communicating with one another, task accomplishment typically suffers—for the short run at least.

Be sure you can ☑ define *team effectiveness* ☑ identify inputs that influence group effectiveness ☑ discuss how membership diversity influences team effectiveness ☑ list five stages of group development ☑ define *group norm* and list ways to build positive group norms ☑ define *cohesiveness* and list ways to increase group cohesion ☑ explain how norms and cohesiveness influence team performance ☑ differentiate between task, maintenance, and disruptive activities ☑ describe use of decentralized and centralized communication networks

Learning Check

Study Question 3
How do teams work?

DECISION MAKING IN TEAMS

Decision making, discussed extensively in Chapter 7, is the process of making choices among alternative possible courses of action. It is one of the most important group processes, and the best teams will use a variety of methods over time as they face different kinds of problems.[53] But decision making in teams can also go off track as members deal with one another and struggle with basic group dynamics.[54]

● **Decision making** is the process of making choices among alternative possible courses of action.

WAYS TEAMS MAKE DECISIONS

Edgar Schein, a respected scholar and consultant, notes that teams use at least six methods to make decisions: lack of response, authority rule, minority rule, majority rule, consensus, and unanimity.[55]

In *decision by lack of response*, one idea after another is suggested without any discussion taking place. When the team finally accepts an idea, all others have been by-passed by simple lack of response rather than by critical evaluation.

In *decision by authority rule*, the leader, manager, committee head, or some other authority figure makes a decision for the team. This can be done with or without discussion and is very time-efficient. Whether the decision is a good one or a bad

Small Teams Connect at Amazon.com

Amazon.com's founder and CEO Jeff Bezos views the firm's "two-pizza" teams as a way of fighting bureaucracy and decentralizing, even as a company grows large and very complex. By keeping team size small enough for two pizzas to feed, about 5–8 members, he believes teams gain speed and become "innovation engines." Bezos is also a fan of what he calls fact-based decisions. He says they help to "overrule the hierarchy by allowing even the most junior person in the company to win an argument with senior executives if they have the right facts."

one, however, depends on whether the authority figure has the necessary information and expertise, and on how well this approach is accepted by other team members.

In *decision by minority rule*, two or three people are able to dominate or "railroad" the team into making a decision that they prefer. This is often done by providing a suggestion and then forcing quick agreement by challenging the team with such statements as "Does anyone object? No? Well let's go ahead, then."

One of the most common ways teams make decisions, especially when early signs of disagreement arise, is *decision by majority rule*. Formal voting may take place, or members may be polled to find the majority viewpoint. Although this method parallels the democratic political process, it is often used without awareness of its potential problems. The very process of voting can create coalitions as some people become "winners" and others "losers." Those in the minority—the "losers"—may feel left out or discarded without having had a fair say. They may be unenthusiastic about implementing the decision of the "majority," and lingering resentments may impair team effectiveness in the future. Such possibilities are well illustrated in the political arena, where candidates receiving only small and controversial victory margins end up struggling against entrenched opposition from the losing party.

Teams are often encouraged to achieve *decision by consensus*. This is where full discussion leads to one alternative being favored by most members, and the other members agree to support it. When a consensus is reached, even those who may have opposed the decision know that their views have been heard by everyone involved. Consensus does not require unanimity, but it does require that team members are able to argue, engage in reasonable conflict, and still get along with and respect one another.[56] And, it requires the opportunity for dissenting members to know that they have been able to speak and that they have been listened to.[57]

A *decision by unanimity* may be the ideal state of affairs. "Unanimity" means that all team members agree on the course of action to be taken. This is a logically perfect method, but it is also extremely difficult to achieve in actual practice. One of the reasons that teams sometimes turn to authority decisions, majority voting, or even minority decisions, is the difficulty of managing the team process to achieve consensus or unanimity.

Keys to Consensus

1. Don't argue blindly; consider others' reactions to your points.
2. Don't change your mind just to reach quick agreement.
3. Avoid conflict reduction by voting, coin tossing, bargaining.
4. Keep everyone involved in the decision process.
5. Allow disagreements to surface so that things can be deliberated.
6. Don't focus on winning versus losing; seek acceptable alternatives.
7. Discuss assumptions, listen carefully, and encourage inputs by all.

ADVANTAGES AND DISADVANTAGES OF TEAM DECISIONS

When teams take time to make decisions by consensus or unanimity, they gain special advantages over those relying more on individual or minority decision methods.[58]

True team decisions that involve all team members make greater amounts of information, knowledge, and expertise available to solve problems. They expand the number of action alternatives that are examined, and they help to avoid tunnel vision and consideration of only limited options. Team decisions also increase understanding and acceptance by members. And, importantly, team decisions increase the commitments of members to work hard to implement the decisions they have made together.

The potential disadvantages of team decision making trace largely to the difficulties that can be experienced in the group process. When many people are trying to make a team decision, it can be hard to reach consensus and there may be social pressure to conform. Some individuals may feel intimidated or compelled to go along with the apparent wishes of others. There may be minority domination, where some members feel forced or "railroaded" to accept a decision advocated by one vocal individual or small coalition. Also, the time required to make team decisions can sometimes be a disadvantage. As more people are involved in the dialogue and discussion, decision making takes longer. This added time may be costly, even prohibitively so, in certain circumstances.

GROUPTHINK

In considering the potential downsides of team decision making, there is a further issue to recognize. Although it may seem counterintuitive, a high level of cohesiveness can be a disadvantage if strong feelings of team loyalty make it hard for members to criticize and evaluate one another's ideas and suggestions. Members of very cohesive teams may feel so strongly about the group that they may not want to do anything that might detract from feelings of goodwill. This might cause them to publicly agree with actual or suggested courses of action, while privately having serious doubts about them. There can be times when desires to hold the team together at all costs and avoid disagreements may result in poor decisions.

Psychologist Irving Janis calls this phenomenon **groupthink**, the tendency for highly cohesive teams to lose their critical evaluative capabilities.[59] He argues, for example, that groupthink played a role in well-known historical blunders such as the lack of preparedness of U.S. naval forces for the Japanese attack on Pearl Harbor, the Bay of Pigs invasion under President Kennedy, and the many roads that led to the United States' difficulties in the Vietnam War.

Janis also suggests that groupthink can be avoided or minimized if team leaders take actions such as those summarized in Management Smarts 16.2. To help you spot its presence in team decision situations, he identifies the following groupthink symptoms.

- *Illusions of invulnerability:* Members assume that the team is too good for criticism, or beyond attack.
- *Rationalizing unpleasant and disconfirming data:* Members refuse to accept contradictory data or to thoroughly consider alternatives.
- *Belief in inherent group morality:* Members act as though the group is inherently right and above reproach.

● **Groupthink** is a tendency for highly cohesive teams to lose their evaluative capabilities.

Management Smarts 16.2

How to avoid groupthink

- Assign the role of critical evaluator to each team member; encourage a sharing of viewpoints.

- As a leader, don't seem partial to one course of action; do absent yourself from meetings at times to allow free discussion.

- Create subteams to work on the same problems and then share their proposed solutions.

- Have team members discuss issues with outsiders and report back on their reactions.

- Invite outside experts to observe team activities and react to team processes and decisions.

- Assign one member to play a "devil's advocate" role at each team meeting.

- Hold a "second-chance" meeting to review the decision after consensus is apparently achieved.

- *Stereotyping competitors as weak, evil, and stupid:* Members refuse to look realistically at other groups.
- *Applying direct pressure to deviants to conform to group wishes:* Members refuse to tolerate anyone who suggests the team may be wrong.
- *Self-censorship by members:* Members refuse to communicate personal concerns to the whole team.
- *Illusions of unanimity:* Members accept consensus prematurely, without testing its completeness.
- *Mind guarding:* Members protect the team from hearing disturbing ideas or outside viewpoints.

CREATIVITY IN TEAM DECISION MAKING

When creativity is needed in special situations, managers shouldn't hesitate to use the time-tested brainstorming and nominal group techniques.[60] For example, Heather Logrippo, owner and publisher of the magazine *Distinctive Homes*, faced a problem—she needed a creative customer incentive program. To come up with it, she called her staff team together and engaged what might be called "unconventional" brainstorming. Team members were given construction paper and crayons, and asked to come back in 30 minutes with creative program suggestions. She says: "This wasn't a situation where you could just 'Google' the answer. They came out with great ideas."[61]

● **Brainstorming** engages group members in an open, spontaneous discussion of problems and ideas.

Classic **brainstorming** usually asks members to follow strict guidelines, such as: *don't criticize each other*—withhold judging or evaluating ideas as they are being presented; *welcome "freewheeling"*—the wilder or more radical the idea the better; *go for quantity*—the more ideas generated, the greater the likelihood that one or more will be outstanding; *keep building on one another's ideas*—don't hesitate to piggy back and tweak one or more existing ideas into new forms. At the Aloft Group, Inc., a small advertising firm in Newburyport, Massachusetts, for example, President Matt Bowen uses brainstorming to foster creative thinking. He says brainstorming works best if he specifies the goal—ideally in a sentence, which he distributes a day or two ahead of the session. He limits the brainstorming session to an hour, and keeps the group small—ideally five to seven members. He allows no criticisms—there is no such thing as a "bad" idea. He also encourages everyone to build on one another's ideas and is sure to follow up by implementing something from the brainstorming session.[62]

● The **nominal group technique** structures interaction among team members discussing problems and ideas.

By prohibiting criticism, the brainstorming method reduces fears of ridicule or failure among individual participants. This is supposed to generate more enthusiasm and a freer flow of ideas among members. But there are times when differences in opinions and goals are so extreme that a brainstorming meeting deteriorates into antagonistic arguments and harmful conflicts. In such cases, a **nominal group technique** can help.[63] This approach uses a highly structured meeting agenda to allow everyone to contribute ideas without the interference of evaluative comments by others. Participants are first asked to work alone and respond in writing with possible solutions to a stated problem. Ideas are then shared in round-robin fashion without any criticism or discussion, and all ideas are recorded as they are presented. Ideas are next discussed and clarified in another round-robin sequence, with no evaluative comments allowed. Finally, members individually and silently follow a written voting procedure that ranks all alternatives in priority order.

<table>
<tr><td>☑</td><td>**Learning Check**
Study Question 4
How do teams make decisions?</td><td>*Be sure you can* ☑ illustrate how groups make decisions by authority rule, minority rule, majority rule, consensus, and unanimity ☑ list advantages and disadvantages of group decision making ☑ define *groupthink* and identify its symptoms ☑ illustrate how brainstorming and the nominal group technique can improve creativity in team decision making</td></tr>
</table>

Management Learning Review

1 How do teams contribute to organizations?

- A team is a collection of people working together to accomplish a common goal.
- Teams help organizations perform through synergy—the creation of a whole that is greater than the sum of its parts.
- Teams help satisfy important needs for their members by providing sources of job support and social satisfactions.
- Social loafing and other problems can limit the performance of teams.
- Organizations operate as networks of formal and informal groups.

FOR DISCUSSION **Why do people often tolerate social loafers at work?**

2 What are current trends in the use of teams?

- Committees and task forces are used to accomplish special tasks and projects.
- Cross-functional teams bring members together from different departments, and help improve lateral relations and integration in organizations.
- New developments in information technology are making virtual teams commonplace at work, but virtual teams also pose special management challenges.
- Self-managing teams are changing organizations, as team members perform many tasks previously done by their supervisors.
- Team building engages team members in a process of assessment and action planning to improve teamwork and future performance.

FOR DISCUSSION **What are some of the things that virtual teams probably can't do as well as face-to-face teams?**

3 How do teams work?

- An effective team achieves high levels of task performance, member satisfaction, and team viability.
- Important team inputs include the organizational setting, nature of the task, size, and membership characteristics.
- A team matures through various stages of development, including forming, storming, norming, performing, and adjourning.
- Norms are the standards or rules of conduct that influence the behavior of team members; cohesion is the attractiveness of the team to its members.
- In highly cohesive teams, members tend to conform to norms; the best situation is a team with positive performance norms and high cohesiveness.
- Distributed leadership occurs as members share in meeting a team's task and maintenance needs.
- Effective teams make use of alternative communication structures, such as the centralized and decentralized networks, to best complete tasks.

FOR DISCUSSION **What can be done if a team gets trapped in the storming stage of group development?**

4 How do teams make decisions?

- Teams can make decisions by lack of response, authority rule, minority rule, majority rule, consensus, and unanimity.
- Although group decisions often make more information available for problem solving and generate more understanding and commitment, they are slower than individual decisions and may involve social pressures to conform.
- Groupthink is a tendency of members of highly cohesive teams to lose their critical evaluative capabilities and make poor decisions.
- Techniques for improving creativity in teams include brainstorming and the nominal group technique.

FOR DISCUSSION **Is it possible that groupthink doesn't only occur when groups are highly cohesive, but also when they are pre-cohesive?**

Multiple-Choice Questions

1. When a group of people is able to achieve more than what its members could by working individually, this is called _____.

   (a) social loafing   (b) consensus   (c) viability   (d) synergy

2. In an organization operating with self-managing teams, the traditional role of _____ is replaced by the role of team leader.
(a) chief executive officer   (b) first-line supervisor   (c) middle manager   (d) general manager

3. An effective team is defined as one that achieves high levels of task performance, member satisfaction, and _____.
(a) resource efficiency   (b) future viability   (c) consensus   (d) creativity

4. In the open-systems model of teams, the _____ is an important input factor.
(a) communication network   (b) decision-making method   (c) performance norm   (d) set of membership characteristics

5. A basic rule of team dynamics states that the greater the _____ in a team, the greater the conformity to norms.
(a) membership diversity   (b) cohesiveness   (c) task structure   (d) competition among members

6. Groupthink is most likely to occur in teams that are _____.
(a) large in size   (b) diverse in membership   (c) high-performing   (d) highly cohesive

7. Gatekeeping is an example of a _____ activity that can help teams work effectively over time.
(a) task   (b) maintenance   (c) team-building   (d) decision-making

8. Members of a team tend to start to get coordinated and comfortable with one another in the _____ stage of team development.
(a) forming   (b) norming   (c) performing   (d) adjourning

9. One way for a manager to build positive norms within a team is to _____.
(a) act as a positive role model   (b) increase group size   (c) introduce groupthink   (d) isolate the team

10. When teams are highly cohesive _____.
(a) members are high performers   (b) members tend to be satisfied with their team membership   (c) members have positive norms   (d) the group achieves its goals

11. When members of a group share commitments to being on time for all meetings, on-time behavior has become _____.
(a) a symptom of groupthink   (b) synergy   (c) a norm   (d) activity maintenance

12. It would be common to find members of self-managing work teams engaged in _____.
(a) social loafing   (b) multitasking   (c) centralized communication   (d) decision by authority rule

13. The team effectiveness equation states the following:
Team Effectiveness = Quality of Inputs + (_____ − Process Losses).
(a) Process Gains   (b) Leadership Impact   (c) Membership Ability   (d) Problem Complexity

14. A _____ decision is one in which all members agree on the course of action to be taken.
(a) consensus   (b) unanimous   (c) majority   (d) nominal

15. To increase the cohesiveness of a group, a manager would be best off _____.
(a) starting competition with other groups   (b) increasing the group size   (c) acting as a positive role model
(d) introducing a new member

Short-Response Questions

16. How can a manager improve team effectiveness by modifying inputs?
17. What is the relationship among a team's cohesiveness, performance norms, and performance results?
18. How would a manager know that a team is suffering from groupthink (give two symptoms), and what could the manager do about it (give two responses)?
19. What makes a self-managing team different from a traditional work team?

Essay Question

20. Marcos Martinez has just been appointed manager of a production team operating the 11 PM to 7 AM shift in a large manufacturing firm. An experienced manager, Marcos is pleased that the team members really like and get along well with one another, but they also appear to be restricting their task outputs to the minimum acceptable levels. What could Marcos do to improve things in this situation, and why should he do them?

Management Skills and Competencies

Back to Yourself: Team Contributions

If teams and teamwork are a major part of how organizations operate today, **team contributions** have to be considered one of the most essential career skills. We need to be able to contribute as team members in many different ways so that our teams can reach their performance potential. But experience proves time and time again that teams often underperform or, at least, lose time and effectiveness as members struggle with a variety of process difficulties. You can probably confirm this quite easily with a good, hard look at the teams in which you participate. While so doing, make a realistic self-assessment of your team contributions as well as those of others. Ask: How can the insights of this chapter help me build the team leader skills that can help turn teamwork potential into real team achievements? After you complete the following Self-Assessment on Team Leader Skills, don't forget to go online to take the T-P Leadership Assessment.

> **Team contributions** are the things people do to help teams succeed and help their members enjoy the team experience.

Further Reflection: Team Leader Skills

Instructions

Consider your experience in groups and work teams while completing the following inventory. Rate yourself on each item using the following scale (circle the number that applies)[64]

1 = Almost never
2 = Seldom
3 = Sometimes
4 = Usually
5 = Almost always

Ask: "How do I behave in team leadership situations?"

1 2 3 4 5   1. Facilitate communications with and among team members between team meetings.
1 2 3 4 5   2. Provide feedback/coaching to individual team members on their performance.
1 2 3 4 5   3. Encourage creative and "out-of-the-box" thinking.
1 2 3 4 5   4. Continue to clarify stakeholder needs/expectations.
1 2 3 4 5   5. Keep team members' responsibilities and activities focused within the team's objectives and goals.
1 2 3 4 5   6. Organize and run effective and productive team meetings.
1 2 3 4 5   7. Demonstrate integrity and personal commitment.
1 2 3 4 5   8. Have excellent persuasive and influencing skills.
1 2 3 4 5   9. Respect and leverage the team's cross-functional diversity.
1 2 3 4 5   10. Recognize and reward individual contributions to team performance.
1 2 3 4 5   11. Use the appropriate decision-making style for specific issues.
1 2 3 4 5   12. Facilitate and encourage border management with the team's key stakeholders.
1 2 3 4 5   13. Ensure that the team meets its team commitments.
1 2 3 4 5   14. Bring team issues and problems to the team's attention and focus on constructive problem solving.
1 2 3 4 5   15. Provide a clear vision and direction for the team.

Scoring

The inventory measures seven dimensions of team leadership. Add your scores for the items listed next to each dimension below to get an indication of your potential strengths and weaknesses.

    1, 9   Building the Team
    2, 10   Developing People
    3, 11   Team Problem Solving and Decision Making
    4, 12   Stakeholder Relations
    5, 13   Team Performance
    6, 14   Team Process
 7, 8, 15   Providing Personal Leadership

Interpretation

The higher the score, the more confident you are on the particular skill and leadership capability. Consider giving this inventory to people who have worked with you in teams and have them rate you. Compare the results to your self-assessment. Also, remember it is doubtful that any one team leader is capable of exhibiting all the skills listed. More and more, organizations are emphasizing teams that blend a variety of skills, rather than depending on the vision of the single, heroic leader figure. As long as the necessary leadership skills are represented within the membership, it is more likely that the team will be healthy and achieve high performance. Of course, the more skills you bring with you to team leadership situations, the better.

Team Exercise

Work Team Dynamics

Preparation

Think about your course work group, a work group you are involved in for another course, or any other group suggested by your instructor. Use this scale to indicate how often each of the following statements accurately reflects your experience in the group.[65]

1 All the time   2 Very often   3 Sometimes   4 Never happens

1. My ideas get a fair hearing.
2. I am encouraged to give innovative ideas and take risks.
3. Diverse opinions within the group are encouraged.
4. I have all the responsibility I want.
5. There is a lot of favoritism shown in the group.
6. Members trust one another to do their assigned work.
7. The group sets high standards of performance excellence.
8. People share and change jobs a lot in the group.
9. You can make mistakes and learn from them in this group.
10. This group has good operating rules.

Instructions

Form teams as assigned by your instructor. Ideally, this will be the group you have just rated. Have all members share their ratings, and then make one master rating for the team as a whole. Circle the items for which there are the biggest differences of opinion. Discuss those items and try to find out why they exist. In general, the better a team scores on this instrument, the higher its creative potential. Make a list of the five most important things members believe they can do to help groups perform better. Nominate a spokesperson to summarize your discussion for the class as a whole.

Case Study: NASCAR

Go to Management Cases for Critical Thinking to find the recommended case for Chapter 16—
"NASCAR: Fast Cars, Passion, and Teamwork Create Wins."

Communication and Collaboration

17

Learning From Others

Impact Begins with Communication and Collaboration

"My Siamese cat Skimbleshanks is up a tree . . . At Wilco concert—Jeff Tweedy is so cool . . . Home alone . . . Flying to Ireland, wish me luck driving . . . Just saw Todd with Stephanie!"

So who cares? Well it turns out that a lot of people care, just as Evan Williams and Biz Stone, co-founders of Twitter, had anticipated. They are the guys who moved microblogging into the upper limits. And the quick, easy, and ever-present social networking offered through Twitter isn't just for friends and family—companies are using it, radio and television shows are using it, and, of course, celebrities are using it.

According to David Murray, director of social Web communications at Bivings Group, "Twitter is a digital handshake. It's one of the fastest ways you can reach out to people." The Twitter concept of sending 140 character or less "tweets" hit the mark with traffic rising quickly to the 40 million range. "I guess we have a lot of things we think we can prove," Stone says, "to provide the infrastructure for a new kind of communication, and then support the creativity that emerges." For his part, Williams points out: "we're totally focused on making the best user experience possible and building a defensible communications network."

Both Stone and Williams have been part of the Internet business community through many past ventures, including Blogger, which was purchased by Google. Williams is actually credited with coining the word "blog," and Stone has published two books on blogging. From something that Stone calls "the side project that took," the Twitter revolution has had a broad impact. But it's also challenging for the firm and its founders. Twitter is dealing with rapid growth in both users and employees, lack of business expertise on the staff, and the need to turn the Twitter user experience into revenue generation. Williams says: "If it weren't growing nearly as fast, we would be building a lot more things."

do the benchmarking

Are you part of the Twitter community, on Facebook, always juggling multiple windows on your PC, married to your mobile device . . . and more? Technology hasn't just changed how we communicate; it has created a social media revolution that even managers are finding can be a performance asset. **There's no doubt that the ability to achieve positive personal impact through communication and collaboration is a "must-have" management competency.**

Learning About Yourself

Communication and Networking

Speaking about personal development, how strong are your **communication and networking** skills? Recruiters give them high priority when screening candidates for college internships and first jobs. Who wants to hire someone that can't communicate well both orally and in writing, and network well with others for collaboration and work accomplishment? Those are the facts, but, if you're like many of us, there's work to be done to master the challenge.

Compare your communication skills with these data. The American Management Association reports that workers rated their bosses only slightly above average on transforming ideas into words, being credible, listening and asking questions, and giving written and oral presentations. Over three-quarters of university professors in one survey rated incoming high school graduates as only "fair" or "poor" in writing clearly, and in spelling and use of grammar.[1] And when it comes to decorum, or just plain old "good manners," a *BusinessWeek* survey reports that 38% of women complain about "sexual innuendo, wisecracks and taunts" at work.[2]

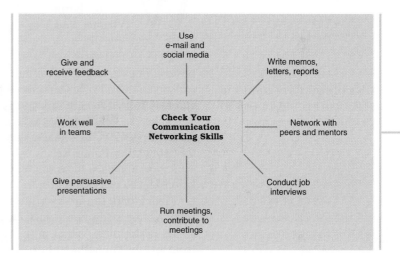

When it comes to networking skills, don't forget that we often do well or poorly at work as a result of how well we use communication to link with other people. Social networking is in on the college campus and among young professionals, as everyone wants to be "linked in." The same skills have to transfer to the workplace. For some of us, networking is as natural as walking down the street, but for others it can be a challenge. A good networker is able to act as a *hub*—connected with others; *gatekeeper*—moving information to and from others; and *pulse-taker*—staying abreast of what is happening.[3]

get to know yourself better

Can you convince a recruiter that you are ready to run effective meetings, write informative reports, deliver persuasive presentations, conduct job interviews, use e-mail and social media well, keep conflicts constructive and negotiations positive, and network well with peers and mentors? The list is long, but every item on it counts. **Make use of the end-of-chapter Self-Assessment feature to further reflect on your communication and networking skills, as well as your use of Conflict Management Strategies.**

Study Question 1	Study Question 2	Study Question 3	Study Question 4
The Communication Process	**Improving Collaboration**	**Managing Conflict**	**Managing Negotiation**
• Effective communication • Persuasion and credibility in communication • Communication barriers • Cross-cultural communication	• Transparency and openness • Interactive management • Use of electronic media • Active listening • Constructive feedback • Space design	• Functional and dysfunctional conflict • Causes of conflict • Conflict resolution • Conflict management styles • Structural approaches to conflict management	• Negotiation goals and approaches • Gaining integrative agreements • Negotiation pitfalls • Third-party dispute resolution
Learning Check 1	**Learning Check 2**	**Learning Check 3**	**Learning Check 4**

Social capital is a capacity to get things done with the support and help of others.

When recruiters are asked what attributes are most important for graduates of business schools, interpersonal skills often top the lists.[4] Whether you work at the top—building support for strategies and organizational goals, or at lower levels—interacting with others to support their work efforts and your own, your career tool kit must include abilities to achieve positive impact through communication and collaboration. They are foundations for something all managers need—**social capital**, the capacity to attract support and help from others in order to get things done.

Whereas intellectual capital is basically what you know, social capital comes from the people you know and how well you relate to them. Pam Alexander, former CEO of Ogilvy Public Relations Worldwide, says: "Relationships are the most powerful form of media. Ideas will only get you so far these days. Count on personal relationships to carry you further."[5]

Think back to the descriptions of managerial work by Henry Mintzberg and John Kotter as discussed in Chapter 1. For Mintzberg, managerial success involves performing well as an information "nerve center," gathering information from and disseminating information to internal and external sources.[6] For Kotter, it depends largely on one's ability to build and maintain a complex web of interpersonal networks with insiders and outsiders so as to implement work priorities and agendas.[7] And when it comes to such capacities for communication and collaboration, most of us probably get it right some of the time but also make our fair share of mistakes. Here are three examples of managers who took steps toward self-improvement by participating in workshops held at the Center for Creative Leadership, or CCL.[8]

Richard Herlich went to the CCL after being promoted to director of marketing for his firm. "I thought I had the perfect style," he said. But role-playing exercises showed that others perceived him as aloof and a poor communicator. Richard made it a point in his new job to meet with his marketing team, discuss his style, and become more involved in their work projects.

Lisa DiTrullio learned from her CCL experiences that "feedback reassures and reenergizes you around what you're doing well and helps you identify areas for development." She gained confidence and says the CCL experience gave her "momentum and energy" to take her to the "next level" of accomplishment. She went on to found her own consulting firm—Lisa DiTrullio & Associates.

Vance Tang learned at CCL that he had an introverted personality, one that might cause others to see him as "cold and distant" in his role as CEO of Kone, Inc. Now he explains his style so people will understand that he isn't slighting them, and he also tries to be more "outgoing" in his relationships.

THE COMMUNICATION PROCESS

Although we can't all attend special training programs like those just described, we can learn from experience and strive to improve how we work with and relate to others. A solid first step is to understand our skills with **communication**, described in Figure 17.1 as an interpersonal process of sending and receiving symbols with messages attached to them. This process can be understood as a series of questions: "Who?" (sender) "says what?" (message) "in what ways?" (channel) "to whom?" (receiver) "with what result?" (interpreted meaning).

● **Communication** is the process of sending and receiving symbols with meanings attached.

The ability to communicate well both orally and in writing is a critical managerial skill and one of the foundation competencies for successful leadership. Through communication people exchange and share information with one another, and influence one another's attitudes, behaviors, and understandings. Managers, for example, use communication to establish and maintain interpersonal relationships, listen to others, deal with conflicts, negotiate, and otherwise gain the information needed to create a high-performance workplace.

EFFECTIVE COMMUNICATION

One problem often encountered in communication is that we take our abilities for granted and end up being disappointed when the process breaks down. Another problem occurs when we are too busy, or too lazy, to invest enough time in making sure that the process really works. These problems raise questions of "effectiveness" and "efficiency" in the communication process. **Effective communication** occurs when the sender's message is fully understood by the receiver. **Efficient communication** occurs at minimum cost in terms of resources expended.

● In **effective communication** the intended meaning is fully understood by the receiver.

● **Efficient communication** occurs at minimum cost.

It's nice for our communications to be effective and efficient. But, as we all know, this isn't always achieved. For one thing, efficiency is sometimes traded for effectiveness. Picture your instructor taking the time to communicate individually with each student about this chapter. It would be virtually impossible. Even if it were possible, it would be costly. This is why managers often leave voice-mail messages and interact by e-mail, rather than visit people personally. These alternatives are more efficient than one-on-one and face-to-face communications, but they may

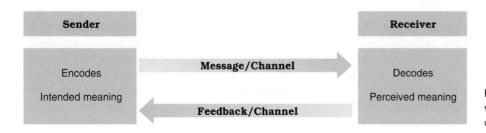

FIGURE 17.1 The interactive two-way process of interpersonal communication.

Wal-Mart Founder Considered the "Great Communicator"

The late Sam Walton, Wal-Mart's founder, was considered a master of persuasive communication. Picture him in a store and wearing a Wal-Mart baseball cap. "Northeast Memphis," he says, "you must have the best floor-cleaning crew in America. This floor is so clean, let's sit down on it." He continues: "I thank you. The company is so proud of you we can hardly stand it. But you know that confounded Kmart is getting better, and so is Target. So what's our challenge?" Walton asks. "Customer service," he replies in answer to his own question, most likely showing a big smile as well.

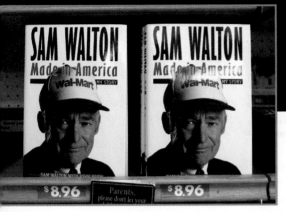

not always be effective. Although an e-mail note to a distribution list may save time, not everyone might get the same meaning from the message.

By the same token, an effective communication may not always be efficient. If a team leader visits each team member individually to explain a new change in procedures, this may guarantee that everyone truly understands the change. But it may also take a lot of the leader's time. In these and other ways, potential trade-offs between effectiveness and efficiency must be recognized in communication.

PERSUASION AND CREDIBILITY IN COMMUNICATION

Communication is not only about sharing information or being "heard." It often includes the intent of one party to influence or motivate the other in a desired way. **Persuasive communication** results in a recipient agreeing with or supporting the message being presented.[9] Managers get things done by working with and persuading others who are their peers, teammates, coworkers, and bosses. They often get things done more by convincing than by giving orders.

Scholar and consultant Jay Conger says that many managers "confuse persuasion with taking bold stands and aggressive arguing."[10] He points out that this often leads to "counterpersuasion" responses and may even raise questions about credibility, something managers can't afford to lose. **Credible communication earns trust, respect, and integrity in the eyes of others.** And without credibility, Conger sees little chance that persuasion can be successful. Conger's advice is to build credibility for persuasive communication through expertise and relationships.

To build credibility through expertise, you must be knowledgeable about the issue in question or have a successful track record in dealing with similar issues in the past. In a hiring situation where you are trying to persuade team members to select candidate A rather than B, for example, you must be able to defend your reasons. And it will always be better if your past recommendations turned out to be good ones. To build credibility through relationships, you must have a good working relationship with the person to be persuaded. And it is always easier to get someone to do what you want if that person likes you. In a hiring situation where you want to persuade your boss to provide a special bonus package to attract top job candidates, for example, having a good relationship with your boss can add credibility to your request.

- **Persuasive communication** presents a message in a manner that causes the other person to support it.

- **Credible communication** earns trust, respect, and integrity in the eyes of others.

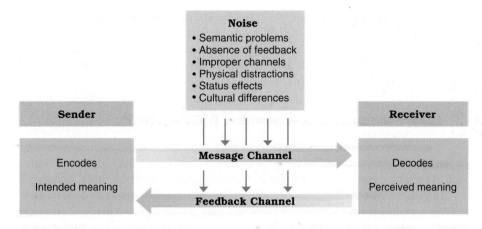

FIGURE 17.2 Downsides of noise, shown as anything that interferes with the effectiveness of the communication process.

COMMUNICATION BARRIERS

When Yoshihiro Wada was president of Mazda Corporation, he once met with representatives of the firm's American joint venture partner, Ford. But he had to use an interpreter. He estimated that 20% of his intended meaning was lost in the exchange between himself and the interpreter, while another 20% was lost between the interpreter and the Americans.[11] When Stephen Martin was head of a firm in England, he once "went underground" for two weeks and posed under an assumed name as an office worker. He says: "They (workers) said things to me that they never have told their managers" . . . "Our key messages were just not getting through to people" . . . "We were asking the impossible of some of them." And when he shared these concerns with his firm's managers, they replied: "They never told us that!"[12]

These examples show the downsides of **noise**, shown in Figure 17.2 as anything that interferes with the effectiveness of the communication process. The potential for noise is quite evident in foreign language situations like Wada's, but perhaps less evident in boss-worker communications like Martin's. And, do you recognize it in everyday conversations and even text messaging, as shown in the boxed exchange between a high-tech millennial and a low-tech baby boomer manager? Common sources of noise that often create communication barriers include information filtering, poor choice of channels, poor written or oral expression, failures to recognize nonverbal signals, and physical distractions.

● **noise** is anything that interferes with the effectiveness of communication.

Millennial text to baby boomer
- Omg sorry abt mtg nbd 4 now b rdy nxt time g2g ttl

Baby boomer text to millennial
- Missed you at meeting. It was important. Don't forget next one. Stop by office.

Information Filtering

"Criticize my boss? I don't have the right to." "I'd get fired." "It's her company, not mine." The risk of ineffective communication may be highest when those at lower and higher levels in organizations are trying to communicate with each other. Consider the "corporate cover-up" once discovered at an electronics company. Product shipments were being predated and papers falsified as salespersons struggled to meet unrealistic sales targets set by the president. At least 20 persons in the organization cooperated in the deception, and it was months before the president found out. What happened in this case was **information filtering**—the intentional distortion of information to make it appear favorable to the recipient.

Tom Peters, management author and consultant, has called information distortion "Management Enemy Number 1." He even goes so far as to say that "once you become a boss you will never hear the unadulterated truth again."[13] The problem most often involves someone "telling the boss what he or she wants to hear."

● **Information filtering** is the intentional distortion of information to make it appear most favorable to the recipient.

Whether the reason behind this is a fear of retribution for bringing bad news, an unwillingness to identify personal mistakes, or just a general desire to please, the end result is the same. The higher-level person receiving filtered communications from below can end up making poor decisions because of a biased and inaccurate information base.

#2 Poor Choice of Channels   *Noise #2*

● A **communication channel** is the pathway through which a message moves from sender to receiver.

A **communication channel** is the pathway or medium through which a message is conveyed from sender to receiver. Good managers choose the right communication channel, or combination of channels, to accomplish their intended purpose.[14]

In general, written channels—paper or electronic memos, letters, and messages—are acceptable for simple messages that are easy to convey and for those that require extensive dissemination quickly. They are also important as documentation when formal policies or directives are being conveyed. Spoken channels such as meetings—virtual or face to face—work best for messages that are complex and difficult to convey and where immediate feedback to the sender is valuable. They are also more personal and can create a supportive, even inspirational, climate.

#3 Poor Written or Oral Expression   *Noise #3*

Communication will be effective only to the extent that the sender expresses a message in a way that can be clearly understood by the receiver. This means that words must be well chosen and properly used to express the sender's intentions. Consider the following "bafflegab" found among some executive communications.

Management Smarts 17.1

How to make a successful presentation

- *Be prepared:* know what you want to say; know how you want to say it; rehearse saying it.

- *Set the right tone:* act audience centered; make eye contact; be pleasant and confident.

- *Sequence and support points:* state your purpose; make important points; give reasons and details; then summarize.

- *Accent the presentation:* use good visual aids; avoid unnecessary "flash;" provide supporting handouts when possible.

- *Add the right amount of polish:* attend to details; have room, materials, and arrangements ready to go.

- *Check your technology:* test out everything ahead of time; make sure it works and then use it smoothly.

- *Be professional:* be on time; wear appropriate attire; act organized, confident, and enthusiastic.

A business report said: "Consumer elements are continuing to stress the fundamental necessity of a stabilization of the price structure at a lower level than exists at the present time." *Translation:* Consumers keep saying that prices must go down and stay down.

A manager said: "Substantial economies were affected in this division by increasing the time interval between distributions of data-eliciting forms to business entities." *Translation:* The division saved money by sending out fewer questionnaires.

A survey of 120 companies by the National Commission on Writing found that over one-third of their employees were considered deficient in writing skills and that employers were spending over $3 billion each year on remedial training.[15] Such training typically covers both written and oral expression. Management Smarts 17.1 offers guidelines on an important communication situation—the executive briefing or formal presentation.[16]

#4 Failure to Recognize Nonverbal Signals   *Noise #4*

● **Nonverbal communication** takes place through gestures and body language.

Nonverbal communication takes place through such things as hand movements, facial expressions, body posture, eye contact, and the use of interpersonal space. It can be a powerful means of transmitting messages, with research showing that up to 55% of a message's impact may come through nonverbal communication.[17] In fact, a potential problem in the growing use of voice mail, text messaging, computer networking, and other electronic communications is that the loss of gestures and other nonverbal signals may lower communication effectiveness.

Think of how nonverbal signals play out in your own communications. The astute observer notes the "body language" expressed by other persons. Gestures, for example, can make a difference in whether someone's speech is positive or negative, excited or bored, or even engaged with or disengaged from you.[18] We can't forget that sometimes our body may be "talking" for us, even as we otherwise maintain silence. And when we do speak, our body may sometimes "say" different things than our words convey.

A **mixed message** occurs when a person's words communicate one message while his or her actions, body language, appearance, or use of interpersonal space communicate something else. Watch how people behave in a meeting. A person who feels under attack may move back in a chair or lean away from the presumed antagonist, even while expressing verbal agreement. All of this may be done quite unconsciously, but it sends a message that will be picked up by those who are on the alert.

> A **mixed message** results when words communicate one message while actions, body language, or appearance communicate something else.

Physical Distractions *Noise # 5*

Any number of physical distractions can interfere with communication effectiveness. Some of these distractions, such as telephone interruptions, drop-in visitors, and lack of privacy, are evident in the following conversation between an employee, George, and his manager.[19]

> Okay, George, let's hear your problem [phone rings, boss picks it up, promises to deliver a report "just as soon as I can get it done"]. Uh, now, where were we—oh, you're having a problem with your technician. She's . . . [manager's assistant brings in some papers that need his immediate signature; assistant leaves] you say she's overstressed lately, wants to leave. I tell you what, George, why don't you [phone rings again, lunch partner drops by] uh, take a stab at handling it yourself. I've got to go now.

Besides what may have been poor intentions in the first place, the manager in this example did not do a good job of communicating with George. This problem could be easily corrected; many communication distractions can be avoided or at least minimized through proper planning. If George has something important to say, the manager should set aside adequate time for the meeting. Additional interruptions such as telephone calls and drop-in visitors could easily be eliminated by good planning.

CROSS-CULTURAL COMMUNICATION *Noise #6*

After taking over as the CEO of the Dutch publisher Wolters Kluwer, Nancy McKinstry initiated major changes in strategy and operations—cutting staff, restructuring divisions, and investing in new business areas. As the first American to head the firm, she first described the new strategy as "aggressive" when speaking with her management team. But after learning the word wasn't well received by Europeans, she switched to "decisive." She says: "I was coming across as too harsh, too much of a results-driven American to the people I needed to get on board."[20]

When the sender and receiver are from different cultures, communicating is a significant challenge, one well recognized by international travelers and executives. To begin, it's hard to communicate when you don't speak each other's languages.

Messages even get lost in translation, as classic advertising miscues such as these demonstrate. A Pepsi ad in Taiwan that intended to say "The Pepsi Generation" came out as "Pepsi will bring your ancestors back from the dead"; a KFC ad in China that intended to convey "finger lickin' good" came out as "eat your fingers off."[21] Cultural differences are also common in nonverbal communication, including everything from the use of gestures to interpersonal space.[22] The American "thumbs-up" sign is an insult in Ghana and Australia; signaling "OK" with thumb and forefinger circled together is not okay in parts of Europe; whereas we wave "hello" with an open palm, in West Africa it's an insult, suggesting the other person has five fathers.[23]

● **Ethnocentrism** is the tendency to consider one's culture superior to any and all others.

One of the major enemies of effective cross-cultural communication is **ethnocentrism**—the tendency to consider one's culture superior to any and all others. Ethnocentrism can hurt communication in at least three major ways. First, it may cause someone to not listen well to what others have to say. Second, it may cause someone to address or speak with others in ways that alienate them. And third, it may lead to the use of inappropriate stereotypes when dealing with persons from other cultures.[24]

☑ **Learning Check** **Study Question 1** What is the communication process?	*Be sure you can* ☑ describe the communication process and identify its key components ☑ differentiate between effective and efficient communication ☑ explain the role of credibility in persuasive communication ☑ list the common sources of noise that inhibit effective communication ☑ explain how mixed messages and filtering interfere with communication ☑ explain how ethnocentrism affects cross-cultural communication

IMPROVING COLLABORATION THROUGH COMMUNICATION

Effective communication is an essential foundation for collaboration as people work together in organizations. And the better the communication, the greater the likelihood of successful collaboration. A number of things can be done to improve the communication process by reducing noise, overcoming barriers, and improving interpersonal connections. They include transparency, interactive management, use of electronic media, active listening, constructive feedback, and space design.

TRANSPARENCY AND OPENNESS

At HCL Industries, a large technology outsourcing firm, CEO Vineet Nayar believes that one of his most important tasks for a CEO is to create a "culture of trust" in the firm. To do that, he says, you have to create transparency. At HCL, transparency means that the firm's financial information is fully posted on the internal Web. As Nayar puts it, "We put all the dirty linen on the table." Transparency also means that the results of 360° feedback reviews for HCL's 3,800 managers are posted on the internal Web, including Nayar's own reviews. And when managers present plans to the top management team, Nayar insists that they too get posted on the internal Web so that others can read and comment on them. By the time a plan is approved it's likely to be a good one, Nayar says, because of the "massive collaborative learning that took place."[25]

● **Communication transparency** involves openly sharing honest and complete information about the organization and workplace affairs.

As just illustrated, **communication transparency** involves being honest and openly sharing accurate and complete information about the organization and workplace affairs. A lack of communication transparency is evident when managers try to hide such information and restrict the access of organizational members to it. The expected result of being transparent and open in communication is a positive impact on employee engagement and greater feelings of trust between them and their managers.

Open communication was one of the hallmarks of how Nucor CEO Daniel R. DiMicco handled the impact of recession on his firm and its employees. Instead of hunkering down behind closed doors talking about the crisis with other executives, DiMicco doubled the time he spent out in the firm's plants talking with employees. He and his managers kept everyone informed about the status of orders for the firm's products. The open communication is well appreciated. One employee sent a card to top management saying, "Thank you for caring about me and my family."[26]

This emphasis on communication transparency is sometimes associated with the notion of **open book management**, in which managers like Vineet Nayar and Daniel DiMicco provide employees with essential financial information about their companies. At Bailard, Inc., a private investment firm, this openness extends to salaries; if you want to know what others are making at the firm, all you need to do is ask the chief financial officer. The firm's co-founder and CEO Thomas Bailard believes this is a good way to defeat office politics. "As a manager," he says, "if you know that your compensation decisions are essentially going to be public, you have to have pretty strong conviction about any decision you make."[27]

⬤ **Open book management** is where managers provide employees with essential financial information about their companies.

INTERACTIVE MANAGEMENT #2 overcome Noise:

One of the ways to pursue transparency is by adopting interactive management practices that keep communication channels open between organizational levels. A popular choice is **management by wandering around (MBWA)**—dealing directly with subordinates or team members by regularly spending time walking around and talking with them. It is basically communicating face to face to find out what is going on. Another interactive management practice involves open office hours whereby busy executives set aside time in their calendars to welcome walk-in visits during certain hours. A rotating schedule of "shirtsleeve" meetings can also bring top managers into face-to-face contact with mixed employee groups throughout an organization. And some organizations form groups such as elected employee advisory councils whose members meet with management on a regular schedule to share information and discuss issues.

⬤ In **management by wandering around (MBWA)**, managers spend time outside their offices to meet and talk with workers at all levels.

Manager Finds Workers' Ideas Really Sweet

Hammond's Candies was in business for 90 years when the Denver, Colorado, business was bought by entrepreneur Andrew Schuman. But the firm was losing money, and Schuman didn't know the candy business. He had what he calls an "aha" moment when learning that Hammond's famous ribbon snowflake candy was the brainchild of an assembly-line worker. "I thought," he says, "wow, we have a lot of smart people back here, and we're not tapping their knowledge." By encouraging a flow of more such ideas, Schuman has been able to move his new company out of the red and into the black.

Today, interactive management also takes many electronic forms creating what might be called *virtual MBWA*. Things like online discussion forums, always-on instant messaging, electronic office hours, executive blogs, and video conferences allow managers to overcome time and distance limitations that might otherwise make communication more difficult and less regular.

#3. USE OF ELECTRONIC MEDIA *overcome Noise #3*

Channel richness is the capacity of a communication channel to effectively carry information.

Today's array of electronic media has lots to offer in management, but its limits also need to be understood.[28] Good, old-fashioned face-to-face communication hasn't gone away and can often be the better choice. Consider, for example, the issue of channel richness—the capacity of a communication channel to carry information in an effective manner.[29] Figure 17.3 shows that face-to-face communication is very high in richness because it allows for two-way interaction and real-time feedback. Written reports, memos, and e-mail are lower in richness because they are more one-way and offer limited opportunity for feedback.

In everyday interactions and at work we are often advised to err on the side of "over communicating," staying in touch, sending information, and expressing gratitude even a bit more than necessary. And electronic media make this pretty easy. But they can be misused as well. Sending a message like "Thnx for the IView! I Wud Luv to Work 4 U!! ;)" isn't the follow-up message most employers like to receive from job candidates. When Tory Johnson, president of Women for Hire, Inc., received a thank-you note by e-mail from an intern candidate, it included "hiya," "thanx," three exclamation points, and two emoticons. She says: "That e-mail just ruined it for me."[30] Even though textspeak and emoticons are the norm in social networks, most staffing professionals consider their use "not professional."

Privacy is also a big issue in the electronic workplace.[31] And when Facebook's CEO, Mark Zuckerberg, says privacy is "no longer a social norm," it's time to take the issue seriously. While employees are concerned that employers are eavesdropping on their computer usage, employers are concerned that too much work time gets spent in personal Web browsing and social networking. They're also concerned about the purpose driving some of that use. Consider this tweet that became an Internet sensation: "Cisco just offered me a job! Now I have to weigh the utility of a fatty paycheck against the daily commute to San Jose and hating the work."[32] What would you do if you were the recruiter who had just made this job offer? When it comes to Web browsing and using electronic media at work, the best advice comes down to this: Find out the employer's policy and follow it. And don't ever assume that you have electronic privacy; chances are the employer is checking or can easily check on you.[33]

Electronic grapevines use electronic media to pass messages and information among members of social networks.

The **electronic grapevine** is now a fact of life as electronic messages fly around our world with great speed as they carry both accurate and inaccurate information. Not too long ago, for example, a law professor told his class that Chief Justice John Roberts was resigning from the U.S. Supreme Court—it was a lesson

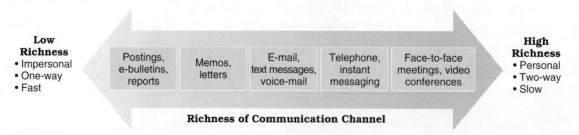

FIGURE 17.3 Channel richness and the use of communication media.

Don't Count on Electronic Privacy

Is electronic "snooping" justified in the employment contract? An American Management Association survey of 304 U.S. companies found the following: 66% monitor Internet connections; 65% block websites, pornography (96%), games (61%), social networking (61%), shopping/auction (27%), sports (21%); 45% track key strokes and keyboard time; 43% store and review computer files; 43% monitor e-mail; 45% monitor telephone time and numbers dialed; and 30% have fired employees for misuse of the Internet.

on checking facts of stories. By the time students realized what he was doing, the false story had been spread by instant messaging and e-mails to the point of almost making the national news.[34]

This power of the electronic grapevine has its upside and downside. On the upside, General Electric started a "Tweet Squad" to advise the rest of the organization how social networking could be used to improve internal collaboration.[35] Domino's Pizza executives felt the downside when a YouTube video showed two Domino's employees doing all sorts of nasty things to sandwiches. It was soon viewed over a million times and by the time the video was pulled (by one of its authors who apologized for "faking"), negative chat created a crisis in customer confidence. Domino's management finally created a Twitter account and posted a YouTube video message from the CEO to present its own view of the story.[36]

#4 ACTIVE LISTENING   Overcome Noise #4

Whether trying to communicate electronically or face to face, managers must be very good at listening. When people "talk," they are trying to communicate something. That "something" may or may not be what they are saying.

Active listening is the process of taking action to help someone say exactly what he or she really means.[37] It involves being sincere and trying to find out the full meaning of what is being said. It also involves being disciplined in controlling emotions and withholding premature evaluations or interpretations. Different responses to the following two questions contrast how a "passive" listener and an "active" listener might act in real workplace conversations.

> *Question 1:* "Don't you think employees should be promoted on the basis of seniority?" Passive listener's response: "No, I don't!" Active listener's response: "It seems to you that they should, I take it?"

> *Question 2:* "What does the supervisor expect us to do about these out-of-date computers?" Passive listener's response: "Do the best you can, I guess." Active listener's response: "You're pretty frustrated with those machines, aren't you?"

These examples help show how active listening can facilitate rather than discourage communication in difficult circumstances. As you think further about what you can do to get better at active listening, keep these rules in mind.[38]

1. *Listen for message content:* Try to hear exactly what content is being conveyed in the message.
2. *Listen for feelings:* Try to identify how the source feels about the content in the message.

● **Active listening** helps the source of a message say what he or she really means.

3. *Respond to feelings:* Let the source know that her or his feelings are being recognized.

4. *Note all cues:* Be sensitive to nonverbal and verbal messages; be alert for mixed messages.

5. *Paraphrase and restate:* State back to the source what you think you are hearing.

#5 CONSTRUCTIVE FEEDBACK Overcome Noise #5

● **Feedback** is the process of telling someone else how you feel about something that person did or said.

The process of telling other people how you feel about something they did or said, or about the situation in general, is called **feedback**. Consider these examples of the types of feedback people receive and deliver to one another.[39]

Evaluative feedback: "You are unreliable and always late for everything."
Interpretive feedback: "You're coming late to meetings; you might be spreading yourself too thin and have trouble meeting your obligations."
Descriptive feedback: "You were 30 minutes late for today's meeting and missed a lot of the context for our discussion."

The art of giving feedback is an indispensable skill, particularly for managers who must regularly give feedback to other people. When poorly done, feedback can be threatening to the recipient and cause resentment. When properly done, feedback—even performance criticism—can be listened to, accepted, and used to good advantage by the receiver.[40] When Lydia Whitefield, a marketing vice president at Avaya, asked one of her managers for feedback, she was surprised. He said: "You're angry a lot." Whitfield learned from the experience, saying: "What he and other employees saw as my anger, I saw as my passion."[41]

There are ways to make sure that feedback is useful and constructive rather than harmful. To begin, the feedback should offer real benefit to the receiver and not just satisfy some personal need of the sender. A supervisor who berates a computer programmer for errors, for example, may actually be angry about failing to give clear instructions in the first place. The sender should also follow those guidelines to make sure that feedback is always understandable, acceptable, plausible, and "constructive."[42]

- Give feedback directly and with real feeling, based on trust between you and the receiver.
- Make sure that feedback is specific rather than general; use good, clear, and preferably recent examples to make your points.
- Give feedback at a time when the receiver seems most willing or able to accept it.
- Make sure the feedback is valid; limit it to things the receiver can be expected to do something about.
- Give feedback in small doses; never give more than the receiver can handle at any particular time.

#6 SPACE DESIGN Overcome Noise #6

● **Proxemics** involves the use of space in communication.

Other important lessons about communication can be found in **proxemics**, the study of how we use space.[43] Simply put, space and how we use it is a form of communication. The distance between people conveys varying intentions in terms of intimacy, openness, and status in interpersonal communications. And the physical layout of an office or room is a form of nonverbal communication. Think about it.

Real Ethics

Blogging Is Easy, but Bloggers Should Beware

It is easy and tempting to set up your own blog, write about your experiences and impressions, and then share your thoughts with others online. So, why not do it?

Catherine Sanderson, a British citizen living and working in Paris, might have asked this question before launching her blog, Le Petite Anglaise. At one point it was so "successful" that she had 3,000 readers. But the Internet diary included reports on her experiences at work—and her employer, an accounting firm, wasn't at all happy when it became public knowledge.

Even though Sanderson was blogging anonymously, her photo was on the site, and the connection was eventually discovered. Noticed, too, was her running commentary about bosses, colleagues, and life at the office. One boss, she wrote, "calls secretaries 'typists.'" A Christmas party was described in detail, including an executive's "unforgivable faux pas." Under the heading "Titillation," she told how she displayed cleavage during a video conference at the office.

It's all out now. News reports said that one of the firm's partners was "incandescent with rage" after learning what Sanderson had written about him. Now Sanderson is upset. She says that she was "dooced"—a term used to describe being fired for what one writes in a blog. She wants financial damages and confirmation of her rights, on principle, to have a private blog.

You Decide

Just what are the ethical issues here, both from the blogger's and the employer's perspective? What rights do employees have with regard to communicating about their work experiences? Is it ethical for a supervisor to fire an employee any time the employee says something negative about the organization? For example, which is the bigger "crime," to get drunk at the office holiday party or to write a blog that reports that your supervisor got drunk at the office party? What obligations do employees have to their employers even when they are off the clock, and, in contrast, where does the employer's ability to control employee behaviors outside of work end?

Offices with chairs available for side-by-side seating convey different messages than offices where the manager's chair sits behind the desk and those for visitors sit facing it in front. An extreme example of space design and communication confronted Tim Armstrong when he became CEO of AOL. One of his first decisions was to remove the doors separating executive offices from other workers. Previously, the only way to open them had been with a company key card.[44]

Architects and consultants specializing in organizational ecology are helping executives build offices conducive to the intense communication needed in today's work environments. When Sun Microsystems built its San Jose, California, facility, public spaces were designed to encourage communication among persons from different departments. Many meeting areas had no walls, and most walls were glass. As manager of planning and research, Ann Bamesberger said: "We were creating a way to get these people to communicate with each other more."[45] At Google headquarters, or "googleplex," telecommuters work in specially designed office "tents." These are made of acrylics to allow both a sense of private, personal space and transparency.[46] And at b&a advertising in Dublin, Ohio, "open space" supports the small ad agency's emphasis on creativity—after all, its Web address is www.babrain.com. There are no offices or cubicles, and all office equipment is portable. Desks have wheels so that informal meetings can take place by people repositioning themselves for spontaneous collaboration. Even the formal meetings are held "standing up" in the company kitchen. Face-to-face communication is the rule; internal e-mail among b&a employees is banned.[47]

MANAGING CONFLICT

Conflict is a disagreement over issues of substance and/or an emotional antagonism.

Substantive conflict involves disagreements over goals, resources, rewards, policies, procedures, and job assignments.

Emotional conflict results from feelings of anger, distrust, dislike, fear, and resentment, as well as from personality clashes.

Among your communication and collaboration skills, the ability to deal with conflicts is critical. **Conflict** is a disagreement between people on substantive or emotional issues.[48] Managers and team leaders spend a lot of time dealing with conflicts of both types. **Substantive conflicts** involve disagreements over such things as goals and tasks, allocation of resources, distribution of rewards, policies and procedures, and job assignments. **Emotional conflicts** result from feelings of anger, distrust, dislike, fear, and resentment, as well as from personality clashes and relationship problems. Both forms of conflict can cause difficulties. But when managed well, they can also be helpful in promoting creativity and high performance.

FUNCTIONAL AND DYSFUNCTIONAL CONFLICT

Functional conflict is constructive and helps task performance.

Dysfunctional conflict is destructive and hurts task performance.

The inverted "U" curve depicted in Figure 17.4 shows that conflict of moderate intensity can be good for performance. This **functional conflict**, or constructive conflict, stimulates people toward greater work efforts, cooperation, and creativity. It helps teams achieve their goals and avoid groupthink, described in the last chapter as a tendency for highly cohesive groups to make bad decisions because members are unwilling to engage in conflict.

At very low or very high intensities, **dysfunctional conflict**, or destructive conflict, occurs. Too much conflict is distracting and interferes with other more task-relevant activities. Too little conflict promotes groupthink, complacency, and the loss of a high-performance edge.

Wacs
Shack

CAUSES OF CONFLICT

When it comes to managing conflict, it helps to understand the antecedent conditions that make the emergence of conflict more likely. *Role ambiguities* set the

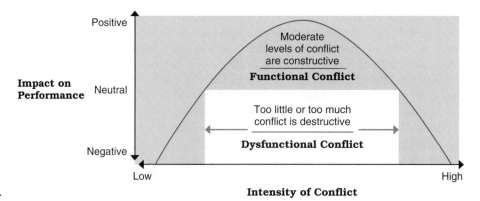

FIGURE 17.4 The relationship between conflict and performance.

stage for conflict. Unclear job expectations and other task uncertainties increase the probability that some people will be working at cross-purposes, at least some of the time. *Resource scarcities* cause conflict. Having to share resources with others or compete directly with them for resource allocations creates a potential conflict situation, especially when resources are scarce. *Task interdependencies* cause conflict. When individuals or groups must depend on what others do to perform well themselves, conflicts often occur.

Competing objectives are also opportunities for conflict. When goals are poorly set or reward systems are poorly designed, individuals and groups may come into conflict by working to one another's disadvantage. *Structural differentiation* breeds conflict. Differences in organization structures and in the characteristics of the people staffing them may foster conflict because of incompatible approaches toward work. And *unresolved prior conflicts* tend to erupt in later conflicts. Unless a conflict is fully resolved, it may remain latent only to emerge again in the future.

CONFLICT RESOLUTION

When conflicts do occur, they can either be "resolved," in the sense that the causes are corrected, or "suppressed," in that the causes remain but the conflict behaviors are controlled. Suppressed conflicts tend to fester and recur at a later time. True **conflict resolution** eliminates the underlying causes of conflict and reduces the potential for similar conflicts in the future.

● **Conflict resolution** is the removal of the substantial and emotional reasons for a conflict.

Real People

Vivian Schiller Deals with Conflict at National Public Radio

Yes, that's right, even at NPR, what *Fast Company* magazine calls "the country's brainiest, brawniest news-gathering giant," there can be a fair amount of conflict behind the scenes as NPR central and its member stations try to work together. And that's precisely what CEO Vivian Schiller knows she has to master.

Money, of course, is the crux of the problem. NPR itself doesn't broadcast anything; it produces several shows like *Morning Edition* and *All Things Considered*. These are sent to local stations that combine them with local programming for their audiences. The nonprofit member stations survive through donations from happy listeners and sponsors, and they pay dues and fees to NPR for rights of affiliation and use of the national shows.

So, what's the problem? Well, NPR now puts its content online. Just about anyone can access it over the Internet; there's even an NPR app for iPhones. In one month alone NPR had 14 million Podcast downloads. And if you can get programs through NPR's website, you don't need to listen to and support the local channel. Right?

One of NPR's own commentators, Paul Farhi, describes the problem this way: "If I'm running a station in Chapel Hill or Bloomington, I pay dues to NPR to get marquee programming

that brings people to my station . . . I don't care about your digital initiative. . . . You're siphoning my dues to build your national brand. That's the essence of the conflict."

With experience at five other major media organizations, most recently the NYTimes.com and previously Discovery Channel, CNN, and TBS, Schiller is confident as CEO. She talks not about conflict and NPR being viewed as a "competitor" to the local stations, but about "opportunity" and says her job is to "figure out a way to work together so that people in every community who go to their local NPR-member-station sites can get the benefit of NPR's international, national, and local coverage in a seamless experience."

But there's a lot to be worked out in the NPR–member station relationships. At KCRW in Los Angeles, general manager Ruth Seymour says: "There is hope on NPR's part that somehow we can work collaboratively online. I am truly dubious about it. In online, everybody is competitive with everybody else."

CONFLICT MANAGEMENT STYLES

People respond to interpersonal conflict through different combinations of cooperative and assertive behaviors.[49] Cooperativeness is the desire to satisfy another party's needs and concerns; assertiveness is the desire to satisfy one's own needs and concerns. Figure 17.5 shows five interpersonal styles of conflict management that result from various combinations of these two tendencies.[50]

- **Avoidance** or *withdrawal*—being uncooperative and unassertive, downplaying disagreement, withdrawing from the situation, and/or staying neutral at all costs.
- **Accommodation** or *smoothing*—being cooperative but unassertive, letting the wishes of others rule, smoothing over or overlooking differences to maintain harmony.
- **Competition** or *authoritative command*—being uncooperative but assertive, working against the wishes of the other party, engaging in win–lose competition, and/or forcing through the exercise of authority.
- **Compromise**—being moderately cooperative and assertive, bargaining for "acceptable" solutions in which each party wins a bit and loses a bit.
- **Collaboration** or *problem solving*—being cooperative and assertive, trying to fully satisfy everyone's concerns by working through differences, finding and solving problems so that everyone gains.[51]

Avoiding or accommodating often creates **lose–lose conflict**. No one achieves her or his true desires, and the underlying reasons for conflict remain unaffected. Although the conflict appears settled or may even disappear for a while, it tends to recur in the future. Avoidance is an extreme form of nonattention. Everyone withdraws and pretends that conflict doesn't really exist, hoping that it will simply go away. Accommodation plays down differences and highlights similarities and areas of agreement. Peaceful coexistence is the goal, but the real essence of a conflict may be ignored.

Competing and compromising tend to create **win–lose conflict** where each party strives to gain at the other's expense. In extreme cases, one party achieves its desires to the complete exclusion of the other party's desires. Because win–lose methods fail to address the root causes of conflict, future conflicts of

---

- **Avoidance**, or withdrawal, pretends that a conflict doesn't really exist.

- **Accommodation**, or smoothing, plays down differences and highlights similarities to reduce conflict.

- **Competition**, or authoritative command, uses force, superior skill, or domination to "win" a conflict.

- **Compromise** occurs when each party to the conflict gives up something of value to the other.

- **Collaboration**, or problem solving, involves working through conflict differences and solving problems so everyone wins.

- In **lose–lose conflict** no one achieves his or her true desires, and the underlying reasons for conflict remain unaffected.

- In **win–lose** conflict one party achieves its desires, and the other party does not.

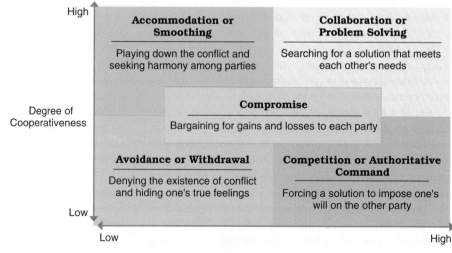

FIGURE 17.5 Alternative conflict management styles.

the same or a similar nature are likely to occur. In competition, one party wins because superior skill or outright domination allows his or her desires to be forced on the other. An example is authoritative command where a supervisor simply dictates a solution to subordinates. Compromise occurs when trade-offs are made such that each party to the conflict gives up and gains something. But because each party loses something, antecedents for future conflicts are established.

Collaborating or true problem solving is a form of **win–win conflict**. It is often the most effective conflict management style because issues are resolved to the mutual benefit of all conflicting parties. This is typically achieved by confronting the issues and by everyone being willing to recognize that something is wrong and needs attention. Win–win outcomes eliminate the underlying causes of the conflict; all relevant issues are raised and discussed openly.

● In **win–win** conflict the conflict is resolved to everyone's benefit.

STRUCTURAL APPROACHES TO CONFLICT MANAGEMENT

Most managers will tell you that not all conflict management in groups and organizations can be resolved at the interpersonal level. Think about it. Aren't there likely to be times when personalities and emotions prove irreconcilable? In such cases a structural approach to conflict management can often help.

When conflict traces back to a resource issue, the structural solution is to *make more resources available* to everyone. Although costly and not always possible, this is a straightforward way to resolve resource-driven conflicts. When people are stuck in conflict and just can't seem to appreciate one another's points of view, *appealing to higher-level goals* can sometimes focus their attention on one mutually desirable outcome. In a student team where members are arguing over content choices for a PowerPoint presentation, for example, it might help to remind everyone that the goal is to impress the instructor and get an "A" for the presentation. An appeal to higher goals offers a common frame of reference for analyzing differences and reconciling disagreements.

When appeals to higher goals don't work, it may be that *changing the people* is necessary. There are times when a manager may need to replace or transfer one or more of the conflicting parties to eliminate the conflict. When the people can't be changed, they may have to be separated by *altering the physical environment*. Sometimes it is possible to rearrange facilities, work space, or workflows to physically separate conflicting parties and decrease opportunities for contact with one another. Organizations also use a variety of *integrating devices* to help manage conflicts between groups. These approaches include assigning people to formal liaison roles, convening special task forces, setting up cross-functional teams, and even switching to the matrix form of organization.

Providing *training in interpersonal skills* can also help prepare people to communicate and work more effectively in situations where conflict is likely. When corporate recruiters list criteria for recruiting new college graduates, such "soft" or "people" skills are often right at the top. In today's horizontal and team-oriented organizations, you can't succeed if you can't work well with other people even when disagreements are inevitable. Finally, by *changing reward systems* it is sometimes possible to reduce conflicts that arise when people feel they have to compete with one another for attention, pay, and other rewards. An example is shifting pay bonuses or even student project grades to the group level so that individuals benefit in direct proportion to how well the team performs as a whole. This is a way of reinforcing teamwork and reducing the tendencies of team members to compete with one another.

Structural ways to manage conflict

- Make resources available
- Appeal to higher goals
- Change the people
- Change the environment
- Use integrating devices
- Provide training
- Change reward systems

MANAGING NEGOTIATION

● **Negotiation** is the process of making joint decisions when the parties involved have different preferences.

● **Substance goals** in negotiation are concerned with outcomes.

● **Relationship goals** in negotiation are concerned with the ways people work together.

● **Effective negotiation** resolves issues of substance while maintaining a positive process.

Situation: Your employer offers you a promotion, but the pay raise being offered is disappointing.

Situation: You have enough money to order one new computer for your department, but two of your subordinates really need one.

Situation: Your team members are having a "cook-out" on Saturday afternoon and want you to attend; your husband wants you to go with him to a neighboring town to visit his mother in the hospital.

Situation: Someone on your sales team has to fly to Texas to visit an important client; you've made the last two trips out of town and don't want to go; another member of the team hasn't been out of town in a long time and "owes" you a favor.

These are examples of the many work situations that lead to **negotiation**—the process of making joint decisions when the parties involved have different preferences. Stated a bit differently, negotiation is a way of reaching agreement. People negotiate over performance evaluations, job assignments, work schedules, work locations, and many other things. And, as pointed out in Management Smarts 17.2, they negotiate over salaries.[52] Any and all such negotiations are susceptible to conflict and negative aftermath, and test the communication and collaboration skills of those involved.[53]

Management Smarts 17.2

"Ins" and "Outs" of negotiating salaries

- *Prepare, prepare, prepare*—do the research and find out what others make for a similar position inside and outside the organization, including everything from salary to benefits, bonuses, incentives, and job perks.

- *Document and communicate*—identify and communicate your performance value; put forth a set of accomplishments that show how you have saved or made money and created value in your present job or for a past employer.

- *Identify critical skills and attributes*—make a list of your strengths and link each of them with potential contributions to the new employer; show how "you" offer talents and personal attributes of immediate value to the work team.

- *Advocate and ask*—be your own best advocate; the rule in salary negotiation is "Don't ask, don't get." But don't ask too soon; your boss or interviewer should be the first to bring up salary.

- *Stay focused on the goal*—your goal is to achieve as much as you can in the negotiation; this means not only doing well at the moment but also getting better positioned for future gains.

- *View things from the other side*—test your requests against the employer's point of view; ask if you are being reasonable, convincing, and fair; ask how the boss could explain to higher levels and to your peers a decision to grant your request.

- *Don't overreact to bad news*—never "quit on the spot" if you don't get what you want; be willing to search for and consider alternative job offers.

NEGOTIATION GOALS AND APPROACHES

Two important goals should be considered in any negotiation. **Substance goals** in negotiation are concerned with outcomes and are tied to content issues. **Relationship goals** in negotiation are concerned with processes. They are tied to the way people work together while negotiating and how they (and any constituencies they represent) will be able to work together again in the future.

Effective negotiation occurs when issues of substance are resolved and working relationships among the negotiating parties are maintained, or even improved, in the process. The three criteria of effective negotiation are:

3 effective Negotiating criteria? (handwritten)

1. *quality*—negotiating a "wise" agreement that is truly satisfactory to all sides;
2. *cost*—negotiating efficiently, using a minimum of resources and time; and
3. *harmony*—negotiating in a way that fosters, rather than inhibits, interpersonal relationships.[54]

The way each party approaches a negotiation can have a major impact on its effectiveness.[55] **Distributive negotiation** focuses on "claims" made by each party for certain preferred outcomes. This emphasis on substance can take a self-centered and competitive form in which one party can gain only if the other loses. In such win–lose conditions, relationships are often sacrificed as the negotiating parties focus only on their respective self-interests.

Principled negotiation, often called **integrative negotiation**, is based on a win–win orientation. The focus on substance is still important, but the interests of all parties are considered. The goal is to base the final outcome on the merits of individual claims and to try to find a way for all claims to be satisfied, if at all possible. No one should lose in a principled negotiation, and positive relationships should be maintained in the process.

> **Distributive negotiation** focuses on win–lose claims made by each party for certain preferred outcomes.

> **Principled negotiation** or **integrative negotiation** uses a "win–win" orientation to reach solutions acceptable to each party.

GAINING INTEGRATIVE AGREEMENTS

When asked by an interviewer to illustrate how the integrative approach to negotiation differs from a distributive one, scholar and consultant William Ury gave this example.[56] A union worker presents a manager with a list of requests. The manager says: "That's your solution, now what's the problem?" The union worker responds with a list of problems. The manager says: "Well, I can't give you *that* solution, but I think we can solve your problem this way."

Can you see the manager's attempt to be "integrative" in the last example?[57] In their book *Getting to Yes*, Roger Fisher and William Ury point out that truly integrative agreements are obtained by following four negotiation rules.[58]

1. Separate the people from the problem.
2. Focus on interests, not on positions.
3. Generate many alternatives before deciding what to do.
4. Insist that results be based on some objective standard.

Proper attitudes and good information are necessary foundations for integrative agreements. The attitudinal foundations involve the willingness of each negotiating party to trust, share information with, and ask reasonable questions of the other party. The information foundations involve both parties knowing what is really important to them and also finding out what is really important to the other party.

Both attitudes and information will come into play during a classic two-party labor–management negotiation over a new contract and salary increase.[59] Look at Figure 17.6 and consider the situation from the labor union's perspective. The union negotiator has told her management counterpart that the union wants a new wage of $15.00 per hour. This expressed preference is the union's initial offer.

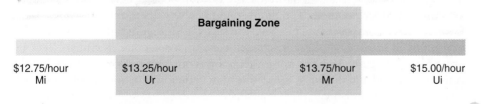

	Bargaining Zone		
$12.75/hour Mi	$13.25/hour Ur	$13.75/hour Mr	$15.00/hour Ui

Mi = Management's initial offer   Mr = Management's maximum reservation point
Ur = Union's minimum reservation point   Ui = Union's initial offer

FIGURE 17.6 The bargaining zone in classic two-party negotiation.

However, she also has in mind a minimum reservation point of $13.25 per hour. This is the lowest that she is willing to accept for the union. Now look at it from the perspective of the management negotiator. His initial offer is $12.75 per hour. And his maximum reservation point, the highest wage he is prepared to eventually offer the union, is $13.75 per hour.

In such a two-party negotiation, the **bargaining zone** is defined as the space between one party's minimum reservation point and the other party's maximum reservation point. The bargaining zone in this case lies between $13.25 per hour and $13.75 per hour. It is a "positive" zone since the reservation points of the two parties overlap. If the union's minimum reservation point was greater than management's maximum reservation point, no room would exist for bargaining. A key task for any negotiator is to discover the other party's reservation point. Until this is known and each party realizes that a positive bargaining zone exists, it is difficult to negotiate effectively.

> A **bargaining zone** is the space between one party's minimum reservation point and the other party's maximum reservation point.

NEGOTIATION PITFALLS

The negotiation process is admittedly complex, and negotiators must guard against common pitfalls. The first is falling prey to the *myth of the "fixed pie."* This involves acting on the distributive and win–lose assumption that in order for you to gain in the negotiation, the other person must give something up. This approach to negotiating fails to recognize the integrative assumption that the "pie" can sometimes be expanded or utilized to everyone's advantage. A second negotiation error is *non-rational escalation of conflict.* The negotiator in this case becomes committed to previously stated "demands" and allows personal needs for "ego" and "saving face" to increase the perceived importance of satisfying them.

A third negotiating error is *overconfidence and ignoring the other's needs.* The negotiator becomes overconfident, believes his or her position is the only correct one, and fails to consider the needs of the other party or appreciate the merits of its position. The fourth error is *too much "telling" and too little "hearing."* The "telling" error occurs when parties to a negotiation don't really make themselves understood to each other. The "hearing" error occurs when they fail to listen well enough to understand what each other is saying.[60]

Another potential negotiation pitfall, and one that is increasingly important in our age of globalization, is *premature cultural comfort.* This occurs when a negotiator is too quick to assume that he or she understands the intentions, positions, and meanings being communicated by a negotiator from a different culture. Scholar Jeanne Brett says, for example, that negotiators from low-context cultures can run into difficulties when dealing with negotiators from high-context cultures. The low-context negotiator is used to getting information through direct questions and answers; the high-context negotiator is likely to communicate indirectly, using nondeclarative language and nonverbal signals, and avoiding explicitly stated positions.[61]

It is also important to avoid the *trap of ethical misconduct.* The motivation to negotiate unethically sometimes arises from an undue emphasis on the profit motive. This may be experienced as a desire to "get just a bit more" or to "get as much as you can" from a negotiation. The motivation to behave unethically may also result from a sense of competition. This is a desire to "win" a negotiation just for the sake of winning it, or because of the misguided belief that someone else must "lose" in order for you to gain. And let's not forget, ethical misconduct can be driven by all-consuming greed and the quest for profits in negotiation situations where financial considerations are at issue.

When unethical behavior occurs in negotiation, the persons involved may try to explain it away with inappropriate rationalizing: "It was really unavoidable." "Oh,

> *Beware of negotiation pitfalls*
> - Myth of fixed pie
> - Escalation of conflict
> - Overconfidence
> - Too much telling
> - Too little listening
> - Cultural miscues
> - Unethical behavior

Words Used Affect Outcomes in Online Dispute Resolution

The Academy
of Management

Journal

The National Consumer League reports that 41% of participants in online trading had problems, often associated with late deliveries. A study of online dispute resolution among eBay buyers and sellers found that using words that "give face" were more likely than words that "attack face" to result in settlement. Jeanne Brett, Mara Olekalns, Ray Friedman, Nathan Goates, Cameron Anderson, and Cara Cherry Lisco studied real disputes being addressed through Square Trade, an online dispute resolution service to which eBay refers unhappy customers. A "dispute" was defined as a form of conflict in which one party to a transaction makes a claim that the other party rejects.

The researchers adopted what they call a "language-based" approach using "face theory," essentially arguing that how participants use language to give and attack the face of the other party will have a major impact on results. For example, in filing a claim an unhappy buyer might use polite words that preserve the positive self-image, or face, of the seller, or the buyer might use negative words that attack this sense of face. Examples of negative words are "agitated, angry, apprehensive, despise, disgusted, frustrated, furious, and hate."

This study examined 386 eBay-generated disputes processed through Square Trade. Results showed that expressing negative emotions and giving commands to the other party inhibited dispute resolution, whereas providing a causal explanation, offering suggestions, and communicating firmness all made dispute resolution more likely. The hypothesis that expressing positive emotions would increase the likelihood of dispute resolution was not supported. The study also showed that the longer a dispute played out, the less likely it was to be resolved.

In terms of practical implications, the researchers say: "Watch your language: avoid attacking the other's face either by showing your anger toward them, or by expressing contempt. Avoid signaling weakness, and be firm in your claim. Provide causal accounts that take responsibility and give face."

Online Dispute Resolution	
Dispute resolution less likely when	**Dispute resolution more likely when**
• Negative emotions are expressed	• Causal explanations given
• Commands are issued	• Suggestions are offered
	• Communications are firm

You Be the Researcher

Why is it that using words that express negative emotions seems to have adverse effects on dispute resolution, but the use of words expressing positive emotions does not have positive effects? How might this result be explained? Also, why is it that using words that communicate "firmness" seems important in resolving disputes? Can you apply these ideas and findings to other contexts? Suppose a student is unhappy about a grade. How does dispute resolution with the course instructor play out? Suppose an employee is unhappy about a performance evaluation or pay raise. How does dispute resolution with the boss proceed?

References: Jeanne Brett, Mara Olekalns, Ray Friedman, Nathan Goates, Cameron Anderson, and Cara Cherry Lisco, "Sticks and Stones: Language and On-Line Dispute Resolution," *Academy of Management Journal*, vol. 50 (February 2007), pp. 85–99.

it's harmless." "The results justify the means." "It's really quite fair and appropriate."[62] Of course these excuses for questionable behavior are morally unacceptable. They can also be challenged by the possibility that any short-run gains will be offset by long-run losses. Unethical negotiators will incur lasting legacies of distrust, disrespect, and dislike, and they can be targeted for "revenge" in later negotiations.

THIRD-PARTY DISPUTE RESOLUTION

Even with the best of intentions, it may not always be possible to achieve integrative agreements. When disputes reach the point of impasse, third-party assistance

● In **mediation** a neutral party tries to help conflicting parties improve communication to resolve their dispute.

● In **arbitration** a neutral third party issues a binding decision to resolve a dispute.

with dispute resolution can be useful. **Mediation** involves a neutral third party who tries to improve communication between negotiating parties and keep them focused on relevant issues. The mediator does not issue a ruling or make a decision, but can take an active role in discussions. This may include making suggestions in an attempt to move the parties toward agreement.

Arbitration, such as salary arbitration in professional sports, is a stronger form of dispute resolution. It involves a neutral third party, the arbitrator, who acts as a "judge" and issues a binding decision. This usually includes a formal hearing in which the arbitrator listens to both sides and reviews all facets of the case before making a ruling.

Some organizations formally provide for a process called *alternative dispute resolution*. This approach utilizes mediation or arbitration, but does so only after direct attempts to negotiate agreements between the conflicting parties have failed. Often an ombudsperson, a designated neutral third party who listens to complaints and disputes, plays a key role in the process.

☑ | **Learning Check**
Study Question 4
How can we negotiate successful agreements? | *Be sure you can* ☑ differentiate between distributive and principled negotiation ☑ list four rules of principled negotiation ☑ define *bargaining zone* and use this term to illustrate a labor–management wage negotiation ☑ describe the potential pitfalls in negotiation ☑ differentiate between mediation and arbitration

Management Learning Review

Study Questions Summary

1 What is the communication process?

● Communication is the interpersonal process of sending and receiving symbols with messages attached to them.

● Effective communication occurs when the sender and the receiver of a message both interpret it in the same way.

● Efficient communication occurs when the message is sent at low cost for the sender.

● Persuasive communication results in the recipient acting as intended by the sender; credibility earned by expertise and good relationships is essential to persuasive communication.

● Noise is anything that interferes with the effectiveness of communication; common examples are poor utilization of channels, poor written or oral expression, physical distractions, and status effects.

FOR DISCUSSION **When is it okay to accept less effectiveness to gain efficiency in communication?**

2 How can collaboration be improved by better communication?

● Transparency in the sense that information conveyed to others is honest, credible, and fully disclosed is an important way to improve communication in the workplace.

● Interactive management through MBWA, such as structured meetings, use of electronic media, and advisory councils can improve upward communication.

● Active listening, through reflecting back and paraphrasing, can help overcome barriers and improve communication.

● Constructive feedback is specific, direct, well-timed, and limited to things the receiver can change.

● Office architecture and space designs can be used to improve communication in organizations.

● Proper choice of channels and use of information technology can improve communication in organizations.

● Greater cross-cultural awareness and sensitivity are important if we are to overcome the negative influences of ethnocentrism on communication.

FOR DISCUSSION **What rules of active listening do most people break?**

3 How can we deal positively with conflict?

● Conflict occurs as disagreements over substantive or emotional issues.

● Moderate levels of conflict are functional for performance and creativity; too little or too much conflict becomes dysfunctional.

● Conflict may be managed through structural approaches that involve changing people, goals, resources, or work arrangements.

● Personal conflict management styles include avoidance, accommodation, compromise, competition, and collaboration.

● True conflict resolution involves problem solving through a win–win collaborative approach.

FOR DISCUSSION **When is it better to avoid conflict rather than engage it?**

4 How can we negotiate successful agreements?

● Negotiation is the process of making decisions in situations in which the participants have different preferences.

● Substance goals concerned with outcomes and relationship goals concerned with processes are both important in successful negotiation.

● Effective negotiation occurs when issues of substance are resolved while the process maintains good working relationships.

● Distributive negotiation emphasizes win–lose outcomes; integrative negotiation emphasizes win–win outcomes.

● Common negotiation pitfalls include the myth of the fixed pie, overconfidence, too much telling and too little hearing, and ethical misconduct.

● Mediation and arbitration are structured approaches to third-party dispute resolution.

FOR DISCUSSION **How do you negotiate with someone who is trapped in the "myth of the fixed pie"?**

Self-Test

Multiple-Choice Questions

1. The use of paraphrasing and reflecting back what someone else says in communication is characteristic of _____.
   (a) mixed messages   (b) active listening   (c) projection   (d) lose–lose conflict

2. When the intended meaning of the sender and the interpreted meaning of the receiver are the same, a communication is _____.
   (a) effective   (b) persuasive   (c) selective   (d) efficient

3. Constructive feedback is _____.
   (a) general rather than specific   (b) indirect rather than direct   (c) given in small doses   (d) given any time the sender is ready

4. When a manager uses e-mail to send a message that is better delivered in person, the communication process suffers from _____.
   (a) semantic problems   (b) a poor choice of communication channels   (c) physical distractions   (d) information overload

5. _____ is a form of interactive management that helps improve upward communication.
   (a) Attribution   (b) Mediation   (c) MBWA   (d) Filtering

6. Cross-cultural communication may run into difficulties because of _____, or the tendency to consider one's culture superior to others.
   (a) selective perception   (b) ethnocentrism   (c) mixed messages   (d) projection

7. An appeal to superordinate goals is an example of a(n) _____ approach to conflict management.
   (a) avoidance   (b) structural   (c) dysfunctional   (d) self-serving

8. The conflict management style with the greatest potential for true conflict resolution involves _____.
   (a) compromise   (b) competition   (c) smoothing   (d) collaboration

9. When a person is highly cooperative but not very assertive in approaching conflict, the conflict management style is referred to as _____.
   (a) avoidance   (b) authoritative   (c) smoothing   (d) collaboration

10. The three criteria of an effective negotiation are quality, cost, and _____.
    (a) harmony   (b) timeliness   (c) efficiency   (d) effectiveness

11. In order to be consistently persuasive when communicating with others in the workplace, a manager should build credibility by _____.
    (a) making sure rewards for compliance are clear   (b) making sure penalties for noncompliance are clear   (c) making sure they know who is the boss   (d) making sure good relationships have been established

12. A manager who understands the importance of proxemics in communication would be likely to _____.
    (a) avoid sending mixed messages   (b) arrange work spaces so as to encourage interaction   (c) be very careful in the choice of written and spoken words   (d) make frequent use of e-mail messages to keep people well informed

13. A conflict is most likely to be functional and have a positive impact on performance when it is _____.
    (a) based on emotions   (b) resolved by arbitration   (c) caused by resource scarcities   (d) of moderate intensity

14. In classic two-party negotiation, the difference between one party's minimum reservation point and the other party's maximum reservation point is known as the _____.
    (a) BATNA   (b) arena of indifference   (c) myth of the fixed pie   (d) bargaining zone

15. The first rule of thumb for gaining integrative agreements in negotiations is to _____.
    (a) separate the people from the problems   (b) focus on positions   (c) deal with a minimum number of alternatives
    (d) avoid setting standards for measuring outcomes

Short-Response Questions

16. Briefly describe how a manager would behave as an active listener when communicating with subordinates.
17. Explain the "inverted U" curve of conflict intensity and performance.
18. How do tendencies toward assertiveness and cooperativeness in conflict management result in win–lose, lose–lose, and win–win outcomes?
19. What is the difference between substance and relationship goals in negotiation?

Essay Question

20. After being promoted to store manager for a new branch of a large department store chain, Kathryn was concerned about communication in the store. Six department heads reported directly to her, and 50 full-time and part-time sales associates reported to them. Given this structure, Kathryn worried about staying informed about all store operations, not just those coming to her attention as senior manager. What steps might Kathryn take to establish and maintain an effective system of upward communication in this store?

Management **S**kills and **C**ompetencies

Self-Assessment

Back to Yourself: Communication and Networking

You might think that **communication and networking** are overdone or over pitched as critical management and career skills, but the reality is they aren't. Recruiters give them high priority when screening candidates for college internships and first jobs. Employers consider it essential that workers can communicate well both orally and in writing, and that they can network with others to find pathways for collaboration and work accomplishment. This is all part of one's social capital, or capacity to enlist the help and support of others when needed. This chapter offers many insights to help you develop communication and networking skills that facilitate positive collaboration, even in conflict and negotiation situations. After you complete the following Self-Assessment on Conflict Management Strategies, don't forget to go online to take the Assertiveness assessment and further examine your tendencies in communication and networking.

> Effective **communication and networking** skills are essential for transforming ideas into actions, being credible, listening and asking questions, and giving written and oral presentations.

Further Reflection: Conflict Management Strategies

Instructions

Think of how you behave in conflict situations in which your wishes differ from those of others.[63] In the space to the left, rate each of the following statements on a scale of "1" = "not at all" to "5" = "very much."

When I have a conflict at work, school, or in my personal life, I do the following:

1. I give in to the wishes of the other party.
2. I try to realize a middle-of-the-road solution.
3. I push my own point of view.
4. I examine issues until I find a solution that really satisfies me and the other party.
5. I avoid a confrontation about our differences.
6. I concur with the other party.
7. I emphasize that we have to find a compromise solution.
8. I search for gains.

9. I stand for my own and the other's goals.
10. I avoid differences of opinion as much as possible.
11. I try to accommodate the other party.
12. I insist we both give in a little.
13. I fight for a good outcome for myself.
14. I examine ideas from both sides to find a mutually optimal solution.
15. I try to make differences seem less severe.
16. I adapt to the other party's goals and interests.
17. I strive whenever possible toward a 50-50 compromise.
18. I do everything to win.
19. I work out a solution that serves my own as well as other's interests as much as possible.
20. I try to avoid a confrontation with the other person.

Scoring

Total your scores for items as follows.

Yielding tendency: 1 + 6 + 11 + 16 = _____.
Compromising tendency: 2 + 7 + 12 + 17 = _____.
Forcing tendency: 3 + 8 + 13 + 18 = _____.
Problem-solving tendency: 4 + 9 + 14 + 19 = _____.
Avoiding tendency: 5 + 10 + 15 + 20 = _____.

Interpretation

Each of the scores above approximates one of the conflict management styles discussed in the chapter. Look back to Figure 17.5 and make the match-ups. Although each style is part of management, only collaboration or problem solving leads to true conflict resolution. You should consider any patterns that may be evident in your scores and think about how to best handle the conflict situations in which you become involved.

Team Exercise

Feedback Sensitivities

Preparation

Indicate the degree of discomfort you would feel in each situation below by circling the appropriate number:[64]

1. high discomfort
2. some discomfort
3. undecided
4. very little discomfort
5. no discomfort

1 2 3 4 5   1. Telling an employee who is also a friend that she or he must stop coming to work late.
1 2 3 4 5   2. Talking to an employee about his or her performance on the job.
1 2 3 4 5   3. Asking an employee for comments about your rating of her or his performance.
1 2 3 4 5   4. Telling an employee who has problems in dealing with other employees that he or she should do something about it.
1 2 3 4 5   5. Responding to an employee who is upset over your rating of his or her performance.
1 2 3 4 5   6. Responding to an employee's becoming emotional and defensive when you tell her or him about mistakes on the job.
1 2 3 4 5   7. Giving a rating that indicates improvement is needed to an employee who has failed to meet minimum requirements of the job.
1 2 3 4 5   8. Letting a subordinate talk during an appraisal interview.

1 2 3 4 5   9. Having an employee challenge you to justify your evaluation during an appraisal interview.

1 2 3 4 5   10. Recommending that an employee be discharged.

1 2 3 4 5   11. Telling an employee that you are uncomfortable having to judge his or her performance.

1 2 3 4 5   12. Telling an employee that her or his performance can be improved.

1 2 3 4 5   13. Telling an employee that you will not tolerate his or her taking extended coffee breaks.

1 2 3 4 5   14. Telling an employee that you will not tolerate her or his making personal telephone calls on company time.

Instructions

Form three-person teams as assigned by your instructor. Identify the three behaviors with which each person indicates the most discomfort. Then each team member should practice performing these behaviors with another member, while the third member acts as an observer. Be direct, but try to perform the behavior in an appropriate way. Listen to feedback from the observer and try the behaviors again, perhaps with different members of the group practicing each behavior. When finished, discuss the overall exercise.

Case Study: Twitter

Go to *Management Cases for Critical Thinking* to find the recommended case for Chapter 17—"Twitter: An Enterprising Opportunity."

Control Processes and Systems

18

Learning From Others

Control Leaves No Room for Complacency

You can get a tasty sandwich at Chick-fil-A, but don't plan on stopping in on a Sunday. All the chain's 1,270 stores are closed. It is a tradition started by 85-year-old founder Truett Cathy, who believes that employees deserve a day of rest. Current President Dan T. Cathy believes the Sunday day off is a statement about that culture. He says: "If we take care of our team members and operators behind the counter, then they are going to do a better job on Monday. In fact, I say our food tastes better on Monday because we are closed on Sunday."[1]

Chick-fil-A, headquartered in Atlanta, GA, where its first restaurant was opened, is wholly owned by Truett's family, and is now headed by his son. It has a reputation as a great business, processing about 10,000 inquiries each year for 100 restaurant franchise opportunities. The president of the national Restaurant Association Educational Foundation says: "I don't think there's any chain that creates such a wonderful culture around the way they treat their people and the respect they have for their employees."

Truett asks his employees to always say "my pleasure" when thanked by a customer. He says: "It's important to keep people happy." He also believes in "continuous improvement," continuing to upgrade menus and stores even after 40 years of increasing sales. Woody Faulk, vice president of brand development, says: "It would be very easy for us to pause after such a successful year, but in doing that, we would be in jeopardy of falling into a trap of complacency." He adds: "Change in the quick-service industry is much like that of the fashion industry. Customer needs are constantly fluctuating, and we have to be intentional about staying ahead of and remaining relevant to those changes."

The results seem to speak for themselves. Chick-fil-A is the 2nd largest chicken restaurant chain in the U.S. Its turnover among restaurant operators is only 3%, compared to an industry average as high as 50%. It is also a relatively inexpensive franchise, costing $5,000, compared to $50,000 that is typical of its competitors.

do the benchmarking

When Truett Cathy asks employees to say "my pleasure" to customer requests, he's confirming the firm's service focus. But you'll also note that he believes well-treated employees will take good care of customers. **At Chick-fil-A, consistent customer service flows not from fear, but from a positive culture that encourages lots of self-control. Isn't this a lesson we should all remember?**

Learning About Yourself

Resiliency

This chapter is about managerial control, and how to make sure that things go right for organizations even as they deal with lots of complexities. We face similar challenges in many ways. We need to be managed, we need to exercise control, and we need the staying power to perform for the long term. A person's career success in the fast-paced and complex worlds of work and personal living today depends significantly on **resiliency**—the ability to call upon inner strength and keep moving forward even when things are tough.

Think of resiliency in personal terms—caring for an aging parent with a terrible disease such as Alzheimer's or Parkinson's, or perhaps balancing single-parenthood with the demands of work and two small children. Think of it also in career terms—juggling multiple responsibilities that are continuously announcing themselves as e-mails, voice mails, instant messages, scheduled and unscheduled meetings.

How capable are you of managing yourself and your demands under these and other similar circumstances? "Resilient people are like trees bending in the wind," says Dr. Steven M. Southwick, professor of psychiatry at Yale University. "They bounce back." Does this description fit you . . . or not?

It certainly fit entrepreneur Tim Baumgartner. He was an independent sales rep for the electronics store Circuit City when it filed for bankruptcy. It caught him totally by surprise, But bounce back he did. Along with his daughter, Baumgartner started an online consumer electronics store within months. He says: "Whining and complaining about how you find yourself here doesn't help. I've refocused my energy on the start-up."

> ### Resiliency Quick Test
> Score yourself 1 (don't at all agree) to 5 (totally agree) on the following items.
> * I am an upbeat person for the most part.
> * Uncertainty and ambiguity don't much bother me.
> * I tend to adapt quickly as things change.
> * I can see positives even when things go wrong.
> * I am good at learning from experience.
> * I am good at problem solving.
> * I am strong and hold up well when times are tough.
> * I have been able to turn bad situations into positive gains.

Resilient people are able to face and identify their challenges, not hide or back away from them. They develop strategies, make plans, and like Baumgartner, act on them to find opportunity even in bad situations.[2]

get to know yourself better

If you score 35 or better on the Resiliency Quick Test, you can consider yourself highly resilient. With any lower score, you should question how well you hold up under pressure. Double-check the results. How do you handle situations like a poor grade at school, a put-down from a friend, a denial letter from a job application, or criticism from a boss or coworker on your job? To what extent do you show resiliency by turning them into opportunities to improve in the future? **Also make use of the end-of-chapter Self-Assessment on After Meeting/Project Remorse and further reflect on your control tendencies.**

18 Control Processes and Systems

Study Question 1	Study Question 2	Study Question 3
Managerial Control	**The Control Process**	**Control Tools and Techniques**
• Importance of controlling • Types of controls • Internal and external control	• Establish objectives and standards • Measure performance results • Compare results with objectives • Take corrective action	• Employee discipline systems • Project management and control • Financial controls • Balanced scorecards
Learning Check 1	**Learning Check 2**	**Learning Check 3**

Keeping in touch . . . Staying informed . . . Being in control. These are important responsibilities for every manager. But "control" is a word like "power." If you aren't careful when and how the word is used, it leaves a negative connotation. Yet, control plays a positive and necessary role in the management process. To have things "under control" is good; for things to be "out of control" is generally bad.

So, you might ask: What happened at Toyota?[3] Something certainly went wrong with quality control when the global giant had to recall over 8 million vehicles to fix throttle problems, and shut down production of models with defects until corrections could be made. It was a major blow to a firm previously praised for its quality vehicles; reputation, sales, and profits were lost immediately. In an attempt to comfort customers, "An Open Letter to Toyota Customers" was published as a full-page ad in major newspapers. In it, Toyota's president and COO Jim Lentz said: "I am truly sorry for the concern our recalls have caused, and want you to know we're doing everything we can—as fast as we can—to make things right . . . We'll continue to do everything we can to meet—and exceed—your expectations and justify your continued trust in Toyota."[4] Still, questions remained unanswered. How did this company known for its product quality lose control? Was it a management lapse, a technology breakdown, or simply the aftermath of growing too fast in too many locations around the world?

WHY AND HOW MANAGERS CONTROL

In the ever-changing technology industry, CEO T. J. Rodgers of Cypress Semiconductor Corp. likes things to be in control. It goes along with his strong emphasis on performance and accountability. Cypress employees work with clear and quantified work goals, which they help set. Rodgers believes that this system identifies problems before they interfere with performance. He says: "Managers monitor the goals, look for problems, and expect people who fall behind to ask for help before they lose control of or damage a major project."[5]

Rodgers is all about planning, or setting goals, and controlling—keeping things on track to accomplish them. Control is important for any organization, and we practice a lot of control quite naturally. Think of fun things you do—playing golf or tennis or Frisbee, reading, dancing, driving a car, or riding a bike. Through activities such as these you've already become quite expert in the control process. How? Most probably by having an objective in mind, always checking to see how well you are doing, and making continuous adjustments to get it right.

IMPORTANCE OF CONTROLLING

Controlling is the process of measuring performance and taking action to ensure desired results.

Controlling is a process of measuring performance and taking action to ensure desired results. Its purpose is straightforward—to make sure that plans are achieved and that actual performance meets or surpasses objectives. The foundation of control is information. Henry Schacht, former CEO of Cummins Engine Company, discussed control in terms of what he called "friendly facts." He stated: "facts that reinforce what you are doing are nice, because they help in terms of psychic reward. Facts that raise alarms are equally friendly, because they give you clues about how to respond, how to change, where to spend the resources."[6]

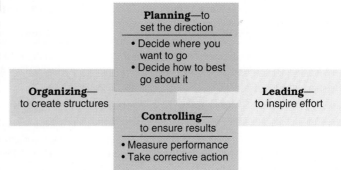

FIGURE 18.1 The role of controlling in the management process.

Figure 18.1 shows how controlling fits in with the other management functions. *Planning* sets the directions and allocates resources. *Organizing* brings people and material resources together in working combinations. *Leading* inspires people to best utilize these resources. *Controlling* sees to it that the right things happen, in the right way, and at the right time. It helps ensure that performance is consistent with plans, and that accomplishments throughout an organization are coordinated in a means–ends fashion. It also helps ensure that people comply with organizational policies and procedures.

Effective control is essential to organizational learning. It is a way of learning from experience. Consider, for example, the program of after-action review pioneered by the U.S. Army and now utilized in many corporate settings. This is a structured review of lessons learned and results accomplished in a completed project, task force assignment, or special operation. Participants answer questions such as: "What was the intent?" "What actually happened?" "What did we learn?"[7] The after-action review helps make continuous improvement a part of the organizational culture. It encourages those involved to take responsibility for their performance efforts and accomplishments. The end-of-chapter self-assessment is modeled on this approach.

Improving performance through learning is one of the great opportunities offered by the control process. However, the potential benefits are realized only when learning is translated into corrective actions. After setting up Diversity Network Groups (DNGs) worldwide, for example, IBM executives learned that male attitudes were major barriers to the success of female managers. They addressed this finding by strengthening controls; senior executives were required to report annually on the progress of women managers in their divisions. This action is credited with substantially increasing the percentage of women in IBM's senior management ranks.[8]

TYPES OF CONTROLS

One of the best ways to consider control is in respect to the open-systems perspective in Figure 18.2. It shows how feedforward, concurrent, and feedback controls link with different phases of this input-throughput-output cycle.[9] Each type of control increases the likelihood of high performance.

Feedforward Controls

Feedforward controls, also called *preliminary controls*, take place before a work activity begins. They ensure that objectives are clear, that proper directions are established, and that the right resources are available to accomplish the objectives. The goal is to solve problems before they occur by asking an important but often neglected question: "What needs to be done before we begin?"

Feedforward controls are preventive in nature. Managers using them take a forward-thinking and proactive approach to control. At McDonald's, for example,

> **Feedforward control** ensures that directions and resources are right before the work begins.

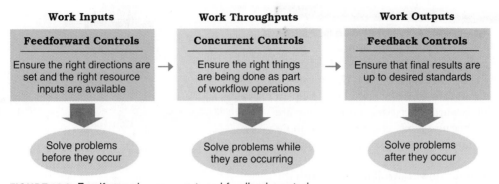

FIGURE 18.2 Feedforward, concurrent, and feedback controls.

preliminary control of food ingredients plays an important role in the firm's quality program. The company requires that suppliers of its hamburger buns produce them to exact specifications, covering everything from texture to uniformity of color. Even in overseas markets, the firm works hard to develop local suppliers that can offer dependable quality.[10]

Concurrent Controls

● **Concurrent control** focuses on what happens during the work process.

Concurrent controls focus on what happens during the work process. Sometimes called *steering controls*, they make sure things are being done according to plan. You can also think of this as control through direct supervision. In today's world, that supervision may be increasingly virtual in nature. Picture this scene at the Hyundai Motor headquarters in Seoul, South Korea, in what the firm calls its Global Command and Control Center.[11]

> "Modeled after the CNN newsroom in Atlanta with dozens of computer screens relaying video and data, it [the Global Command and Control Center] keeps watch on Hyundai operations around the world. Parts shipments are traced from the time they leave the supplier until they reach a plant. Cameras peer into assembly lines from Beijing to Montgomery and keep a close watch on Hyundai's giant Ulsan, Korea, plant, the world's largest integrated auto factory."

The goal of concurrent controls is to solve problems as they occur. The key question is, "What can we do to improve things right now?" In the Hyundai example, operations are monitored in real time and by computer. This allows managers to quickly spot and correct any problems in the manufacturing cycle. The same thing happens at McDonald's, but this time it all takes place face to face as ever-present shift leaders provide concurrent control through direct supervision. They constantly observe what is taking place, even while helping out with the work. They are trained to intervene immediately when something is not done right and to correct things on the spot. Detailed manuals also "steer" workers in the right directions as they perform their jobs.

Feedback Controls

● **Feedback control** takes place after an action is completed.

Feedback controls, also called *post-action controls*, take place after work is completed. They focus on the quality of end results rather than on inputs and activities. Feedback controls are largely reactive; the goals are to solve problems after they occur and prevent future ones. They ask the question: "Now that we are finished, how well did we do?"

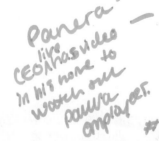

Elsewhere Class Blends Worlds of Work and Leisure

Are you in control, really in control of your life, or are you always thinking about "elsewhere"? You may be at home or out shopping or at a sports event. Yet, you're thinking "it's time to check my messages on my smartphone." Today's young professionals, the "Elsewhere Class," are more and more living in what sociologist Dan Conley describes as "a blended world of work and leisure, home and office." He says: "we feel like we are in the right place at the right time only when in transit, moving from point A to B. Constant motion is a balm to an anxious culture where we are haunted by the feeling that we are frauds, expendable in the workplace because so much of our service work is intangible."

We are all familiar with feedback controls and probably recognize their weak points, especially from a customer service perspective. Restaurants, for example, ask how you liked a meal after it is eaten; course evaluations tell instructors how well they performed after the course is over; a budget summary identifies cost overruns after a project is completed. In these and other circumstances, mistakes may already have been made, but the feedback provided by the control process can help improve things in the future. Perhaps one of the most on-point examples of feedback controls comes from Toyota Motor company and its recent recalls of millions of vehicles with sticky gas pedals. Executives decided to suspend selling eight car models while the problems were studied and solutions implemented. "Helping ensure the safety of our customers and restoring confidence in Toyota are very important to our company," said Group Vice President Bob Carter. "This action is necessary until a remedy is finalized."[12]

INTERNAL AND EXTERNAL CONTROL

Managers have two broad options with respect to control systems. First, they can manage in ways that allow and expect people to control their own behavior. This puts priority on internal control, or self-control. Second, they can structure situations to make sure things happen as planned.[13] This is external control, and the alternatives include bureaucratic or administrative control, clan or normative control, and market or regulatory control. Effective control typically involves a mix of these options.

Self-Control (internal control)

We all exercise internal control in our daily lives; we do so with regard to managing our money, our relationships, our eating and drinking, and more. Managers can take advantage of this human capacity for **self-control** by unlocking and setting up conditions that support it. This means trusting people to be good at self-management, allowing and encouraging them to exercise self-discipline in performing their jobs. Any workplace that emphasizes participation, empowerment, and involvement will rely heavily on self-control.

According to Douglas McGregor's Theory Y perspective, introduced in Chapter 2, people are ready and willing to exercise self-control in their work.[14] But McGregor also points out that they are most likely to do this when they

Self-control is internal control that occurs through self-discipline in fulfilling work and personal responsibilities.

Wikipedia May Need Some Fact Checking

When Larry Sanger and Jimmy Wales started Wikipedia as a user-built online encyclopedia, it was an interesting idea; now it's the fifth most visited website in the world. It's a popular and convenient place for students and others to find "facts," but how accurate is the information it offers? Even though Wikipedia relies on a community of active editors to check and verify entries, no one checks up on them. Sue Garner, head of the Wikipedia Foundation says, "we don't have good, consistent measures, which is a problem for us." And Andrew Lih, author of *The Wikipedia Revolution*, says: "My biggest fear is a slow leakage of the truth, which might not easily be detected."

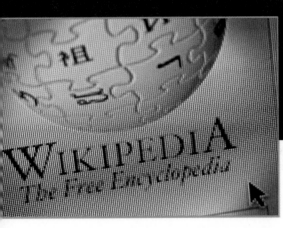

participate in setting performance objectives and standards. Furthermore, the potential for self-control is increased when capable people have a clear sense of organizational mission, know their goals, and have the resources necessary to do their jobs well. It is also enhanced by participative organizational cultures in which everyone treats each other with respect and consideration. An internal control strategy requires a high degree of trust. When people are expected to work on their own and exercise self-control, managers must give them the freedom to do so.

It's also important to consider self-control in the very personal context of work and family. How good are you at taking control of your time and maintaining a healthy work–life balance? Do you ever wonder who's in control, you or your smartphone? It used to be that we sometimes took work home in a briefcase, did a bit, closed the case up, and took it back to work the next day. Now work is always there, on the computer, in our e-mails, and streamed as text messages. And it's habit forming, so much so that some employers are encouraging employees to work less so that they will work better.[15] Consider these somewhat contrasting examples. In San Jose, California, Elizabeth Safran works virtually. That's the way the 13-member public relations firm operates—by e-mails and instant messaging. But she is concerned about work–life balance, saying: "It [technology] makes us more productive, but everybody is working all the time—weekends, evenings. It's almost overkill." In London, England, Paul Renucci is managing director of a systems integration firm. He works at home on Fridays, saving two hours of traffic time and staying connected by computer. At 5 p.m. he turns the machine off, his workday over. He says: "I can work pretty hard, but at 5 p.m. exactly I stop working and the weekend starts."[16]

Bureaucratic Control (external)

● **Bureaucratic control** influences behavior through authority, policies, procedures, job descriptions, budgets, and day-to-day supervision.

A classic form of external control is **bureaucratic control**. It uses authority, policies, procedures, job descriptions, budgets, and day-to-day supervision to make sure that people's behavior is consistent with organizational interests. You can think of this as control that flows through the organization's hierarchy of authority. Organizations typically have policies and procedures regarding sexual harassment, for example, with the goal being to make sure that members behave toward one another respectfully and in ways that offer no suggestion of sexual pressures or improprieties. Organizations also use budgets for personnel, equipment, travel expenses, and the like to keep behavior targeted within set limits.

Another level of bureaucratic control comes from the organization's external environment. Here, laws and regulations may govern the behavior of an organization's top executives. An example is the Sarbanes-Oxley Act (*SOX*), which establishes procedures to regulate financial reporting and governance in publicly traded corporations.[17] The law was passed in response to major corporate scandals that raised serious questions about top management behavior and the accuracy of financial reports provided by the firms. Under SOX, chief executives and chief financial officers of firms must personally sign off on financial reports and certify their accuracy. Those who misstate their firm's financial records can go to jail and pay substantial personal fines.

Clan Control

Whereas bureaucratic control emphasizes hierarchy and authority, **clan control** influences behavior through norms and expectations set by the organizational culture. Sometimes called *normative control* it harnesses the power of group cohesiveness and collective identity. It happens as persons who share values and identify strongly with one another tend to behave in ways that are consistent with one another's expectations. Just look around the typical college classroom and campus. You'll see clan control reflected in dress, language, and behavior as students tend to act consistent with the expectations of peers and groups with whom they identify. The same holds true in organizations, where clan control influences employees and members to display common behavior patterns.

> **Clan control** influences behavior through norms and expectations set by the organizational culture.

Market Control

Market control is essentially the influence of market competition on the behavior of organizations and their members. Business firms show the influence of market control in the way that they adjust products, pricing, promotions, and other practices in response to customer feedback and what competitors are doing. A good example is the growing emphasis on "green" products and practices. When a firm like Wal-Mart starts to get positive publicity from its expressed commitment to eventually power all of its stores with renewable energy, for example, the effect is felt by its competitors.[18] They have to adjust their practices in order to avoid giving up the public relations advantage to Wal-Mart. In this sense the time-worn phrase "keeping up with the competition" is really another way of expressing the dynamics of market controls in action.

> **Market control** is essentially the influence of market competition on the behavior of organizations and their members.

Be sure you can ☑ define *controlling* as a management function ☑ explain benefits of after-action reviews ☑ illustrate how a fast-food restaurant utilizes feedforward, concurrent, and feedback controls ☑ discuss internal control and external control systems ☑ give examples of bureaucratic, clan, and market controls

Learning Check ☑

Study Question 1
Why and how do managers exercise control?

THE CONTROL PROCESS (4 steps followed)

The control process involves the four steps shown in Figure 18.3. They are (1) establish performance objectives and standards; (2) measure actual performance; (3) compare actual performance with objectives and standards; and (4) take corrective action as needed. Although essential to management, these steps apply equally well to personal affairs and careers. Think about it. Without

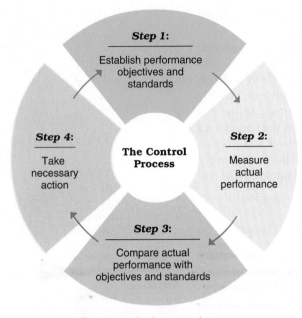

FIGURE 18.3 Four steps in the control process.

career objectives, how do you know where you really want to go? How can you allocate your time and other resources to take best advantage of available opportunities? Without measurement, how can you assess any progress being made? How can you adjust current behavior to improve prospects for future results?

STEP 1: ESTABLISH OBJECTIVES AND STANDARDS control process #1

The control process begins with planning, when performance objectives and standards for measuring them are set. It can't start without them. Performance objectives identify key results that one wants to accomplish; and the word "key" deserves emphasis. The focus in planning should be on describing "critical" or "essential" results that will make a substantial performance difference. Once these key results are identified, standards can be set to measure their accomplishment.

Output Standards (1)

● An **output standard** measures performance results in terms of quantity, quality, cost, or time.

Output standards measure actual outcomes or work results. Businesses use many output standards, such as earnings per share, sales growth, and market share. Others include quantity and quality of production, costs incurred, service or delivery time, and error rates. Based on your experience at work and as a customer, you can probably come up with even more examples.

When Allstate Corporation launched a new diversity initiative, it created a "diversity index" to quantify performance on diversity issues. The standards included how well employees met the goals of bias-free customer service and how well managers met the firm's diversity expectations.[19] When General Electric became concerned about managing ethics in its 320,000-member global workforce, it created measurement standards to track compliance. Each business unit was required to report quarterly on how many of its members attend ethics training sessions and signed the firm's "Spirit and Letter" ethics guide.[20]

How about output standards for other types of organizations, such as a symphony orchestra? When the Cleveland Orchestra wrestled with performance standards, the members weren't willing to rely on vague generalities like "we played well" or "the audience seemed happy" or "not too many mistakes were made." Rather, they decided to track standing ovations, invitations to perform in other countries, and how often other orchestras copied their performance style.[21]

Input Standards (11)

● An **input standard** measures work efforts that go into a performance task.

The control process also uses **input standards** that measure work efforts. These are common in situations where outputs are difficult or expensive to measure. Examples of input standards for a college professor might be the existence of an orderly course syllabus, meeting all class sessions, and returning exams and assignments in a timely fashion. Of course, as this example might suggest, measuring inputs doesn't mean that outputs, such as high-quality teaching and learning, are necessarily achieved. Other examples of input standards at work include conformance with rules, efficiency in the use of resources, and work attendance.

Real People

Roger Ferguson Provides Strategic Leadership for Retirement Security

Leading a huge financial institution with over $70 billion under its management is a big challenge. Doing so when the economy is in recession and the entire financial services industry is in crisis is something else. But as president and chief executive officer of TIAA-CREF, Roger W. Ferguson, Jr., shown here, is well prepared and ready for the job. His firm manages over $402 billion in retirement savings for 3.6 million Americans in the academic, research, medical, and cultural fields.

With a PhD in Economics, Ferguson's prior experience includes Vice Chairman of the Board of Governors of the Federal Reserve System and Chairman of Swiss Re America Holding Corp. And when U.S. President Barack Obama set up a new Economic Advisory Board and charged its members "to meet regularly so that I can hear different ideas and sharpen my own, and seek counsel that is candid and informed by the wider world," Roger W. Ferguson, Jr. was chosen as a member.

In 2009, *Black Enterprise* magazine listed Ferguson as one of the "100 most powerful African Americans in corporate America." And he leads a firm that is committed to managing diversity, claiming "Diversify isn't just smart financial advice. It's a sound hiring policy as well." The firm includes "promoting diversity" in its mission, and states the belief that "all benefit from a work environment that fosters respect, integrity and opportunity for people from a wide variety of backgrounds."

One of Ferguson's current initiatives is retirement security. He points to research that says the average American is presently $250,000 short at retirement time, and says that he wants a retirement system that "is designed to help people through 30 years of retirement, not just 30 years of work," He goes on to add that what he calls a "holistic retirement system" should "combine the best practices of defined benefit and defined contribution plans."

STEP 2: MEASURE PERFORMANCE RESULTS

The second step in the control process is to measure actual performance. It is the point where output standards and input standards are used to carefully document results. When Linda Sanford, currently a senior vice president and one of the highest-ranking women at IBM, was appointed head of IBM's sales force, she came with an admirable performance record earned during a 22-year career with the company. Notably, Sanford grew up on a family farm, where she developed an appreciation for measuring results. "At the end of the day, you saw what you did, knew how many rows of strawberries you picked." At IBM she was known for walking around the factory, just to see "at the end of the day how many machines were going out of the back dock."[22]

Measurements, as in the IBM example, must be accurate enough to spot significant differences between what is really taking place and what was originally planned. Without measurement, effective control is not possible. With measurement tied to key results, however, an old adage often holds true: "What gets measured happens."

STEP 3: COMPARE RESULTS WITH OBJECTIVES AND STANDARDS

Step 3 in the control process is to compare objectives with results. You can remember its implications by this **control equation**:

Need for action = Desired performance − Actual performance

The question of what constitutes "desired" performance plays an important role in the control equation. Some organizations use *engineering comparisons*. One example

● The **control equation** states: Need for action = Desired performance − Actual performance.

Rough Traveling for Privacy and Censorship

Amnesty International claims that Yahoo! and Skype are violating human rights in China by complying with government requests for censorship. The Chinese government expects search engines to block attempts to look for information on topics such as the Tiananmen Square massacre and freedom for Taiwan, as well as sites focused on human rights and democracy.

Amnesty contends that by complying with government demands, corporate values are being compromised in the quest for profits. A spokesperson for Yahoo! China's business, Alibaba.com, counters: "By creating opportunities for entrepreneurs and connecting China's exporters to buyers around the world, Alibaba.com and Yahoo! China are having an overwhelmingly positive impact on the lives of average people in China."

Skype was told by the Chinese government that its software must filter from text messages words that the Chinese leadership considers offensive. If the company doesn't comply,

it can't do business in China. After refusing at first, Skype executives finally agreed. Phrases such as "Falun Gong" and "Dalai Lama" no longer appear in messages delivered through Skype's Chinese joint venture partner, Tom Online.

Skype co-founder Niklas Zennstrom, shown here, says: "I may like or not like the laws and regulations to operate businesses in the UK or Germany or the U.S., but if I do business there I choose to comply."

You Decide

What do you think? Is it ethical for companies who want to do business in China or elsewhere to go along with policies that would clearly be considered to be a violation of human rights in places like the United States or Europe? What determines whether companies should comply with such requests, challenge the status quo, or simply decline to operate in those markets? When should business executives stand up and challenge laws and regulations that are used to deny customers the rights or privacy that they expect?

is United Parcel Service (UPS). The firm carefully measures the routes and routines of its drivers to establish the times expected for each delivery. When a delivery manifest is scanned as completed, the driver's time is registered in a performance log that is closely monitored by supervisors. Organizations also use *historical comparisons*, where past experience becomes the baseline for evaluating current performance. Also used are *relative comparisons* that benchmark performance against that being achieved by other people, work units, or organizations.

STEP 4: TAKE CORRECTIVE ACTION

The final step in the control process is to take the action needed to correct problems or make improvements. **Management by exception** is the practice of giving attention to situations that show the greatest need for action. It saves time, energy, and other resources by focusing attention on high-priority areas.

Managers should be alert to two types of exceptions. The first is a problem situation where actual performance is less than desired. It must be understood so that corrective action can restore performance to the desired level. The second is an opportunity situation where actual performance turns out higher than what was desired. It must be understood with the goal of continuing or increasing the high level of accomplishment in the future.

> **Management by exception** focuses attention on substantial differences between actual and desired performance.

CONTROL TOOLS AND TECHNIQUES

Most organizations use a variety of control systems and techniques. They include employee discipline systems, special techniques of project management, and information and financial controls as discussed here. They also include quality control as discussed in the next chapter on operations and services management.

EMPLOYEE DISCIPLINE SYSTEMS *control technique #1*

Absenteeism, tardiness, sloppy work. The list of undesirable conduct can go on to even more extreme actions—falsifying records, sexual harassment, and embezzlement. All are examples of behaviors that can and should be formally addressed in human resource management through **discipline**—the act of influencing behavior through reprimand.

● **Discipline** is the act of influencing behavior through reprimand.

When discipline is handled in a fair, consistent, and systematic way, it is a useful form of managerial control. And one way to be consistent in disciplinary situations is to remember the "hot stove rules" in Management Smarts 18.1. They rest on a simple understanding: "When a stove is hot, don't touch it." Everyone knows that when this rule is violated, you get burned—immediately and consistently, but usually not beyond the possibility of repair.[23]

Progressive discipline ties reprimands to the severity and frequency of the employee's infractions. Penalties for misbehavior vary according to the significance of the problem. A progressive discipline system takes into consideration such things as the seriousness of the problem, how frequently it has occurred, how long it lasts, and past experience in dealing with the person who has caused the problem. The goal is to achieve compliance with organizational expectations through the least extreme reprimand possible. For example, the ultimate penalty of "discharge" would be reserved for the most severe behaviors (e.g., any crime) or for repeated infractions of a less severe nature (e.g., being continually late for work and failing to respond to a series of reprimands or suspensions).

Management Smarts 18.1

"Hot stove rules" of employee discipline

- A reprimand should be immediate; a hot stove burns the first time you touch it.

- A reprimand should be directed toward someone's actions, not the individual's personality; a hot stove doesn't hold grudges, doesn't try to humiliate people, and doesn't accept excuses.

- A reprimand should be consistently applied; a hot stove burns anyone who touches it, and it does so every time.

- A reprimand should be informative; a hot stove lets a person know what to do to avoid getting burned in the future—"don't touch."

- A reprimand should occur in a supportive setting; a hot stove conveys warmth, but with an inflexible rule: "don't touch."

- A reprimand should support realistic rules. The don't-touch-a-hot-stove rule isn't a power play, a whim, or an emotion of the moment; it is a necessary rule of reason.

● **Progressive discipline** ties reprimands to the severity and frequency of misbehavior.

PROJECT MANAGEMENT AND CONTROL *control technique #2*

It might be something personal, like an anniversary party for one's parents, a renovation to your home, or the launch of a new product or service at your place of work. It might be the completion of a new student activities building on a campus, or the implementation of a new advertising campaign for a sports team. What these examples and others like them share in common is that they are relatively complicated tasks with multiple components that have to happen in a certain sequence, and that must be completed by a specified date. We call them **projects**, complex one-time events with unique components and an objective that must be met within a set time.

Project management is the responsibility for overall planning, supervision, and control of projects. A project manager's job is to ensure that a project is well

● **Projects** are one-time activities with many component tasks that must be completed in proper order and according to budget.

● **Project management** makes sure that activities required to complete a project are planned well and accomplished on time.

Employee Fraud a Costly Problem

Sometimes hard times bring out not the best but the worst in people. In fact, small businesses have suffered as a bad economy fostered increased employee crime. The cost of such bad behavior runs as much as 7% of revenues. Consider these results from a survey of 392 U.S. firms: 20% say workplace theft is a problem, 18% report an increase in money crimes like stolen cash or fraudulent transactions, 24% report an increase in thefts of office supplies and company products, and 17% have tightened security to prevent employee theft.

planned and then completed according to plan—on time, within budget, and consistent with objectives. Two useful techniques for project management and control are Gantt charts and CPM/PERT.

Gantt Charts

A **Gantt chart**, such as the one depicted in Figure 18.4, graphically displays the scheduling of tasks required to complete a project. This approach was developed in the early 20th century by Henry Gantt, an industrial engineer, and it has become a mainstay of project management ever since. In the figure, the left column lists major activities required to complete a new cell phone prototype. The bars extending from the right indicate the time required to complete each activity.

The Gantt chart provides a visual overview of what needs to be done on the project. This facilitates control by allowing progress checks to be made at different time intervals. It also assists with event or activity sequencing, making sure that things get accomplished in time for later work to build upon them. One of the biggest problems with projects, for example, is when delays in early activities create problems for later ones.

A project manager who actively uses Gantt charts is trying to avoid such difficulties. Obviously, the chart in the figure is oversimplified; an actual project to develop a new cell phone, even a product modification such as the newest Blackberry, for example, is very complicated. However, with computer assistance, Gantt charts play a useful role in helping project managers track and control progress—even through high levels of complexity.

● A **Gantt chart** graphically displays the scheduling of tasks required to complete a project.

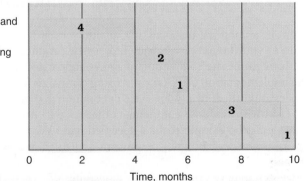

Activities

A Complete research and development work

B Complete engineering design

C Prepare budgets

D Build prototype

E Test prototype

FIGURE 18.4 Simplified Gantt chart for a new cell phone prototype.

#2 **CPM/PERT Techniques** Technique #2 project mgmt

A companion to the Gantt chart is **CPM/PERT**, a combination of the critical path method and the program evaluation and review technique. Project planning based on CPM/PERT uses a network chart like the one shown in Figure 18.5. Such charts are developed by breaking a project into a series of small subactivities, each of which has clear beginning and end points. These points become "nodes" in the charts, and the arrows between nodes indicate in what order things must be completed. The full diagram shows all the interrelationships that must be coordinated during the entire project.

Use of CPM/PERT techniques helps project managers to track and control activities, making sure they happen in the right sequences and on time. The activities can be listed on the arrows for tracking purposes, known as the activity-on-arrows (AOA) diagram; they can also be listed on the nodes, resulting in activity-on-nodes (AON) diagrams. The network in the figure is an AON diagram. If you look again at it, you should notice that the time required for each activity can be easily computed and tracked. The pathway with the longest completion time from start to finish is called the critical path. It represents the best time in which the entire project can be completed assuming everything goes according to plan. In the example, you will find that the critical path is 38 days.

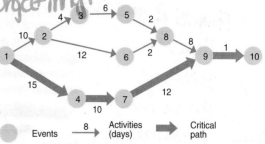

FIGURE 18.5 Sample CPM/PERT Network Activity-on-Node Diagram.

CPM/PERT is a combination of the critical path method and the program evaluation and review technique.

FINANCIAL CONTROLS

The pressure is ever present for all organizations to use their financial resources well. And the global economic recession has left no doubt that an important part of managerial control involves the analysis of financial performance. Control is all about measurement, and there are a number of ways that financial performance can be measured and tracked for control purposes.

The foundation for analysis using financial controls rests with the firm's balance sheet and income statement. The **balance sheet** shows assets and liabilities at a point in time. It will be displayed in an Assets = Liabilities format. The **income statement** shows profits or losses at a point in time. It will be displayed in a Sales − Expenses = Net Income format. You can remember them from an accounting course, or as simply summarized in Figure 18.6.

A **balance sheet** shows assets and liabilities at one point in time.

An **income statement** shows profits or losses at one point in time.

Balance Sheet

Assets	Liabilities
Current Assets	**Current Liabilities**
• Cash	• Accounts payable
• Receivables	• Accrued expenses
• Inventories	• Taxes payable
Fixed Assets	**Long-term Liabilities**
• Land	• Mortgages
• Buildings	• Bonds
Less Depreciation	**Owner's Equity**
	• Outstanding stock
	• Retained earnings
Total Assets =	**Total Liabilities**

Income Statement

Gross Sales
less Returns

Net Sales
less Expenses and Cost of Goods Sold

Operating Profits
plus Other Income

Gross Income
less Interest Expense

Income Before Taxes
less Taxes

Net Income

FIGURE 18.6 Basic foundations of a balance sheet and income statement

Managers should be able to use information from balance sheets and income statements to understand a firm's financial performance. Financial controls of this nature often involve measures of *liquidity*—ability to generate cash to pay bills; *leverage*—ability to earn more in returns than the cost of debt; *asset management*—ability to use resources efficiently and operate at minimum cost; and *profitability*—ability to earn revenues greater than costs. Some of the common financial ratios are listed here.

Liquidity—measures ability to meet short-term obligations
- *Current Ratio* = Current Assets/Current Liabilities
- *Quick Ratio or Acid Test* = Current Assets-Inventories/Current Liabilities

Higher is better: You want more assets and fewer liabilities.

Leverage—measures use of debt
- *Debt Ratio* = Total Debts/Total Assets

Lower is better: You want fewer debts and more assets.

Asset Management—measures asset and inventory efficiency
- *Asset Turnover* = Sales/Total Assets
- *Inventory Turnover* = Sales/Average Inventory

Higher is better: You want more sales relative to assets and inventory.

Profitability—measures ability to earn revenues greater than costs
- *Gross Margin* = Gross Income/Sales
- *Net Margin* = Net Income/Sales
- *Return on Assets* (ROA) = Net Income/Total Assets
- *Return on Equity* (ROE) = Net Income/Owner's Equity

Higher is better: You want more profit relative to sales, assets, and equity.

Financial ratios are useful for historical comparisons within the firm and for external benchmarking. They can also be used to set financial targets or goals to be shared with employees and tracked to indicate success or failure in their accomplishment. At Civco Medical Instruments, for example, a financial report is distributed monthly to all employees. They always know factually how well the firm is doing. This helps them focus on what they can do better to improve on the firm's "bottom line."[24]

BALANCED SCORECARDS

If "what gets measured happens," then managers should take advantage of "scorecards" to record and track performance results. If an instructor takes class attendance and assigns grades based on it, students tend to come to class; if an employer tracks the number of customers each employee serves per day, employees tend to serve more customers. Do the same principles hold for organizations?

Strategic management consultants Robert S. Kaplan and David P. Norton believe they do and advocate using the **balanced scorecard** for management control.[25] It gives top managers, as they say, "a fast, but comprehensive view of the business." The basic principle is that to do well and to win, you have to keep score.

Developing a balanced scorecard for any organization begins with a clarification of the organization's mission and vision—what it wants to be and how it wants to be perceived by its key stakeholders. Next, the following questions are used to develop specific scorecard goals and measures:

- *Financial Performance*—"How well do our actions directly contribute to improved financial performance? To improve financially, how should we appear to our shareholders?" Sample goals: survive, succeed, prosper. Sample measures: cash flow, sales growth and operating income, increased market share, and return on equity.

- A **balanced scorecard** tallies organizational performance in financial, customer service, internal process, and innovation and learning areas.

Research Brief

Restating Corporate Financial Performance Foreshadows Significant Turnover Among Corporate Executives and Directors

The Academy of Management Journal

Control and accountability are core issues in research by Marne L. Arthaud-Day, S. Trevis Certo, Catherine M. Dalton, and Dan R. Dalton. Using a technique known as event history analysis, the researchers say that what happens subsequent to financial misstatements is an "opportunity to study the accountability of leaders for organizational outcomes, independent of firm performance."

Arthaud-Day et al. examined what happened in a two-year period for 116 firms that restated financials, in comparison with 116 others that did not. The firms were chosen from the Financial Statement Restatement Database and matched in pairs by industry and size for control purposes. Results showed that higher turnover of CEOs, CFOs, outside directors, and audit committee members were higher in firms that restated their earnings.

The researchers point out that financial misstatements harm a firm's legitimacy in the eyes of key stakeholders, and this threatens the firm's ability to obtain resources and external support. Because financial misstatements are considered to be direct management failures, executives are more likely to be held accountable for them than for poor performance of an organization overall—even for bankruptcy, which might be explained by adverse external factors.

The researchers note that "companies often couch involuntary departures in nice-sounding clichés (i.e., an executive 'retires'), making it nearly impossible to determine the true reason for turnover." In terms of future research, they recommend looking at what happens after "tainted" leadership is removed. Does the firm regain stakeholder legitimacy and do better in the future, or not?

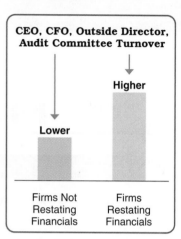

CEO, CFO, Outside Director, Audit Committee Turnover

Higher — Firms Restating Financials
Lower — Firms Not Restating Financials

You Be the Researcher

If one looked not just at financial misstatements, but also at share price declines, profit and loss trends, and product successes and failures, would similar patterns of control and accountability for top managers be found? Given the increased concern for tightening financial controls and holding business executives accountable for performance, are executives in governments, schools, and nonprofits in your community being held accountable as well?

Reference: Marne L. Arthaud-Day, S. Trevis Certo, Catherine M. Dalton, and Dan R. Dalton, "A Changing of the Guard: Executive and Director Turnover Following Corporate Financial Restatements," *Academy of Management Journal*, vol. 49 (December 2006), pp. 119–136.

- *Customer Satisfaction*—"How well do we serve our customers and clients? To achieve our vision, how should we appear to our customers?" Sample goals: new products, responsive supply. Sample measures: percentage sales from new products, percentage on-time deliveries.

- *Internal Process Improvement*—"How well do our activities and processes directly increase the value we provide our customers and clients? To satisfy our customers and shareholders, at what internal business processes should we excel?" Sample goals: manufacturing excellence, design productivity, new product introduction. Sample measures: cycle times, engineering efficiency, new product time.

- *Innovation and Learning*— "How well are we learning, changing, and improving things over time? To achieve our vision, how will we sustain our ability to change and improve?" Sample goals: technology leadership, time to market. Sample measures: time to develop new technologies, new product introduction time versus competition.

When balanced scorecard measures are taken and routinely recorded for critical managerial review, Kaplan and Norton expect organizations to perform better in these four performance areas. Again, what gets measured happens.

Think about the possibilities of using balanced scorecards in all types of organizations. How can this approach be used, for example, by an elementary school, a hospital, a community library, a mayor's office, a fast-food restaurant? How might the performance dimensions and indicators vary among these different organizations? And if balanced scorecards make sense, why is it that more organizations don't use them?

Learning Check

Study Question 3

What are common control tools and techniques?

Be sure you can ☑ explain progressive discipline   ☑ define *project management*   ☑ explain how Gantt charts and CPM/PERT analysis assist in project management   ☑ list and explain common ratios used in financial control   ☑ identify the four main balanced scorecard components

---

Management Learning Review

Study Questions Summary

1 Why and how do managers control?

- Controlling is the process of measuring performance and taking corrective action as needed.
- Feedforward controls are accomplished before a work activity begins; they ensure that directions are clear and that the right resources are available to accomplish them.
- Concurrent controls make sure that things are being done correctly; they allow corrective actions to be taken while the work is being done.
- Feedback controls take place after an action is completed; they address the question "Now that we are finished, how well did we do, and what did we learn for the future?"
- Internal control is self-control and occurs as people take personal responsibility for their work.
- External control is based on the use of bureaucratic, clan, and market control systems.

FOR DISCUSSION **Can strong input and output controls make up for poor concurrent controls?**

2 What are the steps in the control process?

- The first step in the control process is to establish performance objectives and standards that create targets against which later performance can be evaluated.
- The second step in the control process is to measure actual performance and specifically identify what results are being achieved.
- The third step in the control process is to compare performance results with objectives to determine if things are going according to plans.

- The fourth step in the control process is to take action to resolve problems or explore opportunities that are identified when results are compared with objectives.

FOR DISCUSSION **What are the potential downsides to management by exception?**

3 What are the common control tools and techniques?

- Discipline is the process of influencing behavior through reprimand; progressive discipline systems vary reprimands according to the severity of infractions.
- A project is a unique event that must be completed by a specified date; project management is the process of ensuring that projects are completed on time, on budget, and according to objectives.
- Gantt charts assist in project management and control by displaying how various tasks must be scheduled in order to complete a project on time.
- CPM/PERT analysis assists in project management and control by describing the complex networks of activities that must be completed in sequences for a project to be completed successfully.
- Financial control of business performance is facilitated by a variety of financial ratios, such as those dealing with liquidity, leverage, assets, and profitability.
- The balanced scorecard measures overall organizational performance in four areas: financial, customers, internal processes, and innovation.

FOR DISCUSSION **Should all employees of a business be regularly informed of the firm's overall financial performance?**

Self-Test

Multiple-Choice Questions

1. After objectives and standards are set, what step comes next in the control process?
   (a) measure results   (b) take corrective action   (c) compare results with objectives   (d) modify standards to fit circumstances

2. When a soccer coach tells her players at the end of a losing game: "You really played well and stayed with the game plan," she is using a/an _____ as a measure of performance.
   (a) input standard   (b) output standard   (c) historical comparison   (d) relative comparison

3. When an automobile manufacturer is careful to purchase only the highest-quality components for use in production, this is an example of an attempt to ensure high performance through _____ control.
   (a) concurrent   (b) statistical   (c) inventory   (d) feedforward

4. Management by exception means _____.
   (a) managing only when necessary   (b) focusing attention where the need for action is greatest   (c) the same thing as concurrent control   (d) the same thing as just-in-time delivery

5. When a supervisor working alongside an employee corrects him or her when a mistake is made, this is an example of _____ control.
   (a) feedforward   (b) concurrent   (c) internal   (d) clan

6. If an organization's top management visits a firm in another industry to learn more about its excellent record in hiring and promoting minority and female candidates, this is an example of using _____ for control purposes.
   (a) a balanced scorecard   (b) relative comparison   (c) management by exception   (d) progressive discipline

7. The control equation states: _____ = Desired Performance − Actual Performance.
   (a) Problem Magnitude   (b) Management Opportunity   (c) Planning Objective   (d) Need for Action

8. When a UPS manager compares the amount of time a driver takes to accomplish certain deliveries against a standard set through scientific analysis of her delivery route, this is known as _____.
   (a) an historical comparison   (b) an engineering comparison   (c) relative benchmarking   (d) concurrent control

9. Projects are unique one-time events that _____.
   (a) have unclear objectives   (b) must be completed by a specific time   (c) have unlimited budgets   (d) are largely self-managing

10. The _____ chart graphically displays the scheduling of tasks required to complete a project.
    (a) exception   (b) Taylor   (c) Gantt   (d) after-action

11. In CPM/PERT, "CPM" stands for _____.
    (a) critical path method   (b) control planning management   (c) control plan map   (d) current planning method

12. In a CPM/PERT analysis the focus is on _____ and the event _____ that link them together with the finished project.
    (a) costs, budgets   (b) activities, sequences   (c) timetables, budgets   (d) goals, costs

13. A manager following the "hot stove rules" of progressive discipline would _____.
    (a) avoid giving too much information when reprimanding someone   (b) reprimand at random   (c) focus the reprimand on actions, not personality   (d) delay reprimands until something positive can also be discussed

14. Among the financial ratios used for control, Current Assets/Current Liabilities is known as the _____.
    (a) debt ratio   (b) net margin   (c) current ratio   (d) inventory turnover ratio

15. In respect to return on assets (ROA) and the debt ratio, the preferred directions when analyzing them from a control standpoint are _____.
    (a) decrease ROA, increase debt   (b) increase ROA, increase debt   (c) increase ROA, decrease debt   (d) decrease ROA, decrease debt

Short-Response Questions

16. List the four steps in the controlling process and give examples of each.
17. How might feedforward control be used by the owner/manager of a local bookstore?
18. How does Douglas McGregor's Theory Y relate to the concept of internal control?
19. How does a progressive discipline system work?

Essay Question

20. Assume that you are given the job of project manager for building a new student center on your campus. List just five of the major activities that need to be accomplished to complete the new building in two years. Draw an AON network diagram that links the activities together in required event scheduling and sequencing. Make an estimate for the time required for each sequence to be completed and identify the critical path.

Management Skills and Competencies

Self-Assessment

Back to Yourself: Resiliency

The control process is one of the ways through which managers can help organizations best use their available resources and systems to achieve productivity. In many ways our daily lives are similar quests for productivity, and the control process counts there too. We need to spot and understand if things are going according to plan, or going off course; we need to have the courage and confidence to change ways that aren't working well; and, we need to have the **resiliency** to hold on and keep things moving forward even in the face of adversity. The way we utilize, or not, various opportunities to engage in positive self-management probably makes a substantial difference in the results we achieve in work and non-work settings alike. It might be helpful, for example, to pursue personal career development with a strong commitment to both planning—getting the goals clear and right, and controlling—making sure that we are always moving forward to accomplish them. After you complete the following self-assessment on After Meeting/Project Remorse, go online to further assess how well you deal with work-life balance issues.

> In the management of our personal lives we each need the capacity for **resiliency**—the ability to call upon inner strength and keep moving forward even when things are tough.

Further Reflection: After Meeting/Project Remorse

Instructions

Complete the following assessment after participating in a meeting or a group project.[26]

1. How satisfied are you with the outcome of the meeting project?
   Not at all satisfied   1   2   3   4   5   6   7   Totally satisfied
2. How would the other members of the meeting/project group rate your influence on what took place?
   No influence   1   2   3   4   5   6   7   Very high influence
3. In your opinion, how ethical was any decision that was reached?
   Highly unethical   1   2   3   4   5   6   7   Highly ethical
4. To what extent did you feel "*pushed into*" going along with the decision?
   Not pushed into it at all   1   2   3   4   5   6   7   Very pushed into it
5. How committed are you to the agreements reached?
   Not at all committed   1   2   3   4   5   6   7   Highly committed
6. Did you understand what was expected of you as a member of the meeting or project group?
   Not at all clear   1   2   3   4   5   6   7   Perfectly clear
7. Were participants in the meeting/project group discussions listening to each other?
   Never   1   2   3   4   5   6   7   Always
8. Were participants in the meeting/project group discussions honest and open in communicating with one another?
   Never   1   2   3   4   5   6   7   Always
9. Was the meeting/project completed efficiently?
   Not at all   1   2   3   4   5   6   7   Very much
10. Was the outcome of the meeting/project something that you felt proud to be a part of?
    Not at all   1   2   3   4   5   6   7   Very much

Interpretation

This assessment is a chance to look in the mirror and ask: "What are my thoughts about my team and my contributions to the team, now that the project is finished?" Ask what you could do in future situations to end up with a "perfect" score after a meeting, or after the project review.

Team Follow-Up Option

Have everyone in your group complete the same assessment for the project. Share results and discuss their implications (a) for the future success of the group on another project and (b) for the members as they go forward to work with other groups on other projects in the future.

Team Exercise

Defining Quality

Preparation

Write your definition of the word quality here.

QUALITY =

Instructions

Form groups as assigned by your instructor.

1. Have each group member present a definition of the word *quality*. After everyone has presented, come up with a consensus definition of quality. Write down the definition with which everyone most agrees.
2. Use the group's quality definition to state for each organization below a quality objective that can guide the behavior of members in producing high-quality goods and/or services for customers or clients. Make sure that the objective is stated as a "key result" that can be measured for control purposes.
3. Elect a spokesperson to share group results with the class as a whole.

Organizations

1. university
2. community hospital
3. online retail store
4. gourmet restaurant
5. U.S. post office branch
6. coffee shop
7. student apartment rental company
8. used textbook store
9. grocery store
10. fitness center

Case Study: Electronic Arts

Go to *Management Cases for Critical Thinking* to find the recommended case for Chapter 18— "Electronic Arts: Inside Fantasy Sports."

Operations and Services Management

19

Learning From Others

Speed and Flexibility Rule Global Competition

Even in the world of high fashion you can't be competitive if you aren't fast and flexible. Pressures from retailers like Zara International and others that excel at "fast fashion"—getting new designs into stores quickly—have even brought changes to Louis Vuitton. The maker of high-fashion handbags and other accessories has revamped production techniques to increase speed without sacrificing quality.

A Louis Vuitton tote bag used to take up to 30 craft persons some 8 days to make. The bag was passed from hand to hand, with each worker performing a separate and highly specialized task.

That all changed when Vuitton executives, advised by consultants from McKinsey & Company, turned to the automobile industry, believe it or not, for ideas. They benchmarked Toyota's production processes and decided that things at the fashion house could be done a lot faster. The company reorganized workers into teams of 6 to 12 people, working at U-shaped workstations. Workers in each team perform more than one task and pass the in-process tote bag back and forth. They complete a tote bag in just one day.

Vuitton calls its production system "Pégase" after the mythical flying horse that is a symbol of speed and power. Since Pégase was introduced, Louis Vuitton has been able to ship new designs every six weeks, more than twice as fast as previously shipped. Says Patrick Louis Vuitton of the founding family: "It's about finding the best ratio between quality and speed." Yves Carcelle, chief executive officer for the Pégase brand, also points out that "Behind the creative magic of Louis Vuitton is an extremely efficient supply chain." To compete today with fast rivals and global competitors, even Louis Vuitton has now recognized that without the best execution, even a great design can't guarantee success.[1]

do the benchmarking

Workers in Louis Vuitton's Pégase teams are less specialized than before, working on a broader set of individual jobs and as part of a team. They swap tasks and team roles while making different kinds of bags, allowing production to switch quickly from one design to another. **Take a look around the next time you are in a service establishment or in a production facility. How much productivity could be gained by following similar ideas?**

Learning About Yourself

Strength and Energy

As just pointed out in the example of Louis Vuitton, there's a lot to master when it comes to managing the operations of complex organizations. It's a continuous task of identifying players and processes, examining relationships, performing analyses, making decisions, and acting in ways that streamline behavior for maximum efficiency and performance. And at first it might strike you as odd to talk here about personal **strength** and **energy**. But the fact is that it isn't always easy to keep up with fast-paced work and personal responsibilities.

One national survey of American workers found 54% feel overworked, 55% feel overwhelmed by their workloads, 56% say they do not have enough time to complete their work, 59% do not have enough time for reflection, and 45% have to do too many things at once. The Mayo Clinic points out that in our often "frenetically paced world" the boundaries between work and home have blurred.

> **Mayo Clinic on Work–Life Balance**
> * *Learn to say no*—don't do things out of guilt or false obligation
> * *Leave work at work*—set boundaries between work and personal affairs
> * *Manage time*—be efficient and set priorities
> * *Fight guilt*—remember it's okay to have a job and a family
> * *Nurture yourself*—do something relaxing and enjoyable every day
> * *Protect your day off*—spread chores so that a day off is free time
> * *Get enough sleep*—give your system the chance to replenish its energy

We work longer hours and stay constantly in touch with work with information technology. Combined with nonwork responsibilities, these pressures take their tolls and create problems with fatigue—sheer physical breakdown, family—missing life events, friends, not nurturing friendships, and expectations—the more you work the more is expected of you.

Just as is true of playing tennis or some other sport, we have to get and stay in shape, physically and mentally so that we can not only perform well at work, but also maintain positive work–life balance. This means building strength and energy to best handle the inevitable strains and anxieties of conflicts between work demands and personal affairs.[2]

get to know yourself better

Check the Mayo Clinic tips in the box. How good are you, right now as a student, at satisfying both work and nonwork demands? The chances are that present behavior is a good predictor of how you'll do in the future. What are the lessons of a frank self-assessment? Do you have the strength and energy to do well at work and also have a healthy home life? **Also make use of the end-of-chapter Self-Assessment feature to further check on your personal numeracy, a critical life and career skill.**

Study Question 1	Study Question 2	Study Question 3	Study Question 4
Operations Management Essentials	**Value Chain Management**	**Service and Product Quality**	**Work Processes**
• Productivity and competitive advantage • Operations technologies	• Value chain analysis • Supply chain management • Inventory management • Break-even analysis	• Customer relationship management • Quality management • Statistical quality control	• Work process analysis • Process reengineering
Learning Check 1	**Learning Check 2**	**Learning Check 3**	**Learning Check 4**

As the opening example of Louis Vuitton suggests, organizations today operate in a world that places a premium on productivity, technology utilization, quality, customer service, and speed. Businesses large and small are struggling and innovating as they try to succeed in a world of intense competition, continued globalization of markets and business activities, and rapid technological change. Just how top executives approach these challenges differs from one organization to the next, but they all focus on moving services and products into the hands of customers in ways that create loyalty and profits.

At BMW, where customers are foremost, a major thrust is on continuous innovation. CEO Norbert Reithofer says: "We push change through the organization to ensure its strength. There are always better solutions." One of those solutions is state-of-the-art manufacturing: the firm's facilities produce 1.3 million customized vehicles a year. And when Ann Taylor stores were struggling to reassert its women's clothing brand and market position, newly appointed CEO Kay Krill started with a 54-point action plan. It covered everything from processes to products to marketing. Although criticized for identifying so many things to address, she said: "There were 54 things we needed to fix. We fixed every one of them. All 54 were important to me."[3]

OPERATIONS MANAGEMENT ESSENTIALS

Look in at the Roush & Yates Racing Engines facility in Mooresville, North Carolina. As the NASCAR season begins, the shop is a beehive of activity as it supplies Ford engines to several racing teams. It's staffed with engineers and technicians of many skills; the work has to be precise, and the shop also has to run with a strong eye on its bottom line. That's where Mary Ann Mauldwin comes in. She is Roush's director of operations and in just five years has completely overhauled the way things are done. CEO Doug Yates says: "We were a good engine company; Mary Ann has made us a world-class engine-building company."

How did Mauldwin transform Roush's engine shop? She brought in new inventory controls—previously only 48% of parts were accounted for, and now audits account for 100%. Materials were organized and arranged efficiently at workstations, cutting time required to find parts; work processes were standardized to improve consistency across engines under construction. Old parts are now refurbished and sold to other racing teams; some parts previously purchased are now made in-house to improve availability and quality control. The costs saved have generated more available monies for research and development, something

Efficiency Drives Success with Top Racing Engines

With a degree in both mechanical engineering and English, Mary Ann Mauldwin has had a varied and interesting career—from middle school teacher to operations management consultant to director of operations for Roush & Yates. How does a woman succeed in a racing engine shop? "I didn't know a piston from a connecting rod" when I started here, she says. But she soon earned her credibility by restructuring operations to improve inventory control, streamline workflows, standardize engine-building processes, and organize the supply chain for efficiency and quality.

that CEO Yates believes is a key to keeping his firm in front of the NASCAR pack.[4]

In one way or another, all organizations must master the challenges of **operations management**—getting work done by managing the systems through which organizations transform resources into finished products, goods, and services for customers and clients.[5] The span of operations management covers the full input–throughput–output cycle. Typical operations management decisions address such things as resource acquisition, inventories, facilities, workflows, technologies, and product quality.

The essentials of operations management apply to all types of organizations, both manufacturing and services. Xerox transforms resource inputs into quality photocopy machines; BMW transforms them into attractive, high-performance automobiles; and Ann Taylor stores transform them into fashionable clothing and accessories. They are **manufacturing organizations** that produce physical goods, and this process of goods creation has to be well managed. By contrast, Southwest Airlines transforms resource inputs into low-cost, dependable air travel; American Express transforms them into financial services; the Mayo Clinic transforms them into health care services; and governments transform them into public services. They are examples of **service organizations** that produce services rather than physical goods, and this process of creating services must also be well managed.

- **Operations management** is the process of managing productive systems that transform resources into finished products.

- **Manufacturing organizations** produce physical goods.

- **Service organizations** produce nonphysical outputs in the form of services.

PRODUCTIVITY AND COMPETITIVE ADVANTAGE

The core issues in operations and services management boil down to how "productivity" and "competitive advantage" are achieved. This focuses management attention on the various processes and activities that turn resources—in the form of people, materials, equipment, and capital—into finished goods and services.

Productivity

Operations management in both manufacturing and services is very concerned with **productivity**—a quantitative measure of the efficiency with which inputs are transformed into outputs. The basic **productivity equation** is: Productivity = Output/Input.

- **Productivity** is the efficiency with which inputs are transformed into outputs.

- The **productivity equation** is: Productivity = Output/Input.

If, for example, a local Red Cross center collects 100 units of donated blood in one 8-hour day, its productivity would be 12.25 units per hour. If we were in charge of centers in several locations, the productivity of the centers could be compared on this measure. Alternatively, one might compare the centers using a productivity measure based not on hours of inputs, but on numbers of full-time staff. Using this input measure, a center that collects 500 units per week with two full-time staff members (250 units per person) is more productive than one that collects 600 units per week with three workers (200 units per person).

When Microsoft studied the productivity of office workers in an online survey of 38,000+ people across 200 countries, results showed a variety of productivity shortfalls.[6] Although people reported working 47 hours per week, they were unproductive during 17 of the hours; 69% said time spent in meetings was unproductive. Productivity obstacles included unclear objectives and priorities, as well as procrastination and poor communication.

Competitive Advantage

Inefficiencies like those reported by Microsoft are costly; lost productivity by any measure is a drain on organizational competitiveness. Operating efficiencies that increase productivity, by contrast, are among the ways organizations may gain competitive advantage—defined earlier in the book as a core competency that allows an organization to outperform competitors.[7] Potential drivers of competitive advantage include the ability to outperform based on product innovation, customer service, speed to market, manufacturing flexibility, and product or service quality. But regardless of how competitive advantage is achieved, the key result is the same: an ability to consistently do something of high value that one's competitors cannot replicate quickly or do as well.

Consider the example of Matsushita Electric Industries—maker of telephones, fax machines, security cameras, and other electronics. When productivity at Matsushita's plant in Saga, Japan, doubled in a four-year period, the executives didn't sit back and celebrate. They wanted still more. A huge set of conveyers was removed and robots were brought in along with sophisticated software to operate them. Plant manager Hitoshi Hirata says: "It used to be 2.5 days into a production run before we had our first finished product. But now the first is done in 40 minutes." And one might be tempted to compliment Hirata on a job well done and sit back to watch the results. Not so. He says: "Next year we'll try to shorten the cycle even more."[8]

OPERATIONS TECHNOLOGIES

The foundation of any transformation process is technology—the combination of knowledge, skills, equipment, and work methods used to transform resource inputs into organizational outputs. It is the way tasks are accomplished using tools, machines, techniques, and human know-how. The availability of appropriate technology is a cornerstone of productivity, and the nature of the core technologies in use is an important element in competitive advantage.

1 Manufacturing Technology *#1 operation technology*

When you think manufacturing, the first thing that might come to mind is an automobile assembly line. It is a good example, but are you aware of how much that assembly line has changed in the new workplace? Picture this scene from Ford's assembly plant in northeastern Brazil.[9]

Instrument panels made by Visteon in one part of the factory are carried on overhead conveyors to be lowered neatly into car bodies passing underneath. The plant

● **Competitive advantage** is the ability to outperform one's competitors due to a core competency that is difficult to copy or imitate.

● **Technology** is the combination of knowledge, skills, equipment, and work methods used to transform inputs into outputs.

"Henry Ford of Heart Surgery" Saves Lives with Economies of Scale

Would you believe that a hospital can thrive by increasing productivity through old-fashioned economies of scale? The principle is being proven in India by heart surgeon Dr. Devi Shetty, formerly Mother Theresa's cardiologist. Dr. Shetty has shown that by increasing volume for delicate procedures, costs go down while maintaining quality. "Japanese companies reinvented the process of making cars," he says, "that's what we are doing in health care." Not only do his teams of specialized surgeons perform more operations, the sophisticated testing equipment is used up to five times more in a day than in U.S. hospitals. The *Wall Street Journal* calls Dr. Shetty the "Henry Ford of Heart Surgery."

makes three models—Ford's Fiesta hatchback, Fiesta Saloon and EcoSport utility vehicle—each to various specifications, all passing together along the same assembly line, all receiving components for Ford itself and from 13 suppliers inside the final assembly building and a further 11 suppliers in other parts of the 4.7m square meter site.

This is a high-tech and ultra-modern management version of **mass production** where a manufacturing organization produces a large number of uniform products in an assembly-line system. Workers are highly dependent on one another as the product passes from stage to stage until completion. Equipment may be sophisticated as in the Ford example, and workers often follow detailed instructions while performing simplified jobs.

> **Mass production** manufactures a large number of uniform products with an assembly-line system.

There are two other common manufacturing technologies, small-batch production and continuous-process production.[10] In **small-batch production**, such as in a racing bicycle shop, a variety of custom products are tailor-made to order. Each item or batch of items is made somewhat differently to fit customer specifications. The equipment used may not be elaborate, but a high level of worker skill is often needed. Organizations using **continuous-process production** continuously feed raw materials—such as liquids, solids, and gases—through a highly automated production system with largely computerized controls. Such systems are equipment-intensive, but they can often be operated by a relatively small labor force. Classic examples are oil refineries and power plants.

> **Small-batch production** manufactures a variety of products crafted to fit customer specifications.

> In **continuous-process production**, raw materials are continuously transformed by an automated system.

Appropriate use and innovation in manufacturing technology can be a major source of competitive advantage for today's manufacturers. In fact, operations like the Ford plant in Brazil have to be continually updating to stay up with and hopefully ahead of the competition.[11] As you consider what is happening in manufacturing technologies, the following trends are among the most evident.[12]

- There is increased use of *robotics*, where computer-controlled machines perform physically repetitive work with consistency and efficiency. If you visit any automobile manufacturer today, chances are that robotics is a major feature of the operations.
- There is increased use of *flexible manufacturing systems* that allow automated operations to quickly shift from one task or product type to another. The goal is to combine flexibility with efficiency, allowing what is sometimes called *mass customization*—efficient mass production of products meeting specific customer requirements.

#1

#2

Manufacturing ←Trends ↓

#3

- There is increased use of *cellular layouts* that place machines doing different work together, so that the movement of materials from one to the other is as efficient as possible. Cellular layouts also accommodate more teamwork on the part of machine operators.

#4

- There is increased use of *computer-integrated manufacturing* (CIM), in which product designs, process plans, and manufacturing are driven from a common computer platform. Such CIM approaches are now integrated with the Internet, so that customer purchasing trends in retail locations can be spotted and immediately integrated into production schedules at a manufacturing location.

#5

- There is increased focus on *lean production* that continuously innovates and employs best practices to keep simplifying processes, reducing costs, and increasing production efficiencies."[13]

#6

- There is increased attention to *design for disassembly*. The goal here is to design and manufacture products in ways that consider how their component parts will be recycled at the end of their lives.

#7

- There is increased value to be found in *remanufacturing*. Instead of putting things together, remanufacturing takes used items apart and rebuilds them as products to be used again. One estimate is that using remanufactured materials saves up to 30% on costs.

Service Technology

When you think of services, think of the airlines you travel on. What counts for you as a customer? Most likely your customer experience begins with the company's website and how efficient and easy it might be to use. It continues with the process of check-in and how well and efficiently you are treated. It continues further during boarding and then in-flight as the pilots and flight attendants take care of you. And it doesn't end until you arrive safely, hopefully on time, and are able to retrieve all of your check-in bags in a timely manner. At each point in this process things can go wrong or right, with consequences for your satisfaction and loyalty to the airline.

It is in the latter sense that something called the **service-profit chain** becomes important in service organizations. You can think of it as the activities involved in the direct link between an organization's service providers and customers or clients. When the service-profit chain is well managed and executed from an operations perspective, it should result in satisfied and loyal customers for the organization, and, ideally, it should do so with an efficient and productive use of the organization's resources.

As in manufacturing settings, the nature of the service organization's core technology is an important input to the service-profit chain.[14] In health care, education, and related services, **intensive technology** focuses the efforts of many people with special expertise on the needs of patients, students, or clients. In banks, real estate firms, insurance companies, employment agencies, and others like them, **mediating technology** links together parties seeking a mutually beneficial exchange of values—typically a buyer and a seller. And, **long-linked technology** can function like mass production, where a client is passed from point to point for various aspects of service delivery.

The **service-profit chain** consists of all activities involved in the direct link between an organization's service providers and customers or clients.

Intensive technology focuses the efforts and talents of many people to serve clients.

Mediating technology links people together in a beneficial exchange of values.

In **long-linked technology** a client moves from point to point during service delivery.

Learning Check
Study Question 1
What are the essentials of operations management?

Be sure you can ☑ define *operations management* ☑ state the productivity equation ☑ define *competitive advantage* ☑ list alternative types of manufacturing and service technologies ☑ discuss several trends in manufacturing technologies

No Frills Airline Thrives by Cutting Costs

Ryanair's CEO Michael O'Leary argues that the way to profit while running an airline is to keep cutting costs with "imagination and passion." And so Ireland-based Ryanair cuts costs, and it does so aggressively and continuously. A model of the "no frills" airline, it is able to offer spectacularly low fares to customers and still make money. It carries more international travelers than any other airline in the world. Ryanair flies to regional airports (lower fees), has no reclining seats (saves on maintenance), no on-board services (pay if you want a coffee), and even charges passengers to check in at the airport (human contact costs extra).

VALUE CHAIN MANAGEMENT

Whereas productivity may be considered the major efficiency measure in both manufacturing and services, "value creation" should be the target effectiveness measure. In this sense, **value creation** means that the end result of a task or activity or work process is worth more than the effort and resources invested to accomplish it. In a manufacturing operation, for example, value is created when a raw material such as copper wire is combined with transistors and other electrical components to create a computer chip. In a service setting, value is created when a trained financial analyst provides a customer with advice that leads to profitable brokerage transactions in a stock portfolio.

> **Value creation** occurs when the result of a work task or activity makes a product or service worth more in terms of potential customer appeal than at the start.

VALUE CHAIN ANALYSIS

You should recall from earlier discussions in this book that an organization's **value chain**, as shown in Figure 19.1, is the specific sequence of activities that result in the creation of products or services with value for customers. The value chain includes all *primary activities*—from inbound logistics to operations to outbound logistics to marketing and sales to after-sales service, as well as *support activities*—such as procurement, human resource management, technology development and support, and financial and infrastructure maintenance.[15]

> The **value chain** is the specific sequence of activities that creates products and services with value for customers.

Organization as a transformation system

Resources and materials flow in → Materials received and organized for use → People and technology create products → Finished products distributed → Customers served

Management of the value chain

FIGURE 19.1 Elements in an organization's value chain.

Real Ethics

"Not in My Backyard" Dilemma Makes Things Personal

A major grocery store chain has decided to build a supercenter in your town. The store will be open 24/7, and the local economy is expected to benefit greatly. In fact, the company announced that it would hire 40 full-time and more than 100 part-time employees to staff the store. It also intends to use several local construction companies to build the center. City commissioners are excited about the additional tax revenue that will be generated because otherwise they were going to have to cut back on some services. This seems like very positive news.

But, the site selected for the new store is right at the edge of your neighborhood. Home prices are already falling because of the announcement. Neighbors are worried about the nuisances that will result from such a large store. Light pollution is a concern since the store will be open 24 hours a day and the parking lot lights are really bright. Noise will also be an issue because delivery trucks will be arriving at all hours of the day and night. Finally, traffic will certainly increase, and the streets will become more dangerous for the neighborhood children.

As the city manager, you will play a major role in determining whether the grocery store will be given final permission to build the new store. You clearly recognize how much the community can gain from this development. However, it seems that the benefits to the town as a whole will come at a cost to your particular neighborhood.

Your family, friends, and neighbors expect you to put a stop to this development plan. Simply suggesting that the grocery store build elsewhere is not a viable option. The grocery chain has targeted this particular site for years and is only willing to build in the community if it can do so at this location.

You Decide

What will you do? The new store would help the struggling local economy by providing jobs and increasing tax revenues, but why should your family and neighbors have to pay such a high price to support the rest of the community? You probably have the power to break off the negotiations and deny the grocery store permission to build. But is it the right thing to do? What are the ethical considerations that go into making decisions when professional obligations and personal obligations collide?

Analysis of any organization's value chain will show an intricate sequence of activities that step by step adds value to inputs, right up to the point at which finished goods or services are delivered to customers or clients. The essence of value chain management is to manage each of these steps for maximum efficiency and effectiveness.

Part of the logic of being able to identify and diagram a value chain is to focus management attention on three major questions. First: what value is being created for customers in each step? Second: how efficient is each step as a contributor to overall organizational productivity? Third: how can value creation be improved overall? As the customer of an online retailer such as Amazon.com, for example, you can think of this value in such terms as the price you pay, the quality you receive, and the timeliness of the delivery. From the standpoint of value chain management, Amazon's value creation process can be examined from the point where books are purchased to their transportation and warehousing, to electronic inventorying and order processing, and to packaging and distribution to the ultimate customer.

SUPPLY CHAIN MANAGEMENT

An essential element in any value chain is the relationship between the organization and the many people and businesses that supply it with needed resources and materials. All of these supplier relationships on the input side of the input–throughput–output action cycle must be well managed for productivity. Perhaps no company knows this lesson better right now than Boeing. Its new 787 Dreamliner was delayed over two years due to problems with a complex supply chain that required coordinated production from firms located in diverse locations such as Italy, Sweden, Korea,

Japan, Australia, and the United States. Although cost saving was the goal of moving from in-house production to substantial outsourcing of components, the resulting coordination and delivery problems wreaked havoc with the Dreamliner's production schedules. This hurt both costs and customer goodwill. Boeing's CEO Jim McNerney says: "The initial plan outran our ability to execute it."[16]

The concept of **supply chain management**, or SCM, involves strategic management of all operations linking an organization and its suppliers, including such areas as purchasing, manufacturing, transportation, and distribution.[17] The goals of supply chain management are to achieve efficiency in all aspects of the supply chain while ensuring on-time availability of quality resources and products. Wal-Mart is still considered a master of supply chain management. For example, the firm uses an advanced information system that continually updates inventory records and sales forecasts based on point-of-sale computerized information. Suppliers access this information electronically, allowing them to adjust their operations and rapidly ship replacement products to meet the retailer's needs.

> **Supply chain management** strategically links all operations dealing with resource supplies.

Purchasing plays an important role in supply chain management. Just as any individual tries to control how much they spend, a thrifty organization must be concerned about how much it pays for what it buys. To leverage buying power, more organizations are centralizing purchasing to allow buying in volume. They are trimming supply chains and focusing on a small number of suppliers with whom they negotiate special contracts, gain quality assurances, and get preferred service. They are also finding ways to work together in supplier–purchaser partnerships. It is now more common, for example, that parts suppliers maintain warehouses in their customer's facilities. The customer provides the space; the supplier does the rest. The benefits to the customer are lower purchasing costs and preferred service; the supplier gains an exclusive customer contract and more sales volume.

INVENTORY MANAGEMENT

Another important issue in the value chain is management of **inventory**, the amount of materials or products kept in storage. Organizations maintain a variety of inventories of raw material, work in process, and finished goods. Whenever anything is held in inventory, there is cost associated with it, and controlling these costs is an important productivity tool.

> **Inventory** is an amount of materials or products kept in storage.

Inventory management is an area where developments in computer and information technologies play an increasingly important role. For example, it is increasingly common today to find *radio-frequency identification* (RFID) tags to electronically track the movement of goods, parts, and even people through various steps in the value chain. You see this in hospitals and amusement parks, which use wrist bands to track customer progress through the service-profit chain, and in various retail and service settings, ranging from retail and grocery stores to airline baggage handling, as RFID tags assist with supply chain and inventory management.

> Inventory control by **economic order quantity** orders replacements whenever inventory level falls to a predetermined point.

Economic Order Quantity

The goal of inventory control is to make sure that an inventory is just the right size to meet performance needs, thus minimizing the cost. The **economic order quantity** (EOQ) method of inventory control involves ordering a fixed number of items every time an inventory level falls to a predetermined point. When this point is reached, as shown in Figure 19.2, a decision is automatically made (typically by computer) to place a standard order to replenish the stock. The order sizes are mathematically calculated to minimize

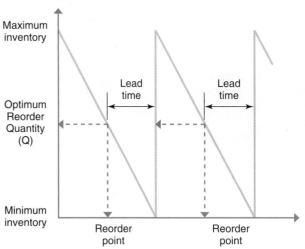

FIGURE 19.2 Inventory control by economic order quantity (EOQ).

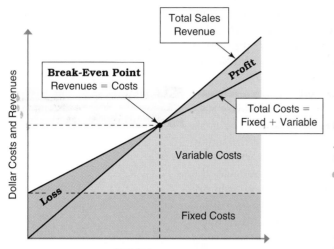

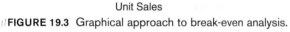

FIGURE 19.3 Graphical approach to break-even analysis.

costs of inventory. The best example is the local supermarket, where hundreds of daily orders are routinely made on this basis.

Just-in-Time Systems

Another approach to inventory control is **just-in-time scheduling** (JIT), made popular by the Japanese. JIT systems reduce costs and improve workflow by scheduling materials to arrive at a workstation or facility "just in time" to be used. Since almost no inventories are maintained, the just-in-time approach is an important productivity tool. When a major hurricane was predicted to hit Florida, for example, Wal-Mart's computer database anticipated high demand for, of all things, strawberry Pop-Tarts. JIT kicked in to deliver them to the stores "just in time" for the storm.[18]

● **Just-in-time scheduling** minimizes inventory by sending out materials to workstations "just in time" to be used.

● The **break-even point** is where revenues = costs.

● **Break-even analysis** calculates the point at which revenues cover costs under different "what if" conditions.

BREAK-EVEN ANALYSIS

Another important value chain management issue relates to capacity planning for the production of products or services, and the pricing of them for sales. In basic business terms too much capacity raises costs, and too little capacity means unmet sales; too low a price fails to deliver revenues that cover costs, and too high a price drives away customers. Thus, when business executives are deliberating new products or projects, a frequent question is: "What is the 'break-even point'?"

The graph in Figure 19.3 shows that the **break-even point** is where revenues just equal costs. You can also think of it as the point where losses end and profit begins. The *formula for calculating break-even points* is:

$$\text{Break-even point} = \text{Fixed costs}/(\text{Price} - \text{Variable Costs})$$

Managers use **break-even analysis** to improve control and perform "what if" calculations under different projected cost and revenue conditions. See if you can calculate some break-even points, doing the types of analyses that business executives perform every day. Suppose the proposed target price for a new product is $8 per unit, fixed costs are $10,000, and variable costs are $4 per unit. What sales volume is required to break even? (Answer: The break-even point is at 2,500 units.) What happens if you are good at cost control and can keep variable costs to $3 per unit? (Answer: The break-even point is at 2,000 units.) Now, suppose you can only produce 1,000 units in the beginning and at the original costs. At what price must you sell them to break even? (Answer: $14.)

Learning Check **Study Question 2** What is value chain management?	*Be sure you can* ☑ define *value creation* ☑ describe the value chain for an organization ☑ explain supply chain management ☑ define *economic order quantity* ☑ explain JIT ☑ define *break-even point* and *break-even analysis* ☑ use the formula to calculate break-even points

SERVICE AND PRODUCT QUALITY

Some years ago, at a time when American industry was first coming to grips with fierce competition from Japanese products, American quality pioneer J. M. Juran challenged an audience of Japanese executives with a prediction. He warned them against complacency, suggesting that America would bounce back in business competitiveness and that the words "Made in America" would once again symbolize world-class quality.[19] American businesses have since done a lot to live up to Juran's prediction. Indeed, when Toyota had its highly public quality crisis, two of the chief beneficiaries were its old-time U.S. rivals Ford and General Motors. Both had already gained reputations for building quality cars, and Toyota's problems gave them added advantage.

A *Harvard Business Review* survey reports that American business leaders rank customer service and product quality as the first and second most important goals for the success of their organizations.[20] But even with the goals, there is often a disconnection between intentions and results. In a survey by the market research firm Michelson & Associates, poor service and product dissatisfaction ranked number 1 and number 2 as reasons why customers abandon a retail store.[21] Just look at the wait lines at some service establishments. How long does it take you to get to the car rental counter or get served at a restaurant? Many service establishments these days are cutting back so far on staff that there are too few people left to actually serve their customers. Don't you wonder how much could be added to the bottom lines of these firms if they would just pay more to add staff at levels that customers would appreciate?

When pursued relentlessly, the twin goals of providing great service and quality products can be an important source of competitive advantage. Bill Gates once said: "Your most unhappy customers are your greatest source of learning." Just imagine what would happen if every customer or client contact for an organization was positive. Not only would these customers and clients return again and again, but they would also tell others and expand the customer base.

Real People

Bob Kidder Brings Change Leadership to Chrysler

Bob Kidder, chairman of Chrysler, is no stranger to the top job. Prior to taking over he was retired, having already been CEO of two Fortune 500 firms—Duracell International and Borden, Inc. And it wasn't like he was bored. Kidder was on several boards, including Morgan Stanley and Merck, and was serving as the chairman of the Ohio University board of trustees. He was also used to getting and rejecting calls from executive headhunters who wanted to land him a new position. But when the call came about Chrysler, "Without hesitation, I said, 'Yes,'" he points out.

Chrysler went into bankruptcy during the economic crisis that saw the U.S. government providing "bail-out" monies to save it and General Motors. When it emerged from bankruptcy, Fiat bought 20%; other major owners are the U.S. and Canadian governments and the pension fund of the United Auto Workers Union. At the time Kidder took over, Chrysler was operating 28 plants and employed over 49,000 workers. And it was still in trouble.

Kidder's job at Chrysler is leading change in a large manufacturing firm. "We're changing a lot of things," he says, "and we're doing so with a cadence that is substantially accelerated versus the past." Problems ranged from a breakup with former parent Daimler of Germany, prior ownership by the private capital firm Cerebus, and a line-up that included so many unpopular vehicles the dealers were forced into

heavy discounting in order to make sales.

In his new role Kidder has been working with Chrysler's board and Fiat CEO Sergio Marchionne to change things. In fact, he claims that the dealers need to get ready because there is so much high-quality new product ready to come their way.

A graduate of the University of Michigan with a degree in industrial engineering, Kidder is described by his alma mater's website as "a vintage businessman, entrepreneur and non-stop supporter of education and the underprivileged." With regard to his leadership style, Kidder's friends describe him as "a very engaging personality," "friendly," "cares about people," "hands-on," and "moves very quickly and very decisively." He'll need all these qualities and more as he continues with the job ahead. Though confident in his own leadership and the Chrysler workforce, Kidder admits that things won't change overnight. "We've got some catching up to do, and you don't do that in 30 days or 60 days or 90 days," he's quick to remind us.

CUSTOMER RELATIONSHIP MANAGEMENT

Without any doubt, customers put today's organizations to a very stiff test. Like you, most want three things: (1) high quality, (2) low price, and (3) on-time delivery of the goods and services they buy. They don't always get them, as these customer stories show.[22]

> *Dell Computer* suffered a major customer backlash when some 3,000 callers to its customer service lines during one week had to wait at least 30 minutes before being able to speak with a real person.
>
> *Northwest Airlines* had a lot to explain to potential customers after leaving passengers stranded inside a plane for 8 hours because of a snowstorm in Detroit.
>
> *Home Depot* saw customer satisfaction fall 8.2% while sales surged at its rival Lowe's, known for its top customer service.

Essentials of CRM

● **Customer relationship management** strategically tries to build lasting relationships with and to add value to customers.

Many organizations now use the principles of **customer relationship management** to establish and maintain high standards of customer service.[23] Known as CRM, this approach uses the latest information technologies to maintain intense communication with customers as well as to gather and utilize data regarding their needs and desires. At Marriott International, for example, CRM is supported by special software that tracks information on customer preferences. When you check in, the likelihood is that your past requests for things like a king-size bed, no smoking room, and computer modem access are already in your record. Says Marriott's chairman: "It's a big competitive advantage."[24]

In your experiences as a customer you probably often wonder why more managers don't get this message. Consider, for example, the case of Mona Shaw, a 76-year-old retired nurse. After arriving at a Comcast office to complain about poor installation of cable service to her home, she sat on a bench for two hours waiting to see a manager. She then left and came back with a hammer. She smashed a keyboard and telephone in the office, yelling: "Have I got your attention now?" It cost Shaw an arrest and $375 fine, but she became a media sensation and a rallying point for unhappy customers everywhere. As for Comcast, a spokesperson said: "We apologize for any customer service issues that Ms. Shaw experienced."[25]

Comcast's apology is nice, but did the system change as a result of this incident? Was customer relationship management activated so that service improved for Shaw and other customers in the future? Was the experience of this branch incident reviewed by top management and the learning disseminated throughout Comcast operations nationwide? Or, did things quickly slide back into business as usual?

External and Internal Customers

Customer relationship management applies equally well to external and internal customers. Figure 19.4 expands the open-systems view of organizations to depict the complex internal operations of the organization, as well as its interdependence with the external environment. In this figure the organization's *external customers* purchase the goods produced or utilize the services provided. They may be industrial customers—other firms that buy a company's products for use in their own operations—or they may be retail customers or clients who purchase or use the goods and services directly. *Internal customers*, by contrast, are found within the organization. They are the individuals and groups who use or otherwise depend on one another's work in order to do their own jobs well.

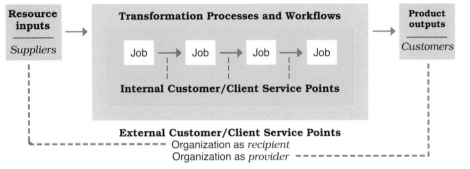

FIGURE 19.4 The importance of external and internal customers.

QUALITY MANAGEMENT

When the quality theme was first introduced in Chapter 2 on the history of management thought, we discussed how "world-class organizations" embed quality in all aspects of their operations.[26] **ISO certification** by the International Standards Organization in Geneva, Switzerland, serves as a major indicator of quality accomplishments. Another benchmark is the **Malcolm Baldrige award**. It is given by the president of the United States to business, health care, education, and nonprofit organizations that meet quality criteria in the following areas: leadership, strategic planning, customer and market focus, measurement and knowledge management, human resource focus, process management, and results.[27]

The work of W. Edwards Deming is a cornerstone of the quality movement. His approach to quality emphasizes constant innovation, use of statistical methods, and commitment to training in the fundamentals of quality assurance. One outgrowth of his work is **total quality management**, or TQM. This is a process that makes quality principles part of the organization's strategic objectives, applying them to all aspects of operations and striving to meet customers' needs by doing things right the first time.

Most TQM approaches insist that the total quality commitment applies to everyone in an organization and throughout the value chain—from resource acquisition and supply chain management, through production and into the distribution of finished goods and services, and ultimately to customer relationship management. Both TQM and the Deming approach are also closely tied to the emphasis on **continuous improvement**—always looking for new ways to improve on current performance. Again, this applies throughout the value chain.[28] The basic notion driving continuous improvement is that one can never be satisfied; something always can and should be improved on.

> **ISO certification** indicates conformance with a rigorous set of international quality standards.

> The **Malcolm Baldrige award** is given to business, health care, education, and nonprofit organizations that meet quality criteria.

> **Total quality management** is managing with an organization-wide commitment to continuous improvement, product quality, and customer needs.

> **Continuous improvement** involves always searching for new ways to improve work quality and performance.

STATISTICAL QUALITY CONTROL

For Deming, quality principles are straightforward: tally defects, analyze and trace them to the sources, make corrections, and keep records of what happens afterwards.[29] He championed statistical quality control that takes samples of work, measures quality in the samples, and determines acceptability of results. Unacceptable results trigger investigation and corrective action.

The task of tallying and analyzing defects can be done with a variety of sophisticated statistical techniques. One involves the Greek letter Σ (sigma), which in statistics is used to identify estimated standard deviation from a norm. In respect to statistical quality control, this would be a measure of defects in a work process, and the higher the Sigma the lower the number of defects. Many manufacturers now use a **Six Sigma program**, meaning that statistically the firm's quality performance standard is set at the Six Sigma level. That is, the quality goal is to

> A **Six Sigma program** sets a quality standard of 3.4 defects or less per million products or service deliveries.

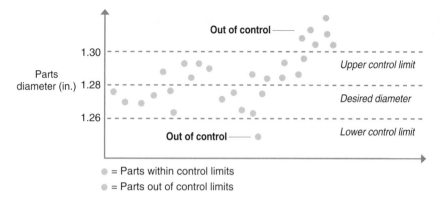

FIGURE 19.5 Sample control chart showing upper and lower control limits.

● **Statistical quality control** measures work samples for compliance with quality standards.

● **Control charts** graphically plot quality trends against control limits.

have no more than 3.4 defects per million units of goods produced or services completed.[30] This translates to a perfection rate of 99.9997 percent.

Another way to tackle **statistical quality control** is shown in Figure 19.5. Such **control charts** are graphical ways of displaying trends so that exceptions to quality standards can be identified for special attention. In the figure, for example, an upper control limit and a lower control limit specify the allowable tolerances for measurements of a machine part. As long as the manufacturing process produces parts that fall within these limits, things are "in control." As soon as parts fall outside the limits, it is clear that something is going wrong that is affecting quality. The process can then be investigated—even shut down—to identify the source of the errors and correct them.

WORK PROCESSES

● **Process reengineering** systematically analyzes work processes to design new and better ones.

The emphasis on productivity and competitive advantage through operations management includes business **process reengineering**.[31] This is defined as the systematic and complete analysis of work processes and the design of new and better ones.[32] The goal is to break old work habits and focus operations management attention on better ways of doing things.

WORK PROCESS ANALYSIS

● A **work process** is a related group of tasks that together create a value for the customer.

In his book, *Beyond Reengineering*, Michael Hammer defines a **work process** as "a related group of tasks that together create a result of value for the customer."[33] These tasks are what people do to turn resource inputs into goods or services for customers. Hammer highlights the following key words as essential elements of his definition: *group*—tasks are viewed as part of a group rather than in isolation; *together*—everyone must share a common goal; *result*—the focus is on what is accomplished, not on activities; *customer*—processes serve customers, and their perspectives are the ones that really count.

● **Workflow** is the movement of work from one point to another in a system.

The concept of **workflow**, or the way work moves from one point to another in manufacturing or service delivery, is central to the understanding of processes.[34]

Research Brief

How Do You Improve the Productivity of a Sales Force?

That's the question asked by Dianne Ledingham, Mark Kovac, and Heidi Locke Simon. Writing in the *Harvard Business Review*, they use a series of case examples to illustrate how companies have used data and analytical methods to raise sales. They contrast the newer, data-driven approaches with what they call a "wing-and-a-prayer" style, in which salespersons are given goals and then simply told to go out and meet them.

One case involves U.S. Equipment Financing, a division of GE Commercial Finance headed by Michael Pilot. Pilot's approach was to focus on raising the performance of existing sales representatives by helping them sell more—the "productivity improvement approach"—in contrast to simply hiring more reps—the "capacity increase approach." Pilot attributes some $300 million in new business to his scientific approach to sales force productivity. He began with a new database that inventoried past transactions. He then asked sales reps to come up with criteria that would indicate the likelihood of a customer doing business with GE. He next ran regression analyses that tested these criteria against the past transactions. The result was a set of six criteria that correlated well with past successes.

When new prospects were scored using the criteria, Pilot found 50% more top-prospect sales candidates than had previously been identified. Using this set of top prospects, he redesigned the sales force to maximize attention to those prospects, and he provided reps with information and tools to better deal with their customers. The result was a 19% increase in the "conversion" rate, or sales closings.

Researchers consider Pilot's scientific method a "best-practice" approach to improving sales force productivity. They recommend the TOPSales approach, focusing on (1) targeted offerings by market segment, (2) optimized technology tools and procedures, (3) performance management metrics and systems, and (4) systematic sales force deployment.

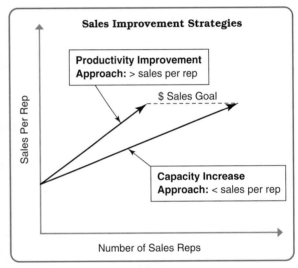

You Be the Researcher

This article, by Ledingham et al., describes a vigorous productivity improvement approach to reaching a higher sales goal. Can you find examples in your experience or community where goals are reached, but the costs of doing so are very high? What would you propose so that the same goals could be reached with lower costs and higher productivity?

Reference: Dianne Ledingham, Mark Kovac, and Heidi Locke Simon, "The New Science of Sales Force Productivity," *Harvard Business Review*, vol. 84 (September 2006), pp. 124–33.

The various parts of a work process must all be completed to achieve the desired results, and they must typically be completed in a given order. An important starting point for a reengineering effort is to diagram or map these workflows as they actually take place. Then each step can be systematically analyzed to determine whether it is adding value, to consider ways of eliminating or combining steps, and to find ways to use technology to improve efficiency.

PROCESS REENGINEERING

Process reengineering can be used to regularly assess and fine-tune work processes to ensure that they directly add value to operations. Through a technique called **process value analysis**, core processes are identified and carefully evaluated for their performance contributions. Each step in a workflow is examined. Unless a

● **Process value analysis** identifies and evaluates core processes for their performance contributions.

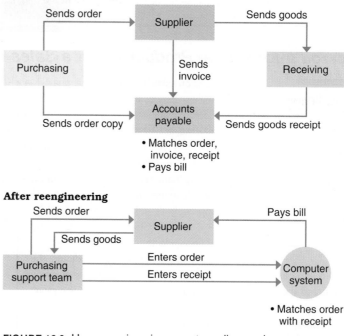

FIGURE 19.6 How reengineering can streamline work processes.

step is found to be important, useful, and contributing to value-added results, it is eliminated. Process value analysis typically takes place as follows.[35]

1. Identify the core processes.
2. Map the core processes with respect to workflows.
3. Evaluate all core process tasks.
4. Search for ways to eliminate unnecessary tasks or work.
5. Search for ways to eliminate delays, errors, and misunderstandings.
6. Search for efficiencies in how work is shared and transferred among people and departments.

Figure 19.6 shows an example of how reengineering and better use of computer technology can streamline a purchasing operation. Ideally, a purchase order should result in at least three value-added outcomes: order fulfillment, a paid bill, and a satisfied supplier. For this to happen, things like ordering, shipping, receiving, billing, and payment must all be well handled. A traditional business system might have purchasing, receiving, and accounts payable as separate functions, with each function communicating with each other and with the supplier. As the figure shows, there are lots of inefficiencies here. Alternatively, process value analysis might result in reengineering the workflow and redesigning it to include a new purchasing support team. Its members can handle the same work more efficiently with the support of the latest computer technology.[36]

Management **L**earning **R**eview

1 What are the essentials of operations and services management?

- The challenges of operations management relate to managing productive systems that transform resources into finished goods and services for customers and clients.
- Manufacturing organizations produce physical goods, while service organizations produce nonphysical outputs in the form of services.
- Productivity measures the efficiency with which inputs are transformed into outputs: Productivity = Output/Input.
- Technology, including the use of knowledge, equipment, and work methods in the transformation process, is an important consideration in operations management.

FOR DISCUSSION **Does the concept of productivity apply equally well in all types of organizations?**

2 What is value chain management?

- The value chain is the sequence of activities that create value at each stage involved in producing goods or services.
- Value chain analysis identifies and examines each step in the value chain to ensure it is efficient.
- Supply chain management, or SCM, is the process of managing all operations linking an organization and its suppliers, including purchasing, manufacturing, transportation, and distribution.
- Efficient purchasing and inventory management techniques such as just-in-time and economic order quantities are important forms of cost control.
- Break-even analysis identifies the point where revenues will equal costs under different pricing and cost conditions.

FOR DISCUSSION **Can value chain analysis be helpful in service organizations such as banks?**

3 How do organizations manage customer service and product quality?

- Customer relationship management builds and maintains strategic relationships with customers.
- Quality management addresses the needs of both internal customers and external customers.
- To compete in the global economy, organizations seek to meet ISO 9000 quality standards.
- Total quality management tries to meet customers' needs—on time, the first time, and all the time.
- Organizations use control charts and statistical techniques such as the Six Sigma system to measure the quality of work samples for quality control purposes.

FOR DISCUSSION **Is it realistic to speak of "total" quality management?**

4 How can work processes be designed for productivity?

- A work process is a related group of tasks that together create value for a customer.
- Process engineering is the systematic and complete analysis of work processes and the design of new and better ones.
- In process value analysis all elements of a process and its workflows are examined to identify their exact contributions to key performance results.
- Reengineering eliminates unnecessary work steps, combines others, and uses technology to gain efficiency and reduce costs.

FOR DISCUSSION **Can process reengineering be overdone to the point where efficiency overwhelms effectiveness?**

Multiple-Choice Questions

1. Productivity in a typical organization is computed using the formula Productivity = _____/Input.
   (a) Profit   (b) Cost   (c) Output   (d) Revenue

2. If you conducted a value chain analysis of a business, you would study _____.
   (a) customer satisfaction with products   (b) how much TQM affects profits   (c) the flow of activities that transform resources into goods and services   (d) the links between performance and rewards

3. New computer technologies have made possible _____ that quickly and efficiently produces individualized products for customers.
   (a) flexible manufacturing   (b) mass production   (c) mass customization   (d) design for disassembly

4. In remanufacturing the focus is on _____.
   (a) breaking down used products and using the parts to make new ones (b) arranging machines in cellular layouts
   (c) mass customization (d) replacing people with robots

5. Wal-Mart's suppliers electronically access inventory data and sales forecasts in the stores and automatically ship replacement products. This is an example of IT utilization in _____.
   (a) supply chain management (b) customer relationship management (c) total quality management (d) strategic constituencies analysis

6. An economic order quantity approach to inventory control _____.
   (a) uses computer control to accomplish JIT scheduling (b) reorders inventory automatically when a certain point is reached (c) allows for inventory to be purchased only when suppliers grant quantity discounts (d) means that inventory levels never exceed a preset reorder amount

7. In a break-even analysis, the break-even point occurs when _____.
   (a) fixed costs = variable costs (b) profits = expenses (c) assets = liabilities (d) revenues = total costs

8. Benchmarking, continuous improvement, and reduced cycle times are examples of organizational practices that show a commitment to _____.
   (a) affirmative action (b) total quality management (c) cost containment (d) supply chain management

9. A quality standard that has become essential for world-class companies competing in global markets is _____.
   (a) the Deming prize (b) upper control limit (c) CRM (d) ISO certification

10. _____ is an example of a statistical quality control technique.
    (a) Design for disassembly (b) SCM (c) Six Sigma (d) Quality circle

11. A work process is defined as a related group of tasks that together create value for _____.
    (a) shareholders (b) customers (c) workers (d) society

12. The first step in process value analysis is to _____.
    (a) look for ways to eliminate unnecessary tasks (b) map or diagram the workflows (c) identify core processes
    (d) look for efficiencies in transferring work among people and departments

13. In addition to operating efficiency, competitive advantage is often pursued through operations management initiatives that _____.
    (a) increase use of minimum-wage workers (b) provide for customer service improvements (c) cut product quality to allow for lower pricing (d) use the same product designs over and over again

14. A major difference between operations management in manufacturing and in services is that _____.
    (a) service organizations don't measure productivity (b) manufacturing organizations don't offer services (c) service organizations often use different technologies than do manufacturing organizations (d) supply chain management doesn't work in services

15. The techniques of operations management are closely aligned with the concept of the organization as a/an _____.
    (a) open system (b) closed system (c) top-down pyramid (d) machine-driven rather than people-driven system

Short-Response Questions

16. What operating objectives are appropriate for an organization seeking competitive advantage through improved customer service?
17. What is the difference between an organization's external customers and its internal customers?
18. Why is supply chain management considered important in operations management?
19. If you were a reengineering consultant, how would you describe the steps in a typical approach to process value analysis?

Essay Question

20. What would be possible productivity measures for the following organizations?
    (a) United States Postal Service (b) university (c) hospital (d) amusement park (e) restaurant

Management Skills and Competencies

Self-Assessment

Back to Yourself: Strength and Energy

Operations management tries to help organizations of all types best use resources and systems to achieve productivity. Managers are continually updating, making adjustments, and maintaining the technologies and other resources that drive organizational performance. When it comes to us and managing our human systems, the same notions apply. And, that's where the importance of **strength and energy** comes in. Work-life balance, for example, can be helped and hindered by smart phone and computer technologies. This really hits home when you consider how easy it is to now take our work with us anywhere we go, 24 hours a day and seven days a week. We need to take charge and better manage the operations of lives. We need vibrant and healthy human systems so that we are always up to the challenges. After you complete the following self-assessment on Personal Numeracy, look back at the many other assessments available in this book and think about their insights.

> Today's intense work environments and hectic lifestyles require lots of **strength and energy**. We have to stay in shape, physically and mentally, so that we can not only perform well at work, but also maintain positive work–life balance.

Further Reflection: Personal Numeracy

Instructions

In operations management and in other aspects of managerial and personal problem solving we have to deal with numbers. But many of us struggle with basic math. How strong are your "numeracy" skills? Complete the following quiz.[37] Compare your results with those of nearby classmates. Work together until you believe you have all the correct answers. Then, join in a class discussion addressing the question: "Why is personal numeracy so important as a life and career skill?"

1. How many zeros does it take to make a "googol"?
2. If there are two red, four green, and six blue M&Ms left in a packet, what is the probability of next picking a green one?
3. What is "pi" rounded to 4 decimal places?
4. How is a billion written in numbers?
5. What is 1/40 as a decimal?
6. If $7x + y = 9$ and $3x - y = 7$, what are x and y?
7. What is the perimeter of a triangular campus green if the bordering walkways measure 150, 540, and 450 feet, respectively?
8. Two angles in a triangle are 37 degrees and 64 degrees. What is the third angle?
9. Evie has $10,000 invested in a tax-free money-market account. The account pays 1.75% interest, and her marginal tax rate is 28%. If this account was taxable, what would Evie's rate of interest be?
10. Salmah needs money for textbooks. She can get a paycheck loan of $200 for a fee of $30 every two weeks. What annual rate of interest is she paying for this loan?

Team Exercise

Straw Towers

Materials Needed

One box of straws per group

Procedure

1. Form groups as assigned by the instructor. The mission of each group or temporary organization is to build the tallest possible straw tower. Each group should determine worker roles: at least four students will be builders, two others will be consultants who offer suggestions, and any remaining students will be observers.[38]

2. Rules for the exercise:

- Ten minutes allowed for planning for the tower.
- Only 60 seconds can be used to build the tower.
- No straws can be put together during the planning.
- All straws must be put back in the box before the competition begins.
- The completed tower must stand alone.

3. Discussion: What lessons for operations and services management are learned from this exercise?

Case Study: Toyota

Go to *Management Cases for Critical Thinking* to find the recommended case for Chapter 19–"Toyota: Hitting the Brakes."

Management Cases for Critical Thinking

Case 1   Trader Joe's: Keeping a Cool Edge

The average Trader Joe's stocks only a small percentage of the products of local supermarkets in a space little larger than a corner store. How did this neighborhood market grow to earnings of $7.2 billion, garner superior ratings, and become a model of management? Take a walk down the aisles of Trader Joe's and learn how sharp attention to the fundamentals of retail management made this chain more than the average Joe.

From Corner Store to Foodie Mecca

In more than 300 stores across the United States, hundreds of thousands of customers are treasure hunting. Driven by gourmet tastes but hungering for deals, they are led by cheerful guides in Hawaiian shirts who point them to culinary discoveries such as ahi jerky, ginger granola, and baked jalapeño cheese crunchies.

It's just an average day at Trader Joe's, the gourmet, specialty, and natural-foods store that offers staples such as milk and eggs along with curious, one-of-a-kind foods at below-average prices in twenty-odd states.[1] With their plethora of kosher, vegan, and gluten-free fare, Trader Joe's has products to suit every dietary need.[2] Foodies, hipsters, and recessionistas alike are attracted to the chain's charming blend of low prices, tasty treats, and laid-back but enthusiastic customer service. Shopping at Trader Joe's is less a chore than it is immersion into another culture. In keeping with its whimsical faux-nautical theme, crew members and managers wear loud tropical-print shirts. Chalkboards around every corner unabashedly announce slogans such as, "You don't have to join a club, carry a card, or clip coupons to get a good deal."

"When you look at food retailers," says Richard George, professor of food marketing at St. Joseph's University, "there is the low end, the big middle, and then there is the cool edge—that's Trader Joe's."[3] But how does Trader Joe's compare with other stores with an edge, such as Whole Foods? Both obtain products locally and from all over the world. Each values employees and strives to offer the highest quality. However, there's no mistaking that Trader Joe's is cozy and intimate, whereas Whole Foods' spacious stores offer an abundance of choices. By limiting its stock and selling quality products at low prices, Trader Joe's sells twice as much per square foot than other supermarkets.[4] Most retail megamarkets, such as Whole Foods, carry between 25,000 and 45,000 products; Trader Joe's stores carry only 1,500 to 2,000.[5] But this scarcity benefits both Trader Joe's and its customers. According to Swarthmore professor Barry Schwartz, author of *The Paradox of Choice: Why Less Is More*, "Giving people too much choice can result in paralysis. . . . [R]esearch shows that the more options you offer, the less likely people are to choose any."[6]

David Rogers of DSR Marketing Systems expects other supermarkets to follow the Trader Joe's model toward a smaller store size. He cites several reasons, including excessive competitive floor space, development costs, and the aging population.[7]

Trader Joe's didn't always stand for brie and baguettes at peanut butter and jelly prices. In 1958, the company began life in Los Angeles as a chain of 7-Eleven–style corner stores called Pronto Markets. Striving to differentiate his stores from those of his competitors in order to survive in a crowded marketplace, founder "Trader" Joe Coulombe, vacationing in the Caribbean, reasoned that consumers are more likely to try new things while on vacation. In 1967 the first Trader Joe's store opened in Pasadena. Mr. Coulombe had transformed his stores into oases of value by replacing humdrum sundries with exotic, one-of-a-kind foods priced persuasively below those of any reasonable competitor.[8] In 1979, he sold his chain to the Albrecht family, German billionaires and owners of an estimated 7,500 Aldi markets in the United States and Europe.[9]

The Albrechts shared Coulombe's relentless pursuit of value, a trait inseparable from Trader Joe's success. Recent annual sales are estimated at $7.2 billion, landing Trader Joe's in the top third of *Supermarket News's* Top 75 Retailers.[10] Because it's not easy competing with such giants as Whole Foods and Dean & DeLuca, the company applies its pursuit of value to every facet of management. By keeping stores comparatively small—they average about 10,000 square feet—and shying away from prime locations, Trader Joe's keeps real estate costs down.[11] The chain prides itself on its thriftiness and cost-saving measures, proclaiming, "Every penny we save is a penny you save" and "Our CEO doesn't even have a secretary."[12,13]

Trader Giotto, Trader José, Trader Ming, and Trader Darwin

Trader Joe's strongest weapon in the fight to keep costs low may also be its greatest appeal to customers: its stock. The company follows a deliciously simple approach to stocking stores: (1) search out tasty, unusual foods from all around the world; (2) contract directly with manufacturers; (3) label each product under one of several catchy house brands; and (4) maintain a small stock, making each product fight for its place on the shelf. This common-sense, low-overhead approach to retail serves Trader Joe's well, embodying its commitment to aggressive cost-cutting.

Most Trader Joe's products are sold under a variant of their house brand—dried pasta under the "Trader Giotto's" moniker, frozen enchiladas under the "Trader Jose's" label, vitamins under "Trader Darwin's," and so on. But these store brands don't sacrifice quality—readers of *Consumer Reports* awarded Trader Joe's house brands top marks.[14] The house brand success is no accident. According to Trader Joe's President Doug Rauch, "the company pursued the strategy to put our destiny in our own hands."[15]

But playing a role in this destiny is no easy feat. Ten to fifteen new products debut each week at Trader Joe's—and the company maintains a strict "one in, one out" policy. Items that sell poorly or whose costs rise get the heave-ho in favor of new blood, something the company calls the "gangway factor."[16] If the company hears that customers don't like something about a product, out it goes. In just such a move, Trader Joe's phased out single-ingredient products (such as spinach and garlic) from China. "Our customers have voiced their concerns about products from this region and we have listened," the company said in a statement, noting that items would be replaced with "products from other regions until our customers feel as confident as we do about the quality and safety of Chinese products."[17]

Conversely, discontinued items may be brought back if customers are vocal enough, making Trader Joe's the model of an open system. "We feel really close to our customers," says Audrey Dumper, vice president of marketing for Trader Joe's East. "When we want to know what's on their minds, we don't need to put them in a sterile room with a swinging bulb. We like to think of Trader Joe's as an economic food democracy."[18] In return, customers keep talking, and they recruit new converts. Word-of-mouth advertising has lowered the corporation's advertising budget to approximately 0.2% of sales, a fraction of the 4% spent by supermarkets.[19]

Customer Connection

Trader Joe's connects with its customers because of the culture of product knowledge and customer involvement that its management cultivates among store employees. Each employee is encouraged to taste and learn about the products and to engage customers to share what they've experienced. Most shoppers recall instances when helpful crew members took the time to locate or recommend particular items. Despite the lighthearted tone suggested by marketing materials and in-store ads, Trader Joe's aggressively courts friendly, customer-oriented employees by writing job descriptions highlighting desired soft skills ("ambitious and adventurous, enjoy smiling and have a strong sense of values") as much as actual retail experience.[20]

A responsible, knowledgeable, and friendly "crew" is critical to Trader Joe's success. Therefore, it nurtures its employees with a promote-from-within philosophy, and its employees earn more than their counterparts at other chain grocers. In California, Trader Joe's employees can earn almost 20% more than counterparts at supermarket giants Albertsons or Safeway.[21] Starting benefits include medical, dental, and vision insurance; company-paid retirement; paid vacation; and a 10% employee discount.[22] Assistant store managers earn a compensation package averaging $94,000 a year, and store managers' packages average $132,000. One analyst estimates that a Wal-Mart store manager earning that much would need to run an outlet grossing six or seven times that of an average Trader Joe's.[23]

Outlet managers are highly compensated, partly because they know the Trader Joe's system inside and out (managers are hired only from within the company). Future leaders enroll in training programs such as Trader Joe's University that foster in them the loyalty necessary to run stores according to both company and customer expectations, teaching managers to imbue their part-timers with the customer-focused attitude shoppers have come to expect.[24]

If Trader Joe's has any puzzling trait, it's that the company is more than a bit media-shy. Executives have granted no interviews since the Aldi Group took over. Company statements and spokespersons have been known to be terse—the company's

leases even stipulate that no store opening may be formally announced until a month before the outlet opens![25]

The future looks bright for Trader Joe's. More outlets have opened on the East Coast and in the Midwest, and the company continues to break into markets hungry for reasonably priced gourmet goodies. But will Trader Joe's struggle to sustain its international flavor in the face of rising fuel costs and shrinking discretionary income, or will the allure of cosmopolitan food at provincial prices continue to tempt consumers?

CASE QUESTIONS

1. **DISCUSSION**—In what ways does Trader Joe's demonstrate the importance of each responsibility in the management process—planning, organizing, leading, and controlling?

2. **DISCUSSION**—This is a German company operating in America. What are the biggest risks that international ownership and global events pose for Trader Joe's performance effectiveness and performance efficiency?

3. **PROBLEM-SOLVING**—At the age of 22 and newly graduated from college, Hazel has just accepted a job with Trader Joe's as a shift leader. She'll be supervising 4 team members who fill part-time jobs in the produce section. Given Trader Joe's casual and nontraditional work environment, what should she do and what should she avoid doing in the first few days of work to establish herself as an effective manager of this team?

4. **FURTHER RESEARCH**—Study news reports to find more information on Trader Joe's management and organization practices. Look for comparisons with its competitors and try to identify whether or not Trader Joe's has the right management approach and business model for continued success. Are there any internal weaknesses or external competitors or industry forces that might cause future problems?

At the announcement of her engagement to Spain's Crown Prince Felipe, Letizia Ortiz Rocasolano wore a chic white pant suit. Within a few weeks, hundreds of European women sported the same look. Welcome to fast fashion, a trend that sees clothing retailers frequently purchasing small quantities of merchandise to stay on top of emerging trends. In this world of "hot today, gauche tomorrow," no company does fast fashion better than Zara International. Shoppers in over 70 countries are fans of Zara's knack for bringing the latest styles from sketchbook to clothing rack at lightning speed and reasonable prices.

In Fast Fashion, Moments Matter

Because style-savvy customers expect shorter and shorter delays from runway to store, Zara International employs a creative team of more than 200 professionals to help it keep up with the latest fashions.[1] It takes just two weeks for the company to update existing garments and get them into its stores; new pieces hit the market twice a week.

Defying the recession with its cheap-and-chic Zara clothing chain, Zara's parent company Inditex posted strong sales gains. Low prices and a rapid response to fashion trends are enabling it to challenge Gap, Inc., for top ranking among global clothing vendors. The improved results highlight how Zara's formula continues to work even in the economic downturn. The chain specializes in lightning-quick turnarounds of the latest designer trends at prices tailored to the young—about $27 an item.[2] Louis Vuitton fashion director Daniel Piette described Zara as "possibly the most innovative and devastating retailer in the world."[3]

Inditex Group shortens the time from order to arrival by utilizing a complex system of just-in-time production and inventory reporting that keeps Zara ahead. Their distribution centers can have items in European stores within 24 hours of receiving an order, and in American and Asian stores in under 48 hours.[4] "They're a fantastic case study in terms of how they manage to get product to their stores so quick," said Stacey Cartwright, CFO of Burberry Group PLC. "We are mindful of their techniques."[5]

Inditex's history in fabrics manufacturing made it good business sense to internalize as many points in the supply chain as possible. Inditex controls design, production, distribution, and retail sales to optimize the flow of goods, without having to share profits with wholesalers or intermediary partners. Customers win by having access to new fashions while they're still fresh off the runway. During a Madonna concert tour in Spain, Zara's quick turnaround let young fans at the last show wear Madonna's outfit from the first one.[6]

Twice a week Zara's finished garments are shipped to logistical centers that all simultaneously distribute products to stores worldwide. These small production batches help the company avoid the risk of oversupply. Because batches always contain new products, Zara's stores perpetually energize their inventories.[7] Most clothing lines are not replenished. Instead they are replaced with new designs to create scarcity value—shoppers cannot be sure that designs in stores one day will be available the next.

Store managers track sales data with handheld computers. They can reorder hot items in less than an hour. This lets Zara know what's selling and what's not; when a look doesn't pan out, designers promptly put together new products.

According to Dilip Patel, U.K. commercial director for Inditex, new arrivals are rushed to store sales floors still on the black plastic hangers used in shipping. Shoppers who are in the know recognize these designs as the newest of the new; soon after, any items left over are rotated to Zara's standard wood hangers.[8]

Inside and out, Zara's stores are specially dressed to strengthen the brand. Inditex considers this to be of the greatest importance because that is where shoppers ultimately decide which fashions make the cut. In a faux shopping street in the basement of the company's headquarters, stylists craft and photograph eye-catching layouts that are e-mailed every two weeks to store managers for replication.[9]

Zara stores sit on some of the world's glitziest shopping streets—including New York's Fifth Avenue, near the flagship stores of leading international fashion brands—which make its reasonable prices stand out. "Inditex gives people the most up-to-date fashion at accessible prices, so it is a real alternative to high-end fashion lines," said Luca Solca, senior research analyst with Sanford C. Bernstein in London. That is good news for Zara as many shoppers trade down from higher-priced chains.[10]

Catfights on the Catwalk

Zara is not the only player in fast fashion. Competition is fierce, but Zara's overwhelming success (recent sales were over $13 billion) has the competition scrambling to keep up.[11] San Francisco-based Gap, which had been the largest independent clothing retailer by revenue until Zara bumped them to second place in 2009, recently posted a 23% decline in full-year sales and had plans to open a modest 50 new stores.[12] Only time will tell if super-chic Topshop's entry into the American market causes a wrinkle in Zara's success.

Some fashion analysts are referring to all of this as the democratization of fashion: bringing high(er) fashion to low(er) income shoppers. According to James Hurley, a senior research analyst with New York-based Telsey Advisory Group LLC, big-box discount stores such as Target and Wal-Mart are emulating Zara's ability to study emerging fashions and knock out look-a-likes in a matter of weeks. "In general," Hurley said, "the fashion cycle is becoming sharper and more immediately accessible."[13]

A Single Fashion Culture

With a network of over 1,600 stores around the world, Zara International is Inditex's largest and most profitable brand, bringing home 77% of international sales and nearly 67% of revenues.[14] The first Zara outlet opened shop in 1975 in La Coruña.[15] It remained solely a Spanish chain until opening a store in Oporto, Portugal, in 1988. The brand reached the United States and France in 1989 and 1990 with outlets in New York and Paris, respectively.[16] Zara went into mainland China in 2001 and expanded into India in 2009.[17]

Essential to Zara's growth and success are Inditex's 100-plus textile design, manufacturing, and distribution companies that employ more than 80,000 workers.[18] The Inditex group began in 1963 when Amancio Ortega Gaona, chairman and founder of Inditex, got his start in textile manufacturing.[19] After a period of growth, he assimilated Zara into a new holding company, Industria de Diseño Textil.[20] Inditex has a tried-and-true strategy for entering new markets: start with a handful of stores and gain a critical mass of customers. Generally, Zara is the first Inditex chain to break ground in new countries, paving the way for the group's other brands, including Pull and Bear, Massimo Dutti, and Bershka.[21]

Inditex farms out much of its garment production to specialist companies, located on the Iberian Peninsula, which it often supplies with its own fabrics. Although some pieces and fabrics are purchased in Asia—many of them not dyed or only partly finished—the company manufactures about half of its clothing in its hometown of La Coruña, Spain.[22]

H&M, one of Zara's top competitors, uses a slightly different strategy. Around one quarter of its stock is made up of fast-fashion items that are designed in-house and farmed out to independent factories. As at Zara, these items move quickly through the stores and are replaced often by fresh designs. But H&M also keeps a large inventory of basic, everyday items sourced from cheap Asian factories.[23]

Inditex CEO Pablo Isla believes in cutting expenses wherever and whenever possible. Zara spends just 0.3% of sales on ads, making the 3–4% typically spent by rivals seem excessive in comparison. Isla disdains markdowns and sales as well.[24]

Few can criticize the results of Isla's frugality. Inditex recently opened 439 stores in a single year and was simultaneously named Retailer of the Year during the World Retailer Congress meeting, after raking in net profits of almost $2 billion.[25,26] Perhaps most important in an industry based on image, Inditex secured bragging rights as Europe's largest fashion retailer by overtaking H&M.[27] According to José Castellano, Inditex's deputy chairman, the group plans to double in size in the coming years while making sales of more than $15 billion. He envisions most of this growth taking place in Europe—especially in trend-savvy Italy.[28]

Fashion of the Moment

Although Inditex's dominance of fast fashion seems virtually complete, it isn't without its challenges. For instance, keeping production so close to home becomes difficult when an increasing number of Zara stores are far-flung across the globe. "The efficiency of the supply chain is coming under more pressure the farther abroad they go," notes Nirmalya Kumar, a professor at London Business School.[29]

Inditex plans to launch its Zara online store in the United States in 2011. There is every indication that it will do well. A Zara application for the iPhone has been downloaded by more prospective clients in the United States than in any other market, according to chief executive Pablo Isla—more than a million iPhone users in just three months. In 2010 Zara rolled out its online store in six European countries and plans to progressively add the remaining countries where Zara operates.[30]

Analysts worry that Inditex's rapid expansion may bring undue pressure to its business. The rising number of overseas stores, they warn, adds cost and complexity and is straining its operations. Inditex may no longer be able to manage everything from Spain. But Inditex isn't worried. By closely managing costs, Inditex says its current logistics system can handle its growth until 2012.[31]

José Luis Nueno of IESE, a business school in Barcelona, agrees that Zara is here to stay. Consumers have become more demanding and more arbitrary, he says—and fast fashion is better suited to these changes.[32] But does Zara International have what it takes to succeed in the hypercompetitive world of fast fashion? Or is the company trying to expand too quickly?

CASE QUESTIONS

1. **DISCUSSION**—In what ways are elements of the classical management and behavioral management approaches evident at Zara International?

2. **DISCUSSION**—How can systems concepts and the notion of contingency thinking explain the success of some of Zara's distinctive practices?

3. **PROBLEM-SOLVING**—Zara's CEO has asked your management consulting firm for advice on how the firm can make immediate improvements to stay ahead of competition. You must choose one of five consultants for this job—Frederick Taylor, Max Weber, Mary Parker Follett, Chris Argyris, or Jeffrey Pfeffer. Which one would you assign to Zara, and why?

4. **FURTHER RESEARCH**—Gather the latest information on competitive trends in the apparel industry, and on Zara's latest actions and innovations. Is the firm continuing to do well? Is it adapting in ways needed to stay abreast of both its major competition and the pressures of a changing global economy? Is Inditex still providing worthy management benchmarks for other firms to follow?

Yvon Chouinard wanted to be a fur trapper when he grew up. Instead he founded Patagonia, a clothing and outdoor gear company that revolutionized the climbing industry while pioneering corporate consciousness and sustainability. Putting the Earth first, questioning growth, ignoring fashion, and telling customers to buy less isn't the usual recipe for success. So how did this antibusinessman's little company become a $270 million corporation and the gold standard for green business?

Chouinard believes he may have climbed before he learned how to walk. Cultural and linguistic differences, along with defending his name, meant Yvon spent much of his time alone and outdoors. Rappelling down from cliff-top falcon nests fueled his love of mountain climbing. When Yvon began climbing, the pitons used to secure climbing ropes were made from soft iron and were meant to be used only once. The son of a blacksmith, Yvon saw his first opportunity for recycling. In 1957, Yvon began to make hard steel pitons that could be used again. His pitons were stronger and more elegant than their predecessors, a triumph of minimalistic engineering. He sold them out of the back of his car for $1.50 and tried to live on the meager proceeds.[1,2]

Soon Yvon discovered that if you tried to remove the steel pitons, the very rock you were climbing was being destroyed. Although his pitons were in high demand, Yvon felt that his business was causing problems to the planet and that he had a responsibility to do something about it. Instead he offered aluminum "chalks" that could easily be put in and taken out with a climber's fingers and that were just as safe as pitons but caused no damage to the rock. "People protect what they love," said Chouinard. "If you love nature, then you want to protect nature. If you love unspoiled rivers and mountains, then you want to protect them."[3]

Over the years, Chouinard Equipment grew and morphed, existing mainly to fund its owner's wilderness adventures.[4] In 1968, the recently married Chouinard and a group of friends began their "Fun Hog Expedition." They surfed, skied, and drove their way to the tip of South America, where they would climb Fitz Roy, a daunting mountain that had been climbed only twice before. According to Chouinard, "The experience led to an unlikely fate for a couple of dirtbags. We became philanthropists." But before you can become a philanthropist, you must first become rich.[5]

In 1972, Chouinard and his wife Malinda branched out into clothing, selling, then making, clothing rugged enough for the harsh conditions Yvon endured in South America. They launched a new company called Patagonia whose name and logo paid homage to Chouinard's historic expedition.[6]

Yvon and Malinda agreed that the growth of this company would be on their terms. Their products wouldn't release toxins into rivers, the business wouldn't cause nervous breakdowns, nor would it chase endless growth. It wouldn't make disposable garments that people didn't really need. Anything it produced would be of the highest quality and manufactured in the most responsible way. When the surf was up or the snow drifted down, employees would be where they ought to be: outside. The biggest lesson Chouinard learned scaling mountains was that reaching the summit had nothing to do with where you arrived and everything to do with how you got there. The same values held true in his business. The point wasn't to focus on making money. He thought the focus should be on doing things right, and then the profits would come. Eventually, they did.[7]

In 1977, Patagonia created its breakthrough product, a jacket made of polyester pile that repelled moisture while retaining body heat. It was stiff and awkward but worked like a charm in harsh conditions in which looking odd was preferable to succumbing to hypothermia. Modifications continued until Patagonia created a finer, softer version called Synchilla in sought-after colors such as sea foam green and garnet red. Sales exploded, and the company became known for the "fleece jacket."[8]

But, as Patagonia discovered, no manufacturing process is environmentally friendly. If you make things, you end up leaving the Earth worse off. While other businesses tried to dodge and deny their impacts, Patagonia chose to openly disclose this information and solicited outsiders' advice in finding better solutions. Patagonia began assigning each of its products a grade, disclosing its environmental impact.[9] So began the Footprint Chronicles that examine Patagonia's life and habits as a company. Through its website anyone can trace the production path from source materials to store shelves, measure Patagonia's manufacturing impacts, water consumption, energy use, waste, carbon emissions, and distance traveled for its chronicled projects.[10]

When Patagonia discovered it could make Synchilla using discarded soda bottles, Chouinard saw a way to reconcile his expanding business with his angst over manufacturing's destructive effects. Materials underwent an "environmental assessment" to determine whether recycled material could be used in a product. They asked questions like: Could the product itself be recycled? Which materials caused the most harm to the environment, and which the least? "We didn't have any of the answers," Chouinard said. "There was no book you could pick up and say, here's what we need to do. We didn't know that making clothes out of a synthetic was better than making them out of a natural material." For instance, wool can be good or bad: "If you get it from sheep grazing in alpine meadows, that's damaging as hell." Conventionally grown cotton was especially monstrous due to noxious pesticides, insecticides, and defoliants. "To know this and not switch to organic cotton would be unconscionable," said Chouinard. In 1994, he gave his managers 18 months to make the change. Given that organic cotton was rare at the time, that it cost at least 50% more, and that a fifth of Patagonia's business came from cotton products, this was quite a risk. Chouinard's ultimatum: Make it happen or we'll never use cotton again.[11]

The gamble paid off. Patagonia's cotton sales rose by 25% and established an organic-cotton industry. As demand grew and prices decreased, other companies followed suit. By 2006, Wal-Mart had become the world's largest purchaser of organic cotton.[12]

In the early 2000s, the fabric company Teijin—a Patagonia partner in Japan—invented a process by which used polyester can be almost endlessly recycled. Patagonia, which makes a line of polyester base layers known as Capilene, encouraged customers to send back their worn-out underwear. Today Patagonia also accepts products made from fleece, nylon, and organic cotton. For Chouinard, recycling polyester is a no brainer. "We use 76 percent less energy than if we'd made it out of virgin petroleum."[13]

Patagonia became the first California company to use renewable resources such as wind and solar energy to power all of its buildings and was one of the first to print catalogs on recycled paper. When it discovered that airfreight requires at least eight times more energy than shipping by ground or sea, the company encouraged customers to "ask yourself if you really need that pair of pants sent overnight." Still, Patagonia does offer that option, which brings up an inconvenient truth: No matter how careful the choice of materials or methods, all companies leave a footprint. This is Chouinard's challenge. "Patagonia will never be completely socially responsible," he writes gloomily at the end of his book. "It will never make a totally sustainable, non-damaging product. But it is committed to trying."[14,15]

As it states on the front door of Patagonia's headquarters, "There is no business to be done on a dead planet." To that end, in 2001 Yvon Chouinard created One Percent for the Planet, an international organization whose members contribute at least 1% of their annual sales to environmental causes—to keep the Earth in business. Their mission is to "use market forces to drive positive environmental change by inspiring companies to give." This growing global movement of 1,252 companies has given them an opportunity not only to see their self-worth rise but also to see their net worth climb.[16,17]

In response to the Crisis in the Gulf, the worst environmental disaster in the U.S., Patagonia provided emergency funding to environmental organizations such as the Louisiana Bucket Brigade and the Gulf Restoration Fund.[18]

In 2004, Patagonia launched its Vote the Environment campaign. Without advocating any individual, Patagonia encouraged voters to investigate candidates' environmental records and helped voters register online and in its retail stores, while asking customers to make the environment their number one priority.[19]

Every one to two years Patagonia chooses an environmental crisis to which it devotes itself. Freedom to Roam is Patagonia's current environmental campaign. Its goal is to create, restore, and protect "corridors" between habitats so that animals can migrate between shifting habitats and survive.[20] Chouinard's philosophy is simple: "It has to start with each and every one of us to make change in our lives. It's up to each individual to lead an examined life."[21]

Will economic challenges make it hard for Chouinard and Patagonia to hold fast to their principles in the future? As more businesses jump on the green bandwagon, will Patagonia's reputation for commitment to the environment and ethical business practices be enough to sustain them?

CASE QUESTIONS

1. **DISCUSSION**—Does the Patagonia experience prove that anyone can do business with principles, or are there business realities that make it hard for others to copy this principled management model?

2. **DISCUSSION**—What examples and incidents from this brief history of Patagonia illustrate how the personal ethics and values of founders can positively influence an organization as it deals with the challenges of start-up and growth?

3. **PROBLEM-SOLVING**—Where are conflicts and controversies most likely to occur among the interests of Patagonia's many stakeholders? How might Chouinard prepare to best deal with them?

4. **FURTHER RESEARCH**—Find news items reporting on what has happened at Patagonia recently. After decades of growth, how has the economic downturn influenced its business decisions?

After hurricanes Katrina and Rita devastated New Orleans, many focused on the damage and despair. But the non-profit organization Global Green USA saw the opportunity to revitalize the region—from the inside out. For over 15 years, Global Green USA has led the charge for advancing green building as a solution to climate change; creating healthy, affordable green homes, schools and communities in cities across the country, benefiting millions of people. Since 1994, Global Green USA's innovative research and cutting edge projects have been focused on solving some of the world's most difficult challenges. As the American arm of Green Cross International, Global Green is one of 31 affiliates worldwide fostering a global shift in values toward a sustainable and secure future by reconnecting humanity with the environment.[1] Eliminating weapons of mass destruction, ensuring clean drinking water for all, and stemming global climate change are major challenges. An ambitious company might wage war on one of these. Can Global Green USA take on all of them?

Jazz, Great Food, and Creating a Model for the Future

Global Green USA is leading the eco-friendly building revolution in New Orleans and slowly creating a clean, green model for the nation. "We want to create a different future" for New Orleans said Matt Petersen, Global Green's president and CEO. The city "was going to be rebuilt, so why not make it a model? Why not create a center of expertise in a city that had no green building or energy efficiency experience?"[2]

As part of Global Green USA's commitment to the sustainable rebuilding of New Orleans and to demonstrate green building as a solution to global warming nationally, Global Green USA sponsored an international design competition during the summer of 2006. Capitalizing on the media frenzy and public interest that surrounds celebrities today, they collaborated with actor Brad Pitt, who acted as jury chairman. More than 125 entries competed to design a net zero energy affordable housing and community center development in the Holy Cross neighborhood of the Lower 9th Ward, an impoverished area that had been particularly hard hit. The group's showcase Holy Cross Project is building five single-family energy-efficient homes, an 18-unit apartment building, and a community center.[3]

It was estimated that if 50,000 of the homes destroyed by Hurricane Katrina were rebuilt according to the green standards set by the design competition, residents of New Orleans would save $38 million to $56 million in energy bills every year and eliminate over a half million total tons of carbon dioxide—the equivalent of taking 100,000 cars off the road.[4]

Overall Global Green has brought in about $15 million in grants and funding for recovery efforts in New Orleans and it has helped other groups seeking sustainable and renewable energy change. "Our role as a catalyst has been tremendous," Petersen says. "There's been a good ripple effect."[5]

Time magazine says that "no organization is doing more to green New Orleans" than Global Green. With the model LEED Silver Wilson School opening and three new LEED Platinum homes completed at the Holy Cross Project, Global Green continues to lead the way. Elsewhere in New Orleans, Global Green is weatherizing homes of low income families. Global Green says the project is also an educational tool—its model home has already received visits from 4,500 people looking for ways to improve energy efficiency in their own homes.[6]

The Case for Building Green

Typical buildings contribute substantially to environmental problems. In the United States, buildings account for 36% of total energy use, 65% of electricity consumption, 30% of greenhouse gas emissions, 30% of raw materials use, 30% of waste output (equal to 136 million tons annually), and 12% of drinkable water consumption. A typical 1700-sq.-ft wood frame home requires the equivalent of clear cutting en entire acre of forest.[7]

Despite all this data, most contractors are not constructing healthy buildings. More than 30% of buildings in the United States have poor indoor air quality, a serious problem given that most people spend about 90% of their time indoors. The American Medical Association and the U.S. Army found that indoor air quality problems cost U.S. businesses 150 million workdays and about $15 billion in productivity losses each year. The World Health Organization puts the losses at close to $60 billion.[8]

The use of non-toxic materials in residential construction is especially important in protecting children from respiratory and other diseases. In commercial settings, green building results in overall health and comfort, which in turn leads to higher productivity, less absenteeism, and reduced insurance costs and liability risk.[9]

By following Global Green's example and building green, natural habitats, watersheds, and ecosystems can be preserved, air and water quality protected, and greenhouse gas emissions and solid waste reduced, all while conserving natural resources and creating healthier indoor and outdoor environments.[10]

Global Green's Green Buildings initiative has been responsible for the greening of over $20 billion in schools, housing, and municipal buildings. As a direct result of their Green Schools initiative, thousands of students from overcrowded and rundown schools now attend classes in healthy classrooms in energy- and water-saving buildings. These state-of-the-art green schools are helping to raise students' test scores, reduce sick days, and save money.[11]

Think Globally

Global Green educates hundreds of millions of people annually, leverages billions of dollars for environmental initiatives, implements ground-breaking environmental policy, and improves the lives of those in low-income communities.[12]

Across the nation, Global Green USA creates sustainable urban environments and combats global warming through their focus on green affordable housing, green schools, community education, solar energy, and sustainable city programs. In the

United States, Global Green's work is primarily focused on stemming global climate change by creating green buildings and cities. Internationally Global Green and their affiliates are working toward eliminating weapons of mass destruction that threaten lives and the environment, and providing clean and safe drinking water for the billions of people.

Global Green USA's philosophy is that water is neither a privilege nor a commodity; it's a right. However, for 2.4 billion people, access to clean drinking water is not a matter of simply turning on the faucet. By taking action on the individual and political levels, Global Green is educating the masses on conservation and cleanup. Worldwide, agriculture accounts for more than 70 percent of freshwater consumption, mainly for the irrigation of agricultural crops. Therefore, Global Green is educating farmers to make changes in how they use irrigation water, and advocating the switch to drip irrigation which reduces water usage from 30 to 70%.[13]

Global Green's focus this year raises the profile of water quality at the political level so that considerations concerning water quality are made alongside those of water quantity. Global Green's initiatives encourage governments to invest in smart water infrastructure and technologies, and increase environmental regulations of polluting industries, while urging government leaders to fulfill financial pledges for clean water.[14]

Pollution in oceans is not overlooked. Global Green USA is working on the issue of Sea-dumped Chemical Weapons, an important part of the larger problem of thousands of tons of weapons that have been dumped into the world's oceans over the years. Since the end of WWII, underwater chemical munitions have been a growing concern, threatening human and marine life. Global Green USA is developing a series of projects to assess the hazards posed by toxic underwater conventional and chemical weapons worldwide, prioritizing risks and dangers among sites by developing a comprehensive database, bringing these threats to light in international dialogues, and examining possible mitigation strategies.[15]

Small Changes Add Up to Great Impact

Little changes can mean a lot. For their part, consumers are encouraged by Global Green to seek out local farmers markets and eat less meat. Global Green asks us to consider this the next time we order a soda or cup of coffee: Every year, 58 billion paper cups are used in the United States at restaurants, events, and homes. If all paper cups in the U.S. were recycled, 645,000 tons of waste would be diverted from landfills each year, reducing greenhouse gas emissions to the equivalent of removing 450,000 cars from the road. If successful, Global Green's pilot project to influence the design of all paper food packaging potentially increases these benefits ten-fold.[16]

Commercially, Global Green USA's Coalition for Resource Recovery helps businesses increase profits by transforming waste into assets. The Coalition identifies and promotes effective waste diversion technologies and programs and is currently conducting pilots in New York City.[17]

Global Green USA's goals are to improve lives, educate the masses, put in place real solutions to global warming, turn trash into cash, and create sustainable futures. It's an ambitious list of goals. Is Global Green USA up to the challenge?

CASE QUESTIONS

1. **DISCUSSION**—Among all of Global Green USA's activities and initiatives, which ones appear to have the most immediate potential for positive impact on sustainability and the natural environment?

2. **DISCUSSION**—Based on this case, can we say that Global Green USA has the right strategy and culture to perform as a highly innovative organization? Why or Why not?

3. **PROBLEM-SOLVING**—Who are the key stakeholders of Global Green USA? As an advisor to its CEO, Matt Petersen, what would you point out as possible conflicts among the key stakeholder interests and what steps would you recommend that he take to best deal with them?

4. **FURTHER RESEARCH**—How well is Global Green USA doing? See what data you can find to assess how the nonprofit has been performing in the current national and global economies. What do its critics, if any, say? Is this organization a role model that others with interests in environment and sustainability might follow? Or is it just another example of a good idea that doesn't really live up to expectations?

Harley-Davidson celebrated a century in business with a year-long International Road Tour. The party culminated in the company's home-town, Milwaukee.[1] Harley is a true American success story. Once near death in the face of global competition, Harley reestablished itself as the dominant maker of big bikes in the United States. However, as a weak economy tightened credit lending, consumers shied away from the purchase of luxury items, including Harley's high-end heavy-weight motorcycles. Can a new CEO with a revised vision help Harley-Davidson weather the economic storm?

Harley-Davidson's Roots

When Harley-Davidson was founded in 1903, it was one of more than 100 firms producing motorcycles in the United States. The U.S. government became an important customer for the company's high-powered, reliable bikes, using them in both world wars. By the 1950s, Harley-Davidson was the only remaining American manufacturer.[2] But by then British com-petitors were entering the market with faster, lighter-weight bikes. And Honda Motor Company of Japan began marketing lightweight bikes in the United States, moving into mid-dleweight vehicles in the 1960s. Harley initially tried to com-pete by manufacturing smaller bikes but had difficulty making them profitably. The company even purchased an Italian motor-cycle firm, Aermacchi, but many of its dealers were reluctant to sell the small Aermacchi Harleys.[3]

Consolidation and Renewal

American Machine and Foundry Co. (AMF) took over Harley in 1969, expanding its portfolio of recreational products. AMF increased production from 14,000 to 50,000 bikes per year. This rapid expansion led to significant problems with quality, and better-built Japanese motorcycles began to take over the market. Harley's share of its major U.S. market–heavyweight motorcycles–was only 23%.[4] A group of 13 managers bought Harley-Davidson back from AMF in 1981 and began to turn the company around with the rallying cry "The Eagle Soars Alone." As Richard Teerlink, former CEO of Harley, explained, "The solution was to get back to detail. The key was to know the business, know the customer, and pay attention to detail."[5] The key elements in this process were increasing quality and im-proving service to customers and dealers. Management kept the classic Harley style and focused on the company's traditional strength–heavyweight and super heavyweight bikes.

In 1983, the Harley Owners Group (H.O.G.) was formed; H.O.G. membership now exceeds 1 million members, and there are 1,400 chapters worldwide.[6,7] Also in 1983, Harley-Davidson asked the International Trade Commission (ITC) for tariff relief on the basis that Japanese manufacturers were stockpiling inventory in the United States and providing unfair competition. The re-quest was granted, and a tariff relief for five years was placed on all imported Japanese motorcycles that were 700 cc or larger. By 1987, Harley was confident enough to petition the ITC to have the tariff lifted because the company had improved its ability to compete with foreign imports. Once Harley's image had been restored, the company began to increase production.[8] The firm opened new facilities in Franklin, Milwaukee, and Menomonee Falls, Wisconsin; Kansas City, Missouri; and York, Pennsylvania; and opened a new assembly plant in Manaus, Brazil.[9]

In the 1980s, the average Harley purchaser was in his late thirties, with an average household income of over $40,000. Teerlink didn't like the description of his customers as "aging" Baby Boomers: "Our customers want the sense of adventure that they get on our bikes. . . . Harley-Davidson doesn't sell trans-portation, we sell transformation. We sell excitement, a way of life."[10] However, the average age and income of Harley riders has continued to increase. Recently, the median age of a Harley rider was 47, and the median income exceeded $80,000.[11] The company also created a line of Harley accessories available online, by catalog, or through dealers, all adorned with the Harley-Davidson logo. These jackets, caps, t-shirts, and other items became popular with nonbikers as well. In fact, the cloth-ing and parts had a higher profit margin than the motorcycles; nonbike products made up as much as half of sales at some dealerships.

International Efforts

Although the company had been exporting motorcycles ever since it was founded, it was not until the late 1980s that Harley-Davidson management began to think seriously about interna-tional markets. Traditionally, the company's ads had been translated word for word into foreign languages. New ads were developed specifically for different markets, and rallies were adapted to fit local customs.[12] The company also began to ac-tively recruit and develop dealers in Europe and Japan. It pur-chased a Japanese distribution company and built a large parts warehouse in Germany. Harley learned a great deal from its in-ternational activities. Recognizing, for example, that German motorcyclists rode at high speeds–often more than 100 mph–the company began studying ways to give Harleys a smoother ride and emphasizing accessories that would give riders more protection.[13]

Harley continues to make inroads in overseas markets. At one time, it had 30% of the worldwide market for heavyweight motorcycles–chrome-laden cruisers, aerodynamic rocket bikes mostly produced by the Japanese, and oversize touring motor-cycles. In Europe, Harley ranked third, with only 10.7% of the market share behind Honda and Suzuki.[14] However, in the Asia/Pacific market, where one would expect Japanese bikes to dominate, Harley had the largest market shares in the early part of the decade. Harley had 21.3% of the market share, com-pared to 19.2% for Honda.[15]

Harley motorcycles are among America's fastest-growing exports to Japan. Harley's Japanese subsidiary adapted the company's marketing approach to Japanese tastes, even pro-ducing shinier and more complete tool kits than those available in the United States. Harley bikes have long been considered symbols of prestige in Japan; many Japanese enthusiasts see themselves as rebels on wheels.[16]

The company has also made inroads into the previously elusive Chinese market, with the first official Chinese Harley-Davidson dealership opening its doors just outside downtown Beijing. To break into this emerging market, Harley partnered with China's Zongshen Motorcycle Group, which makes more than 1 million small-engine motorcycles each year.[17] Like other Harley stores, the Chinese outlet stocks bikes, parts and accessories, and branded merchandise, and offers post-sales service. Despite China's growing disposable income, the new store has several hurdles ahead of it, including riding restrictions imposed by the government in urban areas.

The Future

Although its international sales have grown, the domestic market still represents almost 75% of Harley's sales.[18,19] Given the climbing price of gas, Harley is uniquely positioned to take advantage of this economic factor. Many riders report in-town fuel consumption rates in excess of 40 miles per gallon.[20] Analyst Todd Sullivan notes, "I know plenty of F150, Suburban, and Silverado drivers who ride Harleys. They are doubling or even tripling their gas mileage and savings by making the switch."[21] Executives attribute Harley's success to loyal customers and the Harley-Davidson name. "It is a unique brand that is built on personal relationship and deep connections with customers, unmatched riding experiences, and proud history," said Jim Ziemer, Harley's former president and chief executive.[22]

However, Harley-Davidson has been in a fight not just with its competitors, but also with the recession and a sharp consumer spending slowdown, with the aging of its customer base, and with a credit crisis that has made it difficult for both the motorcycle maker and its loyal riders to get financing.[23] For the first time in 16 years, the company posted a loss–$218.7 million in 2009. As part of the strategy put into place by Harley's new CEO Keith E. Wandell, the company has laid off workers, closed factories, and begun selling brands. In early 2010 Harley discontinued its Buell product line and divested its MV Agusta unit. Considering all that turmoil and transition, some loyalists felt they had been taken for a ride when Wandell, who took over the motorcycle maker part-way through 2009, received a $6.4 million pay package during his first eight months on the job.[24]

Wandell's compensation may be justified, however, if he's successful in his plan to drive growth through a single-minded focus of efforts and resources on the unique strengths of the Harley-Davidson brand, and to enhance productivity and profitability through continuous improvement. Part of his approach focuses company resources on Harley-Davidson products and experiences, global expansion, demographic outreach, and commitment to core customers.[25] Through Harley's demographic outreach, Garage Party Events have been developed specifically for women–creating an intimidation–free zone where female riders can connect with one another. Harley-Davidson's global expansion into the small but fast-growing luxury market in India may help offset tough times at home.[26,27]

Having survived the Great Depression, only time and customers' wallets will determine whether Harley-Davidson will make it through the Great Recession.

CASE QUESTIONS

1. **DISCUSSION**–If you were CEO of Harley-Davidson, how would you compare the advantages and disadvantages of using exports, joint ventures, and foreign subsidiaries as ways of expanding international sales?

2. **DISCUSSION**–In America and Japan Harley's positioning has shifted from providing a product (motorcycles) toward providing a service (way of life). Will this positioning succeed in Asia, Africa, and South America?

3. **PROBLEM-SOLVING**–Assume the CEO of Harley has decided to set up new manufacturing facilities in both China and India. Which of the general environment conditions should be analyzed before Harley makes strategic investments in each country? And to get started there, should Harley set up wholly owned subsidiaries to do the manufacturing, or would it be better off entering into joint ventures with local partners?

4. **FURTHER RESEARCH**–Is it accurate to say that Harley is "still on top" of its game? How is the company doing today in both domestic and global markets? Who are its top competitors in other parts of the world, and how is Harley faring against them?

Most people think of cupcakes as either homemade snacks or prepackaged Hostess treats. But Candace Nelson's cupcake-only bakery, Sprinkles, proved that high-end ingredients in a stylish setting could challenge the low-carb craze and inspire food fans to wait in long lines for a bite-sized taste of heaven.

When Oprah Calls . . .

Candace Nelson's big break came courtesy of two of the world's most famous women, 300 cupcakes, and a sleepless red-eye flight. It started when Barbra Streisand bought a dozen cupcakes from Nelson's new bakery, Sprinkles, for her friend Oprah Winfrey. Soon after, Nelson received a 2 p.m. call from one of Winfrey's producers with a last-minute order: bring 300 cupcakes to Chicago for an appearance the next morning on *Breakfast with Oprah.*

"You can't say no to Oprah," Nelson jokes. So the investment-banker-turned-baker manned her ovens for six hours before catching an overnight flight to the Windy City. She arrived at Oprah's studios with shopping bags full of her gourmet cupcakes—coconut, red velvet, and Madagascar vanilla, topped with Sprinkles' requisite half-inch-thick sheet of buttercream frosting. Like many before her, Nelson soon benefited from Oprah's magic touch—cupcake sales at the Beverly Hills bakery jumped 50% to 1,500 per day.[1] And at $3.25 per cupcake—nearly as much as a half-dozen Krispy Kreme donuts—it was sweet news for Nelson and her husband, Charles, who co-owns the Sprinkles chain.

Reinventing a Classic

No longer relegated to birthday parties and grade-school classrooms, cupcakes are experiencing a major resurgence as sweet-starved adults rediscover one of childhood's sweetest treats. In a rebound from the low-carb craze that swept calorie-conscious dieters, cupcakes now have their own blogs, baking cups, and presentation stands—Amazon.com even sells a baker's dozen of cookbooks devoted to the bite-sized indulgences.

According to Ruth Reichl, former editor of the now defunct *Gourmet* magazine, "The rise of the cupcake is very much about going back to our national identity in food, which is all about comfort. In these times fraught with war and a tough economy, people want to think about when they and their country were innocent." When *Gourmet* devoted a cover to cupcakes, impassioned readers sent letters for nearly a year, some reprimanding the magazine for elevating the snack to epicurean standard but others sharing their fondest cupcake moments. "We actually got pictures of people's cupcakes," Reichl fondly reflected. "It's a very emotional dessert."[2]

Not everyone is so philosophical. "Why do I like cupcakes? Wow, a million reasons," said San Francisco cupcake lover Yoli Anyon. "There's less guilt about eating them because they're small. They're also kind of gourmet. And it just feels much more special than eating a candy bar."[3] Model Tyra Banks put her passion about Sprinkles more succinctly. "I'm addicted," she wryly confessed.[4]

At Sprinkles, the line stretches out the door and around the block. Tourists and locals alike often wait well over a half-hour—longer than a cupcake takes to bake and cool—for a taste of one of Sprinkles' 24 custom flavors, only 14 of which are offered each day. Favorites such as dark chocolate and red velvet are available every day, but specialty flavors such as chai latte, carrot cake, and peanut butter chocolate appear sporadically throughout the week. To distinguish her cakes from grocery-store look-alikes capped with piped flowers or blocky writing, Nelson decorates with a minimalist's touch—a sleek buttercream frosting and little decoration.[5]

Though the nine Sprinkles locations also sell bottled soda, coffee, and 75-cent frosting shots, cupcakes—regular, vegan, and gluten free—are their main attraction. If one cupcake isn't enough, Sprinkles will deliver a dozen cupcakes for $46 in a specially designed box, edged with the color band of your choice, to customers who live near a store. Although Sprinkles doesn't yet ship its luscious wares, that didn't stop one fan from taking matters into her own hands. Actress Katie Holmes, whose affinity for Sprinkles has been reported in the popular press, sent hundreds of specially designed boxes of Sprinkles cupcakes to friends and associates as a Christmas gift.[6] But if you're not lucky enough to have famous friends or to live within snacking distance of a Sprinkles, don't fret—Williams-Sonoma stores now sell canisters of Sprinkles cupcake mix for $14.

From Dream to Buttercream

Setting aside two lucrative careers, Candace and Charles Nelson traded long hours of financial-sector work in San Francisco for long hours in the kitchen after Candace concluded a pastry course at the top-shelf Bay Area cooking school Tante Marie. "I found the one job where the hours are worse than investment banking," Nelson joked.[7] "From our research, a cupcake bakery had the highest risk for failing and a low potential for return, but we went ahead and did it anyway," she says.[8] The couple opened the first Sprinkles location in Beverly Hills in April 2005, believing that an all-cupcake bakery could make it in Los Angeles's fickle "hot or not" environment. "It was time for cupcakes to stop being the backup dancer to cakes," said Candace.[9]

In contrast to the cutesy, bubblegum-pink interiors of other cupcake shops, noted local architect Andrea Lenardin Madden developed a crisp, regimented visual style for Sprinkles. Stores sport custom-made white oak built-in cabinets, strategically located skylights, contemporary and simplified whitewashed walls, a glass-topped bar, and even coordinating benches outside. Each cupcake has its own special location in the display case. "What's distinctive about this store is that it is refined," Nelson noted.[10] Critics agree—Sprinkles Beverly Hills won two Los Angeles restaurant design awards.

It wasn't an easy time to bring the cupcake concept to L.A. With the United States still deep in the throes of the *South Beach Diet Cookbook*-inspired low-carb craze, Nelson faced skepticism from her earliest customers, wedding-shower guests who turned away from her cupcakes in fear of overloading on carbs.[11] Even the Nelsons' landlord doubted, asking, "But what else will you be selling?"[12]

The second Sprinkles outlet opened in the nearby glitzy town of Corona del Mar, a location well suited to its high-end concept. "Because this is purely discretionary spending on food," noted retail consultant Greg Stoffel, "it would require a higher-income area. And in Orange County, you can't get much higher than Corona del Mar."[13]

Cupcake Entrepreneurs

Noted New York bakery Magnolia opened its shutters in 1996, kicking off the cupcake-only trend. *Sex and the City's* Sarah Jessica Parker's love for Magnolia is credited for bringing attention to the palm-sized treat. Fast-forward 10 years, and suddenly a number of aspiring cupcake creators were stepping up to get a taste of sweet success.

Kirk Rossberg, owner of L.A.'s Torrance Bakery and president of the California Retail Bakers Association, found himself over-whelmed with prospective interns. Of the 30 he accepted recently, he estimated that 90% had left salaried professions in the hopes of open-ing bakeries. "Until last year, I never had people asking to work for free," he said.

Rebecca Marrs, director of career services at the California School of Culinary Arts in Pasadena, noted a jump in the number of older applicants hoping for a career switch, when en-rollment in the school's baking program recently grew by nearly a third.[14]

Rachel Kramer Bussel, author of the blog *Cupcakes Take the Cake*, receives approxi-mately one e-mail each week from someone hoping to open a new cupcake bakery. She estimates there are about 75 such shops in the United States right now. "I keep waiting for this to die down," she said, "and instead it keeps mushrooming."[15]

Not Everyone Gets It

Not everyone gets it, though. Georgene Fairbanks, visiting Sprinkles from nearby Mission Viejo on the basis of Oprah's recommendation, couldn't comprehend the fuss. "It's not that I didn't like it," Fairbanks said. "I've just had cupcakes from Betty Crocker that were just as good."[16]

And even worse for Sprinkles, there's a very real concern that too many people might get it—with the skyrocketing num-ber of cupcake-only bakeries opening and consumers' fickle food tastes, the cupcake craze might be over before stores have a chance to switch gears and rebrand themselves.

Nonetheless, cupcakes still have their allies. Pulitzer-winning food critic Jonathan Gold observed that "in a town where people say no to you all the time and you rarely have the sim-ple satisfaction of getting something made, being able to make a sweet simple thing that makes people happy is really compelling."[17]

Candace Nelson agreed. "That's why I went into the cupcake business. I'm in this little cupcake bubble where every-one is smiling ear to ear."[18] And with many more Sprinkles out-lets scheduled to open, Nelson has a lot to smile about.

CASE QUESTIONS

1. **DISCUSSION**—What entrepreneurial characteristics did Candace and Charles Nelson display in this case? What other traits and personal characteristics may be necessary for people to succeed as owners of new Sprinkles' franchises?

2. **DISCUSSION**—With many stores scheduled to open, in what stage of its life cycle is Sprinkles, and what are the major management challenges Nelson faces in keeping the firm successful as it grows?

3. **PROBLEM-SOLVING**—How would you assess the potential for a new venture on your campus called "Sweet Bites," a cupcake-only eatery? What would you include in a business plan to make this new venture an attractive candidate for start-up funding from an angel investor or a university-based venture capital fund?

4. **FURTHER RESEARCH**—How far can a cupcake-only busi-ness grow? Gather current information on Sprinkles and do a "venture capitalist" analysis. Looking to the future, what makes the firm attractive to a venture capital investor, and what are its downsides? Is Sprinkles a good bet for the future?

Amazon.com has soared ahead of other online merchants. What the firm can't carry in its 25 worldwide fulfillment centers, affiliated retailers distribute for it. Not content to rest on past laurels, CEO Jeff Bezos has introduced a number of new services to keep customers glued to the Amazon site. His latest investments are upgrades to the Kindle book reader. The acquisition of online retailer Zappos.com cost Amazon over $900 million. But will the investments pay off?

The Rocket Takes Off

Like a rocket propelled by jet fuel, Internet commerce has shot off the launch pad. No matter what the product is that may set a shopper's heart aflutter, some up-and-coming marketer has likely already set up a specialty e-store selling it. But one online vendor has grander aspirations: Why stop at selling one line of products—or two, or twenty—when customers can instead be offered the equivalent of an online Mall of America?

From its modest beginning in Jeff Bezos's garage in 1995, Amazon.com has quickly sprouted into the most megalithic online retailer. Once Bezos saw that Amazon could outgrow its role as an immense book retailer, he began to sell CDs and DVDs. Even its logo was updated to symbolize that Amazon.com sells almost anything you can think of, from A to Z.

And that only takes into account Amazon's U.S. presence. At latest count, customers in six other countries, including China, Japan, and France, can access Amazon sister sites built especially for them.[1] Amazon's 25 "fulfillment centers" around the world enclose more than 12 million square feet of operating space.[2,3]

So what's next? Growth. Bezos continues to diversify Amazon's product offerings and broaden its brand by partnering with existing retailers to add new product lines. It's a win-win proposition for a multitude of companies—including Target, Toys 'R' Us, and Wine.com. The companies profit from the additional exposure and sales (without undercutting their existing business), and Amazon's brand thrives from the opportunity to keep customers who might otherwise shop elsewhere.

Traditional Content, Layers of Value

Not forgetting its roots, Amazon enhanced its media offerings by making several key acquisitions. Its purchase of on-demand book self-publisher BookSurge reinforces Amazon's literary heritage: Customers publishing memoirs or first books of poetry may, for a small fee, have their work made available for sale via Amazon's website.[4] Considering how many sets of eyes visit the site in the average week, this is a very compelling offer to a writer who may be considering other on-demand services. Readers appreciate the expanded range of literary offerings, and Amazon wins by having more products to sell—products it is paid to stock.

Beyond simply finding more and more products to sell, Bezos realized that to prevent his brand from becoming stagnant, he would have to innovate, creating new levels of service to complement existing products. "We have to say, 'What kind of innovation can we layer on top of that that will be meaningful for our customers?'" explains Bezos.[5]

So far, much of this innovation has come from the depth of the free content available to Amazon customers. Far from being a loss leader, Amazon's free content spurs sales and reinforces customers' perception of Amazon's commitment to customer service.

As David Meerman Scott put it in *eContent*, "Here is the flip side of free in action—a smart content company figuring out how to get people to contribute compelling content for free and then building a for-profit business model around it. Amazon.com has built a huge content site by having all of the content provided to it for no cost. Of course, Amazon.com makes money by selling products based on the contributed content on the site—another example of the flip side of free."[6]

Entering Busy Markets

Time and time again, Amazon has squared off against tech industry giant Apple—first, by launching its Amazon MP3 music downloading service and then, in a move of digital one-upmanship, offering all of its tracks from the Big 4 record labels without proprietary digital rights management (DRM) software, allowing the files to be played on any MP3 player.[7] Amazon also bought top-shelf audio book vendor Audible.com for $300 million, adding more than 80,000 audio titles to its arsenal; it bought the rival online merchant Zappos.com for $928 million.[8] Although Amazon already had its own shoe and handbag site, endless.com, Zappos's brand recognition and market perception is unparalleled. But is that worth the $900 million price tag?

The company introduced the Amazon Unbox, which allows customers to purchase or rent thousands of movies and television shows from most major networks. In another snub to Apple, Unbox files initially could only be played on Windows-compatible devices, putting Apple's computers and TV set-top device out of the action. Amazon touts the content as roughly that of DVD quality, though occupying only half as much space. Using a cable broadband connection, Unbox subscribers can expect to download a two-hour movie in approximately two hours—and can begin to watch it after five minutes or so of downloading.[9]

Although Amazon still sells a considerable number of Apple's iPods, it is the Amazon Kindle that is revamping the publishing industry. Sales of the books for the Kindle recently outnumbered Amazon's sales of hardcover books.[10] Part e-book reader, part wireless computer, the Kindle can download and store e-books, RSS feeds, Microsoft Word documents, and digital pictures in most major formats. Bezos sees this as a natural evolution of technology. "Books are the last bastion of analog," he said to *Newsweek*. "Music and video have been digital for a long time, and short-form reading has been digitized, beginning with the early Web. But long-form reading really hasn't."[11]

But will Amazon continue to hold on to its market share now that Barnes & Noble's Nook and Apple's popular iPad, with its own e-bookstore, continue to make inroads in the e-book market?

Apple played the same game to perfection with the iPhone App Store by unleashing its own e-reader application, Stanza. Apple seems to have a knack for balancing the benefits of both open and closed architectures. Any Web page can act as an application for the iPhone.[12] By May 2009, Amazon realized the benefit of allowing readers to read books on a variety of devices and introduced the free application "Kindle for iPhone and iTouch."[13] Its acquisition of Touchco, a start-up that specializes in touchscreen technology, is a signal that Amazon wants to upgrade its Kindle e-reader to compete with Apple's iPad.[14]

Already among the largest sellers of DVDs and VHS tapes, Amazon is considering allowing customers to download movies for a fee and burn them to DVDs. In 2010 Amazon began advanced negotiations with three Hollywood studios. If the negotiations are successful, Amazon's service will position itself in the media world alongside rivals like Apple Computer's iTunes as a place where people go not just to order goods to be sent by mail, but to instantly enjoy digital wares as well. An Amazon downloading service would be certain to send waves through both the media and retail worlds. Players are racing to offer new ways to give tech-savvy audiences instant access to their favorite shows and songs, in a field crowded with potential rivals using Internet and on-demand technologies.[15] Only time will tell what innovations the Apple–Amazon rivalry will produce next.

Despite Amazon's success in so many new markets, some critics question whether Amazon.com, let alone the Internet, is the best place to make high-involvement purchases. Once again, Bezos is upbeat. "We sell a lot of high-ticket items," he counters. "We sell diamonds that cost thousands of dollars and $8,000 plasma TVs. There doesn't seem to be any resistance, and, in fact, those high-priced items are growing very rapidly as a percentage of our sales."[16]

Looking Ahead

It seems difficult to catch Bezos *not* being upbeat. Even as Amazon's stock values fluctuate, he still believes that customer service and anticipating customers' needs, not the stock ticker, define the Amazon experience. "I think one of the things people don't understand is we can build more shareholder value by lowering product prices than we can by trying to raise margins," he says. "It's a more patient approach, but we think it leads to a stronger, healthier company. It also serves customers much, much better."[17]

In less than two decades, Amazon.com has grown from a one-man operation into a global giant of commerce. By forging alliances to ensure that he has what customers want and making astute purchases, Jeff Bezos has made Amazon the go-to brand for online shopping. But with its significant investments in new media and services, does the company risk spreading itself too thin? Will customers continue to flock to Amazon, the go-to company for their every need?

CASE QUESTIONS

1. **DISCUSSION**—In what ways does Bezos's decision to develop and deliver the Kindle show systematic and intuitive thinking?

2. **DISCUSSION**—How do you describe the competitive risk in Amazon.com's environment as Wal-Mart, Barnes and Noble, and other retailers strengthen their online offerings?

3. **PROBLEM-SOLVING**—Apple's iPad is here and Amazon's Kindle now has a strong rival in the market for eReaders. As CEO Bezos addresses the strategic threat from Apple, he calls on you for decision-making advice. What decision error and traps might cause him to make the wrong decisions in face of the iPad's popularity, and why? What can he do to best avoid these mistakes?

4. **FURTHER RESEARCH**—What are the latest initiatives coming out of Amazon? How do they stack up in relation to actual or potential competition? How has the Zappos acquisition turned out? Is Bezos making the right decisions as he guides the firm through today's many business challenges?

What's so interesting about a company that just wants to be nice? Longevity and year-after-year success, for starters. From a no-questions-asked return policy to patient, limitless customer support, Lands' End has developed a solid business model around treating customers the way they'd like to be treated. See how this former retailer of sailing products turned good manners into healthy profits.

Customers Come First

Lands' End, a clothing retailer out of Dodgeville, Wisconsin, is known for its generous return policy. But no customer request tested this more than a car collector who asked to return a taxicab his wife had purchased for him more than 20 years before. In a novel departure from its normal trade, Lands' End had featured the vintage taxi on the cover of its 1984 holiday catalog and sold it to the woman for $19,000. In 2005, the man contacted Lands' End and inquired about a refund on the car. Cheerfully, Lands' End obliged and returned the woman's full purchase price.

This sort of humble business practice seems unusually generous in today's hypercompetitive retail market. But Lands' End has built a cult following—and consistently strong profits—on the basis of Midwestern kindness and durable, high-quality clothes. When online retail sales top $131 billion, companies need any edge they can get.[1] Lands' End gets its edge simply by living in accordance with the Golden Rule. All business practices—customer service, phone support, return procedures, employee treatment, and even relationships with suppliers—flow from the company's principled ideals. Lands' End refers to this philosophy in one simple notion: "What is best for our customer is best for all of us."[2]

Lands' End's customer-first policies are necessary to distinguish the company amid such catalog-based competitors as Maine's L.L. Bean, a company that has been around more than 50 years longer and has deeper brand equity. And the firm's inimitable customer experience has long been a shopper's favorite, especially during the holiday season. Though more and more customers order via the company's website, many still prefer to work with the well-trained phone staff, who receive 70–80 hours of product, customer service, and computer training when hired. They also respond to e-mails with a personal response, in most cases within three hours.[3]

Jeanne Bliss, author of *Chief Customer Officer* and a 25-year customer service veteran, started her career at Lands' End. She noted, "You've got to do reliability first: 24-hour delivery and answering the phone on the second ring 99.9% of the time. Then you've earned the right to do more." If you're Lands' End, "doing more" means adding fun touches, such as including holiday poems or instructions for turning shipping cartons into barnyard animals.[4]

Born from Boating

Lands' End began in 1963 when founder Gary Comer established the company to sell racing sailboat equipment, along with a handful of sweaters and raincoats. Comer, a 10-year copywriting veteran at the Chicago office of Young & Rubicam, sought a change of pace after leaving the ad industry and struck up a partnership with like-minded sailing enthusiasts.[5] For several years, the company focused on sailing-related products until it became clear that what had been its peripheral merchandise—clothing, canvas luggage, and shoes—was in fact its most profitable.[6]

As the company's focus shifted to the casual, durable clothing it is known for today, its size and its profits continued to grow. By the spring of 1977, the company discontinued carrying sailing equipment altogether. One year later, Comer moved operations from Chicago to Dodgeville, Wisconsin. "I fell in love with the gently rolling hills and woods and cornfields, and being able to see the changing seasons," Comer said. He also likely fell in love with the substantially lower cost of operations.[7]

Lands' End continued to grow and diversify its clothing line for the next 20 years, culminating in a sale to Sears in 2002 for $1.9 billion. Sears planned to expand on the relatively small number of Lands' End stores (only 12 outlet stores existed at the time) by creating a store-within-a-store concept. Some analysts considered this a brilliant move, especially because Lands' End was the top specialty catalog and top specialty online retailer at the time. But the execution floundered when Sears failed to promote the integration. And when faithful Lands' End customers did come to Sears, they found the stock scattered throughout the store.[8]

Lands' End shops are now distinguished in Sears by navy blue signs and columns and occupy an average of 10,000 square feet per store. According to Sears spokesman Christian Brathwaite, "The idea is to enhance the customer experience and make it easy for customers to shop for Lands' End apparel, coupled with the Lands' End service model. We've seen a very positive customer response."[9]

It's a solid bet for Sears, according to Christopher T. Shannon, managing director at the investment bank Berkery, Noyes & Co., who perceived that the store-within-a-store model is gaining steam. He noted a "rise in demand from the public for more specialty retailers. I believe the goal is to have more of a one-on-one relationship with the end-buyer and offer as many different ways to make a purchase as possible."[10]

Standing Out from the Crowd

Lands' End has made Fortune's "Top 100 Best Companies to Work For" for three consecutive years. The company is recognized as a top-performing e-commerce company by the E-Tailing Group and ranks number 9 on *BusinessWeek's* list of "Customer Service Champs." Lands' End has been recognized in the 2007, 2008, and 2009 National Retail Federation Foundation/American Express Customer Service Survey, which asks, "Which retailer delivers the best customer service?" In 2009, Lands' End was named a service winner in the E-Tailing Group's 11th annual Mystery Shopping Study of the top 100 online retailers.[11]

To maintain this competitive presence in the crowded retail clothing market, Lands' End employs a number of creative strategies to stay at the forefront of customers' minds and wallets. Its website was the first to offer a feature called "My Virtual Model," a tool that uses customer-supplied measurements to generate a 3-D likeness that can be used to "try on" merchandise. To answer customers' questions as they occur, while maintaining a seamless Web shopping experience, Lands' End installed a chat module called "Lands' End Live."

Banking on the durability and conservative styling of its clothes, Lands' End branched out of the traditional retail model to market directly to businesses, institutions, and schools. LEBO—the company's business outfitting division—strives to free organizations from the monotony of stuffy, starched uniforms. To attract attention to this program, LEBO provided a free apparel makeover to three companies, partnering to develop new looks that were eventually highlighted in the LEBO catalog.[12]

As part to their plan to attract younger customers, Land's End recently introduced contemporary clothing lines that feature fitted shirts, low rise pants, and dressier suits. They also updated classic items with new colors and materials. The company's web site highlights the new clothing lines and is using social media sites such as Facebook and Twitter to promote their products.[13] Tom Julian, president of brand-consulting firm Tom Julian Group, says it is almost mandatory for older brands to incorporate contemporary touches but he warns against them becoming too trendy and alienating existing customers.[14]

When the annual holiday shopping season approaches, Lands' End kicks its customer-retention efforts into high gear. In a recent holiday season, one customer service representative from each of the company's three call centers is chosen to serve as Elf of the Day from November 28 to December 18 and given the discretion to offer randomly selected customers complementary upgrades, such as free gift boxing or monogramming. "It's a way to spread a little extra surprise and happiness to customers," said Lands' End spokesperson Amanda Broderick.[15]

But as other clothing retailers follow suit and improve their customer service skills, Lands' End may begin to find itself with stiff competition and pinched profit margins. Does the company have what it takes to distinguish itself in the crowded apparel marketplace?

CASE QUESTIONS

1. **DISCUSSION**—What factors internal to Lands' End and in its external environment seem most important to consider as the firm develops plans for the future?

2. **DISCUSSION**—If you were hired by Lands' End to help benchmark its customer service performance, which three companies would you choose and why?

3. **PROBLEM-SOLVING**—As a consultant, what steps would you recommend be taken at Lands' End to build a clear hierarchy of objectives, improve goal alignment, and otherwise help with the implementation of plans in the customer services area?

4. **FURTHER RESEARCH**—Browse the Lands' End website and check the business news for updates to learn as much as you can about the company. Do the same for L.L. Bean. Does one firm or the other have any special advantage in planning for future success? Why or why not?

Once a niche company operating in the northeast, Dunkin' Donuts is opening hundreds of stores and entering new markets. At the same time, the java giant is broadly expanding both its food and its coffee menus to ride the wave of fresh trends, appealing to a new generation of customers. But is the rest of America ready for Dunkin' Donuts? Can the company keep up with its own rapid growth? With Starbucks rethinking its positioning strategy and McDonald's offering a great tasting coffee at a reasonable price, Dunkin' Donuts is hoping they "Kin Do It."

Serving the Caffeinated Masses

There's a lot more to a coffee shop than just change in the tip jar. Some 400 billion cups of coffee are consumed every year, making it the most popular beverage globally. Estimates indicate that more than 100 million Americans drink a total of 350 million cups of coffee a day.[1] And with Starbucks driving tastes for upscale coffee, some customers may wonder whether any coffee vendors remember the days when drip coffee came in only two varieties—regular and decaf. But Dunkin' Donuts does, and it's betting dollars to donuts that consumers nationwide will embrace its reputation for value, simplicity, and a superior Boston Kreme donut.

Winning New Customers

Most of America has had an occasional relationship with the Dunkin' Donuts brand through its almost 6,400 domestic outlets, which have their densest cluster in the northeast and a growing presence in the rest of the country.[2] But the brand has also managed to carve out an international niche with 2,440 international shops in 31 countries. The shops are not only found in expected markets such as Canada and Brazil, but also in some unexpected ones, including Qatar, South Korea, Pakistan, and the Philippines.[3]

If the company has its way, in the future you won't have to go very far to pick up a box of donuts. "We're only represented large-scale in the northeastern market," said Jayne Fitzpatrick, strategy officer for Dunkin' Brands, mentioning plans to expand "as aggressively" as possible. "We're able to do that because we're a franchise system, so access to operators and capital is easier."[4] How aggressively? According to John Fassak, vice president of business development, the company plans to expand to 15,000 outlets by 2020. Sample cities in the Midwest reveal heavy investment: 50 more stores planned in Milwaukee, more than 100 in St. Louis, and 30 in central Ohio.[5]

What Would Consumers Think?

None of Dunkin' Donuts' moves makes much difference unless consumers buy into the notion that the company has the culinary imperative to sell more than its name suggests. If plans prove successful, more customers than ever may flock to indulge in the company's breakfast-to-go menu. If they don't, the only thing potentially worse for Dunkin' Donuts than diluted coffee could be a diluted brand image. After 60 years, the company has a reputation for doing two things simply and successfully—coffee and donuts. Even when consumers see the line of products expand into what was once solely the realm of the company's competitors, they may be unconvinced that Dunkin' Donuts is the shop to go to for breakfast.

For most of its existence, Dunkin' Donuts' main product focus has been implicit in its name: donuts, and coffee in which to dip them. First-time customers acquainted with this simple reputation were often overwhelmed by the wide varieties of donuts stacked end-to-end in neat, mouthwatering rows. Playing catch-up to the rest of the morning market, Dunkin' Donuts has only recently joined the breakfast sandwich game.[6]

According to spokesperson Andrew Mastroangelo, Dunkin' Donuts sells more than one billion cups of coffee a year, for 62% of the company's annual store revenue.[7,8] Considering that coffee is the most profitable product on the menu, it's a good bet that those margins give the company room to experiment with its food offerings.

Changing Course to Follow Demand

Faced with the challenge of maintaining a relevant brand image in the face of fierce and innovative competition, Dunkin' Donuts pursued a time-honored business tradition—following the leader. The company now offers a competitive variety of espresso-based drinks complemented with a broad number of sugar-free flavorings, including caramel, vanilla, and Mocha Swirl.[9] Ever-increasing competition in the morning meal market made an update to Dunkin' Donuts' food selection inevitable. The company currently focuses on bagel and croissant-based breakfast sandwiches, as well as its new Oven-Toasted line, including flatbread sandwiches and personal pizzas.

On Every Corner

Starbucks is known for its aggressive dominance of the coffee marketplace. When competitors opened a new store in town, Starbucks didn't worry. It just opened a new store across the street, in a vigorous one-upmanship that conquered new ground and deterred competitors. But many who have struggled to compete with Starbucks have had to do so with limited resources or only a few franchises. Not so with Dunkin' Donuts. Its parent brand, Dunkin' Brands, also owns Baskin-Robbins.[10]

Simple Food for Simple People

Dunkin Donuts' history of offering simple and straightforward morning snacks has given it the competitive advantage of distinction as *the* anti-Starbucks—earnest and without pretense. Like Craftsman tools and Levi's jeans, the company appeals to unpretentious people who enjoy the little things in life.

The Sweet Spot Has a Jelly Center

Dunkin' Donuts is trying to grow in all directions, reaching more customers in more places with more products. Achieving proper retail placement can be a delicate balance.

Although Dunkin' Donuts often partners with a select group of grocery retailers—such as Stop & Shop and Wal-Mart—to create a store-within-a-store concept, the company won't set up shop in just any grocery store. "We want to be situated in supermarkets that provide a superior overall customer experience," he said. "Of course, we also want to ensure that the supermarket is large enough to allow us to provide the full expression of our brand . . . which includes hot and iced coffee, our line of high-quality espresso beverages, donuts, bagels, muffins, and even our breakfast sandwiches." Furthermore, the outlet's location within the supermarket is critical for a successful relationship. "We want to be accessible and visible to customers, because we feel that gives us the best chance to increase incremental traffic and help the supermarket to enhance their overall performance," Fassak said.

But why stop at grocery stores? Taking this philosophy a step further, Dunkin' Donuts has also entered the lodging market with their first hotel restaurant at the Great Wolf Lodge® in Concord, North Carolina—one of North America's largest indoor water parks. Dunkin' Donuts offers a variety of store models to suit any lodging property, including full retail shops, kiosks, and self-serve hot coffee stations perfect for gift shops and general stores, snack bars, and convention registration areas.[11] Who knows where they'll pop up next?

The launch into the lodging market coincides with Dunkin' Donuts' worldwide expansion program. Steadily and strategically expanding, Dunkin' Donuts unveiled the brand's first-ever theme park restaurant at Hershey Park, new coffee kiosks at sporting venues such as Fenway Park, Yankee Stadium, and the TD Banknorth (Boston) Garden, and new stores at airports including Boston, Dallas-Fort Worth, and New York City.[12]

The company is banking on these mutually beneficial partnerships to help it achieve widespread marketplace prominence. Dunkin' Donuts is a nationally known brand with a long reputation for quality, giving the company the benefit of not having to work hard to earn many customers' trust. And if Dunkin' Donuts can find the sweet spot by being within most consumers' reach while falling just short of a Big Brother-like omnipresence, the company's strategy of expansion may well reward it handsomely. But this strategy is not without its risks. In the quest to appeal to new customers, offering too many original products and placements could dilute the essential brand appeal and alienate long-time customers who respect simplicity and authenticity. On the other hand, new customers previously unexposed to Dunkin' Donuts might see it as "yesterday's brand."

If Dunkin' Donuts' executives focus too narrowly on franchising new stores, they might not be aware of issues developing in long-standing or even recently established stores. Some older franchises seem long overdue for a makeover, especially when compared to the Starbucks down the block. To combat the perception that many of Dunkin' Donuts' stores are outdated, the company unveiled a new prototype restaurant design in Pawtucket, Rhode Island providing a glimpse into the future look and feel of the brand. The contemporary design includes retro elements inspired by the very first shop built in 1950.[13]

Keeping up with the latest health concerns as well, it has reformulated its food and beverages according to its DDSMART criteria so that they meet at least one of these criteria: 25% fewer calories, or 25% less sugar, fat, saturated fat, or sodium than comparable fare.[14] The company has even begun shifting its donut production from individual stores into centralized production facilities designed to serve up to 100 stores apiece.

For the time being, Dunkin' Donuts seems determined in its quest for domination of the coffee and breakfast market. Will Dunkin' Donuts strike the *right* balance of products and placement needed to mount a formidable challenge against competitors?

CASE QUESTIONS

1. **DISCUSSION**—What does a Porter's Five Forces analysis reveal about the industry in which Dunkin' Donuts and Starbuck's compete, and what are its strategic implications for Dunkin' Donuts?

2. **DISCUSSION**—Is Dunkin' Donuts presently using strategic alliances to full advantage? How could cooperative strategies further assist with its master plan for growth?

3. **PROBLEM-SOLVING**—The Starbucks brand is known around the world, much more so than Dunkin' Donuts. As Dunkin's CEO, what global strategy—globalization, multidomestic, or transnational—would you follow to position Dunkin' as a real challenge to Starbucks in the international markets, and why?

4. **FURTHER RESEARCH**—Gather information on industry trends, as well as current developments with Dunkin' Donuts and its competitors. Use this information to build an up-to-date SWOT analysis for Dunkin' Donuts. Based on implications of this analysis, is Dunkin's top leadership doing the right things when it comes to strategic management, or not?

Nike is indisputably a giant in the athletics industry. But the Portland, Oregon, company has grown large precisely because it knows how to stay small. By focusing on its core competencies—and outsourcing all others—Nike has managed to become a sharply focused industry leader. But can it stay in front?

What Do You Call a Company of Thinkers?

It's not a joke or a Buddhist riddle. Rather, it's a conundrum about one of the most successful companies in the United States—a company known worldwide for its products, none of which it actually makes. This begs two questions: If you don't make anything, what do you actually do? If you outsource everything, what's left? A whole lot of brand recognition, for starters. Nike, famous for its trademark Swoosh[TM], is still among the most recognized brands in the world and is an industry leader in the $79 billion U.S. sports footwear and apparel market.[1] And its 33% market share dominates the global athletic shoe market.[2]

Since captivating the shoe-buying public in the early 1980s with legendary spokesperson Michael Jordan, Nike continues to outpace the athletic shoe competition while spreading its brand through an ever-widening universe of sports equipment, apparel, and paraphernalia. The ever-present Swoosh graces everything from bumper stickers to sunglasses to high school sports uniforms.

Not long after Nike's introduction of Air Jordans, the first strains of the "Just Do It" ad campaign sealed the company's reputation as a megabrand. When Nike made the strategic image shift from simply selling products to embodying a love of sport, discipline, ambition, practice, and all other desirable traits of athleticism, it became among the first in a long line of brands to represent itself as aiding customers in their self-expression as part of its marketing strategy.

Advertising has played a large part in Nike's continued success. The largest seller of athletic footwear and apparel in the world, Nike recently spent $2.35 billion annually on advertising.[3] Portland ad agency Wieden & Kennedy has been instrumental in creating and perpetuating Nike's image—so much so that the agency has a large division in-house at Nike headquarters. This intimate relationship between the two companies allows the agency's creative designers to focus solely on Nike work and gives them unparalleled access to executives, researchers, and anyone else who might provide advertisers with their next inspiration for marketing greatness.

What's Left, Then?

Although Nike has cleverly kept its ad agency nestled close to home, it has relied on outsourcing many nonexecutive responsibilities in order to reduce overhead. It can be argued that Nike, recognizing that its core competency lies in the design—not the manufacturing—of shoes, was wise to transfer production overseas.

But Nike has taken outsourcing to a new level, barely producing any of its products in its own factories. All of its shoes, for instance, are made by subcontractors. Although this allocation of production hasn't hurt the quality of the shoes at all, it has challenged Nike's reputation among fair-trade critics.

After initial allegations of sweatshop labor surfaced at Nike-sponsored factories, the company tried to reach out and reason with its more moderate critics. But this approach failed, and Nike found itself in the unenviable position of trying to defend its outsourcing practices while withholding the location of its favored production shops from the competition.

Boldly, in a move designed to turn critics into converts, Nike posted information on its Web site detailing every one of the approximately 700 factories it uses to make shoes, apparel, and other sporting goods.[4] It released the data in conjunction with a comprehensive new corporate responsibility report summarizing the environmental and labor situations of its contract factories.[5]

"This is a significant step that will blow away the myth that companies can't release their factory names because it's proprietary information," said Charles Kernaghan, executive director of the National Labor Committee, a New York-based anti-sweatshop group that has been no friend to Nike over the years. "If Nike can do it, so can Wal-Mart and all the rest."[6]

Jordan Isn't Forever

Knowing that shoe sales alone wouldn't be enough to sustain continued growth, Nike decided, in a lateral move, to learn more about its customers' interests and involvement in sports, identifying what needs it might be able to fill. Nike's success in the running category, for example, was largely driven by the Apple iPod-linked Nike Plus, which now ranks as the world's largest running club. The technology not only motivates runners with music and tracking their pace, but it also uploads their times and distances into a global community of runners online, creating a social-networking innovation that lets runners race in different countries.[7]

Banking on the star power of its Swoosh, Nike has successfully branded apparel, sporting goods, sunglasses, and even an MP3 player made by Philips. Like many large companies who have found themselves at odds with the possible limitations of their brands, Nike realized that it would have to master the one-two punch: identifying new needs and supplying creative and desirable products to fill those needs.

In fitting with the times, Nike's VP of Global Design, John R. Hoke III, is encouraging his designers to develop environmentally sustainable designs.[8] This may come as a surprise to anyone who has ever thought about how much foam and plastic goes into the average Nike sneaker, but a corporate-wide mission called "Considered" has designers rethinking the materials used to put the spring in millions of steps. The company even launched a line of environmentally sustainable products under the same name, all of them built under the principle established in the Considered program. "I'm very passionate about this idea," Hoke said. "We are going to challenge ourselves to think a little bit differently about the way we create products."[9]

Nike first stepped into sustainability in 1993 when it began grinding up old shoes and donating the material and other scraps from the manufacturing process to builders of sports surfaces like tracks and basketball courts.[10] While the original program continues, the company has shifted from one of a kind initiatives to a long-term plan that will "achieve zero waste throughout the supply chain and have products and materials that can be continuously reused—no pre or post consumer waste."[11] In fact, when the world's greatest soccer players stepped on the field at the FIFA World Cup hosted by South Africa in 2010, many were wearing Nike jerseys made almost entirely from plastic bottles salvaged from landfills in Japan and Taiwan.[12]

Nipping at Nike's Heels

Despite Nike's success and retention of its market share, things haven't been a bed of roses in the past few years. When CEO Phil Knight decided to step down, he handed the reins to Bill Perez, former CEO of S.C. Johnson and Sons, who became the first outsider recruited for the executive tier since Nike's founding in 1968. But after barely a year with Perez on the job, Knight, who remained in the inner circle in his position as chairman of the board, decided Perez couldn't "get his arms around the company." Knight accepted Perez's resignation and promoted Mark Parker, a 27-year veteran who was then co-president of the Nike brand, as a replacement.[13]

And pressures are mounting from outside its Beaverton, Oregon, headquarters. German rival adidas drew a few strides closer to Nike when it purchased Reebok for approximately $3.8 billion.[14] Joining forces will collectively help the brands negotiate shelf space and other sales issues in American stores and will aid the adidas group in its price discussions with Asian manufacturers. With recent combined global sales of almost $15 billion,[15] the new supergroup of shoes isn't far off from Nike's $19.1 billion.[16]

According to Jon Hickey, senior vice president of sports and entertainment marketing for the ad agency Mullen, Nike has its "first real, legitimate threat since the '80s. There's no way either one would even approach Nike, much less overtake them, on their own." But now, adds Hickey, "Nike has to respond. This new, combined entity has a chance to make a run. Now, it's game on."[17]

But when faced with a challenge, Nike simply knocks its bat against its cleats and steps up to the plate. "Our focus is on growing our own business," said Nike spokesman Alan Marks. "Of course we're in a competitive business, but we win by staying focused on our strategies and our consumers. And from that perspective nothing has changed."[18]

Putting It All Together

Nike has balanced its immense size and tremendous pressures to remain successful by leveraging a decentralized corporate structure. Individual business centers—such as research, production, and marketing—are free to focus on their core competencies without worrying about the effects of corporate bloat.

A recent organizational change is part of a wider Nike restructuring that may result in an overall reduction of up to 5% of the company's workforce.[19] "This new model sharpens our consumer focus and will allow us to make faster decisions, with fewer management layers," said Charlie Denson, President of the Nike Brand.[20]

It looks like his plan may have worked: Shares of Nike jumped to an all time high in 2010. The company has found continued marketplace success by positioning itself not simply as a sneaker company but as a brand that fulfills the evolving needs of today's athletes. Will Nike continue to profit from its increasingly decentralized business model, or will it spread itself so thin that its competition will overtake it?

CASE QUESTIONS

1. **DISCUSSION**—When Nike CEO Phil Knight stepped down and handed the top job to Bill Perez, he stayed on as chairman of the board. In what ways could Knight's continued presence on the board have created an informal structure that prevented Perez from achieving full and complete leadership of Nike?

2. **DISCUSSION**—Given the problems Nike has had with sweatshop labor being used by some of its foreign contractors, are there parts of the firm that need to be run with a mechanistic rather than organic design? Give examples to support your answer.

3. **PROBLEM-SOLVING**—Do you understand the network structure? Draw one that Nike could use to gain efficiency in operations while still selling high quality and top design shoes?

4. **FURTHER RESEARCH**—Gather information on Nike's recent moves and accomplishments, and those of its rivals. Are the firms following the same strategies and using the same structures to support them? Or is one doing something quite different from the others? Based on what you learn, what do you predict for the future? Can Nike stay on top, or is some other firm destined to be the next industry leader?

Over a span of more than 30 years, Apple Computer paradoxically existed both as one of America's greatest business successes and as a company that sometimes failed to realize its potential. Apple Inc. ignited the personal computer industry in the 1970s,[1] bringing such behemoths as IBM and Digital Equipment almost to their knees; stagnated when a series of CEOs lost opportunities; and rebounded tremendously since the return of its cofounder and former CEO, Steve Jobs. The firm represents a fascinating microcosm of American business as it continues to leverage its strengths while reinventing itself.

Corporate History

The history of Apple Inc. is a history of passion, whether on the part of its founders, its employees, or its loyal users.[2] It was begun by a pair of Stevens who, from an early age, had an interest in electronics. Steven Wozniak and Steven Jobs initially put their skills to work at Hewlett Packard and Atari, respectively. But then Wozniak constructed his first personal computer—the Apple I—and, along with Jobs, created Apple Computer on April 1, 1976. Right from the start, Apple exhibited an extreme emphasis on new and innovative styling in its computer offerings. Jobs took a personal interest in the development of new products, including the Lisa and the first, now legendary, Macintosh, or "Mac."

The passion that Apple is so famous for was clearly evident in the design of the Mac. Project teams worked around the clock to develop the machine and its operating system, Mac OS. The use of graphical icons to create simplified user commands was an immensely popular alternative to the command-line structure of DOS found on IBM's first PCs. When Apple and IBM began to clash head-on in the personal computer market, Jobs recognized the threat and realized that it was time for Apple to "grow up" and be run in a more businesslike fashion. In early 1983, he persuaded John Sculley, at that time president of Pepsi-Cola, to join Apple as president. The two men clashed almost from the start, with Sculley eventually ousting Jobs from the company.

The launch of the Mac reinvigorated Apple's sales. However, by the 1990s, IBM PCs and clones were saturating the personal computer market. Furthermore, Microsoft launched Windows 3.0, a greatly improved version of the Wintel operating system, for use on IBM PCs and clones. Although in 1991 Apple had contemplated licensing its Mac operating system to other computer manufacturers, making it run on Intel-based machines, the idea was nixed by then chief operating officer Michael Spindler in a move that would ultimately give Windows the nod to dominate the market.

Innovative Design to the Rescue

Apple continued to rely on innovative design to remain competitive in the 1990s. It introduced the very popular PowerBook notebook computer line, as well as the unsuccessful Newton personal digital assistant. Sculley was forced out and replaced by Michael Spindler. He oversaw a number of innovations, including the PowerMac family—the first Macs based on the PowerPC chip, an extremely fast processor co-developed with IBM and Motorola. In addition, Apple finally licensed its operating system to a number of Mac-cloners, although never in significant numbers.

After a difficult time in the mid-1990s, Spindler was replaced with Gil Amelio, the former president of National Semiconductor. This set the stage for one of the most famous returns in corporate history.

Jobs's Return

After leaving Apple, Steven Jobs started NeXT computer, which produced an advanced personal computer with a sleek, innovative design. However, the computer, which entered the market late in the game and required proprietary software, never gained a large following. Jobs then cofounded the Pixar computer-animation studio, which coproduced a number of movies with Walt Disney Studios, including the *Toy Story Series, Monsters, Inc., Finding Nemo, Ratatouille*, and *Up*.[3] When Jobs was running Pixar and it was struggling, his cofounder Alvy Ray Smith says: "We should have failed, but Steve just wouldn't let it go."[4]

In late 1996, Apple purchased NeXT, and Jobs returned to Apple in an unofficial capacity as advisor to the president. When Amelio resigned, Jobs accepted the role of "interim CEO" of Apple Computer and wasted no time in making his return felt. He announced an alliance with Apple's former rival, Microsoft. In exchange for $150 million in Apple stock, Microsoft and Apple would share a five-year patent cross-license for their graphical interface operating systems. He revoked licenses allowing the production of Mac clones and started offering Macs over the Web through the Apple Store.

Beginning with the iMac and the iBook, its laptop cousin, Jobs has continually introduced a series of increasingly popular products that have captured the buying public's imagination. Upon their release, the iPod, MacBook, Apple TV, and iPhone instantly spawned imitators that mimicked the look of these products, but they couldn't duplicate Apple's acute ability to integrate design with usability. Once again, Apple became an industry innovator by introducing certifiably attractive—and powerful—consumer electronics products. Its recent successes have included growing to command approximately 35% of operating profits in the computer market and a 66% of the market share for computers priced over $1,000.[5] It also tends to earn more revenue per computer sold than its value-priced competitors. Apple's integrated hardware and software system make it the most valuable personal computer maker in the world.[6]

What Does the Future Hold?

Whenever critics argued that Apple should reinvent itself again, it did just that—and then some. Now it is setting standards with new corporate strategy, taking advantage of the explosion of personal electronic devices. In its first week, iTunes sold 1.5 million songs and captured 80% of the market share of legal music downloads. And now we're into new generation iPhones, wondering just what Apple will next bring to the market.

Casting an ominous shadow on the company was Steve Jobs' announcement in early 2009 of a six-month medical leave. True to his word, Jobs, a pancreatic cancer survivor, officially returned to work that summer following a liver transplant and months of speculation about his health and his future with the company he co-founded more than 30 years ago. While Jobs was on leave, Chief Operating Officer Tim Cook handled Apple's day-to-day operations. Some analysts thought Jobs might transition into an advisory role, focusing on products and strategy and Cook would formally become CEO. Collins Stewart analyst Ashok Kumar said investors were reassured that Jobs would be back at the helm of the company he helped resuscitate over the past decade, with successful products such as the iPod, iPhone, and the iPad.[7]

For most companies, such information is not crucial because they are not as closely associated with one person. But Apple may be an exception. Since he helped found Apple, Steve Jobs has been inextricably linked to the company and its brand.[8] And there was a lot of concern expressed over Apple's ability to stay on its creative course without Jobs at the helm.

Although able to quietly work miracles, Mr. Cook was not credited with the long-term vision or showmanship of Steve Jobs, who appears capable of peering around corners into the future of technology, and can whip crowds into a frenzy merely by taking something new out of his pocket.[9]

Well, as we all know, Jobs did come back, even though his health remained a concern. The stock markets greeted him with share price rises and consumers eagerly awaited Apple's next new product announcements. The "Jobs effect" was positive and evident, and that's due to his unique reputation.

The iPad Era and Beyond

In April 2010, the iPad was launched in the U.S. and sold 300,000 units on the first day; two million in the first two months.[10] The hype began four months earlier, when Apple began touting the iPad as a revolutionary device for browsing the Web, reading and sending email, enjoying photos, watching videos, listening to music, playing games, reading e-books and more. The iPad features a responsive high-resolution touch-screen which let users physically interact with applications and content.[11] Two things that you won't find, however, are Adobe's FlashPlayer or Google's advertisements, causing rifts, rivalries, and SEC involvement. Upon the announcement that the iPad wouldn't support Adobe Flash, Apple's share price dropped 3%.[12]

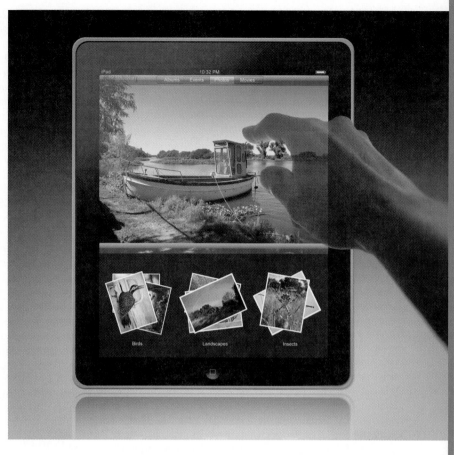

So let's look into the future. Will Steve Jobs' limitations on software developers create enough backlash to threaten the success of his new products? If Jobs is the key to Apple's achievements, how well can the firm do without him? And, what should Jobs himself be doing now to help prepare the firm for this eventuality?

CASE QUESTIONS

1. **DISCUSSION**—Apple sells stylish and functional computers as well as a variety of electronic devices, and it operates retail stores. How does Apple's organization culture help the firm keep its creative edge?

2. **DISCUSSION**—At this point in time, should Steve Jobs push transformational change, incremental change, or both?

3. **PROBLEM-SOLVING**—Leadership succession is a big question mark at Apple—at some point Steve Jobs will have to be replaced. If you were on Apple's board of directors, what personal qualities and skills would you want the next CEO to have, and why?

4. **FURTHER RESEARCH**—Review what the analysts are presently saying about Apple. Make a list of all of the praises and criticisms, organize them by themes, and then put them in the priority order for a change leadership agenda? What does Apple most have to fear in its quest for sustainable competitive advantage?

How is the company that revolutionized the way we rent movies reinventing itself? By making the movie-watching experience even more hassle-free. Netflix is utilizing superior customer service, emerging technologies, strategic partnerships, and an ever-growing subscriber base to transform the traditional video-rental model into a 21st-century on-demand concept.

No More Waiting

For only $8.99 a month, Netflix's 12 million customers can instantly watch any of its 17,000 movies and TV episodes streamed to their TVs and computers and can also receive any of its 100,000 titles delivered quickly to their homes. Netflix members can exchange DVDs as often as they want using a postage-paid return envelope.[1] There are never any due dates or late fees. Everything is hassle-free and picture perfect!

Netflix was founded in 1997 and has truly revolutionized the way we rent movies. It launched its online subscription service in 1999 and has now become the world's largest online movie rental service. The company has more than 55 million discs and, on average, ships 1.9 million DVDs to customers each day.[2] On February 25, 2007, Netflix announced its billionth DVD delivery.[3] Two years later, on April 2, 2009, the company announced that it had mailed its two billionth DVD. The company recently announced the availability of a free Netflix app for the iPhone and iPad allowing users to instantly watch TV episodes and movies.[4] The company is experiencing amazing growth in subscribers and revenues. For fiscal year 2009, revenues exceeded $1.6 billion with net income rising above $123.5 million.[5]

Keys to Success

What accounts for Netflix's success? Co-founder and CEO Reed Hastings believes the key to the sustained growth of the Los Gatos, California-based company is no secret at all—it thrives and stays ahead of competitors because of its renowned customer service.[6] Beating out such heavyweight competition as Amazon, Apple, and Target, Netflix was crowned Number 1 in online retail customer satisfaction by independent surveys from Nielsen Online as well as in nine consecutive surveys by ForeSee/FGI Research.

Netflix's continued focus on providing customers with what they want allows the company to differentiate itself from the competition. More than 97% of Netflix's subscribers live within one day of delivery from the company's 58 distribution centers or 50 shipping points.[7] For example, Netflix has seven shipping centers in Florida, six in California, and six in the state of New York. Netflix even provides customers with movie recommendations based on the customer's own reviews, renting habits, and location. A Netflix subscriber can check to see what movies and television programs are popular in their town.

Another key success factor for Netflix has been the quick adoption of emerging technology and the formation of strategic partnerships. According to Hastings, "Netflix's differentiated service, which combines DVDs delivered quickly by mail and movies streamed instantly over the Internet, is a key element driving our growth."[8]

In order to accomplish this, Netflix has partnered with consumer electronics companies to bring to market a range of devices that can instantly stream movies and TV episodes from Netflix directly to members' TVs. These devices currently include Blu-ray disc players and new Internet TVs from LG Electronics; Blu-ray disc players from Samsung; the Roku digital video player (a palm-sized box to set on top of a TV); Microsoft's Xbox 360 game console; TiVo digital video recorders; and, soon, Internet TVs from Sony and VIZIO.[9] Netflix is even shipping instant streaming discs for the Wii enabling viewers to catch their favorite TV episodes and movies on their Wii consoles.[10]

Putting People First

But has Netflix's ability to attract and retain a dynamic, high-performance workforce also been an important factor that has propelled the company to such success?

Yes, in order to succeed in this business, Hastings is betting as much on people as he is on technology and his business vision. The company does not act like other large employers when it comes to its human resources management and culture. Instead, Netflix has created a very interesting organizational culture based on freedom and responsibility, innovation, and self-discipline.[11]

Patty McCord, Netflix's chief talent officer, understands that deftly managing the talent mix at Netflix is paramount to the success of the company.[12] Netflix is committed to hiring and retaining the best talent in the industry. One of their recruitment and retention practices is to pay top salaries. Netflix believes that one outstanding employee does more and costs less than two adequate performers. Thus they pay at the top of the market and strive to hire only outstanding employees.[13]

Interestingly, pay isn't linked with performance in the sense of annual "merit" reviews. Annual compensation reviews are market-based as well. Salaries are pegged to job markets to ensure that Netflix's pay packages are always the best around.

Freedom with Accountability

If you are identified as a top performer, you get top salary and are given the freedom to put your talents to work making Netflix's strategy successful. But if you're something less than a top performer, say just "average," there isn't room at the company. "At most companies," says Hastings, "average performers get an average raise. At Netflix they get a generous severance package."[14]

The Netflix focus on large salaries is coupled with the freedom to spend it as employees think it is best. Employees choose how much of their compensation is paid in cash and how much in stock or stock options.

Flexibility Rules a Productive Work Environment

Netflix not only hires carefully, it offers a unique and highly productive work environment rich in features that appeal to today's high-tech and high-talent workers. They believe in freedom and responsibility, not rules. Since 2004 Netflix has not had a vacation policy. Instead, the company encourages employees to take time off when they need to.[15] Similarly, they do not have a 9-to-5 work schedule but measure people by how much, how quickly, and how well they get their work done, not by how many evenings or weekends they are in their cube.[16]

Netflix has a lot riding on its human resource strategy. Will it continue to pay off?

CASE QUESTIONS

1. **DISCUSSION**—What are the limitations and risks of Netflix's human resource management practices?

2. **DISCUSSION**—What performance appraisal methods would be most consistent with the organizational culture surrounding Netflix's HRM practices?

3. **PROBLEM-SOLVING**—Could you work for Netflix? Write a letter of application for a full-time position with the firm. What can you say in this letter that shows why you will perform well under Netfilx's unique HRM practices?

4. **FURTHER RESEARCH**—Check up on Hastings and Netflix. How is the firm doing right now? How has it changed since the case information was prepared? Are the human resource management practices described here still active at the firm? What else is Netflix doing to create human capital for sustained competitive advantage?

To say that the airline industry has had problems is an understatement. The largest carriers have lost billions of dollars. But Southwest Airlines has weathered the financial storm better than its rivals. How did a little airline get so big and do so well? Its success springs from its core values, developed by Herb Kelleher, cofounder and former CEO, and embraced daily by the company's 35,000 employees: humor, altruism, and "LUV" (the company's NYSE stock ticker symbol).[1]

Unique Character and Success

One thing that makes Southwest Airlines unique is its short-haul focus. The airline does not assign seats; tickets are mostly bought online, with prices varying by how far ahead the flight is booked. The only foods served are snacks, but passengers don't seem to mind. Serving Customers (always written at Southwest with a capital C) is the focus of the company's employees. When Colleen Barrett, until recently Southwest's president and chief operating officer (COO), was the executive vice president for customers, she said, "We will never jump on employees for leaning too far toward the customer, but we come down on them hard for not using common sense."[2] Southwest's core values produce highly motivated employees who care about customers and each other.

At Southwest Airlines, they believe that low costs are crucial, change is inevitable, innovation is necessary, and leadership is essential—particularly during troubling economic times. "Our competitors take drastic/short-sighted measures to compete with us on the price level . . . They make draconian reductions in their employees' salaries, wages, benefits, and pensions. In doing so, they ultimately sacrifice their most important assets—their employees and their employees' goodwill."[3]

The recent merger of United-Continental has put Southwest on a path to increase their services as well as their profits as United-Continental will lease slots to Southwest as a condition of the Department of Justice's approval of the merger.[4]

Southwest applies this philosophy in an organizational culture that respects employees and their ideas. As executive vice president, Colleen Barrett started a "culture committee" made up of employees from different functional areas and levels. The committee meets quarterly to brainstorm ideas for maintaining Southwest's corporate spirit and image. All managers, officers, and directors are expected to "get out in the field," meeting and talking with employees to understand their jobs. Employees are encouraged to use their creativity and sense of humor to make their jobs, and the customers' experiences, more enjoyable. Gate agents are given books of games to play with passengers waiting for delayed flights. Flight agents might imitate Elvis or Mr. Rogers when making announcements.[5]

The "Luv" Factor

Kelleher, currently chairman emeritus of the board, knows that not everyone would be happy as a Southwest employee: "What we are looking for, first and foremost, is a sense of humor. Then we are looking for people who have to excel to satisfy themselves and who work well in a collegial environment."

To encourage employees to treat one another as well as they treat their customers, departments examine linkages within Southwest to see what their "internal customers" need. The provisioning department, for example, whose responsibility is to provide the snacks and drinks for each flight, selects a flight attendant as "customer of the month." The provisioning department's own board of directors makes the selection decision.

Other departments have sent pizza and ice cream to their internal customers. Employees write letters commending the work of other employees or departments that are valued as much as letters from external customers. When problems occur between departments, employees work out solutions in supervised meetings.

Employees exhibit the same attitude of altruism and "luv" (also Southwest's term for its relationship with its customers) toward other groups as well. It is the job of Fred Taylor, also known as the Chief Apology Officer, and his staff to learn about a situation where something went wrong during a flight, and then apologize to passengers as quickly as possible.[6] A significant portion of Southwest employees volunteer at Ronald McDonald Houses throughout Southwest's service territory.[7] When the company purchased a small regional airline, employees sent cards and company T-shirts to their new colleagues to welcome them into the Southwest family.

Profits to Share

For the thirty-seventh consecutive year, Southwest has posted a profit. Acting in the company's best interests is also directly in the interest of the employees. Southwest has a profit-sharing plan for all eligible employees—and, unlike many of its competitors, Southwest consistently has profits to share. Employees can also purchase Southwest stock at 90% of market value; employees now own about 8% of the total company stock. Although approximately 83% of employees are unionized, the company has a history of good labor relations.[8]

Southwest Airlines is a low-cost operator. But, according to Harvard University professor John Kotter, setting the standard for low costs in the airline industry does not mean Southwest is *cheap*. "Cheap is trying to get your prices down by nibbling costs off everything . . . [Firms such as Southwest Airlines] are thinking 'efficient,' which is very different. . . . They recognize that you don't necessarily have to take a few pennies off of everything. Sometimes you might even spend more."[9] By using only one type of plane in its fleet, Southwest saves on pilot training and aircraft maintenance costs.[10] The *cheap* paradigm would favor used planes, but Southwest's choice for high productivity over lower capital expenditures has given it the youngest fleet of aircraft in the industry.

By using each plane almost 12 hours daily, Southwest is also able to make more trips with fewer planes than any other airline. It has won the monthly "Triple Crown" distinction—Best On-Time Record, Best Baggage Handling, and Fewest Customer Complaints—more than 30 times.

Sometimes the Voyage Is Better than the Destination

Despite its impressive record of success, Southwest Airlines has pressing concerns to address. Management worries about the effects that limited promotion opportunities will have on morale. The company has created "job families" with different grade levels so that employees can work their way up within their job. But after five or six years, employees still begin to hit the maximum compensation level for their job. Another issue is maintaining the culture of caring and fun while expanding rapidly into new markets. Southwest's success has been built with the enthusiasm and hard work of its employees. As Kelleher has said, "The people who work here don't think of Southwest as a business. They think of it as a crusade."[11] Cultivating that atmosphere is a continuing company priority.

From its roots as a regional Texan carrier, Southwest Airlines has grown into one of the most profitable—and most beloved—airlines in American history. The company has created employee satisfaction by focusing on its internal "Customers," who are then positively motivated to show the same degree of concern for external customers. Southwest's perpetual profitability stems not from miserliness but from attention to value and sensible cost savings.

As Colleen Barrett wrote in the company's *Spirit Magazine*: ". . . our steadfast determination remains unbroken to provide the high-spirited Customer Service, low fares, and frequent nonstop flights that Americans want and need."[12] Southwest Airlines continues to be recognized by *Fortune* magazine as America's most admired airline and one of the most admired companies in America.

Leadership Transitions

When Herb Kelleher relinquished his role as Southwest's CEO, investors worried, because so much of Southwest's success came from Kelleher's unique management and leadership. But events showed that Kelleher's successor, Colleen Barrett, was well prepared to handle the challenges of maintaining Southwest's culture and success. Now, Barrett has retired and 23-year employee of the firm, Gary Kelley, has taken the helm.

Kelley is now navigating Southwest Airlines through one of the industry's most turbulent periods by expanding into new markets, adding flights to heavily trafficked domestic airports, and seeking cross-border alliances with foreign carriers. The airline has remained steadfast against charging customers for checking in suitcases and using pillows, as competitors have done. Some analysts question if management has made the right call by not charging for these services, which are generating hundreds of millions of dollars for rivals.[13]

As fuel prices climb and airlines consolidate for security, can Kelley keep Southwest ahead of the airline pack?

CASE QUESTIONS

1. **DISCUSSION**—Does the history of Southwest Airlines indicate that Herb Kelleher was a visionary leader, a servant leader, or both? Why?

2. **DISCUSSION**—What leadership style or styles predominate at Southwest Airlines, and how has this influenced the firm's organizational culture and management practices?

3. **PROBLEM-SOLVING**—Has Southwest Airlines reached the point where something "new" is needed by and from its top leadership? From all the theories, models, and insights of this chapter, what is the best advice you can give Gary Kelley as a guide for successfully following Kelleher and Barrett to lead Southwest today?

4. **FURTHER RESEARCH**—Gary Kelley has had time to bring his personal leadership to Southwest Airlines. But, he has certainly faced some trying times with the economic recession. How well is Kelley doing? Has he demonstrated that he has what it takes to lead Southwest to future success in the turbulent environment of the airline industry?

Social networking web sites are a dime a dozen these days, so how does Facebook stay at the top? By expanding its user base and working with developers and advertisers to create fresh content that keeps users at the site for hours on end. But can Facebook handle the challenges of international expansion and stereotypes about its leadership?

Perception Counts

Mark Zuckerberg wants you to think differently about Facebook. Unlike most other young Silicon Valley CEOs, he's got experience in managing the kind of changes in perception he hopes to bring about. In 2006 he opened Facebook to users of all ages to convince advertisers—and developers—that social networking was more than kids' stuff. Zuckerberg hopes to persuade these same two groups that Facebook is firmly seated at the top and successfully expanding into global markets.

Although users of Facebook and its social networking rival MySpace might trade barbs over whose site has the best features or the widest selection of friends, there's no denying that Facebook has been a runaway success. It is the fourth-most-trafficked site on the Web, according to Internet research company comScore; it is also the most popular social networking site, having usurped that honor from MySpace. Facebook now accounts for 6% of all time spent online In the U.S.[1]

Applications for Every User

Regardless of age or profession, what keeps users coming back to Facebook? The site relies on a host of internally and externally developed applications that integrate directly into the site to keep visitors' eyes glued to Facebook for hours on end. Games and a bevy of trivia contests give users entertaining ways to engage repeatedly with each other.

Commercial marketers are taking note more closely than ever of Facebook's propensity for attracting page views, hoping to benefit from the halo effect surrounding such a successful brand. Companies are integrating their logos and brands into Facebook's built-in culture of sharing and sending. Users can send one another a Wal-Mart–branded ghost, a Ben & Jerry's ice cream cone, virtual birthday bouquets, or even their dream cars. According to Derek Dabrowski, Sunkist brand manager at Dr. Pepper Snapple Group, it's a success. In a promotion to give away 250,000 virtual Sunkist sodas: "We got 130 million brand impressions through that 22-hour time frame. A Super Bowl ad, if you compare it, would have generated somewhere between 6 to 7 million."

More Growth

Facebook sees the bleak economy as reason to press ahead with its plans for aggressive growth. The company is gearing up for more acquisitions, hiring rapidly, and rolling out new advertising programs. Moving beyond traditional online ads—the text and pictorial banners that show up on most Web sites—they believe that they can stand out among the crowd. Facebook began rolling out "engagement ads" encouraging users to respond to the pitches by commenting, sharing virtual gifts, or becoming fans of the ads themselves. Facebook's online advertising accounts for an esti-mated \$200–225 million in revenue, and its digital goods sell for \$1 apiece–generating another \$30–40 million.[2]

But the best potential for amassing page views and click-throughs lies in Facebook's ability to integrate applications. The site's photo viewing app, for example–the number-one photo sharing application on the Web–receives more than 3 billion photos uploaded to the site each month. Some 1,000,000 developers and entrepreneurs from over 180 countries are involved in developing the Facebook Platform. More than 500,000 apps have been developed so far.[3] More than 95% of its members have used at least one application built on the Facebook Platform, and advertisers are betting that they can improve that statistic.[4]

Bet on Advertising

As much as advertisers need Facebook users' page views, Facebook needs those advertisers as loyal customers to make money. A privately held company, Facebook declines to disclose its financials. However, last year board member Marc Andreeson predicted the company would break the \$500 million mark and said that it has the potential to be a billion-dollar company already but that it is acting conservatively.

Rather than use banner advertisements, Facebook is choosing to experiment with "engagement ads" which are "smarter" and integrated into the social-networking experience. When a woman changes her relationship status to "engaged," for example, her Facebook page will likely include advertisements for bridal salons, beauty products, and gyms. Putting "pizza" in a status message can instantly turn up an ad for online-ordering company Seamless Web accompanied by a photo of a pizza.

The Facebook "fan page" and complementary ad space to promote it are the hottest ticket in brand marketing right now. They won't always be, and Facebook will have to maintain that front-runner status in plenty of advertising innovations down the road as the industry evolves faster than ever.[5] Facebook's strategic partnership with PayPal makes it quicker and easier to run campaigns on Facebook, especially for small and international companies. However, the pressure is on Facebook to continue to differentiate itself from other social networking sites, according to Jeff Ratner, a managing partner at WPP's MindShare Interaction. If not, "Facebook doesn't look that different," he said. "It just becomes another buy, and there are cheaper, more efficient ways to reach eyes."[6]

Changing Perceptions

On several occasions during his reign at Facebook, the youthful Zuckerberg has fought the common Silicon Valley stereotype of young CEOs who are brash and unripe to lead. His flat rejection of Yahoo!'s \$1 billion bid to buy Facebook was criticized by some as a lost opportunity, so he's working to create a professional impression for his company by hiring some experienced Web personalities. Zuckerberg persuaded Sheryl Sandberg to leave Google, where she had developed cash cows Adwords and Adsense, to join Facebook as chief operating officer. Fourteen years older than her boss, Sandberg is charged with bringing a mature personality to the laid-back, collegiate work environment. To do this, she's integrated performance reviews, refined the recruiting model, and developed a mature, sustainable advertising program that will support Facebook as it evolves. "I'm hopeful that we play a significant role in pushing the envelope [with] awareness building," Sandberg said.[7]

Noting that visitors to the site tripled after Facebook unveiled its international presence, the company is continuing its international growth.[8] Facebook has translated its content into 70 different languages. This is critical, because more than 70% of Facebook's 400 million users live outside the United States[9]— double MySpace's percentage. Whereas MySpace specializes in locally themed subsites, Facebook has opted to simply translate its entire site for non-English speakers. "Through the translations we are seeing mass adoption in those markets," said Javier Olivan, an international manager at Facebook, adding that because the site is by its nature a tool for communication, Facebook doesn't need to spend much energy localizing it. "The translation approach allows us to support literally every language in the world," Olivan said.[10]

And to head off the efforts of other social networking sites, Facebook makes data available to users from outside of the site with its Facebook Connect program. Like MySpace's Data Availability (which was announced one day before Facebook's data-sharing concept), Facebook Connect allows users to import their Facebook profiles into other Web sites and synchronize their friend lists. Changes appear in real time as users modify their Facebook profiles, and users have "total control" of Web site permissions to access Facebook data, according to the company.[11] But will the new social networking site, Tumblr, which has been described as "a space between Twitter and Facebook," attract a younger crowd looking for a hipper place to socialize? Tumblr allows users to upload images, videos, audio clips and quotes to user's pages in addition to bursts of text.[12,13]

With its hundreds of millions of users and dollars, you would think Facebook was worry free. But controversy continues to follow the company. Complaints range from erosion of privacy and cyber-bullying, to susceptibility of worms and viruses.

What Do You Think?

Despite all of its successes, the management team of Facebook knows that they have serious work ahead in order to change the perception of advertisers, developers, and even some users regarding their ability to lead Facebook successfully and profitably into the future of social networking. Will adding experienced management alter advertisers' stereotypes about youthful Silicon Valley CEOs? Can Facebook overcome the bad impression being communicated by some disgruntled users?

To add insult to injury, *The Social Network,* a movie about Facebook's controversial founding, recently hit theaters. Based on the book, *The Accidental Billionaires* by Ben Mezrich, it describes Zuckerberg in less than flattering terms.[14] What does Zuckerberg think about the movie? "Honestly, I wish that when people tried to do journalism or write stuff about Facebook, they at least try to get it right," said Zuckerberg. He called the book the movie was based on a work of "fiction."[15]

CASE QUESTIONS

1. **DISCUSSION**—In what ways can attribution error cause problems for Mark Zuckerberg as he wrestles with decisions that will determine the future of Facebook?

2. **DISCUSSION**—What personality types does Facebook most appeal to, and how does that affect its potential to broaden and diversify its user base?

3. **PROBLEM-SOLVING**—Sheryl Sandberg is under pressure to bring a mature edge to Facebook. What are the most significant challenges that she faces when communicating with her "young" boss and the firm's "younger" workforce? How might she best deal with them?

4. **FURTHER RESEARCH**—Find as much information as you can about Mark Zuckerberg. Does he have what it takes to lead Facebook at this stage in its life? Use the Big Five Model to analyze his personality. How has his personality influenced, positively and negatively, his behavior as founder and CEO of Facebook?

Sampson Davis, George Jenkins, and Rameck Hunt discovered early in their friendship that they shared one disturbing trait: As children, they had to navigate life in crime-infested, inner-city Newark without a father's support and guidance. While each young man dealt with the turmoil caused by an absent father, with no male role model to turn to for advice, each veered dangerously close to a life of delinquency and crime. Despite great odds, the three overcame the statistics. In high school, they formed the Pact, promising one another that they would become doctors. It kept them dedicated to one another and to their dream, and it helped put them on the road to successful careers as physicians.[1] Along the way they made mistakes and faced disappointments, but by working hard, finding the right mentors, separating themselves from negative influences, and supporting each other, they achieved their goals—and more.[2]

Starting Out

In 1975, two years after the three doctors were born, *Harper's* analyzed the 50 largest cities and declared that Newark, New Jersey, "stands without serious challenge as worst of all." Although the downtown area was undergoing what officials called a "renaissance," Newark remained one of the most violent cities in the United States. Per capita, its murder rate was three times higher than New York's.[3]

At 16 years of age, Rameck Hunt had an altercation with a crack-addict and was arrested for assault. In his jail cell that day, Rameck discovered his fear of confinement and vowed that it would never happen again.[4] He recalls "I was in a lot of trouble as a youngster because I had no course for my life. I made many mistakes but eventually learned from them and recognized what I needed to achieve; something different than what I was exposed to—determination and direction." He found that direction with his two friends, George Jenkins and Sampson Davis.[5]

Rameck, Sampson, and George could easily have followed their childhood friends into drug dealing, gangs, and prison. Like their peers, they came from poor, single-parent homes in the urban neighborhoods of Newark where survival, not scholastic success, was the priority. When the three boys met in a magnet high school, they recognized each other as kindred spirits who wanted to overcome the incredible odds against them and reach for opportunity.[6]

Making a Pact

During their senior year of high school the boys cut class to play basketball but were discovered by the principal and a security guard. They fled into the library where Seton Hall University was holding a seminar about careers in health and science. Each young man knew he wanted more out of life and paid attention. Soon after, they made a pact: They would stick together, go to college, graduate, and become doctors. Surrounded by negative influences and having few positive role models made this a difficult endeavor.[7] Together they found the courage to try.

Determined not to become victims of their environment, the trio stood firm in their mission. Today, Dr. Rameck Hunt is a Board-certified internist at University Medical Center at Princeton and assistant professor of medicine at Robert Wood Johnson Medical School. Dr. George Jenkins serves as assistant professor of clinical dentistry at Columbia University. Dr. Sampson Davis is a Board-certified emergency medicine physician at St. Michaels Medical Center and Raritan Bay Medical Center. Davis is also consultant for the Violence Prevention Institute focusing on gang awareness and preventative medicine in Essex County.[8]

Collectively, they became one of the most remarkable success stories of inspiration, dedication, and determination. Dr. Davis asserts, "Strength comes from knowing that the power to overcome adversity and prevail lies within one's self and you have to first realize that. Once realized, you have to accept accountability for your life and take the necessary steps to turn hopes and dreams into realities."[9]

Giving Back

Upon completion of medical and dentistry school, the group initiated their second pact: to give back to their communities, not only in Newark but also across the country. They created The Three Doctors Foundation whose mission is to inspire and motivate youth through education, and achieve leadership and career success in their community through the formation of positive peer and mentor relationships. The Three Doctors Foundation stands on the premise that "Our Children Can Not Aspire to Be What They Can Not See."[10]

Their vision is to serve as positive role models for inner-city youths and families across the nation utilizing their experience, status, and programs as platforms to encourage community development, volunteerism, and leadership. They empower community members to improve the quality of life for themselves and others. Promoting respect and diversity, the three doctors act as advocates for the underprivileged. The Three Doctors Foundation also provides financial assistance and overall support to help individuals in attaining their goals.[11]

The doctors are active participants in the Foundation's activities, including a walkathon for Sickle Cell awareness; a Mentor Day that offers career and educational enrichment for more than 300 children in grades 6 through 12; and a Holiday Spirit of Giving community basketball event. The three doctors were recognized with a Community Humanitarian Honor at the BET Awards in 2009.[12]

Spreading Hope

Although each is successful in his own right, the trio is fondly and collectively known as "The Three Doctors." Davis, Jenkins, and Hunt tour the country as motivational speakers, serving as extraordinary models of leadership for anyone who's been through challenges or hardships. Knowing at first hand the pressures and struggles of life in the inner city, and how difficult it can be going it alone, enables them to speak authentically and in relatable terms. Dr Hunt explains, "We have a compelling passion for speaking and telling our story. This is not to boast or brag, we just recognize that we are in head-to-head combat with drugs, mental and physical illnesses, teenage pregnancy and all kinds of abuse and we accept the responsibility of making a difference by being role models and touching lives."[13]

Doctors George Jenkins, Rameck Hunt, and Sampson Davis deliver well-needed and urgent messages of hope and inspiration everywhere they go. *"Never underestimate the power of self-reliance and inner strength. Attach a timeline & devise a strategy for achieving your goals. Surround yourself with like-minded people who are in line with your aspirations."*[14]

Their effect on their communities has indeed been tremendous. The Three Doctors received the prestigious Essence Award for their accomplishments and leadership. In addition to their award, their groundbreaking television special aired on Lifetime Television during a special segment entitled *"Things We Do for Love."*[15]

Their books, *The Pact: Three Young Men Make a Promise and Fulfill a Dream* and *We Beat the Streets*, were *New York Times* Best Sellers. *The Pact* is being used at high schools, colleges, and universities all over the country. The book motivates young people who feel that they have come to the end of possibility, offers encouragement to those who need a boost, and blends perfectly with others who feel they are on the right path. "Their life is like a social study," one professor commented. "Children can identify with them, adults, and at-risk teens—everybody."[16]

In their latest book, *The Bond: Three Young Men Learn to Forgive and Reconnect with Their Fathers*, the trio has again turned their fatherless childhoods into an opportunity to inspire others and heal themselves.[17] To reach an even younger and wider audience, a cartoon has also been made based on their lives. The Pact Power Kids are the cartoon characters who wonderfully mirror the positive image of Drs. Davis, Hunt, and Jenkins. The illustrated characters engage in fun and exciting adventures to show younger audiences the importance of health, education, and even the positive aspects of peer pressure.[18]

Bill Cosby emphasized the value these men bring to their communities, saying, "They are an inspiration to young people everywhere, and their message is one that can transform the world." This assessment is further supported by their inclusion in *Essence: 50 of The Most Inspiring African Americans*, a book published by *Essence Magazine*. In 2007, Oprah Winfrey featured them on her show and remarked—"You guys are bigger than Rock Stars!" She then added, "I think you guys are the premier role models of the world!"[19]

The Three Doctors are visionaries who bring hope with them wherever they go. They are among the most sought-after motivational speakers, spreading their inspirational messages across the country. They are frequently asked their formula for becoming prominent, successful men, and doctors at that, and while their lists are long, Drs. Jenkins, Hunt, and Davis are certain that success comes in many different forms.[20]

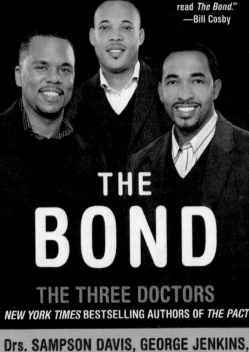

Three Young Men Learn to Forgive and Reconnect with Their Fathers

"Every parent should read *The Bond*."
—Bill Cosby

THE BOND
THE THREE DOCTORS
NEW YORK TIMES BESTSELLING AUTHORS OF *THE PACT*

Drs. SAMPSON DAVIS, GEORGE JENKINS, and RAMECK HUNT
with Margaret Bernstein

CASE QUESTIONS

1. DISCUSSION—Choose two needs theories. How do they explain what motivated the childhood behavior of Davis, Hunt, and Jenkins—both on the positive and negative sides?

2. DISCUSSION—How can the expectancy theory of motivation help explain the success of these men?

3. PROBLEM-SOLVING—Can you turn the Three Doctors story into a positive reinforcement strategy to help problem youth in one of your local schools? What would this program look like? How would it put reinforcement principles to best use in reducing problem behavior by these young people?

4. FURTHER RESEARCH—The Three Doctors Foundation is set up to inspire and empower inner-city youth. What are its current programs and priorities? Is it staying true to the hopes of the doctors? What's new in the "Three Doctors" story? And, what are the possible lessons for dealing with the youth in our communities?

By only his second full year of NASCAR Winston Cup Series racing, the young Ryan Newman was rapidly becoming a racing phenomenon. He has since had spectacular consecutive racing seasons, including winning the Daytona 500. What accounts for the success of a top NASCAR driver?

Racing Passion

In a sport that measures victory in hundredths of a second, NASCAR drivers need every competitive edge they can get. But after years of growth, NASCAR is experiencing a decline in interest and attendance. How will this recent challenge affect NASCAR's young, talented drivers? Will NASCAR be able to restart its engine? Ryan Newman, one of today's most successful NASCAR drivers, claims a unique advantage among his racing peers: his education.[1] Ryan graduated from Purdue University with a degree in vehicle structural engineering. He studied part-time while driving race cars. And did it make a difference? The season he graduated, Ryan earned almost $500,000 in NASCAR winnings. One year later, he'd earned nearly ten times as much.

A self-admitted car buff, Ryan Newman loves to drive cars and work on them.[2] His passion for fast cars developed at an early age. Encouraged by his parents, he started racing quarter midgets when he was only four-and-a-half years old. Newman amassed more than 100 midget car victories. Later he raced midget cars and sprint cars, achieving extraordinary success there as well.[3]

Mentored at NASCAR

When Newman joined the Penske Racing Team, the co-owners hired Buddy Baker, a former top race car driver, to work with Newman. Being very selective about the drivers he works with, Baker insisted on meeting Newman and his family before accepting the job offer. Baker says: "When I started talking to Ryan, I could feel the energy that he had, and the passion he had for the sport. Then, I met his dad, and right there I knew, OK, he's got a good background. His father's been with him in go-carts, midgets. He turned the wrenches for his son. It was an automatic fit for me."

Baker thinks of Newman as though he were one of his own sons, both of whom briefly tried racing but neither of whom had a passion for it. Baker says that he never wanted to do anything but race, and Newman is just like him. Referring to Newman, Baker says: "From the time he was 5 years old until now, he's never wanted to be anything else."[4]

Racing with a Team

About his pre-Winston Cup racing days, Newman says: "I always worked on my own cars and maintained them, did the set-ups, things like that. Obviously, I also drove them so I was always a hands-on, involved, seat of the pants driver." As a Winston Cup driver, Newman acknowledges that he "misses working on the cars, but when you have great guys doing that work, you don't feel like you have to do it yourself."[5]

"For all my life, my family has been my crew," Newman also says. "To come to an organization like Penske, and have so many more people behind you fighting for the same goals, it's like being in a bigger family. When you're with people you like, you have the confidence to do things well."[6] Most of the people who work on Newman's crew are engineers, and all of them are computer whizzes—significant talents for building and maintaining today's race cars.[7]

Newman and the crew try to learn from the problem situations that they encounter so they can "keep the freak things from happening."[8] Newman asserts that his racing team does the best job it can with what they have. "When there's an opportunity to try and stretch it to the end, we're going to try to stretch to the end," says Newman.[9] He enters every race with the attitude that he can and will win it.[10]

Career on the Move

Unfortunately you can't win them all. After years of drought, Newman won the Daytona 500 in 2008 and decided to leave the Penske racing team. "For me, coming to Stewart-Haas Racing is a great opportunity," Newman said. "I had seen the shop and the backbone, the foundation that Haas had laid with their efforts. When I talked to Tony [Stewart] and his people, I knew immediately that it was the best place for me for the right reasons."[11]

High-Performance Team Building

Although great teams can be inherited, they don't happen by chance. Instead, they're the result of good recruiting, meticulous attention to learning every detail of the job, and must be maintained. As good as the Stewart-Haas racing team was, there was still room for improvement. Ryan Newman's crew chief Tony Gibson said the team focused on pit stops, where it felt it lost possible victories. April 2010 was Newman's first Sprint Cup victory since he won the Daytona 500, and it validated just how far the second-year team had come since it was formed. Communication and teamwork were instrumental to the victory, according to Gibson. "We have chemistry," seconds Newman. "We have time together. We have an understanding of attitudes and personalities, which is a big part of confidence. Nothing has really changed. We've just developed."

According to Newman, "from a team standpoint, from a performance standpoint, it's important that we move forward and progress." He adds, "How we do that is honestly a people thing. It's teamwork. It's building better race cars, communicating, all those things that the 48 team has done for the last four years straight. We've got a lot of work ahead of us to get to that point, but I think that our organization has done a lot of great things in the offseason for our people and for our race cars to be stronger, and we'll prove that."[12]

Driving in the Spotlight

When Newman moved to the Stewart-Haas team in 2009, the U.S. Army moved with him as a sponsor for his No. 39 NASCAR Sprint Cup Chevrolet. Lt. Gen. Benjamin C. Freakly says that Newman is not only an outstanding driver, but a "powerful and effective" advocate for men and women in the Army. "It's an honor driving the No. 39 U.S. Army Chevrolet and representing the men and women who serve and protect our country," says Newman. He adds, "And much like them, we're never satisfied. We want to achieve more, and the dedication, teamwork and passion of the soldiers who defend our country is all the inspiration we need to deliver on the race track."[13] He adds that "in racing we stress speed, power, technology and teamwork" and it is "the same in the U.S. Army. That's one of the really neat things about having the Army as a partner."[14]

Working together as a team and optimizing every mechanical advantage, Ryan Newman and his teams have beat the odds to generate a successful record in the ultracompetitive NASCAR circuit. And though victory brings the loyalty of fans and big prize winnings, it can also create tension among fellow racers, many of whom have been racing decades longer than Newman. What does it take for a young driver with talent, know-how, and commitment to create a NASCAR team that can win over the long haul?

CASE QUESTIONS

1. **DISCUSSION**—How can a NASCAR owner use insights from the open systems model of team effectiveness to build a true high performance racing team?

2. **DISCUSSION**—In what ways can a driver's behavior help with or hinder a crew chief's efforts to build the right norms and a high level of cohesiveness in a pit crew team?

3. **PROBLEM-SOLVING**—NASCAR teams change drivers and driver-pit crew relationships must be good. What teamwork and team building approaches could be used to create synergy when a new NASCAR driver joins an established racing team and pit crew?

4. **FURTHER RESEARCH**—Pit crews are often in the news. See what you can find out about pit crew performance. Ask: What differentiates the "high performance" pit crews from the "also rans?" If you were to write a class lesson plan on "Pit Crew Insights for Team Success," what would you include in the lesson and why?

A generation of employees is growing up online which is reshaping the way we do business. Tremendous opportunity and competitive advantage exist for those who embrace new tools for communication and collaboration. Technologies such as wikis, blogs, prediction markets, and social utility websites are being used within and between organizations with powerful results. This isn't an all or nothing engagement. Increasing the reach of a small company to a global audience can be as simple as answering the question "What's happening?"

Enterprise 2.0

Professor Andrew McAfee, formerly of Harvard Business School and currently with MIT, coined the phrase Enterprise 2.0 to describe the technologies and business practices that liberate workforces—by moving beyond traditional tools such as email.[1] New technologies are revolutionizing the way we think about communication and collaboration, product development, customer relationship management, marketing, operations, and business productivity solutions.[2] Just as the original spreadsheet changed business, Enterprise 2.0 is finding its place in the corridors of some of America's largest companies such as Nokia, Kodak, and IBM.[3]

Consider how a company works with its network of partners: suppliers, distribution partners, or service providers. Companies that are more collaborative, participatory, efficient, user-driven, and action-oriented are recognized as the most successful. Many companies are now using wiki-based solutions to increase collaboration and finding more success than through traditional intranet tools. Wikis work the way a smart team does, allowing people to bounce ideas off of each other and expand on each other's knowledge. IBM, for example, holds "Innovation Jams" where thousands of IBM employees are encouraged to simultaneously participate in virtual chat rooms on a given day. IBM has uncovered transformative business ideas through these virtual discussions. Their online conversations and technology allow over 150,000 employees to bring ideas to the table. With the help of sophisticated software, analysts and managers identify and nurture ideas which IBM CEO Samuel J. Palmisano said he believes result in "catalytic innovations" that lead to new business for IBM.[4,5]

It's a Small World After All

Armed with only a computer or a server and Internet access, customers are able to download an application and run software. Users are no longer obligated to purchase hardware and software. Take Google's spreadsheet application—users soon discover that it includes the most-used functionality of Microsoft Excel and something unique. Click on the "share this spreadsheet" link, and suddenly you're collaborating in real time. This can be invaluable now that companies' business units are separated not just by buildings but by countries.[6]

Enterprise 2.0 technologies are making the world smaller and more accessible. It is no longer necessary to bring entire sales forces together for training. Instead they're plugging in their iPods and downloading podcasts to learn about products, communication strategies, training, and industry statistics.

National Semiconductor recently issued iPods to all 8,000 of its employees for this purpose.[7]

Everybody Tweets

When Twitter's success as an instant communication network during shared events like earthquakes, conferences, and festivals was realized, Twitter began to grow. Research reported in *New Scientist*[8] found that blogs, maps, photo sites, and instant messaging systems like Twitter did a better job of getting information out during emergencies than either the traditional news media or government emergency services. Organizations that support relief efforts, such as The American Red Cross, are also using Twitter to exchange minute-to-minute information about local disasters including statistics and directions.[9]

During the 2008 Mumbai attacks, eyewitnesses sent an estimated 80 tweets every 5 seconds. Twitter users on the ground helped compile a list of the dead and injured. In addition, users sent out vital information such as emergency phone numbers and the location of hospitals needing blood donations. CNN called this "the day that social media appeared to come of age" since many different groups made significant use of Twitter to gather news and coordinate responses.[10]

With everyone from President Obama to astronauts in outer space using Twitter, Twitter users are more geographically diverse than ever. Over 60% of registered Twitter accounts come from outside the U.S. By March 2010, Twitter recorded a 1,500 percent growth in the number of registered users, the number of its employees had grown 500 percent, while over 70,000 registered apps had been created for the microblogging platform.[11]

Tweets throughout History

Since Twitter began, billions of tweets have been created. Today, fifty-five million tweets a day are sent via Twitter and that number is climbing sharply. A tiny percentage of accounts are protected but most of these tweets are created with the intent that they will be publicly available. Over the years, tweets have become part of significant global events around the world—from historic elections to devastating disasters. In 2010, Twitter donated access to the entire archive of public tweets to the Library of Congress for preservation and research. After a six-month delay, tweets can be used for internal library use, for non-commercial research, public display by the library itself, and preservation. Through the Library of Congress or Google Replay, anyone can reach back to the very first tweets ever created, becoming a virtual time traveler.[12]

Driving Business

In April 2010, the service, which had been known for having no advertisements on the site, announced a plan for including advertising on the site. Companies are able to purchase 'promoted tweets', which would be targeted at certain people, depending on their searches on the site, an idea famously used by Google. Brands such as Sony Pictures, Red Bull, Best Buy, and Starbucks have already signed up.[13]

While some services, notably Twitter, make it fairly easy to build services that can sort through, process, and analyze the flow of social media to derive real intelligence and insight, most do not.[14] By combining messages that are quick to write, easy to read, public, controlled by the recipient and exchangeable anywhere, Twitter has established a powerful, real-time way to communicate which is turning out to be ground-breaking for users and businesses alike.

Twitter is an instantaneous medium, which has additional implications for businesses: You can ask questions, float ideas, and solicit feedback on Twitter—and usually expect quick replies. When a business launches a product, they're able to ask users what they think or search for real-time tweets from people talking about their product. Businesses can ask or search for feedback on new ad campaigns they've launched, stores they've opened, or murky issues they have to address.[15]

One of Twitter's key benefits is that it gives you the chance to communicate casually with customers on their terms, creating friendly relationships along the way—tough for corporations to do in most other mediums. Businesses and organizations of all shapes and sizes are now able to stay connected to their customers. It can be used to quickly share information with people interested in your company, gather real-time market intelligence and feedback, and build relationships with customers, partners, and other people who care about your business. Customers can use Twitter to tell a company (or anyone else) that they've had a great—or disappointing—experience with your business, offer product ideas, and learn about great offers they've selected to be notified of.[16]

From local stores to big brands, and from brick-and-mortar to Internet-based or service sector, people are finding great value in the connections they make with businesses on Twitter. When people working in the Empire State Building twittered that they were craving ice cream delivery, New York local chain Tasti D Lite was there to listen and meet their need. When electronics buyers look for good deals, the Dell Outlet Twitter account helps them save money with exclusive coupons. When Houston's coffee drinkers decide where to get their daily dose, many choose Coffee Groundz, which lets them order via Twitter.[17]

Although it can be tricky to add up the value of relationships, Twitter does lend itself to measurement in a few ways. When companies offer deals via Twitter, they can use a unique coupon code to tell how many people take them up on a particular Twitter-based promotion. Those with an online presence can also set up a landing page for a promotion, to track not only click-throughs but additional behavior and conversions. Finally, use of third-party tools can be utilized to figure out how much traffic websites are receiving from Twitter.[18]

Does Twitter really help generate business? Absolutely. Not only do coupons get retweeted and picked up by coupon sites—both of which spread the brand name—they also drive sales. Dell Outlet has booked more than $3 million in revenue attributable to its Twitter posts. In addition, the division has done research

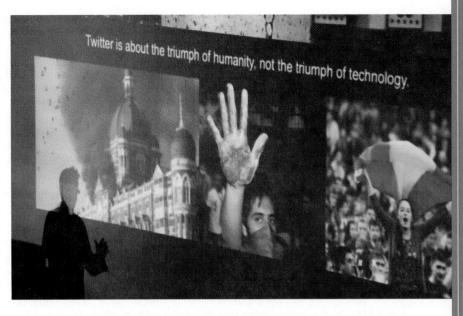

showing that awareness of the outlet has grown, too. "The uplift has been more than we dreamed," says Stephanie Nelson, manager of demand generation at Dell Outlet.[19]

Maintaining Focus

Independent analyst, Jonathan Yarmis, advises clients to stay away from the "Kumbaya Zone"—where we all sit around the campfire, singing odes to social media, and how important it is to engage in the conversation. Instead, he suggests that we apply social media strategies with a sound business strategy in mind. Asking ourselves questions like: Why should I do this? Which conversations do I want to engage in? What outcomes do I hope to achieve from engaging in those conversations?[20]

Many companies still block access to social utility sites such as Twitter. Their haunting question is how to leverage the benefits of Enterprise 2.0 while keeping employees' focus where it belongs—on business.

CASE QUESTIONS

1. **DISCUSSION**—Describe the richness of Twitter as a communication channel. Illustrate the factors that may enhance communication and those that can create barriers.

2. **DISCUSSION**—Explain Twitter's potential as an electronic grapevine, including possible positive and latent negative outcomes.

3. **PROBLEM-SOLVING**—Now you're a manager and supervising a team of high-tech digital natives. They use social networking sites such as Twitter all the time. But, how do you deal with this behavior at work? What lines would you draw on appropriate and inappropriate use?

4. **FURTHER RESEARCH**—Review recent articles about Twitter and its open dissemination of public tweets to the Library of Congress and Google Replay. Has there been any backlash from users? Are they concerned about their privacy?

Electronic Arts is one of the largest and most profitable third-party video game makers. Exclusive contracts with professional sports teams have enabled it to dominate the sports gaming market. Struggling with high development costs and revamping an aging lineup of games, EA's position began to waver and the company looked to acquire a chief competitor to invigorate sales. Can EA maintain the pole position in a crowded and contentious market?

Fantasy Rules

It seems that one company has cornered the market on fantasy. Electronic Arts' customers pay modest prices to make gridiron glory with Super Bowl champions, hunt gangsters with Michael Corleone, create "Sims" and a whole new world in a strategic life simulation—all from the comfort of their sofas or desks. Call it a dream maker, call it a magician of make-believe, but above all, call Electronic Arts profitable.

The Redwood City, California, video game maker holds some 60% of the sports video gaming market and is well known around the world for its incredibly realistic sports titles.[1] Led by the perpetually successful *Madden NFL* games, Electronic Arts has built an empire around putting gamers shoulder to shoulder with their favorite athletes. At last check, EA posted $4.2 billion in annual sales.[2] EA's explosion into digital has propelled the company and increased revenue by thirty percent. It's acquisition of social games company Playfish extends their reach and allows users to play on platforms such as Facebook, MySpace, Bebo, iPad, iPhone, and Android. EA's Pogo is number one in online gaming, and EA Mobile is the leading publisher of games for cell phones, generating at least $57 million in this year's first quarter alone.

Founded in 1982 by William "Trip" Hawkins, an early director of strategy and marketing for Apple Computer, EA gained quick distinction for its detail-oriented sports titles compatible with the Nintendo and Sega platforms. Although EA has also received good reviews for its strategy and fighting games, it left its heart on the gridiron, diamond, court, or any other playing field long ago. Says EA Sports marketing chief Jeffrey Karp, "We want to be a sports company that makes games."[3]

Ad Revenue In, Ad Revenue Out

Word of mouth may still be the most trusted form of advertising, and EA has always depended on fans to spread its gaming gospel. But in a highly competitive—and lucrative—gaming market, EA knows better than to skimp on brand building. According to TNS Media Intelligence, Electronic Arts spent $34 million in a recent year advertising the EA Sports division and its games.[4] EA knows its audience, and it promotes as heavily to *Game Informer* readers as it does to subscribers of *ESPN The Magazine.*

The realism of EA's graphics set it apart from competitors long ago, but the energy and talent used to depict that realism might be wasted if EA games didn't include the one element fans most want to see: their favorite players. However, top athletes aren't cheap, and neither are their virtual depictions.

Players such as Tim Tebow, Donovan McNabb, and Dwight Howard expect a tidy sum to promote any product, including video games that use their likenesses. EA spends $100 million annually—three times its ad budget—to license athletes, players' associations, and teams. It's a complex dance: the *FIFA Soccer* game requires 350 different licenses from a total of 18 club leagues, 40 national teams, and 11,000 players.[5] Cheap? Anything but. EA knows that, simply put, players got game.

Locking Down the Gridiron

With such incredible budgets allocated to promotion and locking in players, competing video game makers have found it difficult to challenge EA's pole position—and a recent string of alliances with sports associations might make it next to impossible. Electronic Arts laid out an estimated $300 million for the exclusive rights to publish National Football League (NFL) titles until 2009, and then announced an extension through the 2012 season. EA, whose Madden series is the most commercially successful sports title of all time, faced stiff competition from worldwide competitors seeking NFL exclusivity. The EA team recognized that losing its NFL license—and its star player—was not a feasible play. The NFL saw that the partnership would be mutually beneficial, and it initiated the negotiations with EA. "Because of the deal, we have more access to players, coaches, teams, and other NFL assets than ever before, which allows us to create a more entertaining experience," says Jeff Karp, vice president of marketing for EA Sports.[6]

Securing the likenesses of these major personalities left rival 2K Sports, the sports label of Take-Two Interactive Software, with only one option: to go after retired players. EA rushed to lock up the rights to the most valuable retired players' rights. But in their effort to score another great deal, EA may have stirred up a lawsuit with angry hall of famers who believe the rights to their likenesses are worth much more than $400,000 per year.[7]

The deal also delivered a crushing blow to competing franchises, such as the otherwise successful *ESPN NFL Football* series from Sega Sports/Visual Concepts. Determined not to be completely outdone, 2K Sports dropped an estimated $90 million to secure a similar deal with Major League Baseball for the next seven years.

But is this what fans really want? Not all fans, it seems. Two gamers filed a lawsuit in Oakland, California, alleging that EA's exclusive contracts to use the names and likenesses of groups such as the NCAA and the NFL players' association violates U.S. antitrust laws. Not only does this keep other gaming companies from signing similar agreements, thus forcing them out of the market, the suit alleges, but it also allows EA to unfairly raise the price of such games, with no real competition to keep pricing in check.[8]

Paying to Be Seen

Even the most dedicated Madden fans may wonder whether the sports video gaming market has enough muscle to shoulder EA's gargantuan costs. Enter the promotional alliance. Just as

EA pays to license the use of NFL logos in its games, big-name sports companies such as Nike and Reebok pay to the tune of $3.5 million a year to get their logos on digital players.[9] One game, *NBA Live*, offers players the opportunity to switch up the color and style of players' logo-friendly footwear. The shoe styles may be virtual, but the value of brand recognition is very real for companies that pony up for sponsorship.

Such brand reinforcement isn't limited to sports games either. EA's *Need for Speed Underground 2*, a fast-paced racing game, took endorsement beyond the omnipresent billboard ads and vehicle logos found in typical driving simulators. Here players received "text messages" on the screen suggesting game hints, each bearing the AT&T logo. The significance may be lost on adults, but for a younger generation raised on instant messaging, the placement makes perfect sense.

It makes financial sense, too. A poll by Nielsen Entertainment and Activision indicates that this kind of placement may result in notable improvements in both brand recall and favorable brand perception. "I think truly that no other media type can deliver the persuasion that in-game ads can if executed properly," said Michael Dowling, general manager at Nielsen Entertainment, Los Angeles.[10]

In-game advertising accelerated to the point of distraction, stirring up resentment from gamers. Beginning with Madden NFL11, EA will move part of the ad operation in-house and hopes in-game ads will be an effective marketing tool, not obtrusive to the user's experience.

Quest for New Blood

In its quest to own the video game market, Electronic Arts made an unsolicited $2 billion cash offer to buy rival Take-Two. EA took the offer public after Take-Two executives privately dismissed the proposal. The offer came at a critical time for both gaming houses: EA's market share had been slowly flagging because of the underperformance of some of its chief titles, and Take-Two was still recovering from having its directors purged by dissident shareholders in a proxy fight.

Corporate consolidation is a fact of life in the cutthroat gaming industry, and EA needs new blood in order to contend with the recent merger of Activision (Guitar Hero III) and the games unit of Vivendi SA (World of Warcraft). EA claimed that it could offer Take-Two, whose *Grand Theft Auto* series has sold more than 65 million copies, more extensive foreign distribution networks and the ability to bring Take-Two titles to other formats, such as mobile devices. According to analyst Michael Pachter, an acquisition of Take-Two would help EA protect its crucial sports gaming franchises. Because Take-Two is one of the "few credible competitors in sports games,"

EA could choose to either cherry pick Take-Two's top programmers or simply end production of Take-Two games that rival EA products.[11]

Playing for Keeps

Despite its wild success in the video game market, Electronic Arts faces substantial challenges to its power by competing game companies, the cost of doing business, and even dissatisfied gamers. Can EA overcome these threats and continue producing the sports franchises that brought the company considerable success?

CASE QUESTIONS

1. DISCUSSION—How can feedforward, concurrent, and feedback controls help Electronic Arts meet its quality goals for video games?

2. DISCUSSION—What output standards and input standards would be appropriate for the control process as applied to video game production?

3. PROBLEM-SOLVING—If you were the head of a project to create and commercialize a new sports video game for teaching math to primary students, how could you use CPM/PERT to make sure that everything needed to create a high quality and popular game gets done in a timely and cost-efficient way?

4. FURTHER RESEARCH—What is the latest in Electronic Arts' strategic acquisitions? How well is EA positioned for future competitive advantage? Overall, is EA's executive team still on "top of its game?"

By borrowing the best ideas from American brands and innovating the rest itself, Toyota became a paragon of auto manufacturing efficiency. Its vehicles were widely known for their quality and longevity—and Toyota's sales numbers were the envy of the American Big Three. By early 2010, however, Toyota found itself in the hot seat—the target of investigations by Congress and the National Highway Traffic Safety Administration and facing billions of dollars in lawsuits. As the carmaker recalled millions of its vehicles, CEO Aiko Toyoda focused on damage control and figuring out what sent his company into this tailspin.

Quality By Design

Toyota's success and growth in the American auto market was no accident. The company has used strategies honed since the 1950s to earn and retain customer satisfaction by producing superior vehicles within a highly efficient production environment. From the home office to factories to showrooms, two core philosophies guided Toyota's business: (1) creating fair, balanced, mutually beneficial relationships with both suppliers and employees, and (2) strictly adhering to a just-in-time (JIT) manufacturing principle.

The Pressure Skyrockets

Toyota's reputation for quality and safety has been tarnished as 9 million of its cars have been recalled since November 2009. Evidence amassed that Toyota drivers had been involved in accidents, been injured, and even died because of defects in their cars.

After sixty years of progress, Toyota's stance as the model of operational excellence waivered. Problems began for Toyota seemingly overnight as it announced recall after recall of eight of its most popular models. In actuality, the problems were years in the making.

As early as 2000, complaints about floor mats possibly jamming accelerators and causing unintentional acceleration led to internal investigation. Based on five consumer complaints about pedal entrapment in the Lexus ES350, the National Highway Transportation Safety Administration (NHTSA) opened a preliminary investigation in March 2007. All-weather floor mats were identified as the probable cause. After years of complaints, the automaker had concluded "that while accelerator feeling can change under certain conditions, Toyota considered it to be a drivability issue unrelated to safety."[1]

Time would tell just how wrong they were. In November 2007, a Toyota Camry driver was injured when the accelerator pedal became entrapped in his all-weather floor mat, causing him to crash into another vehicle, killing its driver. The NHTSA informed Toyota that a recall was required and thousands of optional floor mats were recalled in 2007–2008 Toyota Camry and Lexus ES models. The NHTSA case was closed until another deadly crash occurred, this time involving a 2005 Camry.[2]

Accident reports continued to come flooding in. Moments before a Lexus ES350 crashed into another vehicle at more than 120 mph, killing four people, one of its passengers called 911 reporting that the driver could not stop because the pedal was stuck. This prompts an investigation into the electronic systems that controls the throttle and engine speeds; Toyota adamantly denied a problem with such systems. After speeding out of control, a Toyota Avalon driver cleverly switched in and out of neutral and managed to get his car into the dealership where, despite being parked, the car continued to race its motor. Toyota finally woke up to their deadly problem when another Toyota Avalon sped off the road, into a pond, killing four more people; this time police found the floor mats in the Avalon's trunk.[3]

Paying the Price

"I hate to break this to you," Irving A. Miller—then a group vice president for Toyota Motor Sales USA—wrote to a colleague, "but we have a tendency for mechanical failure in accelerator pedals of a certain manufacturer on certain models. The time to hide on this one is over. We need to come clean." "We are not protecting our customers by keeping this quiet," wrote Mr. Miller, a tireless defender of Toyota who for years was its public face in this country.[4]

In 2010, Democrats on the House Energy and Commerce Committee said Toyota relied first on a flawed study when dismissing the notion that computer issues could be at fault for sticking acceleration pedals, and then Toyota made misleading statements about the repairs. Allegations arose that the company known for its opaque corporate culture deliberately kept information about possible defects from the US government.[5]

Ray LaHood, Transportation Secretary, went so far as to describe Toyota as "safety deaf." Toyota's pattern of dragging its feet on safety issues came as an alarming surprise to the public. Toyota's now-infamous internal "safety wins" presentation—in which it boasted of having saved $100 million by averting a full-blown recall of 50,000 sedans—has only helped fuel the tar-and-feather-them attitude that many have adopted.[6]

Toyota agreed to pay a $16.4 million fine, the largest government penalty ever against an automaker, for concealing information related to its sticking pedal recall. The fine is the maximum amount allowed by law. If not for that cap, Toyota could have been ordered to pay up to $13.8 billion.[7]

"Toyota has accepted responsibility for violating its legal obligations to report any defects promptly," Ray LaHood said. However, the carmaker did not admit wrongdoing, and the fine levied by the National Highway Traffic Safety Administration does not release Toyota from civil or criminal actions. Numerous lawsuits have been filed against the carmaker, by crash victims and relatives of people killed in crashes, seeking billions of dollars. Toyota's actions are also under investigation by the Justice Department and the Securities and Exchange Commission.[8]

In a recent statement, Toyota said it disagreed with the penalty, but decided not to fight it "in order to avoid a protracted dispute and possible litigation, as well as to allow us to move forward fully focused on the steps to strengthen our quality assurance operations."[9]

Return to Its Roots

In Japan, there is no mistaking the significance of Akio Toyoda, the grandson of Toyota Motor's founder, taking over as the carmaker's president. After Toyota announced the move, local media referred to it as *taisei hokan*, a historical reference to the Meiji Restoration in 1867, when Japan's emperor took back power from the shoguns who had been ruling the country.[10]

Appearing before Congress, the company's president, Akio Toyoda, said his company had "pursued growth over the speed at which we were able to develop our people and our organization." He told lawmakers, "I am deeply sorry for any accidents that Toyota drivers have experienced." Since then, Toyota has shifted its public posture toward blaming miscommunication for its problems. Documents and chronologies show the company had ample knowledge of incidents of sticking pedals well before its recall. "Once we thoroughly explored and tried to identify the root cause, we came to realize the problem was rather with communications than with quality itself," Mr. Toyoda told investment analysts.[11]

"Toyota's critical mistake was thinking about the issue as an engineering problem rather than a management problem," according to Daniel Diermeier of the Kellogg School of Management. The fact that the company president apologized and talked about personally heading a task force that would deal with quality issues was the company's first step in the right direction. They are finally responding to the true nature of the problem. Said Diermeier, "They have conceptualized the whole problem as an engineering one. This isn't about the accelerator, or the brakes. It's about a much more fundamental question: Has the company lost its way with respect to quality? It's a management problem, not an engineering problem."[12]

Looking to the Future

By January 2010, Toyota temporarily halted building and selling eight of its models including the immensely popular Camry and Corolla sedans. The company hoped the move would restore confidence in its brand and safety in its products. Toyota began running television ads publicizing their safety measures, showing its dealers and mechanics as well as owners, whom the company thanked for their patience.[13] "We are fundamentally overhauling Toyota's quality assurance process . . . from vehicle planning and design to manufacturing, sales, and service," Shinichi Sasaki, an executive vice-president, told a Senate committee. To give a manager proper control, controls must satisfy a number of criteria, including several that Toyota seems to be zeroing in on. For example, the company has pledged to increase its collection of consumer complaints and to then respond to them more quickly than in the past by deploying "SWAT teams" of technicians. It has also vowed to give its executives in the U.S. and other regions across the globe a greater voice in safety-related decisions.[14]

In fact, Akio Toyoda has promised to push his senior managers to actually drive those cars in which troubles have surfaced. "I believe that only by examining the problems on-site can one make decisions from the customer perspective," Toyoda said. "One cannot rely on reports or data in a meeting room."[15]

In his testimony on Capitol Hill and in other remarks, Toyoda acknowledged that his company became preoccupied with precisely the wrong metrics: market share and short-term

profitability. By enhancing its controls around safety and dependability, the automaker is sending a powerful message to all of its employees about what really matters. What's most significant about the overhaul that the company is undertaking is that Toyota recognizes that regaining control of the company's gas pedals and brakes cannot be achieved without also regaining control of its values.[16]

CASE QUESTIONS

1. **DISCUSSION**—How might Toyota's recent quality debacle help the company capitalize on its concept of *kaizen*?

2. **DISCUSSION**—Toyota was immersed in lean culture. Is it difficult to maintain lean manufacturing and quality control while introducing new products, especially during an economic downturn?

3. **PROBLEM-SOLVING**—Be the consultant. What operating objectives should be set by Toyota as it attempts to regain competitive advantage? How can customer relationship management be used by the firm to reestablish strong customer relationships and service, and regain customer confidence?

4. **FURTHER RESEARCH**—Toyota's turbulence shook up the U.S. car industry. Do some investigation; how are Detroit's big three faring? Who else is in the picture and what countries are they from? Are the other automakers using operations techniques and values similar to those found at Toyota, or are they bringing new ones into play?

Management: New Ways to a Better Town

Greensburg, Kansas had been struggling for years. Located along Highway 54, a major trucking route, the town was merely a pit stop for people on their way somewhere else. It did have a few tourist attractions: the Big Well, the world's largest hand-dug well, and a 1,000-pound meteorite that fell from the sky in 2006.

Lonnie McCollum, the town's mayor, had been looking into ways to breathe new life into the town. McCollum wanted to add a little vintage charm to its quaint Main Street, but could not raise the money. He had launched a campaign to

put the "green" back in Greensburg by promoting green building technology. However, the idea, which many residents associated with hippies and tree-huggers, did not go over well.

Then everything changed. "My town is gone," announced Town Administrator Steve Hewitt on May 5, 2007, after surveying the damage caused by a devastating tornado. An EF-5 tornado—the highest level on the standard meteorological scale used to estimate wind strength—demolished Greensburg, an agricultural community of about 1,400 in south-central Kansas. With 205-mph winds, the tornado cut a swath 1.5 miles

wide and 22 miles long through the community. "I believe 95 percent of the homes are gone. Downtown buildings are gone, my home is gone," said Hewitt.

With a clean slate and 700 homes to replace, Hewitt vowed to rebuild Greensburg using sustainable materials. He believed the town had a unique opportunity to control its environmental impact and reduce operating costs through increased energy efficiency. Hewitt told the mayor, "Every problem, every issue this town has ever had—this is our chance to make it right."

Just one week after the tornado, while residents were still surrounded by debris from shattered buildings, 500 people attended a town meeting to figure out how to rebuild their community. Residents came together in a spirit of collaboration and hope.[1]

"It was a good time for the community to reexamine things," according to resident Daniel Wallach. "One of the things that was often talked about is the fact that, like rural communities elsewhere, with so many elders in the population, Greensburg was dying. Agriculture has become so centralized, so mechanized, that there are very few jobs left in it. It is said now that the average farm has to be 2,000 acres to be viable economically. How can you have any kind of community when you've got one family every 2,000 acres? It doesn't work. The people of Greensburg understood that their way of life was dying, and they were clinging to philosophies that were contributing to their demise." So what could Greensburg do to reverse that?[2]

"When we talk about the green initiative, we are very well embraced by youth," explains Wallach. "It gives them enthusiasm and a vision of living within a community in the future. For 40 years that hasn't happened in this community. Young people just moved away. And they didn't come back, because they couldn't afford to."[3]

"Greensburg's is a story of being stripped bare of everything you thought you knew and having to start over. Here was an opportunity to work with a community that was experiencing the kind of loss and suffering that my wife and I know firsthand—relatively few people really know that in the same way we do," said Wallach. "And that is important; it is important that we have experienced loss, too. We thought we had something to give."[4]

"What if we turned this tragedy into something beautiful?" Daniel Wallach asked in a new business plan he wrote shortly after the disaster. He and his wife had long been interested in sustainable Green living. Using their experience in developing nonprofits, the two launched Greensburg GreenTown, an organization designed to support Greensburg's green building efforts through education, fund-raising, and public relations management.[5]

Very few people understood what the new proposals meant and there was a lot of resentment and prejudices to overcome. There was no "green" movement to build on. By May 2008, the town had seen a lot of transition. In fact, Greensburg was on its third mayor since the disaster.

"I discovered that people out here in rural areas are far more connected to nature and to their roots," says Wallach. Early Kansans lived with the sun. They collected rainwater. They were the first to use the windmill. They're innovative. They're conservationist. They hate waste. They're the original recyclers. All of these things make them environmentalists. They won't call themselves that because it was politicized, yet it is what they are." What resonated most with the townspeople was learning about the long-term savings. Many were put off by the initial higher cost of going green. Once they learned how harnessing the wind or the sun could provide low-cost power that would never run out; how the bricks from old buildings that had been leveled by the tornado could be reused; how capturing rainwater in cisterns could cut their water usage and lower their bills, they began to see the benefits.[6]

One of Wallach's favorite new projects was BTI Greensburg, the local John Deere dealership. Owners Kelly and Mike Estes had decided to replace their ruined building with an energy-efficient, technologically state-of-the-art showroom featuring radiant heat, solar energy, passive cooling, and wind power. With corporate support from John Deere, BTI Greensburg would become a flagship green dealership.

Advocacy for green technologies within the community grew from a handful of people to include essentially all the city leaders, the business community, and a majority of the residents.

Long-term plans for Greensburg included a business incubator to help displaced businesses get back on their feet and bring new businesses to town; a green industrial park, green museum, and green school system; green building codes and zoning restrictions; and a community of green homes and businesses.

The new factory needed to manufacture ultra green modular homes in Greensburg expected to employ 225 people, creating an employment base for a town that had virtually none. New building codes and zoning restrictions require trained builders who are able to think creatively. Therefore, training sessions were held at the business incubator. Several regional builders and architectural and engineering firms working in Greensburg benefited from technical assistance and training, which increased their knowledge and competency in green building projects. These firms are now designing or constructing green, high-efficiency buildings throughout their customer base in Kansas, Missouri, and beyond.[7]

"In the not-too-distant future, all development will be green" according to William S. Becker of the Department of Energy. "Developers, builders and buyers will discover that green not only enhances their pocketbooks, but also their health and the quality of their lives. The developers who grasp this first will have an edge in a massive, emerging market."[8]

The wind that tore Greensburg apart could also be part of its future. Renewable energy resources are abundant in Greensburg and within a 50-mile radius. Overall, Kansas is rated as the third-highest state for wind potential. Consider Wallach's pet project BTI Equipment in Greensburg. This local John Deere dealership has become the North American distributor for a Canadian wind turbine company. In their first nine months of business, they built a North American dealer network across 32 states and 4 Canadian provinces, resulting in 120 new wind-related jobs including wind specialists, service technicians, and installers; and nearly 300 existing sales representatives are learning the new business of wind energy.[9] The towers provide power not only to Greensburg, but also to over 30 other communities and will serve an estimated 4,000 homes in all.[10]

With their town stripped bare, many simply would have packed up whatever they could and left for good. But the people of Greensburg proved they are made of tougher stuff and focused on making their town a better, greener place to live. "The biggest success story in Greensburg, to me, has been the resiliency and determination of our citizens to make a difference in their world. We're new pioneers in the sustainability movement," said Greensburg's current mayor Bob Dixson.[11]

CASE QUESTIONS

1. DISCUSSION—In terms of future progress, how might it help the mayor and community leaders of Greensburg to view the town as a business that needs to be managed for high performance?

2. DISCUSSION—How did Greensburg's history influence the adoption of its current goal of being a socially responsible and "green" community?

3. PROBLEM SOLVING—How can the mayor use the management process of planning, organizing, leading, and controlling to best deal with the possible impact of the town's new green building guidelines on residents, local businesses, and the regional economy?

4. FURTHER RESEARCH—How is Greensburg's rejuvenation holding up in today's economy? What are the town's major challenges at this point in time? If you were a news reporter, how successful on a scale from 1 to 10 would you rate what has been accomplished, and why?

Environment: A Great Place to Start

Buildings were, and are, the largest users of energy in Greensburg, KS. Established in 1886, Greensburg grew rapidly from 1900 to 1910, and its population peaked at 1,988 in 1960. When the infamous tornado struck in 2007, the city was home to about 1,400 people in 515 single-family residences and 215 rental properties, most having been built during that boom period around 1960. The homes have been described as having very poor energy efficiency measures, which was common at the time of their construction. Greensburg also had a school, many businesses, and city offices. As the seat of Kiowa County, Greensburg housed the county courthouse, Kiowa County Memorial Hospital, the county library, and other county functions.[1]

In the first few months after the tornado, everyone focused on regaining the stability of the community. Greensburg's first priority was to care for the needs of its citizens and restore services as quickly as possible. FEMA and Southern Pioneer Electric worked rapidly to make emergency electricity generators and phone service available.[2]

FEMA brought temporary trailers for those who indicated an intention to stay or move back into Greensburg, and to support school functions as well as the county services including City Hall, police dispatch centers, and emergency crews.[3] Trailers became the storefront for many local businesses.

Ashley Petty was job hunting when the tornado hit her hometown of Greensburg, KS. Ashley had started taking massage therapy classes while studying for her business degree. After

graduating, she worked for several years as a massage therapist, until the spa where she worked closed. Watching volunteers, residents, and relief workers exhaust themselves cleaning up the devastated town, she saw an opportunity. She would return home to start her own spa in Greensburg.

It was definitely a risky venture—a spa was the last thing she would have expected to find in Greensburg before the storm. Armed with a business plan she had written in college, Ashley applied for one of the temporary trailers that were brought in to house displaced businesses. She got her trailer—a 1970s singlewide, complete with imitation wood paneling, stinky carpet, and a leaky roof. Not exactly the luxe spa she had envisioned in her business plan, but a good enough start. With a fresh coat of paint, some scented candles, and new drapes, she opened Elements Therapeutic Massage and Day Spa.

Ashley had expected that her spa would be a hard sell. The storm had destroyed the town's communications, so traditional advertising was out. To build a client base, Ashley turned to word of mouth. She went to town meetings, talked to old friends, met with volunteers from all over the country. Still, months went by and she still had barely enough clients to pay her expenses.

Then winter hit. It was cold, the ancient furnace ran constantly, drafts blew in the new curtains, and rain soaked the freshly steamed carpet. Elements was the last place anyone would want to go to escape the stress of rebuilding—even Ashley couldn't stand to be there. Under normal circumstances, she would have considered more extensive capital improvements, but the trailer was only temporary and she was out of money.

At one town meeting, green architecture firm BNIM presented a plan for the new Downtown Greensburg, including a business incubator to sustain old businesses and promote new ones. Traditionally, a business incubator is reserved for start-ups, but in Greensburg, once-successful businesses needed help getting back on their feet. The incubator would be housed in a totally energy-efficient retail/office building with space for approximately ten new businesses. The rent would be reasonable, and the utility costs next to nothing.

Business owners would be able to share space and resources. Additional training in marketing, finance, planning, and networking would also be offered. Ashley jumped at the chance to apply for a place in the building.

"I think the Business Incubator is a great economic-development tool," explains city administrator Steve Hewitt. "We stepped in and we found a way to build this facility to get our local businesses and new businesses back into Greensburg, get them started, get them back on their feet."[4]

The Sun Chips Business Incubator in Greensburg is designed to offer affordable spaces for businesses getting back on their feet, as well as for new retail ventures. This building received a major funding boost from Frito-Lay Sun Chips division, a company known for its environmental advocacy, and additional help from actor Leonardo DiCaprio, a well-known sustainability advocate. The incubator is an LEED Platinum certified building, which is practically unheard of in a rural community, so that notoriety is an attraction on its own.

The incubator was also a sanctuary for Tim and Kari Kyle, who grew up together in Greensburg and were high school sweethearts. They got married and, like most young couples, moved to a bigger town after high school for economic opportunities. But the Kyles never got over leaving their hometown and longed to return.[5]

When the tornado hit, the Kyles were living in Arkansas where Tim worked in construction. They followed the path of the tornado closely as it zeroed in on Greensburg, where Tim's entire family still lived. There was no way for Tim to contact his family so he got in his truck and drove the hundreds of miles from Arkansas to Greensburg. What he saw devastated him. He was shocked that the town was destroyed; but relieved that his family was safe.[6]

Soon after returning to Arkansas, Tim lost his job and worried about how he would support his wife and new baby. Inspiration struck. When Tim had last been in Greensburg, he saw how much construction was already underway. Tim and Kari realized that they wanted to go back home to Greensburg and raise their son, Andy, around their extended family. All that new construction would mean Tim would have plenty of work, so it was possible to make that dream come true.[7]

The journey home was full of opportunities for Tim's wife, too. Kari had always wanted to have a coffee shop, and when she found a space in the business incubator, the "Green Bean' was born. Brewing organic coffee has become a big hit in Greensburg, and the reception has been so great that Kari feels like she never left home at all. Green Bean has already expanded and moved out of the incubator and onto the new mall on Main Street.[8]

At its peak, Greensburg had 228 trailers which provided temporary housing for residents and businesses; now there are only 18. The remaining families and businesses are moving on. City administrator Steve Hewitt finds this a very good sign and says moving out the FEMA trailers represents the town's progress: "We're building homes. We're finding new places to go. It's exciting times."[9]

If people like Ashley, Tim, and Kari continue to flock to Greensburg to find opportunities and to put down roots with their young families, the town will move out of recovery and into growth. Exciting times indeed.

CASE QUESTIONS

1. **DISCUSSION**—What could the mayor of any other small town learn about "sustainable development" from the Greensburg experience?

2. **DISCUSSION**—What major challenges did entrepreneur Ashley Petty face in starting her business in this particular community?

3. **PROBLEM SOLVING**—As mayor, would you be satisfied that Greensburg's business incubator is capable of stimulating the economic development needed by the town? What else can be done to bring businesses with good jobs into the community?

4. **FURTHER RESEARCH**—Is Greensburg living up to its commitment to being "green" and operating as a model sustainable community? Have any other communities in the United States and elsewhere in the world taken a similar approach to transforming themselves for a sustainable future?

Planning: No Time to Micromanage

CITY HALL

"This is a stepping stone for me," thought Steve Hewitt, Greensburg's town administrator. Standing in what was left of his kitchen on the night of Friday, May 4, 2007, he realized he was getting more than he bargained for. His town looked like a war zone.

Across town, Mayor Lonnie McCollum and his wife had survived by clinging to a mattress as the storm ravaged their home. A write-in candidate in the past election, McCollum had accepted the job and set out to revive the dying town. Among his many ideas, the most innovative had been green building. McCollum was no tree-hugger; he was simply looking for a way to save money on fuel and utilities, to conserve the town's resources.

Like many people in town, Hewitt and McCollum had no idea of the extent of the damage. They would later learn that an EF-5 tornado drove right through town. By the end of the weekend, though, they knew that Greensburg, as they knew it, was gone.

Before the storm, McCollum had been exploring ways for Greensburg to be a better town; looking at ways to be more efficient, more effective, and to produce less waste. There wasn't a lot of building going on in this rural Kansas town at the time, new construction or otherwise, so their options were limited. Plus, many townsfolk were reluctant to embrace McCollum's green building ideas.

After the storm, the town was presented with a blank canvas to work on. A whole new direction was possible for Greensburg. But how could this small town with limited resources best take advantage of the situation? The idea to rebuild the community in a sustainable way started to take hold. In a history-making decision, the local council voted to build all city buildings at a LEED Platinum level, the highest standard of green building. At a press conference, McCollum announced that the town would rebuild, and would do it using the greenest technology available.[1]

Greensburg had to act fast but it also needed a plan. Planning took place in stages, first with a Long-Term Community Recovery Plan led by FEMA. The entire community of Greensburg gained an understanding of integrated energy planning. Townspeople and leaders collaborated with a number of partners to successfully develop a new *Greensburg Sustainable Comprehensive Plan.*[2]

Usually an integrated energy plan would be completed before implementing any energy-related projects; however, this simply was not possible in Greensburg's extreme disaster recovery situation. In stark contrast to a disaster that affects isolated parts of a community, the nearly total devastation in Greensburg made long-range and comprehensive community planning imperative before any substantial rebuilding could begin.[3]

Phase I of the comprehensive plan, which focused on land use and downtown design, began in September 2007 and was delivered in January 2008—an extremely short period of time for this type of plan. Phase II of the plan, adding implementation options and more details, was delivered and approved by the Greensburg City Council in May 2008. "Blessed with a unique opportunity to create a strong community devoted to family, fostering business, working together for future generations" is Greensburg's community vision. It emphasizes key values that affect the community's energy goals which were twofold; to "promote a high level of efficiency in new construction and look to renewable options for generation. Greensburg's vast wind resources are part of an emerging economy and should be harvested."[4]

With energy guidelines based largely on the National Renewable Energy Laboratory's studies and recommendations, the plan contains strong energy goals for the community and documents a possible reduction of 36% of pre-tornado carbon dioxide emissions if the plan's energy goals are met. The community has learned a great deal about residential energy efficiency. Under the city's new regulations, residents are able to put solar panels and, where feasible, individual wind turbines on their businesses or homes.

In all, 180 new homes were permitted after the tornado and before March 6, 2009. A number of homeowners volunteered to have their homes rated for energy efficiency, representing approximately 52% of the new homes permitted. Of these, nine townhome rental units in Prairie Point Townhomes were rated. On average, these 106 single-family homes and townhome units are projected to use 41% less energy than a standard home built to the International Energy Conservation Code (IECC) 2003 (with 2004 Supplement). Another 33 homes were renovated and measured. Their ratings indicate that these homes should use, on average, 25% less energy than a similar home built to the IECC code.[5]

At times some individual projects had to proceed while studies and discussions were shaping the overall energy plan. Under the real pressures of rebuilding a community and restarting a local economy, compromises and adjustments had to be made throughout the process to seize opportune moments as they arose. Greensburg's ultimate goal was to become a model green community.[6]

The symbol of Greensburg's initiative and vitality became City Hall. As the first LEED Platinum city hall project in the United States, it epitomizes Greensburg's successful planning—from the ground up. Debris such as bricks retrieved after the storm were reused, and at the front of the building stands a vertical axis wind turbine which generates clean power for the community.[7]

Greensburg's Sustainable Comprehensive Master Plan maps out strategies for the town's next 20 years. As the plan itself states, "A truly sustainable community is one that balances the economic, ecological, and social impacts of development." This balance is visible in the community's goals which clearly represent solid Midwestern values: "Be progressive while remaining unassuming. Open doors to newcomers while maintaining traditional cultural heritage. Provide opportunities for young people—education, jobs, a future back home. Value the natural environment, balanced with growth and economic development. Build a variety of durable, healthy, energy-efficient houses and buildings. Look to renewable sources of energy, such as Greensburg's plentiful wind. Treat each drop of water as a precious resource. Remain affordable."[8]

Greensburg operates as any other business, according to city administrator Steve Hewitt, and must plan for its future and think about investments and the rate of return on those investments. He says, "by having all of these green facilities, and by doing that, we're in a better position financially to do the things that help us to exceed our growth, to grow in the future, and to be more prosperous. And the only direction we can take is to be focused on the business-minded community, not simply patching things together."[9]

Steve is committed to Greensburg and to seeing the town through to the end: becoming the first eco-town in U.S. history. "We took our time," he said. "We created a plan that was sustainable and good for our future. "We didn't want to just put a Band-Aid on this thing. We wanted to fix it and make it better."[10]

If 2007 was a year of recovery and planning for Greensburg, then 2008 to 2010 could be described as a time to "build, build, build." City Hall is complete, the new hospital is open, a wind farm is producing 100% renewable power to Greensburg and surrounding communities, churches are open for worship, and the new school opened in the Fall of 2010. In the time of unthinkable disaster, the fierce community of Greensburg fought back by establishing a long-term community recovery plan—which did more in the first 12 months than most towns can accomplish in 20 years.[11]

CASE QUESTIONS

1. **DISCUSSION**—How did the five steps in the decision-making process come into play as the mayor and community leaders set out to deal with the situation after the full impact of the tornado became clear?

2. **DISCUSSION**—How does the decision making by the mayor and community leaders in the aftermath of the tornado hold up when subjected to a strong ethics analysis?

3. **PROBLEM SOLVING**—There's still a lot left to accomplish in Greensburg. What does a SWOT analysis of the current situation suggest in terms of future strategy and planning?

4. **FURTHER RESEARCH**—Is the strategic intent of Greensburg still clear and compelling to residents? What changes in strategy are evident at this point? From the standpoints of governance and strategic control, is the community leadership meeting its responsibilities? What do things look like from the vantage points of key stakeholders?

Organizing: Think Green, Go Green, Save Green

Greensburg's near-total destruction had a silver lining; it represented a unique opportunity for the town to change. Greensburg was able to try alternative energy solutions on a community-wide scale, for which there are few precedents in the world. Energy affects all aspects of a community, and that was abundantly clear to the people of Greensburg as they began to think about rebuilding after their disaster.[1]

"We need to think about how we build, recycle, etc. Sustainability is the ability to endure for future generations. Don't let the realities of today get in the way of a future vision," advised current mayor, Bob Dixon. "You need a vision and hope, and you need to identify what you can change."[2]

Greensburg's initial primary mission was to help the town choose to rebuild as a model and make it as easy as possible to do that. Town leaders wanted to position the town as a giant science museum where the new buildings and projects, such as the LED streetlights and the community wind farm, would be like exhibits in a museum where visitors, or anyone studying the town, could learn in a very real way about sustainable building and living in harmony with our natural environment.[3]

Greensburg's leaders knew this would be a powerful teaching experience. It would also give the town a much-needed source of income with eco-tourism. With that in mind they created a visitors' center, offer guided tours, cell phone audio tours, tour maps of the town, and a major online resource highlighting the

features of the town so that anyone, either in person or online, can learn from the town's experiences. To immerse themselves in green living, visitors can even stay in model homes which have been turned into bed-and-breakfasts. Though their population may be small, Greensburg's goal isn't; they hope to benefit the world by sharing their experience.

Once the people of Greensburg realized that in the long run, going green would save them a lot of green, they began to embrace change. Citizens looked at potential savings of town-wide initiatives, such as the LED streetlights that will save the town $100,000, and the clean, unlimited potential of the community wind farm. Individuals began to look for other ways to become more cost-effective, eco-friendly, and sustainable in their daily lives.

It wasn't long before their focus turned to their mode of transportation. Traditionally, most of the vehicles in Greensburg have been powered by fossil fuel, primarily gasoline and diesel, major greenhouse gas contributors. Most drivers in Greensburg drive alone to work or school. Greensburg's tight knit community makes it an ideal town for cooperative transportation solutions—but they were thinking beyond simply carpooling. Through neighborly cooperation, their own individual efforts, and by utilizing new technologies and alternative fuels, Greensburg citizens learned that they can dramatically lower their dependence on fossil fuels, reduce their carbon footprint, and cut their transportation costs.[4]

Not too long ago, the phrase "hybrid SUV" would have seemed like an oxymoron. But in just a few years, fuel-efficient hybrids of all shapes and sizes have appeared in showrooms. This new generation of vehicles combines fuel-efficient gas engines, natural gas engines, and hydrogen fuel cells. As gas prices soar and concern over the environment grows, consumers are becoming more and more interested in them.

Enter Lee Lindquist, Alternative Fuels Specialist at Scholfield Honda in Wichita, Kansas. A passionate environmentalist, Lee was researching alternative-fuel vehicles when he learned that Honda had been selling a natural gas

Civic GX in New York and California since 1998. Originally marketed to municipalities and corporations as a way of addressing air quality issues, the Civic GX seemed the perfect way for cost-conscious Kansans to combat rising fuel prices. It was also a way to highlight local resources, because Kansas is a major producer of natural gas.

When the tornado hit Greensburg in May 2007, the idea of going green took on a whole new life at Scholfield Honda. One of the problems with offering the Civic GX had been the lack of natural gas fueling stations, as well as the high cost of constructing one. Well aware of the media attention surrounding Greensburg, owner Roger Scholfield decided to donate a natural gas Civic to the town, along with a fueling station.

Scholfield was up-front about the decision to donate the car. The investment was a costly one, and there were many less expensive ways of reaching his customers in Wichita. Scholfield admits he questioned his decision even as he drove into Greensburg for the presentation. But the bottom line was that it was the right thing to do. Today, when customers come into Scholfield's dealership, they are more interested in alternative-fuel and high-efficiency vehicles.

If you want to buy a Civic GX from Scholfield Honda today, get in line, because the staff can't keep them in stock. While patrons wait, they can enjoy a nice cup of coffee served in a compostable, corn-based disposable cup. And before they leave, customers are offered a com-plimentary Scholfield Honda reusable green shopping bag and water bottle.

Pursuing this wide range of sustainable initiatives and new energy solutions throughout the city has placed Greensburg in a leadership position, not only among Kansas communities but also among communities throughout the United States and the world. Becoming known as a leader in sustainable development is adding to Greensburg's economic competitiveness and allowing the community to take advantage of the upsurge of interest in green initiatives from many residents and businesses in the surrounding communities.[5]

Just over a year after Greensburg's infamous tornado, an earthquake shook Sichuan province in China. The quake, which was measured as an 8.0 magnitude, killed more than 69,000 people and left 4.8 million homeless. People were displaced, families separated, the community was shattered. Clearly, the region needed help rebuilding.[6]

That is why Steve Hewitt was sent to China—to establish an Eco-Partnership. Steve and other visionaries helped implement sustainable design and green building practices along the way. This experience, the United States Treasury Department recognized, would be a huge asset to the people and recovery workers in Sichuan, China.[7]

The two towns have worked together to rebuild green, sharing experiences and lessons along the way. As Bob Dixon explained, "Two countries, two nationalities that at some times have been diametrically opposed to each other are coming together in a common cause of equal partnerships because we know we have to take care of our planet."[8]

Because, as Roger Scholfield said, it is the right thing to do.

CASE QUESTIONS

1. **DISCUSSION**—How did the town "culture" of Greensburg influence how the community responded to this crisis and the goals that were set to rebuild the town in a new and sustainable model?

2. **DISCUSSION**—How did resistance to change affect what happened in Greensburg, and how was it managed by the mayor and community leaders?

3. **PROBLEM SOLVING**—If you were the mayor, what organization structure would you suggest for the community so that the strategy and goals for the future can best be achieved? What key positions would you create and how would you link the various positions together to ensure good cooperation and coordination among the many people and units?

4. **FURTHER RESEARCH**—Evaluate the planned change that has been taking place in Greensburg. What change strategies have been used, what types of changes have been pursued, and who have been the major change leaders? Overall, how would you rate the effectiveness of this attempt at large-scale community change? And finally, what possible lessons in change leadership might business executives learn from this case?

Leading: The Dog Ate My Laptop

Between the war on terror, the collapse of the U.S. economy, the shock of New Orleans, and dealing with the aftermath of the BP oil spill, America has been struggling. In these troubling times, the town of Greensburg, Kansas has become a symbol of American strength, ingenuity, promise, and perseverance. Says Mayor Bob Dixon, "People are seeing that there is hope after a disaster. They want to see some success stories and hope in the forefront. People can see that there is hope in the future in the midst of everything that's going on in the United States right now."[1]

Greensburg's accomplishments in rebuilding green in the first three years after its disastrous tornado are extraordinary. Armed with strong leadership and committed citizens, the small rural town proved they could indeed rebuild greener, better, stronger.

Moments after the tornado, city administrator Steve Hewitt rushed to the command center to coordinate rescue activities, and to safeguard and restore utilities. Taking the lead seemed to come naturally to Hewitt, and it was a role he never really relinquished. Although first-year mayor Lonnie McCollum announced that they would put the green back in Greensburg, he didn't have the staying power to see his vision through to the end. By May 2007, Lonnie had decided that he wasn't the right person to handle the massive rebuilding project; he resigned his post.

Daniel Wallach, founder of Greensburg GreenTown, describes Lonnie as a passionate, inspiring, emotional guy. He paints a very different picture of Steve Hewitt. Wallach likened him to "a cold-blooded athlete, the one who you'd want taking the last shot in the basketball game. He's calculating and strategic. He has a big heart and does connect to people that way but he has an analytical capacity and endurance." Those qualities suited Greensburg and enabled them to bring their town back from the ashes and rubble.

By May 2008, Greensburg was on its third mayor since the disaster—but Steve Hewitt was still the town administrator. He had expanded his staff from 20 to 35 people, established a full-time fire department, a planning department, and a community development department.

"He's very open as far as information," said Recovery Coordinator and Assistant Town Administrator Kim Alderfer. "He's very good about delegating authority. He gives you the authority to do your job. He doesn't have time to micromanage."

Steve Hewitt has to rely on his staff. New departments were established, positions created, and people were hired to fill them. While his team members tried to rebuild their town, they were also picking up the pieces of their own lives and trying to rebuild their own homes. During that time Steve learned that he had to be not just a team leader, but also a counselor and a friend. But he knew that you also have to be tough sometimes when you're the boss. His philosophy: we've got to get this done—get it done now. To do so, you have to trust and allow department heads to be department heads, to take their teams and lead them. You have to give them a true direction, and a true play, and say these are our goals. And then step back to allow them to meet those goals.

"We've got to be focused and dedicated," said Hewitt, "We've got to have goals and got to have a plan. While I'm here, we're going in this [green] direction because it's the right thing to do."

Residents Janice and John Haney rebuilt their family farm on the outskirts of town. Although their new home, an earth berm structure, is full of energy-efficient features, Janice wasn't convinced that the plan to rebuild Greensburg using green technology was the right one. "I personally don't think the persons that are living in Greensburg right now are really committed to it. We didn't have a choice. You MUST go green. That's really not everybody's option."

In retrospect, Lonnie said he feels that if they'd been able to slow down, they would have had more success winning the townspeople over. But for Hewitt, it was full steam ahead.

For years Hewitt and his peers have had everyone from Oprah Winfrey to

Barack Obama talking about the town. "I have learned that hope is found in unlikely places, that inspiration often comes not from those with the most power or celebrity, but from the dreams and aspirations of ordinary Americans who are anything but ordinary," said President Obama in an address to Congress. "I think about Greensburg, Kansas, a town that was completely destroyed by a tornado, but is being rebuilt by its residents as a global example of how clean energy can power an entire community—how it can bring jobs and businesses to a place where piles of bricks and rubble once lay."[2]

Echoed Rick Fedrizzi, President, CEO, & Founding Chair, U.S. Green Building Council, "The city of Greensburg has taken the extraordinary step of committing to rebuild their community to a new vision, not settling for simply recreating what had gone before. By committing to a recovery plan based on green building, the community's leadership has set a path that will result in a healthier, more livable city for its citizens, turning a crisis into an opportunity that is an example for us all."[3]

Countless articles have been written about Greensburg, a documentary and a reality television series created. Greensburg: A Story of a *Community Rebuilding* aired for three seasons on Planet Green, a Discovery Channel network, documenting Greensburg's rise from the ruins. An ABC film, *Earth 2100*, suggested a fictionalized, future Greensburg as a model showing how American towns can successfully implement green technology, and become a beacon of hope.[4]

Despite his tenacity and ambition, Steve Hewitt could not have done it alone. There are many heroes in the Greensburg story. The many and rapid accomplishments of the community were helped by Greensburg's broad and sustained media exposure and by the extraordinary support of the Kansas state government, the U.S. Department of Agriculture, and Department of Energy. Greensburg's visibility on the international stage is due in part to Governor Kathleen Sebelius' advocacy while governor of Kansas.[5]

Superintendent of Schools Darin Headrick boldly committed to opening in time for the new school session in August, a mere three months after the storm. His confidence and assurance inspired others to make their own commitments to stay in town and rebuild. John Janssen replaced Lonnie McCollum as mayor and helped energize and focus the town on its immediate goals of rebuilding as green as possible. His successor, Bob Dixon, implemented city resolutions that laid the groundwork to transfer the town to 100 percent wind power and bring all government buildings to a LEED Platinum standard. The groundbreaking work of Tim Lenz and Professional Engineering Consultants allowed Greensburg to lay claim as the first community in the country with all LED street lights.

Scott Brown single-handedly raised $960,000 to build the downtown business district.[6] Daniel Wallach, Greensburg GreenTown's staff and board of directors have supplied the most consistent leadership and focus on sustainability opportunities throughout the community. They realized that Discovery

Channel advocates would come and go, and the support of federal agencies would eventually end. The team has become vital to continue to carry and promote the green vision for Greensburg.[7]

Even after everything was stripped away, Greensburg was able to rebuild, to survive and thrive, by virtue of the strength and leadership of its people. Together they made miracles happen.

CASE QUESTIONS

1. **DISCUSSION**—What "style" of leadership was evident in the behavior and decisions of Steve Hewitt, and was it the best style under the crisis circumstances that Greensburg faced?

2. **DISCUSSION**—It's clear that not everyone agreed on the directions to be taken in the aftermath of the crisis. What were the sources and types of conflict faced in this situation, and in what ways were the conflicts functional and dysfunctional?

3. **PROBLEM SOLVING**—If you were to become a member of a search committee formed to select the successor to Steve Hewitt as Greensburg's mayor, what personal traits, characteristics, and qualifications would you like most to see in the job candidates? How would you describe to other members of the search committee the type of leader you believe will best meet the town's needs in the future?

4. **FURTHER RESEARCH**—What role did incentives play in creating motivation among community members to rebuild the community and to do so using a sustainable "green" model?

Controlling: So Much to Do, So Little Cash

The night of the tornado, Superintendent of Schools Darin Headrick heard the storm sirens go off on his way home from work. He stopped at the home of high school Principal Randy Fulton and the two men headed for the basement, just in case. The next thing they knew, from the buildings to their contents, the entire school system was demolished. Classroom materials were scattered everywhere; all the computers were destroyed.

For the first few months after the storm, no one could live in town. People stayed in shelters or with friends and family outside of town. No one had a home phone anymore, but people were eager to connect with each other and find out what was happening. The Federal Emergency Management Agency (FEMA) was distributing information at checkpoints on the edges of town and people had to go and get it.

Like 95 percent of the town's 1,500 residents, Headrick himself was homeless. With just four months to rebuild an entire school system, all he had was his laptop and a cell phone, so he got into his truck and began searching for a wireless signal. Taking a lesson from his students, he used text messaging to distribute information. Although few people still had computers, almost everyone had a cell phone. With help from the non-profit group Greensburg GreenTown, residents who subscribed to the text service could receive updates and instant messages over the phone, wherever they were.

Rebuilding the schools was a monumental task. Headrick secured temporary trailers for grades K–12 and received generous donations of desks and school supplies. By August 15, he had the basics needed to start the school year but he still lacked textbooks. It was decided that technology would have to fill in the gaps so the students didn't fall behind.

One of the school system's existing programs was Interactive Distance Learning Network, or ITV. ITV allowed Greensburg's rural schools to log in to classrooms around the state via Web cam. This type of real-time distance learning is referred to as *synchronous learning,* as opposed to the asynchronous online courses given on college campuses. After the tornado, all that was needed to get the program up and running again was a computer, an Internet connection, and a Web cam.

Early in the winter of 2007, each of Greensburg High's students received an unexpected gift: a laptop computer containing e-books, handwriting recognition software, and a tablet screen for note taking. The new laptops replaced their tattered textbooks. Students could hand in their assignments via e-mail and receive feedback from their teachers via instant messaging.

While the rebuilding was taking place, residents who were spread out across the state were kept up to date by Greensburg GreenTown via e-mail. When Dan Wallach started the organization, he knew it wouldn't be easy. A self-proclaimed idea guy, he admits that the details of high finance elude him. What he is good at is rallying people around a cause and getting them to write a few big checks. This time, though, Wallach decided to involve the largest number of people possible. Greensburg GreenTown's One Million $5.00 Donations campaign was the result.

The money raised has been used to cover GreenTown's operating expenses, as well as to fund gaps in municipal projects, build model green homes, and educate residents about green building practices. Another aspect of GreenTown's work is to provide information and access to media organizations. Shortly after the tornado, the Planet Green cable channel began production on a television series that would chronicle the town's rebuilding. Wallach thought the exposure created by that show and others like it would be valuable in his fund-raising efforts.

As a not-for-profit organization, Greensburg GreenTown is heavily regulated by the IRS, because the donations it receives are fully tax deductible. It falls into the same category as religious organizations and educational institutions, which are exempt from federal income taxes but must pay other federal taxes, such as employment taxes. Because working through the red tape required to obtain this IRS status can take time, many organizations, GreenTown included, work through an approved intermediary while their applications are processed.

Although Greensburg GreenTown supports and educates Greensburg's residents, the town itself must rely on other sources of funding. All towns have budgets for repairs and improvements, but no one expected to have to rebuild the entire town. After the tornado, Greensburg had no roads, no hospital, no school system, no utilities, or any of the other services one might expect to find in a town. Money was tight even before the tornado, so rebuilding seemed an impossible task.

Luckily, various government and corporate organizations chipped in. The Federal Emergency Management Agency (FEMA) and the U.S. Department of Agriculture (USDA) provided aid in the form of grants. Various city leaders have given dozens of high-level briefings all around the country

about Greensburg and its green initiative. City leaders have briefed the Kansas state legislature, provided congressional testimony, and given presentations around the country and the world on Greensburg. President George W. Bush visited the community immediately following the tornado, and again a year later to give the high school commencement address. Greensburg was also acknowledged in President Obama's nationwide address on the state of the nation in February 2009.

"The city of Greensburg has had to make a lot of partnerships with agencies, charitable organizations," says Kim Alderfer, recovery coordinator. "We have to have partnerships in order to do all the projects that we need to." The town's businesses and the municipality were eligible for disaster funding, which provided only 75 percent of a building's previous value before the disaster. Residents who had no insurance were eligible to receive only $26,000. That left a huge gap in funding to rebuild—let alone to build with improvements in energy efficiency that cost more up front but save money later on.

Corporations like Frito-Lay donated significant amounts of money to support the town's innovative business incubator. AT&T, Caroma, Mother Earth News, Natural Home Magazine, York, Honda, Sears, Office Depot, Vizio, Cisco, and dozens of other companies were also very generous.

With millions of dollars at stake and hundreds of projects under way at once, Assistant Town Administrator and Recovery Coordinator Kim Alderfer say the hardest part is keeping track of it all.

CASE QUESTIONS

1. **DISCUSSION**—How might the mayor and town leaders utilize some basic operations management approaches, such as value chain management, supply chain management, and customer relationship management?

2. **DISCUSSION**—Given their respective roles and the circumstances they faced in this case, how well did Darin Headrick and Dan Wallach utilize controls and the control process as they tried to get things done?

3. **PROBLEM SOLVING**—Greensburg has done well, but let's assume it's time to make sure some solid management controls are in place. What would you set up as an appropriate "balanced scorecard" template to measure results accomplished in the process of rebuilding Greensburg?

4. **FURTHER RESEARCH**—If you were to use your balanced scorecard and assess the current status of Greensburg today, what would the score reveal? How are the initiatives described so far in the case working out? What isn't working? What directions for future improvement are evident based on your analysis?

Case Endnotes

Chapter 1

[1]www.traderjoes.com/history.html
[2]www.traderjoes.com/static/lists.html
[3]Deborah Orr, "The Cheap Gourmet," *Forbes* (April 10, 2006).
[4]*BusinessWeek Online.* February 21, 2008.
[5]Kerry Hannon. "Let Them Eat Ahi Jerky," *U.S. News & World Report* (July 7, 1997).
[6]Marianne Wilson, "When Less Is More," *Chain Store Age* (November 2006).
[7]supermarketnews.com/retail_financial/food-retailing-0301/index3.html
[8]Orr.
[9]Hannon.
[10]*Supermarket News*'s Top 75 Retailers January 12, 2009.
[11]Hannon.
[12]www.traderjoes.com/value.html
[13]www.traderjoes.com/how_we_do_biz.html
[14]"Win at the Grocery Game," *Consumer Reports* (October 2006), p. 10.
[15]Orr.
[16]ww.traderjoes.com/tjs_faqs.asp#DiscontinueProducts
[17]www.latimes.com/business/la-fi-tj12feb12,1,1079460.story
[18]Jena McGregor, "2004 Customer 1st," *Fast Company* (October 2004).
[19]Orr.
[20]Irwin Speizer, "The Grocery Chain That Shouldn't Be," *Fast Company* (February 2004).
[21]Heidi Brown, "Buy German," *Forbes* (January 12, 2004).
[22]www.traderjoes.com/benefits.html
[23]Irwin Speizer, "Shopper's Special," *Workforce Management* (September 2004).
[24]Ibid.
[25]"Retailer Spotlight," *Gourmet Retailer* (June 2006).

Chapter 2

[1]Inditex Press Dossier: www.inditex.com/en/press/information/press_kit (accessed March 2010).
[2]"Zara Grows as Retail Rivals Struggle." *Wall Street Journal* (March 26, 2009).
[3]Zara, a Spanish Success Story. CNN June 15, 2001
[4]Inditex Press Dossier.
[5]Cecile Rohwedder and Keith Johnson, "Pace-setting Zara Seeks More Speed to Fight Its Rising Cheap-Chic Rivals," *Wall Street Journal* (February, 20, 2008), page B1.
[6]"The Future of Fast Fashion."
[7]Zara: Taking the Lead in Fast-Fashion. *BusinessWeek.* (April 4, 2006).
[8]Rohwedder and Johnson.
[9]Ibid.
[10]"Zara Grows as Retail Rivals Struggle." *Wall Street Journal.* (March 26, 2009).
[11]Ibid.
[12]Ibid.

[13]Diana Middleton, "Fashion for the Frugal," *The Florida Times Union* (October 1, 2006).
[14]Inditex Press Dossier.
[15]"Our Group," www.inditex.com/en/who_we_are/timeline (accessed May 18, 2008).
[16]"Who We Are," www.inditex.com/en/who_we_are/timeline (accessed May 18, 2008).
[17]Inditex Press Dossier.
[18]"Our Group."
[19]Inditex Press Dossier.
[20]Ibid.
[21]Ibid.
[22]"Shining Examples." *Economist* (June 17, 2006).
[23]Inditex Press Dossier.
[24]"The Future of Fast Fashion."
[25]"Westfield Looks to Zara for Fuller Figure of $1bn Australian," *The Australian* (September 3, 2007), p. 3.
[26]Inditex Press Dossier.
[27]"Ortega's Empire Showed Rivals New Style of Retailing," *The Times* (United Kingdom) (June 14, 2007).
[28]"The Future of Fast Fashion."
[29]Rohwedder and Johnson.
[30]Christopher Bjork. Zara Has Online Focus for US Expansion Inditex Says. *Dow Jones Newswires.* (Accessed March 8, 2010) online.wsj.com/article/BT-CO-20100317-709288.html?mod=WSJ_World_MIDDLEHeadlinesEurope
[31]Zara Grows as Retail Rivals Struggle. *Wall Street Journal.* (March 26, 2009).
[32]"The Future of Fast Fashion."

Chapter 3

[1]Yvon Chouinard, *Let My People Go Surfing: The Education of a Reluctant Businessman* (Penguin, 2006).
[2]Susan Casey, "Patagonia: Blueprint for Green Business," *Fortune*, May 27, 2007. (money.cnn.com/magazines/fortune/fortune_archive/2007/04/02/8403423/index.htm).
[3]www.youtube.com/watch?v=SrewYdAxyaI&feature=player_embedded.
[4]Casey, op. cit.
[5]Michael J. Ybarra, "The 'Fun Hog Expedition' Revisited," *Wall Street Journal*, February 19, 2010.
[6]Casey, op. cit.
[7]Ibid.
[8]Ibid.
[9]Allison Coffin, "Review of 'The Responsibility Revolution: How the Next Generation of Businesses Will Win,'" *The CSR Digest* (accessed March 15, 2010. www.csrdigest.com/2010/03/the-responsibility-revolution).
[10]www.patagonia.com/web/us/contribution/patagonia.go?assetid=23429 (accessed March 18, 2010).
[11]Casey, op. cit.
[12]Ibid.
[13]Ibid.
[14]Chouinard., op. cit.

[15]www.good2work.com/article/6039 (accessed March 18, 2010).

[16]Casey, op. cit.

[17]www.onepercentfortheplanet.org/en/aboutus/(accessed March 18, 2009).

[18]www.patagonia.com/us/contribution/patagonia.go? assetid=54730.

[19]Amanda Griscom Little. "Don't Get Mad, Get Yvon," *Grist*, October 22, 2004 (accessed March 18, 2009. www.grist.org/article/little-chouinard).

[20]www.patagonia.com/web/us/patagonia.go?assetid=1865.

[21]Little, op. cit.

Chapter 4

[1]Global Green USA, About, www.globalgreen.org/about/(accessed April 4, 2010).

[2]Katie Howell. A Sustainable New Orleans Slowly Rises in Katrina's Wake. *The New York Times*. July 14, 2009. www.nytimes.com/gwire/2009/07/14/14greenwire-a-sustainable-new-orleans-slowly-rises-in-katr-27129.html

[3]Global Green USA, News, www.globalgreen.org/news/265

[4]www.globalgreen.org/neworleans/holycross/

[5]Katie Howell.

[6]www.globalgreen.org/news/greenurbanism/

[7]Global Green USA, Green Urbanism, Why Build Green? www.globalgreen.org/greenurbanism/whybuildgreen/

[8]Ibid.

[9]Ibid.

[10]www.globalgreen.org/greenurbanism/whybuildgreen/

[11]Global Green USA, Green Urbanism, Green Schools (accessed at www.globalgreen.org/greenurbanism/schools).

[12]About Global Green USA (accessed at www.globalgreen.org/about).

[13]Global Green USA: What You Can Do (accessed at www.globalgreen.org/water/whatyoucando).

[14]www.globalgreen.org/news/442

[15]Ibid.

[16]www.globalgreen.org/climate/

[17]www.thecorr.org/

Chapter 5

[1]www.harley-davidson.com/wcm/Content/Pages/ Events/100th_anniversary.jsp?locale=en_US (accessed May 25, 2009).

[2]Malia Boyd, "Harley-Davidson Motor Company," *Incentive* (September 1993), pp. 26–27.

[3]Shrader et al., "Harley-Davidson, Inc.—1991," in Fred David (ed.), *Strategic Management*, 4th ed. (New York: Macmillan, 1993), p. 655.

[4]Ibid.

[5]Marktha H. Peak, "Harley-Davidson: Going Whole Hog to Provide Stakeholder Satisfaction," *Management Review*, vol. 82 (June 1993), p. 53.

[6]www.harley-davidson.com/wcm/Content/Pages/HOG/about_hog.jsp ?locale=en_US (accessed May 18, 2008).

[7]www.motorcyclistonline.com/calendar/122_0709_hog_members_adirondacks/index.html (accessed May 18, 2009).

[8]Harley-Davidson, 1992 Form 10K, p. 33.

[9]Harley-Davidson home page.

[10]Peak, op. cit.

[11]www.harley-davidson.com/wcm/Content/Pages/Student_Center/student_center.jsp?locale=en_US&request_key=-126553922&bmLocale=en_US#demographics (accessed March 23, 2010).

[12]Kevin Kelly and Karen Miller, "The Rumble Heard Round the World: Harley's," *BusinessWeek* (May 24, 1993), p. 60.

[13]Ibid.

[14]www.harley-davidson.com/en_US/Media/downloads/Annual_Reports/2007/10k_2007.pdf?locale=en_US&bmLocale=en_US.

[15]Harley Davidson home page.

[16]Sandra Dallas and Emily Thornton, "Japan's Bikers: The Tame Ones," *BusinessWeek* (October 20, 1997), p. 159.

[17]www.motorcyclistonline.com/newsandupdates/harley_davidson_chinese_motorcycle_market/index.html.

[18]"H-D Cautiously Upbeat over Beijing Dealer," *Dealer News* (May 2006), p. 67.

[19]Harley-Davidson Motorcycles and Customer Data: Registrations (accessed May 20, 2008, at investor.harley-davidson.com/registrations.cfm?locale=en_US&bmLocale=en_US).

[20]www.cyclespot.com/forums/showthread.php?t=10328 (accessed May 21, 2008).

[21]seekingalpha.com/article/75695-high-gas-prices-may-help-harley-davidson-more-evidence (accessed May 21, 2008).

[22]www.businessweek.com/investor/content/apr2009/pi20090416_239475_page_2.htm.

[23]www.businessweek.com/investor/content/apr2009/pi20090416_239475.htm?chan=rss_topEmailedStories_ssi_5.

[24]www.google.com/hostednews/ap/article/ALeq M5hu2rSpkXHX8Vhb-H_9JM0Nh3fOEgD9EDCVPG0.

[25]www.harley-davidson.com/wcm/Content/Pages/HD_News/Company/newsarticle.jsp?locale=en_US&articleLink=News/0581_press_release.hdnews&newsYear=2009&history=news (accessed March 22, 2010).

[26]www.harley-davidson.com/wcm/Content/Pages/HD_News/Company/newsarticle.jsp?locale=en_US&articleLink=News/0669_press_release.hdnews&newsYear=2010&history=news (accessed March 22, 2010).

[27]online.wsj.com/article/SB125135162394762877.html (accessed March 22, 2010).

Chapter 6

[1]Nancy Luna, "Sprinkles Bakery to Open in Corona del Mar," *Orange County Register* (May 18, 2006).

[2]Marco R. della Cava, "Cupcake Bakeries Cater to the Kid in Us," *USA Today* (September 18, 2007).

[3]Ibid.

[4]"Cupcake Crazy!" *People in Touch* (July 31, 2006).

[5]www.sprinkles.com/flavors.html (accessed March 30, 2010).

[6]"TomKat's Tasty Holiday Treats," *OK Magazine* (December 21, 2007).

[7]Audrey Davidow. "So, Sweetie, I Quit to Bake Cupcakes," *New York Times* (June 3, 2007).

[8]houston.bizjournals.com/houston/stories/2010/06/14/story2.html, *Houston Business Journal* (June 11, 2010).

[9]"Cupcake Bakeries," *USA Today*, op. cit.

[10]"Sprinkles Cupcake Bakery" (accessed May 25, 2008, at www.dmagazine.com).

[11]"So, Sweetie," *New York Times*, op. cit.
[12]"Cupcake Bakeries," *USA Today*, op. cit.
[13]"Sprinkles Bakery," *Orange County Register*, op. cit.
[14]"So, Sweetie,"*New York Times*, op. cit.
[15]"Cupcake Bakeries," *USA Today*, op. cit.
[16]"Sprinkles Bakery," *Orange County Register*, op. cit.
[17]"So, Sweetie," *New York Times*, op. cit.
[18]Joel Stein, "Cupcake Nation," *Time* (August 28, 2006).

Chapter 7

[1]www.amazon.com.
[2]www.jumpstart-it.com/jumpstart-it_on_amazon.html.
[3]Sean O'Neill. "Indulge Your Literary Urge." *Kiplinger's Personal Finance*, vol. 59, no. 8 (August 2005).
[4]"Amazon CEO Takes Long View." *USA Today*, July 6, 2005.
[5]Scott, David Meerman. "The Flip Side of Free." *eContent*, vol. 28, no. 10 (October 2005).
[6]"New Amazon MP3 Clips Widget Adds to Suite of Digital Product Widgets!" Accessed at top40-charts.com/news.php?nid=40273 May 29, 2008.
[7]Thomas Ricker. "Amazon adds Audible to its digital empire." Accessed at www.engadget.com/2008/01/31/amazon-adds-audible-to-its-digital-empire/May 28, 2008.
[8]Ibid.
[9]"Amazon Unbox on TiVo." Accessed at www.amazon.com/gp/video/tivo May 29, 2008.
[10]www.nytimes.com/2010/07/20/technology/20kindle.html, *New York Times* (July 19, 2010).
[11]Steven Levy. "The Future of Reading," *Newsweek*, November 26, 2007.
[12]"10 Questions."
[13]"Long View."
[14]www.nytimes.com/2006/03/10/technology/10iht-web.0310skilos.html?_r=1.
[15]www.nytimes.com/2010/02/04/technology/04amazon.html?scp=2&sq=amazon&st=cse.
[16]"10 Questions."
[17]"Amazon CEO Takes Long View."

Chapter 8

[1]Barry Silverstein, "Lands' End: Hard Landing?" *Brand Profile* (October 7, 2007).
[2]"The Lands' End Principles of Doing Business" at www.landsend.com (accessed April 4, 2010).
[3]"About Lands' End" at www.landsend.com (accessed April 4, 2010).
[4]David Lidsky, "Basic Training," *Fast Company*, issue 108 (September 2006).
[5]"History" at www.landsend.com (accessed May 26, 2008).
[6]www.fundinguniverse.com/company-histories/Lands-End-Inc-Company-History.html (accessed May 27, 2008).
[7]Ibid.
[8]Kelly Nolan, "Sears Gives Lands' End New Beginning," *Retailing Today*, vol. 45, no. 18 (October 9, 2006).
[9]Jim Tierney. "Sears Stores Find a Fit for Lands' End," *Multichannel Merchant* (October 2007).
[10]"Dressed for Success?" *Uniforms* (May/June 2007), p. 50.
[11]www.landsend.com/aboutus/company_info/awards/index.html

[12]"Lands' End Elfs It Up," *Multichannel Merchant* (February 2006), p. 44.
[13]online.wsj.com/article/NA_WSJ_PUB:SB10001424052748703510304574626740978607998.html, *Wall Street Journal* (January 8, 2010).
[14]Ibid.
[15]Ibid.

Chapter 9

[1]dunkindonuts.com/aboutus/company/products/CoffeeConsFacts.aspx?Section=company
[2]www.dunkindonuts.com/aboutus/company/
[3]www.dunkindonuts.com/aboutus/company/Global.aspx
[4]Susan Spielberg. "For Snack Chains, Coffee Drinks the Best Way to Sweeten Profits," *Nation's Restaurant News* (June 27, 2005).
[5]www.bizjournals.com/boston/gen/company.html?gcode=3AF1302DF8B5463AA3EA890B32D5B9C2
[6]dunkindonuts.com/aboutus/company/products/BreakfastSandFacts.aspx?Section=company
[7]www.dunkindonuts.com/downloads/pdf/DD_Press_Kit.pdf
[8]Kara Kridler. "Dunkin Donuts to Add 150 Stores in Baltimore-Washington Area," *Daily Record* (Baltimore) (May 26, 2005).
[9]dunkindonuts.com/aboutus/products/HotCoffee.aspx
[10]Clair Cain Miller. "Starbucks to Close 300 Stores and Open Fewer New Ones." *The New York Times*, January 28, 2009 (accessed at www.nytimes.com/2009/01/29/business/ 29sbux.html April 4, 2010).
[11]www.dunkindonuts.com/aboutus/press/PressRelease.aspx?viewtype=current&id=100140 (Accessed April 4, 2010).
[12]www.dunkindonuts.com/aboutus/press/PressRelease.aspx?viewtype=current&id=100157 (Accessed April 4, 2010).
[13]www.dunkindonuts.com/downloads/pdf/DD_Press_Kit.pdf (Accessed April 4, 2010).
[14]www.dunkindonuts.com/aboutus/BreakfastChoices/ (Accessed April 4, 2010).

Chapter 10

[1]www.apparelandfootwear.org/Statistics.asp
[2]"NIKE 2008 10-K, Item 6, pg. 20.
[3]NIKE 2009 10-K, p. 8 (accessed April 9, 2010 at media.corporate-ir.net/media_files/irol/10/100529/AnnualReport/nike-sh09-rev2/docs/Nike_2009_10-K.pdf).
[4]nikeresponsibility.com/#workers-factories/active_factories
[5]Aaron Bernstein, "Nike Names Names," *BusinessWeek Online*, April 13, 2005.
[6]Ibid.
[7]Stanley Holmes, "Green Foot Forward," *BusinessWeek*, November 28, 2005. Issue 3961.
[8]"Nike Replaces CEO After 13 Months," *USA Today*, January 24, 2006.
[9]"Just Doing It," *Economist*, August 6, 2005. Vol. 376, Issue 8438.
[10]www.nikebiz.com/responsibility/ (accessed August 29, 2010).
[11]www.nytimes.com/2010/06/12/business/energy-environment/12sustain.html?_r=1, *New York Times* (June 11, 2010).
[12]Ibid.

[13]findarticles.com/p/articles/mi_m0EIN/is_2008_March_5/ai_n24363712

[14]premium.hoovers.com/subscribe/co/factsheet.xhtml?ID-14254

[15]Adidas Annual Report 2009.

[16]Nike 2009 Annual Report. Select Financials accessed at media.corporate-ir.net/media_files/irol/10/100529/AnnualReport/nike-sh09-rev2/index.html#select_financials April 6, 2010).

[17]"Deal Sets Stage."

[18]"Adidas-Reebok Merger."

[19] www.nikebiz.com/media/pr/2009/05/14_NikeRestructuringStatement.html (April 6, 2010).

[20]Adidas-Reebok Merger."

Chapter 11

[1]Apple Inc. home page: www.apple.com

[2]Ibid.

[3]Pixar home page: www.pixar.com

[4]www.businessinsider.com/chart-of-the-day-revenue-vs-operating-profit-share-of-top-pc-vendors-2010-3

[5]apple20.blogs.fortune.cnn.com/2008/05/19/report-apples-market-share-of-pcs-over-1000-hits-66/

[6]www.businessinsider.com/chart-of-the-day-revenue-vs-operating-profit-share-of-top-pc-vendors-2010-3

[7]Peter Burrows, "The Improbable Heroes of Toontown," *BusinessWeek* (May 26, 2008), pp. 81–82.

[8]Brad Stone, "Apple's Chief Takes a Medical Leave."

[9]Ibid.

[10]www.apple.com/pr/library/2010/04/05ipad.html

[11]www.apple.com/pr/library/2010/01/27ipad.html

[12]Ben Worthen and Yukari Iwatani Kane. "New iPad Puts Focus on Apple's Flash Feud: New iPad Puts Focus on Apple's Flash Feud." *The Wall Street Journal*. February 10, 2010. Accessed at online.wsj.com/article/SB10001424052748703455804575057672717271784.html

Chapter 12

[1]Netflix Consumer Press Kit at ir.netflix.com (accessed on January 4, 2010).

[2]Information from "Netflix Passes 10 Million Subscribers," retrieved from netflix.mediaroom.com.

[3]Information from "Netflix Delivers 1 Billionth DVD," MSNBC, February 25, 2007, retrieved from www.msnbc.msn.com/id/17331123.

[4]blog.netflix.com/ (August 26, 2010).

[5]Data from Press Release "Netflix Announces Q3 2009 Financial Results," October 22, 2009, retrieved from files.shareholder.com/downloads/NFLX/817845784x0x325825/b0fd694d-3bad-4841-9ab5-39e665d9aa1f/3Q09_Earnings_Release_102209_final.pdf.

[6]Jennifer Netherby, "Netflix Builds Profit, Subs," *Video Business* (January 21, 2008).

[7]Information from Reed Hastings, "Reference Guide on Our Freedom and Responsibility Culture," August 2009, retrieved from www.slideshare.net/reed2001/culture-1798664?from=share_email.

[8]Michelle Conlin, "Netflix: Flex to the Max," *BusinessWeek* (September 4, 2007), p. 74.

[9]blog.netflix.com/ (August 26, 2010).

[10]www.moviesinhouse.com/articles/netflix-shipping-centers.html.

Chapter 13

[1]Southwest Airlines Corporate Fact Sheet, at www.swamedia.com/swamedia/factsheet.html (accessed April 11, 2010); see also James Campbell Quick, "Crafting an Organizational Culture: Herb's Hand at Southwest Airlines," *Organizational Dynamics*, vol. 21 (August 1992), p. 47.

[2]Richard S. Teitelbaum, "Where Service Flies Right," *Fortune* (August 24, 1992), p. 115.

[3]Colleen Barrett, "Pampering Customers on a Budget," *Working Woman* (April 1993), pp. 19–22.

[4]blogs.wsj.com/deals/2010/08/27/southwest-is-the-sweetheart-of-united-continental-deal/tab/print/, *Wall Street Journal* (August 27, 2010).

[5]Justin Martin, "So, You Want to Work for the Best . . ." *Fortune* (January 12, 1998), p. 77.

[6]www.dispatch.com/live/content/business/stories/2010/08/29/when-things-go-bad-he-offers-an-apology.html?sid=101, the *Columbus Dispatch* (August 29, 2010).

[7]Southwest Airlines Corporate Fact Sheet, op. cit.

[8]Ibid.

[9]"Did We Say Cheap?" *Inc.* (October 1997), p. 60.

[10]Southwest Airlines Corporate Fact Sheet, op. cit.

[11]Teitelbaum, op. cit., p. 116.

[12]"Colleen's Corner" (June 27, 2003), www.southwest.com.

[13]Adapted from Mike Esterl. "Southwest Airlines CEO Flies Unchartered Skies." *The Wall Street Journal* (March 25, 2009), p. B1.

Chapter 14

[1]www.comscore.com/Press_Events/Press_Releases/2009/11/Microsoft_Sites_Captures_Largest_Share_of_Time_Spent_Online_Worldwide/(language)/eng-US

[2]Facebook Press Room, Statistics at www.facebook.com/press/info.php?statistics (accessed April 18, 2010).

[3]Ibid.

[4]Jessi Hempel, "Finding Cracks in Facebook," *Fortune* (May 26, 2008).

[5]Caroline McCarthy. Facebook's $1B Revenues: Now Keep It Up. *CNet News* (Accessed April 10, 2010 at news.cnet.com/8301-13577_3-10462824-36.html).

[6]Hempel, op. cit.

[7]Ibid.

[8]Ibid.

[9]www.facebook.com/press/info.php?timeline

[10]Catherine Holahan, "Facebook's New Friends Abroad," *BusinessWeek Online* (May 14, 2008).

[11]Bill Greenwood, "MySpace, Facebook, Google Integrate Data Portability," *Information Today*, vol. 25, issue 6 (June 2008).

[12]www.nytimes.com/2010/08/02/technology/02tumblr.html, *New York Times* (August 2, 2010).

[13]www.fastcompany.com/blog/chris-dannen/techwatch/what-hell-tumblr-and-other-worthwhile-questions, *Fast Company* (May 12 2000).

14www.newsweek.com/blogs/techtonic-shifts/2010/05/13/
as-facebook-takes-a-beating-a-brutal-movie-is-set-to-make-
things-much-worse.html, *Newsweek* (May 13, 2010).
15blogs.forbs.com/velocity/2010/07/22/mark-zuckerbergs-
take-on-the-facebook-movie/, *Forbes* (July 22, 2010).

13www.autoracingdaily.com/news/nascar-sprint-cup-
series/nascar-driver-ryan-newman-visits-fort-bragg-for-an-army-
101/, *Auto Racing Daily* (January 14, 2009).
14www.scenedaily.com/news/articles/sprintcupseries/US_
Army_to_continue_sponsorship_of_Ryan_Newman_with_15_races_
in_2010.html, SceneDaily.com (November 13, 2009).

Chapter 15
1www.threedoctors.com/thebond.php.
2www.threedoctors.com/ourbooks.php.
3www.usatoday.com/life/books/news/2007-10-02-three-
doctors_N.htm.
4www.threedoctorsfoundation.org/bet-timeline.
5www.threedoctorsfoundation.org/RameckHunt.
6www.threedoctors.com/ourbooks.php.
7www.threedoctorsfoundation.org/bet-timeline.
8www.threedoctorsfoundation.org/ourstory.php.
9www.threedoctorsfoundation.org/3Drs.
10www.threedoctorsfoundation.org/about.
11Ibid.
12www.threedoctorsfoundation.org/sites/default/files/
Letter-V3.jpg, The Three Doctors Foundation website (accessed
August 29, 2010).
13www.threedoctors.com/ourstory.php.
14www.threedoctorsfoundation.org/3Drs.
15www.threedoctors.com/ourstory.php.
16www.aetna.com/diversity/aahcalendar/2006/mayprofile.
html.
17Audrey J. Bernard, "Oprah Hails Trio of Medically Correct
Doctors Who Empower, Educate and Continue to Make House
Calls," *New York Beacon*, December 6–December 12, 2007
(accessed April 3, 2010 at newyorkbeacon.com).
18www.threedoctors.com/ourstory.php.
19Bernard, op. cit.
20www.threedoctorsfoundation.org/3Drs.

Chapter 16
1"Ryan Newman: Career Statistics," Yahoo! Sports at
racing-reference.info/driver?id=newmary01 (accessed
April 17, 2010).
2Mike Harris, "Baker: Newman the Perfect Protégé,"
Associated Press (April 10, 2003).
3"Ryan Newman Biography" at www.penskeracing.com/
newman.
4Ibid.
5Dave Rodman, "Conversation: Ryan Newman," Turner
Sports Interactive (June 9, 2003) at www.nascar.com.
6"Ryan Newman Biography," op. cit.
7Harris, op. cit.
8Rodman, op. cit.
9Ibid.
10"Newman Looking Forward to Speedweeks Experience" at
www.nascar.com.
11Stewart Haas Racing, Drivers, Ryan Newman, Biography
www.stewarthaasracing.com/drivers/ryanbio01.php
(accessed April 17, 2010).
12www.motorsport.com/news/article.asp?ID=355147,
Motorsport.com (January 15, 2010).

Chapter 17
1blogs.zdnet.com/projectfailures/?p=4370
2Dion Hinchcliffe, "Ten emerging Enterprise 2.0 technologies
to watch." February 22nd, 2010. (Accessed April 26, 2010 at
blogs.zdnet.com/Hinchcliffe/?p=1224).
3Shiv Singh, "A Web 2.0 Tour for the Enterprise." Boxes and
Arrows. Accessed April 25, 2010 at
www.boxesandarrows.com/view/a_web_2_0_tour_
4Ibid.
5sloanreview.mit.edu/the-magazine/articles/2008/fall/
50101/an-inside-view-of-ibms-innovation-jam/
6Op cit Singh, Shiv.
7Ibid.
8Palmer, Jason. "Emergency 2.0 is Coming to a Website Near
You." *New Scientist*. May 2, 2008. (Accessed April 25 at
www.newscientist.com/article/mg19826545.900-
emergency-20-is-coming-to-a-website-near-you.html).
9twitter.com/RedCross
10Stephanie Busari (November 27, 2008). "Tweeting the terror:
How social media reacted to Mumbai." CNN. (Accessed April 25,
2010. edition.cnn.com/2008/WORLD/asiapcf/11/27/
mumbai.twitter/index.html).
11www.newstatesman.com/digital/2010/03/twitter-
registered-created
12blog.twitter.com/
13blog.twitter.com/2010/04/hello-world.html
14blogs.zdnet.com/Hinchcliffe/?p=1152
15business.twitter.com/twitter101/print
16Ibid.
17Ibid.
18Ibid.
19business.twitter.com/twitter101/case_dell
20blogs.zdnet.com/projectfailures/?p=4370

Chapter 18
1"EA Reports Fourth Quarter and Fiscal Year 2008 Results"
(accessed July 9, 2008, at media.corporate-ir.net/media_files/
IROL/88/88189/Q4Release.pdf).
2EA Reports Third Quarter Fiscal Year 2010 Results
news.ea.com/portal/site/ea/index.jsp?ndmViewId=news_
view&newsId=20100208006734&newsLang=en
3David Whelan, "Name Recognition," *Forbes* (June 20, 2005).
4Ibid.
5Ibid.
6Martin McEachern, "The Only Game in Town," *Computer
Graphics World* (October 2005).
7Owen Good, "Lawsuit: Retired NFLers Cheated by EA,
Union" (accessed May 23, 2009, at kotaku.com/5059011/
lawsuit-retired-nflers-cheated-by-ea-union).

[8]"Anti-trust lawsuit over exclusive license contract" (accessed July 9, 2008, at www.aolcdn.com/tmz_-documents/ 0611_nfl_ea_wm.pdf).

[9]Whelan, op. cit.

[10]Kenneth Hein, "Gaming Product Placement Gets Good Scores in Study," *Brandweek* (December 5, 2005).

[11]Nick Wingfield, "Electronic Arts Offers $2 Billion for Take-Two," *Wall Street Journal* (February 25, 2008).

Chapter 19

[1]www.nytimes.com/interactive/2010/02/10/business/ 20100210_TOYOTA_TIMELINE2.html

[2]Ibid.

[3]Ibid.

[4]Micheline Maynard. "Toyota Delayed a U.S. Recall, Documents Show." *The New York Times*. April 11, 2010. (Accessed April 25, 2010 at www.nytimes.com/2010/04/12/business/ 12gap.html)

[5]Ibid.

[6]www.businessweek.com/managing/content/ mar2010/ca2010034_000939_page_2.htm

[7]Nick Buckley. "Lexus to Recall S.U.V. in Another Black Mark to Reputation." *The New York Times*. April 20, 2010. Accessed April 25, 2010 at www.nytimes.com/2010/04/21/business/ global/21iht-toyota.html

[8]Ibid.

[9]Nick Buckley. "Lexus to Recall GX 460." *The New York Times*. April 19, 2010. Accessed April 25, 2010 at www.nytimes.com/2010/04/20/business/global/20toyota.html

[10]www.businessweek.com/globalbiz/content/jun2009/ gb20090625_571664.htm

[11]Micheline Maynard.

[12]www.businessweek.com/managing/content/feb2010/ ca2010029_503075.htm

[13]Micheline Maynard.

[14]Rick Wartzman. Toyota's Management Challenge. March 5, 2010 accessed April 25, 2010 at www.businessweek.com/ managing/content/mar2010/ca2010034_000939.htm

[15]Toyota, Press Room. pressroom.toyota.com/pr/tms/ document/A._Toyoda_Testimony_to_House_Committee_on_ Oversight_and_Government_Reform_2-24-10.pdf

[16]Rick Wartzman.

Part II Case Endnotes

Part 1

[1] www.blueplanetgreenliving.com/2009/10/15/rebuilding-after-disaster---greensburg-becomes-a-green-town/.

[2] Ibid.

[3] Ibid.

[4] www.blueplanetgreenliving.com/tag/daniel-wallach/.

[5] Ibid.

[6] Ibid.

[7] Energy Efficiency and Renewable Energy Information Center. Accessed April 28, 2010 at www1.eere.energy.gov/buildings/greensburg/pdfs/45135-1.pdf.

[8] Greensburg Sustainable Comprehensive Plan. May 18, 2008 Accessed April 28, 2010 at www.greensburgks.org/recovery-planning/Greensburg%20Comprehensive%20Master%20Plan%2001-16-08%20DRAFT.pdf.

[9] www1.eere.energy.gov/buildings/greensburg/pdfs/45135-1.pdf.

[10] apps1.eere.energy.gov/buildings/publications/pdfs/corporate/45086.pdf.

[11] Ibid.

Part 2

[1] www1.eere.energy.gov/buildings/greensburg/pdfs/45135-1.pdf.

[2] Ibid.

[3] Ibid.

[4] Discovery Channel Documentary, Planet Green. Accessed April 27, 2010 at planetgreen.discovery.com/tv/greensburg/greensburg-slideshow.html.

[5] Ibid.

[6] Ibid.

[7] Ibid.

[8] Ibid.

[9] planetgreen.discovery.com/tv/greensburg/discover-greensburg-special-anniversary.html.

Part 3

[1] Planet Green Documentary Series. Accessed April 27, 2010 at planetgreen.discovery.com/tv/greensburg/greensburg-slideshow.html.

[2] Greensburg Sustainable Comprehensive Plan. Accessed April 27, 2010 at www.greensburgks.org/recovery-planning/Greensburg%20Comprehensive%20Master%20Plan%2001-16-08%20DRAFT.pdf to download the plan.

[3] www1.eere.energy.gov/buildings/greensburg/pdfs/45135-1.pdf.

[4] Greensburg Sustainable Comprehensive Plan.

[5] EERE www1.eere.energy.gov/buildings/greensburg/pdfs/45135-1.pdf.

[6] Greensburg Sustainable Comprehensive Plan.

[7] Ibid.

[8] Ibid.

[9] planetgreen.discovery.com/tv/greensburg/.

[10] www.kansas.com/2010/05/04/1297999/3-years-later-greensburg-truly.html.

[11] planetgreen.discovery.com/tv/greensburg/.

Part 4

[1] N. Carlise, J. J. Elling, T. Penney. *A Renewable Energy Community: Key Elements*. NREL/TP-540-42774. Golden, CO: National Renewable Energy Laboratory, January 2008.

[2] N. Carlise, J. J. Elling, T. Penney.

[3] secretaryofinnovation.com/2010/04/13/from-greensburg-kansas-to-greentown-usa/.

[4] Greensburg Sustainable Comprehensive Plan. Accessed April 27, 2010 at www.greensburgks.org/recovery-planning/Greensburg%20Comprehensive%20Master%20Plan%2001-16-08%20DRAFT.pdf.

[5] www1.eere.energy.gov/buildings/greensburg/pdfs/45135-1.pdf.

[6] planetgreen.discovery.com/tv/greensburg/sneak-peak-greensburg-china.html.

[7] Ibid.

[8] Ibid.

Part 5

[1] planetgreen.discovery.com/tv/greensburg/discover-greensburg-main-street.html.

[2] Transcript of President Obama's Address to Congress. *The New York Times*. February 29, 2009. Accessed April 25, 2010 at www.nytimes.com/2009/02/24/us/politics/24obama-text.html?pagewanted=8.

[3] www.sustainablebusiness.com/index.cfm/go/news.display/id/15006.

[4] abcnews.go.com/.

[5] www1.eere.energy.gov/buildings/greensburg/pdfs/45135-1.pdf.

[6] www.greensburggreentown.org/green-initiative-awards/.

[7] www1.eere.energy.gov/buildings/greensburg/publications.html.

Self-Test Answers

Chapter 1

1. d **2.** c **3.** a **4.** b **5.** a **6.** a **7.** c **8.** a **9.** b

10. b **11.** c **12.** a **13.** b **14.** c **15.** c

16. Managers must value people and respect subordinates as mature, responsible, adult human beings. This is part of their ethical and social responsibility as persons to whom others report at work. The work setting should be organized and managed to respect the rights of people and their human dignity. Included among the expectations for ethical behavior would be actions to protect individual privacy, provide freedom from sexual harassment, and offer safe and healthy job conditions. Failure to do so is socially irresponsible. It may also cause productivity losses due to dissatisfaction and poor work commitments.

17. The manager is held accountable by her boss for performance results of her work unit. The manager must answer to her boss for unit performance. By the same token, the manager's subordinates must answer to her for their individual performance. They are accountable to her.

18. If the glass ceiling effect were to operate in a given situation, it would act as a hidden barrier to advancement beyond a certain level. Managers controlling promotions and advancement opportunities in the firm would not give them to African American candidates, regardless of their capabilities. Although the newly hired graduates might progress for a while, sooner or later their upward progress in the firm would be halted by this invisible barrier.

19. Globalization means that the countries and peoples of the world are increasingly interconnected and that business firms increasingly cross national boundaries in acquiring resources, getting work accomplished, and selling their products. This internationalization of work will affect most everyone in the new economy. People will be working with others from different countries, working in other countries, and certainly buying and using products and services produced in whole or in part in other countries. As countries become more interdependent economically, products are sold and resources purchased around the world, and business strategies increasingly target markets in more than one country.

20. One approach to this question is through the framework of essential management skills offered by Katz. At the first level of management, technical skills are important, and I would feel capable in this respect. However, I would expect to learn and refine these skills through my work experiences.

Human skills, the ability to work well with other people, will also be very important. Given the diversity anticipated for this team, I will need good human skills. Included here would be my emotional intelligence, or the ability to understand my emotions and those of others when I am interacting with them. I will also have a leadership responsibility to help others on the team develop and utilize these skills so that the team itself can function effectively.

Finally, I would expect opportunities to develop my conceptual or analytical skills in anticipation of higher-level appointments. In terms of personal development, I should recognize that the conceptual skills will increase in importance relative to the technical skills as I move upward in management responsibility. The fact that the members of the team will be diverse, with some of different demographic and cultural backgrounds from my own, will only increase the importance of my abilities in the human skills area.

It will be a challenge to embrace and value differences to create the best work experience for everyone and to fully value everyone's potential contributions to the audits we will be doing. Conceptually I will need to understand the differences and try to utilize them to solve problems faced by the team, but in human relationships I will need to excel at keeping the team spirit alive and keeping everyone committed to working well together over the life of our projects.

Chapter 2

1. c **2.** b **3.** d **4.** a **5.** a **6.** b **7.** a **8.** c

9. a **10.** a **11.** c **12.** a **13.** d **14.** c **15.** b

16. Theory Y assumes that people are capable of taking responsibility and exercising self-direction and control in their work. The notion of self-fulfilling prophecies is that managers who hold these assumptions will act in ways that encourage workers to display these characteristics, thus confirming and reinforcing the original assumptions. The emphasis on greater participation and involvement in the modern workplace is an example of Theory Y assumptions in practice. Presumably, by valuing participation and involvement, managers will create self-fulfilling prophecies in which workers behave this way in response to being treated with respect. The result is a positive setting where everyone gains.

17. According to the deficit principle, a satisfied need is not a motivator of behavior. The social need will only motivate if it is not present, or in deficit. According to the progression principle, people move step-by-step up Maslow's hierarchy as they strive to satisfy needs. For example, once the social need is satisfied, the esteem need will be activated.

18. Contingency thinking takes an "if-then" approach to situations. It seeks to modify or adapt management approaches to fit the needs of each situation. An example would be to give more customer contact responsibility to workers who want to satisfy social needs at work, while giving more supervisory responsibilities to those who want to satisfy their esteem or ego needs.

19. The external environment is the source of the resources an organization needs to operate. In order to continue to obtain these resources, the organization must be successful in selling its goods and services to customers. If customer feedback is negative, the organization must make adjustments or risk losing the support needed to obtain important resources.

20. A bureaucracy operates with a strict hierarchy of authority, promotion based on competency and performance, formal rules and procedures, and written documentation. Enrique can do all of these things in his store, since the situation is probably quite stable and most work requirements are routine and predictable. However, bureaucracies are quite rigid and may deny employees the opportunity to make decisions on their own. Enrique must be careful to meet the needs of the workers and not to make the mistake—identified by Argyris—of failing to treat them as mature adults. While remaining well organized, the store manager should still be able to help workers meet higher-order esteem and self-fulfillment needs, as well as assume responsibility consistent with McGregor's Theory Y assumptions.

Chapter 3

1. b **2.** a **3.** d **4.** c **5.** c **6.** d **7.** b **8.** a **9.** c
10. d **11.** c **12.** d **13.** b **14.** d **15.** c

16. The individualism view is that ethical behavior is that which best serves long-term interests. The justice view is that ethical behavior is fair and equitable in its treatment of people.

17. The rationalizations are believing that: (1) the behavior is not really illegal, (2) the behavior is really in everyone's best interests, (3) no one will find out, and (4) the organization will protect you.

18. The socioeconomic view of corporate social responsibility argues that socially responsible behavior is in a firm's long-run best interest. It should be good for profits, it creates a positive public image, it helps avoid government regulation, it meets public expectations, and it is an ethical obligation.

19. Management scholar Archie Carroll describes the immoral, ammoral, and moral manager this way. An immoral manager does bad things on purpose, choosing to behave unethically. The ammoral manager does bad things sometimes, but this is not intentional or calculated; it happens because the ammoral manager just doesn't incorporate ethics into his or her analysis of the situation. The moral manager, by contrast, always includes ethics as a criterion for evaluating his or her approach to decisions and situations. This manager strives to act ethically and considers ethical behavior a personal goal.

20. The manager could make a decision based on any one of the strategies. As an obstructionist, the manager may assume that Bangladesh needs the business and that it is a local matter as to who will be employed to make the gloves. As a defensive strategy, the manager may decide to require the supplier to meet the minimum employment requirements under Bangladeshi law. Both of these approaches represent cultural relativism. As an accommodation strategy, the manager may require that the supplier go beyond local laws and meet standards set by equivalent laws in the United States. A proactive strategy would involve the manager in trying to set an example by operating in Bangladesh only with suppliers who not only meet local standards, but also actively support the education of children in the communities in which they operate. These latter two approaches would be examples of universalism.

Chapter 4

1. a **2.** b **3.** c **4.** b **5.** d **6.** a **7.** b **8.** b **9.** a
10. c **11.** d **12.** d **13.** a **14.** d **15.** c

16. When it comes to organizational stakeholders, the list should always begin with customers and suppliers to establish the output/input players in the value chain. Employees should be included as well as shareholders/investors to identify the interests of the "producers" and the "owners." Given the importance of sustainability it is important to include society at large and future generations in the stakeholder map; it is also important to include the local communities in which the organization operates. Beyond these basic map components the stakeholders for any given organization will include a broad mix of people, groups, and organizations from regulators to activist organizations to government agencies, and more.

17. To make "sustainability" part of any goal statement or objective for an organization the basic definition should reflect the concept of sustainable development. That is: the organization should act in ways that while making use of the environment to produce things of value today the potential for that environment to meet the needs of future generations is also being protected and ideally being enhanced.

18. Product innovations affect what goods and services an organization offers to its customers. Process innovations affect how the organization goes about its daily work in producing goods and services. Business model innovations affect the way the organization makes money and adds value to society.

19. Reverse innovation means finding innovations in alternative settings such as emerging markets and moving them into uses in established markets. An example would be portable and low cost medical diagnostic equipment developed in markets like India and China and then brought to the U.S. and sold there.

20. First of all it sounds like a good idea to have a Chief Sustainability Officer, or CSO, in order to focus attention on sustainability goals and also bring some point of accountability at the senior executive level for their accomplishment. In terms of the job description I would argue that things like this would need to be reflected. First, there should be some acknowledgement of the "triple bottom line" of economic, social, and environmental performance. Second there should be a clear focus on sustainable development in respect to moving the organization forward in ways that while making use of the environment and its resources, the capacity of the environment to nurture and serve future generations is also being protected. This sets the foundation for further priorities or objectives to be set in the areas of pushing for green management practices that support sustainability in all aspects of an organization's operations. And finally there should be a responsibility to serve as the "champion" for sustainable innovations that advance the capability of the organization to be sustainable by green products, green processes and even green business models.

Chapter 5

1. c **2.** c **3.** b **4.** d **5.** a **6.** a **7.** d **8.** c **9.** a
10. d **11.** d **12.** a **13.** c **14.** c **15.** c

16. The relationship between an global corporation and a host country should be mutually beneficial. Sometimes, however, host countries complain that MNCs take unfair advantage of them and do not include them in the benefits of their international operations. The complaints against MNCs include taking excessive profits out of the host country, hiring the best local labor, not respecting local laws and customs, and dominating the local economy. Engaging in corrupt practices is another important concern.

17. The power-distance dimension of national culture reflects the degree to which members of a society accept status and authority inequalities. Since organizations are hierarchies with power varying from top to bottom, the way power differences are viewed from one setting to the next is an important management issue. Relations between managers and subordinates, or team leaders and team members, will be very different in high-power-distance cultures than in low-power-distance ones. The significance of these differences is most evident in international operations, when a manager from a high-power-distance culture has to perform in a low-power-distance one, or vice versa. In both cases, the cultural differences can cause problems as the manager deals with local workers.

18. In Project GLOBE the cultural dimension of institutional collectivism describes the degree to which members of a society emphasize and reward group actions, rather than individual actions. In-group collectivism describes a society in which members take pride in family and their group or organizational memberships.

19. For each region of the world you should identify a major economic theme, issue, or element. For example: Europe—the European Union should be discussed for its economic significance to member countries and to outsiders; the Americas—NAFTA should be discussed for its current implications, as well as its potential significance once Chile and other nations join; Asia—the Asia-Pacific Economic Forum should be identified as a platform for growing regional economic cooperation among a very economically powerful group of countries; Africa—the new nonracial democracy in South Africa should be cited as a stimulus to broader outside investor interest in Africa.

20. Kim must recognize that the cultural differences between the United States and Japan may affect the success of group-oriented work practices such as quality circles and work teams. The United States was the most individualistic culture in Hofstede's study of national cultures; Japan is much more collectivist. Group practices such as the quality circle and teams are natural and consistent with the Japanese culture. When introduced into a more individualistic culture, these same practices might cause difficulties or require some time for workers to get used to them. At the very least, Kim should proceed with caution; discuss ideas for the new practices with the workers before making any changes; and then monitor the changes closely, so that adjustments can be made to improve them as the workers gain familiarity with them and have suggestions of their own.

Chapter 6

1. c   **2.** a   **3.** b   **4.** b   **5.** b   **6.** a   **7.** d   **8.** a   **9.** b
10. a   **11.** b   **12.** d   **13.** c   **14.** b   **15.** d

16. Entrepreneurship is rich with diversity. It is an avenue for business entry and career success that is pursued by many women and members of minority groups. Data show that almost 40% of U.S. businesses are owned by women. Many report leaving other employment because they had limited opportunities. For them, entrepreneurship made available the opportunities for career success that they had lacked. Minority-owned businesses are one of the fastest-growing sectors, with the growth rates highest for Hispanic-owned,

Asian-owned, and African American-owned businesses, in that order.

17. The three stages in the life cycle of an entrepreneurial firm are birth, breakthrough, and maturity. In the birth stage, the leader is challenged to get customers, establish a market, and find the money needed to keep the business going. In the breakthrough stage, the challenges shift to becoming and staying profitable, and managing growth. In the maturity stage, a leader is more focused on revising/maintaining a good business strategy and more generally managing the firm for continued success, and possibly for more future growth.

18. The limited partnership form of small business ownership consists of a general partner and one or more "limited partners." The general partner(s) play an active role in managing and operating the business; the limited partners do not. All contribute resources of some value to the partnership for the conduct of the business. The advantage of any partnership form is that the partners may share in profits, but their potential for losses is limited by the size of their original investments.

19. A venture capitalist, often a business, makes a living by investing in and taking large ownership interests in fledgling companies, with the goal of large financial gains eventually, when the company is sold. An angel investor is an individual who is willing to make a financial investment in return for some ownership in the new firm.

20. My friend is right—it takes a lot of forethought and planning to prepare the launch of a new business venture. In response to the question of how to ensure that I am really being customer-focused, I would ask and answer for myself the following questions. In all cases I would try to frame my business model so that the answers are realistic, but still push my business toward a strong customer orientation. The "customer" questions might include: "Who are my potential customers? What market niche am I shooting for? What do the customers in this market really want? How do these customers make purchase decisions? How much will it cost to produce and distribute my product/service to these customers? How much will it cost to attract and retain customers?" After preparing an overall executive summary, which includes a commitment to this customer orientation, I would address the following areas in writing up my initial business plan: a company description—mission, owners, and legal form—as well as an industry analysis, product and services description, marketing description and strategy, staffing model, financial projections with cash flows, and capital needs.

Chapter 7

1. c   **2.** c   **3.** c   **4.** a   **5.** c   **6.** c   **7.** b   **8.** a   **9.** c
10. b   **11.** c   **12.** a   **13.** a   **14.** b   **15.** d

16. An optimizing decision is one that represents the absolute "best" choice of alternatives. It is selected from a set of all known alternatives. A satisficing decision selects the first alternative that offers a "satisfactory" choice, not necessarily the absolute best choice. It is selected from a limited or incomplete set of alternatives.

17. The ethics of a decision can be checked with the "spotlight" question: "How would you feel if your family found out?" "How would you feel if this were published in the local newspaper?" Also, one can test the decision by evaluating it on four criteria: (1) Utility—does it satisfy all stakeholders? (2) Rights—does it respect everyone's rights? (3) Justice—is it consistent with fairness and justice? (4) Caring—does it meet responsibilities for caring?

18. A manager using systematic thinking is going to approach problem solving in a logical and rational fashion. The tendency will be to proceed in a linear, step-by-step fashion, handling one issue at a time. A manager using intuitive thinking will be more spontaneous and open in problem solving. He or she may jump from one stage in the process to another and deal with many different things at once.

19. It almost seems contradictory to say that one can prepare for crisis, but it is possible. The concept of crisis management is used to describe how managers and others prepare for unexpected high-impact events that threaten an organization's health and well-being. Crisis management involves both anticipating possible crises and preparing teams and plans ahead of time for how to handle them if they do occur. Many organizations today, for example, are developing crisis management plans to deal with terrorism and computer "hacking" attacks.

20. This is what I would say in the mentoring situation: continuing developments in information technology are changing the work setting for most employees. An important development for the traditional white-collar worker falls in the area of office automation—the use of computers and related technologies to facilitate everyday office work. In the "electronic office" of today and tomorrow, you should be prepared to work with and take full advantage of the following: smart workstations supported by desktop computers; voice messaging systems, whereby computers take dictation, answer the telephone, and relay messages; database and word processing software systems that allow storage, access, and manipulation of data, as well as the preparation of reports; electronic mail systems that send mail and data from computer to computer; electronic bulletin boards for posting messages; and computer conferencing and videoconferencing that allow people to work with one another every day over great distances. These are among the capabilities of the new workplace. To function effectively, you must be prepared not only to use these systems to full advantage, but also to stay abreast of new developments as they become available.

Chapter 8

1. d **2.** a **3.** a **4.** d **5.** b **6.** c **7.** a **8.** d **9.** a
10. b **11.** a **12.** c **13.** c **14.** d **15.** c

16. The five steps in the formal planning process are: (1) define your objectives, (2) determine where you stand relative to objectives, (3) develop premises about future conditions, (4) identify and choose among action alternatives to accomplish objectives, (5) implement action plans and evaluate results.

17. Benchmarking is the use of external standards to help evaluate one's own situation and develop ideas and directions for improvement. The bookstore owner/manager might visit other bookstores in other towns that are known for their success. By observing and studying the operations of those stores and then comparing her store to them, the owner/manager can develop plans for future action.

18. Planning helps improve focus for organizations and for individuals. Essential to the planning process is identifying

your objectives and specifying exactly where it is you hope to get in the future. Having a clear sense of direction helps keep us on track by avoiding getting sidetracked on things that might not contribute to accomplishing our objectives. It also helps us to find discipline in stopping periodically to assess how well we are doing. With a clear objective, present progress can be realistically evaluated and efforts refocused on accomplishing the objective.

19. Very often plans fail because the people who make the plans aren't the same ones who must implement them. When people who will be implementing are allowed to participate in the planning process, at least two positive results may happen that help improve implementation: (1) through involvement they better understand the final plans, and (2) through involvement they become more committed to making those plans work.

20. I would begin the speech by describing the importance of goal alignment as an integrated planning and control approach. I would also clarify that the key elements are objectives and participation. Any objectives should be clear, measurable, and time-defined. In addition, these objectives should be set with the full involvement and participation of the employees; they should not be set by the manager and then told to the employees. That understood, I would describe how each business manager should jointly set objectives with each of his or her employees and jointly review progress toward their accomplishment. I would suggest that the employees should work on the required activities while staying in communication with their managers. The managers, in turn, should provide any needed support or assistance to their employees. This whole process could be formally recycled at least twice per year.

Chapter 9

1. a **2.** b **3.** c **4.** c **5.** d **6.** b **7.** c **8.** a **9.** b
10. a **11.** d **12.** c **13.** d **14.** b **15.** a

16. A corporate strategy sets long-term direction for an enterprise as a whole. Functional strategies set directions so that business functions such as marketing and manufacturing support the overall corporate strategy.

17. A SWOT analysis is useful during strategic planning. It involves the analysis of organizational strengths and weaknesses, and of environmental opportunities and threats.

18. The focus strategy concentrates attention on a special market segment or niche. The differentiation strategy concentrates on building loyalty to a unique product or service.

19. Strategic leadership is the ability to enthuse people to participate in continuous change, performance enhancement, and the implementation of organizational strategies. The special qualities of the successful strategic leader include the ability to make trade-offs, create a sense of urgency, communicate the strategy, and engage others in continuous learning about the strategy and its performance responsibilities.

20. Porter's competitive strategy model involves the possible use of three alternative strategies: differentiation, cost leadership, and focus. In this situation, the larger department store seems better positioned to follow the cost leadership strategy. This means that Kim may want to consider the other two alternatives.

A differentiation strategy would involve trying to distinguish Kim's products from those of the larger store. This might involve a "made in America" theme, or an emphasis on leather, canvas, or some other type of clothing material. A focus strategy might specifically target college students and try to respond to their tastes and needs, rather than those of the larger community population. This might involve special orders and other types of individualized service for the college student market.

Chapter 10

1. b **2.** a **3.** b **4.** a **5.** b **6.** c **7.** b **8.** b **9.** a
10. d **11.** c **12.** b **13.** b **14.** c **15.** b

16. The functional structure is prone to problems of internal coordination. One symptom may be that the different functional areas, such as marketing and manufacturing, are not working well together. This structure is also slow in responding to changing environmental trends and challenges. If the firm finds that its competitors are getting to market faster with new and better products, this is another potential indicator that the functional structure is not supporting operations properly.

17. A network structure often involves one organization "contracting out" aspects of its operations to other organizations that specialize in them. The example used in the text was of a company that contracted out its mailroom services. Through the formation of networks of contracts, the organization is reduced to a core of essential employees whose expertise is concentrated in the primary business areas. The contracts are monitored and maintained in the network to allow the overall operations of the organization to continue, even though they are not directly accomplished by full-time employees.

18. The term "contingency" is used in management to indicate that management strategies and practices should be tailored to fit the unique needs of individual situations. There is no universal solution that fits all problems and circumstances. Thus, in organizational design, contingency thinking must be used to identify and implement particular organizational points in time. What works well at one point in time may not work well at another, as the environment and other conditions change. For example, the more complex, variable, and uncertain the elements in the environment, the more difficult it is for the organization to operate. This situation calls for a more organic design. In a stable and more certain environment, the mechanistic design is appropriate, because operations are more routine and predictable.

19. Several options for answering this question are described in the chapter.

20. Faisal must first have confidence in the two engineers—he must trust them and respect their capabilities. Second, he must have confidence in himself, trusting his own judgment to give up some work and allow the others to do it. Third, he should follow the rules of effective delegation. These include being very clear on what must be accomplished by each engineer. Their responsibilities should be clearly understood. He must also give them the authority to act in order to fulfill their responsibility, especially in relationship to the other engineers. And he must not forget his own final accountability for the results. He should remain in control and, through communication, make sure that work proceeds as planned.

Chapter 11

1. b **2.** a **3.** b **4.** c **5.** c **6.** b **7.** a **8.** c **9.** d
10. d **11.** a **12.** d **13.** b **14.** a **15.** b

16. Core values indicate important beliefs that underlie organizational expectations about the behavior and contributions of members. Sample values for high-performance organizations might include expressed commitments to honesty and integrity, innovation, customer service, quality, and respect for people.

17. Subcultures are important in organizations because of the many aspects of diversity found in the workforce. Although working in the same organization and sharing the same organizational culture, members differ in subculture affiliations based on such aspects as gender, age, and ethnic differences, as well as in respect to occupational and functional affiliations. It is important to understand how subculture differences may influence working relationships. For example, a 40-year-old manager of 20-year-old workers must understand that the values and behaviors of the younger workforce may not be totally consistent with what she or he believes in, and vice versa.

18. Lewin's three phases of planned change and the relevant change leadership responsibilities are: unfreezing-preparing a system for change; changing- moving or creating change in a system; and refreezing-stabilizing and reinforcing change once it has occurred. In addition, we might talk about an additional or parallel phase of "improvising." This calls for change leadership that is good at gathering feedback, listening to resistance, and making constructive modifications as the change is in progress to smooth its implementation and make sure what is implemented is a best fit for the circumstances and people involved.

19. Use of force-coercion as a strategy of planned change is limited by the likelihood of compliance being the major outcome. People "comply" with force only so long as it remains real, visible, and likely, but they have no personal commitment to the behavior. So, when the force goes away, so does the behavior. Also, a manager who relies on forcing people to get changes made is likely to be viewed negatively by them and suffer from additional negative halo effects in other work with them. Rational persuasion and shared power are likely to have more long-lasting impact on behavior since the person responds to the change strategy by internalization of the value of the behavior being encouraged. Because of this commitment the influence on their actions is more likely to be long-lasting rather than temporary as in the case of force-coercion.

20. I disagree with this statement, because a strong organizational or corporate culture can be a positive influence on any organization, large or small. Also, issues of diversity, inclusiveness, and multiculturalism apply as well. In fact, such things as a commitment to pluralism and respect for diversity should be part of the core values and distinguishing features of the organization's culture. The woman working for the large company is mistaken in thinking that the concepts do not apply to her friend's small business. In fact, the friend—as owner and perhaps founder of the business—should be working hard to establish the values and other elements that will create a strong and continuing culture and respect for diversity. Employees of any organization should have core organizational values to serve as reference points for their attitudes and behavior. The rites and rituals of everyday organizational life are also important ways to recognize positive accomplishments and add meaning to the employment relationships. It may even be that the friend's roles as diversity leader and creator and sponsor of the corporate culture are more magnified in the small business setting. As the owner and manager, she is visible every day to all employees. How she acts will have a great impact on any "culture"

Chapter 12

1. a   **2.** b   **3.** c   **4.** d   **5.** b   **6.** c   **7.** d   **8.** b   **9.** b
10. c   **11.** d   **12.** a   **13.** b   **14.** a   **15.** b

16. Internal recruitment deals with job candidates who already know the organization well. It is also a strong motivator because it communicates to everyone the opportunity to advance in the organization through hard work. External recruitment may allow the organization to obtain expertise not available internally. It also brings in employees with new and fresh viewpoints who are not biased by previous experience in the organization.

17. Orientation activities introduce a new employee to the organization and the work environment. This is a time when the individual may develop key attitudes and when performance expectations will also be established. Good orientation communicates positive attitudes and expectations and reinforces the desired organizational culture. It formally introduces the individual to important policies and procedures that everyone is expected to follow.

18. The graphic rating scale simply asks a supervisor to rate an employee on an established set of criteria, such as quantity of work or attitude toward work. This leaves a lot of room for subjectivity and debate. The behaviorally anchored rating scale asks the supervisor to rate the employee on specific behaviors that had been identified as positively or negatively affecting performance in a given job. This is a more specific appraisal approach and leaves less room for debate and disagreement.

19. Mentoring is when a senior and experienced individual adopts a newcomer or more junior person with the goal of helping him or her develop into a successful worker. The mentor may or may not be the individual's immediate supervisor. The mentor meets with the individual and discusses problems, shares advice, and generally supports the individual's attempts to grow and perform. Mentors are considered very useful for persons newly appointed to management positions.

20. As Sy's supervisor, you face a difficult but perhaps expected human resource management problem. Not only is Sy influential as an informal leader, he also has considerable experience on the job and in the company. Even though he is experiencing performance problems using the new computer system, there is no indication that he doesn't want to work hard and continue to perform for the company. Although retirement is an option, Sy may also be transferred, promoted, or simply terminated. The latter response seems unjustified and may cause legal problems. Transferring Sy, with his agreement, to another position could be a positive move; promoting Sy to a supervisory position in which his experience and networks would be useful is another possibility. The key in this situation seems to be moving Sy out so that a computer-literate person can take over the job, while continuing to utilize Sy in a job that better fits his talents. Transfer and/or promotion should be actively considered, both in his and in the company's interest.

Chapter 13

1. d   **2.** d   **3.** b   **4.** a   **5.** c   **6.** a   **7.** b   **8.** c   **9.** b
10. a   **11.** b   **12.** a   **13.** d   **14.** a   **15.** b

16. Position power is based on reward; coercion, or punishment; and legitimacy, or formal authority. Managers, however, need to have more power than that made available to them by the position alone. Thus, they have to develop personal power through expertise and reference. This personal power is essential in helping managers to get things done beyond the scope of their position power alone.

17. Leader-participation theory suggests that leadership effectiveness is determined in part by how well managers or leaders handle the many different problem or decision situations that they face every day. Decisions can be made through individual or authority, consultative, or group-consensus approaches. No one of these decision methods is always the best; each is a good fit for certain types of situations. A good manager or leader is able to use each of these approaches and knows when each is the best approach to use in particular situations.

18. The three variables used in Fiedler's model to diagnose situational favorableness are: (1) position power—how much power the leader has in terms of rewards, punishments, and legitimacy; (2) leader-member relations—the quality of relationships between the leader and followers; and (3) task structure—the degree to which the task is either clear and well defined, or open-ended and more ambiguous.

19. Drucker says that good leaders have more than the "charisma" or "personality" being popularized in the concept of transformational leadership. He reminds us that good leaders work hard to accomplish some basic things in their everyday activities. These include: (1) establishing a clear sense of mission; (2) accepting leadership as a responsibility, not a rank; and (3) earning and keeping the respect of others.

20. In his new position, Marcel must understand that the transactional aspects of leadership are not sufficient to guarantee him long-term leadership effectiveness. He must move beyond the effective use of task-oriented and people-oriented behaviors and demonstrate through his personal qualities the capacity to inspire others. A charismatic leader develops a unique relationship with followers, in which they become enthusiastic, highly loyal, and high achievers. Marcel needs to work very hard to develop positive relationships with the team members. In those relationships he must emphasize high aspirations for performance accomplishments, enthusiasm, ethical behavior, integrity and honesty in all dealings, and a clear vision of the future. By working hard with this agenda and by allowing his personality to positively express itself in the team setting, Marcel should make continuous progress as an effective and moral leader.

Chapter 14

1. c   **2.** b   **3.** d   **4.** a   **5.** c   **6.** d   **7.** b   **8.** c   **9.** a
10. b   **11.** d   **12.** d   **13.** c   **14.** a   **15.** c

16. A psychological contract is the individual's view of the inducements he or she expects to receive from the organization in return for his or her work contributions. The contract is healthy when the individual perceives that the inducements and contributions are fair and in a state of balance.

17. Self-serving bias is the attribution tendency to blame the environment when things go wrong—"It's not my fault; 'they' caused all this mess." Fundamental attribution error is the tendency to blame others for problems that they have—"It's something wrong with 'you' that's causing the problem."

18. All the Big Five personality traits are relevant to the workplace. Consider the following basic examples. Extraversion suggests whether or not a person will reach out to relate and work well with others. Agreeableness suggests whether or not a person is open to the ideas of others and willing to go along with group decisions. Conscientiousness suggests whether or not someone can be depended on to meet commitments and perform agreed-upon tasks. Emotional stability suggests whether or not someone will be relaxed and secure, or uptight and tense, in work situations. Openness to experience suggests whether or not someone will be open to new ideas or resistant to change.

19. The Type A personality is characteristic of people who bring stress on themselves by virtue of personal characteristics. These tend to be compulsive individuals who are uncomfortable waiting for things to happen, who try to do many things at once, and who generally move fast and have difficulty slowing down. Type A personalities can be stressful for both themselves and the people around them. Managers must be aware of Type A personality tendencies in their own behavior and among others with whom they work. Ideally, this awareness will help the manager take precautionary steps to best manage the stress caused by this personality type.

20. Scott needs to be careful. Although there is modest research support for the relationship between job satisfaction and performance, there is no guarantee that simply doing things to make people happier at work will cause them to be higher performers. Scott needs to take a broader perspective on this issue and his responsibilities as a manager. He should be interested in job satisfaction for his therapists and do everything he can to help them to experience it. But he should also be performance-oriented, and should understand that performance is achieved through a combination of skills, support, and motivation. He should be helping the therapists to achieve and maintain high levels of job competency. He should also work with them to find out what obstacles they are facing and what support they need—things that perhaps he can deal with in their behalf. All of this relates as well to research indications that performance can be a source of job satisfaction. And finally, Scott should make sure that the therapists believe they are being properly rewarded for their work, because rewards are shown by research to have an influence on both job satisfaction and job performance.

Chapter 15

1. c **2.** d **3.** d **4.** b **5.** b **6.** d **7.** c **8.** d **9.** a
10. b **11.** c **12.** a **13.** b **14.** a **15.** b

16. People high in need for achievement will prefer work settings and jobs in which they have (1) challenging but achievable goals, (2) individual responsibility, and (3) performance feedback.

17. Participation is important to goal-setting theory because, in general, people tend to be more committed to the accomplishment of goals they have helped to set. When people participate in the setting of goals, they also understand them better. Participation in goal setting improves goal acceptance and understanding.

18. Maslow, McClelland, and Herzberg would likely find common agreement in respect to a set of "higher order" needs. For Maslow these are self-actualization and ego; they correspond with Alderfer's growth needs, and with McClelland's needs for achievement and power. Maslow's social needs link up with relatedness needs in Alderfer's theory and the need for affiliation in McClelland's theory. Maslow's safety needs correspond to Alderfer's existence needs. Herzberg's "satisfier-factors" correspond to satisfactions of Maslow's higher needs, Alderfer's growth needs, and McClelland's need for achievement.

19. The compressed work week, or 4-40 schedule, offers employees the advantage of a three-day weekend. However, it can cause problems for the employer in terms of ensuring that operations are covered adequately during the normal five workdays of the week. Labor unions may resist, and the compressed workweek will entail more complicated work scheduling. In addition, some employees find that the schedule is tiring and can cause family adjustment problems.

20. It has already been pointed out in the answer to question 16 that a person with a high need for achievement likes moderately challenging goals and performance feedback. Participation of both manager and subordinate in goal setting offers an opportunity to choose goals to which the subordinate will respond, and which also will serve the organization. Furthermore, through goal setting the manager and individual subordinates can identify performance standards or targets. Progress toward these targets can be positively reinforced by the manager. Such reinforcements can serve as indicators of progress to someone with a high need for achievement, thus responding to their desire for performance feedback.

Chapter 16

1. d **2.** b **3.** b **4.** d **5.** b **6.** d **7.** b **8.** b **9.** a
10. b **11.** c **12.** b **13.** a **14.** b **15.** a

16. Input factors can have a major impact on group effectiveness. In order to best prepare a group to perform effectively, a manager should make sure that the right people are put in the group (maximize available talents and abilities), that these people are capable of working well together (membership characteristics should promote good relationships), that the tasks are clear, and that the group has the resources and environment needed to perform up to expectations.

17. A group's performance can be analyzed according to the interaction between cohesiveness and performance norms. In a highly cohesive group, members tend to conform to group norms. Thus, when the performance norm is positive and cohesion is high, we can expect everyone to work hard to support the norm—high performance is likely. By the same token, high cohesion and a low performance norm will yield the opposite result—low performance is likely. With other combinations of norms and cohesion, the performance results will be more mixed.

18. The textbook lists several symptoms of groupthink, along with various strategies for avoiding groupthink. For example, a group whose members censor themselves from contributing "contrary" or "different" opinions and/or whose members keep talking about outsiders as "weak" or the "enemy" may be suffering from groupthink. This may be avoided or corrected, for example, by asking someone to be the "devil's advocate" for a meeting, and by inviting in an outside observer to help gather different viewpoints.

19. In a traditional work group, the manager or supervisor directs the group. In a self-managing team, the members of the team provide self-direction. They plan, organize, and evaluate their work, share tasks, and help one another develop skills; they may even make hiring decisions. A true self-managing team does not need the traditional "boss" or supervisor, because the team as a whole takes on the supervisory responsibilities.

20. Marcos is faced with a highly cohesive group whose members conform to a negative, or low-performance norm. This is a difficult situation that is ideally resolved by changing the performance norm. In order to gain the group's commitment to a high-performance norm, Marcos should act as a positive role model for the norm. He must communicate the norm clearly and positively to the group and should not assume that everyone knows what he expects of them. He may also talk to the informal leader and gain his or her commitment to the norm. He might carefully reward high-performance behaviors within the group and may introduce new members with high-performance records and commitments. And he might hold group meetings in which performance standards and expectations are discussed, with an emphasis on committing to new high-performance directions. If his attempts to introduce a high-performance norm fail, Marcos may have to take steps to reduce group cohesiveness so that individual members can pursue higher-performance results without feeling bound by group pressures to restrict their performance.

Chapter 17

1. b   **2.** a   **3.** c   **4.** b   **5.** c   **6.** b   **7.** b   **8.** d   **9.** c
10. a   **11.** d   **12.** b   **13.** d   **14.** d   **15.** a

16. The manager's goal in active listening is to help the subordinate say what he or she really means. To do this, the manager should carefully listen for the content of what someone is saying, paraphrase or reflect back what the person appears to be saying, remain sensitive to nonverbal cues and feelings, and not be evaluative.

17. The inverted "U" curve of conflict intensity shows that as conflict intensity increases from low to moderate levels, performance increases. This is the zone of constructive conflict. As conflict intensity moves into extreme levels, performance tends to decrease. This is the zone of destructive conflict.

18. Win-lose outcomes are likely when conflict is managed through high-assertiveness and low-cooperativeness styles. In this situation of competition, the conflict is resolved by one person or group dominating another. Lose-lose outcomes occur when conflict is managed through avoidance (where nothing is resolved), and possibly when it is managed through compromise (where each party gives up something to the other). Win-win outcomes are associated mainly with problem

solving and collaboration in conflict management, which result from high assertiveness and high cooperativeness.

19. In a negotiation, both substance and relationship goals are important. Substance goals relate to the content of the negotiation. A substance goal, for example, may relate to the final salary agreement between a job candidate and a prospective employer. Relationship goals relate to the quality of the interpersonal relationships among the negotiating parties. Relationship goals are important, because the negotiating parties most likely have to work together in the future. For example, if relationships are poor after a labor-management negotiation, the likelihood is that future problems will occur.

20. Kathryn can do a number of things to establish and maintain a system of upward communication for her department store branch. To begin, she should, as much as possible, try to establish a highly interactive style of management based upon credibility and trust. Credibility is earned by building personal power through expertise and reference. In regard to credibility, she might set the tone for the department managers by using MBWA—"managing by wandering around." Once this pattern is established, trust will build between her and other store employees, and she should find that she learns a lot from interacting directly with them. Kathryn should also set up a formal communication structure, such as bimonthly store meetings, where she communicates store goals, results, and other issues to the staff and listens to them in return. An e-mail system whereby Kathryn and her staff could send messages to one another from their workstation computers would also be beneficial.

Chapter 18

1. a   **2.** b   **3.** d   **4.** b   **5.** b   **6.** b   **7.** d   **8.** b   **9.** b
10. c   **11.** a   **12.** b   **13.** c   **14.** c   **15.** c

16. The four steps in the formal planning process are: (1) establish objectives and standards, (2) measure actual performance, (3) compare actual performance with objectives and standards, and (4) take necessary action.

17. Feedforward control involves the careful selection of system inputs to ensure that outcomes are of the desired quality and up to all performance standards. In the case of a local bookstore, one of the major points of influence over performance and customer satisfaction is the relationship between the customers and the store's employees who serve them. Thus, a good example of feedforward control is exercising great care when the manager hires new employees and then trains them to work according to the store's expectations.

18. Douglas McGregor's concept of Theory Y involves the assumption that people can be trusted to exercise self-control in their work. This is the essence of internal control—people controlling their own work by taking personal responsibility for results. If managers approach work with McGregor's Theory Y assumptions, they will, according to him, promote more self-control—or internal control—by people at work.

19. A progressive discipline system works by adjusting the discipline to fit the severity and frequency of the inappropriate behavior. In the case of a person who comes late to work, for example, progressive discipline might involve a verbal warning after three late arrivals, a written warning after five, and a pay-loss penalty after seven. In the case of a person who steals money from the business, there would be immediate dismissal after the first such infraction.

20. There are a very large number of activities required to complete a new student center building on a college campus. Among them, one might expect the following to be core requirements: (1) land surveys and planning permissions from local government, (2) architect plans developed and approved, (3) major subcontractors hired, (4) site excavation completed, (5) building exterior completed, (6) building interior completed and furnishings installed. Use Figure 18.5 from the chapter as a guide for developing your AON diagram.

Chapter 19

1. c **2.** c **3.** c **4.** a **5.** a **6.** b **7.** d **8.** b **9.** d
10. c **11.** b **12.** c **13.** b **14.** c **15.** a

16. Possible operating objectives reflecting a commitment to competitive advantage through customer service include: (1) providing high-quality goods and services, (2) producing at low cost so that goods and services can be sold at low prices, (3) providing short waiting times for goods and services, and (4) providing goods and services meeting unique customer needs.

17. External customers are the consumers or clients in the specific environment who buy the organization's goods or use its services. Internal customers are found internally in the workflows among people and subsystems in the organization. They are individuals or groups within the organization who utilize goods and services produced by others who are also inside the organization.

18. Supply chain management is important due to the cost of resources, the costs of holding things in inventory, and all the costs of transporting resources and supplies for the organization. SCM uses the latest technologies and systematic management to oversee all aspects of inbound logistics so that the various elements and activities in the organization's supply chains operate as efficiently and as effectively as possible.

19. The focus of process reengineering is on reducing costs and streamlining operations efficiency while improving customer service. This is accomplished by closely examining core business processes through the following sequence of activities: (1) identify the core processes; (2) map them in a workflows diagram; (3) evaluate all tasks involved; (4) seek ways to eliminate unnecessary tasks; (5) seek ways to eliminate delays, errors, and misunderstandings in the workflows; and (6) seek efficiencies in how work is shared and transferred among people and departments.

20. Although the appropriateness of the measure would vary by department or area of each organization that one is addressing, possible productivity measures are:

(a) U.S. Post Office—# letters delivered per day / # letter carriers on payroll

(b) University—# students enrolled / (# full-time 1 part-time faculty)

(c) Hospital—# patients per day / # available hospital beds

(d) Amusement park—# paid admissions per day / # available rides

(e) Restaurant—# meals served per day / # servers on payroll

Glossary

A

3 Ps of organizational performance are Profit, People, and Planet.

360-degree appraisals includes superiors, subordinates, peers, and even customers in the appraisal process.

Accommodation or smoothing, plays down differences and highlights similarities to reduce conflict.

Accommodative strategy accepts social responsibility and tries to satisfy economic, legal, and ethical criteria.

According to the **deficit principle** a satisfied need does not motivate behavior.

According to the **progression principle** a need is activated only when the next lower level need is satisfied.

Accountability is the requirement to show performance results to a supervisor.

Active listening helps the source of a message say what he or she really means.

Adaptive organization operates with a minimum of bureaucratic features and encourages worker empowerment and teamwork.

Administrator is a manager in a public or nonprofit organization.

Affirmative action is an effort to give preference in employment to women and minority group members who have traditionally been underrepresented.

Agenda setting develops action priorities for accomplishing goals and plans.

Agreeableness is being good-natured, cooperative, and trusting.

Ambidextrous organization uses integrated creative teams to simultaneously be good at both producing and creating.

Amoral manager fails to consider the ethics of her or his behavior.

Analytics is the systematic use and analysis of data to solve problems and make informed decisions.

Anchoring and adjustment bias bases a decision on incremental adjustments from a prior decision point.

Angel investor is a wealthy individual willing to invest in a new venture in return for equity in a new venture.

Assessment center examines how job candidates handle simulated work situations.

Attitude is a predisposition to act in a certain way.

Attribution is the process of explaining events.

Authentic leadership activates positive psychological states to achieve self-awareness and positive self-regulation.

Authoritarianism is the degree to which a person tends to defer to authority.

Authority decision is made by the leader and then communicated to the group.

Autocratic leader acts in a command-and-control fashion.

Automation is the total mechanization of a job.

Availability bias bases a decision on recent information or events.

Avoidance, or withdrawal, pretends that a conflict doesn't really exist.

B

Balance sheet shows assets and liabilities at one point in time.

Balanced scorecard tallies organizational performance in financial, customer service, internal process, and innovation and learning areas.

Bargaining zone is the space between one party's minimum reservation point and the other party's maximum reservation point.

Base compensation is a salary or hourly wage paid to an individual.

BCG matrix analyzes business opportunities according to market growth rate and market share.

Behavioral decision model describes decision making with limited information and bounded rationality.

Behavioral interviews ask job applicants about past behaviors.

Behaviorally anchored rating scale uses specific descriptions of actual behaviors to rate various levels of performance.

Benchmarking uses external and internal comparisons to plan for future improvements.

Best practices are things people and organizations do that lead to superior performance.

Biculturalism is when minority members adopt characteristics of majority cultures in order to succeed.

Biodata methods collect certain biographical information that has been proven to correlate with good job performance.

Bona fide occupational qualifications are employment criteria justified by capacity to perform a job.

Bonus pay plans provide one-time payments based on performance accomplishments.

Boundaryless organization eliminates internal boundaries among subsystems and external boundaries with the external environment.

Bounded rationality describes making decisions within the constraints of limited information and alternatives.

Brainstorming engages group members in an open, spontaneous discussion of problems and ideas.

Break-even analysis calculates the point at which revenues cover costs under different "what if" conditions.

Break-even point is where revenues = costs.

Budget is a plan that commits resources to projects or activities.

Bureaucracy is a rational and efficient form of organization founded on logic, order, and legitimate authority.

Bureaucratic control influences behavior through authority, policies, procedures, job descriptions, budgets, and day-to-day supervision.

Business incubators offer space, shared services, and advice to help get small businesses started.

Business model innovations result in ways for firms to make money.

Business plan describes the direction for a new business and the financing needed to operate it.

Business strategy identifies how a division or strategic business unit will compete in its product or service domain.

C

Centralization is the concentration of authority for most decisions at the top level of an organization.

Certain environment offers complete information on possible action alternatives and their consequences.

Chain of command links all persons with successively higher levels of authority.

Change leader takes initiative in trying to change the behavior of another person or social system.

Changing is the phase where a planned change actually takes place.

Channel richness is the capacity of a communication channel to effectively carry information.

Chapter 11 bankruptcy under U.S. law protects a firm from creditors while management reorganizes to restore solvency.

Charismatic leader inspires followers in extraordinary ways.

Child labor is the employment of children for work otherwise done by adults.

Clan control influences behavior through norms and expectations set by the organizational culture.

Classic entrepreneur is someone willing to pursue opportunities in situations others view as problems or threats.

Classical decision model describes decision making with complete information.

Classical view of CSR is that business should focus on profits.

Coaching occurs as an experienced person offers performance advice to a less experienced person.

Code of ethics is a formal statement of values and ethical standards.

Coercive power is the capacity to punish or withhold positive outcomes as a means of influencing other people.

Cognitive dissonance is discomfort felt when attitude and behavior are inconsistent.

Cognitive intelligence is the ability to think systematically and identify cause-effect patterns in data and events.

Cognitive styles are shown by the ways individuals deal with information while making decisions.

Cohesiveness is the degree to which members are attracted to and motivated to remain part of a team.

Collaboration, or problem solving, involves working through conflict differences and solving problems so everyone wins.

Collective bargaining is the process of negotiating, administering, and interpreting a labor contract.

Committee is designated to work on a special task on a continuing basis.

Communication channel is the pathway through which a message moves from sender to receiver.

Communication is the process of sending and receiving symbols with meanings attached.

Communication transparency involves openly sharing honest and complete information about the organization and workplace affairs.

Commutative justice is the degree to which an exchange or a transaction is fair to all parties.

Comparable worth holds that persons performing jobs of similar importance should be paid at comparable levels.

Comparative management studies how management practices differ among countries and cultures.

Competition, or authoritative command, uses force, superior skill, or domination to "win" a conflict.

Competitive advantage is the ability to outperform one's competitors due to a core competency that is difficult to copy or imitate.

Complacency trap is being carried along by the flow of events.

Compressed workweek allows a full-time job to be completed in less than five days.

Compromise occurs when each party to the conflict gives up something of value to the other.

Computer competency is the ability to understand computers and to use them to their best advantage.

Conceptual skill is the ability to think analytically to diagnose and solve complex problems.

Concurrent control focuses on what happens during the work process.

Confirmation error occurs when focusing only on information that confirms a decision already made.

Conflict is a disagreement over issues of substance and/or an emotional antagonism.

Conflict resolution is the removal of the substantial and emotional reasons for a conflict.

Conscientiousness is being responsible, dependable, and careful.

Constructive stress acts in a positive way to increase effort, stimulate creativity, and encourage diligence in one's work.

Consultative decision is made by a leader after receiving information, advice, or opinions from group members.

Contingency planning identifies alternative courses of action to take when things go wrong.

Contingency thinking tries to match management practices with situational demands.

Contingency workers are employed on a part-time and temporary basis to supplement a permanent workforce.

Continuous improvement involves always searching for new ways to improve work quality and performance.

Continuous reinforcement rewards each time a desired behavior occurs.

Control charts graphically plot quality trends against control limits.

Control equation states: Need for action = Desired performance − Actual performance.

Controlling is the process of measuring performance and taking action to ensure desired results.

Co-opetition is the strategy of working with rivals on projects of mutual benefit.

Core competency is a special strength that gives an organization a competitive advantage.

Core culture consists of the core values, or underlying assumptions and beliefs that shape and guide people's behaviors in an organization.

Core values are broad beliefs about what is or is not appropriate behavior.

Corporate governance is the oversight of top management by a board of directors.

Corporate governance is the system of control and performance monitoring of top management.

Corporate social responsibility is the obligation of an organization to serve the interests of society in addition to its own interests.

Corporate strategy sets long-term direction for the total enterprise.

Corporation is a legal entity that exists separately from its owners.

Corruption involves illegal practices to further one's business interests.

Cost leadership strategy seeks to operate with low cost so that products can be sold at low prices.

Cost-benefit analysis involves comparing the costs and benefits of each potential course of action.

CPM/PERT is a combination of the critical path method and the program evaluation and review technique.

Creativity is the generation of a novel idea or unique approach that solves a problem or crafts an opportunity.

Credible communication earns trust, respect, and integrity in the eyes of others.

Crisis decision occurs when an unexpected problem can lead to disaster if not resolved quickly and appropriately.

Critical-incident technique keeps a log of someone's effective and ineffective job behaviors.

Cross-functional team operates with members who come from different functional units of an organization.

Cultural intelligence is the ability to accept and adapt to new cultures.

Cultural relativism suggests there is no one right way to behave; ethical behavior is determined by its cultural context.

Culture is a shared set of beliefs, values, and patterns of behavior common to a group of people.

Culture shock is the confusion and discomfort a person experiences when in an unfamiliar culture.

Customer relationship management, or **CRM**, uses information technologies to communicate with customers and gather data tracking their needs and desires.

D

Data are raw facts and observations.

Debt financing involves borrowing money that must be repaid over time, with interest.

Decentralization is the dispersion of authority to make decisions throughout all organization levels.

Decentralized communication network allows all members to communicate directly with one another.

Decision is a choice among possible alternative courses of action.

Decision making is the process of making choices among alternative possible courses of action.

Decision-making process begins with identification of a problem and ends with evaluation of implemented solutions.

Defensive strategy seeks protection by doing the minimum legally required.

Deficit principle states that a satisfied need does not motivate behavior.

Delegation is the process of distributing and entrusting work to other persons.

Demand legitimacy indicates the validity and legitimacy of a stakeholder's interest in the organization.

Democratic leader emphasizes both tasks and people.

Departmentalization is the process of grouping people and jobs into work units.

Destructive stress impairs the performance of an individual.

Differentiation strategy offers products that are unique and different from the competition.

Discipline is the act of influencing behavior through reprimand.

Discrimination actively denies minority members the full benefits of organizational membership.

Disruptive activities are self-serving behaviors that interfere with team effectiveness.

Distributed leadership is when all members of a team contribute helpful task and maintenance behaviors.

Distributive justice focuses on the degree to which outcomes are distributed fairly.

Distributive negotiation focuses on win–lose claims made by each party for certain preferred outcomes.

Divestiture sells off parts of the organization to refocus attention on core business areas.

Divisional structure groups together people working on the same product, in the same area, with similar customers, or on the same processes.

Downsizing strategy decreases the size of operations.

Dysfunctional conflict is destructive and hurts task performance.

E

Early retirement incentive programs offer workers financial incentives to retire early.

Ecological fallacy assumes that a generalized cultural value applies equally well to all members of the culture.

Effective manager helps others achieve high performance and satisfaction at work.

Effective negotiation resolves issues of substance while maintaining a positive process.

Effective team achieves high levels of task performance, membership satisfaction, and future viability.

Efficient communication occurs at minimum cost.

Electronic grapevines use electronic media to pass messages and information among members of social networks.

Emotional conflict results from feelings of anger, distrust, dislike, fear, and resentment, as well as from personality clashes.

Emotional intelligence is the ability to manage ourselves and our relationships effectively.

Emotional stability is being relaxed, secure, and unworried.

Emotions are strong feelings directed toward someone or something.

Employee assistance programs help employees cope with personal stresses and problems.

Employee benefits are nonmonetary forms of compensation such as health insurance and retirement plans.

Employee engagement is willingness to help others do extra, and feeling positive about the organization.

Employee involvement team meets on a regular basis to help achieve continuous improvement.

Employee stock ownership plans help employees purchase stock in their employing companies.

Employment-at-will means that employees can be terminated at anytime for any reason.

Empowerment allows others to make decisions and exercise discretion in their work.

Enterprise 2.0 is the use of social networking and blog technologies in the workplace.

Entrepreneurship is risk-taking behavior that results in new opportunities.

Environmental capital or **natural capital** is the storehouse of natural resources—atmosphere, land, water, and, minerals, that we use to sustain life and produce goods and services for society.

Environmental uncertainty is a lack of information regarding what exists in the environment and what developments may occur.

Equal employment opportunity is the requirement that employment decisions be made without regard to race, color, national origin, religion, gender, age, or disability status.

Equity financing involves exchanging ownership shares for outside investment monies.

Escalating commitment is the continuation of a course of action even though it is not working.

Ethical behavior is "right" or "good" in the context of a governing moral code.

Ethical dilemma is a situation that offers potential benefit or gain and that may also be considered unethical.

Ethical framework is a personal rule or strategy for making ethical decisions.

Ethical imperialism is an attempt to impose one's ethical standards on other cultures.

Ethics establish standards of good or bad, or right or wrong, in one's conduct.

Ethics intensity or **issue intensity** indicates the degree to which an issue or a situation is recognized to pose important ethical challenges.

Ethics training seeks to help people understand the ethical aspects of decision making and to incorporate high ethical standards into their daily behavior.

Ethnic subcultures or **national subcultures** form among people who work together and have roots in the same ethnic community, country, or region of the world.

Ethnocentrism is the tendency to consider one's culture superior to others.

Euro is now the common European currency.

European Union is a political and economic alliance of European countries.

Evidence-based management involves making decisions based on hard facts about what really works.

Existence needs are desires for physical well-being.

Expectancy is a person's belief that working hard will result in high task performance.

Expert power is the capacity to influence other people because of specialized knowledge.

External recruitment seeks job applicants from outside the organization.

Extinction discourages behavior by making the removal of a desirable consequence contingent on its occurrence.

Extraversion is being outgoing, sociable, and assertive.

F

Family business is owned and controlled by members of a family.

Family business feud occurs when family members have major disagreements over how the business should be run.

Family-friendly benefits help employees achieve better work–life balance.

Feedback is the process of telling someone else how you feel about something that person did or said.

Feedback control takes place after an action is completed.

Feedforward control ensures that directions and resources are right before the work begins.

First-mover advantage comes from being first to exploit a niche or enter a market.

Flat structures have short spans of control and few hierarchical levels.

Flexible benefits programs allow employees to choose from a range of benefit options.

Flexible working hours give employees some choice in daily work hours.

Focus strategy concentrates on serving a unique market segment better than anyone else.

Focused cost leadership strategy seeks the lowest costs of operations within a special market segment.

Focused differentiation strategy offers a unique product to a special market segment.

Force-coercion strategy pursues change through formal authority and/or the use of rewards or punishments.

Forecasting attempts to predict the future.

Foreign Corrupt Practices Act (FCPA) makes it illegal for U.S. firms and their representatives to engage in corrupt practices overseas.

Foreign subsidiary is a local operation completely owned by a foreign firm.

Formal structure is the official structure of the organization.

Formal team is officially recognized and supported by the organization.

Framing error is trying to solve a problem in the context in which it is perceived.

Franchise is when one business owner sells to another the right to operate the same business in another location.

Frustration-regression principle states that an already satisfied need can become reactivated when a higher-level need is blocked.

Functional chimneys problem is a lack of communication and coordination across functions.

Functional conflict is constructive and helps task performance.

Functional managers are responsible for one area such as finance, marketing, production, personnel, accounting, or sales.

Functional plans indicate how different operations within the organization will help advance the overall strategy.

Functional strategy guides activities within one specific area of operations.

Functional structure groups together people with similar skills who perform similar tasks.

Functional subcultures form among people who work together in the same functional area, such as marketing, sales, and finance.

Fundamental attribution error overestimates internal factors and underestimates external factors as influences on someone's behavior.

G

Gain-sharing plans allow employees to share in cost savings or productivity gains realized by their efforts.

Gantt chart graphically displays the scheduling of tasks required to complete a project.

Gender similarities hypothesis holds that males and females have similar psychological properties.

Gender subcultures form among persons who work together and share the same gender identities.

General environment is comprised of economic, legal-political, technological, sociocultural, and natural environment conditions.

General managers are responsible for complex, multifunctional units.

Generational cohorts consist of people born within a few years of one another and who experience somewhat similar life events during their formative years.

Generational subcultures form among persons who work together and share similar ages, such as Millennials and Baby Boomers.

Geographical structure groups together people and jobs performed in the same location.

Glass ceiling is an invisible barrier to advancement by women and minorities in organizations.

Global corporation is a multinational enterprise (MNE) or multinational corporation (MNC) that conducts commercial transactions across national boundaries.

Global management involves managing operations in more than one country.

Global manager is culturally aware and informed on international affairs.

Global strategic alliance is a partnership in which foreign and domestic firms share resources and knowledge for mutual gains.

Globalization is the worldwide interdependence of resource flows, product markets, and business competition.

Globalization strategy adopts standardized products and advertising for use worldwide.

Graphic rating scale uses a checklist of traits or characteristics to evaluate performance.

Green management is managing people and organizations in ways that achieve responsible stewardship of the natural environment.

Group decision is made by group members themselves.

Groupthink is a tendency for highly cohesive teams to lose their evaluative capabilities.

Growth needs are desires for personal growth and development.

Growth strategy involves expansion of the organization's current operations.

Growth through **concentration** is within the same business area.

Growth through **diversification** is by acquisition of or investment in new and different business areas.

Growth through **vertical integration** is by acquiring suppliers or distributors.

H

Halo effect occurs when one attribute is used to develop an overall impression of a person or situation.

Hawthorne effect is the tendency of persons singled out for special attention to perform as expected.

Heuristics are strategies for simplifying decision making.

High-context cultures rely on nonverbal and situational cues as well as on spoken or written words in communication.

Higher-order needs are esteem and self-actualization needs in Maslow's hierarchy.

Human capital is the economic value of people with job-relevant abilities, knowledge, ideas, energies, and commitments.

Human relations leader emphasizes people over task.

Human relations movement suggested that managers using good human relations will achieve productivity.

Human resource management is a process of attracting, developing, and maintaining a talented work force.

Human resource planning analyzes staffing needs and identifies actions to fill those needs.

Human skill or interpersonal skill is the ability to work well in cooperation with other people.

Hygiene factor is found in the job context, such as working conditions, interpersonal relations, organizational policies, and salary.

I

Immoral manager chooses to behave unethically.

Importing involves the selling in domestic markets of products acquired abroad.

Impression management is the systematic attempt to influence how others perceive us.

Improvisational change makes continual adjustments as changes are being implemented.

In a **centralized communication network**, communication flows only between individual members and a hub, or center point.

In a **free-agent economy** people change jobs more often, and many work on independent contracts with a shifting mix of employers.

In a **hierarchy of goals** or **hierarchy of objectives,** lower-level goals and objectives are means to accomplishing higher-level ones.

In a **licensing agreement** a local firm pays a fee to a foreign firm for rights to make or sell its products.

In a **restricted communication network** subgroups have limited communication with one another.

In a **strategic alliance**, organizations join together in partnership to pursue an area of mutual interest.

In **arbitration** a neutral third party issues a binding decision to resolve a dispute.

In **bottom-up change**, change initiatives come from all levels in the organization.

In **continuous-process production**, raw materials are continuously transformed by an automated system.

In **effective communication** the intended meaning is fully understood by the receiver.

In **exporting,** local products are sold abroad to foreign customers.

In **franchising,** a fee is paid to a foreign business for rights to locally operate using its name, branding, and methods.

In **global sourcing**, materials or services are purchased around the world for local use.

In **job rotation** people switch tasks to learn multiple jobs.

In **long-linked technology** a client moves from point to point during service delivery.

In **lose–lose conflict** no one achieves his or her true desires, and the underlying reasons for conflict remain unaffected.

In **management by wandering around (MBWA)** managers spend time outside their offices to meet and talk with workers at all levels.

In **mediation** a neutral party tries to help conflicting parties improve communication to resolve their dispute.

In **monochronic cultures** people tend to do one thing at a time.

In **polychronic cultures** time is used to accomplish many different things at once.

In the **global economy,** resources, markets, and competition are worldwide in scope.

In the **individualism view** ethical behavior advances long-term self-interests.

In the **justice view** ethical behavior treats people impartially and fairly.

In the **moral rights view** ethical behavior respects and protects fundamental rights.

In the **utilitarian view** ethical behavior delivers the greatest good to the most people.

In **top-down change,** the change initiatives come from senior management.

In **unstructured interviews** the interviewer does not work from a formal and preestablished list of questions that is asked of all interviewees.

In **win–lose** conflict one party achieves its desires, and the other party does not.

In **win–win** conflict the conflict is resolved to everyone's benefit.

In **work sampling**, applicants are evaluated while performing actual work tasks.

Income statement shows profits or losses in a Sales − Expenses = Net Income format.

Incremental change bends and adjusts existing ways to improve performance.

Independent contractors are hired as needed and are not part of the organization's permanent workforce.

Individualism–collectivism is the degree to which a society emphasizes individuals and their self-interests.

Informal group is unofficial and emerges from relationships and shared interests among members.

Informal structure is the set of unofficial relationships among an organization's members.

Information is data made useful for decision making.

Information competency is the ability to gather, analyze, and use information for decision making and problem solving.

Information filtering is the intentional distortion of information to make it appear most favorable to the recipient.

Information systems use IT to collect, organize, and distribute data for use in decision making.

Initial public offering, or IPO, is an initial selling of shares of stock to the public at large.

Innovation is the process of taking a new idea and putting it into practice.

Input standard measures work efforts that go into a performance task.

Insourcing is job creation through foreign direct investment.

Instrumental values are preferences regarding the means to desired ends.

Instrumentality is a person's belief that various outcomes will occur as a result of task performance.

Intellectual Capital Equation states: Intellectual Capital = Competency × Commitment.

Intellectual capital is the collective brainpower or shared knowledge of a workforce.

Intensive technology focuses the efforts and talents of many people to serve clients.

Interactional justice is the degree to which others are treated with dignity and respect.

Interactive leadership leaders are strong communicators and act democratic and participative with followers.

Intermittent reinforcement rewards behavior only periodically.

Internal recruitment seeks job applicants from inside the organization.

International business conducts for-profit transactions of goods and services across national boundaries.

Internet censorship is the deliberate blockage and denial of public access to information posted on the Internet.

Internet entrepreneurship is the use of the Internet to pursue an entrepreneurial venture.

Internet entrepreneurship through the **advertising model** creates a website attractive to visitors and then advertisers pay to be displayed on.

Internet entrepreneurship through the **intermediary model** creates a website that collects a fee for bringing buyers and sellers together.

Internet entrepreneurship through the **subscription model** creates a website offering value that visitors are willing to pay to view.

Internet entrepreneurship through the **transaction model** creates a website to sell something that customers are willing to buy.

Intrapreneurs display entrepreneurial behavior as employees of larger firms.

Intuitive thinking approaches problems in a flexible and spontaneous fashion.

Inventory control by **economic order quantity** orders replacements whenever inventory level falls to a predetermined point.

Inventory is an amount of materials or products kept in storage.

ISO 14001 is an international quality standard requiring organizations to set environmental objectives and targets, account for environmental impacts, and continuously improve environmental performance.

ISO certification indicates conformance with a rigorous set of international quality standards.

Issue urgency indicates the extent to which a stakeholder's concerns need immediate attention.

J

Job analysis studies exactly what is done in a job, and why.

Job burnout is physical and mental exhaustion from work stress.

Job description details the duties and responsibilities of a job holder.

Job design is arranging work tasks for individuals and groups.

Job enlargement increases task variety by combining into one job two or more tasks previously done by separate workers.

Job enrichment increases job depth by adding work planning and evaluating duties normally performed by the supervisor.

Job involvement is the extent to which an individual is dedicated to a job.

Job rotation increases task variety by periodically shifting workers between different jobs.

Job satisfaction is the degree to which an individual feels positive or negative about a job.

Job sharing splits one job between two people.

Job simplification employs people in clearly defined and specialized tasks with narrow job scope.

Job specifications list the qualifications required of a job holder.

Joint venture operates in a foreign country through co-ownership by foreign and local partners.

Just-in-time scheduling minimizes inventory by sending out materials to workstations "just in time" to be used.

K

Knowledge management is the process of using intellectual capital for competitive advantage.

Knowledge worker is someone whose mind is a critical asset to employers.

L

Labor contract is a formal agreement between a union and an employer about the terms of work for union members.

Labor union is an organization that deals with employers on the workers' collective behalf.

Lack-of-participation error is failure to involve in a decision the persons whose support is needed to implement it.

Laissez-faire leader has a "do the best you can and don't bother me" attitude.

Law of effect states that behavior followed by pleasant consequences is likely to be repeated; behavior followed by unpleasant consequences is not.

Leaders show **integrity** by acting with honesty, credibility, and consistency in putting values into action.

Leadership is the process of inspiring others to work hard to accomplish important tasks.

Leadership style is the recurring pattern of behaviors exhibited by a leader.

Leading is the process of arousing enthusiasm and inspiring efforts to achieve goals.

Lean startups use things like open-source software, while staying small and striving to keep operations as simple as possible.

Learning is a change in behavior that results from experience.

Learning organization continuously changes and improves, using the lessons of experience.

Least-preferred co-worker scale, LPC, is used in Fiedler's contingency model to measure a person's leadership style.

Legitimate power is the capacity to influence other people by virtue of formal authority, or the rights of office.

Lifelong learning is continuous learning from daily experiences.

Limited liability corporation is a hybrid business form combining the advantages of the sole proprietorship, partnership, and corporation.

Line managers directly contribute to producing the organization's goods or services.

Liquidation is where a business closes and sells its assets to pay creditors.

Locus of control is the extent to which one believes that what happens is within one's control.

Long-term plans typically look three or more years into the future.

Low-context cultures emphasize communication via spoken or written words.

Lower-order needs are physiological, safety, and social needs in Maslow's hierarchy.

M

Machiavellianism describes the extent to which someone is emotionally detached and manipulative.

Maintenance activity is an action taken by a team member that supports the emotional life of the group.

Malcolm Baldrige award is given to business, health care, education, and nonprofit organizations that meet quality criteria.

Management by exception focuses attention on substantial differences between actual and desired performance.

Management development is training to improve knowledge and skills in the management process.

Management information systems meet the information needs of managers in making daily decisions.

Management process is planning, organizing, leading, and controlling the use of resources to accomplish performance goals.

Management science and operations research use quantitative analysis and applied mathematics to solve problems.

Management with analytics involves systematic gathering and processing of data to make it useful as information.

Manager is a person who supports, activates, and is responsible for the work of others.

Managing diversity is a leadership approach that creates an organizational culture that respects diversity and supports multiculturalism.

Manufacturing organizations produce physical goods.

Market control is essentially the influence of market competition on the behavior of organizations and their members.

Masculinity–femininity is the degree to which a society values assertiveness and materialism.

Mass production manufactures a large number of uniform products with an assembly-line system.

Matrix structure combines functional and divisional approaches to emphasize project or program teams.

Mechanistic design is centralized, with many rules and procedures, a clear-cut division of labor, narrow spans of control, and formal coordination.

Mediating technology links people together in a beneficial exchange of values.

Members of a **board of directors** or board of trustees are supposed to make sure an organization is run right.

Members of a **self-managing work team** have the authority to make decisions about how they share and complete their work.

Members of a **virtual team** work together and solve problems through computer-based interactions.

Mentoring assigns early-career employees as protégés to more senior ones.

Merit pay awards pay increases in proportion to performance contributions.

Middle managers oversee the work of large departments or divisions.

Mixed message results when words communicate one message while actions, body language, or appearance communicate something else.

Modeling uses personal behavior to demonstrate performance expected of others.

Mood contagion is the spillover of one's positive or negative moods onto others.

Moods are generalized positive and negative feelings or states of mind.

Moral leadership is always "good" and "right" by ethical standards.

Moral manager makes ethical behavior a personal goal.

Most favored nation status gives a trading partner most favorable treatment for imports and exports.

Motion study is the science of reducing a task to its basic physical motions.

Motivation accounts for the level, direction, and persistence of effort expended at work.

Multicultural organization has a culture with core values that respect diversity and support multiculturalism.

Multiculturalism in organizations involves inclusiveness, pluralism, and respect for diversity.

Multidimensional thinking is an ability to address many problems at once.

Multidomestic strategy customizes products and advertising to best fit local needs.

Multiperson comparison compares one person's performance with that of others.

N

NAFTA is the North American Free Trade Agreement linking Canada, the United States, and Mexico in an economic alliance.

Necessity-based entrepreneurship takes place because other employment options don't exist.

Need for achievement is the desire to do something better, to solve problems, or to master complex tasks.

Need for affiliation is the desire to establish and maintain good relations with people.

Need for power is the desire to control, influence, or be responsible for other people.

Need is a physiological or psychological deficiency that a person wants to satisfy.

Negative reinforcement strengthens behavior by making the avoidance of an undesirable consequence contingent on its occurrence.

Negotiation is the process of making joint decisions when the parties involved have different preferences.

Networking is the process of creating positive relationships with people who can help advance agendas.

Noise is anything that interferes with the effectiveness of communication.

Nominal group technique structures interaction among team members discussing problems and ideas.

Nonprogrammed decision applies a specific solution crafted for a unique problem.

Nontariff barriers to trade discourage imports in nontax ways such as quotas and government import restrictions.

Nonverbal communication takes place through gestures and body language.

Norm is a behavior, rule, or standard expected to be followed by team members.

O

Objectives and **goals** are specific results that one wishes to achieve.

Observable culture is what one sees and hears when walking around an organization as a visitor, a customer, or an employee.

Obstructionist strategy avoids social responsibility and reflects mainly economic priorities.

Occupational subcultures form among persons who share the same professions and skills.

Offshoring is the outsourcing of jobs to foreign locations.

Onshoring or **reshoring** is the return of jobs from foreign locations as companies establish new domestic operations.

Open book management is where managers provide employees with essential financial information about their companies.

Open system interacts with its environment and transforms resource inputs into outputs.

Openness to experience is being curious, receptive to new ideas, and imaginative.

Operant conditioning is the control of behavior by manipulating its consequences.

Operating objectives are specific results that organizations try to accomplish.

Operational plan identifies short-term activities to implement strategic plans.

Operations management is the process of managing productive systems that transform resources into finished products.

Optimizing decision chooses the alternative giving the absolute best solution to a problem.

Organic design is decentralized, with fewer rules and procedures, open divisions of labor, wide spans of control, and more personal coordination.

Organization is a collection of people working together to achieve a common purpose.

Organization chart describes the arrangement of work positions within an organization.

Organization structure is a system of tasks, reporting relationships, and communication linkages.

Organizational behavior is the study of individuals and groups in organizations.

Organizational citizenship is a willingness to "go beyond the call of duty" or "go the extra mile" in one's work.

Organizational commitment is the loyalty of an individual to the organization.

Organizational culture is the system of shared beliefs and values that guides behavior in organizations.

Organizational design is the process of creating structures that accomplish mission and objectives.

Organizational effectiveness is a measure of how well an organization performs while using resources to accomplish mission and objectives.

Organizational subcultures are groups of people who share similar beliefs and values based on their work or personal characteristics.

Organizing is the process of assigning tasks, allocating resources, and coordinating work activities.

Orientation familiarizes new employees with jobs, coworkers, and organizational policies and services.

Output standard measures performance results in terms of quantity, quality, cost, or time.

P

Participatory planning includes the persons who will be affected by plans and/or those who will implement them.

Partnership is when two or more people agree to contribute resources to start and operate a business together.

Perception is the process through which people receive, organize, and interpret information from the environment.

Performance appraisal is the process of formally evaluating performance and providing feedback to a job holder.

Performance effectiveness is an output measure of task or goal accomplishment.

Performance efficiency is an input measure of resource cost associated with goal accomplishment.

Performance management system sets standards, assesses results, and plans for performance improvements.

Performance opportunity is a situation that offers the chance for a better future if the right steps are taken.

Performance threat is a situation in which something is obviously wrong or has the potential to go wrong.

Personal wellness is the pursuit of one's full potential through a personal health-promotion program.

Personality is the profile of characteristics making a person unique from others.

Person–job fit is the extent to which an individual's skills, interests, and personal characteristics are consistent with the requirements of their work.

Person–organization fit is the extent to which an individual's values, interests, and behavior are consistent with the culture of the organization.

Persuasive communication presents a message in a manner that causes the other person to support it.

Plan is a statement of intended means for accomplishing objectives.

Planning is the process of setting objectives and determining what should be done to accomplish them.

Policy is a standing plan that communicates broad guidelines for decisions and action.

Political risk is the potential loss in value of a foreign investment due to instability and political changes in the host country.

Political-risk analysis tries to forecast political disruptions that can threaten the value of a foreign investment.

Positive reinforcement strengthens behavior by making a desirable consequence contingent on its occurrence.

Power is the ability to get someone else to do something you want done or to make things happen the way you want.

Power distance is the degree to which a society accepts unequal distribution of power.

Prejudice is the display of negative, irrational attitudes toward members of diverse populations.

Principled negotiation or **integrative negotiation** uses a "win–win" orientation to reach solutions acceptable to each party.

Proactive strategy meets all the criteria of social responsibility, including discretionary performance.

Problem solving involves identifying and taking action to resolve problems.

Procedural justice is concerned that policies and rules are fairly applied.

Procedure is a rule describing actions that are to be taken in specific situations.

Process innovations result in better ways of doing things.

Process of commercializing innovation turns new ideas into actual products, services, or processes to increase profits through greater sales or reduced costs.

Process reengineering systematically analyzes work processes to design new and better ones.

Process structure groups jobs and activities that are part of the same processes.

Process value analysis identifies and evaluates core processes for their performance contributions.

Product innovations result in new or improved goods or services.

Product structure groups together people and jobs focused on a single product or service.

Productivity equation is: Productivity = Output/Input.

Productivity is the quantity and quality of work performance, with resource utilization considered.

Profit-sharing plans distribute to employees a proportion of net profits earned by the organization.

Programmed decision applies a solution from past experience to a routine problem.

Progressive discipline ties reprimands to the severity and frequency of misbehavior.

Project management makes sure that activities required to complete a project are planned well and accomplished on time.

Project team or **task force** is convened for a specific purpose and disbands when its task is completed.

Project teams are convened for a particular task or project and disband once it is completed.

Projection is the assignment of personal attributes to other individuals.

Projects are one-time activities with many component tasks that must be completed in proper order and according to budget.

Protectionism is a call for tariffs and favorable treatments to protect domestic firms from foreign competition.

Proxemics involves the use of space in communication.

Psychological contract is the set of individual expectations about the employment relationship.

Punishment discourages behavior by making an unpleasant consequence contingent on its occurrence.

Q

Quality circle is a team of employees who meet periodically to discuss ways of improving work quality.

Quality of work life is the overall quality of human experiences in the workplace.

R

Rational persuasion strategy pursues change through empirical data and rational argument.

Realistic job previews provide job candidates with all pertinent information about a job and an organization, both positive and negative.

Recency bias overemphasizes the most recent behaviors when evaluating individual performance.

Recruitment is a set of activities designed to attract a qualified pool of job applicants.

Referent power is the capacity to influence other people because of their desire to identify personally with you.

Refreezing is the phase at which change is stabilized.

Relatedness needs are desires for good interpersonal relationships.

Relationship goals in negotiation are concerned with the ways people work together.

Reliability means that a selection device gives consistent results over repeated measures.

Restructuring changes the mix or reduces the scale of operations.

Reward power is the capacity to offer something of value as a means of influencing other people.

Risk environment lacks complete information but offers "probabilities" of the likely outcomes for possible action alternatives.

S

Satisficing decision chooses the first satisfactory alternative that comes to one's attention.

Satisfier factor is found in job content, such as a sense of achievement, recognition, responsibility, advancement, or personal growth.

Scenario planning identifies alternative future scenarios and makes plans to deal with each.

Scientific management emphasizes careful selection and training of workers and supervisory support.

Selection is choosing individuals to hire from a pool of qualified job applicants.

Selective perception is the tendency to define problems from one's own point of view.

Self-control is internal control that occurs through self-discipline in fulfilling work and personal responsibilities.

Self-efficacy is a person's belief that she or he is capable of performing a task.

Self-fulfilling prophecy occurs when a person acts in ways that confirm another's expectations.

Self-management is the ability to understand oneself, exercise initiative, accept responsibility, and learn from experience.

Self-monitoring is the degree to which someone is able to adjust behavior in response to external factors.

Self-serving bias explains personal success by internal causes and personal failures by external causes.

Serial entrepreneur starts and runs businesses and nonprofits over and over again, moving from one interest and opportunity to the next.

Servant leadership is follower-centered and committed to helping others in their work.

Service organizations produce nonphysical outputs in the form of services.

Sexual harassment is behavior of a sexual nature that affects a person's employment situation.

Shamrock organization operates with a core group of full-time long-term workers supported by others who work on contracts and part-time.

Shaping is positive reinforcement of successive approximations to the desired behavior.

Shared power strategy pursues change by participation in assessing change needs, values, and goals.

Short-term plans typically cover one year or less.

Situational interviews ask job applicants how they would react in specific situations.

Six Sigma program sets a quality standard of 3.4 defects or less per million products or service deliveries.

Skill is the ability to translate knowledge into action that results in desired performance.

Skunkworks are special units given separate locations, special resources, and their own managers so that they can succeed with innovation.

Small business has fewer than 500 employees, is independently owned and operated, and does not dominate its industry.

Small Business Development Centers founded with support from the U.S. Small Business Administration provide advice to new and existing small businesses.

Small-batch production manufactures a variety of products crafted to fit customer specifications.

Social business innovation finds ways to use business models to address important social problems.

Social capital is a capacity to get things done with the support and help of others.

Social entrepreneur takes risks to find new ways to solve pressing social problems.

Social entrepreneurship is a unique form of ethical entrepreneurship that seeks new ways to solve pressing social problems.

Social loafing is the tendency of some people to avoid responsibility by "free-riding" in groups.

Social network analysis identifies the informal structures and their embedded social relationships that are active in an organization.

Social responsibility audit assesses an organization's accomplishments in areas of social responsibility.

Socialization is a process of learning and adapting to the organizational culture.

Sole proprietorship is an individual pursuing business for a profit.

Span of control is the number of subordinates directly reporting to a manager.

Staff managers use special technical expertise to advise and support line workers.

Staff positions provide technical expertise for other parts of the organization.

Stakeholder power refers to the capacity of the stakeholder to positively or negatively affect the operations of the organization.

Stakeholders are the persons, groups, and other organizations that are directly affected by the behavior of the organization and that hold a stake in its performance.

Startup is a new and temporary venture that is trying to discover a profitable business model for future success.

Statement of mission expresses the organization's reason for existence in society.

Statistical quality control measures work samples for compliance with quality standards.

Stereotype occurs when attributes commonly associated with a group are assigned to an individual.

Stock options give the right to purchase shares at a fixed price in the future.

Strategic alliance is a cooperation agreement with another organization to jointly pursue activities of mutual interest.

Strategic analysis is the process of analyzing the organization, the environment, and the organization's competitive position and current strategies.

Strategic control makes sure strategies are well implemented and that poor strategies are scrapped or modified.

Strategic human resource management mobilizes human capital to implement organizational strategies.

Strategic intent focuses and applies organizational energies on a unifying and compelling goal.

Strategic leadership inspires people to continuously change, refine,and improve strategies and their implementation.

Strategic management is the process of formulating and implementing strategies.

Strategic opportunism focuses on long-term objectives while being flexible in dealing with short-term problems.

Strategic plan identifies long-term directions for the organization.

Strategy formulation is the process of crafting strategies to guide the allocation of resources.

Strategy is a comprehensive plan guiding resource allocation to achieve long-term organization goals.

Strategy implementation is the process of putting strategies into action.

Stress is a state of tension experienced by individuals facing extraordinary demands, constraints, or opportunities.

Stressor is anything that causes stress.

Stretch goals are performance targets that we have to work extra hard and stretch to reach.

Structured problems are straightforward and clear with respect to information needs.

Substance goals in negotiation are concerned with outcomes.

Substantive conflict involves disagreements over goals, resources, rewards, policies, procedures, and job assignments.

Substitutes for leadership are factors in the work setting that direct work efforts without the involvement of a leader.

Subsystem is a smaller component of a larger system.

Succession plan describes how the leadership transition and related financial matters will be handled.

Supply chain management, or **SCM**, involves management of all operations linking an organization and its suppliers, such as purchasing, transportation logistics, and inventory management.

Sustainability in management means acting in ways that support a high quality of life for present and future generations.

Sustainable business both meets the needs of customers and protects the natural environment for future generations.

Sustainable competitive advantage is the ability to outperform rivals in ways that are difficult or costly to imitate.

Sustainable development makes use of environmental resources tosupport societal needs today while also preserving and protecting them for future generations.

Sustainable innovations or **green innovations** help reduce the carbon footprints and environmental impacts of organizations, their practices, and products.

Sweatshops employ workers at very low wages for long hours in poor working conditions.

SWOT analysis examines organizational strengths and weaknesses and environmental opportunities and threats.

Symbolic leader uses symbols to communicate values that help create a desired organizational culture.

Synergy is the creation of a whole greater than the sum of itsindividual parts.

System is a collection of interrelated parts working together for a purpose.

Systematic thinking approaches problems in a rational andanalytical fashion.

T

Tactical plan helps to implement all or parts of a strategic plan.

Tall structures have narrow spans of control and many hierarchical levels.

Tariffs are taxes governments levy on imports from abroad.

Task activity is an action taken by a team member that directly contributes to the group's performance purpose.

Team is a collection of people who regularly interact to pursue common goals.

Team building is a sequence of activities to analyze a team and make changes to improve its performance.

Team diversity is the differences in values, personalities, experiences, demographics, and cultures among the membership.

Team Effectiveness Equation states: Team effectiveness = Quality of inputs + (Process gains − Process losses).

Team leaders report to middle managers and supervise nonmanagerial workers.

Team process is the way team members work together to accomplish tasks.

Team structure uses permanent and temporary cross-functional teams to improve lateral relations.

Teamwork is the process of people actively working together to accomplish common goals.

Tech IQ is ability to use technology and commitment to stay informed on the latest technological developments.

Technical skill is the ability to use expertise to perform a task with proficiency.

Technology is the combination of knowledge, skills, equipment, and work methods used to transform inputs into outputs.

Telecommuting involves using IT to work at home or outside the office.

Terminal values are preferences about desired end states.

Termination is the involuntary dismissal of an employee.

The **progression principle** states that a need isn't activated until the next lower-level need is satisfied.

The **representativeness bias** bases a decision on similarity to other situations.

The **service-profit chain** consists of all activities involved in the direct link between an organization's service providers and customers or clients.

The **socioeconomic view of CSR** is that business should focus on broader social welfare as well as profits.

The **specific environment,** or **task environment,** includes the people and groups with whom an organization interacts.

The **spotlight questions** test the ethics of a decision by exposing it to scrutiny through the eyes of family, community members, and ethical role models.

The **succession problem** is the issue of who will run the business when the current head leaves.

The **triple bottom line** assesses the economic, social, and environmental performance of organizations.

The **upside-down pyramid** view of organizations shows customers at the top being served by workers who are supported by managers.

The **value chain** is the specific sequence of activities that creates products and services with value for customers.

The **virtuous circle** occurs when CSR improves financial performance, which leads to more CSR.

Theory X assumes people dislike work, lack ambition, act irresponsibly, and prefer to be led.

Theory Y assumes people are willing to work, like responsibility, and are self-directed and creative.

Time orientation is the degree to which a society emphasizes short-term or long-term goals.

Top managers guide the performance of the organization as a whole or of one of its major parts.

Total quality management is an organization-wide commitment to continuous improvement, product quality, and customer needs.

Traditional recruitment focuses on selling the job and organization to applicants.

Training provides learning opportunities to acquire and improve job-related skills.

Transformational change results in a major and comprehensive redirection of the organization.

Transformational leadership is inspirational and arouses extraordinary effort and performance.

Transnational corporation is a global corporation or MNE that operates worldwide on a borderless basis.

Transnational strategy seeks efficiencies of global operations with attention to local markets.

Turnaround strategy tries to fix specific performance problems.

Type A personality is a person oriented toward extreme achievement, impatience, and perfectionism.

U

Unbranding occurs when stores owned by major national and global chains are advertised with local nonbranded names.

Uncertain environment lacks so much information that it is difficult to assign probabilities to the likely outcomes of alternatives.

Uncertainty avoidance is the degree to which a society tolerates risk and uncertainty.

Unfreezing is the phase during which a situation is prepared for change.

Universalism suggests ethical standards apply absolutely across all cultures.

Unstructured problems have ambiguities and information deficiencies.

V

Valence is the value a person assigns to work-related outcomes.

Validity means that scores on a selection device have demonstrated links with future job performance.

Value creation occurs when the result of a work task or activity makes a product or service worth more in terms of potential customer appeal than at the start.

Value-based management actively develops, communicates, and enacts shared values.

Values are broad beliefs about what is appropriate behavior.

Venture capitalists make large investments in new ventures in return for an equity stake in the business.

Virtual organization uses IT and the Internet to engage a shifting network of strategic alliances.

Vision clarifies the purpose of the organization and expresses what it hopes to be in the future.

Visionary leadership brings to the situation a clear sense of the future and an understanding of how to get there.

W

Whistleblower exposes the misdeeds of others in organizations.

Withdrawal behaviors occur as temporary absenteeism and actual job turnover.

Work process is a related group of tasks that together create a value for the customer.

Workflow is the movement of work from one point to another in a system.

Workforce diversity describes differences among workers in gender, race, age, ethnicity, religion, sexual orientation, and able–bodiedness.

Work–life balance involves balancing career demands with personal and family needs.

Workplace privacy is the right to privacy while at work.

Workplace rage is aggressive behavior toward coworkers or the work setting.

Workplace spirituality creates meaning and shared community among organizational members.

World Trade Organization member nations agree to negotiate and resolve disputes about tariffs and trade restrictions.

Wrongful discharge is a doctrine giving workers legal protections against discriminatory firings.

Z

Zero-based budget allocates resources as if each budget were brand new.

Endnotes

Chapter 1

Endnotes

[1]Quotes from Jessi Hempel, "How LinkedIn Will Fire Up Your Career," *Fortune*, Kindle Edition (April 13, 2010).

[2]See monster.com; linkedin.com; Bridget Carey, "Old Resume Just the Start These Days," *The Columbus Dispatch* (March 16, 2008), p. D3; Joseph De Avila, "CEO Reorganizes Job-Search Pioneer, *Wall Street Journal* (May 12, 2008), p. B1.

[3]Information from John Tozzi, Stacy Perman, and Nick Leiber, "America's Best Young Entrepreneurs 2009," *BusinessWeek* (October 12, 2009).

[4]For a good discussion see Pino Audia, "A New B-School Specialty: Self-Awareness," *Forbes* (December 4, 2009): www.forbes.com.

[5]The Johari Window was originally described by Joseph Luft and Harry Ingham, "The Johari Window, a Graphic Model of Interpersonal Awareness," *Proceedings of the Western Training Laboratory in Group Development*. (Los Angeles: UCLA, 1955).

[6]James O'Toole and Edward E. Lawler III, *The New American Workplace* (New York: Palgrave Macmillan, 2006).

[7]Thomas A. Stewart, *Intellectual Capital: The Wealth of Organizations* (New York: Bantam, 1998).

[8]Charles O'Reilly III and Jeffrey Pfeffer, *Hidden Value: How Great Companies Achieve Extraordinary Results with Ordinary People* (Boston: Harvard Business School Press, 2000), p. 2.

[9]Thomas A. Stewart, *Intellectual Capital: The Wealth of Organizations* (New York: Bantam, 1998); and, Dave Ulrich, "Intellectual Capital = Competency × Commitment," *Harvard Business Review* (Winter 1998), pp. 15–26.

[10]Max DePree's books include *Leadership Is an Art* (New York: Dell, 1990) and *Leadership Jazz* (New York: Dell, 1993). See also Herman Miller's home page at www.hermanmiller.com.

[11]See Peter F. Drucker, *The Changing World of the Executive* (New York: T.T. Times Books, 1982), and *The Profession of Management* (Cambridge, MA: Harvard Business School Press, 1997); and Francis Horibe, *Managing Knowledge Workers: New Skills and Attitudes to Unlock the Intellectual Capital in Your Organization* (New York: Wiley, 1999).

[12]Daniel Pink, *A Whole New Mind: Moving from the Information Age to the Conceptual Age* (New York: Riverhead Books, 2005).

[13]Gary Hamel, "Gary Hamel Sees 'More Options . . . Fewer Grand Visions," *Wall Street Journal*, Special Advertising Section (October 6, 2009), p. Akl16.

[14]Diana Middleton, "Landing a Job of the Future," *Wall Street Journal* (December 29, 2009), p. D4.

[15]Jeffrey Zaslow, "The Greatest Generation (of Networkers)," *Wall Street Journal* (November 4, 2009), pp. D1, D2; and, Jessica E. Vascellaro, "Why Email No Longer Rules . . . ," *Wall Street Journal* (October 12, 2009), pp. R1, R3.

[16]Information from Sarah E. Needleman, "A New Job Is Just a Tweet Away," *Wall Street Journal* (September 6, 2009), pp. B7, B12.

[17]Handel, op. cit

[18]Hemnel, op. cit.

[19]Middleton, op. cit.

[20]Kenichi Ohmae's books include *The Borderless World: Power and Strategy in the Interlinked Economy* (New York: Harper, 1989); *The End of the Nation State* (New York: Free Press, 1996); *The Invisible Continent: Four Strategic Imperatives of the New Economy* (New York: Harper, 1999); and *The Next Global Stage: Challenges and Opportunities in Our Borderless World* (Philadelphia: Wharton School Publishing, 2006).

[21]Information from Micheline Maynard, "A Lifeline Not Made in the USA," *The New York Times* (October 18, 2009): nytimes.com (accessed April 15, 2010).

[22]Quote from Alfred E. Eckes Jr. and Thomas W. Zeiler, *Globalization and the American Century* (Cambridge, UK: Cambridge University Press, 2003), pp. 1, 2. See also Thomas L. Friedman, *The Lexus and the Olive Tree: Understanding Globalization* (New York: Bantam Doubleday Dell, 2000); Joseph E. Stiglitz, *Globalization and Its Discontents* (New York: W.W. Norton, 2003); and Joseph E. Stiglitz, *Making Globalization Work* (New York: W.W. Norton, 2007).

[23]Michael E. Porter, *The Competitive Advantage of Nations: With a New Introduction* (New York: Free Press, 1998).

[24]Thomas L. Friedman, *The World Is Flat: A Brief History of the Twenty-First Century* (New York: Farrar, Straus & Giroux, 2005), p. 15.

[25]Esmé E. Deprez, "Madoff Sentenced to Maximum 150 Years," *Business Week* (June 29, 2009): businessweek.com (accessed April 15, 2010).

[26]For discussions of ethics in business and management see Linda K. Trevino and Katherine A. Nelson, *Managing Business Ethics* (Hoboken, NJ: John Wiley & Sons, 2006); and Richard DeGeorge, *Business Ethics, 5th ed.* (Englewood Cliffs, NJ: Prentice-Hall, 2005).

[27]Daniel Akst, "Room at the Top for Improvement," *Wall Street Journal* (October 26, 2004), p. D8; and Herb Baum and Tammy King, *The Transparent Leader* (New York: Collins, 2005).

[28]Workforce 2000: *Work and Workers for the 21st Century* (Indianapolis, IN: Towers Perrin/Hudson Institute, 1987); Richard W. Judy and Carol D'Amico (eds.), *Work and Workers for the 21st Century* (Indianapolis, IN: Hudson Institute, 1997). See also Richard D. Bucher, *Diversity Consciousness: Opening Our Minds to People, Cultures, and Opportunities* (Upper Saddle River, NJ: Prentice-Hall, 2000); R. Roosevelt Thomas, "From Affirmative Action to Affirming Diversity," *Harvard Business Review* (March–April 1990), pp. 107–17; and *Beyond Race and Gender: Unleashing the Power of Your Total Workforce by Managing Diversity* (New York: AMACOM, 1992).

[29]June Dronholz, "Hispanics Gain in Census," *Wall Street Journal* (May 10, 2006), p. A6; Phillip Toledano, "Demographics: The Population Hourglass," *Fast Company* (March 2006), p. 56; June Kronholz, "Racial Identity's Gray Area," *Wall Street Journal* (June 12, 2008), p. A10; "We're Getting Old," *Wall Street Journal* (March 26, 2009), p. D2; Les Christie, "Hispanic Population Boom Fuels Rising U.S. Diversity," *CnnMoney*: www.cnn.com; Betsy Towner, "The New Face of 50+ America," *AARP Bulletin* (June 2009), p. 31; and, Kelly Evans, "Recession Drives More Women in the Workforce," *Wall Street Journal* (November 12, 2009), p. A21.

[30]Information from "Women and Work: We Did It!" *Economist* (December 31, 2009).

[31]Information from Eric Shurenberg, "Salary Gap: Men vs. Women," moneywatch.com (accessed April 15, 2010).

[32]Information from "Racism in Hiring Remains, Study Says," *The Columbus Dispatch* (January 17, 2003), p. B2.

[33]Survey data reported in Sue Shellenbarger, "New Workplace Equalizer: Ambition," *Wall Street Journal* (March 26, 2009), p. D5.

[34]Judith B. Rosener, "Women Make Good Managers. So What?" *BusinessWeek* (December 11, 2000), p. 24.

[35]*BusinessWeek* (August 8, 1990), p. 50.

[36]Thomas, op. cit.

[37]Charles Handy, *The Age of Unreason* (Cambridge, MA: Harvard Business School Press, 1990); Also see Charles Handy, *A Business Guru's Portfolio Life* (New York: Amacom, 2008), and *Myself and Other Important Matters* (New York; Amacom, 2008).

[38]Peter Coy, Michelle Conlin, and Moira Herbst, "The Disposable Worker," *BusinessWeek* (January 18, 2010), pp. 33–39.

[39]See Gareille Monaghan, "Don't Get a Job, Get a Portfolio Career," *Sunday Times* (April 26, 2009), p. 15.

[40]Tom Peters, "The New Wired World of Work," *BusinessWeek* (August 28, 2000), pp. 172–73.

[41]Quote from Stephen Moore, "The Conscience of a Capitalist," *Wall Street Journal* (October 3–4, 2009), p. A11; see also www.wholefoods.com/company.

[42]For an overview of organizations and organization theory, see W. Richard Scott, *Organizations: Rational, Natural and Open Systems*, 4th ed. (Englewood Cliffs, NJ: Prentice-Hall, 1998).

[43]Information from Paul F. Nunes, Geoffrey Godbey, and H. James Wilson, "Bet the Clock," *Wall Street Journal* (October 26, 2009), p. R6; and Steve Hamm, "The King of the Cloud," *BusinessWeek* (November 30, 2009), p. 77.

[44]Includes ideas from Jay A. Conger, *Winning 'em Over: A New Model for Managing in the Age of Persuasion* (New York: Simon & Schuster, 1998), pp. 180–81; Stewart D. Friedman, Perry Christensen, and Jessica DeGroot, "Work and Life: The End of the Zero–Sum Game," *Harvard Business Review* (November–December 1998), pp. 119–29; Chris Argyris, "Empowerment: The Emperor's New Clothes," *Harvard Business Review* (May–June 1998), pp. 98–105; and John A. Byrne, "Management by Web," *BusinessWeek* (August 28, 2000), pp. 84–98. See also emerging reports such as O'Toole and Lawler, op. cit.; Jon Nicholson and Amanda Nairn, *The Manager of the 21st Century: 2020 Vision* (Sydney: Boston Consulting Group, 2008); and, Jeffry Pfeffer, "Building Sustainable Organizations: The Human Factor," *Academy of Management Perspectives*, vol. 24 (February 2010), pp. 34–45.

[45]Jeffrey Pfeffer and John F. Veiga, "Putting People First for Organizational Success," *Academy of Management Executive*, vol. 13 (May 1999), pp. 37–48; Jeffrey Pfeffer, *The Human Equation: Building Profits by Putting People First* (Boston: Harvard Business School Press, 1998).

[46]George Anders, "Drucker's Teachings Find Following in Asia," *Wall Street Journal* (June 18, 2008), p. B2.

[47]Henry Mintzberg, "The Manager's Job: Folklore and Fact," *Harvard Business Review*, Vol. 53 (July–August 1975), p. 61. See also his book *The Nature of Managerial Work* (New York: Harper-Row, 1973: HarperCollins, 1997).

[48]Ellen Byron, "P&G's Lafley Sees CEOs as Link to World," *Wall Street Journal* (March 23, 2009), p. B6; and Stefan Stern, "What Exactly Are Chief Executives For?" *Financial Times* (May 15, 2009).

[49]For a perspective on the first-level manager's job, see Leonard A. Schlesinger and Janice A. Klein, "The First-Line Supervisor: Past, Present and Future," pp. 370–82 in Jay W. Lorsch (ed.), *Handbook of Organizational Behavior* (Englewood Cliffs, NJ: Prentice-Hall, 1987). Research reported in "Remember Us?" *Economist* (February 1, 1992), p. 71.

[50]David Whitford, "A Human Place to Work," *Fortune* (January 8, 2001), pp. 108–20.

[51]Quote from "GM Shakes Up Management Team Three Days after Sacking Its Chief," *Financial Times* (December 5, 2009); see also "Boardroom Battles Are Breaking Out All Over," *Financial Times* (December 8, 2009).

[52]Pfeffer, op. cit.

[53]George Anders, "Overseeing More Employees—With Fewer Managers," *Wall Street Journal* (March 24, 2008), p. B6.

[54]This running example is developed from information from "Accountants Have Lives, Too, You Know," *BusinessWeek* (February 23, 1998), pp. 88–90; Silvia Ann Hewlett and Carolyn Buck Luce, "Off-Ramps and On-Ramps: Keeping Talented Women on the Road to Success," *Harvard Business Review* (March 2005), reprint 9491; and the Ernst-Young website: www.ey.com.

[55]Mintzberg (1973/1997), op. cit., p. 30.

[56]See Mintzberg (1973/1997), op. cit., Henry Mintzberg, "Covert Leadership: The Art of Managing Professionals," *Harvard Business Review* (November–December 1998), pp. 140–47; and Jonathan Gosling and Henry Mintzberg, "The Five Minds of a Manager," *Harvard Business Review* (November 2003), pp. 1–9.

[57]Mintzberg (1973/1997), op. cit., p. 60.

[58]For research on managerial work see Morgan W. McCall Jr., Ann M. Morrison, and Robert L. Hannan, *Studies of Managerial Work: Results and Methods. Technical Report #9* (Greensboro, NC: Center for Creative Leadership, 1978), pp. 7–9. See also John P. Kotter, "What Effective General Managers Really Do," *Harvard Business Review* (November–December 1982), pp. 156–57.

[59]Kotter, op. cit., p. 164. See also his book *The General Managers* (New York: Free Press, 1986) and David Barry, Catherine Durnell Crampton, and Stephen J. Carroll, "Navigating the Garbage Can: How Agendas Help Managers Cope with Job Realities," *Academy of Management Executive*, vol. II (May 1997), pp. 43–56.

[60]Robert L. Katz, "Skills of an Effective Administrator," *Harvard Business Review* (September–October 1974), p. 94.

[61]Ibid.

[62]See Daniel Goleman's books *Emotional Intelligence* (New York: Bantam, 1995) and *Working with Emotional Intelligence* (New York: Bantam, 1998); and his articles "What Makes a Leader," *Harvard Business Review* (November–December 1998), pp. 93–102, and "Leadership That Makes a Difference," *Harvard Business Review* (March–April 2000), pp. 79–90; quote from p. 80.

[63]See Daniel Goleman, Richard Boyatzis, and Annie McKee, *Primal Leadership: Realizing the Power of Emotional Intelligence* (Boston: Harvard Business School Press, 2002).

[64]See Richard E. Boyatzis, *The Competent Manager: A Model for Effective Performance* (New York: Wiley, 1982); Richard E. Boyatzis, "Competencies in the 21st Century," *Journal of Management Development*, vol. 27 (1) (2008), pp. 5–12; and, Richard Boyatzis (Guest Editor), "Competencies in the EU," *Journal of Management Development*, vol. 28 (2009), special issue.

[65]Audia, op cit.

[66]Suggested by and some items included from *Outcome Measurement Project, Phase I and Phase II Reports* (St. Louis: American Assembly of Collegiate Schools of Business, 1986).

Feature Notes

Real Ethics—Based on incident reported in "FBI Nabs 3 over Coca-Cola Secrets," cnn.com (retrieved July 6, 2006); Betsy

McKay, "Coke Employee Faces Charges in Plot to Sell Secrets," *Wall Street Journal* (July 6, 2006), p. B1; and "Man Gets Two Years in Coke Secrets Case," *Wall Street Journal* (June 7, 2007), p. A12.

Real People—Information from Kate Klonick, "Pepsi's CEO a Refreshing Change" (August 15, 2006): www.abcnews.go.com; Diane Brady, "Indra Nooyi: Keeping Cool in Hot Water," *BusinessWeek* (June 11, 2007), special report; Indra Nooyi, "The Best Advice I Ever Got," CNNMoney (April 30, 2008), www.cnnnmony.com; "Indra Nooyi," *Wall Street Journal* (November 10, 2008), p. R3; Andrew Hill, "The Women Who Mean Business, *Financial Times*, Kindle Edition (September 26, 2009); and, "PepsiCo's Nooyi on 'New Capitalism'," money. cnn.com (accessed April 16, 2010).

Photo Essays Notes

Salesforce.com—Information from Jessica Hodgson, "Selling and Software," *Wall Street Journal* (December 17, 2009), p. A25; and Steve Hamm, "The King of the Cloud," *BusinessWeek* (November 30, 2009), p. 77. Teach for America—Information from teachforamerica.org; and "Wendy Kopp's Mission: Ensure Educational Opportunity for All Students," *VOANews.com* (November 2, 2009).

Chapter 2

Endnotes

[1]Information from Venture Capital Dispatch, "Facebook and Zappos's Different Views on Worker Retention," *Wall Street Journal* (October 29, 2009): wsj.com.

[2]See David A. Kolb, *Experiential Learning: Experience as the Source of Learning and Development* (Englewood Cliffs, NJ: Prentice-Hall, 1984); and David A. Kolb, "Experiential Learning Theory and the Learning Style Inventory," *The Academy of Management Review*, vol. 6, 1981, pp. 289–96.

[3]Quote from Allan H. Church, *Executive Commentary, Academy of Management Executive* (February 2002), p. 74.

[4]A thorough review and critique of the history of management thought, including management in ancient civilizations, is provided by Daniel A. Wren, *The Evolution of Management Thought*, 4th ed. (New York: Wiley, 1993).

[5]Pauline Graham, *Mary Parker Follett—Prophet of Management: A Celebration of Writings from the 1920s* (Boston: Harvard Business School Press, 1995).

[6]For a time line of 20th-century management ideas, see "75 Years of Management Ideas and Practices: 1922–1997," *Harvard Business Review*, supplement (September–October 1997).

[7]For a sample of this work, see Henry L. Gantt, *Industrial Leadership* (Easton, MD: Hive, 1921; Hive edition published in 1974); Henry C. Metcalfe and Lyndall Urwick (eds.), *Dynamic Administration: The Collected Papers of Mary Parker Follett* (New York: Harper-Brothers, 1940); James D. Mooney, *The Principles of Administration*, rev. ed. (New York: Harper-Brothers, 1947); Lyndall Urwick, *The Elements of Administration* (New York: Harper-Brothers, 1943); and *The Golden Book of Management* (London: N. Neame, 1956).

[8]*Frederick W. Taylor, The Principles of Scientific Management* (New York: W.W. Norton, 1967), originally published by Harper-Brothers in 1911. See also the biography, Robert Kanigel, *The One Best Way* (New York: Viking, 1997).

[9]For criticisms of Taylor and his work, see Charles W. Wrege and Amedeo G. Perroni, "Taylor's Pig-Tale: A Historical Analysis of Frederick W. Taylor's Pig Iron Experiments," *Academy of Management Journal*, vol. 17 (March 1974), pp. 6–27; Charles W. Wrege and Richard M. Hodgetts, "Frederick W. Taylor's 1899 Pig Iron Observations: Examining Fact, Fiction and Lessons for the New Millennium," *Academy of Management Journal*, vol. 43 (2000), pp. 1283–91; and Jill Lepore, "Not So Fast," *The New Yorker* (October 12, 2009); www.newyorker.com.

[10]For a discussion of the contemporary significance of Taylor's work, see Edwin A. Lock, "The Ideas of Frederick W. Taylor: An Evaluation," *Academy of Management Review*, vol. 7 (1982), p. 14.

[11]Information from Raymund Flandez and Kelly K. Sports, "Tackling the Energy Monster," *Wall Street Journal* (June 16, 2008), p. R1.

[12]Frank B. Gilbreth, *Motion Study* (New York: Van Nostrand, 1911).

[13]Ben Worthen, "Do You Need to Work Faster? Get a Bigger Computer Monitor," *Wall Street Journal* (March 25, 2008), p. B8; and "Plant Seeks Savings with Shot-Clock Approach," *The Messenger, Athens, Ohio* (November 15, 2009), p. A3.

[14]Available in English as *Henri Fayol, General and Industrial Administration* (London: Pitman, 1949); subsequent discussion is based on M. B. Brodie, *Fayol on Administration* (London: Pitman, 1949).

[15]A. M. Henderson and Talcott Parsons (eds. and trans.), *Max Weber: The Theory of Social Economic Organization* (New York: Free Press, 1947).

[16]Ibid., p. 337.

[17]For classic treatments of bureaucracy, see Alvin Gouldner, *Patterns of Industrial Bureaucracy* (New York: Free Press, 1954); and Robert K. Merton, *Social Theory and Social Structure* (New York: Free Press, 1957).

[18]M. P. Follett, *Freedom and Coordination* (London: Management Publications Trust, 1949).

[19]Judith Garwood, "A Review of Dynamic Administration: The Collected Papers of Mary Parker Follett," *New Management*, vol. 2 (1984), pp. 61–62; eulogy from Richard C. Cabot, *Encyclopedia of Social Work*, vol. 15, "Follett, Mary Parker," p. 351.

[20]The Hawthorne studies are described in detail in F. J. Roethlisberger and William J. Dickson, *Management and the Worker* (Cambridge, MA: Harvard University Press, 1966) and G. Homans, *Fatigue of Workers* (New York: Reinhold, 1941). For an interview with three of the participants in the relay–assembly test–room studies, see R. G. Greenwood, A. A. Bolton, and R. A. Greenwood, "Hawthorne a Half Century Later: Relay Assembly Participants Remember," *Journal of Management*, vol. 9 (1983), pp. 217–31.

[21]The criticisms of the Hawthorne studies are detailed in Alex Carey, "The Hawthorne Studies: A Radical Criticism," *American Sociological Review*, vol. 32 (1967), pp. 403–16; H. M. Parsons, "What Happened at Hawthorne?" *Science*, vol. 183 (1974), pp. 922–32; and B. Rice, "The Hawthorne Defect: Persistence of a Flawed Theory," *Psychology Today*, vol. 16 (1982), pp. 70–74. See also Wren, op. cit.

[22]This discussion of Maslow's theory is based on Abraham H. Maslow, *Eupsychian Management* (Homewood, IL: Richard D. Irwin, 1965) and Abraham H. Maslow, *Motivation and Personality*, 2nd ed. (New York: Harper-Row, 1970).

[23]Douglas McGregor, *The Human Side of Enterprise* (New York: McGraw-Hill, 1960).

[24]This notion is also discussed in terms of the "pygmalion effect." See Dov Eden, *Pygmalion in Management* (Lexington, MA: Lexington Books, 1990) and Dov Eden, Dvorah Geller,

and Abigail Gerwirtz, "Implanting Pygmalion Leadership Style through Workshop Training: Seven Field Experiments," *Leadership Quarterly*, vol. 11 (2) (2000), pp. 171–210.

[25] Gary Heil, Deborah F. Stevens, and Warren G. Bennis, *Douglas McGregor on Management: Revisiting the Human Side of Enterprise* (New York: Wiley, 2000).

[26] Information from Terry Stephan, "Honing Her Kraft," *Northwestern* (Winter 2000), pp. 22–25.

[27] Chris Argyris, *Personality and Organization* (New York: Harper-Row, 1957).

[28] Stefan Stern, "Smarter Leaders Are Betting Big on Data," *Financial Times*, Kindle edition (March 9, 2010). See also Thomas H. Davenport, Jeanne G. Harris, and Robert Morison, *Analytics at Work: Smarter Decisions, Better Results* (Cambridge, MA: Harvard Business Press, 2010).

[29] Scott Morrison, "Google Searches for Staffing Answers," *Wall Street Journal* (May 19, 2009), p. B1.

[30] The ideas of Chester I. Barnard, *Functions of the Executive* (Cambridge, MA: Harvard University Press, 1938), and Ludwig von Bertalanffy, "The History and Status of General Systems Theory," *Academy of Management Journal*, vol. 15 (1972), pp. 407–26, contributed to the emergence of this systems perspective on organizations. The systems view is further developed by Daniel Katz and Robert L. Kahn in their classic book, *The Social Psychology of Organizations* (New York: Wiley, 1978). For an integrated systems view see Lane Tracy, *The Living Organization* (New York: Quorum Books, 1994). For an overview, see W. Richard Scott, *Organizations: Rational, Natural, and Open Systems*, 4th ed. (Upper Saddle River, NJ: Prentice-Hall, 1998).

[31] For an overview, see Scott, op. cit., pp. 95–97.

[32] See, for example, the classic studies of Tom Burns and George M. Stalker, *The Management of Innovation* (London: Tavistock, 1961, and republished by Oxford University Press, London, 1994) and Paul R. Lawrence and Jay W. Lorsch, *Organizations and Environment* (Boston: Division of Research, Graduate School of Business Administration, Harvard University, 1967).

[33] W. Edwards Deming, *Quality, Productivity, and Competitive Position* (Cambridge, MA: MIT Press, 1982); and Rafael Aguay, *Dr. Deming: The American Who Taught the Japanese about Quality* (New York: Free Press, 1997).

[34] See Howard S. Gitlow and Shelly J. Gitlow, *The Deming Guide to Quality and Competitive Position* (Englewood Cliffs, NJ: Prentice-Hall, 1987).

[35] See Joseph M. Juran, *Quality Control Handbook*, 3rd ed. (New York: McGraw-Hill, 1979) and "The Quality Trilogy: A Universal Approach to Managing for Quality," in *Total Quality Management*, ed. H. Costin (New York: Dryden, 1994).

[36] Stephen Miller, "Joseph M. Juran: 1904–2008," *Wall Street Journal* (March 8–9, 2008), p. A7.

[37] Peter F. Drucker, "The Future That Has Already Happened," *Harvard Business Review*, vol. 75 (September–October 1997), pp. 20–24; and Peter F. Drucker, Esther Dyson, Charles Handy, Paul Daffo, and Peter M. Senge, "Looking Ahead: Implications of the Present," *Harvard Business Review*, vol. 75 (September–October 1997).

[38] See, for example, Thomas H. Davenport and Laurence Prusak, *Working Knowledge: How Organizations Manage What They Know* (Cambridge, MA: Harvard Business School Press, 1997).

[39] Peter Senge, *The Fifth Discipline* (New York: Harper, 1990).

[40] Eric Schmidt and Hal Varian, "Google: Ten Golden Rules," *Newsweek* (December 2, 2005).

[41] Thomas J. Peters and Robert H. Waterman Jr., *In Search of Excellence: Lessons from America's Best-Run Companies* (New York: Harper-Row, 1982).

[42] For a retrospective on *In Search of Excellence*, see William C. Bogner, "Tom Peters on the Real World of Business" and "Robert Waterman on Being Smart and Lucky," *Academy of Management Executive*, vol. 16 (2002), pp. 40–50.

[43] See *Good to Great: Why Some Companies Make the Leap . . . and Others Don't* (New York: HarperCollins, 2001).

[44] See Bruce G. Resnick and Timothy L. Smunt, "From Good to Great to . . . " *Academy of Management Perspectives* (November 2008), pp. 6–12; and "Bruce Niendorf and Kristine Beck, "Good to Great, or Just Good?" *Academy of Management Perspectives* (November 2008), pp. 13–20.

[45] Jim Collins, *How the Mighty Fall: And Why Some Companies Never Give In* (New York: HarperCollins, 2009).

[46] See Gordon Binder, *Science Lessons: What the Business of Biotech Taught Me about Management* (Boston: Harvard Business School Press, 2008).

[47] Jeffrey Pfeffer and Robert I. Sutton, *Hard Facts, Dangerous Half-Truths, and Total Nonsense: Profiting from Evidence-Based Management* (Boston: Harvard Business School Press, 2006); and Jeffrey Pfeffer and Robert I. Sutton, "Management Half-Truths and Nonsense," *California Management Review*, vol. 48(3) (2006), 77–100; and Jeffrey Pfeffer and Robert I. Sutton, "Evidence-Based Management," *Harvard Business Review* (January 2006), reprint R0601E.

[48] Definition from Rob B. Viner, David Denyer, and Denise M. Rousseau, "Evidence-Based Management: Concept Cleanup Time?" *Academy of Management Perspectives*, vol. 23 (November 2009), pp. 19–28. For debate on the EBMgt concept, see the exchange between ibid. and Trish Reay, Whitney Berta, and Melanie Kazman Kohn, "What's the Evidence on Evidence-Based Management?" *Academy of Management Perspectives*, vol. 23 (November 2009), pp. 5–18.

[49] See Denise M. Rousseau, "On Organizational Behavior," *BizEd* (May/June, 2008), pp. 30–31; and David G. Allen, Phillip C. Bryant, and James A. Vardaman, "Retaining Talent: Replacing Misconceptions with Evidence-Based Strategies," *Academy of Management Perspectives*, vol. 24 (May, 2010).

[50] Jeffrey Pfeffer, The *Human Equation: Building Profits by Putting People First* (Boston: Harvard Business School Press, 1998); and Charles O'Reilly III and Jeffrey Pfeffer, *Hidden Value: How Great Companies Achieve Extraordinary Results with Ordinary People* (Boston: Harvard Business School Press, 2000).

[51] Developed from Sara L. Rynes, Tamara L. Giluk, and Kenneth G. Brown, "The Very Separate Worlds of Academic and Practitioner Periodicals in Human Resource Management: Implications for Evidence-Based Management," *Academy of Management Journal*, Vol. 50 (October 2008), p. 986; and, David G. Allen, Phillip C. Bryant, and James M. Vardaman, "Retaining Talent: Replacing Misconceptions with Evidence-Based Strategies," *Academy of Management Perspectives*, vol. 24 (May, 2010).

Feature Notes

Real Ethics—This situation was reported in *the Columbus Dispatch* (March 8, 2006), p. D2.

Real People—Information from "Chapter 2," *Kellogg* (Winter 2004), p. 6; David Pilling, "Establishing Libraries to Help Children Gain a Love of Books," *Financial Times* (December 8, 2009); *Leaving Microsoft to Change the World*

(New York: HarperCollins), 2006; and, David Pilling, "Establishing Libraries to Help Gain a Love of Books," *Financial Times*, Kindle edition (December 8, 2009).

Photo Essays Notes

Cisco Systems—Adam Bryant, "Bouncing Back Is What Sets a Leader Apart," *The Global Edition of the New York Times* (August 3, 2009), p. 17. The Outliers—See Malcolm Gladwell, *Outliers* (New York: Little, Brown, 2009). Jim Collins—Jim Collins, *How the Mighty Fall: And Why Some Companies Never Give In* (New York: HarperCollins, 2009).

Chapter 3

Endnotes

[1] Information and quotes from www.interfaceglobal.com, accessed January 3, 2010.

[2] J. J. Graafland, "Do Markets Crowd out Virtues? An Aristotelian Framework," *Journal of Business Ethics*, vol. 91 (2010), pp. 1–19.

[3] R. M. Ryckman, M. Hammer, L. M. Kaczor, and J. A. Gold, "Construction of a Hypercompetitive Attitude Scale," *Journal of Personality Assessment*, vol. 55 (1990), pp. 630–39.

[4] Ibid.

[5] Desmond Tutu, "Do More Than Win," *Fortune* (December 30, 1991), p. 59.

[6] For an overview, see Linda K. Trevino and Katherine A. Nelson, *Managing Business Ethics*, 3rd ed. (New York: Wiley, 2003).

[7] M. J. O'Fallon and K. D. Butterfield, "A Review of the Empirical Ethical Decision-making Literature: 1996–2003," *Journal of Business Ethics*, vol. 59 (2005), pp. 375–413; and, S. J. Vitell and E. R. Hidalgo, "The Impact of Corporate Ethical Values and Enforcement of Ethical Codes on the Perceived Importance of Ethics in Business: A Comparison of U.S. and Spanish Managers," *Journal of Business Ethics*, vol. 64 (2006), pp. 31–43.

[8] D. Lyons, *Ethics and the Rule of Law* (Cambridge: Cambridge University Press, 1984).

[9] See, for example, James Oliver Horter and Lois E. Horton, *Slavery and the Making of America* (New York: Oxford University Press, 2004).

[10] Trevino and Nelson, op. cit.

[11] Milton Rokeach, *The Nature of Human Values* (New York: Free Press, 1973). See also W. C. Frederick and J. Weber, "The Values of Corporate Executives and Their Critics: An Empirical Description and Normative Implications," in W. C. Frederick and L. E. Preston (eds.), *Business Ethics: Research Issues and Empirical Studies* (Greenwich, CT: JAI Press, 1990).

[12] Philip Delves Broughton, "MBA Students Sway Integrity for Plagiarism," *Financial Times* (May 19, 2008), p. 13.

[13] Case reported in Michelle Conlin, "Cheating—Or Postmodern Learning?" *BusinessWeek* (May 14, 2007), p. 42.

[14] See Gerald F. Cavanagh, Dennis J. Moberg, and Manuel Velasquez, "The Ethics of Organizational Politics," *Academy of Management Review*, vol. 6 (1981), pp. 363–74; Justin G. Locknecker, Joseph A. McKinney, and Carlos W. Moore, "Egoism and Independence: Entrepreneurial Ethics," *Organizational Dynamics* (Winter 1988), pp. 64–72; and Justin G. Locknecker, Joseph A. McKinney, and Carlos W. Moore, "The Generation Gap in Business Ethics," *Business Horizons* (September–October 1989), pp. 9–14.

[15] Raymond L. Hilgert, "What Ever Happened to Ethics in Business and in Business Schools?" *The Diary of Alpha Kappa Psi* (April 1989), pp. 4–8.

[16] The Universal Declaration of Human Rights was adopted by General Assembly resolution 217 A (III), December 10, 1948, in the United Nations. See un.org/ Overview/rights.html.

[17] Jerald Greenburg, "Organizational Justice: Yesterday, Today, and Tomorrow," *Journal of Management*, vol. 16 (1990), pp. 399–432; and Mary A. Konovsky, "Understanding Procedural Justice and Its Impact on Business Organizations," *Journal of Management*, vol. 26 (2000), pp. 489–511.

[18] For a review see Russell Cropanzano, David E. Bown, and Stephen W. Gilliland, "The Management of Organizational Justice," *Academy of Management Perspectives* (November 2007), pp. 34–48.

[19] Interactional justice is described by Robert J. Bies, "The Predicament of Injustice: The Management of Moral Outrage," in L. L. Cummings and B. M. Staw (eds.), *Research in Organizational Behavior*, vol. 9 (Greenwich, CT: JAI Press, 1987), pp. 289–319. The example is from Carol T. Kulik and Robert L. Holbrook, "Demographics in Service Encounters: Effects of Racial and Gender Congruence on Perceived Fairness," *Social Justice Research*, vol. 13 (2000), pp. 375–402.

[20] M. Fortin and M. R. Fellenz, "Hypocrisies of Fairness: Towards a More Reflexive Ethical Base in Organizational Justice Research and Practice," *Journal of Business Ethics*, vol. 78 (2008), pp. 415–33; and, W. Sadurski, "Social Justice and Legal Justice," *Law and Philosophy*, vol. 3 (1984), pp. 329–54.

[21] Robert D. Haas, "Ethics—A Global Business Challenge," *Vital Speeches of the Day* (June 1, 1996), pp. 506–9.

[22] This discussion is based on Thomas Donaldson, "Values in Tension: Ethics Away from Home," *Harvard Business Review*, vol. 74 (September–October 1996), pp. 48–62.

[23] Thomas Donaldson and Thomas W. Dunfee, "Towards a Unified Conception of Business Ethics: Integrative Social Contracts Theory," *Academy of Management Review*, vol. 19 (1994), pp. 252–85.

[24] Donaldson, op. cit.

[25] Reported in Barbara Ley Toffler, "Tough Choices: Managers Talk Ethics," *New Management*, vol. 4 (1987), pp. 34–39. See also Barbara Ley Toffler, *Tough Choices: Managers Talk Ethics* (New York: Wiley, 1986).

[26] See, for example, Steven N. Brenner and Earl A. Mollander, "Is the Ethics of Business Changing?" *Harvard Business Review*, vol. 55 (January–February 1977).

[27] Survey results from Del Jones, "48% of Workers Admit to Unethical or Illegal Acts," *USA Today* (April 4, 1997), p. A1.

[28] Reported in Adam Smith, "Wall Street's Outrageous Fortunes," *Esquire* (April 1987), p. 73.

[29] Lawrence Kohlberg, *The Psychology of Moral Development: The Nature and Validity of Moral Stages* (*Essays in Moral Development*, Volume 2) (New York: HarperCollins, 1984). See also the discussion by Linda K. Trevino, "Moral Reasoning and Business Ethics: Implications for Research, Education, and Management," *Journal of Business Ethics*, vol. 11 (1992), pp. 445–59.

[30] See Thomas M. Jones, "Ethical Decision Making by Individuals in Organizations: An Issue Contingent Model," *Academy of Management Review*, vol. 16 (1991), pp. 366–95; Sara Morris and Robert A. McDonald, "The Role of Moral Intensity in Moral Judgments: An Empirical Investigation," *Journal of Business Ethics*, vol. 14 (9) (1995), pp. 715–26; and Tim Barnett, "Dimensions of Moral Intensity and Ethical Decision Making: An Empirical Study," *Journal of Applied Social Psychology*, vol. 31 (2001), pp. 1038–57.

[31] The Body Shop came under scrutiny over the degree to which its business practices actually live up to this charter and the company's

self-promoted green image. See, for example, John Entine, "Shattered Image," *Business Ethics* (September–October 1994), pp. 23–28.

[32]The company story and information on Dame Anita Roddick from thebodyshopinternational.com/about+us.

[33]Information on this case from William M. Carley, "Antitrust Chief Says CEOs Should Tape All Phone Calls to Each Other," *Wall Street Journal* (February 15, 1983), p. 23; "American Air, Chief End Antitrust Suit, Agree Not to Discuss Fares with Rivals," *Wall Street Journal* (July 15, 1985), p. 4; "American Airlines Loses Its Pilot," *Economist* (April 18, 1998), p. 58.

[34]Saul W. Gellerman, "Why 'Good' Managers Make Bad Ethical Choices," *Harvard Business Review*, vol. 64 (July–August 1986), pp. 85–90.

[35]Items from news headlines. See also Blake E. Ashforth, Dennis A. Gioia, Sandra C. Robinson, and Linda K. Trevino, "Special Topic Forum on Corruption in Organizations," *Academy of Management Review*, vol. 33 (July 2008), pp. 670t.

[36]Information from the Lockheed Martin Company website retrieved from http://www.lockheedmartin.com/aboutus/ethics/index.html.

[37]Alan L. Otten, "Ethics on the Job: Companies Alert Employees to Potential Dilemmas," *Wall Street Journal* (July 14, 1986), p. 17; and "The Business Ethics Debate," *Newsweek* (May 25, 1987), p. 36.

[38]Information from corporate website: www.gapinc.com/communitysourcing/vendor_conduct.htm.

[39]Information from Joseph Pereira and Steve Stcklow. "Wal-Mart Raises Bar on Toy-Safety Standards," *Wall Street Journal* (May 14, 2008), p. B1.

[40]Archie B. Carroll, "In Search of the Moral Manager," *Business Horizons* (March/April 2001), pp. 7–15.

[41]Kohlberg, op. cit.

[42]See "Whistle-Blowers on Trial," *BusinessWeek* (March 24, 1997), pp. 172–78, and "NLRB Judge Rules for Massachusetts Nurses in Whistle-Blowing Case," *American Nurse* (January–February 1998), p. 7.

[43]For a review of whistleblowing, see Marcia P. Micelli and Janet P. Near, *Blowing the Whistle* (Lexington, MA: Lexington Books, 1992); see also Micelli and Near, "Whistleblowing: Reaping the Benefits," *Academy of Management Executive*, vol. 8 (August 1994), pp. 65–72; and, M. J. Gundlach, S. C. Douglas, and M. J. Martinko, "The Decision to Blow the Whistle: A Social Information Processing Framework." *Academy of Management Review*, vol. 28, no. 1 (2003), pp. 107–23.

[44]"A Tip for Whistleblowers: Don't," *Wall Street Journal* (May 31, 2007), p. B6.

[45]Information from Ethics Resource Center, "Major Survey of America's Workers Finds Substantial Improvements in Ethics," www.ethics.org/releases/nr_20030521_nbes.html.

[46]James A. Waters, "Catch 20.5: Mortality as an Organizational Phenomenon," *Organizational Dynamics*, vol. 6 (Spring 1978), pp. 3–15.

[47]Definition from www.pgsupplier.com/environmental-stustainability-scorecard (accessed: May 12, 2010).

[48]Alfred A. Marcus and Adam R. Fremeth, "Green Management Matters Regardless," *Academy of Management Perspectives*, Vol. 23 (August, 2009), pp. 17–26.

[49]Jeffrey Pfeffer, "Building Sustainable Organizations: The Human Factor," *Academy of Management Perspectives*, Vol. 24 (February, 2010), pp. 34–45.

[50]Joe Biesecker, "What Today's College Graduates Want: It's Not All about Paychecks," *Central Penn Business Journal* (August 10, 2007).

[51]Ibid. Sarah E. Needleman, "The Latest Office Perk: Getting Paid to Volunteer," *Wall Street Journal* (April 29, 2008), p. D1.

[52]Examples are from Dancing Deer Bakery website retrieved from http://www.dancingdeer.com/index.cfm?page_id=45; "Growing Green Business," *Northwestern* (Winter 2007), p. 19; Regina McEnery, "Cancer Patients Getting the White-Glove Treatment," *The Columbus Dispatch* (March 1, 2008); and, Nanett Byrnes, "Heavy Lifting at the Food Bank," *BusinessWeek* (December 17, 2007), pp. SC08–SC09.

[53]See Thomas Donaldson and Lee Preston, "The Stakeholder Theory of the Corporation," *Academy of Management Review*, vol. 20 (January 1995), pp. 65–91.

[54]R. K. Bradley, R. Agle, and D. J. Wood, "Toward a Theory of Stakeholder Identification and Salience: Defining the Principle of Who and What Really Counts," *Academy of Management Review*, vol. 22 (1997), pp. 853–86.

[55]See Joel Makower: *Putting Social Responsibility to Work for Your Business and the World* (New York: Simon & Schuster, 1994), pp. 17–18.

[56]Michael E. Porter and Mark R. Kramer, "Strategy & Society: The Link between Competitive Advantage and Corporate Social Responsibility," *Harvard Business Review* (December 2006), Reprint R0612D.

[57]The historical framework of this discussion is developed from Keith Davis, "The Case for and against Business Assumption of Social Responsibility," *Academy of Management Journal* (June 1973), pp. 312–22; Keith Davis and William Frederick, *Business and Society: Management: Public Policy, Ethics*, 5th ed. (New York: McGraw-Hill, 1984). The debate is also discussed by Makower, op. cit., pp. 28–33. For further perspective on this debate see, for example, Marcus and Fremeth, op cit., and, Donald S. Siegel, "Green Management Matters Only if It Yields More Green: An Economic/Strategic Perspective," *Academy of Management Perspectives*, Vol. 23 (August, 2009), pp. 5–16.

[58]The Friedman quotation is from Milton Friedman, *Capitalism and Freedom* (Chicago: University of Chicago Press, 1962). See also Henry G. Manne, "Milton Friedman Was Right," *Wall Street Journal* (November 24, 2006), p. A12. The Samuelson quotation is from Paul A. Samuelson, "Love That Corporation," *Mountain Bell Magazine* (Spring 1971). Both are cited in Davis, op. cit.

[59]Davis and Frederick, op. cit.

[60]Herb Greenberg, "How Values Embraced by a Company May Enhance That Company's Value," *Wall Street Journal* (October 27–28, 2007), p. B3.

[61]See James K. Glassman, "When Ethics Meet Earnings," *International Herald Tribune* (May 24–25, 2003), p. 15.

[62]See Makower, op. cit. (1994), pp. 71–75; Sandra A. Waddock and Samuel B. Graves, "The Corporate Social Performance—Financial Performance Link," *Strategic Management Journal* (1997), pp. 303–19; Michael E. Porter and Mark R. Kramer, "Strategy-Society: The Link between Competitive Advantage and Corporate Social Responsibility," *Harvard Business Review* (December 2006), pp. 78–92.

[63]The "compliance–conviction" distinction is attributed to Mark Goyder in Martin Waller, "Much Corporate Responsibility Is Box-Ticking," *The Times Business* (July 8, 2003), p. 21.

[64]Archie B. Carroll, "A Three-Dimensional Model of Corporate Performance," *Academy of Management Review*, vol. 4 (1979), pp. 497–505. Carroll's continuing work in this area is reported in Mark S. Schwartz and Archie B. Carroll, "Corporate Social Responsibility: A Three Domain Approach," *Business Ethics Quarterly*, vol. 13 (2003), pp. 503–30.

[65]See the discussion by Porter and Kramer, op. cit.

[66]Elizabeth Gatewood and Archie B. Carroll, "The Anatomy of Corporate Social Response," *Business Horizons*, vol. 24 (September–October 1981), pp. 9–16.

[67]Judith Burns, "Everything You Wanted to Know about Corporate Governance . . . But Didn't Know How to Ask," *Wall Street Journal* (October 27, 2003), pp. R1, R7.

[68]Ibid.

[69]"Warming to Corporate Reform," *Wall Street Journal* (October 25, 2005), p. R2.

[70]Adapted from James Weber, "Management Value Orientations: A Typology and Assessment," *International Journal of Value Based Management*, vol. 3, no. 2 (1990), pp. 37–54.

Feature Notes

Real Ethics—Information from Cheryl Soltis, *Wall Street Journal* (March 21, 2006), p. B7.

[1]Real People—Information from the company website retrieved from http://www.stonyfield.com/about_us; company videos retrieved from http://www.stonyfield.com/yotube/index.jsp; Gary Hirshberg biography retrieved from http://www.notablebiographies.com/ newsmakers2/2007-Co-Lh/ Hirshberg-Gary.html#ixzz0dfM0qduA; and, "25 Rich Ass Greenies Who Made Their Fortune Saving the Environment", Earthfirst.com, August 25, 2008 retrieved from http://earthfirst.com/

Chapter 4

Endnotes

[1]Information and quotes from Jessica Hodgson, "Selling and Software," *Wall Street Journal* (December 17, 2009), p. A25; Steve Hamm, "The King of the Cloud," *BusinessWeek* (November 30, 2009), p. 77. See also Marc Benioff, *Behind the Cloud: The Untold Story of How Salesforce.com Went from Idea to Billion-Dollar Company and Revolutionized an Industry* (San Francisco, CA: Jossey-Bass, 2009).

[2]See "Risk," *Psychology Today* (October 1, 2009), www.psychologytoday.com (accessed February 3, 2010); Nathan Washburn, "Hard Times Can Inspire Wrong Type of Risk Taking," http://knowledgenetwork.thunderbird.edu (accessed January 12, 2010).

[3]Opening quotes from Joseph B. White and Peter Landers, "Toyoda is Wary Star of Kabuki at Capitol," *Wall Street Journal* (February 25, 2010), pp. A1, A7; and, Associated Press, "U.S. May Require Accelerator Override in New Cars," www.clickondetroit.com/automotive/22711707/detail.html (accessed March 8, 2010).

[4]See Kris Maher and Bob Tita, "Caterpillar Joins 'Onshoring' Trend," *Wall Street Journal* (March 10, 2010), pp. B1, B7.

[5]Kimberly Weisul, "Why More Are Buying into 'Buy Local'," *BusinessWeek* (March 1, 2010), pp. 57, 60.

[6]"Neighbor: Starbucks Stole My Ambiance," *Seattle Post Intelligencer* (July 16, 2009), retrieved from www.seattlepi.com.

[7]Josh Mitchell, "U.S. Weighs Stricter Car-Safety Rules," *Wall Street Journal* (March 12, 2010), p. B4.

[8]Charles Forelle, "EU Fines Microsoft $1.35 Billion," *Wall Street Journal* (February 28, 2008), p. B2.

[9]Data in table from "List of the 13 Internet Enemies," Reporters without Borders (July 11, 2006), retrieved from www.rsf.org (August 27, 2008).

[10]See Jane Spencer and Kevin J. Delaney, "YouTube Unplugged," *Wall Street Journal* (March 31, 2008), p. BIB2.

[11]Ibid; and, Ben Worthen and Siobhan Gorman, "Google Prepares to Stop Censoring in China," *Wall Street Journal* (March 12, 2010), p. B1.

[12]Example from Jena McGregor, "Customer Service Champs: USAA's Battle Plan," *Bloomberg BusinessWeek* (March 1, 2010), pp. 40–44.

[13]Information from Martin Giles, "Online Social Networks Are Changing the Way People Communicate," *Economist*, Kindle Edition (February 4, 2010).

[14]Bobby White, "The New Workplace Rules: No Video-Watching," *Wall Street Journal* (March 4, 2008), pp. B1, B3.

[15]Giles, op. cit.

[16]Ibid.

[17]"The Smart Way to Hire Workers," *Economist*, Kindle Edition (February 4, 2010).

[18]See, for example, "America's Changing Workforce: Recession Turns a Graying Workforce Grayer," *Pew Research Center* (September 3, 2009); persocialtrends.com.

[19]Jean M. Twenge, Stacy M. Campbell, Brian J. Hoffman, and Charles E. Lance, "Generational Difference in Work Values: Leisure and Extrinsic Values Increasing, Social and Intrinsic Values Decreasing," *Journal of Management Online First* (March 1, 2010): www.jom.sagepub.com.

[20]See, for example, Sharon Jayson, "'iGeneration' Has No Off Switch," *USA Today* (February 10, 2010), pp. D1, D2.

[21]For a debate on CEO compensation see "Exchange: CEO Compensation," *Academy of Management Perspective*, vol. 22 (May 2008), pp. 5–33. See also "The Gold-Plated Boardroom," *Bloomberg Businessweek* (February 22, 2010), pp. 72–73; and, "Jessica Silver-Greenberg, Tara Kalwarsi, and Alexis Leondis, "CEO Pay Drops, But . . . Cash is King," *Bloomberg Businessweek* (April 10, 2010), pp. 50–56.

[22]Rob Walker, "Sex vs. Ethics," *Fast Company* (June 2008), pp. 73–78.

[23]Information from Remi Trudel and June Cotte, "Does Being Ethical Pay?" *Wall Street Journal* (May 12, 2008), p. R4.

[24]Heather Green and Kerry Capell, "Carbon Confusion," *BusinessWeek* (March 17, 2008), pp. 52–56; and, "Business Begins to Stir," *The Economist*, Kindle Edition (May 29, 2010).

[25]See, for example, "Lessons," *Bloomberg BusinessWeek* (May 10–16, 2010), pp. 49–53.

[26]Definition from www.sustainablebusiness.com.

[27]Alfred A. Marcus and Adam R. Fremeth, "Green Management Matters Regardless," *Academy of Management Perspectives*, vol. 23 (August 2009), pp. 17–26.

[28]See Thomas Donaldson and Lee Preston, "The Stakeholder Theory of the Corporation," *Academy of Management Review*, vol. 20 (January 1995), pp. 65–91.

[29]"Ivory Tower: How an MBA Can Bend Your Mind," *BusinessWeek* (April 1, 2002), p. 12.

[30]Quotation from a discussion by Richard J. Shonberger and Edward M. Knod Jr., *Operations Management: Serving the Customer*, 3rd ed. (Plano, TX: Business Publications, 1988), p. 4.

[31]Quote from *The Vermont Teddy Bear Company Gazette*, op. cit., p. 3.

[32]Rosabeth Moss Kanter, "Transcending Business Boundaries: 12,000 World Managers View Change," *Harvard Business Review* (May–June 1991), pp. 151–64.

[33]"How Marriott Never Forgets a Guest," *BusinessWeek* (February 21, 2000), p. 74.

[34]Roger D. Blackwell and Kristina Blackwell, "The Century of the Consumer: Converting Supply Chains into Demand Chains," *Supply Chain Management Review* (Fall 1999).

[35]See Michael E. Porter, *Competitive Strategy: Techniques for Analyzing Industries and Competitors* (New York: Free Press, 1980); and *Competitive Advantage: Creating and Sustaining Superior Performance* (New York: Free Press, 1986); see also Richard A. D'Aveni, *Hyper-Competition: Managing the Dynamics of Strategic Maneuvering* (New York: Free Press, 1994).

[36]Michael E. Porter, "Strategy and the Internet," *Harvard Business Review*, vol. 79, no. 3 (March 2001).

[37]James D. Thompson, *Organizations in Action* (New York: McGraw-Hill, 1967); and Robert B. Duncan, "Characteristics of Organizational Environments and Perceived Environmental Uncertainty," *Administrative Science Quarterly*, vol. 17 (1972), pp. 313–27. For discussion of the implications of uncertainty see Hugh Courtney, Jane Kirkland, and Patrick Viguerie, "Strategy under Uncertainty," *Harvard Business Review* (November–December 1997), pp. 67–79.

[38]Based on Gaerth N. Jones, *Organization Theory and Design*, 3rd ed. (Upper Saddle River, NJ: Prentice-Hall, 2001).

[39]Quote from "Toyoda-*San* Speaks," *BusinessWeek* (March 8, 2010), p. 6.

[40]See Alan Ohnsman, Jeff Green, and Kae Inoue, "The Humbling of Toyota," *BusinessWeek* (March 22&29, 2010), pp. 33–36.

[41]"Indra Nooyi of PepsiCo," View from the Top, *Financial Times*, www.ft.com (February 1, 2010): retrieved March 11, 2010.

[42]Marcus and Fremeth, op. cit.

[43]From www.iso.org.

[44]See "Principles for Responsible Management Education," www.unprme.org/the-6-principles; and, Jose M. Alcaraz and Eappen Thiruvattal, "The United Nations' Principles for Responsible Management Education: A Global Call for Sustainability in Management Education. An Interview with Manuel Escudero," *Academy of Management Learning & Education*, in press (March 2010).

[45]Information from Margot Roosevelt, "Protection Money," *Columbus Dispatch* (March 10, 2010), pp. A1, A9.

[46]Quotes from Ibid.

[47]See, for example, "The Long Road to an Alternative Energy Future," *Wall Street Journal* (February 22, 2010), p. R4.

[48]www.wbcsd.org.

[49]Economics—Creating Environmental Capital," *Wall Street Journal* (March 8, 2010), p. R1.

[50]"Clean-Tech Companies: Ranking the Top Venture-Backed Firms," *Wall Street Journal* (March 8, 2010), p. R4.

[51]"Call for Submissions," 2009 Annual Meeting of the Academy of Management, www.meeting.aomonline.org/2009; and Marcus and Fremeth, op. cit., and Donald S. Siegel, "Green Management Matters Only if It Yields More Green: An Economic/Strategic Perspective," *Academy of Management Perspectives*, vol. 23 (August 2009), pp. 5–16.

[52]See William M. Bulkeley, "Print Outsourcing Gives Boost to Xerox, H-P," *Wall Street Journal* (December 22, 2009), p. B5.

[53]"Tapping into a New Generation," *Wall Street Journal* (March 8, 2010), p. R4.

[54]See Thomas L. Friedman, "Daring to Dream Can Pay Off Big," *Columbus Dispatch* (March 9, 2010), p. A11.

[55]Quote and example, "Tapping into a New Generation; op cit.

[56]Jeffrey Pfeffer, "Building Sustainable Organizations: The Human Factor," *Academy of Management Perspectives*, Vol. 24 (February, 2010), pp. 34–45.

[57]Quotes from Ibid.

[58]Management Smarts 4.2 suggested in part by Pfeffer's discussion in Ibid, pp. 36–40.

[59]Tom Peters, *The Circle of Innovation* (New York: Knopf, 1997).

[60]Quote from Jena McGregor, "The World's Most Innovative Companies," *BusinessWeek* (April 24, 2006), pp. 63–74.

[61]Ibid; "Innovation: The View from the Top," *BusinessWeek* (April 3, 2006), pp. 52–53; "The Enemies of Innovation," *BusinessWeek* (April 24, 2006), p. 68.

[62]See, for example, Michael Arndt and Bruce Einhorn, "The 50 Most Innovative Companies," *Bloomberg Businessweek* (April 25, 2010), pp. 34–40.

[63]David Cooperrider, "Sustainable Innovation," *BizEd* (July/August, 2008), pp. 32–38.

[64]See Ellen Byron, "The American Soap Overdose," *The Wall Street Journal* (January 27, 2010), pp. D1, D8.

[65]"Green Business Innovations," *BusinessWeek* (April 28, 2008), special advertising section; and, cooperrider, op. cit.

[66]Quote from "How to Measure Up," *Kellogg* (Summer 2009), p. 17.

[67]Peter F. Drucker, *Management: Tasks, Responsibilities, and Practices* (New York: Harper-Row, 1973), p. 797.

[68]Gary Hamel, *Leading the Revolution: How to Thrive in Turbulent Times* (Boston: Harvard Business School Press, 2002).

[69]"The Joys and Perils of 'Reverse Innovation'," *BusinessWeek* (October 5, 2009), p. 12.

[70]Ibid. Also, example and quotes from "How to Compete in a World Turned Upside Down," *Financial Times*, Kindle edition (October 6, 2009).

[71]"New Life for Old Threads," *BusinessWeek* (April 28, 2008), special advertising section.

[72]Information and quotes from Nancy Gohring, "Microsoft: Stodgy or Innovative? It's All about Perception," *PC World* (July 25, 2008).

[73]Kenneth Labich, "The Innovators," *Fortune* (June 6, 1988), pp. 49–64.

[74]Information and quote from Cuckoo Paul, "In Full Flight," *Forbes India* (February 19, 2010), pp. 36–38.

[75]Information and quotes from Yukari Iwatani Kane, "Sony CEO Urges Managers to Get 'Mad'," *Wall Street Journal* (May 23, 2008), p. B8.

[76]Reena Jana, "Brickhouse: Yahoo's Hot Little Incubator," *BusinessWeek* (November, 2007), p. IN 14.

[77]Charles O'Reilly III and Michael Tushman, "The Ambidextrous Organization," *Harvard Business Review* (2004), Reprint # R0404-D.

[78]Information from Steve Hamm, "International Isn't Just IBM's First Name," *BusinessWeek* (January 28, 2008), pp. 36–40.

[79]Jeff Jarvis, "The Buzz from Starbucks Customers," *BusinessWeek* (April 29, 2008), pp. 73–75.

[80]"How Google Fuels Its Idea Factory," *BusinessWeek* (May 12, 2008), pp. 54–55.

[81]See Jack and Suzy Welch, "Finding Innovation Where it Lives," *BusinessWeek* (April 21, 2008), p. 84.

[82]Based on Budner, S. "Intolerance of Ambiguity as a Personality Variable," *Journal of Personality*, Vol. 30, No. 1, (1962), pp. 29–50.

Feature Notes

Real People—Information from Jeffrey D. Sachs, *The End of Poverty* (New York: Penguin, 2005); Muhammad Yunus, *Creating a World Without Poverty: Social Business and the Future of Capitalism* (New York: Public Affairs, 2008); "Executive MBA Students Learn about Micro-Lending from Its Founder, Nobel Laureate Muhammad Yunus," *Stern Business* (Spring/Summer 2008), p. 41; New Steve Hamm, "When the Bottom Line Is Ending Poverty," *Business Week* (March 10, 2008), p. 85; Yunus, op cit.; Daniel Pimlott, "Bangladeshi's Aid for US Poor," *Financial Times* (February 16/17, 2008), p. 4; and Simon Hobbs, "Big Payback," *CNBC European Business* (January/February, 2009), pp. 36–38.

Real Ethics—Information from Jim Phillips, "Business Leaders Say "Green" Approach Doable," *The Athens News* (March 27, 2008), From www.athensnews.com.

Photo Essay Notes

Airline Industry—Information from Mike Esterl, "More Lucrative Business Travelers Now Teleconference, Fly Coach," *Wall Street Journal* (February 18, 2010), p. B.1. Pennies for Peace—See

"Greg Mortensen Delivers 2009 Ashok C. Sani Scholar-in-Residence Lecture," *STERNbusiness* (2009), p. 6; and, Greg Mortensen, *Stones into Schools: Promoting Peace with Books, Not Bombs, in Afghanistan and Pakistan* (New York: Viking, 2009) and *Three Cups of Tea: One Man's Mission to Promote Peace . . . One School at a Time* (New York: Penguin, 2007). Infosys Technologies—Information from Reena Jana, "From India, the Latest Management Fad," *Business Week* (December 14, 2009), pp. 54–56.

Chapter 5

Endnotes

[1]Quotes from www.limited.com/feature.jsp and www.limited.com/who/index.jsp. pp. 40–43: and, limitedbrands.com.

[2]Richard D. Lewis, *The Cultural Imperative: Global Trends in the 21st Century* (Yarmouth, ME: Intercultural Press, 2002).

[3]China examples from Emily Parker, "The Roots of Chinese Nationalism," *Wall Street Journal* (April 1, 2008), p. A17. For more on boxed material see Makoto Ohtsiv, *Inside Japanese Business: A Narrative History 1960–2000* (Armonk, NY: M.E. Sharpe, 2002).

[4]See, for example, Dan Gearino, "Made in This Hemisphere," *Columbus Dispatch* (January 11, 2010), pp. A10, A11; and David Welch, "One Man, One Car, One World," *BusinessWeek* (January 25, 2010), pp. 48–49.

[5]Sample articles include "Globalization Bites Boeing," *BusinessWeek* (March 24, 2008), p. 32; "One World, One Car, One Name," *BusinessWeek* (March 24, 2008), p. 32; Eric Bellman and Jackie Range, "Indian-Style Mergers: Buy a Brand, Leave it Alone," *Wall Street Journal* (March 22–23, 2008), pp. A9, A14; Bruce Emhorn, "Alan Mulally's Asian Sales Call," *Bloomberg Businessweek* (April 12, 2010), pp. 41–43.

[6]See, for example, Kenichi Ohmae's books *The Borderless World: Power and Strategy in the Interlinked Economy* (New York: Harper, 1989); *The End of the Nation State* (New York: Free Press, 1996); *The Invisible Continent: Four Strategic Imperatives of the New Economy* (New York: Harper, 1999); and *The Next Global Stage: Challenges and Opportunities in Our Borderless World* (Philadelphia: Wharton School Publishing, 2006).

[7]See, for example, Gregg Easterbrook, *Sonic Boom: Globalization at Mach Speed* (New York: Random House, 2009).

[8]Pietra Rivoli, *The Travels of a T-Shirt in the Global Economy*, 2nd ed. (Hoboken, NJ: John Wiley & Sons, 2009).

[9]Rosabeth Moss Kanter, *World Class: Thinking Locally in the Global Economy* (New York: Simon and Schuster, 1995), preface.

[10]Thomas L. Friedman, *Hot, Flat, and Crowded: Why We Need a Green Revolution—and How It Can Renew America* (New York: Farrar, Straus and Giroux, 2008).

[11]Information from Mark Niquette, "Honda's 'Bold Move' Paid Off," *Columbus Dispatch* (November 16, 2002), pp. C1, C2.

[12]Information from Mei Fong, "Chinese Refrigerator Maker Finds U.S. Chilly," *Wall Street Journal* (March 18, 2008), pp. B1, B2.

[13]Quote from John A. Byrne, "Visionary vs. Visionary," *BusinessWeek* (August 28, 2000), p. 210.

[14]Information from newbalance.com/corporate; and, "Nike Strategy Leaves It Room to Run," *The Wall Street Journal* (March 16, 2010), P. C10.

[15]Steve Hamm, "Into Africa: Capitalism from the Ground Up," *BusinessWeek* (May 4, 2009), pp. 60–61.

[16]Information on hour wage costs reported in "Breaking a Taboo, High Fashion Starts Making Goods Overseas," *Wall Street Journal* (September 27, 2005), pp. A1, A10.

[17]Information in box from "Factory to the World," *National Geographic* (May 2008), p. 170. For how Chinese firms are being affected by the global economic slowdown see Dexter Roberts, "China's Factory Blues," *BusinessWeek* (April 7, 2008), pp. 78–82.

[18]Information from Geoff Dyer, "iPod Points to Struggle Ahead," *Financial Times* (December 30, 2009).

[19]Information from Michael A. Fletcher, "Ohio Profits from Exports," *Columbus Dispatch* (December 30, 2007), p. B3.

[20]"Survey: Intellectual Property Theft Now Accounts for 31 Percent of Global Counterfeiting," Gieschen Consultancy, February 25, 2005.

[21]Information from "Not Exactly Counterfeit," *Fortune* (April 26, 2006): money.cnn.com/magazines/fortune.

[22]Matthew J. Slaughter, "What Tata Tells Us," *Wall Street Journal* (March 27, 2008), p. A15; and, Michelle Maynard, "A La Feline Not Made in the USA," *The New York Times* (October 18, 2009): www.nytimes.com.

[23]Criteria for choosing joint venture partners developed from Anthony J. F. O'Reilly, "Establishing Successful Joint Ventures in Developing Nations: A CEO's Perspective," *Columbia Journal of World Business* (Spring 1988), pp. 65–71; and "Best Practices for Global Competitiveness," *Fortune* (March 30, 1998), pp. S1–S3, special advertising section.

[24]See James T. Areddy, "Danone Pulls Out of Disputed China Venture," *Wall Street Journal* (October 1, 2009), p. B1.

[25]Karby Leggett, "U.S. Auto Makers Find Promise—and Peril—in China," *Wall Street Journal* (June 19, 2003), p. B1; "Did Spark Spark a Copycat?" *BusinessWeek* (February 7, 2005), p. 64.

[26]"Best Practices for Global Competitiveness," *Fortune* (March 30, 1998), pp. S1–S3, special advertising.

[27]Quote from Charles Forelle and Don Clark, "Intel Fine Jolts Tech Sector," *Wall Street Journal* (May 14, 2009), pp. A1, A14.

[28]See Cliff Edwards, "HP Declares War on Counterfeiters," *BusinessWeek* (June 8, 2009), pp. 44–45.

[29]Information and quote from Dan Molinski and Norihiko Shirouzu, "Venezuelan President Threatens Toyota, GM," *Wall Street Journal* (December 26–27, 2009), pp. A1, A6.

[30]www.wto.org/English/thewto_e/whatis_e/tif_e/fact3_e.htm (March 25, 2008).

[31]Information and quotes from Dexter Roberts, "Closing for Business?" *Bloomberg Businessweek* (April 5, 2010), pp. 32–37

[32]Information and quote from "WTO Takes Up U.S. Complaint against China Patent Regime," *AFP* (September 7, 2007): afp.google.com/article/ALeqM5hASBbePC8gtbmtfzExtmfkdNDvKQ.

[33]Pete Engardio, Geri Smith, and Jane Sasseen, "Refighting NAFTA," *BusinessWeek* (March 31, 2008), pp. 55–59.

[34]Kevin Brown, "Chinese Deal Tops Busy Year for Asean Southeast Asia," *Financial Times* (January 2, 2010).

[35]The *Economist* is a good weekly source of information on Africa; and "Embracing Africa," *BusinessWeek* (December 18, 2006), p. 101.

[36]See Robert Farzad, "Can Greed Save Africa?" *BusinessWeek* (December 10, 2007), pp. 46–54; "The Big Bounce," *Bloomberg BusinessWeek* (May 17–23, 2010), pp. 48–57; and, Will Connors and Sarah Childress, "Africa's Local Champions Begin to Spread Out," *The Wall Street Journal* (May 26, 2010), p. B8.

[37]Information from Chris Tomlinson, "Africa's New Hope: Entrepreneurs Lead Economic Growth," *Columbus Dispatch* (December 9, 2007), p. G3.

[38]www.sadc.int/about_sadc/vision.php.

[39]Data from "By Mac Index 2010," www.wallstcheatsheet.com. accessed April 23, 2010.

[40]Information from "Fortune Global 500," Fortune.com; "FT Global 500 2008," *FT Weekend* (June 28/29, 2008), pp. 34–41:

‍

and, "The Rise of New Business Powers," *FT Weekend* (June 28/29, 2008), p. 14.

[41]See Peter F. Drucker, "The Global Economy and the Nation-State," *Foreign Affairs*, vol. 76 (September–October 1997), pp. 159–71.

[42]Information from Steve Hamm, "IBM vs. TATA: Which Is More American?" *BusinessWeek* (May 5, 2008), p. 28; and, Greg Farrell, "McDonald's Continues to Rely on European Restaurants for Growth," *Financial Times*, Kindle edition (April 20, 2010).

[43]Michael Mandel, "Multinationals: Are They Good for America?," *BusinessWeek* (February 28, 2008): businessweek.com.

[44]See, for example, www.corpwatch.org/article.php?id=377.

[45]Developed from R. Hall Mason, "Conflicts between Host Countries and Multinational Enterprise," *California Management Review*, vol. 17 (1974), pp. 6, 7.

[46]Mandel, op. cit.; Engardio, op. cit.

[47]Devon Maylie, "Alcoa Invests Near Planned Mines," *Wall Street Journal* (March 24, 2008), p. B4; Tom Wright, "Indonesia's Commodity Boom Is a Mixed Bag," *Wall Street Journal* (March 24, 2008), p. A8; and James T. Areddy, "Tibet Unrest May Deter Foreign Investors," *Wall Street Journal* (March 24, 2008), p. A3.

[48]See transparency.org. See also Blake E. Ashforth, Dennis A. Gioia, Sandra L. Robinson, and Linda K. Trevino, "Special Topic Forum on Corruption," *Academy of Management Review*, vol. 33 (July 2008), pp. 670t.

[49]Quote from Carol Matlack, "The Peril and Promise of Investing in Russia," *BusinessWeek* (October 5, 2009), pp. 48–51.

[50]Transparency International, "Corruption Perceptions Index 2009," www.transparency.org: accessed April 23, 2010.

[51]See Dionne Searcey, "U.S. Cracks Down on Corporate Bribes," *Wall Street Journal* (May 26, 2009), pp. A1, A4.

[52]Ibid.

[53]Information and quote from David Crawford and Donne Searcy, "U.S. Joins H-P Bribery Investigation, "*The Wall Street Journal* (April 16, 2010), pp. B1, B5.

[54]See, for example, Jason Dean and Ting-I Tsai, "Suicides Spark Inquiries," *The Wall Street Journal* (May 27, 2010), pp. B1, B7.

[55]Information and quote from Andrew Morse and Nick Wingfield, "Apple Audits Labor Practices," *The Wall Street Journal* (March 1, 2010), p. B3.

[56]Information and quote from Andrew Morse and Nick Wingfield, "Microsoft will Investigate Conditions at Chinese Plant," *The Wall Street Journal* (April 16, 2010), p. B7.

[57]Examples reported in Neil Chesanow, *The World-Class Executive* (New York: Rawson Associates, 1985).

[58]For alternative definitions of culture, see Martin J. Gannon, *Paradoxes of Culture and Globalization* (Thousand Oaks, CA: Sage, 2008), Chapter 2.

[59]P. Christopher Earley and Elaine Mosakowski, "Toward Cultural Intelligence: Turning Cultural Differences Into Workplace Advantage," *Academy of Management Executive*, vol. 18 (2004), pp. 151–57.

[60]For a good overview of the practical issues, see Lewis, op. cit.; and Martin J. Gannon, *Understanding Global Cultures* (Thousand Oaks, CA: Sage, 1994).

[61]Example from Fong, op. cit.

[62]Edward T. Hall, *The Silent Language* (New York: Anchor Books, 1959).

[63]Edward T. Hall, *Beyond Culture* (New York: Doubleday, 1976).

[64]Edward T. Hall, *The Hidden Dimension* (New York: Anchor Books, 1969) and *Hidden Differences* (New York: Doubleday, 1990).

[65]Ibid.

[66]Information from Hiroko Tabuchi, "In Japan, an Odd Perch for Google: Looking up at Leader," *New York Times* (November 30, 2009), pp. B4, B5.

[67]Geert Hofstede, *Culture's Consequences* (Beverly Hills, CA: Sage, 1984), and *Culture's Consequences: Comparing Values, Behaviors, Institutions and Organizations across Nations*, 2nd ed. (Thousand Oaks, CA: Sage, 2001). See also Michael H. Hoppe, "An Interview with Geert Hofstede," *Academy of Management Executive*, vol. 18 (2004), pp. 75–79.

[68]Geert Hofstede and Michael H. Bond, "The Confucius Connection: From Cultural Roots to Economic Growth," *Organizational Dynamics*, vol. 16 (1988), pp. 4–21.

[69]See Geert Hofstede, *Culture and Organizations: Software of the Mind* (London: McGraw-Hill, 1991).

[70]For another perspective see Harry Triandis and M. Gelfand, "Convergent Measurement of Horizontal and Vertical Collectivism," *Journal of Personality & Social Psychology*, vol. 74, pp. 118–28.

[71]This dimension is explained more thoroughly by Geert Hofstede et al., *Masculinity and Femininity: The Taboo Dimension of National Cultures* (Thousand Oaks, CA: Sage, 1998).

[72]Information for "Stay Informed" from "The Conundrum of the Glass Ceiling," *Economist* (July 23, 2005), p. 634, and "Japan's Diversity Problem," *Wall Street Journal* (October 24, 2005), pp. B1, B5.

[73]See Hofstede and Bond, op. cit.

[74]See, for example, Nancy Adler and Allison Gundersen, *International Dimensions of Organizational Behavior*, 5th ed. (New York: Thomson South-Western, 2008).

[75]Geert Hofstede, "Motivation, Leadership, and Organization: Do American Theories Apply Abroad?" *Organizational Dynamics* (1980), p. 43; Geert Hofstede, "The Cultural Relativity of Organizational Practices," *Journal of International Business Studies* (Fall 1983), pp. 75–89. See also Hofstede's "Cultural Constraints in Management Theories," *Academy of Management Review*, vol. 7 (1993), pp. 81–94.

[76]Haier, op. cit.

[77]Geert Hofstede, "A Reply to Goodstein and Hunt," *Organizational Dynamics*, vol. 10 (Summer 1981), p. 68.

[78]Robert J. House, Paul J. Hanges, Mansour Javidan, Peter W. Dorfman, and Vipin Gupta, eds., *Culture, Leadership and Organizations: The GLOBE Study of 62 Societies* (Thousand Oaks, CA: Sage., 2004). Further issues on Project GLOBE are developed in George B. Graen, "In the Eye of the Beholder: Cross-Cultural Lessons in Leadership from Project GLOBE: A Response Viewed from the Third Culture Bonding (TCB) Model of Cross-Cultural Leadership," *Academy of Management Perspectives*, vol. 20 (November 2006), pp. 95–101; and Robert J. House, Mansour Javidan, Peter W. Dorfman, and Mary Sully de Luque, "A Failure of Scholarship: Response to George Graen's Critique of GLOBE," *Academy of Management Perspectives*, vol. 20 (November 2006), pp. 102–14.

[79]This summary is based on Mansour Javidan, P. Dorfman, Mary Sully de Luque, and Robert J. House, "In the Eye of the Beholder: Cross-Cultural Lessons in Leadership from Project GLOBE," *Academy of Management Perspectives* (February 2006), pp. 67–90.

[80]Summary in "Universals" box from Gannon, op. cit., p. 52.

[81]For additional cultural models and research, see the summary in House, op. cit., as well as Fons Trompenaars, *Riding the Waves of Culture: Understanding Cultural Diversity in Business* (London: Nicholas Brealey Publishing, 1993); Harry C. Triandis, *Culture and Social Behavior* (New York: McGraw-Hill, 1994); Steven H. Schwartz, "A Theory of Cultural Values and Some Implications for Work," *Applied Psychology: An International Review*, vol. 48

(1999), pp. 23–47; and Martin J. Gannon, *Understanding Global Cultures*, 3rd ed. (Thousand Oaks, CA: Sage, 2004).

[82]Developed from "Is Your Company Really Global?" *BusinessWeek* (December 1, 1997).

Feature Notes

Real People—Information and quotes from Matthew Saltmarsh, "A Staunch Advocate of Globalization and Trade," *International Herald Tribune* (March 20, 2009): www.iht.com; and, Anne Lee, "2009 Fast 50: The Most Innovative Companies in China," *Fast Company* (February 11, 2009): www.fastcompany.com/fast_50; and Bruce Einhorn, "How Not to Sweat the Retail Deals," *Business Week* (May 25, 2009), pp. 52–59.

Photo Essays Notes

Coffee Roasters—Information from "Green Mountain Coffee's 'Be Fair' Campaign Celebrates Fair Trade Month in October," press release: www.justmeans.com/press-releases/ (October 1, 2009). BMW—Information from "Auto Maker Plans to Build a Second Plant in China," *Wall Street Journal* (November 13, 2009), p. B3. Yahoo Japan—Information from Hiroko Tabuchi, "In Japan, an Odd Perch for Google: Looking up at Leader," *New York Times* (November 30, 2009), pp. B4, B5. McDonald's—Information from Daisy Nguyen, "McBack and Relax," *Columbus Dispatch* (March 28, 2008), pp. C12, C10.

Chapter 6

Endnotes

[1]Information from Douglas MacMillan, Peter Burrows, and Spencer E. Ante, "The App Economy," *BusinessWeek*, (November 2, 2009), pp. 44–49; zynga.com/about; and, Douglas MacMillan, "Zynga and Facebook. It's Complicated, "*Bloomberg Businessweek* (April 26–May 2, 2010), pp. 50, 51.

[2]Stephen Covey, "How to Succeed in Today's Workplace," *USA Weekend* (August 29–31, 1997), pp. 4–5.

[3]Information and quotes for these examples from Alison Damasi, "No Job? Create One," *Bloomberg Businessweek* (March 22 & 29, 2010), p. 89; Laura Lorber, "Older Entrepreneurs Target Peers," *The Wall Street Journal* (February 16, 2010), p. B6; and Dale Buss, "The Mothers of Invention," *The Wall Street Journal* (February 8, 2010), p. R7.

[4]Information from "Women Business Owners Receive First-Ever Micro Loans Via the Internet," *Business Wire* (August 9, 2000); Jim Hopkins, "Non-Profit Loan Group Takes Risks on Women in Business," *USA Today* (August 9, 2000), p. 2B; and "Women's Group Grants First Loans to Entrepreneurs," *Columbus Dispatch* (August 10, 2000), p. B2.

[5]Quote from "Working for Somebody Else Never Amounted to Anything—Wayne Huizenga," http://www.youngentrepreneur.com (accessed Janaury 22, 2010).

[6]Speech at the Lloyd Greif Center for Entrepreneurial Studies, Marshall School of Business, University of Southern California, 1996.

[7]Information from Thomas Heath, "Value Added: The Nonprofit Entrepreneur," voices.washingtonpost.com/washbizblog/2009/03.

[8]Information from the corporate websites; Entrepreneur's Hall of Fame at www.1tbn.com/halloffame.html; and Josh Quittner, "The Flickr Founders," *Time* (April 30, 2006): www.time.com (accessed May 17, 2010); and, www.hunch.com.

[9]Examples from "America's Best Young Entrepreneurs 2008," *BusinessWeek* (September 8, 2009): www.businessweek.com.

[10]For the top-selling franchises, see "Top 10 Franchises for 2009," *Entrepreneur Magazine* (January 2009): www.entrepreneur.com.

[11]For a review and discussion of the entrepreneurial mind, see Jeffry A. Timmons, *New Venture Creation: Entrepreneurship for the 21st Century* (New York: Irwin/McGraw-Hill, 1999), pp. 219–25.

[12]See the review by Robert D. Hisrich and Michael P. Peters, *Entrepreneurship*, 4th ed. (New York: Irwin/McGraw-Hill, 1998), pp. 67–70; and Paulette Thomas, "Entrepreneurs' Biggest Problems and How They Solve Them," *Wall Street Journal Reports* (March 17, 2003), pp. R1, R2.

[13]Based on research summarized by Hisrich and Peters, op. cit., pp. 70–74.

[14]Information from Jim Hopkins, "Serial Entrepreneur Strikes Again at Age 70," *USA Today* (August 15, 2000).

[15]Timothy Butler and James Waldroop, "Job Sculpting: The Art of Retaining Your Best People," *Harvard Business Review* (September–October 1999), pp. 144–52.

[16]This list is developed from Timmons, op. cit, pp. 47–48; and Hisrich and Peters, op. cit., pp. 67–70.

[17]"Smart Talk: Start-Ups and Schooling," *Wall Street Journal* (September 7, 2004), p. B4.

[18]Quote from www.anitaroddick.com/aboutanita.php (accessed: April 24, 2010).

[19]*Paths to Entrepreneurship: New Directions for Women in Business* (New York: Catalyst, 1998) and Eve Hayek, "Report Shatters Myths about U.S. Women's Equality" (October 1, 2005); both available on the National Foundation for Women Business Owners website: www.nfwbo.org/key.html.

[20]Data from *Paths to Entrepreneurship: New Directions for Women in Business* (New York: Catalyst, 1998), as summarized on the National Foundation for Women Business Owners website: www.nfwbo.org/key.html.

[21]National Foundation for Women Business Owners, *Women Business Owners of Color: Challenges and Accomplishments* (1998).

[22]Data in the table are reported by Karen E. Klein, "Minority Start Ups: A Measure of Progress," *BusinessWeek* (August 25, 2005), retrieved from www.businessweekonline; and press release, Minority Business Development Agency (March 5, 2009): www.mbda.gov.

[23]Data reported by Karen E. Klein, "Minority Start Ups: A Measure of Progress," *BusinessWeek* (August 25, 2005), retrieved from www.businessweekonline.

[24]David Bornstein, *How to Change the World: Social Entrepreneurs and the Power of New Ideas* (Oxford, UK: Oxford University Press, 2004).

[25]"The 10 Best Social Enterprises of 2009," *Fast Company* (December 1, 2009): www.fastcompany.com/magazine (accessed April 24, 2010).

[26]Examples are from Byrnes and "Growing Green Business," *Northwestern* (Winter 2007), p. 19; and Byrnes, op. cit.; and Regina McEnery, "Cancer Patients Getting the White-Glove Treatment,"*Columbus Dispatch* (March 1, 2008).

[27]See U.S. Small Business Administration website: www.sba.gov; and *Statistical Abstract of the United States* (Washington, DC: U.S. Census Bureau, 1999).

[28]The White House, "Small Business Week, 2009," News Release (May 15, 2009):www.sba.gov/idc/groups/public/documents.

[29]Information reported in "The Rewards," *Inc. State of Small Business* (May 20–21, 2001), pp. 50–51.

[30]Information from Sue Shellenbarger, "Plumbing for Joy? Be Your Own Boss," *Wall Street Journal* (September 16, 2009), pp. D1, D2.

[31]Information and quotes from Steve Lohr, "The Rise of the Fleet-Footed Start-Up," *The New York Times* (April 23, 2010): www.nytimes.com.

[32]Reported in Mitchell Baker and John Lilly, "Net Neurtrality: Spur to Entrepreneurship . . . ," *Wall Street Journal* (October 30, 2009), p. A23.

[33]"Small Business Expansions in Electronic Commerce," U.S. Small Business Administration, Office of Advocacy (June 2000).

[34]Information from Will Christensen, "Rod Spencer's Sports-Card Business Has Migrated to Cyberspace Marketplace," *Columbus Dispatch* (July 24, 2000), p. F1.

[35]Information and quotes from Tracy Turner, "Smooth Transition: Three Sisters Take over Family's Velvet Ice Cream Business," *Columbus Dispatch* (September 25, 2009), pp. A12, A13.

[36]Data reported by The Family Firm Institute: www.ffi.org/looking/factsfb.html.

[37]Conversation from the case "Am I My Uncle's Keeper?" by Paul I. Karofsky (Northeastern University Center for Family Business) and published at: www.fambiz.com/contprov.cfm? ContProvCode=NECFB[ANGELO]ID=140.

[38]Survey of Small and Mid-Sized Businesses: Trends for 2000 (Arthur Andersen, 2000).

[39]Ibid.

[40]See U.S. Small Business Administration website: www.sba.gov.

[41]George Gendron, "The Failure Myth," *Inc.* (January 2001), p. 13.

[42]Discussion based on "The Life Cycle of Entrepreneurial Firms," in Ricky Griffin, ed., *Management*, 6th ed. (New York: Houghton Mifflin, 1999), pp. 309–10; and Neil C. Churchill and Virginia L. Lewis, "The Five Stages of Small Business Growth," *Harvard Business Review* (May–June 1993), pp. 30–50.

[43]Anne Field, "Business Incubators Are Growing Up," *BusinessWeek* (November 16, 2009), p. 76.

[44]See www.sba.gov/aboutsba.

[45]Developed from William S. Sahlman, "How to Write a Great Business Plan," *Harvard Business Review* (July–August 1997), pp. 98–108.

[46]Marcia H. Pounds, "Business Plan Sets Course for Growth," *Columbus Dispatch* (March 16, 1998), p. 9; see also the firm's website: www.calcustoms.com.

[47]Standard components of business plans are described in many text sources such as Linda Pinson and Jerry Jinnett, *Anatomy of a Business Plan: A Step-by-Step Guide to Starting Smart, Building the Business, and Securing Your Company's Future*, 4th ed. (Dearborn Trade, 1999); and on websites such as American Express Small Business Services, Business Town.com, and Bizplanlt.com.

[48]Example from Matt Golsinski, "Entrepreneurs Score on 'Shark Tank'," *Kellogg* (Winter 2009), p. 9.

[49]Information and quote from "Thriving Small Businesses Still Struggling to Get Loans," CNN.com (December 12, 2009): www.cnn.com/2009/Politics.

[50]"You've Come a Long Way Baby," *BusinessWeek Frontier* (July 10, 2000).

[51]Adapted from Norman M. Scarborough and Thomas W. Zimmerer, *Effective Small Business Management*, 3rd ed. (Columbus, OH: Merrill, 1991), pp. 26–27. Used by permission.

[52]Quote from http://www.woopidoo.com/businessquotes/authors/michaelgerber/index.htm (retrieved September 16, 2006); see also Michael Gerber, The *E-Myth Revisited: Why Most Small Businesses Don't Work and What to Do about It* (New York: HarperCollins, 2001).

Feature Notes

Real People—Information and quotes from Joe Higgins, "Athens Business Owner Presented State Award," *The Athens Messenger* (November 18, 2009), p. 3; and Samantha Pirc, "A Local Success Story: Q&A with Michelle Greenfield of Third Sun," *OHIO Today* (Fall/Winter, 2009), pp. 14, 15.

Management Smarts 6.2—Information from Colleen DeBaise, "Why You Need a Business Plan," *Wall Street Journal* (September 27, 2009): www.wsj.com.

Real Ethics—Information from Jessica Shambora, "The Story Behind the World's Hottest Shoemaker," *Financial Times*, Kindle Edition (March 21, 2010); and, www.toms.com/movement-one-for-one; and, John Tozzi, "The Ben & Jerrys' Law: Principles before Profit," *Bloomberg Businessweek* (April 26–May 2, 2010), pp. 69, 70.

Photo Essays Notes

Roger the Plumber—Information from Sue Shellenbarger, "Plumbing for Joy? Be Your Own Boss," *Wall Street Journal* (September 16, 2009), pp. D1, D2. DiFara's Pizza—Information from Kelly Greene, "Tapping Talent, Experience of Those Age 60-Plus" *Wall Street Journal* (November 29, 2005), p. B7; Manny Fernandez, "Straight Out of Brooklyn, the $5 Slice," *New York Times* (July 31, 2009): www.nytimes.com.

Chapter 7

Endnotes

[1]Information from David A. Price, "From Dorm Room to Wal-Mart," *Wall Street Journal* (March 11, 2009), p. A13; "Huddler.com Interview with CEO and Founder Tom Szaky," www.greenhome.huddler.com/wiki/terracycle; and Tom *Szaky*, *Revolution in a Bottle* (Knoxville, TN: Portfolio Trade, 2009).

[2]Situation from Carol Hymowitz, "Middle Managers Are Unsung Heroes on Corporate Stage," *Wall Street Journal* (September 19, 2005), p. B1.

[3]Ram Charan, "Six Personality Traits of a Leader," career-advice.monster.com/leadership-skills (retrieved August 6, 2008).

[4]Example and quotes from Carol Hymowitz, "Independent Program Puts College Students on Leadership Paths," *Wall Street Journal* (January 14, 2003), p. B1.

[5]See Stefan Stern, "Smarter Leaders Are Betting Big on Data," *Financial Times*, Kindle edition (March 9, 2010); and, Thomas H. Davenport, Jeanne G. Harris, and Robert Morison, *Analytics at Work: Smarter Decisions, Better Results* (Cambridge, MA: Harvard Business Press, 2010).

[6]Richard Tedlow, "Toyota Was in Denial. How About You?" *Bloomberg Businessweek* (April 19, 2010), p. 76.

[7]Peter F. Drucker, "Looking Ahead: Implications of the Present," *Harvard Business Review* (September–October 1997), pp. 18–32. See also Shaker A. Zahra, "An Interview with Peter Drucker," *Academy of Management Executive*, vol. 17 (August 2003), pp. 9–12.

[8]See "Time for Communication to Move Towards Centre Stage," *Financial Times* (December 29, 2009).

[9]Information from John A. Byrne, "Visionary vs. Visionary," *BusinessWeek* (August 28, 2000), pp. 10–14.

[10]Jaclyn Fierman, "Winning Ideas from Maverick Managers," *Fortune* (February 6, 1995), pp. 66–80.

[11]See Susan G. Cohen and Don Mankin, "The Changing Nature of Work: Managing the Impact of Information Technology," Chapter 6 in Susan Albers Mohrman, Jay R. Galbraith, Edward E. Lawler III, and Associates, *Tomorrow's Organization: Crafting Winning Capabilities in a Dynamic World* (San Francisco: Jossey-Bass, 1988), pp. 154–78.

[12]Noel M. Tichy and Warren G. Bennis, *Judgment: How Winning Leaders Make Great Calls* (Knoxville, TN: Portfolio Hardcover, 2007).

[13]Noel M. Tichy and Warren G. Bennis, "Judgment: How Winning Leaders Make Great Calls," *BusinessWeek* (November 19, 2007), pp. 68–72.

[14]Henry Mintzberg, *The Nature of Managerial Work* (New York: Harper Collins, 1997).

[15]For a good discussion, see Watson H. Agor, *Intuition in Organizations: Leading and Managing Productively* (Newbury Park, CA: Sage, 1989); Herbert A. Simon, "Making Management Decisions: The Role of Intuition and Emotion," *Academy of Management Executive*, vol. 1 (1987), pp. 57–64; Orlando Behling and Norman L. Eckel, "Making Sense Out of Intuition," *Academy of Management Executive*, vol. 5 (1991), pp. 46–54.

[16]See, for example, William Duggan, *Strategic Intuition: The Creative Spark in Human Achievement* (New York: Columbia Business School, 2007).

[17]Alan Deutschman, "Inside the Mind of Jeff Bezos," *Fast Company*, Issue 85 (August 2004); www.fastcompany.com.

[18]See Susan Berfield, "The Limits of Going with Your Gut," *BusinessWeek* (December 21, 2009), p. 90. See also Michael J. Mauboussin, *Think Twice: Harnessing the Power of Counterintuition* (Boston: Harvard Business, 2009).

[19]Daniel J. Isenberg, "How Senior Managers Think," *Harvard Business Review*, vol. 62 (November–December 1984), pp. 81–90.

[20]Daniel J. Isenberg, "The Tactics of Strategic Opportunism," *Harvard Business Review*, vol. 65 (March–April 1987), pp. 92–97.

[21]Quote from Susan Carey, "Pilot 'in Shock' as He Landed Jet in River," *Wall Street Journal* (February 9, 2009), p. A6.

[22]Based on Carl Jung's typology as described in Donald Bowen, "Learning and Problem-Solving: You're Never Too Jung," in Donald D. Bowen, Roy J. Lewicki, Donald T. Hall, and Francine S. Hall, eds., *Experiences in Management and Organizational Behavior*, 4th ed. (New York: Wiley, 1997), pp. 7–13; and John W. Slocum Jr., "Cognitive Style in Learning and Problem Solving," ibid., pp. 349–53.

[23]Paul Ingrassia, "How GM Lost Its Way," *Wall Street Journal* (June 2, 2009), p. A21. See also Paul Ingrassia, *Crash Course: The American Automobile Industry's Road from Glory to Ruin* (New York: Random House, 2010).

[24]"They Don't Teach This in B-School," *BusinessWeek* (September 19, 2005), pp. 46–47.

[25]Developed from Anna Muoio, "Where There's Smoke It Helps to Have a Smoke Jumper," *Fast Company*, vol. 33, p. 290.

[26]For scholarly reviews, see Dean Tjosvold, "Effects of Crisis Orientation on Managers' Approach to Controversy in Decision Making," *Academy of Management-Journal*, vol. 27 (1984), pp. 130–38; and Jan I. Mitroff, Paul-Shrivastava, and Firdaus E. Udwadia, "Effective Crisis Management," *Academy of Management Executive*, vol. 1 (1987), pp. 283–92.

[27]Quotes from Jeff Kingston, "A Crisis Made in Japan," *The Wall Street Journal* (February 6–7, 2010), pp. W1, W2; and Kate Linebaugh, Dionne Searcey and Norihiko Shirouzu, "Secretive Culture Led Toyota Astray," *The Wall Street Journal* (February 10, 2010), pp. A1, A16.

[28]Information from Paul Farhi, "Behind Domino's Mea Culpa Ad Campaign," *The Washington Post* (January 13, 2010): www.washingtonpost.com, accessed June 5, 2010; and J. Patrick Doyle, "Hard Choices," *Bloomberg BusinessWeek* (May 3–9, 2010), p. 84.

[29]Information and quotes from Terry Kosdrosky and John D. Stoll, "GM Puts Electric-Car Testing on Fast Track to 2010," *Wall Street Journal* (April 4, 2008), p. B2.

[30]Paul Glader, "GE's Immelt to Cite Lessons Learned," *Wall Street Journal* (December 15, 2009), p. B2.

[31]See George P. Huber, *Managerial Decision Making* (Glenview, IL: Scott, Foresman, 1975). For a comparison, see the steps in Xerox's problem-solving process as described in David A. Garvin, "Building a Learning Organization," *Harvard Business Review* (July–August 1993), pp. 78–91; and the Josephson model for ethical decision making described at www.josephsoninstitute.org.

[32]Peter F. Drucker, *Innovation and Entrepreneurship: Practice and Principles* (New York: Harper Row, 1985).

[33]Joseph B. White and Lee Hawkins Jr., "GM Cuts Deeper in North America," *Wall Street Journal* (November 22, 2005), p. A3.

[34]For a sample of Simon's work, see Herbert A. Simon, *Administrative Behavior* (New York: Free Press, 1947); James G. March and Herbert A. Simon, *Organizations* (New York: Wiley, 1958); Herbert A. Simon, *The New Science of Management Decision* (New York: Harper, 1960).

[35]This figure and the related discussion are developed from conversations with Dr. Alma Acevedo of the University of Puerto Rico at Rio Piedras, and her articles "Of Fallacies and Curricula: A Case of Business Ethics," *Teaching Business Ethics*, vol. 5 (2001), pp. 157–70; and, "Business Ethics: An Introduction," Working Paper (2009).

[36]Based on Gerald F. Cavanagh, *American Business Values*, 4th ed. (Upper Saddle River, NJ: Prentice-Hall, 1998).

[37]Josephson, op. cit.

[38]See Daniel Kahneman and Amos Tversky, "Psychology of Preferences," *Scientific American*, vol. 246 (1982), pp. 161–73.

[39]This presentation is based on the discussion in Max H. Bazerman, *Judgment in Managerial Decision Making*, 6th ed. (Hoboken, NJ: Wiley, 2005).

[40]Barry M. Staw, "The Escalation of Commitment to a Course of Action," *Academy of Management Review*, vol. 6 (1981), pp. 577–87; and Barry M. Staw and Jerry Ross, "Knowing When to Pull the Plug," *Harvard Business Review*, vol. 65 (March–April 1987), pp. 68–74.

[41]See, for example, Amy Saunders and Matzer Rose, "Skybus Throttles Back on Growth," *Columbus Dispatch* (March 13, 2008).

[42]Information from "Lonnie Johnson," *USAA Magazine* (Fall 2007), p. 38; and www.johnsonrd.com.

[43]See, for example, Roger von Oech, *A Whack on the Side of the Head* (New York: Warner Books, 1983); and *A Kick in the Seat of the Pants* (New York: Harper & Row, 1986).

[44]Teresa M. Amabile, "Motivating Creativity in Organizations," *California Management Review*, vol. 40 (Fall 1997), pp. 39–58.

[45]Developed from discussions by Edward De Bono, *Lateral Thinking: Creativity Step-by-Step* (New York: HarperCollins, 1970); John S. Dacey and Kathleen H. Lennon, *Understanding Creativity* (San Francisco: Jossey-Bass, 1998); and Bettina von Stamm, *Managing Innovation, Design & Creativity* (Chichester, England: Wiley, 2003).

[46]Example from Dayton Fandray, "Assumed Innocent: Hidden and Unexamined Assumptions Can Ruin Your Day," *Continental.com/Magazine* (December 2007), p. 100.

[47]Josephson, op. cit.

[48]Information from Stephen H. Wildstrom, "Video iPod, I Love You," *BusinessWeek* (November 7, 2005), p. 20; "Voices of Innovation," *BusinessWeek* (December 12, 2005), p. 22.

[49]Developed from Donald Bowen, "Learning and Problem-Solving: You're Never Too Jung," in Donald D. Bowen, Roy J. Lewicki, Donald T. Hall, and Francine S. Hall, eds., *Experiences in Management and Organizational Behavior*, 4th ed. (New York:

Wiley, 1997), pp. 7–13; and John W. Slocum Jr., "Cognitive Style in Learning and Problem Solving," Ibid., pp. 349–353.

[50]Adapted from "Lost at Sea: A Consensus-Seeking Task," in the *1975 Handbook for Group Facilitators*. Used with permission of University Associates, Inc.

Feature Notes

Real People—Information from Rachel Farrell, "Clean and Green," Kellogg (Winter 2009), p. 31; and "Mission Statement," http://www.ecos.com/mission.html.

Real Ethics—Information from *Economist*, vol. 379, no. 8482, (June 17, 2006), pp. 65–66, 2p, 1c.

Photo Essays Notes

Infosurv—Information and quote from Teri Evans, "Entrepreneurs Seek to Elicit Workers' Ideas, *Wall Street Journal* (December 22, 2009), p. B7. Tropicana—See "The O. J. Trial," *BusinessWeek* (December 28, 2009 & January 4, 2010), p. 41. Fisker Automotive—Information and quotes from Josh Mitchell and Stephen Power, "Gore-Backed Car Firm Gets Large U.S. Loan," *Wall Street Journal* (September 25, 2009), p. B6; and Josh Mitchell, "Fisker Automotive: U.S. Site Chosen to Build Family Hybrid," *Dow Jones Newswires* (October 20, 2009): www.wsj.com.

Chapter 8

Endnotes

[1]Information and quotes from the Associated Press, "Oprah Opens School for Girls in S. Africa," "Lavish Leadership Academy Aims to Give Impoverished Chance to Succeed," MSNBC.com (January 2, 2007); "Oprah Winfrey Leadership Academy for Girls—South Africa Celebrates Its Official Opening," www.oprah.com/about; Jed Dreben, "Oprah Winfrey: 'I Don't Regret' Opening School," www.people.com (December 12, 2007); and, "Givson Foundation Builds Relationship with Oprah Winfrey Leadership Academy to Support Music Education," news release (April 14, 2009), www.gibson.com (accessed January 26, 2010).

[2]Data from "Hurry Up and Decide," *BusinessWeek* (May 14, 2001), p. 16; and *BusinessWeek* (June 23, 2008), p. 56.

[3]Eaton Corporation Annual Report, 1985.

[4]Paul Ingrassia, "The Right Stuff," *The Wall Street Journal* (April 18, 2005), p. D5.

[5]Quote from Stephen Covey and Roger Merrill, "New Ways to Get Organized at Work," *USA Weekend* (February 6–8, 1998), p. 18. Books by Stephen R. Covey include *The 7 Habits of Highly Effective People: Powerful Lessons in Personal Change* (New York: Fireside, 1990); and Stephen R. Covey and Sandra Merril Covey, *The 7 Habits of Highly Effective Families: Building a Beautiful Family Culture in a Turbulent World* (New York: Golden Books, 1996).

[6]See Stanley Thune and Robert House, "Where Long-Range Planning Pays Off," *Business Horizons*, vol. 13 (1970), pp. 81–87. For a critical review of the literature, see Milton Leontiades and Ahmet Teel, "Planning Perceptions and Planning Results," *Strategic Management Journal*, vol. 1 (1980), pp. 65–75; and J. Scott Armstrong. "The Value of Formal Planning for Strategic Decisions," *Strategic Management Journal*, vol. 3 (1982), pp. 197–211. For special attention to the small business setting, see Richard B. Robinson Jr., John A. Pearce II, George S. Vozikis, and Timothy S. Mescon, "The Relationship between Stage of Development and Small Firm Planning and Performance," *Journal of Small Business Management*, vol. 22 (1984), pp. 45–52; and Christopher Orphen, "The Effects of Long-Range Planning

on Small Business Performance: A Further Examination," *Journal of Small Business Management*, vol. 23 (1985), pp. 16–23. For an empirical study of large corporations, see Vasudevan Ramanujam and N. Venkataraman, "Planning and Performance: A New Look at an Old Question," *Business Horizons*, vol. 30 (1987), pp. 19–25.

[7]"McDonald's Tech Turnaround," *Harvard Business Review* (November 2004), p. 128.

[8]Information from Carol Hymowitz, "Packed Calendars Rule over Executives," *Wall Street Journal* (June 16, 2008), p. B1.

[9]Quote from *BusinessWeek* (August 8, 1994), pp. 78–86.

[10]See William Oncken Jr. and Donald L. Wass, "Management Time: Who's Got the Monkey?" *Harvard Business Review*, vol. 52 (September–October 1974), pp. 75–80, and featured as an HBR classic, *Harvard Business Review* (November–December 1999).

[11]Dick Levin, *The Executives Illustrated Primer of Long Range Planning* (Englewood Cliffs, NJ: Prentice-Hall, 1981).

[12]See Elliot Jaques, *The Form of Time* (New York: Russak-Co., 1982). For an executive commentary on his research, see Walter Kiechel III, "How Executives Think," *Fortune* (December 21, 1987), pp. 139–44.

[13]Information from "Skype: How a Startup Harnessed the Hoopla," *BusinessWeek* (September 26, 2005), p. 35.

[14]Information from "Avoiding a Time Bomb: Sexual Harassment," *BusinessWeek*, enterprise issue (October 13, 1997), pp. ENT20–21.

[15]Data from "Car Crazy," *National Geographic* (May 2008), p. 142.

[16]Paul Glader, "BE's Immelt to Cite Lessons Learned," *Wall Street Journal* (December 15, 2009), p. B2.

[17]For a thorough review of forecasting, see J. Scott Armstrong, *Long-Range Forecasting*, 2nd ed. (New York: Wiley, 1985).

[18]Information and quotes from Guy Chazan and Neil King, "BP's Preparedness for Major Crisis is Questioned, "*The Wall Steeet Journal* (May 10, 2010), p. A6; and Ben Casselman and Guy Chazan, "Disaster Plans Lacking at Deep Rigs," *The Wall Street Journal* (May 18, 2010), p. A1.

[19]The scenario-planning approach is described in Peter Schwartz, *The Art of the Long View* (New York: Doubleday/Currency, 1991).

[20]See Arie de Geus, *The Living Company: Habits for Survival in a Turbulent Business Environment* (Boston, MA: Harvard Business School Press, 1997).

[21]Information and quote from "The No. 2 Killer in Africa by Parasite," *Fast Company* (June 2008), pp. 102–103. See, for example, Robert C. Camp, *Business Process Benchmarking* (Milwaukee: ASQ Quality Press 1994); Michael J. Spendolini, *The Benchmarking Book* (New York: AMACOM, 1992); and Christopher E. Bogan and Michael J. English, *Benchmarking for Best Practices: Winning through Innovative Adaptation* (New York: McGraw-Hill, 1994).

[22]David Kiley, "One Ford for the Whole World," *BusinessWeek* (June 15, 2009), pp. 58–59.

[23]Rachel Tiplady, "Taking the Lead in Fast-Fashion," *BusinessWeek Online* (August 29, 2006); and Cecile Rohwedder and Keith Johnson, "Pace-Setting Zara Seeks More Speed to Fight Its Rising Cheap-Chic Rivals," *Wall Street Journal* (February 20, 2008), pp. B1, B6.

[24]Information from Peter Burrows and Manjeet Kripalani, "Cisco: Sold on India," *BusinessWeek* (November 28, 2005), pp. 50–51.

[25]Quote from Kenneth Roman, "The Man Who Sharpened Gillette," *Wall Street Journal* (September 5, 2007), p. D8.

[26]T. J. Rodgers, with William Taylor and Rick Foreman, "No Excuses Management," *World Executive's Digest* (May 1994), pp. 26–30.

[27]Example from Roman, op. cit.

[28]See Dale D. McConkey, *How to Manage by Results*, 3rd ed. (New York: AMACOM, 1976); Stephen J. Carroll Jr. and Henry J. Tosi Jr., *Management by Objectives: Applications and Research* (New York: Macmillan, 1973); and Anthony P. Raia, *Managing by Objectives* (Glenview, IL: Scott, Foresman, 1974). See also Steven Kerr, "Overcoming the Dysfunctions of MBO," *Management by Objectives*, vol. 5, no. 1 (1976).

[29]"How Classy Can 7-Eleven Get?" *BusinessWeek* (September 1, 1997), pp. 74–75; and Kellie B. Gormly, "7-Eleven Moving Up a Grade," *Columbus Dispatch* (August 3, 2000), pp. C1–C2.

[30]The work on goal-setting theory is well summarized in Edwin A. Locke and Gary P. Latham, *Goal Setting: A Motivational Technique That Works!* (Englewood Cliffs, NJ: Prentice Hall, 1984). See also Edwin A. Locke, Kenneth N. Shaw, Lisa A. Saari, and Gary P. Latham, "Goal Setting and Task Performance 1969–1980," *Psychological Bulletin*, vol. 90 (1981), pp. 125–52; Mark E. Tubbs, "Goal Setting: A Meta-Analytic Examination of the Empirical Evidence," *Journal of Applied Psychology*, vol. 71 (1986), pp. 474–83; and Terence R. Mitchell, Kenneth R. Thompson, and Jane George-Falvy, "Goal Setting: Theory and Practice," Chapter 9 in Cary L. Cooper and Edwin A. Locke, eds., *Industrial and Organizational Psychology: Linking Theory with Practice* (Malden, MA: Blackwell Business, 2000), pp. 211–49.

[31]Suggested by a discussion in Robert E. Quinn, Sue R. Faerman, Michael P. Thompson, and Michael R. McGrath, *Becoming a Master Manager: A Contemporary Framework* (New York: Wiley, 1990), pp. 75–76.

[32]Developed in part from Roy J. Lewicki, Donald D. Bowen, Douglas T. Hall, and Francine S. Hall, *Experiences in Management and Organizational Behavior*, 3rd ed. (New York: Wiley, 1988), pp. 261–67. Used by permission.

Feature Notes

Real People—Information from Julie Bennitt, "Don Thompson Engineers Winning Role as McDonald's President," *Franchise Times* (February 2008): www.franchisetimes.com. Real Ethics—Information from "Trial and Error," *Forbes* (June 19, 2006), pp. 128–30; Drake Bennett, "Measures of Success," *Boston Globe Online* (July 2, 2006).

Photo Essays Notes

Office Romance Policies—Information from Phred Dvorak, Baob Davis, and Louise Radnofsky, "Firms Confront Boss-Subordinate Love Affairs," *Wall Street Journal* (October 27, 2008), p. B5, with survey data from Society for Human Resource Management. Wars Cola—Information and quotes from Julia Day, "'Protest' Drinks Range Targets Muslims," *MediaGuardian* (April 23, 2003), www.guardian.co.uk/media/2003, accessed December 14, 2009; and, www.qiblacola.com. Coach—Information and quotes from "Coach's New Bag," *BusinessWeek* (June 29, 2009), pp. 41–43.

Chapter 9

Endnotes

[1]Information and quotes from Ethan Smith and Lauren A. E. Schuker, "Disney Nabs Marvel Heroes," *Wall Street Journal* (September 1, 2009), pp. A1, A14; and Ronald Grover, "Disney Remakes the Movie Studio," *BusinessWeek* (November 9, 2009), pp. 50–51.

[2]Examples from Edward De Bono, *Lateral Thinking: Creativity Step by Step* (New York: Harper & Row, 1970).

[3]For an overview of Wal-Mart see Charles Fishman, *The Wal-Mart Effect* (New York: Penguin, 2006).

[4]See Michelle Conlin, "Look Who's Stalking Wal-Mart," *BusinessWeek* (December 7, 2009), pp. 30–33.

[5]See Anne D'Innocenzio, "Walmart.com CEO Aims to Dominate Web Retail," *Columbus Dispatch* (December 20, 2009), p. D6.

[6]Jackie Crosby, "Retail Makeover," *Columbus Dispatch* (December 30, 2009), pp. A10, A12.

[7]See, for example, Walter Kiechel III, *The Lords of Strategy* (Cambridge, MA: Harvard Business Press, 2010).

[8]Michael E. Porter, *Competitive Strategy: Techniques for Analyzing Industries and Competitors* (New York: Free Press, 1980).

[9]Robert D. Hof, "Can Google Stay on Top of the Web?" *BusinessWeek* (October 12, 2009), pp. 45–49.

[10]See Porter, op. cit., Michael E. Porter, *Competitive Advantage: Creating and Sustaining Superior Performance* (New York: Free Press, 1986); and Richard A. D'Aveni, *Hyper-Competition: Managing the Dynamics of Strategic Maneuvering* (New York: Free Press, 1994).

[11]Jim Collins, "Bigger, Better, Faster," *Fast Company*, vol. 71 (June 2003), p. 74; and www.fastcompany.com/magazine/71/walmart.html.

[12]Information and quotes from Marcia Stepanek, "How Fast Is Net Fast?" *BusinessWeek E-Biz* (November 1, 1999), pp. EB52–EB54.

[13]Gary Hamel and C. K. Prahalad, "Strategic Intent." *Harvard Business Review* (May–June 1989), pp. 63–76.

[14]www.pepsico.com/PEP_company.

[15]For research support, see Daniel H. Gray, "Uses and Misuses of Strategic Planning," *Harvard Business Review*, vol. 64 (January–February 1986), pp. 89–97.

[16]Peter F. Drucker, *Management: Tasks, Responsibilities, Practices* (New York: Harper-Row, 1973), p. 122.

[17]For more on the Patagonia story see Yvon Chouinard, *Let My People Go Surfing: The Education of a Reluctant Businessman* (New York: Penguin Press HC, 2005).

[18]Peter F. Drucker, "Five Questions," *Executive Excellence* (November 6, 1994), pp. 6–7.

[19]See Laura Nash. "Mission Statements—Mirrors and Windows," *Harvard Business Review* (March–April 1988), pp. 155–56; James C. Collins and Jerry I. Porras, "Building Your Company's Vision," *Harvard Business Review* (September–October 1996), pp. 65–77; and James C. Collins and Jerry I. Porras, *Built to Last: Successful Habits of Visionary Companies* (New York: Harper Business, 1997).

[20]Gary Hamel, *Leading the Revolution* (Boston: Harvard Business School Press, 2000), pp. 72–73.

[21]Values quote from www.patagonia.com/web/us/patagonia.go?assetid=3351.

[22]www.patagonia.com/web/us/patagonia.go?assetid=2047&ln=24.

[23]Steve Hamm, "A Passion for the Plan," *BusinessWeek* (August 21/28, 2006), pp. 92–94; quote in box from "Yvon Chouinard: Patagonia's Founder Turned His Passion into Profit," *Spirit* (August, 2008), p. 40.

[24]www.patagonia.com.

[25]Terrence E. Deal and Allen A. Kennedy, *Corporate Cultures: The Rites and Rituals of Corporate Life* (Reading, MA: Addison-Wesley, 1982), p. 22. For more on organizational culture see Edgar H. Schein, *Organizational Culture and Leadership*, 2nd ed. (San Francisco: Jossey-Bass, 1997).

[26]www.patagonia.com.

[27]Peter F. Drucker's views on organizational objectives are expressed in his classic books: *The Practice of Management* (New York: Harper-Row, 1954) and *Management: Tasks, Responsibilities,*

Practices (New York: Harper-Row, 1973). For a more recent commentary, see his article, "Management: The Problems of Success," *Academy of Management Executive*, vol. 1 (1987), pp. 13–19.

[28]Hamm, op. cit., 2006.

[29]C. K. Prahalad and Gary Hamel, "The Core Competencies of the Corporation," *Harvard Business Review* (May–June 1990), pp. 79–91.

[30]See D'Aveni, op. cit.

[31]For a discussion of Michael Porter's approach to strategic planning, see his books *Competitive Strategy* and *Competitive Advantage*; and his article, "What Is Strategy?" *Harvard Business Review* (November–December 1996), pp. 61–78; and Richard M. Hodgetts's interview, "A Conversation with Michael E. Porter. A Significant Extension toward Operational Improvement and Positioning," *Organizational Dynamics* (Summer 1999), pp. 24–33.

[32]See Jonathan Welsh, "The Long Goodbye for Dying Brands," *Wall Street Journal* (December 23, 2009), pp. D1, D3.

[33]Richard G. Hammermesh, "Making Planning Strategic," *Harvard Business Review*, vol. 64 (July/August 1986), pp. 115–120; and Richard G. Hammermesh, *Making Strategy Work* (New York: Wiley, 1986).

[34]See Gerald B. Allan, "A Note on the Boston Consulting Group Concept of Competitive Analysis and Corporate Strategy," Harvard Business School, Intercollegiate Case Clearing House, ICCH9-175-175 (Boston: Harvard Business School, June 1976).

[34]Ibid.

[35]Hammermesh, op cit.

[36]The four grand strategies were described by William F. Glueck, in *Business Policy: Strategy Formulation and Management Action* (New York: McGraw-Hill, 1976).

[37]Information from Vauhini Vara, "Facebook CEO Seeks Help as Site Suffers Growing Pains," *Wall Street Journal* (March 5, 2008), pp. A1, A14.

[38]See Mariko Sanchanta, "Starbucks Plans Big Expansion in China," *The Wall Street Journal* (April 14, 2010), p. B10.

[39]Information and quote from Rajesh Mahapatra, "Tata Group Catapults into Global Marketplace," *Columbus Dispatch* (April 3, 2008), pp. C1, C9.

[40]Liam Denning, "Vertical Integration Isn't Just for Christmas," *Wall Street Journal* (December 30, 2009), p. C12.

[41]See William McKinley, Carol M. Sanchez, and A. G. Schick, "Organizational Downsizing: Constraining, Cloning, Learning," *Academy of Management Executive*, vol. 9 (August 1995), pp. 32–44.

[42]See Harry R. Weber, "Higher Fuel Costs Prompt Delta to Cut Jobs," *Huffington Post* (April 6, 2008).

[43]Kim S. Cameron, Sara J. Freeman, and A. K. Mishra, "Best Practices in White-Collar Downsizing: Managing Contradictions," *Academy of Management Executive*, vol. 4 (August 1991), pp. 57–73.

[44]Information and quote from Steven Musil and Jonathan E. Skillings, "Sold! eBay Jettisons Skype in $2 Billion Deal," *CNET News* (September 1, 2009): www.news.cnet.com (accessed April 25, 2010).

[45]Information from Janet Adamy, "Coffee Clutch: McDonald's Brews a Test for Weakened Starbucks," *Wall Street Journal* (January 8, 2003), pp. 16–17.

[46]This strategy classification is found in Hitt et al., op. cit.; the attitudes are from a discussion by Howard V. Perlmutter, "The Tortuous Evolution of the Multinational Corporation," *Columbia Journal of World Business*, vol. 4 (January–February 1969). See also Pankaj Ghemawat, "Managing Differences," *Harvard Business Review* (March 2007), Reprint R0703C.

[47]Adam M. Brandenburger and Barry J. Nalebuff, *Co-Opetition: A Revolutionary Mindset that Combines Competition and Cooperation* (New York: Bantam, 1996).

[48]For a discussion of Michael Porter's approach to strategic planning, see his books *Competitive Strategy and Competitive Advantage*, and his article, "What Is Strategy? *Harvard Business Review* (November/December, 1996), pp. 61–78; and Richard M. Hodgetts' interview "A Conversation with Michael E. Porter: A Significant Extension Toward Operational Improvement and Positioning," *Organizational Dynamics* (Summer 1999), pp. 24–33.

[49]Information from www.polo.com.

[50]Porter, op. cit. (1996).

[51]www.patagonia.com/web/us/patagonia.go?assetid=3351.

[52]For research support, see Daniel H. Gray, "Uses and Misuses of Strategic Planning," *Harvard Business Review*, vol. 64 (January–February 1986), pp. 89–97.

[53]See Judith Burns, "Everything You Wanted to Know about Corporate Governance . . . But Didn't Know How to Ask," *Wall Street Journal* (October 27, 2003), pp. R1, R7.

[54]Quote from Stephen Moore, "The Conscience of a Capitalist," *The Wall Street Journal* (October 3-4, 2009), p. A11.

[55]Quote from Joann S. Lublin, "Boards Flex Their Pay Muscles," *Wall Street Journal* (April 14, 2008), p. R1.

[56]Josh Levs, "Big Three Auto CEOs Flew Private Jets to Ask for Taxpayer Money," www.cnn.com (retrieved November 21, 2008). See also David Kiley, "Auto Execs in the Hot Seat," *BusinessWeek* (November 19, 2008): www.businessweek.com.

[57]Paul Ingrassia, "The Auto Makers Are Already Bankrupt," *Wall Street Journal* (November 21, 2008), p. A23.

[58]See R. Duane Ireland and Michael A. Hitt, "Achieving and Maintaining Strategic Competitiveness in the 21st Century," *Academy of Management Executive*, vol. 13 (1999), pp. 43–57.

[59]Hodgetts, op. cit.

[60]*AIM Survey* (El Paso, TX: ENFP Enterprises, 1989), Copyright (c)1989 by Weston H. Agor. Used by permission.

[61]Suggested by an exercise in John F. Veiga and John N. Yanouzas, *The Dynamics of Organization Theory: Gaining a Macro Perspective* (St. Paul, MN: West, 1979), pp. 69–71.

Feature Notes

Real People—Information and quotes from William M. Bulkeley, "Xerox Names Burns Chief as Mulcahy Retires Early," *Wall Street Journal* (May 22, 2009), pp. B1, B2; Nanette Byrnes and Roger O. Crockett, "An Historic Succession at Xerox," *Business Week* (June 9, 2008), pp. 18–21; Ben Baker and Geoff Colvin, "Less Than a Year Into the Job, the Xerox CEO Is Already Transforming the Company," *Fortune*, Kindle Edition (April 19, 2010).

Photo Essay Notes

Patagonia—Information and quotes from www.patagonia.com/web/us. Chrysler—Information and quotes from Shawn Langlois, "A Familiar Road," *Columbus Dispatch* (December 15, 2009), p. A11. Dell Computer—Information and quotes from Cliff Edwards, "Dell's Do-Over," *BusinessWeek* (October 26, 2009), pp. 37-40.

Chapter 10

Endnotes

[1]Information and quotes from "Build-A-Bear Workshop, Inc., Funding Universe," www.fundinguniverse.com/company-histories/BuildABear-Workshop-Inc (accessed March 9, 2009); and, www.buildabear.com. See also Maxine Clark and Amy Joyner, *The Bear Necessities of Business: Building a Company with Heart* (Hoboken, NJ: Wiley, 2007).

[2]Henry Mintzberg and Ludo Van der Heyden, "Organigraphs: Drawing How Companies Really Work," *Harvard Business Review* (September–October 1999), pp. 87–94.

[3]The classic work is Alfred D. Chandler, *Strategy and Structure* (Cambridge, MA: MIT Press, 1962).

[4]See Alfred D. Chandler, Jr., "Origins of the Organization Chart," *Harvard Business Review* (March–April 1988), pp. 156–57.

[5]"A Question of Management," *Wall Street Journal* (June 2, 2009), p. R4.

[6]Information from Jena McGregor, "The Office Chart that Really Counts," *BusinessWeek* (February 27, 2006), pp. 48–49.

[7]See David Krackhardt and Jeffrey R. Hanson, "Informal Networks: The Company Behind the Chart," *Harvard Business Review* (July–August 1993), pp. 104–11.

[8]Information from Dana Mattioli, "Job Fears Make Offices All Ears," *Wall Street Journal* (January 20, 2009): www.wsj.com.

[9]See Kenneth Noble, "A Clash of Styles: Japanese Companies in the U.S.," *New York Times* (January 25, 1988), p. 7.

[10]For a discussion of departmentalization, see H. I. Ansoff and R. G. Bradenburg, "A Language for Organization Design," *Management Science*, vol. 17 (August 1971), pp. B705–B731; Mariann Jelinek.

[11]"A Question of Management," *Wall Street Journal* (June 2, 2009), p. R4.

[12]Information and quotes from Luis Garicanco and Richard A. Posner, "What Our Spies Can Learn from Toyota," *Wall Street Journal* (January 13, 2010), p. A23.

[13]"Organization Structure: The Basic Conformations," in Mariann Jelinek, Joseph A. Litterer, and Raymond E. Miles, eds., *Organizations by Design: Theory and Practice* (Plano, TX: Business Publications, 1981), pp. 293–302; Henry Mintzberg, "The Structuring of Organizations," in James Brian Quinn, Henry Mintzberg, and Robert M. James, eds., *The Strategy Process: Concepts, Contexts, and Cases* (Englewood Cliffs, NJ: Prentice-Hall, 1988), pp. 276–304.

[14]Norihiko Shirouzu, "Toyota Plans a Major Overhaul in U.S.," *Wall Street Journal* (April 10, 2009), p. B3.

[15]Information and quotes from "Management Shake-Up to Create 'Leaner Structure'," *Financial Times* (June 11, 2009).

[16]Information and quote from "Revamped GM Updates Image of Core Brands," *Financial Times* (June 18, 2009).

[17]The focus on process is described in Michael Hammer, *Beyond Reengineering* (New York: Harper Business, 1996).

[18]Excellent reviews of matrix concepts are found in Stanley M. Davis and Paul R. Lawrence, *Matrix* (Reading, MA: Addison-Wesley, 1977); Paul R. Lawrence, Harvey F. Kolodny, and Stanley M. Davis, "The Human Side of the Matrix," *Organizational Dynamics*, vol. 6 (1977), pp. 43–61; and Harvey F. Kolodny, "Evolution to a Matrix Organization," *Academy of Management Review*, vol. 4 (1979), pp. 543–53.

[19]Developed from Frank Ostroff, *The Horizontal Organization: What the Organization of the Future Looks Like and How It Delivers Value to Customers* (New York: Oxford University Press, 1999).

[20]The nature of teams and teamwork is described in Jon R. Katzenbach and Douglas K. Smith, "The Discipline of Teams," *Harvard Business Review* (March–April 1993), pp. 111–20.

[21]Information and quotes from Nick Wingfield, "To Rebuild Windows, Microsoft Razed the Walls," *Wall Street Journal* (October 20, 2009), p. B9.

[22]Susan Albers Mohrman, Susan G. Cohen, and Allan M. Mohrman Jr., *Designing Team-Based Organizations* (San Francisco: Jossey-Bass, 1996).

[23]See Glenn M. Parker, *Cross-Functional Teams* (San Francisco: Jossey-Bass, 1995).

[24]Information from William Bridges, "The End of the Job," *Fortune* (September 19, 1994), pp. 62–74; Alan Deutschman, "The Managing Wisdom of High-Tech Superstars," *Fortune* (October 17, 1994), pp. 197–206.

[25]See the discussion by Jay R. Galbraith, "Designing the Networked Organization: Leveraging Size and Competencies," in Susan Albers Mohrman, Jay R. Galbraith, Edward E. Lawler III, and associates, *Tomorrow's Organizations: Crafting Winning Strategies in a Dynamic World* (San Francisco: Jossey-Bass, 1998), pp. 76–102. See also Rupert F. Chisholm, *Developing Network Organizations: Learning from Practice and Theory* (Reading, MA: Addison-Wesley, 1998).

[26]See the discussion by Michael S. Malone, *The Future Arrived Yesterday: The Rise of the Protean Corporation and What It Means for You* (New York: Crown Books, 2009).

[27]See Jerome Barthelemy, "The Seven Deadly Sins of Outsourcing," *Academy of Management Executive*, vol. 17 (2003), pp. 87–98.

[28]Paulo Prada and Jiraj Sheth, "Delta Air Ends Use of India Call Centers," *Wall Street Journal* (April 18–19, 2009), pp. B1, B5.

[29]See Ron Ashkenas, Dave Ulrich, Todd Jick, and Steve Kerr, *The Boundaryless Organization: Breaking the Chains of Organizational Structure* (San Francisco: Jossey-Bass, 1996).

[30]Information from "Scott Livengood and the Tasty Tale of Krispy Kreme," *BizEd* (May/June 2003), pp. 16–20.

[31]Information from John A. Byrne, "Management by Web," *BusinessWeek* (August 28, 2000), pp. 84–97; see the collection of articles by Cary L. Cooper and Denise M. Rousseau, eds., *The Virtual Organization: Vol. 6, Trends in Organizational Behavior* (New York: Wiley, 2000).

[32]For a classic work, see Jay R. Galbraith, *Organizational Design* (Reading, MA: Addison-Wesley, 1977).

[33]This framework is based on Harold J. Leavitt, "Applied Organizational Change in Industry," in James G. March, *Handbook of Organizations* (New York: Rand McNally, 1965), pp. 1144–70; and Edward E. Lawler III, *From the Ground Up: Six Principles for the New Logic Corporation* (San Francisco: Jossey-Bass Publishers, 1996), pp. 44–50.

[34]Max Weber, *The Theory of Social and Economic Organization*, A. M. Henderson, trans., and H. T. Parsons (New York: Free Press, 1947).

[35]Ibid.

[36]For classic treatments of bureaucracy, see Alvin Gouldner, *Patterns of Industrial Bureaucracy* (New York: Free Press, 1954); and Robert K. Merton, *Social Theory and Social Structure* (New York: Free Press, 1957).

[37]Tom Burns and George M. Stalker, *The Management of Innovation* (London: Tavistock, 1961; republished by Oxford University Press, London, 1994). See also, Paul R. Lawrence and Jay W. Lorsch, *Organizations and Environment* (Boston: Division of Research, Graduate School of Business Administration, Harvard University, 1967).

[38]See Henry Mintzberg, *Structure in Fives: Designing Effective Organizations* (Englewood Cliffs, NJ: Prentice-Hall, 1983).

[39]See Rosabeth Moss Kanter, *The Changing Masters* (New York: Simon & Schuster, 1983). Quotation from Rosabeth Moss Kanter and John D. Buck, "Reorganizing Part of Honeywell: From Strategy to Structure," *Organizational Dynamics*, vol. 13 (Winter 1985), p. 6.

[40]See, for example, Jay R. Galbraith, Edward E. Lawler III, and associates, *Organizing for the Future* (San Francisco: Jossey-Bass, 1993); and Mohrman, Galbraith, Lawler, and associates, *Tomorrow's Organizations*.

[41]Peter Senge, *The Fifth Discipline: The Art and Practice of the Learning Organization* (New York: Doubleday, 1994).

[42]www.nucor.com/aboutus.htm

[43]David Van Fleet, "Span of Management Research and Issues," *Academy of Management Journal*, vol. 26 (1983), pp. 546–52.

[44]Information and quotes from Ellen Byron and Joann S. Lublin, "Appointment of New P&G Chief Sends Ripples through Ranks," *Wall Street Journal* (June 11, 2009), p. B3.

[45]Burns and Stalker, op. cit.

[46]Questionnaire adapted from L. Steinmetz and R. Todd, *First Line Management*, 4th ed. (Homewood, IL: BPI/Irwin, 1986), pp. 64–67. Used by permission.

Feature Notes

Real People—Information and quotes from Stacy Perman, "Scones and Social Responsibility," *BusinessWeek* (August 21/28, 2006), p. 38; and www.dancingdeer.com

Photo Essays

Cisco Systems—Information and quote from Peter Burrows, "Cisco's Extreme Ambitions," *BusinessWeek* (November 30, 2009), p. 26. Macy's—Information from Matthew Boyle, "A Leaner Macy's Tries Catering to Local Tastes," *BusinessWeek* (September 14, 2009), p. 13.

Chapter 11

Endnotes

[1]Information and quotes from Daniel Roth, "Netflix Everywhere: Sorry Cable, You're History," *Wired Magazine* (September 21, 2009): www.wired.com.

[2]Michael Beer and Nitin Nohria, "Cracking the Code of Change," *Harvard Business Review* (May–June 2000), pp. 133–41.

[3]Quote from John A. Byrne, "Visionary vs. Visionary," *BusinessWeek* (August 28, 2000), p. 210.

[4]Information from David Welch, "GM: His Way or the Highway," *BusinessWeek* (October 5, 2009), pp. 62–63.

[5]See the discussion of Anthropologie in William C. Taylor and Polly LaBarre, *Mavericks at Work: Why the Most Original Minds in Business Win* (New York: William Morrow, 2006).

[6]Edgar H. Schein, "Organizational Culture," *American Psychologist*, vol. 45 (1990), pp. 109–19. See also *Schein's Organizational Culture and Leadership*, 2nd ed. (San Francisco: Jossey-Bass, 1997) and *The Corporate Culture Survival Guide* (San Francisco: Jossey-Bass, 1999).

[7]James Collins and Jerry Porras, *Built to Last* (New York: HarperBusiness, 1994).

[8]Information and quotes from Christopher Palmeri, "Now for Sale, the Zappos Culture," *BusinessWeek* (January 11, 2010), p. 57. See also Tony Hsieh, *Delivering Happiness! A Path to Profits, Passion, and Purpose* (New York: BusinessPlus, 2010).

[9]Jena McGregor, "Zappos' Secret: It's an Open Book," *BusinessWeek* (March 23/30, 2009), p. 62.

[10]Quotes from Dean Foust, "Where Headhunters Fear to Tread," *BusinessWeek* (September 14, 2009), pp. 42–43.

[11]In their book *Corporate Culture and Performance* (New York: Macmillan, 1992), John P. Kotter and James L. Heskett make the point that strong cultures have the desired effects over the long term only if they encourage adaptation to a changing environment. See also Collins and Porras, op. cit.

[12]John P. Wanous, *Organizational Entry*, 2nd ed. (New York: Addison-Wesley, 1992).

[13]Scott Madison Patton, *Service Quality, Disney Style* (Lake Buena Vista, FL: Disney Institute, 1997).

[14]This is a simplified model developed from Schein, op. cit. (1997).

[15]Schein, op. cit. (1997); Terrence E. Deal and Alan A. Kennedy, *Corporate Cultures: The Rites and Rituals of Corporate Life* (Reading, MA: Addison-Wesley, 1982); Ralph Kilmann, *Beyond the Quick Fix* (San Francisco: Jossey-Bass, 1984).

[16]James C. Collins and Jerry I. Porras, "Building Your Company's Vision," *Harvard Business Review* (September–October 1996), pp. 65–77.

[17]David Rocks, "Reinventing Herman Miller," *BusinessWeek eBiz* (April 2, 2000), pp. E88–E96; www.hermanmiller.com.

[18]James Collins and Jerry Porras, *Built to Last* (New York: HarperBusiness, 1994).

[19]This case is reported in Jenny C. McCune, "Making Lemonade," *Management Review* (June 1997), pp. 49–53.

[20]See Mary Kay Ash, *Mary Kay: You Can Have It All* (Roseville, CA: Prima Publishing, 1995).

[21]See Robert A. Giacalone and Carol L. Jurkiewicz (eds.), *Handbook of Workplace Spirituality and Organizational Performance* (Armonk, NY: M. E. Sharpe, 2005).

[22]McCune, op. cit.

[23]R. Roosevelt Thomas Jr., *Beyond Race and Gender* (New York: AMACOM, 1992), p. 10. See also R. Roosevelt Thomas Jr., "From 'Affirmative Action' to 'Affirming Diversity,'" *Harvard Business Review* (November–December 1990), pp. 107–17; R. Roosevelt Thomas Jr., with Marjorie I. Woodruff, *Building a House for Diversity* (New York: AMACOM, 1999).

[24]Taylor Cox Jr., *Cultural Diversity in Organizations* (San Francisco: Berrett Koehler, 1994).

[25]Survey reported in "The Most Inclusive Workplaces Generate the Most Loyal Employees," *Gallup Management Journal* (December 2001), retrieved from http://gmj.gallup.com/press_room/release.asp?i=117.

[26]Thomas Kochan, Katerina Bezrukova, Robin Ely, Susan Jackson, Aparna Joshi, Karen Jehn, Jonathan Leonard, David Levine, and David Thomas, "The Effects of Diversity on Business Performance: Report of the Diversity Research Network," reported in *SHRM Foundation Research Findings*, retrieved from www.shrm.org/foundation/findings.asp. Full article published in *Human Resource Management* (2003).

[27]See Joseph A. Raelin, *Clash of Cultures* (Cambridge, MA: Harvard Business School Press, 1986).

[28]See Anthony Robbins and Joseph McClendon III, *Unlimited Power: A Black Choice* (New York: Free Press, 1997), and Augusto Failde and William Doyle, *Latino Success: Insights from America's Most Powerful Latino Executives* (New York: Free Press, 1996).

[29]Barbara Benedict Bunker, "Appreciating Diversity and Modifying Organizational Cultures: Men and Women at Work," Chapter 5 in Suresh Srivastava and David L. Cooperrider, *Appreciative Management and Leadership* (San Francisco: Jossey-Bass, 1990).

[30]See Gary N. Powell, *Women-Men in Management* (Thousand Oaks, CA: Sage, 1993) and Cliff Cheng (ed.), *Masculinities in Organizations* (Thousand Oaks, CA: Sage, 1996). For added background, see also Sally Helgesen, *Everyday Revolutionaries: Working Women and the Transformation of American Life* (New York: Doubleday, 1998).

[31]See, for example, Richard Donkin, "Caught Somewhere between the Ys and the Boomers," *Financial Times*, Kindle Edition (December 31, 2009).

[32]Tips in box—See "Reality Check for Gen Y and Its Managers," *Financial Times*, Kindle Edition (May 14, 2009).

[33]See "Women and Work: We Did It!" *The Economist*, Kindle Edition (December 31, 2009); and, "Women CEOs," *Fortune*: money.cnn.com/magazines/fortune/ global500/2007/womenceos.

[34]Laurie Landro, "Of Women and Working," *The Wall Street Journal*, online edition (December 5, 2009). See also Karine Moe and Dianna Shandy, *Glass Ceilings and 100-Hour Couples* (Athens, GA: University of Georgia Press, 2009).

[35]Michael Skapinker, "Companies Need to Recruit the Older Woman," *The Financial Times*, Kindle Edition (February 2, 2010).

[36]"Bias Cases by Workers Increase 9%," *Wall Street Journal* (March 6, 2008), p. D6.

[37]Sue Shellenbarger, "More Women Pursue Claims of Pregnancy Discrimination," *Wall Street Journal* (March 27, 2008), p. D1; and Rob Walker, "Sex vs. Ethics." *Fast Company* (June 2008), pp. 73–78.

[38]Ibid.

[39]Thomas, op. cit. (1992).

[40]Ibid.

[41]For a review of scholarly work on organizational change, see Arthur G. Bedian, "Organizational Change: A Review of Theory and Research," *Journal of Management*, vol. 25 (1999), pp. 293–315; and W. Warner Burke, *Organizational Change: Theory and Practice*, 2nd ed. (Thousand Oaks, CA: Sage, 2008).

[42]Quote from Pilita Clark, "Delayed, not Cancelled," *Financial Times* (December 19, 2009).

[43]Reported in G. Christian Hill and Mike Tharp, "Stumbling Giant—Big Quarterly Deficit Stuns Bank America, Adds Pressure on Chief," *Wall Street Journal* (July 18, 1985), pp. 1–16.

[44]Beer and Nohria, op. cit.; and "Change Management: An Inside Job," *Economist* (July 15, 2000), p. 61.

[45]Information and quote from Adam Bryant, "Xerox's New Chief Tries to Redefine Its Culture," *The New York Times* (February 21, 2010): www.nytimes.com.

[46]See Bedian, op. cit.

[47]Based on John P. Kotter, "Leading Change: Why Transformation Efforts Fail," *Harvard Business Review* (March–April 1995), pp. 59–67.

[48]Jack and Suzy Welch, "Finding Innovation Where It Lives," *BusinessWeek* (April 21, 2008), p. 84.

[49]This is based on Rosabeth Moss Kanter's "Innovation Pyramid," *BusinessWeek* (March 2007), p. IN 3.

[50]For a discussion of alternative types of change, see David A. Nadler and Michael L. Tushman, *Strategic Organizational Design* (Glenview, IL: Scott, Foresman, 1988); Kotter, op. cit; and W. Warner Burke, *Organization Change* (Thousand Oaks, CA.: Sage, 2002).

[51]GM information and quote from David Welch, "Ed Whitacre's Battle to Save GM from Itself," *Bloomberg Businessweek* (May 3–May 9, 2010), pp. 47–55.

[52]Kurt Lewin, "Group Decision and Social Change," in G. E. Swanson, T. M. Newcomb, and E. L. Hartley, eds., *Readings in Social Psychology* (New York: Holt, Rinehart, 1952), pp. 459–73.

[53]See Wanda J. Orlikowski and J. Debra Hofman, "An Improvisational Model for Change Management: The Case of Groupware Technologies," *Sloan Management Review* (Winter 1997), pp. 11–21.

[54]Ibid.

[55]This discussion is based on Robert Chin and Kenneth D. Benne, "General Strategies for Effecting Changes in Human Systems," in Warren G, Bennis, Kenneth D. Benne, Robert Chin, and Kenneth E. Corey (eds.), *The Planning of Change*, 3rd ed. (New York: Holt, Rinehart, 1969), pp. 22–45.

[56]The change agent descriptions here and following are developed from an exercise reported in J. William Pfeiffer and John E. Jones, *A Handbook of Structured Experiences for Human Relations Training*, vol. 2 (La Jolla, CA: University Associates, 1973).

[57]Ram N. Aditya, Robert J. House, and Steven Kerr, "Theory and Practice of Leadership: Into the New Millennium," Chapter 6 in Cary L. Cooper and Edwin A. Locke, *Industrial and Organizational Psychology: Linking Theory with Practice* (Malden, MA: Blackwell, 2000).

[58]Information from Mike Schneider, "Disney Teaching Excess Magic of Customer Service." *Columbus Dispatch* (December 17, 2000), p. G9.

[59]Teresa M. Amabile, "How to Kill Creativity," *Harvard Business Review* (September–October 1998), pp. 77–87.

[60]For an overview see Jeffrey D. Ford, Laurie W. Ford, and Angelo D'Amoto "Resistance to Change: The Rest of the Story," *Academy of Management Review*, vol. 33, no. 2 (2008), pp. 362–77; and, Jeffrey D. Ford and Laurie W. Ford, "Decoding Resistance to Change," *Harvard Business Review* (April 2009), pp. 99–103.

[61]Sue Shellenbarger, "Some Employers Find Way to Ease Burden of Changing Shifts," *Wall Street Journal* (March 25, 1998), p. B1.

[62]These checkpoints are developed from Everett M. Rogers, *Communication of Innovations*, 3rd ed. (New York: Free Press, 1993).

[63]John P. Kotter and Leonard A. Schlesinger, "Choosing Strategies for Change," *Harvard Business Review*, vol. 57 (March–April 1979), pp. 109–12. Example from *Fortune* (December 1991), pp. 56–62; additional information from corporate website: www.toro.com.

[64]Based on an instrument developed by W. Warner Burke. Used by permission.

Feature Notes

Real Ethics—Information from "Can Business Be Cool?" *Economist* (June 10, 2006), pp. 59–60; and Aubrey Henretty, "A Brighter Day," *Kellogg* (Summer 2006), pp. 32–34; Competitive Enterprise Institute, http://www.cei.org/pages/co2.cfm (retrieved September 29, 2006); Joseph Stiglitz, *Making Globalization Work* (New York: Norton, 2006), p. 172; and, Jim Phillips, "Business Leaders Say 'Green' Approach Doable," *Athens News* (March 27, 2008), from www.athensnews.com.

Real People—Information and quotes from David Kiley, "Ford's Savior?" *BusinessWeek* (March 16, 2009), pp. 31–34; and Alex Taylor III, "Fixing Up Ford," *Fortune* (May 14, 2009).

Photo Essay Notes

Herman Miller—David Rocks, "Reinventing Herman Miller," *BusinessWeek eBiz* (April 2, 2000), pp. E88–E96; www.hermanmiller.com. IDEO—Information and quotes from Tim Brown, "Change by Design," *BusinessWeek* (October 5, 2009), pp. 54–56. See also Tim Brown, *Change by Design* (New York: HarperBusiness, 2009).

Chapter 12

Endnotes

[1]Quotes from information from workingmother.com (retrieved January 10, 2010).

[2]See William E. Snizek, "Hall's Professionalism Scale: An Empirical Reassessment," *American Sociological Review*, vol. 37 (February 1972), pp. 109–14.

[3]Information from "SHRM Code of Ethical and Professional Standards in Human Resource Management," retrieved from www.shrm.org/ethics/code-of-ethics.asp.

[4]Jeffrey Pfeffer, *The Human Equation: Building Profits by Putting People First* (Boston: Harvard University Press, 1998), p. 292.

[5]Quote from William Bridges, "The End of the Job," *Fortune* (September 19, 1994), p. 68.

[6]Edward E. Lawler III, "The HR Department: Give It More Respect," *Wall Street Journal* (March 10, 2008), p. R8.

[7]*Dictionary of Business Management* (New York: Oxford University Press, 2006).

[8]T. Sekiguchi, "Person–Organization Fit and Person–Job Fit in Employee Selection: A Review of the Literature," *Osaka Keidai Ronshu*, vol. 54, no. 6 (2004), p. 179.

[9]Information from "New Face at Facebook Hopes to Map Out a Road to Growth," *Wall Street Journal* (April 15, 2008), pp. B1, B5.

[10]James N. Baron and David M. Kreps, *Strategic Human Resources: Framework for General Managers* (New York: Wiley, 1999).

[11]Quotes from Kris Maher, "Human-Resources Directors Are Assuming Strategic Roles," *Wall Street Journal* (June 17, 2003), p. B8.

[12]Ibid.

[13]Information from ADA National Network retrieved from www.adata.org/whatsada-definition.aspx.

[14]Information from the U.S. Equal Employment Opportunity Commission retrieved from www.eeoc.gov/laws/types/ages.cfm.

[15]Information from the U.S. Equal Employment Opportunity Commission retrieved from www.eeoc.gov/laws/types/pregnancy.cfm.

[16]The U.S. Equal Employment Opportunity Commission, "Pregnancy Discrimination Charges EEOC & FEPAs Combined: FY1997-FY2009," retrieved from http://www1.eeoc.gov//eeoc/statistics/enforcement/pregnancy.cfm?renderforprint=1.

[17]Information from the U.S. Department of Labor, retrieved from http://www.dol.gov/whd/fmla/index.htm.

[18]Dr. Mary Curtis and Dr. Christine H.B. Grant, University of Iowa, retrieved from http://bailiwick.lib.uiowa/ge/aboutRE.html.

[19]For a discussion of affirmative action see R. Roosevelt Thomas Jr., "From 'Affirmative Action' to 'Affirming Diversity,'" *Harvard Business Review* (November–December 1990), pp. 107–17.

[20]See the discussion by David A. DeCenzo and Stephen P. Robbins, *Human Resource Management*, 6th ed. (New York: Wiley, 1999), pp. 66–68 and 81–83.

[21]Ibid., pp. 77–79.

[22]See Frederick S. Lane, *The Naked Employee: How Technology Is Compromising Workplace Privacy* (New York: AMACOM, 2003).

[23]Quote from George Myers, "Bookshelf," *Columbus Dispatch* (June 9, 2003), p. E6.

[24]See Ernest McCormick, "Job and Task Analysis," in Marvin Dunnette, ed., *Handbook of Industrial and Organizational Psychology* (Chicago: Rand McNally, 1976), pp. 651–96.

[25]See John P. Wanous, *Organizational Entry: Recruitment, Selection, and Socialization of Newcomers* (Reading, MA: Addison-Wesley, 1980), pp. 34–44.

[26]Theresa Feathers, *Three Major Selection and Assessment Techniques, Their Popularity in Industry and Their Predictive Validity*, December 2000.

[27]See Michael A. D. McDaniel, Deborah L. Whetzel, Frank L. Schmidt, and Steven Maurer, "The Validity of Employment Interviews: A Comprehensive Review and Meta-analysis," *Journal of Applied Psychology*, vol. 79, no. 4 (August 1994), pp. 599–616.

[28]Information from "Biodata: The Measure of an Applicant?" *New York Law Journal* (May 21, 2007).

[29]Information from "Google Answer to Filling Jobs Is an Algorithm," *New York Times* (January 3, 2007).

[30]Quote from Ronald Henkoff, "Finding, Training, and Keeping the Best Service Workers," *Fortune* (October 3, 1994), pp. 110–22.

[31]For a scholarly review, see John Van Maanen and Edgar H. Schein, "Toward a Theory of Socialization," in Barry M. Staw, ed., *Research in Organizational Behavior*, vol. 1 (Greenwich, CT: JAI Press, 1979), pp. 209–64; for a practitioner's view, see Richard Pascale, "Fitting New Employees into the Company Culture," *Fortune* (May 28, 1984), pp. 28–42.

[32]This involves the social information processing concept as discussed in Gerald R. Salancik and Jeffrey Pfeffer, "A Social Information Processing Approach to Job Attitudes and Task Design," *Administrative Science Quarterly*, vol. 23 (June 1978), pp. 224–53.

[33]Boxed material developed from Alan Fowler, "How to Decide on Training Methods," *People Management*, vol. 25 (1995), pp. 36–38.

[34]Gouri Shukla, "Job Rotation and How It Works," April 27, 2005 retrieved from http://www.rediff.com/money/2005/apr/27spec1.htm.

[35]See Larry L. Cummings and Donald P. Schwab, *Performance in Organizations: Determinants and Appraisal* (Glenview, IL: Scott, Foresman, 1973).

[36]Dick Grote, "Performance Appraisal Reappraised," *Harvard Business Review Best Practice* (1999), Reprint F00105.

[37]See Gary P. Latham, Joan Almost, Sara Mann, and Celia Moore, "New Developments in Performance Management," *Organizational Dynamics*, vol. 34, no. 1 (2005), pp. 77–87.

[38]See Edward E. Lawler III, "Reward Practices and Performance Management System Effectiveness," *Organizational Dynamics*, vol. 32, no. 4 (November 2003), pp. 396–404.

[39]"Information from Ilana DeBare, "360 Degrees of Evaluation—More Companies Turn to Full-Circle Job Reviews," *San Francisco Chronicle* (May 5, 1997).

[40]Latham, op. cit.

[41]Timothy Butler and James Waldroop, "Job Sculpting: The Art of Retaining Your Best People," *Harvard Business Review* (September–October 1999), pp. 144–52.

[42]Information from "What Are the Most Effective Retention Tools?" *Fortune* (October 9, 2000), p. S7.

[43]See Betty Friedan, *Beyond Gender: The New Politics of Work and the Family* (Washington, DC: Woodrow Wilson Center Press, 1997); and James A. Levine, *Working Fathers: New Strategies for Balancing Work and Family* (Reading, MA: Addison-Wesley, 1997).

[44]Study reported in Ann Belser, "Employers Using Less-Costly Ways to Retain Workers," *Columbus Disptach* (June 1, 2008), p. D3.

[45]Information from Sue Shellenbarger, "What Makes a Company a Great Place to Work Today," *Wall Street Journal* (October 4, 2007), p. D1.

[46]Examples from Amy Saunders, "A Creative Approach to Work," *Columbus Dispatch* (May 2, 2008), pp. C1, C9; Shellenbarger, op. cit.; and, Michelle Conlin and Jay Greene, "How to Make a Microserf Smile," *BusinessWeek* (September 10, 2007), pp. 57–59.

[47]A good overview of trends and issues is found in the special section on "Employee Benefits," *Wall Street Journal* (April 22, 2008), pp. A11–A17.

[48]See Kaja Whitehouse, "More Companies Offer Packages Pay Plans to Performance," *Wall Street Journal* (December 13, 2005), p. B6.

[49]Ibid.

[50]Erin White, "How to Reduce Turnover," *Wall Street Journal* (November 21, 2005), p. B5.

[51]Information from Susan Pulliam, "New Dot-Com Mantra: 'Just Pay Me in Cash, Please,'" *Wall Street Journal* (November 28, 2000), p. C1.

[52]White, op. cit.

[53]Information from Andrew Blackman, "You're the Boss," *Wall Street Journal* (April 11, 2005), p. R5.

[54]Information from www.intel.com and "Stock Ownership for Everyone," Hewitt Associates (November 27, 2000).

[55]For reviews see Richard B. Freeman and James L. Medoff, *What Do Unions Do?* (New York: Basic Books, 1984); Charles C. Heckscher, *The New Unionism* (New York: Basic Books, 1988); and Barry T. Hirsch, *Labor Unions and the Economic Performance of Firms* (Kalamazoo, MI: W. E. Upjohn Institute for Employment Research, 1991).

[56]"Verizon Labor Talks Continue, Beyond Deadline," Reuters (August 3, 2008), www.reuters.com.

[57]Developed in part from Robert E. Quinn, Sue R. Faerman, Michael P. Thompson, and Michael R. McGrath, *Becoming a Master Manager: A Contemporary Framework* (New York: Wiley, 1990), p. 187. Used by permission.

[58]Developed from Eugene Owens, "Upward Appraisal: An Exercise in Subordinate's Critique of Superior's Performance," *Exchange: The Organizational Behavior Teaching Journal*, vol. 3 (1978), pp. 41–42.

Feature Notes

Real People—http://zappos.com; http://about.zappos.com/ meet-our-monkeys/tony-hsieh-ceo; http://www.mahalo.com/ tony-hsieh; and, Tony Hsieh, *Delivering Happiness: A Path to Profits, Passion, and Purpose* (New York: BusinessPlus, 2010).

Photo Essay Notes

Google—See Bernard Girard, *The Google Way: How One Company Is Revolutionizing Management as We Know It* (San Francisco: No Starch Press, 2009).

Chapter 13

Endnotes

[1]List developed from S. Bartholomew Craig and Gigrid B. Qustafson, "Perceived Leader Integrity Scale: An Instrument for Assessing Employee Perceptions of Leader Integrity," *Leadership Quarterly*, vol. 9 (1998), pp. 127–45; Drucker quotes from Robert Lenzner and Stephen S. Johnson, "Seeing Things As They Really Are," *Forbes* (March 10, 1997), retrieved from: http://www.forbes.com/forbes/1997/0310/5905122a.html.

[2]Quote from Marshall Loeb, "Where Leaders Come From," *Fortune* (September 19, 1994), pp. 241–42. For additional thoughts, see Warren Bennis, *Why Leaders Can't Lead* (San Francisco: Jossey-Bass, 1996).

[3]Barry Z. Posner, "On Leadership," *BizEd* (May–June 2008), pp. 26–27.

[4]Tom Peters, "Rule #3: Leadership Is Confusing as Hell," *Fast Company* (March 2001), pp. 124–40.

[5]See Jean Lipman-Blumen, *Connective Leadership: Managing in a Changing World* (New York: Oxford University Press, 1996), pp. 3–11.

[6]Abraham Zaleznick, "Leaders and Managers: Are They Different?" *Harvard Business Review* (May–June 1977), pp. 67–78.

[7]Rosabeth Moss Kanter, "Power Failure in Management Circuits," *Harvard Business Review* (July–August 1979), pp. 65–75.

[8]For a good managerial discussion of power, see David C. McClelland and David H. Burnham, "Power Is the Great Motivator," *Harvard Business Review* (March–April 1976), pp. 100–10.

[9]The classic treatment of these power bases is John R. P. French Jr. and Bertram Raven, "The Bases of Social Power," in Darwin Cartwright, ed., *Group Dynamics: Research and Theory* (Evanston, IL: Row, Peterson, 1962), pp. 607–13. For managerial applications of this basic framework, see Gary Yukl and Tom Taber, "The Effective Use of Managerial Power," *Personnel*, vol. 60 (1983), pp. 37–49; and Robert C. Benfari, Harry E. Wilkinson, and Charles D. Orth, "The Effective Use of Power," *Business Horizons*, vol. 29 (1986), pp. 12–16; Gary A. Yukl, *Leadership in Organizations*, 4th ed. (Englewood Cliffs, NJ: Prentice-Hall, 1998); includes "information" as a separate, but related, power source.

[10]James M. Kouzes and Barry Z. Posner, "The Leadership Challenge," *Success* (April 1988), p. 68. See also their books *Credibility: How Leaders Gain and Lose It; Why People Demand It* (San Francisco: Jossey-Bass, 1996); *Encouraging the Heart: A Leader's Guide to Rewarding and Recognizing Others* (San Francisco: Jossey-Bass, 1999); and *The Leadership Challenge: How to Get Extraordinary Things Done in Organizations*, 3rd ed. (San Francisco: Jossey-Bass, 2002).

[11]Burt Nanus, *Visionary Leadership: Creating a Compelling Sense of Vision for Your Organization* (San Francisco: Jossey-Bass, 1992).

[12]Lorraine Monroe, "Leadership Is about Making Vision Happen—What I Call 'Vision Acts,'" *Fast Company* (March 2001), p. 98; School Leadership Academy website: www.lorrainemonroe.com.

[13]Quote from Andy Serwer, "Game Changers: Legendary Basketball Coach John Wooden and Starbucks' Howard Schultz Talk about a Common Interest—Leadership," *Fortune* (August 11, 2008): www.cnnmoney.com.

[14]Loeb, op. cit.

[15]A classic work is Robert K. Greenleaf and Larry C. Spears, *The Power of Servant Leadership: Essays* (San Francisco: Berrett-Koehler, 1996).

[16]Jay A. Conger, "Leadership: The Art of Empowering Others," *Academy of Management Executive*, vol. 3 (1989), pp. 17–24.

[17]Greenleaf and Spears, op. cit., p. 78.

[18]Max DePree, *Leadership Is an Art* (New York: Doubleday, 1989 and 2004) and *Leadership Jazz* (New York: Doubleday, 1992 and 2008).

[19]Monroe, opcit., p. 98; School Leadership Academy website: www.lorrainemonroe.com.

[20]The early work on leader traits is well represented in Ralph M. Stogdill, "Personal Factors Associated with Leadership: A Survey of the Literature," *Journal of Psychology*, vol. 25 (1948), pp. 35–71. See also Edwin E. Ghiselli, *Explorations in Management Talent* (Santa Monica, CA: Goodyear, 1971); and Shirley A. Kirkpatrick and Edwin A. Locke, "Leadership: Do Traits Really Matter?" *Academy of Management Executive* (1991), pp. 48–60.

[21]See also John W. Gardner's article, "The Context and Attributes of Leadership," *New Management*, vol. 5 (1988), pp. 18–22; John P. Kotter, *The Leadership Factor* (New York: Free Press, 1988); and Bernard M. Bass, *Stogdill's Handbook of Leadership* (New York: Free Press, 1990).

[22]Kirkpatrick and Locke, op. cit., 1991.

[23]This work traces back to classic studies by Kurt Lewin and his associates at the University of Iowa. See, for example, K. Lewin and R. Lippitt, "An Experimental Approach to the Study of Autocracy and Democracy: A Preliminary Note," *Sociometry*, vol. 1 (1938), pp. 292–300; K. Lewin, "Field Theory and Experiment in Social Psychology: Concepts and Methods," *American Journal of Sociology*, vol. 44 (1939), pp. 886–96; and

K. Lewin, R. Lippitt, and R. K. White, "Patterns of Aggressive Behavior in Experimentally Created Social Climates," *Journal of Social Psychology*, vol. 10 (1939), pp. 271–301.

[24]The original research from the Ohio State studies is described in R. M. Stogdill and A. E. Coons, eds., *Leader Behavior: Its Description and Measurement*, Research Monograph No. 88 (Columbus: Ohio State University Bureau of Business Research, 1951); see also Chester A. Schreisham, Claudia C. Cogliser, and Linda L. Neider, "Is It 'Trustworthy'? A Multiple-Levels-of-Analysis Reexamination of an Ohio State Leadership Study with Implications for Future Research," *Leadership Quarterly*, vol. 2 (Summer 1995), pp. 111–45. For the University of Michigan studies, see Robert Kahn and Daniel Katz, "Leadership Practices in Relation to Productivity and Morale," in Dorwin Cartwright and Alvin Alexander, eds., *Group Dynamics: Research and Theory*, 3rd ed. (New York: Harper-Row, 1968).

[25]See Bass, op. cit., 1990.

[26]Robert R. Blake and Jane Srygley Mouton, *The New Managerial Grid III* (Houston: Gulf Publishing, 1985).

[27]See Lewin and Lippitt, op. cit., 1938.

[28]For a good discussion of this theory, see Fred E. Fiedler, Martin M. Chemers, and Linda Mahar, *The Leadership Match Concept* (New York: Wiley, 1978); Fiedler's current contingency research with the cognitive resource theory is summarized in Fred E. Fiedler and Joseph E. Garcia, *New Approaches to Effective Leadership* (New York: Wiley, 1987).

[29]See Pino Audia, "A New B-School Specialty: Self-Awareness," Forbes.com (December 4, 2009).

[30]Paul Hersey and Kenneth H. Blanchard, *Management and Organizational Behavior* (Englewood Cliffs, NJ: Prentice-Hall, 1988). For an interview with Paul Hersey on the origins of the model, see John R. Schermerhorn Jr., "Situational Leadership: Conversations with Paul Hersey," *Mid-American Journal of Business* (Fall 1997), pp. 5–12.

[31]See Claude L. Graeff, "The Situational Leadership Theory: A Critical View," *Academy of Management Review*, vol. 8 (1983), pp. 285–91; and Carmen F. Fernandez and Robert P. Vecchio, "Situational Leadership Theory Revisited: A Test of an Across-Jobs Perspective," *Leadership Quarterly*, vol. 8 (Summer 1997), pp. 67–84.

[32]See, for example, Robert J. House, "A Path–Goal Theory of Leader Effectiveness," *Administrative Sciences Quarterly*, vol. 16 (1971), pp. 321–38; Robert J. House and Terrence R. Mitchell, "Path–Goal Theory of Leadership," *Journal of Contemporary Business* (Autumn 1974), pp. 81–97. The path–goal theory is reviewed by Bass, op. cit. A supportive review of research is offered in Julie Indvik, "Path–Goal Theory of Leadership: A Meta-Analysis," in John A. Pearce II and Richard B. Robinson Jr., eds., *Academy of Management Best Paper Proceedings* (1986), pp. 189–92. The theory is reviewed and updated in Robert J. House, "Path–Goal Theory of Leadership: Lessons, Legacy and a Reformulated Theory," *Leadership Quarterly*, vol. 7 (Autumn 1996), pp. 323–52.

[33]See the discussions of path–goal theory in Bernard M. Bass, "Leadership: Good, Better, Best," *Organizational Dynamics* (Winter 1985), pp. 26–40.

[34]See Steven Kerr and John Jermier, "Substitutes for Leadership: Their Meaning and Measurement," *Organizational Behavior and Human Performance*, vol. 22 (1978), pp. 375–403; Jon P. Howell and Peter W. Dorfman, "Leadership and Substitutes for Leadership Among Professional and Nonprofessional Workers," *Journal of Applied Behavioral Science*, vol. 22 (1986), pp. 29–46.

[35]An early presentation of the theory is F. Dansereau Jr., G. Graen, and W. J. Haga, "A Vertical Dyad Linkage Approach to Leadership Within Formal Organizations: A Longitudinal Investigation of the Role-Making Process," *Organizational Behavior and Human Performance*, vol. 13, pp. 46–78.

[36]This discussion is based on Yukl, op. cit., pp. 117–22.

[37]Ibid.

[38]Victor H. Vroom and Arthur G. Jago, *The New Leadership: Managing Participation in Organizations* (Englewood Cliffs, NJ: Prentice-Hall, 1988). This is based on earlier work by Victor H. Vroom, "A New Look in Managerial Decision-Making," *Organizational Dynamics* (Spring 1973), pp. 66–80; and Victor H. Vroom and Phillip Yetton, *Leadership and Decision-Making* (Pittsburgh: University of Pittsburgh Press, 1973).

[39]Vroom and Jago, op. cit.

[40]For a related discussion, see Edgar H. Schein, *Process Consultation Revisited: Building the Helping Relationship* (Reading, MA: Addison-Wesley, 1999).

[41]For a related discussion, see Schein, op. cit.

[42]For a review, see Yukl, op. cit.

[43]See the discussion by Victor H. Vroom, "Leadership and the Decision-Making Process," *Organizational Dynamics*, vol. 28 (2000), pp. 82–94.

[44]The distinction was originally made by James McGregor Burns, *Leadership* (New York: Harper-Row, 1978), and was further developed by Bernard Bass, *Leadership and Performance Beyond Expectations* (New York: Free Press, 1985) and Bernard M. Bass, "Leadership: Good, Better, Best," *Organization Dynamics* (Winter 1985), pp. 26–40.

[45]Among popular books are Warren Bennis and Burt Nanus, *Leaders: The Strategies for Taking Charge* (New York: Harper Business, 1997); Max DePree, *Leadership Is an Art*, op. cit.; Kotter, *The Leadership Factor*, op. cit.; Kouzes and Posner, *The Leadership Challenge*, op. cit., 2002.

[46]This list is based on Kouzes and Posner, op. cit.; Gardner, op. cit.

[47]Daniel Goleman, "Leadership That Gets Results," *Harvard Business Review* (March–April 2000), pp. 78–90. See also his books *Emotional Intelligence* (New York: Bantam Books, 1995) and *Working with Emotional Intelligence* (New York: Bantam Books, 1998).

[48]Daniel Goleman, "What Makes a Leader?" *Harvard Business Review* (November–December 1998), pp. 93–102.

[49]Goleman, op. cit., 1998.

[50]Information from "Women and Men, Work, and Power," *Fast Company*, issue 13 (1998), p. 71.

[51]Jane Shibley Hyde, "The Gender Similarities—Hypothesis," *American Psychologist*, vol. 60, no. 6 (2005), pp. 581–92.

[52]A. H. Eagley, S. J. Daran, and M. G. Makhijani, "Gender and the Effectiveness of Leaders: A Meta-Analysis," *Psychological Bulletin*, vol. 117 (1995), pp. 125–45.

[53]Research on gender issues in leadership is reported in Sally Helgesen, *The Female Advantage: Women's Ways of Leadership* (New York: Doubleday, 1990); Judith B. Rosener, "Ways Women Lead, "*Harvard Business Review* (November/December 1990), pp. 119–25; and Alice H. Eagley, Steven J. Karau, and Blair T. Johnson, "Gender and Leadership Style Among School Principals: A Meta Analysis," *Administrative Science Quarterly*, vol. 27 (1992), pp. 76–102; Jean Lipman-Blumen, *Connective Leadership: Managing in a Changing World* (New York: Oxford University Press, 1996); Alice H. Eagley, Mary C. Johannesen-Smith, and Marloes L. van Engen, "Transformational, Transactional and Laissez-Faire Leadership: A Meta-Analysis of Women and Men, *Psychological Bulletin*, vol. 124, no. 4 (2003), pp. 569–91; and Carol Hymowitz, "Too Many Women Fall for Stereotypes of Selves, Study Says," *Wall Street Journal* (October 24, 2005), p. B.1.

[54]Ibid.

[55]Eagely et al., op cit.; Hymowitz, op cit.; Rosener, op. cit.; Vroom, op cit.; Herminia Ibarra and Otilia Obodaru, "Women and the Vision Thing," *Harvard Business Review* (January, 2009): Reprint R0901E.

[56]Ibarra and Obodaru, op. cit.

[57]Rosener, op. cit.

[58]For debate on whether some transformational leadership qualities tend to be associated more with female than male leaders, see "Debate: Ways Women and Men Lead," *Harvard Business Review* (January–February 1991), pp. 150–60.

[59]Quote from "As Leaders, Women Rule," *BusinessWeek* (November 2, 2000), pp. 75–84. Rosabeth Moss Kanter is the author of *Men and Women of the Corporation*, 2nd ed. (New York: Basic Books, 1993).

[60]Hyde, op. cit.; Hymowitz, op. cit.

[61]Julie Bennett, "Women Get a Boost Up that Tall Leadership Ladder," *Wall Street Journal* (June 10, 2008), p. D6.

[62]Based on the discussion by John W. Dienhart and Terry Thomas, "Ethical Leadership: A Primer on Ethical Responsibility," in John R. Schermerhorn Jr., *Management*, 7th ed. (New York: Wiley, 2003).

[63]Schein, op. cit.

[64]Vroom and Jago, op. cit.

[65]James MacGregor Burns, *Transforming Leadership: A New Pursuit of Happiness* (New York: Atlantic Monthly Press, 2003); information from Christopher Caldwell, book review, *International Herald Tribune* (April 29, 2003), p. 18.

[66]Fred Luthans and Bruce Avolio, "Authentic Leadership: A Positive Development Approach," in K. S. Cameron, J. E. Dutton, and R. E. Quinn, eds., *Positive Organizational Scholarship* (San Francisco: Berrett-Koehler, 2003), pp. 241–58.

[67]Doug May, Adrian Chan, Timothy Hodges, and Bruce Avolio, "Developing the Moral Component of Authentic Leadership," *Organizational Dynamics*, vol. 32 (2003), pp. 247–60.

[68]Peter F. Drucker, "Leadership: More Doing than Dash," *Wall Street Journal* (January 6, 1988), p. 16. For a compendium of writings on leadership, sponsored by the Drucker Foundation, see Frances Hesselbein, Marshall Goldsmith, and Richard Beckhard, *Leader of the Future* (San Francisco: Jossey-Bass, 1997).

[69]Quotes from ibid.

[70]Fred E. Fiedler and Martin M. Chemers, *Improving Leadership Effectiveness: The Leader Match Concept*, 2nd ed. (New York: Wiley, 1984). Used by permission.

[71]Victor H. Vroom and Arthur G. Jago, *The New Leadership* (Englewood Cliffs, NJ: Prentice-Hall, 1988). Used by permission.

Feature Notes

Opener—Information and quotes from Irene Rosenfeld, "Irene Rosenfeld Drives Change with 'Rules of the Road'," *Wall Street Journal*, Special Advertising Section (October 6, 2009), p. A17; David Kesmodel and Ceccilie Rohwedder, "Sugar and Spice: A Clash of Two Change Agents," *Wall Street Journal* (September 8, 2009), p. A17; Ilan Brat, "A Jar of New Vegmite, a Window into Kraft," *Wall Street Journal* (September 30, 2009), pp. B1, B2; and Susan Verfield and Michael Arndt, "Kraft's Sugar Rush," *BusinessWeek* (January 25, 2010), pp. 37–39.

Real People—Information and quotes from Lorraine Monroe, "Leadership is about Making Vision Happen—What I Call 'Vision Acts,'" *Fast Company* (March 2001), p. 98; Lorraine Monroe Leadership Institute website: www.lorrainemonroe.com. See also, Lorraine Monroe, *Nothing's Impossible: Leadership Lessons from Inside and Outside the Classroom* (New York: PublicAffairs Books, 1999), and *The Monroe Doctrine: An ABC Guide to What Great Bosses Do* (New York: PublicAffairs Books, 2003).

Photo Essay Notes

César Conde—Information and quotes from Laur Wides-Muñoz, "Miami-born César Conde to Take Over Univisión Networks, *The Miami Herald* (September 29, 2009): www.miamiherald.com; and, David Adams, "César Conde: Univision's Big Bet," www.news.newamericamedia.org (September 17, 2009), accessed May 11, 2010. Martin Luther King, Jr.—Full texts of the I Have a Dream speech are available online; see for example, www.usconstitution.net/dream.html. Mahatma Gandhi—Information from "140 Years Ago: Civil but Disobedient," *Smithsonian* (October 2009), p. 20; and data from "Many U.S. Employees Have Negative Attitudes to Their Jobs, Employers and Top Managers," Harris Poll #38 (May 6, 2005), retrieved from www.harrisinteractive.com.

Chapter 14

Endnotes

[1]Information from Andrew Ward, "Spanx Queen Firms Up the Bottom Line," *Financial Times* (November 30, 2006), p. 7; and Simona Covel, "A Dated Industry Gets a Modern Makeover," *Wall Street Journal* (August 7, 2008), p. B9.

[2]See, for example, Ram Charan, *Know-How: The 8 Skills that Separate People Who Perform from Those that Don't* (New York: Crown Business, 2007); and Ram Charan, "Six Personality Traits of a Leader," www.career-advice.monster.com (accessed August 6, 2008).

[3]Ibid.

[4]Quotes from Charan, op. cit., 2008.

[5]Max DePree, "An Old Pro's Wisdom: It Begins with a Belief in People," *New York Times* (September 10, 1989), p. F2; Max DePree, *Leadership Is an Art* (New York: Doubleday, 1989); David Woodruff, "Herman Miller: How Green Is My Factory," *BusinessWeek* (September 16, 1991), pp. 54–56; and Max DePree, *Leadership Jazz* (New York: Doubleday, 1992); quote from www.depree.org/html/maxdepree.html.

[6]This example is reported in *Esquire* (December 1986), p. 243. Emphasis is added to the quotation. *Note:* Nussbaum became director of the Labor Department's Women's Bureau during the Clinton administration and subsequently moved to the AFL–CIO as head of the Women's Bureau.

[7]degree.org, op. cit.

[8]See H. R. Schiffman, *Sensation and Perception: An Integrated Approach*, 3d ed. (New York: Wiley, 1990).

[9]John P. Kotter, "The Psychological Contract: Managing the Joining Up Process," *California Management Review*, vol. 15 (Spring 1973), pp. 91–99; Denise Rousseau, ed., *Psychological Contracts in Organizations* (San Francisco: Jossey-Bass, 1995); Denise Rousseau, "Changing the Deal While Keeping the People," *Academy of Management Executive*, vol. 10 (1996), pp. 50–59; and Denise Rousseau and Rene Schalk, eds., *Psychological Contracts in Employment: Cross-Cultural Perspectives* (San Francisco: Jossey-Bass, 2000).

[10]A good review is E. L. Jones, ed., *Attribution: Perceiving the Causes of Behavior* (Morristown, NJ: General Learning Press, 1972). See also John H. Harvey and Gifford Weary, "Current Issues in Attribution Theory and Research," *Annual Review of Psychology*, vol. 35 (1984), pp. 427–59.

[11]See, for example, Stephan Thernstrom and Abigail Thernstrom, *America in Black and White* (New York: Simon & Schuster, 1997); and David A. Thomas and Suzy Wetlaufer, "A Question of Color: A Debate on Race in the U.S. Workplace," *Harvard Business Review* (September–October 1997), pp. 118–32.

[12]Information from "Misconceptions about Women in the Global Arena Keep Their Numbers Low," Catalyst Study: www.catalystwomen.org/home.html.

[13]These examples are from Natasha Josefowitz, *Paths to Power* (Reading, MA: Addison-Wesley, 1980), p. 60. For more on gender issues, see Gray N. Powell, ed., *Handbook of Gender and Work* (Thousand Oaks, CA: Sage, 1999).

[14]Survey reported in Kelly Greene, "Age Is Still More Than a Number," *Wall Street Journal* (April 10, 2003), p. D2.

[15]The classic work is Dewitt C. Dearborn and Herbert A. Simon, "Selective Perception: A Note on the Departmental Identification of Executives," *Sociometry*, vol. 21 (1958), pp. 140–44. See also J. P. Walsh, "Selectivity and Selective Perception: Belief Structures and Information Processing, *Academy of Management Journal*, vol. 24 (1988), pp. 453–70.

[16]Quotation from Sheila O'Flanagan, "Underestimate Casual Dressers at Your Peril," *Irish Times* (July 22, 2005). See also Christina Binkley, "How to Pull Off 'CEO Casual'," *Wall Street Journal* (August 7, 2008), pp. D1–D8.

[17]See William L. Gardner and Mark J. Martinko, "Impression Management in Organizations," *Journal of Management* (June 1988), p. 332.

[18]Sandy Wayne and Robert Liden, "Effects of Impression Management on Performance Ratings," *Academy of Management Journal* (February 2005), pp. 232–52.

[19]See M. R. Barrick and M. K. Mount, "The Big Five Personality Dimensions and Job Performance: A Meta-Analysis," *Personnel Psychology*, vol. 44 (1991), pp. 1–26.

[20]Ibid.

[21]For a good summary see Stephen P. Robbins and Timothy A. Judge, *Organizational Behavior*, 12th ed. (Upper Saddle River, NJ: Prentice-Hall). 2007, p. 112.

[22]Adrienne Carter, "Leading Indicators: Doug Conant," *STERNbusiness* (Spring/Summer 2008). pp. 22–24.

[23]Carl G. Jung, *Psychological Types*, H. G. Baynes trans. (Princeton, NJ: Princeton University Press, 1971).

[24]I. Briggs-Myers, *Introduction to Type* (Palo Alto, CA: Consulting Psychologists Press, 1980).

[25]See, for example, William L. Gardner and Mark J. Martinko, "Using the Myers-Briggs Type Indicator to Study Managers: A Literature Review and Research Agenda," *Journal of Management*, vol. 22 (1996), pp. 45–83; Naomi L. Quenk, *Essentials of Myers-Briggs Type Indicator Assessment* (New York: Wiley, 2000).

[26]See the discussion in John R. Schermerhorn, Jr., James G. Hunt, Richard N. Osborn, and Mary UhlBlen, *Organizational Behavior*, 11th Edition (Hoboken, N.J.: John Wiley & Sons, 2010), pp. 31–37.

[27]J. B. Rotter, "Generalized Expectancies for Internal versus External Control of Reinforcement," *Psychological Monographs*, vol. 80 (1966), pp. 1–28; see also Thomas W. Ng, Kelly L. Sorensen, and Lillian T. Eby, "Cocos of Control at Work: A Meta-Analysis," *Journal of Organizational Behavior*, 2006).

[28]T. W. Adorno, E. Frenkel-Brunswick, D. J. Levinson, and R. N. Sanford, *The Authoritarian Personality* (New York: Harper-Row, 1950).

[29]Niccolo Machiavelli, *The Prince*, trans. George Bull (Middlesex, UK: Penguin, 1961).

[30]Richard Christie and Florence L. Geis, *Studies in Machiavellianism* (New York: Academic Press, 1970).

[31]See M. Snyder, *Public Appearances/Private Realities: The Psychology of Self-Monitoring* (New York: Freeman, 1987).

[32]The classic work is Meyer Friedman and Ray Roseman, *Type A Behavior and Your Heart* (New York: Knopf, 1974).

[33]Information and quote from Joann S. Lublin, "How One Black Woman Lands Her Top Jobs: Risks and Networking," *Wall Street Journal* (March 4, 2003), p. B1.

[34]Martin Fishbein and Icek Ajzen, *Belief, Attitude, Intention and Behavior: An Introduction to Theory and Research* (Reading, MA: Addison-Wesley, 1973).

[35]See Leon Festinger, *A Theory of Cognitive Dissonance* (Palo Alto, CA: Stanford University Press, 1957).

[36]Timothy A. Judge and Allan H. Church, "Job Satisfaction: Research and Practice," Chapter 7 in Cary L. Cooper and Edwin A. Locke, eds., *Industrial and Organizational Psychology: Linking Theory with Practice* (Malden, MA: Blackwell Business, 2000); and Timothy A. Judge, "Promote Job Satisfaction through Mental Challenge," Chapter 6 in Edwin A. Locke, ed., *The Blackwell Handbook of Organizational Behavior* (Malden, MA: Blackwell, 2004).

[37]The Job Descriptive Index was developed by Dr. Patricia C. Smith, Department of Psychology, Bowling Green University. The Minnesota Satisfaction Questionnaire was developed at the Industrial Relations Center and Vocational Psychology Research Center, University of Minnesota.

[38]See ibid; Timothy A. Judge, "Promote Job Satisfaction through Mental Challenge," Chapter 6 in Edwin A. Locke, ed., *The Blackwell Handbook of Organizational Behavior* (Malden, MA: Blackwell, 2004); "U.S. Employees More Dissatisfied with Their Jobs," Associated Press (February 28, 2005), retrieved from www.msnbc.com; and "U.S. Job Satisfaction Keeps Falling, The Conference Board Reports Today," The Conference Board (February 28, 2005), retrieved from www.conference-board.org.

[39]Data reported in Jeannine Aversa, "Happy Workers Harder to Find," *Columbus Dispatch* (January 5, 2010), pp. A1, A4. Data from "U.S. Job Satisfaction the Lowest in Two Decades," press release, The Conference Board (January 5, 2010), retrieved January 6, 2010 from: http://www.conference-board.org.

[40]The Conference Board, op. cit.

[41]Judge and Church, op. cit., 2000; Judge, op. cit., 2004.

[42]Reported in "When Loyalty Erodes, So Do Profits," *BusinessWeek* (August 13, 2001), p. 8.

[43]Data reported in "When Loyalty Erodes, So Do Profits," *BusinessWeek* (August 13, 2001), p. 8.

[44]Tony DiRomualdo, "The High Cost of Employee Disengagement" (July 7, 2004): www.wistechnology.com.

[45]See "The Things They Do for Love," *Harvard Business Review* (December 2004), pp. 19–20.

[46]Information from Sue Shellenbarger, "Employers Are Finding It Doesn't Cost Much to Make a Staff Happy," *Wall Street Journal* (November 19, 1997), p. B1. See also "Job Satisfaction on the Decline," The Conference Board (July 2002).

[47]See Mark C. Bolino and William H. Turnley, "Going the Extra Mile: Cultivating and Managing Employee Citizenship Behavior," *Academy of Management Executive*, vol. 17 (August 2003), pp. 60–67.

[48]Dennis W. Organ, *Organizational Citizenship Behavior: The Good Soldier Syndrome* (Lexington, MA: Lexington Books, 1988).

[49]These relationships are discussed in Charles N. Greene, "The Satisfaction-Performance Controversy," *Business Horizons*, vol. 15 (1982), p. 31. Michelle T. Iaffaldano and Paul M. Muchinsky, "Job Satisfaction and Job Performance: A Meta-Analysis," *Psychological Bulletin*, vol. 97 (1985), pp. 251–73; Judge, op. cit., 2004; and, Michael Riketta, "The Causal Relation between Job Attitudes and Performance: A Meta-Analysis of Panel Studies," *Journal of Applied Psychology*, vol. 93, no. 2 (March, 2008), pp. 472–81.

[50]This discussion follows conclusions in Judge, op. cit., 2004.

[51]Damon Darlin and Matt Richtel, "Chairwoman Leaves Hewlett in Spying Furor," *Wall Street Journal* (September 23, 2006), pp. A1, A9.

[52]Daniel Goleman, "Leadership That Gets Results," *Harvard Business Review* (March–April 2000), pp. 78–90. See also his books *Emotional Intelligence* (New York: Bantam Books, 1995) and *Working with Emotional Intelligence* (New York: Bantam Books, 1998).

[53]Goleman, op. cit., 1998.

[54]See Robert G. Lord, Richard J. Klimoski, and Ruth Knafer (eds.), *Emotions in the Workplace; Understanding the Structure and Role of Emotions in Organizational Behavior* (San Francisco: Jossey–Bass, 2002); and Roy L. Payne and Cary L. Cooper (eds.), *Emotions at Work: Theory Research and Applications for Management* (Chichester, UK: Wiley, 2004); and, Daniel Goleman and Richard Boyatzis, "Social Intelligence and the Biology of Leadership," *Harvard Business Review* (September 2008), Reprint R0809E.

[55]Joyce E. Bono and Remus Ilies, "Charisma, Positive Emotions and Mood Contagion," *Leadership Quarterly*, vol. 17 (2006), pp. 317–34; and Goleman and Boyatzis, op. cit.

[56]Bono and Ilies, op. cit.

[57]See "Charm Offensive: Why America's CEOs Are So Eager to Be Loved," *BusinessWeek* (June 26, 2006): retrieved from businessweek.com (September 20, 2008).

[58]See Arthur P. Brief, Randall S. Schuler, and Mary Van Sell, *Managing Job Stress* (Boston: Little, Brown, 1981), pp. 7, 8.

[59]Robert B. Reich, *The Future of Success* (New York: Knopf, 2000), p. 8.

[60]Data from Michael Mandel, "The Real Reasons You're Working So Hard," *BusinessWeek* (October 3, 2005), pp. 60–70; "Many U.S. Employees Have Negative Attitudes to Their Jobs, Employers and Top Managers," The Harris Poll #38 (May 6, 2005), retrieved from www.harrisinteractive.com.

[61]Data from Sue Shellenbarger, "If You Need to Work Better, Maybe Try Working Less," *Wall Street Journal* (September 23, 2009), p. D1.

[62]Sue Shellenbarger, "Do We Work More or Not? Either Way, We Feel Frazzled," *Wall Street Journal* (July 30, 1997), p. B1.

[63]Michael Mandel, "The Real Reasons You're Working So Hard," *BusinessWeek* (October 3, 2005), pp. 60–70; "Many U.S. Employees Have Negative Attitudes to Their Jobs, Employers and Top Managers," The Harris Poll #38 (May 6, 2005), retrieved from www.harrisinteractive.com.

[64]Carol Hymowitz, "Impossible Expectations and Unfulfilling Work Stress Managers, Too," *Wall Street Journal* (January 16, 2001), p. B1.

[65]Hans Selye, *Stress in Health and Disease* (Boston: Butterworth, 1976).

[66]Carol Hymowitz, "Can Workplace Stress Get Worse?" *Wall Street Journal* (January 16, 2001), pp. B1, B3.

[67]See Steve M. Jex, *Stress and Job Performance* (San Francisco: Jossey-Bass, 1998).

[68]See "workplace violence" discussed by Richard V. Denenberg and Mark Braverman, *The Violence-Prone Workplace* (Ithaca, NY: Cornell University Press, 1999).

[69]See Daniel C. Ganster and Larry Murphy, "Workplace Interventions to Prevent Stress-Related Illness: Lessons from Research and Practice," Chapter 2 in Cooper and Locke (eds.), op. cit., 2000; Long working hours linked to high blood pressure," www.Gn.com/2006/Health (retrieved August 29, 2006).

[70]Quote from Shellenbarger, op. cit., 2009.

[71]Reported in Sue Shellenbarger, "Finding Ways to Keep a Partner's Job Stress from Hitting Home," *Wall Street Journal*, (November 29, 2000), p. B1.

[72]Information and quote from Shellenbarger, op. cit., 2009.

[73]Instrument from Julian P. Rotter, "External Control and Internal Control," *Psychology Today* (June 1971), p. 42. Used by permission.

[74]Adapted from Roy J. Lewicki, Donald D. Bowen, Douglas T. Hall, and Francine S. Hall, "What Do You Value in Work?" *Experiences in Management and Organizational Behavior*, 3rd ed. (New York: Wiley, 1988), pp. 23–26. Used by permission.

Feature Notes

Real People—Information from Leigh Buchanan, "Life Lessons," *Inc.* (June 6, 2006): retrieved from www.inc.com/magazine; "A Fortune Coined from Cheerfulness Entrepreneurship," *Financial Times* (May 20, 2009); and, www.lifeisgood.com/about.

Real Ethics—Information from Victoria Knight, "Personality Tests as Hiring Tools," *Wall Street Journal* (March 15, 2006), p. B3C.

Photo Essay Notes

BakBone Software—Information and quotes from "When Three Generations Can Work Better than One," *Financial Times* (September 16, 2009). Root Learning—Information and quote from Kelly K. Spors, "Top Small Workplaces 2009," *Wall Street Journal* (September 28, 2009), p. R7. Violins—Data from Michael Mandel, "The Real Reasons You're Working So Hard," *BusinessWeek* (October 3, 2005), pp. 60–70; "Many U.S. Employees Have Negative Attitudes to Their Jobs, Employers and Top Managers," The Harris Poll #38 (May 6, 2005), retrieved from www.harrisinteractive.com.

Chapter 15

Endnotes

[1]Information and quotes from David A. Kaplan, "#1 SAS: The Best Company to Work For," *Fortune* (January 26, 2010), Kindle edition.

[2]Conference Board research reported in Patricia Soldati, "Employee Engagement: What Exactly Is It?" *Management Issues* (March 8, 2007): www.managementissues.com (retrieved August 10, 2008). Yum Brands information from Erin White, "How Surveying Workers Can Pay Off," *Wall Street Journal* (June 18, 2007), p. B3.

[3]Information from "Executive Briefing: A New Approach for Airlines," *Wall Street Journal* (May 12, 2008), p. R3. See also Greg J. Bamber, Jody Hoffer Gittel, Thomas A. Kochan, and Andrew Von Nordenflycht, *Up in the Air: How the Airlines Can Improve Performance by Engaging Their Employees* (Ithaca, NY: Cornell University Press, 2009).

[4]See Philip Delves Broughton, "More Thank a Paycheck," *Wall Street Journal* (February 2, 2010), p. A17; and Daniel Pink, *Drive; The Surprising Truth about What Motivates Us* (New York: Riverhead Books, 2009).

[5]Information from Melinda Beck, "If at First You Don't Succeed, You're in Excellent Company," *Wall Street Journal* (April 29, 2008), p. D1.

[6]Information from Jerry Krueger and Emily Killham, "At Work, Feeling Good Matters," *Gallup Management Journal* (December 8, 2005): gmj.gallup.com; and, Ellen Wulfhorst, "Morale Is Low, Say Quarter of Employers in Poll," *Reuters Bulletin* (November 17, 2009): reuters.com.

[7]See Paul Glader, "Firms Move Gingerly to Remove Salary Cuts," *The Wall Street Journal* (March 1, 2010), pp. B, B7.

[8]See Abraham H. Maslow, *Eupsychian Management* (Homewood, IL: Richard D. Irwin, 1965); Abraham H. Maslow,

Motivation and Personality, 2d ed. (New York: Harper-Row, 1970). For a research perspective, see Mahmoud A. Wahba and Lawrence G. Bridwell, "Maslow Reconsidered: A Review of Research on the Need Hierarchy," *Organizational Behavior and Human Performance*, vol. 16 (1976), pp. 212–40.

[9]Teresa M. McAleavy, "Worker Dissatisfaction Up, Survey Finds," *Columbus Dispatch* (September 3, 2006), p. F2.

[10]See Clayton P. Alderfer, *Existence, Relatedness, and Growth* (New York: Free Press, 1972).

[11]Examples and quotes from Jane Hodges, "A Virtual Matchmaker for Volunteers," *Wall Street Journal* (February 12, 2009), p. D3; Dana Mattioli, "The Laid-Off Can Do Well Doing Good," *Wall Street Journal* (March 17, 2009), p. D1; Elizabeth Garone, "Paying It Forward Is a Full-Time Job," *Wall Street Journal* (March 17, 2009), p. D4.

[12]The two-factor theory is in Frederick Herzberg, Bernard Mausner, and Barbara Block Synderman, *The Motivation to Work*, 2d ed. (New York: Wiley, 1967); Frederick Herzberg, "One More Time: How Do You Motivate Employees?" *Harvard Business Review* (January–February 1968), pp. 53–62, and reprinted as an HBR classic (September–October 1987), pp. 109–20.

[13]Critical reviews are provided by Robert J. House and Lawrence A. Wigdor, "Herzberg's Dual-Factor Theory of Job Satisfaction and Motivation: A Review of the Evidence and a Criticism," *Personnel Psychology*, vol. 20 (Winter 1967), pp. 369–89; Steven Kerr, Anne Harlan, and Ralph Stogdill, "Preference for Motivator and Hygiene Factors in a Hypothetical Interview Situation," *Personnel Psychology*, vol. 27 (Winter 1974), pp. 109–24.

[14]Frederick Herzberg, "Workers' Needs: The Same around the World," *Industry Week* (September 21, 1987), pp. 29–32.

[15]For a collection of McClelland's work, see David C. McClelland, *The Achieving Society* (New York: Van Nostrand, 1961); "Business Drive and National Achievement," *Harvard Business Review*, vol. 40 (July–August 1962), pp. 99–112; David C. McClelland and David H. Burnham, "Power Is the Great Motivator," *Harvard Business Review* (March–April 1976), pp. 100–10; David C. McClelland, *Human Motivation* (Glenview, IL: Scott, Foresman, 1985); David C. McClelland and Richard E. Boyatsis, "The Leadership Motive Pattern and Long-Term Success in Management," *Journal of Applied Psychology*, vol. 67 (1982), pp. 737–43.

[16]Information from Nanette Byrnes and Jena McGregor, "CEO Pay: Is It Still Out of Synch?" *BusinessWeek* (September 7, 2009), pp. 22–24.

[17]Jeanne Sahadi, "CEO Pay: 364 Times More than Workers," *CNNMoney* (August 29, 2007): money.cnn.com/2007/08/28 (retrieved August 10, 2008); "2007 Trends in CEO Pay," AFL-CIO: aflcio.org/corporatewatch (retrieved August 10, 2008).

[18]See, for example, J. Stacy Adams, "Toward an Understanding of Inequity," *Journal of Abnormal and Social Psychology*, vol. 67 (1963), pp. 422–36; J. Stacy Adams, "Inequity in Social Exchange," in L. Berkowitz, ed., *Advances in Experimental Social Psychology*, vol. 2 (New York: Academic Press, 1965), pp. 267–300.

[19]See, for example, J. W. Harder, "Play for Pay: Effects of Inequity in a Pay-for-Performance Context," *Administrative Science Quarterly*, vol. 37 (1992), pp. 321–35.

[20]Victor H. Vroom, *Work and Motivation* (New York: Wiley, 1964; republished by Jossey-Bass, 1994).

[21]Ibid.

[22]The work on goal-setting theory is well summarized in Edwin A. Locke and Gary P. Latham, *Goal Setting: A Motivational Technique That Works!* (Englewood Cliffs, NJ: Prentice Hall, 1984). See also Edwin A. Locke, Kenneth N. Shaw, Lisa A. Saari, and Gary P. Latham, "Goal Setting and Task Performance

1969–1980," *Psychological Bulletin*, vol. 90 (1981), pp. 125–52; Mark E. Tubbs, "Goal Setting: A Meta-Analytic Examination of the Empirical Evidence," *Journal of Applied Psychology*, vol. 71 (1986), pp. 474–83; Gary P. Latham and Edwin A. Locke, "Self-Regulation Through Goal Setting," *Organizational Behavior and Human Decision Processes*, vol. 50 (1991), pp. 212–47; and Terence R. Mitchell, Kenneth R. Thompson, and Jane George-Falvy, "Goal Setting: Theory and Practice," Chapter 9 in Cary L. Cooper and Edwin A. Locke (eds), *Industrial and Organizational Psychology: Linking Theory with Practice* (Malden, MA: Blackwell Business, 2000), pp. 211–49.

[23]Albert Bandura, *Social Learning Theory* (Englewood Cliffs, NJ: Prentice-Hall, 1977); and Albert Bandura, *Self-Efficacy: The Exercise of Control* (New York: W. H. Freeman, 1997).

[24]Quote from www.des.emory.edu/mfp/self--efficacy.html.

[25]Beck, op. cit.

[26]Bandura, op. cit., 1977 and 1997.

[27]E. L. Thorndike, *Animal Intelligence* (New York: Macmillan, 1911), p. 244.

[28]See B. F. Skinner, *Walden Two* (New York: Macmillan, 1948); *Science and Human Behavior* (New York: Macmillan, 1953); *Contingencies of Reinforcement* (New York: Appleton-Century-Crofts, 1969).

[29]Fred Luthans and Robert Kreitner, *Organizational Behavior Modification* (Glenview, IL: Scott, Foresman, 1975); and Fred Luthans and Robert Kreitner, *Organizational Behavior Modification and Beyond* (Glenview, IL: Scott, Foresman, 1985); see also Fred Luthans and Alexander D. Stajkovic, "Reinforce for Performance: The Need to Go Beyond Pay and Even Rewards," *Academy of Management Executive*, vol. 13 (1999), pp. 49–57.

[30]Knowledge@Wharton, "The Importance of Being Richard Branson," Wharton School Publishing (June 3, 2005): www.whartonsp.com.

[31]Information and quote from Frederik Broden, "Motivate Without Spending Millions," *Fortune*, Kindle edition (April 13, 2010).

[32]Richard Gibson, "Pitchman in the Corner Office," *Wall Street Journal* (October 24, 2007), p. D10. See also David Novak, *The Education of an Accidental CEO: Lessons Learned from the Trailer Park to the Corner Office* (New York: Crown Business, 2007).

[33]Broden, op cit.

[34]For a review, see Arne L. Kalleberg, "The Mismatched Worker: When People Don't Fit their Jobs," *Academy of Management Perspectives* (February 2008), pp. 24–40.

[35]See Frederick W. Taylor, *The Principles of Scientific Management* (New York: W.W. Norton, 1967), originally published by Harper-Brothers in 1911; and, Robert Kanigel, *The One Best Way* (New York: Viking, 1997).

[36]Greg R. Oldham and J. Richard Hackman, "Not What It Was and Not What It Will Be: The Future of Job Design Research," *Journal of Organizational Behavior*, vol. 31 (2010), pp. 463–479.

[37]See Frederick Herzberg, Bernard Mausner, and Barbara Block Synderman, *The Motivation to Work*, 2d ed. (New York: Wiley, 1967). The quotation is from Frederick Herzberg, "One More Time: Employees?" *Harvard Business Review* (January–February 1968), pp. 53–62, and reprinted as an HBR Classic in September–October 1987, pp. 109–20.

[38]For a complete description of the core characteristics model, see J. Richard Hackman and Greg R. Oldham, *Work Redesign* (Reading, MA: Addison-Wesley, 1980). See also, Oldham and Hackman, op. cit. (2010).

[39]See Allen R. Cohen and Herman Gadon, *Alternative Work Schedules: Integrating Individual and Organizational Needs* (Reading,

MA: Addison-Wesley, 1978), p. 125; Simcha Ronen and Sophia B. Primps, "The Compressed Work Week as Organizational Change: Behavioral and Attitudinal Outcomes," *Academy of Management Review*, vol. 6 (1981), pp. 61–74.

[40]Sue Shellenbarger, "What Makes a Company a Great Place to Work," *Wall Street Journal* (October 4, 2007), p. D1.

[41]Information from Lesli Hicks, "Workers, Employers Praise Their Four-Day Workweek," *Columbus Dispatch* (August 22, 1994), p. 6; and Walsh, op. cit., 2001.

[42]For a review, see Wayne F. Cascio, "Managing a Virtual Workplace," *Academy of Management Executive*, vol. 14 (2000), pp. 81–90.

[43]Quote from Phil Porter, "Telecommuting Mom Is Part of a National Trend," *Columbus Dispatch* (November 29, 2000), pp. H1, H2.

[44]Information and quotes from Sudeep Reddy, "Wary Companies Rely on Temporary Workers," *The Wall Street Journal* (March 6–7, 2010), p. A. 4; and, Peter Coy, Michelle Conlin, and Moira Herbst, "The Disposable Worker," *BusinessWeek* (January 18, 2010), pp. 33–39.

[45]Kris Maher, "Slack U.S. Demand Spurs Cut in Work Hours," *Wall Street Journal* (January 8, 2008), *Career Journal*, p. 29.

[46]Michael Orey, "They're Employees, No, They're Not," *BusinessWeek* (November 16, 2009), pp. 73–74.

[47]This survey was developed from a set of "Gallup Engagement Questions" presented in John Thackray, "Feedback for Real," *Gallup Management Journal* (March 15, 2001), retrieved from http://gmj.gallup.com/management_articles/employee_engagement/article.asp?i=238&p=1, June 5, 2003; data reported from James K. Harter, "The Cost of Disengaged Workers," *Gallup Poll* (March 13, 2001).

[48]Developed from Brian Dumaine, "Why Do We Work?" *Fortune* (December 26, 1994), pp. 196–204.

Feature Notes

Real Ethics—Information from Jared Sandberg, "Why You May Regret Looking at Papers Left on the Office Copier," *Wall Street Journal* (June 20, 2006), p. B1.

Real People—Information from "HopeLab Video Games for Health," *Fast Company* (December 2008/January 2009), p. 116; Oliver J. Chang, "Apps and Videogames to Keep You Healthy," www.forbes.com/2010/01/20 (accessed February 6, 2010); and www.hopelab.org.

Photo Essays

Rockwell Collins—Information and quotes from Dana Mattioli, "Rewards for Extra Work Come Cheap in Lean Times," *Columbus Dispatch* (January 4, 2010), p. B7. Quarterback Coach—Information and quotes from Tim May, "Life's Calling for Siciliano," *Columbus Dispatch*, *Game Day* (October 24, 2009), pp. 12–14. Pitney Bowes—Information and quote from Samantha Critchell, "Change Likely to Be Incremental as New Year Unfolds," *Columbus Dispatch* (January 2, 2010), p. D1.

Chapter 16

Endnotes

[1]Information and quotes from Allen St. John, "Racing's Fastest Pit Crew," *Wall Street Journal* (May 9, 2008), p. W4; and, Bonnie Berkowitz, "Pit Crews Keep NASCAR Racers on Track," *Columbus Dispatch* (May 28, 2008), p. D6.

[2]Information from Scott Thurm, "Teamwork Raises Everyone's Game," *Wall Street Journal* (November 7, 2005), p. B7.

[3]Ibid.

[4]Chambers quote from Charles O'Reilly III and Jeffrey Pfeffer, *Hidden Value: How Great Companies Achieve Extraordinary Results through Ordinary People* (Boston: Harvard Business School Publishing, 2000), p. 4; other quotes from www.quotegarden.com.

[5]For a discussion, see Jon R. Katzenbach and Douglas K. Smith, *The Wisdom of Teams: Creating the High Performance Organization* (Boston: Harvard Business School Press, 1993).

[6]Lynda C. McDermott, Nolan Brawley, and William A. Waite, *World-Class Teams: Working across Borders* (New York: Wiley, 1998), p. 5; "White Collar Workers Shoulder Together—Like It or Not," *BusinessWeek* (April 28, 2008), p. 58.

[7]See, for example, Edward E. Lawler III, Susan Albers Mohrman, and Gerald E. Ledford Jr., *Employee Involvement and Total Quality Management: Practices and Results in Fortune 1000 Companies* (San Francisco: Jossey-Bass, 1992); Susan A. Mohrman, Susan A. Cohen, and Monty A. Mohrman, *Designing Team-based Organizations: New Forms for Knowledge Work* (San Francisco: Jossey-Bass, 1995).

[8]Katzenbach and Smith, op. cit.

[9]Joe Lindsey, "Nine Riders, and Nearly as Many Jobs." *Wall Street Journal* (July 9, 2008): www.online.wsj.com.

[10]Harold J. Leavitt, "Suppose We Took Groups More Seriously," in Eugene L. Cass and Frederick G. Zimmer (Eds.), *Man and Work in Society* (New York: Van Nostrand Reinhold, 1975), pp. 67–77.

[11]A classic work is Bib Latané, Kipling Williams, and Stephen Harkins, "Many Hands Make Light the Work: The Causes and Consequences of Social Loafing," *Journal of Personality and Social Psychology*, vol. 37 (1978), pp. 822–32.

[12]John M. George, "Extrinsic and Intrinsic Origins of Perceived Social Loafing in Organizations," *Academy of Management Journal* (March 1992), pp. 191–202; and W. Jack Duncan, "Why Some People Loaf in Groups While Others Loaf Alone," *Academy of Management Executive*, vol. 8 (1994), pp. 79–80.

[13]See Marvin E. Shaw, *Group Dynamics: The Psychology of Small Group Behavior*, 2d ed. (New York: McGraw-Hill, 1976); Harold J. Leavitt, "Suppose We Took Groups More Seriously," in Eugene L. Cass and Frederick G. Zimmer, eds., *Man and Work in Society* (New York: Van Nostrand Reinhold, 1975), pp. 67–77.

[14]For insights on how to conduct effective meetings, see Mary A. De Vries, *How to Run a Meeting* (New York: Penguin, 1994).

[15]Developed from Eric Matson, "The Seven Sins of Deadly Meetings," *Fast Company* (April/May 1996).

[16]Survey reported in "Meetings among Top Ten Time Wasters," *San Francisco Business Times* (April 7, 2003): www.bizjournals.com/sanfrancisco/stories/2003/04/07/daily21.html.

[17]Matson, op. cit., p. 122.

[18]The "linking pin" concept is introduced in Rensis Likert, *New Patterns of Management* (New York: McGraw-Hill, 1962).

[19]See Susan D. Van Raalte, "Preparing the Task Force to Get Good Results," *S.A.M. Advanced Management Journal*, vol. 47 (Winter 1982), pp. 11–16; Walter Kiechel III, "The Art of the Corporate Task Force," *Fortune* (January 28, 1991), pp. 104–6.

[20]Information from Jenny C. McCune, "Making Lemonade," *Management Review* (June 1997), pp. 49–53.

[21]Matt Golosinski, "With Teamwork, Gregg Steinhafel Hits the Bulls Eye at Target," *Kellogg* (Summer 2007), p. 32.

[22]For a good discussion of quality circles, see Edward E. Lawler III and Susan A. Mohrman, "Quality Circles after the Fad," *Harvard Business Review*, vol. 63 (January/February 1985), pp. 65–71.

[23]See Wayne F. Cascio, "Managing a Virtual Workplace," *Academy of Management Executive*, vol. 14 (2000), pp. 81–90; Sheila Simsarian Webber, "Virtual Teams: A Meta-Analysis," http://www.shrm.org/foundation/findings.asp; Stacie A. Furst, Martha Reeves, Benson Rosen, and Richard S. Blackburn, "Managing the Life Cycle of Virtual Teams," *Academy of Management Executive*, vol. 18 (2004), pp. 6–20; and, J. Richard Hackman and Nancy Katz, "Group Behavior and Performance," Chapter 32 (pp. 1208-1251) in Susan T. Fiske, Daniel T. Gilbert, and Gardner Lindzey (Eds.), *Handbook of Social Psychology*, Fifth Edition (Hoboken, NJ: John Wiley & Sons, 2010).

[24]Example from Phred Dvorak, "How Teams Can Work Well Together from Far Apart," *Wall Street Journal* (September 17, 2007), p. B4.

[25]William M. Bulkeley, "Computerizing Dull Meetings Is Touted as an Antidote to the Mouth That Bored," *Wall Street Journal* (January 28, 1992), pp. B1, B2.

[26]R. Brent Gallupe and William H. Cooper, "Brainstorming Electronically," *Sloan Management Review* (Winter 1997), pp. 11–21; Cascio, op. cit; Hackman and Katz, op. cit.

[27]Cascio, op. cit.; Furst et al., op. cit.

[28]See, for example, Paul S. Goodman, Rukmini Devadas, and Terri L. Griffith Hughson, "Groups and Productivity: Analyzing the Effectiveness of Self-Managing Teams," Chapter 11 in John R. Campbell and Richard J. Campbell, *Productivity in Organizations* (San Francisco: Jossey-Bass, 1988); Jack Orsbrun, Linda Moran, Ed Musslewhite, and John H. Zenger, with Craig Perrin, *Self-Directed Work Teams: The New American Challenge* (Homewood, IL: Business One Irwin, 1990); Dale E. Yeatts and Cloyd Hyten, *High Performing Self-Managed Work Teams* (Thousand Oaks, CA: Sage, 1997).

[29]Bradley L. Kirkman and Debra L. Shapiro, "The Impact of Cultural Values on Employee Resistance to Teams: Toward a Model of Globalized Self-Managing Work Team Effectiveness," *Academy of Management Review*, vol. 22 (1997), pp. 730–57.

[30]Edgar Schein, *Process Consultation* (Reading, MA: Addison-Wesley, 1988), pp. 69–75.

[31]A good overview is William D. Dyer, *Team-Building* (Reading, MA: Addison-Wesley, 1977).

[32]Dennis Berman, "Zap! Pow! Splat!" *BusinessWeek*, Enterprise issue (February 9, 1998), p. ENT22.

[33]For a discussion of effectiveness in the context of top management teams, see Edward E. Lawler III, David Finegold, and Jay A. Conger, "Corporate Boards: Developing Effectiveness at the Top," in Mohrman, op. cit. (1998), pp. 23–50.

[34]Quote from Alex Markels, "Money & Business," *U.S. News online* (October 22, 2006).

[35]For a review of research on group effectiveness, see J. Richard Hackman, "The Design of Work Teams," in Jay W. Lorsch (ed.), *Handbook of Organizational Behavior* (Englewood Cliffs, NJ: Prentice-Hall, 1987), pp. 315–42; and J. Richard Hackman, Ruth Wageman, Thomas M. Ruddy, and Charles L. Ray, "Team Effectiveness in Theory and Practice," Chapter 5 in Cary L. Cooper and Edwin A. Locke, *Industrial and Organizational Psychology: Linking Theory with Practice* (Malden, MA: Blackwell, 2000).

[36]Ibid; Lawler et al., op. cit., 1998; Linda Hill and Michel J. Anteby, "Analyzing Work Groups," *Harvard Business School*, 9-407-032 (August 2007).

[37]Example from "Designed for Interaction," *Fortune* (January 8, 2001), p. 150.

[38]See, for example, Lynda Gratton and Tamara J. Erickson, "Eight Ways to Build Collaborative Teams," *Harvard Business Review*, Reprint R0711F (November 2007).

[39]Information from Susan Carey, "Racing to Improve," *Wall Street Journal* (March 24, 2006). pp. B1, B6.

[40]Robert D. Hof, "Amazon's Risky Bet," *BusinessWeek* (November 13, 2006), p. 52.

[41]Information from Carol Hymowitz, "Managers Err If They Limit Their Hiring to People Just Like Them," *Wall Street Journal* (October 12, 2004), p. B1.

[42]Casey Stengel, www.quotegarden.com.

[43]Shaw, op. cit.

[44]See Warren Watson, "Cultural Diversity's Impact on Interaction Process and Performance," *Academy of Management Journal*, vol. 16 (1993); Christopher Earley and Elaine Mosakowski, "Creating Hybrid Team Structures: An Empirical Test of Transnational Team Functioning," *Academy of Management Journal*, vol. 5 (February 2000), pp. 26–49; Jeanne Brett, Kristin Behfar, and Mary C. Kern, "Managing Multicultural Teams," *Harvard Business Review* (November 2006), pp. 84–91.

[45]J. Steven Heinen and Eugene Jacobson, "A Model of Task Group Development in Complex Organizations and a Strategy of Implementation," *Academy of Management Review*, vol. 1 (1976), pp. 98–111; Bruce W. Tuckman, "Developmental Sequence in Small Groups," *Psychological Bulletin*, vol. 63 (1965), pp. 384–99; Bruce W. Tuckman and Mary Ann C. Jensen, "Stages of Small-Group Development Revisited," *Group Organization Studies*, vol. 2 (1977), pp. 419–27.

[46]See, for example, Edgar Schein, *Process Consultation* (Reading, MA: Addison-Wesley, 1988); and Linda C. McDermott, Nolan Brawley, and William A. Waite, *World-Class Teams: Working across Borders* (New York: Wiley, 1998).

[47]For a good discussion, see Robert F. Allen and Saul Pilnick, "Confronting the Shadow Organization: How to Detect and Defeat Negative Norms," *Organizational Dynamics* (Spring 1973), pp. 13–16.

[48]See Schein, op. cit., pp. 76–79.

[49]Ibid.; Shaw, op. cit.

[50]A classic work in this area is K. Benne and P. Sheets, "Functional Roles of Group Members," *Journal of Social Issues*, vol. 2 (1948), pp. 42–47; see also Likert, op. cit., pp. 166–69; Schein, op. cit., pp. 49–56.

[51]Based on John R. Schermerhorn Jr., James G. Hunt, and Richard N. Osborn, *Organizational Behavior*, 9th ed. (New York: Wiley, 2005).

[52]Research on communication networks is found in Alex Bavelas, "Communication Patterns in Task-Oriented Groups," *Journal of the Acoustical Society of America*, vol. 22 (1950), pp. 725–30; Shaw, op. cit.

[53]See Victor H. Vroom and Arthur G. Jago, *The New Leadership: Managing Participation in Organizations* (Englewood Cliffs, NJ: Prentice-Hall, 1988); Victor H. Vroom, "A New Look in Managerial Decision-Making," *Organizational Dynamics* (Spring 1973), pp. 66–80; Victor H. Vroom and Phillip Yetton, *Leadership and Decision-Making* (Pittsburgh: University of Pittsburgh Press, 1973).

[54]Norman F. Maier, "Assets and Liabilities in Group Problem Solving," *Psychological Review*, vol. 74 (1967), pp. 239–49.

[55]Schein, op. cit.

[56]See Kathleen M. Eisenhardt, Jean L. Kahwajy, and L. J. Bourgeois III, "How Management Teams Can Have a Good Fight," *Harvard Business Review* (July–August 1997), pp. 77–85.

[57]Consensus box developed from a classic article by Jay Hall, "Decisions, Decisions, Decisions," *Psychology Today* (November 1971), pp. 55–56.

[58]See Maier, op. cit.

⁵⁹See Irving L. Janis, "Groupthink," *Psychology Today* (November 1971), pp. 43–46; *Victims of Groupthink*, 2d ed. (Boston: Houghton Mifflin, 1982).

⁶⁰These techniques are well described in Andre L. Delbecq, Andrew H. Van de Ven, and David H. Gustafson, *Group Techniques for Program Planning* (Glenview, IL: Scott, Foresman, 1975).

⁶¹Information and quote from Emily Maltby, "Boring Meetings? Get Out the Water Guns," *Wall Street Journal* (January 7, 2010), p. B5.

⁶²Information from Kelly K. Spors, "Productive Brainstorms Take the Right Mix of Elements," *Wall Street Journal* (July 28, 2008): www.wsj.online.com.

⁶³Delbecq et al., op. cit.

⁶⁴Developed from Lynda McDermott, Nolan Brawley, and William Waite, *World-Class Teams: Working across Borders* (New York: Wiley, 1998).

⁶⁵Adapted from William Dyer, *Team Building*, 2nd ed. (Reading, MA: Addison-Wesley, 1987), pp. 123–25.

Feature Notes

Real Ethics—For research see Bib Latané, Kipling Williams, and Stephen Harkins, "Many Hands Make Light the Work: The Causes and Consequences of Social Loafing," *Journal of Personality and Social Psychology*, vol. 37 (1978), pp. 822–32; and W. Jack Duncan, "Why Some People Loaf in Groups and Others Loaf Alone," *Academy of Management Executive*, vol. 8 (1994), pp. 79–80.

Photo Essay Notes

Teamwork and Productivity—Survey data reported in "Two Wasted Days at Work," *CNNMoney.com* (March 16, 2005): www.cnnmoney.com. Reality Team Building—Information from Reena Jana, "Real Life Imitates *Real World*," *BusinessWeek* (March 23 & 30, 2009), p. 42. Amazon.com—Information and quotes from Robert D. Hof, "Amazon's Risky Bet," *BusinessWeek* (November 13, 2006), p. 52; Jon Neale, "Jeff Bezos," *BusinessWings* (February 16, 2007): www.businesswings.com.uk;" Alan Deutschman, "Inside the Mind of Jeff Bezos," *Fast Company* (December 19, 2007); www.fastcompany.com/magazine/85.

Chapter 17

Endnotes

¹Information from American Management Association. "The Passionate Organization Fast-Response Survey," September 25–29, 2000, and organization website: http://www.amanct.org/aboutama/index.htm.

²Data from "Is the Workplace Getting Raunchier?" *BusinessWeek* (March 17, 2008), p. 19.

³"Cultivating Personal Awareness," *BizEd* (May/June 2009), p. 26.

⁴"Ranking the Attributes," *Wall Street Journal* (September 20, 2006), p. R3.

⁵"Relationships Are the Most Powerful Form of Media," *Fast Company* (March 2001), p. 100.

⁶Henry Mintzberg, *The Nature of Managerial Work* (New York: Harper-Row, 1973).

⁷John P. Kotter, "What Effective General Managers Really Do," *Harvard Business Review*, vol. 60 (November–December 1982), pp. 156–57; and *The General Managers* (New York: Macmillan, 1986).

⁸Examples and quotes from *BusinessWeek* (July 8, 1991), pp. 60–61; www.ccl.org/leadership/programs/profiles/lisaDitullio.

aspx (retrieved August 12, 2008); and, Joe Walker, "Executives Learn New Skills to Improve their Communication," *The Wall Street Journal* (May 6, 2010), p. B3.

⁹Jay A. Conger, *Winning 'Em Over: A New Model for Managing in the Age of Persuasion* (New York: Simon & Schuster, 1998), pp. 24–79.

¹⁰Ibid.

¹¹*BusinessWeek* (February 10, 1992), pp. 102–8.

¹²Information and quotes from "Undercover Boss Gets the Communication Message," *Financial Times* (June 9, 2009).

¹³Tom Peters and Nancy Austin, *A Passion for Excellence* (New York: Random House, 1985); and, "Epigrams and Insights from the original Modern Guru," *Financial Times*, Kindle Edition (March 4, 2010). See also Tom Peters, *The Little Big Things: 163 Ways to Pursue EXCELLENCE* (New York: HarperStudio, 2010).

¹⁴See Robert H. Lengel and Richard L. Daft, "The Selection of Communication Media as an Executive Skill," *Academy of Management Executive*, vol. 2 (August 1988), pp. 225–32.

¹⁵Information from Sam Dillon, "What Corporate America Can't Build: A Sentence," *New York Times* (December 7, 2004).

¹⁶See Eric Matson, "Now That We Have Your Complete Attention," *Fast Company* (February–March 1997), pp. 124–32.

¹⁷Martin J. Gannon, *Paradoxes of Culture and Globalization* (Los Angeles: Sage, 2008), p. 76.

¹⁸David McNeill, *Hand and Mind: What Gestures Reveal about Thought* (Chicago: University of Chicago Press, 1992).

¹⁹Adapted from Richard V. Farace, Peter R. Monge, and Hamish M. Russell, *Communicating and Organizing* (Reading, MA: Addison-Wesley, 1977), pp. 97–98.

²⁰Information from Carol Hymowitz, "More American Chiefs Are Taking Top Posts at Overseas Concerns," *Wall Street Journal* (October 17, 2005), p. B1.

²¹Examples reported in Martin J. Gannon, *Paradoxes of Culture and Globalization* (Los Angeles: Sage Publications, 2008), p. 80.

²²Ibid.

²³Information from Ben Brown, "Atlanta Out to Mind Its Manners," *USA Today* (March 14, 1996), p. 7.

²⁴See Edward T. Hall, *The Silent Language* (New York: Doubleday, 1973).

²⁵Information and quotes from Adam Bryant, "Creating Trust by Destroying Hierarchy," *The Global Edition of the New York Times* (February 15, 2010), p. 19.

²⁶Nanette Byrnes, "A Steely Resolve," *BusinessWeek* (April 6, 2009), p. 54.

²⁷Information and quote from Kelly K. Spors, "Top Small Workplaces 2009," *Wall Street Journal* (September 28, 2009), pp. R1–R4.

²⁸See for example John Freeman, *The Tyranny of E-mail* (New York: Scribner, 2009).

²⁹See Lengel and Daft, op. cit. (1988).

³⁰Information and quotes from Sarah E. Needleman, "Thnx for the IView! I Wud Luv to Work 4 U!!)," *Wall Street Journal Online* (July 31, 2008).

³¹For a review of legal aspects of e-mail privacy, see William P. Smith and Filiz Tabak, "Monitoring Employee E-mails: Is There Any Room for Privacy?" *Academy of Management Perspectives*, vol. 23 (November 2009), pp. 33–48.

³²Information and quotes from Michelle Conlin and Douglas MacMillan, "Managing the Tweets," *BusinessWeek* (June 1, 2009), pp. 20–21.

³³"Tread: Rethinking the Workplace," *BusinessWeek* (September 25, 2006), p. IN.

³⁴Information from "'Roberts' Quits Rumor Only a Class Exercise," *The Columbus Dispatch* (March 6, 2010), p. A5.

³⁵Conlin and MacMillan, op. cit.

[36]Stephanie Clifford, "Video Prank at Domino's Taints Brand," *New York Times* (April 16, 2009): www.nytimes.com; and, Deborah Stead, "An Unwelcome Delivery," *BusinessWeek* (May 4, 2009), p. 15.

[37]This discussion is based on Carl R. Rogers and Richard E. Farson, "Active Listening" (Chicago: Industrial Relations Center of the University of Chicago, n.d.); see also Carl R. Rogers and Fritz J. Roethlisberger, "Barriers and Gateways to Communication," *Harvard Business Review* (November–December 2001), Reprint 91610.

[38]Ibid.

[39]Sue de Wine, *The Consultant's Craft* (Boston: Bedford/St. Martin's Press, 2001), pp. 307–14.

[40]A useful source of guidelines is John J. Gabarro and Linda A. Hill, "Managing Performance," Note 996022 (Boston: Harvard Business School Publishing, n.d.).

[41]Carol Hymowitz, "Managers See Feedback from Their Staffers as Most Valuable," *Wall Street Journal* (August 22, 2000), p. B1.

[42]Developed from John Anderson, "Giving and Receiving Feedback," in Paul R. Lawrence, Louis B. Barnes, and Jay W. Lorsch, eds., *Organizational Behavior and Administration*, 3rd ed. (Homewood, IL: Richard D. Irwin, 1976), p. 109.

[43]A classic work on proxemics is Edward T. Hall's book, *The Hidden Dimension* (Garden City, NY: Doubleday, 1986).

[44]Information from Rachel Metz, "Office Décor First Change by New AOI Executive," *Columbus Dispatch* (May 25, 2009), p. A7.

[45]Mirand Weill, "Alternative Spaces Spawning Desk-Free Zones," *Columbus Dispatch* (May 18, 1998), pp. 10–11.

[46]"Tread: Rethinking the Workplace."

[47]Amy Saunders, "A Creative Approach to Work," *Columbus Dispatch* (May 2, 2008), pp. C1, C9.

[48]Richard E. Walton, *Interpersonal Peacemaking: Confrontations and Third-Party Consultation* (Reading, MA: Addison-Wesley, 1969), p. 2.

[49]See Robert R. Blake and Jane Strygley Mouton, "The Fifth Achievement," *Journal of Applied Behavioral Science*, vol. 6 (1970), pp. 413–27; Alan C. Filley, *Interpersonal Conflict Resolution* (Glenview, IL: Scott, Foresman, 1975).

[50]Developed from Alan C. Filley, *Interpersonal Conflict Resolution* (Glenview, IL: Scott, Foresman, 1975).

[51]See Kenneth W. Thomas, "Conflict and Conflict Management," in M. D. Dunnett, ed., *Handbook of Industrial and Organizational Behavior* (Chicago: Rand McNally, 1976), pp. 889–935.

[52]See, for example, Robert Moskowitz, "How to Negotiate and Increase," www.worktree.com (retrieved March 8, 2007); Mark Gordon, "Negotiating What You're Worth," *Harvard Management Communication Letter*, vol. 2, no. 1 (Winter 2005); and Dona DeZube, "Salary Negotiation Know-How," www.monster.com (retrieved March 8, 2007).

[53]Portions of this treatment of negotiation originally adapted from John R. Schermerhorn, Jr., James G. Hunt, and Richard N. Osborn, *Managing Organizational Behavior*, 4th ed. (New York: Wiley, 1991), pp. 382–87. Used by permission.

[54]See Roger Fisher and William Ury, *Getting to Yes: Negotiating Agreement Without Giving In* (New York: Penguin, 1983); James A. Wall, Jr., *Negotiation: Theory and Practice* (Glenview, IL: Scott, Foresman, 1985); William L. Ury, Jeanne M. Brett, and Stephen B. Goldberg, *Getting Disputes Resolved* (San Francisco: Jossey-Bass, 1997).

[55]Fisher and Ury, op. cit.

[56]Matson, op. cit.

[57]Example from Bert Spector, "An Interview with Roger Fisher and William Ury," *Academy of Management Executive*, vol. 18 (2004), pp. 101–12.

[58]Fisher and Ury, op. cit..

[59]Developed from Max H. Bazerman, *Judgment in Managerial Decision Making*, 4th ed. (New York: Wiley, 1998), Chapter 7.

[60]Fisher and Ury, op. cit.

[61]"A Classes Grapher's Care," *Kellogg* (Summer 2006), p. 40.

[62]Roy J. Lewicki and Joseph A. Litterer, *Negotiation* (Homewood, IL: Irwin, 1985).

[63]This instrument is described in Carsten K. W. De Drew, Arne Evers, Bianca Beersma, Esther S. Kluwer, and Aukje Nauta, "A Theory-Based Measure of Conflict Management Strategies in the Workplace," *Journal of Organizational Behavior*, vol. 22 (2001), pp. 645–68. Used by permission.

[64]Feedback questionnaire is from Judith R. Gordon, *A Diagnostic Approach to Organizational Behavior*, 3rd ed. (Boston: Allyn & Bacon, 1991), p. 298. Used by permission.

Feature Notes

Real Ethics—Information from Bridget Jones, Blogger Fire Fury, CNN.com (July 19, 2006).

Real People—Information and quotes from Anya Kamenetz, "Will NPR Save the News?" *Fast Company* (March 18, 2009): www.Fastcompany.com.

Photo Essay Notes

Sam Walton—Quotations from John Huey, "America's Most Successful Merchant," *Fortune* (September 23, 1991), pp. 46–59; see also Sam Walton and John Huey, *Sam Walton: Made in America: My Story* (New York: Bantam Books, 1993).

Hammond's Candies—Information and quotes from Teri Evans, "Entrepreneurs Seek to Elicit Workers' Ideas," *Wall Street Journal* (December 29, 2009), p. B7.

Electronic Privacy—Information from American Management Association, "Electronic Monitoring & Surveillance Survey" (February 8, 2008): www.press.amanet.org/press-releases; and Liz Wolgemuth, "Why Web Surfing is a Nonproblem, *U.S. News & World Report* (August 22, 2008): www.usnews.com/blogs.

Chapter 18

Endnotes

[1]Quotes from, "Chick-fil-A Reaches 20,000[th] Scholarship Milestone" (July 28, 2005), Chick-fil-A press release: www.csrwire.com; Daniel Yee, "Chick-fil-A Recipe Winning Customers," *Columbus Dispatch* (September 9, 2006), p. D1; Tom Murphy, "Chick-fil-A plans aggressive product rollout initiatives," *Rocky Mount Telegram* (May 28, 2008), retrieved from: www.rockymounttelegram.com; and Robert D. Reid, "Ethical Business Leadership in Action," *BGS International Exchange*, Vol. 7 (Summer, 2008), pp. 14, 15.

[2]Information from Beth Howard, "The Secrets of Resilient People," *AARP* (November–December 2009), pp. 26, 37; Resiliency Quick Test developed from "How Resilient Are You?" *AARP* (November–December 2009), p. 37.

[3]The problems with quality and product recalls with Toyota were widely described in the news media during January/February 2010. See, for example, Sharon Terlep and Josh Mitchell, "U.S. Widens Toyota Probe to Electronics," *Wall Street Journal* (February 4, 2010), pp. B1, B12.

[4]Quote from "An Open Letter to Toyota Customers," *Columbus Dispatch* (February 4, 2010), p. A12.

[5]Quote from Gary Hamel, "Today's Companies Won't Make It, and Why?" *Fortune* (September 4, 2000), p. 386.

[6]"The Renewal Factor: Friendly Fact, Congenial Controls," *BusinessWeek* (September 14, 1987), p. 105.

[7]Rob Cross and Lloyd Baird, "Technology Is Not Enough: Improving Performance by Building Institutional Memory," *Sloan Management Review* (Spring 2000), p. 73.

[8]Information from Pep Sappal, "Integrated Inclusion Initiative," *Wall Street Journal* (October 3, 2006), p. A2.

[9]Based on discussion by Harold Koontz and Cryril O'Donnell, *Essentials of Management* (New York: McGraw-Hill, 1974), pp. 362–65; see also Cross and Baird, op. cit.

[10]See John F. Love, *McDonald's: Behind the Arches* (New York: Bantam Books, 1986); Ray Kroc and Robert Anderson, *Grinding It Out: The Making of McDonald's* (New York: St. Martin's Press, 1990).

[11]Information and quote from Gregg Segal, "Hyundai Smokes the Competition," *Financial Times* (January 5, 2010).

[12]Information from Jay Miller, "Toyota Halts Sales," *Wall Street Journal* (January 27, 2010), p. B2.

[13]This distinction is made in William G. Ouchi, "Markets, Bureaucracies and Clans," *Administrative Science Quarterly*, vol. 25 (1980), pp. 129–41.

[14]Douglas McGregor, *The Human Side of Enterprise* (New York: McGraw-Hill, 1960).

[15]See Sue Shellenbarger, "If You Need to Work Better, Maybe Try Working Less," *Wall Street Journal* (Septermber 23, 2009), p. D1.

[16]Examples from Alan Cane, "Are Virtual Offices a Benefit or Burden? *Irish Times* (July 14, 2006), p. 12.

[17]For an overview, see www.soxlaw.com

[18]Martin LaMonica, "Wal-Mart Readies Long-Term Move Into Solar Power," *CNET News.com* (January 3, 2007).

[19]Information from Leon E. Wynter, "Allstate Rates Managers on Handling Diversity," *Wall Street Journal* (October 1, 1997), p. B1.

[20]Information from Kathryn Kranhold, "U.S. Firms Raise Ethics Focus," *Wall Street Journal* (November 28, 2005), p. B4.

[21]Example from George Anders, "Management Guru Turns Focus to Orchestras, Hospitals," *Wall Street Journal* (November 21, 2005), pp. B1, B5.

[22]Information from Raju Narisetti, "For IBM, a Groundbreaking Sales Chief," *Wall Street Journal* (January 19, 1998), pp. B1, B5.

[23]The "hot stove rules" are developed from R. Bruce McAfee and William Poffenberger, *Productivity Strategies: Enhancing Employee Job Performance* (Englewood Cliffs, NJ: Prentice-Hall, 1982), pp. 54–55. They are originally attributed to Douglas McGregor, "Hot Stove Rules of Discipline," in G. Strauss and L. Sayles, eds., *Personnel: The Human Problems of Management* (Englewood Cliffs, NJ: Prentice-Hall, 1967).

[24]Information from Karen Carney, "Successful Performance Measurement: A Checklist," *Harvard Management Update* (No. U9911B), 1999.

[25]Robert S. Kaplan and David P. Norton, "The Balanced Scorecard: Measures That Drive Performance," *Harvard Business Review* (July–August 2005); see also Robert S. Kaplan and David P. Norton, *The Balanced Scorecard* (Cambridge, MA: Harvard Business School Press, 1996).

[26]Developed from Roy J. Lewicki, Donald D. Bowen, Douglas T. Hall, and Francine S. Hall, *Experiences in Management and Organizational Behavior*, 4th ed. (New York: Wiley, 1997), pp. 195–97.

Feature Notes

Real People—Information and quotes from "Who's Who on Obama's New Economic Advisory Board," LATimesBlog (February 6, 2009): www.latimesblogs.latimes.com; "'Diversify' Isn't Just Smart Financial Advice," *BlackMBA* (Winter, 2008/2009), p. 54; "*Black Enterprise* Announces 100 Most Powerful African Americans in Corporate America," Press Release (February 5, 2009): TIAA-CREF CEO Roger Ferguson Outlines Measures to Improve Retirement Security, www.tiaa-cref.org (February 3, 2010): accessed May 8, 2010.

Real Ethics—Paul Davidson, "'Climate Has Changed' for Data Privacy," *USA Today* (May 12, 2006), p. B1; Ben Elgin, "The Great Firewall of China," *BusinessWeek* (January 23, 2006), pp. 32–34; Alison Maitland, "Skype Says Text Messages Censored by Partner in China," *Financial Times* (April 19, 2006), p. 15; and, "Web Firms Criticized Over China," CNN.com (July 20, 2006).

Photo Essay Notes

Elsewhere Class—Information from Dalton Conley, "Welcome to Elsewhere," *Newsweek* (January 26, 2009), pp. 25–26.
Wikipedia—Information and quotes from Richard Waters, "Fact and Friction," *Financial Times* (January 2, 2010). See also Andrew Lih, *The Wikipedia Revolution: How a Bunch of Nobody's Created the World's Greatest Encyclopedia* (New York: Hyperion, 2009).
Employee Fraud—Information from Sarah E. Needleman, "Businesses Say Theft by Their Workers Is Up," *Wall Street Journal* (December 11, 2008), p. B8; Michelle Conlin, "To Catch a Corporate Thief," *Business Week* (February 16, 2009), p. 52; and Simona Covel, "Small Businesses Face More Fraud in Downturn," *Wall Street Journal* (February 19, 2009), p. B5.

Chapter 19

Endnotes

[1]Christina Passariello, "Louis Vuitton Tries Modern Methods on Assembly Line," *Wall Street Journal* (October 9, 2006).

[2]Mayo Clinic information from "Work–Life Balance: Ways to Restore Harmony and Reduce Stress," www.mayoclinic.com/heal/work-lifebalance (retrieved August 14, 2008).

[3]Examples from Gail Edmondson, "BMW's Dream Factory," *BusinessWeek* (October 16, 2006), pp. 68–80. Amy Merrick, "Asking 'What Would Ann Do?'" *Wall Street Journal* (September 16, 2006), pp. B1, B2.

[4]Information and quotes from Mark Yost, "At Ford Racing, Quality (Control) Is Job One," *Wall Street Journal* (February 4, 2010), p. D8.

[5]Good overviews are available in R. Dan Reid and Nada R. Sanders, *Operations Management: An Integrated Approach*, 2nd ed. (Hoboken, NJ: Wileys, 2006); and Roberta S. Russell and Bernard W. Taylor III, *Operations Management: Quality and Competitiveness in a Global Environment* (Hoboken, NJ: Wiley, 2005).

[6]"Survey Finds Workers Average Only Three Productive Days Per Week," www.microsoft.com/press/2005/mar05 (retrieved October 20, 2006).

[7]See Michael E. Porter, *Competitive Strategy: Techniques for Analyzing Industries and Competitors* (New York: Free Press, 1998) and *Competitive Advantage: Creating and Sustaining Superior Performance* (New York: Free Press, 1990); see also Richard A. D'Aveni, *Hyper-Competition: Managing the Dynamics of Strategic Maneuvering* (New York: Free Press, 1994).

[8]Information from ibid.

[9]Information and quote from Jonathan Wheatley, "Promise of

Growth Lures Carmakers," *Financial Times* (January 21, 2010). Kindle Edition.

[10]Joan Woodward, *Industrial Organization: Theory and Practice* (London: Oxford University Press, 1965; republished by Oxford University Press, 1994).

[11]Ian Rowley and Makiko Kitamura, "Autos: Why Japan's B-Team Is Hot," *BusinessWeek* (December 28, 2009 and January 4, 2010), p. 33.

[12]Brian Hindo, "Everything Old Is New Again," *BusinessWeek* (September 25, 2006), p. 70.

[13]See for example, Kenji Hall, "No One Does Lean Like the Japanese," *BusinessWeek* (July 10, 2006), pp. 40–41.

[14]This treatment is from James D. Thompson, *Organizations in Action* (New York: McGraw-Hill, 1967).

[15]Porter, op. cit., 1998.

[16]See, for example, Daniel Michaels and Peter Sanders, "Dreamliner Production Gets Closer Monitoring," *Wall Street Journal* (October 7, 2009), pp. B1, B2; and Peter Sanders, "Boeing Settles in for a Bumpy Ride," *Wall Street Journal* (October 7, 2009), p. B1.

[17]See Michael Hugos, *Essentials of Supply Chain Management*, 2nd ed. (Hoboken, NJ: Wiley, 2006).

[18]"Gauging the Wal-Mart Effect," *Wall Street Journal* (December 3–4, 2005), pp. Al, A9.

[19]See Joseph M. Juran, *Quality Control Handbook*, 3rd ed. (New York: McGraw-Hill, 1979) and "The Quality Trilogy: A Universal Approach to Managing for Quality," in *Total Quality Management*, H. Costin, ed. (New York: Dryden, 1994); W. Edwards Deming, *Out of Crisis* (Cambridge, MA: MIT Press, 1986) and "Deming's Quality Manifesto," *Best of Business Quarterly*, vol. 12 (Winter 1990–1991), pp. 6–10. See also Howard S. Gitlow and Shelly J. Gitlow, *The Deming Guide to Quality and Competitive Position* (Englewood Cliffs, NJ: Prentice-Hall, 1987), and Juran, op. cit. (1993).

[20]Rosabeth Moss Kanter, "Transcending Business Boundaries: 12,000 World Managers View Change," *Harvard Business Review* (May–June 1991), pp. 151–64.

[21]Dale Dauten, "Which One Would You Rather Be?" *St. Louis Dispatch* (October 8, 2006), p. C2.

[22]Information from Brian Hindo, "Satisfaction Not Guaranteed," *BusinessWeek* (June 19, 2006), pp. 32–38.

[23]See C. K. Prahalad, Patricia B. Ramaswamy, Jon R. Katzenbach, Chris Lederer, and Sam Hill, *Harvard Business Review on Customer Relationship Management* (Boston: Harvard Business School Publishing, 1998–2001).

[24]Information from "How Marriott Never Forgets a Guest," *BusinessWeek* (February 21, 2000), p. 74.

[25]Example and quote from Jena McGregor, "Customer Service Champs," *BusinessWeek* (March 3, 2008), pp. 37–42.

[26]For the classics, see W. Edwards Deming, *Quality, Productivity, and Competitive Position* (Cambridge, MA: MIT Press, 1982) and Juran, op. cit., 1979.

[27]http://www.nist.gov/public_affairs/factsheet/baldfaqs.htm.

[28]See Edward E. Lawler III, Susan Albers Mohrman, and Gerald E. Ledford Jr., *Employee Involvement and Total Quality Management: Practices and Results in Fortune 1000 Companies* (San Francisco: Jossey-Bass, 1992).

[29]Rafael Aguay, *Dr. Deming: The American Who Taught the Japanese about Quality* (New York: Free Press, 1997); W. Edwards Deming, op. cit. (1986).

[30]For the pros and cons of this approach see "Six Sigma: So Yesterday?" *BusinessWeek* (June 2007), Special Edition, p. IN 11.

[31]Michael Hammer, *Beyond Reengineering* (New York: Harper Business, 1997).

[32]Michael Hammer and James Champy, *Reengineering the Corporation: A Manifesto for Business Revolution*, rev. ed. (New York: Harper Business, 1999).

[33]Hammer, op. cit., p. 5; see also the discussion of processes in Gary Hamel, *Leading the Revolution* (Boston: Harvard Business School Press, 2000).

[34]Thomas M. Koulopoulos, *The Workflow Imperative* (New York: Van Nostrand Reinhold, 1995); Hammer, op. cit.

[35]Ronni T. Marshak, "Workflow Business Process Reengineering," special advertising section, *Fortune* (1997).

[36]A similar example is found in Hammer, op. cit., pp. 9, 10.

[37]Developed in part from "Quiz: How's Your Maths?" BBC News: newsvote.bbc.co.uk (retrieved August 15, 2008).

[38]Adapted from Bonnie McNeely, "Using the Tinker Toy Exercise to Teach the Four Functions of Management, *Journal of Management Education*, vol. 18, no. 4 (November 1994), pp. 468–72.

Feature Notes

Real Ethics—Information and quotes from Susan Chandler, "'Fair Trade' Label Enters Retail Market," *Columbus Dispatch* (October 16, 2006), p. G6; www.fairindigo.com/about.

Real People—Information and quotes from Dan Gearino, "Managing Change," *Columbus Dispatch* (January 24, 2010), p. D1; http://www.allpar.com/corporate/cerberus/kidder.html (accessed January 26, 2010).

Photo Essay Notes

Racing Engines—Information and quotes from Mark Yost, "At Ford Racing, Quality (Control) Is Job One," *Wall Street Journal* (February 4, 2010), p. D8. Dr. Devi Shetty—Information and quote from Geeta Anand, "The Henry Ford of Heart Surgery," *Wall Street Journal* (November 21-22, 2009), pp. A1, A12. Ryanair—Information from Daniel Michaels, "O'Leary Pilots Ryanair into Lead with 'Mad' Ideas for Cost Cuts," *Wall Street Journal* (December 9, 2009), p. B1.

Photo Credits

Chapter 1
Page 1: Mark Evans/iStockphoto. **Page 2:** KRT/NewsCom. **Page 5:** Press-Telegram, Stephen Carr/©AP/Wide World Photos. **Page 6:** Paul Sakuma/©AP/Wide World Photos. **Page 7:** Digital Vision/Getty Images, Inc. **Page 17:** Reuters/Chip East/Landov LLC. **Page 18:** Courtesy Sage Publications. **Page C-3:** Michael Nagle/Getty Images, Inc.

Chapter 2
Page 27: Mark Evans/iStockphoto. **Page 28:** Peter DaSilva/The New York Times/Redux Pictures. **Page 32:** ©AP/Wide World Photos. **Page 35:** Reuters/Steve Marcus/Landov LLC. **Page 36:** Jose Luis Pelaez/Getty Images, Inc. **Page 39:** From Leaving Microsoft to Change the World by John Wood. Copyright © 2006 by John Wood. Reprinted by permission of HarperCollins Publishers. **Page 42:** NewsCom. **Page 45:** Reprinted with permission of the American Psychological Association. **Page 44:** How the Mighty Fall ©2009 by Jim Collins. Reprinted with permission from Jim Collins. **Page C-5:** Gregory Wrona/Alamy.

Chapter 3
Page 51: Mark Evans/iStockphoto. **Page 52:** NewsCom. **Page 57:** Thomas Cockrem/Alamy. **Page 61:** David Montgomery/Getty Images, Inc. **Page 63:** Scott Boehm/Getty Images, Inc. **Page 64:** Timothy A. Clary/AFP/Getty Images, Inc. **Page 67:** ©2010 Interface, Inc. and its subsidiaries. All Rights Reserved. **Page 69:** Courtesy Springer Science and Business Media. **Page C-7:** Ben Baker/Redux Pictures.

Chapter 4
Page 77: Mark Evans/iStockphoto. **Page 78:** Ben Margot/©AP/Wide World Photos. **Page 82:** Barry Barnes/Alamy. **Page 84:** Journal of Management, May 2, 2010, vol. 36, no. 3. Reprinted with permission of Sage Publishing. **Page 90:** Image courtesy of Central Asia Institute. **Page 91:** Thomas Barwick/Getty Images, Inc. **Page 94:** Jean Paul Guilloteau/Express-REA/Redux Pictures. **Page 95:** Glowimages/Alamy. **Page C-9:** Photograph by Sebastian Copeland, ©Spectralq and Global Green USA.

Chapter 5
Page 103: Mark Evans/iStockphoto. **Page 104:** Ramin Talale/Bloomberg/Getty Images, Inc. **Page 109:** Toby Talbot/©AP/Wide World Photos. **Page 112:** LAIF/Redux Pictures. **Page 113:** Charles Pertwee/Bloomberg/Getty Images, Inc. **Page 117:** iStockphoto. **Page 120:** Reprinted with permission of the American Psychological Association. **Page 122:** Robert Gilhooly/Bloomberg/Getty Images, Inc. **Page 123:** Rene Macura/©AP/Wide World Photos. **Page C-11:** NIR ELIAS/Reuters/Landov LLC.

Chapter 6
Page 131: Mark Evans/iStockphoto. **Page 132:** Jim Wilson/The New York Times/Redux Pictures. **Page 135 (center):** Dallas Morning News/NewsCom. **Page 135 (bottom):** Photo by Joi Ito, Creative Commons. **Page 136 (top):** Bebeto Matthews/©AP/Wide World Photos. **Page 136 (center):** AFP/Getty Images, Inc. **Page 139:** Christian Baird Photography. **Page 141:** Steve Hebert Photography. **Page 142:** Michael Y. Park. **Page 143:** Reprinted with permission of the Academy of Management Journal. **Page 148:** Todd Williamson/Getty Images, Inc. **Page C-13:** Marissa Roth/The New York Times/Redux Pictures.

Chapter 7
Page 155: Mark Evans/iStockphoto. **Page 156:** Photo by Dara Seabridge. Courtesy TerraCycle, Inc. **Page 160:** ©Teri Stratford. **Page 163:** NewsCom. **Page 165:** Courtesy John Vlahakis, Earth Friendly Products, www.earthreport.com. **Page 170:** Gary Malerba/©AP/Wide World Photos. **Page 173:** Bobby Model/Getty Images, Inc. **Page 175:** Courtesy Springer Science and Business Media. **Page C-15:** David Strick/Redux Pictures.

Chapter 8
Page 183: Mark Evans/iStockphoto. **Page 184:** Louise Gubb/©Corbis. **Page 188:** Chuck Berman/MCT/Landov LLC. **Page 192:** Courtesy Harvard Business School Publishing. **Page 193:** Henrik Sorensen/Getty Images, Inc. **Page 195:** KPA Hackenberg/NewsCom. **Page 196:** UN Photo/Evan Schneider. **Page 197:** Victor Fraile/Reuters/Landov LLC. **Page C-17:** John Gress/Reuters/Landov.

Chapter 9
Page 205: Mark Evans/iStockphoto. **Page 206:** David Strick/Redux Pictures. **Page 212:** David Young-Woff/PhotoEdit. **Page 218:** Ramin Talaie/Bloomberg/Getty Images, Inc. **Page 219:** Landov LLC. **Page 221:** Lana Sundman/Alamy. **Page 225:** Reuters/Second Life/Landov LLC. **Page 226:** Courtesy Sage Publications. **Page C-19:** Francis Dean/NewsCom.

Chapter 10
Page 233: Mark Evans/iStockphoto. **Page 234:** Susan Van Etten/PhotoEdit. **Page 241:** Courtesy Dancing Deer Baking Company, Inc. **Page 248:** Chris Ratcliffe/Bloomberg/Getty Images, Inc. **Page 250:** iStockphoto. **Page 251:** Imago/Zuma Press. **Page 252:** Victoria Pearson/Getty Images. Reprinted with permission of Simon & Schuster. **Page C-21:** ©AP/Wide World Photos.

Chapter 11
Page 257: Mark Evans/iStockphoto. **Page 258:** Elena Dorfman/Redux Pictures. **Page 263:** Courtesy Herman Miller, Inc. **Page 264:** Laura Rauch/©AP/Wide World Photos. **Page 265:** David Roark/Photoshot/Landov LLC. **Page 271:** Image Source/Alamy. **Page 276:** Michel Euler/©AP/Wide World Photos. **Page 278:** Reprinted by permission of Taylor & Francis Group, http://www.tandf.co.uk/journals. **Page C-23:** SIMON CHAVEZ/dpa/Landov LLC.

Chapter 12

Page 283: Mark Evans/iStockphoto. **Page 284:** Robert Houser/Getty Images, Inc. **Page 288:** Lucas Racasse/Getty Images, Inc. **Page 290:** Chris Jackson/Getty Images, Inc. **Page 297:** Reprinted with permission of the American Psychological Association. **Page 299:** iStockphoto. **Page 301:** Brad Swonetz/Redux Pictures. **Page 303:** Eros Hoagland/Redux Pictures. **Page C-25:** ©AP/Wide World Photos.

Chapter 13

Page 309: Mark Evans/iStockphoto. **Page 310:** John Gress/Reuters/Landov LLC. **Page 315:** Copyright © 2003 by Lorraine Monroe, Reprinted by permission of PUBLICAFFAIRS, a member of Perseus Books Group. All rights reserved. **Page 318:** Pablo Garcia Photography. **Page 321:** Betsie Van der Meer/Getty Images, Inc. **Page 325:** Rolls Press/Popperfoto/Getty Images. **Page 327:** Reprinted from *Leadership Quarterly*, Vol. 17, Issue 2, 2006. Reproduced with permission from Elsevier. **Page 328:** Bettmann/©Corbis. **Page C-27:** William Thomas Cain/Getty Images, Inc.

Chapter 14

Page 335: Mark Evans/iStockphoto. **Page 336:** Courtesy Spanx, Inc. www.spanx.com, http://www.spanx.com. **Page 340:** Teri Stratford. **Page 341:** Courtesy Root Learning. **Page 342:** Erick Jacobs/The New York Times/Redux Pictures. **Page 344:** Kent Larsson/Getty Images, Inc. **Page 349:** Reprinted with permission of the *Academy of Management Journal*. **Page 353:** Stockbyte/Getty Images. **Page C-29:** Kim White/Getty Images, Inc.

Chapter 15

Page 359: Mark Evans/iStockphoto. **Page 360:** Courtesy SAS Institute, Inc. **Page 365:** Courtesy Rockwell Collins. **Page 367:** Siri Stafford/Getty Images, Inc. **Page 368:** Photo by Liz Song, courtesy of HopeLab. **Page 371:** Image supplied by John Wiley & Sons Ltd, publisher of *Journal of Organizational Behavior*. **Page 376:** Rob Tringali/Sportschrome/Getty Images, Inc. **Page 378:** Ross Anania/Getty Images, Inc. **Page C-31:** The Bond by Samson Davis. Reproduced with permission from Penguin Group USA, Inc.

Chapter 16

Page 385: Mark Evans/iStockphoto. **Page 386:** Rusty Jarrett/Getty Images, Inc. **Page 391:** Masterfile. **Page 393:** Eric Audras/PhotoAlto/Getty Images, Inc. **Page 395:** Bob Mahoney/Time & Life Pictures/Getty Images. **Page 398:** Reprinted with permission of the *Academy of Management Journal*. **Page 404:** Jonathan Fickies/Bloomberg/Getty Images, Inc. **Page C-33:** Jeff Willhelm/MCT/Landov LLC.

Chapter 17

Page 411: Mark Evans/iStockphoto. **Page 412:** Peter DaSilva/The New York Times/Redux Pictures. **Page 416:** Gilles Mingasson/Getty Images, Inc. **Page 421:** Courtesy of Hammond's Candies, since 1920, LLC. **Page 423:** Steve Cole/Getty Images, Inc. **Page 425:** PhotoEdit/Alamy. **Page 427:** Stephen Voss/Redux Pictures. **Page 433:** Reprinted with permission of the *Academy of Management Journal*. **Page C-35:** Phil McCarten/Reuters/©Corbis.

Chapter 18

Page 439: Mark Evans/iStockphoto. **Page 440:** Ric Feld/©AP/Wide World Photos. **Page 445:** Kathrin Ziegler/Getty Images, Inc. **Page 446:** PSL Images/Alamy. **Page 449:** Daniel Acker/Bloomberg/Getty Images, Inc. **Page 450:** Mal Langsdon/Reuters/Landov LLC. **Page 452:** James Lauritz/Getty Images, Inc. **Page 455:** Reprinted with permission of the Academy of Management Journal. **Page C-37:** Peter Steffen/dpa/Landov LLC.

Chapter 19

Page 461: Mark Evans/iStockphoto. **Page 462:** Maxpp/Zuma Press. **Page 465:** Reinhold Matay/©AP/Wide World Photos. **Page 467:** Gireesh Gv/The India Today Group/Getty Images, Inc. **Page 469:** Dani Pozo/AFP/Getty Images, Inc. **Page 470:** Stephen St. John/Getty Images, Inc. **Page 473:** Joe Wilssens/Reuters/Landov LLC. **Page 477:** Courtesy Harvard Business School Publishing. **Page C-39:** ©AP/Wide World Photos.

Case, Part II Openers
©iStockphoto.

Organization Index

Name Index

Subject Index

Active Learning and Critical Thinking Features

PHOTO ESSAYS

Teach for America
Salesforce.com
United Parcel Service
Cisco Systems
The Outliers
How the Mighty Fall
Child Labor
Anita Roddick, Body Shop
Bernie Madoff's Ponzi Scheme
Airline Industry
Pennies for Peace
Infosys Technologies
Green Mountain Coffee
BMW
Yahoo! Japan
McDonald's
Roger the Plumber
DiFara's Pizza
Infosurv
Tropicana

Fisker Automotive
Office Romance Policies Vary
Mecca Cola and Quibla Cola
Changing Times at Coach
Patagonia
Chrysler
Dell Computer
Cisco Systems
Macy's
Herman Miller
Disney
IDEO
Recruiting Goes Online
Performance Appraisals
Googling with Benefits
César Conde-Univisión
Martin Luther King, Jr.
Mahatma Gandhi
BakBone Software

Root Learning
Tension Must Be Fine Tuned
Rockwell Collins Inc.
Quarterback Coach
Pitney Bowes
Microsoft
Reality Team Building
Amazon.com
Sam Walton
Hammond's Candies
Electronic Privacy
Elsewhere Class
Wikipedia
Employee Fraud
Roush & Yates Racing
Dr. Devi Shetty
Ryanair

MANAGEMENT SMARTS

Early Career Survival Skills
Ten responsibilities of team leaders
Practical insights from scientific management
Google's principles for management and learning
Checklist for dealing with ethical dilemmas
Strategic goals engaged by ESR practices
Assessing organizational impact on sustainability
Culture shock: Stages in adjusting to a new culture
Challenging the myths about entrepreneurs
Why you need a business plan
Six rules for crisis management
How to avoid the escalation trap
Personal time management tips
Questions for reading an organizations' culture
How to lead organizational change
Why people may resist change
How to succeed in a telephone interview
Five ways for leaders to make decisions
How to make goal setting work for you
Guidelines for positive reinforcement
Guidelines for punishment
Spotting the seven sins of deadly meetings
How to avoid groupthink
How to make a successful presentation
"Ins" and "Outs" of negotiating salaries
"Hot stove rules" of employee discipline

REAL ETHICS

Coke's Secret Formula
CEO Compensation—Is it Excessive?
No Super Bowl Advertisements from Pepsi
Corporate Greens and Global Warming
E-Waste Graveyards
TOMS Shoes
Left to Die
Fighting Poverty
Cutting Costs by Moving Jobs Overseas
Flattened into Exhaustion
Hidden Agendas
Employers are Checking Your Facebook Page
When Your Boss Expects Too Much
Personality Testing
Information Goldmine
Social Loafing
Bloggers Beware
Privacy and Censorship
"Not in My Backyard" Dilemma